THE
NEW
BREED

THE AMERICAN PATRIOT SERIES

BOOK I

THE NEW BREED

DOUGLASS ELLIOT

BALLANTINE BOOKS · NEW YORK

Library of Congress Catalog Card Number: 81–65420

ISBN 0-345-29822-5

Produced by BOOK CREATIONS, INC.
Executive Producer: Lyle Kenyon Engel

This edition published simultaneously in trade and mass market.

Manufactured in the United States of America

First edition: July 1981

9 8 7 6 5 4 3 2 1

Maps by Ron Toelke

Illustrations by Sandy Kossin

The
American
Colonies 1649

Southern England
and Northwestern
France 1649

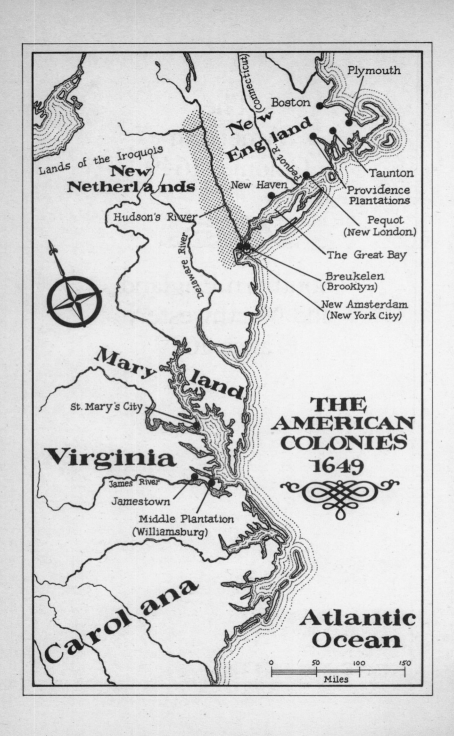

Plymouth

Boston

New England

(Connecticut)

Lands of the Iroquois
New Netherlands

New Haven

Hudson's River

Delaware River

Taunton

Providence Plantations

Pequot (New London)

The Great Bay

Breukelen (Brooklyn)

New Amsterdam (New York City)

Mary land

St. Mary's City

Virginia

James River

Jamestown

Middle Plantation (Williamsburg)

THE AMERICAN COLONIES 1649

Carol ana

Atlantic Ocean

0   50   100   150
Miles

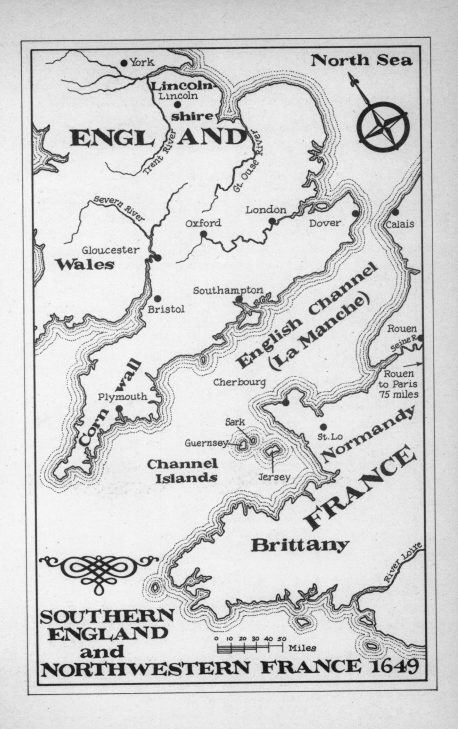

PROLOGUE

BY 1649, *the North American colonies were undergoing a rapid transformation. The new breed of hardy pioneers, settlers whose vision extended far into the future, was rapidly planting roots in the fertile soil of the New World. Farms were productive, towns were burgeoning, and the face of the land was being transformed.*

As befitted the oldest colony, Virginia was the most advanced. Thanks to John Rolfe, tobacco had become the staple and vast fields were devoted to its planting. Now almost forty years old, the original Virginia colony had weathered well; its people knew the climate, the Indians, and the hazards of life, and their culture was spreading to many newer communities. The Virginians, who were closely tied to their homeland across the Atlantic, reflected this in their manners, customs, and even household furnishings.

In contrast, the settlers of Massachusetts Bay and Plymouth colonies led a more rustic existence, largely due to the more difficult climate and their Puritanical beliefs. Boston had few structures that could be termed impressive, and for the most part it was a marshy, hilly town with no trees and muddy roads.

New Haven, although also founded by Puritans, enjoyed a greater prosperity, perhaps because its settlers were less rigorous in following their religious beliefs. Spacious homes surrounded the Green and commercial trade became a stronger investment with each passing year.

Another town whose commerce was based on the waterfront was New Amsterdam, administrated by the Dutch. It was a rousing, rowdy atmosphere with people from many nations coming to trade, staying to live. The director-general, Peter Stuyvesant, was striving to provide order to the town by imposing stringent laws concerning the sale of drinks, and the conduct of citizens and visitors alike. Stuyvesant met with little cooperation among his merchants, who sent a letter of remonstrance to Holland complaining of government's interference with their money-making ability.

Perhaps the most intriguing of settlements was that of Providence Plantations, Rhode Island. Here religious freedom was a fact, not a dream. The residents enjoyed self-rule without their delegates having to swear an oath of allegiance to the British monarch. Roger Williams, founder of the colony, vehemently objected to such oaths.

Men and women breathed the air of freedom in North America, and that in turn gave rise to the new breed which was unique in human annals. For the first time anywhere an individual was judged by accomplishments, not family wealth or personal standing. A new breed truly was arising in this new land.

THE NEW BREED

CHAPTER 1

PRECISELY as England's many soothsayers and fortune-tellers had predicted, the sun did not appear over the British Isles on Tuesday, January 30, 1649. It remained hidden beneath banks of dark gray clouds, and an icy wind that blew in off the North Sea added to the discomfort of a confused and frightened people.

Late in the day, the inclement weather notwithstanding, Londoners by the thousands gathered in the open area outside the great Banqueting Hall at Whitehall Palace, where a black-wreathed platform topped by an executioner's block had been built. The victorious Puritan troops in their drab uniforms, the victors over the Cavaliers, or Royalist forces, in the civil war that had almost destroyed the nation, kept the throngs at a distance. Parliament was supreme, and as the members of the House of Commons filed out of the building and took their places in a special grandstand built for their convenience, a hush settled over the crowd. In the

I

lead was Oliver Cromwell, soon to become Lord Protector of the Realm, his face solemn, his step decorous.

Royalist sympathizers averted their faces, and some murmured the epithet, "Roundheads." But they were careful not to speak aloud. Anyone who opposed Cromwell and his Puritans was in grave danger.

Fifty-nine somber men followed the members of the Commons and took their own seats on the opposite side of the executioner's block. Later to become infamous as the Damned Souls, they constituted the special high court of justice that had placed His Majesty on trial and found him guilty of "treason against Parliament and the nation." Now he would pay the penalty for his alleged crimes.

The black-clad, hooded executioner came through a side door, shouldering his heavy, razor-sharp ax, and many in the crowd shuddered. A number of the Puritans in the grandstand had the sensitivity to appear disconcerted.

The main doors opened wide, and Charles I, head of the house of Stuart, King of Great Britain and Ireland by the grace of God, stood for a moment and looked out at his subjects for the last time. His face was pale, but his emotions were controlled, and he was obviously prepared to meet his Maker. His long Stuart chin jutted forward, his thin nose quivered slightly, and there was cold contempt in his eyes as he glanced first at his judges, then at the Parliamentarians who were responsible for this violent miscarriage of justice.

Waving away two Puritan officers who would have assisted him, he mounted the scaffold alone, and the throngs pressed forward for a glimpse of his fine linen, his cloth-of-gold coat, silk breeches, gold-buckled shoes, and the exquisite fringe of lace at his wrists and neck.

"I need no restraints," Charles said. "I have lived a king, and now I die a king."

Charles looked for an instant at Oliver Cromwell, then faced the crowd. "I do not recognize the right of the Commons," he said in his Scots' accent, "to stand in judgment of their sovereign liege lord." Turning quickly, he bowed to the hooded executioner, then removed a gold coin from his purse and handed it to the man. No matter what his supposed faults, Charles I never lacked the social amenities. The executioner produced a thong to bind the condemned man's wrists and a blindfold to spare him needless agony in his final moments on earth.

"I need no restraints," Charles said. "I have lived a king, and now I die a king." With no one assisting him, he slowly dropped to his knees and placed his head on the block.

No one in the great crowd moved or spoke, but there were many who wept in silence, and even the most implacable of Charles Stuart's foes were compelled to admire his courage.

"I commend my soul to Almighty God," he said. "Executioner, do your masters' duty."

The great ax gleamed as it was raised high over the executioner's shoulder, and then it descended swiftly, making a quiet, almost gentle sound as it severed the head of Charles I, King of Great Britain and Ireland, from his body.

The messenger's footsteps echoed down the long, marbled corridor, interrupted several times by the palace guards. Each time, the messenger was waved by as the sentries became aware of the nature of his mission. At the last chamber, he was asked to be seated in a massive, red velvet chair by the entrance to the office. His instructions were to present the communiqué only to Cardinal Mazarin, and to wait for a reply.

"The messenger has arrived from England, Your Eminence."

"Send him in when I ring. You are excused, Deveaux."

Cardinal Mazarin was unique in Europe, perhaps in the whole world. Like his great flamboyant predecessor, Cardinal Richelieu, he was the first minister of the government as well as a prince of the Church. Promoted to the rank of cardinal for skillfully settling a political dispute, Mazarin had, in fact, never been consecrated priest. Unlike Richelieu, who dressed in gaudy civilian clothes and enjoyed showing off his power, Mazarin lived up to his nickname of the "Gray Spider." He was always dressed in the most modest of clericals, and only the red of his shirt and of his biretta distinguished him from an ordinary priest. He had refined, delicate features that caused him to resemble an intellectual, which he was. What the casual observer did not and could not know, however, was that he was also endowed with an inordinate, soaring ambition for France. He wanted his land to become first in power on all the earth, and he was willing to do anything to further that end.

The assistant turned on his heels and left quickly, closing the gilt double doors quietly. The cardinal turned to his two colleagues. "Be wary of your expressions. This fellow may be trained to read involuntary reactions. This message, on this particular day, can mean only one thing. Cromwell has done it. The King of England is dead."

The cardinal lifted a crystal bell from his desk, summoning the messenger. Reading the parchment, he excused the fellow.

Horace Laing and Jean-Pierre Colbert struggled to control their excitement. This was the moment for which Mazarin's agents had carefully planned. Their machinations could at last be implemented. The cardinal nodded to them: supremacy in Europe and the New World would soon be theirs.

"Your Eminence, do you wish for me to return to Virginia to await the arrival of Lady Dawn?"

"Yes, Monsieur Laing. We will continue as planned regarding the lady. Please, be careful with her face. We want her persuaded, but gently, gently. And control that mad-dog butler of yours. Our last recruit took weeks to heal. Lady Dawn is too precious for such antics. And before you leave, I want you to carry further instructions to Laroche in New Amsterdam."

Lady Dawn was indeed worth special handling. As a member of the highest English aristocracy, she was trusted completely by every man in the king's party. She could come and go at will, she could learn any secret of the machinations being conducted against the Lord Protector, Cromwell, and she was assured of a hearty welcome by almost everyone, even at the court-in-exile. Few other people had such qualifications.

The cardinal paused and jotted some notes to himself, then turned to his other compatriot. "Colbert, please continue with your excellent work. Lady Dawn should be nearing Dover now. Make certain she is not detained in her voyage to the New World by any ignorant Puritan constables. She is too dear to us to be thrown into the Tower to rot. This is your responsibility: make certain she reaches Laing in Virginia. Follow her to America, and use an alias when you book your own passage." The cardinal removed a suede sack of gold coins from his desk and placed it in front of Colbert, who picked it up, tossed it gently to ascertain its weight, and stashed it in his pocket.

"When do you want my next report, Your Eminence?"

"Soon, Colbert, soon. Your ship will be intercepted by one of our officers. You may give him a message for me. He will be in our camp. Do you have any questions?"

The men shook their heads.

"You are excused, then. I will be busy now with the young and impressionable Charles the Second." A slight smile played upon the lips of this man of God.

Sir Richard Dunstable had felt restless all day, and now, as he looked out at the trees on his heavily wooded estate in Lincolnshire, far from London, he decided he needed physical exercise. It was too late in the day to hunt in the royal game preserve, which was his privilege as the King's Forester, an almost meaningless title he had inherited along with his baronetcy from his late father. And he had read until the words melted together on the page, as he had done when he won honors at Oxford University.

But the lack of fresh air stifled him, so he went into his armory and took from their cases his favorite weapons, a riflelike musket and a double-barreled pistol, both made according to his own precise specifications by a London gunsmith. As an afterthought, he buckled on a belt that contained a half-dozen perfectly balanced throwing knives.

Several servants had been given the day and night off, so Richard was attended by a minimal staff in the manor house, but he enjoyed the relative solitude, just as he felt completely at home in the forest of oak, pine, maple, ash, and elm that comprised the royal game preserve. He sat and loaded his weapons, then seemed to uncoil as he stood and headed for the side yard. His gait was that of a natural athlete who had no spare flesh on his rugged six-foot frame, and as he headed toward the fringe of the woods, he inhaled the scent of the pines, faint but still discernible in this season when the snow lay on the ground.

Ladies who saw him often thought that he was wasted in the backwoods of rural England. His hair, naturally crisp and dark brown, was worn fairly short and was gathered in a tie at the nape of his neck. His hazel eyes were alert, reflecting an unusual quickness and intelligence. He was fortunate in that he was endowed with a physical strength and stamina. In the earlier stages of England's civil war when he fought with the king's men against the Parliamentarians, he had been known for his ability to spend twenty-four to forty-eight hours in the saddle without rest, and his feats of strength and of prodigy were legendary.

He had always found accomplishments easy to attain. He had taken honors at Oxford at the age of twenty in a study of England's relationship with France over the centuries; anything connected with the power balance between the two nations fascinated him.

Currently he was annoyed with himself because he had given up the fight against the Puritans too soon. In one battle, near Worcester, he and a group of five scouts had held off an entire battalion of enemy infantry for more than twelve hours, a feat that Cromwell's generals refused to believe. But then, recognizing the hopelessness of the Royalist cause, and aware, too, that there would soon be a price on his head unless he desisted, he had come home, determined to sit out the rest of the war. Sitting of any kind when action promised was very difficult indeed for Richard.

9

Richard halted, took quick aim at a small pine branch thirty paces away, and fired both barrels of his pistol in quick succession, smiling quietly when the acrid smoke cleared sufficiently for him to see that the branch had vanished. He searched for a more difficult target for his rifle shot, ultimately selecting a dead maple leaf that clung tenaciously to a branch on a tree behind the top of the pine. He took careful aim, braced for the recoil, then squeezed the trigger. The single shot echoed through the game preserve, and the leaf was gone. Moving closer to the woods, he threw each of his knives in quick succession at the trunk of a young gray birch, but he felt no satisfaction when he saw all six imbedded in the wood of his target.

Obviously his skill as a marksman gave him no pleasure today, the day the Puritans had sworn they would execute King Charles. A staunch Cavalier who had been a lifelong supporter of the Stuarts, Richard found it difficult to believe that even as arrogant a general as Cromwell would carry out the terrible threat. Certainly, had he known the king would be tried like a common criminal, he would have joined the Royalist Army prior to its last, unsuccessful campaign. He was still sorry he had been dissuaded from that course by the Earl of Newcastle, one of his father's closest friends, who had told him repeatedly in recent years that the Royalist cause was hopeless and that Charles was sure to lose his head because of his unwillingness to compromise with his enemies. Perhaps it would have been better to die honorably in battle than to survive a murdered monarch.

Putting his gloomy thoughts out of his mind, Richard retrieved his knives, returned to the house for his sword, then went out to the stable and saddled his stallion, which he had named Prince Henry, after one of King Charles's sons.

Prince Henry was unique, and he certainly was Richard's most valuable possession. A great stallion, a sleek, jet black, standing eighteen hands tall, with a distinct temper and temperament of his own, he had been trained as a charger by one of the best equestrians in the royal stables. Richard was inclined to believe that the mount was as intelligent as a man, and treated him accordingly.

As dusk settled over Lincolnshire, Richard rode the two miles to the substantial wooden house of a local squire, William Hatcher. Ordinarily, the road was heavily traveled, but few people were abroad today, and Richard, pulling his cloak around him as protection from the raw wind, saw no one as he rode up one hill and down the next. When the Hatcher house appeared ahead, set back from the road, lights were glowing in several rooms, and Richard grinned when he detected a slight ruffling of the curtains in the parlor. His beloved Dorothea knew he would be on time and was waiting for him.

Richard dismounted, looping his reins over the hitching post. The front door opened as he strode toward the house, the aura of the oil lamp that Dorothea Hatcher held in one hand, lighting her hazel eyes and making her brown hair seem to glow. Even in the modest gown that befitted the daughter of the proprietor of a small estate, she looked lovely, and Richard reached for her as he came into the house.

Dorothea was attractive, her regular features and her youth standing her in good stead. A more experienced eye than Richard's would have been aware of the fact that she was beginning to show signs of putting on weight, signs that would be fully revealed in several years.

All Richard knew, to be sure, was that she was tall,

supple, and comely. He lacked both the experience with women and the foresight to be able to see her in long-range terms, much less to realize there were limitations to her beauty. He would have been amazed had someone told him that in a few years Dorothea would become an ordinary-looking woman.

Dorothea evaded his embrace, closed the door, and motioned him into the parlor. As she unfailingly greeted him with a kiss that was his privilege to take as her future husband, Richard was somewhat bewildered by her reserve. "We need to talk quickly," she murmured.

Dorothea placed the lamp on a table and continued to stand as she turned to him. "Papa doesn't want me to marry you," she said, speaking softly but distinctly. "He's afraid that the king's supporters will be executed, or at the very least imprisoned, and he's certain the Roundheads will confiscate your property."

"But that's nonsense," he protested. "I'm protected by English law! We aren't living in the Middle Ages!"

"I'm just telling you what Papa says." Dorothea was deeply troubled.

"If you love me as much as I love you—"

"Papa says survival and the acquisition of worldly goods are more important than love." She paused, then added uncertainly, "Just this afternoon he told me he's selected a more suitable husband for me: a Roundhead county commissioner who stands high in Cromwell's regard. . . ." Her voice trailed away.

"Good evening, Sir Richard." William Hatcher's bulk filled the entrance-hall archway.

Richard turned slowly, struggling for composure, and the thought crossed his mind that the sudden change in

Hatcher's appearance was remarkable. Instead of the swallow-tailed, embroidered coat and pale satin breeches he usually wore, he was dressed in unrelieved black that caused him to resemble an undertaker—or a Roundhead. "Your servant, Master Hatcher."

"Dorothea, be good enough to retire to your room," Hatcher ordered in a deep baritone. "I want a word in private with Sir Richard."

The girl stood uncertainly for a long moment, her eyes filling with tears as she glanced first at her father, then at Richard. Suddenly, she gathered her full skirt and fled.

Richard was not one to dissemble or evade issues, and he immediately took the initiative. "I gather from Dorothea that you no longer regard me as a suitable husband for her."

The heavyset man reddened. "We live in unsettled times, Sir Richard," he replied, apology and defiance mingling in his manner. "In the world that we knew, no bachelor was more eligible than you, a baronet with a fixed income and a fine estate, along with an extra income of three hundred sovereigns in gold each year as the hereditary King's Forester. Ah, you were a man to be envied! Unfortunately, you've been branded with the Stuart mark, and no father who takes his responsibilities seriously could permit his only daughter to marry someone whose future is uncertain."

"No one can look into the future, Master Hatcher," Richard protested. "You lose sight of an all-important fact, sir. Dorothea and I love each other!"

"As a realistic man of the world, I cannot allow myself to be swayed by the feelings of the young. My regret is genuine, Sir Richard, but Dorothea's betrothal to you is ended."

The girl was not yet twenty-one years old, and Richard

knew she would not be married without her father's permission, but he would not give up without a fight. "I'd like to speak with Dorothea, if you please. We have an understanding—"

"Understanding be damned." Hatcher was unyielding. "My daughter is permitted neither to receive you nor to speak with you again." Trying to maintain his dignity, Hatcher led Richard toward the door.

Richard's temper flared, but he managed to hold it in check. If he were dealing with anyone but Dorothea's father, he would have challenged the scoundrel to a duel. But that would not help in the present situation. He was tempted to ask Dorothea to elope with him, but she was so gentle and meek that he knew, without asking, that she could not summon the courage to defy her father. Furthermore, by running away with Dorothea, he would create problems for himself with the Puritans who now held all posts of authority in Lincolnshire, men who already hated him. His only recourse was to find some way to speak privately with Dorothea in the days ahead and ask her to wait for him until the present political frenzy that gripped England died away.

"Your betrothal ring will be returned to you," Hatcher said as he opened the door.

"I prefer that Dorothea keep it," Richard replied stiffly.

As the girl's father well knew, the ring, which had belonged to Richard's late mother, was made of gold and set with diamonds and rubies, so it was valuable, particularly in these uncertain times when money had become scarce. Avarice gleamed in Hatcher's eyes, and he said quickly, "As you wish."

The door closed behind Richard. He stamped down the

steps, mounted his horse, and venting his frustrated rage, he raced home at a gallop.

The front gate, set in two posts of stone that had been worn smooth by the elements over the centuries during which time the Dunstables had owned the estate, stood open. Ahead was the great manor house of solid stone, a dwelling that his ancestors had enlarged and modernized for more than four hundred years, and as Richard looked at it, he smiled grimly. How could the future of the man who owned such a place be uncertain?

He saw a strange gelding tied to the hitching post beyond the side, or family, entrance, so it appeared that Richard had a visitor. Hurrying into the house, he saw a man warming himself at the hearth in the two-story great hall.

William Cavendish, Earl of Newcastle, turned slowly to greet the son of his oldest and closest friend. Inexplicably, the silver-haired nobleman was subduedly dressed in dark riding clothes, with drab boots and tarnished spurs. He looked very tired, but the smile that accented his wrinkles also lighted his face. "I let myself in, Richie," he said. "Luckily, you keep this door unlocked, although that's foolish of you when Roundhead troops are arresting those faithful to the Crown. Lock them out—and you have the talent to shoot down a goodly number of them before they seize you."

"Surely the state of affairs in England won't degenerate that much!" The younger man clung stubbornly to his beliefs that the rights of individuals were inviolable and that every subject of the Crown enjoyed absolute protection under the law.

The earl found it difficult to believe that anyone could be so naive in an era when a bloodthirsty purge was sweeping the country. "King Charles, may God have mercy on his soul," he said, "was beheaded today at Whitehall."

Richard was stunned. He knew, of course, that the monarch had been tried and found guilty by a Puritan-appointed "special high court of justice," but he had refused to believe that the Parliamentarians who had seized power would resort to murder.

"I am on my way to France," Newcastle said briskly. "My arrangements were made well in advance, and a ship is waiting to take me to join Queen Henrietta Maria and her children, particularly young Charles, in exile. I'm traveling with an escort of twenty men who have concealed themselves behind your outbuildings. There's a price on my head now, but I've outwitted Cromwell for years, and I shall have the best of the bargain again."

His mind still reeling, Richard could not allow himself to forget his duties as a host. "Many of my servants won't return until tomorrow, which may be just as well, since I'm uncertain of their sympathies. But let me offer you a supper of cold beef and bread before you go," he said huskily.

"I can't spare the time," Newcastle said, then added pointedly, "and neither can you."

The younger man stared at him.

"The Cavalier planners have been preparing against this day of infamy for three years and more. We've had no illusions about the pious hymn singers who want to drink our blood. And there has been a good reason you haven't been allowed to take part in our more recent military campaigns. We could have used your skills, but we couldn't risk losing you in battle. You've been saved to perform a special task."

"But—"

"Hear me out," the earl said. "You're an accomplished swordsman, and you know firearms better than most. No one is your equal at bringing down a stag or other game. You've stayed away from London because you've preferred the solitude of the royal game preserves, although why you should is something I can't for the life of me understand. Not that your lack of participation in the civil war will save you from the vengeance of the Puritans, you understand. You've made no secret of your Royalist feelings, and you hold the warrant of King's Forester. Our agents in the Puritan camp say you're scheduled to be arrested and thrown into prison tomorrow. If they take you, you'll spend the rest of your days rotting in a cell."

"I'll rid the world of a good many of the scum first," Richard vowed grimly.

Newcastle shook his head. "No, you'll do no such thing, because you won't be here. You're leaving tonight, too."

"With you, Uncle William?"

The earl smiled faintly. "You'll travel in another direction. You'll go to Bristol, where a ship whose master swears allegiance to young Charles the Second awaits you. He'll take you to the New World colonies."

"You're sending me to North America?" Richard could not hide his dismay.

"Yes, lad. The colonies are growing rapidly and are already of enormous importance to us. No matter how long it may take, we intend to place young Charles on the throne that rightfully belongs to him, and we'll need the support of the colonials."

Not yet resigned to his exile in a distant, barbaric land, Richard's heart was heavy as he listened.

"Your duties will not be onerous," Newcastle told him.

17

"You'll assess the sympathies of the colonials, and when possible, you'll work for the formation of a king's party. What's more, you won't be working alone. Our principal agent there is a man called Laroche. He'll be in touch with you, and you'll take your orders from him."

"How will I know where to find him? The colonies occupy a vast territory that stretches from Massachusetts Bay to Virginia."

The earl smiled and shrugged. "To be candid, I don't know. But Laroche has his own means of acquiring information, and he has told the Cavalier high command that he'll locate you. I'd guess that not many men of your stature go to America."

Richard couldn't blame anyone for not wanting to travel to that remote wilderness. "How long must I remain there?"

Newcastle shrugged. "How long will it take the people to see through the hymn singers and clamor for the restoration of young Charles to the throne?" He reached into an inner pocket for a sheet of folded parchment. "Here, lad, is a list of places where you'll stay on your journey to the White Hart Inn at Bristol. Some are private homes, and others are public inns. You'll be welcome at all of them. But avoid the main roads as you would the plague, and don't go near any large towns. The Roundheads are congregated in the cities, while most rural dwellers remain loyal to us."

Richard nodded as he studied the list of stopovers where he would be assured a safe, warm welcome.

"I hate to burden you with something additional," the earl said, "but it can't be helped. Are you acquainted with Lady Dawn Shepherd, the little-known daughter of the late

Earl of Sturbridge? She's an exceptionally outspoken young woman, more's the pity for her. Her father tried to keep her concealed, for her own safety, due to his political situation and her noteworthy beauty. Her friends know her as Mimi."

"I've never had the privilege of meeting her, Uncle William."

Newcastle sighed. "Mimi Shepherd has already arrived at the White Hart in Bristol and is in hiding there. The Puritans are determined to find her and make an example of her, so she desperately needs help. We hope you'll do what you can to assist her."

"In what way?"

"I suggest you work that out with her. She's certain to have ideas of her own which may or may not be valid. We must leave her future to your judgment."

Richard already had enough problems and resented the burden of looking after an earl's spoiled daughter. "How will I know her?"

For the first time Newcastle laughed. "She has red hair, and her appearance is striking, lad, to say the least. You won't need to be a Roundhead informer to recognize her."

"For your sake, I'll do my best."

The earl corrected him gently. "Not for my sake, but for that of the cause that both of us now represent. Write to me of your progress when you're able to do so. The master of the brig *Anne,* who'll carry you to the New World, will tell you which ships' masters can be trusted with correspondence. The letters will be brought to England, then smuggled across the Channel to me. I'll stay for a time with Queen Henrietta Maria at the Louvre and then I'll join my own family in Paris, but I don't yet know where I'll settle. We who are exiles will need to depend on the whims of the French."

A wave of compassion for the older man engulfed Richard. It would not be easy for one of the most prominent noblemen in the realm to live abroad with his wife, their children, and their grandchildren for an indefinite period, perhaps for the rest of their lives.

"I must be on my way." The earl took a purse from his belt. "I wish I could give you more than this, Richie."

"Keep it," Richard told him. "I have ample funds."

"Only the Lord knows when more gold will be available, so take this, along with your own money and valuables. When the Roundheads have discovered you've flown, there is little doubt they'll confiscate your entire estate. All of us are leaving behind precious belongings for the vultures, but it can't be helped," he added bleakly.

Richard accepted the purse, trying to assure himself that he would be expected to earn the money, that he wasn't taking charity. Newcastle went to a sideboard, poured two small glasses of brandy, then indulged in a curious gesture, extending his own glass over a carafe of water, then raising it in a toast. "Remember this sign," he said. "We drink to the king-across-the-water."

The younger man imitated the gesture, then gulped the potent brandy. "I shall not forget," he promised.

They clasped hands, and Newcastle murmured, "We shall meet again in better times." He slipped out through the side door. Moments later Richard heard the pounding of hooves as the fugitive and his escort started northward toward Scotland.

Soon he himself would be a fugitive, and he had no time

to lose. Packing only his tooth-brushing twig, razor, and comb, along with a single change of clothes, he took his rifle, double-barreled pistol, plus a supply of ammunition and powder for both weapons, as well as his belt laden with throwing knives. Hastily packing a saddlebag with money and jewelry, he went to the library where he selected leather-bound volumes of the works of Sir Francis Bacon, several plays by Ben Jonson, and a book of sonnets by William Shakespeare. It was a wrench to leave behind the many hundreds of books he had read and loved, but that could not be helped.

Pausing again, he studied paintings of his father, grand-father, and the earlier ancestors who looked down at him from the walls of the library. Even if he removed some from their frames, they would be too bulky for him to carry and would serve no useful purpose. Standing erect, he raised a gauntlet-gloved hand to his broad-brimmed, plumed hat in salute, then hurried to the kitchen outbuild-ing, where he made up a package of cold meat and bread to take with him on the road. Finally, he filled a feedbag for his stallion. He and Prince Henry had a long journey ahead.

Locking the door of the manor house behind him, he took care to shut the front gate, too, but the knowledge that the Roundheads would be forced to break in when they took possession of his home gave him little satisfaction. Resisting the impulse to look back for a last time, he mounted and started off down to the road toward the southeast.

No lights were burning in the Hatcher house when he passed it, and he bade a silent farewell to Dorothea. It was too much to hope she would have the strength to resist her father's efforts to give her in marriage to some prominent

Puritan. At least Uncle William had verified why their betrothal had been terminated so abruptly; obviously Master Hatcher had been told in confidence that arrest, imprisonment, and confiscation of property awaited Sir Richard Dunstable. He would cherish Dorothea for the rest of his days, of that he was certain.

At the last moment Richard's resolve broke and he knew he could not tolerate the thought of going off without Dorothea. He dismounted, picked up some pebbles from the walk, then stood and, taking a deep breath, threw them up against the leaded pane of her darkened window.

There was a long pause, and when no one replied he was on the verge of repeating his effort. Then, suddenly, the window opened. He caught a glimpse of his beloved Dorothea, her hair hanging loose as she peered out into the night.

"It's Richard," he murmured.

Dorothea was about to shrink back into the room.

"Wait!" he said. "Dorothea, I have no time to explain, but I'm going away—against my own will. I can't leave without you. Please, I beg you, come with me and we'll be married somewhere on our journey."

There was a long silence from above. "Dorothea!" His voice was more urgent. "I don't dare tell you more now, but—"

"It makes no matter," she said faintly, though there was a new resolve in her voice. "I can't go with you, Richard. I can't defy my father, or disobey him. If you go, you must go alone."

He was stunned. He had expected little more, but her refusal was so final that he abandoned all hope. He would have to make his future alone. He had no alternative.

Turning onto a little-used road, Richard made his way through the hills, his great stallion rarely varying the pace. A light, dry snow began to fall, whipped almost horizontal by stiff gusts that blew off the Irish Sea. The particles stung Richard's face, but he shielded his nose and mouth with his cloak, pulled his hat lower on his head, and rode on.

Not until an hour after daybreak did he come to a large, comfortable house, the first on the list that the Earl of Newcastle had given him. As nearly as he could judge, it was the country home of a squire, and a portly, middle-aged man in bathrobe and slippers answered his knock on the front door.

Richard removed his hat. "I am——"

"No names, please," his host replied, cutting him off. "Your horse will be attended, and you shall have breakfast, a warm bed, and another, more substantial meal before you leave. Sleep until you're awakened. We'll take full responsibility for determining when few Puritans will be abroad and it will be safe for you to go."

Richard slept for the better part of the day, and after eating a hearty supper—served by his host, although he could hear women's voices in the house—he tried in vain to pay for his lodging and meals.

"The risks you take are greater than my poor contributions to our mutual cause," the man told him. "All of us must learn to work together and make sacrifices in the long years that lie ahead."

The treatment was typical of the welcome that Richard received everywhere on his journey, and even the proprietors of public inns refused to accept payment from him. Certainly it was heartening to learn that, so soon after the execution of King Charles, a strong network of steadfast

Royalists was already in operation. Riding steadily toward the southwest from his own home, not far from the North Sea to the west, Richard passed through Northampton, then avoided the picturesque villages of the Cotswold hills in Gloucester. He had friends in Oxford who would have welcomed him, but he resisted the desire to stop off for a brief visit. Recognizing the need for strict self-discipline, he followed the Earl of Newcastle's instructions to the letter.

Richard didn't realize it, but in a sense he was fortunate. He was already endowed with the spirit of independence that enabled him to make his own decisions, take his own actions, and accept responsibility for them. Orphaned a decade earlier while in his mid-teens, Richard and his appointed guardian quickly reached a mutual agreement that the lad could make his own decisions. Now, with an assignment in the New World waiting for him, he didn't know that he had already developed the qualities that made for success in the North American colonies.

Finally, late one afternoon, he reached the rough, brawling seaport of Bristol. After stopping to inquire about the location of the White Hart Inn, he made his way toward it through a maze of narrow, cobbled streets. Here he saw Puritans everywhere, distinctive in their suits, cloaks, and hats of black, brown, or gray, their women modestly attired in dark dresses and capes, many of them clutching prayer books as they walked to and from the interminable religious services, hymn-singing, and endless sermons for which their sect was noted. The majority, Richard realized, were honest, plain people, sincere in their beliefs, and it would be wrong to blame them for such outrageous excesses as the killing of King Charles perpetrated by their fanatical leaders.

The White Hart was a substantial three-story building of stone and wood. A stable boy came to take Prince Henry to the rear, and when Richard entered through the front door carrying his saddlebag, he stopped short. The proprietor, who came forward to greet him, was wearing the drab attire of a Roundhead. Richard was so startled that his face mirrored his dismay.

The man, short and swarthy, revealed the absence of several front teeth when he grinned. "I can't say as I blame you for being upset when you see Minter Lucey dressed for a masquerade. But when you're in old Rome, Sir Richard, you wear a toga so you look like the other Romans, if you get my meaning."

"You know me?" Richard was still uncomfortable, ready for violence should it be necessary.

Conscious of his wariness, Minter Lucey tapped a keg of ale in a cubicle off the entrance hall, placed a small container of water on a nearby table, then went through the ritual of passing his mug over the water before returning it to his mouth and gulping the contents. "A friend of yours and mine it's best not to name, if you get my meaning," he said, wiping his lips on his sleeve, "described you to perfection. I wasn't expecting you for at least another day. You did well to get here so fast."

Relaxing with a smile, Richard released his grip on the hilt of his sword.

"I happen to know that Brennan doesn't expect you until late tomorrow at the soonest, Sir Richard."

"Who?"

"Captain James Brennan, master of the brig *Anne*."
Lucey filled the mug, then thrust it at the guest. "Bristol
hospitality, Sir Richard. The day the Roundheads ban
drink—and there's talk of it in their church councils—I'll
have to give up my disguise. Come along, and I'll show you
to your quarters."

Richard sipped his drink as he followed the proprietor up
the stairs to a small, second-floor suite that overlooked a
lane outside the inn. The parlor and bedchamber were tiny
and cramped, furnished with simple essentials that looked
comfortable. The suite was badly in need of paint, and on
one wall of the sitting room was a blank rectangle of a
lighter color where a picture had been displayed.

Minter Lucey saw the visitor's inquiring glance. "A long
time ago," he said, "our mutual friend gave me a copy of a
painting of King Charles, bless him, painted by some artist.
Name of Van Dyke. I felt in my bones what was coming
when the Roundheads made poor Charlie their prisoner,
and ever since then the picture has been hidden in my
cellar." His sigh was lugubrious. "These are hard times,
Sir Richard, and the worst is yet to come."

Richard was forced to agree.

"I gave you these quarters because you have the best view
of the lane from here. Even though I've become as pious a
Puritan as you'll find in Bristol town, all inns are under
suspicion, so at odd times the comings and goings of my
patrons are watched. You'll find this a most useful observation post. Besides," he added with a chuckle, "I'd be afraid
to dislodge the occupant of the grand suite upstairs. As my
pa always said, 'A sharp tongue is more to be feared than a
rapier,' if you get what I mean."

"Indeed," Richard replied politely.

"Now that you're here safe and sound, I'll go off to my own house down the road. The staff will serve your supper in the dining room in an hour. If you're wise, you won't go out of the inn. There will be prayer meetings of thanks for the deliverance from the yoke of King Charlie all over town tonight, and no one is more suspicious of strangers than the faithful."

"I'll follow your advice, Master Lucey."

"For my own sake, as well as yours, I thank you kindly. It's a dangerous, two-faced game I play here, and I want no hymn-chanting constables snooping around my inn." Minter Lucey appeared on the verge of imparting a confidence, but changed his mind abruptly. "We'll talk again early in the morning, before you go off to meet Captain Brennan." He sidled through the door, closing it behind him.

Within moments, a servant in black livery appeared with a bucket of hot water and a basin. After washing away the grim of the road, Richard gratefully changed into his one clean outfit, deciding that if time permitted before he sailed, he would buy some needed additions to his wardrobe.

Strapping on his knife-belt and concealing his pistol beneath his coat, he went down to the ground floor, found the dining room, and seated himself facing the door at a small table. The other two tables were unoccupied.

The same servant appeared with a tureen of a thick mutton and barley soup, and after he placed it on the table, Richard ladled a generous portion into his bowl. Not only was he ravenous, but the small coal fire at the far end of the room was almost dead, and the soup warmed him. As he ate, someone else came into the room, and he couldn't help staring at the most flamboyant beauty he had ever seen.

The woman, who appeared to be in her early twenties, had glowing red hair that cascaded to her waist. Her gown was so daring and her use of cosmetics so lavish that only a courtesan or a great noblewoman—or someone who was both—would have had the courage to display herself in public in a manner certain to attract attention. She was tall, slender, and willowy, her low-cut emerald-green velvet dress revealing the cleavage between her high, full breasts, then nipping in her tiny waist and clinging to her long, firm thighs. Bright rouge accented her provocative lips, and she appeared to have rouged her high cheekbones, too; as if that weren't enough, a velvet beauty patch of emerald green was the focal point on one cheek. But her limpid eyes, which were enormous and matched her gown, were her most arresting feature. They were rimmed in black kohl with a black salve making her long lashes seem even longer, and on her lids was a substance of a delicate green.

She moved past him, hips swaying as she walked to the farthest table, and Richard instantly guessed she was Lady Dawn Shepherd, the late Earl of Sturbridge's daughter. The coal fire was reflected in her long gold earrings, a chain of gold dipped low in her cleavage, and her fingers were covered with rings. If she were truly the fugitive he believed her to be, she was mad for daring to make herself so conspicuous.

Paying no attention to the other guest, acting as if she were the only patron in the dining room, she waved away the soup that the servant brought her. The man reappeared with a roast of rare beef, and she took a slice of the meat, refused the roasted potatoes, and allowed herself to be served a portion of brussels sprouts.

Richard took every dish offered to him. Surely the young

woman was aware of his steady, unwavering gaze, but she looked both past and through him, not once acknowledging his presence.

When the waiter brought glasses of wine, a thought occurred to Richard, and he asked for a carafe of water, too. After it had been served, he observed the ritual of drinking a silent toast to the young king-across-the-water. The woman hesitated for an instant, then went through the same motions. It was her prerogative to speak first, but she remained silent, so he concentrated on his meal, unable to fathom her strange attitude.

When the servant reappeared to clear away their dishes, she raised her voice for the first time, speaking in the clipped soprano of the upper class. "The savory was inedible last night, so I shall have none this evening," she said.

The man bowed and went off to the kitchen for a single portion of oysters and bacon, grilled on toast, which he placed before Richard, then retired.

The woman rose and paused for a moment at Richard's table. "When you're done," she murmured in an almost inaudible tone, "come to my quarters on the third floor." Not waiting for a reply, she swept out of the room.

The savory was delicious, Richard thought, and made a point of asking the servant to give his compliments to the cook.

"I'm the cook, your worship," the man said, bowing. "There's none but me on duty here after dark. Now that we'll have peace, it may be that travelers will start a-coming to Bristol again."

Richard did not pause at his own suite, but went directly to the top floor, stamping his boots on the stairs to announce his approach. When he reached the landing, he saw a door had been opened, so he walked into a sitting room at least three times the size of his own. A jewel-hilted dagger in one hand, the woman appeared from behind the door then quickly closed and bolted it.

"There's no need to carve me, milady," he said as he bowed to her. "Sir Richard Dunstable at your service."

"I am not your lady," she replied coldly, raising her skirt and calmly placing the weapon in a sheath strapped on her calf. "Until further notice, I am to be addressed only as Mimi Shepherd, Sir Richard!"

"As you wish." He watched her as she poured wine from a pewter decanter into two glasses and handed him one. He was amused by her secretive air, just as he was irritated by her arrogance.

She waved him to a high-backed chair with a faded, tapestry-covered seat. "I have spent a full week in this primitive place," she said, taking a chair opposite his. "The only news I've heard in all that time until this morning was that poor, dear Charles is no longer in our midst. I haven't dared to go out-of-doors for fear the rabble will haul me off to one of their frightful gaols. Today, I was informed of your arrival, and you've come just in time to preserve my sanity."

He was less than certain that she was all that sane, but kept his opinion to himself.

"How soon can you make arrangements for my quarters on the ship, Sir Richard?" she demanded.

He knew nothing of her plans and made that fact clear to her.

"I sail to the New World on the brig *Anne*, as do you," she told him impatiently. "The very few I can trust tell me I'm not safe in England any longer, and because Queen

Henrietta Maria dislikes me, I'm not welcome in France."

Richard jumped to the conclusion that the queen probably had no use for her because Mimi had enjoyed a dalliance with King Charles, who had frequently been guilty of indiscretions.

"I haven't chosen the colonies willingly," Mimi Shepherd said. "I regret to say there is nowhere else I can go."

"I hope to visit the ship's master tomorrow morning, and I'll do what I can for you, Mistress Shepherd. Are you expected on board?"

Her shrug was haughty. "I was told only that you would attend to the details. I prefer a spacious cabin on the port side, which will face toward the south crossing the Atlantic and should be warmer at this ghastly season of the year."

Her imperious manner nettled Richard. "I have no idea what accommodations might be available," he said. "I'll pass along your request to the master, but I hope you won't be disappointed if he's unable to provide what you want."

Her green eyes turned as cold as the ice on the eaves beyond the frosted window. "If you're concerned about my ability to pay for what I want, I assure you that I have more than enough money for my needs."

Her haughtiness was similar to that of so many other members of the upper nobility, and he realized that, in spite of her beauty, she would be anything but an ideal traveling companion. "I'll do what I'm able, Lady Dawn, but I make no promises."

"I've already told you, sir, that I prefer to be known as Mimi Shepherd."

His own nerves were raw after his long, hazardous journey. "May I ask why, if you seek anonymity, you dress in a manner that will draw attention to yourself? Any man who even glances in your direction is certain to look a second time!"

She raised a thin eyebrow. "Now you sound like a Puritan, Sir Richard. I dress to please myself, as I've always done. I've remained in hiding here only because I promised poor Charlie that I'd go off to the colonies if anything unpleasant happened to him. If I had my way, I'd flaunt myself before Cromwell and all his mealy-mouthed followers—for the pure joy of watching the hypocrites gape at me!"

She seemed to be confirming his guess that she had been one of King Charles's mistresses. "It appears," he said, coolly polite, "that you fail to recognize the seriousness of your situation—or of mine. I've been charged with your safety. The Roundhead constabulary are searching all of England for you, and although they don't yet know I've come so far from my own home, I'm certain they're maintaining a sharp lookout for Cavaliers in every major seaport. So please stay indoors until I learn the exact hazards we face."

"I haven't shown myself beyond the front door of this horrid little place since I arrived, so your advice is unnecessary. But I reserve the right to change my mind."

Richard stood and bowed. "If you do, Lady Dawn, I shall feel I've been relieved of my obligation to assist you." He unbolted the door and went off to his own quarters. Uncle William had saddled him with a burdensome responsibility.

Sleeping soundly, as he always did, Richard awakened early the following morning. A different manservant brought him hot water for his ablutions and a mug of tea, then he went downstairs for a hearty breakfast of cold ham, cheese, smoked fish, and mild ale.

As he was finishing his meal, Minter Lucey appeared. "I thought you might want advice on how to make your way around Bristol," he said.

"There are parts of town it's wise to avoid, I take it."

"Ah, you get my meaning. Puritan spies lurk in unlikely places."

"I'd be obliged for the most direct route to the water-front."

Lucey gave him careful directions, then added quietly, "You'd be wise not to wear that hat, which advertises you as one of the king's party. Use this instead." He handed the visitor a drab black hat with a domed crown and rounded brim.

The offer was sensible, and Richard accepted it. His rifle would make him conspicuous, but he could hide his pistol and knife-belt under his cloak; only his sword would show, but the Puritan gentry carried sidearms, too.

"Members of the new constabulary carry long staffs and patrol in pairs, so you'll always recognize them. But beware of single loiterers who seem to have no occupation save that of leaning against buildings. Avoid looking directly at any you might encounter, if you get my meaning, and show no hesitation in unfamiliar surroundings. They'll be almost certain to question you if they discover that you're a stranger in Bristol."

Richard thanked the innkeeper, then set out for the waterfront. Following Lucey's instructions, he walked only a short distance down a street that ran parallel to the Avon River before he came to the stream's junction with the smaller Frome River. Together they formed a sheltered harbor at the head of the Severn estuary, and past rows of warehouses he could see the masts of ships tied up at wharves or lying at anchor.

Not slowing his pace, he went briskly past a score of vessels before he came to a weather-beaten brig with the name *Anne* painted in faded gold letters on her hull. She was no more than seventy feet long and, he guessed, did not weigh more than twenty-five hundred tons. Unfamiliar with the sea, Richard felt a knot forming in the pit of his stomach when he contemplated the dangers of making a midwinter Atlantic crossing in such a frail craft.

He was alert to far more immediate dangers: at the foot of the wharf, a man in black, the brim of his hat pulled low, was leaning against a post. Any man who had nothing better to do in this raw, blustery weather undoubtedly was a Roundhead agent. Grateful to Lucey, Richard averted his gaze as he walked boldly past the spy and onto the wharf. The *Anne* was held in place by lines fore and aft, and he halted amidships, a short distance from a partly opened hatch.

"Ahoy, on board," he called.

After a long wait, a middle-aged seaman looked out through the hatch opening.

"I seek a word with your master." Richard knew the Puritan spy was listening.

The sailor's face did not change expression. "Who wants to see him?"

"Isaac Marker." Richard thought the Biblical first name was inspired and might lessen the agent's suspicions.

The seaman vanished, to return a few moments later.

Climbing onto the deck, he placed a plank extending from the deck to the wharf.

Richard went on board, followed the sailor down a narrow ladder, and was conducted aft. The bearded master, James Brennan, wore a look of puzzlement on his lined, weather-beaten face as he stood at the entrance to his cabin, a charcoal brazier glowing behind him. "Master Marker?" he asked uncertainly.

Richard nodded, followed him into the cabin, and closed the door before he said, "I invented a name for the sake of our friend at the foot of the pier. I'm expected, I believe. My real name is Dunstable."

Brennan grinned, his handshake a viselike grip. "You made it here safely, Sir Richard!" He went to a small keg, poured two mugs of foaming porter, handed one to his visitor, and went through the ritual of extending his own over an imaginary water receptacle. Richard did the same, and then they drank in solemn silence.

"I take it you had no troubles on the road, Sir Richard?"

"I avoided main roads whenever possible. One learns quickly how to become a fugitive."

Brennan nodded. "And no one followed you here?"

"Not to my knowledge, Captain."

"Good. There's an agent stationed day and night at the base of the wharf, but they think I'm one of them, and I've already been granted sailing clearance."

"When do we sail?"

"In a few days. You'll be notified about twelve hours in advance. I'll send word to you at Brother Lucey's place. But you can send your sea chests to me at any time, and I'll stash them in your cabin. Would you like to see it?" Not waiting

35

for a reply, he led his passenger down a cramped companionway.

Richard peered into a tiny cabin with upper and lower bunks, a slab of wood that could be lowered from a bulkhead to become a table, and two stools that were fastened to the deck. A single, square window, tightly closed, admitted daylight, and an oil lamp stood on a shelf.

"It's not the most luxurious of quarters," the master said as they returned to his own cabin. "But you'll have privacy, which is more than can be said for those who'll share the general cabin."

"I was asked," Richard said, "to arrange accommodations for a certain lady."

Captain Brennan scowled. "If you refer to the daughter of an earl who died several years ago, there's no place for her on my ship," he said emphatically. "Word leaked out that she would sail with me, and I've been questioned by the new Puritan governor of Bristol himself. Naturally, I swore that I knew nothing about any such lady. They're taking no chances, which is the reason their agents are keeping watch on the *Anne*. They'll not only arrest her and haul her off to prison the moment they set eyes on her, but I'll be thrown into a cell, too, and my ship will be confiscated. There's no man more devoted to the Crown than I am, Sir Richard, but I'll be of no use to the cause if I'm behind bars and lose the *Anne*!"

"I see." Richard saw a great deal, and his mind worked furiously. The Earl of Newcastle had asked him to help Lady Dawn Shepherd, and he could not abandon her, particularly now that he knew the Roundheads were closing in on her. Obviously their plans had to be revised drastically, and the haughty noblewoman's demand for a cabin on the port side now seemed absurd. This new development forced him to take matters into his own hands, and he reacted accordingly. "The lady hasn't come to Bristol yet?"

"No, and I hope she doesn't! I don't know how the Puritans found out she was hoping to sail with me, but that's out of the question now!"

"I quite understand your position, Captain," Richard said. "I noted there are two beds in my cabin, and I wonder if I assume correctly that the second has not been sold."

The master shook his head. "There's no end of people begging for passage, but you're entitled to your privacy."

"Then I'd like to book passage for my serving lad and will pay you a double fare, of course. He's the son of the butler who served my father before me, and I've promised to help the boy launch a new life in the colonies."

Brennan shrugged. "It's of no matter to me, Sir Richard. You'll be stumbling all over each other in that little cabin, but I don't mind, if you don't."

Richard immediately reached for his purse.

"Pay when we sail, not before."

"I insist on giving you an advance now." Anxious to close the agreement, Richard handed the master two gold coins. "I also wonder if you'll have room for my horse. I'll provide his feed and will take care of him."

"There's no space below, but you can quarter him near the fowl pens on the aft deck. Make certain he's supplied with enough blankets. You may pace him only when no one else is on deck. The Atlantic winds are chilly at this time of year, and I won't be held responsible if he becomes ill."

Brennan then added, "I'll have to charge you full fare for your mount, if that's agreeable."

"I accept the arrangement, Captain." Richard gave him another coin.

The master slipped the gold piece into his pocket. "Along with your chests, send along any special foods you may want for a voyage of six weeks. Avoid perishables, and tell the shop clerks you intend the purchases for use on board ship, so they'll pack your goods accordingly." He paused and chuckled. "Mark you, don't bring too many delicacies, Sir Richard. You'll have to store the supplies in your cabin, and what with sharing the room with a boy, you'll scarce have enough space to turn around."

After a final exchange of amenities, Richard went ashore, taking care to pay no attention to the Roundhead agent who continued to loiter at the base of the wharf. Losing no time, he hurried back to the White Hart.

Neither Lucey nor the manservant appeared in the parlor, so he went straight to Lady Dawn's suite on the top floor. He had to identify himself carefully, and not until she recognized his voice did she admit him. She had slept late, and although she had already applied cosmetics to her face, she was clad in a billowing, low-cut silk peignoir.

This touch of intimacy made Richard uneasy, but he knew they would be thrown even closer together if his daring scheme materialized. Mincing no words, he outlined the situation at the harbor and his own plan. The woman brooded in silence for a moment. "You're quite sure the Roundheads are keeping watch for me?"

"There seems little question about it. Someone apparently talked out of turn."

"I daresay that some members of my household staff in London are Roundheads." She sighed lightly. "Well, it can't be helped."

Richard had to admire her for showing no sign of panic.

Her elfin grin was unexpected. "Do you suppose you and I could tolerate living in such close quarters?"

"We'll have no choice if you're going to sail on the *Anne*. It's plain you must leave England. And if you can't go to France, you'd need a refuge somewhere else on the Continent."

"The German states are barbaric, the Dutch are dull, and the Spanish have no use for the English. That leaves only America, I'm afraid." She looked at him, her huge green eyes wide. "Do you actually think I can be disguised as a young boy?"

"We'll have to try," he replied. "I need more clothes myself, so I'll get you some appropriate articles, along with anything special you may want in the way of food. As you've gathered, our space will be severely limited."

"I prefer to take as much of my wardrobe as I can salvage." She gestured toward several large leather boxes in one corner of her sitting room.

Richard made some rapid calculations. "One chest will take care of my needs," he said. "So I estimate we can squeeze in about half of those cases of yours."

"That's all?" She was dismayed, but was resolute. "I prefer saving my head. You realize, I'm sure, that I've placed my future in your hands."

"I've accepted the obligation, and I'll do my best, but I hope you'll remember that this type of problem is as new and strange to me as it is to you."

39

"Somehow we'll manage together, Richard." She smiled and extended her hand.

His hostility toward her melted away. "I wish us good fortune, Mimi," he replied. "We'll need all the luck in the world."

CHAPTER 2

R ICHARD bought enough new clothes for himself to fit into one sea chest, then went shopping for boys' clothes. Mimi Shepherd had told him her measurements, and he purchased shirts, a hat, smock, and breeches. His worst problem was finding boots and shoes for her; footwear worn by aristocrats was custom made by expensive cobblers, but there was insufficient time, so he had to do what he could in the Bristol shops that catered to common people.

His purchases would be delivered later in the day, so, satisfied with his morning's work, he headed back to the White Hart. Somberly clad Puritans were everywhere, but they went about their own business quietly, and none seemed to be aware of the inconspicuously dressed stranger in their midst. No Puritan agents lurked in the street near the entrance to the White Hart, either, so Richard was able to breathe more easily.

Minter Lucey met him in the front hallway. "Our other

guest is being served a meal upstairs," he said, "because we have a visitor, someone who has come here at my invitation to meet you." He led the way into the parlor, where a young man in his early twenties, with pale hair and an athletic build, sat dejectedly in a corner, an untouched mug of ale on a table beside him.

"Sir Richard," Lucey said, "allow me to present Master Dempster Chaney."

Young Chaney tried to smile as they shook hands, but could not quite succeed. Lucey brought Richard a mug of ale, then discreetly withdrew.

Dempster Chaney was unprepossessing at first glance, but first glances were inclined to be deceptive. He appeared slight, but was heavier and more solidly built than he looked and was endowed with wiry muscles as a result of years of hard work on his father's large agricultural estate. His pale hair and eyes gave him a rather nondescript appearance, but as Richard soon learned, a twinkle that appeared often in his eyes indicated there were hidden depths to him. He was dressed like most members of the upper middle class in stout, well-made boots and breeches, a leather jerkin, and an outer cape. Although the middle class was not inclined to carry weapons, a sword hung at Dempster's side with such familiarity that it was obvious he knew how to use it.

"Have I gathered correctly that you wished to meet me?" Richard asked.

The younger man looked despondent. "Lucey insisted, but I know of nothing that you or anyone else can do for me."

He told his story succinctly. His father had been killed while fighting on the Cavalier side in the civil war. Then,

Dempster had been ordered to withdraw from his studies at Edinburgh. Now the victorious Puritans had confiscated his estate and other property, leaving him penniless. And just yesterday the father of his betrothed had terminated the engagement.

Richard was struck by the similarity to his own case. Thinking of Dorothea, he felt sympathy for Chaney's plight.

"Robbin is a girl of great spirit," Dempster said, "and would defy her father. She'd run away with me without hesitation, but I'm virtually bankrupt now. I know of no way to earn a living other than in farming because I was not permitted to complete my medical training. I have no future here: Robbin's father would have no trouble following us, and the Roundheads would send me to prison for corrupting a girl who won't reach her twenty-first birthday for several months."

"You're more fortunate than you realize," Richard said. "Most young women are obedient to their fathers' wishes." He refrained from adding that Dorothea's subservience to her father's will had blighted his own life.

"Robbin would take any risk, Sir Richard, but I can't ask her to run away with me when I have no place to go."

Richard pondered for a time. "Have you thought of emigrating to the colonies in North America?"

"Frequently," Dempster said. "Most people there earn their livings on farms, or so I've read, and I'm prepared to work hard. But passage to the New World costs five sovereigns per passenger, and I don't have ten sovereigns to my name. Nor do I know of a ship that will sail to America in the immediate future. Not that it would be of any help if I did."

Rarely one to make impulsive gestures, Richard nevertheless felt envious of this young man whose sweetheart was self-willed. How different his own life would be if Dorothea had defied her father! "Get your girl," he said brusquely. "Go with her to Captain Brennan of the brig *Anne*. I prefer that you not mention my name, but you have my permission if need be. The only accommodations available are in a general cabin with other passengers—"

"We'll gladly suffer any inconvenience," Dempster interrupted. Slowly the gleam in his eyes faded. "But my basic problem is unsolved. I'd sell my sword, my last remaining possession of value, if I could get ten sovereigns for it."

Richard took two gold coins from his purse and silently handed them to the younger man. A broad smile wreathed Dempster's face as he took the money, then began to unbuckle his sword-belt.

"My own sword serves me well," Richard told him. "You may need your weapon before this adventure ends. Keep it."

"But—but how can I repay you?"

"Give your girl an extra kiss for one who doesn't share your good fortune."

Dempster started to speak, then thought better of it. Something in Sir Richard's troubled countenance told him it would not be wise to ask too many questions about his benefactor's life. "I hope I'll have the chance to show my gratitude to you," he said. "Will we meet again?"

Richard had no intention of admitting, even to a staunch fellow Cavalier, that he, too, intended to sail on the *Anne*. His safety and that of Mimi Shepherd depended on secrecy.

"One often sees friends in this world when least expected," he replied vaguely.

Eager to be on his way, Dempster Chaney thanked him again, then took his leave.

Richard ate cold beef and bread alone in the dining room. His purchases arrived while he was eating, and after his meal he sorted them in his own suite, then went up to the third floor, a bundle under his arm.

"Your own seamstress and bootmaker could do far better for you," he said as the woman made the door secure. "These are the best I could find on short notice."

Mimi looked at the clothes Richard had spread out on a bench and laughed.

"There's no time like the present to find out if our ruse will be effective," Richard told her. "You might start by removing your cosmetics."

"I hadn't thought of that, but it's obvious I must." She went to her bedchamber, returning with her face scrubbed clean. He was startled to see that the absence of rouge, kohl, and other substances in no way detracted from her radiant beauty. For his taste, she looked even lovelier.

"What comes next?" she demanded, making a game of disguising herself.

"Do you have a razor or shears?"

She shook her head. "I have no need for either."

Richard went to his own suite, returning with his razor. He examined her critically, then said, "I dislike having to ask you to sacrifice so many inches of your hair, but I fear there's no choice."

"It will grow again, so that's the least of our problems. Are you a competent barber?"

45

"I've never in my life done anything like this. Hold still, and I'll try to cut it in a straight line." Grasping a handful of the long, red hair that tumbled down her back, he slashed it off at shoulder length.

Mimi sighed gently, but made no comment.

Richard concentrated on the alien task, and when he was done, he was relieved to see that he had cut her hair more or less evenly. Piles of the long strands were now disposed of in a basket.

She hurried into the bedchamber and stared at her reflection in the long pier glass hanging between the windows. "I no longer know myself."

"I must admit there's a change." He refrained from mentioning that she still looked exceptionally attractive.

"So much for minor matters," Mimi said as she turned to face him. "I'm in awe of your efficiency, but what do we do about two major problems?" She cupped her firm, full breasts in her hands.

He tried in vain to hide his discomfort. "This is the best I can manage," he said, and showed her a long strip of unbleached linen several inches wide. "Bind yourself in this to reduce the—uh—protuberances as much as possible."

"You'll have to do it for me. I couldn't make it tight enough." Showing no self-consciousness, she began to unbutton her dress. "You might want to fetch me the boys' smallclothes you bought, too."

Richard hastily went off to the sitting room for the underbreeches he had purchased for her, and when he returned to the bedchamber he saw that she was stark naked, except for a flimsy silk chemise and pantalettes which gave her no apparent concern. She showed no embarrassment, but Richard was very conscious of her appearance and his reaction caused her to giggle. Her slender, feminine body so aroused him that even though he stood at arm's length, color flamed in his face as he handed her the underbreeches.

Mimi was amused as she donned them. "Oh, dear. They're far stiffer than my silks, but I'll try not to scratch or squirm. Now, stand behind me and wrap this strip around my breasts."

He marveled at her tranquility. Dorothea would have been overcome by embarrassment, but Mimi Shepherd seemed unconcerned. He wound the cloth twice around her breasts and tugged gently.

"Much, much tighter," she commanded. "Never fear, I'll tell you quickly enough if you're hurting me."

He pulled harder at the ends of the cloth.

"Enough," she said at last. "Tie off the ends, and cut away what isn't needed."

He did as she had ordered, then finally looked at her. She was examining her reflection critically in the pier glass. "Not long ago young Richard Lovelace promised he'd write an ode that would immortalize my bosom. I'm glad he can't see me now." Her breasts had been reduced to a fraction of their normal size, but no one would have mistaken her for a man.

She climbed into a pair of breeches, stuffing the boys' shirt of coarse wool into it, and then pulled a thick smock over her head. "Not bad," she said after analyzing her reflection again. "What do you think?"

"You should pass muster," Richard told her, and returned to the sitting room for one more item, a cap with a peaked visor. "Pull your hair behind your ears when you wear this," he told her.

The cap did a great deal to assist with her transformation,

but Mimi was not yet satisfied. "Something is still wrong," she said.

Richard laughed for the first time. "I don't believe those diamond earrings are quite suitable," he said. "You'll need to take off your rings, cut your fingernails, and remove that lacquer from them, too."

"When you next see me in this disguise it will be perfect," she said. "How long will I be obliged to wear it on board the ship?"

"That will depend on circumstances," Richard replied.

"We shall have to change the circumstances," Mimi said, wriggling and scratching first her thighs, then her back. "You can't imagine how grateful I am to be a woman. I'd go mad if I had to spend the rest of my days in clothes that itch as if I were being pursued by all of the Puritans' devils."

"It's bad enough," he said, "that the Puritans themselves are hunting for you."

Dempster Chaney waited impatiently until late afternoon, then walked up the path beside the Avon River to a neighborhood of substantial houses and large gardens. These were the homes of Bristol's successful merchants, physicians, and lawyers, all of whom had been unwavering in their loyalty to the Crown prior to the steady series of defeats suffered by the Cavaliers in their war with the Puritans. Now the atmosphere had suddenly changed. No families hosted dinner parties, musical instruments were banished to attics, and a new Nonconformist church was built, which everyone attended in appropriately dark attire.

Dusk was falling as the young man cut through a number of gardens, then paused in what Robbin's father had been fond of calling his grove of statues. Here life-sized reproductions of ancient Greek statues were scattered, and only recently Dempster had remarked to Robbin that soon her father would be obliged to smash the nude figures or clothe them in attire of which the Puritans would approve. This evening they were still in place, however, offering an area of concealment that was useful.

A lamp was lighted in Robbin's second-floor bedroom, and Dempster's heart pounded. He picked up a handful of small pebbles, crept closer to the house, and tossed the stones up against the panes of a leaded glass window.

Elsewhere in the house, a dog barked furiously, then was silenced.

Robbin's father rarely left the place, and if her older brothers had come home from their shop, she would find it difficult to sneak out. Dempster waited as patiently as he could, his temples throbbing, and just as he stooped to pick up more pebbles, the window opened. Robbin appeared, squinting her eyes as she peered out into the darkness.

Dempster caught a glimpse of her blonde hair, paler than his own, and beckoned silently. At last she saw him and understood. The window remained open as she withdrew. He continued to stand, shifting his weight from one foot to the other, until he realized that anyone who glanced out into the garden could see him. Still staring at the open window, he reluctantly withdrew to the grove of statues.

A short time later, a bundle was thrown out of the window, landing with a soft thud on the snow-spotted ground. Dempster resisted the urge to sprint forward and pick it up. Obviously Robbin had been waiting for him and had made her preparations in advance.

A rope made of torn and tied linen sheets was lowered, and a moment later Robbin herself appeared. She climbed to the sill, hampered by her long dress and voluminous cloak, then slowly lowered herself hand under hand down the outside of the ivy-covered wall. The task was almost too great for her, and when she paused for a moment, balanced precariously by resting her foot on the top frame of a window, she appeared to be in danger of falling. Dempster had to curb his instinctive desire to cross the open yard and reach up for her. Overcoming her panic, the girl tightened her grip, then descended more slowly. Dempster's arms ached as he watched her. Ultimately her feet touched the ground, and she snatched her nearby bundle. Knowing where her beloved would be waiting for her, she gathered her skirts and ran as fast as she could to the grove of statues. They embraced, kissing fiercely.

"I won't be missed for about an hour, until I'm called to the dinner table," Robbin whispered. "Then all pandemonium will break loose, and Papa will scour the town for me. Andrew and Theodore are both home tonight—worse luck—so they'll help him."

Robbin was tiny, but her size was belied by her efficiency. She had a nose that was abbreviated and best described as pert, and her figure could have been called pert too, but she moved briskly, with a self-assuredness that more than compensated for the youthful or girlish look that she conveyed. Her hair was as pale a blond as Dempster's and her eyes, which were enormous, were an even more brilliant shade of blue. She was one of those people who seemed to be forever in motion. Even when she was not moving, her features remained animated, and she seemed to exude tremendous energy at all times.

Dempster took the bundle, held Robbin's elbow to guide her as they started across the gardens that would take them to the path beside the Avon, and nodded. Only now did he realize she looked like a Puritan maiden in her black dress with white collar and cuffs, dark bonnet, and ankle-length black cape. "We should have enough time if our luck holds."

"Where are we going?" She took long strides to keep up with him, trusting him completely.

"Wait until we're in the clear," he said.

She was content to accompany him anywhere. "I knew you'd find a way to come for me," she murmured.

Not until they reached the path and it turned into a street nearer the center of Bristol did Dempster explain their situation in full detail.

"Sir Richard must be a wonderful man."

"He appears to be, but we'll discuss him later. We're going straight to the brig, and if I can obtain passage we'll stay on board. I'll find some excuse for the captain so it won't be necessary for us to go ashore again. If our luck is good, your father won't think of having the ships in the harbor searched. He'll probably assume we've gone to London for the help of friends there."

"I think you're right. At least I hope so." Her breath was short, but she managed to ask, "When will we marry, dearest?"

"As soon as possible. But first we need to free ourselves. When did you start dressing like a Roundhead?"

"Today, when I'd hoped you'd come for me. I thought we'd be far less conspicuous if I looked this way."

Dempster nodded in approval. As always, Robbin was a step ahead of him in her thinking.

They were approaching the waterfront now, and having learned the location of the *Anne* before going for the girl, he led her toward it, his grip on her arm tightening when he saw the Roundhead agent on duty at the base of the wharf.

"Who is that man?" Robbin murmured.

He shrugged. "He appears to be watching for someone."

"It won't be you or me," she replied. "So let's walk more slowly and give him enough time to look at us."

Dempster obediently slowed his pace. The Puritan studied them, directing most of his attention to the young woman. He seemed satisfied and averted his gaze.

A seaman, who was coiling a line on the deck, put down the plank that enabled them to board the ship, and they were taken to Captain Brennan's cabin. Dempster introduced himself, then added calmly, "This is my wife, Captain."

Robbin felt as if a bolt of lightning had struck her, but her gentle smile did not waver, even though she realized that she and Dempster would be forced to live a lie until they reached the colonies and could find a clergyman to marry them. But the technical sacrifice of her honor for a time was a small price to pay.

"We're told you sail soon for the colonies, Captain."

"Aye," Brennan replied. "My first port of call will be Boston."

"That's our destination," Dempster said glibly. "Can you find room for us?"

"There are two places left in the general cabin, but you'll share it with three others."

It was not easy for Dempster to say, "We don't mind."

Robbin nodded cheerfully too, although her heart sank. The lack of privacy on board the brig might make it necessary to wait until they reached the New World before she and Dempster slept together.

"I charge five sovereigns a head," Captain Brennan said sternly. "Payable in advance."

Dempster handed him the gold coins. The brig's master held them to the light and bit them before he was satisfied. "You have passage," he said. "Come back at this same time tomorrow for the sailing."

"We wonder," Dempster said, his voice even in spite of his fears, "if we might stay on board until we sail."

Robbin astonished her betrothed by speaking in the thick accent of Northumberland. "We'll save a tidy sum," she said, "and I be weary after spending so many days on the road."

"Stay, if you like," the master told them. "But my cook won't come aboard until dawn, so you'll get no meal before breakfast tomorrow."

"Oh, we've had our supper," Robbin lied. "So we're much obliged to ye."

She was even more extraordinary than Dempster had known.

The master conducted them to the large cabin. "If you decide to stretch your legs ashore," he said, "just remember the sailing hour." Nodding to them, he left the cabin.

"So far so good," Dempster said when they were alone. "Where did you learn that north country accent?"

"There are many things about me that you don't yet know," Robbin replied demurely. "I thought a woman's touch was needed so we could stay on board. That's why I intervened. It's important that we not leave this ship. We've found favor with the gods and goddesses of the Greeks, Romans, and Norsemen who protect lovers, and we're not going to offend them by taking needless chances. We'll be that much hungrier for breakfast after we've fasted tonight."

She was right, as usual. "We'll have a long evening ahead of us, but at least we'll be safe."

The young couple assumed that the other passengers who would occupy the cabin with them would not arrive until the following day, so they could start their honeymoon without delay, even though their wedding necessarily had to be postponed. "The time will pass quickly," Robbin said with a broad smile. "We'll find ways to keep busy."

Richard was eating breakfast when a member of the *Anne*'s crew brought word to the White Hart that the brig would sail on the early-evening tide. Minter Lucey took the word to Lady Dawn, but she remained secluded in her suite. Later in the morning she sent for the manservant, saying her traveling cases were ready.

When Richard saw her three leather boxes, he shook his head. It would be difficult to find a place in the cabin for his one small sea chest, but it was apparent that the daughter of a prominent earl did not think in terms of others' convenience. The day passed slowly, and at noon Richard ate heartily, enjoying his last meal on land for many weeks to come.

Midafternoon he went to the stable himself for Prince Henry and walked the horse beside the cart in which Lady Dawn's many belongings, his few possessions, and the fodder and blankets for his mount were piled. Captain Brennan materialized to supervise the stowing of the various possessions on board, and Prince Henry was penned in an open stall built for him on the aft deck.

Minter Lucey was waiting at the inn when the young

baronet returned, and Richard frowned as he said, "The Roundheads have doubled their watch. There were two agents standing duty at the wharf just now."

"Another is just down the street a short distance, where he can keep an eye on the front door," Lucey said. "I wonder if they've caught wind of something."

"We'll find out soon enough," Richard replied.

The innkeeper nodded dolefully. "Yes, it's too late now to change your plans, if you get my meaning."

"There's no other way to leave," Richard replied, conscious of the mission the Earl of Newcastle had asked him to perform regarding the Royalists in the American colonies.

"You don't think the lady will be recognized?" Lucey asked.

A voice came to them from the staircase. "I don't recognize myself, Master Lucey," Mimi called, approaching them in boys' attire.

The innkeeper, who had known nothing of the scheme, could only gape at her. Richard examined her carefully and could find no fault with her appearance. Her nails, which had been cut short, were free of lacquer, she wore no jewelry of any kind, and her bulky smock, along with the band of linen she had managed to affix by herself, made her prominent breasts inconspicuous.

"I gather you approve," she said to Richard, turning slowly for his benefit.

He told her about the increase in the Puritans' watch. "I have no idea whether they've learned specifics or are just being more careful because they know the *Anne* is sailing this evening. But we can't afford any slips."

Mimi thought for a moment, then went to the hearth and, after drawing a finger across it, added a smudge to the bridge of her nose and one cheek. "I believe I could pass as a boy in the slums of London now," she said.

She might be selfish and indifferent to the rights of others, but Richard had to admire her courage. Oliver Cromwell had been gallant in his treatment of Queen Henrietta Maria, permitting her to go freely to France with her children, in keeping with his frequently quoted statement that Puritans do not wage war against women. But others who had been close to King Charles would be made to suffer for their sins. The daughter of the Earl of Sturbridge, who appeared to have been one of the monarch's mistresses, would spend many years in prison and be subjected to endless humiliations should she be captured.

Lucey was still apprehensive. "What you've done is very clever," he said, "but it may not be enough. I'm sure there's time for me to locate eight or ten Royalists who know how to handle swords. I believe you should have an escort."

Mimi deferred to her protector.

"That wouldn't do," Richard said. "We'd be calling attention to our flight, and a battle would surely develop on the wharf. Even if we succeeded in sailing, it would take time for the brig to make her way out of the Severn estuary and Bristol Channel into the open sea. A swift rider could carry word to the coast, and a warship would overtake us easily. Remember that the Roundheads control the New Model Navy now. Not only would we be captured, but the master of the brig—who is useful to our cause in many ways—would be exposed also. We'll keep to our plan and hope for the best."

Lucey had been overruled and could only bow in resignation. "Let me offer you a drink before you go," he said. "A part of poor King Charles's wine cellar was brought here, and I've been told to use it as my own."

"So you should, Master Lucey," Mimi said as she watched him pour brandy into three glasses. "Richard and I are escaping to a new land, primitive though it may be, but you're staying on here to face countless dangers every day of your life."

The innkeeper smiled and shook his head as he placed a small bowl of water on a table. "If I do say so, your ladyship, I have a rich, strong voice, and as long as I sing the Puritans' hymns loudly enough in their church on Sundays and at their prayer meetings, I'll be safe, if you get my meaning. Most of them squeak like mice when they sing."

He, too, had real courage, Richard thought.

Mimi raised her glass and savored the brandy's bouquet. She was reminded of the brandy-flavored plum pudding that was a staple feature at all family meals at her father's estate in the winter. No dinner would have been complete without it, and she almost succumbed to a nostalgia for a past that could never be retrieved. "What a lovely, familiar aroma," she said, and for a moment threatened to become tearful. But she recovered quickly and went through the ritual of toasting the young king-across-the-water. "To Charles the Second," she said softly. "To you, Master Lucey, and to our success in reaching our destination."

They drank in solemn silence. The brandy, richer and more mellow than any Richard had ever tasted, warmed his throat as it slid down. "We'll be on our way," he said, glancing out of the nearest window at the gathering dusk. After shaking Lucey's hand, he threw his cloak over his shoulders, clapped the detested Puritan hat onto his head, and picked up his rifle. "Boy," he ordered, "carry this for me."

It took a moment for Mimi to realize he was speaking to her. "Is it loaded?" she asked in alarm.

He shook his head. "My other weapons will speak for us if they're needed. Walk a half-step behind me, no more and no less, and keep up the pace. We're not going for a stroll."

"Yes, master," she replied, her tone mocking. "Be good enough to remember that nature made your legs longer than mine, and these shoes are an abomination."

"Come along," he said, and stepped boldly onto the street. He saw the Puritan agent standing in a doorway and pretended to ignore him. The Puritan stared hard at the man and the boy, then lost interest in them.

"We've passed the first test," Richard said as they rounded the corner. "Am I walking too fast?"

"I'm doing my best," Mimi replied grimly. "So far, I'm keeping up with you."

They did not speak again until they drew close to the waterfront. "Steady now," Richard said. "The real test is directly ahead." His companion made no reply.

He emerged from the street closest to the *Anne* and, looking across the street, saw the two Puritan agents. Crew members were busy on the deck of the ship, their bustle indicating they were preparing to sail. The agents looked searchingly at Richard, whom they knew now by sight, and then they devoted their full attention to the boy who was struggling in an attempt not to fall behind.

The half-light of nightfall was deceptive, but an additional diversion was needed, and Richard felt inspired. Without warning he increased his pace. Then, as he approached the two Puritans, he halted abruptly.

"Boy," he roared, "I've warned you for the last time not to lag behind. You have feet and legs! Use them!"

Giving Mimi no chance to reply, he reached out and cuffed her hard with an open hand across the side of the head. She staggered but managed to regain her balance, then half-walked, half-ran as Richard headed for the plank that extended from the wharf to the deck. The agents lost all interest in the pair. They had been warned that Lady Dawn Shepherd might appear in disguise, but it was inconceivable to them that the most celebrated beauty at the court of the late Charles I would be subjected to a severe cuffing.

Ignoring the plank, Richard leaped across the open space onto the deck. Mimi hesitated, the sight of the black water far below making her apprehensive. Richard had intended to let her fend for herself, but every moment's delay was dangerous. "Boy, for tuppence I'd leave you behind," he shouted as he reached for her arm, then hauled her onto the deck so savagely that he sent her sprawling. One of the Roundhead agents snickered.

Allowing Mimi to pull herself to her feet, Richard called, "Good evening, Captain. I trust I haven't kept you waiting."

"You're just in time," the master replied from his quarterdeck. "In another ten minutes you'd have found me gone."

"We'll go below now," Richard told Mimi, and preceding her to the open hatch, he quickly climbed down to the inner passageway.

She followed more slowly, her step tentative on the ladder. He waited, then silently led her to their tiny cubicle, walking ahead of her into the cabin. She closed the door behind her, then said in a cold rage, "You could have warned me that you intended to beat me and knock me down."

"My apologies, but I didn't think of that treatment until the time came. You must admit it was effective. I saw the agents' faces, and they knew you couldn't be the only surviving member of Sturbridge's immediate family."

"My ears are still ringing. Do you frequently beat women?" she demanded sarcastically.

"This was the first time—and, I hope, the last. Besides, I cuffed my stupid servant, not you. Let me make amends. The lower bunk is yours."

She sank onto one of her leather clothes boxes and looked around slowly. "You and I will share this—this wardrobe closet—for the next six to eight weeks?"

He shrugged. "I tried to tell you. Queen Henrietta Maria's accommodations when she sailed to France were little better than this."

"I was intending to avenge myself," she said with a faint smile, "but I'm afraid I'll have to give up my plans. When two people are crammed together like this, they are obliged to make concessions so they don't kill each other."

Richard grinned, then sobered as they heard shouts and pounding footsteps on the deck above. Drawing his double-barreled pistol, he moved quickly to the locked door.

"What's wrong?" Mimi asked, her voice lowered.

"It may be nothing, it may be significant. I'm ignorant of what is and isn't normal on board a ship. But we've come this far unscathed, and I'm taking no chances." He stood still, close to the door, his pistol cocked.

Mimi did not speak until they heard the ship's timbers creak faintly. Then she jumped to her feet and peered out of the square window. "We're moving! We're leaving the wharf!" She sounded ecstatic.

Richard left his post long enough to join her at the window, and saw for himself that the brig was underway, moving at a snail's pace as she threaded a path through the crowded harbor. A feeling of great relief swept over him, but he remained cautious. "This is the start," he acknowledged, "but we're not out of trouble yet."

She looked at him with mischief in her green eyes. "I do declare, sir, you're as determined as Puritan clergymen to stifle joy!" Giving in to a sudden impulse, she threw her arms around his neck and kissed him soundly.

The startled Richard could not help responding, and for some moments he returned the kiss, holding the woman in a firm embrace. Then he disengaged himself and took a single backward step, which was as far as he could go without falling over one of her leather boxes. "Allow me to say something," he said, curbing his desire. "I do not address this remark to my companion, Mimi, or to Lady Dawn Shepherd. I speak as a man whose baronetcy places him at the bottom of the order of nobility and whose blood therefore is far more red than blue. I speak to a very attractive woman with whom circumstances—not of her making or my own—force me to share these cramped quarters. I am not a seducer. I do not engage in idle lovemaking. But my ability to control my natural urges is limited. If such a gesture should be repeated, I shall not be held responsible for the consequences."

"I'll remember your warning, sir," she said with mock gravity, but her ebullience was not to be denied. The danger of capture and imprisonment was fading, and her spirits continued to soar, so she laughed quietly and at length. "Do I have your permission to change into my own clothes and resume my true identity?"

"You may not!" he replied emphatically. "Until we're clear of British territorial waters we could be halted and searched at any time by a New Model Navy warship. You can be sure that detailed descriptions of you—and possibly of me—have been distributed to the captains of the navy. So far we've managed to elude our pursuers, but it would be unfortunate if you were hauled back to England in chains."

"I'd regard it as somewhat worse than misfortune," she murmured, his cold logic quickly restoring her sense of balance. "As much as I hate this uncomfortable disguise, I'll continue to follow your directions."

Her penitence softened him. "It will do no harm," he said, "if we go up to the deck to watch our departure. Just remember, speak to no one, because your voice will give you away."

They went down the companionway to the ladder, which Mimi climbed with some difficulty, and then she meekly followed him to the starboard rail. The *Anne* was still crawling, with only her jib raised, but soon she left the harbor behind, and Captain Brennan called a series of commands, relayed by a mate to the crew. The large sails overhead were unfurled, opening with a cracking sound and filling rapidly in the chilly breeze, and the brig seemed to leap forward through the choppy waters of the Severn estuary.

For some moments the couple looked back at the lights of Bristol, which gradually grew smaller in the distance. A sense of sadness, so deep that it caused him physical distress, crept over Richard. He was leaving the native land he loved, going into exile in a distant country, having committed no crime other than that of being totally loyal to a king whose ancestors had been well served by many generations of Dunstables. The House of Commons supposedly represented the people of the realm, but the present members were bigoted zealots who had killed the monarch, caused thousands to shed blood, and divided the nation.

Richard would do what was required of him in the colonies to rid Britain of the Puritan scourge, but a lump formed in his throat when he realized he might be forced to wait many years before he would be welcome here. Depending on the strength of the Puritan conquest, he might die on alien soil.

Mimi grieved for her England, too. She stood rigidly still, her fists tightly clenched at her sides, and silent tears rolled slowly down her cheeks. Richard could say nothing to comfort her, but he placed a hand on her shoulder for a moment, and he could feel her relax slightly. Neither realized it, but their mutual grief brought them closer together.

Others obviously felt as they did. Some distance down the deck, a short, squat woman in her forties, poorly dressed, was weeping copiously. A youth in his late teens, dark and also short, made clumsy, ineffectual attempts to comfort her.

Then a couple who had been standing at the port rail hastily crossed the deck, and a beaming Dempster Chaney extended his hand. "I didn't know you'd be making this voyage, too, Sir Rich—"

"No titles, if you please, Master Chaney," Richard said, interrupting him. The young man understood and presented a beaming Robbin to his benefactor.

Richard, who made no attempt to introduce the boy at his side, was pleased that he had helped the pair. Robbin was very pretty and young, reminding him of Dorothea, and he felt a fresh stab at what his fealty to the Crown had cost him.

Dempster and the girl related their story briefly, saying they had come on board the previous day and had not gone ashore again. Obviously, their efforts had succeeded, for they had not been found by her father.

"We have only one problem now," Robbin said, "and I'm afraid it can't be solved until we reach the colonies. We had no opportunity to be married before we sailed."

Mimi tugged at Richard's sleeve and whispered to him, "That's no problem. The captain can marry them."

Richard repeated her statement. The young couple, knowing nothing of the customs of the sea, were both astonished and overjoyed. "We'll go to him at once!" Robbin cried.

"He's busy, and he needs to keep watch for warships that could halt us and return all of us to Bristol," Richard said. "I urge you to wait until we put the British Isles behind us."

Further conversation on the subject was delayed by the approach of the short woman, who was still red-eyed. The youth who had stood beside her trailed her. "Mollie Williams is me name, and this here is me son, Bart," she announced. "I've been quiet long enough, and now I'll speak out as loud as I please. God preserve the soul of King Charlie, and may He soon put young Charlie on the throne!"

"Amen," Mimi muttered inaudibly. The others nodded in solemn agreement. All, it was plain, were Cavalier sympathizers.

Mollie Williams lost no time in telling her story to the sympathetic audience. She had served for many years on the staff of Whitehall Palace as a cook, she declared, adding proudly, "Many's the roast I grilled for King Charlie, and many's the sole I poached and boned for him."

"You were discharged?" Richard asked.

She shook her head. "I walked out afore I had trouble. The poor need to be meek, like the Lord said, so I kept me mouth closed tight and stayed at me stove all the while that Charlie was off fighting the Roundheads. But Bart here, he thinks he's as good as a duke or a marquess. He lost his twin brother, me dear son, John, in the fighting. Since that day, he's shot off his fat mouth, telling all who'd listen to him that the Roundheads are scum!"

"So they are," her son pronounced defiantly.

"There's none will deny it, lad," Mollie told him as she shook her head sadly. "But the likes of us can't afford to speak free. When a Puritan investigator came to the Whitehall kitchen and asked me so many questions I scarce knew me own name, it was time for us to be on our way. Every last farthing I'd saved took us to Bristol and bought passage."

"It was worth it, Ma," Bart said, reviving an old quarrel. "Now we're free!"

"The likes of us will never be free," she declared. "But here we be, in this tub that tips and swoops and bounces, so there's naught we can do to turn back the clock."

A gong sounded below.

"I think the passengers are being called to supper," Mimi whispered to Richard.

He repeated her observation, and they obediently trooped down the hatch and made their way forward to the small wardroom, barely large enough for a round table and straight-backed chairs, where the *Anne*'s two mates had already seated themselves. Again, when names were exchanged, Richard carefully refrained from introducing the boy who moved to the place beside him.

The cook appeared with a pot of steaming thick soup, which he placed without ceremony in front of the first mate. Then the officer began to ladle the soup into bowls. "Ladies and gentlemen," he said, "enjoy the fresh foods while you're able. Soon enough we'll live on beans, bacon, hard-tack, salt fish, and bully beef. You'll lose weight before the voyage ends."

"Those of us who like sea fare may gain weight." The speaker was a late arrival who came into the wardroom, bending so he wouldn't hit his head on the bulkhead above the entrance. He was tall and thin, with a balding head and small, piercing eyes; his deep blue velvet coat, cream-colored waistcoat, satin breeches, and ruffled shirt instantly marked him as a Cavalier. His smile, as he took the one vacant chair without apology, resembled a grimace, and looking slowly around the table, he introduced himself only as Robertson.

Richard wondered if the man had dared to walk past the Roundhead agents on the wharf in attire that clearly identified him as a Royalist. If he had, either he was very bold or he lacked common sense.

Mollie Williams chatted at length, Richard made an occasional comment, and Robbin and Dempster joined in the talk, too. But Robertson made it impossible for others to know him. He lapsed into complete silence, saying nothing about himself and making no comment on any other subject. But he was not indifferent to the fellow passengers with whom he would live in close quarters for the next month and a half. On the contrary, he stared intently at each of them in turn.

The man's steady gaze irritated Richard, and he felt uneasy when Robertson concentrated at length on the boy who sat obediently, saying nothing. Mimi seemed to fascinate him, and he scrutinized her repeatedly. She handled the situation with aplomb, eating steadily, never glancing in the man's direction, and pretending to be unaware of his interest.

The main dish was mutton, served with boiled potatoes and greens, and all of the passengers except Robertson took the advice of the first mate and left the hardtack untouched. "You'll have your fill of it soon enough," he told them.

The dessert was pudding so sweet that Richard took only one taste, as did Mimi.

"If you ain't eating your pudding I'll relieve you of it," Bart said. "I were taught never to waste food, weren't I, Ma?" He half-stood and reached for the two plates.

"You was taught manners, too," Mollie said. Her son ignored the remark and quickly gulped the puddings.

After the meal ended, Dempster and Robbin went out to the open deck again, for a time preferring the cold to sharing their cabin with Mollie, her son, and the dour Robertson. Richard and the boy went directly to their own cabin.

Mimi removed her cap and shook out her hair as she sat on a leather box. "If that man had stared at me for one moment longer," she said, "I think I would have screamed. Do you suppose he was trying to memorize my features and every angle in my face?"

"I have no idea," Richard replied. "But I don't like him. Say nothing of any significance in front of him, and we'll keep him under observation, at least until we learn more about him."

"What harm can he do?" She peeled off her smock and began to unbutton her coarse shirt.

Richard turned away from her, deliberately averting his gaze, but he couldn't avoid seeing the frilly silk nightgown she took from a clothing box. Keeping his hands off her when she was easily within reach was going to be an even more difficult problem than he had anticipated.

"What a blessed relief to be rid of that breastband," Mimi said behind his back with a sigh. "You were very clever to think of it, but I can't help wishing you were less ingenious."

He fled to the companionway, waiting there until he felt reasonably certain she had changed into her nightclothes and completed her ablutions. Then, when he returned to the cabin, he deliberately extinguished the oil lamp before undressing and climbing into the upper bunk, which was barely long enough for him. "Good night," he called.

There was silence for a moment, and then Mimi said, "I'd like to ask you something, but you needn't answer my question if it makes you uncomfortable. Are you afraid of me?"

Richard chuckled. "Not of you, but of myself. Only a few days ago I was engaged to marry the prettiest girl in Lincolnshire. Now, through a turn of events, I'm sharing these close quarters with the loveliest woman in all of England. I find the situation disconcerting."

"You think I'd give in to you if you tried to make love to me?"

As always, Mimi knew what she was doing in the realm of sex. She had not been the mistress of the late King Charles, nor had she engaged in any other affairs that had

68

been attributed to her, but that didn't mean she was sexually inexperienced; quite the contrary. Like so many members of her class, she had taken lovers as she chose them, and she had made her selections with great care, enjoying the favors of perhaps a half-dozen distinguished men over the years. Considering the fact that she was in her mid-twenties and that her being of one of Britain's first families offered unlimited opportunities, she could not be considered sexually promiscuous by the standards of the time.

"I hadn't thought of how you'd respond." He was being honest with himself as well as with her.

"Take my word for it, Richard, I'd allow you no liberties, even though the strains in the cabin might become intolerable."

"I'm glad to hear it."

"I'm no angel," Mimi said, "but I'm not promiscuous, either, at least according to my standards. I won't pretend I must be romantically committed before I'll make love to a man. I'm not all that certain I've even been in love. But I must know him well, have confidence in him, and feel close to him."

Richard's relief was mingled with a sense of regret. "You'll be safe with me because we're strangers."

She chuckled. "Do you think Newcastle would believe that?"

"No," he replied slowly, "but Uncle William is a worldly man."

"Poor Charlie would have taken my word. He accepted anything I told him."

Richard did not know what to reply. For a moment Mimi was silent, and then she said, "You think I was

Charlie's mistress." She was stating a fact, not asking a question. "I could read it in your face the first time I mentioned him."

"Your relationship with King Charles is none of my business."

"Nor anyone else's, although half the court was convinced I slept with him." There was a curious, melancholy note in her voice. "Well, I didn't. My father's summer estate was just down the road from Charlie's hunting lodge in Scotland, and I knew him almost as well as I knew my own parents. When I was a little girl, I discovered he had been attentive to my mother before he married that horrid Henrietta Maria. When I was six or seven, I think it was, I had a romantic daydream—a fantasy—that Charlie was actually my father. Poor Mama never looked at any man except my father. Then, when Papa died, Charlie took me under his protection. I was just growing up, men were paying attention to me for the first time, and it was a great help to pretend that Charlie was my lover. I was spared the persistent attention of rakes and fortune hunters. Charlie played the game so enthusiastically, as he did everything, that even the foolish Henrietta Maria snubbed me."

"You needn't have told me any of this," he said, "but thank you."

Her sigh floated up to him. "Ah, well, none of it matters anymore. The Sturbridge estates have been confiscated, and no doubt our possessions will be given to some of Cromwell's cronies. The only funds left to me are in my purse, and when they're gone, I'll be forced to depend on the charity of old family friends. So I needn't worry about fortune hunters. The others I can handle."

"You sound quite sure of yourself."

"You must have seen the dagger I keep strapped to my leg. It has a sobering influence on unwanted advances." She laughed, then said, "Sleep well, Richie."

He was startled by her use of the diminutive version of his name, which was what his parents had called him and was known only by a handful of close family friends. Apparently Uncle William had told Mimi more about him than he had realized.

The cabin was chilly, but it was warm beneath the blankets, and, ordinarily, Richard would have dropped off to sleep almost at once. Instead, he remained wide awake. He could not rid himself of the tensions he had endured since he had been forced to leave Lincolnshire so hastily, and the proximity of the ravishing beauty in the bunk below his further disturbed him. As the brig plowed through the rough waters of the Bristol Channel, rolling and pitching endlessly, she was carrying him farther from Dorothea.

The time had come, he reflected, to try to put dear Dorothea out of his mind for all time. Soon she would be wed to some Puritan functionary whom her father regarded as a suitable mate for her, but even that was irrelevant. She had been forcibly removed from his orbit, and never would she be his. All the same, he told himself, he would continue to love her in spite of his efforts to the contrary.

When he awakened at dawn, Richard felt confused. He realized he had been dreaming, but he couldn't quite decipher whether Dorothea or Mimi had been present in the dream. When he climbed down from his bunk, he saw that Mimi was huddled beneath her blankets, and he could make out only the crown of her red hair. He washed and shaved in very cold water, not learning until later that reasonable quantities of hot water could be obtained from the galley.

Then, he went up to the aft deck to attend to his horse's needs. Prince Henry was frisky, ready for a gallop across rolling fields, and Richard stroked his muzzle softly. "You'll have to be patient, my friend," he said. "I'm allowed to walk you when no one else is on deck, but we won't be able to romp until we reach Boston."

The expression in the mount's alert brown eyes seemed to indicate that he understood what his master was saying to him. In any event, he seemed comforted.

The *Anne* was moving slowly now under reduced sail, and a thick gray-white fog that hid her upper sails from view enveloped the entire ship. It was impossible to see more than a few yards in any direction. Richard walked his stallion for the better part of an hour, pacing up and down the deck. Except for the mate who had the watch and the quartermaster at the wheel, the vessel seemed deserted.

The sounding of the breakfast gong brought the passengers to life. Captain Brennan elected to join them at the table, and Mollie Williams endeared herself to the entire company by offering to help in the galley whenever she might be wanted there. The master promptly accepted, and after she had gone off to consult with the cook, she announced that she would prepare one of her special stews for noon dinner.

The last to appear was Mimi, wearing her boy's attire, and there were no signs of the strain in her face; her eyes were so clear that she could have been a lad in his early teens. The dour Robertson, who answered in monosyllables when remarks were addressed to him, again studied her.

"We're moving through the Bristol Channel," Captain Brennan told the passengers. "A little later this morning, when the fog clears—as it will—you'll see Wales on the horizon to starboard if you look sharp. We're sailing close to Devon and Cornwall on the port side, so land will be much easier to see there."

The entire group laughed when Robbin asked, "If ye please, Captain, which side be port and which be starboard? I'm terribly confused."

Even Robertson smiled.

"Nothing to be ashamed of, missus. Port is left, and starboard is right. You may wish to remember it easily by recalling that port and left have four letters each," answered the ship's master.

At the end of the meal, as the others began to file out, Dempster said, "Captain Brennan, can you spare my wife and me a minute of your time?"

"Several minutes, if you wish," he replied genially, and looked at his fat pocket watch. "I'm not due to relieve the mate on duty for another half-hour."

Suddenly, the scarlet-faced Dempster became tongue-tied. Robbin had to speak for them. "It's this way, Captain," she said, deciding to terminate her north country accent along with their ruse. "Master Chaney—well, he isn't actually my husband yet. We were eloping when we came to the *Anne*—"

"—and because we stayed on board," Dempster cut in, finding his voice, "we had no opportunity to go before a minister. We're told you have the authority to marry us. Will you?"

Brennan looked at the earnest young couple who were holding their collective breath as they awaited his reply.

"Why were you eloping?" As a father with a daughter of his own, for whom he had named his brig, he believed he had the right to inquire.

"Robbin's father forbade us to see each other again," Dempster said, "because I made no secret of my Cavalier sentiments. He became a turncoat, and for his own protection he would have given her to some filthy Roundhead."

"I'd have preferred to die," Robbin said fiercely.

The ship's master made up his mind quickly. "Very well, as a devoted subject of Charles the First, I know your feelings. Come to my cabin, where I keep my *Book of Common Prayer*—well hidden, of course, so the Puritan customs inspectors won't find it and destroy it. I'll have you wed in no time, and this afternoon I'll write out a certificate for you to prove you've legally become man and wife."

When they reached his cabin he raced through the ceremony, halting abruptly only when they discovered that Dempster had no ring to put on his wife's left hand. Robbin solved the problem by taking a plain ring from her right hand.

After they had been pronounced man and wife, the captain said it was time for him to go to the quarterdeck.

"Just one more favor," Robbin said. "Everyone thinks we've been married earlier, and it would be embarrassing if they learned the truth about us."

"Only Sir Rich—ah, Master Dunstable knows our real situation, and I'll explain to him in private," Dempster added.

"I don't talk out of turn," the captain said, and left them.

They wandered hand in hand to the prow, where they found Richard standing with his young servant, both of them straining for a glimpse of land as the fog began to lift.

"We're married now," a happy Dempster said.

"The captain just this minute performed the ceremony in his cabin," Robbin added.

Mimi could keep silent no longer. "How wonderful!" she exclaimed, and impulsively kissed the bride, then the groom.

Her clear soprano could have been that of no one but a young woman, and the honeymoon couple stared at the boy incredulously.

Richard tried to repair the damage as best he could. "There may be more than one secret on this ship that needs keeping," he warned somberly. "Off yonder you see the coast of Devon, crawling with Puritans. Off to the right that smudge is Wales, where there are still more Puritans. We'll be obliged if you'll keep your discovery to yourselves until we're certain that all danger is ended."

CHAPTER 3

THE *Anne* sailed out of the Bristol Channel, leaving Land's End behind and moving into the open Atlantic Ocean beyond the Isles of Scilly. The passengers rejoiced, believing it now unlikely that the brig would be intercepted by a New Model Navy warship. But Richard questioned the master closely on the matter.

"It all depends," Captain Brennan said. "If I happened to be carrying someone the Roundheads really wanted—which I hope I'm not—and they knew he was on board, we wouldn't be safe until we sailed at least another hundred miles from Britain. Then our chances would improve because no ship is easy to find in a sea as vast as the Atlantic."

Richard immediately urged Mimi not to abandon her disguise as yet, and she agreed cheerfully, in spite of the acute discomfort caused by the tightly fitting breastband and her need to keep silent in the presence of others. "I trust your judgment," she said. "If I didn't, I wouldn't have come this far."

Gradually they were getting to know each other better, and in the cramped cabin they established routines that permitted each of them some privacy. To Richard's surprise, Mimi insisted on making up the sheets and blankets on both of their bunks every morning.

"There's no need for you to do a servant's work for me," he told her. "I'm capable of making my own bed."

"You don't understand," she replied proudly. "Never in all my life have I done anything practical like making a bed. I'm hoping that before this voyage ends, I can persuade Mollie to teach me to cook."

He grinned broadly. "Forgive me for smiling," he said, "but I can't picture you settling down into domestic life as a housewife in a colonial town like Boston."

"I have no intention of going to Boston," Mimi replied.

He was surprised. "Oh?"

"You know so much about me already that you may as well hear the rest," she said. "Newcastle and several others told me to go to a town in the Virginia colony called Middle Plantation. Near it is a large plantation owned by a wealthy, devoted Cavalier whose name is Horace Laing."

"I've never heard of Master Laing, but there's no reason he should have been mentioned to me."

"All I know is that he has helped any number of the king's party begin new lives. I can't possibly go back to England until young Charlie gains the throne—if he ever does—so it may be a long while before I go home. Years ago, Captain John Smith, one of the first New World settlers of Virginia, was my parents' guest. They repeated his tales of Virginia to me since I was a child, so perhaps I'll settle there."

"But what will you do?" Richard wanted to know.

78

"If land is still cheap, I hope my funds will be sufficient to buy a small plantation that Master Laing will help me find. Then I'll hire a staff to operate it for me."

"That makes sense," he said. "Certainly help won't be expensive. Why, on this ship alone, Dempster and Robbin don't have a penny, and Mollie Williams admits that she and her son are paupers."

Their talk was interrupted by the shout of the lookout. "Sail ho!"

Richard always carried his knife-belt, but now he also strapped on his sword before they hurried to the open deck.

The other passengers were clustering there, too. "There she is, off the port bow," Dempster Chaney said, and pointed.

Mimi instinctively moved closer to Richard. A thorough New Model Navy search was certain to reveal her identity.

The ship was still little bigger than a white dot on the horizon, but she grew larger moment by moment. Captain Brennan, standing on his quarterdeck, caught Richard's eye and shrugged. He could not outrun a warship, and a battle would be suicidal, so he would be compelled to submit to any indignity imposed on him. As a seasoned commercial mariner, he expected the worst while hoping for the best.

The intruder drew still closer, and it became evident that she was a warship, a frigate of twenty-four guns.

"Sir," one of the mates said, "shall I direct the men to assume their posts?"

"It's not necessary just yet," Captain Brennan replied, and raised his voice. "Bos'n, you may raise our ensign."

"Raise the ensign," the boatswain called.

Within moments, the Union Jack was fluttering at the brig's masthead. The frigate hoisted her colors too, and the passengers were relieved when they saw the gold-and-white lilies of France. Robbin was the first to identify it. "The *fleur-de-lis!*"

Richard smiled at Mimi. "We have nothing to fear now."

She was wildly excited and drew him apart from the others. "You're quite certain she's French? That this isn't a New Model Navy trick of some sort?"

"We can only hope it's not. If it's French, we have nothing to fear."

She nodded, then turned and went below.

Somewhat mystified by her unexplained leave-taking, Richard returned to the deck rail and watched the warship as she bore down on the little brig. He knew that the First Minister of France, Cardinal Mazarin, the guardian of the Boy-King Louis XIV, was a staunch supporter of the House of Stuart. Queen Henrietta Maria was the sister of the late Louis XIII, and Mazarin had given refuge not only to her and her children, but to many nobles who had followed the British royal family into exile. There was no possibility that any of the passengers would be taken prisoner and turned over to the Puritans. Even Mimi, should her identity become known, would be safe; French officers, always aware of the latest gossip, would be delighted to tell Queen Henrietta Maria that the young woman she disliked was en route to the New World.

Ultimately, the frigate sent up a signal that read: *Heave to*. Captain Brennan had no choice and complied with the order. A longboat, manned by eight oarsmen, was lowered from the upper deck of the warship into the water, and a junior officer in a blue-and-white uniform climbed down a ladder to it, followed by a dozen soldiers armed with muskets and bayonets.

"Why in the devil should the French send a party to board me?" Captain Brennan demanded, thinking aloud.

No one could answer his question.

As the longboat started across the open water, Mimi emerged from the hatch. The boy had been transformed into the dazzling Lady Dawn Shepherd, daughter and heiress of the Earl of Sturbridge. Her low-cut gown of pale green velvet hugged her incomparable figure, sandals with towering heels added to her height, and on her head was perched a feathered Cavalier hat, jauntily cocked to one side. Diamonds glittered at her throat, ears, fingers, and wrists. She wore cosmetics suitable for an appearance at a Stuart court.

The brig's officers, crew, and passengers gaped, and Captain Brennan broke the silence. "I'll be damned," he said.

Mollie Williams dropped to the deck in a deep curtsy. "I was sure I knowed you," she cried. "Lady Dawn Shepherd it is, God save us all."

Only the man known as Robertson seemed not particularly surprised, and a tight smile compressed his lips as he stared.

Richard grinned broadly as he bowed and offered Mimi his arm. "You do know how to put on a first-rate show," he said in a low tone.

"I decided to greet our visitors as myself. This dress is rather fetching, don't you think? It's one of my favorites." Seeming impervious to the cold, she was enjoying herself, relishing the sensation she was creating.

The French officer came on deck, his men close behind him, and stopped short when he caught sight of the radiant beauty. Then he remembered his duty and marched stiff-legged to the quarterdeck. His troops, obviously accustomed to such maneuvers, promptly formed a half-circle around the raised quarterdeck platform.

The officer saluted smartly. "Enseigne Le Brun of His Christian Majesty's Navy," he said. "I regret the inconvenience I caused by halting you on the high seas, Captain, but this cannot be helped."

"Why can't it?" Captain Brennan was not intimidated.

"Our countries are close to war, Captain, because your usurper government chose to remove the head of the unfortunate King Charles. Cardinal Mazarin himself has issued a directive to all ships of His Christian Majesty's fleet, ordering them to halt all British merchant ships and to remove any Puritans of consequence. If you understand French, I shall gladly read the order to you."

"I don't know a word of your language, and I assure you there are no Puritans in this company. On the contrary, I'm carrying some Cavalier refugees to the New World."

"I do not doubt your word, sir," the Frenchman replied in his strongly accented English. "But you will not object if I interrogate them myself. Your cabin will be fine for the purpose."

"I prefer you use the saloon." Brennan was retaining what he could of his dignity. "The bos'n will show you the way."

The officer returned to the main deck and doffed his helmet to the little group of passengers. "I offer you my apologies in advance," he said politely, "but together we will make our little chats as brief and as painless as possible.

I shall interview you one at a time. Is it possible that any of you speak French?"

Mimi took a single step forward, her manner beguiling. *"Mais oui, Monsieur l'Enseigne."*

The officer's eyes widened. *"Après vous, mademoiselle,"* he replied. She nodded, then preceded him to the hatch, quickly disappearing.

Mimi was unique, Richard thought, grinning and shaking his head. Within moments, the officer would forget his reason for questioning her.

The others quickly surrounded him. "We knew your boy-servant was a woman," Robbin said excitedly. "But is she really Lady Dawn Shepherd?"

"Indeed."

"Is it true that she and King Charles—"

"Mistress Chaney," Richard said, "there are matters I shall not discuss with anyone."

Dempster scowled at his wife. "You knew there was and still is a price on her head? The Roundheads are anxious to capture her."

"So I gleaned," Richard replied dryly.

Captain Brennan beckoned him. "I regret, Sir Richard, that you didn't take me into your confidence. As captain of this ship, I have a right to know the true identities of my passengers. I further regret that it's too late to change the cabin arrangements."

Richard had to bite back a smile.

There was nothing more the ship's master could say, but at least he had the satisfaction of knowing that the most prominent Cavalier he had ever carried on the *Anne* was being safely transported through England's waters.

Mimi remained in the saloon for more than a quarter of

an hour, and when she returned to the deck, her smile indicated that all was well.

Richard was summoned by the French officer and had no difficulty in establishing his credentials. The post he had been forced to abandon as the King's Forester clearly defined his loyalties, and his examination was cursory. He carefully made no mention of the assignment that awaited him in the New World, and after a brief conversation, he was excused.

Dempster and Robbin were of little interest to Enseigne Le Brun, and soon were dismissed, as were Mollie Williams and her belligerent son. Somewhat to Richard's surprise, however, Robertson spent an inordinately long time below with the French officer.

"I wonder what they're talking about," he said to Mimi.

"I can't imagine," she replied. "Did you notice that Robertson didn't seem in the least surprised when I appeared as myself? He acted as if he had known or guessed my identity from the onset."

When the enigmatic Robertson finally returned to the deck, his face was expressionless. He was accompanied by Enseigne Le Brun, who made it his business to question the ship's officers briefly. These interviews took place on the quarterdeck because it would have been an unpardonable insult to ask Captain Brennan and his mates to go below for the purpose. Even though the search was illegal, the French officer was observing the proprieties.

At last, Le Brun and his troops departed, the officer bowing low over Mimi's hand and flirting gallantly with her before he climbed down the waiting ladder. But the *Anne* was not yet free to resume her voyage and had to wait until Le Brun gave his report to the *capitaine* of the frigate.

Then signal flags were raised on the warship: *You may proceed.*

"The French may be the allies and supporters of the Cavaliers in our time of need," the fuming Captain Brennan said after giving the order to weigh the anchor and hoist the sails, "but I can't abide their arrogance. I'd be tempted to make common cause with the Roundheads if we go to war with them."

Bart Williams felt the same way. "When that fop was a-talking to me," he said, a knife sliding down into his hand from beneath his sleeve, "it was all I could do to keep from carving him."

Mollie shook her head. "The sailors would have hanged you from their warship's yardarm. Will you never learn to curb your bad temper?"

"I didn't do it, Ma," he said, then added under his breath, "more's the pity."

The passengers dispersed, and Mimi asked Richard to wait for her on deck. Going below, she made a bundle of the boys' clothes she had worn. Then, returning to the deck, she ceremoniously threw them overboard. "May I never be forced to disguise myself again."

Richard was about to reply when he saw Robertson watching them from the opposite side of the deck. Mimi saw him, too. "He makes my flesh crawl," she said. The angry Richard started to cross the deck, intent on forcing a confrontation, but Robertson bolted, hurrying to the hatch, and disappearing from sight.

"He can't go very far," Richard said, returning to Mimi's side. "Sooner or later we're going to find out why he's so interested in every move you make."

*   *   *

When the *enseigne* returned to the French frigate, he moved directly to the *capitaine*'s quarters, as he had been instructed. From a pocket inside his uniform, he removed a parchment envelope and placed it on the desk before his superior officer. Then he stepped back and stood silently at attention.

"Thank you. You are excused. Please inform the crew to prepare to sail for France. I assume this communiqué is from Monsieur Colbert?"

"Oui, Monsieur le Capitaine."

"You have done well." The *capitaine* waved away his junior officer, then opened the envelope from Colbert. Mazarin's agent's message was brief:

> *Dawn Shepherd is on board, without incident. She is sharing a cabin with Sir Richard Dunstable, who is acting as her watchful escort. It will be necessary for me to eliminate him at my earliest convenience. I will keep you informed of our progress upon reaching Boston, then will follow the lady to Virginia.*
>
> *C.*

The *capitaine* smiled as he leaned back in his chair. The cardinal would be pleased with the message, and having been the catalyst, perhaps there would be a reward in it for him. He refolded the report and locked it in a small chest, still reflecting on fantasies of himself wearing, perhaps, the rank of *amiral*.

A new atmosphere prevailed that evening at the supper table in the saloon. Mollie was obsequious, Dempster and Robbin were deferential, young Bart seemed awed, and even Captain Brennan treated Mimi with great respect.

Only the enigmatic Robertson remained silent, as always.

Mimi, who was in high spirits, knew she could not tolerate their formality for the duration of the long voyage. "I'm the same person I've always been," she said, "and the only difference is that now I can speak without fear of giving myself away. This adventure wasn't of our making, but we're comrades, and we're going to a land where, I'm told, the highborn enjoy no special privileges. So, for all our sakes, let's try to remember this is a ship, not the audience chamber at Whitehall!"

The ice was broken, but the others still found it difficult to relax. Mimi realized she had to go still further. "Robbin," she said, "I envy your long hair. It will take years for mine to grow that long again. Since I miss having my own to arrange, perhaps we could spend some time tomorrow fashioning yours in a new style." The younger girl was delighted and flattered.

"Mollie," Mimi continued, "the next time you make your wonderful stew, please take me into the galley and show me how you do it. I've never boiled a kettle of water, but there's no telling how much I'll be forced to fend for myself in America, and it's time I learned how to be more self-sufficient."

Richard nodded in silent approval. Even Mimi herself failed to realize how profoundly her tribulations were changing her nature. She always would be an aristocrat, as would he, but her escape and life on board the cramped ship were making her far less arrogant and selfish. Her friends in London, whoever they might be, would be surprised to see her chatting amiably with a middle-class girl and a cook, smiling genially at a sea captain who in status was far beneath her, and making small talk with Dempster, who only months earlier would have been overwhelmed to have been given a post on her household staff.

Richard knew that he himself had changed. It was impossible to maintain the barriers demanded by protocol and custom when he and Mimi lived in such confined quarters. Worst of all, she was so lovely, so naturally seductive that he knew he wanted her, but was troubled because he realized at the same time that by no stretch of the imagination was he in love with her. Dorothea remained his ideal, and although she was unattainable, Mimi was too sure of herself for him to lose his heart to her. Something in his own nature demanded a soft, yielding woman. It did not occur to him that he was not the product of a typical Cavalier family. Indeed, he would have been stunned had he known that his moral standards were remarkably similar to those of the Puritans he despised.

After supper Mimi remained behind in the saloon to teach an eager Robbin and Dempster how to play cards. Richard stopped in the cabin for his cloak, then went up to the deck to walk Prince Henry, who had been more restless than usual that day. Thick clouds concealed the stars and moon, and the sea was rough, with water breaking over the bow as the brig dipped into a trough, then climbed to the crest of the next wave. The mate who had the watch and the sailor at the wheel on the quarterdeck were fully occupied with their duties. The *Anne* was tossing and pitching violently and erratically, which created problems with walking the horse. The steed was unsteady on his feet, which made it necessary for Richard to hold the reins taut and move slowly. The spray soaked the deck, making the task even more hazardous, so after a few minutes he returned Prince Henry to the stall, groomed and fed him, then covered him with blankets. The horse was withstanding the rigors of the voyage well.

Emerging from the stall, Richard stood for a time at the fantail. The night was so dark that he could see the ship's wake for no more than a few yards, and the waves that loomed above the brig were black and menacing. But the cold sea air was invigorating, so Richard lingered, unwilling to return to the stuffy wardroom. Only the instincts developed and sharpened during the years he had spent in the forest of the royal hunting preserve saved his life. He heard nothing, but sensed the presence of someone behind him, and turned just as Robertson, a sword in hand, lunged at him. Richard barely managed to sidestep in time, and the blade missed his body by inches. Robertson grimaced, poised for another thrust. The moonlight broke through a rift in the clouds, enabling Richard to distinguish his opponent's blazing eyes.

Richard's first thought was that it was almost impossible to defend himself. His own sword and pistol were stored below in the cabin because there had appeared to be no need to carry them to the deck. His only weapons were the throwing knives in the belt that he habitually wore.

The wind howled through the lines above from prow to stern, making it unlikely that the pair on the quarterdeck would hear him if he shouted, and the horse's stall blocked their view of what was happening. Robertson, whatever the reason for his seemingly inexplicable attack, had chosen the right time and place for it.

"Have you lost your reason?" Richard demanded.

"You've been in the way long enough," the man said. "Now that Lady Dawn has come into the open, it's time to be permanently rid of you."

The statement made no sense to Richard, but there was no opportunity to analyze it. Robertson lunged again, balancing as best he could on the heaving deck. The erratic movement of the ship saved Richard this time. The sword aimed for his heart just missed him, and Robertson's momentum carried him to the rail beyond Richard, forcing him to grip it in his free hand so he wouldn't be thrown overboard. This momentary respite gave Richard the chance to collect himself. He drew one of his knives, aware that he could not afford to miss.

Robertson laughed harshly at the sight of the knife. "Would you duel with toys, Sir Richard?" Lifting his blade to the guard position, its tip at eye level, he advanced slowly, carefully, his elbow bent, making certain that his next thrust would be effective.

Richard did not move. Continued evasion would result in his death, and he realized he had to find his target with a single knife, throwing it before the man could strike for a third time.

Their eyes met, and each could read death in the other's grim gaze. This was a duel, however unfair, in which no quarter would be given. Robertson poised for his thrust. Exerting no visible effort, Richard utilized his many years of training as he released his knife. The blade flew through the air before Robertson could lunge, penetrating the man's left eye and embedding itself in his brain. He toppled backward onto the deck, dying without making a sound. At the same instant, his sword flew from his hand, clattered onto the deck as the ship lurched, then vanished overboard.

Richard stood for a long moment, his entire body bathed in cold sweat. His skill had prevented his own murder, but the realization dawned on him that he was confronted by a

grave problem: if he went to the officer of the watch and
Captain Brennan came on deck, it would appear that he had
cold-bloodedly killed Robertson. It would be difficult for
anyone to believe he was telling the truth when his attacker's
weapon had vanished into the sea.

Leaping forward, Richard dropped to one knee and with
great effort managed to draw his knife from the dead man's
head. Wiping the blade on Robertson's breeches, he saw
that little blood had been shed, which was all to the good.
The sea spray was becoming heavier, and the salt water was
washing away the blood.

Desperately wanting to learn the reason for the attack,
Richard made a swift, thorough search of the man's pockets. His fingers closed over a small, leather-bound notebook, but the night was too dark for him to read the
contents here. Besides, he could not take the time now. The
man's other pockets were empty.

It was necessary to dispose of Robertson's body. Still on
one knee, Richard pushed it close to the edge of the deck,
and the movement of the ship did the rest. A savage lurch
sent the body overboard, and it slid into the black sea
below, disappearing from sight.

Standing again, Richard made an effort to compose himself. Only a few minutes had passed since he had emerged
from his horse's stall, and he knew of no reason to believe
that the men on the quarterdeck would point a finger of
suspicion at him when Robertson failed to appear. He
started forward along the wet deck, walking slowly, and
paused to call a greeting to the mate.

"You'd best go below, Master Dunstable," the officer
called.

"I was attending to my horse."

"Fair enough, but don't tempt the sea. The deck isn't safe for an evening stroll."

Richard nodded in pleasant agreement and went below. Mimi hadn't yet returned to the cabin, so he sought her in the saloon.

She looked up from her card game, saw his troubled eyes and pale face, and immediately excused herself.

"We'll play again tomorrow," she told Robbin and Dempster, then silently went with Richard to the cabin. Something in his manner prompted her to ask no questions. He bolted the door behind them, then told her what had happened in the duel and its aftermath, omitting no detail. She, too, was puzzled by Robertson's single, enigmatic remark.

Color drained from her face, but she remained seemingly calm. "You were right to act as you did," she said. "Captain Brennan may be a loyal Cavalier, but he would have been obliged to place you under arrest and hand you over to the authorities in Boston for a trial that would have been very difficult to win. Are you sure the sea washed away the blood?"

"It was gone by the time I left the deck. Now, let's see what this notebook tells us."

They sat side by side on the lower bunk and opened the little leather-bound volume.

"It's written in French," Richard said in surprise.

"So it is. And it seems to be a dated diary, started a year ago in London."

"I'm afraid my French isn't very good, and Robertson's handwriting is only partially legible to me."

"I'll translate—" Mimi broke off and gasped. "It's all

about me! He kept a journal, and I am the subject." She was silent for a time as she scanned the pages. "Robertson had me under observation for a full year. Charlie was off fighting the Roundheads, and, as you know, he surrendered to the Scots, who handed him over to Cromwell. There was almost no activity at Whitehall. I was living quietly in my family's town house, and he has recorded every move I made: the names of my guests, the people at whose homes I dined, my companions on horseback rides and at the theater. This is incredible."

Not wanting to interrupt her reading, Richard remained silent.

Mimi was flushed now. "His facts are remarkably accurate, but he also speculates outrageously. He suspects that Newcastle, the Lord Chamberlain, and the Earl of Lindsey were my lovers! Really! All of them friends of my father who were keeping watch over me!"

He smiled quietly.

Again she gasped. "Robertson followed me to Bristol and knew I was at the White Hart. He records your arrival, and he realized what was afoot when you went down to the docks to see Captain Brennan. He admired my disguise, but it didn't fool him for a minute. By that time he had already arranged his own passage on the *Anne*."

Robertson had been no fool, Richard thought.

"You seem to have infuriated him. Listen to this: 'Dunstable has become her protector and must be removed. His presence can prove very harmful.' What do you suppose that means?"

He thought hard, then shrugged. "I'm afraid we'll never know. Was he vindictive toward any other man?"

"Only the Earl of Lindsey, whom he seems to have forgotten after his first visit to my house."

"How odd. Perhaps Robertson was in love with you and resented the proximity of anyone who appeared to be close to you."

"That's possible," Mimi said, "but his tone doesn't indicate it. The flavor of these notes is—strictly objective. Only the comment about you is in the least emotional, and even then his dislike seems more professional than personal. How I wish I'd known that every move I made was being watched for months and months!" She shuddered, then instinctively rested against his shoulder. Richard put an arm around her for comfort.

"I've had no private life for a full year. How awful!"

"Well, no harm has been done."

"You could have been killed tonight!"

"I must admit I find it odd that Robertson would go to extremes to get rid of me. I can only think he wanted no one nearby who would be able to help you."

"But why, Richie?"

"I'm not sure. I find many entries in this journal strange," he said. "Robertson knew we met and saw through your disguise, but he made no attempt to prevent us from boarding the *Anne*. A single, quiet word to the Roundhead agents at the pier would have resulted in our immediate arrest."

"The worst part is remembering that his eyes seemed to cut through me." Mimi was working herself into a highly emotional state.

Richard continued to deal with realities. "What I find even more puzzling is that he elected to write this diary in French, since I assume he was an Englishman. I can't imagine the Puritans hiring a French agent to keep watch on any Cavalier's movements."

"Nor can I. I like to think of myself as resourceful, but this is too much." Again she shivered.

His grasp tightened. "Robertson, whoever he may have been, never will be able to harm you in any way."

Mimi looked up at him, her green eyes troubled. "I'm still frightened. I suppose it's knowing that everything I did, every move I made for a whole year was being recorded, and presumably reported to someone who was Robertson's superior."

"You're safe now," he said, "especially with Robertson himself gone."

"But why did the Roundheads choose me as the subject for such a careful watch? Why me?"

"How actively were you involved in Cavalier politics, Mimi?"

"I wasn't. In this past year when the Royalist cause was declining so severely and London became a dangerous place for Cavaliers to gather, many meetings took place at my town house. I believed, as did Charlie's principal supporters, that it was a safe place. I didn't dream the Puritans knew when people like the Earl of Lindsey sneaked into London for a day or two."

"If they had known, they could have arrested every last man who was trying to restore King Charles to his rightful place on the throne. They could have advanced their eventual victory, and Cromwell, with all his faults, is wise enough to have known it."

"Yet no active steps were taken."

"I keep coming back to the fact that this journal was written in French," Richard said. "Now I can't help wondering whether Robertson may have been an agent in the employ of France—or on the personal payroll of Queen Henrietta Maria."

"The stupid woman disliked me intensely—for reasons you know. But I didn't set eyes on Charlie during this past year, and she knew there was no way we could have come together. Even if I had been his mistress at one time, she would have accomplished nothing by having my movements watched. Besides, as she must have guessed, he really did sleep with two ladies at the court, and both of them visited him in Scotland. Henrietta Maria has never been one to squander money."

"That leaves the French government," he said.

She shook her head wearily. "Mazarin knows who is and who was powerful in England. Surely a man that shrewd had no false illusions about me."

"We're reduced to one last possibility," Richard said. "For the sake of argument, let's assume that Cardinal Mazarin learned that secret meetings of the Cavalier high command were being held at your house. By keeping you under surveillance, he could have easily learned the identities of every active Royalist leader."

Mimi brooded in silence for some moments, then said, "Logical enough. That sort of operation would be typical of Mazarin. But why would his agent continue to follow me after I became a helpless refugee, and then try to kill you when you became my sole source of protection?"

"I have no idea." He placed both hands on her shoulders. "All I know is that we've experienced a nightmare. Fortunately, we knew nothing about any of it until tonight, and now it's ended. We'll keep the notebook, and tomorrow I'll ask you to read it to me, word by word, to see if we find any additional clues. But no matter what we learn, if anything, the problem has been solved. I'm still alive, and you're free to live as you please."

She absorbed what he said, closed her eyes for an instant, and then returned his unblinking gaze. Neither of them knew why it was happening, but he embraced her, she slid her arms around his neck, and as they embraced, they kissed fervently. Their ardor increased, Mimi's lips parted, and soon only their mutual desire mattered. They disrobed in almost unseemly haste, then began to make love in earnest. Mimi, suffering no inhibitions, was as forthright as a lover as she was in every other aspect of her life. Richard no longer cared that he did not love her. He wanted her desperately and reveled in the knowledge that she was willing.

The tiny cabin became still smaller, and the lower bunk was their whole world. Their caresses became urgent, and when they ultimately mated, their explosive frenzy culminated in a burst of ecstasy.

Not until they grew calmer did they become aware of the chill in the cabin, and Richard drew the bedclothes around them.

"I knew it would be like this," Mimi murmured as they became locked in a fresh embrace.

"You knew it would happen?"

"Well," she said with a smile, "I play a fair game of whist because I know the odds. And I couldn't imagine that a healthy man and a healthy woman, both compatible in many ways, could stay apart when they're spending the entire voyage in a space this cramped."

"I fought it," he admitted.

"Why?"

He hesitated.

"Why, Richie?" Mimi insisted.

"Since you force me to be less than a gentleman, I'll tell you. You're not only beautiful beyond compare, but you're lovely in many ways. You're honest and good. In spite of an inborn arrogance, you mean harm to no one. Yet, with all of these qualities, I don't think I love you. However," he added hastily, "I'm not certain I really know the meaning of love."

Her laugh was full-throated. "Be comforted, my dear. I'm not in love with you, either." She snuggled closer, her body pressing against his. "But I do enjoy our relationship more than any other."

They made love again in a more leisurely manner, exploring and arousing, postponing their climax until they could wait no longer.

The wind shrieked, and the little brig rocked and pitched in violent spasms, her timbers groaning in protest. But all was serene in the cramped cabin.

"Do you want me to go to the upper bunk?" Richard asked at last.

"Don't you dare!" Mimi said. "After this, I intend to make only one bed in the mornings."

"So be it," he replied with a grin.

"You know," she said drowsily as she nestled in his arms, "we'll have no trouble passing the time for the rest of this long voyage."

Young Charles II stared at the canopy of his lavish bed. He was unable to sleep again tonight, and his bedclothes were wrapped uncomfortably around his legs, resulting from his futile efforts to find a suitable position for slumber.

There were so many weighty concerns rolling around in his mind, all seeming to defy attempts for resolution. His life was out of control. He grieved for his father, he felt himself to be politically adrift and financially dependent, and his mother was thriving in her homeland of France and seemed none too anxious to return to England with her son on the throne.

Giving up all hopes of sleep, young Charles sat up in bed, pulled aside the bed curtains, and lit the candle on the night table. He considered ringing for his manservant, but decided against it. There was no need for two people to go without sleep.

He was surprised to hear a light tapping at the door of his bedchamber. Had his servant heard him thrashing around the bed?

"Yes, you may enter," young Charles called.

The door opened slowly. Standing in the doorway was a young and radiant woman, holding a candle that softly illuminated her face. Charles sat transfixed, looking at her. Neither one moved nor spoke for several moments.

"May I come in, Your Majesty? I am Anne-Louise. I have been sent to you by the Prime Minister of France." The woman moved toward Charles's bed and sat at its foot. He looked at her closely, mesmerized by her beauty.

She was satisfied to let him gaze upon her, giving him time to acclimate himself. "You see, Your Majesty, there are many levels, many aspects to our hospitality. It has been noted by your hosts that you look tired. The cardinal suggested I help you to pass the long hours of the night."

The cardinal had suggested more than that. He had closely supervised her selection from among a number of women for this specific duty. She had her long, blonde hair

loosely arranged atop her head so it would fall past her
shoulders by removing a single hairpin. Her first meeting
with young Charles was orchestrated so his first glimpse of
Anne-Louise would be softened by candlelight.

"Your Majesty, may I pour you something to drink?"

"Yes, I would like that."

Anne-Louise stood and moved slowly toward the decanter and crystal snifters. She poured a drink for the young
man and brought it and her candle to his bed. Handing him
the brandy, she placed her candle carefully beside his own,
then sat next to him on the bed. She must proceed slowly so
Charles would consider the conquest his.

"You wish nothing to drink?"

"No, thank you, Your Majesty. I have come here for
your own pleasure, and to serve your needs." Anne-Louise
had been warned not to join Charles in his drinking.

Anne-Louise sat quietly by Charles, aware of his decreas-
ing suspicion and tension. He sipped the brandy in silence,
without taking his eyes from her face. When he had
finished, she took the snifter from his hands and placed it
on the table. She blew out one of the candles, came back to
Charles, and removed the pin from her hair.

When Robertson failed to appear at the breakfast table,
the first mate observed that in all probability he was suffering from seasickness.

"I feel none too hearty meself," Mollie Williams declared.

"We were a little queasy during the night," Robbin said,
"but we appear to have found our sea legs."

"How long do you suppose this storm will last?" Richard
asked coolly.

The mate shrugged. "We should see our way through the worst of it in a few more hours. But this is just a taste of what's to come. This is the season for gales in the Atlantic, and the next one could well stay with us for a week."

Mimi's hand found Richard's beneath the table. If the other passengers knew from the way they looked at each other and touched that they had become lovers, no one was disturbed. Robbin had slept with Dempster before they were married, Mollie had long enjoyed a scullery-eye view of the upper class, and the temperamental Bart was of an age when only his own feelings mattered.

Ever since Mimi had revealed her real identity, all had assumed that she and Richard were lovers, and neither the passengers nor the officers thought less of them for it. The crew envied Richard but respected Mimi, while Robbin and Mollie condemned neither. It was taken for granted that bluebloods made their own rules and were responsible only to themselves, and that even the nobles who had joined the Puritan cause would not alter their personal habits.

Late in the morning, Captain Brennan became mildly concerned and sent a crew member to the general cabin. The seaman reported that Robertson's bunk, concealed behind boxes of cargo for which there had been no room in the hold, had not been used the previous night. The entire ship was searched, but no sign of the missing man was found.

Captain Brennan made a laconic notation in his log: "Passenger Robertson lost overboard last night during gale." That was the end of the matter. Robertson had been so aloof that no one missed him.

His disappearance had not only changed the lives of Mimi and Richard, it made a difference to the Chaneys, too. They rearranged the location of their own bunks. Captain Brennan, aware of their situation, had several crew members move the cargo boxes, which were filled with the iron skillets and kettles eagerly sought after by those in the New World. After the crates were lashed to the nearest bulkhead for security, Robbin and Dempster finally had a private corner. They kept their voices down at night because otherwise Mollie and Bart might be disturbed from their rest, but the young couple soon learned there was little need for conversation.

Mimi and Richard spent the better part of two days reviewing every word in Robertson's diary, but could find no clues that explained his behavior or indicated the identity of his employers.

"If you don't mind," Richard said, "I'll send the notebook to Newscastle, in France, via Captain Brennan at the end of the voyage. It may be of more significance to him than it is to either of us."

"Please do," Mimi told him. "There's nothing in those pages that I care to hide from the people who are struggling to put young Charlie on the throne." A sudden thought struck her. "How does it happen that you're going to America rather than to France? I know Lindsey has a great need for officers who are skilled swordsmen and who know how to use firearms."

Not even to her could Richard reveal his mission. "I'm being sent to the colonies," he said, his voice unintentionally curt.

Mimi knew enough about Cavalier politics not to press him. "I just wish they had given me something useful to do," she said, and dropped the subject, refraining from bringing it up again.

* * *

Dempster volunteered for the formidable task of teaching Mollie and her son to read and write, and devoted the better part of each morning to instruction. Mollie was a surprisingly apt and devoted student.

"Just imagine me being able to read a book!" she exclaimed enthusiastically. "Just like the Duke of Buckingham!"

Bart, on the other hand, showed no interest in learning. "I've never knowed nobody who could write a word or even read his name," he said. "Why should I bother? It ain't going to help me earn a living."

Every afternoon Mimi played cards with the Chaneys, who were becoming increasingly proficient, but Richard did not join them. Games bored him, and he confessed that his father had not been able to kindle his enthusiasm for chess, either. He preferred to spend his afternoons reading various volumes borrowed from Captain Brennan's small library.

Mimi became increasingly fond of the Chaneys, and one evening she seemed disturbed, but said nothing until she and Richard retired to their cabin. "I'm only slightly older than Robbin and Dempster," she said, "but I can't help thinking of them as naive. I don't think you'll believe what I've just learned today. They're traveling to the New World without a penny between them."

"I know," he said, and told her he had provided the funds that had enabled Dempster to buy their passage.

"They'll need money after we land," she said. "They don't seem in the least concerned, but they'll need funds for food and lodging until they find work. I'm going to find some way, without embarrassing them, to make them a gift of cash before we reach Boston."

"I've fully intended from the start to help them," Richard said, "so I wish you'd leave it to me. Dempster is a proud and sensitive lad, and it would mortify him if anyone offered him charity. He'll take money from me more readily because I'll offer it to him as a loan."

"I see." It was obvious she was disappointed, if not annoyed, at not having her own way.

"If you wish," he suggested, "you might make a gift to Mollie. I believe her purse is more or less empty, too, and it would help her if someone gave her a start."

"I'll do it." Her quick smile forgave him. "What about Bart?"

"Helping his mother will be enough."

"You don't like the boy?"

"I neither like nor dislike him," Richard said. "This afternoon I grew tired of reading, and when the garbage was being thrown overboard I went up to the deck with my pistol to keep my eye and hand sharp. Bart coveted my pistol and actually wanted to know what price I'd ask for it. He's a volatile lad, with no notion of good sense. I'm afraid he'd spend a gift on a weapon that could create problems for himself and his mother."

"You're the only man I've ever known who has valid reasons for everything that should or shouldn't be done. Do you have any other suggestions, Richie?"

"Indeed I do, my lady. Stop talking so much and get undressed—or I'll be forced to remove your clothes myself."

"What a lovely idea," she said.

The final weeks of the voyage seemed endless. The brig was buffeted almost incessantly by strong winds, the seas ran high, and the sun rarely appeared in the dreary, leaden sky. Crew members worked day and night in the open, their clothes rarely dry, their meals abominable, and yet their attitude was unfailingly cheerful. They did what was required of them, and if they complained, it was not in the presence of the passengers.

"As one who grew up near Bristol," Dempster said, "I've always taken seamen for granted, more or less. I wish I had the stamina of the civilians who sail on merchantmen and those in the old Royal Navy, too."

"Oh, you do, darling," Robbin assured him.

"I don't mind spending fourteen or more hours a day in the fields," he said, shaking his head, "but I've had enough of the sea to last me for the rest of my life."

"I so hope we will make good lives for ourselves in the colonies," his bride said.

"I intend to succeed," he told her, "if for no other reason than because I'll never have to sail back to England. Once we make a home, we'll stay there—even when young Charles gains the throne!"

Perhaps the worst of the voyage was the monotony of the diet. The hardtack was soggy, the bully beef had lost its taste, and the boiled beans needed seasoning to make them palatable. The mere thought of salt fish caused passengers and crew alike to shudder. Even the inventive Mollie Williams, who continued to assist the cook in the galley every day, could no longer invent ways to make the meals more appetizing. "There's just so much a body can do to bully beef and salt fish," she said. "If we had more spices and herbs it would help a mite, but we don't." So the same dishes were served at virtually every meal, and passengers and crew members lost their appetites. The seamen, having known what to expect, continued to eat in order to keep up their strength, and the civilians, for want of anything better to eat, followed their example.

As the *Anne* drew nearer to Massachusetts Bay, the need to make specific plans for the future became more urgent. Dempster and Robbin tentatively decided to stay in the colony, go west to the frontier country, and establish a homestead of their own if they could find sufficiently attractive land for farming. Captain Brennan told them that free acreage was available, but made it plain they would encounter difficulties.

"The American wilderness isn't like English farm country," he said. "You'll have to build your house, uproot trees, and clear the land. That could take months of hard work. By the time you're ready to start planting, it might be too late to reap a harvest in the coming season."

Dempster refused to feel discouraged. "If I must," he said, "I'll find work with someone else this year, which will give us time to find the right property for ourselves. All I know for sure is that I can grow crops in just about any kind of soil."

Mollie Williams was overwhelmed by the gift of cash made to her by Mimi. "This will give me a chance to look around and find what's best for me. I want to settle in some place where Bart will be able to make a good life for himself, too. If we like Boston, maybe we'll stay there. If not, we had a scullery maid at Whitehall who went to Providence Plantations, so maybe I'll look her up."

The plans made by Richard and Mimi were more complicated. He intended to remain in the capital of Massachusetts Bay long enough to make his own soundings regarding the feelings of the people about the relative merits of the Cavaliers and Puritans. Mimi, however, would stay only for four days and then sail to New Amsterdam before going on the last leg of her voyage, which would end at her destination, Middle Plantation.

"We'll have a few days together in Boston, at least," Richard said.

She nodded. "But we'll need to be careful. If we share the same quarters, there's certain to be talk that will find its way back to London."

He had no intention of allowing her to become involved in a scandal. "There's only one inn of substance in Boston, Captain Brennan tells me. The Sign of the Bear, it's called. I'm hoping they'll give us accommodations near each other."

"I'd like that," she replied with a smile.

"I've been doing a great deal of thinking about you and me, Mimi," he said. "Are you quite sure you want to go on to the plantation of this Horace Laing in Virginia?"

"I believe so. From what I've gathered, the winters in New England are even worse than in Scotland."

"I don't know where I'll make my permanent headquarters," he told her. "It depends on the way my—uh—mission works out. But you may want to reconsider your own arrangements."

She didn't understand what he was trying to tell her, and raised an eyebrow. He had thought of many ways to say what he had in mind, but had discarded all of them. "If you wish," he said bluntly, "we could be married."

She was so startled that she had no immediate reply.

"I realize," Richard said uncomfortably, "that it would be a step down, a long step down, for the daughter of a belted earl, who already has a title in her own right, to become the wife of a mere baronet, but I nevertheless extend to you my offer."

Mimi began to chuckle, then halted herself sharply. "I beg your pardon, Richie," she said. "I didn't mean to laugh, and I'm not making sport of you. The truth of the matter is that I'm overwhelmed."

He bowed, still waiting for her reply.

"Do I gather correctly that you've recovered from your love for the girl you left behind in Lincolnshire?" There was no flippancy in her manner.

"I'm no longer certain of what I feel for her." He had done his best to put Dorothea out of his mind and had not been completely successful. "What I do know is that you and I have been living together all this time, and we're compatible."

Mimi wondered if he had been overcome by shyness, which wasn't like him. "Are you trying to say you've fallen in love with me?" she asked, prompting him.

Richard frowned and shrugged. "I'm confused by our intimacy," he said. "Ask me that same question with a sword pointed at my heart, and I'd be forced to say that I don't know. I honestly don't think I am in love with you, but I can't swear to it."

"If this is any comfort to you," she said with a broad smile, "I don't believe I love you, either."

"That relieves my conscience somewhat."

She looked hard at him. "Yet you'd do this for me?"

"Of course, if it's what you'd want."

An expression of wonder crept into her eyes. "I don't think there are many gentlemen of your caliber in our world these days. Buckingham gives a girl an expensive bauble and goes on to the next, and there are dozens like him."

"I had only a nodding acquaintance with Buckingham. I know nothing about his private life."

"What I know is only hearsay, I'm pleased to report." Her smile faded. "First, I thank you with all my heart for your proposal, but my own conscience forces me to reject it."

"The offer remains open if you change your mind."

"That's unlikely," Mimi said, and slid her arms around his neck. "I suggest we enjoy to the hilt the time we have left together—and let the future take care of itself."

CHAPTER 4

BOSTON, the capital of Massachusetts Bay Colony, was a strange town, unlike any place that either Richard or Mimi had ever seen. It had a population of almost three thousand inhabitants and was growing rapidly, but it bore little resemblance to any community in England. Perhaps the proximity of the endless North American wilderness, a vast sea of trees that extended for many hundreds—perhaps thousands—of miles to the north, south, and west, was responsible for its unique qualities.

Already a major seaport and the largest town of Britain's colonies on the continent, it nevertheless was only recently becoming influenced by cosmopolitan sophistication. Few taverns that catered to seamen were to be seen in the port area, and as Richard would learn when he made inquiries to satisfy both Mimi's curiosity and his own, there were no bordellos within the town limits, although night walkers were apprehended without warrant and presented to the courts for punishment.

The main portion of the town, which extended from the harbor past Beacon Hill, was still growing rapidly, with only a few buildings of stone or brick. Most, including a majority of the churches, shops, and dwellings, were made of wood, preferably oak. That made sense, since trees were the New World's least expensive commodity, but what was surprising was the relative absence of large homes. Even those who already had become well-to-do lived modestly in simple houses of one or two stories, many of them little more pretentious than log cabins.

Although founded nineteen years earlier, Boston had few public gathering places of consequence other than the churches. The court was housed in the First Church, and the governor's mansion, a two-story house of white painted clapboard, stood between the Common and Fort Field. There were no meeting houses, no theaters, and no other places of entertainment. Only three streets had been cobbled, although a few more would be paved when the warmer weather came, and most roads were rutted, with ice and snow caking the frozen mud. Several roads were pebble-paved down their center strip, making use of the round stones from the area's shorelines.

Many residents were attired in drab clothes, as Mimi noted immediately. Men and women alike dressed in blacks, dark browns, and grays, and the children were smaller versions of their elders. Only a very few wore clothes imported from England. Most wore suits, dresses, and cloaks of a locally made material known as linsey-woolsey, a mixture of wool and linen or cotton that was durable but shapeless.

The only note of color was provided by the copper-skinned American Indians, who roamed through the streets in large numbers, the men painting their faces with streaks of color that identified their various tribes. The Wampanoags, in particular, under the leadership of Massasoit, had long enjoyed friendly relations with the colonists of the Bay Colony. Indian men and women alike wore clothes of supple animal skins, and the costumes of the women were decorated with dyed porcupine quills and beads of many hues.

A huge area that extended from Beacon Hill toward the waterfront was known as the Common. From spring through late fall this was a carefully tended pasture, dotted with relatively few trees, as was the case in all of Boston, where milk-producing cows were permitted to graze. All citizens had the right to entrust their cows to William Hudson, the herder for the town, who would drive the animals to the Common each morning and return them at the sunset. Many families owned at least one milk-producing cow.

The Sign of the Bear looked as primitive as the rest of Boston, but the interior, although simply furnished, proved to be surprisingly comfortable. Richard and Mimi were given adjoining second-floor rooms without asking for such quarters; later, they would discover that they had been assigned the only private rooms in the place. All other quarters were dormitories, each of which housed as many as a half-dozen visitors.

While Mimi luxuriated in a hot bath, the water having been poured into a tub four feet long, Richard exercised his horse. Prince Henry celebrated his release from the shipboard pen by cantering spiritedly through the muddy roads, and Richard soon found himself in the open countryside. This was an area in which farms predominated, most of them small, interspersed with patches of deep woods. The man and his mount felt at home in the forests, and Richard reflected that, while Boston seemed alien, this taste of the American wilderness buoyed his spirits.

He returned to the Sign of the Bear after a brisk, two-hour ride that did wonders both for the stallion and for the rider. Then, after bathing quickly, he joined Mimi in her room. Already dressed for the evening in a form-fitting gown of emerald silk, she sat at a small table, applying cosmetics with the aid of two smoking pine knots and an oil lamp. "I'll be ready as soon as I can manage," she said. "The lights here are dreadful, and apparently smokeless French tapers are too expensive for the colonials."

Richard sat in a straight-backed chair while he waited for her. "The weather is so raw and cold," he said, "that I suggest we eat right here in the inn this evening. I did a bit of scouting and saw a few taverns in the neighborhood, but none of them looked very appetizing."

When the woman completed her toilet, they descended to the ground floor, and there the proprietor approached them hurriedly, a look of alarm on his face. "Lady Dawn!" he said, obviously concerned. "Surely you don't intend to appear in public looking as you do!"

Richard bristled, but controlled himself sufficiently to speak quietly. "Do you find something objectionable in Lady Dawn's appearance?"

"Not I, Sir Richard," the man protested. "I worked in a London public house for years before I came to Massachusetts Bay and built this place. But this is Boston. When a woman makes an exhibition of herself with her arms bare and her chest—uh—exposed, she's placed under arrest and is forced to spend two days sitting in the stocks. No exceptions are made, and I'd hate to see Lady Dawn in trouble."

Mimi made no attempt to conceal her amusement.

"Perhaps," Richard said, "we could be served our dinner in Lady Dawn's room."

"I'm afraid that can't be done, either, Sir Richard. I could spend a month in prison for fostering personal relations between unmarried persons of opposite sexes."

Richard and Mimi exchanged incredulous glances. The innkeeper drew himself up to his full height. "Lady Dawn, Sir Richard," he said, "this is Boston!"

"I would venture a guess that the Puritans control this community," Mimi said.

"Your ladyship, Boston was founded by Puritans. I'm sure that no city in England is as firmly in the Puritan camp. Those who are of other persuasions," the man added, "soon move. Some have founded new towns elsewhere in Massachusetts Bay, and a good many are now making their homes in Providence Plantations and other portions of Rhode Island. The Boston Town Council, made up exclusively of churchgoers, tolerates no dissent and no disobedience of its laws."

"You've convinced me I'd be wise to conform," Mimi said.

The innkeeper walked beside her to the staircase. "I'm grateful for your understanding, your ladyship. If you appeared in my dining room as you're now dressed, I could be arrested."

"I have a strange notion," Richard said as he and Mimi ascended the stairs to the second floor, "that I won't be tarrying overlong in this town myself. I just want to assure myself that our host isn't exaggerating."

Mimi found a jacket with a high ruffled collar and long sleeves among her belongings, and she donned it over her dress. Then, laughing at the local customs, they went down to the dining room. There they ate before a roaring log fire, and new surprises awaited them. The oxtail soup was delicious, the venison steak, which had been marinated in wine and herbs, was extraordinary, and the apple pie, enclosed in a crust rather than served in a deep dish as it was in England, was unlike anything they had ever eaten. The portions were so large, Richard could eat only part of what was placed in front of him. With their meal, they were served drinks of hard cider that had been produced locally.

The other guests were even more fascinating than the unusually good food. Two young, bearded French fur traders in buckskins appeared to have returned recently to the comparatively civilized atmosphere of the town from a hunting and trapping expedition in the northwest. Loud and uncouth, they drank enormous quantities of liquor, and they used language that would have made a London slum inhabitant blush. Three other men, who seemed to be local merchants, were clearly offended by the traders, first viewing them with disdain, then turning their backs to the rustics.

"It is a wonder to me that such conduct hasn't resulted in their arrest," Mimi said after she and Richard returned surreptitiously to her chamber.

"Well," he replied, "the Puritan standards of this colony, at least, aren't those we knew at home. I'd guess that allowances must be made here for the concentration of the Puritan population."

"I predict that as the wilderness settlements grow and become stronger, the clergymen here will lose their control over the people. Until then, I'm glad I won't be living here. Why, the way all those men were staring at me, I'd swear they've never seen a woman wearing rouge or rimming her eyes with kohl. I'll need to use cosmetics lightly while I'm here, or I might be sent to gaol for wearing too much."

He grinned as he watched her disrobe, then followed her example. "I guess I'd be horsewhipped if they caught me going to bed with you."

"I shudder to think of what they'd do to me. I just hope the other colonies are less prim, or I'll have to buy an entire new wardrobe."

Richard made certain the bolt that kept the door locked was firmly in place before he and Mimi went to bed.

Taking no chances in the morning, Richard made his own bed look as if he had slept in it. After changing his clothes and shaving, he went for a ride on his horse before joining a demure Mimi for breakfast. Her face was bare of cosmetics and her attire was modest, but the other patrons, all of them male, nevertheless gaped at her. She had an inner quality, Richard reflected, that drew men to her.

After breakfast he went on a long, solitary walk to acquaint himself with the town, and many of his earlier guesses were confirmed. In spite of the overlay of Puritanism that was evident everywhere, the shopkeepers and others with whom he conversed were earthy people. A few disliked the overzealousness that had been imposed on them, but were afraid to speak their minds as they pleased. Some cautiously admitted, in response to Richard's casual, leading remarks, that although they were Puritan sympathizers, they condemned the brutal execution of Charles I, of which they had learned from the officers and crew of a ship that had reached port only a few days earlier.

"The Puritan leaders here are serious, right enough," a cobbler said, "but the day we kill somebody here for his beliefs, I will pack up my family and move to another area. I go to our church, sing our hymns, and listen to sermons that last all through the Sabbath. But if our Puritan leaders go too far, my conscience will suffer for it. I came here to be free, I did, and no one is going to push me into corners!"

Reviewing his estimates of Boston's loyalties, Richard visited as many local establishments as he could until it was almost time to return to the Sign of the Bear to meet Mimi for the noon dinner. A watery light from the sun was shining in a pale sky, the wind had died away, and he took his time, strolling down a cobbled street.

"Richard!"

He was startled to hear someone call his name.

"Richard!" The deep voice came from an unpainted, single-story wooden building.

He hurried toward the window reinforced with metal bars about six inches apart, stretching from top to bottom.

A haggard Dempster Chaney stared out at him. "Thank God you happened to walk past this awful place. Robbin and I have been thrown into the Boston gaol, and they're holding us in separate cells!"

"What in the devil did you do to be arrested?"

"The devil's own work, or so they told us. We were wandering around, seeing the sights of the town—such as they are—when we were arrested for committing a sin."

"You and Robbin?" Richard was stunned. "What sin could you have possible committed?"

"We were holding hands," Dempster said bitterly, "and when we stopped at the edge of the Common, we kissed. A constable took us straight to the church, and when the justice learned we had only ten sovereigns, the money you gave us before we landed, he took it from us. He also sentenced us to thirty days' imprisonment because the fine for this offense was more than we had. I haven't seen Robbin since yesterday, and I'm going out of my mind with worry."

"Don't despair," Richard said. "I'll do what I can for you."

He raced back to the inn, and when he told Mimi what had happened, they promptly postponed dinner. Instead, they asked for directions, then walked quickly to the Strangers' Court, which was two town squares away.

Justice Platt had just concluded his morning session in court and was about to return to his house for a two-hour dinner recess. But his bailiff, impressed by the refined appearance of Sir Richard and Lady Dawn, went directly to the magistrate to convey the visitors' names. The magistrate immediately consented to see them.

Clad conservatively, like almost all Puritans, he nevertheless bowed from the waist when the couple came into his tiny office, where several books of law sat on a wall shelf. "What progress Boston is making when people of your stature visit our fine city. Welcome, milady. Welcome, Sir Richard."

Richard decided to soften the harsh approach he had intended to take. "We're overwhelmed by Boston, Your Honor," he said. "But we are saddened, too. We have just learned that two shipmates of whom we're very fond have run afoul of the law and have been imprisoned."

"I think it unlikely that friends of yours would have committed a serious crime," Justice Platt replied gallantly. "Their names?"

"Master and Mistress Dempster Chaney."

The judge opened a ledger and moved a forefinger down a closely written page.

Richard's quick, warning glance told Mimi to control her temper.

"Here we are," Justice Platt said, and frowned. "Dear me. It grieves me to tell you that your friends committed no ordinary crime. They have sinned."

"What was the nature of their sin?" Mimi asked sweetly.

"They dared to embrace and kiss in a public place!"

It was Richard who had to make the effort to speak calmly. "You realize, Your Honor, that they are legally man and wife."

"No matter, Sir Richard. In fact, all the more reason for them to behave in a seemly manner in public. When married couples feel the need to embrace—which is discouraged but not forbidden—they are expected to do it in strict privacy. The Chaneys might well have contributed to the corruption of the single men and maidens of Boston."

Mimi knew how to handle this bigoted representative of the Massachusetts Bay law. "They are so young themselves, Your Honor, that they were no doubt carried away by passions they couldn't curb. As you say, their conduct was unseemly, at best. But forgiveness is a virtue that all of us strive to acquire, so I do hope you can show forgiveness to these poor sinners."

"The law requires justice, not forgiveness, milady," Justice Platt said severely.

"What are the specific penalties of the law for this couple's grave offense?" Richard asked, his serene façade beginning to slip.

The judge crossed the room and picked up a law book.

"This volume just arrived from London, where it was published by some of our dear colleagues. I find it both useful and enlightening. I don't suppose you're familiar with it?"

"As a country dweller," Richard murmured, "I've had little to do with the law."

Mimi carefully refrained from adding that, until recently, a member of her household staff took care of legal matters on her behalf.

Justice Platt took his time thumbing through the book, at last finding the citation he was seeking. "Here we are. The suggested fine is twenty-five sovereigns. Since few sinners can afford to pay that sum, they cool their ardor behind prison bars. The practice hasn't yet been established in London or other cities in England, although soon the unholy there will learn their lessons, too. Here we find it much easier to keep them under control."

Richard was struggling with his anger now, so Mimi took the initiative. "We understand the Chaneys have already paid a fine of ten sovereigns. May we be permitted to supply the funds necessary to terminate their incarceration?"

"That's generous of you, milady."

She opened her purse and quickly had the gold coins in hand.

"I must make my acceptance of the fine conditional. I shall order this errant couple released into your custody and Sir Richard's, but there is no proper place here for people of that sort. They must leave Boston no later than sundown tonight!"

"It's you who show true generosity, Your Honor!" Mimi placed the gold coins on his desk.

Richard marveled at her seeming sincerity and told himself that her high position in the peerage had robbed the theater of a superb actress.

Justice Platt scribbled a few lines on a sheet of parchment with a quill pen, signed his name with a flourish, sprinkled the ink with talc and, after dripping tallow from a burning candle onto the page, affixed his seal. "I hope it will be my pleasure to see both of you again," he said. "Mistress Platt will regard it as a privilege if you will pay our humble home a visit."

"I'm afraid the visit will need to wait for a short time," Mimi said, picking up the sheet of parchment and waving it in the air to dry. "I sail very soon for Virginia."

"I'm leaving Boston in the immediate future myself," Richard said, then forced himself to add, "but I shall call on you without delay when I next come to town."

"I look forward to that day, Sir Richard." The judge bowed them out.

When they reached the street, Mimi breathed in the cold air deeply. "I thought I'd suffocate in there."

"I was afraid I'd create a real problem by slicing off his buttons with my sword. If the penalty a married couple must pay for the sin of embracing in a public place is twenty-five sovereigns, the Puritans are mad indeed! Once they try to enforce laws like that in England, there aren't enough ships in all of the country's ports to accommodate the emigrants who'll be clamoring to come to the New World."

"But not to Boston," Mimi said as they started toward the prison.

"No, not to Boston while the Roundheads rule here, that's sure. I don't dare stay more than a short time myself, or I'm certain to be in trouble. But the situation here isn't totally as it appears on the surface. I started to test the temper of the people this morning, and I was pleasantly surprised." He had no intention of going into detail until they were alone.

The gaoler who sat behind a desk in the bare prison office was eating a slab of meat between two chunks of bread when the pair arrived. He did not rise, and they saw no need to identify themselves as, continuing to eat, he very slowly read Justice Platt's order. It occurred to Richard that the man had difficulty in making out the meaning of the written word.

The gaoler finished his meal, wiped his mouth on the back of his linsey-woolsey sleeve, and hauled himself laboriously to his feet. "Wait ye here," he grumbled, and shuffled out.

Within moments he returned with a tearful Robbin Chaney, who sobbed as she threw herself into Mimi's arms. "I knew it had to be you two who saved us," she cried. "I've never known such a horrid nightmare."

The gaoler smirked, then went off again.

Robbin was eager to learn how the rescue had been arranged. "What did you—"

"Later," Mimi said.

The gaoler returned, leading a dejected Dempster, whose ankles and wrists were chained. He brightened immeasurably when he saw his wife and their benefactors, and when his chains were removed, he started toward Robbin.

Richard clamped a restraining hand on his shoulder. "Patience," he said. "You sinners never learn, but we'll take you to dinner and try to teach you the error of your ways." He led the still-dazed younger man into the street, and Mimi followed with Robbin, whose weeping had turned to wild laughter.

"Hush," Mimi told her. "It may be against the law to laugh in this barbarous Roundhead town, too."

A few minutes later they were seated at a snug corner table in the dining room of the Sign of the Bear. "Bring our friends a sample of everything on the menu, if you please," Richard said to the proprietor, who hovered over them himself.

"You must have guessed," Dempster said, "that I was given only stale bread and water in gaol."

"I had something the gaoler called soup," Robbin said, "and the sanctimonious fraud promised me anything I wanted to eat if I— Needless to say, I refused."

"I'll kill him," Dempster stormed.

"You'll do no such thing," Richard declared firmly. "The longer you stay here, the more troubles you'll create. You're leaving Boston before sundown today." He told the Chaneys the whole story of their visit to Justice Platt, and at the end of his recital, he handed Dempster two five-sovereign pieces. "See if you can use these more judiciously."

"We can never repay either of you," Dempster said. "I'm afraid we'll be indebted to both of you for years to come."

"You owe us nothing," Mimi said.

"But we do." Robbin was wide-eyed. "It would be wrong to accept so much money as a gift."

"Establish a solid place for yourselves, and we'll be satisfied," Richard replied. "You may repay the loan as you're able."

"Where should we go?"

Dempster shrugged helplessly as he looked at his wife.

"I've hardly become an expert on the New World in this short a time," Richard said. "But I kept my ears open wide this morning, and as I see it, you have two choices. Either you'll go south to a new colony called Rhode Island, and you'll find work there in a town called Providence Plantations, where they need masons and bricklayers. Or you can go on to another town called Newport, where most men catch fish for a living. There's also the start of a new shipbuilding industry there."

"I know nothing about bricks or masonry, fishing, or building ships."

"Then your only alternative is to start out toward the west. There are many villages and hamlets, most of their inhabitants people who couldn't tolerate the more unyielding attitudes of Boston's Roundheads." They were the only diners in the room, but Richard nevertheless took the precaution of speaking in a low tone. "You'll find someone who will give you supper and a bed tonight for a few pennies. Keep walking until you come to farm country that appeals to you, then stake a claim there. Just this morning a baker told me that's what he intends to do. He also told me his nephew has a working farm of one hundred and sixty acres somewhere to the west."

"What a huge estate," Robbin murmured.

"Not in the New World," Richard said with a grin. "Plus, reports claim that wheat, oats, rye, and barley grow here with greater success than in England."

"I'd need to let part of my property lie fallow while I cultivate thirty or forty acres," Dempster said thoughtfully. "But that's all right. I guess I've got to start thinking of farming on a larger scale."

Their first course consisted of shellfish largely unknown in England or Europe. Called clams, because of their tightly closed shells, these sea creatures had been steamed until the shells had opened from the heat, and as they were eaten, one by one, they were dipped first in broth, then in melted butter. Then came bear steak, which had been pounded to tenderize it. The spirits of all four rose as they ate.

"I was afraid of the food we'd find here," Mimi confessed, "but I've changed my mind."

Richard had to agree. "There's no need for anyone to starve here," he said.

After the meal, Dempster and Robbin bid good-bye to their benefactors, promising that they would meet again, and started off on foot toward the frontier. Both were cheerful, suppressing any doubts or fears they may have been feeling, and although they did not realize it, they were following in the steps of others who had come before them.

"They have courage," Richard said as they watched the young couple go off down the road.

"And confidence in themselves," Mimi added.

It was that spirit of self-assured optimism that Richard encountered again and again in the next two days as he spoke with people from every walk of life in Boston. The frontier beckoned, and anyone who could no longer tolerate the narrow-mindedness of those who were trying to create a society in their own image was free to go into the wilderness and make his own rules.

Writing a long report to the Earl of Newcastle, Richard concluded that although Boston was in the firm grip of the Puritans and could not be relied on for help in the restoration of young Charles II to the throne of his father, the same could not be said of the rest of Massachusetts Bay.

> *Ultimately,* he wrote, *the frontier here, which creates a love of liberty in all men, will surely prevail. This colony cannot be judged by English standards, and in the short time I have been here, I have already seen the influence that the wilderness exerts on all but the most rigid of Puritans.*

He also reported all he knew about the man who had called himself Robertson, and after hesitating momentarily, he related the true account of the man's attack on him and its grisly climax. He enclosed the man's journal, adding his own speculation and Mimi's as to the reason it had been written in French.

When he accompanied Mimi to the brig, he closeted himself briefly with Captain Brennan, to whom he gave the packet containing his letter and Robertson's diary. "You know to whom this is addressed," he said. "I thought it safer to write no name on the outside of the package."

"Rest assured that it will be forwarded to the man to whom you wrote," the master of the *Anne* replied. "It will be in safe hands at all times and will not fall into the possession of the enemy."

It was strange to think of fellow Englishmen as enemies, but that was what they had become, Richard knew.

"Are you familiar with the system we use for the transmission of communications?" Captain Brennan wanted to know.

Richard shook his head. "I was told only that I would be informed at the appropriate time."

"Well, that time is at hand. Come with me." The captain led him from the cabin to the main deck, and nodded in the direction of the yardarm. "Do you see anything out of the ordinary up there?" he asked.

Richard looked up, but saw nothing.

"Ordinarily," Brennan said, "a ship doesn't fly her nation's colors in port. It isn't done, and the custom has been observed for many years. Whenever you see the Union Jack flying from a ship's yardarm when she is anchored or tied to a wharf, you'll know that her master shares our political sentiments. This signal was chosen because of its ambiguity: to those unaware of this system, it appears that the captain is perhaps sloppy or forgetful about hauling in his colors. It would be difficult for a Roundhead to prove that the captain is letting it be known that he is willing to take messages back to England with him."

"I won't forget," Richard said, and after shaking hands with the captain, went off to the cabin he had shared with Mimi on the long voyage to the New World. They had agreed they would part there, in private, rather than on the open deck, where their embrace would create troubles.

They kissed, then stood at arm's length. "I know we shall meet again," Mimi said.

"I'm sure of it," Richard replied. "I shall make it my first order of business to see Horace Laing when I come to Virginia, as I intend to do. I'll find you, no matter where you may be."

With one accord they kissed again, and Mimi clung to him. "I hate to admit this," she said, "but I shall miss you."

"It isn't too late to change your mind and stay with me," he told her.

"No, it's right that we go our separate ways," she replied, her voice firm.

"Just remember that my offer of marriage remains open," Richard said.

She nodded, smiled, and pushed him away.

Her insistence on leading her own life as she saw fit was similar to the feelings he had heard expressed by many Bostonians, Richard thought as he took his leave. Her independence was a sign that she would do well in the New World.

He stood on the wharf as the lines were released, and the seamen began hoisting the brig's sails. Then, as the vessel edged away from the pier, Mimi came on deck and waved.

Removing his hat and returning her wave, Richard told himself she was unique. He could not help contrasting her attitudes with those of Dorothea, who did only what she was told. Perhaps he was being too harsh in his judgment of Dorothea, but he knew himself sufficiently well to realize that he would miss Mimi far more.

He stayed on in Boston for only a few more days after the *Anne* sailed, and learning nothing additional of consequence, he started out for Rhode Island. His horse was frisky in spite of the saddlebags and sleeping blankets Richard had secured, and had to be curbed to be prevented from tiring himself too quickly. When they left Boston behind, the man and his mount entered a deep forest of maple, pine, ash, elm, and oak, and Richard breathed more freely. Boston had depressed him, but now he could forget the Puritans who made life so miserable for themselves and for everyone around them.

What astonished him was the difference between the col-

onies and England. Here, the wilderness intruded everywhere, and although he passed the log cabins and cleared
fields that marked the presence of farms, the forest soon
closed in again, enveloping him. Familiar, rustling sounds
that the untrained ear could not detect told him of the
proximity of game, and he knew that even though a thin
blanket of snow still covered areas of the ground, spring
soon would come to this country of rolling hills and unexpected level areas.

In the afternoon, he came to a salt lick near a stream that
meandered through the deep woods, and halting upwind of
it, he waited; with any luck he might eat fresh venison
before the day ended. At last his patience was rewarded
when a doe appeared, and he brought down the creature
with a single rifle shot, the sound echoing through the
forest. Richard's rifle was one of a handful of similar hand-
tooled weapons in England and in France that were perhaps
unique. Certainly they fired accurately and lived up to their
reputations and hence were infinitely more valuable than
the ordinary musket available to everyone. That night he
feasted on a venison steak at a fire he made in the open, and
for the first time since coming to the New World, he was
content.

He had taken the precaution of reloading his rifle as soon
as he had fired it, a practice he had followed ever since he
had first learned to handle firearms, and as he finished his
meal, he reached for the weapon beside him, then leaped to
his feet. Prince Henry sensed the approach of strangers,
too, and whinnied softly.

Soon, two Indians appeared on foot, their faces smeared
with dye, their buckskins worn. Their bows remained on
their shoulders, and neither of the pair reached for an

arrow; their whole manner convinced Richard that they were curious rather than hostile. He lowered his rifle.

The taller of the pair, a brave of about thirty, raised an arm in greeting, then in his own language said something incomprehensible to Richard.

Richard returned the gesture, and saw both of the Indians staring at the remains of the doe's carcass, far more meat than he alone could possibly eat. "Help yourselves," he said, and when they did not understand, he told them in broad pantomime that they were free to use the meat as they saw fit.

They promptly built up his fire, carved chunks of meat, and placed them on a crude but effective spit. Then, as their meal cooked, they carefully separated the animal's hide from the flesh beneath it. They were using primitive but finely chiseled stone knives, and Richard marveled at their dexterity. This was his first direct experience with the copper-colored natives, and they interested him because these forests were their natural home.

Feeling more at ease with the white man, the Indians did their best to communicate with him while they devoured their meal. Ultimately, Richard was able to convey the message that he was traveling south, and the Indians, it developed, were going in the same direction. Returning his hospitality, they offered to guide him. Not until he indicated by his acceptance that he trusted them, did they smile.

Richard's horse fascinated the two braves, and both inspected the great beast at length, taking care not to approach Prince Henry too closely. The realization dawned on Richard that horses were alien to them, that there were no such animals in their tribe's possession.

That night, the two Indians slept in the dry clearing on

one side of the fire while Richard, wrapped in a blanket, stretched out on the other, his rifle close at hand, as always. In spite of their apparent friendliness, he remained cautious, uncertain whether they would try to steal his horse or his equally precious rifle, which was much superior to the conventional muskets that were so unreliable. Therefore, he slept lightly, but the Indians did not betray him, and in the morning he felt more secure in their company.

The pair demonstrated their gratitude by cooking more venison for him, as well as for themselves. The shorter of the pair cut a line of tendon from the doe, made a hook with a long, spiked thorn, then astonished the young Englishman by using this primitive equipment to catch a fish in a stream that passed close to the campsite. Skewering the fish on a branch, the man roasted it over the coals, and when it was done, he offered it to Richard.

Already surfeited, Richard indicated that he appreciated the gesture, but preferred that the Indians eat it. This they did, splitting the fish with their stone knives and removing the bones swiftly and easily. Richard watched them, reflecting that anyone who wanted to live in the wilderness had a great deal to learn from these people.

He discovered that he himself had much to learn about Indians. When he mounted Prince Henry for the resumption of the journey, the two braves led him, both walking tirelessly for the entire morning, never pausing to rest, never showing the slightest sign of fatigue.

After traveling for another day through the forest, they halted at noon, and one of the Indians pointed through an opening in the trees. Peering ahead, Richard saw a stockade fence, with clusters of log cabins and more substantial buildings of brick on the far side and cleared fields on the near side. This, it appeared, was Providence Plantations, the core of the community that a clergyman named Roger Williams had founded a decade and a third earlier after his banishment from Boston, when he also had discovered his inability to tolerate the stern, unyielding ways of the Puritans.

One moment the Indians were there, and the next they were gone, vanishing silently through the trees. Richard could hear them as they went their own way only because of his lifelong training, and he made up his mind to learn their language as soon as he could. No one, he told himself, could understand America without knowing the natives of this rugged country.

He rode slowly down the hill toward Providence Plantations, aware of the sentries who were watching his every move from the tower that dominated the palisade. From the heights, too, he could make out the small boats that rode at anchor in the half-circle of harbor that formed the inner rim of the town, and he assumed these were fishing craft. What struck him most forcibly was the diversity of Providence Plantations' architecture: dwellings and larger buildings were constructed in a bewildering variety of styles. There were simple log cabins, buildings made of stone, and several handsome houses of brick. The total population could not be greater than one thousand persons at the most, but it was plain that the citizens of the town had planted strong roots here and planned to stay.

The gates opened as Richard rode toward them, and a stocky man, clad in a buckskin shirt, linsey-woolsey breeches, and footgear of soft leather like that of the two Indians Richard had encountered, waved his musket in welcome.

"We figured you wasn't no Indian when we saw your horse and clothes," he called, "but we had to see the color of your skin to make certain. It don't pay to take risks these days. We permit entrance to Indians only when they are in the company of a white man."

Richard drew to a halt beside him. "Having troubles with the Indians?"

"Oh, a friendly little fuss with the Narraganset, you might say," the man replied. "Reverend Williams bought the land from them before he started Providence Plantations, but now we're a-bustin' at the seams, and the more farmland we claim for ourselves beyond the palisade, the more the Narraganset carry on. We're a-hopin' there won't be a shootin' dispute with them because we be a peace-lovin' people. But it don't hurt none to keep our powder dry."

"Where can I find lodging?"

The sentry took careful note of the cut and fabric of the stranger's clothes and the fit of his expensive boots. "For the likes o' you," he said, "you'll do best at Miz Gertie's, down to the waterfront. Just keep a-ridin' until you come to the water, and then turn left. You can't miss the place." He busied himself shutting the gates.

Richard followed the man's directions, wondering how he could identify Miss Gertie's, but instinct telling him to ask the sentry no more questions. People he passed en route to the waterfront kept themselves occupied with whatever they were doing and paid scant attention to the new arrival. A man mending a fishing net in his yard barely glanced at the rider, then returned to his task. A young woman dragging a cart filled with shiny new cooking utensils seemed unaware of his existence. She continued to trudge up the middle of the dirt road, forcing Richard to pull as far as he

could to the side to make a path for her. Only two small
boys throwing a ball to each other paused in their game long
enough to wave.

After proceeding a short distance down the waterfront,
Richard saw a hand-lettered sign, swinging from a post in
front of a shingled, unpainted two-story building:

ROOMS TO LET
Only Genteel Folk Accepted
G. Allen, Prop.

Standing in the yard was a gray-haired woman wearing
trousers under her skirt, energetically chopping down a tree
with a long-handled ax. "The trouble with paper birch,"
she announced, "is that you need to keep the grove thinned
out, or before you know it, you'll have a whole forest."

"You can't use the wood for much except kindling,"
Richard replied in the same easy, conversational tone. "But
I understand the Indians use it for building canoes."

Apparently his demeanor pleased the woman, because she
rewarded him with a smile. But her eyes remained sharp,
and she absorbed every detail of his appearance.

"I was told to apply to you for temporary quarters," he
said.

He took great care to speak politely, to smile, and to treat
her with great respect. He knew the type, understood how
she would react, and was taking no chances on having her
regard him as glib.

"I get sixpence per day, payable in advance," Miss Gertie said. "Dinner is at noon sharp, supper is half-past five,
and you get two candles every forty-eight hours you spend
here—no more. Breakfast is whatever is left over from the
night before."

135

Richard dismounted and handed her a silver half-crown. "This will take care of the basics for five days," he said. "I assume the stabling of my horse and feed for him will be extra, am I right?"

"You're wrong," Miss Gertie replied testily. "I run an honest hostelry. Beside, I don't know when I've seen a better-looking horse."

To Richard's surprise, Prince Henry, who disliked being touched by strangers and normally reacted by stomping and snorting, allowed himself to be petted and admired.

Soon the horse was at home in the stable behind the main building, munching on some apples that Miss Gertie gave him, and Richard was shown to a room dominated by a huge, four-poster bed. "Are you quite certain you want to charge only sixpence per day?" he wanted to know.

"I'll thank you not to mock me, young man!"

He changed the subject hastily. "I wonder if a friend of mine has settled here in recent days. Her name is Mollie Williams, and she—"

"Not here," Miss Gertie replied. "She applied to me for a position as my cook, but I don't have enough guests here to hire anyone." She peered even more sharply at the new arrival. "You must be Master Dunstable."

He bowed.

"Mollie Williams told me about the voyage from England and how a certain lady gave her enough money for her to take time finding the place she wants. She couldn't find it here. Providence grows slowly. Everyone in Rhode Island is entitled to his own opinion, but folks hereabouts keep their thoughts to themselves, so Mollie's boy would have had problems in Providence. He speaks too freely for his own good. They went on to Connecticut, the next colony down the line."

Richard thanked her, wondering if he had correctly gleaned that the woman had Cavalier sympathies. "Mollie told you the cause of her predicament?"

Miss Gertie nodded. "You won't find sympathy here for Puritans," she said. "We accept anyone whose beliefs are sincere, provided he doesn't try to cram his views down the throats of others. Lapsed Puritans are welcome in Rhode Island, but those who try to make others feel the way they do are invited to leave the colony before they lose their good health. We don't hold with violence, you know, but those who preach that the only road to eternal salvation is their road have been known to suffer accidents in Rhode Island. We value our freedom!"

Richard chuckled, then said, "There must be a strong Cavalier feeling in the colony."

She shook her head. "Mollie bragged how smart you are, but I see little sign of it, Master Dunstable. People in this colony don't do much of the bowing and scraping that kings expect of their subjects. All we want is to be left to ourselves." She walked to the nearest window and pointed. "What do you see out there, beyond the stockade?"

"The forest?" Richard asked.

"The forest, sir!" Miss Gertie said severely. "In a hundred years that forest will be gone, cleared by men who love their freedom. Rhode Island isn't Massachusetts Bay, where the population is expanding every year. To get along in Rhode Island you need to love liberty and be willing to die for it! That's why we say to the Roundheads and the Cavaliers—a pox on both your houses. We want no Old World quarrels here. We have enough to keep us occupied, taming the wilderness, maintaining a difficult friendship with the Narraganset, and trying to keep our young from being tainted with the bigotry and hatreds of outsiders. We don't give a hang whether England is ruled by a king or by Parliament. All we want is to be left alone to live as we see fit!"

In the days that followed, Richard discovered that Miss Gertie's thoughts were shared by virtually everyone he encountered. Religious freedom was guaranteed to the residents of the colony in a covenant made five years earlier with Parliament, and Rhode Islanders were so conscious of their liberties they carried a large chip on their collective shoulder, daring any and all outsiders to knock it off.

During the course of Richard's brief stay in the colony, representatives came from Newport and Warwick, the other principal Rhode Island towns, for the purpose of joining Providence in discussing the tensions between the Puritans and the Niantic and Narraganset tribes. The entire colony was dedicated to Roger Williams's commitment to friendship with the Narraganset; therefore, the visiting Englishman had the opportunity to learn of the whole colony's views.

A dozen of the Rhode Island leaders gathered at Miss Gertie's on Saturday night for a dinner of boiled lobster, which started with a fish soup that everyone present called a chowder, and Richard was surprised when toasts were offered in home-brewed beer.

"To liberty!" Providence's delegate to the council declared, rising at his place and lifting his glass.

"To liberty," the others echoed, and drained their glasses.

"We don't tell the Puritans of Boston what prayers to recite, what hymns to sing, or what man-made rules to obey," the Warwick representative explained to the silent, observing Richard. "We expect the same courtesy from them in return, and when they refuse to reciprocate, which happens more often than not, we run them off our soil."

"Our ships sail as far as the West Indian Islands to trade," the Providence representative added. "We do business with New Haven, New Amsterdam, and the Indians. We go anyplace where we can earn a profit. But I'll be damned if our captains will put into Boston, no matter how much they might be able to earn there."

"It's been my observation that the Roundheads are a vindictive lot," Richard said. "Don't they try to even the score when you snub them?"

The representative from Newport looked at his red, work-roughened hands and chuckled. "Oh, they try," he said. "Frequently they claim the border needs redefinition, that we're extending the boundaries of Rhode Island. But we have a map that was approved by King Charles and was ratified by the Long Parliament. So we show it to them every year, and they can't say much when they see the great seal of Parliament on the bottom of the map, right next to that of King Charles."

"I would think the royal governors would solve such problems," Richard said, and discovered that everyone at the table was staring at him.

"Some colonies may choose to take guidance from England," the Warwick representative said haughtily. "But

Rhode Island doesn't entertain that particular attitude. We govern ourselves, and we swear no allegiance to either the Crown or to Parliament. We swear allegiance only to God, and we pray to Him to preserve our independence."

Richard was confused. "You do regard yourselves as an English colony?"

"Of course." The man from Newport was impatient. "You can tell for yourself that we aren't French or Spanish or Portuguese, sir!"

"Then you pay British taxes?" Richard asked.

Everyone in the room, including Miss Gertie, who presided at the table and ladled out the food, burst into loud, sustained laughter.

"You might say, Master Dunstable," the Providence representative said dryly, "that we pay when we must. With great reluctance."

The man from Newport grinned, revealing two rows of yellow teeth. "It's all a matter of pride," he said. "I do believe our Rhode Island sea captains are more adept at avoiding the payment of duties than those of any other British possession."

Richard began to grasp what these Rhode Islanders were trying to tell him. Independence—the right to do as they wished—was an obsession with them, so he said, "The Cavaliers are firm believers in the Church of England, while the Roundheads have developed the teachings of Calvin and Knox. But presumably they worship the same God. Would you permit a godless man to settle in your colony?"

They looked at each other in silence, and then the man from Warwick said quietly, "We wouldn't know he was godless, Master Dunstable, because we don't ask a man about his faith. That is something we regard as a private matter, to be determined by an individual's own conscience. We don't pry into matters that concern only a man and his Maker."

CHAPTER 5

RICHARD spent a full week in Providence Plantations, and when he left the town he felt a grudging admiration for the people of Rhode Island, who practiced the liberties in which they believed so fervently. Certainly their concept of freedom was new and unique. England and most nations of Europe had an official state religion which the people were required to observe; alliances were based on the system of government and religion being intertwined. Even colonies were founded on that same principle.

But the pioneers of little Rhode Island, few in number and trying to eke out a living in the wilderness of North America, were living according to a revolutionary concept: a man's religion was his own private business, and it was his right—not his privilege—to believe and practice his faith as he alone saw fit. Freedom of conscience was a novel, daring idea, and the more that Richard pondered the matter, the more he approved.

Only in the free world of America, where men faced

dangers every day of their lives with a determined calm, could such an idea come into being and grow. His report to the Earl of Newcastle would necessarily indicate that neither the Cavaliers nor the Parliamentarians could expect much active support in Rhode Island, and Richard guessed that officially he would have to disapprove of the new concept. But in actuality, he found he secretly admired the Rhode Islanders. If one of the powerful nations of the world, like Great Britain or France, ever adopted such an idea, that nation would be greatly strengthened. And if the concept spread to other colonies from Rhode Island, the appeal of the New World would become irresistible to those people of the Old World who were reduced to second-class citizenship because their way of worshiping God did not happen to be the same as that of their rulers.

Mounted on Prince Henry, he headed toward the southwest, occasionally catching a glimpse of the high seas and angry surf of the Atlantic from the crest of a hill. The Rhode Islanders had provided him with a crude map of the area between Providence Plantations and the small town called Pequot, urging him to go on to New Haven colony. One curious fact impressed itself on Richard's mind: there was no marker, no definition of any kind to tell him when he left Rhode Island and entered Connecticut. "The area is so sparsely settled," he was told, "that the problem of drawing a precise boundary won't become urgent for years to come."

In other words, Richard thought, someone who carved a home for himself and his family in these boundless forests would not necessarily know whether he was a resident of Rhode Island or Connecticut. Even more significant, that lack of knowledge would have no bearing on the man's life.

As nearly as the newcomer could determine, only in Boston did the geographical location of a man's dwelling have an effect on his way of life. Elsewhere he was free to do as he pleased, the colony in which he lived neither contributing to nor demanding service from him.

This was a life that Richard truly relished. He loved sleeping in the open, bringing down game, and catching fish for his meals, and what he did not already know about life in the wilderness, he was quick to teach himself. Through constant experiments he learned which roots and plants were edible, and once he found some forest produce he enjoyed, he invariably recognized it when he saw it again.

His clothes could not tolerate the strain of wilderness traveling, so he paid a tailor in Providence Plantations to cure the skins of several bucks that he shot, then to fashion trousers and shirts for him out of the stout leather that could withstand the punishment of rain and brambles. He was so much in his element that the problems of England seemed almost unreal to him, and frequently he had to remind himself not to dawdle on the trail. He still had a mission to perform.

One day, in the vicinity of the poorly defined Rhode Island—Connecticut border, Richard made out the sounds of human voices somewhere ahead. At almost the same instant, Prince Henry lifted his ears and became alert. Riding warily, Richard checked his rifle and pistol to make certain they were loaded, ready for use.

The trees thinned as he neared the crest of a rounded hill, and he drew to a halt in the shadows of a patch of evergreens, shading his eyes as he stared ahead. Five Indian braves were slowly circling some object on the ground.

Two jabbed at it with pointed sticks, while the others applied flaming brands they brought to life repeatedly in a nearby fire. Every time one of them jabbed at the object, he laughed and spoke aloud. Richard could not understand a word that was said, but he recognized the tone of voice as taunting.

All at once, he realized that the braves were torturing a fellow human being whom they had spread-eagled and tied to stakes. With his wrists and ankles held firmly in place, the writhing, silent victim could not evade the jabs nor the fire of his foes.

Richard first felt a sick revulsion for the scene he was witnessing, and that sensation gave way to an overwhelming feeling of outrage. No matter what the reason for the punishment, the odds against the victim were insurmountable, and his tormentors were prodding him for the sheer sport of it.

Weighing his own odds, Richard quickly made up his mind to intervene. "Steady, lad," he whispered to his mount, and raising his rifle to his shoulder, he squeezed the trigger. One of the torturers flung his arms high above his head, then collapsed onto the ground.

The other Indians heard the rifle shot, but could not figure out what had happened, perhaps because they were not anticipating the sound of a firearm's discharge, possibly because they had never known such expert marksmanship.

Reloading swiftly, Richard did not take his eyes from the Indians who were staring first at their fallen companion, then at each other. Again he raised his rifle, and he put his bullet between the eyes of a brave who caught a glimpse of the mounted man behind the fringe of trees and opened his

All at once, he realized that the braves were torturing a fellow human being whom they had spread-eagled and tied to stakes. With his wrists and ankles held firmly in place, the writhing, silent victim could not evade the jabs nor the fire of his foes.

mouth to shout a warning to his companions. He died before he could utter a sound.

"Go, Prince Henry!" Richard said, touching his horse's flanks with his heels. The great beast needed no other signal and bounded forward, hooves thundering through the spring mud as he gathered speed, his rider again reloading the rifle.

The braves stared in awe and fright at the unexpected apparition, a white-skinned man riding on the back of a huge mount, bearing down on them with reckless speed. They scattered, running for their lives.

No shot is more difficult than one attempted at a moving target while the marksman himself is in motion, but Richard was equal to the challenge. He knew Prince Henry as well as he knew himself, and adjusted easily to the horse's jarring gallop. Raising his double-barreled pistol, he took aim and squeezed the trigger. A third brave sprawled on the ground.

The remaining pair were heading for the forest on the far side of the open space, and Richard knew they would disappear unless he acted with dispatch. He drew one of his throwing knives, waited until he had gained on the fleeing braves, then hurled it with all of his might. The blade plunged into the Indian's back, vanishing up to the hilt, and the brave went down, his lifeblood soaking his buckskin shirt as he died.

The last surviving member of the group turned to face the onrushing man and horse, his desperation giving him the courage to make a stand. He snatched his tomahawk from his belt, then steadied himself before hurtling it.

Richard had another knife in his hand, but he had no chance to throw it. Prince Henry seemed to understand that this Indian was his master's enemy, and he bore down on the brave, his speed still increasing, a wild fire in his eyes, his teeth bared.

Too late the brave realized the stallion's intent, and turned away hastily after throwing his tomahawk, which sailed harmlessly over Richard's head. There was a thud as the horse ran over the man, but Prince Henry did not slow his pace, and the warrior died under the great steed's relentlessly pounding hooves. The task complete, Prince Henry wheeled abruptly and halted.

Richard surveyed the carnage, aware that five men had been killed within moments and that he had the field of combat to himself. He dismounted hastily, retrieved the knife he had thrown, and hurried to the victim of the quintet. The Indian was alive and conscious, his pain-filled eyes reflecting his gratitude to the white man who had rescued him from torment.

Richard slashed the leather thongs that held the warrior fast. Clad only in a loincloth, the man had suffered some nasty burns and cuts, but had survived his ordeal in relatively good condition. To the white man's astonishment, the Indian addressed him in English. "The leaves of the red plant that grows near the evergreens will heal me and make me well again," he whispered.

Richard ran to the nearest pines, and to his surprise saw a number of small plants with clusters of dark reddish-brown leaves growing up through the last remnants of snow on the forest's floor. He cut them at their base with his knife, then returned to the Indian with them.

The warrior crushed the leaves between his fingers, then rubbed them into his wounds. The procedure must have been excruciatingly painful, but he did not flinch, his face remaining impassively expressionless. When he was done treating himself, however, a great sigh of relief shook through him. "Roaring Wolf owes his life to the white man with the thundersticks and the horse who knows no fear," he said. "Roaring Wolf will serve them well as long as the Great Spirit allows him to live in this world."

The Indian was short and stocky, and the wiriness of his arms and legs indicated that he was capable of great stamina. His most compelling feature was his eyes, which were dark brown and unusually penetrating. They reflected an inner quality Richard was soon able to fathom as wisdom. The Pequot knew a great deal about nature and ways to survive in the wilderness.

Later, when Roaring Wolf came to know his benefactor better, he explained how he had acquired his name. It seems that years earlier when his tribe was at war and badly outmanned by neighbors, he dozed off while standing a long sentry duty. He awakened just in time to see a large band of enemy warriors approaching. Giving no heed to his own safety, he fired arrow after arrow at them, at the same time shouting at the top of his lungs. His colleagues later described his voice as being similar to that of a wolf that roared its displeasure when under attack by enemies. Roaring Wolf was obviously proud of his name, and also obviously had good cause for his pride.

Richard stared at him in fascination. "How do you happen to speak my language?" he demanded.

"It did not happen," the warrior replied. "I was the pupil of one who tried to teach me to love your God." Richard had not known that missionaries had been active in the area.

"I will collect more of the plants with red leaves," Roaring Wolf said, "and in two days my wounds will be healed.

This is a secret known only by the Pequot. Then I will be strong again and will help you in all you wish to do." Reaching out suddenly, he plucked a throwing knife from the startled young Englishman's belt, hauled himself to his feet, and walked to the nearest of the dead braves. Richard had to avert his eyes when he saw Roaring Wolf neatly and expertly scalping the dead warrior.

Soon the brave returned, five scalps clutched in his hand. "You killed them in fair combat," he said. "There are many in my tribe who would claim that one man cannot kill five Narraganset in battle, but I saw this miracle with my own eyes. You have earned the spoils." He offered his savior the scalps.

"I have no use for them," Richard said, feeling queasy.

Roaring Wolf shrugged, then tucked the scalps into the top of his loincloth. Returning the knife with a clumsy bow, he went off again, going from one fallen body to the next. Richard watched him as he took a buckskin shirt from one, trousers from another, and a pair of moccasins from a third. He acquired a knife, a bow and a quiver of arrows, and finally a tomahawk in the same practical, realistic way. He needed these essentials, and it did not seem to bother him that he was robbing the dead.

"Now we will go on your journey," Roaring Wolf announced. "You will lead and I will follow."

Richard wondered how anyone could travel so soon after being subjected to painful torture, but he was anxious to leave the scene and did not argue the point. He mounted Prince Henry, and as he set off again to the southwest, he deliberately walked his horse. The Indian made no complaint, and for more than two hours kept up the pace.

Afraid the brave might collapse at any moment, Richard

finally halted and made camp beside a swift-running stream. Roaring Wolf gathered dead wood, made a fire, and after digging up some roots unknown to his benefactor, he first washed them in the little river, then placed them in the coals at the edge of the fire. Finally, using his new knife with dexterity and speed, he fashioned a spear, which he took to the stream. Lying on his stomach, he peered intently into the water, his body motionless. All at once, his arm flashed, and he grinned happily as he exhibited a large fish on the point of his spear.

As the meal was cooking, Roaring Wolf told his story. He was a warrior of the small Pequot tribe, he said, and was thirty-five summers old. His people had been severely punished by the Great Spirit, and Richard gleaned from his explanation that the tribe had been decimated by a plague of some sort. The Narraganset, the ancient enemies of the Pequot and far more numerous than their foes, had long contested the Pequot's control of superior hunting grounds and were now obtaining possession of them. Pequot braves were isolated, captured, and tortured to death, which had been the fate in store for Roaring Wolf prior to Richard's intervention; the women of the tribe were enslaved and the children were adopted by the Narraganset.

"Soon all the Pequot will be gone," Roaring Wolf said, looking moodily into the fire. "The hunting grounds of my people will become the hunting grounds of the Narraganset. But," he added, his homely face suddenly relaxing as he smiled, "they will not enjoy these lands for long. The fathers will not be able to pass these hunting grounds to their sons."

"Why not?" Richard's curiosity prompted him to interrupt.

The Indian pointed a forefinger at him. "Every moon, ships that look like great white birds bring more men and women with pale skins from far places to the land of my ancestors. Already your towns are larger than the towns of the Narraganset. Your people use thundersticks that kill their foes and bring game to the cooking fires. The Narraganset use the bows and arrows of their fathers, which are no match for the thundersticks." The finger jabbed in the direction of Prince Henry, who was foraging for some tender grass and shoots protruding through the rich spring soil. "The men with pale skins bring beasts who carry them with great speed that the legs of the Narraganset cannot equal. So the greed of the Narraganset will gain them little. Soon, they will join their fathers in the land of spirits, and no man who lives in this land will remember them." He chuckled aloud, the notion giving him great satisfaction. Roaring Wolf interrupted his recital long enough to gather more plants with red leaves, which he rubbed into his wounds.

Richard was astonished to note that the burns and cuts were already far less inflamed and swollen than they had been. It was obvious that the primitive method of treating them was effective.

"It was the will of the Great Spirit that directed you to the place where the warriors of the Narraganset were taking the life of Roaring Wolf," the Indian declared.

Richard was too polite to suggest that sheer happenstance had brought him to the scene.

"So it is plain that the Great Spirit spared the life of Roaring Wolf for a purpose. I will devote the rest of my days to helping you overcome your enemies."

The young Englishman tried to dissuade him. "I became

angry when I saw the odds against you and realized that you were being tormented. But you are not in my debt, and you owe me nothing."

The warrior shook his head stubbornly. "Great evil will come to me if I disobey the will of the Great Spirit. And I would shame my father and his father before him if I did not hold out the hand of friendship to him who saved me from death." Reaching into the fire, he picked up a small coal and, with no sign of feeling pain, crushed it in his hand. Then he dropped the ashes into the palm of Richard's hand. "I will go where you go," he said solemnly, "and I will do as you direct me to do."

For better or worse, Richard knew, he had acquired a companion for the duration of his New World travels.

Richard had long assumed that he was familiar with forests, and even though he could survive in the deep woods, he soon realized how much he could learn from Roaring Wolf. The Indian was not only infallible in noting signs of game, but was equally adept at detecting the recent presence of men in the forest. Richard gratefully listened to the warrior's advice, observing the way leaves that had been scattered and bent blades of grass revealed the proximity of other humans.

He learned, too, how many edible roots there were in the wilderness, and how to distinguish between plants and berries that gave nourishment and those that were poisonous to man. Plants that had medicinal properties were endless, and the young Englishman gave up trying to commit them all to memory, instead concentrating on the most useful and plentiful herbs.

He was also taught by example how to eat after the

fashion of the Indians, wasting nothing. The staple of the Indians' diet was corn, supplemented by other vegetables and plants, he discovered, with meat, fowl, and fish taking a minor role in their nutrition. He found it more difficult to acquire the art of walking for hour after hour without tiring. He began to practice shooting with a bow and arrow, and his eye was so keen he quickly acquired the knack. His talent for throwing a knife made tomahawk-throwing an easy skill to acquire, but he had to admit he never would be able to hurl the clumsy weapon with the accuracy that Roaring Wolf took for granted.

The backgrounds of the two men were dissimilar in every way, but their love for the forest bound them together, and they soon established a solid rapport. Their communication transcended the use of words, and often a look or a hand signal was enough. The thought dawned on Richard that he had gained an ally who could prove of great value to him.

They traveled southward by easy stages until Roaring Wolf's wounds were healed, and after crossing the Pequot River, they came to the town of that same name. The inhabitants of the little port town were struggling to establish a foothold in the wilderness, and the lookout of the garrison seemed upset by the prospect of admitting Roaring Wolf to the town.

"You are welcome here, Master Dunstable," he said, "but we've made it a rule to keep out all Indians."

"Roaring Wolf is my friend," Richard replied, "and he goes where I go."

The guard was still nervous.

"Do you fear he'll steal from you?" Richard demanded.

"I assure you, he already has all that he needs. Are you afraid he'll learn your strength and lead a band of warriors in an attack on your town? His tribe is scattered, and he is responsible to no one—other than to me." With great reluctance the lookout granted permission for Roaring Wolf to enter the town.

No rooms or taverns for visitors were available, but Richard and Roaring Wolf were offered a meal by one of the hospitable residents. Richard wanted to tell the leaders of the little community that they were making a grave error. Pequot had a total of only thirty-six home lots, and the residents were greatly outnumbered by the Indians of the area, according to Roaring Wolf. Common sense dictated the necessity of winning the friendship of the natives, instead of holding them at arm's length. But Richard had learned to keep his opinions to himself.

Pequot, founded by John Winthrop, Junior, he discovered, was surprisingly not a smaller version of Boston. Richard had come to a town directed by its inhabitants, among whom Winthrop held paramount authority. During the few hours he spent in the community, he learned that the citizens of Pequot might be Puritans, but they were not fanatical in their devotion to the cause. The wilderness, he decided, was far more of an active force here than it was in Boston, and consequently, the Puritanism of the inhabitants was tempered by a realistic appraisal of the harsh environment that surrounded the town.

Richard had a private word with a town leader, who was known by the title of constable. "Constable Palmer," he said, "forgive an outsider for interfering, but you'll do far better if you trade with the Indians of the neighborhood rather than deny them the right to enter your town."

"You think so?" the man asked uncertainly. "We debate the question often at town meetings."

"Well," Richard replied, "surely your people know they can catch more bees with sweet pollen than with vinegar."

Constable Palmer's guffaw belied his funereal appearance. "I never thought of it that way, sir, but you may be right! Folks here are inclined to be extremely cautious when their safety is at stake!"

Richard rejected the constable's plea, seconded by others, to remain overnight as his guest. No one offered Roaring Wolf quarters for the night, and Richard refused to accept shelter when his companion would be forced to sleep in the open, even though that was the arrangement the Indian would have preferred.

The journey to New Haven was resumed, with Roaring Wolf leading his friend along the shore of the Great Bay. They spent the night on the beach after feasting on clams, crabs, and oysters they gathered in the shallow salt water, and after beginning their inland march the next day, they came to a relatively narrow bend in the Pequot River, the largest stream by far that Richard had encountered on his travels. Roaring Wolf offered to build a raft that would carry them and Prince Henry to the west bank of the river.

The forest was more dense now, making it necessary for Richard to follow the Indian on foot. Prince Henry brought up the rear and, like a well-trained dog, followed his master of his own accord. They proceeded in this fashion until early afternoon, when Roaring Wolf halted suddenly, raising a hand in warning. Richard moved up beside him, while Prince Henry seemed to realize he could not make his way quietly through the underbrush, and halted, too.

Directly ahead, in a sun-dappled hollow, several young Indian girls were gathering berries, which they tossed into woven baskets. The girls chatted and laughed, and the scene was joyously pastoral, so Richard could not understand the expression of alarm on the warrior's face.

The Indian maidens were enjoying themselves thoroughly and were so carefree, so uninhibited in their movements that it seemed impossible for them to be in danger of any kind. In fact, as Richard watched them, he was struck by their similarity to young English girls at play. They had the same innocent quality, the same bubbling mirth, the same free spirit. But something definitely was amiss.

Roaring Wolf made a circular motion with one hand, indicating his intention of giving the girls a wide berth. He started around the hollow, and Richard accepted the decision, turning away from the scene ahead. As he did, something caught the corner of his eye, and he looked back to see a huge black bear standing upright behind one of the Indian girls who had inadvertently wandered too close to the edge of the forest clearing. She was unaware of her danger until her companions began to scream, and then she was rooted to the spot, terror robbing her of her ability to flee.

Regardless of Roaring Wolf's reason for withdrawing, Richard could not leave now. He raised his rifle to his shoulder, took aim over the head of the endangered young girl, then fired. His bullet caught the bear in the shoulder, sending him down on his side. The beast howled in anger, rolled over, then rose to his hind legs again and lumbered toward his attacker.

Richard was so astonished to see the animal coming toward him that he gaped at the bear for a moment. Then he drew his pistol from his belt and fired, but through carelessness or haste he missed his target, something that rarely happened. Furious with himself, he fired a second time.

His shot found its mark, but the five-hundred-pound bear did not stop. The wound that was inflicted on the bear landed close to the first, and the animal's roar of pain and rage echoed through the forest. Prince Henry answered the challenge, pawing the ground, and his neigh was loud and clear. Richard knew the bear would tear the stallion apart or break the horse's neck with a single swipe of his powerful forefoot. There was no time now to prevent his mount from joining in the combat. The screams and shrieks of the Indian girls mingled with the bear's menacing growls, adding to the confusion.

Richard stepped into the open, blocking Prince Henry's charge, and drew one of his throwing knives. For his own sake, as well as his horse's safety, he could not afford to miss. No encounters with wild animals in the royal game preserve had prepared him for the rush of the gigantic creature bearing down on him now, but he steadied himself, and knowing his life and Prince Henry's depended on his aim, he let fly.

The knife penetrated the bear's skull between the eyes. To Richard's horror, the monster continued to lumber toward him for a few more paces before collapsing in a heap. Making certain the bear was dead before he ventured any closer, Richard retrieved his knife. Only then did he hear Roaring Wolf say urgently, "The maidens are Mohegan. We must go!"

The warning came too late. A party of thirty warriors burst into the open, all of them armed with bows and arrows or tomahawks. The girls all spoke simultaneously, and the leader of the party, a stern-faced man of forty, raised a hand for silence, then pointed first at one maiden, then at another. After each related in turn the story of what had happened, the leader went to the bear, examined the dead beast carefully, and finally turned to Richard, an expression of wonder in his eyes. At last he spoke, saying something curt and stern.

"He wishes us to come with him," Roaring Wolf muttered. "Now I shall surely be killed."

Warriors surrounded the pair, taking care to avoid Prince Henry, and Richard realized that their plight was hopeless. He had no opportunity to reload either his rifle or his pistol, and even if he took the chance and tried, the odds for their escape were minuscule. Perhaps he could leap into the saddle and rely on Prince Henry's powerful, flashing hooves to clear a path for him, but if he escaped he would need to leave Roaring Wolf behind, so he abandoned the plan as quickly as it crossed his mind. He picked up his mount's reins and, surrounded by the warriors, allowed himself to be led off through the forest. For the better part of an hour, he trudged in silence, wondering if he could bear the pain and indignity of torture with the tight-lipped courage that Roaring Wolf had shown.

At last, they came to a cleared field where neat furrows had been hoed for planting. Beyond it stood a circular palisade similar to those that Richard had seen in Providence Plantations and Pequot. Inside the circle, there were oval dwellings covered with woven mats or bark, the smoke of fires within them emanating from crude holes in their roofs. Scores of Indians appeared from nowhere, and women, old men, and half-naked children watched the procession in silence, with small boys and dogs joining the rear of the column. All were careful, Richard saw, to keep beyond the range of Prince Henry's hooves.

The two captives were conducted to an empty hut, and the horse was tethered outside. Air was admitted only through the door-flap of animal skin, and when it was lowered, the interior was as stuffy as it was dismally dark.

Roaring Wolf stoically seated himself cross-legged on the ground. "I tried to warn you," he said, no hint of bitterness in his voice. "How much better it would have been to let the bear send the maiden to her death!"

Richard's eyes smarted, and he blinked them in order to see his companion in the gloom. "I would do the same thing again," he said, "no matter what the consequences. What will happen to us now?"

His friend seemed indifferent to the fate that awaited them. "We will do what the Great Spirit wills," he said. "That which is done to us will be done at the will of the Mohegan, and I prefer not to think about it."

Suddenly weary, Richard seated himself on the hard ground and brooded. The ways of North American savages were inexplicable, he thought. Any other people would be pleased that a daughter of the tribe had been saved from a needless, cruel death, but it appeared that he would be penalized for his interference, perhaps because his skin was white, possibly because his companion was a Pequot.

All at once the door-flap was opened, admitting air and light, and a young woman in doeskins stood in the entrance, holding a wooden bowl in both hands.

Richard recognized her as the maiden he had saved from

the clutches of the bear. She looked older now that he had a chance to study her, and he guessed she was in her late teens or early twenties. Her features were regular and clean-cut, her cheekbones were high, and her full lips parted in a smile when she saw the man who had saved her life. Her huge, dark eyes expressed her gratitude to him as she entered the hut and, still holding the bowl, prostrated herself on the ground. Then, she said something in a singsong voice.

"Take the bowl and drink," Roaring Wolf whispered urgently. Following the instructions, Richard took the receptacle from the girl's hands, raised it to his lips, and drank. The brew was flavored with herbs, and the taste was so bitter, so alien that he shuddered.

Roaring Wolf snatched the bowl from his grasp and noisily drained the contents, then smacked his lips repeatedly in exaggerated approval. Then, he delivered what sounded like an endless address. The girl continued to gaze only at Richard as she listened to the diatribe. There was no way he could mistake the expression in her eyes. She wanted him.

When Roaring Wolf finished speaking, the girl took the bowl from him, rose to her feet and, after replying briefly and succinctly, withdrew. Perhaps she was being careless, but she left the flap open, and for whatever reason, Richard was grateful to her.

"What was all that?" he demanded.

The Pequot sucked in his breath. "It may be that we will not be made to suffer the death of a thousand torments. The girl you saved is Ilia-awi. She is the daughter of the sachem of the Mohegan. She made the drink for you herself." He sounded deeply impressed.

"No matter who made it, I'm glad you took it and drank it. I've never tasted anything worse."

"Your face told the way you felt. That is why I snatched the bowl from you and drank it myself, even though it was intended for you. It would not be wise to arouse the anger of the sachem's daughter. The Mohegan have many faults and are an ignorant, bad people, but they love their children."

"Are you telling me we may not be killed?"

"It is unlikely now." Roaring Wolf folded his arms across his chest and stared into space.

Nothing was more maddening, Richard thought, than Roaring Wolf's present unwillingness to communicate.

The next to arrive was a young warrior with fresh paint smeared on his face. He stood rigidly erect inside the entrance to the hut and raised his arm in greeting, the palm of his hand held perpendicular to the ground. Feeling a trifle foolish, Richard responded with a similar gesture.

The warrior spoke, apparently asking a question. Roaring Wolf replied at length, and the warrior withdrew. Wishing he could understand the language, Richard looked inquiringly at his friend.

"The Mohegan, as I told you, are an ignorant people. They have only seen a horse from a distance, so they think that Prince Henry is a god and that he has magical powers. They wished to know if he eats the food of humans, so I told the stupid warrior that he consents to eat apples."

Richard grinned and had a hard time controlling an urge to laugh when he saw through the entrance to the hut that the warrior had returned, slightly out of breath, carrying a basket filled with apples. He placed the basket on the ground, then pushed it with his foot toward where the horse was tied. Prince Henry sniffed, recognized the scent, and began to eat. The relieved warrior withdrew.

Richard was becoming convinced that no harm would befall him or Roaring Wolf. People who were solicitous of his horse's welfare would not injure or torture them.

A drum began to throb somewhere in the distance, then a second and a third were pounded rhythmically, too.

"Ah, it has started," Roaring Wolf said.

"What has?" Richard's nerves were ragged.

"You have a great surprise in store for you. The drums are summoning all Mohegan to the village." The Pequot chuckled, obviously enjoying the air of mystery he was helping to create.

Richard had already reloaded his rifle and pistol, which had not been taken from him, and he checked them automatically now.

An alarmed Roaring Wolf shook his head. "Do not shoot the Mohegan, I beg you!" he exclaimed. He had no chance to elaborate.

A group of a dozen warriors approached, all with fresh paint smeared on their solemn faces.

Their paint, which had been applied with a heavy hand, consisted of broad strokes of deep red, edged with thinner lines of white. They were attired in loincloths, moccasins, leggings that fastened behind, and fringed shirts that were closed with thonglike contraptions. They looked barbaric in the extreme, but Richard was becoming sufficiently acclimated to the New World to accept them in his stride. They drew to a halt outside the hut, and Richard recognized the leader as the man who had captured him. The warrior made a mercifully brief speech.

"He wants us to come with him," Roaring Wolf said. "I apologize for not answering your questions earlier, but I did not want to lift your hopes if I was wrong. But I am not wrong. The Mohegan are going to honor you."

Richard was relieved, but carried his rifle as he stepped into the open and was surrounded by the warriors. They led him through the strangely vacant town to the palisade gate, and there, in the open, Richard saw a vast crowd—hundreds, perhaps even a thousand men, women, and children gathered around a blazing, roaring fire.

Seated cross-legged at one side of the fire was a man of middle years whose elaborate headdress of feathers set him apart from all the rest. A half-dozen others, some elderly and some middle-aged, all with bonnets only slightly less elaborate, surrounded the man, who rose and extended his arm in greeting as the party approached.

Richard needed no one to tell him that he was meeting the sachem of the Mohegan and his principal aides, whatever they might be called. He returned the greeting.

The drums fell silent, and the sachem, speaking in a loud voice that carried through the twilight to the far edge of the crowd, made an address. Richard, understanding nothing that was said, heard the same words repeated again and again, and it was obvious to him that the chief of the Mohegan enjoyed public speaking. The young Englishman looked obliquely at Roaring Wolf, who stood beside him. The Pequot shook his head, and Richard understood; it would have been bad manners to interrupt the sachem.

The elders picked up the refrain, the drums began to beat again, and gradually the entire assemblage joined in, repeating the same words endlessly.

Roaring Wolf leaned closer to his friend. "The sachem

told his people of your virtues, and now the people of the Mohegan are singing your praises."

Richard stood self-consciously, a half-smile on his lips as he listened to the endless, singsong refrain. How Mimi would laugh if she could see him now! It was strange, he reflected then, that he should think of Mimi rather than of Dorothea.

At last the seemingly interminable chanting came to an end, and the sachem lowered himself to the ground, inviting the guest of honor to follow his example. Richard seated himself in a cross-legged position, which he found uncomfortable.

Ilia-awi approached, carrying something she had taken from the fire, and prostrating herself on the ground, offered the contents of the platter to her father and to Richard.

"This is a very great honor," Roaring Wolf whispered. "You are being given the opportunity to eat the heart and the brains of the bear you killed." Feeling his stomach turn over convulsively, Richard didn't know how he could follow the sachem's example.

"You must eat," Roaring Wolf whispered insistently. "The Mohegan will be insulted if you refuse."

"I am not worthy to eat the heart and mind of my enemy, the great bear," Richard announced, and forced himself to take token amounts of the food on the platter. The Pequot translated his words.

The members of the council beamed. The white man not only had made a fittingly, modest response in the true Indian tradition, but his refusal to eat left more of the delicacy for them. The contents of the platter, to Richard's relief, soon disappeared.

167

Now, dozens of the women were busy ladling out food for the entire crowd, and Richard noted that they worked methodically, in an orderly manner. They carried steaming victuals on wooden platters to the warriors of middle years, obviously the heads of families, and these braves distributed the rations to their wives and children.

Ilia-awi continued to serve her father and the man who had saved her life, her frank gaze burning into Richard whenever she looked at him. The girl could not be accused of being shy.

Richard looked suspiciously at the contents of his serving and was encouraged by the aroma. Taking a deep breath, he lifted it to his mouth, and to his surprise he found the thick, souplike stew to be delicious. The basic contents were corn, which he recognized at once, having eaten it not only in Boston, but in Providence and with Roaring Wolf, and chunks of a meat with a flavor all its own. Not until later was Roaring Wolf able to tell him that the meat was moose, the Mohegan having been fortunate enough to have enjoyed good luck on a recent hunting expedition.

There was no need to identify the main course that followed the stew: the bear had been roasted after being cut into quarters, and there was enough to give everyone present a portion. The taste was strong, Richard discovered, but he entered into the spirit of the occasion, aided by a healthy appetite, and between bites he smacked his lips in the approved manner. Far more to his liking were little corn cakes and steaming squash, served in gourds and sweetened with honey. The Mohegan might be a primitive people, but their cooking was excellent.

After the meal, the sachem wiped his mouth on his sleeve, then rid himself of the grease on his hands by wiping them on his trousers. Richard did the same, glad he had purchased a suit of buckskin, thereby saving the English clothes that would be difficult to replace.

Everyone around him was grinning now, and the strains of strange music floated across the area. Two braves were playing flutelike instruments, hollow reeds with finger holes, and rattles and drums picked up the tempo. The entire assemblage began to stamp and sway to the music.

Ilia-awi approached Richard again, and this time there was no obsequiousness in her manner. She stood boldly before him, her face wreathed in a happy smile, and slowly extended both hands to him.

Richard needed a moment to collect his thoughts, but soon he realized the girl was asking him to dance with her. This was the first time he had seen an Indian dance, and there was no escape, so he grasped her hands in his, and the crowd roared in approval as she led him to an open area at one end of the fire.

Ilia-awi began to dance, her feet stamping in time to the beat of the music, and Richard emulated her, his hands on his hips. At first he was awkward, unsure of himself, but the dance was simple, and he was soon carried away by the spirit behind it. The girl flirted with the man, enticing him, and when he came after her, she retreated. Then, when she grew tired of this game, she made the advances, and he retreated.

Scores of other couples came into the open area and were soon dancing, too. Richard was astonished to discover he was enjoying himself. He forgot that the music was repetitive and simple, that the girl who was flirting with him so expertly was a wilderness dweller who could neither read nor write. The Mohegan, he was learning, knew what they were doing. The very repetitiousness of the dance aroused him, and he pursued Ilia-awi with a mock vengeance that soon became real, then retreated from her in haste when she became aggressive.

Both were laughing and breathless when the music stopped. He and this young Mohegan woman had not been able to exchange a single word, yet he felt that he knew her well. She grasped his hand and led him back to her father. The sachem looked hard at the young couple who stood before him, his eyes bright. Then, folding his arms across his chest, he made a simple, direct speech to them. Ilia-awi averted her gaze and looked off into space.

Roaring Wolf materialized out of the crowd and translated for his friend. "The sachem gives his daughter to the great warrior who preserved her life. The great warrior will be given a hut of his own, and there he will sleep with Ilia-awi until the sun rises in the morning."

Richard's blood ran cold. At this time he could not afford the luxury of a liaison; he was devoting himself completely to the mission he had undertaken on behalf of the Stuarts and his country, and an affair with the Indian girl might well cause complications he could not predict. He had no way of knowing whether the offer was customary under the circumstances, or whether it would be followed by a demand that he marry the girl, which would be disastrous. Yet, in spite of all that his good sense told him, he knew he wanted Ilia-awi, who was making no secret of her willingness to give herself to him. He had to summon his willpower in order to shake his head.

Too late Richard realized he had committed a serious mistake. Roaring Wolf's expression of incredulous horror told him that he had erred, Ilia-awi was insulted, and the

*"The sachem gives his daughter to the great warrior who preserved her life.
The great warrior will be given a hut of his own, and there he will sleep
with Ilia-awi until the sun rises in the morning."*

sachem was enraged. Well knowing that his future depended on the goodwill of the Mohegan, he blocked the girl's path when she would have flounced away.

"Hear me," he said. "Ilia-awi is the loveliest and most desirable of women."

Roaring Wolf translated hastily, and from the length of his statement, it was apparent that he was adding embellishing touches of his own.

"I did not know she was so attractive when I saved her from the death embrace of the bear," Richard continued. "If I were to claim her body as a reward, I would denigrate the deed that I performed. I think too highly of her to sleep with her. I prefer to let my deed speak for itself. In this way it becomes a symbol of all that is good between us."

As Roaring Wolf translated, again adding his own words to the statement, Richard saw the sachem begin to thaw. His daughter was not being rejected, so his own honor remained intact.

Even more important, Ilia-awi accepted the explanation and was mollified by it. Her instinct had told her that this ruggedly handsome stranger, so unlike the warriors of the Mohegan, wanted her as much as she wanted him. But he was holding back because of his ideals, and there was nothing that could have flattered an Indian girl more.

Certain now that his approach was right, Richard bowed to Ilia-awi. "You will be present for all time in my thoughts and in my dreams," he said, knowing he was speaking the truth.

"The Great Spirit who guides and protects the Mohegan brought you to me in my hour of need," she replied, speaking softly. "He will not let us part, never to see each other again. I admire you all the more because you will not sleep with me now. That will await another time. The Great Spirit has not brought us together, only to separate us for all time. We will meet again in this world, of that I am very sure."

Richard continued to look at the girl as Roaring Wolf translated her words, and she gazed at him in return, her eyes steady, her bearing proud. Perhaps, he thought, primitive savages who were close to nature could foretell the future more readily and accurately than those who were too civilized for their own good. He knew, in ways that defied analysis, that she was speaking the truth. Their paths would cross again, and both would have cause to remember the death of the bear and its aftermath.

After spending three days on the trail that led to the southwest, Dempster Chaney estimated that he and Robbin had walked at least thirty miles. Had he been alone, he would have continued his journey, but he knew Robbin was tired, and the prospect of again trudging through forests and past occasional farms was too much for her.

He had not yet found the property that, he was convinced, he would recognize as his. The ten sovereigns that Richard Dunstable had given him were dwindling, and he realized that his dream of establishing a land claim and developing the property would need to be postponed. Robbin, who had led a sheltered life, deserved a roof over her head now, and it was wrong to wander on in search of an unattainable goal.

Dempster knew, too, that they had come far enough from Boston to escape both the Puritan influences and ways of life. The proprietor of the little country inn where they had spent the night was a bluff, hardy man, and the men of the neighborhood who had filled the taproom were hard-working farmers whose talk had indicated they were free from Puritan prejudices. Perhaps this was the area in which to settle and search for work.

So, as he paid the innkeeper for their lodging and food, Dempster asked casually, "Do you happen to know of anyone in these parts who could use the help of two able-bodied people, Master Greenleaf?"

The proprietor looked him up and down slowly, then inspected Robbin, too. "That depends upon what you can do," he replied.

"I was born on a farm in Devonshire and grew up there," Dempster replied, not adding that he had been trained as a gentleman and had planned to be a surgeon, not a laborer. "I daresay I know more about raising crops than most."

"And I'm not afraid to work, either," Robbin added. "I can cook and sew, and I've spun cloth."

The innkeeper instinctively liked the forthright young couple and rubbed his chin reflectively. "Well, now, that does put a different light on the matter. I figured from your dress and manners that you were city folk—that you'd feel more at home in Boston than you would out here in the wilderness."

"May we never see Boston again!" Dempster exclaimed.

"Amen to that," Robbin said.

Greenleaf was lost in thought. "Everybody hereabouts knows that the Widow Browne sure needs help. Mrs. Hester Browne, who has a farm a couple of miles down the creek road. Her husband died two years ago, and she's had a hard struggle trying to farm her land herself."

"We'll go to see her," Dempster replied instantly.

"Hold on for a minute, young fellow," the innkeeper said. "Hester isn't the easiest person to get along with. She has the sharpest tongue in all of Massachusetts Bay, and she wants things done her way. You wouldn't find it easy living under her roof."

Robbin hesitated before she asked, "Is she of the Puritan faith, Master Greenleaf?"

"No more than anybody else in Taunton, young woman! All I said was that she's cantankerous, but she's in her right mind!"

"That's all right, then," Dempster said, and after thanking the innkeeper for his help and directions to the farm, they started out.

The village, which consisted of the inn, a general store, and a small cluster of houses, was soon left behind, and the couple started off on a narrow trail that led through deep woods. "This isn't very promising," Robbin said as she followed her husband. "The lady's farm must be terribly isolated."

Dempster shrugged. "We'll find out soon enough." He was becoming adept at avoiding fallen logs and other obstacles on the path.

Suddenly they emerged into the open, and directly ahead saw a large farm, the ground cleared of trees. The main house was two stories tall, of unpainted clapboard, and behind it stood a stable, a barn, a chicken coop, and a toolshed.

"There she is," Robbin said, indicating a gray-haired woman trying to handle a team of two large, gray work-horses who were pulling a plow through the ground. It was obvious to Dempster that she was fighting the horses rather than giving them their heads, and as a consequence, the plow sometimes was effective in turning over the earth and sometimes was not.

He cut across the open fields toward her, calling, "Mistress Browne?"

The woman halted her team, then wiped perspiration from her leathery, lined face. "Whoever you be, you're trespassing," she declared.

"I suggest you let your horses decide the path they'll take," he said. "They have an instinct for the line of least resistance, and you'll find it much easier to fill in the places they miss, later on. Like this." He moved toward the team, picked up the reins, plowed a straight furrow, then doubled back. As he had indicated, the horses were far more malleable.

Hester Browne watched him, her narrowed eyes bright. "You make it look easy, just like my Eddie did," she said grudgingly.

Dempster halted near her. "You have a large property here," he said. "Do you intend to plow up all of it?"

"All three hundred and twenty acres," Hester replied testily. "I've got to plant the entire property because I never know what crops will take and what crops won't."

"I see." He dropped to one knee, picked up a handful of plowed soil, and let it sift through his fingers. "Depending on the rainfall, which looks good judging by the trees, you'll do best here with wheat. And perhaps maize. I know very little about American corn, though. I presume you grow vegetables too, for your own use?"

"Naturally I do. Who be you, coming nosing around here, and how does it happen you know so much about my farm?"

"I only know what I see," Dempster replied gently, then introduced himself and his wife.

Hester Browne sniffed audibly.

"Green beans, cucumbers, and squash should do nicely here," Dempster said. "And depending on how much of your land you allow to lie fallow, you could raise sheep, too."

"My husband raised sheep, but I don't have the knack." The gray-haired woman stared at him. "You haven't answered my question!"

"Master Greenleaf, at the inn, said you could use some help. My wife and I are looking for work."

The young couple's clothes were travel-soiled but expensive, Mrs. Browne observed. "I can't afford the likes of you, though goodness knows I'm not too proud to admit that I can't earn the living that Eddie made here."

"We'll work for our room and board," Dempster said, "and we'll work out an arrangement to be paid a small share of the profits, too."

The widow laughed harshly. "There have been no profits since Eddie passed away."

"There will be." Dempster took his time looking out across the fields. The soil was rich, there were no tree stumps, boulders, or other obstacles that he could see, and he knew of no reason why hard work shouldn't produce bumper crops.

"You show up out of the forest, as bold as you please, and you expect to be hired. Just like that. How do I know you're not a pair of rogues who will murder me in my sleep?"

"Do we look like rogues and murderers?" Robbin knew she should be civil, at the very least, but her indignation was too great.

"I'm none too friendly with folk of that ilk," Hester Browne replied, a hint of a smile appearing at the corners of her compressed mouth. "You and I will go to the house, where you'll tell me all about yourselves, young woman. Meantime your husband can finish what's been started here." Not waiting for a reply, she walked briskly toward the farmhouse. Robbin looked at her husband, shrugged, and followed. She had been given no choice.

Dempster removed his coat, folded it carefully, and addressed the workhorses. "You two," he told them, "are going to earn your feed today!"

He plowed rapidly, the team responding to his confident handling, and in an hour he turned up much more soil than Mrs. Browne had managed in all her previous efforts. He had been aware of her peering out of the window at him from time to time, and he had given her enough of a sample. He unhitched the horses, giving them the opportunity to graze freely in the unplowed areas, and as he started toward the house, he saw the fence needed repair and that the barn door had been torn from its hinges. There was enough to be done to keep a man occupied here.

When he walked into the kitchen, where two partly consumed cups of tea rested on a table that needed to be scraped and sanded, he was startled to see Hester Browne laughing heartily while Robbin stared at her indignantly.

"I told her the truth about us," Robbin explained, "and when I came to the part about Boston and what happened to us there, she started to laugh. She just won't stop."

"As the Puritans would say," Hester declared, stifling her laughter, "the Lord works in mysterious ways. You two deserved punishment for sleeping together before you were properly married. Oh, I understand the circumstances," she went on, giving Robbin no chance to interrupt, "but you could have been strong enough to resist temptation. You didn't, so you got what you deserved when the Boston constables threw you into prison for kissing in public!"

Dempster could see the point she was making, but nevertheless thought her sense of humor odd.

"I thought my Eddie and I were brave, coming out to the wilderness ten years ago and claiming this property," Hester said, "but at least we had our tools and our equipment and enough saved to buy whatever else we might need. You two came out this way armed only with your courage."

"It was necessity, not courage, that brought us out here, Mistress Browne," Robbin said firmly, dropping the cloth soaked in vinegar she had been using to clean a copper pan while they talked. "We had no choice."

"What will you do if I refuse to take you in?" Hester demanded.

"We'll search until we find someone who will," Dempster replied. "I can't believe that a man with my knowledge of how to operate a farm won't be able to find honest work."

"This isn't relevant," Robbin said as she peered into the parlor that adjoined the kitchen, "but you have a bench in there that badly needs a new cover."

"Don't I know it," Hester replied with a sigh. "But cloth is dear these days. Everything we can buy comes all the way from England."

"Do you have any flax?" Robbin wanted to know.

"The barn is half-filled with last year's crop. Everyone in the region had the same idea, and there was no market for all of it."

"In that case, I'll make you a new linen cover. I see you

have a wheel." Robbin indicated a spinning wheel that stood in a kitchen corner.

"Aye, and no time to use it." Hester was silent for a moment, trying to make up her mind. "I suppose I have naught to lose by seeing how you'll do here. You're hired. For your room, board—and five percent of the profits."

"Make it ten percent," Dempster said quietly. "You said you've had none at all in the past couple of years, so you can see that ten percent of something is better than five percent of nothing."

"You have a bargain." Hester extended a bony hand. "But don't try to flummox or fool me, and don't—" She broke off as Dempster headed toward the door. "Where do you think you're going, young man?"

"There's plowing to be done," he said, "and with this spring weather, we need to be ready for planting." The door closed behind him.

She turned and saw Robbin energetically scrubbing the copper pan, so she muttered something about being behind in her mending as she headed for the stairs. It was true, she thought, that the Lord did His work in mysterious ways, and she felt ashamed of herself for being so flippant. She had been desperate, near the end of her rope when this young couple had appeared out of the blue, and if they lived up to their promise, she would never again doubt the Almighty's ability to work miracles.

CHAPTER 6

MOLLIE Williams was tired after the long journey to New Amsterdam from Providence Plantations, and after kicking off her shoes beneath the table at the Thorn and Thistle, she sat back gratefully, soaking in the atmosphere and enjoying the cold mug of ale that Angus MacNeill, the proprietor, had brought her.

"What I tell you is God's truth, Master MacNeill," she said. "The Puritans of Boston are as mad as those in England—nay, madder—and I fled from them as though Beelzebub hisself was hauling at me petticoats. Providence Plantations may become a fine town in time, and I've naught against it, but the birds made so much noise in the first hour of dawn, they had me wide awake. I'm a Londoner born and bred, I am, and I despaired of finding a civilized nook in this wild country until I saw New Amsterdam. Now then, I said to meself, here's a town for you, Mollie, me girl!"

Angus MacNeill grinned at her, revealing gaps where

there used to be front teeth, then he absently smoothed his thinning, sandy hair. "Come to the windows with me, Mistress Williams. I feel as you do, and it's no accident that New Amsterdam is unique in all this land, even though we have a population far less than that of Boston."

Mollie searched frantically for her shoes, found them, and dutifully accompanied her host to the window. She was applying for a position here, so she was in no way able to refuse the invitation, much as she wanted to stay seated.

"Look yonder, to the right of the windmill, and what do you see?" he demanded.

"The fort, sir?"

"Yes, the little fort with the useless Dutch cannon that will blow up in the face of the man who has the nerve to fire them," he replied. "And over yonder, past Hudson's River?"

"It looks like chalk cliffs to me, Master MacNeill," she said dubiously.

"Ah, the Palisades, we call them. The beginning of a godforsaken wilderness that stretches all the way to the Pacific Ocean. Or so I'm told, though I don't intend to find out. And what do you see to the left of the fort? Long Island, another wilderness, save for the little town of Breukelen, where some who would farm want their own land so bad they're willing to risk their lives. And right here, surrounded by wilds, is New Amsterdam!" Beaming with pleasure, he led her back to the table.

Mollie followed, again disposing of her shoes, and took a swallow of her ale.

"New Amsterdam is like Holland, all right, but it's better," he said, beginning to laugh before he finished telling his little joke. "The Dutch, you see, are a minority here."

Mollie laughed dutifully.

"You think I jest." He began to enumerate on his thick, callused fingers. "The Dutch are reluctant to leave the prosperity in Holland to make the difficult ocean voyage. But we have Swedes from New Sweden who couldn't tolerate the wilds of the land. We have French Huguenots who were persecuted by Richelieu, then by Mazarin, damn his French soul. We have Jews who wanted a country where they could worship freely. We have West Indian planters who could not tolerate the hot climate, and we have a smattering of folk from Bohemia and Brandenburg, not to mention a boatload of settlers from the Kingdom of Naples."

Mollie was impressed, but tried not to show it. "That's most unusual, Master MacNeill."

"Aye, and it's what makes New Amsterdam the best and liveliest town in all of the New World. Do you know why, Mistress Williams? Because we have a philosophy here of live and let live. We accept a man for what he is, not for his religion or his nationality. We have British colonists who are fleeing the rigidity of the Puritans in England and in the New World, so that's why we laugh at the Puritans and thumb our noses at the Cavaliers!"

"Aren't the English who live in New Amsterdam loyal to the Stuarts?" Mollie was shocked.

"Why should we be? What did poor Charlie or his pa before him ever do for us? I built this inn with my own hands. I worked for years to save the money to be able to build it. I owe no debt to any man on earth, so I say to the Puritans and the Royalists, go on, chop off each other's heads. I'll have no pains in my neck as a result of their squabbling!"

Mollie nodded thoughtfully, and could see the man's point of view, which she wouldn't have understood before coming to America herself. The New World was physically removed from the Old World by thousands of miles, and the bitter disputes that had resulted in Britain's civil war were of little consequence to a people who now were trying to earn a living in a town controlled by the Dutch and surrounded by wilderness.

"I tell you all this for a reason, Mistress Williams," Angus MacNeill said soberly. "When I first planned this place, I thought I'd act as my own principal cook and barman. But I find I don't have the time. I've tried out three men for the job, one who couldn't cook and two who drank my best beer. You're a gift from Heaven, and I'd be a fool to let you get away. What wages do you want?"

Mollie shrugged. "I know nothing of what's paid here. At Whitehall I got all I wanted to eat, food to take home to me son, and three shillings per week."

"The Stuarts have a collection of marvelous gems, Mistress Williams, because they robbed the poor. You'll cook and tend the bar for me, and you'll get every other Sunday to yourself. I'll give you all your meals, wages of six shillings per week, and you'll keep the tips the patrons give you. You'll have your own snug quarters, too, with a fireplace of your own."

Mollie was overwhelmed. "You're most generous, Master MacNeill."

"Nay, I have need of you. Just remember what I told you about New Amsterdam. Don't encourage talk among the patrons about Cavaliers and Puritans. Keep in mind that New Netherland doesn't care what happens to England or the rest of the world, and you'll do fine."

"You can depend on it, sir. I'll weep for poor Charlie in me own snug quarters as I sit before me own hearth."

"When can you begin?"

"Now," she said. "Just tell me how many you expect to sup here tonight, and I'm off to the market."

"I've already bought all we'll need for tonight. You'll find the larders are filled. And Mistress Williams—the Thorn and Thistle isn't Whitehall, I hardly need tell you. We serve wholesome meals here, but I've been in the habit of buying what's cheapest at the market."

"I'll tell you a secret, Master MacNeill," Mollie replied. "The Stuart jewels didn't come only from the money they saved on the wages they paid me. Old King Jamie went over the food bills hisself, and poor Charlie picked up the habit from him."

Angus MacNeill grinned at her. They had achieved a perfect understanding.

"There's just one more question to be settled," she said. "It concerns me son."

His cheerful smile faded rapidly. "That young Bart is a troublemaker."

"I beg to contradict you. He don't mean to cause a fuss. He has a hot temper and too big a mouth, but he's always surprised when there's trouble."

"Well," MacNeill said firmly, "I've heard him going on and on about King Charles, goading and poking and pushing until he can strike an argument. And I tell you plain, Mistress Williams, there's no room for the likes of that lad in my taproom. People come here to eat because they like the food and because the atmosphere is peaceful. The place would be in an uproar if I hired young Bart to wait on tables!"

Mollie hesitated. She didn't want to lose the post that had been offered to her, but she had to look out for her son's future, too. "What would you do if you was in me shoes, Master MacNeill?" she asked.

The proprietor of the Thorn and Thistle didn't want to lose the services of an experienced cook who could also attend to drink orders, so he relented. "There happens to be a place he might fit in. Does he know horses?"

"No more and no less than most," she said cautiously.

"Then he'll learn much about them. There's an opening in the stables for an ostler who will attend the guests' horses. I'll pay him two shillings per week, you can feed him his meals—which you'd do in any event—and he can sleep in the loft above the horses' stalls. That's the best I can offer him."

"On Bart's behalf, I accept with great pleasure," the relieved Mollie said quickly.

So the bargain was struck, and MacNeill took his new cook to the extensive kitchen, an outbuilding connected with the main portion of the Thorn and Thistle by a passageway. Mollie quickly asked questions as she familiarized herself with the hearth, utensils, and contents of the larder, and MacNeill, equally brisk, replied succinctly.

"How much say will I have in working out a menu?" she wanted to know.

"Well, I urge you to check your plans for meals with me for a couple of weeks until you learn what our patrons like," he said. "Then you'll be on your own. With as many as a dozen guests spending the night, I'm too busy to bother. Your kitchen will be your own kingdom, Mistress Williams."

Nothing he could have said would have made Mollie happier. She threw some bones into a pot to make stock for soup, and as she busied herself, she began to hum under her breath.

"I haven't heard you sing for a long time, Ma." Bart had come in behind her.

Mollie turned to him with a frown. "Where have you been, lad?"

"If you must know," he replied defiantly, "a fine gentleman bought me two pints of ale, all for the pleasure of me company."

"What grand gentleman would seek the company of the likes of you?" she demanded.

Bart was short, but managed to look towering as he drew himself up haughtily. "His name is Laroche."

Had Richard Dunstable been present, he would have recognized the name as that of the principal Cavalier agent in the colonies, the man to whom he would report at the appropriate time. But Mollie remained blank. "And why did Master Laroche buy you two pints of ale, lad?"

"I was having a bit of a dispute with a pair of locals on the subject of King Charlie," he said proudly. "I lost me temper a mite when they said they couldn't care less what had befallen him. Master Laroche heard me light into them, and the ale followed, just like that. He says he wants to know you, too. He was impressed to no end when he heard you was on the staff at Charlie's palace."

"You'll keep your big mouth shut from now on," Mollie said. "I've arranged a job for you, courtesy of Master Mac-Neill—"

"He's sweet on you, Ma."

"Never you mind that, young man!" She told him in detail about the position she had obtained for him and the stipulations concerning Bart's behavior. "So you'll go to the stables right now. Report to the chief groom for work. And don't bother me again with your tales of grand gentlemen and pints of ale!"

Bart went off sulking, not bothering to thank her for intervening successfully on his behalf.

Mollie overcame her irritation with him by devoting herself totally to her work. She enjoyed cooking, and the new position was a challenge she intended to meet. It was true, as Bart had said, that Angus MacNeill was attracted to her. She was flattered and had to admit she was drawn to him, too. But he had hired her because of his need for the services she could perform at the Thorn and Thistle, not because of the potential of their personal relationship, so she would do her best to justify his faith in her.

The supper hour came, and as the dining room filled with guests the atmosphere in the kitchen became frenzied. Two waiters came in and out with orders, and Mollie was everywhere at once. She ladled soup, broiled steaks, put fresh fish on the fire, and served portions of potatoes, vegetables, and salad greens with speed and expertise. The kitchen was her domain, and the waiters were brisk and businesslike in their dealings with her, recognizing her aura of command. Gradually the hubbub subsided, and as she sat down at last to eat her own supper, Angus MacNeill came into the kitchen, a broad smile lighting his square face.

"That was grand," he said, helping himself to a large portion of beef stew and sitting opposite her at the hardwood table. "I thought I was the only person alive who could keep the orders moving, but you're better at it than I am!"

Mollie thanked him with a smile and a nod. She well knew the praise was deserved, and having passed her first test with flying colors, she realized that she had made a secure place for herself.

"If you're too weary," Angus told her, "I'll take charge in the taproom tonight."

Mollie savored the taste of the fish she was eating before she replied. The flavor was delicate, unlike any fish she had ever prepared in London, and she wanted to commit the taste to memory. "I thank you most kindly for the offer, Master MacNeill," she said, "but—as you well know—the serving of drinks to them as wants relaxation before bedtime is child's play."

He remained solicitous. "Whenever you grow weary, then, close the taproom for the night."

She grinned and shook her head. "While there's an honest penny to be made, I'll earn it!"

He had been fortunate to find someone with her experience and capacity for hard work, he knew. "We'll go to the market together in the morning. I'll go with you until you come to know the butchers, fishmongers, and greengrocers." With Mollie relieving him of the chores that had tied him down, he would have the time to make the Thorn and Thistle the finest inn in New Amsterdam, and he would be in a position to construct the annex he had envisioned far sooner than anticipated.

When Mollie finished her meal, she went to the taproom, where she took up her place behind the long bar. Customers soon began to drift in, and she served them deftly, making small talk. Apparently the evening clientele included a number of locals, as well as travelers who had rented quarters at the Thorn and Thistle, and two of the former became involved in a loud argument while consuming their third mugs of strong ale.

Mollie promptly rapped a tumbler with a spoon, and everyone in the place looked at her. "I'll tolerate no blasphemy in my taproom," she announced, aware of the need to set a tone for the establishment if she hoped to maintain order. "And you'll take yourself elsewhere if you're having a dispute."

One of the men who had been quarreling, a brawny fisherman, glowered at her. "Who are you to tell me how loud I can talk and what I'm to say?"

Mollie's expression became cold. "I happen to be mistress of this here room," she said. "I don't tolerate cursing, or those disturbing others who have paid for a pint and want to drink it in peace. If you can't abide by me rules, you will be asked to leave."

The fisherman hauled himself to his feet. "Who will run me out of here?" he demanded. "You?"

Mollie promptly picked up a bar knife and pointed it at the man, using it to underscore her authority. "I could call the constables and have you locked up for creating a nuisance, but that won't be needful. Mind your manners, and you'll be welcome here. Create a fuss, and I'll be obliged to run you off the property meself!" She emerged from behind the bar, the knife still pointed accusingly at the disturber of the peace.

To her surprise, the other half-dozen patrons applauded, none more vehemently than a dark, well-dressed man of indeterminate age who sat quietly at a corner table by himself. The fisherman flushed. This determined woman would cause him a great deal of trouble before he could subdue her, and he knew that if he tried, the law would be on her side.

"Sit you down!" she commanded.

The man sat.

Mollie went to him and picked up his mug. "You shall have some free ale, courtesy of the management, in return for behaving like a gentleman." She bustled back to the bar and refilled his mug.

The fisherman looked at her sheepishly as she placed it in front of him. "I—I didn't mean to cause a disturbance, ma'am," he said. "And I thank you for the ale."

Her smile indicated that she forgave him, while at the same time warning him not to forget his place again. She had not only won the encounter, but she knew the word of her victory would spread through the town, and that, consequently, she would have fewer problems in the future.

The dark, well-dressed man moved from his table to the bar and ordered a glass of sweet sack. "You handled that ruffian well," he said. "Forgive my curiosity, but would you have used that knife to drive him out?"

Mollie considered the question. "Aye," she replied laconically.

"You're an unusual woman, Mistress Williams," he observed.

Mollie peered at him sharply. His shrewd eyes were

studying her, but she felt certain she had never set eyes on him until he had appeared in the taproom a quarter of an hour earlier. "You know me name," she said.

"I happen to know more than that," he replied. "I know where you worked in London—and why you left to come to the New World."

She felt uncomfortable. "I'm an ordinary woman," she said. "Why should the likes of me be of interest to a grand gentleman?"

"Because," he said, speaking so softly she had to strain in order to hear him, "we share the same sentiments." He went through the motions of drinking a toast to the king-across-the-water, a gesture she hadn't seen since her voyage across the Atlantic. Mollie continued to stare at him as she awaited a fuller explanation.

"I had the good fortune to engage your son in conversation," he said. "He made no secret of his sentiments, and he told me of your great good fortune. We serve the cause in different ways, but you enjoyed the privilege of preparing the very meals that His Majesty ate. What satisfaction you must have felt!"

He actually made her work in the Whitehall kitchen sound far more important and rewarding than it had been. She had held the position because of the need to earn a living for her son and herself, and her loyalty to the Crown had nothing to do with her employment. In fact, she had disapproved of much that she had seen of King Charles and his way of life.

The man knew he was failing in his attempt to impress her. "My name is Laroche," he said.

As Mollie nodded, she knew she disliked Master Laroche. Something in his manner set her teeth on edge, but he was a patron of the Thorn and Thistle, and he had said and done nothing untoward, so it was her place to treat him with civility.

"I assume that you'd be willing to work for the restoration of the Stuarts to the throne. I know you'd be delighted to return to your former place of employment."

He was assuming far too much. "For the privilege of serving Charlie," she said tartly, "I worked me fingers to the bone and was paid a pittance. You can have the privilege, Master Laroche. This is me first day here, but I tell you plain, I prefer an honest day's wages for an honest day's work."

"No one can fault you for that, Mistress Williams." He paid for his glass of sack, then made a point of leaving a half-crown on the bar.

"Don't forget your change, Master Laroche," she reminded him.

His smile was cheerless. "That's for you, Mistress Williams." Mollie well knew that she didn't deserve that large a tip, and even as she thanked him, she felt suspicious of him. In her experience, those who seemingly gave something for nothing had ulterior motives.

"What do you think of the French?" he asked suddenly.

The unexpected question bewildered her. "They've been the enemies of England as far back as anybody can remember. I suppose we should be thankful to them for giving young Charlie a roof over his head, and not go looking gift horses in the mouth. But I don't rightly trust the French, and I say no good will come out of this friendship they're showing the queen and her young son."

Her attitude did not surprise Laroche. The hatred of the English lower classes toward the nation that lay on the far side of the English Channel was deep-rooted. "I believe you're mistaken, but we'll let that pass," he said. "Mistress Williams, you're in a position to do the cause of the Stuarts much good."

"Am I now? A simple body like me?" She put her hands on her hips and challenged him, no longer hiding her suspicions. "How would I do that?"

"The Thorn and Thistle is the best inn in New Amsterdam," Laroche replied calmly. "Men of substance from England and from other colonies are guests here. And as you surely know, liquor loosens men's tongues. You'll hear a good many conversations not intended for your ears in your new position here."

"If I hear anything that's none of me affair," Mollie replied indignantly, "you can count on it that it will pass through me mind like a sieve. I'm hired to tend bar here, not to gossip about things that are none of me concern!"

"You may pick up tidbits that could be valuable to the cause of young King Charles. It's your duty to repeat them to those who serve him!" His manner became stern.

"I—I didn't think of it that way." She felt less sure of herself.

"I'll be grateful for anything of importance that you can pass along to me—sufficiently grateful to reward you accordingly." He picked up the half-crown that he had left on the bar, then spun it on the polished surface.

Somehow, it didn't seem right to Mollie to be taking pay for the performance of what Laroche had termed a patriotic duty.

The coin clattered as it fell, and Laroche pushed it toward her. "We need to know our friends in the New World," he said. "And our enemies. It will take a great concentration of effort on the part of many good, devoted people to bring Charles the Second to the throne of his father and grandfather."

Her confusion growing, Mollie could only nod.

"You're not being disloyal to MacNeill by repeating anything of interest you may hear," he assured her. "And keeping your ears open, staying alert, will not interfere with the duties for which MacNeill is paying you. On the other hand, it isn't everyone who has your opportunity to serve the monarch—and to be handsomely paid in the bargain."

She knew Laroche was applying pressure, but she didn't know what to reply.

"I'll drop in from time to time, and we can have a little chat that will be mutually beneficial." He bowed, smiled faintly, and left the taproom quickly, not looking at any of the patrons.

Mollie was flattered by the thought that she had been enlisted, even involuntarily, as a spy for the Crown. All the same, she trusted her instincts, and she knew she neither liked nor trusted the smooth-talking Laroche.

New Haven was the most attractive and well-established town in the American colonies that Richard had as yet visited. The homes were substantial, the port area was busy, and although there was a Green similar to the Boston Common, the inhabitants of the affluent town preferred to keep their livestock at home and use the Green as a public park.

Less than an hour after Richard and Roaring Wolf arrived in New Haven, they were dining at a licensed tavern facing the Green. As they sat at their table, they were approached by a plump, smiling man of middle years. "I take it you're strangers here," he said, and the men exchanged introductions and background information. Richard soon learned that Adam Burrows owned a thriving fleet of merchant ships engaged in the encouraged intercolonial coastal trade, and that as the head of the colony's militia, he preferred to be addressed as Colonel.

· "I migrated here from Lincolnshire a good many years ago," he said. "I wonder, do you by chance know Sir William Dunstable?"

"He was my father," Richard said.

"I knew him well, and we were good friends," Colonel Burrows replied. "I gather he's no longer alive?"

Richard nodded.

"In that event, you're Sir Richard! I insist that you and your friend stay at my home as my guests!"

Refusing to listen to Richard's polite protests, he supervised their move to his impressive waterfront house of red brick.

Roaring Wolf was relieved when he saw a large yard behind the house. "I will sleep there, in the open," he said. "The houses of white men are like boxes, and I feel shut up inside them."

Familiar with the ways of Indians, Colonel Burrows calmly agreed. Then he led Richard to his library for a chat, while Roaring Wolf took Prince Henry to the stable.

"You have a remarkable collection of books here, Colonel," Richard observed.

"I was fortunate, Sir Richard. When I first came to America, not too many people were settling in New Haven, so I took advantage of a half-empty ship to bring my entire library with me. What brings you to the New World?"

Richard became cautious. "If you knew my father, you

must have been aware of the hereditary Crown post he held."

"Of course. As King's Forester. Ah, I see." Colonel Burrows folded his hands across his paunch. "I can guess the rest. The Parliamentarians abolished the position, as they have so many royal sinecures. And you're searching for a place to settle."

"Something like that." It was easiest not to admit too much.

"I hope you'll look long and hard at New Haven. Our sea trade doesn't equal that of either Boston or New Amsterdam, but we do a lively business nonetheless, exporting corn, beaver skins, and livestock. And our people are far friendlier."

"Then the Puritan influence isn't strong here?"

"It is a way of life for the older generation, Sir Richard. Our children, people your age, are devising their own codes of conduct and beliefs. We're all too busy, young and old alike, building our own trade and buying land from the Indians to let those generational differences disrupt peace and cooperation in our homes. Recently we had a request from Cromwell, asking us to pledge our allegiance to Parliament. So Tom Clayton, our leading merchant, and I signed the papers he sent us and shipped them right back to London. I doubt if Tom's son would have signed such a pledge. He's not so involved with the politics of England as is his father." He chuckled, then winked.

Richard was startled when an exceptionally attractive young woman opened the door and swept in. She was tall and blue-eyed, with long, blonde hair streaming down her back, and her gown of pale silk made no secret of her lithe figure. "I should have guessed you'd be cooped up here, talking business as usual, Papa," she said. "Didn't you smell and feel spring in the air today? If I were you, I'd leap at the opportunity to spend the whole day on the waterfront docks. Anything to stay out-of-doors!"

"My daughter, Eliza," Colonel Burrows said proudly. "Sir Richard Dunstable."

As Richard bowed he could feel the girl's appraising glance, and he knew she was attracted to him, just as he was drawn to her.

Eliza Burrows would have attracted attention anywhere, in any country. Her hair, to be sure, was an unusual shade, and her eyes were an intense blue that was startling. Her figure, at least at first glance, appeared to be virtually flawless. She had a long neck, naturally square shoulders, a high firm bosom, a tiny waist, round but firm hips, and long thighs. But these were merely the externals; what caused her to be striking was an intangible quality: she seemed to give off an air, an electric current, an aura—something that called attention to her.

She had lived with her beauty sufficiently long that she did not rely on it and seemed to take it for granted. Rather, she depended on the vibrant inner warmth that exuded from her, that surrounded her and seemed almost to explode, so intense was it.

Richard had never encountered anyone quite like her. He was willing to acknowledge her beauty, but it was the extra dimension that utterly fascinated him from the moment he first set eyes upon her. He had no idea what this quality might be, or how it was affecting him; all he knew was that he found Eliza utterly captivating.

"Don't tell me you're content to sit behind closed windows on a glorious spring day, Sir Richard," she said.

"That must be your horse I saw in the stable just now. A magnificent brute! If I were his master, nothing would prevent me from going out for a canter in the hills."

"As I was telling you, Sir Richard," the colonel said, "my daughter has her own ideas of how people should and shouldn't behave."

"I approve of Papa's regiment because they go on long marches to keep the frontier pacified," Eliza said with a laugh. "Otherwise, he leads too sedentary a life, and as you can see for yourself, he's toting some extra weight."

"I know the ways of this wench," Adam Burrows said, "having brought her up alone since early childhood, after my dear wife's death. I can tell you right now that she's planned on taking you for a ride down one of her favorite trails, and somewhere along the way she'll offer to change horses with you. She has it in her mind to ride your stallion, Sir Richard."

"Papa does have an uncanny ability to read my mind on occasion," she admitted cheerfully. "Will you ride with me, sir?"

Richard had little choice, so he bowed his assent. Eliza went off to change, reappearing shortly in a riding dress, gloves, and boots. She led Richard to the stable, where she saddled a gelding, and then she walked to Prince Henry, patted him, and offered him some sugar.

The great stallion looked at her for a long moment, then took the sugar from her hand, and Richard had to admire his horse's instinct. Prince Henry seldom lost his dignity in the presence of strangers, but Eliza Burrows had made him an easy conquest.

The girl led the way inland on a trail through the forest, and Richard had to admit she was an expert horsewoman.

She kept her seat well, and the gelding was under control at all times.

At last she turned. "There's an open meadow ahead, a perfect area for a race, if you're game."

Richard smiled and shook his head. "I'd hate to take unfair advantage of you," he said, "but your horse simply isn't a match for mine." He was too polite to add that Eliza wasn't in his class as a rider, either.

She grinned at him, a light dancing mischievously in her blue eyes. "You could equalize the odds by changing horses with me," she said, gathering her long hair into a ribbon, obviously preparing for an unencumbered ride.

Her father had been right, divining her intent from the outset. "It's all right with me," Richard replied, "but my mount usually has his own ideas, and I'm not so certain he'll allow you to ride him."

"We'll soon find out," she replied, and instantly dismounted.

He jumped to the ground too, and patted Prince Henry. "Boy," he said, "this young lady has it in her mind to ride you. She means well, and she admires you, so don't mistreat her. What do you say?" The stallion pawed the ground and returned his master's gaze.

Eliza Burrows came up to the beast and murmured something that Richard could not hear. Then, without hesitation, she hoisted herself into the saddle. Prince Henry was as surprised as his master, and reacted instantly by bucking and kicking violently. The girl clung to her seat, even though the horse was plunging, then rearing back, running a few paces, and halting abruptly. Eliza had no intention of being thrown. The color was high in her face, her lips were compressed, and the light in her eyes showed that she was as determined as the stallion.

Richard was afraid she would be hurt if she were thrown, but he knew better than to interfere. The girl had forced herself on Prince Henry, and the battle was between them. If the stallion had persisted, he would have won the engagement, but he neighed loudly, then stood still. Obviously he had decided that the stubborn young woman was worthy of riding him.

Richard was surprised. "He likes you," he said.

She had won the first round against heavy odds, and it would have been natural for her to gloat. Instead she leaned forward, stroked the mount's neck, and murmured, "Good lad."

She had a real understanding of horses, Richard thought as he mounted the gelding.

"We'll start here," she said as they rode into the open. "In order to make it a fair race, I suggest we go to the line of elms over yonder—about two hundred and fifty yards— and then double back to the starting line. Is that agreeable?"

"Very," Richard replied. "But I suggest you allow me to signal the start. My stallion won't cut loose for you unless I give him the word."

"Oh, no," Eliza said quickly. "That would remove all the sport from the race. I'll count to three, slowly, and then each of us will be responsible for him—or herself—and his or her horse."

"Fair enough." He was sure Prince Henry would refuse to budge unless he gave the order, but the headstrong young woman would have to learn all that for herself.

"Ready?" she called. "One—two—three!"

As Richard spurred forward, shooting past her, he could see her whispering to Prince Henry. It was unfair to humiliate her, so he held the gelding in check. Suddenly his own mount roared past him. Prince Henry had reached an understanding with Eliza Burrows and was out to win the race.

A strange sensation of jealousy welled up within Richard. He alone had trained his horse, and no one else had ever ridden the great beast. Very well then, he would be forced to teach the wench and Prince Henry a lesson! The gelding responded to his touch and gradually regained the lost ground.

He drew even as they approached the line of huge elm trees, and Richard caught a glimpse of Eliza, her face flushed with exertion and pleasure, her blonde hair streaming behind her. It was apparent that she was relishing every moment of the experience.

Unfamiliar with the gelding's ways, Richard nevertheless managed to maneuver the steed into a sharp turn, and when Eliza had difficulty in turning Prince Henry, he gained about two lengths. For all practical purposes, that ended the race. He gave the gelding his head, and the animal ran freely, gaining yet another half-length. Richard could hear Prince Henry thundering behind him, and knew the mistake that Eliza was making. There would be ample time to tell her when they were done. He reached the finish line, then gently slowed the winning gelding to a walk.

Prince Henry was outraged at having been defeated, and angrily tried again to throw his rider, bucking and plunging, halting for an instant, then rearing high into the air, his front hooves flailing wildly. Richard maneuvered the gelding close enough to seize the reins from the struggling girl. "Behave yourself this instant, sir!" he told Prince Henry. Responding to his master's command, the great beast became quiet and stood still.

"He's not accustomed to losing," Richard said, his tone apologetic.

"What did I do wrong?" Eliza asked quietly. "I could feel his power, but he didn't go all out for me."

"You should have given him his head, and he would have done the rest."

"I see. I'll know better next time—if there is a next time—and he won't be compelled to lose his temper with me. I'm sorry, lad," she told Prince Henry. "I should have realized that a horse of your intelligence would have known what needed to be done."

"Ride him back to your father's house, if you like," Richard told her. "He's feeling ashamed of himself, and he'll be convinced you've abandoned him if we change mounts now."

"Thank you, I shall continue to ride him with great pleasure. I'd give my soul to own a horse like this."

"He's not for sale."

"I should think not!" She sounded shocked. "Have you had him long?"

"I claimed him four years ago, the day he was born. His mother had been my favorite mare, and I knew the moment I saw him that there was no other horse like him."

"I knew it too, when I saw him in our stable. I'm sorry I tricked you, but I couldn't help it."

"Your father warned me what to expect. You ride well. I've never known a woman who has your understanding of horses."

"That's what comes of being reared by a father who had always wanted a son."

Richard's curiosity was aroused as they rode side by side through the deep woods on the trail back to New Haven. "Are you also familiar with firearms?"

Eliza laughed. "It's plain you're a stranger to the New World," she said. "For our own protection, parents teach their children to handle firearms as soon as they can lift a musket and handle the recoil. My father has made some good treaties with the Indians who live hereabouts, and they've learned to respect our militia regiment in recent years. But—until about two years ago, if that long—it wasn't safe in these woods. You never knew when you might be attacked. In fact, it was right about here, three years ago, that Ezekiel and I had the devil's own time fighting our way clear of an ambush."

What astonished him about her recital was her matter-of-fact tone. She seemed to take Indian ambushes for granted. "Who is Ezekiel?"

"Ezekiel Clayton. The son of my father's oldest friend and business associate. We grew up together. I'm sure the Claytons will be coming to supper tonight. Papa will want them to meet you."

Richard silently marveled at her lack of fear in the wilderness. The musket she carried as a matter of course was familiar to her, she had proved her ability to handle any horse, and the forest held no terrors for her. Yet she was feminine in every way, conscious of her beauty and willing to use it in order to achieve her ends, even the simple goal of riding Prince Henry.

"I enjoyed our outing very much," Richard told her as

they dismounted, led the horses into the stable, and removed the saddles.

"I'm grateful to you for tolerating a spoiled brat's whims," she replied. "But this is a day I won't soon forget, I promise you that." Eliza's smile was angelic.

Later, changing for supper in his guest bedchamber in the Burrowses' spacious house, Richard had to warn himself to be careful. This girl was as lovely as Mimi Shepherd, and her self-reliance was an added magnet that made her even more attractive to him. He thought of Dorothea and wondered how she would fare in the New World. But such speculation was nonsensical, so he put her out of his mind.

When he came downstairs he found the Clayton family had already arrived. Thomas Clayton was a tall, spare man who had the self-assurance of someone who had fought for his place in the world and won it fairly. His wife, Mary, exuded charm and obviously had been a great beauty in her younger days. She, too, seemed sure of herself. Their son, Ezekiel, was a few years younger than Richard, with his father's dignity and his mother's bubbling nature.

Richard was totally unprepared for his introduction to the younger Clayton. "This," Colonel Burrows said, "is Eliza's betrothed."

So she was engaged to be married to the man! Surely she could have referred to him as her betrothed when she had mentioned being caught with him in an Indian ambush. Disappointed that her hand was promised, Richard was nevertheless relieved that he had not been overbold in displaying his own interest in her.

Ezekiel wore his clothes with an air and seemed very much in command of himself. He had good cause for his self-assurance; he was tall, his regular features gave him a handsome appearance, and he was athletic in build. Obviously he could give a good account of himself in hand-to-hand combat. Obviously, too, he spent a great deal of time out-of-doors because he was heavily tanned or wind-burned, which set off his dark hair and eyes to good advantage. Certainly he knew that he was attractive to the opposite sex.

Eliza chose that moment to make her appearance in an off-the-shoulder gown of ivory that would have been far more appropriate at a Whitehall assembly than in a New Haven house set on the fringe of the wilderness.

"Aha!" Ezekiel declared, bowing over her hand with mock gravity. "Sir Richard, I must warn you for your own good to beware of this charmer. It's apparent from the way she is dressed tonight that she intends to bedazzle you."

"She is succeeding," Richard admitted.

"Ezekiel," Eliza said severely, "I've heard your father tell you a hundred times that you talk too much. You should take to heart the advice he gives you."

"Well, everyone knows you're a flirtatious jade who collects admirers, the way that Sir Richard's warrior friend who is sleeping out in the yard collects scalps," Ezekiel replied.

She made a face, sticking her tongue out at him, before she escaped to the kitchen to check on the preparations for supper.

Richard was puzzled by the relationship. Eliza and Ezekiel obviously knew each other well and enjoyed their mutual teasing, but they did not behave like a betrothed couple. He had no chance to dwell on the matter, however, as Colonel Burrows handed him a glass of what appeared to be dry sack.

"Would you care to propose a toast, Tom?" the host asked.

"I drink to next year!" the elder Clayton said promptly, and raised his glass.

Richard took a small sip from his tumbler and almost choked on it: he had been served a fiery rum. Yet even Mary Clayton sipped with aplomb and seemed able to handle the potent drink. "May I ask the significance of your toast?" Richard asked as soon as he composed himself.

The others smiled, and Mary explained. "We live very near to the wilderness," she said, "and close to the forces of nature. Our towns, even a settled place like New Haven, are subject to Indian raids. We're at the mercy of the weather, and if it's bad, people starve because our lives depend on our crops. What we mean when we drink to next year is that we hope we'll all be alive, well, and prosperous in another year."

"That's true," Eliza said, coming into the quietly furnished parlor and accepting a small tumbler of rum from her father. "Richard asked me this afternoon whether I could handle firearms, and he seemed surprised when I told him I've used them all my life."

"In England, Sir Richard," Tom Clayton declared, "you take the law for granted, and the enforcement of it is almost automatic. That's why the people of the British Isles were so surprised by the beheading of King Charles."

"Here, we live with violence. We expect it in every aspect of our lives." Colonel Burrows motioned the guests to the dining room. Richard was surprised when Eliza took his arm, rather than her betrothed's, and led him to the table, where she seated him on her right.

"Every time I send one of my little tubs out to sea," Colonel Burrows continued, "I wonder if it will return safely. You need to know the fury of a West Indian hurricane to understand what I mean. It's enough for me to say that the officers and seamen on every ship in my fleet take their lives in their hands every time they go to sea."

A serving maid brought in a large tureen of soup, which Eliza ladled into bowls at the table. It was a chowder of whole clams, onions, and potatoes in a clear broth.

"They ruin this dish in Boston by cooking it in cream," Mary said. "A good chowder should contain the natural clam juice, with nothing added."

Richard thought the chowder was delicious.

"This soup is a good example of what we're talking about," the elder Clayton said. "There must be twenty towns along the shore of New England now, and every one has a different recipe for this dish. What matters is that the clams are here for the taking. We've followed the example of the Indians, and we use what nature provides us."

"Well, I've eaten some unusual dishes since I've come to the New World," Richard said. "But I've discovered that my palate has adjusted rapidly to them."

The colonials nodded. "Bison meat is an acquired taste," Mary Clayton said, "but when you have a choice between bison or no meat at all, you quickly learn to like the taste."

"We live on bison, turkey, moose, venison, and fish," Eliza added. "Ezekiel and I have grown up here, and we scarcely know the taste of beef."

Ezekiel nodded, grinning at his parents and at Colonel Burrows. "On the rare occasions when beef is served, we try to show our appreciation of the luxury, but the truth of the matter is that we don't much care for the taste. Our cows are too valuable as milk producers to be slaughtered for their meat."

Richard drank in the information and began to understand the New World way of life for the first time. The main course was bison steak that had been marinated for two days in dry sack, oil, and herbs to make it less tough, and he had to admit he enjoyed the taste.

"Our principal concern," Colonel Burrows told him, "is our security. I estimate there are fifty thousand to one hundred thousand colonists on the seaboard, from New Somersetshire being claimed by Massachusetts Bay to the territory south of Virginia that has no name as yet. We cling to the Atlantic coast, where we've established a toehold, and we either trade with the Indians when we're fortunate or fight them when we must. I've heard many estimates of their numbers, but no one really knows how many are out there in the forests. All I know for certain is that we're obliged to live side by side with them in peace—or perish."

"How do you manage to maintain peaceful relations with them?" Richard wanted to know.

"They may be savages, but they understand justice," the colonel replied. "Here in New Haven we fine any man who tries to cheat or cozen them. The colony makes it a practice to pay for any land we acquire, and we give value received for furs and corn and other products we obtain from the Indians."

"Would that the Indians were our only worry," the elder Clayton said. "The Old World transfers its problems to the New. France and Spain understood the value of North America long before the British became aware of the potentials here, and both nations have thriving colonies to the north, the west, and the south of us. Naturally, they covet our growing civilization here. And frankly, it makes me nervous to see the hospitality that France is showing the Cavaliers. Cardinal Mazarin exacts what he deems to be appropriate reciprocity when he does a favor or extends a hand in friendship."

"The French, Dutch, and Spanish don't try to take your territory by force?" Richard asked.

Colonel Burrows shook his head. "No, we'd fight to the last man if they invaded us. But they use other, more subtle means. The French and Spanish offer bribes to our Indian neighbors to stir up trouble. They know the New Model Navy is preoccupied and going through changes at home, so they send privateers—unofficial ships over which they supposedly have no control—to prey on our shipping and destroy our lifelines to the islands of the West Indies and England itself. Every last one of my trading brigs is heavily armed, and my men know how to use their cannon."

Richard had been unaware of the colonists' struggle for the right to make their homes in the New World.

"Another great concern of ours is how to best utilize the services of the immigrants who are pouring into the colonies," the elder Clayton declared. "It was difficult for a number of years because we had a shortage of trained craftsmen and unskilled laborers. Inevitably, this forced wages up beyond accustomed levels in England. The court here in New Haven decreed specific wage and profit controls to prevent economic exploitation. We're getting more than our fair share of townsmen these days, but unfortunately they know nothing about carving homesteads for themselves out of the wilderness and then farming for a living. It's our responsibility to help them settle here, and perhaps to re-adjust our economic guidelines."

"Yes, the problems are increasing," Colonel Burrows agreed. "When a stonemason, shoemaker, bricklayer, carpenter, or tailor comes to the colonies, he's looking forward to the practice of the one trade he knows. It's a necessity to help him find his place in our society."

"That's why," Eliza said bluntly, "we don't give a hang for England's problems. We have enough of our own."

Ezekiel nodded emphatically. "Precisely so! The quarrels of the Puritans and the Cavaliers mean nothing to me. All I know is that we're required to pay duties to the mother country, regardless of whether a king sits on the throne or Parliament is the supreme authority in the land. We're worried about our own survival, and we'd like something in return for our money: troops to help us hold off the Indians—or arms, at the very least. We need protection of our merchant fleets."

"You can't expect automatic loyalty," Eliza said firmly. "England takes our furs, lumber, and other products, and charges us an export duty for the privilege. In addition, we pay an import tax on every skillet, every bolt of cloth we buy from England."

"Those of us who were born and bred in England have ties to her, naturally," Mary Clayton explained. "But the younger generation—your generation, Sir Richard—has grown up in the colonies. They take the rights of native-born Englishmen for granted, and they're far more outspoken than anyone would dare to be in the Old World in these trying times."

"I hadn't thought of it that way, but what you say is true, Aunt Mary," Eliza said. "I'm loyal to New Haven colony.

I can also sympathize with the problems of Connecticut or Rhode Island or New Netherland because they're similar to our own, so I can understand them. I know that eventually all of us must stand together or fall separately. If I were a man I'd march to defend our neighbors because their fall would threaten our own survival. But I wouldn't lift a finger to put Charles the Second on the throne of England any more than I'd take up arms on behalf of the Puritans." The others obviously agreed with her, and the whole group looked at Richard, awaiting his reaction.

"I don't feel as you do because my background is different," he said. "I despise the Roundheads because they drove me from my country and confiscated my property, when the only crime I committed was that of being steadfast in my loyalty to the Crown." He looked at Eliza, then at Ezekiel. "But if I had grown to manhood here, I'm sure I'd resent having to pay a tax on every barrel of salt fish I sent back to England."

Eliza rewarded him with a dazzling smile. "You don't yet know it," she said, "but you're already becoming a colonial. We're a new breed."

What she said was valid. A new breed was being formed in the wilderness of North America, where men breathed the clean, fresh air of personal freedom, and an individual was judged by his accomplishments, not by his family's standing.

CHAPTER 7

RICHARD repeatedly extended his stay in New Haven. The gracious hospitality of Adam Burrows was one reason, and he felt that he was learning more about the colonies here each day than he had gleaned in all of the time he had so far spent in North America. He was forced to admit, too, that he was reluctant to part company with Eliza Burrows, even though she was betrothed.

To his consternation, Eliza flirted with him openly, frequently in the presence of Ezekiel Clayton, who seemed either not to know or care what she was doing. As an honorable man, Richard could not respond, but he knew he was strongly attracted to the girl. On several occasions, he made up his mind to go on to New Amsterdam, only to change his mind at the last minute.

Somehow, he reflected, he had to find the strength to resist the temptation to form a more intimate relationship with Eliza. His protracted stay in New Haven was helping him to understand the minds and hearts of British colonials, and he could perform no greater service for the cause he represented than to portray conditions as he found them to the Earl of Newcastle and the other members of the Cavalier high command.

He suspected that Eliza was amusing herself at his expense, and one day, when her father was called to a conference of the New England Federation, he became sure of it. It would have been difficult enough for him to dine with her alone at noon, but she invited Ezekiel Clayton to join them, then seemed to go out of her way to create an awkward situation by devoting most of her attention to Richard.

Eliza lowered her voice and spoke huskily, with a personal immediacy whenever she addressed Richard, and she spoke to him almost exclusively. Her eyes widened whenever she smiled up at him, her lashes fluttered deliciously, and she seemed unable to illustrate her remarks without constantly touching his sleeve. She was aware of all the tricks of a professional flirt and obviously relished using them.

Ezekiel became aware of the young Englishman's discomfort, and said, "Behave yourself, Eliza!"

She sobered at once and stared down at her plate, but the corners of her mouth twitched suspiciously.

"The girl is a vixen, and I apologize for her, Richard," Ezekiel said. "Remember, Eliza, that Richard doesn't understand."

She nodded, then turned back to the guest. "Forgive me for teasing you. Ezekiel and I have been wondering if we might confide in you."

"Of course," Richard muttered, bewildered by the seemingly complex situation.

"You tell him, then," Eliza said to Ezekiel.

"As best I'm able. Our fathers have been close friends and business partners ever since they helped found New Haven. Eliza and I grew up together."

"You might say we had a sibling relationship," the girl interjected. "I can't remember a time when Ezekiel wasn't present in my life. We fought incessantly when we were younger."

"We did, indeed," Ezekiel confirmed, then laughed wryly. "Until I discovered that she wouldn't fight fairly. She'd kick, scratch, and bite, and if I became so exasperated that I hit her, she'd tattle to my parents and my backside would be tanned."

Eliza looked demurely innocent, but Richard knew that Ezekiel was telling him the truth.

"When we grew older," Ezekiel continued, "our fathers took it for granted that we'd be married. So did we, I guess."

"Ezekiel never formally proposed, and I never formally accepted," Eliza said. "We drifted into an engagement two years ago."

"And since that time we've been finding reasons—excuses, really—to postpone the wedding. I'd feel as if I were marrying my own sister."

"It's an impossible situation," Eliza declared. "We haven't wanted to hurt our fathers by telling them the truth, but they've been nagging at us lately to be married this spring, so we may be forced to tell them we want to go our separate ways."

"There you have it," Ezekiel said. "At the risk of embarrassing Eliza, I knew she was attracted to you from the day you came to New Haven. Now you know why she has behaved as she has toward you."

"I was trying to convey to my father—in a none-too-subtle fashion—that Ezekiel isn't the only man on earth for me. Quite the contrary. But you've been such a gentleman that you've refused to take the bait."

It annoyed Richard to discover that a baldly deliberate attempt had been made to use him, but he couldn't help laughing. "If I had given in to my natural inclinations, Colonel Burrows would have accused me of taking advantage of his hospitality and he'd have been justified to ask me to leave this house!"

"We wouldn't have allowed it to go that far," Eliza assured him.

"It strikes me," he said, "that you two have no choice. Go to Colonel Burrows and Master Clayton and tell them the truth."

Eliza and Ezekiel exchanged a long, despairing look. "He doesn't understand," the girl said. "Richard, we've tried to talk to them, but they won't listen. They've been looking forward to our marriage for so long that it's a fact to them. They're wonderful fathers, but they're headstrong men who believe only what they want to believe."

Ezekiel nodded in corroboration. "For once, Eliza isn't exaggerating," he said. "When I've tried to make my father see reason, he cuts me off by saying I simply don't know my own mind."

"There seems to be nothing we can do, short of refusing to go through with a ceremony," Eliza added.

"Surely there must be some way you can convince them," Richard said.

"Well," the girl replied, "I think Aunt Mary knows how we feel."

"We've gone to her, separately and together," Ezekiel

went on. "She's influenced by my father, so she won't take us seriously, either."

"In time I could convince her," Eliza said. "But we don't have much time. Papa has even had a new house built for us, and now he and Uncle Tom have ordered furniture from England for it."

Richard found it inconceivable that the two fathers were so determined to go through with the wedding, but he sympathized with the young couple. "Would they listen to Mistress Clayton?"

"Oh, yes, provided she believed we really meant what we said," Eliza replied.

"And you think that you could persuade her that you're serious?"

"She's more inclined to listen to me than to Ezekiel," the girl said. "If I could win her support, it would be a big help."

"Then what you need is time." Richard turned to the young man. "Are you familiar with the wilderness, Ezekiel?"

Ezekiel grinned at him. "I grew up in the forest. I'm more at home there than I am at my desk in Uncle Adam's shipyard, I can tell you."

"I'm making two major stops in my journey through the colonies," Richard said. "I'm going first to New Amsterdam, then on to Middle Plantation, in Virginia. You'd be welcome to come with me, if that would help. During your absence, it would be up to Eliza to convince your mother that neither of you wants to marry."

"Nothing would give me greater pleasure than to go with you," Ezekiel replied eagerly. "I'll need an excuse to travel, of course—"

"That's simple enough," Eliza said, interrupting him. "Tell Papa—and your own father too—that you believe you can arrange some business deals for them in New Netherland and Middle Plantation. They'll send you off with their blessings."

"That's precisely what I'll do," Ezekiel said. "It happens to be true that we have few trade agreements in either colony. I'm sure I can return with enough new business to make the trip worth my while."

Richard began to appreciate Eliza's cleverness.

"I'll go to my father right now, and I'll speak to Uncle Adam when he comes back from his conference. I appreciate this, Richard." Ezekiel was confident, and grasped Richard's hand.

"So do I," Eliza said. "You could have refused to help us."

"I haven't solved your problem," Richard said. "Only you can do that."

"I shall," she said. "I can be far more blunt with Aunt Mary than I can with Papa and Uncle Tom."

Ezekiel went to the front hall for his hat and musket. "Wish me well," he said. "With any luck you and I will soon be free of each other at last, Eliza."

They watched him from the parlor window as he rode off toward the harbor offices. Then Eliza looked up at Richard, her manner suddenly diffident. "You're kind to bear no grudge after what I did," she said. "I flirted with you outrageously."

"I enjoyed it," he replied candidly.

"I—I wasn't just trying to take advantage of you," the girl confessed. "It's true that you attract me—a great deal."

"Well, I didn't keep my reactions to you as much under

control as I would have liked," he replied. "I didn't grasp the situation because I wouldn't have dreamed that any man would be reluctant to marry you."

She smiled slowly. "That's the nicest compliment I've ever been paid," she said.

"I mean it. It would be exceedingly easy to fall in love with you."

"That's because you don't really know me. I'm as headstrong as my father, and I always manage to have my own way. I know that I'm spoiled, and I freely admit I'm selfish."

Her frankness was disconcerting. "It may be your faults aren't truly as grave as they appear to you to be," he said.

"Don't humor me, sir. These past days haven't been as simple for me as you might think."

"That just goes to prove that you have a conscience," Richard said.

"I'd say that you know far too much about women," Eliza said.

"How can you tell?" he countered uncomfortably.

"You watched me as I flirted with you, and I could perceive you weighing my motives, speculating on whether I was trying to tempt you to bed me."

"Were you?"

"No, I'd have become frightened, and I'd have found some reason to hold you at arm's length."

"That's the way I had you figured," he said.

"But I knew from the way you were observing and measuring me that you've had experience, that you've had at least one serious affair."

His loyalty to Mimi kept him silent.

"It doesn't matter in the least," Eliza said lightly, seating herself on a small bench and spreading her full skirt. "I've always believed a husband should be more experienced in matters of love than his wife."

Richard was so startled he could only gape at her.

"Why don't you sit down?" she asked him sweetly.

He sank into a chair opposite her, still staring.

"I thought it only fair to give you warning, Richard. If Ezekiel and I break free of each other, I'm setting my cap for you. And not for the reasons you think. Your bride will become Lady Dunstable, but your title means nothing to me. In case you need reminding, I'm a new-breed American. With a little encouragement you could become one of the new breed yourself," she said with a smile. "Now, sir, since I've been honest with you, I think you owe it to me to be honest in return. What exactly are you doing in the colonies?"

"I explained all that the day we met. I'm traveling from one to another, becoming acquainted with all of them before I decide where to settle."

"You're concealing something from me, but no matter. It isn't any of my business, is it? For your own good, though, I think it only fair to tell you that you're a most unconvincing liar."

He raised an eyebrow.

"Something in your manner gives you away. I'm not certain I can pinpoint it, and I don't know if I'd tell you, even if I could. It helps a wife to know when her husband lies to her."

"You can't be seriously contemplating marriage to me," he protested.

"I've never been more serious in my life," Eliza replied, her blue eyes bright. "I've been waiting all my life for you.

I know what I feel, and that satisfies me." She smoothed her skirt absently. "I hope you like New Haven and decide to settle here. I'll go elsewhere, if you wish, but my roots are here, and I don't like the thought of leaving Papa alone."

As far as she was concerned, their future together was settled. She was amazing. "I haven't yet seen New Netherland or Virginia," he said slowly, "but—so far, at least— New Haven is the only place I've visited where I feel at home."

Eliza was delighted. "Oh, I'm so glad!"

"Let me make a few basics clear to you, however," he went on grimly. "Please don't take it for granted that you and I will marry. I'm very much drawn to you, but I haven't fallen in love with you—"

"You will," she said, calmly interrupting him. "You held back your feelings because of the relationship you naturally assumed I had with Ezekiel. Now that you understand, it's just a question of time before you realize that you love me."

"My funds are limited, and I haven't yet decided how I intend to earn my living in the colonies. I'm not the sort who would live on his wife's income."

"It never crossed my mind that you would. A man who refuses to let a headstrong woman win a simple horse race isn't the sort who would accept favors from anyone."

She knew him better than he had realized, and the knowledge made him all the more uncomfortable.

Eliza sensed his lack of ease, and rose to her feet. "You've been wanting to kiss me for days," she said. "You may."

Everything else was blotted from Richard's mind. Before he quite knew what he was doing, he was on his feet.

sweeping her into an embrace. Eliza clasped his head in both of her hands and returned his kiss with a sincerity and passion that told him she had meant every word. Suddenly he stepped back, afraid his own desire would get the better of him. "This is premature," he said huskily. "You're still engaged to be married to Ezekiel."

She was shaken too, but recovered quickly. "I've now confirmed what I guessed—or divined—about you and me. Never fear, my dear, my betrothal to Ezekiel will be terminated, no matter how badly our fathers may be hurt. I have a reason now to be free, and free I shall be!"

Ezekiel Clayton won enthusiastic support from his father and Colonel Burrows for his plan to go to New Netherland and Virginia with Richard in an attempt to obtain new shipping contracts for the growing merchant firm. Plans for the journey were concluded quickly, and Ezekiel gathered his gear, intending to take his own gelding from the family stable.

No one was happier than Roaring Wolf that the journey would be resumed. The Pequot warrior had waited patiently, sleeping and eating in the Burrowses' yard, and he accepted the addition of another member of the party with resignation. "If the brave can shoot and follow a trail," he said, "he will be welcome."

Richard and Ezekiel said their good-byes at a supper given by the elder Claytons, arranging to meet at the Green at dawn the next day. Adam Burrows spoke for all three of the elders when he said, "We hope you'll return to New Haven and make your home here, Richard. There's a need in the colony for men of your caliber."

Richard thanked the colonel for his hospitality, said he

would give serious thought to the prospect of settling in New Haven, and promised solemnly that he would return. His unfinished business with Eliza demanded it.

Richard did not dare look directly at Eliza, but glanced at her surreptitiously as he acknowledged her father's gracious remark. She was looking off into space, her expression dreamy.

He was awake long before dawn the next morning, and when he went down to the kitchen to prepare a predeparture cup of tea for himself, he was surprised to find Eliza already standing at the hearth over a kettle that was just starting to steam.

"You didn't think I'd let you go without saying a private farewell, did you?" she asked as she poured his tea into a cup.

"You make this more difficult for both of us," he replied.

"I daresay I do, but we'll be glad later. I've already told Aunt Mary that I'm coming to see her this morning, so I hope to have the issue settled before you even reach New Netherland."

"I hope you don't intend to bring me into the problem," he said. "I'd hate to have your father think that I abused his hospitality by making advances to his daughter behind his back."

Eliza could be forceful when she chose. "Trust me," she said abruptly.

"I do."

"And think of me—often."

"It will be difficult not to think of you." He hesitated, then took a major step. "I was betrothed before I left England," he said. "The engagement was ended by the girl's father because I was a Cavalier with a dubious future, and he already had a suitable Roundhead selected for her."

"She didn't elope with you?"

"She wasn't the type." Even now, he could not damn Dorothea. "The reason I'm telling you this is because she's been in my thoughts until you came into my life. Now I find it hard even to conjure up a mental picture of her."

"I'm glad," Eliza said simply. "And thank you for telling me. It will make this separation easier to bear."

He gulped his tea and glanced out of the window, where he saw the first streaks of dawn appear in the dark sky. "It's time for me to be on my way."

"I wish you Godspeed," she said. "May your endeavors, whatever they be, end successfully. And may you come back to me soon." She lifted her face to his.

Richard kissed her tenderly, then gazed at her for a long moment as he continued to hold her in his arms. "I'll have no trouble remembering the way you look," he said, and releasing her abruptly, walked out into the dawn.

Eliza stood silently at the window, watching him as he went to the stable for Prince Henry, then set out for his rendezvous with Ezekiel at the Green. His Indian friend trotted happily beside the stallion.

Drawing her dressing gown around her more tightly, Eliza sighed, then drank her own cup of tea. Somehow, she would have to make Aunt Mary understand. And she could not mention Richard. It was a miracle that they had sparked to each other, and she knew, in spite of their brief acquaintance, that a real romance would flourish if they had the time and the opportunity. It was up to her to create both.

Carefully rinsing out the teacups, she went upstairs to her own chamber, where she took her time dressing for the day.

Her father was just starting his breakfast when she came down to the dining room.

"Bless my soul," he said. "It isn't often that I'm graced with your presence this early in the day."

"I have a busy day ahead," she said.

Colonel Burrows chuckled indulgently as he boned his broiled fish, which he ate with bread smeared with honey. "The house will seem empty without Richard Dunstable here," he said.

"Very empty," Eliza replied carefully.

"He'll be back," he said. "He doesn't give his word lightly, and he promised solemnly that he'll see New Haven again."

"I'm sure he will, Papa."

"I hope so. The town needs men of his caliber. He's still devoted to the Cavalier cause, which is natural, but time and three thousand miles of the Atlantic should soften and change his perspectives. We've seen it happen to others."

Eliza nodded, unable to carry on the conversation. Too tense to eat breakfast herself, she drank another cup of tea, and after her father went off to his waterfront office, she dawdled for an hour, killing time. Then she donned her lightweight cape of unbleached wool and walked the short distance to the Clayton house.

The dirt road was rutted, but it was so familiar to Eliza that there was no need for her to pick a path for herself. The stately elm trees that lined both sides of the road were budding, and she took that as a hopeful sign. Slowing her pace as she neared the house with the white portico, she quickly rehearsed what she intended to say, then raised the brass knocker on the door and released it.

Mary Clayton answered the summons herself. "Well,"

she said. "I was expecting you, but not this early. Come in, dear." She led the way to her sewing room. "You're just in time to help me measure the cloth for a new dress."

"Gladly, but first I want to talk to you, Aunt Mary." Eliza's throat was dry. "I don't quite know how to begin. It's a subject that Ezekiel and I have tried to discuss, but Papa and Uncle Tom are deaf to it, and I can only hope you'll understand and act as our ally."

The older woman looked at her calmly. "I understand far more than you think. You're going to tell me that your betrothal is a mistake, that you and Ezekiel don't love each other and never have."

Eliza swallowed hard and stared at her.

Mary smiled. "The reason your fathers haven't listened to either of you in the past is because they've wanted your marriage very badly. They saw the founding of a New World dynasty, and inasmuch as neither of you was interested in anyone else, they hoped against hope that proximity would take care of the problem. Well, it hasn't, obviously, and now the situation is changed —drastically."

Eliza's head swam.

"You and Richard Dunstable have found each other. Or think you have, which amounts to the same thing. Your father is no ogre, Eliza, and neither is my husband. They won't force either you or Ezekiel to go through with an unwanted marriage. They may be crochety about it for a time, but I can promise you they'll understand and relent." Mary reached for a bolt of cloth. "This arrived from Leeds the other day. Rather attractive, isn't it? I thought of making it into a dress with a high neck and a straight skirt. What do you think?"

"Wait," Eliza said, and discovered she was short of breath. "How do you—know so much?"

"Dear Eliza, I'm almost fifty years old, but I'm not blind! The way you and Sir Richard avoided looking at each other last night was painful. And Ezekiel's idea of going off to New Netherland and Virginia to gain new business had to have been your idea, not his. I know my son, and his mind doesn't function that way."

Eliza laughed ruefully. "If you only knew the speech I'd practiced to convince you that Ezekiel and I aren't right for each other."

The older woman's smile faded, and she reached to pat the girl's face. "You'll never know how much I shall regret not having you for a daughter-in-law."

"I'm sorry, too." Eliza's eyes filled with tears. "You've been a mother to me, the only mother I've ever known."

Mary Clayton quickly recovered her composure. "It does no good to weep over what might have been," she said. "The breaking of your engagement won't end our relationship. My feelings for you aren't changed."

Eliza hugged her impulsively. "You won't mind if I still come to you for advice and help?"

"Mind? I'd be hurt if you didn't." The older woman became reflective. "It's always easier to see one's mistakes after they've been made. Adam, Tom, and I shouldn't have pushed you and Ezekiel together. If we had left you to your own devices, I daresay you'd have found each other."

"I don't think so. We feel as if we're related."

"So you are, even though you aren't blood kin. Now, tell me about you and Richard Dunstable. Are you sure in your own mind that you love him?"

"Very sure," Eliza said. "I didn't plan it, and it wasn't gradual. The moment I met him I knew he was the man I've been waiting for all of my life. And I was so unfair to him, Aunt Mary! I tried to force the issue by flirting with him, but the more I showed him my feelings, the more restrained he became. That made me admire him that much more!"

"Does he love you?" Mary asked quietly.

"I—I think so. He's too honorable to tell me in so many words until my engagement to Ezekiel is broken, and he's so self-contained that he doesn't show his feelings. But I can tell by the way he looks at me. I can't explain it, but I know what's in his mind and heart before he realizes it himself. I sense it, somehow."

Mary nodded gravely. "A rapport of that kind is unusual, and you're fortunate to have experienced it."

"What I find strange is that we've talked very little about things that matter. I know, for instance, that Richard has some reason other than finding a place to settle that's causing him to travel through our colonies, but he hasn't confided in me, and I've hesitated to ask him outright. I don't want him to think I'm prying into business that's none of my concern."

"I worry about you, not about Richard. He appears to be an upright, honest man, but you have no real understanding with him. Suppose he decides to make his home in New Netherland or Virginia. Suppose he doesn't come back here for you. I'm afraid you'd be badly hurt."

"Yes, I would," Eliza said, then smiled confidently. "But I can't imagine him just disappearing. If I'm sure of anything in this world, it's that I know he'll return to New

Haven. Richard and I have too much unfinished business that needs to be settled!"

The journey to New Amsterdam was uneventful for two days and nights. Ezekiel Clayton proved himself adept at wilderness travel, and even Roaring Wolf approved of his expertise. Certainly he was a welcome addition to the little party, his presence contributing to security in the forest. "The danger of Indian attacks is slight in this neighborhood," he said. "The real danger is encountering a band of robbers."

"There are highwaymen in the vicinity?" Richard was surprised.

"Not exactly, but they're outlaws, all the same. They roam in packs of up to a half-dozen men, and they make it a practice to halt and rob the unwary who travel between New Amsterdam and New England. We'll have to keep our eyes and ears open."

In spite of the precautions the trio took, however, robbers struck late one afternoon, when camp was being made on the bank of a small stream that flowed into the Great Bay. Richard and Ezekiel had dismounted and turned their horses loose to graze, and Roaring Wolf had gone down to the shore to gather shellfish for supper while his companions built a fire. Prince Henry gave the first warning, lifting his ears, pawing the ground, and neighing softly. Richard immediately reached for his rifle, which lay on the ground beside him. Ezekiel, equally alert, picked up his musket.

They didn't have long to wait. A party of five roughly clad men came into the open on foot, all of them armed with pistols and clubs. "Do what you're told and you won't be hurt," the leader called. "We're a-goin' to help ourselves to your horses. Just throw your purses on the ground, and we'll soon be on our way."

One of his confederates made the mistake of approaching Prince Henry, intending to take hold of his bridle. But the great stallion apparently sensed what was happening; snorting and baring his teeth, he reared, then brought his flailing front hooves down on the luckless bandit. The man tried to escape but was crushed, and Prince Henry ended his fury by stomping on his victim.

The incident, which took no more than a few seconds, distracted the attention of the other robbers long enough for Richard to raise his rifle and fire. He severely wounded the leader, whose scream of pain echoed down the deserted beach.

Ezekiel Clayton took careful aim with his musket and fired, too, his shot striking another of the thieves. Ordinarily a musket was not that accurate a weapon, but Ezekiel was close enough to make his shot good.

The remaining robbers started to retreat, and their rout was complete when an arrow sang out from the direction of the beach and caught one of them in the shoulder. The band had been unaware of Roaring Wolf's presence in the party, and they fled the scene, the wounded helping each other as they crashed through the forest. One of their number was dead, three others were injured, and only one escaped unscathed.

Richard calmly reloaded his rifle, then indicated the body of the dead robber. "We'll be wise to move our campsite, I believe," he said quietly, going to his stallion and calming him. Roaring Wolf insisted on cutting away the scalp of the dead robber before moving on.

Richard congratulated his companions on their quick responses and the accuracy of their respective musket and arrow fire, and after the camp had been moved, he ate with great relish his crabs, which had been baked in wet leaves. "I was hungrier tonight than I realized," he said.

Ezekiel looked at him curiously. "I've never seen anyone remain so cool in an emergency," he said.

Richard grinned as he tossed the remains of a baked crab into the fire. "I believe in doing what needs to be done," he replied. "When a man gets excited he loses his ability to think clearly."

"You act as if you've spent your whole life in the wilderness," Ezekiel said admiringly.

Roaring Wolf, squatting on his haunches, laughed aloud. "Richard," he said, "is a mighty warrior."

The accolade was the highest praise that a man could receive, and Richard was pleased. "It's good to know I'm traveling with friends who don't panic, either," he said. Fishing another crab from the fire, he separated it from the wet leaves, then quietly returned to his meal.

No other violence marred the journey, and the following day at about noon, the trio reached New Amsterdam, a ferryman taking them across the East River to the wilderness of upper Manhattan. By midafternoon they reached the bustling town itself, and after inquiring of a passerby where to find lodging, they were directed to the Thorn and Thistle. While Ezekiel attended to their mounts, turning them over to a groom, Richard engaged a room from the amiably talkative Angus MacNeill.

"Our Indian friend isn't comfortable in white man's accommodations," Richard told him. "Can you suggest a place where he'll feel more at home?"

"Aye, sir, it's a common complaint of the redmen," Angus replied. "He'll be safer if he'll stay close by you. New Netherland and the Indians have had, to all our grief, a very difficult and bloody relationship. He'll be welcome to stay in the cellar, provided you'll pay for his space. Your friend will also be welcome in my kitchen—provided you'll pay for his meals."

"That I'll gladly do." Richard was pleased with the arrangements, because they satisfied Roaring Wolf. Ezekiel was eager to set up appointments for himself with various companies of merchants, so he set out for their offices on Hudson's River, a few blocks away. Richard decided to follow his usual custom of wandering around a city to begin his acquaintance with it.

He had to pass through the taproom in order to reach the street, and he was startled when he heard someone shout his name. He turned to see an overjoyed Mollie Williams emerging from behind the bar. She threw herself at him, kissing him soundly on both cheeks.

"What a wonderful surprise!" he exclaimed. "I traced you only as far as Providence Plantations."

"The life there wasn't for Bart and me," Mollie replied, still grinning broadly. "Ah, you look like a New World trapper in your buckskins. That's why I was so startled when I first saw you. I had to make sure it really was you."

Richard became conscious of Angus MacNeill standing a short distance away, scowling at him and at Mollie. "We crossed the Atlantic together," he explained.

"That we did, and it was the kindness of Master Dunstable that gave me the courage to travel from Boston all the way to New Amsterdam."

Richard was relieved by her care in avoiding any mention of his title.

"There are no customers here now, and none are likely to wander in at this hour," Mollie said, "so we can sit and tell each other the news. Do you know what's become of the Chaneys?"

Following her to a table in the empty taproom, Richard noted that Angus MacNeill's scowl deepened until, suddenly, he turned on his heel and stalked out.

"I believe I've made the proprietor jealous," Richard said with a chuckle.

Color flamed in Mollie's face. "He'll get over it soon enough when he realizes we're naught but old friends. And if he stops to think about it, you're near young enough to be me son."

"I'd hate to be the cause of trouble between you and your employer, Mollie."

"The only trouble will be of his making," she said with a satisfied smile. "I need the work, but Master MacNeill needs me even more!" There was pride in her voice as she went on to tell him of her success at the Thorn and Thistle.

"I'm delighted for you. And how is Bart faring?"

The happiness faded from her face. "Still fighting the good fight for King Charlie. Master MacNeill made a place for him in the stable as an ostler, but he argues with one and all, even though most of the folk here wouldn't know the difference between a Cavalier and a Roundhead, and wouldn't care one way or t'other. I've warned the lad

235

until I'm hoarse, but he won't listen. He's responsible for one strange happening, though." Lowering her voice, she told him about her encounter with the Royalist agent who had called himself Laroche. "I don't know what his game may be, so I've given him no information."

The Earl of Newcastle had told Richard he would report to a man named Laroche. "I believe he's what he says he is, Mollie."

Her eyes widened. "You'll vouch for him?"

"I haven't yet met him, so I wouldn't go that far. But I'm glad to learn he's in town, and I'm eager to make his acquaintance. Do you happen to know where he lives?"

Mollie shook her head. "Nay, but he drops in here near every night around ten o'clock for a glass of sack. In the time I've been here, I haven't known him to miss a night, so I'll arrange that you meet him this very evening, if you like."

"That won't be necessary," Richard said, not wanting to use her as a go-between. "Just point him out to me, and I'll attend to the rest."

"And you'll tell me whether I should accept some of the good money he's offered me?"

He could readily understand her wariness. Having worked hard for every penny she had ever earned, she was suspicious of Laroche's generosity. "After I've met him, Mollie, I'll give you my opinion of the fellow—for whatever it may be worth."

They continued to chat until Mollie had to return to the kitchen to prepare supper for the evening's guests. Her news that Laroche was in New Amsterdam, making a meeting possible that very night, altered Richard's plans. He returned to his room, where he wrote a long letter to Newcastle, telling him of the indifference to the Cavalier cause that he had found in Providence, Pequot, and New Haven.

Sealing the communication with a blob of wax, Richard set out for the waterfront on Hudson's River, hoping he could find a ship's captain with Cavalier sympathies who would carry the letter to Uncle William in France. New Amsterdam residents, he noted as he made his way down the cobbled streets filled with carts drawn by horses and mules, bustled far more than did the people of any other colony. Elsewhere, they strolled casually, but here everyone was in a hurry, darting between carts and needlessly endangering lives by boldly stepping in front of rapidly moving horsemen. If New Amsterdam citizens represented the new breed, they were a breed apart.

Slowing his own pace to a stroll when he reached the wharves, he could not believe his good fortune: a brig tied up at one of the first docks he saw was flying the Union Jack, a signal that her master was willing to act as a courier—unless, of course, the flying of the ensign in port was a careless accident.

He walked down the dock, saw the ship appeared deserted, and, cupping his hands, called, "Ahoy!"

A bearded man with thick, dark eyebrows emerged from a hatch. "What do you want?" he asked, his tone and manner surly.

"A word with the master of this vessel."

"I'm Captain Wardell." The man hooked his thumbs in his belt.

"A word in private, if you please, sir."

"Come aboard, then." The master's manner did not change.

Richard leaped onto the deck, and Captain Wardell led him below to a cluttered cabin.

Looking around, Richard found a dirty glass, and went through the ritual of extending it over water.

The seafaring man's attitude changed abruptly. He grinned as he went through the same gesture. "Why didn't you say so in the first place?" he demanded.

"It isn't the sort of information that one shouts across the wharf," Richard replied. "You sail soon for England?"

"Soon enough," Captain Wardell replied.

Trying to remain civil, Richard removed the bulky letter from the pocket of his buckskin shirt. "This won't add too much weight to your cargo."

The ship's master took the letter, saw it bore Newcastle's name, and frowned. "The earl is in France," he said.

"I know."

"I sail to Southampton."

"I was led to believe that communications could be forwarded to him through appropriate, safe channels."

"So they can, but the cost is dear. I'll have to charge you a gold sovereign."

The price was so high that Richard wondered if he was being cheated. "A gold sovereign buys many things."

"In this instance, it buys safety," Captain Wardell replied bluntly. "The owners of fishing craft that smuggle letters across the English Channel lose their heads if they're caught by the Roundheads, you know."

Richard realized he had to pay the fee, and took a gold sovereign from his purse.

The master's eyes gleamed as he held the coin up to the light of a small oil lamp, then bit it to satisfy himself that it was genuine. "Your letter will be safe, and you can bet it

will reach the Earl of Newcastle. I enjoy doing business
with you, sir, and for your information, I'll return here in
late July if you have more letters to send to good friends."

"I'll keep that in mind." Richard went ashore again as
quickly as he could. Captain Wardell was motivated by
greed, not a devotion to the Royalist cause, and Richard felt
deep disgust for anyone who sought personal gain from a
situation in which others risked their lives.

He strode briskly back to the Thorn and Thistle, uncon-
sciously adapting himself to the pace of New Amsterdam,
and the smell of clean sea air put him in a better mood. He
found Ezekiel had already returned, much encouraged by
his own venture.

"I was amazed to find how many merchants here know of
Burrows and Clayton," he said. "It will be far easier than I
thought to work out trade agreements with them. Trust
Eliza to have thought of a clever way to expand the business. She's unique."

"That she is." Richard was reluctant to discuss her virtues with the man to whom she was still betrothed. "I
suggest we go to supper, and I give you my word you'll be
served a meal you won't soon forget. The cook here was on
board ship with me crossing the Atlantic, and you'll search
long and hard before you find her culinary equal."

The meal lived up to his expectations. The soup was thick
with vegetables, the broiled cod was delicately flavored with
herbs that neither of the hungry young men could identify,
and the roast was so tender that Ezekiel found it difficult to
believe he was eating shoulder of venison. The final course
was a triumph, a pie of fresh spring berries cooked colonial-
style, in a crust.

Angus MacNeill made it his business to be present in the

dining room at the supper hour, and Richard hailed him. "I can't remember eating a meal I enjoyed so much," he said. "Give Mollie my compliments."

The innkeeper glared at him. "Tell her yourself!" he said curtly.

Richard knew how to rid the man of his unwarranted jealousy. "I shall do more than that. I'm traveling to Virginia to see the young lady who was Mollie's benefactress, and she'll be very happy—as I am—to learn that Mollie has found a position worthy of her talents."

Angus peered at him more closely, and then he became sheepish. "It may be I jumped to the wrong conclusions when I saw you and Mistress Williams a-hugging and a-kissing. You're not sweet on her?"

"Oh, I would be if I were older," Richard replied gallantly. "But she needs—and deserves—someone more mature."

Angus beamed at him. "I'll take your compliments to her myself," he announced, and headed toward the kitchen.

"Did he really regard you as a rival?" Ezekiel wanted to know after the proprietor was no longer within earshot.

"So it seems. People in love aren't quite sane, you know, at least according to my observations of them."

Ezekiel nodded. "Like the way Eliza flirted with you, trying to force a confrontation with her father and mine."

"I'd like to make a pact with you," Richard said. "As far as I am concerned, you and Eliza are still engaged to be married."

"But you and she are—"

"That's irrelevant. The facts of the existing situation are at odds with the potentials of my own relationship with her.

You and I work together effectively, as we proved yesterday when we were attacked by bandits. We're going to be on the trail together for a long time to come when we go to Virginia, and I suggest, for the sake of harmony, that we exclude Eliza from our discussions."

"Surely, if that's what you want." Ezekiel could not understand his companion's rigid code of honor.

Richard saw that the dining room was emptying. "Come along to the taproom, and I'll buy you a drink of ale." He made no mention of the meeting he hoped to have with Laroche, but thought it wise to remain inconspicuous.

The taproom was crowded, but the two young men were able to obtain one of the few empty tables. Most of the patrons were businessmen wearing brightly decorated suits and shirts with squared collars and deep cuffs. Mollie, busily taking orders and serving drinks, was the only woman in the room aside from a pair of obvious trollops who pouted when Richard and Ezekiel ignored them.

Mollie came to their table at once. "You set Master MacNeill on the straight road again!" she said. "I don't rightly know what you told him, but the storm has passed and the sun shines again, so that's good enough for me. I'm forever in your debt, Master Dunstable."

"I wish you all the happiness you want and deserve, Mollie," he replied.

"When I think of all you've done for me, I just wish I could find some way to repay you." She went off to the bar with their order.

Ezekiel was curious. "You say you crossed with her on the same ship, but she didn't call you Sir Richard."

"She was being discreet."

"I don't understand."

"I don't want to sound mysterious, Ezekiel, but there are aspects of my life it's best not to question."

He looked so somber that the younger man was abashed. "I didn't mean to pry—"

"No harm done."

Mollie approached with two tankards of ale, and as she placed one before Richard, she nodded in the direction of a table in the far corner.

He followed her gaze and saw a dark, inconspicuous man who could have been thirty or fifty, dressed in a suit of black. Only his multicolored waistcoat prevented him from resembling a Puritan.

Richard thanked Mollie, paying her for the ale, and tipping her generously. "I'm afraid I'll have to leave you to drink your ale alone," he said to the surprised Ezekiel as he stood, picked up his tankard, and made his way quickly across the room.

Dark eyes studied him intently as he approached. Richard took a seat opposite the solemn, dark man and quickly made the sign of drinking to the king-across-the-water. Then he waited until the man did the same. "I'm told you're Laroche," he said. "I'm Dunstable."

Laroche was surprised by the appearance of this rugged young man in buckskins. "Sir Richard?"

Richard nodded in confirmation.

"Judging by the way you look, I'd have sworn you were a hunter and trapper who has just come to town from the deep forests."

"That's where I've been, Master Laroche. Let's say I adapt to my surroundings."

"Well, you don't look as I pictured you." Laroche pursed his lips. "How did you know me?"

Not wanting to create trouble for Mollie, Richard merely shrugged.

A gleam of sardonic humor appeared in the man's dark eyes. "It's obvious, now that I think about it. You and Mistress Williams were shipmates."

Richard had to admit the man was sharp-witted. "I sent off a report today to our mutual friend in France."

"Ah, via Captain Wardell, no doubt." Laroche seemed to know everything. "And he charged you an outrageous fee for his services."

"That he did. A sovereign."

Laroche whistled under his breath, then shrugged. "We must build our house with the tools we have at hand," he said. "And speaking of money, do you have enough?"

"More than enough. I've lived frugally."

"Good." Laroche was relieved. "We're forced to live on the charity of the few who smuggled fortunes out of England, and funds for my operations aren't easy to obtain."

"Well, I shall impose no burden on you." Richard sipped his ale, reflecting that he could not warm to the gimlet-eyed man.

"I'm glad to hear it. Where have you been, and what was the nature of your report?"

"None too encouraging, I fear. Boston is a nest of Puritans. Providence Plantations, Pequot, and New Haven are too wrapped up in their own concerns to give a hang for our cause."

Laroche did not seem surprised. "You'll find most colonials react with indifference to anything that doesn't directly concern them. They fail to realize how much the restoration of the Stuart line will benefit them. I have it on good authority that when young Charles gains the throne, he intends to encourage migration to the colonies."

"He'll win a loyal following far more quickly if he lowers the taxes the colonies are forced to pay on everything they import and export."

"Ah, you've been listening to local merchants."

"Their argument seems valid."

"It isn't our place to debate royal policy. We do what we're told."

Richard made no reply, but the thought occurred to him that the man chosen to lead the Royalists in North America was going out of his way to be unpleasant.

Laroche seemed to relent a trifle. "You'll find Virginia far different from the other colonies. The Puritans have established no foothold of any kind there, and the Cavalier sentiment is strong, or so I've been informed. I'll be anxious to learn your reactions." He delicately sipped his sack. "There will be no need for you to tarry here. I know New Amsterdam well, and the people here have no concern for either Cavaliers or Puritans. They are actively protesting the actions of their own Dutch authorities who place restrictions on their God-given right to earn as much money as they can in the shortest possible time. They refuse to give any assistance to the Royalist cause."

He spoke with an intense loathing that surprised Richard. "They can't be blamed for that. The English and Dutch have never been on easy terms, due to colonial land disputes and commercial competition."

Laroche's face remained expressionless. "After you've

visited Virginia, come back here to me. By that time, I shall have other work for you to do."

His manner was so arbitrary that Richard wanted to remind him he was dealing with a volunteer who not only was paying his own way, but ultimately would be forced to earn a living. Instead he changed the subject. "Have you heard anything about the welfare of Mimi Shepherd?"

"All I can tell you is that she reached the colonies safely, which you already know. For whatever their reasons, the high command didn't see fit to recruit her for the—uh—special services you and I perform, so I have no cause to check on her well-being." Laroche looked as if the subject bored him.

Richard guessed that a spymaster, by definition, had to be cold-blooded and impersonal. Laroche was the first of that occupation he had ever encountered, and he was glad they would be going their separate ways in the foreseeable future.

All at once the man seemed to grow tense as he asked, "In your travels so far, what have you noted in regard to the relations of the various colonies with the French?"

"People here seem to think like people back in England, as nearly as I can judge." Richard shrugged. "In New Haven and Providence Plantations, they keep a wary eye on what's happening to the north, and they seem to believe the French can't be trusted. They think Mazarin covets the English colonies and wouldn't be above bribing the Indian nations of the area in an effort to stir up trouble."

"Do they offer any proof of the theory?"

"Not to me, but I feel precisely as they do. It's common knowledge that before his death, Richelieu lured German peasants into the French army and commissioned the construction of large carts for supplies. He spent money on the development of artillery, and whenever that happens, there's always trouble for us. Besides, they always demand a price, and there's bound to be some reason for the French to have offered a refuge to young King Charles."

"It's only natural that they would," Laroche replied. "After all, Queen Henrietta Maria was a princess of France."

"So she was, but the hospitality they've offered her and her children is a shade too convenient for my own taste. France has been our natural, principal enemy for more than five hundred years, and although she may hesitate to invade England despite the fact we've been weakened by the civil war, Mazarin well may believe he can occupy our colonies in North America and the West Indian Ocean without fear of starting a major war."

"That's an interesting conjecture," Laroche replied coldly, "but I can't give it much credence unless you substantiate it with facts. The economy of New France appears to be sound, young King Louis is earning large sums from the fur trade on the St. Lawrence River, and I'd be surprised if they took the risk of expanding. I could be mistaken, of course, so keep your eyes and ears open, and let me know if you find any hard evidence to indicate that they have designs on the English colonies." His tone and expression indicated that he refused to take the threat from Quebec seriously.

Richard merely nodded. He was surprised that the spymaster, who should have been alert to dangers from every source, should show so little concern for the possibility of a threat from Quebec.

CHAPTER 8

AT Mollie Williams's request, Richard made it a point to speak privately with her son before leaving New Amsterdam. He found young Bart in the stable of the Thorn and Thistle and deliberately took him off to a waterfront tavern for a drink of ale.

"You look as if your work agrees with you, lad," Richard said with a smile.

"It ain't too bad. The work I do is easy, and I collect a heap of tips." Bart was cocky. "Ma got me the job, you know. Just about the whole staff at the Thorn and Thistle believes that Angus MacNeill is sweet on her, but she won't even talk to me about him."

"From what I've observed, they're developing an interest in each other. I think it's wonderful that your mother not only has a position that suits her talents, but has a chance to find personal happiness as well. She's worked hard for many years, Bart—for herself and for you—and she deserves all the good things in life."

"That she does, Sir Richard." The youth eyed him a trifle suspiciously, now suspecting the true purpose of this conversation.

"It would be a shame if her opportunities were spoiled for her," Richard said pointedly.

Bart gulped his ale. "Ma asked you to have a talk with me, didn't she?"

"You might say I volunteered to have a word or two with you. Your mother tells me you've taken up with a gang of rough Cavaliers."

"I have the courage of me convictions, Sir Richard, and so do the boys who have become me friends."

"I'm not so sure that's wise, Bart. Director-General Stuyvesant has imposed heavy fines for violent disruption of the peace. The city has hired an interpreter to aid British merchants. This is a climate for enhancing the peace, not disturbing it. Such indiscretions won't be tolerated."

"They can't scare me none! I ain't afraid of them!" Bart spoke defiantly.

"You know where my own sympathies lie. But I don't make an issue of them."

"Well, I don't hold with keeping me views secret!"

"It's true, then, that you and your new friends go looking for Puritan sympathizers and then beat them?"

"They have a beating coming to them, Sir Richard. It was their kind who took off old King Charlie's head, it was. They killed me brother, John. And it was their kind that made life so miserable for Ma that she had to leave England and travel three thousand miles to start life all over again in the New World!"

"Where her son seems determined to create new messes for her." Richard was quietly emphatic. "Surely you know

I hold no warmth for the Roundheads. I had to flee from my home to escape imprisonment, and property that belonged to my family for many generations was confiscated, all because I was loyal to the Crown. I have my own valid reasons to hate the Puritans, but I serve neither the cause of young King Charles nor my own case if I flaunt my sympathies. The Roundheads have won, at least for the present, so we've got to be patient until the clock pendulum swings back in our direction."

"I'm no coward, Sir Richard!"

"Do you think I am one?"

"You belong to the gentry. Your ways and me ways are different."

"Not as different as you may think. See here, Bart—most people in America wash their hands of the quarrels between the Cavaliers and the Puritans. I'm not asking you to change your views, merely to keep them to yourself. You and your friends are going to force the authorities to take notice of you. You're making it necessary for them to send you to prison for disturbing the peace—"

"We'll bash in a few heads good and proper before they can take us, I'll tell you that."

"Every head you bash will add time to the sentence you'll serve. Your mother will be disgraced and might well lose her new position, no matter how much Angus MacNeill needs her. And you may well ruin her chance for personal happiness, too. A public innkeeper like MacNeill must stay in the good graces of the authorities, you know."

"Just because he bows and scrapes to the authorities so he can make his money don't mean I've got to follow his example."

"For your mother's sake, Bart, I urge you to stay out of trouble."

"I ain't a little boy no more, Sir Richard. I've become a man, and I've got to act like one!"

Richard knew he was wasting his breath. Bart Williams had no understanding of the power struggle between the Cavaliers and the Puritans, and instead saw the complex problems only as they related to him. It was apparent that he would cause troubles for his hardworking mother as well as for himself in his misguided efforts to prove his manhood.

Dempster Chaney labored in the fields of Hester Browne's farm from dawn until dusk seven days a week, as if motivated by an unrelenting, supernatural force. Robbin felt compelled to prove herself too, scouring the house until it shone, preparing meals, and spinning cloth. Neither uttered a complaint about their long hours, and their employer, dubious of the young couple at first, gradually softened.

"You two make me feel tired just watching you!" she told them at supper one evening. "My Eddie and I worked hard all our lives, but I feel downright lazy when I compare my efforts to what you do!"

Dempster paused in his eating of the roast turkey. "When there's chores to be done, ma'am," he said, "there's only one way to do them, so we pitch in."

"That you do." Suddenly, the gaunt woman's smile vanished, and she gasped and clutched her right side, grimacing in pain.

"Is something wrong, Mrs. Browne?" Robbin asked solicitously.

"I—I don't rightly know. Maybe I got me a touch of

indigestion, but it's an odd place for it." She touched the lower portion of her abdomen.

"Perhaps we should call in a physician," Robbin suggested.

Hester Browne forced a smile. "That's easier said than done, child. Old Doc Carey lived on the other side of the pond, but he passed away the year I lost my Eddie. Now, I don't rightly think there's a physician between here and Boston." She gasped again, the color draining from her face. It was obvious that her distress was genuine.

Dempster cleared his throat. "Ma'am," he said diffidently, "I was a student at the Royal College of Surgeons in Edinburgh until the Roundheads ruined my chances of becoming a doctor. If you don't object, maybe I might examine you."

"I reckon you'd best do it," the tight-lipped woman replied. "I get these pains that shoot through me like a knife was being stuck into my innards."

The meal was forgotten. Encouraging the older woman to lean heavily on her, Robbin assisted Hester to the parlor, and there she stretched out on the sofa. Dempster bent over the patient, gently probing the area she indicated. Every time he released the pressure of his palpating hand, she winced.

At last he straightened. "It appears," he said, "that you have an infection of some sort in your appendix. Fortunately it's a simple enough ailment to diagnose. Less fortunate is the fact that the appendix must be removed."

"In the medicine chest near the hearth," Hester said, "I keep some phials of herb medicines for emergencies. You know where to find them, Robbin."

"Indeed I do." Robbin started to leave the room.

Dempster called her back. "Don't bother," he said. "All the herbs in the world won't rid Mrs. Browne of the infection. I'm sorry, ma'am, but that is the truth."

"What needs to be done?" Hester bit her lower lip.

"The appendix must be cut out," he replied firmly. "It's an operation for a surgeon." He shook his head, then added grimly, "But there is no surgeon between the farm and Boston. Even if we rigged up a cart to carry you to town, the jouncing on the road would worsen your condition, and the appendix might rupture. In that event—you'd die. The infection would spread to all of your internal organs, and there would be no way to save you."

"You're sure, Dempster?" Robbin demanded anxiously.

"Very sure. This is one of the first things we learned at Edinburgh."

"Can you perform the surgery on me, young man?" Hester demanded, pausing between phrases as pains shot through her.

"I've removed two appendixes in my time, both under the direction of a senior staff surgeon. I've never tried doing it alone, and I can only hope I remember all that needs to be done."

"If this . . . infected organ isn't removed, you say—I'll not live?"

"Your chances won't be good, ma'am."

There was a long silence, and they could hear the ticking of the clock that stood on the parlor mantel.

"Then I have no choice, and neither do you, young man. Operate, and do your best!"

Dempster made no move for a time, then he suddenly squared his shoulders. "Do you happen to have any laudanum in your medicine chest?"

"The appendix must be cut out," he replied firmly. "It's an operation for a surgeon." He shook his head, then added grimly, "But there is no surgeon between the farm and Boston. Even if we rigged up a cart to carry you to town, the jouncing on the road would worsen your condition, and the appendix might rupture. In that event—you'd die."

"I—I think so." Hester gasped and shuddered. "Doc Carey gave us a supply when Eddie needed it, and it hasn't been touched since he passed on."

"Show me," Dempster said to Robbin, who led him to the kitchen and opened a cupboard that stood above the stove.

She scanned the contents quickly, then removed a phial containing an opaque liquid. Removing the stopper, he sniffed the contents, touched a bit to his tongue, then nodded. "We're in luck so far. Robbin, thread a slender needle with the thinnest silk thread you can find. Get me some clean cloths, and a bottle of brandy."

"You're sure that you know what you're doing, Dempster?"

"I'd best be very sure. Hurry." He cleaned off the kitchen table, scrubbed it with a brush and then, while it dried, hurried back to the parlor. "Don't try to walk. Just clasp your hands around my neck."

Hester Browne obeyed silently, and he carried her to the kitchen, placing her on the table. Robbin returned with the various items he had demanded. Dempster busied himself sharpening two kitchen knives on a whetstone. One was a small utility knife that could be used as a scalpel; the other was a long, heavy carving knife that Robbin had used to cut the turkey they had been eating, and its appearance suddenly became sinister, threatening.

Hester Browne, suffering spasm after spasm of intense pain and nausea, averted her gaze.

Dempster could not tolerate the worry he saw in his wife's eyes. "Now go to the woodpile," he told her, "and bring back a small slab about an inch deep. Hardwood, preferably. And while you're at it, you'd best fetch several more oil lamps. I'll want as much light as we can produce. I'll need some clothespins too, the kind you use to hold wash on the line."

His requests seemed odd to Robbin, but he seemed to know what he was doing, so she asked no questions as she hurried off to do his bidding.

Dempster measured a dose of laudanum in a glass, added water, and handed it to Hester, raising her head with one hand. "Drink this right down," he told her. "It has a very bitter taste, so don't stop drinking until you've drained the last drop."

"What is it?" she asked faintly.

"An opiate," he replied. "What I'm about to do won't be easy for either of us, but the laudanum will dull the pain for you." He refrained from telling her that, even with the aid of the medication, the surgery would be excruciatingly painful. She dutifully accepted the drink, almost gagging twice, but somehow getting it down.

Robbin returned with the various items that her husband had requested. He pulled over a small table, and laid them out after rinsing them in brandy. The strong odor of the potent liquor filled the room and added to Robbin's sense of growing queasiness.

Dempster rearranged the lights to his satisfaction, then rolled up his sleeves and washed his hands with soft, yellow soap. "Stand up there, behind Mrs. Browne's head," he told his wife. "Can you hear me, Mrs. Browne?"

The laudanum had taken effect quickly, and the gray-haired woman nodded groggily.

"Put this chunk of wood in your mouth, and when I start, bite down hard on it. It will help you to withstand the pain. I promise you I'll work as fast as I can."

She understood him, the expression in her eyes indicating that she trusted him implicitly, even though her life was at stake.

Robbin closed her eyes and swayed on her feet. "We'll have none of that," Dempster told her firmly. "I'll need your help, so you can't afford to faint. Take a cloth and use it to wipe perspiration from her brow. If need be," he added in a lower tone, "you'll have to hold her arms at her sides and prevent her from thrashing around on the table. That's paramount. I prefer not to tie her down, so you'll need to stay alert."

Robbin got a firm grip on her emotions. Never had she seen her husband so earnest, so determined.

"All right," he said. "Give her the block of wood. Mrs. Browne, the incision will be the worst of it."

Robbin placed the block of wood in the patient's mouth, and as she did, she saw her husband standing with his eyes closed, his lips moving. She realized he was praying, so she prayed too, not knowing what to expect and calling on Divine Providence to guide him.

Dempster bent lower over the patient's abdomen, probed with two fingers, then picked up the utility knife. Robbin held her breath. Moving swiftly, he made an incision about four inches long. Hester Browne shuddered, emitting a sound that was part scream, part moan.

In order to reduce the patient's bleeding, Dempster used the clothespins to clamp the exposed flesh. They were far less effective than the surgical clamps he had known in Edinburgh.

To Robbin's horror, he seemed to be digging deeper, so she concentrated her attention on Hester Browne, who was sweating heavily, her wide-open eyes reflecting her agony.

There was no sound in the room but the crackle of logs in the kitchen fire as Dempster worked, trying to recall all he had been taught so long before. His instructors had told him that he had a natural feel for surgery, and he was relying on that sixth sense to see him and his patient through the crisis. He labored quickly, his fingers surprisingly nimble as well as strong, and he paused only once to wipe away beads of his own perspiration that were stinging his eyes and threatening to blind him.

"Aha," he said at last, "I've got it."

Robbin could not look at the small, bloated object that he deposited in a bowl. Hester Browne was moaning continuously now as her teeth sank into the hardwood gag in her mouth. The worst was over, Dempster knew. He tied off blood vessels and removed the clothespins one by one, pausing occasionally to wipe away blood with a cloth soaked in brandy. At last he picked up the needle and thread, closed the lips of the incision, and sewed it. Then, pouring more brandy on a clean cloth, he wiped the patient's skin. "We're done, Mrs. Browne," he said wearily, and removed the wood from her mouth.

She understood the gesture to indicate that the operation was ended. "It—still—hurts," she managed to say.

Quickly washing his hands again, he mixed a smaller dose of laudanum and gave it to her. "This should put you to sleep," he said. "When you wake up tomorrow, you should be feeling much better." He turned to Robbin. "We'll wait until she's asleep before we move her to her bed. It will be far less painful for her that way."

His wife indicated that she concurred.

"Tell me—before the opiate takes effect," Hester

Browne whispered. "Did you rid me . . . of the diseased part?"

"I did, Mrs. Browne. You'll be fit and fine again in a matter of days."

In spite of her pain, she managed to smile at him. "I'm not Mrs. Browne," she said. "Not to you. Call me . . . Aunt Hester." She drifted off to sleep, the smile still on her face.

Dempster helped Robbin carry her to her bedchamber, where Robbin dressed her in a nightgown, and then they returned to the kitchen to clean up the room. They worked in silence for a time, with Robbin scrubbing energetically. "I've never been so frightened in all my life," she said. "How did you manage to remain so calm?"

Dempster grinned at her. "If I'd allowed myself to be scared," he replied, "I couldn't have done what was necessary."

"You missed your calling, my dear. You seemed to know exactly what you were doing every minute. Somehow we've got to save the money for you to go back and finish surgeons' school. You have a talent that shouldn't be wasted."

He felt shaken inside, but when he extended his hands he discovered they were steady. "I won't be welcome at Edinburgh as long as the Roundheads are in power," he said. "And by the time they're out, it will be too late. No, Robbin, I seem destined to live as a farmer, like my father and grandfather before me. I don't wear my religion on my sleeve, the way the Puritans do, but I still put my faith in the Almighty, and I'm content to live as He directs." Smiling at her, he went to a cupboard and took out two glasses, into which he poured a small quantity of brandy. "I prescribe a little of this for internal use," he said. "We used quite a bit of it."

"Why did you wipe all the instruments you used with brandy?" she asked, taking a glass from him.

Dempster shrugged. "No one knows why," he said, "but they discovered at Edinburgh that patients suffer fewer fevers and infections after surgery when brandy is used liberally during an operation. I just did what I've been taught."

She raised her glass to him. "You've accomplished one thing tonight, Dr. Chaney. Our days of being on trial here are over. I believe you've guaranteed us a home here for as long as we want to stay."

"God bless Hester Browne," he said, and drained the contents of his glass.

Robbin drank too, but reflected that she would not be content to let her husband spend the rest of his life as a farmer. In some way she could not yet foresee, she would make certain he returned to school to earn his degree as a surgeon. His performance tonight proved where his real talents lay, and she was determined that he would have a chance to develop them to the full.

The holding of Horace Laing, outside Middle Plantation, was an extensive estate devoted to the growing of tobacco, for which there was an ever-increasing demand in England. Obviously the plantation was a profitable enterprise. The main house was constructed of red stone, with the upper stories shingled in wood, and virtually all of the handsome furnishings had been imported from England. A large staff, which included a cook, a butler, and several housemaids, attended to the needs of the host and his guests.

Certainly Mimi Shepherd felt completely at home here. Laing had been absent from the plantation when she had first arrived, but he had left orders to make her welcome, and this the staff had done, expertly attending to her needs. She could close her eyes and imagine herself back in her own London town house.

Now Horace Laing had come home, and they were dining together by candlelight for the first time. A burly man in his early forties, with the healthy tan of one who spent most of his days out-of-doors, he was endowed with a rugged charm. Only his accent was a trifle strange: he spoke so precisely, so deliberately that he sounded as if he were speaking English with the care of one to whom the language was alien.

Expensively attired in a suit of nubby raw silk, he was at ease in his surroundings. The tablecloth and napkins were of thick, creamy damask, the dinner service was made of fine bone china, and the flatware was gleaming silver. Even the goblets and glasses were fashioned of sparkling crystal, worth a fortune in England and far more in the distant land to which they had been transported.

Certainly, Horace Laing was not impervious to feminine beauty. Mimi had elected to wear a strapless gown for her first dinner alone with him, and she knew by the expression in his eyes that he appreciated her appearance.

"I owe you an apology, Lady Dawn," he said. "Had I known when you were arriving, I'd have altered my business arrangements accordingly. I didn't expect you to spend weeks here unattended."

"Oh, I assure you I was very well attended, Master Laing," she replied. "Your staff is superb, and I wouldn't have guessed that any help could be that well trained in the New World. I went out for a long canter every day, and I've even explored the wilderness beyond your property. What's more, your library is marvelous, and I've availed myself freely of your books."

"You relieve my concern," Horace Laing replied gallantly. "I hope you exercised caution in your explorations of the wilderness. The forests here aren't as innocent as they seem. I've tried hard to bring civilization as I know it to the New World, but beyond my cultivated fields lies another realm. As recently as five years ago, it was explosively dangerous and cruel. Thankfully, the treaty approved three years ago seems to have completely subdued the tribes, but one cannot be too careful."

"I saw no one when I went for rides," she assured him. "Your chief groom told me to keep watch for Indians who might be hostile, but I didn't see any. Thank you for your concern."

A serving maid came into the dining room and filled their wineglasses. Horace Laing went through the ritual of drinking a toast to the king-across-the-water. Mimi instantly did the same.

"I understand that the Roundheads were eager to prevent your departure from England," he said.

"Apparently so. They boast that they don't wage war against women, but I appear to have been a special case."

"Because of your father's rank, I assume."

"Partly that," she replied candidly. "But also, I'm sure, because there were rumors about King Charles and me."

"I see." He was too much of a gentleman to inquire whether there was any substance to the story.

"But it worked out well for me, thanks to Sir Richard Dunstable."

"I've had good reports about Sir Richard. He appears to be competent."

"If it weren't for Richard," Mimi said with a smile, "I wouldn't be here today."

"Then I owe him my gratitude as well. Do you think our cause is doomed in England, Lady Dawn?"

"For the present I can see little hope for us. Parliament has been ruthless in crushing the opposition, and Cromwell has proved clever in playing on the sentiments of the people."

"Then our only hope rests with the French, I take it," Laing declared.

"The French? Hardly." She made no attempt to hide her scorn.

"Young Charles is the guest of Mazarin, and Queen Henrietta Maria, after all, is the aunt of the Boy-King Louis the Fourteenth. It strikes me that we'd be wise to accept all the help that Paris offers," Laing said earnestly.

"You can be sure there are conditions tied to French help. I may be prejudiced, of course, because I'm not welcome in France myself these days. Queen Henrietta Maria is none too fond of me. But I don't base my opposition of the French on personal grounds. In all the years my father was a member of the Privy Council, he argued successfully against forming any close alliance with France. He always said they'll throw one arm around your shoulder and pick your pocket with their free hand."

"With all due respect to Sturbridge, who was a distinguished diplomat, if he were alive today I'm sure he'd sing a different tune."

"You didn't know my father," Mimi replied firmly. "His mistrust of France was basic."

"Well, as I see our situation, the Cavalier party is disorganized and has no funds. If we're to put young Charles on the throne, we'll certainly need the assistance of the French navy, and it may be we'll require help from their army, too."

"I don't know how long it has been since you spent any appreciable amount of time in England, Master Laing," Mimi said heatedly, "but you misjudge the temperament and the patriotism of the English public. Let one French warship sail into English waters, let one battalion of French troops land on our soil, and the people will become united behind Cromwell and Parliament. Not only will the Roundheads win the complete support of the vast mass of people who have taken no part in the quarrel between the Cavaliers and the Puritans, but most of the Royalists will rally behind Cromwell's banner, too."

"Do I gather correctly that you would be one of the first to change sides?"

Mimi shrugged prettily. "I'm relieved that it's a decision I don't need to make. Let's just say I'd be sorely tempted."

Horace Laing nodded thoughtfully, then changed the subject. "I hope you'll join me in a glass of port, Lady Dawn. I usually reserve port for the men, totally ignoring the fact that a lady might appreciate the bouquet and taste of a rare old port, too."

"Kind sir, I'd be delighted to join you," she said, convinced that he was charming.

By use of a bellpull, he summoned a serving maid who had anticipated his desires, appearing with a decanter of port wine and two glasses. She placed them on the table before him, then stood back while he served the beverage.

Calling Mimi's attention to the floral centerpiece on the table, Laing reached surreptitiously into a waistcoat pocket and removed a packet containing a gray powder, which he slipped into his guest's glass before he filled it with port. Mimi was busily inspecting the floral arrangement and noted nothing untoward.

The serving maid could not help but realize what her master was doing, but she stared off into space, her face wooden, and when he nodded to her, she placed the silver glass in front of the guest, then silently withdrew. Whatever Laing's motive, she was familiar with his routine.

He solemnly went through the ritual of offering a silent toast to the king-across-the-water. Inasmuch as they had started the meal in the same way, Mimi thought that here was a man truly devoted to the Cavalier cause, so she followed his example before sampling the sweet wine.

"There are two schools of thought about port," he said. "Some prefer it served in a clear glass so they can enjoy holding it to the light and seeing the color of the wine. I prefer a silver cup because I'm convinced it enhances the taste. I import it from a vineyard in the north of Portugal. It takes a bit of doing to bring it across the Atlantic because its importation has not officially been approved, but I import it in bulk, so I don't mind paying a premium to a shipper for my pipes of wine."

Mimi listened to him politely, but found herself becoming so drowsy she could scarcely hold up her head. In an attempt to rouse herself, she took another large swallow of her port. She knew her smile was fixed and hoped her eyes didn't look as glassy as she feared they were. She could never forgive herself for falling asleep at her first dinner with a host who was doing everything in his power to please her.

Laing continued to talk at length about his method of bringing the wine to the New World from Portugal. He saw his guest struggling but slowly losing the battle to remain awake, and his voice droned on steadily.

Not until Mimi slumped in her chair, her breathing deep and even, did he fall silent and reach for the bellpull.

The serving maid did not appear to notice that the Lady Dawn was fast asleep.

"Tell Simms I'm ready for him," Laing directed.

The woman disappeared, and a heavyset man in butler's livery came into the room, glanced at Mimi, and grinned. "I wondered how long this one would last after you came home," he said. "You wasted no time."

"There's none to waste, is there?" Laing demanded. "You may remove her to the cellar, Simms."

The man scooped Mimi up into his arms. "What's the treatment to be this time?"

"Lady Dawn is more self-reliant and headstrong than the others. I believe she'll require a special treatment in order to break her spirit quickly. Tell Anna to strip her."

The butler nodded, his eyes gleaming.

"No, Simms," Horace Laing said sharply. "I forbid you to go near her. Your techniques may be effective with some, but Lady Dawn is of very high rank, and she'd be so outraged by your—uh—devotion to her that she would become all that much more difficult to break down. Tell

"You may remove her to the cellar. Lady Dawn requires special treatment to break her spirit. Tell Anna to strip her."

Anna I said she's to receive no visitors and is to be given the silent treatment."

"As you wish," Simms said sulkily, and made his way out of the room, easily managing the dead weight of the unconscious woman in his arms.

Alone at the table now, Laing refilled his glass with port, twirled it, and drank. A hint of a smile appeared at the corners of his mouth, but his eyes remained dark and hard.

Mimi's first conscious thought was that she was thirsty, that never before had she craved water so badly. She sat up, startled to discover that she was reclining on a small cot instead of the four-poster bed in her guest suite. Then she realized she was completely nude. But her thirst came first, and she poured water from a carafe that stood on a crude bedside table into a glass, and not until she drained the contents did she look around.

Scarcely able to believe what she saw, she realized she was in a cell, a chamber no more than twelve feet long and eight feet wide, illuminated by a small oil lamp with the wick burning low. The walls appeared to be of solid stone and were sweating; that fact, combined with the absence of a window, convinced her that her place of detention was underground. Between her and freedom stood a heavy door of solid oak, and she knew even before she raised the latch that it was locked.

Conquering the panic that threatened to overwhelm her, Mimi sat shivering on the cot, and as she tried to reconstruct what had happened, she wrapped herself in the single, thin blanket that had covered her. Gradually she began to recall the previous night's events: she had been dining with Horace Laing, and as she had been drinking her port wine, he had told her in boring detail about his trials in importing it.

Of course! The port! Now that she recalled it, the wine had tasted curiously metallic. She had attributed that to the silver goblet. But why should Laing have gone to the trouble of drugging her and making her a prisoner? The strange dilemma in which she found herself made no sense. The removal of her clothes had made her vulnerable, but she was not prepared to tolerate this outrage. Wrapping the blanket around her as best she could, she picked up the slop jar, the only weapon in the cell, then rattled the latch hard.

After a time Mimi heard footsteps on the stone floor outside her cell, and when a key was inserted into the lock, she raised the slop jar over her head, intending to hurl it at an attacker.

Instead a broad-faced woman in nondescript attire came into the cell, barely glancing at the prisoner. In one hand she carried a tray, which she deposited on the little table.

There was food on the tray, but Mimi was too angry to care. "I demand to know why I've been made captive!" she cried. "And how dare you take my clothes! I hold Horace Laing responsible, and I demand to see him at once!"

The woman calmly ignored the prisoner's outburst, and picked up the carafe and empty water glass.

Mimi thought of hurling the slop jar at the woman, but the rumble of male voices in the corridor outside the cell accented her helpless state. One man—or a dozen—could assault her, and there was nothing she could do to protect herself.

Slowly she lowered the jar. "Please," she begged, "why am I being treated this way?"

The woman did not reply. Instead she withdrew with the carafe and the water glass, and a key grated harshly in the lock.

Mimi was so furious that she trembled violently, and no longer able to stand, she sat abruptly on the edge of the cot. Her common sense told her to control her temper; there had to be a reason she had been imprisoned, a reason for the woman's silence. As she grew calmer she became aware of the aroma of food and realized she was ravenously hungry.

Whisking a cloth from the tray, she realized that at least her captors had no intention of starving her. On a platter were thick slices of ham, cheese, and smoked whitefish. Beside the plate was a loaf of bread, still warm from the oven, a crock of fresh butter, and a wooden tankard filled with a mild ale.

Forcing herself to eat slowly, Mimi analyzed her situation. It was difficult to believe that a man who lived as ostentatiously as Horace Laing would have gone to all this bother in order to rob her. Surely her money wasn't worth the effort, although her jewels—which had been in the family for generations—were worth a king's ransom. If he had coveted them, how much simpler it would have been to kill her and dispose of her body in the nearby wilderness. No, she was being kept alive for a reason.

It was difficult to judge the passage of time, and after Mimi ate her fill she crawled back onto the cot. Perhaps an hour or two later, the woman gaoler returned to remove the tray and fill the lamp with oil.

Mimi deliberately remained silent. The woman appeared surprised by her prisoner's change in demeanor, but made no comment as she removed the serving tray and the dishes.

Perhaps, Mimi reflected, she was employing the wrong

tactics. Nothing ventured, nothing gained. It was a long, tedious wait until the next meal was brought to the cell, but this time she unleashed her frustration in a rage, demanding an explanation for the way she was being treated. The woman paid no heed to her, and might well have been deaf and mute.

Only the serving of meals marked the passage of time. Mimi slept and daydreamed, then deliberately called to mind the puzzles that had been the rage at the court of Charles I a few years earlier. Puzzles had always bored her, but solving them now helped to maintain her sanity.

She was held captive for about three days and nights before there was a sudden change in her routine. One day, the female in charge brought Mimi a complete set of her own clothes, a hand mirror, and her cosmetics case. Washing as best she could in the tub of cold water that the woman had also dragged into the cell, she dressed quickly. The gown that had been selected for her was unsuitable for a prison cell, and Mimi couldn't help grinning at her reflection in the mirror. She looked incongruously frivolous in a dress with wide, frilly cuffs of organdy and a matching collar that framed a deep neckline. The mere fact that she was dressed restored a measure of her confidence, and after she used her cosmetics and brushed her hair, she felt better able to cope with whatever might lie ahead. She suspected that her incarceration was entering a new phase.

The woman reappeared to remove the tub of water, and when she deposited a bottle of wine and two glasses, Mimi knew she was due to receive a visitor. She registered no surprise when Horace Laing appeared and bowed formally. "You'll forgive me if I occupy the only seat," she said coldly.

"I don't mind standing," he replied, leaning against the wall.

"Apparently the wine has been served to celebrate our reunion," she continued, filling the two glasses, "but if you don't mind, you'll drink first. The last time we drank together I suffered rather extraordinary consequences."

Obviously admiring her spirit, he raised his glass to her. Mimi went through the ritual of drinking to the king-across-the-water. The gesture surprised Laing, but he recovered and did the same.

"Now, sir, the time has come for an explanation of the horrendous treatment to which I have been subjected!" she said.

Laing looked uncomfortable. In similar circumstances, the earlier prisoners had been cowed and sullen, enabling him to take the lead and direct the conversation into channels he wanted to explore. But this bold aristocrat had a will and a mind of her own, so he was forced to talk on her terms. "I am not what I seem," he told her.

Mimi's high-pitched laugh echoed from the stone walls of the cell. "You, sir, have a most profound grasp of the obvious. Tell me you're in the personal employ of Oliver Cromwell, and I swear to you I shall not be surprised."

"I am not employed by Puritans, and I am no Cavalier, either. I have the honor of serving His Christian Majesty, Louis the Fourteenth, and I report directly to Cardinal Mazarin himself."

Mimi stared at him without blinking. "I'll be damned," she said softly.

"Whether you are, or whether you accept the salvation that is offered to you, remains to be seen." Little by little, Laing was gaining control of the situation. "My real identity is irrelevant to your situation. It is enough that you know me as Horace Laing."

"You wouldn't be flattered, sir, if you knew what I'm thinking of you!" she retorted. "What astonishes me is that you've gone to so much trouble to maintain a false front."

"The stakes are enormous, and Mazarin plays only to win. Think of Europe, my dear Lady Dawn. With England safely under French control, France can spread her influence and bring Spain, the German states, and the Low Countries under her wing. It is not too farfetched to say that even the Archduke in Austria will be forced to conclude a treaty of peace and friendship with France, as will Russia and the Ottomans. As for North America, all of it will be absorbed into New France."

"A wonderful dream, sir, and I envy you the sweep, the scope of it. The American colonies will be French. France will stand astride all of Europe, and every head will bow to your boy-monarch. But reality has a way of upsetting dreams. You can accomplish Mazarin's goal only by first subduing the English. But they're as indigestible today as they were at Agincourt long before your day and mine!" Mimi faced him proudly.

"It is not Mazarin's intention to fight the English," Laing replied somberly. "He well knows and respects their valor in battle. Wars are expensive, and he can accomplish his ends far more cheaply, with no loss of life. England has met her match in Mazarin!"

"I'm sure he'd be pleased to know how much you admire him, but I fail to recognize his many accomplishments, aside from causing me great distress and embarrassment."

Laing refused to be distracted by her sarcasm. "Hear me, Lady Dawn," he said. "At the moment Cromwell reigns triumphant over a divided, bitter England. Only a king can reunite the country—the legitimate monarch, Charles the Second. Do you agree?"

"So far, sir, we have little cause for argument." She looked across the cell at him, challenging him.

"Young Charles suffers from the familiar Stuart weakness, a liking for beautiful, exciting women. His cravings are already being cultivated and indulged. Mark my words, when he returns to the throne of his father, he will be accompanied by at least one mistress in the pay of France, and others will follow her. He will be a marionette manipulated by a puppeteer in Paris."

Mimi was aghast. "Damnable, but clever," she admitted.

"First, however, he must be restored to the throne. Mazarin needs able assistants to accomplish that goal, and you have long held the place of honor at the top of his list of potential recruits. Your qualifications are unique, after all. You are capable of gathering information available to virtually no one else, so your value to Cardinal Mazarin, therefore, is extraordinary."

She hadn't been aware that Cardinal Mazarin even knew of her existence, and she stared at him incredulously. It was obvious to her that he was sincere.

"In certain fields of endeavor, particularly as an agent who will influence the thinking of a nation, one woman can be as effective as one hundred men. Your credentials are impeccable. As the sole surviving member of one of England's greatest families, you have access to the entire nobility. Your beauty and charm speak for themselves. Even I have been impressed by them."

He was so much in earnest that her blood ran cold. The

French seemed prepared to go to any lengths to obtain her services.

"You appear to be intelligent, and it is our understanding that you speak French fluently, which is also helpful to us. The one quality you lack is ruthlessness, a determination to allow nothing to stand between you and the goals we have set, but you can be taught that quality."

"By you, no doubt."

"I have been selected to act as your instructor," he replied gravely. "There are many nobles in England who care nothing for the causes of the Puritans and the Cavaliers. They are your first targets, and their defection to France must receive the first priority."

"I loathe the Roundheads with all my being," Mimi said, "but I prefer to see England ruled by Oliver Cromwell than to see her become a pawn of France!"

"Your patriotism is misguided. Mazarin decided long ago that you were necessary to the fulfillment of his aims, and he always gets what he wants. You have been under observation for a long time, Lady Dawn. We don't know what became of the agent, a man known to the English as Robertson, who was keeping watch over you. He sailed with you from England, but he was not on board the ship when you anchored in Boston."

Realizing that Laing was scrutinizing her carefully in order to assess her reaction, Mimi concealed her shock. So the man Richard had killed on board the brig had been in the employ of France rather than the Puritans, as she and Richard had assumed. Now she knew why he had written his journal in French. "He was washed overboard during a storm, the captain told us. That's all I know about the matter."

He couldn't determine whether she was telling the truth. "Poor Jean-Pierre," he said. "He was a devoted servant of France. But no matter. If you are willing, your instructions will begin at once. I neglected to mention that you will have no financial concerns if you cast your lot with us. I know your funds are limited because I have taken the liberty of counting the gold in your purse. But I have been authorized to assure you that no limits will be placed on the sums you will be privileged to draw from the royal treasury of France. There will be no need for you to change your style of living, Lady Dawn."

"Suppose I decline to accept Cardinal Mazarin's generosity. What then?" she demanded.

"I urge you to think twice before rejecting such an opportunity," Laing said.

"You haven't answered my question."

"Think of your situation," he told her. "Surely you don't enjoy your confinement in this miserable cell. Surely you must recognize the helplessness of your predicament. I have seen to it that you've been served edible food, and as a special favor I allowed some clothes to be returned to you today."

"I find your generosity overwhelming."

"Not at all," he said seriously. "You have a mind of your own, and I far prefer to have your voluntary cooperation than to force you to work with us. A reluctant agent is not the best agent. You'll continue to be served the same meals that I myself eat, and I shall have your clothing boxes brought to you, even though they'll make this cell far more cramped. I'm prepared to be patient, Lady Dawn. Think about all I've said to you today, and I'm sure you'll see the wisdom of working loyally with us."

Mimi bit back an angry reply.

Laing strolled to the door. "Take your time. You have little else to occupy yourself, so choose wisely. Although I don't like to threaten, the privileges of enjoying your wardrobe and eating fine food can be withdrawn." He bowed and left the cell.

Mimi faced the door defiantly until the key grated in the lock, then she crumpled onto the cot. It was one thing to maintain a brave pose in front of her captor, but now that she was alone, despair overwhelmed her.

She knew now that she had become a pawn in an international conspiracy being devised for the highest of stakes, the domination of Europe and the bloodless conquest of the British colonies in North America. Pitted against her was the wily first minister of France, who had all of the resources of a powerful nation to back him up. Charles I, her protector and friend, was dead, and his forces had been scattered and rendered impotent.

She had spoken the truth when she had said that she preferred to see Oliver Cromwell rule England than to watch a proud nation become an instrument of France. She could see no way out of the trap. Laing would continue to hold her prisoner until she agreed to become an agent of France, and he would apply pressures that would become intolerable.

Worst of all, she stood alone. In fact, no one in a position to help her even knew of her predicament. The Earl of Newcastle was in France, presumably near young Charles II, who was himself being corrupted by the French. And on this side of the Atlantic only Richard Dunstable knew where she had gone, and he had no reason to suspect that she had fallen victim to foul play.

In spite of the odds against her, she had no intention of giving in. Fighting back tears, she clenched her fists and glared at the closed door. "Never!" she vowed aloud. "Never!"

CHAPTER 9

THE American wilderness was a land of bounty to those who knew how to benefit from it. Game was plentiful, with deer and rabbits everywhere, and spring added northward-bound ducks and geese to the larder. Fish abounded in clear, swift-running streams, and Roaring Wolf taught Richard a new trick in forest living. The Pequot packed fish in green leaves and then suspended it over a low fire in a hammocklike contraption fashioned of vines. The result was beautifully steamed food. At times during the cooking, Roaring Wolf added small amounts of water to the leaves to retain moisture. There were enough wild berries for a man to eat his fill, and Richard learned to distinguish edible plants and roots at a glance. Never had he enjoyed food more.

He was fortunate, too, in his choice of companions. Roaring Wolf was in his natural environment and made all aspects of wilderness living seem easy. Ezekiel Clayton was familiar with the endless forests, too, and seemed never to tire. The trio moved southward through New Sweden and Maryland at a relatively leisurely pace, making steady progress in their journey to Virginia.

The wilderness was considerably different from the woods of Lincolnshire that Richard had known and loved. There were no poachers here, no civilized intruders greedy for forbidden game. The sweet, resinous scent of pines was everywhere, and often, when there was a break in the stands of towering oak, maple, and ash, the effect created by the sunlight slanting down into the open space was like that of sun streaming through a cathedral window.

As Richard became more familiar with the North American wilderness, his awe at the very size of the forests gradually led to an understanding of the fierce love the colonists felt for their new homeland. The quarrels of the Old World seemed petty here, and the man who cooperated with the natural forces lacked nothing. The forest provided him with food and drink, clothing, and a healthy body. Above all else, it gave him a sense of peace that was unique in Richard's experience.

"I can see the attraction of the wilderness for men like your father and Adam Burrows," he said to Ezekiel one night as they sat at their campfire, feasting on broiled venison and trout. "I wondered how men of their caliber could be content living so far from English civilization. Now I wonder how anyone in his right mind could be content anywhere else than here."

"We have a saying we've borrowed from the Indians," Ezekiel replied. "The sap that runs in the trees finds its way into a man's bloodstream."

"This is true," Roaring Wolf said. "White men who come to the forest know nothing of its ways. They learn from warriors, and soon they act more like Indians than Indians themselves." The uninhibited laughter of all three was a reflection of the comradeship that bound them together.

"I came to the New World not knowing what to expect here," Richard said. "Now that I know, I'll never willingly live in England again. I feel more at home here than I do in the house where I was born and reared—which is just as well, seeing that it's been taken from me." He laughed again, without bitterness.

They rolled themselves up in their blankets to sleep, and at dawn they awakened, washed in a creek, and ate cold venison and fish for breakfast before resuming their journey. As always, Richard was excited by the challenges that a new day on the trail would offer.

As they started to break camp, however, Roaring Wolf suddenly raised a hand in warning, then bent low, with one ear close to the ground. Richard did the same and heard the approaching thumping of many footsteps. He looked at Roaring Wolf for guidance.

"Large party of braves comes this way," the Pequot said. "Too many warriors for us to hide. Better to stay here and let them see us."

Richard promptly checked his rifle and pistol, and the other two made ready their own weapons.

Soon they could clearly hear the sound of a rapidly approaching party, and from the crest of the hill near their campsite, they saw a band of braves making their way rapidly toward the east, all armed with bows, arrows, and tomahawks, all with red and purple paint smeared on both their faces and bare torsos.

Roaring Wolf courageously stepped into the open, and

while the others covered him with their firearms from their hiding places, he raised his hand, palm outward in a gesture of friendship.

The column halted, and a weary, middle-aged brave, whose bonnet identified him as the leader of the group, came forward. They spoke for some time in low tones. Richard, whose deficiencies in the languages of the Indians made it impossible for him to understand exactly what was being said, tried to deduce the meaning from the Indians' gestures, posture, and expressions. Ezekiel strained to hear, but could pick up only an occasional word or phrase.

Suddenly, Roaring Wolf turned and beckoned to his companions. They came into the open too, and Richard took care to cradle his rifle under one arm while he raised the other in the traditional greeting of Indian friendship.

"This," Roaring Wolf explained, "is Sha-wa-na, sachem of the Conestoga. He leads one hundred warriors, and he is troubled. The Conestoga are being chased by a band of their ancient enemies, the Iroquois, who have three warriors for each of the Conestoga. The Iroquois know that most warriors of the Conestoga have gone far into the wilderness to hunt. It is that time of year. The Iroquois will attack the main town of the Conestoga, burn it to the ground, and make slaves of the women and children. Only Sha-wa-na and his braves stand between the Iroquois and their bloody goal."

Richard looked at the exhausted, worried sachem, and impulsively reached a decision. "You say there are three Iroquois warriors for each of the Conestoga?"

Roaring Wolf nodded.

"Perhaps we can make the odds more equal with the aid of our firesticks," Richard said.

Ezekiel Clayton grinned broadly. "I'm going to enjoy this," he said. "The Iroquois are noted for their viciousness toward their captives. They deserve being taught a lesson they won't forget."

Roaring Wolf translated the offer for the sachem, who promptly reached out and grasped Richard's forearm as he spoke solemnly.

"The Conestoga," Roaring Wolf translated, "will never forget the friendship their white brother offers them in their hour of need. Tell us what needs to be done."

A battle plan had already formed in Richard's mind, and he spoke quickly, decisively. "Divide the warriors into three groups, with one double the size of the others. Let the smaller parties conceal themselves on the flanks in the forest—there, and there. The large group will hide in the forest here, on the side of this hill. None will open fire on the enemies until I give the word."

As Roaring Wolf translated, the Conestoga warriors, bewildered and eager for leadership, obeyed with alacrity.

"Roaring Wolf," Richard said, "the success or failure of that which we will attempt depends on you. For many days you have seen Ezekiel and me using our firesticks. You have examined them often. Do you think you can reload them swiftly? Do you think you can teach a Conestoga brave to do the same?"

The Pequot nodded solemnly. "I will do this for you. I will ask Sha-wa-na to help. My fingers are not as nimble as your fingers, but the Great Spirit will help us."

"Good. Now listen carefully. You too, Ezekiel. I want the Iroquois to think they're facing a large company of white men who carry firearms. Shoot your musket, and Roaring Wolf will reload it while you discharge your pistol. Sha-wa-na will do the same with my weapons. My idea is to establish and maintain a steady stream of fire at the Iroquois. I want to convince them that they face a whole company of marksmen, so you'll both have to reload quickly, Roaring Wolf. And Ezekiel, you and I will be obliged to make every shot count."

Sha-wa-na nodded in approval when Roaring Wolf, who was examining the firearms critically, explained to him what Richard had in mind. "The Iroquois," the sachem declared, "have no fear of other nations. But no Indian can stand up to the magic of the white man's firesticks."

Roaring Wolf and Sha-wa-na were given a supply of powder and lead, and while they practiced the reloading operation, Richard and Ezekiel led their horses to the far side of the hillcrest and tethered them there. The coming battle would be better waged on foot.

A random thought flickered through Richard's mind and caused him to smile at himself. He, who should be concerning himself with the conflict between the Cavaliers and the Roundheads, felt so at home in the American wilderness that he was committing himself to a fight between two tribes of whose very existence he had been unaware only a short time earlier. He had promised his support to the outnumbered Conestoga, however, so he was determined that they win a victory.

As he and Ezekiel returned to their place of concealment behind a thick stand of oaks and brambles, Roaring Wolf raised a hand in warning. The Iroquois were approaching.

Richard had to admire the stealth of the native braves. One moment, the wooded section directly ahead appeared deserted; the next, it was swarming with Iroquois warriors, their faces and bodies streaked with bright green paint.

Obviously this was the enemy's vanguard or scouting party, and the braves advanced cautiously.

To open fire now would be to give away his entire plan of action before the main bodies were joined. So he turned to Sha-wa-na and drew a finger across his throat. The sachem understood at once and reacted accordingly, silently signaling to his own men.

Richard would never forget the astonishing spectacle that followed. One by one, the twelve to fifteen Iroquois scouts seemed to be swallowed up by the earth itself. The waiting Conestoga struck with swift brutality, making no sound, and their knives disposed of the entire advance party. Not until later did Richard become conscious of the discipline the Conestoga were exercising; aware of the need for continuing secrecy, they refrained from their customary removal of the scalps of the dead.

Now the main body of the Iroquois came into sight, the brawny, copper-skinned braves making no attempt to conceal themselves because they had no reason to suspect that they were walking into a trap.

"Now, Ezekiel," Richard muttered. "Fire at will—and keep firing."

The rifle and musket spoke almost at the same instant, the former killing one Iroquois warrior in the front rank, the latter wounding another. Dropping his rifle to the ground beside the tense, waiting Sha-wa-na, Richard took aim with his pistol and fired twice. When he saw yet another Iroquois drop to the ground, he decided not to keep count of the casualties. Dropping his still-smoking pistol, he reached for his rifle again, and had to wait only a moment for it to be reloaded.

Thanks to the skill of the sweating Roaring Wolf and

Sha-wa-na, who paid no attention to the enemy and concentrated solely on the vital task they had been given, the rifle, musket, and pistols were reloaded steadily, enabling Richard and Ezekiel to keep up an uninterrupted fire. Troops familiar with firearms would have understood the nature of the hoax and been quick to pinpoint the enemy fire, but the Iroquois had never before encountered sustained gunfire in battle and had no idea they faced only two men.

The war chief of the Iroquois came forward, resplendent in a feathered bonnet, and Richard felt a grim satisfaction as he put a bullet between the man's eyes. The Iroquois, leaderless and confused, gave in to a sudden panic and began to withdraw from the field.

"Now!" Richard yelled. "Let the Conestoga attack!"

Roaring Wolf barely had time to translate before the Conestoga, whooping loudly, let fly at their foes with a hail of arrows, then fell in behind the retreating Iroquois.

It was too dangerous now to continue the gunfire for fear of striking down a friend rather than a foe. "Continue your fire," Richard told Ezekiel, "but aim over their heads."

Ezekiel was quick to grasp the principle at stake, and obeyed the order.

Sha-wa-na followed in the wake of his warriors, who were relishing the unusual experience of driving the Iroquois off through the forest and, consequently, were fighting even more ferociously than they otherwise would have done. The sounds of combat became fainter in the distance.

No quarter was given and none was expected. The Conestoga, showing no mercy to their foes, scalped the living who had been wounded, as well as the braves who had been killed.

Sha-wa-na returned to the command post. "My brothers," he said, "there is a rich harvest of scalps that awaits you."

Roaring Wolf looked at Richard, silently entreating for permission to share in the spoils that his efforts had helped to create. Richard waved him forward. "Go ahead," he said. "You're welcome to any scalps I might claim."

"Mine, too," Ezekiel called after him, and calmly began to clean his musket and pistol.

Sha-wa-na and Roaring Wolf soon returned, with bloody, dripping scalps hanging from their belts. It was plain that both were gratified with the results of the battle.

The Conestoga warriors drifted back, their war chiefs reporting to Sha-wa-na, who finally allowed his wooden features to relax in a smile. "More than ten times ten Iroquois warriors lost their lives this day," he announced proudly. "The sons of the Conestoga and their sons after them will sing songs in praise of this great day in the history of our nation." He raised his voice and summoned his warriors, who clustered around Richard and Ezekiel.

"Let all who fought in this battle mark the faces of the Pequot and the white brothers whose firesticks broke the power of the Iroquois," he said in a loud voice. "Let their likenesses be engraved in your hearts, my children, as you would chisel them in stone or wood. They are our brothers for all time and will always be welcome wherever the Conestoga live and hunt. We are a proud people who do not wish to be in debt to anyone. So our medicine men will offer prayers to the Great Spirit that the day will come when we will be able to repay the debt we owe to the white brothers and the Pequot whose help made it possible for us to defeat the mighty Iroquois in battle!"

Hester Browne sat in an armchair, a blanket keeping her warm, a mug of steaming tea on the table beside her. She seemed lost in thought as she stared out at the fields where Dempster Chaney's industry had spread a mantle of green crops. She seemed preoccupied, so Robbin did not disturb her, and instead was content to remain nearby in case she was needed.

"Ah, he's through with work at last," Hester muttered to herself.

Dempster came cheerfully into the house. "The bean crop looks even better than I thought," he announced. "We'll have at least one hundred bushels more than I expected to send off to the Boston markets."

Robbin knew how important the size of the produce yield had become to him. "Wonderful!" she said.

Hester did not react, and it was plain she hadn't heard him.

Dempster looked at her in concern. "You're not suffering a setback after all the fine progress you've been making, Aunt Hester?"

She jerked her mind back to the present. "Indeed I'm not. I'm stronger every day, and by the end of the week, I hope to make those new scarecrows you want for the west forty." She smiled, then sobered. "I want a word with you, young man. With you too, Robbin."

"Let me wash up, and I'll be right back," Dempster said as he went off to the kitchen.

Hester nodded vaguely, then once again peered out at the gathering dusk that enveloped the Massachusetts Bay farm. Her behavior was strange, and Robbin felt a stab of apprehension, even though she told herself there was no cause for concern.

Dempster returned to the parlor, rubbing his hands together. "I see you're cooking venison stew with dumplings and brown gravy tonight," he said with a grin. "How did you know I had my mouth set on that very dish?"

"Because," Robbin replied with a laugh, "you've mentioned it day and night for almost a week."

"Sit down, both of you," Hester commanded.

Her tone was so abrupt that they sat, and Robbin's laugh died away.

"Young man," the proprietress of the farm said gravely, "I owe my life to you. You showed skill as well as courage when you took the diseased part from my body, and those are qualities I admire. If it wasn't for you, and for all that Robbin did for me too, I wouldn't be sitting here now, as chipper as you please."

Dempster was embarrassed by her praise. "I did what was needed, that's all," he said.

"Nonsense and fiddlesticks! Now, I'm not a wealthy woman, not by any means, but I can't see letting a natural talent like yours go to waste. I've decided to pay your way at the surgeon school in Edinburgh so you can complete your training."

Dempster was stunned. "I'm more grateful than I'll ever be able to tell you for the offer, Aunt Hester," he said. "But how will you get along here without me?"

"I'll be able-bodied again as soon as my strength returns. Robbin is healthy and strong. Between us we'll manage."

Dempster leaned forward in his chair and put his hand over hers. "Your generosity overwhelms me, Aunt Hester, but I wouldn't dream of accepting. Not only do I refuse to beggar you, but surgeon school belongs to my past, not my present or my future. I doubt that the Roundheads would even permit me to register."

"We'll see about that," she snapped. "There are some Puritan clergymen in Boston who call themselves friends, so we'll see how much influence they can muster on your behalf."

"This may be difficult for you to understand," the young man replied, "but even if my entrance at Edinburgh were guaranteed, I wouldn't accept. Once, I had a dream of becoming a surgeon, but the Roundheads shattered the dream. They did me a favor because I've rediscovered the soil, which is my true love."

"You aren't just saying it because you're reluctant to accept my money?" the woman demanded suspiciously.

"I'll prove it to you." He turned to his wife. "I did what we discussed last night."

"I'm glad for you," Robbin replied softly. "I knew it was right when you mentioned it."

Hester Browne was perplexed. "I dislike mysteries, and I can't abide talk I don't rightly understand."

"Aunt Hester, I've found myself," Dempster told her. "I've planted my own roots in the soil of New England, they're spreading. This is my homeland now. I've put England behind me for all time, and that includes surgeon school. The militia has been campaigning for recruits, so I went into the village today and signed up."

"Did you now?" Hester was startled. "Fancy that!"

"I proved to the recruiting sergeant that I can handle firearms and a sword," he continued, "and my education being what it is, the sergeant seemed to think I'll be awarded a commission, at the very least as an ensign. He said the decision would be made by the Massachusetts Bay high command, but I'll be notified in due time. By early summer, at the latest."

Robbin jumped from her chair and kissed him. "I'm proud of you," she said.

"Well, the way I see it, what with the Indians of the neighborhood getting restless, I'd be less than a man if I didn't live up to my obligations to you two."

"What obligations do you have to me?" Hester demanded, sounding angry.

"I live under your roof and I eat your food," he replied. "It seems to me the least I can do in return is to protect you from Indian attacks!"

Hester blew her nose loudly in a handkerchief she took from her sleeve, and then, still flustered, she sipped her tea. "If there's anything I can't abide it's cold tea!"

Robbin immediately rose again. "The pot is on the stove," she said. "I'll bring you a fresh cup."

"You'll do no such thing, young woman! Land o' Goshen! You'd think I was an invalid the way you pop up like a jack-in-the-box! You'll stay seated until I tell you that you're excused!"

Robbin sank slowly back into her chair, thinking that the older woman's convalescence was making her crochety.

"I knew, deep down," Hester said, "that you wouldn't accept my offer to send you to Edinburgh, young man. You're too proud for your own good, and you forget that we're taught pride cometh before a fall. Well, I have another scheme in mind, and this time I intend to have my way. Is that understood?"

"Yes, ma'am," Dempster replied meekly, knowing how to mollify her.

She settled back in her chair. "With my Eddie gone, I'm

alone in the world," she said. "The Almighty didn't see fit for me to bring children into being, and I have no other relatives. Then the Lord sent me you two, out of the blue."

Robbin started to speak.

"Don't interrupt, young woman!" Hester glowered at her. Never had Robbin seen her in such a foul mood.

"Mind you, what I tell you now is what will be. There will be no arguments, no discussions. Tomorrow morning, first thing, you'll ride over to Solicitor Burnham's and ask him to call on me, Robbin. Tell him I'll appreciate the courtesy, seeing as how I've been ailing and haven't the strength to call on him. I want him to prepare two documents for me. One is a new Last Will and Testament, in which I leave all my earthly goods to you two. The other is a property agreement that makes us equal partners. From now on we'll share equally the profits of this farm." She glared at them. "Do I make myself clear?"

"Very clear, Aunt Hester," Robbin said, and tears came to her eyes.

"We'll have none of that. You should know by now that I can't tolerate sniveling!" Robbin couldn't help laughing through her tears.

Hester turned to Dempster, her manner still ferocious. "I haven't heard you say a word, young man!"

"For one thing, you've given me no chance to get a word in edgewise, Aunt Hester. And for another, I'm so surprised that I've run out of breath."

"A body has a right to deal with what's hers any way she sees fit, so I'll stand for none of your arguments to the contrary, Dempster Chaney. Not only did you save my life by performing surgery on me, as cool as you please, but you work your fingers to the bone around here. Not even my

Eddie, may the Lord have mercy on his soul, worked as hard as you do. That's why we'll share, and share alike from now on!"

"Aunt Hester," he replied huskily, "you're an old fraud. You remind me of a poodle I had when I was a boy. He was old and toothless, but he raised such a storm, barking and growling whenever a stranger came to the door, that people thought he was a mastiff or a sheep dog, at the very least."

Hester Browne opened her mouth to protest further, thought better of it, and merely muttered, *"Hmph!"*

"You've made it clear that we have no choice, that you've made a final decision in matters that concern all three of us. Very well, I won't embarrass you by telling you how grateful we are. That will spare us another scolding." Dempster grinned as he stood and went to her. "But you forget that love and affection flow two ways at the same time. You've adopted us. Fair enough. Robbin and I are now adopting you, too." He went to her and hugged her gently.

Robbin followed him, kissing the woman's leathery cheeks. "If we don't stop all this chatter and eat supper soon," she said, "my dumplings will be as hard as the rocks I've been digging out of my kitchen garden."

That night Aunt Hester's appetite improved sharply and she devoured every scrap of food on her plate.

Mary Clayton elected to wait until a Sunday noon, after church services, to break Eliza Burrows's news to her husband and the young woman's father. She invited Adam and Eliza to dinner, telling the daughter in advance to arrive at least a half-hour late.

Colonel Burrows lost no time apologizing for his daughter's tardiness. Accepting a hot buttered rum from Tom

Clayton, he said, "Eliza doesn't understand the value of promptness, no matter how much I lecture her. She was still primping when I stopped at home for her just now. Seeing she didn't even have the decency to come to church with me, you'd think she could have been ready on time."

"Eliza is late," Mary replied immediately, "because I requested it. You two gentlemen are the victims of a female conspiracy." Adam and Tom looked at each other, then at the smiling Mary.

"Have a swallow—a large swallow—of your drinks and brace yourselves."

"What in thunderation has gotten into you?" her husband demanded irritably.

"One step at a time, if you please." She deliberately seated herself on a cushioned stool and faced the two men who stood together at the hearth, facing her suspiciously.

"Why should you have asked Eliza to be late?" Colonel Burrows wanted to know.

"I wanted an opportunity to talk freely and frankly with both of you," Mary replied, her smile fading. "You've nurtured a dream for many years, and it's painful when a dream bubble bursts. You forced Eliza and Ezekiel to become betrothed. Between the two of you, you gave them no choice. As a dutiful wife and a loyal friend I tried to accept your plans, even though I knew in my heart they would never materialize. Having grown up together, they regard their relationship as that of a brother and sister. There's no spark of romance that flows between them."

"There will be plenty of time for romance after they're married," Tom Clayton growled.

"Agreed," Adam Burrows said emphatically. "They're young, and they don't know what they want."

"They know they don't want each other, as they've tried to tell you many times," Mary said forcefully. "Ezekiel may not know what he wants, but he's relieved—beyond measure—that Eliza has lost her heart to someone else."

Colonel Burrows looked as if he had been slapped across the face. "How could that be?" he asked in bewilderment.

"All I find surprising is that it didn't happen a long time ago—to both of them. I swear, Adam, some men are blind. There was a lovely romance budding, right under your nose, and you refused to recognize it."

"Who is the man?"

"Sir Richard Dunstable. I gather he's very much interested in Eliza too, but refrained from expressing his feelings because she was betrothed to Ezekiel."

The colonel drained his drink. Tom Clayton refilled both glasses.

"It could be worse, I suppose," Adam said at last. "Young Dunstable could be useful to us in the business."

"Yes, it would be easy to find a spot for him," Tom agreed.

Mary lost her temper. "Business! Is that your only reaction? Two young people tried hard to please—and submit to the will of—their fathers at the cost of their personal happiness until the strain became too great. I'm proud of Eliza, and I'm proud of my son! And to the devil with what all this does to your precious business plans!"

Eliza had the misfortune to arrive at that moment. She glanced uncertainly at her father, then looked at Mary.

"They know now," Mary told her.

"I'm sorry, Papa," the young woman said. "I tried to tell you, but you wouldn't listen to me. Uncle Tom, I hope you understand, as Aunt Mary does, that my feelings are no reflection on Ezekiel. He's a wonderful person, my best friend, and I wish him all the happiness I want for myself."

The elder Clayton made a gallant attempt to smile. "I've thought of you as a member of the family for so long that it won't be easy to get out of the habit."

"Don't try," Eliza said, and impulsively hugged him.

Adam was still in a whirl. "Why Dunstable?" he demanded.

"I suppose I could tell you a hundred reasons, Papa," Eliza said earnestly. "But it should be enough that I didn't fall in love with him on purpose. It just happened."

"He's established no roots in the New World," her father replied. "That isn't necessarily a handicap, of course. And he is a baronet, so you'd become Lady Dunstable if and when you marry him."

"As if that mattered," Eliza said scornfully. "I know it means nothing to Richard. He prefers not to use his title."

"Life in the colonies is already influencing him," Mary said. "That's all to the good."

Adam walked slowly to a chair and sank into it. "I'll need time to digest all this," he said, shaking his head.

Eliza went to him. "I didn't flout your will deliberately, Papa, and the last thing I wanted was to hurt you. But there are some things that can't be controlled. I know you meant well and were thinking of my welfare."

He looked up at her, his eyes revealing his inner turmoil. "I've got to admire your spirit, Eliza," he said. "I brought you up to be independent, so I suppose I should have expected something like this." He hauled himself to his feet, then embraced his daughter. "Does Ezekiel know how you feel?"

"Of course!"

"And Dunstable?"

"I didn't keep my feelings secret," she replied defiantly.

"Does he reciprocate?"

"I—I have reason to believe he does."

"Well," Adam said, "he hasn't seen fit to ask me for your hand. So, until he does, you can only surmise he feels as you do. Don't count on a marriage to him, Eliza. You can't know him all that well after so brief an acquaintance, so you have no way to judge the permanence of his feelings for you."

The young woman shook her head vigorously, causing her long, blonde hair to dance. "I know he loves me as much as I love him."

"Your father is right, dear," Mary said, "and he doesn't want you to be hurt. Richard may have commitments or relationships you know nothing about, and until you're formally engaged to him, he has every right to change his mind."

The incident began innocently enough. A delegation of three Puritan commissioners arrived in New Amsterdam from Boston at the request of Director-General Stuyvesant to discuss the New Englanders' charges that the Dutch endeavored to stir up an Indian revolt against them. The meetings were not scheduled to start until the following day, so the trio went to the Thorn and Thistle for supper. There Bart Williams saw them and could not resist the temptation to amuse himself at their expense.

His own workday at an end, Bart hastily summoned several like-minded youths, and they waited for the trio. When the commissioners emerged from the inn after supper, they were subjected to a barrage of eggs, fruit, and rotten fish. Several small children joined in the fun, chanting, "Dirty Roundheads," while a number of sympathetic citizens came to the aid of the besieged Puritans.

A full-scale riot ensued, and only the arrival of the local constabulary on the scene prevented serious injuries and property damage. A dozen men were arrested, Bart among them, and all were charged with inciting a riot. All twelve were held pending trial the following day.

Director-General Stuyvesant had committed himself to reform and had forbade sabbath-breaking, brawling, and drunkenness in the disorderly town of New Amsterdam. The senseless, unjustified attack infuriated him. He sent to Magistrate Pieter van Dijk, the justice who would hear the case, a personal note in which he declared that the honor of New Netherland was at stake.

The courthouse, located only a stone's throw from the scene of the crime, was crowded to capacity the next morning, and among those in attendance was Mollie Williams, who was badly upset. Angus MacNeill, who had accompanied Mollie, tried to soothe her.

"The defender appointed by the court for Bart and the other lads is competent," he said. "You can be certain he'll do his best."

Everyone stood when Magistrate van Dijk came into the courtroom and took his place on the bench. The shackles worn by the defendants were removed in an antechamber, and the entire group looked sheepish as they filed into the chamber under the watchful gaze of constables armed with six-foot staffs of heavy wood. Mollie noted at once that the new shirt she had only recently made for Bart was torn.

The facts of the case were soon established. The visitors

from Boston told their story, saying they had been subjected to an unprovoked attack after dining at the Thorn and Thistle. A parade of witnesses described the development of the riot, and an officer of the constabulary told the court how order had been restored.

Bart was identified as the leader of the band of attackers, and when he was called to the witness stand, Magistrate van Dijk himself questioned him.

"Are you acquainted with the plaintiffs?"

"I never saw them in me life until last night, Your Honor."

"Then why did you attack them?"

"Because they're Roundheads." Bart smirked.

"And you consider that a cause for assault?"

"I sure do, Your Honor. We live as we please here, and we don't need these hypocrites telling us to pray. Let them keep their long noses out of our affairs!"

Bart was excused, and the official statement in Bart's defense pointed out that no one had been seriously harmed and no property damaged.

Magistrate van Dijk was not impressed by the argument. "I do not happen to hold the beliefs of those who call themselves Puritans," he said, "but that does not give me the right to ridicule those who do, to subject them to abuse, or to try to harm them. It has been suggested that Boston tries to impose its principles on all who go to that city, but that is Boston's business, and Boston is not New Amsterdam. This city is unique in all the colonies. Living in our midst are people of many nationalities and faiths. All of us are citizens of New Netherland. It is our duty to live together in harmony. Tolerance of the views of others, tolerance of what sets them apart from us is what causes us to be different from the savages who inhabit the neighboring wilderness. If we are tolerant, we shall flourish; if we are not, then we are doomed."

The defendants were called to the bench for sentencing. The court took their youth into account and was prepared to be lenient, but order had to be preserved in the streets of a town that took pride in its new desire for civility. Bart, as the ringleader, was fined thirty guilders, and each of his confederates was fined fifteen guilders. Those who could not pay would work off their fines in gaol at a rate of one guilder per day. Bart, who spent his wages as rapidly as he earned the money, faced twenty-one days of imprisonment.

Mollie blinked back the tears that threatened to erupt. "Master MacNeill," she said, "I've never in my life been in debt to anyone, but I'll be forever obliged to you if you'll advance me the amount of Bart's fine."

"That I will not, Mistress Williams," Angus replied firmly. "I know how your heart must ache for your one and only child, but you'll do him no favor if you buy his freedom for him."

Mollie was too proud to beg; she stood rigidly erect, the color drained from her face.

"You heard what Magistrate van Dijk said about tolerance," Angus went on. "I happen to agree with him, and so do you. What your son thinks—if there's any thought at all that enters his mind—is hard to tell. But give him twenty-one days on bread and water to digest the magistrate's words, and he'll think twice afore he attacks strangers who have committed no crime worse than that of appearing in our streets dressed in black."

Mollie knew in her heart that he was right, but could not admit it. "Think of the disgrace a prison term will cast on Bart."

"Think of how fortunate he is that none of the Puritans was killed or maimed. Then he'd swing on a gibbet, Mistress Williams."

She drew in a sharp breath and, unable to speak, could only nod.

"This could be the making of the lad," Angus said. "I swear I won't hold this against him, and he'll have his post as an ostler at the Thorn and Thistle waiting for him when he's released."

"You're good to him, and I won't forget your kindness. Do you think they'll allow me a word with Bart afore they haul him off to gaol?"

"We'll soon find out." Angus piloted her to the front of the courtroom and identified her to the sergeant of the constabulary. A moment later, Mollie stood facing her son in an anteroom.

Bart grinned at her. "I knowed you'd come for me, Ma," he said. "But there's no need for you to bear the expense. I'll pay you back at a rate of a shilling per week."

"I've not paid your fine, boy," she told him.

He looked at her in astonished dismay. "They'll give me naught to eat and drink for three weeks but bread and water. And I'll work from dusk until nightfall breaking stones to be used in making new roads."

"Then, me lad," she replied, tight-lipped, "mayhap you'll learn to appreciate that eggs, apples, pears, and peaches are grown for folk to eat and aren't intended to be thrown." Her head high, she marched back to the courtroom where Angus awaited her. "I'm in your debt, Master MacNeill, for showing me the error of me ways. The boy was as brazen as you please, expecting me to pay the fine! A diet of bread and water will be the best of medicine for him."

Angus was relieved that she took no offense at his refusal, but a principle had been at stake, so it had been impossible for him to compromise.

They walked in silence back to the Thorn and Thistle, and finally Angus said, "You might like the day to yourself, Mistress Williams."

"And who would cook dinner and supper for them as will come crowding into the taproom?"

"I'll stand in for you myself."

"You'll do no such thing, Master MacNeill, I thank you for being so thoughtful. With naught to do but brood, I'd soon feel sorry for meself, when me only real sorrow is for the day I brought that useless boy into this world."

"Well," Angus said with a smile, "it will do no harm if I lend you a hand."

Mollie returned the smile. "It isn't easy for me to say this to one who pays me wages, but you're a darling man, Master MacNeill."

Angus turned scarlet. Mollie was equally embarrassed, and they compensated for their feelings by working furiously when they returned to the kitchen. Pots and pans clattered, Mollie threw ingredients into a bowl and stirred vigorously, while Angus kneaded a shell of dough in which to wrap a venison roast. Both were on the verge of declaring their feelings, yet both were too shy, so they took refuge in the bustle.

The kitchen door swung open, and Bart swaggered in, his walk as brazen as his expression. "A good day to you both," he said. "Ma, I hope you'll be a-cooking plenty of victuals for dinner. The bread they gave me in gaol was stale. And Master MacNeill, there's no need to hire a replacement for me. I'm on me way to the stables this very minute." He began to strut toward the back door.

Mollie and Angus stared at the youth as if he were an apparition, and then the woman found her voice. "Wait!" she commanded.

Bart halted and turned, his grin insolent.

"The last we knew, you were on your way to prison for three weeks. But here you be, as bold as you please. What happened?"

"It seems there are folk in New Amsterdam who feel the same way I do about Roundheads. The very sight of the hypocritical psalm singers makes them sick."

"What happened?" she demanded, her knuckles whitening on the ladle she held in a tight grasp.

"A fine gentleman showed up and paid me fine so I was set free, that's what!"

Mollie glared at her son suspiciously. "And just who was this fine gentleman, pray tell?"

"Master Laroche, that's who! Friends do favors for each other, he told me, and he paid out me penalty in gold as quick and easy as if it was threepenny bit!"

Trim, healthy, and in high spirits after their journey through the wilderness, Richard, Ezekiel, and Roaring Wolf arrived at Horace Laing's estate outside Norfolk. As they started up the long driveway, lined on both sides by

305

graceful linden trees, Ezekiel stared hard at the portico supported by four ornately carved Corinthian columns, then paused.

"Maybe Roaring Wolf and I had best find ourselves lodging elsewhere," he muttered.

The Pequot felt as he did, and nodded. "Too fancy here," he said.

"Rubbish," Richard replied briskly. "I wouldn't insult Master Laing's hospitality by having you go somewhere else. Just look at the house, and you know he has plenty of room for all three of us. Besides, from what I have heard of him, he'll be delighted to have us here! Come along!"

Not waiting for a reply, he rode up to the front door, dismounted, and knocked. Simms, the stone-faced butler, led the trio into the house and alerted his master of their arrival.

Horace Laing greeted his guests in the library, an impressive room lined with bookshelves that stretched from floor to ceiling. "Sir Richard, you've been expected for some time, ever since you first landed in Boston. Master Clayton, I know of your father by repute, although I've never had the pleasure of doing business with him. And Roaring Wolf, an honorable warrior is always welcome here."

"I will sleep in the yard," Roaring Wolf replied, "and I will get food from your kitchen. The beds of white men are too soft, the tables where they eat are too clumsy."

"Of course," Laing replied urbanely. "I sometimes have Powhatan guests, and they feel just as you do. Sir Richard, I can offer you and Master Clayton adjoining chambers, and I hope you're prepared to stay with me long enough to have made your journey worth your effort. Your horses have been attended?"

"Indeed they have, and I've taken the liberty of warning your chief groom to provide my stallion with a stall of his own."

"You may be certain that we'd treat a stallion in no other way," the still-smiling Laing replied. "Hot water will be brought to your rooms at once, gentlemen. Roaring Wolf, I trust the pond behind the stables will be sufficient for your needs. We'll gather here for a cup of cheer before dinner at noon, gentlemen." He bowed them out, and Simms waited to conduct them to their rooms.

Horace Laing's genial smile vanished as he closed the door of his library behind the guests. He threw himself into a leather armchair behind his desk, then picked up a quill pen, and chewed thoughtfully on the end. Here was an unexpected obstacle to his neatly made plans.

It was true that Sir Richard's visit had been anticipated, and Laing had been looking forward to the arrival of the promising new recruit. Dunstable, like Lady Dawn, was a special prize. The young man was in robust health, an expert shot, a fair enough swordsman, and as the King's Forester who had lost his hereditary position when the Puritans had taken full control of England, he was certain to arouse sympathy in Cavalier circles. Mazarin himself had marked Dunstable's file for Laing's personal attention.

Horace Laing had expected to handle the recruiting of Dunstable in his usual manner, just as he was now doing with Lady Dawn, and as he had done with all who had gone before her. A few drops of the apothecary's special powder in a glass of port, a stay of long or short duration in one of the cells below, and another agent would join the ranks of the English who were working for France. After all, Dunstable had no ties to anyone in the New World, and his disappearance would not create even a ripple of excitement or interest.

The presence of Ezekiel Clayton caused many complications. He was of no use to France and, consequently, would have to be eliminated. But that would prove awkward. His father was a prominent New England merchant and was associated in business with a wide network of influential officials. If he vanished into thin air, an inquiry might be launched, and Laing wanted no colonial militia probing into dark corners. He himself might slip, and there was always the possibility that the members of his staff, no matter how much he trusted them, might blunder. If the militia of the English colonies learned of his plans to bring all of their territory under the French flag, the task would become far more involved, and the chance of success would be lessened drastically. Yes, he would need to find a way to neutralize young Clayton.

As for the Indian, Laing dismissed him from mind. He felt only contempt for savages, whom he regarded as stupid brutes, and a knife neatly inserted between the ribs of the warrior called Roaring Wolf would dispose of him.

Unfortunately, he would need time now to work out a foolproof scheme. Very well, he would make the best of the situation while he played to the hilt his role of jovial host.

When Richard and Ezekiel reappeared in the library at noon, he prepared stiff drinks of brandy for his guests, thinking the strong liquor would affect them quickly and forestall questioning on subjects he would prefer to avoid.

But Richard politely took a single sip of his drink, then

left it untouched. "Tell me how Lady Dawn is faring," he said. "I've been eager to hear about her."

Laing was prepared for the inquiry. "A charming young lady, isn't she? I enjoyed her stay with me, although her lack of interest in political affairs was somewhat surprising."

"She is like so many of us," Richard replied. "She took it for granted that people would remain loyal to the Crown, and she didn't dream that Parliament would try to usurp King Charles's royal prerogatives. Where is she these days?"

"She became interested in the new colony being formed to our south, Carolana," Laing replied glibly. "A number of new settlements are being formed down there by Cavaliers, and she went off to join them."

"Really?" Richard couldn't picture Mimi making her home in a frontier community totally lacking in the comforts of civilization she not only enjoyed, but took for granted.

Laing didn't want him to become too curious about the woman's whereabouts. Realizing by Richard's attitude that he had erred in some way, he tried to compensate. "I had a number of guests while Lady Dawn was visiting here," he said. "Among them was a nobleman whom she had known at Whitehall, and I believe he influenced her decision to join the party that was planning to establish a new settlement."

Richard shook his head. The story didn't quite ring true, but he had no reason to doubt Horace Laing's word.

"I expect to receive word on their progress at any time now, Sir Richard. Perhaps I'll be fortunate enough to get a letter while you're still here." The best way to allay Dunstable's unformed suspicions would be to nip them in the bud. Later in the day, Laing would forge a note from a leader of the Carolana settlers. He would present it to Dunstable in the morning, making certain it contained a reference to Lady Dawn, stressing that she was well and content with her life on the frontier.

Laing realized he was walking a tightrope, that his hitherto foolproof operation was in jeopardy. He would be obliged to proceed with great care.

CHAPTER 10

ROARING WOLF needed few comforts to make himself at home anywhere. The overhanging roof of a little smokehouse in the yard behind Horace Laing's mansion provided him with shelter in case of rain, the kitchen staff had been notified that he was to be provided with food, and his blanket was the only bed he required.

The main house was the largest private dwelling he had ever seen, and the coming and going of a large staff fascinated him. Sitting motionless in the sun, his back propped against the smokehouse wall, a pipe clamped in his teeth, Roaring Wolf amused himself by observing and identifying the hired help. The cook who had given him his noon meal was already familiar to him, and he wondered why both the groom in charge of the stable and the handyman carried knives and pistols in their belts. It seemed odd to him, too, that the butler, whose name was Simms, exerted so much authority over the others. They appeared to fear him, and when he gave an order they jumped to obey.

The ways of whites were strange. First Simms came stealthily to the backyard and, taking a key from a ring, unlocked a heavy door. When he opened it, Roaring Wolf caught a glimpse of stairs that descended into a cellar. The groom and the handyman stationed themselves outside the door.

Then a grim-faced serving maid in a starched uniform that looked uncomfortable came from the kitchen outbuilding carrying a tray of food. She marched past the groom and handyman, disappearing down the cellar stairs.

Roaring Wolf had nothing better to occupy him, so he was content to remain propped against the wall of the smokehouse. After a wait of about a half-hour, as white men counted time, the maidservant reappeared, and the food on the tray was gone. Then Simms carefully closed and locked the door again, and the groom and handyman went off about their business.

Removing the pipe from his mouth and absently tapping the bowl against the palm of his hand to empty it, the Pequot pondered what he had just witnessed. He came to the conclusion that the cellar had an entrance of its own, separate from the main portion of the house, and that a meal had been served to someone who either lived or was hiding there. But why had the door been locked? And why did the groom and the handyman stand guard when it was open?

Unable to answer the questions, Roaring Wolf became restless. Curious about whites and the way they lived, he made up his mind to investigate further, but he knew better than to attempt to force the locked door. He was enjoying the game he had devised for himself, so he waited with the utmost patience until all members of the staff had taken themselves elsewhere.

Then, needing an excuse to approach the building, he drew his tomahawk from his belt and hurled it at a small silver birch that stood at one side of the cellar. The blade imbedded itself in the trunk, and he strolled to retrieve it, never once looking in the direction of the cellar.

Ah! At ground level was a window that had not been washed in many months; the pane of glass was filthy, rendering it opaque. That window was perfect for his purposes, so Roaring Wolf made his way slowly back to the smokehouse wall, propped himself against it, and fell asleep.

He awakened shortly before sundown, stood and stretched, then went off to the kitchen.

"It's you again," the cook muttered, carving a thick slice of ham, then placing it on a board with a slab of corn bread and thrusting the food at the Indian, her eyes angry and resentful.

Roaring Wolf's face remained expressionless as he accepted the food. Taking it to his resting place, he consumed it slowly. When he was finished he licked his fingers, wiped his mouth on the sleeve of his buckskin shirt, and went off to the pond for a drink of water.

By now night had fallen, and the Pequot no longer moved lethargically. The yard was dark, but he took no chances, creeping toward the house. He approached the window and, drawing his knife from his belt, pried it open silently. His guess had been right: it had not been locked from the inside; the dirt caked on it indicated that the butler and the rest of the staff had forgotten its existence. Opening the window gently so he wouldn't dislodge the dirt, Roaring Wolf lowered himself to the ground, slithered through the opening, then silently closed the window again, using his knife blade to ease it shut. Now he found himself in a stone-lined corridor with a stone floor. The odor was musty, indicating a lack of fresh air. Momentarily closing his eyes in order to acclimate himself to the dark, the Pequot saw an open door on one side of the short corridor, and hurried to it. Beyond it stood a cell, furnished only with a cot, and he knew for certain now that this place was a prison of some sort. There was a rusty key in the lock which he removed with some difficulty, guaranteeing that he could not be locked inside the cell should his presence be discovered.

On the opposite side of the corridor stood another door similar to the one that stood ajar. It was closed, and a crack of light made by a burning candle or an oil lamp showed on the floor. Roaring Wolf concluded that the cell was occupied.

All at once the Pequot heard the outer door being unlocked, so he drew back farther into the cell. Then he heard two sets of approaching footsteps. Peering out from his place of concealment, he saw Simms, toting an oil lamp, followed by the serving maid, who carried a tray of cooked food.

By the light of the lamp Roaring Wolf saw a key protruding from the lock of the door opposite him, and he guessed that it could not be removed. The metal used by whites grew rusty in damp weather, and it was uncomfortably damp in this cellar. The door was opened, and the serving maid entered silently.

Roaring Wolf was astonished to see a young woman in a dress of shimmering silk in the cell. Her skin was fair, and he took note of her shoulder-length red hair and her eyes, which were a startling shade of green. Obviously she was a captive, even though she was dressed for a party of some sort.

As the fascinated Pequot, his presence still undetected, continued to watch, the red-haired young woman sat on the cot in her cell and ate her meal, totally ignoring the serving maid. Neither spoke a word. Then the maid withdrew, Simms closed and locked the door, and the maidservant walked ahead of him into the open. The experience was so extraordinary, so eerie that Roaring Wolf almost imagined he had been dreaming. But the hair and eyes of the prisoner had been so vivid that he knew what he had seen had not been a fantasy.

The retreating footsteps halted, the outer door was relocked, and the Pequot heard no sound but his own breathing. He was tempted to unlock the cell door opposite him, but the ways of whites were so contrary to his own that he didn't want to inadvertently offend his host or Richard. He would report what he had seen to Richard, who would interpret the incident for him. First, however, he had to exercise still more patience and wait until he was certain the way was clear.

He listened outside the closed door of the cell, but could hear nothing, although the light continued to show under the door. He waited for a long time, then departed as he had entered the cellar, first assuring himself that Simms, the groom, and the handyman were no longer loitering outside.

Now he faced the problem of how to convey what he had learned to Richard. Laing and his guests were still at supper, so Roaring Wolf walked purposefully to the side door of the house, slipped inside, and then rapidly climbed the inside stairs. There were so many rooms in the house that he became confused, but he looked in them one at a time, until finally he recognized Richard's rifle and saddlebag in a corner of a chamber on the third floor.

Relaxing and grinning, he seated himself cross-legged on the floor, folded his arms, and waited patiently in the dark for his friend to appear. After a long time he heard voices on the stairs, listened intently, and nodded when he recognized Richard's and Ezekiel's voices deep in conversation. Rising to his feet, he moved out into the corridor.

Richard, who was saying something to his companion, broke off abruptly when he saw the silent Indian awaiting him. Roaring Wolf raised a hand in warning. The baffled pair followed him into the bedchamber, and Richard closed the door behind them. Knowing the Pequot was not given to melodrama, he looked at him and waited.

Roaring Wolf quickly described what he had seen in the cellar, explaining how he had made his way there and relating what had aroused his curiosity.

"Describe the prisoner again," Richard said, his mind whirling.

"Young. Very pretty. With very red hair. And eyes the color of young oak leaves in the spring."

Richard drew in his breath as he turned to Ezekiel. "This makes no sense, but Horace Laing appears to be holding Lady Dawn Shepherd captive!"

Ezekiel didn't know what to reply.

"You're sure, Roaring Wolf?" Richard demanded incredulously.

"Very sure," the Pequot replied.

"I'm damned well going to get to the bottom of this!" Richard started toward the door.

Ezekiel remained level-headed. "Wait!" he said, grabbing hold of Richard's arm. "Whatever is responsible for all this, it's a serious business. I heard Laing lie to you today about Lady Dawn going off to Carolana. He has a considerable household staff—not to mention the field hands who may or may not be loyal to him. In any event, we're outnumbered, and we could find ourselves in a nasty situation."

"You're right, of course," Richard said, halting abruptly. "Why Mimi is a prisoner isn't relevant at the moment. We've got to rescue her first, and then we can ask questions."

"Precisely so," Ezekiel Clayton replied. "If you go to Laing with what we've just learned, we lose the element of surprise."

Richard thought rapidly. "Roaring Wolf, can you lead us to the lady?"

The Pequot's broad grin was sufficient reply.

"Are there enough horses in the stables for all of us?"

"Plenty of horses," Roaring Wolf assured him.

"And there are no guards stationed outside the cellar now?"

"Guards come only at mealtime."

"It seems to me there's no time like the present," Richard said. "I see nothing to be gained by waiting until tomorrow night. I propose to rescue Mimi right now, get our horses and whatever additional mounts we may need from the stable—and then make a break for freedom." Richard picked up his rifle, checked it and then his pistol. "All right. We'll sneak out and let Roaring Wolf show us the way. Bring your saddlebag, Ezekiel, because we won't be

317

coming back up here." He hesitated for a moment. "It's a dark night, but I suggest we use no candles or lamps. We'd be asking for problems if we show any lights."

"We don't need lights," Roaring Wolf said.

Ezekiel agreed. "We got along fine in the wilderness without oil lamps."

"So be it, then." Richard loosened his knives in his belt. "Once we set Mimi free, I suggest we head straight for Middle Plantation and swear out a warrant for Laing's arrest."

"Let's rescue the prisoner first," Ezekiel said as he went off for his own saddlebag and weapons.

They met in the corridor and, with Roaring Wolf in the lead, crept down the stairs.

What they did not know—and could not have known—was that Horace Laing was still in his library, writing the letter he intended to produce the following day to prove that Lady Dawn was thriving in Carolana. He heard the soft footsteps on the stairs, then stole after the trio after first alerting Simms and sending him to rouse the other men on the household staff.

The Pequot led his companions into the side yard, then made his way directly to the cellar window. Richard followed Roaring Wolf deep into the dark cellar, with Ezekiel Clayton close behind. Roaring Wolf pointed toward the closed prison door with the light showing beneath it.

At that moment they heard a key turning in the lock and the door creaking open. Several dark shapes loomed at the top of the stairs.

Roaring Wolf braced himself, and Richard drew his

pistol. "Fetch Mimi," he told Ezekiel softly. "We'll hold them off here."

"Who goes there?" Horace Laing called. "Come out with your hands over your heads now!"

Richard replied by firing his pistol twice, first at the taper that Simms held, then at the armed man himself. The landing suddenly became dark, and the butler stumbled and screamed, pitching headlong down the stairs.

Ezekiel Clayton hurried down the dark corridor, guided by the light he saw beneath the door. He tried turning the key in the rusted lock, but in his haste he wedged it more securely. "Stand away from the door!" he commanded, and blew off the lock with his pistol, then raised the latch.

Mimi Shepherd stood facing him in the light of her oil lamp, wide-eyed and bewildered, but even in this moment of crisis showing no fright.

Never had he seen anyone so lovely. "I'm Ezekiel Clayton. I've come with Richard to get you out of here," he said.

Mimi unhesitatingly opened a clothing box and removed her jewel case. "I'm ready," she said.

Ezekiel hastily reloaded his pistol. "Don't take the lamp. It makes too good a target. Stay close behind me."

Asking no questions, she followed his orders, and they crept down the corridor, halting when they saw the activity directly ahead.

As Richard reloaded in the dark, Roaring Wolf detected a movement near the open cellar door. He hurled his tomahawk at the shadow, and a man's howl echoed through the stone vault, indicating that the Pequot's aim had been accurate.

Yet another figure appeared at the top of the steps, and Richard saw the burly groom, armed with a musket. His pistol spoke twice more, and the man slumped to the ground.

"Dunstable," Horace Laing seethed, "you've interfered in matters of state that are none of your concern!"

Richard turned to see the outraged Laing bearing down on him, a sword in one hand. There was no chance to reload his pistol, and knowing his rifle was useless at such close range, he retreated hastily before the onrushing Laing, stumbling over the body of Simms. On the stone floor beside the butler was the sword he had dropped. Richard bent down, snatched it, and straightened just in time to deflect a wicked thrust from Laing's blade.

"No!" Mimi shuddered, and Ezekiel, a pistol in one hand, encircled the woman's shoulders with his free arm, shielding her.

Roaring Wolf fitted an arrow into his bow, but the duelists were dancing back and forth so quickly and erratically in the uncertain half-light that the Pequot was afraid to release it.

The corridor was narrow, the damp stone flooring underfoot was slippery, and the light was bad. Horace Laing was an expert swordsman, and in his rampant fury he was determined to kill the man who had spoiled his carefully conceived plans.

Richard knew when their swords clashed that he had more than met his match. His touch with a blade was less skilled than that of his foe, his reflexes slower. He parried a vicious thrust just in time to save himself, and was pressed backward step by step to the inner end of the corridor.

Then, suddenly, Horace Laing was gone, appearing to have vanished into thin air.

But Roaring Wolf, whose night vision was superior to that of his companions, was not fooled. He saw Laing leap up onto a stone block, preparing to demolish his enemy from the greater height. The Pequot unhesitatingly unloosed his arrow, the twang of his bow echoing faintly down the length of the underground chamber. The arrow penetrated Laing's chest, and he toppled to the stone floor.

"All enemies are dead now," Roaring Wolf declared.

"We don't know how many others may be around," Richard said. "Are you all right, Mimi?"

"I—I think so, Richie," the shaken woman gasped.

"All right. Let's get out of here." Suddenly belying his own words, Richard snatched one of his throwing knives from his belt and hurled it with full force at the prone body of Horace Laing. A pistol that had been pointed at Mimi slipped from Laing's grasp as he died.

The full impact of her captivity was suddenly felt by Mimi, and she found it difficult to breathe. She buried her face in Ezekiel's shoulder, leaning on him for support.

Richard retrieved his knife. "I saw him just in time," he said. "We have no way of knowing how many male retainers may be at large here. Certainly the serving maids have heard the sounds of pistol shots. Roaring Wolf, take the lead. Ezekiel, you shield Mimi and follow close behind me."

They hurried to the stable where Prince Henry greeted his master by whinnying. Losing no time, they saddled the stallion and Ezekiel's gelding, found a mare for Mimi to ride, and another gelding for Roaring Wolf. Within a short time they were on the road that would take them to Middle Plantation.

"My money is gone," Mimi said, on the verge of tears, "and I've had to leave all my clothes behind. All I've managed to salvage are my jewels."

"You're safe now, and that's all that matters," Ezekiel said, trying to comfort her as he rode close beside her.

"What I want to know is why Laing was holding you prisoner, Mimi," Richard said.

She told her story, her voice breaking as she related her helplessness and frustration. Ezekiel's expression indicated that he found her story unbelievable, but Richard accepted every word literally. He clearly recalled how Robertson had conferred at length and in private with the French *enseigne* when the brig bringing him and Mimi to the New World had been halted on the high seas, and that Robertson's journal had been written in French. Obviously a great conspiracy that threatened the future of England and her colonies had been exposed.

"I might have guessed it would be you who would find me, Richie," Mimi said tremulously.

He stared hard at her and petted her hand. "You've held up well during your ordeal," he told her. "I don't know anyone else who would have your courage."

They looked hard at each other and what they did not say was far more significant than the words they spoke. Somehow, for reasons neither of them understood, their mutual attraction had vanished; they were no longer interested in each other as man and woman, although as colleagues bound together in a great adventure with enormous stakes, their ties were still indissoluble.

"Your captivity wasn't in vain," he said. "You've done a

great service for England, and you've accomplished even more for her colonies here. All of us are in Roaring Wolf's debt for being so observant."

The Pequot, clinging to his saddle, was in no mood to accept praise.

"We've left at least four dead men behind us at Laing's estate, and your story will be hard to prove, Mimi," Richard said. He carefully refrained from saying that by making the conspiracy public the French would be alerted to their own activities. He had surmised enough about espionage to know that the advantage lay with the nation that knew what to expect from its foes. "I've changed my mind about going to the local authorities in Middle Plantation. Laing was a personage of consequence in the community here, and we might spend days being questioned about tonight's events. I suggest we leave the area as rapidly as possible." Richard added to himself: *And give me the chance to report these developments to colonial leaders I know I can trust.*

"I won't need much persuasion," Mimi said, "but where I'll go, I can't imagine."

"Let me worry about that," Ezekiel told her. "I'm sure my family will give you a warm welcome."

"We'll go straight to the waterfront and see if we can find a ship that will take us north," Richard said, reflecting that travel through the wilderness would take too long.

Smudges of the early, false dawn streaked the sky as he rode at the head of the little party as they approached the Kecoughtan harbor, where, in spite of the early hour, there was a great deal of activity. Fishermen were heading out into Chesapeake Bay for their day's work, their torches glowing brightly at a half-dozen docks, and Richard felt encouraged when he saw a merchant ship's crew on deck, obviously making ready to put out to sea.

Dismounting hastily, he left his companions waiting for him while he went to confer with the master of the ship. "May I ask your destination, sir?"

"New Amsterdam." The captain looked askance at this man who smelled of burned gunpowder.

"Can you take four passengers—and four horses?" Richard knew he had to make the offer interesting. "You'll be paid a sovereign in gold for your trouble."

A gold sovereign would substantially increase the master's personal profit on this three-day voyage, and he brightened. "I have stalls on board for the animals, so they'll be no problem," he said. "But I have no quarters available for you. I can feed you in the cabin, that'll offer no problem, either. But you'll have to sleep on deck."

Richard unhesitatingly reached into his purse for a gold sovereign.

A short time later, with the horses snugly penned in the hold, he and his companions gathered on the aft deck where they tried to stay out of the busy crew's way. "You'll be roughing it on deck for three days, Mimi, but the sea air should bring some color to your face. How long did you spend in that confounded cell?"

"It felt like forever, but actually it was about two weeks." The girl rubbed her arms and smiled. "The most welcome sound in the world was the shot that Ezekiel fired when he blasted the lock."

"I'll never forget the way you looked," Ezekiel replied with a grin. "As cool as you please, accepting my introduction as if we had just met at a lawn party."

She joined in his enjoyment. Richard noted absently that

they had struck a good rapport, and he was glad. It was odd, he thought, but he could look at Mimi without thinking that they had ever been intimate. His relationship with Eliza had supplanted Mimi in his thoughts; come to think of it, he no longer yearned for Dorothea, either.

Waiting until the ship sailed and the excitement died away, Richard sat down with Mimi and told her to recount every word of the talk she'd had with Horace Laing in her cell. It was important, he said, that she remember every detail.

The woman realized he was in dead earnest and did her best to methodically comply with the request. Ezekiel listened to her narrative with great sympathy, but could not understand why Richard remained stone-faced, memorizing every detail.

The voyage was uneventful, marred only by the seasickness of Roaring Wolf, who was badly frightened to find himself sailing on one of the great white birds that he had viewed previously only from a safe distance. The wilderness held no terrors for him, but the rolling blue-green ocean, with its mountainous waves that caused the frail vessel to pitch and toss, made him miserable.

Richard spent the better part of the voyage analyzing the information that he had gleaned from Mimi. As nearly as he could judge, the French conspiracy obviously was not confined to Laing and the members of his household. The man who called himself Laroche had to be in the pay of Cardinal Mazarin of France, too, as did one or more high-placed Cavaliers who had either followed young Charles II into exile or were living inconspicuously in England. Richard thought of his dear friend the Earl of Newcastle and wondered how he would react to this knowledge.

Preoccupied with the problem and its many implications, Richard was only vaguely conscious of the growing intimacy of Mimi and Ezekiel. They spent literally all of their time together, conversing at great length, and at night when they slept on deck, Ezekiel took care to place himself adjacent to Mimi, ready to protect her with the loaded pistol he kept close at hand.

On the last morning of the voyage, Richard revealed something of his plans to his companions. "We'll go straight to the Thorn and Thistle Inn," he said, "because I have some unfinished business with a gentleman there. Ezekiel, you'll scour the waterfront and arrange a sailing for us tomorrow on a ship that will take us to New Haven without delay. It's urgent that I see Colonel Burrows."

"Will there be time for me to attend to some errands of my own?" Mimi wanted to know. "I'm traveling in the only clothes I have to my name, and I'm sick of them. It's important that I look presentable when I meet Ezekiel's parents, you know."

Richard nodded, but the significance of her statement escaped him.

"I've decided to sell a ruby ring that has no particular sentimental value. That will give me enough money to buy some clothes and cosmetics in New Amsterdam."

"Very well," Richard said. "But Roaring Wolf and Ezekiel will go with you everywhere."

The others looked at him blankly.

"Horace Laing may be dead," he said somberly, "but you have other, far more important enemies, ruthless people who will stop at nothing to gain their ends—one of which is the recruitment of Lady Dawn Shepherd to the cause of France. Ezekiel, I charge you and Roaring Wolf with protecting Mimi. Don't allow her out of your sight for a single minute on shore. Where she goes, you two will go. And when you search the waterfront for a ship to take us to New Haven, Mimi will accompany you."

"It's that serious?" Mimi asked gravely.

"It's more serious than you know," Richard assured her. "Just do what I ask, and you'll be all right."

They landed at noon, their horses were led from the hold, and the party went straight to the Thorn and Thistle. There, Richard engaged two rooms, one for himself, the Pequot, and Ezekiel, the other for Mimi. Then, while they went off on their errands, he turned with a smile to Angus MacNeill, who had been loitering in the vicinity, obviously seeking a word with him.

"How is our Mollie?"

"She has news for you, both good and bad, and it'll be best if she tells you herself. Will you come to the kitchen with me?"

Richard accompanied him to the kitchen, where Mollie, wrapped in an apron, was testing a cake with a long straw. She put down the straw, wiped her hands on her apron, and hurriedly approached, her face wreathed in smiles. "Me prayers have been answered, Master Dunstable," she said. "You're the very man I've been aching to see." She turned to Angus. "What have you told him?"

"Nothing. All I said is that you have news both good and bad."

"The good first, then," she said, and smiled shyly at the balding innkeeper. "Master MacNeill has done me the honor of proposing marriage, and I've accepted him," she said.

Richard kissed her on the cheek and grasped MacNeill's

hand. "My best wishes to both of you! You'll have a wonderful life together, and the Thorn and Thistle will become the best inn on the entire seaboard."

"That it will," Angus MacNeill assured him.

"But there's bad news to temper the good." Mollie lowered her voice so the assistant cook and waiters could not hear her. "Me Bart has disappeared."

Richard was startled.

"Mistress Williams ain't saying it right, sir," MacNeill declared. "The lad didn't vanish into the blue, like you might say. One day he was gone, but he left a note for his ma, he did. He said he was going off to Quebec to make his fortune."

"Why Quebec?" Richard tried to conceal his surprise, but guessed that young Bart had been recruited in the service of France.

"He took us by surprise, he did," Mollie replied with a deep sigh. "Me and Master MacNeill, we didn't know he had as much as a nodding acquaintance with anyone up there. Seeing as how you wasn't around to give us advice, we consulted Master Laroche, and he told us not to worry, that Bart is sure to do fine there."

Laroche again! Richard's eyes narrowed as he said, "I'm intending to have a little chat with Laroche this very evening. I assume he still comes here for a late-evening drink."

"He's as regular as the tide," Angus assured him.

"I'll find out what I can for you," Richard said. "I'm interested in his reasons for thinking Quebec offers opportunities to the lad."

Mollie and Angus insisted that he dine as their guest, then piled his plate high with food, which embarrassed him. He took his time, dawdling over the meal, and it was late afternoon when Mimi and her escorts returned, all three laden with packages containing clothes she had purchased.

The woman was in high spirits, the first time since her ordeal that she seemed like herself. "Now I can feel presentable when I meet Ezekiel's parents!" she said enthusiastically.

Richard wondered why the meeting was so important to her, but Ezekiel's news obliterated everything else from his mind.

"We're in luck, Richard! One of Uncle Adam's coastal brigs is in port and will have her cargo loaded in time to sail on the morning tide tomorrow. We're welcome on board, and although we'll be a mite cramped for space, we'll reach New Haven in far less time than we'd need on an overland march through the forest."

Only Roaring Wolf was gloomy over the prospect of another sea voyage.

Mimi deposited her packages, then went off to the kitchen for a joyful reunion with Mollie.

"You didn't tell me what a remarkable person Mimi is," Ezekiel said to Richard.

A light slowly dawned. "Are you smitten?"

"From the moment I saw her, and she feels the same way! What I find astonishing is that she puts on no airs, and she doesn't give a hang about her rank."

"As you say, she's remarkable," Richard replied, feeling infinite relief. With Ezekiel in love with the daughter of the late Earl of Sturbridge, whom his parents were certain to welcome warmly, he would have no obstacle in his wooing of Eliza Burrows. But he could not allow himself to dwell at length on the mercurial Eliza. The future of the colonies was at stake and required his complete concentration.

That evening the party dined at leisure, and Richard gave specific instructions to Mimi and Ezekiel. "Ask no questions, but do as I say," he told them. "Wait about five minutes, no more, and then follow me into the taproom. You'll find me at a table with a dark-haired man who looks as if his supper disagreed with him. Take a table at the far end of the room and make sure you sit where he can see you. Most important, pay no attention to me or to him."

"There is obviously some reason for all this," Mimi said.

He nodded. "You were Horace Laing's prisoner for two weeks, and that's reason enough. When you want to be rid of vermin, you smoke them out." Richard refused to say anything more. Stifling their curiosity, they agreed to do his bidding.

Angus MacNeill came to the table, and as he had been asked, he told Richard that Laroche had arrived and was seated at his usual corner table.

Richard rose abruptly, then made his way into the taproom by a roundabout route, so Laroche would not see him as he approached. He halted at the man's table, then said quietly, "Good evening, Master Laroche. May I join you?"

The agent's training stood him in good stead, but he nevertheless gaped at Richard for a moment, his face registering astonishment before a mask again covered his face. "By all means," he said.

The shock he displayed so plainly, if briefly, convinced Richard that the same fate Mimi had suffered had been in store for him, too. He believed that Laroche was working for France, and soon he would be able to put that theory to the test.

"You stayed only a short time in Virginia, I take it," Laroche said.

"Circumstances made it unnecessary for me to prolong my visit there." Richard did not elaborate.

"You saw Horace Laing?"

"A charming man. He takes his duties as a host seriously." That, Richard reflected, was an understatement. From the corner of his eye, he watched Mimi and Ezekiel make their way to a table directly in Laroche's line of vision. "By the way, I encountered an old friend at Laing's plantation. You aren't acquainted with Lady Dawn Shepherd, I believe you said."

The man nodded.

"There she is, in the blue gown—the woman with red hair. Once you've seen her, you aren't likely to forget her. Don't you agree?"

Laroche's jaw dropped as he stared at Mimi. Recovering his aplomb quickly, he managed to murmur, "She's very lovely." Obviously something had gone amiss with Laing's recruiting operation, but he could ask no questions of the sharp-eyed young baronet who was studying him so intently.

The last doubts vanished from Richard's mind. Laroche had been a party to Laing's recruiting scheme, which meant that the supposed chief of New World operations for the Cavaliers was actually in the employ of France. Richard found it difficult to hold his anger in check, while Laroche seemed to be calculating his next move.

"I'm pleased you've returned at this particular time," Laroche said briskly. "Our friends in England want a personal report, and so do our principals in France. If you're willing, I'd like you to sail in about ten days, when a safe ship will go off to England."

"I'm not sure I can afford the luxury of making another journey this soon," Richard temporized.

"Your fare and other expenses will be paid," Laroche replied quickly. "The voyage will cost you nothing but your time."

"In that case, I might be able to arrange it." Richard wondered if he would be entering another trap.

"Are you acquainted with Lord Blankenship?"

"Slightly." Richard had gone to London every year to receive his pay as King's Forester from Blankenship, who had served as assistant secretary of dispensing of funds at the court of Charles I.

"Good. You'll find him awaiting you in England at the Royal Arms Inn, at Dover. Return here nine days from today, and your passage will be waiting for you. Master MacNeill will be given a packet for you."

"A round-trip passage, I trust?" Richard asked quietly.

"Naturally," Laroche replied quickly, almost too quickly. "You've become familiar with the colonies during your stay in the New World, so you're more valuable to the king's party here than you were previously."

Richard knew it could prove dangerous to make an immediate decision. "If I can't settle my own affairs in time to make the voyage, I'll be in touch with you."

"I hope you'll see fit to go. You're better able to give a comprehensive report than anyone else."

Richard nodded, rose to his feet, then said casually, "Mollie Williams tells me you approved of her son's going off to Quebec to seek his fortune there."

"Indeed I did," the man replied smoothly. "The future of the English colonies depends on Anglo-French trade, and any man who knows Quebec will be valuable to the exporters."

"I see." What Richard saw was that Laroche would be difficult to back into a corner. The man was as clever as he was lethal.

The little coastal ship ran her owner's pennant to the yardarm as she entered the New Haven harbor, and the unusual gesture brought both Tom Clayton and Colonel Adam Burrows to the dock. The partners tried in vain to conceal their surprise as Ezekiel came ashore escorting a red-haired beauty, both of them beaming. "Lady Dawn Shepherd," he said, "allow me to present my father and his partner, Colonel Burrows."

Mimi's smile was devastating. "I'd have known you anywhere, Master Clayton," she said. "Ezekiel looks so very much like you."

Richard, watching from the deck, where he was supervising the debarkation of the horses, knew from the elder Clayton's broad smile that Mimi had made another conquest.

Following the couple ashore, with Roaring Wolf at his heels, Richard immediately sought Colonel Burrows. "I need to confer with you in private at once, sir."

Adam Burrows nodded as he led the way to his sparsely furnished office. He assumed that Richard intended to ask him for permission to court Eliza, and he had to admit to himself that the young Englishman was wasting no time.

"Colonel," Richard said as soon as they were seated, "when I came to the New World I accepted an assignment from the Earl of Newcastle as a Cavalier agent, and in that capacity I fear I have discovered a conspiracy that threatens the very foundations of the English colonies."

Adam's smile faded.

Richard launched into a detailed recital, beginning with the vessel that had brought him to the New World having been halted on the high seas, followed by the attack launched on him by the man who had called himself Robertson. He described Laroche, then gave a crisp account of Mimi's harrowing experience under Horace Laing's roof. The colonel hitched forward in his chair as he listened to the story of the woman's rescue.

"Finally," Richard said, "I saw Laroche again in New Amsterdam the night before last." He gave a full account of their talk.

The commander of the New Haven artillery company leaned back in his chair as he assimilated the information. "Obviously you believe that this Laroche is secretly in the employ of the French, and obviously you have ample evidence for that belief."

"I couldn't prove it in a law court, but I'm convinced of it, sir!"

"Well, it sounds likely. We've had indications of late that the French in Quebec are stirring up the Indian tribes on our entire frontier. They're being bribed with blankets, whiskey, iron cooking utensils, and trinkets, that much we know. But not firearms. The French are too clever to arm allies as unreliable as tribes that will favor anyone who gives them gifts. Putting all of the facts together convinces me that our frontier settlements are going to be inundated with Indian raids this summer."

"What will you do about it, Colonel?"

"Pass the word to our sister colonies, of course," Adam replied firmly. "I was reluctant to alarm them, especially when men are needed to bring in the crops. But there's no longer any choice. Massachussetts Bay, Rhode Island, and Connecticut will be wise to follow the example I intend to set. I'm calling the council of war regiment to duty. It's too bad your stay in Virginia was cut short, but I'll notify the authorities there too, so they can be prepared for a summer of hard fighting."

"I see." Richard was silent for a moment. "Now, sir, I'd like your advice in a personal matter. I don't know if Laroche suspects I know too much and is setting a trap for me by suggesting that I go to England and possibly to France."

The colonel pressed his fingertips together. "It seems to me you have no choice. In England and in France, too, there are men posing as representatives of the Cavalier party who are actually in the pay of France. Give them free reign and Mazarin will achieve his ends. England would become a helpless French possession, and the *fleur-de-lis* banner soon would fly over the capitals of every English colony in North America. You're in a unique position to prevent those catastrophes. You can uncover the identity of the traitors. I can't force you to expose yourself to danger. No one can. But I urge you to take the risks."

"You confirm my own decision," Richard replied quietly. "I'd made up my own mind to go."

All at once, Adam grinned at him. "There are ways to reduce the risks to a minimum, but we'll speak of that later. If I don't take you home with me now, Eliza will be furious with both of us. You've never faced her when she loses her temper, or you'd know the rage I'd prefer to avoid."

All at once Richard's self-confidence vanished. "Do I gather correctly that Eliza has spoken to you about me, sir?"

"At length," the colonel replied drily.

"I hope you don't mind, Colonel."

"I'm a realist, or try to be. And what with Ezekiel so obviously in love, it does simplify matters."

"Then I have your permission to pay court to Eliza?"

Adam Burrows grinned broadly. "Neither of us has an alternative," he said. "Eliza has set her cap for you, and what she wants she usually succeeds in getting!"

Prince Henry was so lively after being cooped up on board ship again that he had to be restrained on the short ride to the Burrows house.

Eliza looked indignant as she came to the door. "The very idea!" she exclaimed. "The least you could have done, Papa, was to let me know that Richard was expected. My hair is a mess, I've been wearing this old gardening dress all day, and I don't even have on a smidgen of lip rouge."

"Richard, maybe you can handle her better than I," the colonel said, and hastily went off into the house.

Roaring Wolf was eager to escape from the irate young woman, and took the horses off to the stable.

"You look fine to me," Richard said mildly. "Exactly as I've pictured you in my mind."

"Is that a compliment or an insult?"

"I intended my observation as a compliment."

"In that case," she replied, her mood changing swiftly, "I forgive you." She threw herself into his arms.

They embraced and kissed sincerely, and both were shaken by the depth of their emotions now that their separation had come to an end. "Your father has granted permis-

sion for me to court you," he said, "and your worries over
Ezekiel are at an end." He told her what he deemed
appropriate for her to know about Mimi, making no mention of his own affair with her.

"Then there are no obstacles in our path," Eliza said.

"No obstacles, but there are complications," he replied.
"My stay here is limited."

"But you've just come back!" she cried. "What must I do
to persuade you to stay?"

"There's nothing you or anyone else can do," Richard
told her.

"You may find this hard to believe, Eliza," Colonel
Burrows said as he came into the parlor, "but there are
matters in this world more important than what you do or
don't want."

"Do you know about his new travel plans, Papa?"

The colonel nodded, but had no intention of taking her
into his confidence. Eliza turned to Richard for an explanation, but he took his clue from her father and offered no
elaboration, either.

She looked at one, then at the other. "I suppose," she
said, her tone scathing, "that your secret is connected with
the precious security of New Haven."

"Something of the sort," her father admitted.

"Well, I'll tell you one thing, and don't forget it, either
of you! I've worried myself sick over Richard for the last
time. You're not going anywhere without me again,
Richard Dunstable!" She swept out of the room, partly to
indicate a conclusion to the discussion, but also to make
herself more presentable.

Later, attired in a silk gown of deep red, with her hair
piled high on her head, she enjoyed a far better mood, and

was delighted when a servant brought a supper invitation from Mary Clayton. "Good," she said. "I'm anxious to meet the woman who has captivated Ezekiel."

"His taste is impeccable," Richard said. "I'm sure you and she will become fast friends."

Eliza was on her best behavior when she accompanied Richard and her father to the Clayton house. She was quick to appreciate Mimi's patrician beauty and seemed pleased by Ezekiel's choice.

The elder Claytons made it plain they were delighted with Mimi, and Ezekiel had an announcement to make before supper. "I've been waiting for Mimi all of my life," he said, "and now that I've found her, I intend to lose no time. The banns will be posted tomorrow, and after three days we'll be married."

Richard gallantly offered a toast to the bride and groom. The newlyweds, it developed, would take up residence in the new house that had been built for Eliza and Ezekiel.

"That is, if Eliza doesn't object," Mimi interjected quickly. "Ezekiel has told me all about his relationship with you, and I'm well aware that you have a vested interest in the house, which I haven't even seen as yet."

"You're welcome to it, Mimi," Eliza said. "I hope you'll be as happy there as I would have been miserable. Anyway," she added, glancing at Richard, "my own plans aren't really settled yet. It appears that I'm going to be doing some traveling before I settle down." Richard laughed, as did Colonel Burrows, and Eliza took care not to mention that she wasn't joking.

Before the party went in to supper, Mimi contrived to have a moment alone with Richard. "Thank you for your discretion," she told him.

"You can rely on me."

"I know," she said, and squeezed his hand before turning back to her betrothed and smiling radiantly at him.

Never before, Richard reflected as he sat at the supper table, had he been so aware of the power of seeming adversity to change people in a positive way. Mimi, the complete aristocrat, had begun such a transformation from the moment she fled England, and it was apparent that she would be content to spend her days in a middle-class New Haven home as the wife of a young merchant. She seemed so sure of her destiny, and so did Ezekiel, neither of them questioning whether she could be happy in a life so unlike that for which her whole previous experience had prepared her.

Mimi seemed to read Richard's mind. "In all the days and nights I was cooped up in that cell of Horace Laing's," she said slowly, looking around the supper table, "I had nothing to read, nothing to do except review my life. I realized that most of my values were artificial, most of my precepts false. I did what was expected of me at court, and I really think the Puritans did me a favor to strip me of my inheritance. I knew then that all I wanted was a relationship in which I could place my trust. And in came Ezekiel, spoiling for a fight, his pistol still smoking after he shot out the lock!"

"I've always believed the poets exaggerated when they wrote about love at first sight," Ezekiel added, looking affectionately at his betrothed, "but the moment I first saw Mimi I realized how wrong I had always been."

"I'll take some of the credit," Eliza said. "I told you for years that you'd know the real from the superficial."

They lingered for a long time at the supper table, and

when Colonel Burrows adjourned to the study with his host for a private discussion, he suggested that Richard escort Eliza home. "I want to tell Tom about our talk earlier in the day, Richard," he said.

Richard held Eliza's cape of light silk for her, and after saying good-night to everyone present, they started back to the Burrows house, walking hand in hand down the street lined with lindens. "You didn't tell me you and Mimi had slept together," she said calmly.

He stared at her. "Whatever prompted you to say that?"

"Really," she said with a light laugh. "I knew it the instant you greeted each other. It was obvious."

"Only to you," Richard replied. "You'll do Ezekiel a disservice if you mention it to anyone else."

"Believe it or not, I know when to keep my mouth shut. When are you going to confide in me—or must I continue to ferret out your secrets?"

"We'll see what your father has to say."

"Then I'll never know. And now that I'm free, when do you intend to propose to me? We were reunited ten hours ago, and I had no idea you could be so backward."

"The question has been very much on my mind," he admitted. "But it would be unfair to propose now. I have a delicate, dangerous, and complex mission still to perform, and I won't become my own master until it's done."

"You're as bad as Papa with your military secrets. Very well, sir, I don't require a proposal, though I'd have enjoyed one. I shall simply take it for granted that we're going to be married. When shall it be?"

"Wait until I return. We'll discuss it then."

"Oh, how I envy Ezekiel and Mimi. Just think, in three

340

days they'll be husband and wife. Aren't you jealous of them?"

He shook his head, unable to explain to her that he would be risking his life on his journey to the Old World, and consequently could not tie her down to an advance commitment.

"You force me to behave rashly, sir. I want you to remember that." Eliza looked up at him, her blue eyes shining in the pale moonlight.

"You're a hussy," Richard told her. "You know how much I want you."

Eliza's quiet smile told him the issue was far from settled.

The church that faced the New Haven Green was crowded with guests attending the wedding of Lady Dawn Shepherd and Ezekiel Clayton. The citizens of the town took advantage of this rare opportunity to wear their finery. Most men would be reporting for duty with their battalions and separate companies later in the day, but Colonel Burrows had demonstrated his compassion by signing an order that permitted Ezekiel to report for duty one week late. Eliza Burrows attended the bride, at the latter's request, and this simple act stifled the gossip of the many who had assumed that Eliza harbored ill will for the woman who married Ezekiel. Richard Dunstable stood up with the bridegroom and looked so distinguished that the mothers of eligible daughters stared at him. But they changed their minds when they saw the proprietary look in Eliza's determined eyes when she and Richard followed the bride and groom down the aisle at the end of the ceremony. Roaring

Wolf observed the ceremony and festivities with his continued interest in the ways of the white man.

A lavish reception was held in the garden behind the Clayton home, and roasted meats, fritters, vegetables, and a variety of fresh shellfish were served. There was a potent rum punch, and a milder version for those so inclined. Innumerable toasts were offered to the health and longevity of the bride and groom.

The only reminder of Mimi's past were her earrings of diamonds and sapphires, which she wore with a matching necklace. Regal in a gown of ivory satin and lace, she looked every inch the daughter of an earl.

"I wish you a life of great joy," Richard told her as he kissed her lightly after the ceremony. "Ezekiel, my congratulations. You're the most fortunate man in the world."

"I'm forever grateful to you for suggesting I travel through the colonies with you—and for ordering me to fetch Mimi when we were attacked in Laing's cellar," Ezekiel replied. "You changed my life."

Eliza delighted in presenting Richard to more people than he could remember. Her hand firmly grasping his arm, she made the rounds of the garden beside him, and he was pleased that she introduced him as Master Dunstable rather than Sir Richard. She knew he preferred not to use his title, and that was good enough for her.

At last, after everyone had eaten and Richard, in his capacity as the groom's attendant, had offered a formal toast to Mimi and Ezekiel, the bridal couple departed for their own new home. Now the atmosphere became more relaxed, and as Eliza chatted vivaciously with her friends, Richard couldn't help thinking that the lives of the young colonials depended on what he could learn about the French conspiracy. It did not matter whether they were men or women, young or old, Cavaliers or Puritans. They were an integral part of the new breed of which Eliza was so proud: they were committed to new lives in a new land, and their future rested in his hands.

Colonel Burrows threaded his way through the crowd, approached his daughter, and asked, "Do you suppose I could borrow Richard for a time?"

The girl's grasp on Richard's arm tightened. "Not today, Papa! I forbid it!"

"You may forbid all you please, but it's necessary all the same. I'm leaving at dawn tomorrow to muster the council of war up and down the length of New Haven Colony, and it's urgent that I speak to Richard in private. Now."

The disgruntled Eliza reluctantly released her hold on Richard's arm, and he followed the colonel into the house. They went to Tom Clayton's study, and Adam closed the door behind them.

"I took my partner into my confidence," he said, "and we believe we've worked out a scheme that will offer you maximum protection while taking as few risks as possible. First, I suggest you write tomorrow to Laroche and give your letter to Tom, who'll send it straight to New Amsterdam by intercolonial rig. Tell Laroche you'll arrive at the Royal Arms in Dover in approximately a month, and that you're providing your own transportation. Supply him with no details. The less he knows, the safer you'll be."

"How will I provide my own transport, Colonel?"

"Through Tom and me," Adam replied with a smile. "We have a one-thousand-ton frigate in the West Indian trade, the *Bonnie Anne*, that's big enough for an Atlantic crossing. We've taken Captain Hooper, the most reliable of our ship's masters, into our confidence. He'll carry a cargo of furs and lumber so the voyage will be legitimate, and what with the ironware he'll bring back, we'll make a handsome profit. What's important is that he'll sail you to Dover and wait for you. If you're sent to France, he'll take you there and will wait again to bring you back here."

"I see. That's clever of you. And convenient for me."

"It is the least we can do for you—and for ourselves. Not even Mazarin will dare to abduct you and either do away with you or force you in some way to serve France—not when you have your own means of transportation. Mazarin may be smart, but a pair of old colonials can prove themselves smarter. What Mazarin might have forgotten is that most of us have had military training in England where men had a military obligation to fulfill for the homeland. This is our home now, and we are ready to pass on our military experience and knowledge to benefit our children and our children's children. The younger men—like you, like Ezekiel—are building a life of seemingly limitless opportunities and rewards. Our experience, teamed with your youth, strength, and emotional ties to the New World, is a combination no one can conquer. God be with you, young man. The future of the new breed depends upon your courage and success."

CHAPTER 11

RICHARD wrote a carefully worded letter to Laroche in New Amsterdam, and Tom Clayton saw to it that the communication was dispatched without delay. Clayton introduced the young Englishman to Captain Hooper, a bluff, hearty giant, who wrung his hand.

"Be ready to sail in two days' time, Master Dunstable," he said. "And don't worry your head none. I'll see you safely to England, to France if need be, and back home again. I've been told your situation, and you'll come to no harm traveling with me."

Richard could not keep his departure a secret from Eliza Burrows and braced himself for a confrontation with her. "I'm leaving in two days' time," he told her as they sat together at noon dinner in the Burrows house.

"You're leaving sooner than Papa led me to expect. May I know where you're going?" Her calm was astonishing.

"To England, possibly to France. I won't tarry long in either country."

"Is England safe for a Cavalier these days?"

"Not for this Cavalier. That's one of the risks I'm obliged to take."

She nodded thoughtfully. "Papa is providing a ship for you, I suppose."

"How did you guess?"

"I know Papa. The only ship in his fleet big enough for an Atlantic crossing is the *Bonnie Anne*."

He saw no need to conceal that fact from her. "You're right again."

She smiled serenely. "You'll like Captain Hooper. I've know him since I was a little girl. I was frightened to death of him for years, but then I realized that his gruff ways are just a front. Well, we'll need to get you ready for the voyage. If there's anything you want me to get for you, just put it on a list and give it to me."

Richard studied her for a moment. "Thank you, Eliza," he said. "You're taking this news like a lady, and you're asking me no embarrassing questions that I'd be reluctant to answer."

"You don't know me as well as you may think. I can be practical when it's necessary. You'll leave Roaring Wolf here?"

"Yes, and Prince Henry, too. I hope you'll exercise him occasionally."

"Every day," she said solemnly. "And when you return, we'll make our marriage plans."

"I—I can't afford the luxury of looking that far ahead," he said. "I'm not avoiding the question, and my reluctance has nothing to do with you. I'm on the trail of something that's vital to the future of the colonies, and if certain people—unscrupulous, ruthless people—learn that I have uncovered their schemes, my life won't be worth a ha'penny."

"I honestly wasn't trying to trick you into proposing to me now. You told me of your own volition about Dorothea, and I found out about Mimi on my own. I know there is no one else in your life now, and I also know from the way you look at me how much you love me. That's quite good enough for me. We'll wait until the appropriate time to talk about marriage."

He covered her hand with his. "To think that I dreaded telling you I'm sailing in two days!"

Her smile was soft. "You have enough on your mind, and I just wish I could help you in some way."

"Your attitude is a great help."

"I meant doing something active. Ah, well. You'll sail on the late-afternoon tide, I presume?"

"Yes, that's when Captain Hooper wants me on board."

"In that case I'll be very busy collecting good foods for you to eat on the voyage. Trust me."

"I do," Richard said.

He had just enough time to organize his belongings for his departure: he had a new suit made, appropriate for presentation if he should be called to the court of young King Charles II. He bought new powder for his guns and spent as much time as possible with Eliza, who was happy to accompany him on his errands.

On the day of his departure he found a large cloth-covered hamper awaiting him in the front vestibule, and he knew that Eliza was keeping her promise to provide him with delicacies. He went to the stable to bid farewell to Prince Henry, and the stallion seemed to sense the pending separation. Finally, he piled his belongings into a wheelbarrow, which Roaring Wolf insisted on pushing, and they made their way to the harbor together. There his gear and the hamper of food were transferred to the ship, which lay at anchor in the harbor, and he was surprised and pleased when the newlyweds appeared to see him off.

"I have a fair idea of what may be in store for you," Mimi told him. "Be careful. Horace Laing was fanatical in his beliefs, and others of the same stripe must be equally devoted to the cause of France."

"I wish I were going with you," Ezekiel said. "We make a good team."

"So we do," Richard replied, "but you have other responsibilities now."

"Where is Eliza?" Mimi wanted to know. "I thought she'd be here to say good-bye."

Richard concealed his disappointment. "So did I, but her nose must be out of joint because I'm making this voyage."

Ezekiel sympathized with him. "Handling Eliza is like trying to stuff quicksilver into a bottle. You never know from one moment to the next what she's going to think or do."

The gig from the *Bonnie Anne* was waiting, and the boatswain signaled to Richard that the time had come for them to leave.

Mimi reached up and kissed him. "May you be alert to treachery," she said. "Our colony's future depends on you."

Ezekiel grasped his friend's hand. "Good luck and good hunting," he said.

Richard went up to Roaring Wolf, who was standing quietly by the emptied wheelbarrow. He extended his hand to the Pequot, who grasped his wrist.

"This may be my most difficult farewell, my friend. We have grown close and have enjoyed a most unusual friendship. You call me your leader, but you are my teacher. I am grateful to you for your loyalty, bravery, and company. I hope you will be here in New Haven when I return, but I do not want to insist that you stay." Richard scanned the Indian's inscrutable face, hoping to read an indication of the Pequot's plans.

"I will be here when you return. You are my white brother. The Great Spirit has intended your path and mine to run side by side. I will honor the wishes of the Great Spirit always," the warrior assured him.

Richard and Roaring Wolf stood silently for several moments, savoring the closeness and feelings of mutual respect they were unable to express. Then Richard turned and moved toward the *Bonnie Anne*, glancing briefly over his shoulder with hopes of seeing Eliza. His effort was unrewarded.

As soon as the passenger came on board, Captain Hooper weighed anchor, and the ship threaded a path for herself through the crowded harbor, her jibs filling.

Richard stood at the starboard rail and watched the New World recede. When he had sailed from England, he had felt sad and uncertain of what was in store for him. But now he knew America, and he was surprised by his reactions. The communities that clung to the edge of the forest had become his home, and he was determined to return to this land of promise. He had found his true self in the wilderness, and he realized that he identified with the sturdy, independent, and self-reliant people who were creating a new way of life for themselves in a place where a person was judged solely by accomplishments, character, and ability to cope with adversity.

He had joined the new breed, and for their sake he would

do his best to get to the bottom of the international conspiracy that threatened the colonies. Only the failure of Eliza Burrows to say good-bye to him marred his mood, and though he tried to accept her behavior, he did not succeed.

Feeling frustrated and annoyed, he abruptly turned away from the rail and went below, where a pleasant surprise awaited him. His quarters were spacious, he had a real bed rather than a bunk, and there were several chairs, a table, and a rug on the deck, all making his cabin seem like a living room. Thanks to Adam Burrows, he would travel in real comfort.

That night at supper, Richard discovered that the ship's cook was competent and the two mates were intelligent young men, so the voyage promised to be pleasant. "The Atlantic is calmer now than at any other time of year," Captain Hooper told him, "and we should have tailwinds all the way across. I expect to reach Dover in four to five weeks."

After supper Richard went for a stroll on deck, but the lights of New Haven, twinkling and fading in the distance, reminded him of Eliza, so he returned to his cabin before his mood became too melancholy. Opening the hamper, he discovered that Eliza had packed several books for him, so he read for a time before retiring.

The next day he found they were out of sight of land, and he settled in for the long voyage. American seamen, he soon found, were unlike their British counterparts in that they needed neither goading nor strict discipline. Every man knew the performance level expected and understood the reasons his tasks were important. The men worked well together, and there was no need for the boatswain to patrol the decks with a length of knotted rope to prod the sloppy, the lazy, or the recalcitrant.

The winds remained favorable, as the master had predicted, and the sea was calm, so the ship cut rapidly and smoothly through the green-blue water. The days were so much alike that Richard made a small chart for himself to mark the passage of time. On the fourth day of the voyage, Captain Hooper invited him to his great cabin for dinner at noon, and proved to be well informed about the New World.

"The colonies are just beginning to live up to their potential," he said. "New England is more self-sufficient than Virginia for sustaining a chosen way of life, but that will change as our population grows and we continue to develop our colonial unity. We have waterpower and all the wood we need, and there's sure to be coal under the ground, so it's just a matter of time before we develop our strength. Then we'll be truly independent, able to stand on our own feet."

He was interrupted by a tap at the door, and one of the mates stood on the threshold, scowling unhappily. "I hate to spoil your dinner, Captain," he said, "but we've just found a stowaway on board."

Eliza Burrows came forward, the mischievous expression in her eyes belying her demure manner. "I apologize for any inconvenience that my presence may cause," she said.

Captain Hooper was on his feet, and so was Richard, both of them staring at her apparent nonchalance.

"I told you that I didn't intend to be separated from you again, Richard," she said. "You didn't believe me."

He nodded and swallowed hard, still unable to accept the fact that she was actually on board the ship.

Captain Hooper groaned and ran a hand through his thinning hair. "I've worked for your father for twenty years, but this will cost me my job," he said. "We're too far out in the Atlantic to turn back now!"

"That's why I waited until today to come out of hiding," Eliza replied blithely. "I know the *Bonnie Anne* as well as I know my own house, so it was easy to hide myself and my clothing boxes in the hold, although I must admit I'm tired of the cold meat and bread I've been eating. Aren't you going to invite me to join you for dinner?"

Captain Hooper could only sputter helplessly.

Eliza took pity on him. "I left a note for my father," she said. "I took full responsibility for what I've done, and I made it very clear to him that neither you nor Richard had any idea of what I was going to do. Papa is a fair and just man, and he won't blame either of you."

"But why have you done this?" Richard found his voice.

"I've already told you. I refused to be separated from you again. Besides, I can help you. We have much to discuss."

Captain Hooper turned to the mate and said in a constricted voice, "Be good enough to ask the cook to prepare a plate of food for Mistress Burrows."

"Please, Captain, hold the food for the time being. If you will excuse us, Miss Burrows and I seem to have several matters to discuss," Richard said as he took Eliza's elbow and guided her swiftly and none too gently to his cabin.

Eliza was surprised at Richard's brusqueness as he shoved her into his cabin and closed the door behind them, then turned to glare at her.

"Your audacity knows no bounds. You have placed Captain Hooper's professional standing in jeopardy. You have made my own mission even more dangerous, if that is possible!"

Eliza stared at Richard, and her high spirits vanished. She had misjudged his reaction.

"You may," he continued, "find it possible to gain easy forgiveness from your father, but you will not from me. If it had been convenient for you to accompany me on this voyage, you most assuredly would have been invited. But no, I said it was impossible, and here you are nonetheless."

"Richard, I——"

"You must have everything your own way, is that it, Eliza? Is that how it's always been for you? Is that how it always must be? Well, I am sorry. And your future husband, whoever he may be, also has my deepest sympathies."

Richard had exhausted his fury, and sank into a chair.

Eliza felt as if she had been knocked off a horse and couldn't regain her breath. Her heart was pounding wildly and she felt a depth of regret and remorse previously unexperienced in her young life. *Could he mean this?* she thought. *Could he really be through with me?*

"Please, Richard. I only did this out of love for you. I cannot bear to be away from you, not knowing where you are, but knowing that you are in danger. I can help. That's why I came, so I can help. Your enemies will be my enemies."

He lifted his gaze and found her face. She sank to her knees in front of him, afraid to touch him, but unable not to. She placed her hands on his knees, and looked up at him imploringly.

"Eliza, this is no pleasure cruise. When we reach England, I will arrange passage for you directly back to your father. He seems to be able to deal with your obstinacy more calmly than I. I am sorry, Eliza, but I will move my belongings out of this cabin so you may have your privacy and your reputation. I will move elsewhere as soon as Captain Hooper can find the space."

"Richard, please listen to me. Now your enemies will have two people to deal with. It's bound to be twice as safe for you that way. I was not raised to be like your women in England. I have been taught to deal with danger, to protect myself, and to think quickly. I am capable of assisting you. I will go where you tell me, I will stand by you just as I would if we were attacked by Indians in New Haven—or in a frontier fort. That's how I was brought up."

Richard, having vented his spleen, was beginning to calm down, and her words were making some sense. If the French tried to convert him to their cause, they would have to convert Eliza, as well. Order began to be created out of chaos. Although she was impulsive, she was also intelligent. If he could curb her behavior, it could work.

"You would be placing yourself in danger. Your father would never forgive me for this," Richard said.

Eliza began to take heart. He was speaking to her again, and his color was returning to normal. "I left my father a note, I told you, assuming all responsibility for my actions. I knew it could be dangerous, Richard; I could draw that from the little you were willing to discuss with me. I will stand beside you. How better could I prove my love?"

He melted; placing his hand on the back of her head, he stroked her long, blond hair. She leaned her head against his knee and tried to regain her equilibrium. Clearly, he was considering what she had said. She waited silently for his verdict.

"Eliza, you deserve a sound spanking. Your behavior is reprehensible. However, I feel your intentions were honorable. Because of that, I will reciprocate in kind. I will ask the captain to perform a marriage ceremony immediately, so I can make an honest woman of you."

Her hair danced as she shook her head vigorously. "I am grateful to you for your offer, but I must decline. I owe it to my father to be married only in his presence."

"Be realistic," Richard said hoarsely. "How can you and I sleep apart in the same bed?"

"We'll let nature take its course. You are an honorable man, and I am quite sure you'll marry me when we return to New Haven. A wedding ceremony is only a technicality. Papa would never forgive me if I married in his absence."

She was too much for him. "Let's return to Captain Hooper. I am sure he is anxious to know how you are faring."

Back in the captain's quarters, they briefly explained the arrangements.

"For my own protection," Captain Hooper said, "you'll sign a statement to the effect that you insist on moving in with Master Dunstable, but you refuse to marry him."

"Word it as you please, and I'll gladly sign it." She smoothed her skirt. Obviously she had changed her clothes before revealing to the crew that she was a stowaway. "I'll be obliged to you if you'll have my clothing boxes moved to the cabin from the forward hold, Captain."

Captain Hooper shrugged helplessly. He knew how headstrong she could be.

They were interrupted by the steward, who appeared with Eliza's meal. Announcing that she was ravenously hungry, Eliza began to eat. The steward was instructed to remove Mistress Burrows's wardrobe chest to Master Dunstable's cabin.

Captain Hooper sensed that a great deal had transpired between the two passengers, and he was greatly relieved when they excused themselves after the meal to return to their now-shared cabin.

Richard closed the door and bolted it shut. He sat down on the chair and watched Eliza as she unpacked her belongings. He reflected with interest that he had condemned Dorothea for her inability to control her own life. Now, he was confounded by Eliza's behavior at the opposite end of the spectrum.

When her organizing was completed, she turned to face him.

"I've gone to a great deal of trouble to arrange this rendezvous," she said. "Do you find me so much less attractive than Dorothea, so much less desirable than Mimi?"

He was goaded, as she had known he would be, and when he came to her, taking her in his arms, her lips parted for his kiss. Their differences immediately became irrelevant, and whether they were married or unmarried had no bearing on their present situation. They had curbed their desires long enough, and now, suddenly, all restraints were removed.

Eliza's lovemaking was as frank, as natural as her approach to Richard had been. She wanted him urgently, and she cast aside her inhibitions, responding to his caresses with an all-devouring passion that further inflamed him. She gave herself to him totally, holding back nothing, and he was overwhelmed by the need to conquer her.

As their desire expanded, they became unaware of their surroundings, and seemed to float freely from dizzying heights. They acted and reacted instinctively, giving and taking, demanding and yielding. They became one, and Eliza's scream of ecstasy mingled with Richard's moan of sheer gratification.

"Richard, you know how much I love you," she murmured, her eyes shining.

He did not reply in words, but instead made love to her again, then for a third time. Her insatiable desire matched his, and each existed only for the other. Richard no longer wondered whether his love for this fascinating vixen was genuine; it was proof enough that she had the power to arouse him repeatedly.

The afternoon passed, and at last he rose to light the oil lamp that was held in place by a bracket beside the bed.

Eliza giggled. "I wonder what I could have been thinking when I packed some books in the food hamper," she said. "Who'd want to read when we could be making love?"

Richard grinned at her. "I wonder why you go out of your way to make shocking remarks," he said.

She shrugged. "I don't know why," she replied. "I say whatever comes into my head, and sometimes I'm surprised myself at what comes out."

"That," he told her, "is a tendency you'll learn to curb, my love. You've elected to play a dangerous game, and a single slip could prove fatal for both of us."

"Never fear," she said, her smile fading. "I'm Adam Burrows's daughter, and now I've become your woman. I'll be equal to any test."

They made love all the way across the Atlantic, with the master and crew of the *Bonnie Anne* discreetly ignoring their impropriety. No one on board had forgotten that Eliza was the daughter of the ship's owner, no matter how unorthodox her conduct.

The mood changed abruptly one night at supper when Captain Hooper told the couple, "We'll put into the English Channel later this evening, and we should reach Dover by noon tomorrow."

Later, in the privacy of their cabin, Richard's mood was grim as he cleaned his rifle and pistol. "Take your lead from me," he told Eliza. "Say as little as possible, keep your eyes and ears open, and if danger threatens, do as I tell you without argument or discussion."

"I'm prepared for any emergency myself," she replied, and showed him a little poniard, razor-sharp, that fitted into the palm of her hand.

"That's a lethal weapon, not a toy," he said. "Have you ever used it?"

"No, but I'm prepared to do whatever is needed," she said seriously.

In the morning they packed their belongings before breakfast, and after eating they stood together on the deck, looking at the coast of England. Captain Hooper joined them.

"I'll need about twelve hours to dispose of my cargo, no more," he said. "Then I'll be available whenever I'm needed. If there's time I'll pick up a cargo of kitchen utensils and pots, but only if you don't need me to sail away quickly. Just remember I'm at your disposal. Your requirements receive my first attention."

"We won't forget," Richard told him.

Shortly before noon they saw the white chalk cliffs of Dover ahead, the heights above it dominated by an ancient castle, frequently rebuilt, that dated back to the time of the Roman conquerors. Sail was reduced as the *Bonnie Anne* eased her way into the small, cramped harbor, and after her anchor was dropped, the Puritans' harbor officials came on board. Somber men attired in unrelieved black, they studied the ship's manifests, then gave Captain Hooper the approval that made it possible for him to engage in trade.

"Take ashore with you only what you'll need for a day or two," Richard told Eliza. "And make certain your clothes are inconspicuous, even drab. You're in the land of the Roundheads now."

"I've packed a dress with long sleeves and a high neckline, and I'll hide my hair under a linen cap similar to what women in Boston wear."

He nodded in approval, hesitated, and decided to leave his rifle on board the ship. His sword and pistol, together with the throwing knives concealed beneath his dark coat, should be sufficient protection. In the New World it was taken for granted that a man would carry his rifle or musket wherever he went, but this was England, and different behavior was in order.

"We'll stay at an inn called the Royal Arms," Richard told Captain Hooper before they disembarked. "We'll register there as Master and Mistress Burrows, and you can expect to hear from me within the next twenty-four hours."

"If there's no word from you, I'll come in search of you," the ship's master promised.

They went ashore in the master's gig. Richard had expected to experience a rush of emotion, but he felt nothing when he stepped onto the solid ground. England was no longer his home and had become alien soil.

He hired a carriage and driver, then placed their one small clothing box in the rack on top of the coach himself.

"Be ye strangers to Dover?" the driver asked.

"Aye, that we are," Richard replied, broadening his accent. "We're from Lincolnshire."

"Be ye troubled there by snooping Roundheads?"

"We have no complaints," Richard replied diplomatically. "In the North we've found that those who tend to their own affairs are left in peace."

"Would it were that way here," the coachman muttered. "What with laws against this and laws prohibiting that, we may as well all be dead."

Uncertain whether the man was speaking in earnest or was in the hire of the Puritans, Richard nodded vaguely, but made no reply. England was obviously still permeated by fear and uncertainty.

On the drive to their inn, Eliza stared out of the carriage window, drinking in the sights of the mother country. Every road was cobbled, which impressed her, and many of the buildings of stone and brick were very old. And she was fascinated by the people who filled the narrow streets. Without exception they were attired in black, gray, or brown; they stared straight ahead as they walked sedately, and the children looked like miniature versions of the adults.

The proprietor of the Royal Arms not only resembled a clergyman, but had a minister's grave manner, and as soon as he departed after seeing "Master and Mistress Burrows" to their room, Eliza asked, "Now that we're here, what do we do next?"

"Well," he said, "it was useless to ask for Lord Blankenship, who, if he is here, is sure to be using an assumed name. The Roundheads would be keeping a close watch on the assistant secretary of funds of King Charlie's court. Let's go to the dining room and see if he is there."

Eliza busied herself at a mirror, tucking her blonde hair under a close-fitting cap. "How do I look?"

"Far too pretty for a Puritan," he replied, and kissed her. "If we should meet Blankenship, watch and judge him closely. The fact that Laroche set up the meeting with him makes me suspect him of being a French agent."

Eliza nodded, then preceded him down the stairs to the inn's dining room, her manner appropriately grave. They found a table near an open window that overlooked the harbor and were conscious of being studied by other diners. Eliza, Richard noted with satisfaction, played her role perfectly, sitting with downcast eyes, her hands folded in her lap.

He glanced casually around the room, then stiffened. Seated several tables away was a Roundhead with a bony, angular face, dressed in solid black; a chill shot up Richard's spine when he recognized Lord Blankenship posing as a Puritan.

Their eyes met for an instant, and Richard knew he had been recognized in return.

"He's here," Richard said quietly. "Three tables away, directly behind you. The next move is his."

Eliza nodded casually, and studied the bill of fare.

Both ordered steak-and-kidney pie, which had long been one of Richard's favorite dishes, but he was surprised to discover it had lost its savor. He preferred the game of the New World.

Blankenship finished his meal, paid for it, and stood. As he walked past Richard's table, a small pellet of folded paper dropped from his hand, landing near Eliza.

Continuing to eat with one hand, she scooped up the pellet in the other and dropped it into her purse, her motions so swift, natural, and fluid that even someone watching would have been unsure of what he had seen.

Blankenship was gone, and Richard did not turn in his chair. He and Eliza finished their own food, then returned to their room, where she removed the pellet and stared at what was written there: "Olde Tavern, six," she read.

"I gather he wants us to meet him at six o'clock this evening at a place called the Olde Tavern. I do believe we'll go for a stroll and see if we can find the Olde Tavern."

"Wouldn't it be simpler to inquire of the proprietor?"

He shook his head. "Never. That would be revealing too much."

They went out for a walk and soon discovered the location of the Olde Tavern, a modest establishment that occupied the first floor of a Tudor-style house. It was located only a few minutes' walk from the Royal Arms, and Richard strolled past it without halting. "Now," he murmured, "just in case we're being watched, we'll go into a shop nearby and buy something."

"That will be easy," she said, and led him to a shop directly across the road from the tavern, where she purchased a collar and a set of cuffs in stiff, white lawn. "Tonight," she told Richard, "I shall look like every other Puritan woman in this dismal town."

It was true that the collar and cuffs caused her to resemble the women of Dover. She was a chameleon, and her scrubbed face, modest gown, and demure manner made

Richard, by association, less conspicuous. He had to admit that her presence was a bigger help to him than he had anticipated.

Precisely at six o'clock that evening, they walked into the Olde Tavern, where Lord Blankenship awaited them at a table set for three. "God be with you, niece," he said loudly, kissing Eliza on the cheek. "And with you, nephew," he added as he bowed and shook Richard's hand.

The lively expression in Eliza's eyes indicated her appreciation of the charade.

"We can speak freely here until the place fills up," Lord Blankenship said softly. "The proprietor is one of us, even though the Roundheads come here in large numbers." He stared at Richard accusingly. "I expected you to come alone."

"Permit me to present you to my wife, sir," Richard replied.

The courtier raised an eyebrow. "Laroche mentioned no wife."

"I wasn't married when I last saw Laroche. My wife's loyalties are identical to my own."

Blankenship studied the woman. "Well, she's handsome, and she certainly looks like a Puritan. You could be useful to the cause, ma'am."

"You're kind to say so, sir," she replied smartly.

"We'll waste no time on the amenities," Lord Blankenship said after they had been served with glasses of ale. "I await your report, sir."

Richard told him in detail about conditions in the colonies, stressing the indifference to the quarrel between Cavaliers and Puritans everywhere but in Boston. As he talked he had the feeling that Blankenship already had a thorough understanding of the position taken by the colonies, and he wondered if he had been sent across the Atlantic on a fool's errand.

When he finished his recital, Blankenship downed his glass of ale, coughed slightly, and turned to Eliza. "As a colonial, I daresay you're grateful to France for the support she gives to the young king."

"I am not, sir," she responded at once. "The French never give anything without demanding full payment in return."

"You may change your mind," Blankenship said with a genial smile, and ordered their meal from a waiter who approached the table.

The oxtail soup was fragrant, and as Richard ate it slowly he awaited a fuller explanation of the courtier's cryptic remark.

"You have a singular honor in store. As soon as passage to Cherbourg can be arranged for you, you'll be received by the young king so you can report to him in person."

So they would be going to France! "We already have a ship at our disposal. Tell me when we're expected, and we'll be there," Richard said.

Blankenship artfully concealed his surprise. "That's convenient, I must say. You'll be met by someone you know and have reason to trust. He'll await you at the stone quay inside the Cherbourg breakwater the day after tomorrow."

"We'll be there," Richard promised, thinking that in France it might be easier to distinguish a traitor who appeared in the guise of a patriotic Cavalier.

"I trust you'll have suitable attire for your presentation," Blankenship said to Eliza. "His Majesty doesn't appreciate a Roundhead appearance." He looked up, his face darken-

ing when he saw a party in somber attire approach a nearby
table. "Uh oh. Be careful to speak softly. Here is the
Warden of the Port, damn the luck."

The Warden of Dover was the most powerful official in
the town, and Richard glanced up casually at a pudgy,
waxen-faced, self-important man clad in black. He was
escorting a woman, and they were followed by three other
men. The woman also wore the black of a Puritan, but she
was young and exceptionally pretty. Richard's heart skipped
a beat, then pounded furiously when he saw her. It was
Dorothea!

Eliza looked at him curiously, aware that the color had
drained from his face.

"Dorothea!" he muttered.

Eliza turned slowly, and saw the shock in the other girl's
eyes when she spotted Richard. She sat facing him, unable
to tear her gaze from him as she replied absently to a
remark made by her husband.

Richard was aware of his danger—and Eliza's. He was
on the proscribed list, and if Dorothea revealed his identity,
he would be imprisoned, then held indefinitely without a
trial. Eliza could expect the same fate.

But his alarm faded when it dawned on him that
Dorothea had no intention of betraying him. The expression in her limpid eyes was tender, and she continued to
stare at him as if he had risen from the dead.

Eliza also knew there was no danger. As the proprietor
came forward obsequiously to greet the honored guest, she
studied the dark-haired girl and knew her love for Richard
was still a living force.

Richard became conscious of the concern in Dorothea's
eyes, too, and he felt as if he were suffocating. Here, almost

within reach, was the girl he had idealized and worshiped from afar. Beside him sat his mistress, whom he felt honor-bound to marry. Never had he felt so disoriented.

Blankenship was still speaking, but neither of the others at the table heard a word he said.

Dorothea's focus widened to include those at Richard's table, especially Eliza, who returned her gaze. Richard realized that, in ways too subtle for him to grasp, the girl from his past and the girl who represented his present and his future, were communicating. Eliza raised a hand, placed it on Richard's sleeve for no more than an instant in a proprietary gesture, then withdrew it. Dorothea understood, bowing her head for a moment in recognition of the gesture. Then she put her past behind her, turned to her husband, and spoke to him with animation. Richard turned away from Dorothea, looked at Eliza, and grinned at her.

She stared deeply into his eyes and knew that all was well between them. He had buried a ghost that had haunted him, and his clear smile indicated his present feelings.

"Is this good beef?" Eliza asked lightly. "I've eaten it so seldom that I can't judge it."

"It's very good," Richard assured her. She refrained from hugging him and creating a spectacle.

"You'll see the future in a new light after your visit with our friend," Blankenship continued.

"The future," Eliza replied, "couldn't be more promising than it is at this moment."

"Amen to that," Richard said.

Blankenship looked at his dinner companions, unable to understand their coded comments. He concluded that the proximity of the Warden of the Port was responsible, and he decided to bring the evening to a conclusion. His purpose in holding the meeting had been to arrange for Richard's reception at the court-in-exile, and it would serve no useful purpose to prolong the session.

"I suggest we leave separately," he murmured, then stood. "Good-bye, niece. May God be with you. Until we meet again, nephew, may the Lord watch over you." He watched them as they made their way out of the tavern, both of them avoiding looking in the direction of the table occupied by the Warden of the Port and his party. Trained to observe human conduct, he thought it odd that the pretty young brunette at the Warden's table studiously averted her eyes when the departing couple brushed past her.

Richard made no mention of the encounter with Dorothea. "It struck me that Blankenship was anxious for us to gain a good impression of France. But that isn't proof that he's in the pay of France."

"Perhaps we'll learn more when we visit the court."

That night their lovemaking was more impassioned and more tender than it had ever been. The accidental meeting with Dorothea had sealed their own relationship.

The *Bonnie Anne* threaded her way through the harbor of Cherbourg, the low-lying hills of France in the background, and Richard knew this was truly foreign soil. The dock area was patrolled by soldiers in the gold-and-white uniforms of France, heavily booted, all carrying cumbersome sabers; riding herd over the merchant ships in the harbor were two frigates of the French navy, their powerful cannon more than compensating for the clutter on their decks that no British officer would tolerate.

Captain Hooper came and stood beside Richard. "I don't like this situation," he said. "You'll be at the mercy of the French every minute you're ashore here."

Richard shrugged. "I've calculated the risks, and I have no real choice. All that worries me is Eliza's safety. I've tried to persuade her to stay on board until I return, but she refuses."

"She's been headstrong all her life, accustomed to having her own way," the captain replied. "I don't envy you. Colonel Burrows will be wild if something happens to her."

"I can look after myself," someone behind them said.

Richard turned and was astonished by Eliza's appearance. She was wearing a gown of shimmering pale silk that hugged her torso tightly, then was elegantly decorated with cascades of ruffles from her hips to the hem. The most dramatic feature of her gown was its neckline, which plunged daringly and was adorned by insets of lace. The crew gaped at her. Eliza thoroughly enjoyed the sensation she was creating, and lightly fingered a long, dangling earring. "I've been saving this dress for a special occasion, and I thought I'd give the young king cause to remember me," she said with a smile.

"You're tempting fate," Richard told her, hurriedly enveloping her in a lightweight cloak of matching silk. "I'm not sure this is wise."

"There are times," she replied archly, "when a woman's natural assets are more potent weapons than a man's firearms. This is such a time."

He knew it would be impossible to persuade her to change into more modest attire.

The *Bonnie Anne* inched toward a berth inside the stone breakwater, then tied up at a dock. A squad of French soldiers appeared, taking up positions at the foot of the dock, but no harbor officials came to the ship for the customary examination, so it was plain that the vessel was being accorded special treatment.

"I'll wait for you right here until hell freezes," Captain Hooper confirmed.

"I hope we won't be obliged to stay in France that long," Richard replied, gripping the master's hand, then escorting Eliza ashore.

As he started down the dock, a familiar, gray-haired figure, resplendent in a plumed helmet and beribboned waistcoat, appeared at the foot of the dock. "Uncle William?" he cried.

The lines in the Earl of Newcastle's wrinkled face deepened when he smiled. "Welcome to France, Richie," he called.

Richard presented Eliza as his wife, and she surprised him by dropping in a deep curtsey, which was so graceful that it seemed like second nature to her.

Newcastle studied her openly, nodding in approval. "You've outdone yourself, boy," he said. "Now I know that His Majesty will give you a hearty welcome."

He conducted them to a luxurious carriage that bore the Stuart crest, and Richard noted at once that a troop of French soldiers, fifty strong, surrounded the vehicle. Obviously they would not only travel in style, but were under the protection of the government of France.

Newcastle chatted easily as the team of matched bays drew the carriage at a rapid clip down a road of crushed gravel lined with manicured trees. The queen was well, he said, and at present was paying a visit to the court of the Boy King, Louis XIV. "She is given every privilege of her rank here, and her grief over her husband's martyrdom has been assuaged." Charles II, now twenty years old, was grateful to his hosts and was saved from overwhelming French influences by receiving a steady stream of visitors from England. "We may fool ourselves, of course," Newcastle mused, "but we think the tide is turning in His Majesty's favor. We feel, and so does Cardinal Mazarin, that it won't be too long before King Charles is restored to the throne."

"You see Mazarin yourself?" Richard asked.

"Regularly," Newcastle replied proudly. "He takes a keen interest in our affairs."

A little too keen an interest, Richard told himself.

The earl continued to gossip about the court-in-exile. James, Prince of Wales, the younger brother of Charles II, was moody and unpredictable, inclined to spend his time reading English history rather than availing himself of the pleasures that were his for the taking. "You wouldn't know that he and Charles were brothers," he said.

Richard had the feeling that the Stuart court was a world of its own, far removed from reality, and what surprised him was Newcastle's deep involvement in it. That was to be expected, however, since the earl's own fate was so closely tied to the fortunes of the young monarch.

After an hour's drive they approached a château that stood high on a hill, its medieval towers and buttresses dominating the productive farms in the valley below, as it had done for centuries.

"When you make your report to King Charles," Newcastle said, "don't ramble. Be concise. His Majesty is easily bored by details."

French sentries armed with sabers and muskets stood guard duty outside the château, and the security precautions were thorough, the carriage halting repeatedly while an officer checked the identities of those inside. "We take no risks here," Newcastle explained. "We take no chance that Roundhead fanatics will try to assassinate or kidnap him."

It was a simple matter for the French to keep Charles II isolated, Richard reflected, allowing him to see only those of whom Mazarin approved. The realization made him uneasy, and he wondered how the young monarch managed to keep in touch with day-to-day affairs in England.

When they reached the château, a servant in Stuart livery—who, it rapidly developed, spoke not one word of English—conducted Richard and Eliza to a suite where they could refresh themselves before being presented to the king. Richard paced the chamber restlessly, paying no attention to the spectacular view of the valley below, while Eliza sat before a mirror arranging her hair. "I have the strange feeling here that we're cut off from the whole world by the French troops," he said.

The Earl of Newcastle conducted them to the great hall of the château, where, even though the sun stood high overhead, scores of French tapers were burning, casting their reflections on the huge, priceless tapestries that covered the stone walls.

Groupings of ladies and gentlemen, all elegantly attired, sat at small tables, amusing themselves at cards or with dice, occasionally pausing to take silver wine cups from one of the many servants in attendance. Richard's presence created no stir whatever, but the gentlemen looked up from their games to inspect Eliza, while the ladies scrutinized every detail of her appearance, their eyes measuring their own looks against the standard created by the newcomer.

Lolling on a bench set on a dais at the far end of the great

371

hall was an athletic-looking young man with long, brown hair, informally attired in a shirt of white silk, open at the throat, and snug-fitting black breeches. Reclining on a mound of pillows beside him was an almond-eyed girl of about the same age, who fed him tidbits from a tray of sweets and occasionally lifted a cup to his lips.

Richard instantly recognized Charles II. He had the long Stuart chin and thin, almost Roman nose of his father and grandfather, his forehead was high, and, although he was totally preoccupied with the young woman whom he was fondling, his brown eyes were sharp and penetrating. But what was Charles doing here? He had moved from France to the island of Jersey months ago.

The Earl of Newcastle cleared his throat in order to gain his monarch's attention. "Your Majesty," he said, "I have the honor to present your loyal subjects, Sir Richard and Lady Dunstable."

Richard bowed low, and Eliza, smiling because she had been called Lady Dunstable for the first time, sank to the floor in a deep curtsey.

King Charles took another sip of wine, then forcibly removed his attention from his companion. His eyes were slightly glazed as they slid past Richard, but he came to life as he gazed at Eliza. "Have something to drink," he said in French, much to their astonishment.

Richard accepted a cup from a servant, and went through the ritual of drinking to the king-across-the-water. His gesture amused King Charles, who chuckled as he reached for the pliant playmate beside him on the divan.

Somehow Richard managed to give his report on conditions in the colonies, his voice sounding hollow in his own ears. He was prepared to swear that the man who would become the master of the New World when he regained the throne did not hear a word. Charles studied Eliza with obvious relish, then busied himself fondling the breasts of his unidentified companion, who wriggled in pleasure at his touch.

Richard spoke briefly, poignantly, knowing he was wasting his time.

"We appreciate your loyalty to our person and our cause," Charles said automatically when Richard finished his recital. "Rest assured you will be duly rewarded when we return to England." He smiled, then added in French, "Stay to dinner, why don't you?" Not waiting for a reply, he embraced the girl beside him.

Newcastle signaled to Richard, and they backed out of the hall as King Charles devoted himself to serious love-making. Richard could not conceal his revulsion, drawing a deep breath of fresh air in the corridor.

"Who is the wench?" Eliza asked contemptuously.

The earl shrugged. "Her identity doesn't matter. His Majesty's appetite is insatiable, and he's kept well supplied. He comes back to France from Jersey periodically just for relaxation of this type. I should have warned you what to expect."

"It seems to me," Richard said, "that I've traveled three thousand miles in vain."

Newcastle shook his head. "Not at all," he replied gently. "The purpose of your journey soon will become evident to you."

Richard knew only that he was glad to put the château behind him, and he could tell that Eliza felt as he did. He was serving a monarch whose corruption by the French made him unworthy of the risks taken and the sacrifices made in his name.

Not until the carriage started toward the south after moving down the hill did it occur to Richard that Cherbourg was not their destination. "Where are you taking us, Uncle William?" he asked.

Newcastle's smile was enigmatic. "Trust me."

They rode in silence for a time, and Richard dared to think the unthinkable: was it possible that the Earl of Newcastle, the inheritor of one of the greatest and most distinguished English titles, could have sold out his country's interests? Was it conceivable that he was in the pay of France?

Newcastle's voice intruded on his thoughts. "I'm sorry your dinner has been delayed," he said, "but you'll find the wait well worth the increase in your appetites." He seemed pleased with himself.

After a drive of another hour or two, still surrounded by the cavalry escort, the carriage rumbled into the sleepy market town of Saint-Lô, its ancient walls and towers, which dated back to Roman times, reminding Eliza and Richard of the wooden palisades that protected the communities of the New World from the dangers of the wilderness.

A few farmers driving carts that had been emptied of their produce at the open-air market stared at the carriage and troops, but otherwise the dusty street was deserted. In the center of Saint-Lô, in between the town hall and an imposing church, lay several one-story buildings, the weather-beaten sign on the front gate identifying them as a monastery. Richard was surprised when the gate was opened by smartly uniformed sentries, and the carriage drew to a halt before what appeared to be the main building. Several brown-robed monks glanced up from their work in a vegetable garden, then returned to their labors.

Newcastle led the young couple down a silent corridor, and there was no sound but that of their heels clicking on the tile floor. At last the earl paused before a closed door and tapped tentatively.

"Come in, William," a deep voice boomed from within. "I've been expecting you."

Richard and Eliza found themselves in the presence of a gray-haired priest who was seated behind a desk piled high with papers in an otherwise bare room. A smile lighted his gentle face as he stood and extended both hands. "Ah, Sir Richard, we meet at last," he said. "And this is Lady Dunstable. I commend your eye for beauty, Sir Richard."

The priest's manner and appearance suggested sophistication and worldliness, and Richard was not shocked when he was presented to Jules Cardinal Mazarin, Regent and Principal Minister of the Realm. Here was the man who had never been consecrated as priest but had risen to the rank of cardinal through nepotism, general lack of public interest, and shrewd diplomacy.

"You haven't dined as yet?" Mazarin asked. "Good! I bring my chef with me whenever I'm called away from Paris, so I can offer you a passable meal." Gathering his habit closely around him, he led them down the corridor to the refectory, a bare room with whitewashed walls, and seated himself on a bench at a scrubbed table.

The meal was one of the most memorable that Richard

had ever eaten, although he was too dazed to fully enjoy the rich soup and dishes of fish, fowl, and meat that followed in profusion, served by silent monks.

Very much at his ease, Mazarin conversed fluently on many subjects, surprising Eliza and Richard with his wealth of knowledge of the English New World colonies. He seemed familiar with the business affairs of Burrows and Clayton, he knew the New England Federation militia had been called to duty only five weeks earlier, and he made a passing reference to the recent marriage of Lady Dawn Shepherd. It was obvious that he kept himself well informed.

At the conclusion of the meal he had their wine glasses refilled, then glanced meaningfully at Newcastle.

"His Eminence has kept you under observation for a long time, Richie," he said, "and concluded that a personal meeting was in order. We apologize for wasting your time with Blankenship in Dover, and for the charade to which you were subjected today, but both were necessary for you to grasp the situation in which we find ourselves."

So it was true, Richard thought, his heart sinking. Newcastle was a traitor who was betraying England for French influence and gold.

Cardinal Mazarin laced his slender fingers together. "Politics imitates nature," he said in his gentle, cultured voice, "and like nature, she abhors a vacuum. For generations France and England have been Europe's greatest powers, each balancing the other. Now Cromwell has destroyed that equilibrium. Consequently Spain has been stirring, the Holy Roman Emperor in Vienna dreams of extending his realm, and even the Czar of Russia thinks of increasing his power. That is not to be. France and England are the two most civilized nations in the West, and if they are not to share the rule, then one or the other must dominate. Thanks to the blunders of Cromwell, it is the good fortune of Louis the Fourteenth to become the master of Europe and of the New World."

"It was not accidental that you met Charles the Second," Newcastle interjected. "An amiable enough young man, but I watched your faces, and I know you have judged him for yourselves."

Richard felt ill, and a glance at Eliza told him she too was stunned.

"The common people of any nation are ill-informed in matters of politics," Mazarin said, "and must be led. You have qualities of leadership that have called you to my attention, Sir Richard. And you have chosen a mate worthy of you. Together you will be instrumental in bringing the English colonies of the New World into the fold of France."

Eliza expected Richard to protest and refuse, but to her astonishment he said nothing. A few moments of reflection explained his prudent silence: no force had been used, but they were the prisoners of France, isolated in a little market town far from the ship that awaited them at Cherbourg. Mazarin, with a troop of his own guards at his disposal, could eliminate them from the face of the earth with a wave of his patrician hand. He had placed them completely in his power.

"The man you know as Laroche is exceptionally able and understands both our goals and our methods," Mazarin continued. "You will operate under his jurisdiction. Naturally, France will be grateful for your efforts."

"And France is generous," Newcastle said with a faint smile.

"Your rewards will be ample," Mazarin declared. "I am not niggardly in my dealings with those who show loyalty to our ideals, just as I am severe in my treatment of those who betray us." Nothing in his expression or tone indicated that he was threatening the couple. "We must strike while England is disorganized and confused. Earthly power and glory are the just spoils of the bold and the swift." He paused, then asked quietly, "May we count on your help, Sir Richard?"

Richard knew that only one reply was possible if he and Eliza hoped to leave Saint-Lô alive. "You may, Your Eminence."

"I applaud your good judgment," Mazarin said. "And you, Lady Dunstable?"

Unable to trust her voice, Eliza could only nod. She and Richard had been maneuvered into becoming French puppets.

"Splendid," Mazarin said, rising quickly to his feet. "Much work of importance remains to be done, and I shall anticipate glowing reports of your progress from Laroche."

The cardinal was a man who prided himself on his subtlety, and never would he do anything so crass as to issue threats blatantly and openly. Having made his position clear, he reached into the girdle that encircled his waist, and there, adjacent to his ivory rosary beads, was a short, exceptionally sharp double-bladed knife that he plucked out and held carelessly. He flipped it over in the palm of his hand, then grasped it and absently sliced a sheet of parchment with it. The knife was so sharp that it instantly cut through the sheepskin without making a sound. Smiling benignly, Mazarin tested the blade with his thumb as if thinking of something else, but his meaning was very clear. Either

Richard and Eliza did precisely what they were told, or they had only a short time to live. His threat was all the more brutal because it was indirect. Still smiling and nodding, he left the refectory.

"Both of you have displayed wisdom beyond your years," Newcastle said when the door closed behind the principal minister. He drew two bags of gold from his belt and placed them in front of the young couple. "The wealth of France is as unlimited as her gratitude to those who serve her."

Richard wanted to hurl the gold into his face, but instead he took the bag and slipped it into his own belt. This was not a time for heroics. Eliza hesitated, then followed Richard's example.

"There is no choice, really, in selecting the path I now follow," Newcastle said. "Oliver Cromwell is despicable. Young Charles is unfit to rule. So France offers the only hope of salvation."

It was so easy to rationalize, to believe what one wanted to believe, Richard thought bitterly. Perhaps there was no choice in the Old World, but America offered an alternative, the freedom to live according to the principles of liberty espoused by the new breed.

"You have been privileged to meet and break bread with a great man," Newcastle said, then smiled as he stood. "You'll be back at your ship in time to sail for the New World on the evening tide."

Ashamed of the commitment he had been forced to make, and despairing for the loss of an old family friend, Richard's greatest regret was that he had pulled Eliza with him into ruin and disgrace.

CHAPTER 12

THE summer weather was benign and the sun shone brightly on the green-blue Atlantic, so the westward voyage should have been carefree. But Richard and Eliza were miserable.

"I should have known better than to try to outsmart the shrewdest man in France," he said in self-disgust. "For all the good it does, I know the identities of the traitors to England, and I recognize the dangers to the colonies. But my own hands are tied: either I cooperate with France, or I'll be knifed in my sleep."

"Don't feel too badly," Eliza said bravely. "We were amateurs playing professionals' games."

"The worst of it is that you've become involved," he said. "I should have seen the pitfalls when they tried to recruit Mimi, but instead I delivered you into their hands."

"You can't blame yourself for my involvement," she replied. "I went into this with my eyes open and I gave them the opportunity to use me, too."

"There is a way out for you," he said. "When we reach New Haven, you can refuse to have anything more to do with me. Just drop me permanently. Then I'll report to Laroche that you were too flighty to be reliable, and you should be safe."

Eliza's blue eyes blazed as she stared at him. "Are you trying to get rid of me?"

"For your own welfare and protection, yes," Richard told her.

"What a convenient excuse!"

"You're wrong," he said earnestly. "But I prefer to give you up to seeing you suffer the degradation of being forced to act as an agent for France. If I loved you less, it would be simple enough to drift with the tide."

"Did I hear you correctly?" she demanded. "Did you say that you love me?"

"Of course! Why should that surprise you?"

She looked at him and slowly shook her head. "In all the weeks we've been living together, this is the first time you've said you love me."

"I thought you knew." Richard was defensive.

"I guessed it," Eliza said. "I even assumed it. But I still like to be told."

His smile was a trifle sheepish.

"That settles the matter," she said decisively. "I've been frightened by the depth of our commitment to France and our inability to wriggle out of a menacing situation. If you didn't care for me, I might have been willing to accept your suggestion that we part, even though I know Papa would be terribly upset. But it happens that I love you too, and nothing in this world is going to separate us. That includes Cardinal Mazarin!"

He realized she had tied his hands, making it impossible for him to protect her. "Then we'll simply have to do our best to outwit Mazarin and his people, impossible though that may seem."

"Together we can do anything!" Eliza said confidently, and embraced him.

It was true, he knew, that he had come to love this woman with her fiercely independent mind and will. Somehow he would have to shield her from the ruthless foes who were determined to make England a mere puppet of France and to gain possession of the New World colonies for themselves.

Captain Hooper was not looking forward to his ship's return to her home port. "Colonel Burrows will nail my hide to a wall," he said on the last night of the voyage as he entertained the young couple at supper in his cabin.

"Leave Papa to me," Eliza said. "I'll take care of calming him."

The following day, as the ship eased into her berth at the New Haven port, the ship's master nodded in the direction of the dock. Adam Burrows was pacing there, a frown on his face, his eyes angry.

Eliza insisted on going ashore alone. "You can't blame Richard or Captain Hooper for what's happened, Papa," she said as she embraced and kissed him. "I accept full responsibility."

"Are you married?" Adam demanded.

She shook her head and smiled. "Not yet, but I soon will be. Richard offered to marry me the instant he discovered I stowed away, and I refused only because it wouldn't have been right to hold the ceremony unless you were there."

She had succeeded in disarming him, as she had known

she would, and his anger melted away into relief and joy at having his daughter home again. Her behavior no longer shocked him. He had been her father too long for that.

A short time later, at dinner in the Burrowses's house, Richard gave the colonel a full report on their meeting with Lord Blankenship, their reception at the court-in-exile of King Charles II, and their climactic session with Cardinal Mazarin. "I've offered to part with Eliza so she won't become involved with the French, but she refuses."

"It's too late for that," she said. "Besides, our love is more important than the dangers to which we may be subjected."

Colonel Burrows's reaction surprised them. "You've wanted a life of adventure for a long time, Eliza," he said, "and now you've taken a bigger bite than you may be able to digest. But the situation may not be as bad as it seems."

They looked at each other, then at him.

"Every able-bodied man in the colonies has been mobilized for what promises to be the fight of our lives," Adam Burrows explained. "The French have been smarter than I gave them credit for being. We've had reports that the two biggest Indian nations of the border country, the Algonkian and the Micmac, are moving hundreds of warriors down the Pequot River. They intend to split Connecticut and New Netherland from Massachusetts Bay and Rhode Island, and gobble us piecemeal. Indians don't think in such terms, so the maneuver is French-inspired, but our scouts—and Roaring Wolf is worth his weight in gold to us—report that there are no French troops on the march against us, only a handful of mercenaries. We're badly outnumbered, but the threat of a common enemy has served one purpose: it has united the British and Dutch colonials in a military action of common defense. Therefore, I have every confidence that we'll give a good account of ourselves. What has worried me is that even if we beat back the attackers, France won't give up. It will be convenient, to say the least, to have a daughter and son-in-law who can keep the colonies informed on what new schemes the French may be devising."

Richard felt better than he had at any time since he and Eliza had been dragooned into service by Mazarin. "You're suggesting we become triple agents, sir. I'm supposedly working for the Cavaliers, although I have no heart for their cause after seeing the young king."

Eliza nodded in emphatic agreement.

"We've been forced to work for the French," he went on. "Now you're suggesting that we go along with them so we can report their plans to you."

"That's the general idea," Adam Burrows replied. "It won't be too easy, I daresay, and you'll be in danger every minute. But we've been given an opportunity to learn the long-range thinking and planning of the French, so I'm compelled to urge you to take the risks."

"I'll do it gladly," Richard said. "But I still hesitate to let Eliza become too involved."

"You can't stop me," she said with spirit. "And neither can Papa. I have an investment here too: I am concerned for both of your welfares and for the security of my home. You can't expect me to withdraw my active support."

Her father nodded and sighed. "All right, Eliza, Richard—we'll have to move one step at a time," he said. "I came to New Haven to move every available ship to the mouth of the Pequot River. It's coincidental that I happened to be here when you landed. The first order of business is your marriage, and then I've need to rejoin the combined colonial militia."

"I hope you'll let me come with you, Colonel," Richard said. "I'm a fair shot, and I cannot bear to do nothing while others fight for the freedom of the colonies. This trip to England and France has taught me what to put first, and the colonies have become my home."

"You'd leave your bride behind?" Eliza demanded.

"You'll stay right here," Richard told her firmly.

The rector of the New Haven church agreed to waive the customary three-day waiting period following the posting of banns because of the wartime situation. Adam hastily rounded up the senior Claytons as witnesses, and the wedding was conducted in much haste. But the rush in no way detracted from the solemnity of the occasion.

This was no ordinary marriage, and Richard was conscious of the bride's need to be sheltered and protected from influential, unscrupulous foes in this international conspiracy that would stop at nothing to achieve power and wealth. Eliza, in spite of her eagerness to do her share, was far more vulnerable than she realized.

At the end of the ceremony the newlyweds kissed, then accepted the good wishes of the Claytons and of Mimi, who was delighted by the marriage. "I'm so glad that circumstances have worked out for you as they have," she said. "I don't know of any two people—except Ezekiel and me—who are so well suited."

The bridal couple's honeymoon consisted of sharing a glass of wine at the Burrows house. "If you're coming with me," the colonel told his new son-in-law, "you'll have to leave right now."

Richard nodded, then took his bride in his arms. "Stay out of mischief while I'm gone," he told her.

"I shall," she promised, "provided you'll come back to me so I can enjoy being Mistress Dunstable." She clung to him for only a moment, then made their parting easier for him by smiling impudently.

Richard knew nothing of the military situation that faced the colonies, but understood why he had been so prompt in volunteering his services. He was going off to fight to preserve a way of life that was unique, and someday, when he and Eliza had a family, he wanted their children to enjoy the benefits of a new kind of civilization, a world in which all were born equal and had equal opportunity to make of their lives what they wanted.

Prince Henry whinnied and pawed the ground in pleasure at the sight of his master, and as Richard started off with Colonel Burrows along the coast trail, he had to hold the stallion in check.

As they rode, Adam Burrows briefed his son-in-law. "Our scouts tell us that the Algonkian and Micmac are traveling downriver by canoe, and if their estimates are accurate, we'll face at least one thousand warriors. The bulk of our defending force will be my own regiment, about three hundred and fifty strong. New Netherland has sent us one hundred British volunteers living in the Dutch colony, Rhode Island and Connecticut have contributed fifty, and Plymouth and Massachusetts Bay, which have recognized the dangers to all of us, have sent two hundred."

"Then we're outnumbered by several hundred."

"Unfortunately we are. I hope to block the mouth of the river with cannon on board a half-dozen ships that will force the enemy to land. But we're handicapped by a lack of Indian allies of our own—warriors who will understand what the enemy will do next."

"I can see where they'd be useful," Richard said. "You have no alliances with any neighboring tribes?"

"The French have proved far more shrewd in their dealings with the natives. We've paid them for land we've taken, but we haven't actively cultivated their friendship. The French have made them welcome in Quebec and ply them with gifts, and their policy pays off. Now, when we need the advice of war chiefs, there's no time to develop a relationship."

Richard's mind worked rapidly. "Do I assume we're riding straight through to your camp area?"

"It's only forty-five miles," the colonel replied. "It shouldn't unduly tax our horses."

"Do you speak any of the Indian languages? I've learned a little from Roaring Wolf, but I'm far from fluent."

"I've picked up enough to make myself understood," his father-in-law said. "What do you have in mind?"

"The Mohegan are indebted to me," Richard replied. "I'm wondering if the time hasn't come to cash in that debt. We'll be riding only a few miles from one of their main towns. It might be worth our while to pay them a visit."

"Well," Adam Burrows said, "at the rate the Algonkian were leading the enemy, they won't reach our defense lines for at least another forty-eight hours. I suppose we have nothing to lose by trying."

So, late in the day, they made a detour inland, and as they had anticipated, two Mohegan sentries appeared out of the bush. Richard promptly raised a hand in friendly greeting, and the colonel addressed the braves in their own tongue. "We wish to meet with your sachem on a matter important to him and to us," he said. The request was unusual, and the warriors hesitated.

"You do not remember me?" Richard asked quickly. "The Mohegan are noted for their memories, but they have already forgotten the man who saved the life of Ilia-awi."

Adam translated his words dutifully, and the attitude of the braves changed at once. They peered hard at Richard, then professed to remember him, and one of them raced ahead to a sentry outpost. Soon Richard and the colonel, following at a more stately pace with the other sentry, heard the beat of drums echoing through the wilderness, announcing their arrival.

Adam glanced at his new son-in-law, then decided to trust him completely. Ordinarily he would have hesitated to ride to the village of one of the most warlike of the New England tribes, but Richard showed no fear, so the visit must be worth the risks.

As they drew near the town, they discovered that the entire community was turning out to greet them, with warriors old and young, staid women, and hordes of children pouring out of the palisade gates and inundating the fields of corn and squash.

At last Richard saw the familiar figure of the sachem, surrounded by his war chiefs, medicine men, and the tribe's elders, with Ilia-awi, wearing a dress and leggings of beaded doeskin, half-concealed behind them.

Richard dismounted promptly, surprising himself by delivering a long speech, translated by the colonel, in which he stressed his friendship with the tribe.

The sachem replied in kind, making it clear that he whose skill with a firestick was unequaled anywhere was welcome.

Not to be outdone, Richard introduced his father-in-law as the most illustrious of white war chiefs.

His exaggeration embarrassed Colonel Burrows, who nevertheless translated the younger man's remarks literally, and was rewarded when the Indians raised their arms in salute to him.

The Mohegan considered the occasion adequate excuse for a feast, and scores of volunteers dug a large pit, filled it with firewood, and, after lighting it, went off to their storehouse for several sides of buffalo. The whole town seemed eager to participate in the preparation of the feast.

Richard, meanwhile, removed his hat, then bowed low to Ilia-awi. The girl obviously was pleased by his attentiveness to her, and several of the older women nudged each other slyly. But Richard had no intention of taking unfair advantage of Ilia-awi's still-obvious interest in him.

Richard bided his time, having learned the ways of Indians. He could see Colonel Burrows becoming restless, aware that the hour of attack by the Algonkian and Micmac was drawing closer, but he refused to become agitated. Just as one survived in the wilderness by patiently flowing with the forces of nature, so one dealt with the natives of the wilderness.

At last the food was prepared, and Ilia-awi herself served her father and the two guests. She was appropriately reserved in her manner toward Adam Burrows, but cast aside restraint and eyed Richard boldly. He knew he would cause far more harm than good if she gained the wrong impression, so he only nodded to her politely as she handed him each dish, doing nothing that would cause her to believe he was personally interested in her.

At last the meal came to an end, and the sachem rose to his feet. Relishing his role as a public speaker and proud of his ability to play on the emotions of his people, he spoke at great length, extolling the virtues of the white war chief and particularly those of the unselfish friend of his people.

The night was advancing, and Colonel Burrows was finding it difficult to curb his impatience.

Then Richard stood and offered a reply, which his father-in-law duly translated for him. His opening words were so unexpected that he captured the attention of the Mohegan people. "My brothers," he said, "we sit side by side in peace for the last time. Soon these forests and hunting grounds, which we share in peace, will be soaked with blood.

"Even as I speak to you, the land is about to be invaded. The mighty Algonkian and the ferocious Micmac have sent forces of invaders to drive the English and Dutch settlers from the soil. Rest assured that the colonists will resist! Oh, yes! Their firesticks are ready, and they will stand bravely to the challenge, even though the invaders number as many as the trees in the forest."

The unexpected sobriety of his alarming speech had fully shocked his hosts. The sachem's face revealed nothing, but his knuckles turned white as he gripped the bowl of the long pipe he held in his hand. Others, including the tribe's medicine men and war chiefs who sat directly behind him, were less able to hide their feelings, and stared in fascinated horror at Richard.

Making up his speech as he went along, Richard decided to simplify. These Indians had no understanding of European politics, were untouched by the rivalries of the English and French, and would not understand that the warriors who were about to invade their homeland had responded to French goading. It was enough that the Algonkian and Micmac were bent on conquest far from their own homeland. Everyone knew, he declared, that the invaders were ruthless men who showed no mercy to their foes. Warriors who dared to oppose them would be killed and scalped. Women and children would be dragged off to the north to become the slaves of the rapacious Micmac, the servants of the dreaded Algonkian.

He and the white war chief should be at their posts at this very moment, Richard continued, rallying and preparing their men for combat. But they had stopped off in the land of the Mohegan in order to warn their friends and neighbors of the impending danger.

As he spoke, the traditional cold indifference of the warriors gradually gave way to indignation, then to outright anger. A young warrior broke the spell by uttering a fierce war cry that echoed through the nearby forest. "Death to the Algonkian!" he shouted, brandishing a tomahawk. "Death to the Micmac!"

All at once dozens of braves were on their feet, uttering similar cries, and in the bedlam it was impossible for Richard to finish his address.

"I reckon you've accomplished your purpose," the colonel told him. "I've never seen anyone communicate with Indians any better!"

The sachem conferred briefly with his elders, medicine men, and war chiefs, then raised a hand for silence. "My brothers," he said as the crowd gradually became quiet, "the Mohegan, who hunt where their fathers and the fathers of their fathers hunted, thank you for the warning you have brought to us. How soon do you march against the invaders?"

"Now," Colonel Burrows replied promptly, not bothering to consult Richard first. "At once!"

The sachem nodded, then turned back to the throng. "How many warriors will march beside our white brothers to defeat the strangers who invade our sacred soil?"

The fighting men of the tribe responded with one voice, their suspicion of the English and Dutch settlers in abeyance in light of this greater, more immediate peril.

A war party was organized with dispatch. A total of one hundred twenty-five warriors daubed their faces and torsos with fresh paint, filled rawhide bags with strips of sun-dried venison and a few handfuls of parched corn, and shouldered quivers of arrows, then pronounced themselves ready to depart. Their leader, a hawk-faced war chief named Ro-an, gripped the forearms of the two visitors to demonstrate his fealty to them. Soon the party was on the trail, led by Colonel Burrows and Richard, who rode while the warriors trotted tirelessly behind them.

"You've brought us reinforcements of the best kind when they were desperately needed," Adam Burrows said.

"If we had more time, I think I could persuade the Conestoga to march north to join the defenders."

"I knew you were resourceful," his father-in-law said, "but I'll never understand how you've made allies of at least two tribes in no time at all!"

They traveled the better part of the night, and it was still dark when they stood their mounts at the crest of a hill and looked down at the broad mouth of the Pequot River. No campfires were burning, and the only signs of a defense force were the small ships riding at anchor, their unlimbered cannon shimmering in the pale moonlight.

Colonel Burrows cupped his hands over his mouth, then gave a credible imitation of an owl.

There was an answering owl cry from the thick foliage ahead, and then a sentry in buckskins appeared, his musket ready for use. "Ah, it's you, Colonel," he said. "Some of the men was getting jittery because you hadn't showed up yet."

"I was delayed," Adam Burrows replied. "Show our good allies to a place where they can conceal themselves."

The sentry stared in astonishment as the half-naked warriors of the Mohegan filed forward silently. Shaking his head in wonder, the sentinel quickly led them down the hill.

The colonel conducted Richard to his own command post, a small clearing with a view up the river. There they turned their tired horses loose to graze, and an orderly brought them a cold breakfast of corn bread and fish, which they washed down with a bitter ale.

Adam Burrows took no time to rest. "Pass the word that I'm back," he told an aide. "We'll hold a meeting of the high command here in an hour's time. Meanwhile I want a report from the scouts." Using the knife that he carried in his belt, he removed the bones from his fish and began to eat.

Admiring his calm at a time when extreme danger threatened, Richard could better understand and appreciate Eliza. She, like her father, couldn't help responding to a challenge.

The first to arrive was Roaring Wolf, who was so overjoyed when he saw Richard that he emitted a low cry of pleasure, then embraced his friend. "I was afraid you would miss the battle!" he said.

"Never fear," Richard assured him, "I have a nose for a good fight."

Ezekiel Clayton appeared, clad in buckskins that camouflaged him so completely that he wasn't visible until he stepped from the screen of trees into the clearing. "Well, well," he said. "You've come back from Europe just in time!"

"Richie hasn't been idle since he landed yesterday," the colonel said with a chuckle. "He and Eliza were married less than two hours after they came ashore, and on our way here from New Haven we stopped off long enough to pick up a hundred twenty-five Mohegan warriors."

Ezekiel pumped Richard's hand. "I'm so glad you and Eliza married," he said simply.

"I had little choice," Richard replied. "She decided to become my wife, and that was that."

Ezekiel joined in his laugh, then asked, "Are the Mohegan reliable?"

Roaring Wolf frowned. "Mohegan are cowards," he declared flatly.

Richard had no intention of becoming engaged in a dispute with the Pequot. "We'll find out soon enough," he said.

The colonel had exercised patience, but now he asked sharply, "What reports do you have on the enemy's progress?"

"A scout came in less than an hour ago." Ezekiel glanced at Roaring Wolf for confirmation.

"He is a Pequot, so he can be trusted," he said. "The Algonkian and Micmac are in no great hurry. They stop to

395

hunt and fish whenever they need fresh food. If they keep up their present pace, they will reach the mouth of the great river before the sun sets tonight."

"Good. We'll give them a suitable reception. Did the Pequot scout count their numbers?"

"There are many," Roaring Wolf replied with a shrug. "With them are ten or twelve white men who speak in the tongue of New Haven."

Colonel Burrows was incredulous. "They speak English rather than French?"

Again Roaring Wolf shrugged. "The Pequot is an honest man, and was close enough to the white men to touch them. He swears they spoke English, and I believe him."

Adam Burrows was baffled, but wasted no time on conundrums that he couldn't solve. "We'll find out the meaning of this mystery soon enough," he said.

The leader of the New Netherland contingent arrived with the captain in command of the Rhode Island troops, and they were soon followed by the captain of the Connecticut militia and the colonels commanding the Massachusetts Bay and Plymouth colony regiments, accompanied by two aides. One of them, a lieutenant, was compactly built and tanned, his manner reflecting the self-confidence of a man who knew what he wanted in life and was well on his way to achieving that goal.

Richard stared at him, then stared again. "Dempster! Dempster Chaney!"

Equally startled, Dempster grasped the hand of the benefactor who had made it possible for him to establish himself in the New World.

As they chatted, bringing each other up to date on the developments in their lives, Richard reflected on the remarkablè changes in his protégé. When they had first met, Dempster had been timid and confused, hoping for success in America but unsure of how to achieve his ends. Now he was a man whose brains and brawn had given him a solid base, and his devotion to the cause of liberty marked him as a member of what Eliza called the new breed.

"Robbin had mixed emotions when I volunteered to join this expedition," he said. "She'll be lonesome, but saw the need for me to come. If we can teach the Algonkian and the Micmac that they'll pay a high price for aggression, the Mohawk and the other powerful tribes that live to the west of us will leave us in peace. There are some who argue that New Netherland has no business interfering in the British colonials' quarrels, but they're shortsighted. There are too few of us on these shores, so we stand or fall together."

Colonel Burrows sent Roaring Wolf for Ro-an, the Mohegan war chief, for whom he would translate, and when they arrived together he called the meeting to order. "Gentlemen," he said, "our situation is much improved in the past forty-eight hours. First, I was able to assemble the fleet of brigs, barques, and frigates that you see blockading the mouth of the river. Every last one of those ships is armed with two or three cannons, and although their marksmanship might not qualify them as experts by British or French standards, their guns can make one whale of a racket when they're fired. I'm confident they'll persuade the enemy to come ashore on the west bank of the river, where we'll be waiting for them. If the ships do that much for us, they'll be accomplishing their purpose.

"Our other need was equally urgent," the colonel went on. "My son-in-law, Master Dunstable, stepped into the breach and persuaded the Mohegan to send a strong war party to aid us in the fight. I ask Ro-an, their war chief, to station himself beside me during the coming battle to predict how the enemy will react."

Roaring Wolf translated rapidly, and Ro-an smiled, obviously pleased that he would play a key role.

"Tell the braves of the Mohegan," Colonel Burrows continued, speaking to the war chief in his own tongue, "that they must be patient. I intend to hold them in reserve, then send them into battle only when the time is ripe. We face a cruel and determined foe, but the Mohegan will gather a rich harvest of scalps if they follow orders."

"The braves of the Mohegan," Ro-an replied solemnly, "have not only the courage and strength of the bear, but also the cunning of the wolf. They will do as they are told, and will win glory as well as scalps."

"I intend to deploy the units in depth on the near bank of the river," the colonel told his associates. "We'll keep ourselves well concealed in the forest so the enemy won't be able to learn our strength. It is imperative that all militia units hold their fire until the last possible moment and then make every shot count."

"Apparently, sir, you're relying on our ability to cause the enemy to panic," the Massachusetts Bay commander said.

"Exactly so." Colonel Burrows's expression was grim. "As I understand Indian tactics, their aim, always, is to overwhelm their enemies. But neither the Algonkian nor the Micmac has ever faced massed musket fire, which can be a terrifying experience for them, provided your troops hold steady when they're rushed. There you have my basic battle plan, gentlemen. Feel free to discuss it and suggest modifications."

Dempster Chaney cleared his throat. "It strikes me you're relying on the element of surprise, at least to some extent, Colonel. But the cannon fire you'll utilize in order to drive the war canoes ashore should tell the Algonkian and Micmac that a land force will be waiting for them in the forest."

"So it will, Lieutenant," Adam Burrows replied. "But they've undoubtedly been told that we have few settlements in New Haven and Connecticut, and they'll expect to meet a far inferior force. Our numbers are not equal to theirs, but I'm relying on their losing the desire to fight when they realize they're not going to roll us back and send us fleeing from the field. What do you think, Ro-an?"

The Mohegan war chief listened to Roaring Wolf's translation and was lost in thought for a time, his arms folded across his chest. "The war chief of the colonists," he said at last, "also has the cunning of the wolf. The enemy will fear for their lives when you do not run, and then they will wish only to withdraw from the field with honor."

"That brings up an interesting point," the New Netherland commander said when the war chief's comment was translated. "By working together we've been able to accumulate a force to effectively challenge the enemy. But next time we may not be so fortunate. The Indian nations of this continent can send thousands of warriors into battle against us, while the best we can do is muster hundreds. Every sachem and every war chief in America, regardless of his tribe, will hear of this battle and will judge us accordingly. I say that we show the enemy no mercy, that we kill as many as we can. Other tribes will recognize the power of our firearms, and we'll be left in peace."

Richard was strongly inclined to agree with him. There

was no place for the chivalry of the Old World in the wilderness of North America.

But the colonel from Plymouth was shocked by the suggestion. "Surely you won't lower our standards to those of the barbarians we're going to meet in battle!" he declared.

"That's exactly what I propose," the New Netherland officer replied. "The Mohawk, the Seneca, and the other tribes of the Iroquois Confederation, the most powerful Indian force anywhere, make their homes in territory claimed by my colony. If we turn soft, no farm, no village, and no town in New Netherland will be safe. Savages understand only the language of brute force."

"You're right Major," Colonel Burrows said. "The survival of our civilization on the shores of the New World is at stake today, so we're obliged to be as ruthless as our foes. This is not the time to consider the moral niceties of the situation. I want every militiaman under your command to realize that once he opens fire, he's to keep firing as long as one enemy warrior is still alive. We expect no quarter—and we'll give none!"

Shortly after noon the grim-faced militiamen deployed, taking up the positions in the forest that they would occupy when the fighting started. A peaceful beach, curved like a half-moon, stood on the near shore, with sand dunes behind it and the forest moving down to the scrub vegetation behind the dunes, and here Colonel Burrows massed his greatest strength.

"The way I see it," he said, "the strip of beach promises the braves a safe landing, so they're almost certain to come ashore here. We'll prepare a welcome for them accordingly."

He gave the honor of first emplacement in the line of battle to his own troops from New Haven, and then Connecticut, explaining his reasoning to Richard. "They'll be defending their own soil," he said, "so they'll fight harder than anyone else."

The Massachusetts Bay and Plymouth regiments were assigned a position directly behind that of the men from Connecticut, with the New Netherland volunteers, the Rhode Islanders, and the restless Mohegan being held in reserve, deep in the forest to the rear. Ezekiel Clayton demanded the right to station his company of veteran Indian fighters in the vanguard, directly behind the crests of the dunes, and Colonel Burrows could not deny him the privilege. His men, being the most experienced, would be least likely to panic or confuse orders in the heat of combat.

Then, when the colonel was satisfied, he withdrew to his command post at the crest of the hill from which he could see the whole field spread out below, and calmly ate parched corn and sun-dried venison. Richard followed his example, and although the food was dry, he discovered he enjoyed the taste. Perhaps, after going without sleep all night, he was hungrier than he had realized.

"Now that everything else is settled," he said quietly, "perhaps you can devote a moment or two to deciding what part I'm to play in the battle."

Colonel Burrows blinked in surprise. "I've assumed you'd stay right here with me," he replied.

Richard shook his head. "I'm a civilian with no training in strategy or tactics," he said. "I'd be of little use to you here other than as a messenger."

His father-in-law hesitated and frowned.

"I know what you have in mind," Richard said. "You

don't want to run the risk of seeing me killed or badly wounded in the fight. It wouldn't be easy for you to face Eliza. But I have a responsibility to myself to do my fair share. Remember, sir, that I have a quarrel with the French, who are responsible for this invasion. They've tricked my wife and me into working for them as spies, so I have a private score to settle with them."

The colonel sighed. "I might have known you'd feel this way," he said. "What do you have in mind?"

"I want to join Ezekiel's company," Richard said.

"But they're in the most exposed, dangerous position of any troops in the entire force!"

"I assure you, sir, that I'm not being heroic. I just want to be stationed where I can do the greatest amount of good. I've fought Indians only once, when we helped the Conestoga in a battle with a superior force of Iroquois. I don't pretend to be an expert in the Indian style of warfare, just as I don't pretend to have a military mind. But—if I do say so—you don't have a marksman in your whole command who is my equal. Turn me loose to do what I do best, and I promise you I won't disgrace you—or Eliza."

It would be wrong to shelter him, Adam knew, and the request could not be denied. "Go ahead," he said with a sigh as he extended his hand. "I can't stop you. And I'm forced to admit I admire my daughter's choice!"

Richard grinned at him, then started down the slope toward the Pequot River, his rifle cradled in one arm. It was odd, he thought as he threaded his way past troops who were sprawled on the ground on the forest, that he felt nothing. He had volunteered for an exposed position in a battle for his wife's homeland—his adopted homeland now—yet he felt neither fear nor an anticipatory tingle of excitement. Perhaps the sunlight gleaming on the broad ribbon of water below him was lulling him into a false sense of security. Crouching low as he left the shelter of trees, he made his way to the crest of a high dune where Ezekiel Clayton was at ease. "I figured you could use some help," Richard said.

Ezekiel chuckled. "I made a private bet with myself that you'd show up here, Richard," he said. "I couldn't imagine you missing all the fun." His smile faded slowly. "I'm damned glad you're here. We'll need all the help we can get."

Richard carefully surveyed the scene. The dunes were about one hundred yards from the inner rim of the beach, and he estimated that if the enemy charged, he would be able to fire and reload his rifle at least twice, perhaps three times before being forced to use his pistol, so the odds were favorable.

Certainly the veterans who made up Ezekiel's command were unflustered by the imminence of a fight for their lives. Some ate parched corn and sun-dried venison, a few dozed, and several sat quietly, lost in thought as they contemplated the almost pastoral scene.

There was a stir in the forest underbrush, and scores of hard-eyed men watched Roaring Wolf emerge from cover and stroll forward nonchalantly, his quiver filled with arrows, his bow slung over one shoulder.

"Too many moons have passed since we have faced an enemy together," he told Richard as he dropped to his haunches, plucked a blade of grass, and chewed on it.

"Does the colonel know you've joined us?" Ezekiel wanted to know.

The Pequot shrugged. "Roaring Wolf does not serve the colonel."

Richard and Ezekiel exchanged a quick glance, and both appreciated Roaring Wolf's presence with their unit. Ro-an would interpret the enemy movements for Colonel Burrows, but they would also have an Indian who would know and understand any sudden shifts in the tactics of the Algonkian and Micmac.

The afternoon wore slowly, endlessly on. Occasionally the hum of a mosquito, the call of a gull, or the buzz of a yellow jacket sounded loudly in the silence, with a slight breeze ruffling the waters of the Pequot River as it flowed toward the Great Bay. The ships of the little flotilla anchored at the mouth of the river rocked gently, and the gunners on the decks sat beside their cannons and dozed.

Then, in late afternoon, the lookout on the tallest of the ships silently signaled the quarterdeck. A moment later a red signal flag fluttered as it was hoisted to the yardarm.

The enemy had been sighted, and the defenders came to life. The gunners on the ships struggled to their feet, and there was a rustling sound in the forest as the militia braced for action. Richard calmly checked his rifle and pistol, even though he knew they were loaded. The veterans yawned, then stretched out on their stomachs behind the crest of the high dune.

At last, after a wait that seemed interminable, the lead canoe of the enemy flotilla came into sight as it swept around a bend, the paddlers bending to their tasks in unison.

All at once the river was filled with war canoes, some carrying Algonkian warriors with purple paint on their faces and bodies, others filled with Micmac, who wore blue paint. One of the frail craft in particular caught Richard's attention. Although it was being rowed by Algonkian, its occupants were white men, clad in buckskins. Apparently these were the white leaders of the expedition who had been identified by a scout as English-speaking.

The river was at least a half-mile wide at its mouth, and seemed to be alive with the formidable force sent by the French to harass and conquer the English and Dutch colonies.

As the warriors became aware of the presence of the merchant ships at anchor, they faltered, then slowed dramatically. The white men conferred, an order was shouted, and the lead canoe gathered speed again, apparently intending to break through the cordon.

The roar of a cannon sent seagulls by the hundreds rising high into the air, their wings flapping frantically. One by one the other guns joined in the ragged salvo. The aim of the cannoneers was erratic, to say the last. Most shots fell short, with iron balls falling into the water at least fifty feet from the lead canoe, while several others sent their shots sailing high over the heads of the invaders.

Any New Model Navy officer who had witnessed the scene would have regarded the marksmanship of the gunners as deplorable, but, as Colonel Burrows had predicted, the steady cannon fire had the desired effect. The warriors knew they were the targets of these huge weapons that belched fire and smoke, and realizing there was no way they could retaliate, they turned their frail craft toward the beach that lay on the western shore.

The gunners obeyed the orders they had been given and kept up a steady fire, their aim not improving in spite of their efforts to sink the canoes.

The occupants of the canoes, much to their credit, retained their composure, and the craft hesitated offshore until several could approach the beach simultaneously. Then they were propelled toward the beach at top speed, the warriors leaping out into waist-high water and fitting arrows into their bows as they waded ashore in unison.

The well-disciplined men concealed behind the dune watched the enemy land and group together on the beach, none of them revealing his presence by firing prematurely. But Ezekiel Clayton twisted around, his gaze fastened on a clearing at the crest of the highest hill behind him. He was waiting for a direct order to repel the invaders.

The warriors were forming in ranks on the beach, with the buckskin-clad white men urging them to open their ranks and spread out.

All at once the enemy was in motion, and while canoe after canoe discharged its passengers, a force of at least two hundred sturdy Algonkian headed at a trot toward the sand dunes.

A red flag attached to a stick swept toward the ground at Colonel Burrows's command post. Ezekiel Clayton felt infinite relief, knowing he could not have restrained his men much longer. "Fire at will!" he called.

A number of his wilderness fighters were proud of their speed as well as their skill, but none could match the marksmanship of Richard Dunstable. His rifle spoke sharply at least a full second before any other gun was discharged, and an Algonkian whose feathered headgear marked him as a war chief pitched forward, then lay face down in the sand. Other Algonkian were dropping, too, as the marksmen took a deadly toll.

But the warriors soon demonstrated their courage, proving it was not accidental they were universally feared. The survivors of the first salvo held their places, other braves came forward to fill the gaps in the line, and then the entire body was on the move again, sending a hail of arrows sailing over the crest of the dune at their unseen enemies.

Reloading coolly but hastily, Richard got off a second shot, then a third. By now the warriors in the lead were close enough for him to see their faces clearly, and they were not panicking, even though their enemies were armed with firesticks that were taking a heavy toll.

Richard expected to be engaged in hand-to-hand combat at any moment, but suddenly the line halted, and then the wave receded, with the warriors still sending arrows over the top of the dune.

An arrow grazed Roaring Wolf's arm, then embedded itself in the hard-packed sand of the dune only inches from his face. He plucked it out, then studied the craftsmanship of its maker. "Algonkian are good fighters," he said in grudging admiration. "They fight like Pequot."

"They're hard to discourage," Ezekiel admitted. "If they hadn't retreated when they did, they'd have been right on top of us."

"It looks like we have a day's work ahead, that's sure," Richard said, aware that he had come to life when the battle had started. He watched the enemy regroup on the shore, exhorted by the white men in buckskins. Something vaguely familiar about one caught his attention, and he peered intently at the man, then was almost overcome by astonishment. He was staring at Bart Williams!

Now he understood the enormity of the crimes being perpetrated by the French. Young men who were courageous but whose intelligence was limited were being recruited from the English colonies by the French, to act as the invasion's leaders. In that way, should any one of them be captured, he would be regarded as a traitor to the English colonies. France would not become involved. The scheme was both audacious and clever.

"What's wrong?" Ezekiel asked him. "You look as if you've just seen a ghost."

"I believe I have," Richard muttered, and thought of Mollie Williams, who had sacrificed so much in order to bring her son to America, where he could have an opportunity to make something of himself.

"When they charge again," Ezekiel said, "pick off their white leaders. Pass the word."

Even as Richard repeated the order to the men beyond him, he knew he didn't have the heart to kill Mollie's son. The directive that Ezekiel had just given was sound, to be sure, for without the guidance of the whites who commanded them, the Algonkian and Micmac well might falter. But knowing Bart's background made a difference. The lad was a confused Cavalier, not a traitor, and the real villains were men like Cardinal Mazarin, the Earl of Newcastle, and Laroche, who took advantage of the Bart Williamses of the world for their own purposes. Hating France with all his being, Richard braced for the next assault.

The purple-smeared Algonkian advanced again over a broader front, and this time they held their fire.

Roaring Wolf recognized their tactics at once. "Algonkian will wait until they see us before they shoot arrow," he said.

The maneuver made no difference to Ezekiel. "This time," he said, "we'll wait until we can count their teeth before we open fire."

Three white men were accompanying the advancing

braves, and Richard felt a wave of nausea sweep over him when he recognized Bart Williams as one of them. He wanted to shout a warning to the stupid lad, but instead he peered down the length of his rifle. His heart hammered, and cold sweat beaded on his forehead, which he wiped angrily with his sleeve.

The onrushing Algonkian were no more than a stone's throw away when Ezekiel called again, "Fire at will!"

Richard took aim at Bart, then suddenly changed his target, instead bringing down the warrior beside him.

Ezekiel Clayton didn't know Bart, was unfamiliar with his story, and felt no sympathy for him. Taking careful aim, he squeezed the trigger of his musket.

Bart Williams halted, a look of utter astonishment on his face as he pitched forward on the side of the dune, his blood turning the yellow sand a bright shade of crimson.

"Now all enemies come," Roaring Wolf said.

Again he proved accurate. The Micmac formed a blue wave behind the wall of purple as the invaders hurled their entire force at the one point.

The woods came to life behind Ezekiel Clayton's New Haven and Connecticut companies as the Massachusetts Bay and Plymouth volunteers charged to the aid of their comrades who held such an exposed position.

Richard reloaded and fired, reloaded and fired, his every movement faultless. Had he stopped to think of the overwhelming odds against him, he would have been numbed by fear, but the mere act of shooting down one warrior after another was sufficient to keep him rooted to the spot.

Recklessly ignoring their own casualties, the braves continued to advance. Ezekiel knew his exposed position on the dune soon would be overwhelmed. "Retreat!" he called above the din of battle. "Draw back to the main line in the forest!"

Richard brought down a warrior, then reloaded and fired again at another who was in the act of throwing a tomahawk at him. The sharp blade missed him by a hair's breadth, then buried itself in the sand behind him.

The senseless death of Bart Williams so infuriated him that he gave no thought to his own safety. These savages had been sent by France to crush and humiliate the English and Dutch colonies, and he had no intention of retreating. "I'm taking my stand right where I am," he declared, making himself heard above the blood-curdling whoops of the advancing Indians.

Roaring Wolf heard him and quietly stood beside him. So did three other members of Ezekiel's band, all of them firing and reloading as rapidly as they could.

Ezekiel Clayton and the bulk of his company reached the safety of the concealed front ranks in the forest before they realized that five of their band had refused to budge, becoming an island in a sea of surging Algonkian and Micmac. Before Ezekiel could react, however, a company of Massachusetts Bay militiamen raced forward into the open, led by Dempster Chaney, who knew only that the man responsible for his happiness was in grave danger.

Richard had no chance to reload his rifle now. He fired both barrels of his pistol point-blank at two warriors, then began to hurl his throwing knives at the foes who surrounded him, his companions using their muskets as clubs to ward off the enemy.

Ezekiel Clayton could not allow strangers from Mas-

Richard had no chance to reload his rifle now. He fired both barrels of his pistol point-blank at two warriors, then began to hurl his throwing knives at the foes who surrounded him, his companions using their muskets as clubs to ward off the enemy.

sachusetts Bay to rescue members of his own unit. "Forward again, lads!" he called.

Colonel Burrows was in despair as he watched the unorthodox scene unfolding below him. Ezekiel had been right to order his band to retreat, and the Algonkian and Micmac would have been decimated had they followed into the heart of the defenders' formation. But his stubborn son-in-law had refused to move; a handful of others had followed his example, and the situation was rapidly degenerating into chaos.

His alarm increased as he watched Lieutenant Chaney's men engage in hand-to-hand combat with the foe, followed quickly by Ezekiel Clayton's veterans. He knew he was losing control of the situation, his superior arms nullified by the inability to fire into the midst of the swirling, charging masses of men engaged in hand-to-hand combat. He had to act quickly to restore some semblance of order—or at least contribute to the mass pandemonium.

Turning to the eager Ro-an who stood beside him, he said, "Go! Lead your warriors into battle!"

The war chief needed no urging, and within moments the Mohegan, anxious to prove their valor, hurled themselves into the fray.

Richard knew that his personal situation had eased a trifle. Braves painted purple and braves painted blue were falling through no effort of his own. Roaring Wolf stood behind him, wielding a tomahawk with deadly efficiency, and as Richard bent to pick up his rifle, he found himself face to face with Dempster Chaney.

"At last! I finally have a chance to help you," Dempster shouted above the din.

The bulk of the New Haven, Plymouth, Connecticut, and Massachusetts Bay militia watched the struggle helplessly, unable to intervene, until several young men conceived the same idea at the same moment. Breaking ranks, they raced into the open to join the free-for-all. Scores of their comrades followed them, and Colonel Burrows laughed aloud. The techniques of Indian-fighting he would describe to his colleagues in his report on the fray would make mighty strange reading.

Now it was the turn of the Rhode Islanders and the British volunteers from New Netherland to surge forward, and the fight spread quickly over the dunes and onto the beach. Refusing to be deprived of their share of glory, these militiamen eagerly brought down every foe they could find.

Richard felt no concern for his own safety. Every time he clubbed down a warrior wearing purple or blue paint, he was ridding himself of frustration. Every enemy was a representative of France, which had not only maneuvered him and Eliza into bondage, but had caused the needless death of Mollie Williams's son. He had no idea that bodies were piled around him, that the Indians who saw him in action would write songs about his ferocity and prowess. He knew only that he was obtaining vengeance, and the taste in his mouth was sweet, even though there was a hard core of bitterness within him that would not dissolve.

The surviving Algonkian and Micmac were bewildered by the turn of events. Never before had they engaged in combat with a foe so eager to meet its enemies face to face, and as the realization dawned on the braves from the north that they were losing the battle, they rapidly lost their appetite for combat. Their war chiefs had lost none of their skill, and somehow they managed to form the remnants of their battered force into cohesive units that gradually retreated toward the water.

But the wild white man—whose refusal to retreat had been responsible for the turn of battle—would not allow the enemy to escape without further punishment. Richard had the opportunity to reload his rifle at last, and calling, "After them, lads!" he fired, reloaded, and started down the dune in pursuit.

Hundreds followed him, firing into the ranks of the desperate savages who were trying to reach their canoes. The Mohegan ran amok, scalping indiscriminately, and Colonel Burrows knew he would never be able to write a report that would describe the scene accurately. When the canoes of the invaders were launched, and weary Algonkian and Micmac bent low over their paddles straining every muscle in their efforts to leave the site of their defeat, they left behind more than half of their total force.

Colonel Burrows had ordered that no quarter be shown the enemy, and none was given. The Mohegan reaped a rich harvest of scalps, a reward sufficient to cause them to sign a treaty of alliance with the men of New Haven and Connecticut. And it was no accident that the Micmac and Algonkian never again waged war so far from their homes. The white men whom they had faced in battle were not only armed with magical firesticks, but they fought with a deadly ferocity that put even the dreaded Seneca and Huron to shame.

Feeling faintly cheated now that the battle had ended so abruptly, Richard returned to the spot where he had taken his stand and methodically began to collect his throwing knives. He was still engaged in the grim task when Ezekiel Clayton found him.

"I wonder if Eliza knows she has married a madman," he said as he pumped his friend's hand. "I've heard of people going berserk in battle, but watching you in action is the first time I've ever seen such madness."

Richard thought he was exaggerating. "All I knew," he said, "was that I'd been insulted enough by the French, and I was damned if I was going to retreat." He hailed Roaring Wolf and they clasped forearms. "Well done, my friend!"

The Pequot looked at him proudly. "I knew from the day you saved my life that you are the greatest of warriors. The sons of our sons will sing your praises!" He hurried off to collect still more scalps.

Richard went in search of the Massachusetts Bay regiment, and finally located Dempster Chaney. "I'm much obliged to you for your help," he told the young farmer. "It didn't occur to me at the time that I was taking such risks."

"What set you off?" Dempster wanted to know. "You looked and acted demented."

Richard told him about the death of Bart Williams.

"So that's the game that France plays. Poor Mollie."

"I'll have to write her a letter, and it's a task I dread," Richard said. "I'll have to be truthful with her, but I'll omit mentioning that I saw a Mohegan scalp him."

"Yes, there's no reason to cause her needless pain. You're going to settle in New Haven, Richard?"

"I imagine I will, although I've had no chance to think about the future. I have a wife now, and I have no intention of living on the charity of my father-in-law."

"We'll meet again, I'm sure of it," Dempster said. "I don't know when or where it will happen, but our paths are sure to cross."

"Until they do, give my love to Robbin, and tell her that Mimi thinks of her often, too."

As they parted company, Dempster wondered how it had happened that Richard had married someone other than Mimi, who was now married herself. But he was too polite to ask, which was just as well, because Richard could not have offered him a logical explanation. It was enough that he had lost his heart elsewhere, as had Mimi.

At Colonel Burrows's direction, the dead were buried. The casualties suffered by the defenders were surprisingly light; most injuries were incurred during the hand-to-hand melee, so their wounds were superficial.

Hunting parties were sent into the wilderness, and they returned with enough game for a feast. Campfires were lighted, and that night the victorious celebrated. Colonel Burrows set an example for intercolonial cooperation by inviting all of the officers to dine with him, and making a point of asking Ro-an and the subordinate Mohegan war chiefs to be present, too. So the militia leaders of New Haven, Connecticut, New Netherland, Massachusetts Bay, Plymouth, and Rhode Island dined together, and as they talked they were surprised to find they held similar aspirations and goals. More alike than they had realized, they learned that all were devoted to the principle of independence and were determined to lead their own lives without interference from their European governments. They were united, too, by their fervent desire to prevent France from gaining control of their rapidly expanding towns and farms.

A smiling Colonel Burrows refused to reveal where he obtained the wine he served that night. Richard assumed he had stored quantities of it on board the merchant ships that had played such a decisive role at the onset of the battle. But he knew his father-in-law was enjoying the bewilderment of his pleased guests, so he made no mention of his guess.

"I offer a toast to every man who fought today," Colonel Burrows said, raising his cup at the end of the meal. "The Algonkian and the Micmac—and, above all, their French masters—did us a great favor. No one colony could have repelled them alone. But we have learned from our victory that by standing together, shoulder to shoulder, we are invincible. We and our brave allies, the Mohegan, have struck a blow for liberty that will long be remembered."

"To liberty!" the colonel from Massachusetts Bay cried, and the officers rose spontaneously to their feet, then drained their cups in silence.

"It is appropriate on an occasion such as this," Colonel Burrows declared, "to mention those who distinguished themselves in battle. But the list is too long, so I shall save those mentions for the reports I shall send to the governors of the individual colonies. I cannot resist, however, calling your attention to one fact for which I am grateful. It is fortunate that my son-in-law is a civilian and holds no commission in the militia of New Haven or of any other colony. His civilian status saves me from the need to solve an impossible dilemma, whether to order him tried by a court-martial for refusing to obey orders, or whether to promote him for gallantry in action beyond the call of duty."

A roar of laughter erupted, and some of the officers cheered.

Richard had the grace to flush, and felt he had to respond. "I publicly apologize to Captain Clayton for my refusal to obey his orders to retreat," he said, "but my hatred for the French and my contempt for their methods interfered with my better judgment. As I intend to apply for a militia commission in the immediate future, I promise my conduct will be more orthodox hereafter."

Again he was cheered, and Dempster Chaney embarrassed him by proposing a toast to "the man who wouldn't retreat."

The celebration ended on that convivial note, and the officers went off to their own camp area. Early the following morning the army disbanded, with the various units heading for their homes. The troops from New Haven marched with the New Netherland militia and were accompanied by the Mohegan, who were proud of the role they had played.

At Colonel Burrows's request, Richard rode with him at the head of the column, and as they made their way down the trail that cut through the wilderness near the shoreline, the older man asked, "What are your plans for the future?"

"I'm not sure," Richard replied. "I'll want to discuss the matter with Eliza, although she knows no more than I about how much time we'll be obliged to spend on missions for the French. I just wish we could tell them to go to the devil."

"The connection you've established with them is too valuable for that," the colonel told him. "You can be certain that the failure of the Algonkian and Micmac to crush us will cause Cardinal Mazarin to redouble his efforts to gain control of the English colonies. I can appreciate the satisfaction you'd enjoy by thumbing your nose at them, and I know you want to protect Eliza, but you can't afford to neglect an opportunity to learn from the inside what France may be plotting against us."

"I don't have the temperament for espionage work, but I'll do my duty," Richard said.

"The very fact that you and Eliza are unlikely double agents increases your value to us. That's why I prefer not to give you a commission in the militia at present. You'd place yourself in even greater jeopardy if the French learned that you were reporting their activities to me."

"I suppose you're right, sir," Richard conceded grudgingly. "I reckon I'll need time to adjust to the role that I'm going to play. Meantime I'm thinking of establishing a land claim on some wilderness property and developing it."

"Have you had any experience in farming?"

"Not really, but—"

"Neither has Eliza, and in my opinion neither of you is suited to farm life. Tom Clayton and I will be delighted if you'll accept a post in our business."

"I must decline, sir, with thanks."

It was not difficult for Adam Burrows to read his mind. "You're rejecting my offer," he said, "because you think I'd be creating a place for my daughter's husband."

Richard nodded.

"I wonder what you'd say," the colonel declared, his voice quiet, "if you knew that Tom and I discussed ways of tempting you to join us long before I had any idea that you and Eliza were interested in each other."

Richard was startled, and could only stare at him.

"I'll grant you know nothing about ships and nothing about trade," Adam said, "but you could learn. Look at the problems from our point of view. Tom and I are growing older, and there's no one but young Ezekiel to succeed us. Meanwhile the colonies are growing so rapidly that the volume of our business has more than doubled in the past two years. And if the present pace of immigration is maintained, which is likely as people in England and Scotland become disillusioned by the power struggle between the Puritans and Cavaliers, it will multiply again in the years ahead. We need someone who knows men and enjoys their respect. You'll become famous as the hero of yesterday's battle. So all I can tell you is that even if you weren't my son-in-law, I'd ask you to name your own price."

Richard studied him closely. "You mean what you say, sir? You aren't just making work for me because I'm Eliza's husband?"

"I'd be doing her a disservice and insulting you, as well," Adam said firmly.

Richard's objections crumbled. "In that case, sir, you have a new hired hand. As to wages, pay me what you think I'm worth."

They clasped hands, and the issue was settled.

The column spent two days on the wilderness trail, the Mohegan warriors taking their leave and heading inland at noon of the second day after exchanging vows of friendship with the colonel.

The merchant ships had already brought the news of the victory to New Haven, and the town prepared a celebration worthy of heroes for the conquerors of the Algonkian and Micmac. Huge bonfires lighted the Green, where tables were spread with food contributed by the grateful citizens, and a fife-and-drum corps welcomed the militiamen. Virtually the entire population of the town and surrounding countryside was on hand to cheer the troops, who straightened their ranks and marched proudly in time to the beating drums.

Colonel Burrows doffed his hat repeatedly as people

raised their voices to acclaim him and his men. Richard felt an unfamiliar thrill of excitement as he searched the crowds that lined the cobbled street, looking for the face of the woman he loved. He had to admit that Eliza had been absent from his mind for days, but now the realization flooded him that she was actually his wife.

At last he saw her, standing arm in arm with Mimi Clayton at the edge of the Green, the light of the huge fires playing on their hair. Others were cheering lustily, but Eliza stood silently, one hand at her throat, her glowing eyes fixed on the hero who was her husband.

Colonel Burrows halted the column, and it seemed like an eternity before he gave the order to break ranks. Richard leaped to the ground and embraced Eliza, only vaguely aware that Ezekiel had brushed past him and lifted Mimi off her feet. Eliza showed no reluctance to return her husband's embrace, and their kiss was so prolonged that the crowd cheered.

Eliza caught her breath when he released her. "I'm told, sir, that you did your best to be killed in action!"

"Something like that," Richard said, realizing that the story of the anger he had felt when he had seen Bart Williams leading the enemy savages would have to await a more appropriate time.

"I don't know whether to be proud of you or whether to scold you," she said. "But I'm so relieved to find you well that I'll do neither."

Ezekiel Clayton turned to them, his arm encircling Mimi's slender waist. "A reception like this," he said with a grin, "makes fighting a battle worth the while."

Only when well-wishers engulfed Richard, with the men anxious to shake his hand and women congratulating him, did he realize how renowned he had become. He and Eliza were separated repeatedly by the crowd, and he was offered more food than he could eat, more ale and mead and rum than he could drink.

He shared Colonel Burrows's concern for the reception being accorded the New Netherland militiamen, and was relieved when he discovered they were being inundated by the hospitable people of New Haven, too. The rivalry between colonies was forgotten, and all who had fought and won the battles were being honored equally.

Eliza came to Richard's rescue when he was surrounded by an admiring throng of young women. "Pardon me, ladies," she said sweetly, her hold on his arm firm, "but I've come to claim my husband."

"It strikes me I've done my duty now," he told her as she led him away. "How much longer are we obliged to attend this reception?"

"That decision is entirely yours, sir," she replied demurely.

"In that case," Richard said, sweeping her off her feet and carrying her to the waiting Prince Henry, "we're leaving now." Her happy sigh as she curled her arms around his neck indicated that she did not object.

The Burrows house was deserted when they arrived there, and together they removed Prince Henry's saddle, then fed and watered the stallion.

"It seems as if we've been married forever," Richard said as they started toward the house.

"No, not quite that long. I've waited patiently for my honeymoon, Master Dunstable."

"Your wait has ended, Mistress Dunstable," he replied huskily.

Their lovemaking followed their usual pattern, at first swift and savage, then prolonged and tender. Not until they were satiated did they talk.

"Your father has persuaded me to work for him," Richard said. "He swears he would have offered me the post even if we weren't married."

"He means it, and with good cause," Eliza replied. "You'll receive offers from every man of business in the colony after your exploits in battle. But I'm glad you'll work for Papa. I'll enjoy knowing that our children will inherit a thriving business one day." She paused, then told him news of her own. "I wasn't inactive while you were off at war. I've found us a house of our own. It's just right for our needs, and we can have it for five hundred sovereigns. I'll use my dowry to pay for it."

"You'll do no such thing. I can scrape together five hundred sovereigns, although we'll be short of cash for a time."

Eliza started to protest, then thought better of it. Her husband's homecoming was too important to be spoiled by a marital disagreement.

The next morning they went together to see the house, and Richard was well pleased with the property. The rambling structure was solidly built of gray fieldstone and was situated on extensive land only a short distance from Colonel Burrows's home. It was modest, as were the furnishings that came with it, compared to the estate that Richard had been forced to abandon in Lincolnshire, but he truly was sinking his roots here. He and his wife had acquired a vested interest in the New World.

That same day, while Eliza supervised the move of their personal belongings, even riding Prince Henry to his new stable behind the main dwelling, Richard went to work. He had long meetings with Colonel Burrows and the elder Clayton, then he studied the all-important ledgers, and finally Ezekiel took him on a tour of the company's docks and warehouses.

"My head is spinning, Ezekiel," he said at last. "But the principles of the operation are simple enough. We buy as cheaply as possible, we sell for as much as the market will bear, and we hold merchandise in storage for as short a time as possible."

That evening, the first in his new home, Eliza met him at the front door with a kiss. His wages were sufficiently generous for her to hire a cook and a serving maid, but she prepared their first supper herself. Although the menu was simple, he found the meal delicious.

They quickly established routines, and a few evenings later they invited Eliza's father and the Claytons to supper.

Mimi Clayton offered a toast that fit the occasion. Lifting her glass, she said, "May all of us flourish in the New World!"

Soon after they were seated at the table, there was a pounding at the front door, and Richard excused himself to answer the summons.

A stranger stood on the threshold, the dust of the road thick on his boots and cloak. "Be this the home of Sir Richard Dunstable?" he demanded.

Richard nodded, his heart sinking. Only the French called him Sir Richard. "I am he."

The man thrust a square of parchment into his hands, then returned to his waiting mount and clattered off into the night.

The communication was addressed to "Sir Richard and

Lady Dunstable," and Richard broke the seal with reluctance. The message itself was succinct: *"Meet me at your earliest convenience on a matter of urgent importance. L."*

The hope that he and Eliza could lead normal, peaceful lives vanished abruptly. They were being summoned to duty by their French masters.

Putting the communication into an inner pocket, Richard returned to the supper table, where he tried to carry off the pretense that nothing out of the normal had occurred. Eliza knew from his expression that he was disturbed, but she asked no questions. Her guess was confirmed when the Claytons prepared to leave after the meal, and Richard asked his father-in-law, in an undertone, to stay.

They saw the Claytons off, and then Richard handed Eliza the square of parchment. "The life we hoped to lead here is too good to be true," he said. "Reality has caught up with us."

Eliza read the brief message in silence, then gave the parchment to her father.

"The 'L' stands for Laroche, no doubt," Colonel Burrows said.

"So I assume, Colonel."

"I must hand it to the French. They're wasting no time after the defeat of the Algonkian and Micmac. Very well, you'll sail to New Amsterdam on one of our coastal brigs that leaves in the morning. This journey will give you the chance to become acquainted with our customers in New Netherland."

"I'll go, but I'm sailing alone," Richard replied. "I refuse to allow Eliza to become embroiled."

Eliza squared her shoulders. "This order was addressed to me as well as to you. I couldn't do battle against the forces sent by France to subdue us, but I can fight them in my own way. And I shall."

"I'll find a valid excuse to leave you here," Richard said.

Her blonde hair danced as she slowly shook her head. "We're engaged in a war of wits with the French, and the whole New World is the prize that will be taken by the winner. I insist upon my right to insure that the just are victorious."

Her father smiled in approval. "I knew you'd feel that way," he said.

Richard shrugged bleakly. He had done his best to prevent Eliza's involvement, but had failed, and now she would be obliged to share whatever risks he faced. "So be it," he said.

THE AMERICAN PATRIOT SERIES
Volume II
THE GREAT DECEPTION

The year is 1650. Peter Stuyvesant and the Dutch colonists in the New World are now threatened by the English settlers, who perceive America as a permanent home in which to live, worship, and grow toward a more secure future.

War is imminent as the English colonials expand toward Dutch settlements, and as Stuyvesant provides the Indians with firearms and the inspiration to use them.

Richard and Eliza Dunstable, forced to act as espionage agents for France, are now involved with the wily Peter Stuyvesant. They travel to many parts of the New World, gathering information for the Dutch, French, and British colonials with whom their sincere loyalties rest.

As they practice the deeply felt belief that they represent a "new breed"—free thinking, free acting, responsible only to their vast and promising new land—Richard and Eliza face danger, intrigue, and the possibility their marriage will not survive the challenges they have undertaken in service of their great new land . . .

THE GREAT DECEPTION

COMING SOON FROM BALLANTINE BOOKS

IN COUNTRY

THE ILLUSTRATED ENCYCLOPEDIA OF THE VIETNAM WAR

EDITED BY
JAMES S. OLSON

METRO BOOKS
NEW YORK

Metro Books
122 Fifth Avenue
New York, NY 10011

ISBN-13: 978-1-4351-1184-4

Printed and bound in China

10 9 8 7 6 5 4 3 2 1

Jacket photographs:

Front (top row left to right): © Bettmann/Corbis;
SSgt Batchelor/National Archives; © Jack Kightlinger/Corbis;
PH2 Stanley C. Wycoff/National Archives; © Wally McNamee/Corbis

Front (bottom): courtesy of D.M. Giangreco

Back (top row left to right): National Archives; PFC Freddie M.
Duncan/National Archives; SSgt Alfred Batungbacal/National Archives;
© Barry Sweet/Landov; SP6 Samuel L. Swain/National Archives

Back (bottom): Cpl M.J. Coates/National Archives

Background map courtesy of John Rossie/www.vietvet.org

Front flap from the Collection of Bradford Edwards,
photographed by Hans Kemp, © 2007 Asia Ink
and Visionary World

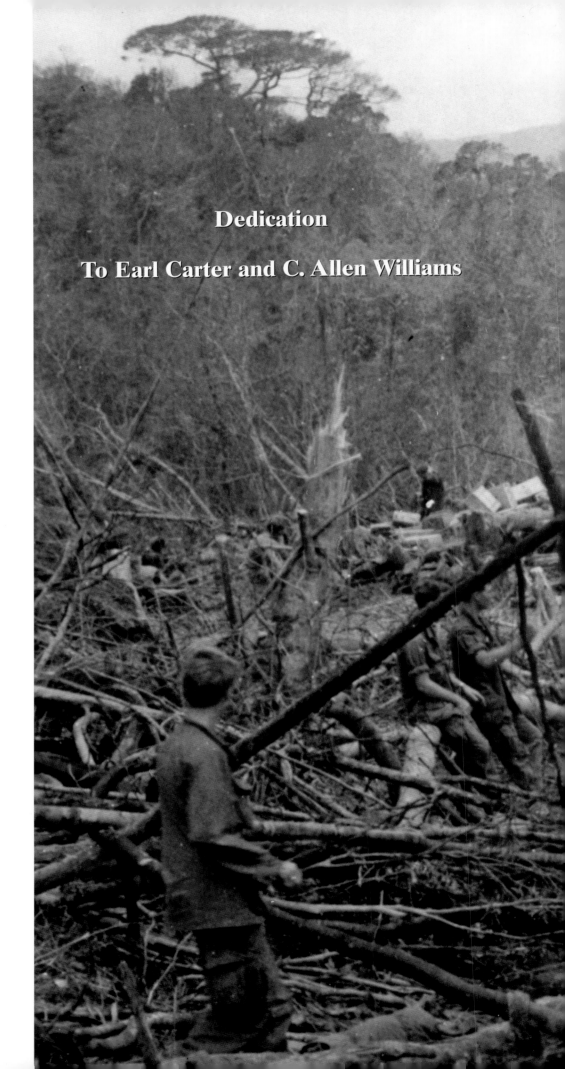

Dedication

To Earl Carter and C. Allen Williams

Contents

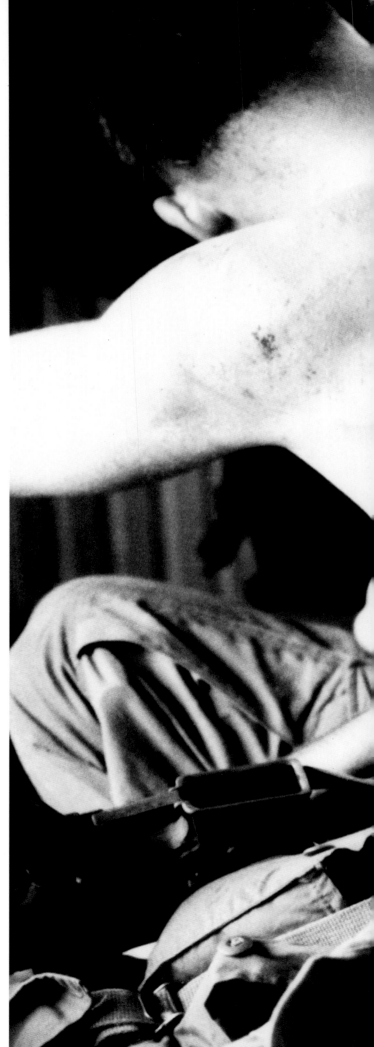

The last U.S. combat troops left Indochina in 1972, but the Vietnam War still pulsates in the American memory. The successful capitalist revolution—finally embraced by the ruling Communists—sweeping Vietnam in 2008 was termed a veritable "economic miracle," with Vietnam becoming one of Asia's fastest-developing countries after two decades of Communist oppression. Americans debate whether the war in Iraq will become "another Vietnam." Historians will, no doubt, continue to debate the origins of the conflict and, with 20/20 hindsight, suggest what might have been. No one, however, will question that the Vietnam War was a seminal event in modern American history— a watershed against which the past will be measured for generations. In a sense, the war ended "the American century," that period of unrivaled power and virtue the United States enjoyed between 1918 and 1965. During the Vietnam years, liberalism gave way to cynicism, internationalism to isolationism, and naïve innocence to cold reality. Quite simply,

America was a different place in 1975 than it had been in 1964; life would never be the same again, and the Vietnam War was responsible.

In Country: The Illustrated Encyclopedia of the Vietnam War is designed to provide a ready reference tool for students and scholars. Its major focus is the thirty years between 1945 and 1975, although critically important individuals and events from earlier years are also discussed. *In Country* provides brief descriptive essays on most of the people, legislation, military operations, and controversies important to American participation in the Vietnam War. References at the end of each entry provide sources of additional information for those wishing to pursue the subject further. Entries are arranged in alphabetical order. Cross-references within the text of most entries, designated by an asterisk, will help the reader find related items. Appendixes provide a description of the minority groups of South Vietnam in 1970, the population of South Vietnam in 1971, a glossary of acronyms and slang expressions, a selected bibliography of the Vietnam War, and a chronology of the Vietnam War.

I wish to express my thanks to the scholars who contributed essays to *In Country*. Their initials appear at the end of the entries they wrote. All unsigned entries were written by me. I would also like to thank the librarians who assisted me in locating hard-to-find material. I am especially grateful to J. Larry Murdock, Ann Holder, Paul Culp, and Bill Bailey, all of the Newton Gresham Library at Sam Houston State University. Ruth O'Brien, *In Country's* editor, has been patient, persistent, and endowed with good judgment in seeing the book to completion.

Kevin Ullrich and Andrei Koribanics have designed a beautiful book. Finally, I am indebted to my wife, Judy, for her patience in tolerating what has seemed an endless task in producing this volume.

—James S. Olson

Staff Sergeant Clarence Neitzel, squad leader of Company D, 2d Battalion, 173d Airborne Brigade, prepares for the final assault on Hill 875, 15 miles southwest of Dak To, on November 22, 1967.

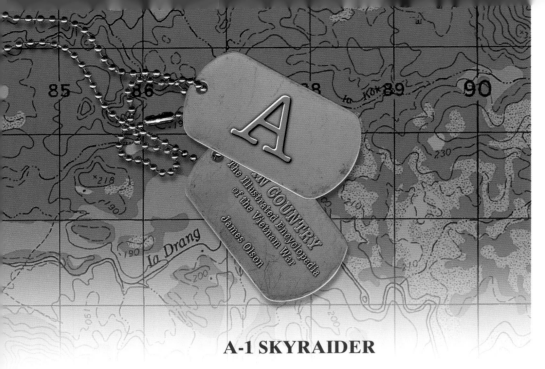

the A-1 could remain airborne over targets much longer than jet aircraft, and it was also highly accurate delivering its bomb loads. During the Korean War the A-1 had been widely used on naval aircraft carriers, but by the early 1960s the Navy was replacing the A-1 with the A-4 Skyhawk* jet. The A-1s were transferred to the United States Air Force* and the Vietnamese Air Force,* where they were first employed in Operation Farmgate.* By 1968 the A-1 Skyraider was the backbone of close air support operations in the Vietnamese Air Force.

Source: Wayne Mutza, *The A-1 Skyraider in Vietnam: The Spad's Last War*, 2003.

A-1 SKYRAIDER

During the Vietnam War fighter-bombers (*see* Fighters) played a critical role in providing close air support to American and South Vietnamese soldiers. The propeller-driven A-1 Skyraider was frequently the battlefield choice of commanders who needed fighter-bomber support. Nicknamed the Spad, the A-1 had been operational since 1946, and could deliver up to 8,000 pounds of explosives, including napalm,* phosphorus, and cluster bomb* units. The A-1 could fire rockets and carry four 20mm cannons that together could fire more than 2,000 rounds a minute. Although its maximum airspeed was only 318 miles an hour,

A-4 SKYHAWK

The A-4 Skyhawk flew more missions in Vietnam than any other naval aircraft. Developed in the mid-1950s by Douglas, the A-4 could carry a maximum payload of 8,200 pounds and a functional payload of 5,000 pounds. Its maximum airspeed was 685 miles an hour and it had a range of 700 miles. Its built-in armament consisted of two 20mm cannons. The A-4 Skyhawk was propelled by either a 7,700-pound-thrust Wright J65 engine or an 8,500-pound-thrust Pratt and Whitney J52 engine.

Source: Jim Winchester, *Douglas A-4 Skyhawk: Attack and Close-Support Fighter Bomber*, 2005.

Right: Two U.S. Air Force A-1 Skyraiders—one named the *Nancy Lou*—head out on a 1970 mission with a mixed bomb load. As well as being nicknamed the Spad, the trusty Skyraiders also had such names as Destroyer, Hobo, Old Faithful, Fat Face, Flying Dumptruck, and Crazy Water Buffalo.

A-6 INTRUDER

Manufactured by Grumman, the A-6 Intruder was equipped with two 9,300-pound Pratt and Whitney J52 turbojets and had a maximum airspeed of 640 miles an hour. The A-6 could carry up to 15,000 pounds of ordnance and had a range of 1,077 miles (3,100 miles when equipped with external fuel tanks). Its advanced navigation system, known as DIANE (Digital Integrated Attack Navigation Equipment), had a terrain avoidance radar capability and allowed the A-6 to fly long distances at low altitudes, regardless of weather conditions. Its forte was pinpoint attacks at night or in poor weather conditions.

Source: Dennis R. Jenkins, *Grumman A-6 Intruder*, 2002.

Left: Three A-4E Skyhawks and one A-6A Intruder fly in formation over Vietnam. Skyhawks were favored for maneuverability and payload. Intruders routinely carried twenty-eight 500-pound bombs.

Below: An A-6 Intruder preparing to launch from the USS *Forrestal* around 1968. The A-6 Intruder played an important role in the ability of the U.S. military to efficiently deliver enormous amounts of firepower throughout Indochina.

Right: During the Vietnam War, the U.S. Navy deployed a number of aircraft carriers to the South China Sea. From carriers like the USS *Constellation*, where an A-7 Corsair is coming in for a landing on April 26, 1972, U.S. naval aircraft provided tactical air support for American, South Vietnamese, and South Korean soldiers. The carrier-based aircraft also participated widely in strategic air operations.

Below: The A-7 Corsair, a naval jet aircraft powered by a 13,500-pound-thrust TF30 turbofan, first deployed to Vietnam in December 1967 aboard the carrier USS *Ranger.* The A-7 Corsair packed enormous punch, with an ordnance load of up to 15,000 pounds, more than the World War II-era B-29. The A-7 Corsair had a maximum speed of 679 miles an hour and a maximum range of 700 miles.

A-7 CORSAIR II

The Vought A-7 Corsair II was first deployed to Vietnam aboard the USS *Ranger* in December 1967. It was powered by an 11,350-pound-thrust TF30 turbofan and had a maximum airspeed of 679 miles an hour, a range of 700 miles, and an ordnance capacity of 20,000 pounds. A later version, the A-7E, which entered combat in 1970, had a 15,000-pound-thrust Allison TF41 engine and a 20mm M61 Vulcan rapid-fire cannon. Its weapons-delivery system was highly accurate, and the A-7 was especially useful in attacking the Ho Chi Minh Trail* and making night assaults on Hanoi* and Haiphong.

Source: Peter Mersky, *U.S. Navy A-7 Corsair II: Units of the Vietnam War,* 2004.

ABRAMS, CREIGHTON

Creighton Abrams was born in Springfield, Massachusetts, on September 16, 1914. Described as "tough," "crusty," and "gruff," Abrams graduated from West Point in 1936. Considered one of the great combat officers of World War

II, Abrams served in General George Patton's Third Army and took part in the relief of Bastogne. Upon assuming command of Military Assistance Command, Vietnam* (MACV) in July 1968, after General William Westmoreland* left, Abrams shifted American tactics in the direction of small-unit operations in an attempt to keep pressure on Vietcong* and North Vietnamese Army* (NVA) forces while avoiding the heavy American casualties that often resulted from Westmoreland's large-scale "search and destroy"* sweeps. Also, in the latter half of 1968, Abrams launched the Accelerated Pacification Campaign,* in which the United States and South Vietnam committed a major share of their military resources to controlling the Vietnamese countryside. The campaign enjoyed only short-term success.

As MACV commander, Abrams was responsible for implementing the Vietnamization* program, which had originated in the Johnson* administration and which was announced with much public fanfare in 1969 by President Richard M. Nixon.* Abrams viewed the Cambodian incursion of 1970 (*see* Operation Binh Tay) as a means of keeping Vietcong and NVA pressure off the gradual American withdrawal mandated by Vietnamization. Although Abrams privately doubted the ability of the South Vietnamese Army to replace U.S. troops effectively, he was successful in carrying out the American troop withdrawal called for by Vietnamization. During his tenure as MACV commander, Abrams saw American strength reach its peak (543,482) in April 1969, and also witnessed the departure of the last United States Army* combat unit (3d Battalion, 21st Infantry) from Vietnam in August 1972. Abrams was promoted to chief of staff of the U.S. Army in 1972, a post he held until his death on September 4, 1974. SAK

Sources: Mackubin Thomas Owens, *Thunderbolt: General Creighton Abrams and the Army of His Time*, 1998; *New York Times*, September 5, 1974.

Left: The Commanding General of the American effort in Vietnam, Creighton Abrams, congratulates the 2d Ranger Battalion, 21st Infantry, of the South Vietnamese army on receiving the Second Oak Leaf Cluster to their Presidential Unit Citation in 1968. Abrams was charged with shifting more of the fighting from American units to South Vietnamese ones.

AC-47 GUNSHIP

Technological developments have always been among the results of war, and the era of American involvement in Vietnam was no exception. One of the most exciting was the development of fixed-wing gunships.* The theory behind the development of gunships was simple; it involved the placement of rapid-fire weapons on one side of a large aircraft to fire at ground targets as the firing platform circled an area at a constant altitude and speed. The development of this idea in Vietnam stemmed directly from unique battlefield situations in the theater of operations and eventually evolved into an effective and impressive weapons system.

The selection of the C-47 as the first gunship during the early years of the Vietnam War married the new 7.62mm minigun to one of the Air Force's oldest operational aircraft. The first flight of a Douglas DC-3, the civilian version of the C-47, took place on December 18, 1935, but the aircraft earned a reputation as a versatile performer during World War II when the armed forces had nearly 10,000 in service. Although most of the C-47s had been retired by

1960, Air Force personnel realized that it was the ideal platform for the mounting of weapons with which to attack ground targets.

The formation of the first AC-47 gunship squadron began in May 1965 when Headquarters, United States Air Force* (USAF) directed the Air Force Logistics Command (AFLC) to prepare a feasibility study on the installation of 7.62mm guns on twenty C-47s. This study demonstrated the practicality of such a modification, and during the summer of 1965 the Warner-Robins Air Materiel Area, Robins Air Force Base (AFB), Georgia, undertook the work, adding not only three miniguns to the port side but also attaching flare launchers to make the aircraft capable of night operations.

Even as these modifications were under way at Robins AFB, crews for these aircraft were being trained at Forbes AFB, Kansas, by the Tactical Air Command (TAC). Early in November 1965 the USAF activated the 4th Air Commando Squadron as the operational unit for these crews and aircraft and began deployment to Vietnam. During the remainder of 1965 this squadron flew 1,441 hours and 277 combat missions. It expended 137,136

Below: A U.S. Air Force AC-47 at Tan Son Nhut Air Base in 1965. Machine guns protrude through the fuselage of the plane just forward of the door. AC-47s could be used at night, when North Vietnamese and Vietcong liked to attack. The aircraft would light up the area with flares then set their deadly 7.62mm miniguns to work.

rounds of ammunition and 2,548 flares and received credit for 105 Vietcong* killed. Most of its operations were conducted during the hours of darkness in support of fort and village defense.

These operations demonstrated the effectiveness of the AC-47 gunship not only as a powerful destructive force but also as an instrument of terror. Its capability to strike quickly in far-flung parts of Southeast Asia and the tremendous firepower it possessed was thought by American commanders a valuable tool in deterring Vietcong activity. It could be used for both air defense and air interdiction. The AC-47 gunship also flew reconnaissance and forward air control missions at night. So successful were combat operations that the USAF increased the number of AC-47s operated by the 4th Air Commando Squadron to twenty-two, and on October 25, 1967, it activated the 14th Air Commando Squadron with a complement of sixteen

additional AC-47s. Later a third squadron operating AC-47 aircraft was activated, and the three units were redesignated Special Operations Squadrons.

During 1969 the AC-47 gunships flew their last operational missions in Vietnam. They were being replaced by AC-130 gunships* and helicopter gunships* that were more versatile, speedy, and less aged. For four years the AC-47 had been an integral part of the Vietnam War, recognized as both an offensive and defensive weapon. A total of fifty-three AC-47s had been built at a cost of about $6.7 million, many of which had been in operation for three or more years. As the gunship pioneer, the AC-47 was the progenitor of a second generation of improved gunships and tactics that followed between 1970 and 1973. RDL

Source: Jack S. Ballard, *The United States Air Force in Southeast Asia: Development and Employment of Fixed-Wing Gunships, 1962–1972*, 1982.

Above: The crew of an Action C-47 fires rounds from interior-mounted miniguns in 1965. The AC-47 was a fixed-wing gunship with rapid-fire weapons mounted on one side of the aircraft. The aircraft would circle a ground target at a constant altitude and at a constant speed, firing with devastating effect on enemy troops. The AC-47 represented the marriage of a 7.62mm minigun with a civilian DC-3, one of the Air Force's oldest operational aircraft.

Right, inset: A Lockheed AC-130 shows its two portside 20mm Vulcan multibarreled machine guns. As did the earlier AC-47, the AC-130 circled an area in a slow turn, pouring down lethal fire from its machine guns.

Below: A Lockheed AC-130 parked in a revetment at Ubon Air Base in Thailand. The AC-130 first arrived in Vietnam in 1967 and, because it could carry more and heavier weapons, took over many of the gunship duties from the smaller AC-47s.

AC-130 GUNSHIP

The AC-130s were fixed-wing gunships introduced to the Vietnam War in 1968. They were C-130* transport aircraft converted to AC-130s by equipping them with two multi-barreled machine guns, four 20mm Vulcan multibarreled guns, and a 40mm Bofors cannon, along with infrared sensors, radar, low-light television, and laser target designators. The AC-130s were used both to provide ground support and to interdict supplies being shipped along the Ho Chi Minh Trail.* RSB III

Sources: Jack Ballard, *The United States Air Force in Southeast Asia: Development and Employment of Fixed-Wing Gunships, 1962–1972*, 1982; Kevin J. Fitzpatrick, *Flying Gunship*, 2000.

ACCELERATED PACIFICATION CAMPAIGN

After the Tet Offensive* of February 1968 the United States renewed its commitment to a stronger military and political position in the Republic of Vietnam,* and that became especially important later in the year when Vietcong* repre-

sentatives at the Paris peace talks* began hinting at their willingness to accept a "cease-fire in place." If that really was a possibility, it was important for the United States to gain control of the countryside through more aggressive pacification programs. On November 1, 1968, the United States launched the Accelerated Pacification Campaign, with an objective of expanding government control over 1,200 villages currently controlled by the Vietcong. The

Accelerated Pacification Campaign was placed under the control of William Colby,* who was given a ninety-day time frame for the program. The United States had high hopes for the program because the Vietcong had been badly drained by the Tet Offensive and had essentially adopted a defensive strategy. The Phoenix Program* was launched simultaneously.

The Accelerated Pacification Campaign was basically a "clear and hold"* strategy using Regional Forces* (RF) and Popular Forces* (PF). Operating in or near their home villages, the RF and PF were familiar with the countryside as well as the people, knew how to differentiate between Vietcong and nonpolitical families, and built some confidence among locals because the villagers knew they would remain in the area. After destroying or at least expelling the Vietcong infrastructure, Accelerated Pacification then turned its attention to economic development, and included clearing roads, repairing bridges, building schools, and increasing farm production. The Americans also tried to train villagers in free election and then trained elected

officials in village administration. Finally, Accelerated Pacification tried to bring about land reform by distributing land to peasant farmers.

The results of Accelerated Pacification were mixed at best. By March 1970 more than 1 million hectares of land had been redistributed, and the number of RF and PF engaged in pacification had increased to 500,000 men. They were armed with M16 rifles* and had received improved training. But destruction of the Vietcong infrastructure was never achieved, nor did Accelerated Pacification really change the way most South Vietnamese looked upon the government of Nguyen Van Thieu.* Nor could Accelerated Pacification really survive the withdrawal of American troops that President Richard Nixon* began implementing in the summer of 1969. As the U.S. military presence declined, the South Vietnamese were unable to fill the vacuum.

Sources: Robert W. Komer, "Pacification: A Look Back," *Army* (June 1970): 20–29; Edward P. Metzner, *More Than a Soldier's War: Pacification in Vietnam*, 1995.

Above: During the war, U.S. Marines operated primarily in I Corps, the tactical area of operations in the northern reaches of South Vietnam. Marine Combined Action Platoons conducted a variety of pacification projects to improve living conditions, none more important than providing potable water to peasants. The Marines completed this village well in 1967. In doing so, the Marines hoped to win the political loyalties of villagers and wean them away from the Vietcong.

Above: Dean Acheson (in a photo from 1965), a prominent Democrat and one of the premier architects of U.S. cold war foreign policy, served as secretary of state to President Harry Truman and an advisor to presidents John F. Kennedy and Lyndon B. Johnson. During the late 1960s he served as one of the so-called Wise Old Men, a small group of senior advisors who recommended escalation of the Vietnam War to Johnson and then changed their minds after the Tet Offensive of 1968 and suggested to the president that it was time to disengage.

ACHESON, DEAN GOODERHAM

Dean Acheson was born on April 11, 1893, in Middletown, Connecticut. Coming from a prosperous New England family, he graduated from Yale in 1915 and the Harvard Law School in 1918. Acheson served as private secretary to Supreme Court Justice Louis Brandeis until 1921, practiced law privately in Washington, D.C., until 1933, and then joined the New Deal as undersecretary of state. Acheson resigned that post in opposition to the gold-buying program of 1933, practiced law again, but then returned to the Franklin D. Roosevelt* administration in 1941 as an assistant secretary of state. He became undersecretary of state in August 1946 and secretary of state under Harry S. Truman* in July 1949. Acheson left the State Department in 1953 and returned to his law practice. During the 1960s he advised both the Kennedy* and Johnson* administrations on foreign policy, and became part of the informal policy group known as the Wise Old Men* in 1965. By 1966 Acheson began expressing serious reservations about the American presence in South Vietnam, and by 1967 he was urging Lyndon B. Johnson to de-escalate the conflict. Acheson was present at the March 1968 meeting in which the Wise Old Men told Johnson that the war was lost. Dean Acheson died on October 12, 1971.

Sources: Dean Acheson, *Present at the Creation*, 1969; *New York Times*, October 13, 1971; Walter Isaacson and Evan Thomas, *The Wise Men: Six Friends and the World They Made*, 1986.

ADAMS–WESTMORELAND CONTROVERSY

In 1965 Sam Adams was an intelligence officer with the Central Intelligence Agency* working on Vietnam. Using captured enemy documents and interrogations of enemy personnel, Adams found support for Pentagon estimates of enemy killed, wounded, captured, and deserted—figures that the news media believed were inflated. Adams also found support for a far higher estimate of the number of enemy in South Vietnam, for the infiltration* rate of regular troops from North Vietnam to the South, and a higher capability for supplying those larger numbers than the U.S. Army intelligence estimates coming out of Military Assistance Command, Vietnam* headquarters in Saigon.*

Adams gradually became the center of a growing controversy. He was unable to gain upper-level support within the CIA for his revisions of the size of the enemy; meetings between intelligence officials of the CIA and various military commands could not reach a compromise figure. General William C. Westmoreland* was unwilling to change enemy totals, although he was willing to reallocate figures within various categories. With the Tet Offensive* of 1968, Adams felt the battle weakened the enemy less than Army officers claimed, since he believed the enemy was stronger originally.

In 1975 Adams made his charges public in *Harper's* magazine, and in January 1982 in a CBS News documentary. The documentary charged General Westmoreland with a conspiracy to report low figures for the enemy. After Westmoreland sued, the resulting court trial in 1985 seemingly found support for Adams's original contention and vindication for his lonely vigil. Westmoreland and CBS settled their suit out of court.

Source: Bob Brewin and Sydney Shaw, *Vietnam on Trial: Westmoreland vs. CBS*, 1986.

AD HOC TASK FORCE ON VIETNAM

The Tet Offensive* of 1968 dealt a deathblow to the American war effort in Vietnam by undermining the political atmosphere at home. Doubtful congressmen began evaluating their positions, while the military was requesting greater investment of resources in the conflict. Late in February 1968 General William C. Westmoreland* asked President Lyndon B. Johnson* for the deployment of 200,000 more troops to Southeast Asia, and the president convened the Ad Hoc Task Force on Vietnam to evaluate Westmoreland's request. The debate was also taking place in the midst of the presidential primary campaign of 1968, in which Lyndon Johnson was facing considerable pressure from Senators Eugene McCarthy* of Minnesota and Robert F. Kennedy* of New York. Clark Clifford,* the new secretary of defense, chaired the group. The debate was wide-ranging, dealing with the Vietnam War in particular and American commitments abroad in general. General Maxwell Taylor* and Walt W. Rostow,* both presidential advisors, supported the commitment, as did General Earle Wheeler,* chairman of the Joint Chiefs of Staff (*see* Chairman, JCS), but the escalation was opposed by other prominent people, including Paul Nitze,* deputy undersecretary of defense, and Paul Warnke,* assistant secretary of defense. Although Clifford took no formal position in the debate, his own doubts about the nature of the war were confirmed. Those opposing the escalation prevailed, and Westmoreland received only 25,000 of the 200,000 troops he requested. Later in March, President Lyndon Johnson announced his decision not to run for reelection and to de-escalate the war effort.

Sources: Harry G. Summers Jr., *Vietnam War Almanac*, 1985; Clark M. Clifford, "A Viet Nam Reappraisal," *Foreign Affairs* (July 1969): 601–22; Clark Dougan and Steven Weiss, *The Vietnam Experience: Nineteen Sixty-Eight*, 1983.

Left: General William C. Westmoreland salutes between visiting U.S. President Lyndon Johnson and Vietnamese Chief of State Lieutenant General Nguyen Van Thieu during the playing of the Vietnamese national anthem in October 1966. Westmoreland commanded the American effort through some of the most tumultuous times of the war, including the Tet Offensive and the My Lai massacre.

Left: U.S. Air Force security police examine the bodies of Vietcong guerillas killed during an attack on the Tan Son Nhut Air Base near Saigon in the first days of the Tet Offensive of early 1968. The fighting devastated the ranks of the Vietcong.

Above: An African American soldier of the 1st Cavalry Division carries a wounded comrade in March 1967. African Americans made up about 11 percent of those who served in Vietnam, but about 12 percent of Americans killed in action. Twenty African Americans were awarded the Congressional Medal of Honor for heroism during the war.

AFRICAN AMERICANS IN VIETNAM

See Black Soldiers

AGENT ORANGE (Defoliants, also Agent Blue, Agent White)

See Defoliants

AGNEW, SPIRO THEODORE

Spiro Agnew was born on November 9, 1918, in Baltimore. Before World War II he attended Johns Hopkins University and the Baltimore Law School, and after serving in an Army armor unit during the war, he graduated from the Baltimore Law School in 1947. Agnew began practicing law and working in local Republican politics, and in 1957 he was appointed to the Baltimore County Zoning Board of Appeals. He won election to the position of county executive in 1962, and in 1966 he won the governorship of Maryland, defeating a segregationist Democrat and earning liberal credentials. During his two terms as governor Agnew became increasingly conservative and strident in his rhetoric. In 1968 he supported Richard Nixon's* candidacy for president, and Nixon rewarded him with the spot of running mate. They won the election over Democrat Hubert Humphrey,* and Agnew became vice president of the United States in 1969.

As vice president, Agnew carried the battle to the opponents and critics of the Nixon administration. Critics of the Vietnam War, whether in Congress* or on campus, were the special targets of Agnew's alliterative verbal assaults. The baiting and buzzwords of the 1950s were dusted off for reuse, together with many new ones of Agnew's invention. But while Agnew carried the cudgels for the administration, his excesses often inflamed an already overheated national debate, and Agnew himself was severely criticized for exacerbating the situation.

Thus, when Agnew's past caught up with him, those who had been the victims of his denunciation could hardly conceal their delight. Faced with the threat of prosecution and impeachment for violation of bribery, conspiracy, and tax laws, on October 10, 1973, Agnew entered into a plea bargaining agreement, pleading no contest (nolo contendere) to one count of income tax invasion, and resigned from the vice presidency. Spiro Agnew died on September 17, 1996. JMR Jr.

Sources: Spiro T. Agnew, *Go Quietly or Else*, 1980; *New York Times*, September 18, 1996.

AGRICULTURAL REFORM TRIBUNALS

By 1954, after the defeat of the French at the Battle of Dien Bien Phu,* Ho Chi Minh* was firmly in control of Vietnam, especially in the north. Although he faced no real political problems, the economy was in a state of disaster, which he proceeded to make worse through the imposition of awkward ideological controls. Determined to wipe out "landlord" elements as a symbol of his devout Marxism, Ho unleashed cadre teams to search out the landlord class,

which he estimated at 2 percent of the rural population. It was a preposterous assumption, since few Vietnamese peasants in the north had more than three to four acres. Nevertheless, by 1955 the cadres had established Agricultural Reform Tribunals in each village to identify the landlords. Accusations, lies, informants, and a vicious neighbor-against-neighbor mentality filled rural villages. Thousands of so-called landlords were killed and thousands more were sent to labor camps. The rural economy was disrupted. The tribunals had quotas of landlords to find and kill, and their justice was quick and capricious. Concerned about the random killings and economic disruption, Ho Chi Minh repudiated the campaigns in August 1956.

Sources: Stanley Karnow, *Vietnam: A History*, 1983; Jean Lacouture, *Ho Chi Minh: A Political Biography*, 1968; Charles Fenn, *Ho Chi Minh: A Biographical Introduction*, 1973.

AGROVILLE PROGRAM

Because of increasing instability and Vietcong* insurgency in rural areas, President Ngo Dinh Diem* launched the Agroville Program in 1959. Its main purpose was to protect Vietnamese peasants from Vietcong terrorism by relocating them to secure areas controlled by the Army of the Republic of Vietnam* (ARVN). The government of South

Left: In 1972, President Richard M. Nixon and Vice President Spiro T. Agnew ran for a second term in office. An outspoken critic of anti-war protestors and criminals, Agnew is pictured here at a campaign rally. Two years later, he would resign the vice presidency in disgrace, pleading no contest to charges of bribery and income tax evasion and adding weight to charges that the Nixon administration had been the most corrupt in U.S. history.

Below left: A chief warrant officer of the 145th Aviation Battalion pulls on his helmet before taking off in his AH-1G Cobra gunship in 1969. He was answering a call from a Ranger Long-Range Patrol Company.

Below right: An AH-1G Cobra gunship rests in a revetment in 1970. An XM35 Vulcan gun is mounted below the stubby "wing" on the fuselage's left side. This Cobra was flown by the 17th Air Cavalry, 1st Aviation Brigade.

Vietnam built several new communities as part of the Agroville Program, complete with schools, medical clinics, and electricity, but financial incentives for peasants were meager and they had no desire to leave their ancestral homelands. In many instances the ARVN had to forcibly remove peasants to the new Agroville communities, and the program inspired bitter resentment against the Diem regime. The Agroville Program was abandoned in 1961 when the government committed its resources to the Strategic Hamlet Program.*

Sources: Denis Warner, *The Last Confucian*, 1963; Douglas S. Blaufarb, *The Counterinsurgency Era: U.S. Doctrine and Performance, 1950 to Present*, 1977; William A. Nighswonger, *Rural Pacification in Vietnam*, 1966.

AH-1G HELICOPTER

The AH-1G helicopter, also known as the Cobra, was first delivered to South Vietnam in 1967 but was not deployed in large numbers until 1968. The AH-1G had a length of 52 feet, 11 inches; a weight of 5,783 pounds; and a payload of 1,993 pounds. Its primary purpose was escort reconnaissance and direct fire support. The AH-1G was an attack vehicle firing grenades, machine guns, and rockets in support of American and South Vietnamese infantry.

Sources: John J. Tolson, *Airmobility, 1961–1971*, 1973; Shelby L. Stanton, *Vietnam Order of Battle*, 1981.

AIKEN, GEORGE DAVID

George D. Aiken was born in Dummerston, Vermont, on August 20, 1892. In keeping with family tradition, he was a farmer and a politician. Running as a Republican, Aiken was elected to the Vermont legislature in 1930, lieutenant governor in 1935, and governor in 1937. During two terms in the governor's mansion, Aiken established a record as a progressive maverick, and in 1940 he was elected to the U.S. Senate and became one of the country's most prominent liberal Republicans. In 1954 Aiken gave up thirteen years of seniority on the Labor and Public Welfare Committee to take a seat on the Foreign Relations Committee.* Had he not exercised his option to do so, the seat would have gone to Senator Joseph McCarthy of Wisconsin, whom Aiken thoroughly disliked. During the next twenty years Aiken became one of the most respected members of the committee.

In the 1960s, when President Lyndon B. Johnson* escalated the Vietnam conflict, Aiken at first supported him. But by 1966 he joined the ranks of the doves. In that year, he gave some widely quoted advice to Johnson. He said that the president should pull American troops out of the fighting, and to save face simply "declare the United States the winner and begin de-escalation." Aiken would later point out that President Nixon* had essentially followed that course in extricating American ground forces from Vietnam. In 1975 Aiken retired from the Senate and returned to his

beloved farm in Vermont. George Aiken died on November 19, 1984. JMR Jr.

Sources: George D. Aiken, *The Aiken Senate Diary*, 1976; *New York Times*, November 20, 1984.

AIR AMERICA

One of the many civilian airlines operating in Southeast Asia, Air America was a Central Intelligence Agency* "proprietary." A proprietary is an entity that appears to be a normal, legitimate enterprise but actually is operated and controlled by the CIA. To maintain its appearance as an independent business, Air America engaged in activities common to air carriers, especially cargo transportation. In Southeast Asia, even during the war, businesses continued to operate normally, and so civilian air transport was a necessary and lucrative venture. Approximately 75 percent of Air America's flights were not related to the war or to the CIA's involvement in the war, so Air America employees may even have been unaware of its connection to the agency. However, the company primarily was used by the CIA for its numerous war-related activities.

The pilots and crews that were involved in the clandestine activities of Air America were often military veterans, many of whom had served previous tours of duty in Southeast Asia. While some of the CIA-related Air America flights were undramatic, such as commonplace transportation of personnel, materiel, and payrolls, often the flights were extremely dangerous. They frequently involved trips to remote areas dominated by the enemy, and for security reasons they were usually flown at night and/or under cover of clouds or fog. Also, they were not confined to Vietnam, since the CIA operated extensively in Cambodia and especially in Laos* throughout the war. Most of the flights did not involve combat action by the Air America planes, although the aircraft available to Air America did include combat-capable types. STT

Sources: John Morrocco, *The Vietnam Experience. Rain of Fire: Air War 1969–1973*, 1984; Christopher Robbins, *Air America*, 1979.

Left: Late in April 1975, the Army of the Republic of Vietnam imploded when North Vietnamese troops launched an invasion that took them to the outskirts of Saigon. With the fall of South Vietnam imminent, tens of thousands of South Vietnamese civilians panicked. They were convinced that North Vietnam would wage a bloodbath throughout South Vietnam, especially against those who had collaborated with the United States. They thronged outside the gates of the U.S. embassy in Saigon, hoping for admittance to the embassy grounds and helicopter evacuation. Air America helicopters also staged evacuations from the roofs of other buildings in Saigon. Here hundreds of civilians are gathered on the roof of a building at 22 Gia Long Street in Saigon, a half mile from the U.S. embassy. From the rooftops, they were flown to U.S. aircraft carriers in the South China Sea. For every South Vietnamese civilian who was rescued, thousands were left behind to suffer their fate at the hands of the North Vietnamese.

Below: A South Vietnamese tank shelters members of the U.S. Air Force 377th Security Police Squadron and adds firepower along the perimeter of the Tan Son Nhut Air Base on the first day of the 1968 Tet Offensive.

AIR BASE DEFENSE

In the early morning of November 1, 1964, Communist Vietnamese forces attacked Bien Hoa* Air Base, outside of Saigon.* Positioning six 81mm mortars about 400 meters north of the base, these forces fired some eighty rounds onto parked aircraft and troop billets. These forces then withdrew undetected and unmolested, after killing four American military advisors, wounding thirty others, and hitting twenty B-57 bombers. Of these, five aircraft were completely destroyed. Increasingly after this time American aerial defense forces became attractive targets for Communist forces. Through 1973 there were 475 enemy attacks on American air bases in Vietnam, resulting in 898 American aircraft damaged and 155 service personnel killed in action. An additional 305 aircraft and 154 personnel assigned to the Republic of Vietnam* Armed Forces were also lost in these attacks.

To counter these attacks the U.S. military directed that forces be deployed to Vietnam to secure these airfields. The first force, the 9th Marine Expeditionary Brigade,* landed at Da Nang* in March 1965. United States Army* and Air Force* air base defense units followed soon thereafter. These units combated several threats present to aircraft in Vietnam: sabotage, sapper infiltration, ground attack, and shelling by standoff weapons. Sabotage was little used. Ground attacks by battalion-size forces took place on only two occasions. Sapper raids posed a more serious threat, but in terms of numbers and damage, standoff rocket and mortar fire presented the greatest hazard. The air base defense forces were partially successful in countering these threats. From 1969 on these attacks decreased every year until the American withdrawal. The casualties and aircraft losses registered similar declines. At the same time, the U.S. air bases in Vietnam were always vulnerable to Communist attack. RDL

Source: Roger P. Fox, *Air Base Defense in the Republic of Vietnam, 1961–1973*, 1979.

Left: U.S. Army artillerists fire on Vietcong positions near the Tan Son Nhut Air Base during the Tet Offensive.

Below: Airmen make repairs on an RF-4C aircraft damaged during a Vietcong mortar attack on Tan Son Nhut Air Base in 1966. Air bases were always tempting targets for the Communist Vietnamese forces.

82d Airborne Division

101st Airborne Division

173d Airborne Brigade

AIRBORNE FORCES

The term "airborne" refers to soldiers who parachute into battle. During the Vietnam War several airborne units—the 101st Airborne Division,* the 3d Brigade of the 82d Airborne Division,* and the 173d Airborne Brigade*—were deployed to Southeast Asia, but they were used as infantry helicoptered into battle. Except for isolated situations, airborne tactics did not play a significant role in the Vietnam War.

Sources: Harry G. Summers Jr., *Vietnam War Almanac*, 1985; Shelby L. Stanton, *Vietnam Order of Battle*, 1981, and *The Rise and Fall of an American Army: U.S. Ground Troops in Vietnam, 1965–1973*, 1985.

Opposite page: Airborne operations were a tactical innovation of World War II, in which large numbers of infantry could be transported long distances and then parachute into an area to engage the enemy in combat. Vietnam's rugged terrain, with heavy jungle canopies covering mountains and ravines, limited the effectiveness of standard airborne operations. Helicopters became the vehicle of choice in delivering soldiers to the battlefield. In this 1963 photograph, some 840 ARVN paratroopers jump from U.S. Air Force C-123 transport planes during Operation Phi Hoa II in Tay Ninh Province.

Top left: Soon after the signing of the Geneva Accords in 1954, the United States commenced direct military assistance to the Army of the Republic of Vietnam, and helicopters immediately proved their utility, especially the UH-1 Huey. Manufactured by Bell and known in the U.S. Army as the Iroquois, this UH-1 ferries ARVN troops on April 19, 1956, to battle the Vietcong near the Cambodian border.

Top right: A view from the ground of American paratroopers dropping into a grassy field near Phan Rang on November 19, 1965. Phan Rang, 50 miles southwest of Cam Ranh, had an airfield that had been in operation since World War II.

Bottom: Soldiers from the 1st Platoon (nicknamed "Champagne Flight") of Company A in the 1st Aviation Battalion of the 1st Infantry Division disembark from a UH-1D Huey. Before signaling to the pilot to take off, the door gunner makes sure that the troops are all on the ground.

Right: A helicopter gunner takes up position just before takeoff, one foot inside and one outside the helicopter body. The drawing was made by a civilian combat artist in late 1969.

Below: Two troopers of the 1st Cavalry Division check their location before searching the area in March 1968. One is acting as an artillery forward observer.

AIR CAVALRY

During the nineteenth century American cavalry units were horse-mounted troops designed to survey enemy positions and provide screens for incoming infantry units. The horse-mounted cavalry gave way during the twentieth century to armored personnel carriers* and tanks. A major innovation of the Vietnam War was the use of air cavalry units where troops are moved into battlefield positions by helicopters. The 1st Cavalry Division* was one of the main air cavalry units in Southeast Asia.

Sources: John J. Tolson, *Airmobility, 1961–1971*, 1973; Shelby L. Stanton, *The Rise and Fall of an American Army: U.S. Ground Troops in Vietnam, 1965–1973*, 1985, and *The 1st Cavalry in Vietnam: Anatomy of a Division*, 1999; Andrew F. Krepinevich Jr., *The Army and Vietnam*, 1986.

Right: A helicopter gunner takes up position just before takeoff, one foot inside and one outside the helicopter body. The drawing was made by a civilian combat artist in late 1969.

Above: Troops from the 1st Cavalry Division jump from a UH-1 to begin a reconnaissance patrol. Because of the helicopter, the troops were transported to the top of the hill and did not have to fight their way up through entrenched enemy positions. They instantly owned the high ground.

Right: Troopers of the 1st Cavalry Division move through smoke during a sweep as part of Operation Jeb Stuart in March 1968.

Below: The aircraft carrier USS *Bon Homme Richard* conducted operations in the South China Sea in March 1967. Here an F-8E Crusader fighter is about to launch from the *Bon Homme* for a bombing run over North Vietnam. Armed with air-to-air Sidewinder missiles, the Crusader also had four 20mm cannons and carried up to 5,000 pounds in bombs. It was a single-seat, single-engine fighter aircraft that became the workhorse of naval air operations in Vietnam.

AIRCRAFT CARRIERS

Between 1964 and 1975 the Seventh Fleet's* Task Force 77 operated off the coast of Vietnam in the South China Sea. Until the summer of 1966 there were usually two to three carriers in Task Force 77, but beginning in mid-1966 three to four carriers were usually deployed there. Each carrier wing consisted of between 65 and 100 aircraft—A-4 Skyhawks,* A-1 Skyraiders,* A-7 Corsair IIs,* A-6 Intruders,* F-4 Phantom IIs,* and F-8 Crusaders. The aircraft were used over North Vietnam, South Vietnam, Laos,* and Cambodia to disrupt enemy supply lines and for close air support of

American and South Vietnamese ground operations. Nineteen aircraft carriers served separate missions off the coast of Vietnam between 1964 and 1975: the *America, Constellation, Ticonderoga,* *Yorktown, Franklin D. Roosevelt, Enterprise, Bon Homme Richard, Coral Sea, Forrestal, Hancock, Hornet, Independence, Intrepid, Kitty Hawk, Midway, Oriskany, Ranger, Saratoga,* and *Shangri-La.*

Sources: Peter Mersky and Norman Polmar, *The Naval Air War in Vietnam: 1965–1975*, 1981; Edward J. Marolda and G. Wesley Pryce III, *A Short History of the United States Navy and the Southeast Asian Conflict, 1950–1975*, 1984.

Left: On April 26, 1972, U.S. Navy pilots prepare to board their planes on the USS *Constellation*. This aircraft is loaded with 500-pound bombs.

Below: USS *Constellation* (CV-64), a *Kitty Hawk*-class supercarrier. Construction began in 1957 at the New York Navy Yard and the ship was launched in October 1960. In 1964, *Constellation* was deployed to the Gulf of Tonkin off the coast of South Vietnam and launched F-4 Phantoms during the Gulf of Tonkin Incident. In 1967, the carrier operated first on Dixie Station with strikes in the Iron Triangle, and then moved north to Yankee Station.

Right: During the Vietnam War, the U.S. Navy patrolled inland waterways in South Vietnam. Known as "riverine" operations, they conducted assault and search-and-destroy missions, ferried supplies to U.S. troops, transported soldiers and Marines to battle sites, and carried out search-and-rescue missions. This Patrol Air Cushion Vehicle (PACV) was capable of speeds up to 75 knots.

Below: An assault air-cushion vehicle prepares to take part in Operation Truong Cong Dinh at the end of June 1968 near Dong Tam, South Vietnam.

AIR-CUSHION VEHICLES

Because of the extensive marshlands of South Vietnam and the frequent difficulty of moving propeller-driven craft through water thick with grass, the United States and South Vietnam had to develop a river craft giving its own troops the mobility enjoyed by Vietcong* using sampans. What they turned to was the air-cushion vehicle, a modified Bell Aerosystem craft that moved on a base of air about four feet thick. It reached speeds of up to 75 knots. United States Navy* and Army Special Forces* personnel used air-cushion vehicles to patrol extensive areas of the Mekong Delta.* Generally, the air-cushion vehicles were plagued with problems, including heavy fuel consumption, noise, and frequent breakdowns.

Sources: Edward J. Marolda and G. Wesley Pryce III, *A Short History of the United States Navy and the Southeast Asian Conflict, 1950–1975*, 1984; Shelby L. Stanton, *Green Berets at War*, 1985; Edgar C. Doleman Jr., *The Vietnam Experience: Tools of War*, 1984.

AIR DEFENSE, NORTH VIETNAM

The North Vietnamese constructed the most elaborate air defense system in the world during the 1960s and 1970s. Beginning in 1965 North Vietnam began installing Soviet SA-2 surface-to-air missiles, or SAMs.* They also employed MiG-17s and MiG-21s to attack American bombers. Finally, North Vietnam used a variety of antiaircraft weapons against American planes: 37mm guns that fired eighty 1.6-pound shells a minute to an altitude of 9,000 feet; 57mm S-60s that fired seventy 6-pound shells a minute to 15,000 feet; 8mm M1944s that fired twenty 20-pound shells a minute to 30,000 feet; 100mm guns that fired fifteen 35-pound shells a minute to 45,000 feet; and 130mm guns that fired twelve 74-pound shells a minute to 45,000 feet. In addition to shooting down American aircraft, the air defense system limited the effectiveness of allied airpower. As North Vietnamese air defense systems became more sophisticated, American pilots spent increasing amounts of time dodging missiles and less time over their targets.

Sources: Paul Burbage et al., *The Battle for the Skies Over North Vietnam, 1964–1972*, 1976; Anthony Robinson, "Air Forces in Vietnam," in John S. Bowman, ed., *The Vietnam War: An Almanac*, 1985; Mark Clodfelter, *Limits of Air Power*, 1989.

Above: Although the United States enjoyed complete air superiority throughout the war, the North Vietnamese countered with one of the most sophisticated air defense systems in the world. In this photograph, North Vietnamese soldiers operate a Type 55 37mm antiaircraft gun. It was similar to the U.S. Navy's 40mm gun. Over time, the North Vietnamese developed considerable expertise with the weapon, employing it against U.S. aircraft attacking fixed targets at predictable angles. Along the Ho Chi Minh Trail and the tri-border region of Laos, Vietnam, and Cambodia, the 37mm gun proved especially effective on slower-moving piston-driven aircraft and helicopters.

Left: NVA gunners operating a Soviet-made M1939 automatic air defense gun or its Type 55 Chinese copy. Although this 37mm weapon had a low rate of fire and its accuracy fell off badly after only about 9,000 feet, it was nevertheless very deadly when sited along known angles of attack, such as at bridges, and its fielding in large numbers in North Vietnam and along the Ho Chi Minh Trail effectively discouraged low-level air strikes.

AIR FORCE, UNITED STATES

The United States Air Force played a major role in the American military effort during the Vietnam War, providing close air support, tactical airlift,* and high-altitude bombing strikes by B-52* bombers. The Seventh Air Force* directed all close air support, tactical airlift, and the Military Air Command, while the Strategic Air Command directed the B-52 strikes. During the war the Air Force had 1,737 personnel killed in action, nearly 3,500 wounded, and lost 2,257 aircraft.

Sources: Carl Berger, ed., *The United States Air Force in Southeast Asia, 1961–1973*, 1977; John Morrocco, *The Vietnam Experience: Thunder from Above*, 1985, and *The Vietnam Experience: Rain of Fire*, 1984; Harry G. Summers Jr., *Vietnam War Almanac*, 1985.

AIR FORCE, VIETNAMESE

See Vietnamese Air Force

Above: The only U.S. Air Force pilot ace of the Vietnam War, Captain Richard "Steve" Ritchie flew an F-4D Phantom and destroyed five MiG 21s during Operation Linebacker I in 1972.

Left: A B-52 in action over Vietnam in 1966. The B-52 first went to war in Vietnam, where its tremendous fire-power intimidated the enemy.

Below: A C-123 "Provider" turns around on the makeshift Mardsen matting runway of an unidentified remote Special Services Camp in 1965.

Below: A helicopter gunner of the 1st Cavalry Division (Airmobile) fires his M60 machine gun on a Vietcong position in 1966.

AIRMOBILE OPERATIONS

Airmobile operations involved the use of helicopters to transport troops into battle and to provide fire support at battle sites. Instead of transporting troops into battle while artillery barrages prepared the way, airmobile operations had transport helicopters move troops simultaneously with artillery and gunship fire, keeping the enemy off guard. During the Vietnam War airmobile operations were used extensively by the United States Army* and Marine Corps,* but the major airmobile unit was the 101st Airborne Division.* Since airmobile operations had not even been tested until the 1950s when reliable helicopters were functioning, Vietnam became the combat breakthrough for airmobile tactics. They proved to be the major tactical innovation of the Vietnam War.

Sources: John J. Tolson, *Airmobility, 1961–1971*, 1973; John H. Hay Jr., *Tactical and Materiel Innovations*, 1975.

AIRMUNITIONS SUPPLY

Beginning in 1965 the United States Air Force* in Southeast Asia began extensive combat operations, requiring the acquisition and shipment to the theater of a vast quantity of conventional bombs, rockets, ammunition, and associated ordnance. The Air Force Logistics Command (AFLC), charged with support of operational weapons used by the Air Force, procured these airmunitions, while the Military Air Transport Service, later renamed the Military Airlift Command,* and the Navy's Military Sealift* Transport System transported the necessary materiel to Southeast Asia. As operations increased in the combat theater during the latter 1960s, these organizations created a pipeline for airmunition movement from American bases to theater dispersal sites. Based on a requirement to maintain a 30-day supply at the forward Southeast Asian bases and a 120-day supply in the Philippines,* the AFLC

was forced to plan for airmunitions resupply seven to eight months ahead of estimated operational usage.

To reduce these excessively long lead times, in 1965 and 1966 the Department of Defense approved a plan for dedicated transport of munitions to Southeast Asia. The Navy made available five cargo ships with a combined capacity of 35,300 tons, and the Air Force developed the Southeast Asia Airlift system, designated by the acronym SEAIR, to move all types of munitions used in Vietnam. In all, more than

1 million tons of airmunitions were moved to Southeast Asia between 1965 and 1973. The system worked effectively from 1966 on as bombs, airmunitions, flares, rockets, missiles, and assorted ordnance were moved to combat areas on a timely basis. RDL

Source: Bernard J. Termena, "Logistics in War and Peace," in *Logistics: An Illustrated History of AFLC and Its Antecedents, 1921–1981* (Wright-Patterson AFB, Ohio: AFLC Office of History, n.d.).

Left: Troops from the 1st Cavalry Division operate an M102 105mm howitzer battery during the Battle of the Ia Drang Valley in November 1965. The M102 was light and easily lifted by most helicopters in the U.S. fleet. It had a maximum range of 12,580 yards. The two M102s here were operated by an eight-man crew. The M102 fired a variety of explosive rounds, none more lethal than the XM546 "Beehive" that, when detonated, released 8,000 small darts. The helicopter in the background lowering supplies is a CH-47 Chinook.

AIRPOWER

Throughout the more than a decade of American involvement in Vietnam, one critical factor allowed the United States to maintain a military superiority: airpower. Airpower is a concept, a philosophy developed over several generations by thoughtful fliers and seemingly validated by the conduct of World War II. At its fundamental level it is the ability of an air force to take and maintain control of the skies over its armies; to strike at enemy resources such as combat forces, transportation facilities, and industrial complexes; and to support ground units through the projection of force over long distances.

A certain tension between United States Air Force* resources allocated to the tactical mission of ground support and air interdiction of enemy forces behind the battle lines and those allocated to the strategic bombing of enemy industrial and transportation resources has been present since the 1930s. The ideal of strategic bombing, developed between the wars and validated during World War II, became the dominant Air Force goal thereafter. The primacy of strategic thinking was reflected in the first postwar division of the nation's air resources into three commands in the late 1940s: Strategic Air Command, Air Defense Command, and Tactical Air Command. The first was given more than 100,000 people, the second 26,000, and the third 7,000.

The use of airpower in Southeast Asia followed patterns established early in American strategic thinking. Believing that airpower alone might succeed in containing the insurgents in South Vietnam, early in the 1960s the U.S. Air Force and Navy* adopted a contingency plan that called for a holding action in South Vietnam using air-strike squadrons positioned around the periphery of China. By relying on technology rather than manpower, planners contended, this approach would avoid getting the United States bogged down on the ground in Asia. But airpower without ground commitment was insufficient, and in April 1965 President Lyndon B. Johnson* sent American ground forces to Vietnam. Other steps followed in rapid succession, and before long the Air Force was fighting four air wars: over North Vietnam, South Vietnam, northern Laos,* and

southern Laos. The bombing campaign against North Vietnam never succeeded as intended, in part because of political decisions to halt operations and in part because of fragmented control by service representatives. The second air war in Southeast Asia, the one fought over South Vietnam, was also less than effective because it was pursued simultaneously by at least six air forces. The Tactical Air Force, the Navy, the United States Marines* and Army,* the Vietnamese Air Force,* and the Strategic Air Force of fifty or so B-52s* each pursued a fragmented strategy of operations. The two air wars over Laos were attempts to interrupt the flow of men and supplies coming out of North Vietnam, westward toward the Plain of Jars, and along the Ho Chi Minh Trail* toward South Vietnam. Once again, politics at both the international and interservice levels hampered effective operations. Indeed, airpower in the Vietnam War suffered from the traditional drawbacks of coalition warfare. RDL

Sources: John Schlight, "The Impact of the Orient on Air Power," in Joe C. Dixon, ed., *The American Military and the Far East: Proceedings of the Ninth Military History Symposium USAF Academy, 1980*, 1980; Mark Clodfelter, *Limits of Air Power*, 1989.

capability meant that accuracy was not a major requirement, thus reducing the training time before a soldier could be sent into combat.

Most armaments analysts judge the AK-47, which normally holds thirty bullets, to be superior to the U.S. M16,* which became the standard weapon of American, Korean, and South Vietnamese troops. The AK-47 was more durable and less adversely affected by the climate* and conditions of Vietnam. There are a number of accounts of cases in which American troops preferred to use the AK-47 and in fact did use it when combat conditions permitted. The continuing popularity of this weapon is illustrated by its use in many military hostilities since the Vietnam War. STT

Sources: Ray Bonds, ed., *The Vietnam War*, 1983; Edward Clinton Ezell, *The Great Rifle Controversy*, 1984; Chris McNab, *The AK-47*, 2001.

Below center: The AK-47 was designed in the Soviet Union shortly after World War II. It required minimal care but was relatively heavy at nine pounds. This example was made in 1954 and captured in 1971. The holes in the top of the receiver cover were caused by high velocity grenade splinters.

AK-47

Right: A member of the Vietcong holding a Soviet AK-47.

The AK-47 was the basic infantry weapon of the North Vietnamese Army* (NVA) and the Vietcong* (VC). Originally manufactured by the Soviet Union,* most of these "assault rifles" used in the war were made in the People's Republic of China,* which was the major supplier of armaments to NVA and VC forces. Also known as the Kalashnikov, after its Russian inventor, this weapon was sturdy, reliable, compact, and relatively lightweight. It fired a 7.62mm bullet in a fully automatic mode (continuous firing, like a machine gun, as long as the trigger was squeezed). The high muzzle velocity (speed of the bullet after firing) and the tumbling action of the bullet at the point of impact contributed to its effectiveness because the results were large entry and exit wounds, severe tissue damage, and extensive trauma in body areas near the wound. The combination of these effects plus its rapid-fire

ALVAREZ, EVERETT JR.

A native of San Jose, California, Lieutenant Everett Alvarez Jr. was stationed on the USS *Constellation* in the South China Sea at the time of the Gulf of Tonkin Resolution* in 1964. Piloting an A-4 Skyhawk,* Alvarez was shot down over North Vietnam on August 5, 1964. He was transferred to the "Hanoi Hilton"* prison and spent the next eight years as a prisoner of war.* Alvarez was the first American pilot taken prisoner by the North Vietnamese.

Source: Terrence Maitland and Steven Weiss, *The Vietnam Experience: Raising the Stakes*, 1982.

Top right: Lieutenant Everett Alvarez is photographed on the flight deck of the USS *Constellation*. The photograph was taken in August 1964 just before he was taken prisoner.

Bottom left: Jon Brenneis of *Life* magazine photographed Mrs. Everett Alvarez with the Navy telegram informing her that her husband was missing in action. She would spend nearly a decade waiting for his return.

Bottom right: At Travis Air Force Base in California in 1973, Lieutenant Everett Alvarez returns to the United States. Air Force Major-General John F. Gonge accompanies Alvarez, who is waving to a crowd assembled to greet him.

Below: An armored personnel carrier of the Americal Division searches for the enemy in 1968. Later known as the 23d Infantry Division, Americal was formed during World War II on the South Pacific Island of New Caledonia as the American New Caledonia Division. It was deactivated but reactiviated in the 1950s and again in Vietnam in 1967. Its patch, shown here (inset), is a depiction of the Southern Cross constellation.

AMERICAL DIVISION

See 23d Infantry Division

AMERICAN FRIENDS OF VIETNAM

Formed in the fall of 1955, the American Friends of Vietnam (also known as the Vietnam Lobby) had its origins in 1950 after a meeting between Wesley Fishel of Michigan State University and Ngo Dinh Diem,* then living in self-imposed exile. At Fishel's urging, Diem came to the United States, where he met Cardinal Spellman, senators Mike Mansfield* and John Kennedy,* and Supreme Court Justice William Douglas, all of whom became Lobby supporters. Friends of Vietnam was an odd aggregation of former leftist intellectuals, conservative generals, and liberal politicians. Their search for a "third way" or "independent nationalist alternative" to "Communist totalitarianism" grew out of the cold war and McCarthyism as many liberals fought to prove their anti-Communism rather than attack red-baiting witch-hunts. To prove his Americanism, Senator Kennedy gave a major speech in April 1954 in which he opposed any negotiated settlement allowing Ho Chi Minh* participation in Vietnamese governance.

Lobby members convinced officials in the Eisenhower* administration that Diem, an anti-Communist untainted by French or Japanese association, was right for premier.

Eisenhower, however, was never really sold on Diem. In 1955 Diem's regime tottered, but he successfully confronted the Binh Xuyen* and the Hoa Hao* and Cao Dai* religious sects, enabling the Friends of Vietnam to use their political power and press contacts to maneuver Eisenhower into reaffirming and increasing his support to "free Vietnam" from Communist

aggression. This required selling Diem to Americans as an Asian democrat, no easy job given Diem's often antidemocratic remarks. The Vietnam Lobby eventually created a number of myths to bolster American support for Diem: (1) the "miracle myth" of political stability, economic development, land reform, and refugee resettlement; (2) the "democratic myth" justifying refusal to hold reunification elections mandated by the Geneva Accords* because Communists would win by subverting the election process; (3) the myth that refugees* moving south were portrayed as peasants "voting with their feet" against "Communist oppression"; and (4) the myth that North Vietnamese aggression necessitated Diem's totalitarian measures and substantial increases in American military assistance.

While possessing grains of truth, these myths created false images. "Stability" resulted from brutal oppression. The local economy was disintegrating, thanks partially to American aid. Land reform was a failure, and Diem's favoritism toward northern refugees created animosity among native southerners. Ho Chi Minh was a hero even in the south and would have defeated Diem in both northern and southern Vietnam in a fair election. Rather than common peasants, northern refugees were almost exclusively Catholics, having served either in the French colonial government or the French Union Forces,* and were urged to migrate by U.S. General Edward Lansdale's* propaganda campaign. The Vietcong* organized resistance to Diem over

the North Vietnamese government's opposition at first. The Lobby's fealty to Diem was short-lived. After his murder, the Lobby sent a congratulatory telegram to the generals. SF

Sources: Frances FitzGerald, *Fire in the Lake: The Vietnamese and the Americans in Vietnam*, 1972; Robert Sheer and Warren Hinckle, "The Vietnam Lobby," *Ramparts*, January 25, 1969: pp. 31–36; Denis Warner, *The Last Confucian*, 1963; Hillaire Du Berrier, *Background to Betrayal: The Tragedy of Vietnam*, 1965.

AMPHIBIOUS FORCES

Task Force 76 of the Seventh Fleet* was responsible for amphibious action during the Vietnam War. Using transport and cargo ships, helicopters, tank landing ships, and dock landing ships, Task Force 76 carried out large numbers of amphibious assaults, especially in I Corps* where the Marine Amphibious Force was operating. Amphibious forces, including Task Force 76 and Task Force 76.8, assisted in the removal of refugees* from Cambodia and South Vietnam, as well as American personnel, during the evacuations of 1975.

Sources: Peter L. Hilgartner, *The Marines in Vietnam, 1954–1973*, 1974; Edward J. Marolda and G. Wesley Pryce III, *A Short History of the United States Navy and the Southeast Asia Conflict, 1950–1975*, 1984; Harry G. Summers Jr., *Vietnam War Almanac*, 1985.

Below: Marines disembark from amphibious tractors during a river crossing near Da Nang in 1967.

Right: LCMs (landing craft, mechanized) exercise off the USS *Denver* in the Gulf of Tonkin. These were meant to land Marine tanks ashore. The amphibious force was often used to extend the allied flank at sea, block Communist movements, land troops in the enemy's rear, or reinforce front-line units. The Seventh Fleet's Amphibious Task Force (Task Force 76) exercised operational control of the Amphibious Ready Group (ARG) and the Special Landing Force (SLF). The powerful, versatile, and mobile formation was capable of striking along the length of the South Vietnamese coast and far inland. The ARG usually consisted of three or four ships, including an amphibious assault ship (LPH), a dock landing ship (LSD), an attack transport (APA) or an amphibious transport dock (LPD), and a tank landing ship (LST).

Right: An amphibian tractor carries Marines and moves alongside soldiers north of Da Nang. A battalion of the 9th Marines was one of the first units to land in Vietnam following the decision to commit Marine forces against the Vietcong. On March 8, 1965, Battalion Landing Team (BLT) 3/9, commanded by Lieutenant Colonel Charles E. McPartllin Jr., landed in Da Nang in central Vietnam as part of the 9th Marine Expeditionary Brigade. Although clearly communicating that the Marines had arrived, the landing was an administrative landing in friendly territory, rather than an assault landing on an enemy-held beach.

Left: An amphibious assault vehicle, known as an LVT, fires in support of Marines in 1969. LVTs (landing vehicle, tracked) were particularly helpful in riverine operations.

Below: Marines prepare to paddle a rubber boat across a water course. The waterways of South Vietnam were not likely to be scenes of battle, but were more often used to provide support and conduct vital reconnaissance or other special operations. The waterways would not be targeted until 1975, when the coastal areas of South Vietnam became the war's main operational theater.

Opposite page: In 1967, poster-bearing women with the antiwar group "Women Strike For Peace" assemble outside the Pentagon. The doors to the building had to be locked and sealed after a group of demonstrators tried to storm their way inside.

Below: In this 1972 photograph, troops from the ARVN 2d Division at Lai Khe, South Vietnam, prepare to board U.S. helicopters of the 1st Air Cavalry Division that will transport them to An Loc.

AN LOC, BATTLE OF (1972)

Between April 13 and July 11, 1972, the siege of An Loc was a major part of the North Vietnamese Eastertide Offensive.* An Loc was the capital of Binh Long Province, an area approximately sixty-five miles north of Saigon.* Combined Vietcong* and North Vietnamese Army* (NVA) forces left their Cambodian bases and captured Loc Ninh, a town fifteen miles north of An Loc. The ARVN 5th Division (*see* Army of the Republic of Vietnam) went up to defend An Loc, and the NVA then surrounded the town and cut off reinforcements. Through more than three months of intense fighting, the South Vietnamese held their ground, enjoying massive support from American B-52* bombing sorties.* On July 11, 1972, the North Vietnamese and Vietcong ended the battle and withdrew from Binh Long Province.

Sources: Ngo Quang Truong, *The Easter Offensive of 1972*, 1980; G.H. Turley, *The Easter Offensive: Vietnam 1972*, 1985; James H. Willbanks, *The Battle of An Loc*, 2005.

ANNAM

Along with Tonkin* and Cochin China,* Annam was the name applied by the French to one of the three major regions of Vietnam. Annam was composed of nearly 57,000 square miles of land joining Cambodia and Laos* to the west and the South China Sea to the east, north, and south of the 17th parallel (*see* Geneva Accords). Its former capital was Hue,* and other principal cities were Binh Dinh, Da Nang,* Quang Tri, and Vinh. Anciently inhabited by the Cham* people, Annam was conquered by the Chinese in the third century BC and remained a colony until the revolution of 986. The Chinese were expelled by invading Annamites, retook the area in 1407, and were expelled again in 1428, after which Annam remained an independent monarchy until 1802, when the French brought it under their control.

Annam was south of the Red River Delta and at several points was only thirty miles wide. Except for the Montagnard* people in the highlands, most of the people of Annam lived along the coast and, in addition to rice cultivation, engaged in a vigorous coastal trade because of the abundance of sheltered bays along the coast.

Sources: Virginia Thompson, *French Indochina*, 1937; Joseph Buttinger, *The Smaller Dragon*, 1958; Henry McAleavy, *Black Flags in Vietnam: The Story of the Chinese Intervention*, 1968.

ANTICOLONIALISM

"Anticolonialism" is opposition to a nation's acquisition of colonies or holding of colonies or a particular colony. It may arise in the home country itself, as in the American opposition to acquiring the Philippines* in 1898 to 1899 and in the later American desire to grant the islands their independence. There was such anticolonialism in Europe as well, especially during the second half of the nineteenth century, the era of rapid colonization.

Anticolonialism also arose in Western nations' colonies, expressed by the National Congress in India, Sarekat Islam and the Indonesian Nationalist party in Indonesia, and Katipunan in the Philippines. Vietnamese anticolonialism first appeared in 1859 when the French captured Saigon* and guerrillas operated in Cochin China* thereafter. In the 1885 rebellion of young Emperor Han Nghi and his chief advisor, Ton That Thuyet, the two were defeated at Hue* and fled to Laos,* where Thuyet organized a resistance movement. Various nationalists and groups existed early in the twentieth century, using Vietnamese reactions to having to recite in school "Our ancestors the Gauls formerly inhabited Gaul." From French schooling, Vietnamese also learned of political and civil liberties and realized that they were denied these by colonialism.

Violence reappeared with the Viet Nam Quoc Dan Dang* (Vietnamese Nationalist Party), organized by the Chinese Nationalists and never quite eradicated by the French. Ho Chi Minh* created the Indochinese Communist Party (see Lao Dong Party) in 1929, in Hong Kong, and eventually it helped to create the Vietnam Independence League, the Vietminh,* which later defeated France. Vietnamese anticolonialism, combined with guerrilla warfare, won victory in the First Indochina War (1946–54) and was crucial to the American failure in the second war when the Saigon government was unable to rally its adherents.

The Communist government of unified Vietnam shares another form of anticolonialism with peoples in many former colonies. Expressed in what has come to be called neutralism, it is the view that economic and cultural colonialism continued after independence and must be overcome. RWS

Sources: Selig S. Harrison, *The Widening Gulf: Asian Nationalism and American Policy*, 1978; David G. Marr, *Vietnamese Anticolonialism, 1885–1925*, 1971; William J. Duiker, *The Rise of Nationalism in Vietnam, 1900–1941*, 1975.

ANTIWAR MOVEMENT

The United States has often experienced antiwar movements, but never did the opposition become as influential, divisive, and widespread as during the Vietnam War. From 1961 to 1963 American troop levels in South Vietnam increased from 685 to 16,000. At first, Americans paid scant attention to U.S. involvement. Beginning in 1965 troop levels increased rapidly, reaching a peak of 543,000 in 1969. The increase, with concomitant increases in casualties, piqued public interest and became a formative factor in the development of the antiwar movement. As the war intensified, the antiwar movement—in reality many movements with diverse goals—emerged, and the National Mobilization to End the War in Vietnam became the most well-known group.

Below: In 1969, antiwar protestors march down Pennsylvania Avenue in Washington, D.C., from the Capitol toward the Washington Monument, for a rally against the Vietnam War.

The antiwar movement owed much to the civil rights movement, borrowing heavily from its direct-action techniques based on civil disobedience. College students became deeply involved, especially those who saw civil rights and the war in Vietnam as directly related. After the Vietcong* attack on Pleiku in 1965, the United States responded with massive air strikes against North Vietnam, and "teach-ins" occurred on many campuses. Protest marches, speeches, and congressional hearings followed.

Even though very small, the antiwar movement disagreed over methods and goals. Activists divided over whether to protest the war or the system producing it. Increasingly, a generation gap developed. Alienated young Americans developed a counterculture to demonstrate their anger—long hair, bizarre dress, communal living, and drug use. Older, more affluent Americans began to develop questions about the war when troop levels and casualties increased and draft* calls began reaching their children. Some people believed the war was morally wrong, some thought it unwinnable, and some criticized it for diverting attention and resources from more important domestic problems. Some hoped to use the antiwar movement as a vehicle for altering America's economic and political system. Many divergent groups constituted the antiwar movement—students, the New Left, the Old Left, pacifists, Communists, church groups, liberals, conservatives, intellectuals, anarchists, utopians, and idealists. When protests failed to alter policies in 1967 and 1968, the movement increasingly split between those advocating nonviolent civil disobedience and those calling for militant, violent confrontation and the use of force. Groups like the Southern Christian Leadership Conference advocated nonviolence, while others like the Students for a Democratic Society* and the Weather Underground became increasingly militant and prone to violent protests. Militant demonstrators attempted to close Selective Service offices, burned or turned in draft cards, destroyed Selective Service files, boycotted and demonstrated against weapons manufacturers, held massive rallies, bombed ROTC buildings, and practiced self-immolation.

In 1968 the antiwar movement rallied behind the political campaigns of Senator Robert Kennedy* of New York and Senator Eugene McCarthy* of Minnesota. The Tet Offensive* in February 1968 energized the antiwar movement, toppled Lyndon B. Johnson's* political hopes, and convinced increasingly large numbers of "middle-Americans" that the Vietnam War was a losing effort. After the assassinations of Robert Kennedy and Martin Luther King Jr.* in the spring of 1968, the antiwar movement temporarily lost some of its momentum, and its frustrations exploded with tempestuous demonstrations at the Democratic National Convention in Chicago.

After Richard Nixon's* election in 1968, the war and protests continued. Nixon began reducing U.S. troop levels but intensified the bombing* of North Vietnam,

Laos,* and Cambodia. A nationwide moratorium, involving more than a million demonstrators, occurred in October 1969, and widespread protests followed the U.S. invasion of Cambodia and the Kent State University* incident in 1970. By 1971 polls showed that 71 percent of Americans believed the war had been a mistake. The antiwar minority had become the majority. Because of Nixon's Vietnamization policy and the Watergate* controversy, the war consumed less and less political energy in 1972 and 1973, and the antiwar movement gradually dissipated. Activists either devoted their time to other counterculture issues, joined the radical underground, or returned to mainstream society. JH

Sources: Thomas Powers, *Vietnam, The War at Home*, 1984; Nancy Zaroulis and Gerald Sullivan, *Who Spoke Up? American Protest Against the War in Vietnam 1963–1975*, 1984; Charles DeBendetti, *An American Ordeal: The Antiwar Movement of the Vietnam Era*, 1990.

AP BAC, BATTLE OF (1963)

The Battle of Ap Bac began to develop in December 1962. Ap Bac was a village in the Mekong Delta,* approximately forty miles southwest of Saigon.* Three Vietcong* companies built defensive positions along a mile-long canal connecting Ap Bac with the village of Ap Tan Thoi. The Vietcong dug in behind trees, grass, and shrubs with clear views of the surrounding rice fields. The Army of the Republic of Vietnam (ARVN) 7th Division attacked the position, and although they outnumbered the Vietcong by ten to one, they were defeated. The ARVN was characterized by incompetent officers and terrible morale. At the end of the battle, on January 2, 1963, the ARVN had lost five helicopters and sixty were dead, while the Vietcong suffered three casualties. Although American military advisors in South Vietnam tried to claim the battle a victory because the Vietcong abandoned their position, the engagement showed how difficult a guerrilla war would be and how much the United States would have to learn about the nature of warfare in Southeast Asia.

Sources: Stanley Karnow, *Vietnam: A History*, 1983; Joseph Buttinger, *Vietnam: A Dragon Embattled*, Vol. 2, *Vietnam at War*, 1967.

AP BIA

See Hamburger Hill

APOCALYPSE NOW

See Rambo and Other Vietnam Films

ARC LIGHT OPERATIONS

The code name for the devastating aerial raids of B-52* Stratofortresses against enemy positions in Southeast Asia, the first B-52 Arc Light raid took place on June 18, 1965, on a suspected Vietcong* base north of Saigon.* For this raid elements of the 2d and 320th Bombardment Wings of the Strategic Air Command had deployed from the United States to Anderson Air Force Base, Guam. Shortly after this strike, the results of which were inconclusive, several Americans began to question the advisability of "swatting flies with sledgehammers." During the eight years of Arc Light operations such criticism became increasingly common.

The B-52s assigned to the Arc Light mission were involved in several types of operations; air interdiction, strategic bombing, and raids on such important targets as Hanoi* and Haiphong were only a few such episodes. For instance, in November 1965 B-52s directly supported American ground forces for the first time, and were used regularly for that purpose thereafter. Perhaps the most important such action involved support of incursions into Cambodia (*see* Operation Binh Tay) and Laos (*see* Lam Son 719) in 1970 and 1971, operations designed to check flows of North Vietnamese personnel and assets from safe havens on South Vietnam's border into the country.

Below: Three B-52s drop 1,000- and 750-pound bombs on Communist targets 25 miles from Bien Hoa Air Base in 1966.

Between June 18, 1965, and August 18, 1973, the effective dates of Arc Light operations, the Strategic Air Command scheduled 126,663 combat sorties* for B-52s, of which 126,615 were actually launched. Of this total, 125,479 sorties actually reached their target areas and 124,532 successfully released their bombs on target. Geographically, 27 percent of the missions were flown in Laos, 12 percent in Cambodia, and 6 percent in North Vietnam. The remainder attacked targets in South Vietnam. These missions expended more than 3.5 million tons of conventional ordnance. Altogether, the Air Force lost thirty-one B-52s during Arc Light operations—eighteen from hostile fire over North Vietnam and thirteen from other operational causes. RDL

Sources: Robert R. Kritt, "B-52 Arc Light Operations," in Carl Berger, ed., *The United States Air Force in Southeast Asia, 1961–1973, An Illustrated Account*, 1977; Mark Clodfelter, *Limits of Air Power*, 1989; Don Harten, *Arc Light One*, 2003.

Below: Australian troops move out in a convoy of armored personnel carriers near Bien Hoa in 1965. From the time of the arrival of the first Australian military advisors in 1962 to 1975, some 50,000 Australians—including ground troops, air force, and navy personnel—served in Vietnam; 520 died as a result of the war and almost 2,400 were wounded.

ARMORED PERSONNEL CARRIERS

Highly adaptable vehicles running on tanklike tracks, the armored personnel carriers, or APCs, proved to be the backbone of armored cavalry formations during the Vietnam War. The M113 was the most important APC, and it could be adapted for use as a carrier for mortars, machine guns, flamethrowers, troops, and command posts. When properly armed and protected with heavy machine guns and secured hatch, they could also be used as assault vehicles. The M113 was lightly armored with aluminum and equipped with a .50-caliber Browning heavy machine gun on its roof. In addition to its driver, the M113 APC carried eleven infantry troops and a machine gunner. It had a speed of forty miles an hour on land and nearly four miles an hour in water. By January 1968 there were more than 2,100 M113 APCs in Vietnam. By that time the APC had even evolved into an ACAV—armored cavalry assault vehicle. Armored cavalry units were reequipped with M113s upon arrival in Vietnam, and they modified the vehicle by building armored shields around the .50-caliber machine gun and adding two 7.62mm M60 machine guns.

Sources: Ian Vhoog, "Land Forces in Vietnam and Their Weapons," in John S. Bowman, ed., *The Vietnam War: An Almanac*, 1985; Shelby L. Stanton, *Vietnam Order of Battle*, 1981; Edgar C. Doleman Jr., *The Vietnam Experience: Tools of War*, 1984.

ARMORED WARFARE

Although jungle fighting has traditionally not been a hospitable environment for armored battle, the Vietnam War provided an exception, with both sides using tanks and armored personnel carriers* (APCs). Before 1965 the United States and the Army of the Republic of Vietnam (ARVN) had only a few M113 APCs, M8 armored cars, and Gage V-100 Commando armored cars. But beginning in 1965 the United States Marines* had a tank battalion* of M48 A-3 Patton tanks with each of its two divisions. Early in 1966 the Army's 1st Infantry Division* also brought a squadron of M48s to Vietnam. In 1969 the M551 Sheridan tanks were deployed to Vietnam, but they suffered from constant electronic, engine, and transmission problems in the wet South Vietnamese climate.* The M48 remained the backbone of American armor. The M113 APCs were important, especially after they were reequipped with new armored shields around the .50-caliber machine gun and new 7.62mm M60 machine guns. Eventually, the United States had three tank battalions in Vietnam, as well as ten battalions of APC mounted infantry, one armored regiment, and five armored cavalry squadrons. By the end of the war the ARVN had three tank battalions and eighteen armored cavalry units.

Above: A flame-throwing tank attacks a Vietcong position during Operation Elliot A in July 1967. This one is being used by the 1st Marine Division.

Below: Marines ride on and march behind their tanks in July 1970.

Right: Troops of the 5th Marines use tanks to assault Communist positions south-west of Da Nang in 1969.

Below: Crews check M42 self-propelled 40mm anti-aircraft guns near An Khe in 1967. Used against ground targets rather than airplanes, the M42s were called "Dusters" for the amount of dust they would stir up on Vietnamese dirt roads. The Communists called them "Fire Dragons" for the amount of tracer bullets they spewed.

Above: 9th Marines move past one of their tanks near Cam Lo in 1967. A CH-46 evacuates wounded in the background.

Left: Marines of the 11th Motor Transport Battalion operate their tracked vehicle south of Da Nang in 1970.

North Vietnam did not employ tanks until later in the conflict. Their tanks first appeared in 1968 with the use of Soviet PT-76 amphibious tanks to attack a Special Forces* camp near Khe Sanh.* Eventually they added Soviet T-34, T-54, and T-59 tanks until their armor totaled 700 vehicles by 1975. Because of inferior training, the North Vietnamese Army* (NVA) armored units were no match for either the U.S. or ARVN groups, but the NVA made effective use of 57mm recoilless rifles, RPG-2 and RPG-7 rocket-propelled grenades, and the Soviet "Sagger" wire-guided missiles. In the Final Offensive (see Ho Chi Minh Campaign) of 1975, the 700 NVA tanks overran the 350 ARVN tanks.

Sources: Simon Dunstan, *Vietnam Tracks: Armor in Battle, 1945–1975*, 1982; Donn A. Starry, *Mounted Combat in Vietnam*, 1979; Ian Vhoog, "Land Forces in Vietnam," in John S. Bowman, ed., *The Vietnam War: An Almanac*, 1985.

ARMY, UNITED STATES

Throughout the Vietnam War, the main burden of battle fell on the United States Army. More than 65 percent of the American personnel wounded or killed in action in Vietnam were serving in the Army. Between 1961 and 1975, 30,868 Army personnel died from hostile action in Vietnam, and 7,193 died nonhostile deaths. A total of 201,536 Army personnel were wounded in action in Vietnam. The commander of the Military Assistance Command, Vietnam* was an Army general. Throughout the course of the war, the Army deployed to Vietnam a total of 81 infantry battalions,* 3 tank battalions, 12 cavalry squadrons,* 70 artillery and air defense artillery battalions, and 142 aviation companies and air cavalry* troops.

Sources: Harry G. Summers Jr., *Vietnam War Almanac*, 1985; Shelby L. Stanton, *Vietnam Order of Battle*, 1981; Andrew F. Krepinevich Jr., *The Army and Vietnam*, 1986.

ARTILLERY

During the Vietnam War the United States Army* deployed sixty-five artillery battalions and five air defense battalions to Vietnam. In addition, there were ten artillery battalions from the United States Marines* and United States naval bombardment* from the Seventh Fleet* in the South China Sea. By the end of the war the Army of the Republic of Vietnam* had sixty-four artillery battalions. South Korea* supplied six artillery battalions, Thailand* three, and the Philippines* and Australia* one each. The primary artillery weapons employed in Vietnam included: (1) the M109, a 155mm self-propelled howitzer with a range of 14,600 meters; (2) the M107, a 175mm gun with a range of 32,600 meters; (3) the M110, an 8-inch self-propelled howitzer with a range of 16,800 meters; (4) the M114A1, a 155mm howitzer with a range of 14,600 meters; (5) the M102, a 105mm howitzer with a range of 11,500 meters; (6) the M108, a 105mm light howitzer with a range of 11,500 meters; and (7) the M101A1, an older 105mm howitzer with a range of 11,000 meters.

Sources: David Ewing Ott, *Field Artillery, 1954–1973*, 1975; Shelby L. Stanton, *Vietnam Order of Battle*, 1981; Edgar C. Doleman Jr., *The Vietnam Experience: Tools of War*, 1984.

ARVN (ARMY OF THE REPUBLIC OF VIETNAM)

See Army of the Republic of Vietnam, p. 60

Opposite page: In 1964, before the introduction of regular U.S. ground troops, U.S. Army Captain Robert Bacon leads an ARVN unit on patrol.

Below: Troops from the 7th Battalion of the 8th Artillery operate an M110 8-inch howitzer in March 1968 near Long Binh, South Vietnam. The M110 was known for its accuracy. Its heavy 203mm, 200-pound projectiles were not affected by wind. In the foreground, a hydraulic spade holds the M110 in place when it fires.

ARMY OF THE REPUBLIC OF VIETNAM (ARVN)

Below: A U.S. Army advisor helps an ARVN soldier with his weapon after a Vietcong ambush in 1964.

Late in the 1940s, as Ho Chi Minh and his Vietminh army gained strength in Vietnam and the French hemorrhaged money and men, France tried to establish a Vietnamese National Army (VNA) in an effort to preserve its colony, all the time portraying the struggle as a noble fight against Communism. The French organized the Vietnamese National Army into divisions, battalions, companies, and platoons, and on paper it appeared worthy of respect. On the battlefield, however, was another story. Vietnamese soldiers drafted into service deserted at the first opportunity, and in combat those who stayed proved thoroughly unreliable. VNA soldiers broke ranks at the first sight of Vietminh troops and avoided firefights to a fault. Despite years of training by battle-hardened officers of the French Expeditionary Corps, VNA officers suffered from a lack of courage, imagination, and perseverance.

The French, of course, found VNA ineptitude appalling, which should have come as no surprise. VNA soldiers were not fools. The Vietminh had nationalism on their side, the French only colonial exploitation. The Vietminh had Ho Chi Minh to admire and follow, while the VNA had only the most recent French colonial administrator. The Vietminh represented the future, the VNA only the past. VNA soldiers had no cause for which to fight, and the prospects of dying in the name of France held little appeal. Early in the 1950s, when the momentum began to shift toward the Vietminh, the Vietnamese National Army disintegrated into an institution known more for its corruption than its bravery. In 1954, the Geneva Accords divided Vietnam at the 17th parallel, with North Vietnam known as the Democratic Republic of Vietnam and South Vietnam as the Republic of Vietnam. The Vietminh became the nucleus of the North Vietnamese Army (NVA), while the VNA constituted the foundation of the Army of the Republic of Vietnam (ARVN).

The ARVN may have had new uniforms and a new flag, but it inherited a lack of identity, willpower, and

commitment. Before soldiers will sacrifice their lives in the name of patriotism, they must possess a national identity. The Republic of Vietnam, however, was of recent diplomatic vintage, a creation of the Geneva Accords of 1954. The vast majority of Vietnamese peasants were illiterate, and if they knew of any Vietnamese leader, it was Ho Chi Minh, not President Ngo Dinh Diem. They had never heard of the Republic of Vietnam, and to expect them to fight valiantly was naive and stupid. Nevertheless, the United States assumed the French mantle and tried to turn the ARVN into a real fighting force. By 1960 the ARVN counted 234,000 troops, but despite billions of dollars in aid from the United States, it could not contend with the Vietcong (VC). The Battle of Ap Bac in 1963 exposed the ARVN's weaknesses and convinced Secretary of Defense Robert McNamara that only U.S. combat troops could defeat the VC. The ARVN was simply not up to the task.

The ARVN's most serious challenge was instability and corruption in the government of South Vietnam. Although the United States heralded South Vietnam as a beacon of democracy in Southeast Asia, its government was closer to a fascist dictatorship dripping in venality. Officials like Ngo Dinh Diem viewed the ARVN more as a weapon to protect their own political power than to fight Communism, and repeated coups d'etat undermined political loyalty. The government shamelessly manipulated elections and crushed dissent. Through conscription, economic incentives, and even kidnapping, the ARVN increased its ranks to 500,000 troops at the end of 1964, 720,000 at the end of 1966, and 800,000 at the end of 1968. During the late 1960s and early 1970s the ARVN identity gradually took shape. A few ARVN units distinguished themselves. During the Tet Offensive ARVN Airborne Division troops fought well, and in 1970 they spearheaded the combined U.S.-ARVN invasion of Cambodia. Almost as successful was the ARVN 1st Infantry Division, which fought valiantly against Vietcong and NVA forces in I Corps. ARVN marines served with distinction in all four corps zones. Along with the Airborne and the 1st Infantry divisions, ARVN marines took heavy casualties during the poorly executed invasion of Laos in 1971.

In 1968, President Richard Nixon announced his Vietnamization program—a concerted effort to turn the war over to the ARVN. At the end of 1969 the ARVN claimed to have 875,000 troops, a number which swelled to 940,000 at the end of 1970 and to more than 1 million at the end of 1972, with a combat strength of 500,000 soldiers—108,000 regular troops, 377,000 Regional and Popular Forces, and 14,000 border rangers. They were divided into 11 infantry divisions, 1 marine division, and 1 air cavalry division. Those divisions contained 18 armored cavalry squadrons, 124 infantry battalions, 9 marine battalions, 55 ranger battalions, 68 artillery battalions, 40 engineer battalions, 16 signal battalions, and 12 military police battalions. By that time, the ARVN had suffered more than 190,000 combat deaths.

Anxious to extract the United States from Vietnam, Nixon accelerated the pace of Vietnamization, handing over to South Vietnam a mountain of war materiel and billions of dollars. By 1972 the ARVN was the largest, most well-equipped army in the world. The South Vietnamese Navy, with more than 1,500 ships, 40,000 officers and sailors, and 13,000 marines, was one of the largest in the world. Size, however, did not translate into success. Desertion rates remained high and morale low, and when U.S. troops left Vietnam, the ARVN was on its own. North Vietnam bided its time, rebuilding after the disastrous Eastertide Offensive of 1972 and restoring the NVA to full battle strength. In April 1975 the NVA attacked South Vietnam. During late March and early April, eighteen NVA divisions settled into place within a forty-mile radius of Saigon. They attacked on April 26. The ARVN fought a retreating action back toward Saigon, and by April 29 NVA troops were inside the city limits. When the last Americans evacuated Saigon on April 30, 1975, the ARVN collapsed. North Vietnamese troops overran the city. The war was over. A total of 223,748 ARVN soldiers were killed during the war, with another 1,169,763 wounded, a testimony to dismal leadership.

Sources: Dong Van Khuyen, *The RVNAF*, 1981; Shelby L. Stanton, *Vietnam Order of Battle*, 1981, and *The Rise and Fall of An American Army: U.S. Ground Troops in Vietnam, 1965-1973*, 1985; Cao Van Vien and Dong Van Khuyen, *Reflections of the Vietnam War*, 1980.

ARVN AIRBORNE DIVISION

The ARVN Airborne Division was first organized into the French Union Forces* as individual battalions.* Four airborne battalions were committed to Dien Bien Phu,* and they distinguished themselves. After the Geneva Conference (*see* Geneva Accords) of 1954, Vietnamese units were integrated into the ARVN, with Vietnamese officers replacing the French. In the mid-1960s the airborne battalions were organized into independent brigades,* and in 1968 into the Airborne Division. They made a number of parachute assaults between 1950 and 1975. The ARVN Airborne Division was widely considered the best unit in the South Vietnamese military and the equal of any military unit in Southeast Asia. In 1966 General Nguyen Cao Ky* sent airborne units to subdue rebellious units in I Corps* during the Buddhist* crisis. Against the North Vietnamese Army* (NVA) and Vietcong,* the airborne troops were used as a "fire brigade." The ARVN Airborne Division was one of the few units to serve in all four tactical zones.

During the Tet Offensive* the division fought extremely well, tenaciously holding key positions. At Tan Son Nhut Air Base,* an airborne training battalion was deployed to close a breach in ARVN lines where NVA-Vietcong forces were entering the base. They closed the breach and decisively defeated the attacking forces. The battalion received numerous decorations. In 1969 the division was paired with the U.S. 1st Cavalry* in joint operations along the Cambodian border, spearheading the 1970 Cambodian invasion (*see*

Below: ARVN soldiers use an M-48 tank to advance near the Dong Ha River in 1972. Note the tank's camouflage. Soldiers often used tree branches and brush to conceal tanks and other weaponry.

Operation Binh Tay). In 1971 the division suffered heavy casualties in the ill-conceived Laotian invasion (Lam Son 719).* During the 1972 Eastertide Offensive,* and again throughout 1974, the division saw heavy combat in I Corps. As the 1975 Final Offensive (*see* Ho Chi Minh Campaign) overran I Corps, the division was withdrawn to defend Saigon,* where they provided the last organized resistance against the NVA.

While other South Vietnamese units proved ineffective, wilting under fire, the Airborne Division and a handful of other elite units fought well, even heroically. They were well trained, well equipped, and well led. The French instilled the airborne esprit de corps, which the division never lost. Division commanders gave troops the security of knowing that the unit took care of their families while they were away and if they were killed, and would take care of the troops if they were disabled. SF

Sources: Dong Van Khuyen, *The RVNAF*, 1980; Cao Van Vien and Dong Van Khuyen, *Reflections of the Vietnam War*, 1980; Robert K. Brigham, *ARVN: Life and Death in the South Vietnamese Army*, 2006.

ARVN 1ST INFANTRY DIVISION

The 1st Infantry Division was second only to the Airborne Division* as an elite ARVN (*see* Army of the Republic of Vietnam) unit. Stationed in I Corps,* the 1st Division was responsible for protecting five northern provinces against Vietcong* attack and North Vietnamese Army* (NVA) infiltration from Laos* and across the Demilitarized Zone* (DMZ). It was a formidable task given the rugged

terrain. The 1st Division was often assisted by other elite ARVN units, including the Airborne Division, marines,* and rangers, as well as by American units, particularly U.S. Marines and the 101st Airborne Division.* The 1st Division saw heavy combat during the war. I Corps was sparsely populated with only two major cities—Hue*

and Da Nang.* Given a strong Vietcong presence in I Corps, and resistance by ARVN troops to serving away from home, it was always difficult to maintain sufficient manpower. Elite ARVN units were used to being shifted around the country. Hue, the imperial capital and always resistive to Saigon's* authority, was a center for Buddhist* opposition to Ngo Dinh Diem* and subsequent rulers of South Vietnam. Da Nang was an important port city often influenced by events in Hue. During the 1966 Buddhist crisis, the 1st Division sided with the Buddhists, and Nguyen Cao Ky* sent the Airborne Division in to restore government authority. American advisors reacted with horror as the ARVN's two best units prepared to battle each other. The disaster was averted when Ky promised elections.

The 1st Division participated in the ill-conceived 1971 Laotian invasion. It bore the brunt of the 1972 Eastertide Offensive,* as well as the "strategic raids" of 1974 that left it in a weakened condition as the Final Offensive approached (*see* Ho Chi Minh Campaign). With I Corps collapsing, Nguyen Van Thieu's* abrupt troop movements and indecisive orders made the situation impossible. The 1st Division was completely exposed and overwhelmed. SF

Source: Robert K. Brigham, *ARVN: Life and Death in the South Vietnamese Army*, 2006.

Left: South Vietnamese trainees learn how to camouflage themselves and set up ambushes.

Below: These National Police Field Force soldiers march back to their training center after a class on defensive combat.

Opposite page: A wounded Marine accepts a light from a buddy following a fight in the A Shau Valley area in 1970. The battle was part of Operation Dewey Canyon.

ARVN MARINES

One of the ARVN's (*see* Army of the Republic of Vietnam) three best units, the marines served in all four Corps Tactical Zones, and most extensively in I Corps.* Organized into six battalions* with one battalion of artillery, the marines were given additional artillery and upgraded to a division in October 1968. Marine units fought well during the Tet Offensive* but were plagued with desertions, and 1969 was devoted to rebuilding. They did not participate in the 1970 Cambodian invasion (*see* Operation Binh Tay), but were involved in the 1971 Laotian invasion (*see* Lam Son 719), being assigned to secure the southern flank. Fighting on unfamiliar and extremely difficult terrain, against a superior enemy force, the marines took heavy casualties. Although some units did not perform up to expectations and panic gripped others during the retreat, it is a testimony to the marines (as well as the 1st Infantry Division* and the Airborne Division*) that they did not surrender and were not wiped out as the North Vietnamese Army* (NVA) made every effort to encircle and annihilate the ARVN's three best divisions.

During the 1972 Eastertide Offensive,* I Corps marines delayed NVA forces, enabling Saigon*—which responded too slowly—to counterattack. While the 3d Infantry Division disintegrated—one regiment surrendered without a fight—no marine unit surrendered or broke ranks. One battalion of 300 was reduced in two days to 69 men. They fought, maneuvered, regrouped, and fought again, continuing to fight as a unit despite decimation. Although badly mauled marine units participated in the counterattack, they ultimately regained Quang Tri City and most of I Corps. In the face of

Below: ARVN Marines train with an American Army captain during field exercises in 1963.

the NVA's 1975 Final Offensive (*see* Ho Chi Minh Campaign), I and II Corps* collapsed. ARVN units evaporated. Nguyen Van Thieu's* interference and indecisive orders prevented any possibility of an effective defense. Marine units that were still operative were redeployed to III Corps* for the futile defense of Saigon.* SF

Source: Robert K. Brigham, *ARVN: Life and Death in the South Vietnamese Army*, 2006.

A SHAU VALLEY

The A Shau Valley is located in Thua Thien Province of I Corps* near the Laotian border. Actually composed of several valleys and mountains, the A Shau Valley was one of the principal entry points to South Vietnam of the Ho Chi Minh Trail.* It was an area that was critical to the North Vietnamese because it was the conduit for supplies, additional troops, and communications for units of the North Vietnamese Army* (NVA) and Vietcong* (VC) operating in I Corps. Because of its importance to the NVA and VC, it was the target of repeated major operations by allied forces, especially the U.S. 101st Airborne Division.* Likewise, it was defended vigorously by the NVA and VC. Consequently, the A Shau Valley was the scene of much fighting throughout the war, and it acquired a fearsome reputation for soldiers on both sides. Being a veteran of A Shau Valley operations became a mark of distinction among combat veterans. Although each American effort to staunch the shipment of men and materiel through the A Shau Valley was successful for only a brief period of time, the net effect was a series of transitory decreases in the flow followed by increases until the next American operation. Since the U.S. strategy for fighting the enemy did not include occupying remote and sparsely populated areas, the enemy often lost military battles but subsequently was able to reinfiltrate an area when the Americans left the battlefield. The most famous battle of the A Shau Valley was Operation Apache Snow,* also known as Hamburger Hill.* STT

Sources: Willard Pearson, *The War in the Northern Provinces, 1966–1968*, 1975; Shelby L. Stanton, *The Rise and Fall of an American Army: U.S. Ground Troops in Vietnam, 1965–1973*, 1985; Larry Chambers, *Death in the A Shau Valley*, 1998.

ATROCITIES

Unlike earlier wars involving the United States, the conflict in Vietnam brought home to most Americans the fact that their country, as well as the enemy, was capable of committing atrocities. The case of William Calley* and the massacre at My Lai* was the most intense example, but the press regularly circulated stories of civilian casualties, torture and

Below left: A soldier of the 2d Royal Australian Regiment keeps watch along a trail during guard duty in 1970. Alongside him is his M60 machine gun.

Below right: Aussies with an M60 machine gun and self-loading rifles use trenches to guard the perimeter of Ben Hoa Air Base in 1965.

executions of Vietcong* prisoners, throwing Vietcong prisoners of war* out of helicopters, and cutting off the ears of Vietcong* and North Vietnamese dead. As a guerrilla war without fronts, and fought in a distant land against a different ethnic group, the Vietnam War was ripe for atrocities. American soldiers, tired and frustrated about the environment and the nature of the conflict, angry about losing comrades and being unable to separate the Vietcong from civilians, came to look upon all Vietnamese as combatants. Approximately 10 percent of all American casualties were caused by booby traps,* and during lulls in formal military engagements that rate was even higher. American soldiers often developed feelings of deep hostility for the Vietnamese. Between 1965 and 1973, 278 Army and Marine soldiers were convicted of serious offenses—murder, rape, and negligent homicide—against Vietnamese civilians, but civilian casualties in the field—from accident and atrocities—were far higher. The press, which was more active in the Vietnam War than in any earlier conflict in American history, was also more able than ever to carry the story of the war back home.

But Americans were not alone in committing atrocities. Terrorism was a major weapon used by the Vietcong in promoting their cause. More than 25,000 people were part of the Vietcong Security Service, and between 1957 and 1972 they were responsible for nearly 37,000 assassinations and nearly 60,000 kidnappings—usually of government officials, religious leaders, civil servants, teachers, and prospective draftees. Vietcong terrorism was also used to guarantee a lack of cooperation among peasants and villagers for the pacification programs of the United States (*see* Rural Reconstruction) and South Vietnam (*see* Accelerated Pacification Campaign).

Finally, civilian atrocities commonly resulted from the indiscriminate bombing or shelling of major cities. The Vietcong and North Vietnamese killed large numbers of civilians in their artillery barrages against Saigon,* Hue,* and Da Nang,* and the United States killed large numbers of civilians in its bombing raids against Hanoi* and Haiphong. Even conservative estimates of civilian deaths in Vietnam total more than 250,000 people during the war. The magnitude of the atrocities, on both sides, during the war in Vietnam helped reinforce in the mind of the American public that the conflict in Southeast Asia was a futile, brutalizing effort from which the United States ought to withdraw.

Sources: Guenter Lewy, *America in Vietnam*, 1978; Michael Bilton and Kevin Sim, *Four Hours in My Lai*, 1993; Christian Appy, *Patriots: The Vietnam War Memories from All Sides*, 2003.

AUGUST REVOLUTION

See Bao Dai

AUSTRALIA

Because of its charter membership in the Southeast Asia Treaty Organization,* Australia found itself drawn into the American sphere of influence in the Pacific. And it was a role it did not resent. After the French defeat at Dien Bien Phu* in 1954, the Australians steadily warned the United States that the fall of South Vietnam would threaten democracies throughout Asia. Australian officials believed the domino theory.* As early as 1962 Australia had sent thirty military advisors to work with the ARVN* on jungle and guerrilla warfare tactics. After the Gulf of Tonkin Resolution* in 1964, Australia increased its troop contingent in South Vietnam to 1,300 people, with a large combat battalion at Bien Hoa.* Under pressure from Washington in 1965 and 1966, Australia increased that commitment, eventually to more than 8,000 troops at its peak in October 1967. Australian prime minister Harold Holt consistently offered his support to Lyndon Johnson,* politically as well as militarily, even to the point of using a conscription system to supply his troop commitment. Next to the South Koreans, Australia provided the most military support to the United States in the conflict.

Sources: Stanley Karnow, *Vietnam: A History*, 1983; Peter King, *Australia's Vietnam*, 1983; Stanley Robert Larsen and James Lawton Collins Jr., *Allied Participation in Vietnam*, 1975.

Left: An American lightweight field jacket carried in the pack of the first Australian killed in Vietnam in the 1960s. Sergeant William Hacking carried the uniform top in his pack when he was killed by friendly fire. Holes are evident near the bottom of the uniform where the grenade fragments passed through the folded garment.

Below: Royal Australian Airmen march off the flight line at the Saigon International Airport in 1964. These were among the first Australians to come to the aid of the South Vietnamese government.

B-52 BOMBER

The B-52 is regarded by experts as the most successful military aircraft ever produced. It began entering service in the mid-1950s, and by 1959 had replaced the awesome but obsolete B-36 as the backbone of the heavy-bomber force of the Strategic Air Command (SAC). While its primary mission was nuclear deterrence through retaliation, the B-52 has been amazingly adaptable. It was initially designed to achieve very high-altitude penetration of enemy airspace. But when that concept was rendered obsolete by the development of accurate surface-to-air missiles (SAMs),* the B-52 was redesigned and reconstructed for low-altitude penetration. It has undergone eight major design changes since first flown in 1952, from the B-52A to the B-52H. Although much the same in appearance, the most recent version is a radically different aircraft, superior in every way to the first models.

When the Vietnam situation began to deteriorate in 1964, key SAC commanders began pressing for SAC to get involved in any U.S. action in Vietnam. But the first problem was one of mission. How could a heavy strategic bomber designed to carry nuclear bombs be used in Vietnam? The answer was to modify the B-52 again. Two B-52 units, the 320th Bomb Wing and the 2d Bomb Wing, had their aircraft modified to carry "iron bombs," i.e., conventional high-explosive bombs. After a second modification, each B-52 used in Vietnam could carry eighty-four 500-pound bombs internally and twenty-four 750-pound bombs on underwing racks, with a 3,000-mile nonstop range. The two bomb wings were deployed to operate from Guam as the 133d Provisional Wing. Later, additional units were

Below: A B-52 is loaded with incendiary bombs at its air base in the western Pacific in 1967. Incendiary bombs were meant to burn wide areas of growth where Communist camps lay hidden.

Left: A B-52 rises into the air from its base in the Pacific for a mission in 1967. B-52s had eight engines and were refueled in the air on long missions by Boeing KC-135 Stratotankers.

deployed to Thailand* and Okinawa to reduce in-flight time, and thus warning time.

The first B-52 raids against a target in South Vietnam (and the first war action for the B-52) took place on June 18, 1965. The target was a Vietcong* jungle sanctuary, and the results were not encouraging. Two B-52s collided in flight to the target and were lost in the Pacific Ocean. The results of the bombing could not be evaluated because the Vietcong controlled the area. Although the press criticized the use of B-52s, ground commanders were much impressed with the potential of the new heavy bomber. Previous attempts to use tactical bombers and fighter-bombers *(see Fighters)* to disrupt enemy troop concentrations and supply depots had not been successful. But the B-52 was a veritable flying boxcar, and the effect of a squadron-size attack was to create a virtual Armageddon on the ground.

Ironically, the most effective use of the B-52 in Vietnam was for tactical support of ground troops. B-52s were called in to disrupt enemy troop concentrations and supply areas with devastating effect. B-52 raids were also flown against targets in North Vietnam, Cambodia, and Laos.* General William Westmoreland* considered the B-52 essential to U.S. efforts in Vietnam. From June 1965 until August 1973, when operations ceased, B-52s flew 124,532 sorties* that successfully dropped their bomb loads on target. Thirty-one B-52s were lost; eighteen were shot down by the enemy (all over North Vietnam), and thirteen were lost to operational problems. JMR Jr.

Sources: Carl Berger, ed., *The United States Air Force in Southeast Asia, 1961–1973*, 1984; Andrew W. Waters, *All the U.S. Air Force Airplanes, 1907–1983*, 1983; R. Bruce Harley, *A Short History of Strategic Bombardment*, 1971.

BA CUT

See Hoa Hao

BAEZ, JOAN

Joan Baez was born on Staten Island, New York, on January 9, 1941. She excelled in music, and after her father began teaching physics at Harvard in the late 1950s, she turned to folk music, singing in local coffeehouses. Baez received several recording contracts after her performance at the 1959 Newport Folk Festival. Her liberal politics and belief in peace and disarmament made her a natural antiwar* leader when the Vietnam conflict escalated in the 1960s. Baez refused to pay her income taxes in 1966 to protest the war and was arrested in Oakland, California, in 1967 for picketing in front of the Northern California Draft Induction Center. Baez married draft* resister David Harris, and together they led a number of protest movements in the late 1960s and early 1970s. In 1973 Baez culminated her antiwar activities with a visit to Hanoi,* and after the visit she reported that American air raids had caused widespread destruction in Hanoi as well as wiping out part of an American POW* camp. SS

Sources: Charles Mortiz, ed., *Current Biography*, 1964; Stanley Millet, *South Vietnam–U.S. Communist Confrontation in Southeast Asia*, 1973; Nancy Zaroulis and Gerald Sullivan, *Who Spoke Up? American Protest Against the War in Vietnam, 1963–1975*, 1984; http://www.joanbaez.com.

BA GIA, BATTLE OF (1965)

On May 29, 1965, a contingent of more than 1,000 Vietcong* attacked three battalions of South Vietnamese troops at the hamlet of Ba Gia near Quang Ngai. The ARVN* troops panicked and fled the battlefield, leaving behind their weapons and uniforms. The Vietcong were driven out of Ba Gia by concentrated rocket and napalm* fire from U.S. F-100 Super Sabres and A-1 Skyraiders.* South Vietnamese troops reoccupied Ba Gia early in June, but on July 4, after only ninety minutes of battle, the Vietcong had driven them out again. Even though his own troops were standing by at the Quang Ngai airfield, General Nguyen Chanh Thi* requested the assistance of U.S. Marines,* who attacked and dislodged the Vietcong. Along with several other engagements in the late spring of 1965, Ba Gia convinced U.S. policymakers that South Vietnamese forces would need massive American military assistance if they were to stave off a Vietcong takeover.

Source: Terrence Maitland and Peter McInerney, *A Contagion of War*, 1983.

BALL, GEORGE WILDMAN

George Ball was born in Des Moines, Iowa, on December 21, 1909. He took both his undergraduate and law degrees at Northwestern University in 1930 and 1933, and then joined the general counsel's office of the Department of the Treasury. Between 1935 and 1942 Ball practiced law in Chicago, and in 1942 he became associate general counsel with the Lend Lease Administration. In 1944 President Franklin D. Roosevelt* named him director of the U.S. Strategic Bombing Survey in London. After the war, Ball returned to private law practice in Washington, D.C., and in 1961 he became undersecretary of state for economic affairs in the Kennedy* administration. Later in the year, Kennedy named him undersecretary of state, and Ball became an influential figure in the American diplomatic establishment. Between 1961 and 1966 Ball was an opponent of American involvement in the Vietnam War. He opposed the troop buildup occurring during the Kennedy administration and repeatedly argued that the regime of Ngo Dinh Diem* in South Vietnam was hopelessly corrupt, that a land war in Indochina* was not in the strategic interests of the United States, and that the objective of creating a viable, democratic nation there was unreachable. After the Gulf of Tonkin incident* in the summer of 1964, Ball opposed the American bombing* of North Vietnam, and he maintained that position throughout 1965 and 1966. From his experience as head of the U.S. Strategic Bombing Survey, Ball was convinced that American bombing would only make the North Vietnamese more committed to their political and military objectives. Frustrated about the drift of

Opposite page: In May 1975, Joan Baez joined other anti-war activists in Central Park to celebrate the end of the Vietnam War. Nearly three years had passed since the last U.S. troops had left Vietnam and since any U.S. military funds had been spent there. At the end of April 1975, the North Vietnamese conquered South Vietnam and reunited Vietnam under a Communist regime. In her 1975 performance, Baez celebrated the end of the Vietnam War; many conservatives, however, saw this as a celebration of the triumph of Communism in Vietnam and the defeat of the United States there.

Left: George Ball served as undersecretary of state in the John F. Kennedy administration and as an advisor in the Lyndon B. Johnson administration. He advised both presidents on foreign policy matters. He consistently argued against the presence of U.S. troops in Vietnam because he considered the region only tangential to U.S. national security interests.

Below: On December 19, 1972, as part of Operation Linebacker II, U.S. B-52 bombers hit targets throughout North Vietnam in the most ferocious aerial attack in the history of the war. Among the targets of the "Christmas bombings" was the international airport near Hanoi. Antiwar activist and folk singer Joan Baez was in North Vietnam at the time to distribute mail and Christmas presents to American prisoners of war. She toured the rubble of the airport.

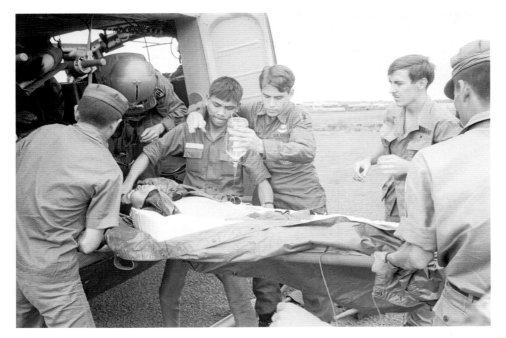

Above: On November 14, 1969, at Ban Me Thuot in South Vietnam, a U.S. jet in tactical air support accidentally bombed a unit of the Army of the Republic of Vietnam. Here an ARVN soldier wounded in the assault is loaded onto a medical evacuation helicopter.

American policy, Ball resigned from the State Department in September 1966 and returned to his law practice. In 1968, after the Tet Offensive,* President Lyndon B. Johnson* appointed Ball a member of the Senior Advisory Group to evaluate American policy in Southeast Asia. Taking their cue from Ball's long-held position, the Senior Advisory Group urged disengagement from Vietnam. In 1969 Ball became a senior partner in the Lehman Brothers investment firm. He wrote a number of books, including *The Discipline of Power* (1968), *Diplomacy in a Crowded World* (1976), and *The Past Has Another Pattern* (1982). George Ball died on May 27, 1994.

Source: James A. Bill, *George Ball: Behind the Scenes in U.S. Foreign Policy*, 1997.

THE BAMBOO BED

The Bamboo Bed is the title of William Eastlake's surrealistic 1969 Vietnam War novel. Beginning with the suicide of Madame Dieudonne after she hears of the death of her American ranger lover Captain Clancy, Eastlake tries to describe the absurdity of the war with implausible fantasy images: peace-loving hippie flower children wandering aimlessly through the Indochinese jungles; helicopter pilots having sex with medevac* nurses* while airborne; and American rangers topped with Roman helmets and accompanied by drummer boys being airlifted into French-Vietnamese villas. Although not altogether successful, the novel was an early literary effort to expose the contradictions inherent in the Vietnam War.

Sources: William Eastlake, *The Bamboo Bed*, 1969; Philip D. Beidler, *American Literature and the Experience of Vietnam*, 1982.

BAN ME THUOT

Ban Me Thuot is the capital city of Darlac Province and the largest urban concentration in the Central Highlands. Its 1970 population was estimated at more than 65,000 people. In 1975 Ban Me Thuot was the central objective in the NVA's (*see* North Vietnamese Army) attempt to seize the Central Highlands during the Final Offensive (*see* Ho Chi Minh Campaign). Known as Campaign 275, the assault on Ban Me Thuot was led by General Van Tien Dung,* commander of ten NVA divisions. On March 10, 1975, Dung had the NVA 10th, 316th, and 320th divisions move on Ban Me Thuot and the ARVN 23d Division (*see* Army of the Republic of Vietnam). Intense fighting lasted for two days, but on March 12, 1975, NVA soldiers were in control of the city. The fall of Ban Me Thuot had great strategic significance because there were no ARVN troops left between the NVA soldiers in Ban Me Thuot and the South China Sea. The North Vietnamese had an unprecedented opportunity to cut South Vietnam in half. Eventually, of course, they abandoned that strategy and concentrated on the massive assault on Saigon* in April.

Sources: Alan Dawson, *55 Days: The Fall of South Vietnam*, 1977; Van Tien Dung, *Our Great Spring Victory*, 1977; Clark Dougan and David Fulghum, *The Vietnam Experience: The Fall of the South*, 1985.

BAO DAI

Bao Dai, the last emperor of Annam,* was born Prince Nguyen Vinh Thuy on October 22, 1913, to the Emperor Khai Dinh. Bao Dai became emperor in 1925 at the age of twelve, but did not actually assume the throne until 1932, after spending ten years in France* receiving an education. The empire of Annam was essentially a powerless entity, however, because the French Treaty of Protectorate in 1884 had limited the powers of the emperor and the Convention of 1925 had stripped away all the rest. But on becoming emperor, Bao Dai hoped to create a modernized imperial government and induce France to establish a true protectorate, with limited independence, over Vietnam. He remained emperor until 1945. During the Japanese occupation of Vietnam, Bao Dai cooperated with the invaders and earned the ire of the anti-French, Communist Vietminh.*

When news of the Japanese surrender reached Vietnam in August 1945, peasants began attacking Japanese installations and food storage facilities, and Vietminh leaders began moving into positions of power. In Hanoi* Ho Chi Minh* formed the National Liberation Committee, named himself president, and hoped to greet the returning Allies from a position of power. Vietminh groups in the southern part of Vietnam battled with the Cao Dai* and Hoa Hao,* and in Annam, at the imperial palace in Hue,* demanded the abdication of Bao Dai. Known as the August Revolution, the transfer of power from the Japanese to various Vietnamese groups toppled Bao Dai from the throne, leaving Ho Chi Minh's Vietminh followers in control.

Bao Dai lived in Paris between 1945 and 1949, but returned to Vietnam in 1949 after a provisional government in 1948 had reunited Cochin China,* Annam, and Tonkin.* But he was little more than a French puppet. After the Battle of Dien Bien Phu* and expulsion of the French in 1954, Bao Dai lost his base of power, and a national referendum in 1955 stripped him of his office as chief of state and turned power over to Ngo Dinh Diem.* Bao was then exiled to France. Bao Dai died on July 31, 1997. TM

Source: Oscar Chapuis, *The Last Emperors of Vietnam: From Tu Duc to Bao Dai*, 2000.

Left: U.S. Admiral Russell S. Berkey confers with Bao Dai, the emperor of Vietnam on April 1, 1950. Bao Dai was emperor in title only; he did the bidding of the French colonial government.

Below: Emperor Bao Dai reviews a company of soldiers of the Vietnamese National Army on December 28, 1951. Note the French military officers following behind Bao Dai and the French advisors to the left of the first row of Vietnamese soldiers.

Below: On September 25, 1965, paratroopers from the 2d Battalion of the U.S. 173d Airborne Brigade had been on a search-and-destroy mission for twelve days without engaging the Vietcong. Here, near Ben Cat, South Vietnam, despite the heavy rain, they lift their weapons high to keep them out of the water during a river crossing.

BATTALION

A battalion is an organizational institution in the United States Army* and Marine Corps.* Commanded by a lieutenant colonel, an infantry battalion usually has around 900 people, and an artillery battalion about 500 people. During the Vietnam War, however, American battalions were usually much smaller than that.

Sources: Shelby L. Stanton, *Vietnam Order of Battle*, 1981; Harry G. Summers Jr., *Vietnam War Almanac*, 1985.

BATTERY

A battery in the United States Army* or Marine Corps* is an artillery unit of approximately 100 people commanded by a captain. In the Vietnam War there were howitzer batteries, searchlight batteries, machine-gun batteries, and target-acquisition batteries.

Sources: Shelby L. Stanton, *Vietnam Order of Battle*, 1981; Harry G. Summers Jr., *Vietnam War Almanac*, 1985.

BAY VIEN

See Le Van Vien

BEEHIVE AMMUNITION

Beehive ammunition was used by U.S. forces in Vietnam as ammunition for rockets, howitzers, and recoilless rifles. The rounds were filled with thousands of small metal fléchettes that exploded in a 30-degree arc.

Source: Edgar C. Doleman Jr., *The Vietnam Experience: Tools of War*, 1984.

BEN HAI RIVER

The Ben Hai River is the frontier boundary between North and South Vietnam, dividing the two countries from July 22, 1954, to April 29, 1975, when South Vietnam fell. Generally paralleling the 17th parallel (*see* Geneva Accords), the Ben Hai River comes out of the Laotian highlands and runs into the South China Sea.

Source: *Webster's Geographical Dictionary*, 1969.

BEN SUC

Ben Suc was a village of perhaps 5,500 people located along the Saigon River in Binh Duong Province. About thirty miles northwest of Saigon,* Ben Suc was in the heart of the Iron Triangle* and a center of activity for the Vietcong.* ARVN (*see* Army of the Republic of Vietnam) soldiers had kept an outpost at Ben Suc between 1955 and 1964 until Vietcong troops ousted them. After that, the Vietcong received the active cooperation of the village inhabitants. Between 1965 and 1967 ARVN troops—assisted by massive American air strikes, phosphorous bombs, napalm,* and B-52* assaults—tried unsuccessfully to retake Ben Suc. Late in 1966 American officials launched Operation Cedar Falls* to wipe out Vietcong resistance in the Iron Triangle. Although Ben Suc lay just beyond the northwestern tip of the Iron Triangle, it was an important objective for American troops in Operation Cedar Falls. In the end, the village of Ben Suc became a notorious example of the futility of American military policy in South Vietnam.

On January 8, 1967, sixty troop-carrying helicopters took off from the Dau Tieng airstrip and deposited 420 U.S.

Above: Late in 1966 and early in 1967, as part of Operation Cedar Falls, U.S. troops attacked Vietcong positions in the Iron Triangle, a 60-square-mile area of rice paddies, jungle, and rubber plantations located approximately 20 miles northwest of the outskirts of Saigon. The region was laced with elaborate tunnel systems, where Vietcong troops concealed themselves. Ben Suc, a village in the Iron Triangle, was destroyed during Cedar Falls and became emblematic of the futility of U.S. military policy in Vietnam. As soon as U.S. soldiers withdrew, Vietcong troops could be seen returning to the area.

Left: U.S. infantrymen motor away from a burning bamboo hut in the village of Ben Suc during Operation Cedar Falls. Americans assaulted this Vietcong stronghold, removed all the inhabitants, and burned the huts. The Vietcong thus lost use of the shelters, but so did many villagers not associated with the Communists.

Below: After the U.S. 9th Division left South Vietnam in 1970, the ARVN 7th Division replaced it in Kien Hoa Province of IV Corps. In this photograph, an ARVN soldier near Ben Tre leads a wounded comrade away from the battlefield.

soldiers right in the middle of Ben Suc. Since Ben Suc was reputedly the headquarters for Vietcong control of the Iron Triangle, the American soldiers expected intense resistance. Instead, they encountered only sporadic small-arms fire. The villagers were evacuated from Ben Suc and taken to a new refugee camp at Phy Loi near Phu Cuong. The 1st Engineer Battalion of the 1st Infantry Division* then moved into Ben Suc and leveled the village with Rome plows,* tank-dozers, and M48 antimine tanks, destroying every home and building and bulldozing all the mango, jackfruit, and grapefruit fields. Miles of tunnels used by the Vietcong were destroyed at the same time. Two days after the end of Operation Cedar Falls on January 26, Vietcong were back in the area. At home the American press reacted to the razing of Ben

Suc with outrage. Less than thirty miles from Saigon, U.S. and ARVN troops, after destroying a village and turning nearly 6,000 people into refugees, had not been able to prevent Vietcong control of the area. Although Operation Cedar Falls was a blow to the Vietcong in the area of the Iron Triangle, it also raised serious doubts among the American press and American policymakers about the effectiveness of both pacification (*see* Rural Reconstruction) and the "search-and-destroy"* strategy.

Sources: Jonathan Schell, *The Village of Ben Suc*, 1967; Bernard William Rogers, *Cedar Falls–Junction City: A Turning Point*, 1974.

BEN TRE

Ben Tre was the capital city of Kien Hoa Province in IV Corps.* South of Saigon,* Kien Hoa Province borders the Vietnamese coast along the South China Sea. Ben Tre became temporarily famous in 1968 when Vietcong* forces captured the city during the Tet Offensive.* Overwhelming American and South Vietnamese forces, bolstered by massive air strikes, recaptured Ben Tre, but the artillery and air strikes all but destroyed the town, killing an estimated 550 people and wounding 1,200 more. The battle for Ben Tre was not much different from countless other struggles during the Vietnam War, except for the famous quote of an American major when asked by journalist Peter Arnett to justify the indiscriminate use of explosives. His remark, "It became necessary to destroy the town in order to save it," was widely quoted in the world press and became a symbol, to antiwar* activists, of the bankruptcy of U.S. policy in Southeast Asia.

Sources: Clark Dougan and Stephen Weiss, *The Vietnam Experience: Nineteen Sixty-Eight*, 1983; Max Hastings, *The Fire This Time: America's Year of Crisis*, 1969; Peter Braestrup, *Big Story: How the American Press and Television Reported and Interpreted the Crisis of Tet 1968 in Vietnam and Washington*, 1983.

BERGER, SAMUEL DAVID

Born in Gloversville, New York, on December 6, 1911, Samuel Berger received his Ph.D. degree from the University of Wisconsin in 1934 and joined the State Department after several years in the field of statistics and labor economics. His first assignment at State was as a labor officer at the U.S. Embassy in London in 1945. After several diplomatic assignments to Japan, New Zealand, and Greece, Berger became ambassador to South Korea in 1961. He was named deputy ambassador to South Vietnam in 1968, and he remained in that post until 1972. Berger's role was to act as liaison between President Nguyen Van Thieu,* the

United States, and the South Vietnamese military. Above all else, Berger wanted to maintain a stable civilian government in South Vietnam, with the military playing only a secondary political role. As such, Berger was a staunch supporter of Thieu and believed that the U.S. military effort in Southeast Asia could lead to a permanent, anti-Communist government in Saigon.* Berger supported the invasion of Cambodia in 1970 and helped plan the disastrous Lam Son 719* ARVN (*see* Army of the Republic of Vietnam) invasion of Laos* in 1971. Berger left Saigon in 1972 and went to work for the Foreign Service Institute. Samuel Berger died on February 12, 1980.

Sources: Department of State, *Biographic Register*, 1974; Clark Dougan and Steven Weiss, *The Vietnam Experience: Nineteen Sixty-Eight*, 1983; *New York Times*, February 13, 1980.

BERRIGAN, DANIEL

Born in Virginia, Minnesota, on May 9, 1921, Father Daniel Berrigan was a prominent figure in the New Catholic Left of the 1960s and a leading opponent of the Vietnam War and Selective Service system. He entered training for the Roman Catholic priesthood in 1939 and was ordained on June 19, 1952, as a member of the Society of Jesus. A prolific writer and poet, Berrigan won the Lamont Prize for his first poetry collection, *Time Without Number*, in 1957. As a professor of New Testament studies at Le Moyne College in

Syracuse, New York, from 1957 to 1963, he encouraged students to become involved in work with civil rights, pacifism, and the poor. One of his students became the first person convicted for burning a draft* card. With James H. Forest, Thomas C. Cornell, and Philip Berrigan,* he founded the Catholic Peace Fellowship in 1964. A year later, he helped found the interdenominational Clergy and Laity Concerned About Vietnam.* In February 1967 he went to Hanoi* with Howard Zinn of Boston University to help gain the release of three captured U.S. pilots. On the afternoon of May 17, 1968, Berrigan, his brother Philip, and seven others entered Selective Service Board 33 at a Knights of Columbus hall in Catonsville, Maryland. There they removed several hundred 1-A draft records from filing cabinets, threw them into trash cans, burned them with homemade napalm* in the parking lot outside, and then awaited arrest. The "Catonsville Nine" were found guilty of conspiracy and destruction of government property. Berrigan was sentenced to three years in prison. He received considerable notoriety, however, when he refused to surrender on April 9, 1970, to begin serving his sentence. He went underground and made periodic public appearances at religious services and antiwar* rallies, and was even interviewed by NBC-TV News on June 4. He was finally apprehended by the FBI on Block Island in the Long Island Sound on August 11, 1970, and sent to the federal prison at Danbury, Connecticut. On January 12, 1971, he was named as an unindicted coconspirator on charges of conspiring to kidnap Henry Kissinger* and to blow up the heating systems of federal buildings in Washington, D.C. Berrigan was paroled on January 26, 1972, because of poor health. After the war, he largely receded from public view but remained supportive of causes associated with pacifism and the poor. He also distressed some followers by voicing opposition to abortion, along with war and capital punishment.

On January 19, 1976, he began serving a sixty-day jail sentence rather than pay a fine for digging a hole in the White House lawn on November 26, 1975, in protest of the proliferation of nuclear weapons. In 1980 he was one of the "Plowshares Eight" who were arrested and convicted for hammering on two nuclear warhead cones and pouring blood on desks and files at the General Electric Re-entry Division plant in King of Prussia, Pennsylvania, on September 9. The convictions were upheld and prison sentences reinstated by the Supreme Court of Pennsylvania in November 1985. On April 10, 1990, the Plowshares Eight were resentenced and paroled in consideration of time already served. Daniel Berrigan has since remained actively dedicated to his cause, taking part in many of the more than seventy Plowshares protests against weapons of war worldwide. JK

Sources: Daniel Berrigan, S.J., *No Bars to Manhood*, 1970; Murray Polner and Jim O'Grady, *Disarmed and Dangerous: The Radical Life and Times of Daniel and Philip Berrigan*, 1998.

Left: The brothers Philip and Daniel Berrigan are featured on the cover of the January 25, 1971, issue of *Time* magazine. Both Roman Catholic priests, the Berrigans protested the Vietnam War in a variety of ways, including acts of civil disobedience, and gradually emerged as the moral conscience of the antiwar movement.

BERRIGAN, PHILIP (FRANCIS)

Born in Two Harbors, Minnesota, on October 5, 1923, Philip Berrigan was a leading member of the New Catholic Left and a prominent opponent of the Vietnam War and Selective Service system. While attending St. Michael's College in Toronto, he was drafted in January 1943. He served with the U.S. Army artillery and infantry in World War II, and received a battlefield promotion to second lieutenant for service in some of the most savage battles on the European front. After earning a B.A. in English at the College of the Holy Cross, Worcester, Massachusetts, he was ordained into the Society of Jesus in 1955. Assigned to New Orleans, he earned a B.S. in secondary education at Loyola University of the South and an M.S. at Xavier University. For six years, he taught at St. Augustine High School in New Orleans' black ghetto.

After he became quite controversial locally for his activity in the civil rights movement, his superiors transferred him to a seminary in Newburgh, New York. There, in 1964, he founded the Emergency Citizens' Group Concerned About Vietnam. He also helped to found the Catholic Peace Fellowship in 1964. Again, his superiors transferred him, this time to St. Peter Claver Church in the black ghetto of Baltimore. He then founded the Baltimore Interfaith Peace Mission.

On October 27, 1967, Berrigan and three other activists entered the Selective Service office at the Baltimore Customs House and, in front of startled workers, poured jars of duck blood onto draft* files. Berrigan thus became the first Roman Catholic priest in the United States to be sentenced to prison for a political crime.

While awaiting sentencing, however, he and eight others, including his brother Daniel,* entered Selective Service Board 33 at a Knights of Columbus hall in Catonsville, Maryland, on the afternoon of May 17, 1968. They removed 1-A records from filing cabinets, carried them out to the parking lot in wire waste baskets, and burned the records with homemade napalm.*

Berrigan was convicted of conspiracy and destruction of government property and sentenced to three and a half years in prison, to be served concurrently with a six-year sentence he had already begun to serve for his first protest action against the draft. He was granted bail but refused to surrender to authorities on April 9, 1970. FBI agents apprehended him on April 21. On January 12, 1971, he and six others were indicated by a federal grand jury for conspiring to blow up the heating systems of federal buildings in Washington, D.C., and to kidnap Henry Kissinger.* The trial jury found Berrigan guilty on one charge of having a letter smuggled out of prison to codefendant Sister Elizabeth McAlister. The jury deadlocked on the other charges—ten for acquittal and two for conviction. Berrigan was sentenced to two years in prison. The conspiracy charges were dismissed upon a motion for mistrial from the U.S. Department of Justice; the smuggling conviction was later overturned by a Circuit Court of Appeals. Berrigan was paroled from the Danbury federal prison on December 20, 1972. On May 30, 1973, he announced that he and Elizabeth McAlister had privately married themselves in 1969. McAlister gave birth to a daughter on April 1, 1974, a son the following year, and another daughter six years later.

On October 4, 1975, Berrigan and twenty-one others were arrested for pouring a red liquid on military aircraft being exhibited at Rentschler Airport in East Hartford, Connecticut. Charges were dropped, however, when Pratt & Whitney Aircraft said that the liquid had been cleaned off the aircraft with soap and water. Berrigan continued to protest U.S. nuclear policies. On November 26, 1975, he and eight others dug a hole in the White House lawn in protest of nuclear weapons proliferation. He served sixty days in jail rather than pay a fine for what he called his "act of conscience." Five years later, he was one of the "Plowshares Eight" who were arrested and convicted for hammering on two nuclear warhead cones and pouring blood on desks and files at the General Electric Re-entry Division plant in King of Prussia, Pennsylvania, on September 9, 1980. The convictions were still on appeal in 1986, but on April 10, 1990, the defendants were paroled and resentenced to time served. Berrigan remained a dedicated activist, spending a total of some eleven years of his life in federal prison for his nonviolent protest activities. Philip Berrigan died on December 6, 2002. JK

Sources: William O'Rourk, *The Harrisburg 7 and the New Catholic Left*, 1972; Charles A. Meconis, *With Clumsy Grace: The American Catholic Left, 1961–1975*, 1979; Murray Polner and Jim O'Grady, *Disarmed and Dangerous: The Radical Life and Times of Daniel and Philip Berrigan*, 1998.

BETTER TIMES THAN THESE

See Literature and Vietnam

BIDAULT, GEORGES

Georges Bidault was born on October 5, 1899, in Moulins, France. During World War II he was president of the National Council of Resistance, and after the war he rose through the conservative political ranks. Between 1949 and 1952 he served as president of the Mouvement Républicain Populaire. Bidault was premier of France* between June and November 1946 and extracted from President Harry Truman* a promise that the United States supported the return of the French to Indochina.* He returned as premier between October 1949 and June 1950. During his years of power Bidault was a strong advocate of the French Empire and took a conservative approach to imperial problems in Indochina and Algeria, insisting that France maintain its commitments there. Throughout the 1950s and early 1960s he was a vigorous supporter of General Charles de Gaulle, but he lost favor after 1962 for demanding the maintenance of French Algeria. Georges Bidault died on January 27, 1983.

Sources: James J. Cooke, *France 1789–1962*, 1975; Georges Bidault, *Resistance: The Political Autobiography of Georges Bidault*, 1967; *New York Times*, January 28, 1983.

BIEN HOA, BATTLE OF (1964)

Bien Hoa, the capital city of Bien Hoa Province, is located approximately twenty miles north of Saigon* on the Dong Nai River. Early in the war, the United States constructed a large airfield and military headquarters just outside Bien Hoa, and on November 1, 1964, Vietcong* sappers attacked the installation, destroying five aircraft and killing four U.S. soldiers. Since the Gulf of Tonkin incident* in August 1964 and the subsequent bombing* of North Vietnam, the Indochinese conflict had been consuming increasing

amounts of time and resources in Washington as well as in the American public mind. Although the Johnson administration did not respond immediately to the attack, it was becoming more and more clear that if the United States were going to conduct an air war over North and South Vietnam, with aircraft and personnel stationed in the South, regular ground troops would be required to defend those installations. Escalation of the conflict became one indirect consequence of the attack on Bien Hoa in 1964.

Sources: *New York Times*, November 2–4, 1964; George W. Ball, "Top Secret: The Prophecy the President Rejected," *The Atlantic*, 230 (July 1972): 35–49.

THE BIG V

See Literature and Vietnam

BINH XUYEN

With their stronghold in the Cholon* section near Saigon,* the Binh Xuyen were drug smugglers who traditionally traded support for legal protection of their rackets, whether they were dealing with the French Empire or the Vietminh* nationalists. Their trade was in prostitution, gambling casinos, and opium dens. In post–World War II Vietnam, the Binh Xuyen became a powerful political faction under the leadership of Bay Vien (*see* Le Van Vien). In 1945 the Binh Xuyen provided terrorists to the Vietminh, who assassinated more than 150 French civilians, including women and children. Emperor Bao Dai,* in order to generate the funds necessary to sustain his government, readily accepted money from the Binh Xuyen, who received legal protection for their rackets in return. Bao Dai made Bay Vien a general in the Vietnamese army and gave him complete authority over the casinos, prostitution, opium traffic, gold smuggling, currency manipulation, and other rackets. The French accepted Bay Vien's authority and even used his private Binh Xuyen army to fight against the Vietminh. By the early 1950s the Binh Xuyen army had more than 40,000 soldiers and was a major political-military faction in southern Vietnam.

In the spring of 1955, after securing control of the new government of South Vietnam, Ngo Dinh Diem* decided to crush the political and religious factions in the South—like the Hoa Hao* and the Cao Dai*—and one of the most powerful was the Binh Xuyen. On April 27, 1955, Diem ordered Bay Vien and the Binh Xuyen to remove their troops from Saigon, and when they refused, Diem attacked. The battle raged inside the city, killing more than 500 people and leaving 25,000 homeless. The French and Bao Dai tried to assist the Binh Xuyen, but Diem prevailed. By the end of May, Bay Vien had fled to Paris and the Binh Xuyen's troops had been driven into the Mekong Delta,* where many of them joined the Vietcong* guerrillas.

Sources: Stanley Karnow, *Vietnam: A History*, 1983; Denis Warner, *The Last Confucian*, 1963; Edward Doyle and Samuel Lipsman, *The Vietnam Experience: Passing the Torch*, 1981; Charles A. Joiner, *The Politics of Massacre: Political Processes in South Vietnam*, 1974.

BLACK SOLDIERS

See Black Soldiers in Vietnam, p. 82

BLUM, LÉON

Léon Blum was born on April 9, 1872, and became one of the leading French socialists. He was elected a deputy in the national legislature in 1919. Blum was Jewish, and that created some political problems for him over the years, but his gentility and commitment to democracy and peaceful change enabled him to succeed politically despite prevailing anti-Semitism. Blum became prime minister in 1936 and again in 1938, and he was responsible for a variety of left wing, social welfare measures. Openly sympathetic with the Communists during the Spanish Civil War, Blum was arrested by the Vichy government in 1940 and deported to Germany, where he was imprisoned. After the war Blum served as president of the Council of Ministers from 1946 to 1947 and generally advocated independence for Vietnam. Léon Blum died on March 30, 1950.

Sources: James J. Cooke, *France 1789–1962*, 1975; Louise Dalby, *Leon Blum: Evolution of a Socialist*, 1963.

"BOAT PEOPLE"

See Indochinese Refugees

BODY COUNT

Because the Vietnam War was a guerrilla conflict without front lines or territorial objectives, and with shifting defensive positions, it became impossible to use geography as a reliable index of progress. Instead, Secretary of Defense Robert McNamara* and General William Westmoreland* came to rely on the "body count"—the number of Vietcong* and North Vietnamese soldiers killed—to evaluate the progress of the war. But a number of factors made the body count figures unreliable. Combat conditions often

BLACK SOLDIERS IN VIETNAM

Right: Three Marine artillery-men raise their fists in a Black Power salute while two others hold a banner proclaiming "Black Power is Number One." They were serving at the large base of Con Thien south of the DMZ in late 1968.

Above: Specialist 4 Charles H. Richey of Baltimore, Maryland, was an Artillery Forward Observer Radio Operator during Operation Jeb Stuart in March 1968. He served in the 1st Cavalry Division.

During the 1960s and early 1970s the antiwar and civil rights movements intersected explosively in the United States, and the role played by black soldiers in Vietnam provided the fuse. In 1965 the introduction of U.S. ground troops escalated rapidly and led to increased draft calls. At the time, the Selective Service exempted several groups of Americans from induction. By far the most controversial exemption went to full-time college students, who could legally escape the draft as long as they were enrolled. The exemption introduced a powerful class bias into the Selective Service. Young men from middle-class and upper-class families were far more likely to go to college and qualify for the exemption. The U.S. Armed Services, therefore, were filled with poor, working-class young men, while well-to-do college students sat out the war in dormitories with paid-up meal plans.

The exemption also introduced a racial bias into draft calls. Because black families were more likely than white families to be poor, relatively fewer young black men attended college. Draft calls, there-fore, fell disproportionate-ly on them. Because the high school dropout rate was higher among blacks than among whites, black men entered the armed forces with fewer job skills and were therefore more likely to end up in infantry units. Because infantry units were more likely to end up in combat-prone forward areas, the rate at which black men were wounded or killed in Vietnam far exceeded their percentage in the American population. In 1965, although blacks made up only 12 percent of the U.S. population, black soldiers constituted nearly 20 percent of American combat deaths.

African American civil rights leaders noticed the discrepancy, and in 1966 Martin Luther King Jr. denounced Vietnam as a racist war. Young black men, he insisted, were more likely to be drafted than whites, more likely to be assigned to infantry units, and within those units more likely to be killed or wounded. King's condemnation of the war stirred deep concern among civil rights activists, who feared a political backlash from conservatives. King's critique grabbed the attention of Presidents Lyndon B. Johnson and then Richard M. Nixon, both of whom ordered the Joint Chiefs of Staff to investigate the charges and, if necessary, take appropriate action. They confirmed the allegations, and all service branches took a careful look at the racial outcomes of combat operations. By 1972, when the last U.S. ground troops left Vietnam, the total number of black soldiers killed in action mirrored the percentage of black people in the U.S. population.

Heavyweight boxing champion Muhammad Ali stood astride the intersection of the antiwar and civil rights movements. In 1964 he took the heavyweight

championship from Sonny Liston and aligned himself with Elijah Muhammad and the Nation of Islam, condemning all whites as "devils" and proclaiming the superiority of black people. Few African Americans held to Ali's religious beliefs, but his pride and rhetoric

thrilled them. In April 1967 Ali refused induction, asking for a conscientious objector deferment and proclaiming, "I ain't got no quarrel with those Vietcong. They never called me nigger." The World Boxing Association then revoked his title, and in June 1967 a federal court convicted him of draft evasion, levying a fine of $10,000 and a prison sentence of five years. Ali had become a hero to antiwar activists as well as to black people. He remained out of jail on appeal until June 1970, when the U.S. Supreme Court overturned his conviction. Ali regained the heavyweight title in 1974. Since then, he has become one of the most beloved athletes in American history, not just because of his talent and persona but also because of his political courage.

Sources: Wallace Terry, *Bloods: An Oral History of the Vietnam War by Black Veterans*, 1984; Stanley Goff and Robert Sandfors, *Brothers: Black Soldiers in Nam*, 1982; Lawrence M. Baskir and William A. Strauss, *Chance and Circumstance: The Draft, the War, and the Vietnam Generation*, 1978; Christian G. Appy, *Working-Class War: American Combat Soldiers and Vietnam*, 1993; James E. Westheider, *African Americans and the Vietnam War*, 1999; Diane Canwell and Jon Sutherland, *African Americans and the Vietnam War*, 2005.

required estimates of enemy killed, often from aerial observation or memory. It was also very difficult to distinguish between Vietcong and civilian Vietnamese casualties. Counts were often duplicated, and American officers, desperate for good efficiency reports, were known to exaggerate the body counts. Until 1968 American military officials accepted "probable kills" as the body count figure. By the time of the Tet Offensive,* however, Defense Department studies indicated that body count figures were probably 30 percent inflated. Civilian officials were also concerned because the Vietcong and North Vietnamese lost only one-sixth as many weapons as they did people, at least according to the body count figures. Such a discrepancy meant either that large numbers of civilians were killed along with the Vietcong, that the body count figures were seriously inflated, or both. At the end of the war, U.S. officials estimated that 666,000 Vietcong and North Vietnamese had died during combat in South Vietnam between 1965 and 1974, and that American air strikes had killed 65,000 people in North Vietnam. Vo Nguyen Giap* estimated that by 1969 his Communist forces had lost 500,000 men killed in action.

Sources: Philip Caputo, *A Rumor of War*, 1977; Guenter Lewy, *America in Vietnam*, 1978; John E. Mueller, "The Search for the 'Breaking Point' in Vietnam: The Statistics of a Deadly Quarrel," *International Studies Quarterly* 24 (December 1980): 497–519.

Left: Two African Americans of the 173d Airborne Brigade advance toward Vietcong positions in 1967. Although blacks were dying at a higher rate than whites in 1965, by the time the war ended, black fatalities almost exactly mirrored their proportion of the population of the United States.

Below: On June 20, 1971, heavyweight boxing champ Muhammad Ali arrived in Houston, Texas, to stand trial for refusing to be drafted. Ali condemned the Vietnam War. He was convicted of draft evasion and sentenced to five years in prison. Using the appeals process in the federal court system, Ali managed to avoid incarceration, and in 1970 the U.S. Supreme Court overturned his conviction.

Opposite page, bottom: An African American member of the 1st Cavalry helps rush a wounded comrade to an evacuation helicopter. This was during Operation White Wing in early 1966.

Opposite page: A Boeing B-52 Stratofortress unleashes a clutch of bombs over Vietcong positions in 1966. Such B-52s could carry 60,000 pounds of bombs.

BODY COUNT

See Literature and Vietnam

BOMBING OF SOUTHEAST ASIA

At the end of World War II, Vietnam was one of several nations that was artificially divided into sectors by the victorious Allies. The United States was instrumental in the creation of the capitalistic Republic of South Vietnam, while the Soviet Union established the leftist nation of North Vietnam. Each portion of Vietnam held differing political beliefs and sought to unify the entire nation under its rule. The United States developed a close relationship with South Vietnam during the 1950s, and as difficulties with leftist North Vietnam grew during the early 1960s, so did American commitments. Eventually, by the late 1960s, the United States had assumed the primary responsibilities of conducting the defense of South Vietnam.

The first clash between North Vietnamese and American forces occurred on August 2, 1964, when a North Vietnamese force attacked an American naval vessel

Right: Ordnance men work on a bomb at base in January 1970. The tonnage of bombs dropped during the Vietnam War was almost triple the tonnage dropped during World War II.

patrolling the Gulf of Tonkin.* Two nights later, American destroyers were attacked along the Vietnamese coast. Following these attacks, President Lyndon B. Johnson* ordered a retaliatory bombing strike against a North Vietnamese supply depot on August 5. The president then requested and Congress approved the Gulf of Tonkin

Below: A U.S. Air Force F-100 Super Sabre fires rockets at enemy positions in the tree-covered terrain below.

Resolution* on August 7, 1964, granting Johnson the authority to use all measures necessary to assist South Vietnam in defending its territory. These actions set the stage for extended bombing operations against enemy targets in North Vietnam.

From the very beginning of bombing operations against enemy targets, the United States Air Force* (USAF) experienced difficulties. Bombardment campaigns in Vietnam were substantially different from those of World War I and II, and even materially different from those of Korea. First, the president was intensely concerned with the complexities and necessities of fighting a limited war, limited both in size and scope, and maintained firm control over all phases of its planning and execution. Coordination of all bombing operations involved not only military planners but also senior State Department, Defense Department, cabinet, and numerous other government officials. Second, USAF bombing doctrine underwent a striking alteration during the war as the practical differences between air interdiction and strategic bombing against North Vietnam were muted. In this conflict, all types of bombers and fighters* worked together to attack transportation, supply, and industrial targets not just in North Vietnam but in the allied South as well. Third, because of the limited nature of the war in Southeast Asia, any bombing activity could never be decisive.

The initial air strikes, code-named Operation Rolling Thunder,* were limited primarily to enemy radar and bridges below the 20th parallel. As the effort expanded, however, President Johnson ordered the bombing of most metropolitan areas in North Vietnam. The first of these expanded attacks took place on May 22, 1965, when USAF F-105s* bombed the North Vietnamese barracks at Quang Soui. While the first strikes were made by tactical aircraft, the most spectacular and destructive aircraft used in the air war were B-52* strategic bombers. These aircraft operated essentially from six large airfields in Thailand.* The USAF bomber and support presence in Thailand grew from about 1,000 personnel and 83 aircraft in early 1965 to a peak of about 55,000 personnel and 600 aircraft by the time of the Tet Offensive* in January and February 1968.

From the first handful of strikes into enemy territory in 1965 until the USAF and Navy* sorties* were halted by presidential decree on October 31, 1968, allied aircraft struck at bridges, vehicles, rolling stock, military posts, assembly plants, supply depots, vessels, antiaircraft and radar sites, railroads, and highways. During nearly four years of bombing, USAF, Navy, Marine,* and South Vietnamese aircraft had flown about 304,000 tactical and 2,380 B-52 sorties and dropped 643,000 tons of bombs on enemy targets.

Although the bombing halt was called off for several months during the winter of 1968 to 1969, after President Richard M. Nixon* assumed office, the bombing would resume. President Nixon was responsible for the most controversial bombing operation of the war, taking place in Cambodia after spring 1969 (*see* Operation Menu). American military leaders had long complained that leftist forces were using Cambodian jungles near the Vietnamese border as safe havens from which to stage hit-and-run attacks against American and South Vietnamese troops. President

Nixon was convinced by military leaders that he could cripple North Vietnam by destroying its Cambodian sanctuaries.*

Accordingly, on March 18, 1969—operating under cover of special security and reporting procedures—a B-52 bombing campaign in Cambodia began. The sorties, all of which were flown at night, were directed by ground control units, ensuring that not even the aircrews were told all directions for the bomb release from the ground control personnel. In all, between March 18, 1969, and May 26, 1970, the B-52s flew 4,308 sorties and dropped 120,578 tons of bombs on enemy base camps in Cambodia.

These bombings temporarily hampered North Vietnamese efforts in Cambodia, but they also expanded the war into Cambodia as the North Vietnamese retaliated. By April 26, 1970, for instance, North Vietnam had taken control of large areas of the country, and appeared on the verge of toppling the Cambodian government. This action prompted an American and South Vietnamese invasion of Cambodia to preserve the friendly government. During a three-month period, April 29 to June 30, 1970, these forces temporarily threw back the North Vietnamese, but upon their withdrawal North Vietnam attacked Cambodia again. Throughout these operations, the USAF provided bombing support to the Cambodian Army in its defensive activity, but it was insufficient. Not long after the withdrawal of the United States from Southeast Asia, the Cambodian government fell, and the puppet state of Kampuchea was created by North Vietnam.

As bombing in Cambodia, Laos,* and North Vietnam continued between 1969 and 1972, so did peace negotiations in Paris.* On January 23, 1973, the Paris negotiators signed a nine-point cease-fire agreement. This agreement provided for a cease-fire of all combat operations, the release of all American and allied prisoners of war, establishment of a commission to supervise the truce, and affirmation of the national rights of South Vietnam, Laos, and Cambodia. The United States also tacitly recognized the presence of about 100,000 North Vietnamese troops in South Vietnam. During the period of the negotiations, the USAF had flown 51,000 tactical and 9,800 B-52 bombing sorties against North Vietnam, dropping 124,000 tons of bombs by tactical air-craft and 109,000 tons by B-52s. During the same period, these forces flew additional sorties against enemy positions in Laos and Cambodia. Cumulatively, between June 1965 and August 1973, the Strategic Air Command's B-52s flew 126,615 bombing sorties and the tactical forces flew more than 400,000 bombing sorties, in the process dropping 6,162,000 tons of munitions on enemy positions. By contrast, the total tonnage of explosives dropped in World War II had been 2,150,000 tons. RDL

Sources: David A. Anderton, *The History of the U.S. Air Force*, 1981; Carl Berger, ed., *The United States Air Force in Southeast Asia, 1961–1973: An Illustrated Account*, 1977; Walter Boyne, *Boeing B-52: A Documentary History*, 1981, and *The Development of the Strategic Air Command: A Chronological History*, 1982; James N. Eastman Jr. et al., eds., *Aces and Aerial Victories: The United States Air Force in Southeast Asia, 1965–1973*, 1976; Stanley Karnow, *Vietnam: A History*, 1983; James Clay Thompson, *Rolling Thunder: Understanding Policy and Program Failure*, 1980.

Below: Vietcong positions burn after being bombed by U.S. Air Force fighter bombers in this attack of January 1966.

Right: Punji sticks stabilized by a board, and barbed so they cannot be easily withdrawn from a foot or leg.

Below: A pit of bamboo punji stakes 30 inches long.

BOOBY TRAPS

Booby traps—ranging from punji stakes* to a variety of grenades, mines, and explosive devices—were a common part of the Vietnam War, primarily because of the guerrilla nature of the conflict. More than one out of ten American battlefield casualties in Vietnam was the result of a booby trap of one kind or another. The most dangerous of the makeshift Vietcong* weapons were the following: a bullet buried straight up with its firing pin on a bamboo stub, activated when someone stepped on the bullet's tip; hollowed-out coconuts filled with gunpowder and triggered by a trip wire; walk bridges with ropes almost cut away so they would collapse when someone tried to cross them; underground and hidden punji stakes; bamboo stakes connected to grenades and planted at helicopter landing sites; the "Malay whip" log, attached to two trees by a rope and triggered by a trip wire, which would sweep down on entire units; and boards studded with iron barbs and buried in streambeds and rice paddies. The common use of booby traps only further alienated American troops from civilian Vietnamese, whom they did not trust and could not distinguish from the Vietcong. During the course of the Vietnam War, booby traps and mines were responsible for the majority of combat injuries and deaths among American troops.

Sources: Edgar C. Doleman Jr., *The Vietnam Experience: Tools of War*, 1984; Peter Goldman and Tony Fuller, *Charlie Company: What Vietnam Did to Us*, 1983.

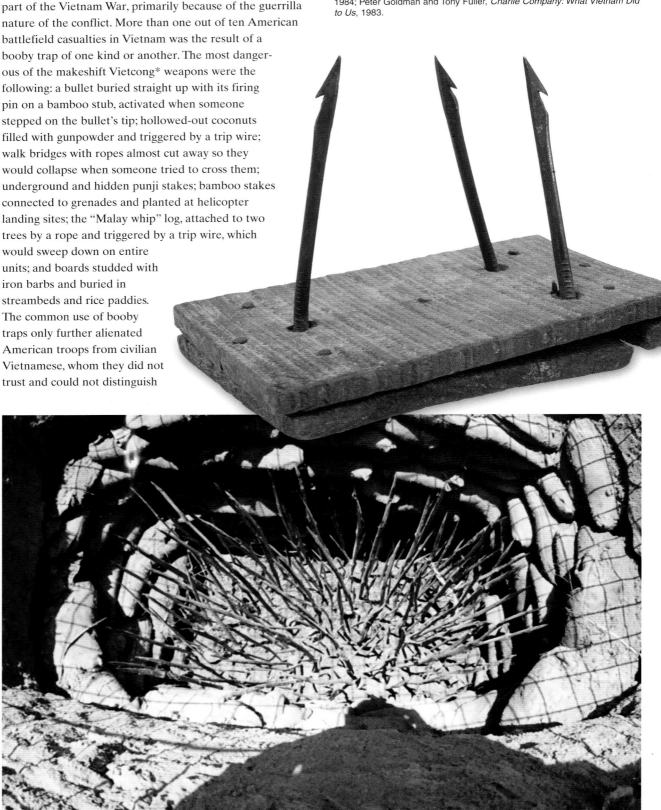

Above left: A punji stick of the type shown opposite top with a fragment of its supporting board still attached.

Above right: A punji stick piercing a man's foot. The barb at the punji stick's tip prevents easy extraction.

Left: South Vietnamese also used bamboo for booby traps, though visible to enemy soldiers. Here, three layers of bamboo defenses circle a guard post in 1962. There is an outer fence, then angled pointed bamboo stakes pointing toward attacking soldiers, and an inner fence of sharpened bamboo stalks.

198th Infantry Brigade

18th Engineer Brigade

18th Military Police Brigade

20th Engineer Brigade

1st Aviation Brigade

1st Signal Brigade

173d Airborne Brigade

44th Medical Brigade

BORN ON THE FOURTH OF JULY

Born on the Fourth of July was published in 1976 and became a national bestseller. Published just one year after the fall of Saigon to North Vietnamese troops, the book recounts the experiences of Ron Kovic, a wounded U.S. Marine who came home from the war in a wheelchair. Born on Long Island, New York, to a devout, patriotic Catholic family, Kovic joined the Marine Corps* soon after graduating from high school. With images of John Wayne and *The Sands of Iwo Jima* dancing in his head, he hoped to serve his country in Vietnam, just as his father had done in World War II. After boot camp and jungle training, Kovic deployed to Vietnam, where he found a war with no heroes, just victims. The GIs could not figure out the reasons for the war, civilians could not comprehend the rationale for the war, and innocent men, women, and children were dying in an orgasm of American firepower. Kovic himself participated in the accidental killing of civilians, and during a firefight with enemy troops he was cut down with a wound to the spinal cord that left him paralyzed below the waist.

Upon his return to the United States, Kovic languished in an underfunded, understaffed, and rat-infested Veterans Administration hospital, and instead of being welcomed home as a wounded war hero, he was treated as a pariah, a man who sacrificed everything for nothing. Amidst his depression, Kovic found hope in the antiwar movement,* where as a paralyzed veteran he enjoyed the credibility reserved only for those who served in Vietnam and then spoke out against the war. Kovic wrote the book in the fall of 1974, in Santa Monica, California. In 1989 Oliver Stone directed the film *Born on the Fourth of July*, starring Tom Cruise and Willem DaFoe.

Source: Ron Kovic, *Born on the Fourth of July*, 1976.

BOWLES, CHESTER BLISS

Chester Bowles was born on April 5, 1901, in Springfield, Massachusetts, and graduated from Yale in 1924. He established a successful advertising firm in 1929 and worked there until 1942, when he joined the Office of Price Administration. Bowles was a member of the War Production Board from 1943 to 1946. Elected governor of Connecticut in 1949, Bowles served one term and became ambassador to India in 1951. He served one term in Congress* between 1958 and 1960, and in 1961 he became undersecretary of state in the Kennedy* administration. He did not last there long. A strong advocate of a negotiated settlement, based on neutrality for Vietnam, Bowles was identified as a "dove" by the Kennedy administration and fired as undersecretary of state in November 1961. He was named an ambassador-at-large and traveled widely until

1963, when he replaced John K. Galbraith* as ambassador to India. He remained there until his retirement from public life in 1969. Chester Bowles died on May 23, 1986.

Sources: Chester B. Bowles, *Promises to Keep: My Years in Public Life, 1941–1969*, 1971; Lee H. Burke, *Ambassador at Large: Diplomat Extraordinary*, 1972; *New York Times*, May 24, 1986.

independent entities. A number of combat support brigades, designed to provide supplies, medical care, and maintenance, also functioned in South Vietnam during the 1960s and 1970s.

Sources: Harry G. Summers Jr., *Vietnam War Almanac*, 1985; Shelby L. Stanton, *Vietnam Order of Battle*, 1981.

THE BOYS OF COMPANY C

See Rambo and Other Vietnam Films

BRIGADE

The term "brigade" defines a basic military organizational institution. During the Vietnam War a division was organized into three brigades, with each brigade commanded by a colonel. A division consists of approximately 20,000 people. There were also separate infantry brigades functioning in the Vietnam War. The 11th,* 196th,* and 198th infantry brigades fought in the war until 1967, when they were brought together to reconstitute the Americal Division, or the 23d Infantry.* The 199th Infantry Brigade* and the 173d Airborne Brigade* continued to fight as

BRINKS HOTEL (SAIGON)

The Brinks Hotel housed some American military officers in Saigon.* On the afternoon of Christmas Eve 1964, two Vietcong* agents placed a bomb in the basement carpark. They had reconnoitered the target painstakingly, and had managed to park a car containing the bomb without being observed or suspected. At 5:45 PM, while the Americans were eating dinner and planning the Christmas Eve party for later that evening, the bomb exploded, while one of the agents, Nguyen Thanh Xuan, casually observed from a restaurant across the street. Two American officers were killed and fifty-eight were wounded. The Brinks Hotel episode is significant for several reasons. It demonstrated the ability of the Vietcong to operate anywhere in South Vietnam, even in the capital of its enemy. It also demonstrated the inability of that enemy to protect its citizens and allies, a vital prerequisite to successful guerrilla or insurgency warfare. Coming soon after the American bombing* of North Vietnam following the Tonkin Gulf incident,* it demonstrated the form of escalation or response that any further

Left: Here is the rubble of several homes destroyed near the Brinks Hotel in downtown Saigon. On December 24, 1964, Vietcong detonated a car bomb in the hotel's basement garage. The hotel was home to 125 U.S. military personnel and civilians. Two Americans died in the blast, and many others — Americans, Australians, and Vietnamese — were wounded.

bombing of North Vietnam would take. Finally, it presented policymakers in Washington with a basic question that would characterize the war throughout its history: Would bombing the North reduce enemy hostilities in the South? President Johnson* overruled his advisors in this instance, arguing that bombing retaliation for the Brinks Hotel attack would be politically unwise during Christmas and militarily unsound as a disproportionate response that might unnecessarily escalate the war.

The attack on the Brinks Hotel epitomized the situation for Americans in Vietnam in the mid-1960s. No place was completely safe from Vietcong acts of terrorism, and the result was uncertainty, confusion, and trepidation for allied forces. The audacity of the Vietcong attack contributed to the escalation of the war during a critical period in Washington's policymaking. STT

Sources: Stanley Karnow, *Vietnam: A History*, 1983; *New York Times*, December 25–28, 1964.

BROWN, GEORGE SCRATCHLEY

George S. Brown was born in Montclair, New Jersey, on August 17, 1918. He graduated from the United States Military Academy in 1941, served with the Eighth Air Force in Europe during World War II, and was director of operations for the Fifth Air Force in Korea. He became Air Force chief of staff in March 1973, after having served as commander of the Seventh Air Force* in 1969 and 1970. In 1974 Brown became chairman of the Joint Chiefs of Staff (*see* Chairman, JCS). He was a controversial figure for a time in 1973 when, during Senate confirmation hearings, his role in the secret bombings of Cambodia (*see* Operation Menu) and Laos (*see* Lam Son 719) was discussed. George S. Brown died on December 5, 1978.

Sources: *New York Times*, December 6, 1978; William Shawcross, *Sideshow: Kissinger, Nixon, and the Destruction of Cambodia*, 1979; Lawrence J. Korb, *The Joint Chiefs of Staff: The First Twenty-Five Years*, 1976.

BROWN, SAMUEL WINFRED

Samuel Brown was born on July 27, 1943, in Council Bluffs, Iowa. He received a bachelor's degree from the University of Redlands in 1965, a master's degree in political science from Rutgers University in 1966, and spent some time at the Harvard Divinity School in 1967 and 1968. In 1968 Brown organized student volunteers for Senator Eugene McCarthy's* presidential bid, and in 1969 he became founder and coordinator of the Vietnam Moratorium Committee. The committee sponsored antiwar* demonstrations throughout the United States in

Above: George S. Brown, chairman of the Joint Chiefs of Staff, in November 1974.

October and November of 1969 (*see* Moratorium Day Demonstrations). The committee disbanded in 1970. Brown was active in support of Senator George McGovern's* presidential campaign in 1972.

Sources: Harry G. Summers Jr., *Vietnam War Almanac*, 1985; Eugene McCarthy, *The Year of the People*, 1969; Nancy Zaroulis and Gerald Sullivan, *Who Spoke Up? American Protest Against the War in Vietnam, 1963–1975*, 1984.

BUDDHISM

See Buddhism, p. 94

BUI DIEM

Bui Diem was born on October 1, 1923, in Phu Ly, North Vietnam. A cousin of South Vietnamese president Nguyen Van Thieu's,* Bui Diem fled to the South in 1954 after the Geneva Accords.* He worked as a journalist until 1964 when he became an advisor to South Vietnamese prime minister Phan Huy Quat.* Between 1966 and 1972 Bui Diem was ambassador to the United States, but he returned home in 1972 to serve as an advisor to President Nguyen Van Thieu. By 1975 Bui Diem was urging Thieu to either resign or launch a major offensive against the North Vietnamese, but Thieu was indecisive. After the fall of South Vietnam in April 1975, Bui Diem fled to the United States and opened a Jewish delicatessen in Washington, D.C.

Sources: *Who's Who in the World, 1974–1975*, 1975; Bui Diem, *In the Jaws of History*, 1987.

BUI PHAT

As part of the Geneva Accords* of 1954 ending the war between the French and the Vietminh* and establishing two Vietnams, a 300-day armistice period allowed Vietnamese to relocate from the North to the South or vice versa. During that period, with the assistance of the U.S. Seventh Fleet,* more than 900,000 people, most of them Roman Catholics* from the dioceses at Phat Diem and Bui Chu in North Vietnam, relocated to South Vietnam. The refugees* became the political base of Ngo Dinh Diem* in South Vietnam. Although most of the refugees ended up in special camps, some of them settled in Saigon* across the river from the French settlement. The name of this tin-roofed ghetto was Bui Phat, a composite title taken from the bishoprics of Phat Diem and Bui Chu. Because the economy of Bui Phat revolved

around money flowing from the American military presence in South Vietnam, the population tended to resist Vietcong* and Buddhist political overtures. Any political movement threatening the American presence also threatened the livelihoods of the people of Bui Phat.

Source: Frances FitzGerald, *Fire in the Lake: The Vietnamese and Americans in Vietnam*, 1972.

BUI TIN

Born in Hue* in 1924, Bui Tin came from an aristocratic family but joined the Vietminh* in 1945. He fought with them in the battles of the Red River Valley and at Dien Bien Phu* in 1954. After the Geneva Accords* of 1954, Bui Tin became one of the leading Communists in Hanoi,* and in 1963 he went to South Vietnam to assist the Vietcong* in their struggle against the government of Ngo Dinh Diem.* Over the next ten years Tin became a colonel in the North Vietnamese Army* (NVA) and deputy editor of *Quan Doi Nhan Dan*, the NVA newspaper. When the NVA entered Saigon* on April 30, 1975, Bui Tin was the ranking NVA officer who accepted the surrender of the South Vietnamese government.

Source: John S. Bowman, ed., *The Vietnam War: An Almanac*, 1985.

Left: In 1991, Bui Tin, a former colonel in the North Vietnamese Army, visits the Vietnam Veterans Memorial in Washington, D.C.

Below: On May 29, 1973, the last American servicemen left Vietnam. In this photograph, North Vietnamese Lieutenant Colonel Bui Tin of the Joint Military Commission greets an unidentified Air Force sergeant. The Joint Military Commission consisted of representatives of the United States, North Vietnam, South Vietnam, and the provisional Revolutionary Government, and worked to bring about the repatriation of all prisoners of war.

BUDDHISM

Buddhism first came to Vietnam in 111 BCE when China conquered the Red River Delta. At the time, most Vietnamese worshipped as animists, and Buddhism fit in nicely, allowing them to remain loyal to older traditions while adopting the new faith. Over time, the animist traditions gradually waned, while Buddhist doctrine waxed more powerful. In the Middle Ages, when Vietnam's imperial dynasty took root, Buddhism acquired a strong political base, evolving into a state religion governed by a hierarchy of Buddhist monks. By the 1400s, Buddhism had entered a period of decline among imperial bureaucrats, intellectuals, and the upper class, which turned

increasingly to Confucianism and Taoism, but Buddhism retained its grip on peasants. In China, Mahayana Buddhism prevailed and spread throughout the Red River Delta. Mahayana Buddhism was dynamic, and held that to achieve Nirvana in the next life, men and women had to perform acts of charity and good deeds. Mahayana Buddhism had a communal spirit that lent itself to political cooperation.

A different Buddhism flourished in the south. Indian migrants had brought Theravada Buddhism to the Mekong

River and delta regions of Cambodia and southern Vietnam. Theravada Buddhism was considerably more conservative, viewing salvation as a distant, abstract concept detached from contemporary concerns. The path to Nirvana, argued Theravada Buddhists, lay in transcending the present and detaching from worldly concerns, including economics and politics. Good deeds played a lesser role on the road to Nirvana. In southern Vietnam, therefore, more individualistic concerns prevailed—not the communal spirit of the north—as did inclinations toward capitalism and private property. The Red River Delta, not the Mekong Delta, became the soil in which the seeds of Vietnamese nationalism and communism first sprouted.

Beginning in the sixteenth century, Roman Catholic missionaries from France, Portugal, and Spain began working the peasant population of Vietnam, and by 1700 they had gathered together more than 1 million converts. A backlash soon gripped Confucians and Buddhists, who correctly identified Roman Catholicism with European imperialism. A small minority of the Vietnamese population, Roman Catholic converts soon found themselves the object of increasingly vitriolic Buddhist persecution. That persecution subsided in the nineteenth century when the French imperial government extended to Catholics the protection of the state. French imperial authorities also encouraged Roman Catholicism as an alternative to Buddhism, which they increasingly viewed as a dimension of Vietnamese nationalism. Buddhist leaders came to resent the heavy hand of French imperialism and its exploitation of Vietnam, a sentiment that gradually spread through the peasant population, where Buddhist-led ancestral villages had become the foundation of society, politics, and religion.

In 1954, after the Geneva Accords split Vietnam at the 17th parallel, South Vietnamese Buddhists found themselves besieged. The United States had installed Ngo Dinh Diem as president of South Vietnam. A fanatically devout Roman Catholic who loathed Buddhists, Diem's approach to governing was enlightened by neither an inclination to compromise nor a sense of democracy. The Geneva Accords of 1954, in addition to partitioning Vietnam, called for free elections in 1956, with Diem running against Ho Chi Minh. U.S. secretary of state John Foster Dulles, worried about the outcome of the election and anxious to strengthen Diem's political base, asked the Central Intelligence Agency to stage a propaganda campaign inside North Vietnam encouraging Roman Catholics there to immigrate to South Vietnam. The CIA crusade persuaded more than 900,000 Roman Catholics to uproot themselves and head south.

Diem then moved ruthlessly against Buddhist leaders. Two Buddhist sects—the Cao Dai and the Hoa Hao—maintained their own independent armies, a condition Diem refused to tolerate. In 1955 South Vietnamese soldiers attacked Cao Dai and Hoa Hao headquarters, closed their temples, jailed their monks, and crushed their armies, driving the remnants into the hands of the Vietminh. Diem further alienated Buddhists by giving choice government jobs to Roman Catholics and summarily resettling new Catholic immigrants on Buddhist land. He prohibited public celebrations of Buddha's birthday, jailed protesting Buddhist monks, and forbade the display of the Buddhist flag. He then canceled village elections and replaced local officeholders, most of whom were Buddhists, with Roman Catholic appointees. In Hue and Da Nang, Thich Tri Quang, a prominent Buddhist monk, began organizing demonstrations against Diem, demanding his resignation, the restoration of traditional ways, and an end to the Catholic domination of the government. He condemned both Catholicism and Communism. On June 11, 1963, Buddhist monk Thich Quang Duc protested the Diem government with self-immolation by gasoline and fire, capturing the attention of the world and convincing the Kennedy administration that Diem had become a political albatross. In November 1963, most Buddhists hailed the demise of the Diem government.

Buddhist activism remained a part of the South Vietnamese political climate throughout the war. In 1965 their opposition to the military government of General Nguyen Khanh in Saigon brought about its downfall. One year later, Thich Tri Quang surfaced again, mobilizing Buddhist protests against the South Vietnamese government of Nguyen Cao Ky. Tri Quang generated enough support to paralyze the government and force Ky to call for elections. Ky survived the elections and then, with U.S. support, crushed the protests militarily and broke the monk's power. Although Buddhists constituted 80 percent of the South Vietnamese population, they never again exercised enough power to threaten the existence of the government. In 1975, after conquering South Vietnam, North Vietnam banished Thich Tri Quang, whom they considered politically dangerous, to a Buddhist monastery, where he lived out his life in obscurity.

Sources: Sukumar Dutt, *Buddhism in East Asia*, 1966; Shawn Frederick McHale, *Print and Power: Buddhism, Confucianism, and Communism in the Making of Modern Vietnam*, 2003; Nguyen Long Thaonh Nam, *Hoa Hao Buddhism in the Course of Vietnamese History*, 2004; Tai th Nguyen, *History of Buddhism in Vietnam*, 2006.

BUNDY, McGEORGE

McGeorge Bundy was born on March 30, 1919, in Boston. He graduated from Yale in 1940 and joined the U.S. Army during World War II. His primary responsibilities were logistics and the planning for the invasions of Sicily and France. Bundy came from an old New England family, and as a result enjoyed contacts with influential people in the American business and political establishments. That he was brilliant only ensured his success. Bundy left the Army in 1946 and became a research assistant to former secretary of state Henry L. Stimson, and was coauthor with Stimson of *On Active Service in Peace and War* in 1948. Also in 1948 Bundy served as a consultant to the Thomas Dewey presidential campaign, to the Marshall Plan implementation group in the State Department, and to the Council on Foreign Relations in New York City. He began lecturing at Harvard in 1949, and in 1953 Bundy became dean of arts and sciences at Harvard. In January 1961 President John F. Kennedy* named Bundy special assistant to the president for national security affairs, where he became a principal architect of the Vietnam escalation.

In 1965 Bundy traveled to South Vietnam for a personal assessment of the situation there, and he returned advocating the large-scale bombing of North Vietnam. His recommendation soon became Operation Rolling Thunder.* One of the "best and the brightest" of the

Below: McGeorge Bundy, here in the White House with President Lyndon B. Johnson on August 23, 1967, played a critical role in shaping U.S. Vietnam policy in the 1960s. He served as a special assistant to the president on national security affairs in the Kennedy and Johnson administrations, and like his brother William, he urged an escalation of the war in Vietnam.

Above: William Bundy served in the Kennedy administration as deputy assistant secretary of defense for international security affairs and in the Johnson administration as assistant secretary of state for Far Eastern affairs. Bundy consistently advised Kennedy and Johnson to escalate the American military presence in Vietnam.

cold warriors, Bundy was convinced that Communism had to be stopped in Southeast Asia if the rest of Asia were to remain free. In 1966 Bundy left the administration to become head of the Ford Foundation, but he continued to serve as a consultant to Lyndon B. Johnson* as a member of the "Wise Old Men"* group. As part of that group, in 1968 Bundy helped Johnson realize that the combination of the antiwar movement* at home and the difficult political and military situation in Vietnam made a negotiated settlement of the war inevitable. Bundy later spent several years as president of the Ford Foundation. McGeorge Bundy died on September 16, 1996.

Source: Kai Bird, *The Color of Truth: McGeorge and William Bundy: Brothers in Arms*, 1998.

BUNDY, WILLIAM

William Bundy was born on September 24, 1917, in Washington, D.C. He graduated from Yale in 1939, served with the U.S. Army during World War II, and earned a law degree from Harvard in 1947. Between 1950 and 1960 Bundy worked for the Central Intelligence Agency.* He became a member of President Dwight D. Eisenhower's* Commission on National Goals in 1960, and in 1961 President John F. Kennedy* appointed him deputy assistant secretary of defense for international security affairs. Along with his brother McGeorge Bundy,* he played an influential role in the development of American policy toward Southeast Asia. Bundy was a strong supporter of the government of Ngo Dinh Diem* in the early 1960s and an advocate of an escalating American presence in South Vietnam. He was the chief author of what became the Gulf of Tonkin Resolution* in 1964. Early in 1964 Bundy had become assistant secretary of state for Far Eastern affairs, and later in the year President Lyndon B. Johnson* asked him to head the National Security Council Working Group and make policy recommendations for the American future in Vietnam. Their recommendations eventually became Operation Rolling Thunder,* in which Bundy and his brother often personally selected the bombing targets in North Vietnam. Bundy continued opposing negotiation and favoring increased bombing of North Vietnam until 1967, when he began to moderate his position. A leading "hawk" for both the Kennedy and Johnson administrations, Bundy left the State Department in 1969 and returned to research and writing, serving for a time as editor of *Foreign Affairs*. William Bundy died on October 6, 2000.

Source: Kai Bird, *The Color of Truth: McGeorge and William Bundy: Brothers in Arms*, 1998.

Above: A U.S. diplomat with the Department of State, Ellsworth Bunker had accepted postings during his career as ambassador to Argentina, Italy, India, and Nepal, and in 1967, President Lyndon B. Johnson appointed him ambassador to South Vietnam. Bunker was a strong supporter of the regime of Nguyen Van Thieu and urged a negotiated settlement to the war that would leave the government of South Vietnam intact.

BUNKER, ELLSWORTH

Ellsworth Bunker was born on May 11, 1894, in Yonkers, New York. He graduated from Yale in 1916, and between his graduation and 1951 he worked for the National Sugar Refining Company, serving as president from 1940 to 1948 and chairman of the board from 1948 to 1951. Bunker's diplomatic career began in 1951 when President Harry S. Truman* appointed him ambassador to Argentina, where he worked diligently and successfully in implementing a rapprochement between the Peronistas and the United States. He was ambassador to Italy between 1952 and 1953, and in 1956 became ambassador to India and Nepal, a post he held until 1961. Bunker played a major role as a troubleshooter, negotiating settlements to the Netherlands-Indonesia controversy over West Irian in 1962 and the Panama crisis in 1964. He was the American representative to the Organization of American States from 1964 to 1966 and also helped calm the angry feelings in Latin America over the American intervention in the Dominican Republic in 1965.

Bunker was appointed ambassador to South Vietnam in 1967, and he remained in that position until his resignation in 1973. Bunker was a strong supporter of the regime of Nguyen Van Thieu,* Vietnamization,* a negotiated settlement to the conflict, and the Cambodian invasion of 1970 (*see* Operation Binh Tay). Bunker became an ambassador-at-large late in 1973 and played a major role in the Panama Canal Treaties, which were signed on September 7, 1977. Ellsworth Bunker died on September 27, 1984.

Sources: *New York Times*, September 28, 1984; Howard B. Schaeffer, *Ellsworth Bunker: Global Troubleshooter*, 2005.

"BUST CAPS"

"Bust caps" was a military slang term meaning "to fire a rifle." Used predominantly by U.S. Marines,* the term refers to the unique sound of the M16 rifle,* which was the standard weapon used by American, South Vietnamese, and South Korean troops after 1964. Unlike the Russian AK-47,* which was commonly used by Communist forces and had a bigger bullet, the relatively narrow bullet of the M16 makes a higher-pitched noise when it is fired and sounds more like a cap pistol. Thus, to "bust caps" meant to fire the M16 rifle, and through repeated usage the term came to mean the firing of any kind of rifle. The term also spawned a number of derivations, such as "capping," which simply meant shooting. STT

Source: Mark Baker, *Nam*, 1981.

Left: Marines from Gulf Company, 5th Marines, their rifles at the ready, assault an enemy machine gun position on Go Noi Island during the opening hours of Operation Allan Brooke on May 7, 1968. Gulf Company was en route to assist a beleaguered patrol when the enemy ambushed the relief column 1 mile from their objective.

Below: Private First Class Howard Oakley of the 5th Marines fires his M16 at Communist snipers in 1968 southwest of Da Nang.

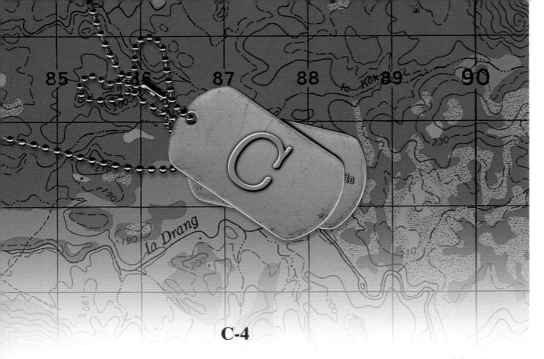

tion devices, even when dropped, beaten, shot, or burned. It was not destabilized by water, an important consideration given the Vietnamese climate.* Because it could be safely burned, C-4 was popular with GIs, who would break off a small piece of it for heating water or C-rations. Sometimes they used it in foxholes to warm hands and feet on chilly nights, and C-4 replaced sterno as the heating fuel of choice. Soldiers in the field could obtain C-4 on a resupply mission, whereas sterno required a trip to the PX, which, of course, was not necessarily possible. SF

Sources: Edgar C. Doleman Jr., *The Vietnam Experience: Tools of War*, 1984; Al Santoli, *Everything We Had: An Oral History of the Vietnam War by Thirty-three American Soldiers Who Fought It*, 1981.

C-4

C-4 was a plastic explosive popular among soldiers in Vietnam because of its various properties. It was easy to carry because of its lightweight, stable nature. It had a potent explosive power, and, malleable with a texture similar to play dough, it could be formed into a shaped charge of infinite configuration. The availability of C-4 reduced the necessity of carrying a variety of explosive charges. C-4 would not explode without the use of detona-

C-5 GALAXY

The gigantic C-5 Galaxy, with its tremendous payload capability, was developed during the 1960s in response to the unprecedented dimensions of inter-theater airlift in support of U.S. forces in Vietnam. Designed as the world's largest aircraft, the C-5 first became operational with the Military Airlift Command* on December 17, 1969, and was assigned to the Transitional Training Unit at Altus Air Force Base,

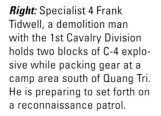

Right: Specialist 4 Frank Tidwell, a demolition man with the 1st Cavalry Division holds two blocks of C-4 explosive while packing gear at a camp area south of Quang Tri. He is preparing to set forth on a reconnaissance patrol.

Oklahoma. The first operational Galaxies were delivered to the 437th Military Airlift Wing, Charleston Air Force Base, South Carolina, in June 1970, followed by delivery to the 60th Military Airlift Wing at Travis Air Force Base, California, in October 1970. The C-5s operated by the 60th Military Airlift Wing became an important force in ensuring the efficiency of the aerial supply pipeline between the United States and Southeast Asia during the latter years of the war in Vietnam.

The C-5 was especially important for Vietnam support because it could carry virtually all equipment in the U.S. Army's inventory at intercontinental ranges and jet speeds. It could, for instance, handle such bulky items as the 74-ton mobile scissors bridge. Additionally, in its test program the C-5 air-dropped four 40,000-pound units—a total of 160,000 pounds—in a single pass over a drop zone. It could also be loaded and unloaded simultaneously at the front and rear cargo openings, and had the capability to "kneel down" to facilitate loading directly from truck-bed levels. All these attributes made the C-5 a transport especially useful in Southeast Asia aerial resupply operations.

The task of moving essential supplies, personnel, and units between the United States and Vietnam was a staggering one, and after 1970 a task in which the C-5 force figured prominently. For instance, the C-5s were instrumental in

supporting the defense of South Vietnam after an invasion from the North in April 1972. Teaming with C-141* aircraft and commercial carriers, C-5s moved 3,195 personnel and 1,600 tons of cargo from the United States to Vietnam between May 6 and 15, 1972. Additionally, when the Communist offensive swept through the provincial capital of Quang Tri and moved southward, the United States Army* turned to the Air Force* to deliver more tanks and armored vehicles to the South Vietnamese. In response, and within twenty-four hours, the C-5 fleet airlifted twenty-six tanks—weighing about 1.6 million pounds—in ten flights directly to Da Nang,* including six that were delivered from a repair depot in the Pacific.

As the Vietnam War drew to a close and American participation in the war was phased out, Military Airlift Command C-5s were necessary to support troop movements. Following the peace agreements in January 1973, for example, C-5 and other transport aircraft were heavily involved in the withdrawal of the remaining American military personnel and materiel from Vietnam. This task involved several thousand tons of materiel and more than 20,000 personnel. RDL

Sources: Kenneth W. Patchin, "Strategic Airlift," in Carl Berger, ed., *The United States Air Force in Southeast Asia, 1961–1973, An Illustrated Account*, 1977; Chris Reed, *Lockheed C-5 Galaxy*, 2000.

Below: A C-5 Galaxy with its nose raised is ready to receive cargo at the Cam Ranh Bay Air Base in 1970. The C-5 was then the largest aircraft in the world.

C-7

See Caribou Aircraft

C-130 HERCULES

One of the principal tactical transport aircraft used in Vietnam, the C-130 Hercules proved remarkably adaptable for in-country tasks. Beginning in 1965 United States Air Force* leaders made the decision to station C-130 units under the operational control of the Pacific Air Forces (PACAF) offshore to provide much of the airlift necessary to support operations in Southeast Asia. These aircraft played a critical role in tactical operations in the theater until 1975, when they were used to assist in the evacuation of American nationals and certain South Vietnamese from Saigon.*

A key aspect of this airlift force's role in Southeast Asia was support of ground forces. For instance, during Operation New Life, beginning November 21, 1965, the 173d Airborne Brigade* of the 101st Airborne Division* made a helicopter assault on a dirt airstrip forty miles east of Bien Hoa* Air Base. To support this operation, within an hour of the initial attack, the first C-130s landed to deliver troops and cargo. In all, some seventy C-130 sorties* brought in critical support resources during the first thirty-six hours of the operation. A second aspect of this type of support involved the aerial resupply of Khe Sanh* during the first four months of 1968. This support was indispensable to the success of the garrison's defense during an enemy siege. Seen by North Vietnam as a second Dien Bien Phu,* the 1954 siege of a northern city in which the French were soundly defeated, Communist forces pressed to crush the 6,000-man Marine garrison at Khe Sanh as part of the 1968 Tet Offensive.* To aid the defenders, C-130s flew daily airdrops and low-altitude parachute extraction (LAPE) deliveries of some 12,400 tons of supplies to the garrison. Between January 21 and April 8, 1968, C-130s flew 496 airdrop, 67 extraction, and 273 landing missions. Without this tactical airlift support provided by C-130s, the Khe Sanh garrison would have been forced to surrender.

Between 1965 and 1973 Air Force C-130s moved more than 5 million tons of passengers and cargo in Southeast Asia. Fifty-three C-130s were lost during these operations, more than half of these losses coming in the North Vietnamese offensives of 1967 and 1968. RDL

Sources: Ray L. Bowers, *The U.S. Air Force in Southeast Asia: Tactical Airlift,* 1983; Peter Smith, *Lockheed C-130 Hercules,* 2001.

Right: C-130s taxi at Tay Ninh during an airlift for Operation Birmingham in 1966. More than 3,000 troops from the 1st Infantry Division were brought in to landing zones near the Cambodian border by C-130s to take part in the operation. The two-brigade operation was launched to locate and destroy Vietcong forces and base camps in the area of operations.

Left: A C-130 delivers a load to the U.S. Army 1st Cavalry Division by means of the Low Altitude Parachute Extraction System (LAPES). The plane would not land, but fly at 150 miles per hour about 10 feet from the ground, then release a parachute that would pull containers out of the rear of the aircraft. Delivery was done this way for speed and where a runway was damaged or nonexistent.

Left: Members of the 101st Airborne Division aboard a C-130 being flown from Phan Thiet Air Base to Phi Troung Air Base during Operation Austin in 1966.

C-141 STARLIFTER

The C-141 Starlifter has been the workhorse of the Military Airlift Command's* strategic airlift fleet since the mid-1960s, and was a major contributor to the successful resupply of American military forces during the conflict in Southeast Asia. It was the first jet aircraft specifically designed, engineered, and built to meet military standards as a strategic troop and cargo carrier. It succeeded admirably in fulfilling the great spectrum of inter-theater airlift requirements that arose because of the Vietnam experience. Used to lift combat forces over long distances, inject those forces either by air-landing or air-dropping activities, resupply those employed forces, and extract the sick and wounded from the hostile area to far-removed medical facilities, the C-141, along with the larger C-5 aircraft,* ensured the capability of the United States to resupply forces in Vietnam on a timely basis.

Indeed, it was a milestone in the modernization of the strategic airlift fleet in April 1965 when the C-141 Starlifter became operational and began flying to Southeast Asia. By 1967 the C-141 fleet had grown to more than 100 aircraft, and in 1968 the 284th and last C-141 was produced. The Starlifter could carry 67,620 pounds of cargo 4,000 miles or 20,000 pounds nonstop from California to Japan at speeds of 440 knots. By comparison the C-124, the principal transport aircraft of the U.S. Air Force* prior to 1965, could carry only 50,000 pounds over a range of 1,000 miles or 25,000 pounds for about 2,300 miles at speeds of only 200 knots.

In responding to the urgent Southeast Asia requirements that arose with the escalation of the American commitment in South Vietnam, the Air Force quickly found that traffic to the Pacific grew from a monthly average of 33,779 passengers and 9,123 tons of cargo in fiscal year 1965 to 65,350 passengers and 42,296 tons of cargo in fiscal year 1967. In flying about 210 million miles during 1967, the Military Airlift Command flew the equivalent of 8,750 aircraft around the world and carried sufficient troops to fill every manpower space in eighty-five Army infantry divisions. The C-141 airlift fleet was the major method of supporting these increases.

On several occasions during the war, the Air Force was called on to undertake the deployment of major Army units under special conditions. The first of these, designated Operation Blue Light, came in response to the need to rush the 3d Brigade, 25th Infantry Division, from Hawaii to Pleiku, Vietnam, to offset a buildup of Communist forces late in 1965 that threatened the area. The Military Airlift Command's C-141 fleet carried the brunt of this activity, flying with C-133 aircraft 231 sorties* over a twenty-six-day period and moving 3,000 troops and 4,700 tons of equipment some 6,000 miles to Pleiku by January 23, 1966. At the height of the airlift, a C-141 or C-133 took off from Hickam every three hours.

In mid-1969 emphasis shifted to the return of units to the United States in accordance with the president's policy of gradual American withdrawal from Vietnam, beginning with 25,000 troops before August 31. The Military Airlift Command's C-141s carried out the first redeployments through a series of operations called Keystone. In the first of these, C-141s airlifted 15,446 of the 25,000 troops plus 47.5 tons of materiel from Vietnam to the United States. As the president directed other incremental withdrawals over the next several years, the C-141 force responded accordingly. RDL

Sources: Kenneth W. Patchin, "Strategic Airlift," in Carl Berger, ed., *The United States Air Force in Southeast Asia, 1961–1973, An Illustrated Account*, 1977; Frederick A. Johnson, *C-141 Starlifter*, 2005.

CAI TANG

A Vietnamese custom widely misunderstood by American soldiers during the war, cai tang is a religious act of exhuming and reburying the bodies of dead relatives. The practice was most likely to occur if the family could not afford a proper burial or if the body was buried in a hurry, a common occurrence in South Vietnam during the late 1960s and early 1970s. Usually several years after the individual's death, the family would locate the bones, wash them, and rebury them in a place more suitable as a resting place.

Sources: Ann Crawford, *Customs and Culture of Vietnam*, 1966; Gustave Dumoutier, *Annamese Religions*, 1955; Jacques Dournes, *God Loves the Pagans*, 1966.

CALLEY, WILLIAM LAWS JR.

See My Lai Massacre

CAMBODIA

Covering nearly 70,000 square miles in Southeast Asia, Cambodia (known as Democratic Kampuchea under Pol Pot and his Khmer Rouge, 1975–1979, People's Republic of Kampuchea under a Vietnamese-sponsored government from 1979–1989, and the Kingdom of Cambodia since the restoration of the monarchy in 1993) had a population in 1985 of 6,180,000; the current estimate is 13,971,000. The country is a great basin composed of one gigantic alluvial floodplain formed by numerous streams. Near the center of the basin is a huge, shallow lake called Tonle Sap. It has hundreds of tributaries flowing in, and the lake drains southeast into the Mekong River via a complex system of distributaries. When the Mekong floods, however, the drainage is reversed and the river backs into Tonle Sap. Three-quarters of Cambodia is heavily forested, and rice is cultivated on 80 percent of the arable land. A growth in the garment industry followed the signing of the Bilateral Textile Agreement by the United States and the Kingdom of Cambodia in 1999. Tourism has also boosted the economy, with more than 1.7 million visitors spending foreign dollars in the former dictatorship for the year ending September 2006.

Above: Lieutenant William Calley arrives at a pre-trial hearing in 1970 before his court-martial owing to his involvement in the My Lai massacre.

Opposite page: Men of the 9th Division debark from a C-141 Starlifter in the summer of 1969. The Starlifter was designed specifically for large passenger loads and cargo hauling.

Below: A UH-1D helicopter lands at Kintum, a remote site near the Cambodian border.

Opposite page: A map of Cambodia with its bordering neighbors, Thailand, Laos, and South Vietnam. The body of water on the southwest coast is the Gulf of Thailand. The geography of Cambodia is dominated by the Mekong River and the Tonlé Sap, the largest freshwater lake in Southeast Asia.

Below: When the Khmer Rouge Communists conquered Cambodia in April and May of 1975, their leader Pol Pot inaugurated a reign of terror equaled by few other genocidal campaigns in the twentieth century. He liquidated intellectuals, priests, professionals, small businessmen, and those who had cooperated with the U.S. backed-Lon Nol government. When the blood had all dried by the end of the 1970s, more than 2 million people had been killed. In this July 1991 photograph taken at the Choeng Ek Memorial south of the capital Phnom Penh, on the site of a Khmer Rouge extermination camp where almost 9,000 bodies were exhumed from mass graves after the fall of the regime, a pile of skulls reminds visitors of the horror and destruction.

Approximately 90 percent of the people are ethnic Khmer.* The vast majority (75 percent) are small farmers raising rice. About 5 percent of the population are ethnic Vietnamese and 1 percent ethnic Chinese,* and both of these groups dominate commerce and industry. Ethnic conflicts between the Khmer and the Vietnamese are fundamental to an understanding of Cambodian history. Anciently, the Khmer occupied much of the Mekong Delta* in southern Vietnam, but as the ethnic Vietnamese expanded out of northern Vietnam in the sixteenth century, they pushed the Khmer west back into Cambodia. Both countries were under French rule until 1954, but even after independence the expansionary pressures of the ethnic Vietnamese on the Khmer continued. That pressure precipitated the 1970 coup d'etat, the 1975 triumph of the Khmer Rouge,* and the genocidal rage of Pol Pot* in the late 1970s.

Prince Norodom Sihanouk* became head of state in Cambodia in 1954, and he walked a neutralist tightrope between the Vietnamese-backed Khmer Rouge Communists and the American-backed South Vietnamese. His prime minister Lon Nol,* however, was bitterly anti-Communist and resented the willingness of Sihanouk to allow Vietcong* and North Vietnamese Army* (NVA) troops to occupy sanctuaries* in eastern Cambodia and to infiltrate supplies and personnel into South Vietnam via the Ho Chi Minh Trail.* Sihanouk tolerated their presence there only because he feared a North Vietnamese invasion and the triumph of the Khmer Rouge if he tried to drive Vietcong and NVA soldiers out. Beginning in 1969 he secretly allowed the United States to begin bombing enemy targets inside Cambodia (*see* Operation Menu). In March 1970 Sihanouk traveled to France, and while he was gone Lon Nol engineered a coup d'etat. The National Assembly displaced Sihanouk, and Lon Nol became the new head of state. Lon Nol then tacitly

agreed to the U.S. invasion of Cambodia in April 1970. Prince Sihanouk fled to the People's Republic of China* and announced his support for the Khmer Rouge.

In October 1970 Lon Nol abolished the monarchy and proclaimed a republic, but in effect he had become the dictator of Cambodia. His administration was marked by extraordinary corruption and ineptitude, and a stroke in 1971 left him unable to maintain control of the government, while Pol Pot and the Khmer Rouge made steady gains in the countryside. In the spring of 1975 the Khmer Rouge surrounded the Cambodian capital of Phnom Penh. Lon Nol fled to Hawaii early in April 1975, and the Khmer Rouge overran the capital later that month. They then renamed the country Kampuchea, its ancient name.

Pol Pot, the leader of the Khmer Rouge, then declared "Year Zero" and began forcibly depopulating all Kampuchean cities, forcing everyone into rural labor camps and murdering anyone and everyone with ties to the French, Norodom Sihanouk, and Lon Nol. The killings assumed genocidal dimensions, with up to 2 million people dying between 1975 and 1979. Astonished by the brutality of Pol Pot, worried about the political stability of the regime, and still interested in their ancient quest for dominance of the Khmer people, the Vietnamese went on the march again as soldiers of the Socialist Republic of Vietnam* invaded Kampuchea in 1979. They drove to the capital, and Pol Pot fled back into the jungles, organizing remnants of the Khmer Rouge into a new guerrilla force fighting against the Vietnamese occupation force, igniting a ten-year struggle and nearly thirteen years of civil war. United Nations–sponsored elections were held in 1993, two years after Paris Peace Accords were signed calling for a cease-fire. The first democratic coalition government dissolved following factional fighting in 1997, and remaining Khmer Rouge elements surrendered in early 1999. After more than a year of contentious negotiations between emerging political parties, a new coalition government was elected in July 2003. GLH

Sources: William Shawcross, *Sideshow: Kissinger, Nixon, and the Destruction of Cambodia*, 1979; Michael Vickery, *Cambodia, 1975–1982*, 1984; William Shawcross, *The Quality of Mercy: Cambodia, Holocaust, and the Modern Conscience*, 1984; Ben Kiernan, "How Pol Pot Came to Power," Ph.D. diss., 1986; Milton Osborne, *Before Kampuchea*, 2004; Central Intelligence Agency, *World Factbook*, 2006.

CAMBODIA, BOMBING OF

See Operation Menu

CAMBODIA, INVASION OF

See Operation Binh Tay

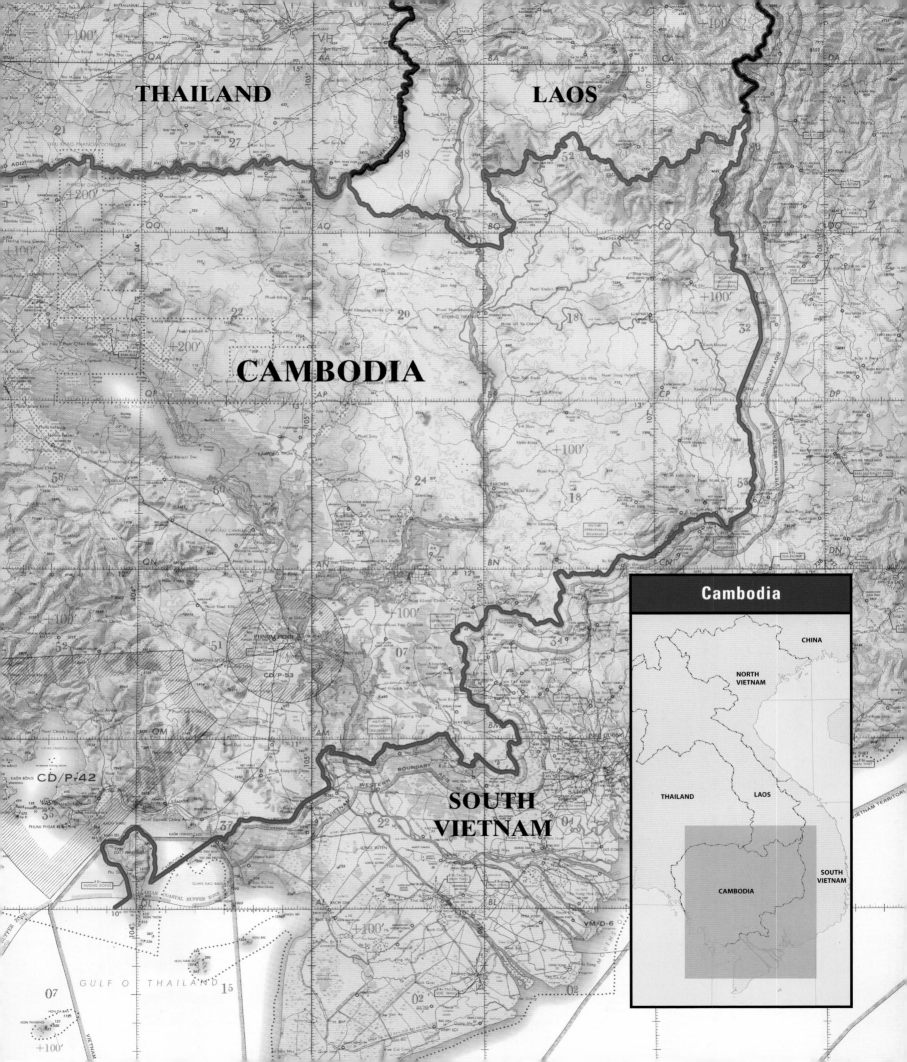

CAMOUFLAGE

Until the twentieth century, soldiers' uniforms and weapons were meant to be seen, the better to awe an enemy and for generals to control a battle. But when bullets could travel a mile and machine guns could mow down rows of men, soldiers preferred being less visible to hostile forces. In a war of patrols, ambushes, night stalking, jungles, and brush, the less seen by your enemy until the last moment the better. This meant blending in with the background—generally vegetation.

When American advisors began assisting South Vietnamese troops in the early 1960s, they adopted a kind of camouflage called "tiger stripes" used by the French in their own Indochina War. The tiger stripe pattern was mainly altering swaths of interlocking horizontal greens and browns. The American Green Berets* used the tiger stripe camouflage as well, though they often secured it on their own because it never became a standard issue uniform.

As regular U.S. troops began to arrive, their camouflage uniforms were what was called the ERDL pattern, for Engineer Research and Development Laboratory. This was a "wine leaf" pattern, not horizontal but still a mix of swirling greens and dark areas. The pattern was repeated on helmets and helmet covers. In addition, the colorful unit patches and name designations of World War II uniforms were converted to

Left: The Vietcong used camouflage as well, generally tying leaves or other vegetation to their clothing.

Below: Soldiers in battle fatigues take shelter below the crest of a grassy hill. Their clothing makes them less obvious to the enemy at a distance.

Below, inset: A helmet with camouflage cloth covering also carries insect repellant and a book of matches.

Right: Two Vietnamese paratrooper jackets and their camouflage patterns. The jacket on the right was worn by American Major Robert Hattler. The unit patches are in subdued colors not meant to detract from the camouflage.

Right: A U.S. Navy SEAL wears tiger stripe camouflaging as he looks for the enemy along the banks of a stream. His forehead and hair are camouflaged with a green head scarf and his face and hands are marked to dull reflection and blend with the vegetation. Above is a sample of tiger stripe camouflage.

Left: On the left is a tiger stripe camouflage jacket worn by a U.S. colonel rated also as a master parachutist. On the right is a jacket of the type worn by ARVN paratroopers and their U.S. advisors. This is the leaf pattern of camouflage.

Left: Vietnamese soldiers wear camouflage in anticipation of a riverine operation against the enemy.

Below left: General William Westmoreland accompanies President Lyndon Johnson on a visit to Cam Ranh Bay in October 1966.

Below right: About a thousand Canadians demonstrate against the war in Canada's capital of Ottawa in 1969.

subdued browns and blacks. Soldiers could add to their camouflage by stuffing vegetation into the bands of their helmets. Snipers often put on ghillie suits, nets or cloths with vegetation attached, to blend in with the surroundings when they were motionless.

American equipment was sometimes painted in camouflage colors, the better to keep them from being spotted by Communist artillery or approaching infantry. A tactic of camouflage paint on vehicles as large as troop carriers and tanks was to disguise the profile of the machine, fooling an enemy eye into not seeing it or incorrectly identifying it.

The Communists used camouflage as well, though in a less sophisticated manner with respect to uniforms. The Vietcong wore the "black pajamas," which provided some camouflage in the jungle and at night, and the NVA uniforms were khaki or dark green. But the Communists put camouflage skillfully to work disguising their punji stake pits and tunnel and bunker entrances—American soldiers might not see them at all until almost directly upon them.

Sources: Wikipedia.org; nchsinc.com; Guy Hartcup, *Camouflage: A History of Concealment and Deception in War*, 1980.

CAM RANH

Cam Ranh was an independent municipality located between Khanh Hoa and Ninh Thuan provinces in South Vietnam. At the peak of the fighting during the Vietnam War, Cam Ranh had a population of nearly 105,000.

Sources: *Webster's Geographical Dictionary*, 1984; Judith Banister, *The Population of Vietnam*, 1985.

CAM RANH BAY

Cam Ranh Bay was the major port of entry for U.S. military supplies and personnel in South Vietnam. Located about 200 miles northeast of Saigon* on the southern bulge of Vietnam, it had been an important way station for navigators since the days of Marco Polo. In June 1965 the U.S. Army Corps of Engineers began improving the port with 70 miles of roads, warehouses, fuel tanks, and larger cargo-handling facilities. A new pier was shipped from South Carolina and assembled at Cam Ranh Bay, enabling the facility to handle six large ships simultaneously. The port was considered so safe that Lyndon Johnson* visited there twice, which made the shock of the Vietcong* raid in 1969 even more severe. The Vietcong attack destroyed a water tower and chapel and damaged the hospital. Most patients were evacuated safely, but two Americans were killed and ninety-eight wounded. The Vietcong escaped without a casualty. Security was tightened, and Cam Ranh Bay continued to be the major supply port for Vietnam, even after the American withdrawal in 1975. It was abandoned without a fight in June 1975. BW

Sources: Harvey H. Smith et al., *Area Handbook for South Vietnam*, 1967; Carroll H. Dunn, *Base Development in South Vietnam, 1965–1970*, 1972.

CANADA

Canada played several important roles in the Vietnam War. Despite some disagreement over figures, it is clear that large numbers of young Americans exercised the option of becoming expatriates in Canada, either temporarily or permanently, in order to avoid the Vietnam War. Canadian immigration officials suggest that approximately 30,000 Americans settled legally there between 1965 and 1972. The American exile organization AMEX argued that the number was closer to 50,000–80,000 illegally and 30,000 legally. Canada was clearly an alternative for men who chose not to aid the war effort, who could not secure deferments, or who found the possibility of jail intolerable.

Canada also served, after the 1954 Geneva Accords,* as a longtime member of the International Commission for Supervision and Control in Vietnam (ICSC), created to monitor

compliance with the accords. Soon the Canadian role in the ICSC changed, especially after it became readily apparent that the 1954 Geneva Accords would not be upheld. With access to North Vietnam, Canadian members also became conveyors of messages from the United States to Hanoi,* especially in terms of threats of escalation unless North Vietnam compromised its position. Critics of the war charged Canada with compliance, but Prime Minister Lester Pearson defended Canadian actions as attempts to bring the war to an end and keep lines of communication open.

Pearson also pointed out that cooperation with American requests helped Canada maintain access to the corridors of power in Washington, and thus enabled Canada to influence American policy. Although Canada steadfastly would not provide material aid to the war effort, it also would not condemn American actions. Harsh criticism would have alienated the Americans, while expressions of cautious support lent credibility to urgings of moderation. That Canadian voice, along with those of other NATO allies, may have prompted more restraint in American policies and hastened the eventual disengagement.

As the United States withdrew from Vietnam, the ICSC was reconstituted in 1972 as the International Commission of Control and Supervision* (ICCS), and again Canada served as a member. The commission had the same weaknesses as its predecessor. Communist forces were uncooperative to the point of taking military action against ICCS helicopters and refusing to allow authorized teams to make required inspections. When Poland and Hungary, also ICCS members, hindered objective reporting on the military situation in South Vietnam, Canada resigned from the commission, in 1973. GMB

Sources: Douglas A. Ross, *In the Interests of Peace: Canada and Vietnam, 1954–1973*, 1984; Daniel S. Papp, *Vietnam: The View from Moscow, Peking, Washington*, 1981; Charles Taylor, *Snow Job: Canada, the United States, and Vietnam (1954–1973)*, 1974.

CAN LAO NHAN VI CACH MANG DANG

Translated as the Revolutionary Personalist Labor Party, the Can Lao was founded in 1954 after Ngo Dinh Diem* took over the government of South Vietnam. Ngo Dinh Nhu,* the brother of Ngo Dinh Diem, was a powerful person in his own right who advised his brother on all political matters. Nhu's political philosophy was known as Personalism, or Nhan Vi, a belief in the power of the state mixed with a strong emphasis on the virtues of humility, submissiveness, and sacrifice. In 1954 Nhu created the Can Lao, or Personalist Labor Party, from the ranks of Catholic refugees.* Eventually the party numbered more than 20,000 people, each of them occupying a position of influence in the bureaucracy and military. Nhu left direction of the Can Lao to Dr. Tran Kim Tuyen,* and together they built a number of secret intelligence organizations in the Can Lao to

keep Nhu informed of traitors, spies, plots, and military news. To finance the Can Lao, Nhu resorted to graft, extortion, currency racketeering, and vice throughout South Vietnam. The Can Lao went into decline after 1963, when Ngo Dinh Diem was assassinated and his regime overthrown. Nhu was killed at the same time. In 1969 many members of the Can Lao returned to power when President Nguyen Van Thieu* dismissed his cabinet and used old Can Lao members to staff his government. The Can Lao were frequently vulnerable to Vietcong* assassination attempts, and those unable to get to the United States after 1975 were imprisoned and killed when Saigon* and South Vietnam fell to the Communists.

Sources: Frances FitzGerald, *Fire in the Lake: The Vietnamese and Americans in Vietnam*, 1972; Denis Warner, *The Last Confucian*, 1963; Joseph Buttinger, *Vietnam: A Dragon Embattled*, Vol. 2, *Vietnam at War*, 1967.

Above: Part of a large floating market at Can Tho, a city on the Mekong River in the Mekong Delta region of Vietnam.

CAN THO

Can Tho, located on Highway 4 between Saigon* and Ca Mau, is the capital city of Phong Dinh Province and the

Below: Worshippers gather for prayer in the large Cao Dai Cathedral near Tay Ninh. This temple was built between 1933 and 1955.

commercial center of the Mekong Delta.* Its population at the height of the Vietnam War was nearly 154,000. Can Tho became one of South Vietnam's autonomous municipalities on September 30, 1970.

Sources: Danny J. Whitfield, *Historical and Cultural Dictionary of Vietnam,* 1976; *Webster's Geographical Dictionary,* 1984.

CAO DAI

Cao Dai is the popular name for the Dai Dao Tam Ky Pho Do religious sect, a group of approximately 1.5 million South Vietnamese. In 1902 a young Vietnamese civil servant, Ngo Van Chieu, became involved in spiritualism and felt that the supreme power of the universe, the Cao Dai, had communicated with him. Cao Dai was organized as a formal religion in 1926. An eclectic faith drawing on Christianity, Vietnamese animism, Buddhism,* and Confucianism, Cao Dai was centered in the city of Tay Ninh, about sixty miles northwest of Saigon.* The largest collection of Cao Dai adherents lived in the Mekong Delta* between the Mekong River and the Song Hau Giang River.

The Cao Dai believed that Buddha, Jesus, and Lao-tzu were all manifestations of one divine power and religious force in the universe, and they had a great pantheon of diverse saints, ranging from Buddha and Jesus to Charlie Chaplin and Joan of Arc.

The new religion grew rapidly in the Mekong Delta, so much so that the French prohibited its export to Annam,* Cambodia, or Tonkin.* Although the sect was more interested in religious proselytizing than political activity, it did take on a general anti-French cast and became a home for many Vietnamese nationalists. Because many Cao Dai leaders had jobs in the French bureaucracy, peasants in Cochin China* became loyal to the movement because it made it easier for them to deal with the empire. In 1938 the Cao Dai established their own private army to protect the property of members, and gradually the Cao Dai formed a semiautonomous state in the Mekong Delta. Stocked with Japanese, French, and American weapons, they literally controlled a large area northwest of Saigon. Generally free of Communist influence, the Cao Dai were among the most stable elements of the South Vietnamese population. Not until 1955, under military pressure, did the Cao Dai yield their independence to President Ngo Dinh Diem* of South

Above: A C-7 Caribou built by de Haviland Canada taxis on a runway.

Vietnam. Pham Cong Tac, leader of the Cao Dai, fled to Cambodia in February 1956, and South Vietnamese forces seized control of Tay Ninh. Most Cao Dai leaders were then incorporated into the South Vietnamese bureaucracy and military.

Sources: Victor L. Oliver, *Cao Dai Spiritualism: A Study of Religion in Vietnamese Society*, 1976; Denis Warner, *The Last Confucian*, 1963; Bernard Fall, "The Political Religious Sects of Vietnam," *Pacific Affairs*, 28 (1955): 235–253; http://www.caodai.org/pages/?pageID=1.

CAO VAN VIEN

Born in Laos* in 1921, Cao Van Vien was trained in the army as a paratrooper. Vien established close relations with General Nguyen Cao Ky* and became his chief of staff in 1966. Vien fled to the United States in 1975.

Source: "Clean-Up Time," *Newsweek*, 69 (February 6, 1967), 44–45.

CAPITAL DIVISION

See Korean Troops

CARIBOU AIRCRAFT

Manufactured by the Haviland Aircraft Corporation in Canada, the Caribou C-7 was first deployed to South Vietnam in 1964. It was a propeller-driven aircraft with a thirty-two-passenger capacity and the ability to rapidly load and unload cargo. The United States Army* had six companies of Caribou aircraft in Vietnam before control of the C-7 was shifted to the U.S. Air Force* early in 1967.

Sources: Harry G. Summers Jr., *Vietnam War Almanac*, 1985; Shelby L. Stanton, *Vietnam Order of Battle*, 1981; Carl Berger, ed., *The United States Air Force in Southeast Asia, 1961–1973*, 1977.

CASE, CLIFFORD

Above: Senator Clifford Case, Republican from New Jersey, was one of the first mainstream Republicans to voice strong opposition to the conduct of the war in Vietnam.

Below: Late in 1967, the 1st Brigade of the 101st Airborne fought a bloody battle in Chu Lai, South Vietnam, as part of Operation Wheeler. This photograph, taken on December 18, 1967, shows a makeshift memorial to the Americans killed in the battle.

Born in 1904 in Franklin Township, New Jersey, Clifford Case was a moderate-liberal congressman who, as the ranking Republican member of the Senate Foreign Relations Committee,* became a critic of the war in Vietnam. A graduate of Rutgers University (1925) and the Columbia Law School (1928), Case practiced corporate law until his election to the New Jersey Assembly in 1942. Two years later he was elected to the House of Representatives. Case resigned his congressional seat in 1953 to become president of the Fund for the Republic, and in 1954 he won election to the U.S. Senate by a margin of only 3,507 votes. He was reelected by wide margins in 1960, 1966, and 1972.

During his Senate career Case was a champion of social and civil rights programs, and in the early 1970s he was the only Republican to be given a zero rating by the conservative Americans for Constitutional Action. His committee assignments included Appropriations, Atomic Energy, Intelligence, and Foreign Relations. Case's questioning of U.S. policy in Southeast Asia began in 1967 following Senate Foreign Relations Committee hearings. He based his criticism on three points: that the war was an unwarranted extension of executive power, that the creation of a viable South Vietnamese government was impossible as U.S. forces increasingly did what the South Vietnamese should have been doing, and that the war was not winnable without the "destruction of South Vietnam and much of American might itself." Case opposed the use of funds to subsidize foreign troops in Laos* and proposed a cap on military and economic assistance to Cambodia.* He was especially critical of the military assistance program that had been used by Presidents Johnson* and Nixon* to extend overseas commitments without congressional concurrence.

In 1978 Case was defeated in the Republican Party primary by conservative Jeffrey Bell, who subsequently lost to Bill Bradley in the general election. Case remained in public life as chairman of Freedom House, a forty-year-old organization dedicated to promoting freedom in the United States and abroad. Clifford Case died on March 6, 1982. DB

Sources: *New York Times*, March 7 and 9, 1982; George Douth, *Leaders in Profile: The United States Senate*, 1975.

CASUALTIES

The question of casualties during the Vietnam War has been a controversial issue, with opponents of the war tending to exaggerate the numbers and proponents minimizing them. In recent years more accurate estimates have been possible because of increased access to American, Soviet, and Vietnamese sources. Today, the most reliable studies estimate that 2 million people died in North Vietnam during the war, with a similar number killed in South Vietnam. Military casualties included 1.1 million North Vietnamese and Vietcong killed in combat and another 600,000 wounded in action. A total of 223,748 ARVN (*see* Army of the Republic of Vietnam) soldiers died in combat and another 1,169,763 were wounded. The remaining dead in both countries, which totaled in the millions, were civilians killed by North Vietnamese, Vietcong, and American military action. Among allied forces, the United States lost 43,378 troops in combat, with another 10,284 killed by disease or in accidents. A total of 304,704 U.S. troops were wounded in action. South Korea counted 4,407 of its soldiers killed in combat and another 17,060 wounded in action. In support of the United States, 371 soldiers from Thailand died in Vietnam, as did 469 Australians and New Zealanders.

Sources: Edward S. Herman, *Atrocities in Vietnam: Myths and Realities*, 1970; Telford Taylor, *Nuremberg and Vietnam: An American Tragedy*, 1971; Guenter Lewy, *America in Vietnam*, 1978; Harry G. Summers Jr., *Vietnam War Almanac*, 1985; http://www.rjsmith.com/kia_tbl.html.

CENTRAL HIGHLANDS

The Central Highlands, a strategically important region of South Vietnam throughout the 1960s and 1970s, is a plateau area at the southern edge of the Truong Son Mountains. Nearly 1 million people, primarily Montagnard* tribesmen, lived in the 20,000 square miles of the Central Highlands in 1968. The region was economically known for its production of coffee, tea, and vegetables.

Source: Gerald Cannon Hickey, *Free in the Forest: An Ethnohistory of the Vietnamese Central Highlands, 1954–1976*, 1982.

CENTRAL INTELLIGENCE AGENCY (CIA)

The Central Intelligence Agency (CIA), an outgrowth of the World War II Office of Strategic Services (OSS), was established by Congress in 1947 to serve as a clearinghouse for all foreign intelligence operations. Subsequent legislation in 1949 allowed the CIA to use secret administrative procedures and even insulated it from the congressional budget process. The CIA's involvement in Vietnam began late in World War II when a special OSS team there allied itself with Ho Chi Minh* in opposing the Japanese occupation forces. After the war the CIA supported first the French and later, until the 1963 coup d'etat, the regime of Ngo Dinh Diem.* Until the Geneva Accords* of 1954, a CIA team led by Colonel Edward Lansdale,* working out of Saigon,* had conducted psychological operations and paramilitary raids against the Vietminh* and North Vietnamese. In 1961 the CIA launched its clandestine campaign in Laos,* recruiting nearly 10,000 Hmong* tribesmen to attack the Ho Chi Minh Trail* and sever the infiltration* route. Throughout the 1960s the CIA worked to destroy the Vietcong* infrastructure, particularly through the Phoenix Program,* which included military operations against the National Liberation Front (*see* Vietcong) as well as targeted assassinations of Vietcong leaders.

Early in the 1970s the CIA came under tremendous pressure from political critics. First, revelations of CIA assassinations of Vietcong leaders raised eyebrows, as did its intervention in the internal affairs of Cuba, Chile, Iran, Laos, and a number of other countries. More severe, however, was the public reaction to President Richard Nixon's* 1967 launching of Operation CHAOS, a program of CIA surveillance of antiwar critics in the United States, a

Above: President Lyndon B. Johnson and Richard Helms, deputy director of the Central Intelligence Agency, meet on April 8, 1965, to discuss the need for more U.S. combat troops in Vietnam.

Below: Vietnamese peasants have cultivated rice for thousands of years in the Central Highlands of South Vietnam, as they do here on January 28, 1994, near An Khe.

directive that violated the CIA charter. In 1974 Congress* amended the Foreign Assistance Act of 1974 to require that the CIA be used only for intelligence operations outside of the United States. Both houses of Congress also established permanent oversight committees to monitor CIA activities.

Sources: William E. Colby and Peter Forbath, *Honorable Men: My Life in the CIA*, 1978; Morton Halperin et al., *The Lawless State: The Crimes of the U.S. Intelligence Agencies*, 1976; Harry Howe Ransom, *The Intelligence Establishment*, 1970; John Prados, *Presidents' Secret Wars: CIA and Pentagon Covert Operations Since World War II*, 1986; Peer da Silva, *Sub Rosa: The CIA and the Uses of Intelligence*, 1978.

CENTRAL OFFICE FOR SOUTH VIETNAM

The Central Office for South Vietnam (COSVN) was the headquarters for North Vietnamese command of Vietcong* forces. Although COSVN was nominally located in Tay Ninh Province, it was highly mobile and quite different from what most American military officials thought of as a command headquarters. COSVN consisted of a small number of senior officers and staff assistants, but it was not a fixed installation resembling U.S. Military Assistance Command, Vietnam* (MACV) headquarters. Throughout the war American officers talked longingly of ending the conflict by capturing the COSVN—crippling the Vietcong and the North Vietnamese Army* (NVA). General Creighton Abrams* in 1970 remarked that the

"successful destruction of COSVN headquarters in a single blow would, I believe, have a very significant impact on enemy operations throughout South Vietnam." The desire to strike at COSVN became the rationale for the bombing of Cambodia in 1969 (*see* Operation Menu) and the invasion of Cambodia in 1970 (*see* Operation Binh Tay). Supposedly it had been located and was vulnerable to B-52* strikes. Because Cambodia was a neutral nation, elaborate steps were taken to maintain secrecy, including the falsification of military records. In the invasion of Cambodia, American and South Vietnamese soldiers captured large amounts of Vietcong supplies, but they never located COSVN. The primary results of the invasion were to push the Vietcong and NVA deeper into Cambodia, increase the flood of refugees* into Phnom Penh, strengthen the Khmer Rouge,* hasten the collapse of the Cambodian military, and undermine the Cambodian government. The American pursuit of COSVN became a symbol of the difficulties of fighting a guerrilla war. SF

Sources: William Shawcross, *Sideshow: Kissinger, Nixon, and the Destruction of Cambodia*, 1979; Malcolm Caldwell and Tan Lek, *Cambodia in the Southeast Asian War*, 1973; Jonathan Grant et al., *The Widening War in Indochina*, 1971.

CH-21 WORKHORSE

Early versions of the Piasecki/Vertol CH-21 "Workhorse" saw action in the Korean War. During the early years of U.S. involvement in Vietnam, the CH-21 lived up to its name, serving as the major component of U.S. helicopter assistance to the Armed Forces of the Republic of Vietnam.* By the time American combat troops began playing a major role in Vietnam in the mid-1960s, the CH-21 had largely disappeared from service with regular units of the U.S. military. The aircraft continued to play a role in the war, however, with Air America,* the Central Intelligence Agency's* covert air arm. One joke going around among GIs in the late 1960s was that you could go clear across Laos* without ever touching foreign soil—you could just jump from the wreck of one CH-21 to the next.

Powered by one 1,425-horsepower Wright R-1820-103 engine, the CH-21 could accommodate twelve stretchers or fourteen fully equipped troops in a passenger-cargo compartment 20 feet long and 5 feet 8 inches wide. Capable of carrying 4,700 pounds of cargo, either internally or slung beneath the fuselage, the CH-21 did yeoman service as the workhorse of the early years of the Vietnam War. NJA

Sources: Stanley Karnow, *Vietnam: A History*, 1983; *Jane's All the World's Aircraft*, 1957.

CH-34 CHOCTAW

The first production model of the CH-34 Choctaw flew on September 20, 1954. The Choctaw was adopted by all branches of the U.S. Armed Services, including the Coast Guard.* Powered by a Wright R-1820-84 radial air-cooled engine rated at 1,525 horsepower, the CH-34 could carry twelve fully equipped combat troops. Equipped with a power winch and a cargo sling, the CH-34 was a versatile aircraft capable of performing in a wide variety of missions. Throughout the 1960s the Choctaw was used in Vietnam as a medium cargo carrier, troop transport, and medical evacuation (*see* Medevac) aircraft. Relatively large in relation to its payload capabilities, and slow and unmaneuverable compared with later helicopters, the CH-34 proved vulnerable to enemy ground fire and was replaced as an assault aircraft by the UH-1, or "Huey." NJA

Source: *Jane's All the World's Aircraft, 1963–64*, 1964.

CH-37 MOJAVE

In late 1962 the United States Army* introduced the CH-37 to Vietnam. One flight platoon of the 19th Transportation Company, stationed in Korea,* was brought to Vietnam to provide heavy helicopter support for forces of the Republic of Vietnam.* While very few aircraft were involved, the introduction of the CH-37 marked an escalation in American involvement in the war. The CH-37 was capable of airlifting heavy equipment, including the largest artillery, into any part of the country in support of Vietnamese ground operations.

Right: Marines of 1st Battalion, 3d Marines are being taken by CH-34 Choctaw to Hill 327, known as Freedom Hill, near Da Nang to relieve 3d Battlion, 9th Marines in April 1965.

When it was introduced into service in 1956, the CH-37 Mojave was the largest, most powerful helicopter in the non-Communist world. With a cabin 30 feet 4 inches long and 7 feet 9 inches wide, the Mojave was comparable in size to the DC-3 transport. Fitted with hydraulically operated clamshell doors, the Mojave could carry three jeeps or three quarter-ton trucks internally. Twenty-three fully equipped combat troops could be carried in the Mojave, or it could be set up to carry twenty-four litter patients and medical attendants. Large, bulky loads could be carried under the aircraft in a sling designed to automatically release its load upon touchdown.

Powered by two Pratt & Whitney R-2800 engines with 4,200 combined horsepower, the CH-37 could carry a 5-ton payload at a cruising speed of 115 miles per hour. This helicopter was one of the first ever built with retractable landing gear and night-flying equipment. With its automatic stabilizing ability, the Mojave was capable of flying under virtually any weather conditions. NJA

Source: *Jane's All the World's Aircraft, 1959–60*, 1960.

CH-47 CHINOOK

The Boeing-Vertol CH-47 Chinook entered service with the United States Army* in the spring of 1963 at Fort Benning, Georgia. First assigned to the 11th Air Assault Division (Airmobile), the Chinook replaced the CH-37* as the main cargo helicopter for the Army. When the Chinook started service with the division, the 11th Air Assault was developing the strategies and techniques that were later to be tried in Vietnam. Redesignated the 1st Cavalry Division*

Left: A CH-37 Mojave helicopter prepares to deliver recently arrived U.S. soldiers to a combat zone on May 8, 1965.

Below: GIs crouch to avoid the debris sent flying by a Chinook helicopter. It is delivering supplies to the U.S. base at Khe Sanh in 1971.

Below top: The Sikorsky CH-53D Sea Stallion was used primarily by the U.S. Marine Corps to ferry soldiers and cargo between rear areas, base camps, and battlefields. It was also used to recover downed aircraft, sweep mined areas, and, if necessary, tow distressed ships.

(Airmobile), this unit was later to play a key role in the Army's helicopter war in Vietnam. The CH-47 was a key component of that role.

The CH-47 was powered by two Lycoming T55 L-7 engines, each delivering 2,200 shaft horsepower, driving two three-bladed rotors. With a cabin 30 feet long, 7 feet 6 inches wide, and 6 feet 6 inches high, the CH-47 had a normal payload of three tons of freight, thirty-three troops,

twenty-seven paratroopers, or twenty-four litters. The rear-loading ramp could be left open or removed to enable the Chinook to transport extra-long cargo or to be used for free-drop delivery of cargo or for paratroop drops. Capable of cruising at 150 miles per hour, the Chinook served very successfully as a major cargo helicopter of the Vietnam War.

The CH-47 was also used as a gunship in Vietnam, with a 20mm Vulcan cannon mounted to fire from the side of the aircraft. The Chinook was less successful in this role, however, as the vibrations from the cannon placed too much stress on the airframe, greatly shortening the useful life of the aircraft. NJA

Source: *Jane's All the World's Aircraft, 1963–64*, 1964.

CH-53

In 1962 the United States Navy* selected the Sikorsky CH-53 as the new heavy assault transport helicopter for the Marine Corps.* The United States Air Force* also selected the Sikorsky to serve in a variety of roles, including transport, medical evacuation (*see* Medevac), and rescue. Deliveries of the CH-53 started in 1965, and the aircraft entered service in Vietnam in 1966.

The CH-53 has a passenger-cargo cabin 30 feet long, 7 feet 6 inches wide, and 6 feet 6 inches high, and is capable of carrying up to 18,000 pounds of freight (overload condition). A typical cargo load would be two jeeps, two Hawk missiles, or a 105mm howitzer. The CH-53 can carry thirty-eight combat-ready troops or twenty-four stretchers.

Powered by two General Electric T64-GE-6 2,850-horsepower shaft-turbine engines, the CH-53 has a normal cruising speed of 172 miles per hour and a normal radius (with a 4-ton load) of 115 miles. NJA

Source: *Jane's All the World's Aircraft, 1963–64*, 1964.

CH-54 SKYCRANE

The CH-54 Skycrane (Tarhe) was first delivered to Vietnam in 1966 and was used to carry heavy payloads. Capable of lifting up to 20,000 pounds, the CH-54 often moved heavy artillery pieces, aircraft, trucks, and Army surgical-center pods. During the course of the Vietnam War, the CH-54, with its two 4,500 shaft horsepower engines, retrieved more than 380 shot-down aircraft.

Sources: Richard O'Neill, ed., *An Illustrated Guide to the Modern US Army*, 1986; Shelby L. Stanton, *Vietnam Order of Battle*, 1981.

CHAIRMAN, JOINT CHIEFS OF STAFF

The Joint Chiefs of Staff was created by the National Defense Act of July 1947. Composed of the senior officer of each of the four branches of the U.S. Armed Services, the Joint Chiefs of Staff operates under the secretary of defense and the president of the United States. Between 1959 and 1975 six men served as chairman of the Joint Chiefs of Staff: Air Force General Nathan F. Twining (1957–60); Army General Lyman L. Lemnitzer (1960–61); Army General Maxwell D. Taylor* (1961–64); Army General Earle G. Wheeler* (1964–70); Admiral Thomas H. Moorer* (1970–74); and Air Force General George S. Brown (1974–78).*

Sources: Edward Luttwack, *The Pentagon and the Art of War*, 1985; Lawrence J. Korb, *The Joint Chiefs of Staff: The First Twenty-five Years*, 1976.

CHAMPA

Champa was an Indianized kingdom in Southeast Asia, located approximately in central Vietnam between the Red River Delta and the Mekong Delta.* To the north were the Vietnamese people; to the south were the Khmers,* or Cambodians. During the Early Han Dynasty, Champa came to the attention of the Chinese, and its recorded history begins; by the fifteenth century, Champa had succumbed to the relentless advance of the Vietnam kingdom down the peninsula.

Champa and Vietnam marked a dividing line of sorts between Indian and Chinese cultural and political influence in Southeast Asia. Champa was a decentralized kingdom, with each coastal fishing village having a measure of independence and power. Champa augmented income and power from fishing—there was virtually no farming land—with piracy against ships operating in the South China Sea and against Vietnamese landed communities.

For a thousand years Champa was able to withstand Vietnamese expansion. Until the collapse of the T'ang Dynasty in the early tenth century, Vietnam faced Chinese

Opposite page, bottom: A CH-54 Skycrane transports a howitzer in 1967. The CH-54 specialized in air-lifting bulky equipment.

Below: In November 1968, the Joint Chiefs of Staff of the U.S. military consisted of, from left to right, General William C. Westmoreland, former commander of U.S. forces in Vietnam; General John P. McConnell, U.S. Air Force; Chairman General Earle G. Wheeler, U.S. Army; Admiral Thomas H. Moorer, U.S. Navy; and General Leonard F. Chapman Jr., U.S. Marine Corps.

Above: General Leonard Fielding Chapman Jr. as the 24th Commandant of the Marine Corps (1968–1972). During his first year in office, General Chapman traveled widely, covering nearly 100,000 miles while visiting Marines stationed around the world. The heavy commitment to Vietnam took him to that country twice in 1968. By the end of his tenure, General Chapman witnessed the III Marine Amphibious Force withdrawal from Vietnam and the strength of the Corps drop from a peak of 289,000 to 198,000.

Opposite page, bottom: The antiwar movement steadily gained influence throughout the early 1960s and peaked in 1968 at the Democratic National Convention in Chicago. Jerry Rubin, Abbie Hoffman, and Rennie Davis were three of the most prominent leaders of the antiwar movement. All three of them were part of the so-called Chicago 8, a group of protestors charged with conspiracy to foment a riot.

imperial power on again (during the Han Dynasty) and off again (during the interregnum) and could not devote its full strength to expansion. Champa paid tribute to Chinese dynasties and hence maintained a measure of independence and power.

The situation began to change after the fall of the T'ang. Vietnam became stronger, and soon began advancing slowly from the Red River Delta down the coastline, reaching approximately the 17th parallel by AD 1000, and the city of Hue* by approximately AD 1400. Along with the advance of the Vietnamese, the Mongol rise to power sapped the vitality and strength of the Champa kingdom. Vietnam and Champa united temporarily to withstand the Mongols and their Chinese and Korean levies, but the centuries of constant warfare proved too great a strain. By 1471 Vietnam had conquered Champa, and the kingdom became part of history. CD

Source: Michael G. Cotter, "Towards a Social History of the Vietnamese Southward Movement," *Journal of Southeast Asian History*, 9 (March 1968): 12–24.

CHAMS

Until the early 1400s the Chams were an Indianized people living along the coast of present-day Vietnam between the Red River Delta and the Mekong Delta.* The Chams reflected the differences between Indian and Chinese cultural influences in Southeast Asia. They were a seafaring people, alternating fishing with piracy, and because of their relatively martial pursuits and despite their small numbers, they were able to withstand the aggression of their neighbors, the Vietnamese and the Cambodians, and for a while even threatened the Vietnam capital of Hanoi.*

For more than a thousand years the Cham people survived along with their kingdom. The Vietnamese always faced Chinese pressure, sometimes Chinese armies, occasionally Chinese control, while the Cambodians were not particularly warlike. The Chams meanwhile benefited from fishing, piracy, and trade with the islands of present-day Indonesia.

Matters considerably worsened after the collapse of the T'ang Dynasty in China. Until AD 900, the Vietnamese expended a considerable amount of their energy resisting the Chinese; after the T'ang collapse, the Vietnamese would have their independence secure, and would begin a thousand-year drive to control all of Indochina.* The Chams formed the first barrier, and hence the first target. Vietnamese pressure crushed the Chams; the slow, inexorable march of Vietnamese farmers down the coast overwhelmed the seafaring Chams, whose hold on their land was weak. By AD 1000, the Vietnamese had secured perhaps a third of old Champa; by the 1400s, Champa had disappeared.

In the 1950s and 1960s a vestige of the old Cham people remained in Vietnam. Around Hue,* the old Champa

kingdom capital, there were up to 20,000 people who made their living from the sea and were descendants of the old Chams. Along with the expulsion of Chinese-ethnic Vietnamese (*see* Chinese) after North Vietnam's May 1975 conquest of the South, presumably the old Chams were expelled as well. CD

Sources: John Frank Cady, *Southeast Asia: Its Historical Development*, 1958; John F. Embree, *Ethnic Groups of Northern Southeast Asia*, 1950.

CHAPMAN, LEONARD FIELDING JR.

Leonard Chapman's tour as commandant of the Marine Corps* (1968–72) coincided with the withdrawal of U.S. forces under President Nixon's* Vietnamization* policy. Born in Florida in 1913, he graduated from the University of Florida with a Reserve Army commission that he resigned in favor of a Marine Corps commission in 1935. Chapman served in the Pacific Fleet before the Vietnam War but instructed artillery classes at Quantico until 1944, when orders sent him to the staff of the 11th Artillery and combat on Peleliu.

Chapman's postwar assignments included staff duty and regimental and barracks commands in Japan and North Carolina. In Washington in the early 1960s, his staff work earned the annual merit award of the Armed Forces Management Association (1966) and the attention of President Johnson,* who promoted Chapman to commandant over the more celebrated Victor Krulak* and Lewis Walt* in 1968.

The first artillery officer to rise to the Marines' top billet and a product of McNamara's* industrialized Pentagon, Chapman became known as the cerebral commandant and an expert in management techniques, logistics, and communications. Candidly admitting, "We've got a problem," Chapman faced morale and racial problems on Okinawa and in Vietnam rear areas during his tour before retiring in January 1972. A year later President Nixon* appointed him commissioner of immigration and naturalization; he retired from that post in May 1977. Leonard Chapman died on January 6, 2000. DA

Sources: *New York Times*, 1968–1977; J. Robert Moskin, *The U.S. Marine Corps Story*, 1982; *Marine Corps Gazette* 84 (March 31, 2000): 19–21.

CHARNER, LEONARD VICTOR JOSEPH

Leonard Charner was born in February 1797 and died in February 1869. He spent his career in the French Navy, and as a result of his efforts in 1861, the French secured their control of Saigon* and controlled the flow of rice into eastern Vietnam from the western provinces. He returned to France in 1862 to become a senator, and he was promoted to the rank of admiral in 1864.

Source: Joseph Buttinger, *Vietnam: A Dragon Embattled*, 2 vols., 1967.

CHIANG KAI-SHEK

Chiang Kai-shek, longtime leader of the Kuomintang and Nationalists in China, was born in 1887. Chiang was trained and served in the Japanese Army between 1909 and 1911, and then joined Sun Yat-Sen in the Chinese nationalist movement. After Sun Yat-Sen's death in 1925, Chiang became leader of the Kuomintang. Although the Nationalists split with the Communists in the Kuomintang in 1927, they later joined to resist Japanese oppression in China, especially after 1937. The civil war with the Communists resumed in 1946, and Chiang, along with the other Nationalists, was expelled from China to Taiwan after the Communist victory in 1949. From 1950 to his death in 1975, Chiang served as president of Taiwan, and although he was willing, and even anxious, to provide troops to assist the American war effort in South Vietnam, U.S. policymakers resisted the idea, worried that it might bring about a large-scale intervention from the People's Republic of China. Chiang Kai-shek died on April 5, 1975.

Sources: Keiji Furaya, *Chiang Kai-shek. His Life and Times*, 1981; William Morwood, *Duel for the Middle Kingdom: The Struggle Between Chiang Kai-shek and Mao Tse-tung for Control of China*, 1980.

THE CHICAGO 8

The "Chicago 8" was the name given to eight persons tried in Chicago in 1969 on charges of criminal conspiracy with intent to start a riot in August 1968. The trial was also called the Chicago Conspiracy Trial. The proceedings were occasioned by the massive anti–Vietnam War demonstrations held in streets and parks around the site of the Democratic Party's 1968 national nominating convention,* which had opened in Chicago on August 26. Considerable violence occurred during the demonstrations; in December, however, the National Commission on the Causes and Prevention of Violence concluded that the unrest was caused by a "police riot," not by the demonstrators. Despite political pressure to prosecute the alleged leaders of the Chicago demonstrations, U.S. attorney general Ramsey Clark concluded that there was no basis for prosecution.

Nevertheless, U.S. District Court judge William J. Campbell, a friend of Chicago mayor Richard Daley's, convened a federal grand jury to investigate the demonstrations. Under the administration of President Richard

M. Nixon,* U.S. attorney general John Mitchell agreed to prosecute the presumed demonstration leaders; an indictment was issued on March 20, 1969. The defendants were charged with violating the so-called Anti-Riot Statute, or "H. Rap Brown Law," a rider that had been attached to the Civil Rights Act of 1968 in an attempt to quell rioting and civil disturbances. David T. Dellinger,* Rennard C. Davis, Thomas E. Hayden,* Abbott H. Hoffman,* Jerry C. Rubin,* Lee Weiner, John R. Froines, and Bobby G. Seale were charged with conspiracy to cross state lines with intent to cause a riot, to interfere with the performance of duties of police officers and firemen, and to teach and demonstrate the use of incendiary devices. Weiner and Froines were also charged with teaching and demonstrating the use of incendiary devices. The other defendants were also charged with actually crossing state lines with intent to cause a riot.

The trial began on September 24, 1969, before seventy-four-year-old U.S. District Court judge Julius Jennings Hoffman, and was itself a raucous and well-publicized event. Judge Hoffman frequently denied defense motions and mispronounced the names of defendants and their attorneys. Insults and epithets were traded between the judge and the defendants and their attorneys. The defendants sought to make the Vietnam War, racism, and domestic repression the central issues of the trial. At one point, the defendants draped Vietcong* and American flags across their defense tables. When Seale's attorney was hospitalized, Seale, the only black defendant, requested a postponement of proceedings and then the right to defend himself. Judge Hoffman denied both requests. Seale protested frequently and called Hoffman a racist, a fascist, and a pig.

Above: In 1949, General Chiang Kai-shek lost his long-running battle with Mao Zedong and the Communists for control of China. Mao's Red Army triumphed over Chiang's forces and drove them across the Straits of Formosa to Formosa (Taiwan). Chiang then proclaimed the Republic of China there. Until his death in 1975, he insisted that his Republic of China was sovereign and governed the People's Republic of China on the mainland.

Above: Admiral Elmo Zumwalt Jr. served as chief of naval operations between 1970 and 1974. This photo was taken on August 1, 1970.

Hoffman ordered Seale to be gagged and chained hand and foot to a metal chair. When Seale banged his chains on the chair, Hoffman placed him in a wooden chair with a larger gag over his mouth. On November 5, Hoffman declared a mistrial for Seale, severed him from the case, and sentenced him to four years in prison on sixteen contempt charges. After the jury retired to deliberate on the case of the remaining defendants, Judge Hoffman found all seven defendants as well as two trial lawyers, William M. Kunstler and Leonard I. Weinglass, guilty of 175 charges of criminal contempt and sentenced them to terms of imprisonment (four years and thirteen days for Kunstler and one year and eight months for Weinglass).

On February 18, 1970, after five days of deliberation, the jury found all defendants not guilty of conspiracy, but found Dellinger, Davis, Hayden, Hoffman, and Rubin guilty on substantive charges of intent to riot. Each defendant was sentenced to five years in prison and fined $5,000. These convictions were overturned on November 21, 1972, by the U.S. Court of Appeals, Seventh Circuit. Contempt and conspiracy charges against Seale were dropped after a new trial. Contempt charges against the remaining defendants and their attorneys were reduced and dismissed during ten years of appeal. JK

Sources: Jason Epstein, *The Great Conspiracy Trial*, 1970; Clark Dougan and Steven Weiss, *The Vietnam Experience: A Nation Divided*, 1984; Nancy Zaroulis and Gerald Sullivan, *Who Spoke Up? American Protest Against the War in Vietnam, 1963–1975*, 1984.

CHIEF OF NAVAL OPERATIONS

The chief of naval operations is the senior officer of the United States Navy.* Between 1959, when Admiral Arleigh Burke held the position, and the end of the Vietnam War in 1975, six men served as chief of naval operations: Admiral Arleigh Burke (1959–61); Admiral George W. Anderson (1961–63); Admiral David L. McDonald (1963–65); Admiral Thomas H. Moorer* (1965–70); Admiral Elmo Zumwalt* (1970–74); and Admiral James L. Holloway (1974–75).

Sources: John M. Collins, *U.S. Defense Planning: A Critique*, 1982; Edward J. Marolda and G. Wesley Pryce III, *A Short History of the United States Navy and the Southeast Asian Conflict, 1950–1975*, 1984.

CHIEF OF STAFF, U.S. AIR FORCE

The senior officer in the United States Air Force* is the chief of staff. Six people occupied that position between 1959 and 1975: General Thomas D. White (1959–61); General Curtis LeMay* (1961–65); General John P. McConnell (1965–68); General John D. Ryan (1968–73); General George S. Brown* (1974); and General David C. Jones (1974 until after the war).

Sources: John M. Collins, *U.S. Defense Planning: A Critique*, 1982; Carl Berger, ed., *The United States Air Force in Southeast Asia, 1961–1973*, 1977.

Right: Admiral David L. McDonald, the chief of naval operations, and Vice Admiral Ephriam P. Holmes on a visit to Vietnam in September 1965.

CHIEF OF STAFF, U.S. ARMY

The Army chief of staff is the senior officer in the United States Army,* and seven people held the position between 1959 and 1975, starting with General Maxwell Taylor.* Taylor was replaced in 1959 by General Lyman L. Lemnitzer, who served until October 1960. General George Decker succeeded Lemnitzer and served until 1962. General Earle Wheeler* became chief of staff in October 1962 and remained in the post until July 1964, when General Harold K. Johnson took over the position. General William Westmoreland* replaced Johnson in 1968 and remained in office until October 1972. General Creighton Abrams* served as chief of staff until his death from cancer in 1974. General Fred C. Weyand* took over after Abrams' death.

Sources: Harry G. Summers Jr., *Vietnam War Almanac*, 1985; James M. Collins, *U.S. Defense Planning: A Critique*, 1982.

CHIEU HOI PROGRAM

Efforts to destroy the National Liberation Front (NLF; *see* Vietcong) included the "Chieu Hoi" (Open Arms) amnesty program initiated at the insistence of American and British advisors, including Sir Robert Thompson.* The program, like all others in Vietnam, generated impressive statistics— nearly 160,000 deserters and 11,200 weapons turned in—but only meager results. The program was conducted in typical American fashion, with leaflets dropped from the air in NLF-controlled areas and Vietnamese psyops (psychological operations) personnel haranguing peasants via bullhorn from hovering helicopters. Those who rallied to the government were usually low-level personnel, many of whom may not have been enthusiastic about the NLF program to begin with. The program, in part because of its failure to develop face-to-face contacts, attracted few members of the NLF political or military cadres. In fact, critics charged that the program was an "R&R" for the NLF, allowing NLF soldiers to "rally" temporarily to recuperate themselves before returning to the NLF. Evidence indicates that some may have "changed sides" as many as five times. Of those who rallied, however, were some who genuinely changed sides and were recruited into the GVN military (*see* Republic of Vietnam), often as "Kit Carson" scouts.* Good Kit Carson scouts were highly prized by American military units because of their familiarity with guerrilla movements, tactics, and booby traps.* Unfortunately, far more of the Chieu Hoi deserters also infiltrated American and ARVN (*see* Army of the Republic of Vietnam) military units and caused serious problems. SF

Sources: Frances FitzGerald, *Fire in the Lake: The Vietnamese and the Americans in Vietnam*, 1972; Tran Dinh Tho, *Pacification*, 1979; Andrew F. Krepinevich Jr., *The Army and Vietnam*, 1986.

Left: General William Westmoreland and President Lyndon Johnson meet in the White House Cabinet Room on October 14, 1968. At the time, Westmoreland was chief of staff of the U.S. Army. The presidential campaign was underway and the number of U.S. troops in Vietnam had reached nearly 550,000 people.

Below: The fall of Saigon to North Vietnamese forces on April 30, 1975, precipitated a mass emigration from South Vietnam. South Vietnamese who had been closely associated with the United States and with the government of the Republic of Vietnam feared bloody reprisals from the Communists. Many South Vietnamese fled in rickety boats, fishing trawlers, and cargo vessels, and became known as "boat people." In this 1978 photograph, a South Vietnamese family is stuck aboard the *Hai Hong* after the Malaysian government refused to allow the freighter to land. The *Hai Hong* carried 2,500 refugees.

CHINA

See People's Republic of China

CHINESE

Ethnic Chinese constituted the largest minority group in South Vietnam. At the peak of the conflict, there were approximately 1 million Chinese living in South Vietnam, most in the Cholon* suburb of Saigon.* They constituted a highly prosperous group active in banking, foreign trade, real estate, and commerce. Because of centuries of conflict between the Chinese and ethnic Vietnamese, the Chinese were often resented by the larger population, but their services and skills were important to the local economy. Large numbers of Vietnamese refugees* entering the United States after 1975 consisted of ethnic Chinese escaping the economic restrictions imposed by the Socialist Republic of Vietnam.*

Sources: F. Raymond Iredell, *Vietnam: The Country and the People*, 1966; Joan Schrock et al., *Minority Groups in the Republic of Vietnam*, 1967.

CHINH PHU CACH MANG LAM THOI CONG HOA MIEN NAM VIETNAM

See Provisional Revolutionary Government of South Vietnam

CHOLON

Cholon is the Chinese* part of the city of Saigon.* It was originally separate from Saigon and populated exclusively by native Chinese living in Indochina* and prospering commercially. Urban growth eventually brought Cholon into the Saigon metropolitan area, and at the height of the Vietnam War the Cholon population exceeded 1 million people.

Sources: *Webster's Geographical Dictionary*, 1984; Joseph Buttinger, *Vietnam: A Dragon Embattled*, Vol. 2, *Vietnam at War*, 1967.

Left: During the Tet Offensive in 1968, Vietcong soldiers attacked ARVN and U.S. troops throughout South Vietnam. The grounds of the ARVN 8th Division were in the middle of Cholon, the Chinese market center in Saigon. This photograph shows two 750-pound bombs being dropped on Vietcong forces that had penetrated the area.

Below: Members of the 38th Ranger Battalion fire into a Vietcong position in Cholon in June 1968.

Above: Noam Chomsky, the MIT professor credited with being the father of modern linguistics, was also a bitter opponent of the Vietnam War, a position he explained in his bestselling book *American Power and the New Mandarins*. In this 2000 photograph, Chomsky is pictured in a classroom at MIT.

Below: During the Vietnam War, the CIA's Phoenix Program assassinated Vietcong leaders as a matter of U.S. policy. Revelations about the program stirred a ferocious political debate in the United States. In this June 1975 photograph, Senator Frank Church, Democrat from Idaho, holds a press conference calling for legislation prohibiting CIA assassination operations.

CHOMSKY, AVRAM NOAM

Noam Chomsky, a leading intellectual critic of the war in Vietnam, was born in Philadelphia on December 7, 1928. He received a B.A. from the University of Pennsylvania in 1949, specializing in language and linguistics, and an M.A. and Ph.D. in 1951 and 1955. Chomsky joined the faculty of the Massachusetts Institute of Technology in 1955 and became a full professor in 1961. He wrote several well-received books in the late 1950s and early 1960s, including *Syntactic Structures* (1957) and *Aspects of the Theory of Syntax* (1965). Chomsky openly opposed the war in Vietnam as early as 1965, speaking widely on the northeastern campus circuit in 1966 and 1967, but he really made his mark on the antiwar movement* with the publication of his *American Power and the New Mandarins* in 1969. There he argued that the United States had become intoxicated with its own military and economic power, had assumed an ideology of superiority in world politics, and was destroying a society in the name of freedom. He also accused American intellectuals of having become stooges of the business and government establishments. After the war, Chomsky continued to write and speak out about American foreign policy and to teach at MIT, where he enjoys a reputation as the father of modern linguistics.

Sources: *Who's Who in America*, 1984–1985, 1985; Noam Chomsky, *American Power and the New Mandarins*, 1969; Nancy Zaroulis and Gerald Sullivan, *Who Spoke Up? American Protest Against the War in Vietnam, 1963–1975*, 1984.

CHRISTMAS BOMBING OF 1972

See Operation Linebacker II

CHU LAI, BATTLE OF (1965)

See Operation Starlite

CHURCH, FRANK FORRESTER

Frank Church was born in Boise, Idaho, on July 25, 1924. During World War II Church served as a military intelligence officer in China, India, and Burma, and in 1947 he graduated from Stanford University. Church attended Harvard Law School for a year, but a bout with cancer brought him back west again, and in 1950 he graduated from the Stanford University Law School. Between 1950 and 1956 Church practiced law in Idaho and was active in Democratic politics, serving as chairman of the statewide

Young Democrats organization. He won the party's nomination for the U.S. Senate in 1956 and went on to upset the Republican incumbent, Herman Welker. At thirty-two, Church was the youngest member of the Senate. He quickly earned a reputation as an outspoken liberal, and by supporting majority leader Lyndon B. Johnson* on civil rights legislation, Church gained favor and was appointed to the prestigious Senate Foreign Relations Committee* in 1959. In 1960 Church supported John F. Kennedy* for the presidential nomination, and he won reelection to the Senate in 1962.

After 1965 Senator Church became increasingly apprehensive about U.S. involvement in Southeast Asia. He warned against American support for repressive regimes such as that in Vietnam unless substantial progress was made toward reform. In 1965 he repeated this warning, contending that the rift in the Communist world between the People's Republic of China* and the Soviet Union* had diminished the threat of "monolithic communism." In 1966 Church broke with the Johnson administration over Vietnam policy by calling for an end to the bombing.* In 1970 Church cosponsored the Cooper-Church Amendment* to prohibit U.S. deployment of ground forces in Cambodia,* setting off a six-month debate in the Senate. In 1972, in reaction to the Nixon* administration's bombing of Hanoi* and Haiphong and the mining of Haiphong Harbor,* Church joined with Senator Clifford Case* of New Jersey in sponsoring a resolution seeking an end to all U.S. military activity in Southeast Asia. The proposal was considered the first step in the eventual adoption of the War Powers Resolution* of 1973.

On the domestic front, Church chaired the Senate Select Committee on Intelligence, which investigated excesses and violations of law by the Central Intelligence Agency,* Federal Bureau of Investigation, and National Security Agency under the Nixon administration. In 1976 Church made a bid for the Democratic presidential nomination, but he lost out to Governor Jimmy Carter of Georgia. In 1980 he was defeated for reelection to the Senate. Frank Church continued to live in Washington, D.C., practicing international law until his death from cancer on April 7, 1984. JMR Jr.

Sources: *Current Biography*, 1978; *New York Times*, April 8, 1984.

"THE CITY"

See Fishhook

CIVILIAN IRREGULAR DEFENSE GROUP

The Civilian Irregular Defense Group, or CIDG, was a Central Intelligence Agency* operation initiated in 1961 to prevent Vietcong* control of Vietnamese minorities. The purpose of the program was to train the indigenous tribes of the Vietnamese interior in self-defense, so the Vietcong would not be able to get control of the Central Highlands,* and to relieve regular South Vietnamese Army forces of the responsibility of controlling the interior. The CIA went to work with the Montagnards* first, and then gradually extended the defensive program out to such other tribes as the Khmers,* Nungs,* Cao Dai,* Hoa Hao,* and some South Vietnamese youth groups. By mid-1963 the CIDG was functioning in more than 200 tribal villages, with 12,000 people participating in the program. The CIDG programs were more popular than later counterinsurgency efforts because they did not involve resettlement of people away from their home villages.

In October 1963 the CIDG programs were removed from the CIA and placed under the control of the Special Forces.* At the same time the Special Forces assumed responsibility for about 600 people in Combat Intelligence Teams and more than 5,000 Border Surveillance personnel and Mountain Scouts. A group of Civilian Airborne Rangers were militarized and worked with the CIDG. The CIDG was under the command of the Luc Luong Dac Biet—South Vietnamese Special Forces. After the switch from the CIA to the Special Forces, the CIDG became more militarily aggressive, although their main purpose remained defensive. At times the CIDG forces were hired on a contractual basis, but usually they functioned as local security units. After 1964 some CIDG units began performing commando hit-and-run raids along the border of Vietnam, Laos,* and Cambodia,* and the Special Forces established twenty-four CIDG camps in the border area to stop North Vietnamese infiltration.* To defend some of the more remote camps, the Special Forces gave some of the CIDG groups more extensive training and named them Mobile Strike Force Commands.* When Vietnamization* took place after Richard Nixon* became president, the CIDG units were changed either into border-patrolling battalions or special units. The Cambodians became part of the Khmer Republic Army and the Nungs,* who were ethnic Chinese,* became part of the Studies and Observation Groups* program. Vietnamese CIDG units joined the South Vietnamese Army. Most of the transfers came in 1970.

Sources: Francis J. Kelly, *U.S. Army Special Forces, 1961–1971*, 1973; Shelby L. Stanton, *Green Berets at War*, 1985; Kevin Generous, "Irregular Forces in Vietnam," in John S. Bowman, ed., *The Vietnam War: An Almanac*, 1985; Ngo Quang Truong, *Territorial Forces*, 1981.

Above: Civilian Irregular Defense Group (CIDG) members man a .50-caliber machine gun on a bunker on the inner flood dikes at a camp in the Mekong Delta in July 1967.

CIVIL OPERATIONS AND REVOLUTIONARY DEVELOPMENT SUPPORT

Throughout the war in Vietnam, the United States paid lip service to the idea of pacification (*see* Rural Reconstruction)—converting the loyalties of South Vietnamese peasants to the government—but the major American effort in Indochina* was always military. In February 1966 Nguyen Van Thieu* and Nguyen Cao Ky* had agreed to strengthen the pacification program, and they renamed it Revolutionary Development. Several months later Ambassador Henry Cabot Lodge* established the Office of Civil Operations to manage State Department–controlled pacification efforts. In May 1967 a new agency named CORDS was established, short for Civil Operations and Revolutionary Development Support. Military Assistance Command, Vietnam* (MACV) was in complete control of CORDS, removing it from State Department direction, but CORDS drew on support from the military, the Central Intelligence Agency,* the State Department, and the U.S. Information Agency. Robert Komer* became director of CORDS and a deputy to MACV commander William Westmoreland.* Komer established unified civilian-military advisory teams in all 44 provinces of South Vietnam and in 250 districts. By 1969 CORDS had more than 6,500 military personnel and 1,100 civilians pursuing pacification objectives in South Vietnam. Although CORDS claimed credit for winning higher loyalties from the peasant population, most of the gains came only from peasant migration from rural areas to the major South Vietnamese cities. Actual gains in converting the population from the Vietcong* were minimal. The Tet Offensive* of 1968 became clear proof of that reality. When President Richard Nixon* came to power in 1969, the United States quickly made its decision to withdraw from Vietnam, and after that point CORDS became an afterthought. Pacification efforts continued, but U.S. officials were more interested in getting out of Vietnam than in bringing about any real reformation of the distribution of power in Vietnam. The combination of the Tet Offensive and CORDS activities in 1968 and 1969 had severely weakened the Vietcong, but the North Vietnamese Army* only filled the vacuum.

Sources: Guenter Lewy, *America in Vietnam*, 1978; Robert Komer, "Clear, Hold, and Rebuild," *Army*, 20 (May 1970): 18–23; Tran Dinh Tho, *Pacification*, 1979; Thomas Scoville, *Reorganizing for Pacification Support*, 1982; J.K. McCallum, "CORDS Pacification Organization in Vietnam: A Civilian-Military Effort," *Armed Forces and Society*, 10 (Fall 1983): 105–122; Larry E. Cable, *Conflict of Myths: The Development of American Counterinsurgency Doctrine and the Vietnam War*, 1986.

CLAYMORE

Widely used in Vietnam, the claymore antipersonnel mine was designed to produce a directionalized, fan-shaped pattern of fragments. The claymore used a curved block of C-4* explosive, shaped to blow all its force outward in a semi-circular pattern. A large number of pellets were embedded in the face of the explosive, creating a devastating blast of fragments similar to the effect of an oversized shotgun.

With their directional pattern, claymores were well suited as a perimeter-defense weapon. Using electronic firing, defenders in bunkers could set claymores in a pattern to cover all approaches and fire them at will. One problem with this was the tendency of the enemy to use infiltrators to sneak into the defense perimeter before an attack and simply turn the claymores around. Then when defenders fired the mine, its fragments peppered their own position.

The Vietcong* liked to use captured claymores as booby traps.* Set off by trip wires, a claymore mounted close to the ground was capable of severing the legs of an unwary enemy. A more unorthodox use was found for claymores by many American GIs. The explosive burned with intense heat, and a small amount of explosive could quickly heat a can of C-rations in the field. While never designed for it, and certainly never sanctioned as such, claymores became one of the most popular field stoves in the war. NJA

Source: John Quick, *Dictionary of Weapons and Military Terms*, 1973.

Right: Sergeant Joseph McKnight of the 5th Special Forces Group demonstrates setting up a claymore mine during a training session at Fort Bragg, North Carolina, in November 1976.

"CLEAR AND HOLD"

Operations termed clear and hold were part of the pacification program (*see* Rural Reconstruction) during the war in Vietnam. Most observers realized that the military sweep operations—temporary efforts to attack Vietcong* and North Vietnamese installations—would not be successful in permanently eliminating the guerrilla structure in South Vietnam. Clear and hold operations involved military attacks on Vietcong strongholds and then permanent stationing of military units in the area after the initial engagements. Local populations would not cooperate with American or South Vietnamese soldiers if they knew they would be departing in a few days. The problem with clear and hold operations, of course, was the personnel requirements. General William Westmoreland* argued that clear and hold strategies would have worked if he had had a larger contingent of U.S. troops at his disposal. As it was,

Westmoreland generally used American troops for the military sweep operations and then relied on South Vietnamese soldiers and Popular Forces* and Regional Forces* to hold those areas. They generally proved, however, to be quite unreliable.

Sources: William C. Westmoreland, *A Soldier Reports*, 1976; Hoang Ngoc Long, *Strategy and Tactics*, 1980; Harry G. Summers Jr., *On Strategy: A Critical Analysis of the Vietnam War*, 1982.

CLERGY AND LAITY CONCERNED ABOUT VIETNAM (CLCV)

Clergy and Laity Concerned About Vietnam (CLCV) was founded in 1965 by an interdenominational group of religious leaders including Reverend John C. Bennett and

Below: Two soldiers of the 101st Airborne relax in a field near Kontum, a remote site near the Cambodian border, during Operation Pickett in 1966.

Above: When Robert McNamara stepped down in 1967 as secretary of defense, President Lyndon B. Johnson replaced him with Clark Clifford, a seasoned Democratic Party operative and advisor to Harry Truman and John F. Kennedy.

Father Daniel Berrigan.* Early co-chairs included Father Berrigan, Rabbi Abraham Heschel, and Dr. Martin Luther King Jr.* Members of CLCV followed a moderate antiwar* course, advocating a negotiated settlement and holding teach-ins, fasts, vigils, and orderly antiwar activities. They sponsored a 2,000-member demonstration at the White House in January 1967 and a February Fast for Peace with more than 1 million reportedly participating. Although CLCV also participated in events with more radical antiwar groups, it consistently resisted radical activities such as draft* card burning and violent protest.

Late in 1966 CLCV commissioned a study entitled *In the Name of America* indicting U.S. involvement in Vietnam. It was published just before the 1968 Tet Offensive.* Drawing heavily on press reports and government documents, it argued that American involvement in Vietnam violated international law, and that the United States and its allies were committing crimes against humanity. It focused on issues including the uses and effects of napalm,* gas, and defoliants;* search and destroy* operations; treatment of prisoners; forced relocation and pacification programs (*see* Rural Reconstruction); and the impact of artillery, aerial, and naval bombardment.

CLCV participated in the umbrella National Mobilization Committee protesting at the 1968 Democratic National Convention* in Chicago. Like other antiwar and peace organizations, CLCV was under surveillance and subject to infiltration by government intelligence and police agencies, including the Central Intelligence Agency's* Operation CHAOS in 1969, which was in violation of the CIA charter prohibiting domestic operations. Reflecting its expanding focus from Vietnam to U.S. military policies in general, CLCV changed its name in 1974 to Clergy and Laity Concerned. After the war the organization protested high schools' allowing armed forces recruiters and ROTC programs on campus without giving equal time to peace organizations; opposed the Nestlé Corporation's marketing of infant formula in developing countries; and called for corporate divestment in South Africa. SF

Sources: Nancy Zaroulis and Gerald Sullivan, *Who Spoke Up? American Protest Against the War in Vietnam, 1963–1975*, 1984; Daniel L. Migliore, "The Crisis of Faith in the Aftermath of Vietnam," *The Christian Century* 90, June 13, 1973: 672–677; January 23, 1980; and March 24, 1982.

CLIFFORD, CLARK MCADAMS

Clark Clifford was born at Fort Scott, Kansas, on December 25, 1906. He attended Washington University in St. Louis and received his law degree there in 1928. Clifford practiced law in St. Louis until World War II, when he became an assistant to Harry S. Truman's* naval aide. In 1946 Clifford was named naval aide to the presi-

dent. He resigned from the U.S. Navy in June 1946 and joined Truman's staff as special counsel. During the next four years he became one of Truman's most trusted aides, playing key roles in the development of the Central Intelligence Agency,* the Department of Defense, the Truman Doctrine, and U.S. policy toward Israel. Clifford resigned and returned to private law practice in 1950, although he remained in Washington, D.C., as a prominent consultant. In 1960 he helped plan John F. Kennedy's* campaign strategy, and when Kennedy was elected president, Clifford headed the transition team. After the election Kennedy named Clifford to the Foreign Intelligence Advisory Board to oversee CIA operations, and in 1963 Clifford became chairman of the board. After the assassination of Kennedy, Clifford soon broke into Lyndon B. Johnson's* inner circle. He planned Johnson's 1964 election campaign, and after the election Clifford advised the president on Vietnam, making frequent fact-finding trips to Southeast Asia and numbering himself among the "hawks."

When Secretary of Defense Robert S. McNamara* resigned in 1968, Johnson persuaded Clifford to accept the cabinet post. He became the president's chief spokesman and defender on Vietnam policy. But after sounding out the generals on the future prospects in Vietnam, Clifford was dismayed that they had no timetable for completing the struggle. They just wanted more money, more men, and more weapons. With that sad prognosis, Clifford persuaded Johnson to put a lid on manpower allocations, limit bombing raids, and start peace negotiations.

In other foreign policy problems, such as the USS *Pueblo** incident, Clifford urged a cautious and restrained response. And he assumed (incorrectly it would seem) that China and not Russia posed the major threat to U.S. interests in the future. He believed that U.S.-Soviet relations would be normalized, given time, through détente. In January 1969 the Nixon administration took office and Clifford was replaced as secretary of defense by Melvin Laird* of Wisconsin. Back in private life, Clifford became increasingly critical of the Nixon administration's policy in Vietnam. In 1970 he branded the invasion of Cambodia (*see* Operation Binh Tay) as "reckless and foolhardy," and said that Nixon's policy of Vietnamization* was "a formula for perpetual war." He advocated an accelerated withdrawal from Vietnam in order to end the U.S. role in ground fighting no later than December 31, 1970. After the war Clifford remained active in Democratic Party politics and consulting on foreign policy. Clark Clifford died on October 10, 1998. JMR Jr.

Sources: *Current Biography*, 1968; Thomas G. Paterson, *American Foreign Policy*, 1983; *Facts on File*, 1970; *New York Times*, October 11, 1998.

CLIMATES OF VIETNAM

Three distinct climatic regions are distinguishable in Vietnam between the Sino-Vietnam border in the north and the south coast along the South China Sea. All three climatic types found in Vietnam are variations of tropical climates. The Koppen climate classification system is used here, and average monthly rainfall and temperature data for three locations—Hanoi,* Hue,* and Ho Chi Minh City*—are used to show major climatic characteristics.

Highland Tropical Savanna Climate (Koppen)

Based on the Koppen climate classification system, Hanoi falls within a climatic zone of Southeastern Asia located in latitudes 20° to 25° north of the equator. This climate is described as temperate, rainy in the spring and summer, with a dry winter and a hot, humid summer. Slightly more than 60 inches of the total precipitation falls in the warmer six months (April–October) of the year. The average annual temperature is 23°F with the warmest monthly average in July and the coolest in January. The Cw, or

"temperate-tropical wet-dry climate," is a poleward extension of the true tropical savanna (Aw). While Hanoi is not in the highlands (elevation 53 feet), it is in a geographical position to be influenced by the highlands west and north of the city. As a result, two months out of the year have average temperatures that cool below 64.4°F and therefore cannot be classified as tropical. As one progresses south of Hanoi toward Hue, the climate becomes both tropical and monsoon in nature.

The distinct wet-dry season results in the development of a vegetation complex identified as "tropical savanna." It is characterized by open expanses of tall grasses, with shrubs, thorn bushes, and scattered trees. True forest exists in areas where a permanent water supply is available. All of this vegetation can be classified under the heading "Raingreen Vegetation." Soils are mostly yellowish or red latisols (Ultisols). Extensive leaching is common, and often the true highland soils are infertile. Frequently, local alluvial soils are quite productive and extensively used. This climatic type (Cwa), "highland tropical savanna," was greatly favored by Europeans who settled in the tropics in the nineteenth century.

Above: Although this photograph was taken in 1991, it reflects a peasant way of life that has existed in the Mekong Delta of Vietnam for thousands of years.

Right: Winter and summer monsoon rains drench Vietnam every year. Here, a soldier from the 1st Infantry Division tries to sleep on top of a pillbox bunker while a fellow soldier keeps guard. They are 35 miles northeast of Phuc Vinh, South Vietnam.

Below: This September 1992 aerial photograph reveals a stretch of the Mekong River in far southern Vietnam. During the war, U.S. Navy riverine patrols engaged Vietcong troops throughout the Mekong Delta.

Tropical Monsoon

Monsoons are found in close association with rainy tropics, generally along coasts where there is a seasonal onshore flow of moist air. In Vietnam the monsoon extends southward along the coast from Vinh, to Dong Hoi, Hue, and south to Quang Ngai. The windshift occurs in September, and from then until early February the wind blows from the northeast across the South China Sea onto the north-central coast of Vietnam.

The climate differs from rainy tropics in that it has a distinct dry season. Storage of soil moisture, however, is generally sufficient to maintain a forest in the dry season. Monsoons can be regarded as transitional between rainy tropics (Aw) and the wet and dry tropics (Cwa), having total rainfall comparable to the true rain forest and a precipitation regime comparable to the Aw's (tropical savanna).

The term "monsoon tropics" does not apply to all climates affected by a monsoonal wind circulation. Its use stems from the characteristic climates of monsoon Asia, but the designation "wet-and-dry tropics" is applied to those regions with less annual precipitation and a distinct dry season.

There is little difference in the temperature characteristics of the monsoon and tropical rain forest. The most noticeable, however, is the occurrence of the maximum temperature prior to the onset of the rain period. The diurnal temperature variations are greater than in the rain forest, with greatest differences occurring in the dry months.

The average precipitation during the monsoons is around 70 inches, but where orographic conditions exist, annual precipitation can be tremendous, running more than 200 inches annually. Most of the precipitation comes as heavy showers, especially where the orographic effect plays a major role.

Soils in the monsoon region are usually lateritic (Ultisols) and red and yellow in color. In some localized areas they can be utilized for tropical plantation agriculture as well as subsistence agriculture.

Tropical Savanna (Koppen)

Described as the tropical wet-dry by Koppen, this climatic type has a wet summer controlled by moist, warm equatorial and maritime tropical air masses and a dry season dictated by continental (dry) tropical air in the winter months. In Vietnam this climatic type extends from approximately 8° to 15° north latitude. A very distinct characteristic of the tropical savanna (Aw) is that the warmest average monthly temperature occurs in the spring, just prior to the onset of the rain season. (See the data for Ho Chi Minh City.*) There is also a distinct dry season in the winter and a wet, humid summer. In the case of Ho Chi Minh City, the annual climatic distribution is isothermal. According to the Koppen system, any location with an annual temperature range of 9°F or less is classified as "isothermal," indicated by the lowercase letter (i). The Asiatic wet-dry climate probably has a stronger monsoon control than other regions of the tropics. The vegetation of the tropical savanna is distinct and consists of coarse-textured, tall grass mixed with scattered trees and tall brush. Permanent and true forests exist along and/or around permanent streams or water bodies. Profitable agriculture is possible in the form of tropical plantations. In the case of Vietnam, rubber plantations were particularly important in the lower Mekong Delta* of the south. In addition, subsistent, riverine agriculture is important in the tropical savanna regions of Vietnam. As with the highland tropical savanna (Cwa) in the north, the vegetation of the tropical savanna (Aw) can be classified as "Raingreen Vegetation." The soils are yellow and red latisols (Ultisols), but more severely leached than those in the highland tropical savanna because of warmer temperatures and more precipitation. GH

Sources: F. Raymond Iredell, *Vietnam: The Country and the People*, 1966; Daniel Hall, *Atlas of Southeast Asia*, 1964.

CLUSTER BOMBS

A major, and controversial, weapons development of the Vietnam War was the appearance of the cluster bomb, an explosive that had a broader impact than standard bombs and was primarily used as an antipersonnel weapon. The CBU-24 contained 600 golf-ball-sized bombs, each containing 300 steel pellets. The CBU-46 had submunition systems with fins that allowed for wider dispersal before exploding. The most common antitank cluster bomb was the MK-20, which released 9-inch darts, each containing armor-penetrating warheads. A mine CBU was the WAAPM (wide area antipersonnel munition) that, when dropped from an aircraft, shot out dozens of fine wires on impact. When touched, the wire triggered the explosion. Finally, the FAE, or fuel air explosive, was used in the end stages of the war. An FAE was a large canister filled with a gaseous explosive.

Left: Major Charles H. Lynch, a chemical officer of the 199th Light Infantry Brigade, sets the timer mechanism of a cluster bomb aboard a Huey in preparation for an aerial mission outside Saigon in December 1968.

Below: Specialist 4 Eloy S. Lopez, chemical specialist with the 199th Light Infantry Brigade, throws the cluster bomb out of the Huey as it circles over the target area during the mission outside Saigon in December 1968.

When dropped from aircraft, the FAEs sprayed out fuel at a preset altitude, creating a huge gasoline cloud that then ignited as it descended. The cluster bomb units generated a good deal of controversy among antiwar groups because of their main purpose: the killing and maiming of people.

Source: Edgar C. Doleman Jr., *The Vietnam Experience: Tools of War*, 1984.

COASTAL SURVEILLANCE FORCE

A major problem facing the United States and South Vietnam was the infiltration* of enemy troops and supplies along the 1,200-mile coastline between the 17th parallel (*see* Geneva Accords) and the border with Cambodia.* It was a difficult task because on any given day literally thousands of small junks were plying the rivers of South Vietnam. A tight blockade of the coast became a major American strategic concept, and the Seventh Fleet* established a Coastal Surveillance Force to maintain the blockade. At first the Navy transferred former destroyer escorts from the North Atlantic to serve as radar picket ships in the South China Sea. A number of coastal surveillance centers were set up along the South Vietnamese coast. Late in 1965 P-5 Marlin seaplanes and P-3A Orion aircraft were patrolling the coast up to 150 miles offshore, while Coast Guard Squadron One, equipped with nearly 100 50-foot "Swift" boats and 26 83-foot cutters, was patrolling closer to shore. Operation Game Warden* involved use of a riverine

force to monitor boat and ship movements on the interior rivers. The Coastal Surveillance Force's work off the coast of South Vietnam was code-named Operation Market Time* beginning in July 1967.

Sources: Victor Croizat, *The Brown Water Navy: The River and Coastal War in Indo-China and Vietnam, 1948–1972*, 1984; Antony Preston, "The Naval War in Vietnam," in John S. Bowman, ed., *The Vietnam War: An Almanac*, 1985.

COAST GUARD, UNITED STATES

The origins of the United States Coast Guard can be traced to the Revenue Cutter Service, a military organization founded shortly after the American Revolution and assigned to cooperation with the U.S. Navy in 1799. The modern Coast Guard was formed in 1915 when the Revenue Cutter Service and the Life-Saving Service were merged. The Lighthouse Service merged with the Coast Guard in 1939, and in 1942 the Bureau of Navigation and the Steamboat Inspection were added to the Coast Guard. The Coast Guard was financed out of the Treasury Department until 1967, when it became part of the Department of Transportation. At the direction of the president of the United States, the Coast Guard serves within the United States Navy.* On April 30, 1965, President Lyndon Johnson* designated Coast Guard Squadron One to be assigned to Vietnam. In 1965 and 1966 twenty-six Coast Guard patrol boats were deployed to the coast of the South China Sea, where they engaged in coastal surveillance using Da Nang,* Qui Nhon,* Nha Trang,* Vung Tau,* and An Thoi as bases. Coast Guard Squadron Three was assigned to South Vietnam in 1967. During the war Coast Guard crews boarded approximately 250,000 small craft, usually sampans and junks, and participated in 6,000 support missions. Their main objective was to stop the infiltration* of supplies to the Vietcong.* In January 1969 South Vietnamese crews began operating the cutters, and in 1971 and 1972 all of the cutters were turned over to South Vietnam.

Sources: Edward J. Marolda and G. Wesley Pryce III, *A Short History of the United States Navy and the Southeast Asian Conflict, 1950–1975*, 1984; Stephen Evans, *The United States Coast Guard, 1790–1915*; Eugene Tulich, *The United States Coast Guard in Southeast Asia During the Vietnam Conflict*, 1975.

Below: The U.S. Navy patrolled rivers throughout South Vietnam during the war. U.S. Navy gunners aboard a Swift boat in 1969 watch for enemy activity as they emerge from the Cao Mao River estuary.

COCHIN CHINA

Geographers divided Vietnam into three general areas: Tonkin,* Annam,* and Cochin China. Cochin China comprises the six southern provinces of Vietnam. In the mid-sixteenth century, Portuguese adventurers referred to

Vietnam as Cauchichina, taking "Cauchi" from Giao Chi, the Chinese term for Vietnam, and then added the word China to differentiate it from Portugal's Cochin colony in India. By the nineteenth century the French were using the term "Cochin China" to refer only to the southern part of Vietnam. The economy of Cochin China was dominated by the Mekong Delta.* Unlike the Red River in Tonkin, the Mekong River is more regular in its flow, not given to flooding, and far more predictable. The largest city of Cochin China was Saigon,* now known as Ho Chi Minh City.* Located approximately forty miles inland from the coast, Saigon is connected to the South China Sea by the tidal Dong Nai River. North and east of the Mekong Delta are the forestlands of the Annamese highlands. Large regions there are still uninhabited because of extensive and malaria-ridden swamps. To the west are the lowland plains of Cambodia,* which constitute an extension of the Mekong Delta. The weather of Cochin China is usually very hot. The dry season extends from November to April, while heavy rains from May to October combine with oppressive heat. Cochin China consists of approximately 26,500 square miles.

Before the second half of the nineteenth century, Cochin China was part of China, the Khmer* Empire of Cambodia, and the Empire of Annam. The French seized Saigon in 1858, and four years later the emperor of Annam ceded the eastern portion of Cochin China to France. In 1887 the rest of Cochin China became part of the French colony. In June 1946 Cochin China became an independent republic in the new Federation of Indochina, but three years later Cochin China voted to become part of Vietnam.

Source: Milton E. Osborne, *The French Presence in Cochin China and Cambodia*, 1969.

COFFIN, WILLIAM SLOANE JR.

William Sloane Coffin, a leading figure in the antiwar movement,* was born in New York City on June 1, 1924. He served in the Army during World War II and later studied at Yale and the Union Theological Seminary. Between 1950 and 1953 he worked as a Soviet expert for the Central Intelligence Agency,* but left the CIA to complete his seminary studies at Yale. Coffin was ordained a Presbyterian minister in 1956 and in 1958 became chaplain of Yale. A political activist committed to civil rights and antipoverty causes, Coffin also became an early opponent of the Vietnam War. He traveled widely around the country calling for draft* resistance and serving as an officer of the National Emergency Committee of Clergy Concerned About Vietnam. In 1968 Coffin was indicted and convicted for conspiring to assist draft resisters, but the convictions were eventually overturned and then dropped by the Department of Justice. Coffin left Yale in 1975 to pursue new interests in lecturing and writing, and he became the senior minister at Riverside Church in upper Manhattan in 1977. After the end of the war, Coffin continued to write and speak about American foreign policy, widely lecturing on the subject in the United States and abroad following his retirement in the early 1990s. William Sloane Coffin Jr. died on April 12, 2006.

Source: Warren Goldstein, *William Sloane Coffin Jr.: A Holy Impatience*, 2004.

Above: One of the tasks of the U.S. Navy was to interdict the smuggling of arms to the Vietcong. On June 16, 1966, a Swift boat patrols in the South China Sea off the coast of South Vietnam.

Below: William Sloane Coffin, chaplain of Yale University, speaks at an antiwar rally on January 28, 1968, just before the outbreak of the Tet Offensive.

Above: The Vietnam War finally came to an end on April 30, 1975, when North Vietnam conquered South Vietnam. CIA activities in country then came under the scrutiny of the House Select Committee on Intelligence, forcing CIA Director William Colby to convene a press conference at CIA headquarters in Langley, Virginia.

Below: J. Lawton Collins commanded the U.S. Army's 25th Infantry Division at Guadalcanal and the VII Corps in the Normandy invasion in 1944. Between 1949 and 1953, he served as U.S. Army chief of staff. President Dwight D. Eisenhower sent Collins to Saigon in 1954 to work with the newly established government of Ngo Dinh Diem. Collins quickly lost faith in Diem, who he came to consider unfit to preside over the country. He recommended in vain that the United States identify another leader for the country.

COLBY, WILLIAM EGAN

William E. Colby was born on January 4, 1920, in St. Paul, Minnesota. He graduated from Princeton in 1940, and after completing officer candidate school for the U.S. Army was assigned to the Office of Strategic Services where he worked with the French resistance. In 1947 the Office of Strategic Services became the Central Intelligence Agency.* Colby earned a law degree at Columbia University and joined the CIA in 1950. In 1959 Colby became station chief for the CIA in Saigon where he supervised the recruitment of Montagnard* tribesmen and the Strategic Hamlet Program.* Colby returned to Washington, D.C., in 1962 as head of the CIA's Far East Division. In that position he directed Air America* and the Phoenix Program.* Colby returned to South Vietnam in 1968 as a deputy to General William Westmoreland,* commander of the U.S. Military Assistance Command, Vietnam.* There Colby was responsible for the Civil Operations and Rural Development Support* program and the Phoenix Program. Congressional investigations into charges of torture and assassination under the Phoenix Program brought Colby before several committees to testify, where he maintained that most of the 20,000 people killed had died in combat situations. He never denied, however, that there had been assassinations under the Phoenix Program. Colby became director of the Central Intelligence Agency in 1973 and retired three years later. William Colby died on April 27, 1996.

Sources: William Colby and Peter Forbath, *Honorable Men: My Life in the CIA*, 1978; John P. Prados, *Lost Crusader: The Secret Wars of CIA Director William Colby*, 2003.

COLLINS, JOSEPH LAWTON

From November 3, 1954, to May 14, 1955, General J. Lawton Collins served as special U.S. representative in Vietnam, a designation that made him the de facto American ambassador in Saigon* during that period. Born on May 1, 1896, Collins graduated from West Point in 1917. After the attack on Pearl Harbor, he commanded the 25th Infantry Division in successful campaigns on Guadalcanal and New Georgia. His soldiers in the Pacific gave him the nickname "Lightning Joe." Transferred to Europe in 1944, Collins commanded the VII Corps during the Normandy invasion and the assault on Germany. From 1949 to 1953 he served with distinction as Army chief of staff, and he was the U.S. representative to the Military Committee and Standing Group of the North Atlantic Treaty Organization (NATO) when President Dwight D. Eisenhower* sent him to Saigon in 1954.

Collins' mission to Vietnam came at a decisive moment in the history of U.S. involvement in Indochina.* In June 1954 Emperor Bao Dai* had selected Ngo Dinh Diem* as prime minister of the state of Vietnam. Since the partitioning of Vietnam under the Geneva Accords* of 1954 was to be only temporary, the hopes of a nationalist alternative to the Communists in the North rested on the prospects of Diem's government in the South. Collins' assignment was to assess Diem's abilities and to seek ways for the United States to assist his government. Working with General Paul Ely,* the French high commissioner in Indochina, Collins made progress in the reorganization and training of the South Vietnamese armed forces, but he soon concluded that Diem lacked the leadership qualities and experience necessary to compete with Ho Chi Minh.* In April 1955 Collins specifically recommended that the United States shift its support from Diem to other South Vietnamese leaders. After direct consultations in Washington between the general and Secretary of State John Foster Dulles,* a decision was reached to accept Collins' judgment. At that moment, however, Diem precipitated a hostile confrontation with his South Vietnamese opponents. The Vietnamese National Army helped Diem survive the crisis, and the prime minister's advocates in Washington sustained Dulles in reversing the decision to dump Diem.

The reaffirmation of American support for Diem wedded Washington to his regime in Saigon. In the years that followed, Collins' assessment of Diem's weaknesses proved tragically correct. Collins left Saigon in May 1955 and returned to duty with NATO. He retired from the Army in 1956 and later served as an executive with Charles Pfizer & Company. J. Lawton Collins died on May 6, 2002. DLA

Sources: J. Lawton Collins, *Lightning Joe: An Autobiography*, 1979; *New York Times*, May 7, 2002.

COLUMBIA UNIVERSITY DEMONSTRATIONS

During the week of April 23 to 30, 1968, Students for a Democratic Society* (SDS) and the Students Afro-American Society (SAS) led 700 to 1,000 Columbia University students in the seizure and occupation of five campus buildings. Among the buildings occupied was Low Library, which contained the office of university president Grayson Kirk. While in control of Low Library the students committed several acts of vandalism including ransacking Kirk's files, ostensibly searching for secret links between the university and the military establishment. Among their demands, the demonstrators called for a halt to construction of a controversial gymnasium at Morningside Park and the severing of university ties with the Institute for Defense Analysis (IDA). The IDA was a Pentagon-sponsored group of universities that advised the government on defense strategies. Other demands dealt with the university's disciplinary policies.

Left: Demonstrators from the Students for a Democratic Society (SDS) clash with New York City police on the quad at Columbia University on April 24, 1968. To the left is the Low Library, which contained the office of Grayson Kirk, the president of Columbia. SDS members stormed the library, occupied and ransacked Kirk's office, and demanded that the university cut its ties to the Department of Defense and cease construction of a gymnasium at nearby Morningside Heights.

The events of April 23 to 30 began with a rally called at the sundial, a gathering place for students, which was to start at noon, by the Columbia chapter of SDS under the leadership of Mark Rudd. The demonstrators had been called to protest disciplinary actions taken against students who had participated in a protest against the university's tie with the IDA and to demand that the university end its involvement with that organization. After an unsuccessful attempt to gain entry to Low Library, the students drifted over to Morningside Park, which had become a symbol of the division between Columbia and the surrounding black community of Harlem. Following a confrontation with police, Mark Rudd, who had arrived later, led the students back to the sundial. The demonstrators then marched into Hamilton Hall to hold a sit-in. While in control of Hamilton the protesters issued their demands. They also took a hostage, Henry Coleman, the acting dean of Columbia College, who was later released unharmed. On April 24, after much discussion, the white students were asked to leave Hamilton by the SAS, which wanted to use this event

to demonstrate black power and discipline. The students who left, including Rudd, occupied Low Library shortly thereafter. Eventually, various student groups occupied Fayerweather, Avery, and Mathematics halls.

Attempts to negotiate a peaceful resolution of the crisis were hampered by distrust on the part of the students and the administration. Finally, on April 30 at 1:30 AM, 1,000 New York City police officers cleared the buildings of demonstrators. Except at Hamilton Hall, from which the black demonstrators had assured police they would leave peacefully, the police used violence to expel the students. The Cox Commission, headed by Harvard law professor Archibald Cox and charged with investigating the events of April 23 to 30, concluded that violence was to be expected when students resisted arrest.

Immediately after the events of April 23 to 30, a university-wide strike was called by the SDS. On May 21 Mark Rudd and about 350 supporters again occupied Hamilton Hall over a dispute concerning disciplinary action against Rudd and others who had participated in the April 23–30

Below: Dickey Chapelle, a photographer for the *National Observer*, at the Don Phuc command post on the Vietnam–Cambodia frontier at the end of 1964. Chapelle resided at this post for thirty-four days, photographing the combat. Chapelle had covered World War II and Korea as a combat photographer and made five trips to Vietnam to cover eleven major campaigns. Over forty years old when she got to Vietnam, she jumped with paratroopers, and was the only American combat photographer fully accredited as a paratrooper by both U.S. and Vietnamese armed forces. She became the first American woman combat photographer to be killed in action when a Marine near her stepped on a land mine in November 1965. Her last moments — receiving last rites — were captured in a photograph by Henri Huet (who himself was killed in action along with photographers Larry Burrows, Keisaburo Shimamoto, and Kent Potter when their helicopter was shot down over Laos). Chapelle was given a full Marine burial.

demonstrations. Again the police were called in to dislodge the protesters. This time the officers used violence not only against the demonstrators but also against innocent bystanders. The Cox Commission characterized the violence as "brutality for which a layman can see no justification unless it be that the way to restore order in a riot is to terrorize civilians."

Following twenty-one days of hearings beginning on May 4, 1968, and after listening to seventy-nine witnesses, the Cox Commission determined that the university's connection with the IDA had become a symbol of Columbia's participation in the Vietnam War. As such, Columbia had become a surrogate for the frustrations students felt over their inability to affect national policy on the war. The Cox Commission further concluded that while the Vietnam War was not the only grievance expressed at Columbia, it was of overriding concern for nearly all students and was a potentially explosive issue. MD

Source: *Crisis at Columbia: Report of the Fact-Finding Commission Appointed to Investigate the Disturbances at Columbia University in April and May 1968*, 1969.

COMBAT PHOTOGRAPHERS

Though the Vietnam War was the first in history to be broadcast on the television sets of the nation, the photographs that were taken of the conflict are unprecedented in the history of modern warcraft, both for their startling immediacy and for the sheer volume produced by the photojournalists who covered the war. America learned about the war its sons and daughters were fighting on the other side of the globe mainly through images, and the iconic images of Vietnam had a profound effect on the course of the war.

The press covering the war in Vietnam had unprecedented freedom of access to combat zones. Though journalists had to be accredited by the Joint United States Public Affairs Operation (JUSPAO), there was no form of censorship. By 1968, more than 600 journalists were in Vietnam. They were daring and aggressive, usually working alone, which gave them the advantage of being able to squeeze into a helicopter ferrying soldiers to the front and become part of the action.

Left: Specialist 6 Maurice Gauchi of the 221st Signal Company (Photographic) films the heliborne assault of the 4th Infantry Division during Operation Francis Marion along the Cambodian border in Pleiku Province in 1967.

Above: Corporal William Thomas Perkins Jr. was a combat photographer attached to Marine Corps Company C in 1967. He was filming Operation Medina southwest of Quang Tri when he was killed after he threw himself on an enemy grenade to spare the lives of three of his fellow Marines. For his gallantry and intrepidity above and beyond the call of duty he was awarded the Medal of Honor posthumously on October 12, 1967.

Above: The camera he was using at the time, damaged by the same grenade that killed Corporal Perkins (see caption above).

Right: Corporal Perkins shooting with his Bell & Howell camera. The spring-wound Bell & Howell "Eyemo" 16mm film camera, with swivel turret-mount for wide-angle, normal, and telephoto lenses, was the workhorse for combat cameramen in World War II, Korea, and into early Vietnam.

Below: Marines of the 3d Marine Division walk along the dikes between flooded rice paddies in 1966.

In documenting the war, the American military also gave its own military photographers wide leeway. Between 1962 and 1975, military photographers for the U.S. Army, Marine Corps, Navy, and Air Force took millions of photographs, about a quarter of which are now in the National Archives. The Army Pictorial Center (APC) first organized the operations, creating Department of the Army Special Photo Office (DASPO) teams, which rotated into Vietnam for three-month tour of duties. Soon after, the Marines were sending their own photographers, and then the Army created its 221st Signal Company (Photographic). The 221st and the DASPO were considered the Army's elite photographic units.

Many of the images transmitted back home influenced public opinion. Associated Press photographer Eddie Adams's photo (*see* Nguyen Ngoc Loan) of South Vietnam's national police chief shooting a Vietcong officer in the head on a street in Saigon in 1968 during the Tet Offensive caused widespread shock and galvanized growing antiwar sentiment in the United States. Sergeant Ronald L. Haeberle's photos of the massacre at My Lai in 1968 outraged people around the world and reduced support in America for the Vietnam War, as did Nick Ut's 1972 image of a naked girl running from her napalmed village. These photographs are unforgettable, an integral part of the visual history of the Vietnam War. They captured the true horror of war and preserved it, making it inescapable.

Source: Norman, B. Moyes, *American Combat Photography*, 2001.

COMBINED ACTION PLATOONS

One of the problems the United States Marines* faced in their combat activities in I Corps* was pacification (*see* Rural Reconstruction) and village security. Although designed as an assault force, the Marines found themselves in static positions trying to defend territory from the Vietcong* and the North Vietnamese. In that sense they were performing a mission that had not historically been part of their function. Since security was the primary prerequisite of any pacification program, the Marines developed the Combined Action Platoons (CAP) program in 1965. Under the CAP program, a Marine rifle squad would operate with a South Vietnamese Regional Forces* (RF) company. Beginning in 1970 the program was changed to Combined Action Groups, in which an entire Marine company was assigned to work with an RF battalion. The theory was that if the Combined Action Platoons or Groups were able to provide security, pacification efforts would succeed in winning the fidelity of South Vietnamese peasants.

Sources: Larry E. Cable, *Conflict of Myths: The Development of American Counter-insurgency Doctrine and the Vietnam War*, 1986; Jack Shulimson, *U.S. Marines in Vietnam: An Expanding War 1966*, 1982.

COMING HOME

See Rambo and Other Vietnam Films

COMMAND AND CONTROL

Problems with lines of authority posed a serious challenge to General William Westmoreland,* commander of Military Assistance Command, Vietnam.* During World War I the United States operated a unified field command in which all military units answered ultimately to General John J. Pershing, who in turn answered to one man— President Woodrow Wilson. In Europe during World War II, particularly during D-Day, General Dwight D. Eisenhower headed a unified field command. In Vietnam, on the other hand, instead of a unified field command Westmoreland led a "subordinate unified command" in which he did not control all of the military units and did not enjoy direct access to the president. Real control of the war was in Hawaii with Admiral Ulysses S. Grant Sharp, Commander in Chief, Pacific Command (CinCPac*). All communication between the president and Westmoreland filtered first through Sharp. Westmoreland's control over air operations was also blurred. Westmoreland controlled Air Force sorties*

over South Vietnam and at the southern reaches of the Ho Chi Minh Trail* in Laos, but CinCPac controlled air strikes over North Vietnam and northern Laos, while the Seventh Air Force controlled B-52 strategic air operations. This divided command and control structure reflected political ambivalence about the war among U.S. policy-makers as well as interservice rivalries.

Source: William Westmoreland, *A Soldier Reports*, 1967.

COMMANDANT, U.S. MARINE CORPS

The Marine Corps commandant is the senior officer in the United States Marine Corps.* Between the time of the first American casualty in Vietnam in 1959 and the end of the war in 1975, five men occupied the office of commandant of the Marine Corps. General Randolph Pate was replaced in 1960 by General David Shoup,* who served until January 1964. Shoup was replaced by General Wallace M. Greene,* who served until January 1968, when General Leonard Chapman* became commandant. Chapman was commandant until January 1972. General Robert Cushman* replaced Chapman and served as commandant until after the Vietnam War.

Sources: Harry G. Summers Jr., *Vietnam War Almanac*, 1985; Shelby L. Stanton, *Vietnam Order of Battle*, 1981; Allan R. Millett, *Semper Fidelis: The History of the United States Marine Corps*, 1980.

COMMANDER, MILITARY ASSISTANCE COMMAND, VIETNAM (MACV)

The Military Assistance Command, Vietnam* (MACV) was established on February 8, 1962, with its headquarters in Saigon.* During the course of the war in Vietnam, four men served as commander of MACV: General Paul D. Harkins* (February 1962–June 1964); General William C. Westmoreland* (June 1964–July 1968); General Creighton W. Abrams* (July 1968–June 1972); and General Frederick C. Weyand* (June 1972 to the end of the conflict).

Sources: George S. Eckhardt, *Command and Control, 1950–1969*, 1974; Shelby L. Stanton, *Vietnam Order of Battle*, 1981.

General Randolph Pate

General David Shoup

General Wallace M. Greene

General Robert Cushman

COMMANDER IN CHIEF, PACIFIC COMMAND (CINCPAC)

Also known as CinCPac, the commander in chief of the Pacific Command changed four times during the Vietnam War. Admiral Harry D. Felt served until June 1964, when he was replaced by Admiral U.S. Grant Sharp.* Sharp stayed in the post exactly four years until Admiral John S. McCain replaced him. In September 1972 Admiral Noel Gayler took over for McCain. Gayler remained as CinCPac until the end of the war.

Sources: U.S. Grant Sharp, *Strategy for Defeat: Vietnam in Retrospect*, 1978; Harry G. Summers Jr., *On Strategy: A Critical Analysis of the Vietnam War*, 1982.

COMMUNIST PARTY OF VIETNAM

The Communist Party of Vietnam was formally established in June 1929, although its true origins predate this official establishment. Ho Chi Minh,* originally named Nguyen Sinh Cung, was really a nationalist prior to the success of the Bolshevik Revolution of 1917. While in Paris young Ho was exposed to Marx and other socialist writers and leaders through his friendship with Jules Raveau, a veteran French Marxist. By this time he had adopted a more militant name—Nguyen Ai Quoc (Nguyen the Patriot)—and joined the Communist Party.

By the 1920s French officials had begun to scrutinize Ho's revolutionary activities. In 1924 Ho went to Moscow, where he met Stalin and attended the University of Oriental Workers. It is from this institution that many Asians learned the fundamentals of Marxist-Leninism. Later in 1924 Ho moved to Canton (now with the name Ly Thuy), where he mobilized and organized Vietnamese students in southern China. Chiang Kai-shek's* betrayal of his Communist associates in 1927 forced Ho to flee. He returned to Moscow, toured Europe, and slipped into Paris secretly under the name of Duong. Ho in 1928 moved to Bangkok, where he established a school and espoused the doctrines he had preached to the Thanh Nien Cach Menh Dong Chi Hoi* (Revolutionary Youth League), an organization he created while in southern China.

The revolutionary climate inside Vietnam was not very good during the 1920s. Many of Ho's students and comrades were imprisoned for revolutionary activities. Finally, in the summer of 1929, Ho organized a meeting in Hong Kong of rival Communist factions from Vietnam. Out of the meeting grew a cohesive Communist Party dedicated to the overthrow of colonial rule in French Indochina. Ho named the new party the Indochinese Communist Party (*see* Lao Dong Party), reflecting the assembled leaders' ultimate goal of extending their control over all of Indochina.* They called for Vietnamese independence and a proletarian government.

The 1930s were a period of both growth and repression for Ho and his comrades. Although Ho eluded imprisonment by the French, his comrades Pham Van Dong* and Le Duc Tho* were not so lucky. Both ended up at the infamous prison island of Poulo Condore.* During this same period thousands of Vietnamese peasants were tortured and killed by French authorities because of their support of Ho's war of liberation. By the late 1930s Ho determined that his party was too limiting and began to press his associates to form a broader movement, which in 1941 resulted in the creation of the Vietminh.* Ho Chi Minh's war against the French did not gain momentum until after World War II, and ended with the surrender of Dien Bien Phu* in May 1954. JSL

Sources: Charles Fenn, *Ho Chi Minh: A Biographical Introduction*, 1973; Peter Wiles, *Ho Chi Minh: A Political Biography*, 1968; William J. Duiker, *The Rise of Nationalism in Vietnam, 1900–1941*, 1976; and *Sacred War: Nationalism and Revolution in a Divided Vietnam*, 2004.

COMPANY

A company is an organizational institution commanded by a captain and consisting of two or more platoons.* It varies widely in size according to its mission. An artillery company is called a battery* and a cavalry company is called a troop.*

Sources: Harry G. Summers Jr., *Vietnam War Almanac*, 1985; Shelby L. Stanton, *Vietnam Order of Battle*, 1981.

CONEIN, LUCIEN

Lucien Conein was born in Paris but grew up in the American Midwest after his mother sent him to live with her sister, who had married a World War I veteran. In 1940 Conein volunteered for the French Army, and when France* surrendered in late June 1940, he deserted and, after some difficulty, made his way to the United States. The newly formed Office of Strategic Services, forerunner of the Central Intelligence Agency,* recruited him, and he parachuted into France to work for the resistance. When the war in Europe ended, he joined a commando group harassing the Japanese in northern Vietnam. Conein entered Hanoi* when Japan surrendered and met Ho Chi Minh* and other Vietminh* leaders. Between 1954 and 1956 Conein was back in Vietnam, this time as part of Edward G. Lansdale's* intelligence mission.

In 1962 Conein was reassigned to Vietnam, this time as an Army lieutenant colonel assigned to the Interior Ministry, but his real assignment was to maintain CIA contacts with Vietnamese generals. Almost all of them

trusted Conein; indeed, some of them trusted only Conein, because he once had been their commanding officer in the 1940s and early 1950s. Conein's code name in 1962 and 1963 was Lulu or Black Luigi. His major role in Vietnam then was in the military coup against Ngo Dinh Diem* in 1963. Conein knew that American support for Diem had all but disappeared, and he worked with the generals in letting them know that the United States would not look unfavorably upon a change in government. The coup, complete with Diem's assassination, took place on November 1, 1963. Conein left Vietnam shortly thereafter and retired from government service early in the 1970s. CD

Sources: Marvin E. Gettleman et al., eds., *Vietnam and America: A Documented History*, 1985; John Prados, *Presidents' Secret Wars: CIA and Pentagon Covert Operations Since World War II*, 1986.

CONFUCIANISM

Confucianism is a religious and moral philosophy based on the teachings of the Chinese sage Confucius, who lived in the sixth century BC. Confucianism emphasizes worship of the family and ancestors and imposes on all people the obligation of accepting their station in life. Personal honor depends on social complacency; one has to behave in accordance with the expectations of society, and the essence of personal behavior is obedience, submissiveness, and peaceful acquiescence in the social hierarchy. As a political philosophy, Confucianism views the state as an extension of the family, with a political leader acting as a father, providing his followers with a good example, protection, and love. A leader who protects and cares for his family can automatically expect complete obedience and reverence from them. When the Chinese subjugated Vietnam in the second and third centuries BC, Confucianism, which was rapidly permeating Chinese culture, came into Vietnam and became the dominant ideological force there. The Vietnamese emperors accepted the Chinese model of bureaucratic government based on a Confucian-trained civil service. That bureaucracy dominated Vietnamese life until the arrival of the French in the nineteenth century.

Although both Confucianism and Buddhism* coexisted in the Vietnamese spiritual world, they came into serious political conflict during the thirteenth and fourteenth centuries. Buddhists resented the control Confucians had over the civil bureaucracy, while the Confucians accused the Buddhists of exploiting peasants through religious superstition. Gradually, the Buddhists were forced to retire from central political influence to their villages, pagodas, and monasteries, where they still exercised considerable authority in Vietnamese cultural life. While Buddhism was the organized religion of Vietnam, Confucianism was the moral philosophy that the Vietnamese used to govern their society.

Sources: Ellen Joy Hammer, *Vietnam, Yesterday and Today*, 1966; Sukumar Dutt, *Buddhism in East Asia*, 1966; John Frank Cady, *Southeast Asia: Its Historical Development*, 1958.

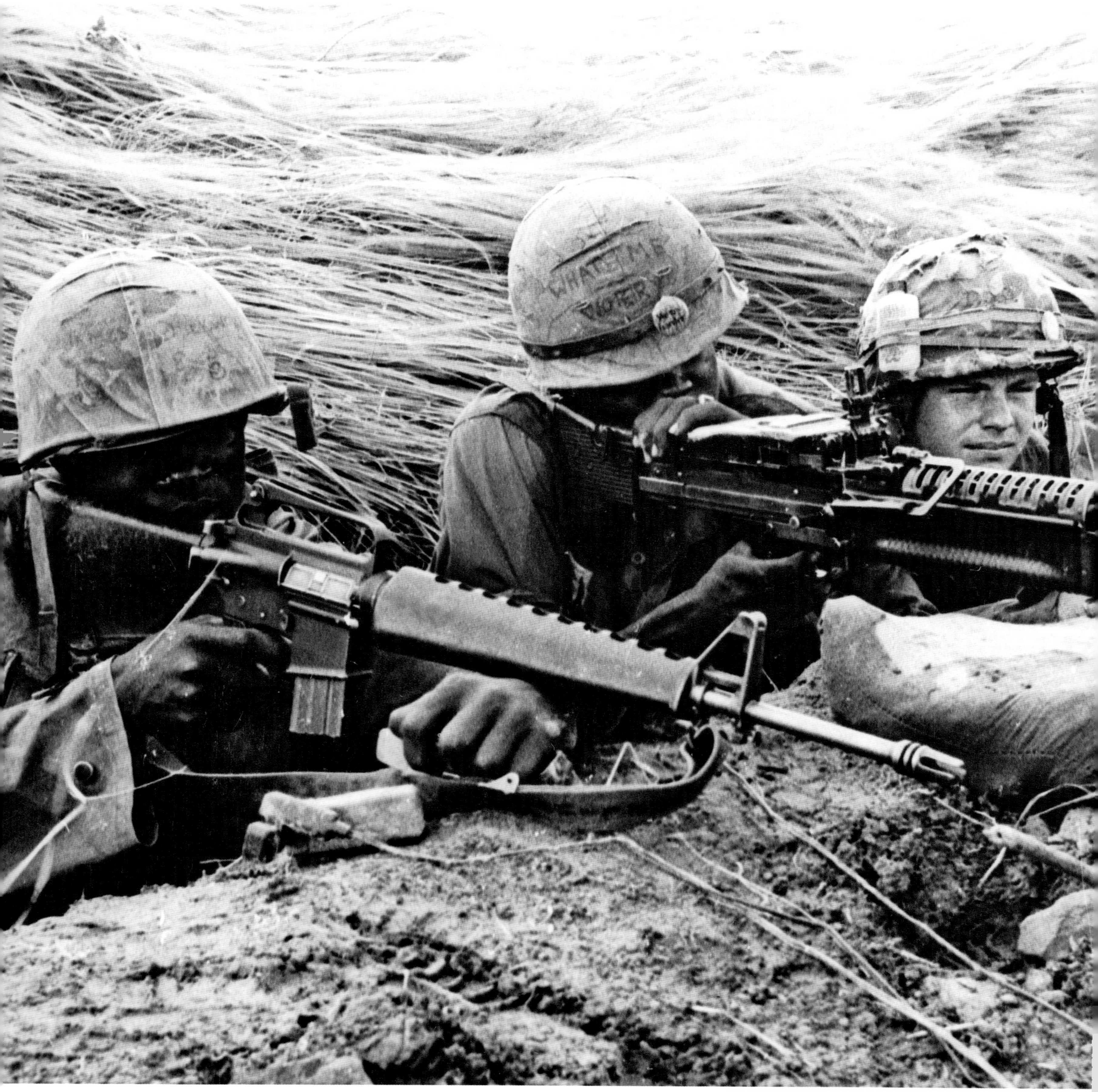

CONGRESS, UNITED STATES

The Vietnam War led to major changes in the foreign policy role of the U.S. Congress. At the beginning of the war, Congress allowed the president a relatively free hand in foreign affairs, including the use of American armed forces abroad. By the end of the war, however, Congress was playing a major role in the conduct of American foreign policy.

The Constitution of the United States divides power in foreign affairs between the president and Congress, but it gives the dominant role to the president. Traditionally, presidents have taken the lead in foreign affairs, with Congress only occasionally using its powers to check presidential initiatives. This pattern continued in the aftermath of World War II. As the United States became involved in the cold war, American foreign policy relations between the president and Congress were characterized by bipartisanship. Congress, arguing that partisan politics were inappropriate in foreign policy, allowed the president a great deal of freedom in the conduct of foreign policy. In the 1950s American presidents committed U.S. military forces in a number of the world's trouble spots, and they generally received the full support of Congress. While American military commitments in Korea* were under the auspices of the United Nations, and were carried out with considerable congressional involvement, most American military commitments during this era were made by the president in his role of commander in chief and involved little congressional input. Early American military involvement in Vietnam occurred within this framework; Congress allowed presidents to take the lead role in determining the size and extent of American involvement. As that involvement grew, President Lyndon Johnson* instructed his assistants to draft plans to punish North Vietnam. William P. Bundy,* assistant secretary of defense, pointed out that taking military action against North Vietnam would normally require a declaration of war, something no one was prepared to make. Yet to proceed without legislative endorsement would be "unsatisfactory." Bundy advocated obtaining a congressional resolution of the sort that had given Eisenhower* a free hand in 1955 when it appeared that the Chinese Communists might attempt to seize the islands of Quemoy and Matsu. Johnson's aides began drafting such a resolution. Five months later a series of circumstances allowed that draft to form the basis of the Gulf of Tonkin Resolution*—a resolution that Johnson's aides called a virtual declaration of war.

The Gulf of Tonkin Resolution resulted from a controversial series of events in July and August of 1964, culminating with the destroyer USS *Maddox** engaging three North Vietnamese PT boats in the Gulf of Tonkin on August 2, sinking one and damaging the other two. When word of the engagement reached Johnson, he purposely downplayed the incident. Dean Rusk,* however, instructed his staff to "pull together" Bundy's draft resolution. Talking to reporters, Rusk warned North Vietnam about any repeated action.

Left: Three Marines man a machine gun nest about 20 miles south of Da Nang in 1967.

Two nights later, during a thunderstorm, the *Maddox* and USS *C. Turner Joy** intercepted messages that gave the impression of an imminent attack by the North Vietnamese. Both ships' radar and sonar were acting erratically due to weather conditions. Both ships' crews recorded what they believed to be torpedo attacks on their sonars, and took evasive action. They opened fire on radar blips, and officers of the *Maddox* reported sinking two or perhaps three Communist craft. By daylight, Captain Herrick, in command of the *Maddox*, was having serious doubts that any engagement had actually occurred, and informed his superiors of his doubts. He suggested that daylight reconnaissance be conducted and completely evaluated before any further action was taken.

While the commander at the scene doubted that he had been attacked, President Johnson had no such doubts, and announced to key Democratic members of Congress that an attack had taken place, that he would retaliate against North Vietnam, and that he would ask Congress for a resolution of support. Not a single congressman present raised an objection. On August 5, 1964, Johnson sent the resolution to Congress. Polls at the time indicated that 85 percent of the American public backed the president on this issue, and Congress passed the resolution, giving the president the power to "take all necessary measures." As Johnson later quipped, the resolution was "like Grandma's nightshirt—it covered everything."

As American military involvement deepened in Vietnam, public support began to wane. The Tet Offensive,* showing the North Vietnamese ability to strike seemingly at will at a time when American leaders were predicting victory, represented a psychological turning point in the war. Although a military disaster for North Vietnam, the Tet Offensive resulted in a public relations coup; after Tet, Americans refused to believe anyone who said that the end was in sight, and began pressing for an end to American involvement. Congress, reflecting this change in the attitudes of the public, began to assert itself in policy debates over Vietnam. In 1969 Congress passed its first restriction on presidential power in Vietnam, prohibiting the use of American combat forces in Cambodia* or Laos.* President Richard Nixon,* ignoring the congressional dictate, launched a secret series of air attacks in Cambodia (*see* Operation Menu) that lasted fourteen months.

In 1973 Congress passed the War Powers Resolution,* limiting the ability of a president to commit American military forces without congressional involvement. That same year Congress voted to stop all bombing throughout Indochina.* By this time American combat forces had been withdrawn, and American prisoners of war* who had been held in Hanoi* had come home.

Throughout the war in Vietnam, Congress reflected public opinion in its actions. When the public was willing to give the president a free hand, Congress did so; when the

public began to oppose American involvement, Congress reflected that opposition. NJA

Sources: Thomas M. Franck and Edward Weisband, *Foreign Policy by Congress*, 1980; P. Edward Haley, *Congress and the Fall of South Vietnam and Cambodia*, 1982.

CON SON ISLAND

See Poulo Condore

CONTAINMENT POLICY

First pronounced by George Kennan* in a 1947 article in *Foreign Affairs*, "containment" was the most important postwar American foreign policy. At first it was designed to keep Soviet expansionism under control, preferably behind its 1945 military boundaries. In the beginning containment was nonmilitary in nature, focusing on economic and technical assistance, and it was embodied in such programs as the Marshall Plan in 1947 and 1948 to rebuild the European economies and the Truman Doctrine to provide the funds Greece and Turkey needed to fight Communist guerrillas. As the cold war escalated in the late 1940s, however, containment took on new global, military dimensions. After the fall of China in 1949, it came to imply the encirclement of the People's Republic of China* and the Soviet Union* using a network of military alliances: the North Atlantic Treaty Organization, the Baghdad Pact, the Southeast Asia Treaty Organization,* and the enormous military buildup of the 1950s and 1960s. When the North Koreans invaded South Korea in 1950, the United States intervened in the conflict in the name of containment. The policy reached its peak during the Eisenhower* years and the tenure of Secretary of State John Foster Dulles* (1953–1959).

When the French were expelled from Indochina* after the Battle of Dien Bien Phu* in 1954, the United States began increasing its commitment there to prevent a Communist takeover. American policymakers were applying the containment doctrine to Vietnam, assuming that Soviet and Chinese aggression were behind the North Vietnamese crusade to reunite the country. The domino theory* and the containment policy fit nicely together in the 1950s and early 1960s. Not until the mid-1960s, however, when American policymakers began to see that Communism was not a single, monolithic movement orchestrated from Moscow, did the application of containment to Vietnam begin to seem counterproductive. By the late 1960s and early 1970s American policymakers had accepted the importance of colonialism and nationalism in the history of the anti-French and anti-American movements in Vietnam. By that time as well American policy-makers realized that Communism was a polycentric movement requiring creative, individual responses.

Sources: John L. Gaddis, "Containment: A Reassessment," *Foreign Affairs*, 55 (July 1977): 873–887; David Allen Mayers, *George Kennan and the Dilemma of American Foreign Policy*, 1988; Douglas S. Blaufarb, *The Counterinsurgency Era: U.S. Doctrine and Performance 1950 to the Present*, 1977.

CON THIEN, BATTLE OF (1967–68)

Also known as the Hill of Angels, Con Thien is a series of three hills, approximately 475 feet high, located south of the Demilitarized Zone* (DMZ) in eastern Quang Tri Province. Elements of the 3d Marine Division* had established fixed positions on Con Thien in hopes of stopping North Vietnamese Army* (NVA) infiltration* across the DMZ and establishing "McNamara's Wall," or Project Practice Nine,* an electronic barrier south of the DMZ. It was a role the Marines did not like. Trained as a rapidly moving assault force, they found themselves holding down a defensive position. From mountains in the DMZ, the NVA regularly shelled the Marine positions with heavy Soviet artillery. In preparation for large-scale infiltration of NVA troops into South Vietnam and an offensive against South Vietnamese cities in 1968, General Vo Nguyen Giap* instigated a series of border battles in 1967 to distract American and ARVN (*see* Army of the Republic of Vietnam) attention away from the most populated areas. These border clashes occurred near the DMZ, the Central Highlands* of the Cambodian-Laotian-South Vietnamese border, and the rubber plantations near the Cambodian border in III Corps.* The siege of Con Thien was the first of these border battles.

Early in September 1967 the artillery barrage against Con Thien intensified. The American media began to portray Con Thien as another Dien Bien Phu,* but General William Westmoreland* launched Operation Neutralize* to relieve the Marines there. Seventh Air Force* commander William M. Momyer* developed the SLAM* campaign, which concentrated B-52* strikes, tactical air support, and naval bombardment on NVA positions surrounding Con Thien. By early October 1967, when the NVA 324B Division abandoned the siege, the United States had flown more than 4,000 sorties* against Con Thien, unloading more than 40,000 tons of bombs. The North Vietnamese could not withstand such firepower and gave up the battle. In the

short term the battle of Con Thien was an American victory that left more than 2,000 North Vietnamese troops dead. But in the long run it did serve Vo Nguyen Giap's purpose in distracting American attention away from the South Vietnamese cities that would soon face the Tet Offensive.*

Sources: Shelby L. Stanton, *The Rise and Fall of an American Army: U.S. Ground Troops in Vietnam, 1965–1973*, 1985; William W. Momyer, *Airpower in Three Wars, 1978*; James P. Coan, *Con Thien: The Hill of Angels*, 2004.

COOPER, CHESTER

Author of *The Lost Crusade: America in Vietnam* (1970) and *In the Shadows of History: 50 Years Behind the Scenes of Cold War Diplomacy* (2005), Chester Cooper was born on January 13, 1917, in Boston. He attended MIT, New York University, and Columbia, and earned a Ph.D. at American University in Washington, D.C. Cooper worked for the Central Intelligence Agency* between 1945 and 1952, and then joined the staff of the National Security Council. Between 1963 and 1964 he served as deputy director of intelligence, and between 1964 and 1966 he was a member of McGeorge Bundy's* staff, where he specialized in Asian affairs. Unlike most men in either the Johnson* or Nixon* administrations, Cooper consistently advocated a political

Below: In 1967, General Vo Nguyen Giap began to stage a series of "border battles" to distract General William Westmoreland while the Vietcong prepared for the Tet Offensive of early 1968. One of the border battles took place at Con Thien. The two Marines pictured here in a church in An Hoa, South Vietnam, were wounded on May 16 when the 1st Battalion, 9th Marines tried to reach the besieged Marine outpost at Con Thien.

I Field Force, Vietnam

II Field Force, Vietnam

XXIV Corps

III Marine Amphibious Force

solution over a military solution to the conflict. He also defended U.S. policies in South Vietnam, however, arguing that the United States did not exert itself more with Ngo Dinh Diem* because it did not want to play the role of colonial master. With prospects for peace negotiations in early 1968, Cooper urged the establishment of communication channels with both the North Vietnamese and the Vietcong* and insisted that South Vietnamese resistance to negotiations must be overcome if negotiations were to succeed. He opposed the Cambodian invasion (*see* Operation Binh Tay) because it widened the war and made it impossible to negotiate a genuine peace settlement in Paris without dealing with Cambodia* and Laos.* One of the first to recognize the plight of Amerasian children, Cooper recommended in 1973 that the United States offer vigorous support for UNICEF's program to care for them. Chester Cooper died on October 30, 2005. SF

Sources: *Contemporary Authors*, vols. 29–32, 1978; Chester L. Cooper, *The Lost Crusade: America in Vietnam*, 1970; *New York Times*, November 8, 2005.

legislature from 1928 to 1930, and then served eight years as a judge in Pulaski County. Cooper was a circuit judge in the 28th Judicial District in Kentucky (1938–46), and won a seat in the U.S. Senate in 1946. He served three terms in the Senate, 1947–48, 1952–55, and 1957–73. Between 1955 and 1956 Cooper was the U.S. ambassador to India. He specialized in foreign affairs, and during the late 1960s he became an increasingly vocal critic of American policy in Vietnam. In 1970, after the invasion of Cambodia (*see* Operation Binh Tay), Cooper openly called for American withdrawal from Cambodia* and condemned the widening of the war. Along with Senator Frank Church,* Cooper sponsored the Cooper-Church Amendment* demanding a withdrawal from or cutting off of all funds for military operations in Cambodia. The amendment succeeded in the Senate but failed in the House. Cooper left the Senate in 1973 and became U.S. ambassador to the German Democratic Republic. He retired from public life in 1976. John Sherman Cooper died on December 21, 1991.

Source: Robert Shulman, *John Sherman Cooper: Global Kentuckian*, 1983.

COOPER, JOHN SHERMAN

John Sherman Cooper was born in Somerset, Kentucky, on August 23, 1901. He graduated from Yale in 1923 and attended the Harvard Law School from 1923 to 1925. He served in the Kentucky

COOPER-CHURCH AMENDMENT

In reaction to the invasion of Cambodia (*see* Operation Binh Tay) ordered by the Nixon* administration in 1970 without consultation with Congress,* Senators John Sherman Cooper* (R-Kentucky) and Frank F. Church* (D-Idaho) proposed an amendment that would prohibit spending funds without congressional approval after June 1, 1970, for the purposes of keeping U.S. troops in Cambodia, for sending U.S. advisors into Cambodia, for providing combat air support for Cambodian troops, or for financing the sending of troops or advisors into Cambodia* by other nations.

Supporters saw the proposed amendment as an overdue attempt by Congress to reassert its constitutional control over the power to make war. The administration and its supporters in Congress denounced the amendment as an unconstitutional intrusion into the president's power as commander in chief. After bitter debate, the Senate adopted the Cooper-Church Amendment on June 30 by a vote of 58 to 37.

The amendment was attached to a foreign military sales bill. That bill also carried another amendment repealing the Gulf of Tonkin Resolution.* But the repeal was not significant because the Nixon administration cited the

president's constitutional powers as commander in chief and not the Gulf of Tonkin Resolution as the basis for his war-making authority. JMR Jr.

Sources: *Facts on File*, 1970; Paul L. Kattenburg, *The Vietnam Trauma in American Foreign Policy, 1945–1975*, 1980.

CORPS

The term "corps" has a dual meaning in the U.S. Armed Services. It can be used to designate any group of military personnel performing a similar function, like the Signal Corps or the Medical Corps. As an organizational element in the military, a corps is a unit made up of at least two divisions.* The corps commander, usually a lieutenant general, controls combat operations by issuing directives to division commanders and coordinating the work of artillery and cavalry groups. There were four corps operating in Vietnam during the war: XXIV Corps;* III Marine Amphibious Force;* II Field Force, Vietnam;* and I Field Force, Vietnam.*

Sources: Shelby L. Stanton, *Vietnam Order of Battle*, 1981; Harry G. Summers Jr., *Vietnam War Almanac*, 1985.

COUNTERINSURGENCY

Counterinsurgency is the strategy and tactics for winning a revolutionary guerrilla war. Guerrilla warfare is ancient, though it takes its name from Spanish resistance to the Napoleonic French occupation. Revolutionary guerrilla war adds a new goal: it seeks not merely to resist another force but to overthrow it and achieve the political goal of seizing control of a country. Examples include the Mexican revolution that overthrew Porfirio Díaz, Mao Zedong's* expulsion of Chiang Kai-shek* from China, and Ho Chi Minh* and Vo Nguyen Giap's* conquest of Vietnam.

British expert Robert Thompson* suggested five basic rules for conducting a successful counterinsurgency: the goal must be clearly that of establishing a unified country that is democratically run and stable politically and economically; one must operate according to the law rather than violating it, avoiding the use of brutality; there must be a coherent plan of operations; the first priority must be to defeat political subversion rather than only guerrillas; and one must make base areas secure before attempting anything else. Uppermost here, as others have warned, is to avoid alienating the local population. As Mao put it, "The guerrilla is the fish; the people are the water." Hence a sixth rule: do not use foreigners, especially in a former colony. Subordinate rules include ensuring reliable intelligence regarding the enemy and cutting him off from outside aid if at all possible.

Above: Senator John Sherman Cooper, R-Kentucky, on January 7, 1955. During the 1960s, his opposition to the course of the war in Vietnam escalated, and in 1970 he openly condemned President Richard Nixon for the U.S. invasion of Cambodia.

Left: On April 14, 1971, the III Marine Amphibious Force leaves South Vietnam for redeployment to Okinawa. Before their departure, they paraded for review at Da Nang, South Vietnam. Their departure reduced the U.S. Marine contingent in Vietnam to a 13,000-man brigade.

Above: CBS television news anchor Walter Cronkite on June 28, 1968, several months after he had declared the war in Vietnam a "stalemate" and a lost cause. Cronkite's defection came as a major political blow to the Johnson administration.

Both the French and the Americans violated these precepts in their wars in Vietnam, and both lost. The French, indeed, ignored the concept of counterinsurgency, and Charles de Gaulle typified this in saying, "I know of two types of warfare: mobile warfare and positional warfare. I have never heard of revolutionary warfare."

The American approach was naive, first in believing that one merely had to instruct peasants in democracy, and then in oversimplifying counterinsurgency into "winning the people over" somehow or another. At best this approach represented the use of unorthodox techniques rather than real political mobilization of a people. Lyndon Johnson* ignored Roger Hilsman's* suggestion to train South Vietnamese to operate as counterguerrillas, though this could have kept out foreigners—American troops. Some U.S. officials were contemptuous of the Vietnamese and hence all too willing to make the war an American one.

President John F. Kennedy* sought to develop "special forces"* capable of counterinsurgency. But his position was weak because of the narrowness of his 1960 victory, because most of his advisors did not understand revolutionary war, and because the United States Army* limited counterinsurgency largely to being an "additional duty" for all regular units. The Army leaders ignored the long-published works of Samuel B. Griffith and, once committed to Vietnam, fought a technological war, highly destructive to civilians and thus arousing anti-American feelings. Members of the Central Intelligence Agency* had some grasp of the situation, but Americans in Vietnam squabbled among themselves about tactics and withheld crucial intelligence from one another.

Pacification efforts (*see* Rural Reconstruction) such as the Strategic Hamlet Program* failed because of South Vietnamese inefficiency combined with Saigon's* wish to use the program as a means of control rather than to help peasants. CORDS (Civil Operations and Revolutionary Development Support)* was organized only when insurrection had progressed too far. Also, CORDS was meant for Saigon's use, but that government was not interested in anything that helped the peasant but not its own power. Hence the U.S. Army took the program over and again ignored the rules of counterinsurgency. The Army could not buy enough time for South Vietnam to become stable and democratic because of the war's destructiveness and also because of Saigon's own antidemocratic tendencies. Most important was the fact that Vietnamese nationalism was on the side of the revolutionary guerrillas. RWS

Sources: Douglas S. Blaufarb, *The Counterinsurgency Era: U.S. Doctrine and Performance 1950 to Present*, 1977; Lawrence E. Grinter, "South Vietnam: Pacification Denied," *Southeast Asia Spectrum* 3 (July 1975): 49–78; Larry E. Cable, *Conflict of Myths: The Development of American Counterinsurgency Doctrine and the Vietnam War*, 1986.

COWARD

See Literature and Vietnam

CREDIBILITY GAP

The term "credibility gap" refers to the discrepancies between the public pronouncements and private policies of American political leaders in the 1960s and 1970s. The idea of the credibility gap first emerged during the Lyndon Johnson* presidency in general but with the Vietnam War in particular. In February 1968 White House staffer Fred Panzer wrote a position paper explaining the psychology of the credibility gap. He blamed the phrase on "antiwar and anti-Johnson forces" who focused on the charge that Johnson lied to the American people in the election of 1964 by promising to stay out of Asian wars. The term was first used by reporter David Wise in a May 23, 1965, article for the *New York Herald Tribune*, and was popularized by a December 5, 1965, article by Murray Marder for the *Washington Post*. Talk about the credibility gap had escalated as doubts appeared about what had actually happened in the Gulf of Tonkin in August 1964 (*see* Gulf of Tonkin Incident); intensified even more after the Tet Offensive* in February 1968; reached a fever pitch with the publication of the Pentagon Papers* in July 1971; and climaxed with the entire series of Watergate* revelations between 1972 and 1974. FF

Sources: David Culbert, "Johnson and the Media," in Robert Divine, ed., *Exploring the Johnson Years*, 1981; Peter Braestrup, *Big Story: How the American Press and Television Reported and Interpreted the Crisis of Tet 1968 in Vietnam and Washington*, 1983.

CRONKITE, WALTER LELAND

Rising through the journalistic ranks, Walter Cronkite became the preeminent media figure of the 1960s and 1970s as correspondent and anchorman for CBS Television. Born in St. Joseph, Missouri, in 1916, Cronkite was a correspondent for United Press in World War II and joined CBS in 1950, serving as anchor and managing editor of the *CBS Evening News*, 1962–81. Cronkite was widely watched and respected, and his coverage and reporting of Vietnam was seen as both reflecting and influencing American public opinion.

On September 2, 1963, in a prime-time interview with Cronkite, President John F. Kennedy* was critical of the South Vietnamese government then headed by Ngo Dinh Diem* and said that changes needed to be made in South Vietnam. Kennedy said, however, "I don't agree with those who say we should withdraw. That would be a great mistake. We must be patient. We must persist." In the following years

Cronkite did not publicly question this position, and his coverage was generally uncritical of later Johnson* administration policies. During the Tet Offensive* of 1968, however, Cronkite made his first visit to Vietnam since 1965. Upon his return, the newsman delivered a somber assessment on February 27, saying that it seemed certain "that the bloody experience of Vietnam is to end in stalemate." Rejection of the administration's optimistic forecasts by Cronkite, who had been called the "most trusted man in America," sent shock waves through the government, according to George Christian, President Johnson's press secretary. Cronkite's comments especially upset Johnson, who viewed them as a turning point in American attitudes toward his administration's Vietnam policies. David Halberstam* later wrote that Johnson said that "if he had lost Walter Cronkite he had lost Mr. Average Citizen," and this development helped to solidify Johnson's decision not to run for reelection. Walter Cronkite retired as anchor of the *CBS Evening News* in 1980. HP

Sources: Kathleen J. Turner, *Lyndon Johnson's Dual War: Vietnam and the Press*, 1985; David Halberstam, *The Powers That Be*, 1979.

C. TURNER JOY

See USS *C. Turner Joy*

CU CHI

See Tunnel Rats

CUONG DE

Cuong De, a direct descendant of Emperor Gia Long,* was born in 1882 in Vietnam but lived most of his life in Japan. The nationalist rebel Phan Boi Chau* came to know Cuong De in the early 1900s, and began to campaign for a royal, nationalist religious movement against the French. Phan Boi Chau had Prince Cuong De study in Japan instead of Europe as part of an Asian pride movement, but Chau eventually abandoned his support of Cuong De when he became convinced of the need for a democratic revolution. Cuong De remained for years in Japan and collaborated with the Japanese during their occupation of Indochina* between 1940 and 1945, hoping they would give him accession to the Vietnamese throne. But after World War II ended and the French returned, Cuong De's hopes were destroyed when Bao Dai* was installed as emperor. Cuong De had strong support among the Hoa Hao* and the Cao

Dai* religious sects, but he never gained the power necessary to take control of the Vietnamese throne. Cuong De died in 1951.

Sources: *Webster's New Biographical Dictionary*, 1893; Joseph Buttinger, *The Smaller Dragon: A Political History of Vietnam*, 1958.

CUSHMAN, ROBERT EVERTON JR.

When Vice President Richard Nixon* chose Robert Cushman as his national security advisor in 1957, he put the combat- and CIA-trained colonel on an inside track for selection as commandant of the Marine Corps* in January 1972. Born in Minnesota in 1914, Cushman graduated tenth in his 1935 Naval Academy class, served in China, and commanded the Marine detachment aboard the battleship USS *Pennsylvania* when the Japanese attacked Pearl Harbor. Decorated for bravery on Bougainville and Iwo Jima, he also received the Navy Cross for valor on Guam and after the war assumed ascending staff positions at Quantico, the Pentagon, and the Central Intelligence Agency,* which he joined in 1949.

Cushman would always speak openly about his friendship with Nixon, but after leaving the White House in 1961 he built an enviable record on his own—taking command of the 3d Marine Division* on Okinawa in 1961, becoming assistant chief of staff of the Marine Corps the following year, and then serving as Camp Pendleton's commander for three years before his selection to command the III Marine Amphibious Force* in April 1967. In Vietnam, from 1967 to 1969, Cushman led 163,000 soldiers and Marines, the largest combat force under a Marine general in history, and was often at the controls of a helicopter, conducting the defense of Khe Sanh* and the battle for Hue,* as well as leading the overall I Corps* counteroffensive in the wake of the 1968 Tet Offensive.*

Nixon appointed Cushman deputy director of the CIA in 1969, and during Watergate* Cushman, then commandant, became briefly entangled in accusations concerning the alleged CIA authorization of a burglary at the offices of Daniel Ellsberg's* psychiatrist; no formal charges were brought and the matter quickly faded in the press. General Cushman served as commandant until his retirement in 1975, stressing mobility as the key to combat success and decrying the "static defense concepts" he believed had undermined the U.S. military involvement in Vietnam. Robert Cushman Jr. died on January 2, 1985.

Sources: *New York Times*, January 3, 1985; Edwin H. Simmons, *The Marines in Vietnam*, 1974.

Above: Lieutenant General Robert Cushman tours the American base at Con Thien in 1967. A decorated Marine in World War II and CIA-trained, Cushman led the Marines in Vietnam from 1967 to 1969, winning more medals for his contribution to the American effort.

DAI VIET QUOC DAN DANG

The Dai Viet Quoc Dan Dang, or Nationalist Party of Greater Vietnam, was known as the Dai Viet and was founded in Hanoi* in 1939 by the followers of Phan Boi Chau,* the pro-Japanese, anti-French, and anti-Communist nationalist. Ho Chi Minh* outlawed the Dai Viet in 1946 and forced its members into exile in South Vietnam. The Dai Viet declined in the South and fractured into several groups, but it still attracted the loyalties of large numbers of civil servants. After the collapse of the Diem* regime in November 1963, the Dai Viet was revived by Phan Thong Thao and Nguyen Ton Hoan. It had a membership of approximately 20,000 people, with its strength concentrated in Hue* and Quang Tri Province in central Vietnam. By 1965 there were three major Dai Viet factions, and their prominent leaders were Ha Thuc Ky, Nguyen Ngoc Huy, Tran Van Xuan, Dang Van Sung, and Phan Huy Quat.* Because of its internal factionalism, the Dai Viet was not able to assume political power in post-Diem South Vietnam, although Dai Viet leaders continued to occupy seats in the national legislature.

Source: Harvey H. Smith et al., *Area Handbook for South Vietnam*, 1967.

DAK TO, BATTLE OF (1967)

Located in Kontum Province in northwestern II Corps,* isolated Dak To sat astride an infiltration route into the Central Highlands* for Vietcong* and North Vietnamese Army* (NVA) forces operating out of Cambodia.* In August 1962 U.S. Special Forces* established a border-monitoring unit at Dak To to be manned by Montagnard* troops organized to watch the border. The Montagnards could not hold the outpost, and the sparsely populated area fell under Vietcong control. As the United States substantially increased its military presence with the introduction of combat units, the Special Forces reestablished a camp there in August 1965.

By May 1967 the 24th NVA Regiment had established a way station and supply area nearby, leading to a series of skirmishes between elements of the regiment and Special Forces–led Civilian Irregular Defense Groups.* In response to the NVA presence, elements of the 173d Airborne Brigade* deployed in late summer to be joined by portions of the 4th Infantry Division.* A series of sharp clashes ensued, culminating in November. The explosion of the 4th Division's ammunition dump virtually leveled the camp, which was reconstructed in December. Throughout early November the American troops attacked highly fortified NVA positions—complete with elaborate tunnels and

Left: Troops from the 173d Airborne Brigade, part of Operation MacArthur in Dak To, use yellow smoke as a screen and so that spotter planes can identify targets for tactical air attacks on November 26, 1967.

Below: Troops from the 173d Airborne Brigade captured Hill 875 near Dak To on November 24, 1967. For seven hours before the assault, U.S. artillery and tactical air subjected Hill 875 to withering fire that left it resembling a "no man's land." In their attack on the hill, U.S. soldiers engaged in bloody, hand-to-hand combat with NVA troops.

Right: On November 21, 1967, these three members of the 173d Airborne Brigade wait to be evacuated from Dak To. Dak To sat astride an NVA and Vietcong infiltration route in the northwestern reaches of II Corps.

bunkers—along the elevated ridgelines. By the third week of November the battle for Dak To was centering on Hill 875, located twelve miles west of the camp. General William Westmoreland* called in more than 300 B-52* missions and 2,000 fighter-bomber sorties* to destroy the defensive positions of the 174th NVA Regiment before American troops began their ascent up the hill. Between November 19 and 23, 1967, the battle for Hill 875 raged, complete with air strikes, napalm* bursts, and hand-to-hand combat. Late in the evening of November 22, the North Vietnamese evacuated the area, and the next morning the American soldiers reached the summit. For 1967, at least, the battle for Dak To was over.

From early May to late June 1969, Dak To and nearby Ben Het were besieged by the 28th and 66th NVA regiments. Although Dak To's perimeter wire was penetrated in May, the Ben Het camp, located to the northwest and closer to the Cambodian border, bore the brunt of the NVA attacks. Manned by irregular forces, the camps were little more than thorns in the side of the NVA, which attacked the camps with token forces while infiltrating the main body of its forces around them. The camps were kept open by the United States primarily for their symbolic political value. SF

Sources: Shelby L. Stanton, *Green Berets at War*, 1985; Stanley Karnow, *Vietnam: A History*, 1983; Lawrence Okendo, *Sky Soldier: The Battles of Dak To*, 1988.

DA LAT

Located in Tuyen Duc Province of II Corps* in the Central Highlands,* Da Lat was one of South Vietnam's six autonomous municipalities with administrative powers similar to those of the provinces. The other cities with such status were Saigon,* Hue,* Da Nang,* Vung Tau,* and Cam Ranh.* Blessed with a cool climate on the plateau of the Central Highlands, Da Lat was a resort town for Vietnamese generals. Its population in the late 1960s was nearly 60,000 people. The Da Lat Military Academy was the Vietnamese "West Point" for officers in the Army of the Republic of Vietnam.*

Sources: Harvey Smith et al., *Area Handbook for South Vietnam*, 1967; Paul Isoart, *Le Phénomene National Vietnamien: De L'Indépendance Unitaire a L'Indépendance Fractionée*, 1961.

DA NANG

Da Nang, a port city in Quang Nam Province, was the second-largest city in South Vietnam. At Western insistence, the 1954 Geneva Conference partitioned Vietnam along the 17th parallel (*see* Geneva Accords) so that South Vietnam would include Da Nang and the imperial city of Hue,* a major concession because the Vietminh*

controlled most of the territory between the 13th and 17th parallels. On March 8, 1965, the first U.S. combat units in Vietnam landed at Da Nang. The city became I Corps* headquarters, and a major military base, port, and resupply area for South Vietnamese and American forces.

As the war ground on, Da Nang became choked with refugees* forced to flee their ancestral homes. With no jobs and limited opportunities, many catered to the desires of military personnel—providing alcohol, drugs, and prostitution. A generation of South Vietnamese were turned into pushers, pimps, and prostitutes as the war tore apart the Vietnamese social fabric.

During the 1966 "Buddhist crisis" Da Nang was the site of massive anti-government demonstrations as rebellious ARVN (*see* Army of the Republic of Vietnam) soldiers sided with the Buddhists.* Premier Nguyen Cao Ky* sent loyal troops to "liberate" Da Nang, though it was secured by U.S. Marines* who averted a confrontation by interpositioning themselves between contentious troops.

In 1967 the Vietcong* mortared and rocketed Da Nang's air base, destroying $75 million worth of aircraft. Da Nang was also attacked by Vietcong and North Vietnamese Army* (NVA) forces during the 1968 Tet Offensive.* Unlike at Hue, which was attacked by much larger forces, Da Nang's defenses held. The 1975 Final Offensive (*see* Ho Chi Minh Campaign) produced total chaos in Da Nang. A million refugees struggled to enter a town besieged by the NVA. Military units evaporated as soldiers sought to assist their families or attempted their own escape. With the city cut off, families loaded on to anything that would float or waded out to sea, many only to drown, as men fought desperately to get on the few aircraft that dared brave NVA antiaircraft fire. Known as Tourane by the French, Da Nang had a population of nearly 450,000 people in 1970. SF

Sources: George McTurnan Kahin and John W. Lewis, *The United States in Vietnam*, 1967; Harvey H. Smith et al., *Area Handbook for South Vietnam*, 1967; *Webster's Geographical Dictionary*, 1984; Carroll H. Dunn, *Base Development in South Vietnam, 1965–1970*, 1972; Richard Tregaskis, *Building the Bases: The History of Construction in Southeast Asia*, 1975.

Above: An aerial view of Da Nang Air Base, South Vietnam, in April 1968.

Above: Captain Georges Thierry d'Argenlieu of the Free French Forces here on January 1, 1941. Between 1945 and 1947, d'Argenlieu served as the first French high commissioner to Indochina. Devoted to the idea of France as an imperial power, he could not abide the Vietminh or any talk of compromise with them.

DANIEL BOONE OPERATIONS

"Daniel Boone" was the code name for U.S. Special Forces* operations into Cambodia.* Teams typically included two or three Americans and about ten indigenous personnel. Operations were authorized in June 1966, but operational permission was delayed until May 1967. Their mission was to penetrate Cambodia on foot or by heliborne insertion, conduct reconnaissance, plant "sanitized self-destruct antipersonnel" mines, sabotage enemy activity, and gather intelligence. Over four years there were 1,835 Daniel Boone missions with twenty-four prisoners captured. Initially the operations were limited to a small section of the Cambodian border but were eventually expanded, encompassing the entire South Vietnam–Cambodian border to a depth of thirty kilometers (about twenty miles). Many missions were detected within hours of insertion, prompting a race to effect extraction before being cornered.

Daniel Boone teams collected information on Vietcong* and North Vietnamese border base camps, providing much of the basis for Military Assistance Command, Vietnam* requests to strike the sanctuaries,* planning the secret bombing of Cambodia (Operation Menu)* beginning in 1969, and planning the 1970 Cambodian invasion (*see* Operation Binh Tay). After the first B-52* raids, Daniel Boone teams were sent in to survey the damage. They were slaughtered. Some teams then refused to go, with Americans being arrested and threatened with court-martial. Some still refused, knowing they could not be court-martialed for refusing to violate Cambodian neutrality.

Daniel Boone operations were authorized and conducted in a manner specifically intended to prevent congressional awareness. Their legality was debatable. International law recognizes "hot pursuit"* and the right of one nation, under attack by irregular forces, to attack those forces in a second nation if the second nation does not prevent cross-border attacks. U.S. law, however, prevents American military and private citizens from attacking nations with which the United States is at peace and has diplomatic relations. Daniel Boone was renamed Salem House in December 1968 and Thot Not (pronounced "Tot Note") in 1971. SF

Sources: William Shawcross, *Sideshow: Kissinger, Nixon, and the Destruction of Cambodia*, 1979; Shelby L. Stanton, *Green Berets at War*, 1985.

DAN VE

The Dan Ve were village militia units organized by the Diem* government in the late 1950s and early 1960s to provide self-defense against Vietcong* attacks. Local supporters of the Diem regime would receive weapons and ammunition, though often antiquated, and a small monthly stipend. Like so many of the programs of the Diem regime, the Dan Ve was riddled with corruption, many of its militiamen using their authority to fleece the peasants, while others actually converted to the Vietcong.

Sources: Denis Warner, *The Last Confucian*, 1963; Ngo Quang Truong, *Territorial Forces*, 1981; Tran Dinh Tho, *Pacification*, 1980.

D'ARGENLIEU, GEORGES THIERRY

Born in France in 1889, Georges d'Argenlieu graduated from the French Naval Academy and served on active duty until 1920, when he entered the Carmelite Order. He eventually became provincial of that order in 1932 but returned to active duty in the navy in 1940. Early in 1941 d'Argenlieu joined Charles de Gaulle in London and became commander in chief of the Free French Naval Forces. He was promoted to admiral in 1943. Between August 1945 and March 1947 d'Argenlieu was the first high commissioner to Indochina.* He was highly committed to the French Empire and adamantly opposed to any negotiated settlement with the Vietminh.* After he returned from Indochina, d'Argenlieu rejoined the Carmelite Order. Georges d'Argenlieu died on December 7, 1964.

Sources: Joseph Buttinger, Vietnam: *A Dragon Embattled.*, Vol. 1, *From Colonialism to the Vietminh*, 1967; *New York Times*, December 8, 1964.

Above: U.S. Special Forces members duck from flying debris as their demolition charge blows up Vietcong bunkers on Tan Dinh Island during Operation Bold Dragon in 1968.

Opposite page, bottom: On January 30, 1968, the Vietcong launched the Tet Offensive, lighting up the sky over the U.S. air base at Da Nang, South Vietnam, during a Vietcong rocket attack.

Above: David Dellinger, one of the earliest critics of the Vietnam War and eventually a leader of the antiwar movement and one of the famed "Chicago 8" is pictured at a news conference at the Federal Building in Chicago on October 2, 1969.

Opposite page, top: In what was later described as a "police riot," Chicago police clash with antiwar demonstrators on Michigan Avenue outside the Conrad Hilton Hotel on August 28, 1968, during the Democratic National Convention.

Opposite page, bottom: During the Vietnam War the U.S. Marines fought throughout I Corps in northern South Vietnam. Here a Marine patrol makes its way through low foliage inside the Demilitarized Zone, where it is engaged in a combat-reconnaissance mission, in February 1968.

THE DEER HUNTER

See Rambo and Other Vietnam Films

DEFENSE ATTACHÉ OFFICE

After the U.S. Military Assistance Command, Vietnam* closed early in 1973, President Richard M. Nixon* established a Defense Attaché Office (DAO) in Saigon* to provide assistance to the South Vietnamese military. Major General John Murray of the United States Army* headed the DAO between January 1973 and June 1974, and Major General Homer Smith directed it from mid-1974 until the final withdrawal of American personnel late in April 1975.

Sources: Harry G. Summers Jr., *Vietnam War Almanac*, 1985; William E. LeGro, *Vietnam: From Ceasefire to Capitulation*, 1981.

DEFOLIATION

See Defoliants, p. 162

DELLINGER, DAVID

David Dellinger was born on August 22, 1915, in Boston, Massachusetts, where his father was a conservative Republican lawyer. Dellinger graduated from Yale in 1936 with a degree in economics, studied at Oxford University and two divinity schools, and served as an associate pastor in 1939 and 1940. A pacifist, Dellinger refused to register for the draft* in 1942 and had to serve a year in prison. When he refused to report for duty in 1943, he was sentenced to two more years in prison. Between 1946 and 1967 Dellinger lived in New Jersey and owned the Libertarian Press. In 1956 he was a founder and editor of the magazine *Liberation*, which became a leading organ for radical pacifism.

In October 1965 Dellinger coordinated the Committee for a Fifth Avenue Peace Parade, the first major antiwar demonstration in New York City. In 1967 he was a judge in Bertrand Russell's unofficial "International War Crimes Tribunal" at Stockholm, which found the United States guilty of war crimes in Vietnam. In 1967 he also became chairman of the National Mobilization Committee to End the War in Vietnam,* which sponsored an antiwar march of about 150,000 people on the Pentagon in October. His passport had been revoked in 1966 when he traveled to Hanoi* to meet with Ho Chi Minh,* but he met with North Vietnamese officials again in 1968 and 1969. He then became a key link between the American peace movement and North Vietnam. As head of the Committee of Liaison

with the Families of Servicemen Detained in North Vietnam, Dellinger arranged for the release of six prisoners of war.

In August 1968 Dellinger was a leading figure in the antiwar demonstrations at the Democratic National Convention in Chicago. At the famous trial of the "Chicago 8"* in February 1970, Dellinger was convicted of inciting to riot and contempt of court, fined $5,000, and sentenced to five years in prison. In 1972 a federal appeals court overturned the convictions. By the early 1970s the antiwar movement* had become national in scope. In 1971, when the "New Mobe"—New Mobilization Committee to End the War in Vietnam—changed its name to the People's Coalition for Peace and Justice, Dellinger became a leader and continued his open opposition to the war. In 1975 he founded *Seven Days* magazine to promote active resistance to war. In Stewart Alsop's words, "For Dellinger, somehow, the truth shines, still, and his ideals … are amazingly unfaded." David Dellinger remained active in antiwar causes until his death on June 25, 2004. JR

Sources: David Dellinger, *More Power Than We Know: The People's Movement Toward Democracy*, 1975; J. Anthony Likas, *The Barnyard Epithet and Other Obscenities: Notes on the Chicago Conspiracy Trial*, 1970; Jason Epstein, *The Great Conspiracy Trial: An Essay on Law, Liberty, and the Constitution*, 1970; Nancy Zaroulis and Gerald Sullivan, *Who Spoke Up? American Protest Against the War in Vietnam, 1963–1975*, 1984; *New York Times*, June 26, 2004.

THE DELTA

See Mekong Delta

DEMILITARIZED ZONE

At the Geneva Conference (*see* Geneva Accords) in 1954, negotiators "temporarily" divided Vietnam into North Vietnam and South Vietnam. From the South China Sea to the village of Bo Ho Su, the demarcation line followed the Ben Hai River,* and from there it headed due west to the border of Laos,* roughly following the 17th parallel. A buffer zone five miles wide surrounded the line, and the entire area was designated the Demilitarized Zone, or DMZ.

Source: Robert F. Randle, *Geneva, 1954*, 1969.

DEMOCRATIC NATIONAL CONVENTION OF 1968

More than anything else, the Democratic National Convention of 1968 exposed the political divisions created by the Vietnam War. After the Tet Offensive* in February 1968 had undermined the credibility of the American war effort, Senator Eugene McCarthy* of Minnesota had almost defeated President Lyndon B. Johnson* in the New Hampshire presidential primary in March. Senator Robert Kennedy* then announced his candidacy, and at the end of March Johnson announced his decision not to seek re-election. Vice President Hubert Humphrey* and Robert Kennedy then became the front-runners for the Democratic presidential nomination. Kennedy's assassination on the night of his June primary victory in California left the campaign in Humphrey's hands. Senator George McGovern* of South Dakota entered the race, and some liberals began touting Senator Edward Kennedy* of Massachusetts, but Humphrey was clearly the leader when the Democratic delegates met in Chicago in August 1968.

Inside the convention hall, the delegates bitterly debated the war, with pro–Johnson-Humphrey forces running the

DEFOLIANTS

Below: Vietnamese soldiers of the 202d Chemical Team, Combat Development Test Center, open barrels of defoliant on a trailer truck in June 1968. The herbicide will be pumped into tank trucks near the maintenance area of the 12th Air Commando Squadron at Bien Hoa Air Base.

During the Vietnam War one of the most difficult challenges facing the United States military was the ability of enemy troops to hide in the jungles of South Vietnam and Cambodia. Often frustrated in their attempts to kill NVA and Vietcong soldiers, the United States decided to kill the jungles hiding them and to destroy the croplands feeding them. In 1961 MACV commander General Paul Harkins secured permission from President Ngo Dinh Diem of South Vietnam to spray herbicides over areas of heavy NVA and Vietcong activity. The chemicals would defoliate the jungles and make it easier for U.S. forces to locate and destroy enemy troops. The U.S. Air Force

dubbed the program Operation Ranch Hand, and President John F. Kennedy endorsed it in November 1961. The Air Force retooled six C-123 transports with crop-dusting technologies and deployed them to Bien Hoa Air Base near Saigon. The first flights commenced on January 13, 1962. Operation Ranch Hand eventually dumped 19.22 million gallons of herbicides on more than 6 million acres in South Vietnam and Cambodia and 417,000 gallons on 325,000 acres in Laos. In South Vietnam, more than 500,000 acres of cropland were

sprayed. Ranch Hand continued in South Vietnam and Laos until mid-1969 and in Cambodia until 1971.

The herbicides consisted primarily of three chemicals, each identified by the color of their shipping containers. The chemical most commonly used was Agent Orange—a mixture of n-butyl esters of 2,4-D and 2,4,5-T. Before being sprayed, Agent Orange was dissolved into such organic compounds as diesel oil and kerosene. Within six weeks of application, leaves began to fall, and the effect continued for seven to twelve months. Many areas were repeatedly sprayed. Agent White, another defoliant, combined picolinic acid with 2,4-D in a low-volatility amine salt formation. It had the advantage of controlling the growth of a wide variety of woody plants and could be more accurately targeted. The third most commonly used herbicide was Agent Blue—a concoction of cacodylic acid, which acted much more quickly than Agent Orange, withering plants in days rather than weeks. The military employed Agent Blue to subdue vegetation along roads and surrounding military bases. Agent Blue destroyed rice fields in areas of heavy enemy activity, supposedly depriving the enemy of food. On political, tactical, and environmental levels, Ranch Hand was controversial and counterproductive. South Vietnamese and Cambodian peasants resented their exposure to the chemicals and the destruction of their rice paddies, to say nothing of the side effects. The use of the herbicides served only to further alienate peasants from the United States and South Vietnamese governments and give the Vietcong and then the North Vietnamese another propaganda tool. Nor did the program make any tactical sense. Vietcong and North Vietnamese troops were not about to operate out of denuded areas, and South Vietnam contained more than 43 million acres, more than enough to hide an enemy. Whenever Ranch Hand sprayed an area, enemy troops simply relocated to nearby jungles. Finally, the program became an environmental and political disaster. In 1961 Rachel Carson had written her best-selling book *Silent Spring*, launching the modern environmental movement. She picked the title because the spraying of DDT for mosquito control had seriously reduced bird populations near her home. The spraying of chemicals over vast regions of Indochina seemed increasingly irresponsible, and a new military term was coined—"eco-warfare."

The greatest controversy surrounding Agent Orange and the other chemical defoliants, however, revolved around their impact on the American soldiers and Marines who regularly patrolled denuded areas in search of enemy troops. Moreover, as early as April 1966 North

Vietnam claimed that the herbicides caused permanent ocular lesions, altered chromosomes, and caused congenital birth defects, as well as permanent damage to affected ecosystems. Sometimes, U.S. troops entered an area soon after a spraying. Many Vietnam veterans can remember wiping the chemicals off their hands and faces after a defoliant spraying. Soon after their return, some exposed veterans began complaining of health problems. For a long period, the Pentagon denied that Agents Orange, White, and Blue had any collateral health effects on those exposed, but veterans' groups maintained enormous political pressure, and in 1992 Congress authorized the Institute of Medicine (IOM) of the National Academy of Sciences to investigate the relationship between exposure to Agent Orange and specific health problems.

Over the course of the next decade, the IOM issued three damning reports, each pilloring the Pentagon's denials with hard evidence that exposure to Agents Orange, Blue, and White explained the high incidence among Vietnam veterans of chloracne, peripheral neuropathy, porphyria cutanea tarda, non-Hodgkin's lymphoma, multiple myeloma, Hodgkin's disease, Type II diabetes, chronic lymphocytic leukemia, soft-tissue sarcomas, and cancers of the prostate, lungs, trachea, and larynx. The chemicals have also been associated with high rates of spina bifada in the children of exposed Vietnam veterans. The Veterans Administration today pays benefits to exposed veterans suffering from these diseases. Tens of millions of South Vietnamese, Cambodians, and Laotians were exposed as well and suffer the same side effects.

Sources: J.B. Neilands, *Harvest of Death: Chemical Warfare in Vietnam and Cambodia*, 1972; William A. Buckingham Jr., *Operation Ranch Hand: The United States Air Force and Herbicides in Southeast Asia, 1961–1971*, 1982; Fred A. Wilcox, *Waiting for an Army to Die: The Tragedy of Agent Orange*, 1983; Philip Jones Griffith, *Agent Orange: Collateral Damage in Vietnam*, 2003.

Above: In July 1965, U.S. naval aviator Jeremiah Denton was shot down 75 miles south of Hanoi. Denton spent the next seven years as a prisoner of war in North Vietnam. In 1976, he published a memoir of his time spent as a POW in Vietnam, which was later made into a movie. In 1980, Denton was elected the first Republican Senator from Alabama since Reconstruction. Here, on May 1, 1981, Denton sits as a member of a sub-committee of the Judiciary Committee.

convention with an iron hand. Outside the convention hall, antiwar* protesters led by people like Tom Hayden* and David Dellinger* demonstrated against the war and against "establishment" control of the Democratic Party. Chicago police, on the orders of Mayor Richard Daley, brutally attacked the crowds. Later dubbed a police riot, the brutality on the streets of Chicago in 1968 stunned a nation watching the battle on television. Hubert Humphrey secured the nomination, selecting Senator Edmund Muskie as his running mate.

Sources: Norman Mailer, *Miami and the Siege of Chicago*, 1969; Theodore White, *The Making of the President, 1968*, 1969.

DEMOCRATIC REPUBLIC OF VIETNAM

The name "Democratic Republic of Vietnam" was the national description of the North Vietnamese government. In mid-August 1945, with the Japanese government reeling under the impact of atomic bombs and the imminent American invasion of the mainland, Ho Chi Minh* and the Vietminh* invaded Hanoi,* and after encountering no resistance they proclaimed the establishment of the Democratic Republic of Vietnam. At the same time, the French moved into Cochin China,* with the assistance of British troops, and announced their intention to return to Tonkin* in the north as well. They returned in force in February 1947, invading Hanoi and pushing more than 100,000 Vietminh into the countryside, where the guerrilla war culminating in the Battle of Dien Bien Phu* in 1954 began. After the French surrender there and the division of the country at the 17th parallel in the Geneva Accords* of 1954, Ho Chi Minh again proclaimed the Democratic Republic of Vietnam as an independent nation-state. This time he was right. The term "Democratic Republic of Vietnam" was used until 1975, when North Vietnamese troops conquered the Republic of Vietnam* (South Vietnam). The reunited country was then given the new name "Socialist Republic of Vietnam."*

Sources: Frances FitzGerald, *Fire in the Lake: The Vietnamese and Americans in Vietnam*, 1972; Joseph Buttinger, *Vietnam: A Dragon Embattled*, Vol. 1, *From Colonialism to the Vietminh*, 1967.

DENTON, JEREMIAH

Born in 1924, Jeremiah Denton had become an outstanding naval pilot by the 1950s. In June 1965 he went to Vietnam, and one month later he was shot down about seventy-five miles south of Hanoi.* He spent the next seven years in North Vietnamese prisons, remaining steadfastly uncooperative with his captors. Denton came to national attention

during a televised interview. While the North Vietnamese were pleased with his verbal answers, Denton was eye-blinking, in Morse code, the word "torture" to the cameras. In 1973 Commander Denton was one of the first American prisoners of war* released after the Paris Peace Accords,* and his smart salute and "reporting for duty" comment after deplaning at Clark Field in the Philippines* endeared him to the American public. In 1980 Denton became the first Republican to win a seat in the U.S. Senate from Alabama since Reconstruction. He was unsuccessful in his bid for reelection in 1986. Jeremiah Denton continues to lecture on national and international affairs and plays an active role in the leadership of the National Forum Foundation.

Sources: Jeremiah A. Denton, *When Hell Was In Session*, 1976; John S. Bowman, ed., *The Vietnam War: An Almanac*, 1985.

DEROS

DEROS is an acronym for Date Eligible to Return from Overseas. Every military individual assigned to duty in Southeast Asia knew in advance how long he or she would be there. For most United States Army* personnel, the normal tour of duty was 365 days, while Marines* usually served 13 months. After that date, the individual would be reassigned, usually to the United States and often to immediate separation from military service (discharge). Because leaving Vietnam safely became the fundamental objective for most troops, each individual's DEROS became a vital statistic for him or her. As an individual's DEROS approached, he/she became a "short-timer," and both anxiety and anticipation increased. STT

Source: Al Santoli, *Everything We Had*, 1981.

DESERTION

During the Vietnam War the highest desertion rates (defined as unauthorized abscence exceeding thirty days) occurred among soldiers of the Army of the Republic of Vietnam* (ARVN). Between 1967 and 1971 more than 57,000 ARVN troops deserted. During the same period the number of North Vietnamese and Vietcong* deserters totaled 87,000 soldiers. Between 1965 and 1973 nearly 7,600,000 Americans served in the military in Vietnam, and the total number of desertions exceeded 550,000. All but 100,000 of those men and women returned to active duty after absences of less than one month. The others were discharged from the armed forces for desertion. Most of those cases involved non–combat-related problems. There were 32,000 cases involving failure to report to duty in Vietnam, refusal to return from rest-and-relaxation breaks, and unauthorized absences after completing a tour of duty in South Vietnam. There were only 5,000 cases of desertion "in-country," and only 24 of those were committed to avoid hazardous duty. When the war ended in 1973, more than 10,000 servicemen and women were still listed as deserters, and more than 7,000 of them received amnesty from Presidents Gerald Ford* and Jimmy Carter.

Sources: Lawrence M. Baskir and William A. Strauss, *Chance and Circumstance: The Draft, the War, and the Vietnam Generation*, 1978; Guenter Lewy, *America in Vietnam*, 1978; Harry G. Summers Jr., *Vietnam War Almanac*, 1985.

DESOTO MISSIONS

"DeSoto Mission" was the code name for covert U.S. naval operations. Ever since the 1950s DeSoto Missions had been carried out against the People's Republic of China,* the Soviet Union,* and North Korea. Intelligence agents or commando units would harass coastal radar transmitters so that American electronic intelligence ships could monitor the transmissions, measure frequencies, and pinpoint locations. In the spring of 1964 the United States Navy* began DeSoto operations off the coast of North Vietnam using South Vietnamese commando units to harass radio transmission units. The destroyer USS *Maddox** was assigned to begin the program, and it was these DeSoto Missions that led to the Gulf of Tonkin Incident* in July and August 1964.

Sources: Anthony Preston, "The Naval War in Vietnam," in John S. Bowman, ed., *The Vietnam War: An Almanac*, 1985; Edward J. Marolda and G. Wesley Pryce III, *A Short History of the United States Navy and the Southeast Asian Conflict, 1950–1975*, 1984.

Below: A sniper team with the 7th Marines in 1967. Though most Army personnel only had to serve one year in Vietnam, the normal tour of duty for a Marine was thirteen months. These Marines would no doubt know their DEROS (Date Eligible to Return from Overseas) by heart and be counting down their time.

Above: Colonel Peter Dewey (shown here as a captain) was the first American soldier to die in Vietnam. Dewey was shot and killed on September 26, 1945, during anti-American rioting in Saigon.

DEWEY, A. PETER

Peter Dewey was the first American serviceman to be killed in Vietnam. Dewey was a member of the U.S. Office of Strategic Services (OSS), a World War II unit. One of the activities of the OSS was to work "behind the lines" with partisan groups fighting against U.S. enemies. In early 1945 an OSS detachment, the "Deer Team," parachuted into Tonkin,* made contact with Ho Chi Minh,* and assisted the Vietminh* in its guerrilla war against the Japanese. A close personal relationship developed between Ho and the Deer Team officers, and the impression resulted that the OSS was an advocate of early independence for Vietnam, under a Vietminh government. In August 1945 Dewey led another OSS detachment into Saigon,* which was then under the control of the British, who had accepted the Japanese surrender in Vietnam south of the 16th parallel. The British commander, Douglas D. Gracey, was faced with the near-impossible task of governing in the midst of turmoil, chaos, and confusion. Rival political and military units were operating throughout the south, and Saigon was the focal point of activity. The major parties in this setting were the British, the French, the Japanese, and various factions of Vietnamese nationalists, religious sects, and warlords. Dewey and his OSS unit were a minor group, but Dewey was sufficiently outspoken and abrasive to anger Gracey repeatedly, especially by giving the appearance of siding with the Vietminh, which the OSS in fact did. One incident in particular summarized the antagonistic relationship between Gracey and Dewey: Dewey wanted to fly an American flag on the fender of his car, but Gracey prohibited it on technical grounds. As a result, Dewey decided to leave Saigon and Vietnam. On his way to Saigon's Tan Son Nhut* Airport, Dewey's jeep, without the flag, was fired on, probably by mistake, by Vietminh soldiers. Dewey was killed instantly, on September 26, 1945.

Ho Chi Minh apologized to the United States. It would be fourteen years before another U.S. soldier would be killed in Vietnam. STT

Source: Edward Doyle and Samuel Lipsman, *The Vietnam Experience: Passing the Torch*, 1981.

DIEN BIEN PHU, BATTLE OF (1954)

See French Forces and the Battle of Dien Bien Phu

DIKES

For more than 2,000 years a system of dikes has regulated water flow in the Red River Delta of northern Vietnam, and the systematic construction of dikes began intensely in the thirteenth century. By the 1970s there were more than 3,000 miles of dikes to protect against the monsoon floods of the Red River. During the Vietnam War there were proposals for large-scale American bombing of the dikes during the monsoon season. Such an attack would have destroyed the system, caused widespread flooding of the Red River Delta, ruined rice crops, and drowned thousands of civilians. Because international law prohibited deliberate attacks on civilian populations, Presidents Lyndon B. Johnson* and Richard Nixon* never adopted the proposal.

Sources: Gerard Chaliand, *The Peasant of North Vietnam*, 1969; Bernard Fall, *The Two Vietnams*, 1967.

"DINK"

"Dink" was a racist reference to enemy forces or to civilians in Vietnam. The difference in usage by Americans in Vietnam of such epithets from similar epithets in previous wars was the generalized application of such words to the civilian population rather than just to enemy forces. It is generally recognized that soldiers usually dehumanize the enemy in order to help accept the reality of killing them. To some extent military training, in preparing soldiers for combat, encourages development of such an attitude. A problem occurs when dehumanization proceeds to the point where the conscience is totally numbed, enabling a soldier to become a wanton killer. Another problem occurs when the soldier begins to generalize such attitudes toward the civilian population. This was very easy to do in Vietnam, where it was so difficult to distinguish the enemy from the civilian population. Such generalization facilitated intentional, indiscriminate killing of civilian noncombatants and lent credit to charges by the war's critics that it was an immoral, racist conflict directed against the Vietnamese people. SF

Sources: Loren Baritz, *Backfire*, 1985; Peter Trooboff, *Law and Responsibility in Warfare*, 1975; Guenter Lewy, *America in Vietnam*, 1978.

DIVISION

A division is a nearly universal military organization consisting of approximately 20,000 troops commanded by a major general. During the Vietnam War the following U.S. divisions or elements thereof participated in the conflict: the 1st Cavalry;* the 1st,* 4th,* 5th,* 9th,* 23d,* and 25th Infantry;* the 82d* and 101st Airborne;* the 1st,* 3d,* and 5th Marines;* and the 2d, 7th,* and 834th Air.*

Source: Shelby L. Stanton, *Vietnam Order of Battle*, 1981.

DIXIE STATION

"Dixie Station" was the place-name for the U.S. Seventh Fleet's* staging area in the South China Sea. During 1965 and 1966 Task Force 77, the carrier strike group in the Seventh Fleet, used Dixie Station as the reference point for its operations. Dixie Station was located at 11°N 110°E off the coast of Cam Ranh Bay.*

Source: Harry G. Summers Jr., *Vietnam War Almanac*, 1985.

DMZ

See Demilitarized Zone

DOMINO THEORY

The domino theory was first proposed by President Harry S. Truman* in the Truman Doctrine in 1946, when he argued that unless the United States provided military aid assistance to Greece and Turkey, both countries and much of the Middle East would fall, like a row of dominoes lined up against one another, to Communist aggression. In April 1954, during the siege at Dien Bien Phu,* President Dwight D. Eisenhower* announced the same idea about Southeast Asia, arguing that if Vietnam fell to Communist guerrillas, the rest of the region, including Cambodia,* Laos,* Thailand,* and Burma, would fall as well, and perhaps much of East Asia. Malaysia, Indonesia, New Zealand,* Australia,* and the Philippines* would also be threatened. Presidents John F. Kennedy* and Lyndon B. Johnson* both used the domino theory to justify the commitment of American resources to Vietnam in the 1960s. America's strategic interests, the theory demanded, required a strong military presence in South Vietnam.

Since the fall of South Vietnam in 1975, the domino theory has really not been fulfilled. Armies from the Socialist Republic of Vietnam* have invaded Cambodia and Laos, both of whom have experienced Communist takeovers, but Thailand, Indonesia, and Malaysia have retained their pro-Western positions; Burma is still neutral; and the integrity of Australia, New Zealand, and the Philippines is still intact.

Sources: Russell H. Fifield, *Americans in Southeast Asia*, 1973; Richard J. Barnet, *Roots of War: The Men and Institutions Behind U.S. Foreign Policy*, 1972; Gabriel Kolko, *The Roots of American Foreign Policy*, 1969.

Below: The USS *General Leroy Eltinge* delivers troops from the 101st Airborne Division to Dixie Station off Cam Ranh Bay in South Vietnam on July 29, 1965. The ship, its deck crowded with soldiers, resembles a World War II ship carrying troops. During the Vietnam War, most U.S. troops were flown to Vietnam.

Below: U.S. soldiers patrol through a village near Dong Ha in South Vietnam on October 11, 1966, inspecting the bodies of several South Vietnamese. Whether the dead were Vietcong soldiers was impossible to tell — one of the many problems the U.S. military faced throughout the war.

DONG HA

Located at the junction of Routes 1 and 9 and less than fifteen kilometers from the southern boundary of the Demilitarized Zone,* Dong Ha was a combat base and supply center for III Marine Amphibious Force* units operating in Quang Tri Province. An ideal site for the 3d Marine Division's* headquarters, established in June 1968, the base also proved crucial to the defense of the Cua Viet River system, through which supplies unloaded at the river's mouth on the South China Sea were taken upstream to Dong Ha's force logistics unit and then distributed to U.S. Marine* and Republic of Vietnam* forces.

Together with Gio Linh north on Route 1, Con Thien to the northwest, and Cam Lo west on Route 9, Dong Ha became the southeast anchor of "Leatherneck Square." In April 1968 enemy forces attacked the base, and intermittent but heavy fighting continued in the area until late summer. Meanwhile, after the Marines abandoned Khe Sanh* and other northern firebases in the same year, Dong Ha retained its role as a command and logistics center, and Marines fanned out from the base to conduct operations as far west as the Laotian border. The Marines turned Dong Ha over to the South Vietnamese Army when the 3d Marine division left northern I Corps* for Okinawa in November 1969. DA

Sources: *The Marines in Vietnam, 1954–1973*, 1974; Willard Pearson, *The War in the Northern Provinces, 1966–1968*, 1975.

DONG HA, BATTLE OF (1968)

In the spring of 1968, after the Tet Offensive* and before the opening of the Paris peace talks,* the North Vietnamese Army* (NVA) and the Vietcong* made a concerted attempt to improve their bargaining position. They conducted 119 attacks on provincial and district capitals, military installations, and major cities in South Vietnam. At Dong Ha in I Corps,* the United States Marines* maintained a supply base; it was in the northeastern area of Quang Tri Province. Late in April and early in May, the NVA 320th Division, complete with 8,000 troops, attacked Dong Ha and fought a concerted battle against an allied force of 5,000 Marines and South Vietnamese troops. The North Vietnamese failed to destroy the supply base and had to retreat back across the Demilitarized Zone,* leaving behind 856 dead. Sixty-eight Americans died in the fighting.

Sources: Clark Dougan and Steven Weiss, *The Vietnam Experience: Nineteen Sixty-Eight*, 1983; Willard Pearson, *The War in the Northern Provinces, 1966–1968*, 1975; *The Marines in Vietnam, 1954–1973*, 1974.

Above: On June 20, 1968, NVA artillery hits the ammunition dump at Dong Ha in the continuing battle.

Below: U.S. Air Force members dispose of damaged and live ordnance in Dong Ha in April 1970.

DONG XOAI, BATTLE OF (1965)

Dong Xoai was a district capital in Phuc Long Province of III Corps.* An American Special Forces* Camp at Dong Xoai was manned by 400 Montagnard* Civilian Irregular Defense Group* troops and 24 U.S. Seebees* and soldiers. Early in the morning of June 10, 1965, approximately 1,500 Vietcong* guerrillas, armed with AK-47* rifles, grenades, and flamethrowers, attacked the camp. The defenders quickly retreated to one area of the installation, and American and South Vietnamese aircraft attacked the Vietcong with napalm* and phosphorous bombs. Soldiers from the ARVN's (*see* Army of the Republic of Vietnam) 42d Ranger Battalion were helicoptered in, and the Vietcong retreated. At the end of the first day's fighting, 20 Americans were killed or wounded, along with 200 Vietnamese civilians and soldiers. Military Assistance Command, Vietnam* reported 700 dead Vietcong. On June 11 and 12, ARVN rangers searched for the Vietcong, but late on June 12 the Vietcong attacked the rangers. ARVN soldiers quickly deserted their positions and ran into the surrounding jungles, and the American advisors were airlifted out. The Battle of Dong Xoai affected American policy by undermining faith in the stability of ARVN troops and making the commitment of large numbers of American ground forces inevitable.

Source: Terence Maitland and Peter McInerney, *The Vietnam Experience: A Contagion of War*, 1983.

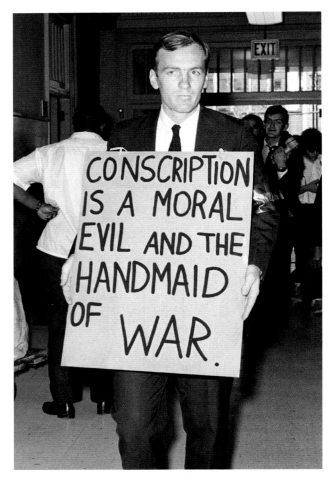

DRAFT

More than 2 million men were inducted into U.S. military service during the Vietnam War period in accordance with the Selective Service Act of 1948 and its ensuing extensions. The draft law provided for the registration of all males on their eighteenth birthday. The president delegated authority in draft matters to the director of the Selective Service System. The director, his staff, and about 4,000 local draft boards throughout the country administered the system. Local draft boards were under the supervision of state directors, but quotas for inductees were set at the national level, which made its decision relative to the number of men from each state already in the military. The Department of Defense initiated draft calls for a given number of men, based on projected enlistments and needs. Draft deferments in terms of essential activities and critical occupations were defined by the Departments of Commerce and Labor. The secretary of defense defined the standards for physical, mental, and moral acceptability for military service. Although the system operated under the regulations and standards drawn up at a national level, where the president could adjust induction numbers to meet changing political and military needs, local draft boards had considerable latitude in

selecting men for service. Major inequities in the Selective Service System and its deferment procedures were recognized by both supporters and critics of the draft, but the majority of recommendations made by President Lyndon Johnson's* National Advisory Commission on Selective Service in 1967 to eliminate most deferments were not incorporated in the 1967 draft extension act. Both the inequities, such that poor, rural, and minority young men were disproportionately drafted and sent to combat, and the increasing number of young men called to the draft made the Selective Service a natural target of the antiwar movement.* Antidraft activity ranged from "Stop the Draft" week in October 1967 to break-ins of draft boards with the symbolic pouring of blood over the draft files. President Richard Nixon* ended all draft calls in December 1972, and President Gerald Ford* issued a proclamation terminating the remaining draft registration requirements in 1975. President Jimmy Carter, on January 21, 1977, pardoned all who had been convicted of violating the Selective Service Act during the Vietnam period. In 1979 President Carter reintroduced draft registration. LKA

Sources: Lawrence M. Baskir and William A. Strauss, *Chance and Circumstance: The Draft, the War, and the Vietnam Generation*, 1978; Stephen M. Kohn, *Jailed for Peace: The History of American Draft Law Violators*, 1986.

DRUGS

Almost inevitably, illegal drugs snaked their way into the U.S. Armed Forces during the Vietnam War, especially in the 1970s when drug use among soldiers became common. Drug culture was gaining traction all through the 1960s in the United States, inspired and encouraged by music and a burgeoning "hippie" culture, and many young men ordered to Vietnam in the late '60s and '70s had already sampled drugs in America. They landed in a country where marijuana, heroin, cocaine, and amphetamines were widely available and cheap.

For several years after 1965, most soldiers in Vietnam were dedicated professionals and volunteers, intent on their mission and unaffected by the rising counterculture in America. They were led by the best officers the military could find. But these rotated out and the newer arrivals included draftees and younger men exposed in the United States to growing skepticism about the war's chances for success. In addition, the most influential music group in the United States—the Beatles—increasingly sanctioned drugs as the decade progressed. Songs like "Norwegian Wood" and "Lucy in the Sky with Diamonds" suggested marijuana and LSD use. Other bands followed suit and by the late '60s the airwaves were filled with songs about the enjoyment of mind-altering drugs. Smoking pot was becoming prevalent among young people of the middle class. Going off to war, the young men took their music with them, as well as their loosened inhibitions about prohibited drugs. In the war zone, like countless soldiers before them, they had a need to relax, recreate, and temporarily forget about their dangerous circumstances; drugs helped meet that need.

The military unwittingly contributed to the drug problem. For one, it often issued amphetamines to soldiers

Below: On December 9, 1967, antiwar protestors organized a series of "Stop the Draft" weeks throughout the United States. In this photograph, thousands of protestors assemble at the Armed Forces Induction Center in New York City. Four thousand policemen descended on the scene to break up the demonstration because of the traffic jam it had created.

to enhance their performance. For another, because it outlawed the sale of alcohol to soldiers under twenty-one, men consequently attempted to find solace in drugs. Then there was the availability. Marijuana could be found for sale in almost any shop in Saigon, where joints cost a dime apiece. Soldiers on the streets were often offered it by curbside "mama-sans." Military surveys found that only a small percentage of soldiers smoked marijuana before 1967, but that by 1968 about one-quarter of the troops were doing so. In the period 1969–71, half the troops were smoking pot either occasionally or regularly. In the early '70s, 80 percent of American soldiers were being offered heroin within a week of arriving in Vietnam. One soldier said that an American serviceman anywhere in Vietnam, no matter whom he was with, was never farther from some sort of drug than ten yards.

By the late '60s, MACV began a campaign against marijuana. It brought in antidrug officers from the U.S. Department of Justice and in 1969 it flew in drug-sniffing dogs. It displayed posters about the detriments of pot smoking. These efforts did curtail marijuana use on American military bases, but did little to curb the drug's

Right: A patrol of U.S. soldiers from the 9th Division with what appears to be drug paraphernalia in a rice paddy field in the Tan An Delta in 1968.

availability outside the installations. And the military made poor headway in its campaign to persuade soldiers that pot was harmful when most of the soldiers' favorite songs and even some of their movies and books told them it wasn't.

More addictive drugs also gained traction among the servicemen. A great deal of opium—then about half the world's supply—came from mountainous regions of Laos, Thailand, and Burma, making opiates and heroin abundant and cheap in Vietnam. Heroin in the region could be 80 to 90 percent pure. Soldiers would bring it back after being on leave in Bangkok. Both Asian and American pilots smuggled narcotics into Vietnam; and corrupt South Vietnamese officials allowed the traffic, some even making large amounts of money off the trade. South Vietnamese teenage girls sold heroin from roadside stands, and street peddlers pushed $2 to $3 vials of almost pure heroin on servicemen walking Saigon streets. Owing to this purity, the soldiers smoked it or inhaled it rather than injected it, and it was easier to conceal from officers than marijuana. Heroin had particular appeal among "short-timers," men who were approaching the end of their tours and scheduled to go home; for some, marijuana tended to give the illusion of slowing time down but heroin tended to make the days seem to go by faster. By 1969, the military estimated that 25 to 30 percent of its servicemen were buying heroin. Two years later, the military estimated that as many as 37,000 Americans in Vietnam were addicted heroin users.

Drug use was more prevalent in the rear areas than near the front lines. Relaxed discipline, time off, peer pressure, and anger at the military all contributed to drug use. The military arrested 8,000 men in 1969 on drug charges and more than 11,000 in 1970, but still the number of users increased. Officers were little inclined to report or punish casual drug use for fear of losing too many men in their units. The military tried an amnesty program, but it was not particularly effective. Senior officers had done too little to anticipate the problem of drug abuse and their efforts when the epidemic raged were of little avail. During 1971, the military treated no more than 5,000 men for combat wounds but more than 20,000 men for serious drug abuse.

Sources: George Donelson Moss, *Vietnam: An American Ordeal*, 1998; Samuel Lipsman and Edward Doyle, *The Vietnam Experience: Fighting for Time*, 1983; Richard Davenport-Hines, *Pursuit of Oblivion: A Global History of Narcotics*, 2002

DRV

See Democratic Republic of Vietnam

DULLES, JOHN FOSTER

Above: John Foster Dulles served as secretary of state under President Dwight D. Eisenhower. An intensely religious man who saw most issues in terms of good and evil, Dulles considered Communism a stalking horse for the antichrist.

John Foster Dulles was born on February 25, 1888, in Washington, D.C. He graduated from Princeton in 1908 and took a law degree from George Washington University in 1911. His grandfather John Foster had been secretary of state to President Benjamin Harrison, so Dulles was raised in a diplomatically conscious family. He specialized in international law and attended the Paris Peace Conference (1919), Washington Conference (1921–22), Reparations Commission (1920s), Berlin Debt Conference (1933), and the San Francisco Conference (1945) to establish the United Nations. President Harry S. Truman* had Dulles negotiate the Japanese peace treaty (1950–51), and in 1953 President Dwight D. Eisenhower* made Dulles secretary of state. Dulles was convinced that the United States had a mission to counteract global Communism, to stop the Soviet Union* from its imperial designs. For Dulles, the world was engaged in a moral struggle between good and evil, and his penchant for such phrases as "massive retaliation," "agonizing reappraisal," and "brinkmanship" alarmed critics.

As far as Dulles was concerned, the struggle in Indochina* was only another example of Soviet evil. There was no doubt in his mind that the Soviets were manipulating Ho Chi Minh* and the Vietminh* and that French control over Vietnam had to be maintained. Dulles also expected, however, that the French would have to invest more resources in the struggle, eventually agree to grant independence to Vietnam, Laos,* and Cambodia in order to eliminate any taint of colonialism, and secure allied support from the English, Australians, and New Zealanders. Early in 1954, when the Vietminh were preparing the assault on French forces at Dien Bien Phu,* Dulles joined Admiral Arthur Radford* in advocating Operation Vulture*—the American air assault on the Vietminh. Dulles was disappointed when President Eisenhower refused to approve the mission, but when Dien Bien Phu fell in 1954, Dulles argued that it would "harden, not weaken, our purpose to stay united" in checking further Communist aggression. Dulles did not live to see the direct American intervention in Vietnam. After a two-year struggle with cancer, he died on May 24, 1959.

Sources: Michael Guhin, *John Foster Dulles: A Statesman and His Times*, 1972; Townsend Hoopes, *The Devil and John Foster Dulles*, 1973.

DUONG VAN MINH

Duong Van Minh, the last president of the Republic of Vietnam,* was born in 1916 in the Mekong Delta,* in what was then the French colony of Cochin China.* Trained by the French, Minh became in 1955 the ranking army officer in Ngo Dinh Diem's* newly proclaimed Republic of Vietnam. He rose to prominence a year later as a result of

Above: General Duong Van Minh served as president of South Vietnam for less than a week. He came to power after the departure of Nguyen Cao Ky and Nguyen Van Thieu in mid-April 1975. Duong Van Minh fled the country at the end of the month when NVA troops overran Saigon.

defeating the Mekong Delta–based Hoa Hao* sect, the leader of which was publicly guillotined. Minh's rising popularity combined with his outspokenness forced Diem to remove him from military command by "promoting" him to a largely honorific advisory position.

General Minh emerged from obscurity seven years later as the leader of a group of Vietnamese generals that staged the November 1963 military uprising, ending the regime of President Ngo Dinh Diem. During the uprising Diem and his brother Ngo Dinh Nhu* were assassinated, reportedly on Minh's orders. The generals replaced the Diem government with a Military Revolutionary Council, with Minh serving as nominal chairman. This remarkably ineffective group governed for only three months. The council, and General Minh, were ousted by a military coup led by General Nguyen Khanh* in January 1964.

After living in exile for several years, Minh returned to South Vietnam in 1968. Once there he came to be regarded as a potential leader of a non-Communist coalition of opponents of President Nguyen Van Thieu.* Minh did in fact enter the 1971 presidential election, but he withdrew from the race when events eliminated any possibility of his defeating Thieu. Minh's last appearance on the Vietnamese political stage occurred in April 1975, during the last days of the crumbling Republic of Vietnam. On April 21 Thieu resigned the presidency. His elderly vice president, Tran Van Huong,* shortly thereafter appointed Minh to the presidency, as North Vietnamese units converged on Saigon.* The Minh administration lasted only two days. On April 29, 1975, Minh was taken into custody, after surrendering unconditionally to the North Vietnamese Army* unit that had occupied the presidential palace. Duong Van Minh, the last president of the Republic of Vietnam, was allowed to immigrate to France in 1983. Duong Van Minh lived the last few years of his life in Pasadena, California, where he died on August 6, 2001. SAK

Sources: Frances FitzGerald, *Fire in the Lake: The Vietnamese and the Americans in Vietnam*, 1972; Stanley Karnow, *Vietnam: A History*, 1983; George C. Herring, *America's Longest War: The United States in Vietnam, 1950–1975*, 1986; *New York Times*, August 7, 2001.

DURBROW, ELBRIDGE

Elbridge Durbrow was born on September 21, 1903, in San Francisco. He eventually went to Yale University, where he obtained a Ph.D. in 1926. Durbrow subsequently joined the foreign service, with which he served in a number of minor posts around the world until after World War II. Between 1948 and 1950, however, he was an instructor at the National War College. After his stint at the War College, he was promoted and named the chief of the Division of Foreign Service Personnel.

Durbrow was a career foreign service officer, and in 1957 Dwight D. Eisenhower* decided to send this seasoned diplomat to the tiny country of South Vietnam. Almost from the outset, Ambassador Durbrow found much to criticize in Ngo Dinh Diem.* Of note, he would later acknowledge that the repression and corruption of the South Vietnamese regime was a catalyst to insurgency. He was also a shrewd diplomat who warned Diem that his brother Ngo Dinh Nhu* and his sister-in-law were damaging the government. Nhu's control of the secret police made him a most powerful man, and he used that power indiscriminately.

Diem apparently did not heed Ambassador Durbrow's warnings, and on December 4, 1960, Durbrow sent a message to Washington indicating that in the not too distant future the United States might be forced to support an alternative regime. Meanwhile, Diem continued to resist American pressures for reform. Most of the aid sent from the United States was used by Diem to enrich his own family and to prop up his regime. Only a very small fraction of the funds were utilized for South Vietnamese economic development.

Durbrow's warnings about the unpopularity of the Diem regime finally bore fruit in November 1960. Lieutenant Colonel Vuong Van Dong staged an abortive military coup against Diem. Dong had revolted in response to Diem's arbitrary rule, his promotion of favorites, and his meddling in military operations against the insurgency. Although he succeeded in surrounding the presidential palace, Dong allowed the telephone lines to remain intact. Diem decided to wait out the dissident soldiers until loyal contingents arrived in Saigon.* Dong even went to Durbrow to gain his assistance in overthrowing Diem. The ambassador, however, refused to assist Dong, knowing that Washington would never accept nor approve of Diem's overthrow with support from a U.S. ambassador. The rebellion was crushed, and Dong and other dissident soldiers fled South Vietnam.

Diem, however, was annoyed with Durbrow's relationship with Dong and did not hesitate to express his displeasure with the ambassador to officials in the new Kennedy administration. John F. Kennedy* was convinced that he could gain Diem's confidence and succeed in ending the Communist threat in South Vietnam. In April 1961 Kennedy replaced Durbrow with the untested Frederick Nolting* as the U.S. ambassador to South Vietnam. Durbrow nonetheless was apparently correct about the intractability of the Diem regime, because in late 1963 the United States assisted in its overthrow. Durbrow returned to the State Department in 1961 and remained there until his retirement in 1968. Elbridge Durbrow died on May 16, 1997. JSL

Sources: John E. Findling, ed., *Historical Dictionary of American Diplomatic History*, 1980; Gabriel Kolko, *Anatomy of a War: Vietnam, the United States, and the Modern Historical Experience*, 1986; *New York Times*, May 17, 1997.

DUSTOFF

"I need a dustoff" became an all-too-familiar call over the airwaves of Vietnam. Dustoff missions were medical evacuation missions (*see* Medevac) using helicopters. While "dustoff" has been used to apply to all medical evacuation missions, GIs reserved the term for missions flown to pick up wounded soldiers in the field, often under fire. When a soldier was hit, the call went out for a dustoff, and any helicopter in the area without a higher-priority mission could respond.

Many of the early helicopters used in Vietnam did not fare well in dustoff missions. The CH-21* and CH-34* were used in this role, but their lack of maneuverability and relatively slow speed, combined with a small door in the case of the CH-21, made them vulnerable to ground fire. During the Tet Offensive* CH-34s flown by the U.S. Marines* in a dustoff role took heavy casualties. The UH-1* "Huey" excelled in this role, with its wide doors and ability to get in and out of battle sites quickly. Still, flying dustoffs took courage on the part of the crew, as ground fire was the rule rather than the exception. The rewards, however, were great. Dustoffs allowed wounded soldiers to be brought to medical facilities much more quickly than in any other war, usually in a matter of minutes, and saved many lives. NJA

Source: Jim Mesko, *Airmobile: The Helicopter War in Vietnam*, 1985.

DYLAN, BOB

Born Robert Zimmerman in Duluth, Minnesota, on May 24, 1941, Bob Dylan (he took his name from the poet Dylan Thomas) soon became one of the most influential folk-rock artists in the world, especially after moving to New York City in the mid-1960s. As a performer Dylan refused to be categorized, be it for his playing style, lifestyle, music, or political opinions. He wrote about injustice, women, drugs, and for a period about topics so obscure that no one knows exactly what he was seeking. Although he never wrote a specific song about Vietnam, Dylan nevertheless became associated with the antiwar movement* because his songs of social consciousness, particularly "The Times They Are A-Changin'" and "Blowin' in the Wind," became anthems of a kind to a generation seeking to change America. In the 1970s Dylan continued to produce albums, but critics charged that he was not as innovative as before.

Nevertheless, Bob Dylan had a strong influence on youth and antiwar movements in the 1960s and early 1970s and enjoyed a revival in popularity in the 1990s. His 2006 album, *Modern Times*, hit #1 and made him the oldest living person to top the charts at age 65. CD

Sources: Theodore Roszak, *The Making of a Counter Culture*, 1969; Richard Flacks, *Youth and Social Change*, 1971; http://www.keno.org/classic_rock/bob_dylan_bio.htm.

Above: Folksinger Bob Dylan became known as one of the unofficial musical voices of the antiwar movement. Here he is pictured during a visit to Great Britain in April 1965.

Left: Troops from the 1st Battalion of the 173d Airborne Brigade race to get a wounded comrade onto a medevac helicopter on June 29, 1965. The fallen soldier had been wounded by sniper fire in War Zone D, 30 miles north of Saigon.

EAGLE FLIGHT

"Eagle Flights" described airmobile strike forces used to ambush, raid, harass, and observe enemy positions. Eagle Flights were first used in 1963 in South Vietnam, but the 5th Special Forces Group* began using them continually in October 1964. An Eagle Flight group consisted of five American soldiers, thirty-six Montagnard* irregular troops, a helicopter airlift, and several UH-1* gunships. Eagle Flights supported Civilian Irregular Defense Group* operations as well as regular operations of the 5th Special Forces Group.

Sources: John S. Bowman, ed., *The Vietnam War Almanac*, 1985; Shelby L. Stanton, *The Green Berets at War*, 1985.

Below: At the time of this photo on May 13, 1972, the NVA had launched the Eastertide Offensive throughout South Vietnam. ARVN artillery soldiers fire on NVA positions in An Loc, South Vietnam.

EASTERTIDE OFFENSIVE
(also known as the Easter Offensive)

Late in 1970, with Vietnamization* in full gear, the North Vietnamese began planning an all-out assault on South Vietnam. Le Duan* visited Moscow in the spring of 1971 to secure heavy weapons supplies. North Vietnam wanted to break the military stalemate in South Vietnam and, with a major victory, perhaps help defeat Richard Nixon's* reelection bid in 1972, leaving the White House open to a more moderate, even anti–Vietnam War Democratic president. Throughout 1971 the Soviet Union* provided heavy supplies—trucks, surface-to-air (SAM)* missiles, tanks, and artillery—to prepare the North Vietnamese Army* (NVA) and Vietcong* for the attack.

The offensive began on March 30, 1972. Three North Vietnamese divisions, strengthened by Soviet T-54 tanks, attacked across the Demilitarized Zone* and along Highway 9 out of Laos,* with Hue* as their objective. Three more North Vietnamese divisions attacked Binh Long Province, captured Loc Ninh, and surrounded An Loc.* Other North Vietnamese troops attacked Kontum* in the Central Highlands.* Finally, two North Vietnamese divisions took control of several districts in Binh Dinh along the coast of the South China Sea. Quang Tri Province was lost by the end of April 1972. But at that point the tide turned. ARVN (*see* Army of the Republic of Vietnam) troops held their positions twenty-five miles north of Hue, and the NVA was unable to take Kontum and An Loc. President Nixon had already begun bombing North Vietnam again, but on May 8, 1972, he mined Haiphong Harbor* and several other North Vietnamese ports as well. Fighting continued throughout the summer, with the ARVN launching a counteroffensive that recaptured Quang Tri Province. The Eastertide Offensive had failed. North Vietnam suffered more than 100,000 killed. But it still controlled more territory in South Vietnam than before and felt it was in a stronger bargaining position at the Paris negotiations.*

Sources: Ngo Quang Truong, *The Easter Offensive of 1972*, 1980; G.H. Turley, *The Easter Offensive: Vietnam 1972*, 1985.

18th ENGINEER BRIGADE

The 18th Engineer Brigade was deployed to the Republic of Vietnam* in September 1965 and remained there until September 1971. It consisted of the 35th, 45th, and 937th Engineer Groups and confined its construction activities to I* and II Corps.*

Source: Shelby L. Stanton, *Vietnam Order of Battle*, 1981.

18th MILITARY POLICE BRIGADE

The 18th Military Police Brigade deployed to Vietnam in September 1966 and was charged with supervision of military police throughout South Vietnam. In addition to traffic control and policing activities, the 18th Military Police Brigade provided security for convoys, highways, and bridges and supervised the evacuation of refugees.*

Source: Shelby L. Stanton, *Vietnam Order of Battle*, 1981.

834th AIR DIVISION

The 834th Air Division, stationed at Tan Son Nhut Air Base* outside Saigon,* provided tactical airlift for Seventh Air Force* operations in South Vietnam. The 834th functioned between its organization in October 1966 to its dissolution in November 1970, by which time most of its aircraft had been handed over to the South Vietnamese Air Force.*

Source: Ray L. Bowers, *The U.S. Air Force in Southeast Asia: Tactical Airlift*, 1983.

Left: During the Vietnam War, comedian Bob Hope continued the practice he had started during World War II of staging shows for U.S. soldiers overseas. In this 1966 photograph, a military police officer stands watch as dancers perform on stage at an amphitheater in Long Binh, South Vietnam.

Below: A GI of the 18th Military Police Brigade on guard on July 28, 1969, at the entrance to Tan Son Nhut Air Force Base outside Saigon. The base also housed the headquarters of the Vietnam National Air Force.

Above: In 1954, President Dwight D. "Ike" Eisenhower refused to provide U.S. military assistance to the besieged French soldiers at Dien Bien Phu. A shrewd military planner who had led the D-Day invasion of Europe in 1944, Eisenhower found the proposed intervention laced with potential problems. Here he is in Great Britain in December 1944.

82d AIRBORNE DIVISION

Although the Joint Chiefs of Staff (*see* Chairman, JCS) considered deploying the entire 82d Airborne Division to Vietnam, only the 3d Brigade ever received such orders, serving in Vietnam between February 18, 1968 and December 11, 1969. Attached to the 101st Airborne Division,* the 3d Brigade fought in I Corps,* primarily in Hue.* Late in 1968 the 3d Brigade was moved down to Saigon* to defend Tan Son Nhut Air Base.*

Sources: Shelby L. Stanton, *Vietnam Order of Battle*, 1981; Leroy Thompson, *The All Americans: The 82nd Airborne*, 1988.

EISENHOWER, DWIGHT DAVID

Dwight D. Eisenhower was born on October 14, 1890, in Denison, Texas. He was a West Point graduate who commanded Allied invasions of Europe during World War II, and was later Army chief of staff, president of Columbia University, and commander of the North Atlantic Treaty Organization's (NATO) forces. Easily defeating Democrat Adlai Stevenson in the 1952 election, Eisenhower saw his presidential role as one of creating equilibrium at home, while keeping the United States involved in world affairs and avoiding nuclear war.

Eisenhower found the stalemate in French Indochina* unacceptable; it would further drain French resources and morale, and undermine the French role in NATO. A French defeat seemed even worse despite Eisenhower's view that France had caused the war by refusing to grant full independence to the Indochinese states; the domino theory* was already current, holding that defeat in Indochina would lead to Communist gains throughout Southeast Asia and the Pacific. Elected on a platform of "liberation" of Communist satellites, Eisenhower had accepted a Korean armistice that left North Korea in Communist hands. He told his cabinet that he could not give Democrats the chance to imitate Republican taunts of "Who lost China?" by demanding "Who lost Vietnam?" There was no way to obtain a French victory without American forces being sent to Vietnam, which Eisenhower opposed. He also vetoed as inflammatory the use of Chinese Nationalist forces from Taiwan (see Chiang Kai-shek). What Eisenhower really wanted was a joint U.S.-British intervention with air support and materiel but no ground troops. The British wanted nothing to do with it, so Eisenhower increased monetary aid to France to about 75 percent of the war's cost.

Despite fervent French requests, Eisenhower limited American military aid to a few aircraft and technicians. He also prepared for a deluge of demands for intervention, which he expected when Dien Bien Phu* fell, by specifying conditions for American involvement: a clear grant of independence to the Indochinese states, British and Southeast Asian participation, congressional approval, and continued French participation under American command. Historians now generally believe that Eisenhower deliberately set conditions that were impossible, believing that the United States must not destroy its anticolonial image. He was thus prepared for pressure from Vice President Richard Nixon,* Secretary of State John Foster Dulles,* and Chairman of the Joint Chiefs of Staff* Admiral Arthur Radford,* even confronting them with the risk of global and nuclear war if the United States were actually to fight in Southeast Asia.

Though Eisenhower avoided direct intervention in 1954, he did not intend to abandon the region, using the domino theory in press conferences to explain Southeast Asia's importance. Trying behind the scenes, but failing, to keep France involved after the fall of Dien Bien Phu, he continued to push his idea of a multilateral effort to save South Vietnam. By September 1954 the United States had created the Southeast Asia Treaty Organization* (SEATO), which Eisenhower hoped would protect the region from further Communist aggression. He also resigned himself to accepting the Geneva Accords* of 1954 partitioning Vietnam, supposedly temporarily. Eventually that "temporary" clause was discarded when the United States refused to participate in the elections promised in the Geneva Accords. U.S. recognition of the government of Ngo Dinh Diem* led to economic and military assistance. Prophetically, while Eisenhower was still in office, a few U.S. advisors went out into the field with the South Vietnamese, exposing themselves to combat and casualties.

Eisenhower's last involvement with Vietnam came as a former president giving advice and support to Lyndon Johnson* during the escalation stage of the conflict. Eisenhower's advice followed his own earlier views: there must be multilateral aid and forces, and the Vietnamese must not depend on American troops but shoulder the bulk of the fighting themselves. While he was consistently a hawk in his approach, urging Johnson to find a way to win, Eisenhower never told Johnson that victory would be easy. He was furious when, in March 1968, Johnson withdrew from the presidential race, ended most bombing, and in effect signaled that he had given up. Dwight D. Eisenhower died on March 28, 1969. RWS

Sources: Stephen E. Ambrose, *Eisenhower*, Vol 2, *President and Elder Statesman*, 1984; Elmo Richardson, *The Presidency of Dwight D. Eisenhower*, 1979; Robert A. Divine, *Eisenhower and the Cold War*, 1981.

Below: On October 29, 1955, a parade in Saigon celebrates the formal establishment of the Republic of Vietnam (South Vietnam). The Geneva Accords of 1954 had provided for the separation of Vietnam. The crowd is marching past the official residence of Ngo Dinh Diem, the newly installed president of the Republic of Vietnam.

ELECTION OF 1955 (SOUTH VIETNAM)

The 1954 Geneva Conference (see Geneva Accords) produced six unilateral declarations, three cease-fire agreements that were signed by the principals, and an unsigned Final Declaration that called for reunification elections to be held between July 1955 and July 1956. Whether any nations present "agreed to" the Declaration or took the election provisions seriously has been hotly debated. What is clear is that Walter Bedell Smith* issued a statement "taking note" of the Declaration and pledging the United States to support it. The Republic of Vietnam* refused to sign, making it clear that it did not consider itself bound by the Declaration.

Neither Ngo Dinh Diem,* the United States, nor France* was enthusiastic about reunification elections, first because northern Vietnam had several million more people than did the South, and second because Ho Chi Minh* had substantial popularity in the South. It was conceivable that he would win a majority vote even in the South. Consequently,

Opposite page: Staff Sergeant Willie Jones, a squad leader with the 82d Airborne Division, keeps watch on the flank during a halt.

Right: During the presidential election of 1967 in South Vietnam, President Nguyen Van Thieu arrested and jailed his political opponent, the lawyer Truong Dinh Dzu, using trumped-up charges of criticizing the "judiciary." In this photograph, Truong Dinh Dzu's wife leads students from the University of Saigon in a demonstration to protest blatant rigging of the election. Dzu had run in the election as the "peace candidate."

Diem, with the strong support of the United States, announced there would be no reunification elections because free elections were impossible. Instead, there would be two plebiscites in the South to decide first whether to abolish the monarchy, and second whether to authorize the drafting of a new constitution. General Edward Lansdale* advised Diem on how to manipulate election machinery to his own benefit, including choosing the color of the ballots— red (signifying good luck) for Diem and green (signifying misfortune) for Emperor Bao Dai.* Lansdale also admonished Diem not to rig the election, stating that receiving 60 percent of the vote would convince Americans that Diem had a legitimate mandate. Such a small winning margin, however, fit neither with Diem's absolutist nature nor with Vietnamese culture. In an election marked by massive fraud, Diem collected 605,000 votes from the 405,000 registered voters in Saigon, and "won" the election with 98.2 percent of the total vote. SF

Sources: George McTurnen Kahin and John W. Lewis, *The United States in Vietnam*, 1967; Stanley Karnow, *Vietnam: A History*, 1983; George C. Herring, *America's Longest War: The United States and Vietnam, 1950–1975*, 1986; John C. Donnell and Charles A. Joiner, eds., *Electoral Politics in South Vietnam*, 1974.

ELECTION OF 1967 (SOUTH VIETNAM)

Justification of U.S. policy in Vietnam often hinged on South Vietnam's being (or becoming) a democracy, necessitating elections for at least a facade of democratic structure. Ironically, Vietnam historically had elected village chiefs, but Ngo Dinh Diem* tampered with this tradition. Nguyen Van Thieu* abolished it—all with American acquiescence. Local elections, however, don't get U.S. headlines like national elections. Although local elections might be more indicative of a meaningful democracy, the United States put its money on national elections. Some argue this "top down" approach made defeat inevitable.

As a result of the Honolulu Conference of 1966,* Nguyen Cao Ky* tried to consolidate power, precipitating the 1966 "Buddhist crisis." Denouncing American imperialism and military rule, Buddhists* brought Ky's government to the verge of collapse, ending the crisis only when they were promised elections for a National Assembly and the presidency. But seeing an electoral structure that would ensure junta control of the National Assembly, the Buddhists boycotted the very elections they had demanded. Ky and Thieu opposed elections because of the remote prospect that the military's candidates would lose, and because both felt the elections were an attempt by the United States to humiliate and depose them. National Assembly candidates and the electorate, despite a large

turnout, were singularly apathetic—possibly because these were the eleventh and twelfth national elections since 1955 and were likely to be no more meaningful than previous ones.

The 1967 presidential election was marked by less voter fraud than the 1955* embarrassment. More accurately, it was "managed" sufficiently to ensure a Thieu-Ky victory (with 35 percent). Buddhist leaders were arrested. Press censorship was tightened. Serious opposition candidates such as General Duong Van Minh* and "neutralists" or "leftists" were banned. All candidates other than Thieu or Ky had to travel together and were at the mercy of the military for transportation. Politically unknown Truong Dinh Dzu,* a semi-peace candidate who got on the ballot by concealing his program until after the screening process, came in second with 17 percent. He was jailed shortly thereafter. There was evidence of coercing voters, multiple voting by military personnel, stuffing ballot boxes, and fraudulent vote counts—a typical "demonstration" election ultimately conducted more for its propaganda value in the United States than anything else. SF

Sources: Frances FitzGerald, *Fire in the Lake*, 1972; Stanley Karnow, *Vietnam: A History*, 1983; Edward Herman and Frank Borhead, *Demonstration Elections*, 1984; John C. Donnell and Charles A. Joiner, eds., *Electoral Politics in South Vietnam*, 1974.

ELECTION OF 1968 (U.S.)

The presidential election of 1968 was one of the stormiest in American history. Although there had been considerable opposition to a third term for President Lyndon B. Johnson,* few people in the Democratic Party had any hope of wresting the presidential nomination from him until after the political disaster of the Tet Offensive* in South Vietnam, when Vietcong* and North Vietnamese troops administered a stunning setback to American forces by proving they still had the will and ability to resist. Senator Eugene McCarthy,* an antiwar Democrat from Minnesota, announced his candidacy for the presidency, and to everyone's surprise won 42 percent of the vote in the New Hampshire primary, an almost unheard-of total against an incumbent president. Four days after the March 12, 1968, New Hampshire primary, Senator Robert F. Kennedy* of New York, another antiwar Democrat, announced his candidacy, and on March 31 Lyndon B. Johnson informed the country in a televised speech that he would not run for reelection.

With Johnson's decision, Vice President Hubert Humphrey* decided to seek the presidency, and the race quickly became a struggle between him and Robert Kennedy. Kennedy's assassination after the California primary on June 6 then left the nomination in Humphrey's hands. He received the nomination after a tempestuous convention in Chicago where Mayor Richard Daley's police brutally attacked antiwar* demonstrators on the streets. Richard M. Nixon* won the Republican nomination after promising a diplomatic solution to the war, and he named Spiro Agnew,* governor of Maryland, as his running mate. Alabama governor George Wallace staged a vigorous third-party campaign based on a military victory in South Vietnam and an end to federal government liberalism. He selected former Strategic Air Command chief Curtis LeMay* as his running mate.

It was a dramatically close election, and Richard Nixon became the next president of the United States. The Democrats had self-destructed because of opposition to the war and the spectacle in Chicago, and George Wallace cut into their strength in the blue-collar districts of the Midwest and Northeast. Nixon received 302 electoral votes and 31,785,480 popular votes, 43.4 percent of the total, to Hubert Humphrey's 191 electoral votes and 31,275,166 popular votes, 42.7 percent of the total. George Wallace took 45 electoral votes, all in the South, and 9,906,473 popular votes, 13.5 percent of the total. Democrats kept control of the House of Representatives by 243 to 192, and the Senate by 58 to 42.

Sources: Richard B. Morris, *Encyclopedia of American History*, 1976; Clark Dougan and Stephen Weiss, *The Vietnam Experience: Nineteen Sixty-Eight*, 1983; Theodore H. White, *The Making of the President, 1968*, 1969.

Below: In the U.S. presidential election of 1968, the Republican candidate Richard M. Nixon defeated the Democratic candidate Vice President Hubert H. Humphrey by a razor-slim margin. On November 6, at his New York City campaign headquarters, Nixon celebrates the victory. To the left of Nixon are daughters Julie and Tricia and Julie's fiancé David Eisenhower. To Nixon's right is his wife Pat.

Above: Daniel Ellsberg, a former U.S. Marine and employee of the Department of Defense during the tenure of Robert McNamara, assembled what became known as the Pentagon Papers and leaked them to the *New York Times.* On July 28, 1971, he testifies against the Vietnam War before a conference of twenty-eight Democratic members of Congress.

Right: Nguyen Van Thieu is inaugurated President of South Vietnam in Saigon on October 31, 1971. Under heavy security, Thieu ignites a ceremonial torch to celebrate the beginning of his second four-year term in office. Representatives from thirty countries attended.

ELECTION OF 1971 (SOUTH VIETNAM)

The South Vietnamese election of 1971 took place in the midst of the Paris peace talks* to end the war. Le Duc Tho,* the representative of the Democratic Republic of Vietnam,* informed Henry Kissinger* that a settlement would be easier to reach if the United States withdrew its support from Nguyen Van Thieu,* president of the Republic of Vietnam.* Vice President Nguyen Cao Ky* and army general Duong Van Minh* were challenging Nguyen Van Thieu for the presidency. The election was scheduled for October 3, 1971. North Vietnam supposed it would be easier to work out a political accommodation with someone other than Thieu. President Richard Nixon,* however, decided to stay with Thieu on the grounds of the need for stability. In the election, Thieu forced the withdrawal of Ky, and Minh then decided not to run, making a sham of the election. Running unopposed, Thieu won another term. Ellsworth Bunker,* the U.S. ambassador, was outraged at Thieu's high-handedness, but there was little he could do about it. The peace negotiations continued to stall over the status of the South Vietnamese government. SF

Sources: Stanley Karnow, *Vietnam: A History*, 1983; George C. Herring, *America's Longest War: The United States in Vietnam, 1950–1975*, 1986; John C. Donnell and Charles A. Joiner, eds. *Electoral Politics in South Vietnam*, 1974.

11th ARMORED CAVALRY

Also known as the Blackhorse Regiment, the 11th Armored Cavalry deployed to Vietnam on September 8, 1966. At peak strength, the 11th Armored Cavalry consisted of a tank troop of 51 tanks, a howitzer battery of 18 155mm howitzers, 296 armored personnel carriers,* and 48 helicopters. By 1970 it had 3,891 personnel attached to it. Most of its efforts took place in III Corps,* especially in War Zone C* in Tay Ninh Province. In January 1969 the 11th Armored Cavalry received its first detachment of M551 Sheridan tanks. Between April 1969 and June 1970 the 11th Armored Cavalry was under the control of the 1st Cavalry Division,* and in 1970 it participated in the Cambodian incursion (*see* Operation Binh Tay). The 11th Armored Cavalry left Vietnam on March 5, 1971.

Sources: Shelby L. Stanton, *Vietnam Order of Battle*, 1981; Michael D. Mahler, *Ringed in Steel: Armored Cavalry, Vietnam, 1967–68*, 1986.

11th INFANTRY BRIGADE

See 23d Infantry Division

ELLSBERG, DANIEL

Daniel Ellsberg was born in Chicago on April 7, 1931. His father was a structural engineer and his mother was a musician. In 1952 he graduated summa cum laude from Harvard with a degree in economics. Two years later he was commissioned a first lieutenant in the Marine Corps,* where, according to Sanford J. Ungar, author of *The Papers and the Papers* (1972), he "developed an authentically military approach to America's international responsibilities." In 1959 Ellsberg joined the Rand Corporation* and became a specialist on game theory and risk in nuclear war. Eager to get in on decisions relating to Vietnam, he moved to Washington in August 1964 and became one of Defense Secretary Robert McNamara's* whiz kids, writing speeches and lobbying in support of the hawkish viewpoint on Vietnam. He later confessed that at times he furnished McNamara "ten alternative lies" to use in tight situations with the press.

In July 1965 Ellsberg volunteered to help Major General Edward Lansdale* evaluate the success of the pacification programs (*see* Rural Reconstruction) in South Vietnam. In 1967 McNamara commissioned Ellsberg as a member of a research task force to write a history of American-Vietnamese relations from 1945 through 1967.

Ellsberg's hypothesis was that President John F. Kennedy* had been led by bad advice to deepen American commitments in Vietnam. However, Ellsberg found that

Kennedy acted against the counsel of many of his top aides. After looking at the whole picture of presidential actions and the advice presidents had received, he concluded that "to a large extent it was an American President's war. No American President, Republican or Democrat, wanted to be the President who lost the war." In 1968 he gave advice in Defense Department meetings that resulted in the bombing halt in November. Ellsberg began going to antiwar meetings and writing Senator Robert F. Kennedy's* policy statements on Vietnam during the 1968 presidential primaries. He also gave advice to president-elect Richard Nixon's* National Security advisor Henry Kissinger.*

Beset with guilty feelings because of his involvement in policy decisions and the pacification program, Ellsberg in the fall of 1969 began using a copying machine to reproduce a Pentagon study. By making it public he hoped that "truths that changed me could help Americans free themselves and other victims from our longest war." Ellsberg gave a copy to Senator William Fulbright,* chairman of the Senate Foreign Relations Committee.* His increasingly public role caused Rand to pressure him to resign, which he did in late 1969, before becoming a senior research associate at MIT's Center for International Studies.

After engaging in a whirlwind of antiwar activity, he became frustrated at how little influence he was able to exert. President Nixon's invasions of Cambodia (*see* Operation Binh Tay) and Laos (*see* Lam Son 719) angered him and in March 1971 triggered his leaking of the Pentagon Papers* to the *New York Times.* The *Times* began publishing excerpts and articles based on the Papers on June 13, 1971. Although the Nixon administration secured an injunction against further *Times* publication, the *Washington Post* and the *Boston Globe* continued to make the documents public. On June 30 the Supreme Court decided in favor of the *Times* and the *Post*, ruling that the First Amendment presumed that there would be no prior restraint on the press.

On June 29, 1971, Ellsberg was indicted for converting government property to his personal use and illegally possessing government documents. Later, the grand jury charged him with conspiracy, theft, and violation of the Espionage Act. In the midst of the proceedings on May 11, 1973, Judge Matthew Byrne Jr. dismissed all charges because of government misconduct, especially illegal wiretapping, breaking into the office of Ellsberg's former psychiatrist, and Nixon's attempt to influence Byrne by offer-

Above: Because of the mountainous jungles and swamps of South Vietnam, armored tank warfare did not play a major role in the Vietnam War until the end stages when the North Vietnamese Army swept down and conquered South Vietnam. In January 1969, a Sheridan tank of the 11th Armored Cavalry moves through heavy woodlands on the Michelin Plantation in South Vietnam.

Above: General Paul Ely, the French commissioner general and supreme commander in Indochina, joins Ngo Dinh Diem, the new president of South Vietnam, in watching the tricolor flag of France descend a flagpole in Saigon and the red-striped yellow flag of Vietnam replace it in 1954.

ing him the directorship of the Federal Bureau of Investigation. Ellsberg remained active in the antiwar movement,* becoming a vocal proponent of strategic arms limitations during the 1980s; today he continues to write and lecture about American foreign policy. JR

Sources: Daniel Ellsberg, *Papers on the War*, 1972, and *Secrets: A Memoir of Vietnam and the Pentagon Papers*, 2002; Peter Schrag, *Test of Loyalty*, 1974.

ELY, PAUL HENRY ROMAULD

Born in France* in 1897, Paul Ely was a highly respected military officer who commanded French forces in Indochina* in 1954 and 1955. Educated at the Lycée de Brest, École Spéciale Militaire de Saint Cyr, and the École Supérieure de Guerre, he worked his way through the military command system. In 1941 to 1942 Ely was a

commanding officer with the Tenth Chasseurs, and served for the rest of the war as representative of the Allied High Command with the resistance movement. In 1945 Ely became commander of the infantry. He became military director to the minister of national defense in 1946, commander of the Seventh Region in 1947, and inspector general of the armed forces in 1948. Between 1950 and 1953, Ely served as the French representative to NATO, and late in 1953 was named commander in chief of the French Armed Forces in Indochina.

It was a lost cause. In 1954, as the final stage of the struggle began, Ely wanted American air support, and on March 20 he flew to Washington, D.C., to request assistance. There he warned Admiral Arthur B. Radford* and other American leaders that the "destruction of Dien Bien Phu* was likely." Direct American assistance was not forthcoming, and French forces at Dien Bien Phu surrendered on May 7, 1954. At the Geneva Accords* in 1954, Vietnam was divided into two countries, and American support replaced the French presence in the South. Ely departed South Vietnam in the spring of 1955. He served as chief general staff marshal until January 1959 and then as chief staff officer for defense until his retirement in 1961. Paul Ely died on January 19, 1975.

Sources: *International Who's Who, 1964–1965*, 1965; Joseph Buttinger, *Vietnam: A Dragon Embattled*, 2 vols., 1967.

ÉLYSÉE AGREEMENT OF 1949

The Élysée Agreement was signed on March 8, 1949, by the puppet emperor Bao Dai* and French president Vincent Auriol in Paris. The agreement declared that Vietnam was an independent nation, but that France* still had authority over defensive, financial, and diplomatic matters there. The agreement also promised to incorporate Cochin China* into a unified Vietnamese nation. Bao Dai realized that the Élysée Agreement really did nothing to promote real independence, while the Vietnamese Communists under Ho Chi Minh* viewed it as a sellout and realized that any real hope of securing independence peacefully from the French was a pipe dream.

Sources: Stanley Karnow, *Vietnam: A History*, 1983; Donald Lancaster, *The Emancipation of French Indochina*, 1961; Joseph Buttinger, *The Smaller Dragon: A Political History of Vietnam*, 1958.

ENCLAVE STRATEGY

The American buildup in Vietnam precipitated a major debate within the Lyndon B. Johnson* administration about strategic commitments in Indochina.* People like Admiral Ulysses Sharp* and General William Westmoreland* wanted

Above: Vincent Auriol, in his Paris office on March 20, 1951, served as president of France from 1947 to 1954. He signed the Élysée Agreement with Vietnamese emperor Bao Dai on March 8, 1949, declaring Vietnam an independent nation, but retaining French authority over financial and diplomatic matters there.

Left: Economist Alain Enthoven, at the blackboard, during a briefing on the Strategic Air Command budget at the Rand Corporation Research Institute in September 1958.

a rapid buildup and independent combat operations by U.S. personnel to "search and destroy"* the enemy in a war of attrition.* Secretary of State George Ball,* on the other hand, was suspicious about the entire American commitment in the region. Edward Lansdale* wanted the major American commitment to be directed at counterinsurgency* and pacification (*see* Rural Reconstruction) efforts. Initially, American forces secured cities and strategic military positions in a static defensive posture, but Westmoreland quickly abandoned that approach for the enclave strategy, which was something of a compromise. Under the enclave strategy, American forces would conduct aggressive patrolling near their defensive enclaves. After gaining experience, U.S. troops would be permitted to conduct offensive operations in support of ARVN (*see* Army of the Republic of Vietnam) forces within a fifty mile radius of their enclaves. Officially that strategy lasted only a year, but it was eroded almost immediately as Westmoreland succeeded in deploying the 173d Airborne* to the Central Highlands* and in initiating limited search-and-destroy operations. In 1967, sensing a stalemate, Paul Warnke,* head of International Security Affairs at the Pentagon, unsuccessfully recommended the readoption of the enclave strategy to reduce casualties and costs, and to return the combat burden to the South Vietnamese. SF

Sources: Peter Poole, *Eight Presidents and Indochina*, 1978; William R. Corson, *The Betrayal*, 1968; Bruce Palmer Jr., *The 25-Year War*, 1984; Andrew F. Krepinevich Jr., *The Army and Vietnam*, 1986; Harold K. Johnson, "The Enclave Concept: A 'License to Hunt,'" *Army* (April 1968).

ENTHOVEN, ALAIN

Alain Enthoven was born in Seattle, Washington, on September 10, 1930. He received a degree in economics from Stanford University in 1952, studied under a Rhodes Scholarship at Oxford in 1954, and received a Ph.D. in economics from MIT in 1956. Enthoven was an economist and systems analyst for the Rand Corporation* between 1956 and 1960, and after the election of John F. Kennedy* he joined the Department of Defense as a deputy assistant secretary. At the height of the Vietnam War, Enthoven was a senior assistant to Secretary of Defense Robert McNamara,* and he continually offered his opinion that the real issue in Vietnam was nationalism, not Communism, and American bombing, money, and personnel would not stem the tide. Enthoven saw the war as a struggle between American public opinion, which was gradually souring on the war, the corruption of the South Vietnamese regime, and the growing strength of the Vietcong* and North Vietnamese. Consequently, Enthoven opposed the American troop buildup as futile. When the Democrats were ousted from the White House in the election of 1968,* Enthoven left Washington and joined Litton Industries as a vice president and later as president of Litton Medical Services. In 1973 he became the Marriner S. Eccles Professor of Management at Stanford Institute for International Studies, where he still teaches.

Sources: *Who's Who in America, 1984–1985*, 1985; Stanley Karnow, *Vietnam: A History*, 1983; Alain C. Enthoven and K. Wayne Smith, *How Much Is Enough? Shaping the Defense Program, 1961–1969*, 1971.

Below: Marine F-4 Phantoms enroute to targets in support of ground-force Marines operating in northern I Corps. The photo was taken from a TA-4F Skyhawk trainer.

F-4 PHANTOM II

The F-4 Phantom II, a twin-engine, all-weather, tactical fighter-bomber (see Fighters), was one of the principal aircraft deployed to Southeast Asia. Capable of operating at speeds of more than 1,600 miles per hour and at altitudes approaching 60,000 feet, the first F-4s were deployed in August 1964 to participate in the air war over Vietnam by the United States Navy.* On August 6, 1964, in response to the Gulf of Tonkin incident,* five F-4Bs from the USS *Constellation* attacked North Vietnamese patrol boat bases. Operating from the USS *Ranger*, the USS *Coral Sea*, and the USS *Hancock*, the F-4 aircraft expanded their operations beginning on April 3, 1965, when fifty F-4Bs attacked a road bridge 65 miles south of Hanoi.

The first United States Air Force* (USAF) F-4s were deployed to Southeast Asia in early 1965. They became involved in significant air operations during the summer. For instance, on July 10, 1965, two F-4Cs shot down two MiG-17 fighters over North Vietnam with Sidewinder missiles. Additionally, in October 1965 the first RF-4s, aircraft equipped with reconnaissance equipment, were deployed to the theater. Operations expanded thereafter; by March 1966 seven USAF F-4 squadrons were in South Vietnam and three were in Thailand.* The buildup of F-4 aircraft and operations continued thereafter.

The air fighting over North Vietnam lasted from spring 1965 to January 1973, but included a long period between April 1968 and March 1972 when strikes in the North were halted or severely restricted by presidential decree. Consequently, regular air fighting by F-4s took place for approximately forty-three months during the seven-and-a-half year conflict. During their operations USAF F-4s were credited with 107.5 air victories, Navy F-4s with 38, and Marine Corps* F-4s with 1. A total of 511 F-4s from all services were lost in Southeast Asia from June 6, 1965, through June 29, 1973. Of these, 430 were combat losses, while 81 resulted from aerial or ground accidents. RDL

Sources: Francis K. Mason, *Phantom: A Legend in Its Own Time*, 1984; *Modern Fighting Aircraft: F-4 Phantom III*, 1984.

F-5

The F-5 was designed for smaller allied nations. Designed late in the 1950s by Northrup, the first production F-5 flew in 1963. Twelve F-5s arrived in Vietnam on October 23, 1965, for combat testing. Most of the F-5 aircraft were used

by the Vietnamese Air Force.* The United States supplied them with fifty-four F-5s, and they leased another eighty from Taiwan, South Korea, and Iran in 1973. The F-5 was armed with two 20mm guns, two AIM-9B Sidewinder missiles at the wing tips, and three 1,000-pound and two 750-pound bombs.

Sources: Ray Wagner, *American Combat Planes*, 1982; Anthony Tambini, *F-5 Tigers Over Vietnam*, 2000.

F-104 STARFIGHTER

The F-104 Starfighter was produced in 1956, after several years of development, by the Lockheed Aircraft Corporation as a lightweight air-superiority jet fighter to replace the aging F-100 force of Korean War–era aircraft. The F-104 entered the operational aircraft inventory of the United States Air Force* on January 26, 1958, and saw service in Southeast Asia throughout the 1960s. The first twenty-four F-104s deployed to Southeast Asia on a temporary basis beginning on April 7, 1965, with one squadron standing alert at Kung Kuan, Taiwan (*see* Chiang Kai-shek), and another at Da Nang,* South Vietnam. From Da Nang these aircraft could strike targets in both South and North Vietnam. The F-104s sustained heavy losses from enemy ground fire. They were relieved of the air defense commitment on November 21, 1965, and redeployed in December 1965. A permanent contingent of F-104s was deployed to Southeast Asia on July 5, 1966, in response to the escalation of the American

commitment there. Accordingly, F-104Cs from the 479th Tactical Fighter Wing were assigned to the 435th Tactical Fighter Squadron at Udorn Royal Thai Air Base, Thailand.* These aircraft were heavily involved in combat operations throughout the theater until they were replaced in July 1967 by more efficient F-4D aircraft. During their operations in Southeast Asia F-104s numbered a maximum of twenty-four aircraft. They flew a total of 7,083 sorties;* eight aircraft were lost, and there were no confirmed MiG victories. RDL

Sources: Marcelle S. Knaack, *Encyclopedia of U.S. Air Force Aircraft and Missile Systems, Vol. 1, Post–World War II Fighters*, 1978; Martin W. Bowman, *F-104 Starfighter*, 2001.

Above: On March 1, 1966, a U.S. F-5 "Skoski Tiger" fighter drops a bombload on a suspected Vietcong position.

Below: An F-104 Starfighter at Tan Son Nhut Air Base in 1965.

Right: Major Ralph L. Kluster directs 20mm fire from his F-105 Thunderchief at a MiG-17 enemy fighter on June 3, 1968. Its left wing badly damaged after taking hits, the MiG then crashed.

Below: Camouflaged F-105 Thunderchiefs armed with white phosphorous rockets and AGM-45 Shrike missiles head to targets in North Vietnam in May 1966.

F-105 THUNDERCHIEF

The F-105 Thunderchief, a supersonic, tactical fighter-bomber (*see* Fighters) capable of delivering conventional and nuclear weapons, was one of the workhorses of the United States Air Force* (USAF) in Southeast Asia. The first F-105 production aircraft was delivered to the Air Force in May 1958; it incorporated the distinctive swept-forward air-intake ducts in the wing-root leading edges that reduced turbulence in front of the tail section. The aircraft also had an internal bomb bay and positions for ordnance on wing pylons, as well as a six-barrel 20mm cannon that fired 6,000 rounds per minute. The F-105 was ultimately modified for several special missions: all-weather and night bombing, air interdiction, aerial reconnaissance, air-superiority operations, and air-to-air and air-to-ground missile operations.

The F-105D, a model of the aircraft that began entering the Air Force inventory in the early 1960s, was the principal aircraft used for strikes on heavily defended ground targets in North Vietnam during the Southeast Asian conflict. These aircraft began to see action in the theater in early 1965, as F-105Ds, flying from Korat Air Base, Thailand,* and striking targets north of the 17th parallel (*see* Geneva Accords). While participating in tactical air strikes over South Vietnam in 1966 and subsequent years, they carried out more strikes against the North than any other USAF aircraft. Operating against ever-stiffening defenses, the F-105Ds also led in battle losses for USAF combat aircraft. These fighter aircraft, as well as the F-105F and F-105G configurations that began arriving in Vietnam in 1966,

operated in the theater until 1973. During the eight years of operations the maximum number of F-105 aircraft in Southeast Asia flew 137,391 sorties* and scored 27.5 confirmed victories over enemy aircraft, while sustaining 334 combat losses. RDL

Sources: J.C. Scutts, *F-105 Thunderchief*, 1981; Larry Davis, *F-105 Thunderchief*, 1998.

F-111

Manufactured by General Dynamics, the F-111 was the most controversial aircraft in the American arsenal during the Vietnam War. Capable of delivering either nuclear weapons or conventional payloads of four 2,000-pound bombs or twelve to twenty-four 750-pound bombs, the F-111 was highly accurate because of its computerized APQ-113 attack radar and AJQ-20 inertial bombing-navigational system. The F-111 had terrain-avoidance capabilities and could fly long distances at low altitudes, avoiding enemy radar contact. General Dynamics produced the F-111 and subcontracted the Navy's F-111B to Grumman. Its top speed was 1,453 miles per hour with a combat ceiling of 56,000 feet and a combat radius of 1,330 miles. On March 17, 1968, six F-111As arrived in Thailand* to attack targets in North Vietnam. After only fifty-five missions and three aircraft losses, operations were halted and the remaining F-111As returned to the United States. Serious doubts existed about the aircraft's structural stability, and all of them were retested. Between September 1972 and February 1973 two squadrons of fifty-two F-111As were redeployed and flew more than 3,000 missions. Seven were lost. All F-111 fighters were retired in 1996.

Sources: Ray Wagner, *American Combat Aircraft*, 1982; Anthony Thornborough, *F-111: Success in Action*, 1990.

FAC

See Forward Air Controller

FALL, BERNARD

Author of *The Viet Minh Regime* (1956), *Le Viet Minh, 1945–1960* (1960), *Street Without Joy* (1961), *The Two Viet Nams* (1963), *Viet Nam Witness* (1966), *Hell in a Very Small Place* (1966), and *Last Reflections on a War* (1967), and editor with Marcus Raskin of *The Viet Nam Reader* (1967), Bernard Fall was a recognized authority on Vietnam and the wars fought there. Born in 1926, Fall served in World War II with the French underground until the liberation, and then with the French Army until 1946. He was a research analyst at the Nuremberg War Crimes Tribunal and worked for the United Nations in the International Tracing Service. He came to the United States in 1951 on a Fulbright Scholarship, earning an M.A. and Ph.D. in political science at Syracuse University. He first went to Vietnam in 1953 to do research for his doctorate and returned for the sixth time in 1966 on a Guggenheim Fellowship. When not in Vietnam, he was a professor of international relations at Howard University.

Above: This F-111 fighter had a variable geometry "swing wing." When the wing was fully extended, the fighter achieved very slow speeds for landing. With its wing swept fully back, the F-111 had a delta-wing configuration that allowed for extremely high speeds at tree-top level. The F-111 carried an enormous bombload, which, during Operation Linebacker and Operation Linebacker II in 1972, included laser-guided weapons. The now retired F-111 was one of the fastest aircraft in the U.S. inventory and was known for its speed, accuracy, and reliability.

Below: A child soldier of the Khmer National Armed Forces (FANK) takes a break, in February 1974. In fourteen more months, the Khmer Rouge would march into Phnom Penh, the capital city of Cambodia, seize control of the government, and defeat FANK. Pol Pot, the new leader of what was then called Kampuchea, would inaugurate a reign of terror that would kill as many as 2 million people.

Fall was a complex man with a passion for Vietnam. He saw both wars there as tragedies. Although deep concern about Communism in Indochina* softened his criticism of both France* and the United States, Fall held to the justice of an Indochina free of foreign domination, whether it be French, American, Chinese, or Russian. A critic of both French colonialism and American intervention, Fall distinguished clearly between the policies of governments and the human beings caught in between. Fall combined meticulous scholarship with a humane writing style. He wanted to see the war as it was experienced by those condemned to fighting it, and he wrote sensitively about their travails. He loved the Vietnamese people and had great respect and admiration for the forces of the Vietminh* and National Liberation Front (NLF; *see* Vietcong). On February 21, 1967, Bernard Fall was killed in the field with a United States Marine Corps* unit when an NLF booby trap* exploded. SF

Sources: *New York Times*, February 22, 1967; Bernard Fall, *Hell in a Very Small Place*, 1966, and *Last Reflections on a War*, 1967.

FANK

The acronym FANK stood for Forces Armées Nationales Khmeres, or the Khmer* National Armed Forces. FANK was the military arm of the pro-American Lon Nol* government that took over Cambodia* after the collapse of Norodom Sihanouk's* neutral government in March 1970. FANK was defeated in 1975 when Pol Pot's* Vietnamese-trained Khmer Rouge* troops seized the Cambodian capital of Phnom Penh.

Sources: Clark Dougan and David Fulghum, *The Vietnam Experience: The Fall of the South*, 1985; William Shawcross, *Sideshow: Kissinger, Nixon, and the Destruction of Cambodia*, 1979.

FELLOWSHIP OF RECONCILIATION

The Fellowship of Reconciliation (FOR) was an important, though not very publicly visible, influence on the civil

rights and antiwar movements of the late 1950s and the 1960s. Formally founded in Great Britain in 1914 and then on November 11, 1915, in the United States, the current worldwide FOR has organizations in twenty-seven countries, with an international secretariat in Brussels. The American FOR, headquartered in Nyack, New York, is a religious, predominantly Christian, pacifist association of persons who "recognize the essential unity of all humanity and have joined together to explore the power of love and truth for resolving human conflict." FOR publishes a magazine called *Fellowship* eight times a year as well as other literature. During World War I, World War II, the Korean War, the Vietnam War, and the years between those wars, FOR opposed conscription and provided support and encouragement for conscientious objectors and others wishing to protest war or refuse participation in the military. For many years, perhaps the leading spokesperson for FOR, and FOR's most well-known pacifist, was A.J. Muste* (1885–1967). Muste was among the early organizers of FOR, along with such notable reformers as Jane Addams, Scott Nearing, and Norman Thomas. In the fall of 1964 Muste and other pacifists issued the first public statement endorsing draft* resistance during the Vietnam War: the Declaration of Conscience Against the War in Vietnam. Muste died in February 1967 while helping to organize large antiwar* demonstrations that were held on April 15.

Throughout its existence, FOR's greatest influence appears to have come from its enduring ability to facilitate, and provide leadership for, the formation of other reform organizations, including, for example, the War Resisters League, American Civil Liberties Union, National Conference of Christians and Jews, Congress of Racial Equality, and American Committee on Africa. During the late 1950s FOR supported the civil rights movement in the South by participating in demonstrations and conducting workshops on nonviolence and civil disobedience. Prominent black civil rights leaders, such as James Farmer, Martin Luther King Jr.,* and Bayard Rustin, were members of FOR. Similarly, FOR supported, provided leadership for, or helped to educate new organizations, such as Clergy and Laity Concerned* and Another Mother for Peace, that were formed to protest the war in Vietnam. After the Gulf of Tonkin incident* in 1964, FOR rallied more than 3,000 clergy to endorse a statement saying, "In the Name of God Stop It." FOR members conducted long-term vigils and mounted hunger strikes against the draft and the war, and in 1970 held a monthlong series of Daily Death Toll "die-ins" in front of the White House. During the war FOR especially sought to establish ties with Buddhist* pacifists and "third force" activists in South Vietnam. Thich Nhat Hanh, a Vietnamese Buddhist monk, first came to the United States in 1965 under FOR sponsorship. FOR supported and housed the U.S.

Liaison Office for the Vietnamese Buddhist Peace Delegation. After the war FOR continued to protest the mistreatment of Buddhist pacifists and other antiwar and antimilitary activists in Vietnam. While most of the youth-based organizations as well as many others of the Vietnam era had disappeared by 1975, FOR remained active, in part because it did not deviate from its nonviolent beliefs, it had always had a reform agenda larger than the Vietnam War, and its members have been, as a group, older and more committed to pacifism as a religious philosophy. FOR membership in 1986 was 33,000 in the United States (up from some 23,000 in 1973), and currently FOR has established groups in more than forty countries and on every continent. JK

Sources: Vera Brittain, *The Rebel Passion*, 1964; Nancy Zaroulis and Gerald Sullivan, *Who Spoke Up? American Protest and the War in Vietnam, 1963–1975*, 1984.

FIELDS OF FIRE

Fields of Fire is the title of James Webb's 1978 novel about Vietnam. The plot follows a platoon of Marines slogging through the rice paddies and jungles outside of An Hoa, suffering violent death, horrible injuries, wretched living conditions, and poor morale because they see no rationale for the sacrifice, no reason to die. The central character is Will Goodrich, a Harvard student who enlists in the Marine Corps* Band only to be assigned by mistake to Vietnam.

Sources: James Webb, *Fields of Fire*, 1978; Philip D. Beidler, *American Literature and the Experience of Vietnam*, 1982.

5th INFANTRY DIVISION

The 1st Brigade of the 5th Infantry Division arrived in Vietnam on July 25, 1968, from Fort Carson, Colorado. The brigade had been involved in riot-control activities in the United States early in 1968, and then had undergone reorganization as a mechanized unit. When the brigade arrived in Quang Tri of I Corps* in July, it had more than 1,300 vehicles. The brigade came under the direction of Lieutenant General Richard G. Stillwell and the XXIV Corps,* and worked closely with the 3d Marine Division* and the 101st Airborne Division* (Airmobile) in the northern provinces of South Vietnam. The 1st Brigade of the 5th Infantry Division left Vietnam on August 27, 1971.

Sources: Shelby L. Stanton, *Vietnam Order of Battle*, 1981, and *The Rise and Fall of an American Army: U.S. Ground Forces in Vietnam, 1965–1973*, 1985.

Below: Lieutenant General Louis W. Walt of the Marine Corps talks to a Marine from the 2d Battalion, 5th Marines, near the Demilitarized Zone. Walt was privately critical of William Westmoreland's strategy of attrition in Vietnam. Walt felt U.S. policy needed to have more emphasis on pacification programs.

5th MARINE DIVISION

In March 1966 the Defense Department reactivated the 5th Marine Division and thus revived a unit that had fought on Iwo Jima, participated briefly in the occupation of Japan, and ceased to exist in early 1946. When the Johnson* administration decided not to call up the 4th Marine Division from the Organized Reserve, Major General Robert E. Cushman Jr.* moved over from his skeletal Reserve headquarters and began drawing on the additional 55,000 volunteers and draftees authorized for the Marine Corps* by Congress* in late 1965.

The first battalion of two regimental landing teams (RLTs) eventually committed to Vietnam landed north of Dong Ha* in September 1966, and by April the other two battalions of the 26th Marines were ashore and under the operational control of the 3d Marine Division.* The 26th Marines (RLT-26) won a Presidential Unit Citation for their role in the defense of Khe Sanh* in 1968 and later that year were attached to the 1st Marine Division* for operations with the 27th Marines (RLT-27), also of the 5th Marine Division, south of Da Nang.* The 27th Marines left I Corps* for Camp Pendleton in September 1968, but RLT-26 remained and conducted ten special landing force operations along the coast of southern I Corps until its return to California in the early fall of 1969. The 5th Marine Division disbanded in November of that year. DA

Sources: Donald L. Evans, "USMC Civil Affairs in Vietnam: A Philosophical History," in *The Marines in Vietnam, 1954–1973*, 1983; Shelby L. Stanton, *Vietnam Order of Battle*, 1981.

5th SPECIAL FORCES GROUP

Various Special Forces* groups had served tours of duty in South Vietnam during the early 1960s; it was not until October 1964 that the 5th Special Forces Group was formally deployed there. The 5th established its headquarters at Nha Trang.* It consisted of groups of A, B, and C teams. Each twenty-man C team was in charge of three B teams, which controlled four twelve-man A teams. The A teams were the operational units used to head Special Forces camps, attack and infiltrate enemy units, reconnoiter enemy positions, and call in air strikes. There were four 5th Special Forces companies, one assigned to each of the four Corps Tactical Zones. The 5th Special Forces Group was also responsible for directing the work of Montagnard* tribal units of the Civilian Irregular Defense Group* (CIDG) camps. Between October 1964 and October 1969 the 5th Special Forces Group grew from 950 U.S. personnel and 19,000 irregular troops to 3,740 U.S. troops and more than 40,000 irregulars. The 5th Special Forces Group also directed the Eagle Flight* program; developed the Long Range Reconnaissance Patrol* program; supervised Projects Delta,* Sigma,* and Omega;* and helped transform many CIDG units into Regional Forces,* Popular Forces,* and South Vietnamese ranger units. The 5th Special Forces Group was withdrawn from South Vietnam in March 1971. At the time of its withdrawal, the 5th had also been responsible for a wide variety of civic action and pacification projects (*see* Rural Reconstruction). The 5th Special Forces

Group claimed to have established 49,902 economic aid projects in Vietnam, 34,334 educational projects, 35,468 welfare projects, and 10,959 medical projects.

Sources: Shelby L. Stanton, *Vietnam Order of Battle*, 1981, and *Green Berets at War*, 1985; Francis J. Kelly, *U.S. Army Special Forces,1961–1971*, 1973; Andrew F. Krepinevich Jr., *The Army and Vietnam*, 1986.

FIGHTERS

A variety of fighters and fighter-bombers were used by the American military forces during the Vietnam War. The mainstay of the United States Air Force* attack was the Republic F-105 Thunderchief,* or the "Thud." F-105s flew more combat missions over North Vietnam than any other Air Force craft, but by the end of the 1960s they were being replaced by the F-4 Phantom II.* The F-4 was also used extensively by the U.S. Marines* and the Navy.* The Navy and the Marines also made wide use of the A-4 Skyhawk* as well as the A-6 Intruder.* The Air Force also used the F-100 Super Sabre and the A-7 Corsair II,* for close air support. In 1967 the Air Force introduced six General Dynamics F-111s* to Southeast Asia, but three of them were lost almost immediately because of severe technical difficulties. They were not ready for widespread use in Vietnam until September 1972. Until the cease-fire in January 1973, the F-111s flew more than 3,000 combat missions over North Vietnam.

Sources: Carl Berger, ed., *The United States Air Force in Southeast Asia, 1961–1973*, 1977; William W. Momyer, *Airpower in Three Wars*, 1978.

FINAL OFFENSIVE

See Ho Chi Minh Campaign

1st AVIATION BRIGADE

Headquartered at Tan Son Nhut Air Base* (May 1966–December 1967 and December 1972–March 1973) and Long Binh* (December 1967–December 1972), the 1st Aviation Brigade carried out aerial reconnaissance, medical evacuations (*see* Medevac), tactical assaults, fire support, and cargo handling. At its peak strength, the 1st Aviation Brigade consisted of 7 aviation groups, 20 aviation battalions, 4 air cavalry squadrons, 641 fixed-wing aircraft, 441 Cobra AH-1G* attack helicopters, 311 CH-47* cargo helicopters, 635 OH-6A observation helicopters, and 2,202 UH-1* utility helicopters. The 1st Aviation Brigade also worked actively with the Rural Development Program in relocating Vietnamese civilians during pacification (*see* Rural Reconstruction).

During its deployment to Vietnam the 1st Aviation Brigade had eight commanders: Brigadier General George P. Seneff (May 1966–November 1967); Major General Robert R. Williams (November 1967–April 1969); Brigadier General Allen M. Burdett Jr. (April 1969–January 1970); Brigadier General George W. Putnam Jr. (January 1970–August 1970); Colonel Samuel G. Cockerham (acting; August 1970); Brigadier General Jack W. Hemingway (August 1970–September 1971); Brigadier General Robert N. Mackinnon (September 1971–September 1972); and Brigadier General Jack V. Mackmull (September 1972–March 1973).

Source: Shelby L. Stanton, *Vietnam Order of Battle*, 1981.

Above: Captain Vernon Gillespie Jr. of the U.S. Army Special Forces questions a captured Vietcong soldier in South Vietnam on January 1, 1964.

Below: A U.S. F-100 fighter fires a Bullpup missile at an enemy position on January 1, 1966.

1st CAVALRY DIVISION (AIRMOBILE)

Originally activated in 1921, the 1st Cavalry Division fought (dismounted) in the Pacific during World War II and later in Korea. In 1965 the division's flag was taken from Korea and presented to the experimental 11th Air Assault Division, which became the 1st Cavalry Division (Airmobile). (The former 1st Cavalry Division, still in Korea, became the new 2d Infantry Division.) The division was deployed to South Vietnam in September 1965 and was the first full division to arrive in-country. It was almost immediately in battle in the Ia Drang Valley.* The division won a Presidential Unit Citation for its fierce fighting. During 1966 and 1967 elements of the division were engaged in numerous actions throughout the II Corps* Tactical Zone. Initially committed to operations in Binh Dinh Province in early 1968, the bulk of the division was hurriedly recommitted to the Battle for Hue* and then to the relief of the Marine position at Khe Sanh.* Later in the year the division served in the A Shau Valley* before being shifted to protect the northern and western approaches to Saigon.* The division was in constant action throughout 1969, and in 1970 was part of the American–South Vietnamese force that invaded Cambodia (*see* Operation Binh Tay). Most of the division left South Vietnam in April 1973. The remaining 3d Brigade returned to Fort Hood, Texas, in June.

As the Army's first airmobile division, the 1st Cavalry Division pioneered air-assault tactics. It was considered one of the Army's elite units in Vietnam, highly valuable because of its extreme mobility. The 1st Cavalry participated in the following operations and battles: Ia Drang Valley* (1965), Masher/White Wing/Thang Phong II,* Paul Revere II,* Davy Crockett, Crazy Horse, Thayer, Irving,* Pershing,* Tam Quan (1967), Hue* (1968), Pegasus/Lam Son #207 (Khe Sanh),* Delaware/Lam Son #216,* Montana Raider, Toan Thang* #43, and Toan Thang #44. The division suffered more than 30,000 casualties during the war. RSB III

Sources: Shelby L. Stanton, *Vietnam Order of Battle*, 1981, and *The Rise and Fall of an American Army: U.S. Ground Forces in Vietnam 1965–1973*, 1985; Edward Hymoff, *The First Air Cavalry Division*, 1985; Kenneth D. Mertel, *Year of the Horse—Vietnam: First Air Cavalry in the Highlands*, 1968.

I CORPS

Also known as "Eye" Corps, I Corps was one of the four major military and administrative units of the South Vietnamese government in the 1960s and early 1970s. In particular, I Corps was the Central Vietnam Lowlands administrative unit and consisted of the five northernmost provinces: Quang Tri, Thua Thien, Quang Nam, Quang Tin, and Quang Ngai. The headquarters of I Corps was located in Da Nang.* The major cities in I Corps were Hue,* Quang Tri City, Da Nang,* and Chu Lai. During the Vietnam War the major military units of the ARVN (see Army of the Republic of Vietnam) were the 1st Airborne Division,* 1st Division, 2d Division, 3d Division, and the 20th Tank Regiment. I Corps was also known as Military Region 1. During the course of the Vietnam War the following U.S. military units fought in I Corps: 9th Marine Amphibious Brigade,* 3d Marine Division,* III Marine Amphibious Force,* 1st Marine Division,* Americal Division,* XXIV Corps,* 1st Cavalry Division (Airmobile),* 101st Airborne Division,* 1st Brigade, 5th Infantry Division,* and 82d Airborne Division.*

An estimated 78,000 enemy troops operated in I Corps. According to allied intelligence, the Communist order of battle included about 49,000 North Vietnamese Army (NVA) regulars, perhaps 6,000 main force Vietcong (VC), over 12,000 VC guerrillas, and about 11,000 supply and administrative personnel. Almost half of these troops, some 42 infantry and 11 support battalions, were believed to be massed along or near the DMZ, while the second largest concentration—16 combat and 4 support battalions—threatened Da Nang in Quang Nam.

Sources: Harvey H. Smith et al., *Area Handbook for South Vietnam*, 1967; Shelby L. Stanton, *Vietnam Order of Battle*, 1981.

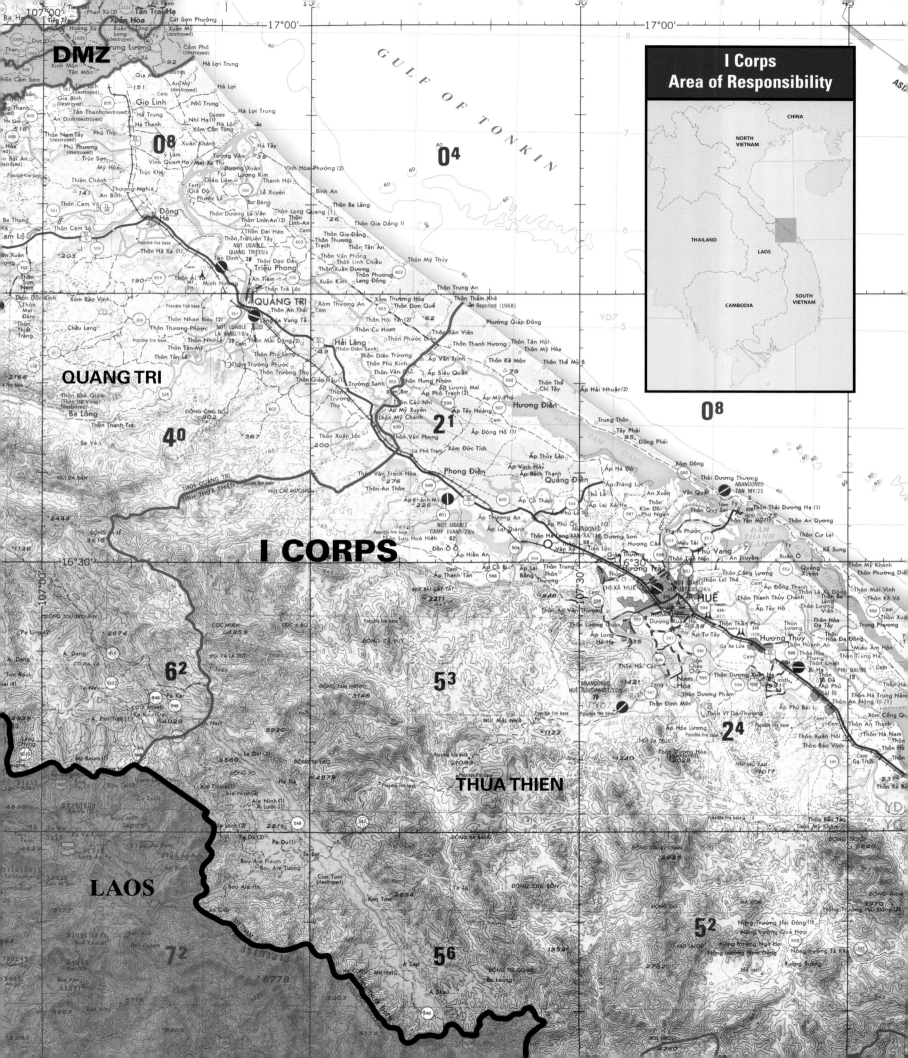

I FIELD FORCE, VIETNAM

Because of the increasing commitment of U.S. combat units in 1965, Military Assistance Command, Vietnam* created a provisional field force in II Corps* on August 1, 1965. It was known as Task Force ALPHA. Field Force, Vietnam grew out of Task Force ALPHA, and it was renamed I Field Force, Vietnam on March 15, 1966. It was a corps*-level military organization, with operational control over United States and allied forces in II Corps, but it did not carry the corps name because it was functioning inside an existing South Vietnamese corps zone. I Field Force, Vietnam was headquartered at Nha Trang.* It left Vietnam on April 30, 1971, and was replaced by the Second Regional Assistance Command. The following individuals commanded I Field Force, Vietnam: Lieutenant General Stanley R. Larsen (March 1966–March 1968); Lieutenant General William R. Peers (March 1968–March 1969); Lieutenant General Charles Corcoran (March 1969–March 1970); Lieutenant General Arthur Collins Jr. (March 1970–January 1971); and Major General Charles P. Brown (January 1971–April 1971).

Source: Shelby L. Stanton, *Vietnam Order of Battle*, 1981.

Below: In 1966, helicopters of the 1st Infantry Division unload troops for a patrol operation in South Vietnam.

1st INFANTRY DIVISION

The 1st Infantry Division, known as the Big Red One, was first organized during World War I and saw extensive action during World War II in Africa, Sicily, Italy, France, Germany, and Czechoslovakia. The division arrived in Vietnam on October 2, 1965, and served in III Corps.* It fought Vietcong* forces in Binh Dinh and Tay Ninh provinces in 1966, fought in War Zone C* during 1966 and 1967 in Operation Attleboro* and Operation Junction City,* and during the Tet Offensive* defended Saigon* against Vietcong attack. The 1st Infantry Division participated in Operations Birmingham, Hollingsworth, Lexington III,* El Paso I and II,* and Toan Thang II.* Throughout much of 1969 the division worked in pacification programs (*see* Rural Reconstruction) and late in 1969 initiated Operation Keystone Bluejay equipment transfers in preparation for departure from Vietnam. The 1st Infantry Division worked closely with the ARVN (*see* Army of the Republic of Vietnam) 5th Division to train its troops for combat operations. The division left Vietnam on April 15, 1970.

Sources: Shelby L. Stanton, *Vietnam Order of Battle*, 1981, and *The Rise and Fall of an American Army: U.S. Ground Forces in Vietnam, 1965–1973*, 1985.

FIRST LOGISTICAL COMMAND

The First Logistical Command arrived in Vietnam from Fort Hood, Texas, on March 30, 1965, and established its headquarters in Saigon.* At first it was responsible for logistical support of all U.S. military units in II,* III,* and IV Corps,* with the United States Navy* in charge of logistics in I Corps.* In 1968, when U.S. Army* units became active in I Corps, the First Logistical Command assumed jurisdiction there as well. Eventually the First Logistical Command moved its headquarters to Long Binh,* and it controlled the major subordinate commands of United States Army Support Commands at Saigon,* Cam Ranh Bay,* Qui Nhon,* and Da Nang.* The First Logistical Command supervised the maintenance of the transportation system in South Vietnam; supervised ammunition, petroleum, and food supply depots; and delivered supplies to American troops on military bases and in the field. The First Logistical Command was consolidated with the United States Army, Vietnam* on June 26, 1970. The First Logistical Command left Vietnam on December 7, 1970, and returned to Fort Bragg. The United States Army, Vietnam assumed control of logistical support.

Sources: Joseph M. Heiser Jr., *Logistic Support*, 1974; Shelby L. Stanton, *Vietnam Order of Battle*, 1981.

Left: Private First Class Milt D. Longstaff of Company B, 2d Battalion, 28th Infantry, 1st Infantry Division, searches a Vietcong tunnel in the Iron Triangle during Operation Cedar Falls in January 1967.

Below: Captain Charles S. Robb of the 1st Marine Division begins his first day of patrol in South Vietnam on May 18, 1968. Robb is the son-in-law of the late President Lyndon B. Johnson. Robb later went on to become a U.S. Senator from Virginia.

1st MARINE AIRCRAFT WING

The 1st Marine Aircraft Wing, which contained nearly 500 aircraft and helicopters, was established at Da Nang* in May 1965 and remained in Vietnam until April 1971. The 1st Marine Aircraft Wing was in charge of all Marine aircraft operations in Vietnam.

Sources: Jack Shulimson, *U.S. Marines in Vietnam: An Expanding War 1966*, 1982; Jack Shulimson and Charles M. Johnson, *U.S. Marines in Vietnam: The Landing and the Buildup 1965*, 1978.

1st MARINE DIVISION

Known as the Old Breed in the Marine Corps,* the 1st Marine Division was widely recognized as one of the best military units in the United States. It was formally activated on February 1, 1941, as the first division in the history of the U.S. Marine Corps. During World War II the 1st Marines saw action on Guadalcanal, New Guinea, New Britain, Peleliu, and Okinawa, and fought in Korea as well in 1950 and 1951. In August 1965 the headquarters of the 1st Marines was moved from Camp Pendleton, California, to Okinawa. Its 7th Marine Regiment deployed to Chu Lai* in I Corps* in August 1965, and the 1st and 2d battalions of its 1st Marine Regiment deployed there in August

Right: In 1968, U.S. troops from the 1st Signal Brigade engage in a reconnaissance mission on the road connecting Tay Ninh and Dau Tieng, South Vietnam. Soldiers nicknamed the road "Ambush Alley" because of the frequency of surprise Vietcong attacks on U.S. forces.

and November 1965. The 1st Marine Division arrived formally in Vietnam on February 23, 1966, and was stationed at Chu Lai. In November 1966 division headquarters was transferred to Da Nang.* By midsummer 1966 1st Marine Division strength exceeded 17,000 men.

During 1966 the 1st Marines fought small engagements and patrolled widely in I Corps, and at the beginning of 1967 the division was evenly divided between Chu Lai and Da Nang. Fighting was especially intense in the Phuoc Ha Valley between Chu Lai and Da Nang. In March and April 1967 the 1st Marines participated in Operations Union I and II* in Quang Nam and Quang Tin provinces, and in September it fought against North Vietnamese Army* (NVA) and Vietcong* forces during Operation Swift in the same region. In 1968 the division fought in the Tet Offensive* and at the Battle of Hue,* patrolled and fought widely along the border of Thua Thien and Quang Nam provinces in Operation Houston, and kept Highway 1 (*see* "Street Without Joy") open, especially along the Hai Van Pass.* It also engaged in Operation Mameluke Thrust in central Quang Nam Province. Early 1969 found the 1st Marine Division fighting the Vietcong and NVA in Operation Taylor Common in Quang Nam Province. It also patrolled widely throughout An Hoa and Que Son valleys, protecting access routes to Da Nang. The 1st Marines had settled into a string of firebases and strongpoints stretching from Da Nang's Monkey and Marble mountains, west to Hill 55, and then on to the An Hoa basin's "Arizona Territory."

The 1st Marine Division received two Presidential Unit Citations, the Vietnamese Cross of Gallantry with Palm, and a Republic of Vietnam* Civil Actions Award. Twenty of the division's Marines, two of its corpsmen, and one Navy chaplain received the Medal of Honor, and President Nixon* appeared at the 1st Marine Division's nationally televised return to Camp Pendleton in April 1971. DA

Sources: *The Marines in Vietnam, 1954–1973*, 1974; R. Robert Moskin, *The U.S. Marine Corps Story*, 1982; Edwin H. Simmons, *The Marines in Vietnam*, 1974; Shelby L. Stanton, *Vietnam Order of Battle*, 1981, and *The Rise and Fall of an American Army: U.S. Ground Forces in Vietnam, 1965–1973*, 1985.

1st SIGNAL BRIGADE

Because of the increasing size and complexity of the U.S. military forces in Vietnam, the Department of the Army created the Strategic Communications Command Signal Brigade, Southeast Asia on April 1, 1966. This unit, which was under the operational control of the United States Army, Vietnam* was redesignated the 1st Signal Brigade on May 26, 1966.

In the fall of 1965 General William Westmoreland* had formally protested the "fragmentation of command and control of Army Signal Units" above the field-force level. The creation of the 1st Signal Brigade solved this problem by bringing all long-lines communications under its control and the control of the theater commander in Vietnam. By the end of 1968 the 1st Signal Brigade was larger than divisional size. It was composed of six signal groups, twenty-two signal battalions, and more than 23,000 men. It was the largest signal organization that the United States had ever deployed to a combat theater.

The 1st Signal Brigade provided a secure voice and message-transmission system throughout all of South Vietnam and linked that system to Thailand* and to the Department of Defense's worldwide communications network. This network provided cable, line-of-sight, tropo-spheric-scatter, and satellite communications support to all U.S. military units—Army,* Navy,* Marine,* Air Force,* and Coast Guard.* By 1970 the communications system was so highly refined that direct-distance dialing was possible even into the most remote areas. DLA

Source: Thomas M. Rienzi, *Vietnam Studies: Communications-Electronics, 1962–1970*, 1972.

FISHHOOK

The "Fishhook" referred to a geographical region in Cambodia* approximately fifty miles northwest of Saigon.* American military and political officials had long suspected that the Central Office for South Vietnam (COSVN), the central headquarters of the Vietcong,* was located in the Fishhook, although the Central Intelligence Agency* and other intelligence officers doubted it. Nevertheless, the Fishhook was a sanctuary for Vietcong and North Vietnamese Army* (NVA) forces attacking South Vietnam, and in 1970 President Richard Nixon* made the region the central thrust of the Cambodian "incursion" (*see* Operation Binh Tay). A major objective of the invasion of Cambodia was to destroy Vietcong and NVA supplies. On May 1, 1970, the invasion of the Fishhook was under way, with tanks and armored personnel carriers* of the 11th Armored Cavalry* crossing the border and helicopters dropping the 1st Air Cavalry* into the area. They established fire-support bases throughout the Fishhook and

then used those bases to launch search-and-destroy* operations, although their major objective was to locate COSVN and major supply caches. During the second week of May the 25th Infantry Division* invaded the "Dog's Head," a region approximately 30 miles southeast of the Fishhook. The 9th Infantry* also joined the invasion. President Nixon ordered American troops to confine themselves to military activity within 35 miles of the Cambodian border. During the invasion U.S. troops captured 15 million rounds of ammunition, 143,000 rockets, 14 million pounds of rice, 23,000 weapons, 62,000 grenades, 5,500 mines, and 200,000 antiaircraft rounds. They also destroyed "The City"—11,700 Vietcong bunkers. Still, they did not locate the COSVN, and the invasion triggered a storm of protest in the United States as well as the Kent State University* disaster. JEW

Sources: Samuel Lipsman et al., *The Vietnam Experience: Fighting for Time*, 1983; William Shawcross, *Sideshow: Kissinger, Nixon, and the Destruction of Cambodia*, 1979.

Below: Tanks and armored personnel carriers from the 11th Armored Cavalry take positions to lead 6,500 U.S. troops and 3,500 ARVN soldiers in an invasion of the Fishhook region of Cambodia, approximately 50 miles northwest of Saigon on May 2, 1970. Unexpectedly, they encountered little resistance.

"FIVE O'CLOCK FOLLIES"

At 5:00 PM daily in downtown Saigon* the Joint United States Public Affairs Office (JUSPAO) briefed reporters on the previous day's events. They were dubbed the Five O'Clock Follies because of the general atmosphere of confusion, difficulties in presenting detailed information providing an overview of the war, and growing suspicion that the briefings overestimated National Liberation Front (*see* Vietcong) losses and understated its successes while doing just the opposite with U.S. gains and losses. Briefing data was compiled at Tan Son Nhut* airfield's "Pentagon East" by the Military Assistance Command, Vietnam* Office of Information (MACOI). Although the briefings were intended to be comprehensive, several problems made the communication of information difficult. First, both MACOI and the press focused almost exclusively on U.S. operations. MACOI usually treated ARVN (*see* Army of the Republic of Vietnam) operations as adjunct to American operations, and the press, if it reported on ARVN at all, usually did so in negative terms. Western reporters seldom attended ARVN briefings held across the street from JUSPAO offices. Second, it was impossible to discuss an unconventional war in the typical terms of "lines," "fronts," and "advances"; yet this was what the military, press, government officials, and public were conditioned to expect. Third, the war was being fought episodically throughout the country, making the development of a comprehensive picture impossible. The media's "spot news" demands produced a war du jour—Khe Sanh* one day, Tay Ninh, My Lai,* or An Loc* the next. Fourth, MACOI was dependent on information from the field, which might be incomplete, inaccurate, or unavailable. Fifth, most MACOI personnel had no field experience in Vietnam and seldom, if ever, ventured outside of Saigon. Sixth, the war was such that reporters generally didn't know which questions to ask. Those who knew did not attend the "Follies." They were in the field getting answers for themselves. Seventh, military personnel, straining already difficult relationships, generally regarded the press as a necessary evil. This became most evident during the Tet Offensive.* Reporters were incredulous at General William Westmoreland standing on the grounds of the American embassy, surrounded by Vietcong* bodies, claiming victory. Since most reporters lived in Saigon's comfortable and previously safe confines feeding off MACOI handouts, they had little experience with actual combat. What they saw was disconcerting, contradicting what they were told in the Follies. SF

Sources: Frances FitzGerald, *Fire in the Lake: The Vietnamese and the Americans in Vietnam*, 1972; Peter Braestrup, *Big Story*, 1983; Daniel C.Hallin, *The Uncensored War: The Media and Vietnam*, 1986.

FLAK JACKET

A heavy, fiberglass-filled vest worn by U.S. troops in the field during the Vietnam War as a protection against shrapnel, the flak jacket became essential to the public image of the American soldier. Because of the heat of the Southeast Asian climate,* soldiers frequently wore the flak jacket while going sleeveless. The picture of the sleeveless, helmeted soldier, chest covered by the bulky flak jacket, was published or broadcast thousands of times during the Vietnam War.

Source: Al Santoli, *Everything We Had: An Oral History of the Vietnam War by Thirty-Three American Soldiers Who Fought It*, 1981.

FLEET MARINE FORCE, PACIFIC COMMAND

Based in Hawaii, Fleet Marine Force, Pacific Command (FMFPac) was responsible for all U.S. Marine* forces in the Pacific theater and immediately subordinate to the U.S. Navy's* commander in chief of the Pacific Command (CinCPac), who in turn was responsible to Washington. Lacking authority to direct particular operations in Vietnam, FMFPac nevertheless influenced the direction of the war and contributed to its planning, while its chief concerns included overseeing the provision of personnel and materiel to the theater's Marines and thus providing the III Marine Amphibious Force* with an administrative and logistical link to CinCPac. During the Vietnam War there were three FMFPac commanders: Lieutenant General Victor H. Krulak* (1964–68); Lieutenant General Henry W. Buse Jr. (1968–70); and William K. Jones (1970–73). DA

Sources: Allan R. Millett, *Semper Fidelis: The History of the United States Marine Corps*, 1980; Victor H. Krulak, *First to Fight: An Inside View of the U.S. Marine Corps*, 1984.

Above: Amtracs (flat-bottomed military vehicles that move on tracks on land or water) deliver Marines from the 2d Battalion, 3d Marines, to a spot on the coast of the South China Sea approximately 15 miles north of Hue on July 20, 1965. Part of Operation Bear Chain fighting against both Vietcong and NVA positions in South Vietnam, it is the thirty-fourth assault that Pacific Fleet Amphibious Force ships have launched since March 1965.

Above: The antiwar actress Jane Fonda earned the eternal enmity of many Vietnam veterans when she visited Hanoi in July 1972. In this photograph on July 18, 1972, she is visiting the Truong Dinh residential center in the Nai Ba Trung District of Hanoi, North Vietnam.

Below: Jane Fonda sings an antiwar song while sitting behind a North Vietnamese 57mm towed antiaircraft gun in July 1972. During her two-week visit to Hanoi, Fonda taped as many as ten propaganda messages, some broadcast live, for her North Vietnamese hosts. She later expressed regrets, but said that "I did not, have not, and will not say that going to North Vietnam was a mistake."

FLIGHT

A basic organizational element in the United States Air Force* is called a flight. A major usually commanded a flight, composed of five aircraft and their crews, during the Vietnam War. An Air Force squadron* consisted of four flights.

Source: Harry G. Summers Jr., *Vietnam War Almanac*, 1985.

FONDA, JANE

Jane Fonda was born on December 21, 1937, in New York City. Her father, Henry, was a well-known actor and her mother, Frances Seymour, was a socialite who in a fit of depression committed suicide in 1950. Fonda attended Vassar College for two years. She appeared in her first stage role opposite her father in a 1954 production of *The Country Girl* in Omaha, Nebraska. In 1958 she studied method acting under Lee Strasberg at the Actors' Studio. In 1964 Fonda went to France,* where she met and married director Roger Vadim, who tried to mold her into a sex symbol like his previous wife, Brigitte Bardot. He starred Fonda in *The Circle of Love* (1964) and *Barbarella* (1968). The publicity posters for these films were popular pinups for American soldiers in Vietnam. Later, she regretted her nude scenes, explaining that she was only "reacting against the attitude of puritanism I was brought up with."

During 1966 and 1967 Fonda became disturbed at reports on French television that American planes were bombing Vietnamese villages and hospitals. Unhappy with her marriage and genuinely concerned about the war, she returned to the United States and worked with the Free Theater Association, which sponsored satirical antimilitary plays and skits in coffeehouses near military bases all over America. She participated in demonstrations against the war throughout 1969 and 1970, and in February 1971 helped financially support the Winter Soldier Investigation* in Detroit, where more than 100 veterans testified about

atrocities and war crimes that they had either committed or witnessed in Vietnam. Also in 1971, Fonda won an Academy Award for Best Actress for her role in *Klute*.

In the summer of 1972 she went to Hanoi* and spoke with selected American prisoners and to all American soldiers in Vietnam during a radio broadcast. She posed next to an antiaircraft gun used to shoot down American pilots, and journalists, comparing her to Tokyo Rose, dubbed her Hanoi Jane. Her visit to North Vietnam earned her the wrath of American conservatives. In 1978 Fonda won another Academy Award for Best Actress, this time for *Coming Home*. During the early 1980s, with husband Tom Hayden,* Fonda was active in a number of social and economic causes,* as well as starring in "socially aware" films and producing her best-selling book and video, *Jane Fonda's Workout Book*. In the 1990s and early 2000s she was married to media tycoon Ted Turner and claimed to be a born-again Christian. All of that aside, she remains extraordinarily unpopular among Vietnam veterans, a virtual pariah more vilified than Tokyo Rose of World War II fame. In a 2005 autobiography, Fonda remained unapologetic about her opposition to the Vietnam War but confessed to regrets about the way she expressed her opposition, especially in posing for the photographs in front of North Vietnamese antiaircraft installations. JR

Sources: Fred Lawrence Guiles, *Jane Fonda*, 1981; Nancy Zaroulis and Gerald Sullivan, *Who Spoke Up? American Protest Against the War in Vietnam, 1963–1975*, 1984; http://www.imdb.com/name/nm0000404/; Jane Fonda, *My Life So Far*, 2005.

FONTAINEBLEAU CONFERENCE OF 1946

When World War II ended and the Japanese withdrew from Indochina,* the Vietnamese, under Ho Chi Minh,* declared their independence, while the French expressed the intention of returning and reestablishing their imperial apparatus and government. Ho Chi Minh wanted an independent Vietnam with Cochin China,* Annam,* and Tonkin* united under one flag, and although the French at first seemed sympathetic to such an arrangement, with a united and independent Vietnam closely tied economically and politically with France,* they renounced the idea in the spring of 1946 when they established the Republic of Cochin China. Ho went to Paris in June 1946 to negotiate the future of Vietnam, and met with French officials in the Fontainebleau forest outside of Paris. At the conference, the new conservative French government under Georges Bidault* favored a French Union of former colonies tightly connected politically to France, while Ho Chi Minh preferred a much more open arrangement similar to the British Commonwealth of Nations. At the conference they also debated the problem of Cochin China, whose independence Ho viewed as a setback. The conference lasted for more than eight weeks, but

Ho had no satisfaction on unification or independence. He initialed an agreement accepting a temporary modus vivendi, but resented the agreement for the rest of his life. His lifelong passion for the unification of Vietnam reached back to the Fontainebleau Conference of 1946.

Source: Joseph Buttinger, *Vietnam: A Dragon Embattled*, Vol. 2, *Vietnam at War*, 1967.

FORCED-DRAFT URBANIZATION

To deprive the Vietcong* "fishes" of their civilian "sea," the United States developed a policy of depopulating rural areas and creating "free-fire zones."* The displaced population was relocated to "Strategic Hamlets,"* "New Life Hamlets,"* "Really New Life Hamlets," or became refugees* in Saigon,* other cities, or the countryside. Other tactics contributing to rural depopulation included chemical warfare, destruction of Vietcong villages, and general fighting. Before the war approximately 15 percent of the South Vietnamese population lived in cities. By 1970, 40 to 50 percent lived in cities, especially Saigon, with 30 to 35 percent of them temporary or permanent refugees. Such massive uprooting of the population bode ill for "winning the hearts and minds* of the people," especially among peasants committed to ancestor worship and family villages who saw leaving their land as a form of death. Samuel Huntington, in a 1968 issue of *Foreign Affairs*, used the term "forced-draft urbanization"* to describe the counterinsurgency* tactic of

rural population movement. One way to counter the rural revolutionary strategy of the Vietcong was to bring about an accelerated modernization of the Vietnamese economy. Supposedly the modernization of the Vietnamese economy—industrialization and urbanization—would destroy the rationale of Mao Zedong's* "people's wars" (*see* Wars of National Liberation). According to Huntington, "In an absent-minded way, the United States ... may well have stumbled upon the answer to 'wars of national liberation.' The effective response lies neither in the quest for a conventional military victory, nor in esoteric doctrines and gimmicks of counterinsurgency warfare. It is instead forced-draft urbanization and modernization which rapidly brings the country in question out of the phase in which a rural revolutionary movement can ... succeed." SF

Source: Samuel Huntington, "The Bases of Accommodation," *Foreign Affairs*, 46 (July 1968): 642–656.

FORD, GERALD RUDOLPH

Gerald R. Ford was born on July 14, 1913, in Omaha, Nebraska, and was raised in Grand Rapids, Michigan. He attended the University of Michigan on a football scholarship. After graduating he turned down several offers to play professional football and instead attended the Yale Law School. After graduating from Yale in 1940, Ford practiced law briefly before joining the Navy after the Japanese attack on Pearl Harbor. Ford served on the aircraft carrier USS *Monterey* in the Pacific. He returned to

Below: Congressman Gerald R. Ford, Republican from Michigan, meets in the White House with President Richard M. Nixon on July 22, 1970. Four years later, after the resignation of Vice President Spiro Agnew, Nixon nominated Ford to become vice president of the United States. Ford would ultimately become president when Nixon stepped down, and would pardon his former boss for his Watergate foibles.

Opposite page, top: A U.S. Army Cessna Bird Dog plane used for low-altitude reconnaissance flights. The Bird Dogs helped identify enemy positions and relayed the information to U.S. air and ground forces. The relatively slow-moving Bird Dogs frequently experienced heavy small arms fire from enemy troops.

Opposite page, bottom: Members of the 44th Medical Brigade give an emergency blood transfusion to a wounded U.S. soldier on board a medical helicopter in February 1968.

Grand Rapids after the war to practice law, became active in Republican politics, and in 1948 won a congressional seat from the Fifth District in Michigan. Ford was a loyal member of the "Republican team" until 1973, when he was named vice president of the United States, filling a vacancy created by the resignation of Spiro Agnew. House minority leader since 1965, Ford had a reputation as a party regular and a reliable "hawk" concerning the Vietnam War. After Richard Nixon's* resignation in August 1974, Gerald R. Ford became the thirty-eighth president of the United States.

Since 1974 the Paris Peace Accords* had long been violated by both sides, and by autumn North Vietnam was stronger than the South. Still, Gerald Ford received overly optimistic reports from Ambassador Graham Martin* and the Defense Attaché Office.* A Congress that was antiwar and controlled by Democrats limited aid to South Vietnam, preventing its forces from using U.S. equipment and bringing on political and economic woes. North Vietnam launched attacks late in 1974 and a major offensive in March 1975. ARVN (*see* Army of the Republic of Vietnam) forces promptly collapsed. Ford requested $300 million in emergency aid in late January and another $722 million on April 10, alienating many congressmen with the hawkish rhetoric accompanying the request. Ford received only $300 million for evacuating Americans and for use toward "humanitarian purposes." As South Vietnam collapsed, President Ford declared that the war was "finished as far as America is concerned." North Vietnamese forces entered Saigon* on May 1, 1975. Shortly thereafter, when the new Khmer Rouge* government of Cambodia* captured the *Mayaguez* (*see* Mayaguez Incident), an American merchant ship, Ford sent in a contingent of U.S. Marines* to rescue the crew, even though Cambodia had already agreed to release them. Both Ford and Secretary of State Henry Kissinger* wanted to prove that although the United States had suffered a debacle in the Vietnam War, its resolve to maintain a position of strength in Asia was still strong. In the presidential election of 1976, Gerald Ford lost narrowly to Democrat Jimmy Carter. Carter and Ford became good friends and served together as honorary co-chairs of the National Commission on Federal Election Reform in 2001. In 1999, Ford was awarded the Presidential Medal of Freedom by Bill Clinton. In 2001, he was presented with the John F. Kennedy Profiles in Courage Award for his decision to pardon Nixon. Gerald R. Ford died on December 26, 2006, at the age of 93. RWS

Sources: Arnold R. Isaacs, *Without Honor: Defeat in Vietnam and Cambodia*, 1983; Robert T. Hartman, *Palace Politics: An Inside Account of the Ford Years*, 1980; Gerald R. Ford, *A Time to Heal: The Autobiography of Gerald R. Ford*, 1979.

FORRESTAL, MICHAEL VINCENT

Michael V. Forrestal was born on November 26, 1927, in New York City. The son of James Forrestal, the first U.S. secretary of defense, he became an aide to W. Averell Harriman,* working on Marshall Plan affairs, and in 1953 he received a law degree from Harvard. Forrestal practiced law in New York until 1962, when he joined the White House National Security staff. In late 1962 President John F. Kennedy* sent Roger Hilsman* and Forrestal on a fact-finding mission to South Vietnam. Their "balanced" report, delivered early in 1963, struck a middle ground between the embassy's optimism and journalists' pessimism. Forrestal and Hilsman had serious reservations about the ARVN's (*see* Army of the Republic of Vietnam) effectiveness, saw flaws in the Strategic Hamlet Program,* felt Ngo Dinh Diem* was increasingly isolated, and concluded that the United States and South Vietnam were "probably winning," but that the war would "probably last longer than we would like" and "cost more in terms of lives and money than we had anticipated." Their report reinforced doubt about the accuracy of official estimates of progress.

In August 1963 the first "Buddhist* crisis" paralyzed Diem's government as ARVN generals plotted coups. Ambassador Henry Cabot Lodge* requested instructions from Washington, but it was a weekend and most of Kennedy's key advisors were out of town. Forrestal drafted a response with Harriman and Hilsman stating that the United States would no longer tolerate Ngo Dinh Nhu's* influence over Diem and called for the removal of Nhu from power. Otherwise, U.S. support for Diem would end. Kennedy approved the cable but was later enraged when he found out that Secretary of Defense Robert McNamara* and Central Intelligence Agency* director John McCone had not seen it before it was sent. During the Johnson* administration, Forrestal was a member of the White House National Security staff. Believing that the military's war reporting was grossly optimistic and supporting a negotiated settlement, Forrestal fell into disfavor with Johnson, was excluded from policy discussions, and resigned in 1965. He then returned to private law practice, and later founded the American Trade Consortium. Michael V. Forrestal died on January 11, 1989. SF

Sources: Nelson Lichtenstein, ed., *Political Profiles. The Kennedy Years*, 1976; Loren Baritz, *Backfire*, 1985; Michael Maclear, *The Ten Thousand Day War*, 1981.

44th MEDICAL BRIGADE

The 44th Medical Brigade deployed to Vietnam in April 1966 and remained there until 1970, when it was dissolved into subordinate units. The 44th Medical Brigade consisted of the 32d Medical Depot at Long Binh;* the 43d and 55th

Medical Groups in II Corps;* the 67th Medical Group in III Corps;* and the 68th Medical Group in III and IV Corps.* The 44th Medical Brigade was responsible for medical evacuation (*see* Medevac), evacuation hospitals, field hospitals, Mobile Army Surgical Hospitals, convalescent centers, and ambulance detachments.

Source: Shelby L. Stanton, *Vietnam Order of Battle*, 1981.

FORWARD AIR CONTROLLER

The forward air controller, or FAC, had the responsibility of calling in air strikes on enemy positions during the Vietnam War. Usually flying a low-level, low-speed aircraft, such as a single-engine Cessna 0-1 Bird Dog spotter plane, the FAC identified Vietcong* or North Vietnamese positions and relayed the information to attack aircraft, helicopter gunships,* or high-altitude bombers. On the ground, a forward air controller would call in similar information.

Source: Terrence Maitland and Peter McInerney, *The Vietnam Experience: A Contagion of War*, 1983.

Opposite page: IV Corps encompassed the southern-most military region of South Vietnam and included the marshy Mekong Delta south of Saigon. The many rivers and canals in the region enabled rice production, and so the area was the breadbasket for the Vietcong. IV Corps had a higher concentration of Vietcong troops and minimal NVA troops, the opposite of I Corps.

Below: At Tan Son Nhut Air Base near Saigon in 1973, representatives of the United States, South Vietnam, North Vietnam, and the National Liberation Front meet in a four-party joint military conference to work out the details for a release of all prisoners of war held at Loc Ninh.

FOUR-PARTY JOINT MILITARY COMMISSION

One of the provisions of the Paris Peace Accords* was establishment of a Four-Party Joint Military Commission (FPJMC) to supervise the withdrawal of American and allied troops from South Vietnam, implement a prisoner-of-war (POW) exchange, and maintain the existing cease-fire. At the time there were still more than 50,000 American, South Korean, Australian,* and New Zealand* troops in South Vietnam and 587 American POWs* in North Vietnamese prisons. The FPJMC formally came into existence at the end of January 1973 and consisted of representatives from South Vietnam, North Vietnam, and the United States, as well as the National Liberation Front (*see* Vietcong), or Provisional Revolutionary Government of South Vietnam.* The FPJMC dissolved on March 29, 1973. By that time the American and allied forces had been removed from South Vietnam and 587 American POWs had been released. The cease-fire, of course, had not been maintained because the South Vietnamese, Vietcong, and North Vietnamese were still struggling for power.

The problem of American military personnel missing in action had not been resolved, however, and on March 29, 1973, a Four-Party Joint Military Team (FPJMT) replaced the dissolved commission, with the same representation. The FPJMT was far less successful than the FPJMC had been. The Vietcong and North Vietnamese, no longer bothered by any American military presence, refused to cooperate. Not until 1974 did the United States receive any real information, and that came only with the release of two

dozen bodies. The U.S. delegation to the FPJMT withdrew from Saigon* on April 10, 1975, just before the occupation of the city by North Vietnamese and Vietcong forces.

Sources: Stuart A. Harrington, *Peace With Honor*, 1984; Walter Scott Dillard, *Sixty Days to Peace*, 1982; Alan Dawson, *55 Days: The Fall of South Vietnam*, 1977.

IV CORPS

In the 1960s and early 1970s, IV Corps was the southern-most of the four major military and administrative units of South Vietnam. Its headquarters was located at Can Tho in the Mekong Delta.* Also known as Military Region 4 (MR 4), IV Corps was the fourth allied Tactical Combat Zone. It consisted of the following provinces: Chau Doc, Kien Phong, Kien Tuong, Hau Nghia, Kien Giang, An Giang, Vinh Long, Dinh Tuong, Long An, Chuong Thien, Phong Dinh, Vinh Binh, Kien Hoa, Go Cong, An Xuyen, Bac Lieu, and Ba Xuyen. The 7th and 9th ARVN divisions (*see* Army of the Republic of Vietnam) played prominent roles in IV Corps military activities. The U.S. 9th Infantry Division* operated widely throughout IV Corps, attacking Vietcong* units in their strongholds in the Plain of Reeds,* the U Minh Forest, and the Seven Mountains areas.

Sources: Shelby L. Stanton, *Vietnam Order of Battle*, 1981, and *The Rise and Fall of an American Army: U.S. Ground Forces in Vietnam, 1965–1973*, 1985.

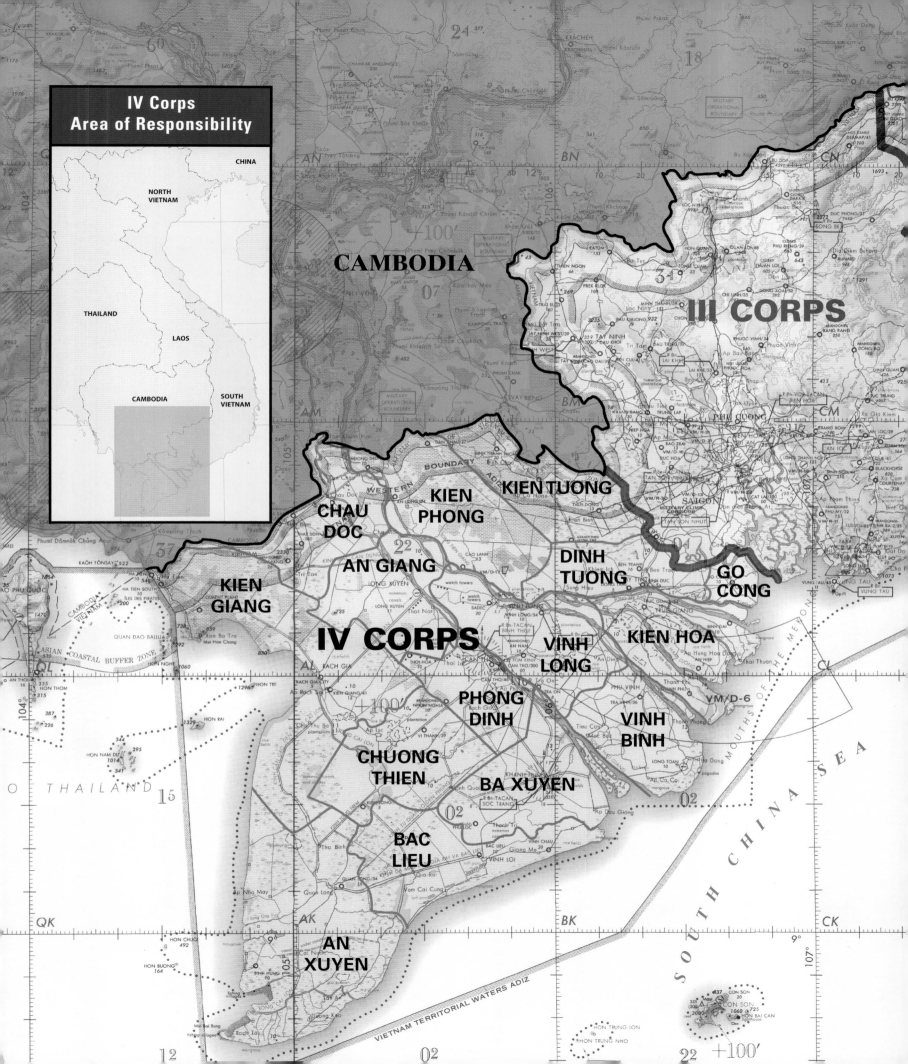

**IV Corps
Area of Responsibility**

CHINA

NORTH
VIETNAM

THAILAND

LAOS

CAMBODIA

SOUTH
VIETNAM

CAMBODIA

III CORPS

SAIGON

KIEN TUONG

KIEN
PHONG

CHAU
DOC

AN GIANG

DINH
TUONG

GO
CONG

KIEN
GIANG

IV CORPS

VINH
LONG

KIEN HOA

PHONG
DINH

VINH
BINH

CHUONG
THIEN

BA XUYEN

BAC
LIEU

GULF OF THAILAND

AN
XUYEN

SOUTH CHINA SEA

VIETNAM TERRITORIAL WATERS ADIZ

Below: A combat tracker team of the 4th Infantry "Ivy" Division climb aboard a UH-1D helicopter in February 1969.

4th INFANTRY DIVISION

Originally formed in 1917, the 4th Infantry Division (nick-named the Ivy Division) served in both World Wars. The division arrived in Vietnam in September 1966 and was immediately committed to action in Operation Attleboro.* During the last months of 1966 and the first half of 1967, most of the division attempted to secure Pleiku and Kontum provinces, while the division's 3d Brigade participated in Operation Junction City.* Later in 1967 the division's 1st and 2d brigades participated in Operation MacArthur* in Kontum Province. In this operation elements of the 4th Division became involved in the bitter Battle of Dak To* in November. The division continued to patrol the Pleiku and Kontum provinces of the western highlands throughout 1968 and 1969. In May 1970 the division entered Cambodia* in support of Operation Binh Tay.* The division left Vietnam in December 1970 as part of the phased American withdrawal. During the course of the Vietnam War, the 4th Infantry Division suffered 16,844 casualties. RSB III

Source: Shelby L. Stanton, *The Rise and Fall of an American Army: U.S. Ground Forces in Vietnam, 1965–1973*, 1985.

4th MARINE DIVISION

The 4th Marines fought at Kwajalein, Saipan, and Tinian, and landed the first waves at Iwo Jima's southern beach-head in 1945. Disbanded in early 1946 but later reactivated as part of the United States Marine Corps* Organized Reserve, the 4th Marine Division was almost completely manned and trained by 1965, and in early February 1966 Major General Robert E. Cushman Jr.* took command of a staff of twenty-nine officers and sixty-nine enlisted men at Camp Pendleton, California, and began planning for mobilization should the Pentagon call the division to active duty. The Johnson* administration, however, gave scant consideration to mobilizing reserve units to fight in Vietnam and in March reactivated the 5th Marine Division,* with its ranks to be filled from the expanding pool of 80,000 volunteers and 19,000 draftees allotted to the Marines that year. DA

Sources: *The Marines in Vietnam, 1954–1973*, 1974; J. Robert Moskin, *The U.S. Marine Corps Story*, 1982.

FRAGGING

During the Vietnam War, "fragging," the murder of overzealous officers and noncommissioned officers (NCOs), was estimated to have taken the lives of 1,016 officers and NCOs. The term arose because the most popular method of eliminating the victim was to roll a fragmentation grenade into his hooch or tent. A fragmentation grenade was preferred because it left no evidence; the murder weapon was destroyed along with the victim. Fragging was not new to the Vietnam War; the mutiny of Roman legions at Pannonia in AD 14 was marked by the murder of unpopular officers, for example. There have been recorded incidences of troops murdering unpopular officers throughout the history of

warfare. In his book *A Soldier Reports*, General William Westmoreland* concluded that fragging "increases when a sense of unit purpose breaks down and esprit de corps fails and when explosives and weapons are loosely controlled."

Except for a brief period in 1967 to 1968, in which soldiers in the Mekong Delta* pooled their money to pay a person to kill a marked officer or NCO, there were few fragging cases until 1969, when there were 96 documented assault cases. That number increased to 209 in 1970 and peaked in 1971 with 333 confirmed fragging incidences and 158 possible fraggings. For the most part, fragging was almost entirely confined to the Army.

By 1969 the war was winding down for American soldiers, who were being pulled out and replaced by South Vietnamese troops in President Richard Nixon's* attempt to "Vietnamize" the war. Many American soldiers failed to see the purpose of dying in a war that their government was presumably abandoning. Many units at the platoon and squad level were refusing to obey orders that they perceived would place their lives in peril. It was this attitude of fear and frustration, combined with drug abuse, racial tension, and the inherent inequality of the military (which afforded some special privileges because of rank), that led to fragging. In some cases, especially in rear areas, there were cases of fragging without apparent provocation. The reason could be as trivial as forcing a soldier to wear his flak jacket,* which could be perceived as harassment. Often the fragging victim would be warned first with the placing of a grenade pin by the entrance of his tent or with an attack using a smoke grenade. If the warning was not heeded, a fragmentation grenade would be used. Fragging was a method soldiers could use to control their officers, who would have to consider the possibility when giving orders. One second lieutenant refused an order to advance on a hill; when his men heard about this, they removed a bounty they had earlier placed on his head. In the end, fragging had become only one symptom of a demoralized Army. MD

Sources: Eugene Linden, "Fragging and Other Withdrawal Symptons," *Saturday Review* (January 1972): 12–17; Richard Holmes, *Acts of War: The Behavior of Men in Battle*, 1985.

FRANCE

France became involved in Vietnam because of the European missionary movement in Asia, which coincided with a rising interest in trade. In the seventeenth century the French founded both a Society of Foreign Missions and an East India Company, two vehicles of *la mission civilisatrice*—the "civilizing mission"—to non-Westerners. In the 1780s a bishop's private expedition restored to power the Nguyen* family, traditional Vietnamese rulers, in the person of Gia Long,* who tolerated Christianity but whose xenophobic heir spurned Western overtures and repudiated

toleration. Incidents in the 1840s and 1850s, combined with religious and business pressure, led to expeditions and the conquest of the Mekong Delta.* After the Franco-Prussian War the French were divided, some arguing that imperialist adventures merely distracted France from recovering Alsace and Lorraine, while others held that colonies could compensate for such losses while providing the raw materials and markets necessary to industry. The latter won, and an 1883 expedition took all of Vietnam amid the disorder following Emperor Tu Duc's death. France even abolished the very name of Vietnam, dividing it into Cochin China,* Annam,* and Tonkin.* Resistance continued into the twentieth century, but the French refused to recognize the depth of Vietnamese nationalism.

Their colonial administration was "direct," using French officials instead of ruling through indigenous institutions. This meant a large French presence, ways of governing that did not fit Vietnam, and Vietnamese mostly only in low-level positions. A few converts collaborated in return for nominal high status. French law destroyed native traditions and was itself discredited by the jailing of political prisoners without trials. France also shifted the fiscal burden to the Vietnamese, imposing taxes and lucrative monopolies on alcohol, rice, and opium. The French and their allies took land, creating a growing and discontented peasantry, and ruthlessly exploited local labor on rubber plantations and in mines. The global depression of the 1930s made the situation worse yet, but on the eve of World War II some 40,000 *colons* ignored the signs of unrest. Their rules for governing were "a lot of subjugation, very little autonomy, a dash of assimilation."

French surrender in 1940 produced a "cataclysm" in Indochina,* undermining the myth of invincibility. Vichy officials, unable to act, were reduced to orating about France as a colonial power. The Free French saw the empire as an integral part of France but could not defend it. French forces in Asia were totally inadequate to resist Japanese advances, which began in June 1940 with the demand that France stop the flow of war supplies through Haiphong to China. Governors had to accept such demands while trying

Above: On July 10, 1954, approximately two months after the fall of Dien Bien Phu, a French soldier and a Vietminh soldier pose together on joint military police duty at Trung-gia, North Vietnam. French and Vietminh representatives were there to work out details of a truce and to arrange for the exchange of prisoners of war.

Above: In 1954, a patrol of French Legionnaires encounters and questions a suspected Vietminh soldier hiding in the jungles near Dien Bien Phu.

to delay the erosion of French control, in July 1941 having to grant bases in southern Vietnam for 50,000 Japanese troops. During the war Japan* encouraged Vietnamese nationalism and, in March 1945, took control of the colony in a coup. Emperor Bao Dai* was persuaded to declare independence, and French rule had ended. The French, however, refused to recognize that fact.

When Japan surrendered in August 1945, the Vietminh* made its play for power, taking Hanoi* and organizing a national congress. Having effective independence, it proclaimed the Democratic Republic of Vietnam* on August 29. Seeking to restore French greatness, de Gaulle in Paris was committed to recovering Indochina and refused to guarantee its independence. He and his officials were ignorant of Vietnam and did not listen to those who understood it. At Japan's surrender he sent what forces he could, shaping future events by his choice of leaders. Jean Sainteny, son-in-law of former governor Albert Sarraut, was a *colon*; High Commissioner Admiral Georges Thierry d'Argenlieu* was rigid; General Jacques Leclerc was ready to fight. The arrival of British troops in the south and the rearming of liberated French soldiers in the north gave Hanoi's *colons* overconfidence; they attacked the Vietnamese and the violence grew. By the end of 1945 Leclerc had regained some control in the south, but the Vietminh ruled the north. It was able to hold elections, even clandestinely in Leclerc's

area. D'Argenlieu's new government in Saigon* included Vietnamese, but the latter had accepted French culture and were unable to rally their countrymen. Yet while Ho Chi Minh,* the Vietminh leader, found no support among French Communists, the United States supported France, and the USSR appeared indifferent. On March 6, 1946, Ho consented to French troops in the north in exchange for independence within the new French Union. But a trip to Paris for confirmation was humiliating; the independence was not real, and he returned to Hanoi to meet militants' anger. That anger and French intransigence made peace impossible. Premier Georges Bidault* allowed d'Argenlieu to use a skirmish at Haiphong late in 1946 as an excuse for a full-scale attack on the Vietminh. Violence escalated, leading to Vo Nguyen Giap's* December 19 call for resistance. The First Indochina War had begun.

Amid changing French cabinets and offers to Ho that would mean his surrender, officials in Paris paid no heed to Leclerc's warning to deal with Vietnamese nationalism. Instead, they bullied Bao Dai into accepting obviously phony independence while ignoring Ho's offer of a neutralist Vietnam. Both sides turned to the battlefield. Vietminh forces operated as guerrillas, and with Mao Zedong's* conquest of China, aid became readily available. As French casualties and costs mounted with no victory in sight, so did discontent at home. Replacement of commanders, even the appointment of renowned General Jean de Lattre de Tassigny,* was of no avail. A deadlock broke when Giap trapped French forces at Dien Bien Phu,* near Laos,* where their supply lines were long and his short. The siege ended in French surrender on May 7, 1954, and, ironically, the next day delegates from nine countries met at Geneva* to begin talks to end the war.

Having suffered more than 90,000 casualties in Vietnam on top of the disasters of World War II, the French were sick of fighting. The diplomatic deadlock ended when Pierre Mendès-France,* dedicated to ending the war, became premier and accepted the Geneva Accords.* These meant a cease-fire, a temporary division of Vietnam at the 17th parallel, and nationwide elections to be held in 1956. The French era in Vietnam had officially ended. RWS

Sources: Joseph Buttinger, *Vietnam: A Dragon Embattled*, 2 vols., 1967; John Cady, *The Roots of French Imperialism in Indochina*, 1954.

FRANCO-VIETNAMESE ACCORDS OF 1946

After World War II, with pressure building in Indochina* for independence as well as anti-imperialist sentiment in France,* representatives of France, Tonkin,* and Annam* signed an agreement on March 6, 1946. This agreement recognized the independence of Tonkin and Annam and admitted them to the French Union, but French troops were not withdrawn. France scheduled elections in Cochin China* to measure public opinion there about unification with Tonkin and Annam. The Franco-Vietnamese Accords of 1946 were followed by the Fontainebleau Conference.*

Sources: James J. Cooke, *France 1789–1962*, 1975; Joseph Buttinger, *Vietnam: A Dragon Embattled*, Vol. 2, *Vietnam at War*, 1967.

FREEDOM BIRDS

"Freedom birds" ("big iron birds") took GIs home to the United States. These were passenger aircraft, most under contract from private charter air services such as World Airways, that ferried troops to and from Vietnam. To Vietnam vets, these freedom birds represented everything desirable in life—home, family, friends, safety, and peace. Soldiers with time left in Vietnam looked upon them longingly and painfully. To those going home, they were the most beautiful sight on earth. Passengers bound for Vietnam were usually neatly dressed, quiet, and somber. A sense of dread and impending doom permeated their plane. Soldiers going home usually had a disheveled look, and many were still dressed in combat fatigues. But the mood was one of relief and celebration.

The rapid passage home has been seen as a contributing force to post-traumatic stress syndrome. In previous wars soldiers had time during the long ocean voyage home to debrief themselves in conversations with other GIs. This enabled them to deal with their war experiences, and allowed them more time to prepare for returning home and

Left and below: French soldiers were still in Vietnam in 1954, eight years after the Franco-Vietnamese Accords were signed. Wounded French soldiers are evacuated from the Battle of Dien Bien Phu in March 1954 (left), and a French Union patrol surveys the enemy's position on April 3.

resuming civilian life. For some Vietnam veterans the return trip was so quick that they literally were in the jungle one day and sitting at home the next, producing profound cultural shock. SF

Sources: Gloria Emerson, *Winners and Losers*, 1976; Rick Eilert, *For Self and Country*, 1983; John Wheeler, *Touched with Fire*, 1984.

FREE-FIRE ZONES

"Free-fire zones," officially designated specified strike zones after 1965, were described by the Defense Department as "specifically designated areas" that had been cleared "by responsible local Vietnamese authority for firing on specific military targets." They were "known enemy strongholds" and "virtually uninhabited by noncombatants." The designation of free-fire zones was an attempt to structure the war along conventional military lines, with enemy forces and friendly forces occupying distinct, separate areas. When forces of the enemy had been thus isolated, they would become the targets of massive American air strikes or artillery fire.

The flaw in the logic of the free-fire-zone concept was that the isolation of enemy forces was accomplished by definition rather than actual physical separation from friendly inhabitants. Longtime strongholds of the Vietcong* were simply defined as being free of noncombatants. Thus anyone residing in these areas was assumed to be the enemy, regardless of sympathies or noncombatant status. In localities not identifiable as Vietcong strongholds, free-fire zones were created by removing noncombatants from the area. Loudspeaker announcements, aerial leaflet drops, and sweeps by infantry units through affected hamlets were among the techniques used, sometimes in combination, to warn inhabitants to evacuate. Forced relocations to create free-fire zones impacted such large numbers of civilians that a senior Agency for International Development official characterized them as "mass movements." Such relocation efforts were rarely effective. Some Vietnamese villagers simply could not read the warning leaflets and others were reluctant to abandon ancestral homes. Nevertheless, once inhabitants had been warned and evacuation efforts made, the affected locality was assumed to be cleared of friendly inhabitants and was designated a free-fire zone. As a military tactic, the use of free-fire zones proved only marginally effective. Much more significant was the impact on American public opinion, where it became synonymous with the indiscriminate use of American artillery and airpower, and thus helped fuel popular doubts concerning America's role in Vietnam. SAK

Sources: Frances FitzGerald, *Fire in the Lake: The Vietnamese and the Americans in Vietnam*, 1972; Raphael Littauer and Norman Uphoff, eds., *The Air War in Indochina*, 1972.

FREE KHMER (KHMER ISSARAK, KHMER SEREI)

The Khmer Issarak (Free Khmer) were anti-French Cambodian guerrillas formed in the western provinces of Battambang and Siem Reap (Angkor) with Thai encouragement. Although loosely affiliated with the Vietminh,* the Khmer Issarak were non-Communist. The significance of the Issarak in opposing French colonialism is debated, but they were considerably weaker than the Laotian Pathet Lao.* In 1954 at Geneva,* the Vietminh tried vainly to have Pathet Lao and Khmer Issarak delegations seated, but both were excluded because of Soviet and Chinese pressure.

Toward the end of World War II, at the request of occupying Japanese forces, Prince Sihanouk* named Son Ngoc Thanh as foreign minister and then premier. With Japan's defeat he attempted to seize power, only to be arrested and exiled by the French, who restored Sihanouk as the nominal head of state. Son Ngoc Thanh joined the Khmer Issarak in Thailand,* but the Issarak dissolved with Cambodia's* independence. Son Ngoc Thanh then formed the Khmer Serei (also meaning "Free Khmer"), an anti-Sihanouk, anti-Communist guerrilla group with operations based in South Vietnam. Throughout the 1960s the Khmer Serei recruited members from non-Communist Phnom Penh elites frustrated by Sihanouk's autocratic rule. Sihanouk's popularity in the countryside, however, made the Khmer Serei, like the Khmer Rouge,* little more than a nuisance for his regime.

Late in 1969 Serei units in South Vietnam "defected" to Sihanouk's army—part of a Central Intelligence Agency* plan to undermine his government, according to Sihanouk. There were contacts between the CIA and the Khmer Serei and American military assistance and training for Khmer Serei troops, but it has not been established that the CIA was behind the defection or Sihanouk's overthrow in 1970. After the coup, Lon Nol* embraced the Khmer Serei, but Son Ngoc Thanh chose initially to remain in the field, receiving Lon Nol's permission to attack Vietcong*/National Liberation Front sanctuaries* in eastern Cambodia. Son Ngoc Thanh then recruited forces from among South Vietnam's Cambodian population. They were trained by U.S. Special Forces* in South Vietnam and flown into Cambodia. Better trained than the Cambodian Army and a potential threat to Lon Nol, these forces were committed to major battles until decimated and eventually wiped out. SF

Sources: William Shawcross, *Sideshow: Kissinger, Nixon, and the Destruction of Cambodia*, 1979; Philippe Devillers and Jean Lacouture, *End of a War*, 1969; Wilfred Burchett, *The Second Indochina War*, 1970; Ben Kiernan, "How Pol Pot Came to Power: A History of Communism in Kampuchea, 1930–1975," Ph.D. diss., Monash University, 1983.

FREE WORLD MILITARY FORCES

"Free World Military Forces" was used to describe those allied nations providing assistance to the Republic of Vietnam* between 1959 and 1975. Including the United States, forty nations provided military and/or economic assistance to South Vietnam. The peak troop commitments from those nations were as follows: 10 from Spain, 30 from Taiwan (*see* Chiang Kai-shek), 550 from New Zealand,* 1,576 from the Philippines,* 7,672 from Australia,* 11,568 from Thailand,* 48,869 from South Korea,* and 540,000 from the United States.

Source: Stanley Robert Larsen and James Lawton Collins Jr., *Allied Participation in Vietnam*, 1975.

FRENCH EXPEDITIONARY CORPS

The French Expeditionary Corps was first sent to Vietnam in the 1880s, ostensibly to protect French Catholic missionaries. Although there were isolated uprisings periodically, France* colonized and controlled Indochina* for more than sixty years with only a few thousand soldiers—70,000 in all of Indochina when World War II began. In 1940 the French Expeditionary Corps fought a brief, bloody war with Japan, but then sat out the war after France surrendered to Germany. At the war's end, Great Britain* quickly rearmed French forces. Although this upset Vietnamese hoping for independence, they were more concerned about their ancient enemy's presence (the Chinese) in northern Vietnam. Consequently, Ho Chi Minh* permitted 15,000 French troops to enter northern Vietnam to hasten the Chinese withdrawal. France, meanwhile, moved to reestablish its Indochina colonies.

Relations between Ho Chi Minh and France deteriorated steadily. On December 6, 1946, the French Navy bombarded Haiphong Harbor and the First Indochina War began. Initially, less than 20,000 French troops confronted fewer than 50,000 Vietminh* guerrillas, but the numbers changed rapidly. French forces increased to 115,000 men in 1947 and 178,000 in 1954 (including about 30,000 Vietnamese who had been integrated into the French Expeditionary Corps). These forces were augmented by 339,000 indigenous forces. Vietminh strength also grew tremendously, to approximately 375,000 by 1954.

In December 1948 General Jean de Lattre de Tassigny* was appointed commander in chief of the French Expeditionary Corps and high commissioner in Indochina. He established the Vietnamese National Army,* which became the largest part of the French Union Forces.* He predicted victory in fifteen months, and in 1950 enjoyed a

FRENCH FORCES AND THE BATTLE OF DIEN BIEN PHU

Below: Vietminh soldiers attack the French military base at Dien Bien Phu in 1954. This photo is now displayed at the Dien Bien Phu museum. The historic Battle of Dien Bien Phu lasted fifty-six days and is considered one of the great battles of the twentieth century. The French defeat led to the signing of the Geneva Accords on July 21, 1954.

Opposite: A wounded Foreign Legion officer leans on sandbags at Dien Bien Phu.

In 1953 General Henri Navarre, commander of French forces in Indochina, made a fateful decision that led to the demise of France's empire there. Tired of fighting the Vietminh in a bloody guerrilla war that drained his army of money and men, and anxious for a conventional, set-piece battle in which overwhelming firepower and superior tactics would prevail, Navarre built an outpost in the mountains near the Laotian border. At the time, Dien Bien Phu was a sleepy village through which Laotian opium traveled on its way to commercial markets, a traffic the Vietminh employed to raise money. Navarre felt confident that if France built an outpost there, he could interdict the opium traffic and deprive the Vietminh of necessary resources. He also anticipated that the Vietminh would launch a direct infantry assault on the base, which he would then repulse with artillery. Navarre expected to inflict massive casualties on General Vo Nguyen Giap's Vietminh army.

From an observation post in the mountains above the valley of Dien Bien Phu, Giap watched dumbfounded as the French built the installation. They seemed to be making every tactical blunder possible. First, they had surrendered the high ground to their enemy. The valley was surrounded by rugged, heavily forested mountains, where Giap began to station his Vietminh troops. The roads into Dien Bien Phu were narrow, exposed, and had little paving or base. Giap would ensure that French supply trucks never reached the base, and his artillery would

rain shells on the French airstrip, making it difficult for aircraft to land. French troops, Giap predicted, would soon find themselves short of food, medicine, and ammunition. Giap could not fathom why Navarre had selected Dien Bien Phu for a base. The Nam Yam River ran through the valley, and rainfall frequently turned the valley floor into a muddy quagmire. After heavy rains, the valley drained slowly. Even in dry weather the valley floor was a thick mesh of heavy, vined brush certain to render French tanks and armored personnel carriers useless. Nor could Giap understand the location of French artillery bases—one was three miles south of the French outpost, a second was one mile to the northeast, and a third was two miles to the north. The French expected the Vietminh to attack in massive human wave assaults, coming out of the mountains and then traversing the valley floor toward the outpost. Navarre was confident that the valley floor would become a killing field where triangulated French artillery and machine guns would decimate the Vietminh.

The entire French strategy, however, rested on a presumption that the Vietminh would have no artillery. Giap surprised them. The Chinese had captured hundreds of American-manufactured 105mm howitzers and 120mm pot-bellied mortars in Korea. They delivered them to Vietminh troops, who disassembled the artillery pieces and had peasant volunteers carry them to the mountains surrounding Dien Bien Phu, where Giap reassembled them. Suddenly, the French at Dien Bien Phu were sitting ducks. Vietminh troops sealed off the highways, while Vietminh artillery turned the airstrip into a lunar landscape of craters. French supplies soon ran thin. On March 12, 1954, Vietminh artillery shells fell on the French artillery posts. Within thirty-six hours, all three French artillery bases had fallen to the Vietminh, leaving the French outpost completely exposed. By that time, Giap had 50,000 combat-hardened troops encircling Dien Bien Phu, with another 100,000 Vietnamese peasant porters keeping them supplied.

Despite their precarious position, the French remained optimistic, confident that the United States would come to their rescue with air strikes on the Vietminh positions. Admiral Arthur Radford, Chairman of the Joint Chiefs of Staff, supported such an intervention, as did Vice President Richard Nixon. They dubbed the proposed rescue Operation Vulture. President Dwight Eisenhower pondered the proposal, but in the end he demurred. The country was war weary after Korea, and Ike could muster little support for intervention in Congress or among American allies. If the air strikes failed, the temptation to introduce U.S. ground troops would intensify, a scenario Eisenhower considered folly—land war in the mountainous jungles of northern Vietnam and Laos. Army Chief of Staff Matthew Ridgway concurred with Eisenhower. An American invasion promised a protracted, bloody conflict with little connection to U.S. national security interests. The French wanted U.S. intervention to save their empire, and Eisenhower did not consent. Vulture was a stillborn operation.

The French failure to secure U.S. intervention guaranteed a Vietminh victory, and Giap had no intention of launching human wave infantry attacks across the valley, where French machine-gun fire would mow them down. In fact, Giap had another surprise for the French. Vietminh soldiers and peasant porters armed with shovels began digging miles of trenches, winding closer and closer to the outpost, rendering French machine guns less and less relevant. Day and night, for months on end, the Vietminh trenches and tunnels inched closer and closer, tightening around the French perimeter and eliminating the open space on which France had based its tactical plan. By April 30, 1954, the French perimeter, at one time longer than fifteen miles, had shrunk to a few thousand yards. Giap's troops outnumbered the French ten to one, and by night the Vietminh trenches had gotten so close that French soldiers could hear small talk and smell cigarette smoke wafting into their bunkers.

On May 6, the same day that the Geneva Conference began to address the Indochina problem, Giap dumped Soviet-made Katyusha rockets on the French position. Amid the explosions, he ordered his infantry to attack. The next day, after bloody hand-to-hand combat, the Vietminh overwhelmed the French outpost and struck the French flag. The Vietminh flag soon fluttered above Dien Bien Phu, and more than 10,000 French soldiers had become prisoners of war. Giap had sustained 22,900 casualties—7,900 killed and 15,000 wounded. French losses were significantly fewer—2,080 dead and 5,613 wounded—but the calculus of victory in combat is rarely statistical. At Dien Bien Phu, France had lost a battle, an army, and its Indochinese empire. The Geneva Conference extended independence to Laos and Cambodia and divided Vietnam at the 17th parallel into two independent nations. Even more significant, colonial peoples around the world celebrated the humbling of a European power.

Sources: Vo Nguyen Giap, *Dien Bien Phu*, 1962; Jules Roy, *The Battle of Dien Bien Phu*, 1965; Bernard Fall, *Hell in a Very Small Place: The Siege of Dien Bien Phu*, 1966; Ralph Wetterhahn, *The Battle of Dienbienphu*, 2002; Howard R. Simpson, *Dien Bien Phu: The Battle That America Forgot*, 2005.

Below: French infantrymen march through the hills near Yen Lao, Vietnam, as part of Operation Seagull to destroy Vietminh outposts and supply dumps in the Ninh Binh region on October 31, 1953.

victory over General Vo Nguyen Giap.* Upon de Lattre's death in January 1952, General Raoul Salan became commander in chief. His command was short-lived but significant, for he reoriented French strategy from maintaining static defensive positions to conducting mobile warfare. He was replaced in 1953 by General Henri Navarre (*see* Navarre Plan), who was perceived as better able to implement this strategy. Navarre had few hopes of winning and simply hoped to keep Laos* and arrange a negotiated settlement. But when Giap invaded Laos, Navarre overextended himself by committing troops to Dien Bien Phu.* Sensing a chance to lure Giap into a pitched battle, Navarre countermanded his mobile-warfare strategy and committed the heart of French forces to a remote, poorly defensible valley surrounded by mountains. Contrary to expectations, the Vietminh hauled in heavy artillery and in 1954 defeated Navarre's French Expeditionary Corps at Dien Bien Phu, destroying the French Empire in Indochina. SF

Sources: Bernard Fall, *Viet Nam Witness, 1953-66*, 1966, and *Hell in a Very Small Place: The Siege of Dien Bien Phu*, 1966; Ellen J. Hammer, *The Struggle for Indochina, 1940–1955*, 1966.

FRENCH UNION FORCES

As World War II began, France* held all of Indochina* with about 70,000 poorly equipped troops. Neither the numbers nor the equipment had changed much by the beginning of the First Indochina War. Trying first to hold its colonies and then to establish (at least in name) autonomous nations within the French Union, France increased the size of the French Expeditionary Corps* (FEC) and, in 1948, established native armies, the largest of which was the Vietnamese National Army* (VNA). FEC and native forces composed the French Union Forces.

By the spring of 1954, when General Navarre (*see* Navarre Plan) ordered the French stand at Dien Bien Phu,* French Union Forces totaled more than 517,000 men, with 178,000 being members of the FEC and the remaining 339,000 being native Indochinese. Building an army of more than 300,000 from scratch in a wartime situation was no small task. Since effective combat leadership cannot be quickly produced, most VNA forces were led by French officers. While this greatly improved their fighting qualities, it hindered French efforts to convince the Vietnamese that France had abandoned its colonialist

intentions. It also dramatized the problem of building independent governments (assuming France was truly willing to do so, which is debatable at best).

The French developed a plan later echoed by American military strategists. French units tied down in pacification, communication, transportation, and static defense postures would be replaced with newly trained VNA units, producing a twofold benefit. Battle-seasoned French soldiers could then carry the fight to the Vietminh* on a larger and more intense scale, and increasing the presence of the Vietnamese officials among the people would improve the Vietnamese sense of independence and will to resist "Communist aggression."

Lack of time and resources doomed the plan to failure. Furthermore, the better units of the VNA were integrated into the FEC to compensate for its shortage in manpower, again undercutting the illusion of Vietnamese independence. Despite limited time and resources, however, the Vietnamese National Army and Vietnamese units in the FEC accorded themselves well in battle, often demonstrating fighting skills and heroism equal to those of their French comrades. SF

Sources: Bernard Fall, *Viet Nam Witness, 1953–66*, 1966, *Hell in a Very Small Place*, 1966, and *Street Without Joy*, 1961; Ellen J. Hammer, *The Struggle for Indochina, 1940–1955*, 1966.

FRIENDLY FIRE

"Friendly fire" was a euphemism used during the war in Vietnam to describe air, artillery, or small-arms fire from American forces mistakenly directed at American positions. The term gained national prominence as the title of C.D.B. Bryan's 1976 book *Friendly Fire*, describing the death of Michael E. Mullen in Vietnam on February 18, 1970. Mullen was killed by an accidental American artillery strike, and the telegram to his parents said that he had been "at a night defensive position when artillery fire from friendly forces landed on the area." In 1983 a television movie starring Carol Burnett further emphasized the term in the public consciousness.

Source: C.D.B. Bryan, *Friendly Fire*, 1976.

FULBRIGHT, JAMES WILLIAM

J. William Fulbright was born on April 9, 1905, in Sumner, Missouri. He graduated from the University of Arkansas in 1925 and then attended Oxford University as a Rhodes scholar. Fulbright took a law degree from the George Washington University Law School in 1934, and then taught law at George Washington and the University of Arkansas between 1934 and 1939. Fulbright became president of the University of Arkansas in 1939, and in 1942 was elected to Congress.* In 1945 he began a stay in the U.S. Senate that lasted for the next thirty years. In 1959 Fulbright became chairman of the Senate Foreign Relations Committee.* Although he helped Lyndon B. Johnson* shepherd the Gulf of Tonkin Resolution* through Congress in 1964, Fulbright soon became an outspoken critic of U.S. policy in Vietnam. Convinced that there was no such thing as "monolithic communism," Fulbright accused Johnson of confusing Communist aggression with nationalism in Vietnam and urged an American withdrawal. Throughout 1967 and 1968 Fulbright held public hearings of the Senate Foreign Relations Committee, giving critics of American policy in Southeast Asia a high-level forum for expressing their views. Fulbright was defeated in the Arkansas Democratic primary for the Senate in 1974 and returned to the private practice of law. J. William Fulbright died on February 9, 1995.

Sources: Tristram Coffin, *Senator Fulbright: Portrait of a Public Philosopher*, 1966; J. William Fulbright, *The Arrogance of Power*, 1966; *Who's Who in America, 1984–1985*, 1985; Randall Bennett Woods, *Fulbright: A Biography*, 1995.

Above: Senator J. William Fulbright, Democrat from Arkansas, was a close friend of President Lyndon B. Johnson. In 1966, however, Fulbright broke ranks with the president and became an outspoken critic of the war in Vietnam. Here Fulbright is photographed as head of the Senate Foreign Relations Committee in 1966.

States should open negotiations with Ho Chi Minh.* In 1967 Galbraith repeated those ideas in his book *How to Get Out of Vietnam*. Also in 1967, Galbraith became the chairman of Americans for Democratic Action, and lobbied against the war from that forum. He endorsed the presidential candidacy of Senator Eugene McCarthy* in 1968. After the war Galbraith continued to be active in Democratic Party politics, spoke on the lecture circuit, and served as a professor emeritus at Harvard. John Kenneth Galbraith died on April 29, 2006. KY

Sources: John Kenneth Galbraith, *A Life in Our Times: Memoirs*, 1981; John S. Gambs, *John Kenneth Galbraith*, 1975; Richard Parker, *John Kenneth Galbraith: His Life, His Politics, His Economics*, 2004; *New York Times*, April 30, 2006.

Above: The Harvard economics professor John Kenneth Galbraith was a key advisor on domestic and foreign policy issues to Democratic presidents John F. Kennedy and Lyndon B. Johnson. After having served as U.S. ambassador to India, Galbraith returned to the United States with a more sophisticated understanding of Asian affairs. During the 1960s, as President Johnson steadily escalated the U.S. presence in Vietnam, Galbraith became increasingly alienated. In 1968 he endorsed Senator Eugene McCarthy of Minnesota for president.

Right: This 1954 image captures a meeting of the Geneva Conference in Switzerland. The delegates represented France, the United States, Great Britain, India, Laos, Cambodia, the Democratic Republic of Vietnam, the State of Vietnam, the Soviet Union, and the People's Republic of China. Their deliberations led to the independence of Laos and Cambodia and the separation of Vietnam at the 17th parallel into the independent Democratic Republic of Vietnam (North Vietnam) and the Republic of Vietnam (South Vietnam).

GALBRAITH, JOHN KENNETH

John Kenneth Galbraith was born on October 15, 1908, on a farm near Iona Station, Ontario, Canada. He graduated from the University of Toronto in 1931 and received a Ph.D. in agricultural economics from the University of California at Berkeley in 1934. Galbraith began teaching at Harvard in 1934, and remained there except for a stint at Princeton (1939–40), government work during World War II, and editorial board of *Fortune* magazine membership (1943–48). He was also U.S. ambassador to India from 1961 to 1963. A prolific writer, Galbraith is the author of *The Affluent Society* (1958), *The New Industrial State* (1967), and *Money* (1977), among other books. A vigorous opponent of the war in Vietnam, Galbraith wrote *A Moderate's View of Vietnam* in 1966, arguing for an enclave* policy of withdrawal to the coastal and urban areas, which the United States could hold with ease. Once those regions were secure, the United

GAVIN, JAMES

James Gavin was born on March 22, 1907, in New York City. He enlisted in the United States Army* in 1924 but the next year was allowed to enroll at West Point, from which he graduated in 1929. Gavin rose through the ranks, and during World War II he won a Silver Star, became an expert in airborne warfare, and was promoted to lieutenant general. In 1961 President John F. Kennedy* named Gavin ambassador to France,* a post he held until 1963. During the Vietnam War Gavin became one of the few American military figures to voice real misgivings about U.S. policy there. In 1966 Gavin testified before the Senate Foreign Relations Committee* and urged the Johnson* administration to adopt the "enclave strategy"*—stop escalating the war and confine American troops to easily defensible positions

in the major Vietnamese cities and coastal locations. In 1968 Gavin published a book, *Crisis Now*, and maintained illusions that he could seek the presidency, but those hopes remained unrealized. Unbowed, he continued to urge a de-escalation of the conflict. James Gavin died on February 23, 1990.

Sources: James Gavin, *Crisis Now*, 1968; Thomas Powers, *Vietnam: The War at Home*, 1984; Thomas Booth, *Paratrooper: The Life of General James M. Gavin*, 1994.

GENEVA ACCORDS OF 1954

After the defeat of French forces at the Battle of Dien Bien Phu* in 1954, an international convention met in Geneva, Switzerland, between May 8 and July 21, 1954, to determine the political future of Indochina.* Delegates from the United States, the Soviet Union,* the People's Republic of China,* Great Britain,* France,* India, the State of Vietnam, the Democratic Republic of Vietnam,* Laos,* and Cambodia* attended the meetings. For a time the conference tried to work out some method of reuniting North and South Korea,* but all efforts failed. What the conference did manage to do was draft a number of complicated political arrangements for Vietnam. The American delegation was headed by W. Bedell Smith.*

The accords divided Vietnam at the 17th parallel into two countries: South Vietnam (Republic of Vietnam*) and North Vietnam (Democratic Republic of Vietnam). With the division in place, the Geneva Accords imposed a cease-fire throughout Vietnam as well as cease-fire provisions for the peaceful withdrawal of French forces from North Vietnam and Vietminh* forces from South Vietnam. New foreign troop placements were prohibited throughout Vietnam, and all troops were to be withdrawn from Laos and Cambodia. Finally, provisions were made for free elections in both North and South Vietnam in 1956, with the goal of reunification and the elimination of the artificial barrier at the 17th parallel. An International Supervisory Commission comprised of representatives from India, Canada, and Poland was established to monitor compliance with the accords. Although the United States did not sign the accords, it did agree with them and promised to avoid the use of military force in the area and to support the principle of self-determination throughout Indochina. South Vietnamese representatives also neglected to sign the accords but nevertheless expressed public support for its major provisions. By not signing the agreement, the United States had the advantage of appearing supportive without being bound by its provisions. Two years after the Geneva Conference, when it appeared that the followers of Ho Chi Minh* had majority support in North as well as South Vietnam, the United States scuttled the free elections and

threw all of its economic and military support behind the South Vietnamese regime.

Sources: Robert F. Randle, *Geneva 1954*, 1969; Arnold R. Isaacs, *Without Honor: Defeat in Vietnam and Cambodia*, 1983.

GENOVESE, EUGENE DOMINICK

Eugene Genovese was born on May 19, 1930, in Brooklyn, New York. He received a B.A. from Brooklyn College in 1955 and the M.A. and Ph.D. from Columbia University in 1956 and 1959. Genovese taught history at the Brooklyn Polytechnic Institute from 1958 to 1963. He joined the faculty of Rutgers University in 1963 and published his first book, *The Political Economy of Slavery*, in 1965. Known as a neo-Marxist, Genovese came to national political attention in 1967 and 1968 when he protested American involvement in the Vietnam War and described the Vietcong* as a nationalistically inspired people trying to liberate their homeland from foreign domination. The ensuing controversy caused Genovese political problems at Rutgers, and he accepted a position at Sir George Williams University in Montreal in 1967. In 1969 he joined the faculty of the University of Rochester. He subsequently became one of the most well-known American historians, not just because of his politics but also because of the quality of his research and writing. Genovese's books *The World the Slaveholders Made* (1969) and *Roll, Jordan, Roll* (1974) helped reshape the way American historians viewed slavery and the South. Later in his career, Genovese became increasingly disenchanted with Marxism, seeing in it less a description of historical reality than a rigid ideology that came crashing down with the collapse of the Soviet Union. Genovese converted to Roman Catholicism in 1996 and became a conservative commentator on modern American political and social life.

Source: http://www.calvin.edu/january/1998/genovese.htm.

GIA LONG

Gia Long was born in 1762 as Nguyen Phuc Anh, and adopted his new name when he became emperor of Vietnam in 1802. With the help of French missionary Pigneau de Behaine, Nguyen Anh escaped Vietnam during the Tay Son Rebellion* and was the only surviving heir to the Nguyen* throne. In 1787 Nguyen Anh secured French assistance in crushing the Tay Son Rebellion. In return he promised unrestricted trade for the French in Cochin China.* After years of struggle, Nguyen Anh's forces defeat-

Above: Major General James Gavin, commanding general of the 82d Airborne Division, before an award ceremony in Belgium in 1945.

Below: Eugene Genovese became a leading figure in the rise of the "New Left History," which criticized the United States for its racist treatment of minorities, its capitalistic exploitation of poor and working-class people, and its aggressive foreign policy. In 1966, Genovese ran for governor of New Jersey and generated considerable animosity by expressing sympathy for the Vietcong and claiming that the United States was "making war on Vietnam, not for it," and planning the physical destruction of China. Later in his career, Genovese did an ideological about-face and became decidedly conservative in his politics and in his interpretation of U.S. history.

ed the Tay Son and seized control of Vietnam in 1802. Nguyen Anh then changed his name and established the Nguyen dynasty, which lasted until the abdication of Bao Dai* in 1955. Gia Long moved the capital of Vietnam from Hanoi* to Hue,* constructed public granaries and a working postal system, repaired the Old Mandarin Road, and brought Cambodia* under control as a vassal state. Gia Long died in 1820.

Sources: *Webster's New Biographical Dictionary*, 1983; Joseph Buttinger, *The Smaller Dragon: A Political History of Vietnam*, 1958.

GOING AFTER CACCIATO

Going After Cacciato is the title of Tim O'Brien's 1978 Vietnam War novel. The central character is Specialist Fourth Class Paul Berlin, who leads a cast of soldiers and Vietnamese civilians (Doc Peret, Sarkin Aung Wan, Corson, Oscar Johnson, Eddie Lazutti, and Stink Harris) on a surrealistic pursuit of Private Cacciato, who leaves their base camp in Quang Ngai Province and goes AWOL. Cacciato then leads his pursuers on a trancelike trek across the Laotian border, through Burma, India, Afghanistan, Iran, Turkey, Greece, Yugoslavia, Austria, East and West Germany,* and France* into Paris. On the way they expose the absurdity of the war.

Sources: Tim O'Brien, *Going after Cacciato*, 1978; Philip D. Beidler, *American Literature and the Experience of Vietnam*, 1982.

GOLDBERG, ARTHUR JOSEPH

As U.S. ambassador to the United Nations from July 1965 to April 1968, Arthur Goldberg believed that the Vietnam War could end only through negotiations, not continued application of force. Born in 1908 in Chicago, he worked his way through Northwestern's undergraduate and law schools and began practicing corporate and labor law in 1929. After service in the OSS during World War II, Goldberg became general counsel of the United Steelworkers and the CIO (the AFL-CIO after the 1955 merger) until tapped by President Kennedy* to serve as secretary of labor in 1961.

Kennedy appointed him to the Supreme Court the following year, and Goldberg voted with the Warren Court's "liberal" bloc until his lifelong interest in foreign affairs and concern with the direction of the war persuaded him to accept President Johnson's* offer of the UN post in July 1965. Uninformed by the White House on many critical decisions and thus often operating at odds with Johnson's Vietnam policy, Ambassador Goldberg focused his attention on finding a way to begin peace talks between Washington and Hanoi.* Although he failed to win administration accommodation to his views in that effort, Goldberg did participate in the March 1968 sessions of the "Wise Old Men,"* who reassessed Vietnam policy, recommended a bombing halt, and persuaded Johnson to announce a de-escalation at the end of the month.

Goldberg left the administration in April 1968, and Johnson responded with a cold letter that failed to praise the ambassador for his UN efforts. Goldberg then publicly broke with U.S. policy and later spoke out vigorously at the October 1969 Moratorium Day demonstrations* in Washington and other rallies. In 1970 Goldberg ran unsuccessfully for governor of New York against Republican Nelson Rockefeller. He then returned to private law practice. In 1977 President Jimmy Carter appointed him U.S. ambassador to the Belgrade Conference on Human Rights. Arthur J. Goldberg died on January 19, 1990. DA

Sources: David Halberstam, *The Best and the Brightest*, 1972; Stanley Karnow, *Vietnam: A History*, 1983; *New York Times*, 1964–1975; *Guide to the U.S. Supreme Court*, 1979; David Stebbene, *Arthur J. Goldberg: A New Deal Liberal*, 1996.

GOLDWATER, BARRY MORRIS

Barry M. Goldwater was born in Phoenix on January 1, 1909. He attended the University of Arizona for a year after leaving high school but then worked in the family department store business. Goldwater saw active duty in the Asian theater with the Army Air Corps as a pilot during World War II. A conservative Republican, Goldwater was elected to the U.S. Senate in 1952, and in 1964 he won the

Republican nomination for president. It was an inauspicious time for conservative Republicans, and Lyndon B. Johnson* defeated Goldwater in a landslide. During the election Goldwater had adopted a very "hawkish" position on the U.S. role in Vietnam, and throughout the course of the war he argued that the United States should be willing to make a major military commitment—whatever it took, short of nuclear weapons—to support American soldiers in the field, or should withdraw from the conflict. Because of the presidential nomination, Goldwater did not run for reelection to the Senate in 1964, but he was reelected in 1968, 1974, and 1980. During his Senate career Goldwater was a vigorous supporter of a strong military effort in Vietnam and the government of South Vietnam. In the closing stages of the conflict, Goldwater called for large-scale bombing* of North Vietnam and increased financial assistance to South Vietnam. In 1986 Goldwater decided not to seek reelection, and he retired from public life in 1987. Barry Goldwater died on May 29, 1998.

Sources: Barry M. Goldwater, *With No Apologies: The Personal and Political Memoirs of United States Senator Barry Morris Goldwater*, 1979; Robert Alan Goldberg, *Barry Goldwater*, 1995.

GO TELL THE SPARTANS

Based on Daniel Ford's novel *Incident at Muc Wa,* *Go Tell the Spartans* is one of the best films on the Vietnam War. Set in 1964 when the U.S. effort was still "advisory," it captures significant issues of the war honestly and accurately. Unlike *The Deer Hunter* and *Apocalypse Now*, *Go Tell the Spartans* presents the racism of American involvement without being racist. Rather than some film producer's imaginings of what the war was like, it presents a view that Vietnam veterans, especially advisors, can relate to as truthful. The film opens with a Vietcong* suspect enduring water torture at a Regional Forces*/Popular Forces* (RF/PF) base camp. Against his better judgment, the senior American advisor is ordered to occupy a former French position at Muc Wa, where more than 300 French soldiers had been killed by the Vietminh* in 1953. The film then centers on the RF/PF forces and their American advisors, who quickly are besieged and overrun. The significant issues captured include American contempt for the French; the role of civilians as Vietcong sympathizers; the patriotic naivete of American forces; the arrogance of senior U.S. officers; the way in which ground was taken one day and given up the next; the emphasis on psychological operations, intelligence reports, and high-tech warfare; the sober realization of some experienced American officers and NCOs who were totally frustrated by the war; the corruption and incompetence of South Vietnamese officials; the mixed quality of South Vietnamese forces; the brutality and heroism of both South Vietnamese and American forces; and the sheer terror of night combat. Released in 1978, *Go Tell the Spartans* starred Burt Lancaster as Major Asa Barker, the commander of a Military Advisory and Assistance Group* in Penang, South Vietnam. SF

Source: http://www.imdb.com/title/tt0077617/.

GRAVEL, MIKE

Mike Gravel was born in Springfield, Massachusetts, on May 13, 1930. He spent one year at American International College before entering the United States Army* in 1951, with which he served in Germany and France. Gravel graduated from Columbia University in 1956 with a degree in economics and moved to Alaska. He won a seat in the Alaska House of Representatives in 1962, and he defeated Senator Ernest Gruening,* one of the earliest critics of the Vietnam War, in the Democratic primary. Ironically, *Time* magazine called Gravel hawkish in the campaign. Gravel won the general election and eventually became an increasingly outspoken critic of the Vietnam War, gaining a reputation as a Senate maverick. In 1971 Gravel tried unsuccessfully to read the Pentagon Papers* in the Senate chamber. Then, on June 29, 1971, Gravel convened a late session of the Building and Grounds subcommittee, which he chaired. For the next three hours he read from the Pentagon Papers, sometimes crying and sobbing. Many senators opposed his actions. Subsequently, he arranged with Beacon Press to publish *The Senator Gravel Edition of the Pentagon Papers* in four volumes. Gravel also made public a copy of National Security Study Memorandum No. 1, which Daniel Ellsberg* had provided him.

Gravel's opposition to the war continued. He opposed extension of the draft* and advocated equal air time from the media to counter the Nixon* administration's position on the war. He worked to organize a War No More group. Gravel criticized Vietnamization* as "a plan to keep on our involvement for decades until we win." In 1972 Gravel tried unsuccessfully to have the Senate vote on a declaration of war against North Vietnam and to persuade the Senate to publish, in the *Congressional Record*, a secret Nixon administration study of U.S. bombing* effectiveness in Vietnam. Gravel won reelection in 1974, but he lost the senatorial primary in 1980 to Clark Gruening, Ernest Gruening's grandson. Mike Gravel announced his 2008 candidacy for U.S. president on April 17, 2006, in Washington, D.C. In March 2008 he left the Democratic Party and joined the Libertarian Party to campaign for the Libertarian presidential nomination. JH

Sources: *Biographical Directory of the American Congress, 1789–1971*, 1972; *New York Times*, November 7, 1980; http//:www.gravel2008.us/.

Above: Senator Barry Goldwater of Arizona captured the Republican nomination for president of the United States in 1964. He campaigned on a platform that included proposals to roll back New Deal entitlement programs, trim Social Security, and shrink the size of the federal government. He also advocated a vigorous, anti-Communist foreign policy and pursuit, through any means necessary, of a military victory in Vietnam. Here, Goldwater stops at O'Hare Airport in Chicago on February 8, 1964, while on the campaign trail.

Below: In 1968 Mike Gravel defeated Alaska Senator Ernest Greuning in the Democratic primary and then went on to win the general election. He soon earned a reputation as a maverick in the Senate and as an outspoken critic of the Vietnam War. Gravel's opposition only intensified during the Richard M. Nixon administration. He is known for having put the Pentagon Papers into public record by entering 4,100 pages of the Papers into his Senate subcommittee in 1971. On July 7, 1972, Gravel announced his candidacy for vice president of the United States, but lost the nomination.

GREAT BRITAIN

Ever since 1945 the British have adopted a policy of relative noninvolvement with Indochina.* They were preoccupied with a contraction of their own responsibilities east of the Suez Canal; bogged down in a counterinsurgency effort in Malaysia; undergoing substantial reductions in defense expenditures because of economic problems; entertaining hopes of expanding trade with Communist-bloc nations; and dealing with a powerful left-wing movement at home that resented military adventures abroad. All of these problems precluded active British intervention in the problems of Vietnam.

In 1945, in order to free American troops for the anticipated invasion of Japan, the British took the Japanese surrender in Indochina, disarmed the enemy, and reestablished the prewar supremacy of the French. The British commander, Major General Douglas Gracey, actually used, however, a combined force of British and Japanese troops to fight the Vietminh,* who were preparing to resist any reimposition of Western control over Vietnam. Still, on March 5, 1946, the British disengaged from the area. Eight years later, when President Dwight Eisenhower* sought British support for an American air strike at Dien Bien Phu,* Prime Minister Winston Churchill refused, pragmatically arguing that air strikes would accomplish little, since most of Indochina was already under Vietminh control. He preferred a diplomatic solution.

In 1954 Great Britain co-chaired the Geneva Conference (*see* Geneva Accords) on Vietnam, where it supported the American proposal for a division of Vietnam at the 17th parallel, with reunification elections to be held in two years. Privately, the British hoped—as did the Americans—that the 17th parallel would become a recognized and permanent international boundary, with the South remaining non-Communist, out of the control of the Vietminh. When it appeared obvious that such elections would endorse the demands of Ho Chi Minh* and the Vietminh, Britain supported the U.S. decision to stall and delay those elections.

As the American involvement escalated during the Johnson* administration, Prime Minister Harold Wilson refused all American requests for military support. The British sense that the United States would not prevail against the Vietcong* persisted. Sensitive to the "special relationship" that Britain had with the United States in the postwar era but also harassed by strongly leftist elements in his own Labor Party who vocally condemned the war, Wilson maintained a delicate balance between 1964 and 1970. His government gave verbal support to American policy in Southeast Asia generally, while privately calling for an end to the bombing of North Vietnam and a negotiated settlement. Wilson's conservative successor, Edward Heath, continued the policy of limited support but no formal participation.

Britain did serve, however, as an important conduit for contact between the United States and the Soviet Union.* Harold Wilson consulted frequently with Soviet leaders. The United States often used the British government as a sounding board, and to either convey negotiating positions to or to try to bring pressure on North Vietnam through the Soviet Union. Such contacts availed little because the United States greatly exaggerated the amount of influence the Soviet Union had with the North Vietnamese. GMB

Sources: Harold Wilson, *A Personal Record: The Labour Government, 1964–1970*, 1971; Max Beloff, *The Future of British Foreign Policy*, 1969; J.H. Weiner and J.H. Plumb, *Great Britain: Foreign Policy and the Span of Empire, 1689–1971. A Documentary History*, 1972; George Rosie, *The British in Vietnam: How the Twenty-five Years War Began*, 1970.

GREAT SOCIETY

"Great Society" became the historical description of the domestic reforms of the Johnson* administration. In his 1964 State of the Union address, Lyndon B. Johnson declared a "war on poverty," and in an address at the University of Michigan in May 1964, Johnson spoke of "the opportunity to move not only toward the rich society and the powerful society but upward to the Great Society." The Great Society, he argued, "rests on abundance and liberty for all. It demands an end to poverty and racial injustice—to which we are totally committed." The Civil Rights Act of 1964, the Voting Rights Act of 1965, the antipoverty campaign of the mid-1960s, and the Civil Rights Act of 1968 were all part of the Great Society. Eventually, Great Society reforms, which were Johnson's favorites, ran up against the demands of the Vietnam War, which Johnson hated. His decision to continue funding domestic reforms along with increased military funding without a tax increase fueled inflation and made him even more politically vulnerable. Lyndon Johnson's Great Society died in the jungles of Vietnam.

Sources: Lawrence S. Wittner, *Cold War America. From Hiroshima to Watergate*, 1974; Doris Kearns, *Lyndon Johnson and the American Dream*, 1976.

GREEN BERETS

See Green Berets, p. 224

Opposite page, bottom: John Wayne and David Janssen in a still from the movie *The Green Berets*.

THE GREEN BERETS

Robin Moore's 1965 novel *The Green Berets* was a naive but temporarily popular novel about the American war effort in Vietnam. In the book U.S. Special Forces* troops appear as the "good guys" out to rescue South Vietnam from its own incompetence and the immoral aggression of the Vietcong* and the North Vietnamese. South Vietnamese Army officers appear cowardly and venal and ARVN (*see* Army of the Republic of Vietnam) troops unreliable and quick to desert when facing combat. The Vietcong and the North Vietnamese are depicted as uniformly venal and evil, bent on torture, murder, and atrocity. The book also celebrates the genius of American technology and the virtues of American democracy and capitalism. In short, *The Green Berets* is a "World War II novel" about the Vietnam War. By 1966, as the antiwar movement* gained momentum in the United States, Robin Moore's novel quickly lost credibility, becoming almost a ludicrous caricature of U.S. policy in Vietnam.

Sources: Robin Moore, *The Green Berets*, 1965; Philip D. Beidler, *American Literature and the Experience of Vietnam*, 1982.

THE GREEN BERETS

Written in 1965 when the Vietnam War was just under way at its escalated level but released in 1968 when the antiwar movement* was at its peak, *The Green Berets* starred John Wayne as the Green Beret colonel, David Janssen as a jaded journalist, and Jim Hutton as the naive, big-hearted American GI out to save the world. The film was loaded with World War II clichés, with the Vietcong* portrayed as universal savages and the Americans and the South Vietnamese characterized as the epitome of goodness and mercy. Of all the films of the Vietnam era, none was a better reflection of U.S. policies in 1965, at the beginning of the conflict.

Source: http://www.imdb.com/title/tt0063035/.

GREENE, WALLACE MARTIN JR.

During his tour as commandant of the United States Marine Corps* (1964–68), Wallace Greene became a strong public advocate of U.S. policy in Vietnam. Born in Burlington, Vermont, in 1907, he attended the University of Vermont for a year before entering Annapolis and taking a Marine Corps commission in 1930. In the 1930s he served aboard ship, on Guam, and in China, then advanced rapidly as a staff officer in the Pacific, receiving the Legion of Merit

for planning the Marshall Islands invasions in 1944. After the war he served as Assistant Chief of Staff, Fleet Marine Force, Pacific Command* (1948–50), then on the staff of the Marine Corps Schools for two years before graduating from the National War College in 1953. Greene next served on the Joint Chiefs of Staff (*see* Chairman, JCS) for two years, becoming assistant commander of the 2d Marine Division in 1955 and commander of Parris Island and Camp Lejeune in 1957. When President Kennedy* selected him to succeed David M. Shoup* as commandant in 1963, Greene had just completed four years as chief of staff of the Marine Corps.

With his troops committed to defensive tactics around Da Nang,* Phu Bai, and Chu Lai* in the late spring of 1965, Greene publicly pushed for an expanded combat role, one in which Marines would not be "sitting around on their diddybox." Thereafter Greene spoke optimistically of U.S. prospects in Vietnam, promoting the Combined Action Platoons,* yet acknowledging that pacification (*see* Rural Reconstruction) would take about a decade to accomplish. Wallace Greene retired from active service on December 31, 1967, a month before the Tet Offensive. Wallace M. Greene Jr. died on March 8, 2003, at the age of 95. DA

Sources: Robert Moskin, *The United States Marine Corps Story*, 1982; Allan R. Millett, *Semper Fidelis: The History of the United States Marine Corps*, 1980; www.arlingtoncemetery.net/wmgreene.htm.

Above: General Wallace M. Greene Jr., Commandant of the U.S. Marine Corps, appears at a press conference on May 26, 1967. He had opposed the use of Marines to defend static positions in Vietnam and promoted a more active combat role for them. General William C. Westmoreland agreed and deployed most Marines to I Corps, where they engaged Vietcong or NVA troops throughout the war.

GREEN BERETS

After World War II the Soviet Union sponsored Communist insurgent movements to overthrow the governments of Turkey and Greece. As the insurgents gained ground, the Truman administration decided to funnel money and military assistance to Greece and Turkey, hoping to block Soviet expansion into the eastern Mediterranean and Middle East. Dubbed the Truman Doctrine, the policy strengthened the governments in Athens and Istanbul, which then crushed the insurgencies. Deeper concern about Communist insurgencies developed in 1949 when Mao Zedong and the

Special Forces groups were organized. The 5th arrived in South Vietnam on October 1, 1964, establishing its headquarters in Nha Trang.

President John F. Kennedy, fascinated by cloak-and-dagger covert operations, had taken a particular liking to the Special Forces, expanding them from 2,500 men to 10,000 men during his administration. Against the wishes of Army brass, the president awarded the Special Forces elite status and allowed its members to wear a distinctive green beret. At the time, to be eligible for the Green Berets, as they became known, an applicant had to be physically fit, airborne- and ranger-qualified, and fluent in at least two languages. They were then trained in explosives and demolitions, hand-to-hand combat, communications, field medicine, mountaineering, and weapons of every kind. Americans fell in love with the Green Berets, soldiers who, in the words of journalist David Halberstam, "were uncommon men, extraordinary physical specimens and intellectual Ph.D.s, swinging through trees, speaking Russian and Chinese, eating snake meat and other fauna, springing counter-ambushes at night on unwary Asian ambushers."

Right: Colonel McAuliffe, commander of the 5th Special Forces Group in Vietnam, visits one of his A-teams at the Buon Ea Yang Special Forces Camp in Darlac Province, South Vietnam, in March 1966. An A-team is a twelve-man Special Forces unit.

Communists seized power in Beijing and proclaimed the People's Republic of China a Communist state. Mao advocated "wars of national liberation" among peasant peoples around the world, and American policymakers and military officials began to develop strategic approaches to that challenge. In 1952 the U.S. Army established the Special Forces to develop anti–guerrilla warfare tactics and counterinsurgency measures. In June 1957, assuming that Asia would be the most critical region for Mao Zedong's wars of national liberation, the Army established the 1st Special Forces Group in Japan. Later in the year, members of the 1st Special Forces Group deployed to Nha Trang, South Vietnam, to train ARVN commandos. Subsequently, the 5th and 7th

In 1965, when the Vietnam War still enjoyed widespread political support, Robin Moore's book *The Green Berets* rocketed onto the *New York Times* bestseller list, hailing the Special Forces as an American antidote to Mao Zedong's wars of national liberation. They were, Moore argued, "a potent new weapon against the Communists," a key to victory in the cold war. One year later, Vietnam veteran Barry Sadler wrote the "Ballad of the Green Berets," which sat for five weeks atop the Billboard charts as the most popular song in the country and was the No. 1 hit for the year. It eventually sold more than 11 million records, adding to the mystique of the Green Berets and reinforcing prevailing beliefs in America's special virtues and mission in the world.

Left: Green Berets guarding Phu Tuc Special Forces Camp in South Vietnam from the lookout post, April 1966.

The Green Berets distinguished themselves in Vietnam. During the late 1950s and early 1960s, the Central Intelligence Agency had engaged in extensive counterinsurgency programs in South Vietnam and Laos—organizing, training, and equipping native Montagnard tribesmen into Civilian Irregular Defense Groups (CIDGs). The CIDGs were essentially militia units, and by 1963 the CIA had 12,000 troops working out of more than 200 villages. That year, the Special Forces assumed control of the CIDG troops, eventually building them up to more than 42,000 men and women defending the border areas of Laos and South Vietnam. The Green Berets also organized what became known as Mobile Strike Teams to attack NVA and Vietcong bases, conduct reconnaissance missions, and maintain thousands of educational, medical, and welfare projects in Laos and South Vietnam.

As American support for the Vietnam War waned in the late 1960s, so did the fascination with the Green Berets. In 1965 John Wayne purchased film rights to Robin Moore's *The Green Berets* and then proceeded to make a patriotic, pro-American, pro–Vietnam War movie of the same name that was released soon after the Tet Offensive of 1968. The film enraged those who opposed the war, and it trivialized the Green Berets. It was, for all intents and purposes, an old-fashioned western, with the Green Berets replacing the U.S. Cavalry and the Vietcong substituting for American Indians. The movie had not an ounce of nuance. Renata Adler, the *New York Times* film reviewer, wrote that *The Green Berets* "is a film so unspeakable, so stupid, so rotten and false … that it passes through being fun, through being funny, through being camp, through everything and becomes an invitation to grieve, not for our soldiers in Vietnam or for Vietnam (the film could not be more false or do a greater disservice to either of them) but for what has happened to the fantasy-making apparatus … Simplicities of the right, simplicities of the left, but this one is beyond the possible. It is vile and insane." Even the *Hollywood Reporter*, the trade journal for the film industry, called *The Green Berets* a "cliché-ridden throwback to the battlefield potboilers of World War II, its artifice readily exposed by the nightly actuality of TV news coverage." One year later, President Richard M. Nixon began the staged withdrawal of American troops from Vietnam. The Special Forces remained in South Vietnam and Laos until March 1971.

Sources: Shelby L. Stanton, *Green Berets at War: U.S. Army Special Forces in Vietnam, 1961–1975*, 1985; Andrew F. Krepinevich Jr., *The Army and Vietnam*, 1986; Francis J. Kelly, *U.S. Army Special Forces, 1961–1971*, 1973; Larry E. Cable, *Conflict of Myths: The Development of American Counterinsurgency Doctrine and the Vietnam War*, 1986.

Below: Psychological warfare officer 1st Lieutenant John B. Salter checks a machine gun field of fire from a bunker at Camp Bu Prang, 1968.

Below: In 1968, elements of the 3d Marine Division participated in Operation Thor 1 mile south of the Demilitarized Zone. A Marine protected by fire from the 3d Tank Battalion tosses a grenade to flush out a group of North Vietnamese soldiers.

GRENADES

Grenades played a dominant role in the largely guerilla style of fighting that typified the Vietnam War and were used by both sides to devastating effect.

ARVN and American soldiers in Vietnam carried hand grenades for use when they could neither hit the enemy with a bullet nor call in mortar fire on the enemy position. A soldier could throw a grenade about 30 yards. The principle grenade used in Vietnam was the M61 Fragmentation or "frag" grenade. It contained a core of TNT mixture surrounded by a metal casing that burst into shrapnel when exploded, inflicting damage within a range of about 15 yards. Jungle growth was found sometimes to snag the safety pins from the grenades of marching soldiers, so the M61s were fitted with a "jungle clip." The clip held the longer safety lever to the grenade if the safety pin was accidentally pulled. Vietnam soldiers also carried smoke grenades, especially used for signaling winged aircraft and helicopters. Yellow marked a safe landing zone for a helicopter, red a "hot" zone, one under enemy fire.

To increase the range of grenades, infantrymen sometimes carried M79 grenade launchers. These were called Thumpers or Bloopers, looked like sawn-off shotguns and could hurl a barrel-loaded (not meant for hand-throwing) 44mm grenade several hundred yards. There might be two

men in a rifle squad with M79s, men who did not carry rifles of their own, only pistols. The M79s could also fire smoke grenades and flares. A later version of the M79 was one that could attach to an M16 assault rifle and was called the M203.

Communist forces also used grenades—Chinese made, or captured ones, or improvised ones using tin can or soda cans—often for booby traps. They fastened them to trip wires near or over trails for exploding automatically or by means of trip wires running to operators out of sight. More soldiers were killed by booby traps, mines, and grenades than by gunfire in Vietnam.

Sources: http://www.pbs.org/wgbh/amex/vietnam/trenches/weapons.html; http://en.wikipedia.org/wiki/United_States_hand_grenades; www.173rdairborne.com/weapons.htm; http://www.1stcavmedic.com/glossary.html

Opposite page, top: During the Vietnam War, the Vietcong and NVA proved highly versatile in their capacity to inflict damage on American forces. More U.S. troops were killed by mines and booby traps than by enemy fire. On November 17, 1968, a Marine from the 1st Marine Division, while searching an enemy 140mm rocket site 8 miles southeast of Da Nang, found a Coca-Cola can transformed into a hand grenade.

Left: Elements of the 1st Cavalry Division participated in Operation Wallowa near Chu Lai, South Vietnam, in late October 1967. Specialist 4 Gary McGhee, a door gunner on a UH-1B gunship, positions his smoke grenades before takeoff.

Below Soldiers stand near a cloud of yellow smoke signaling their position to air support outside Hue, 1968.

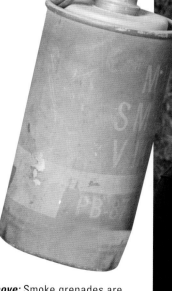

Above: The fragmentation grenade (a "frag") is an antipersonnel weapon that disperses shrapnel upon exploding.

Above: Smoke grenades are ground-to-ground or ground-to-air signaling devices, used to mark landing zones or screen unit movement.

Above: In 1964, Senator Ernest Gruening of Alaska was one of only two members of the U.S. Senate to vote against the Gulf of Tonkin Resolution. Gruening was convinced that President Johnson was exaggerating the alleged North Vietnamese attack on U.S. ships in order to escalate the war. History eventually confirmed Gruening's suspicions.

Below: President Nguyen Van Thieu, President Lyndon B. Johnson, and Premier Nguyen Cao Ky salute as the American and Vietnamese anthems play at the welcome ceremony of the Guam Conference at Guam's International Airport.

GROUP

A group in the United States Army* is a system of command controlling several battalions.* Subordinate to a brigade,* a group is usually part of support commands. Most commonly groups are commanded by a colonel.

Source: Harry G. Summers Jr., *Vietnam War Almanac*, 1985.

GRUENING, ERNEST HENRY

Elected to the U.S. Senate in 1959 when Alaska became a state, Gruening entered the Senate with a diverse background. Born in New York in 1887, he studied medicine but spent much of his career as a journalist, working as an editor and writer for a number of publications, including the *Nation* magazine. A major interest was Latin America; he crusaded against U.S. military intervention and what he saw as financial exploitation in Central and South America. In the mid-1930s he turned to government service, eventually being appointed governor of Alaska by President Franklin Roosevelt.* Gruening became a leader of the Alaskan statehood movement.

In the Senate, Gruening, a liberal Democrat, was one of the first to question U.S. involvement in Vietnam. In a speech on March 10, 1964, Gruening deplored the waste of American lives and resources "in seeking vainly in this remote jungle to shore up self-serving corrupt dynasties or their self-imposed successors, and a people that has

demonstrated that it has no will to save itself." He said that "all Vietnam is not worth the life of a single American boy" and that the loss of any American lives in Vietnam would some day "be denounced as a crime." Later that year he joined Senator Wayne Morse* in casting the only votes against the Gulf of Tonkin Resolution,* which Gruening said subverted the Constitution by giving the president "warmaking powers in the absence of a declaration of war." He remained in the Senate through 1968 and consistently opposed appropriations to support the war. He blamed his defeat by Mike Gravel* in the 1968 Democratic primary on his opposition to the war. Ironically, as a senator, Gravel eventually became an outspoken opponent of the war. After leaving the Senate, Gruening coauthored a book, *Vietnam Folly*, calling for an "end of the folly of America's intervention and the return by the United States to principles which it has long cherished." Ernest Gruening died on June 26, 1974. HP

Sources: Joseph C. Goulden, *Truth Is the First Casualty: The Gulf of Tonkin Affair—Illusion and Reality*, 1969; Ernest Gruening and Herbert B. Beaser, *Vietnam Folly*, 1968; *New York Times*, June 27, 1974; David Robert Johnson, *Ernest Gruening and the American Dissenting Tradition*, 1998.

GUAM CONFERENCE OF 1967

In 1967 President Lyndon B. Johnson* decided to hold a high-level conference on the island of Guam. Guam was secure yet near Saigon,* symbolized American Pacific interests, and represented American power because of the B-52s* stationed there. Johnson, Secretary of State Dean Rusk,* Secretary of Defense Robert McNamara,* and a number of military advisors and reporters made the 16,000-mile trip to the March 20–21, 1967, conference. Ambassador Henry Cabot Lodge,* Premier Nguyen Cao Ky,* and President Nguyen Van Thieu* came from Saigon. They met at the Officers' Club on Nimitz Hill.

The president called the meeting for several reasons. He wanted to demonstrate American resolve in continuing the war effort and to introduce new personnel to the South Vietnamese leaders. In particular, Ellsworth Bunker* would replace Lodge as ambassador; Eugene Locke, a presidential friend and ambassador to Pakistan, would become Bunker's assistant; Robert Komer* would become the new deputy for Civil Operations and Revolutionary Development Support* to direct the pacification effort (*see* Rural Reconstruction); and General Creighton W. Abrams* would become William Westmoreland's* deputy and eventual successor. At the conference, Westmoreland presented his request for 200,000 more troops, but the president, pressured by McNamara to be cautious, agreed to only 55,000 new troops. Ky and Thieu brought the new South Vietnamese

constitution, just completed by the Constituent Assembly, to satisfy Johnson that they were making progress toward democracy. Ky also called for increased bombing sorties* against North Vietnamese and Vietcong sanctuaries* and supply routes in Laos* and Cambodia.* The president refused, and the Guam Conference became little more than a public relations event. JH

Source: *New York Times*, March 21–23, 1967.

GUERRILLAS

See Vietcong

GULF OF TONKIN INCIDENT (1964)

By August 1964 the United States Navy* was supporting South Vietnam's fight against North Vietnam in two programs. Operations Plan (OPLAN) 34 involved South Vietnamese naval and marine forces raiding North Vietnamese coastal installations with American advice and logistical support. Operation DeSoto involved American naval ships patrolling international waters off the coast of North Vietnam to observe the North Vietnamese Navy and probe North Vietnamese radar

capabilities by electronic surveillance. The destroyer USS *Maddox*,* patrolling 28 miles off the North Vietnamese coast as part of DeSoto, came under attack by three North Vietnamese torpedo boats on August 2. An OPLAN 34 raid against the torpedo boat base at Loc Chao had taken place on the night of July 31, and this probably precipitated the attack on the American destroyer. The *Maddox* fired warning shots, but the torpedo boats continued attacking by launching two torpedoes. These were avoided, and fire from the destroyer damaged one of the torpedo boats. Four

Above: Captain John J. Herrick, Commander Destroyer Division 192 (left) and Commander Herbert L. Ogier, Commanding Officer of USS *Maddox* (DD-731), on board on August 13, 1964. They were in charge of the ship during her engagement with three North Vietnamese motor torpedo boats on August 2, 1964.

Below: The USS *Maddox* operating off the coast of Oahu, Hawaii, on March 21, 1964. The ship had recently been refitted with an SPS-40 air search radar.

Above: One of the three North Vietnamese torpedo boats to attack the USS *Maddox* on August 2, 1964.

Vought F-8E Crusaders, on patrol from the carrier USS *Ticonderoga,** came to assist the *Maddox*. The destroyer division commander on board the *Maddox* ordered the aircraft to attack the now-retiring torpedo boats. Several strafing runs with 20mm cannons and rocket attacks with 5-inch Zuni rockets resulted in the sinking of the already-damaged torpedo boat. The destroyer USS *C. Turner Joy** joined the *Maddox*, and the carrier USS *Constellation* proceeded to the area from Hong Kong. The two destroyers retired to an area 100 miles off the coast, and combat air patrols began.

On the evening of August 4, in very poor weather conditions, the *Maddox* identified five high-speed radar contacts as North Vietnamese torpedo boats. The details of the engagement are somewhat confused, but American naval personnel were convinced they were being attacked, reporting several torpedo wakes while maneuvering in the darkness. The *Ticonderoga* sent two Douglas A-1 Skyraiders* to assist, and between the aircraft and destroyers two torpedo boats were reported destroyed and two damaged. President Johnson* ordered retaliatory air strikes against four North Vietnamese torpedo boat bases on August 5. Aircraft from the *Ticonderoga* and *Constellation* destroyed twenty-five boats and severely damaged the support facilities. The boats destroyed amounted to one-half of the total North Vietnamese torpedo boat strength. Two American aircraft were shot down by antiaircraft fire and two were damaged. An A-4* pilot

became the first American prisoner of war* in North Vietnam. On August 7, 1964, both houses of Congress* passed the Gulf of Tonkin Resolution.* CA

Sources: Tom Carhart, *Battles and Campaigns in Vietnam*, 1984; *Jane's Fighting Ships, 1976–1977*, 1978; Joseph C. Goulden, *Truth Is the First Casualty: The Gulf of Tonkin Affair—Illusion and Reality*, 1969; Edwin E. Moise, *Tonkin Gulf and the Escalation of the Vietnam War*, 1996.

GULF OF TONKIN RESOLUTION

On August 4, 1964, the USS *Maddox** and its companion destroyer, the USS *C. Turner Joy,** were ordered to the Gulf of Tonkin for electronic surveillance of North Vietnam. At 9:12 PM the Combat Information Center (CIC) reported the detection of fast-closing targets, apparently the repeat of an attack two days before by three North Vietnamese torpedo boats. The sonar man reported that torpedoes were in the water. At that time the *C. Turner Joy* opened fire, but the *Maddox* found no target, not even the *C. Turner Joy*. Before midnight the *Maddox* was ordered to open fire, but Patrick N. Parks, standing in the main gun director, refused to do so until he heard from the *C. Turner Joy*. The *C. Turner Joy* turned out to be the proposed target of the *Maddox*.

The attack by the North Vietnamese boats on the *Maddox* on August 2, 1964, and the supposed engagement between the *Maddox, C. Turner Joy*, and North Vietnamese ships on August 4, 1964, marked the turning point in the Vietnam War. In retaliation, U.S. bombers swept over North Vietnam for the first time, attacking patrol boat bases and large oil-storage depots.

President Lyndon B. Johnson* found the Gulf of Tonkin incident* politically useful because it justified a large-scale American attack on North Vietnam, boosted South Vietnamese morale, and rallied support back home. On August 7, 1964, Congress* passed a resolution stating that "the Congress approves and supports the determination of the President as Commander in Chief, to take all necessary measures to repel any armed attack against the forces of the United States and to prevent further aggression." The resolution also gave the president authority to provide military assistance to any member or protocol nation of the Southeast Asia Collective Defense Treaty. The power of the resolution would expire when the president had decided that the security of the area was reasonably assured. It passed by a 416–0 vote in the House and by 88–2 in the Senate. President Johnson then used the Gulf of Tonkin Resolution as his congressional authority to conduct the war in Vietnam. Six years later President Richard Nixon* used the Gulf of Tonkin Resolution to justify the invasion of Laos (*see* Lam Son 719) and Cambodia (*see* Operation Binh Tay). During the ensuing political uproar in 1970 Congress repealed the resolution. TM

Sources: Joseph C. Goulden, *Truth Is the First Casualty: The Gulf of Tonkin Affair—Illusion and Reality*, 1969; Eugene Windchy, *A Documentary of the Tonkin Gulf Incidents on August 2 and August 4, 1964, and Their Consequences*, 1971; Edwin E. Moise, *Tonkin Gulf and the Escalation of the Vietnam War*, 1996.

"GUNS AND BUTTER"

"Guns and butter" was used frequently during the Vietnam War to refer to the problem of financing domestic reform programs while conducting an expensive war. President Lyndon B. Johnson's* major preoccupation was with his Great Society* plan to extend the net of social welfare assistance to every needy group in America while eliminating racial, ethnic, and religious discrimination. But the attempt to maintain government spending on behalf of Great Society reforms, when combined with the enormous cost of the Vietnam War, contributed to the severe inflationary cycle of the 1970s and early 1980s. Between 1965 and 1968, when the Vietnam War assumed larger and larger dimensions, defense spending,

Left: In August 1964, selected members of the House of Representatives and the Senate gather to witness President Lyndon B. Johnson sign the Gulf of Tonkin Resolution, greatly expanding the president's power to attack North Vietnam militarily. The president used several pens to sign the document and later gave them as mementos to the Congressmen.

Below: In July and August 1964, the American aircraft carrier USS *Constellation* was on patrol in the Gulf of Tonkin when North Vietnamese patrols boats allegedly attacked a U.S. destroyer. President Johnson used the alleged attack to secure the Gulf of Tonkin Resolution from Congress, which gave him free reign to make war on North Vietnam. Aircraft from the USS *Constellation* were among the first to attack North Vietnam.

Right: In this Air Force photo taken on March 1, 1966, Staff Sergeant John R. Boineau of Adams Run, South Carolina; Staff Sergeant Carl R. Starwalt of Toledo, Illinois; and Master Sergeant Norris W. Johnson of Price, Utah, install three 7.62mm cannons on an AC-47 Dragonship. The cannons can fire 18,000 rounds per minute. On the tarmac are containers of flares and ammunition.

measured in constant dollars, increased 43 percent, while government transfer payments to individuals grew 39 percent. That was "guns and butter" policy. The unemployment rate fell to 3.8 percent in 1966, while the rate of inflation went from 1.7 to 2.9 percent. By 1969 the unemployment rate had dropped again, this time to 3.6 percent, but the inflation rate had increased to 5.4 percent. To deal with rising prices, Congress* enacted a 10 percent income tax surcharge in 1968, but the $6 billion in savings was offset by lenient monetary policies. The money supply grew 2.8 percent in 1966, but 6.4 percent in 1967 and 7.3 percent in 1968. By then the inflation problem was set in place.

President Richard Nixon* came into the White House in 1969 committed to reducing inflation, but he too was baffled by the problem. Defense spending as a percentage of the gross national product began to subside, from 9.5 in 1968 to 5.0 percent in 1978, but the reduction was replaced by concomitant increases in spending for Medicare, Social Security, retirement, and unemployment programs. In August 1971 President Nixon took desperate measures to control inflation by imposing wage and price restrictions and devaluing the dollar. But over the next two years the value of the dollar dropped more than 25 percent, increasing the prices of American imports as well as the inflation rate. The wage and price controls were ineffective. The Arab oil embargo of 1973 and subsequent dramatic increases in the price of OPEC oil only exacerbated the problem, creating the spiraling prices of the 1970s.

Source: Kenneth Bacon, "Vietnam's Legacy," *Wall Street Journal*, April 30, 1985.

GUNSHIPS

During the Vietnam War the United States Air Force* used gunships to attack North Vietnamese and Vietcong* supply lines as well as to provide close air support for American and ARVN forces (*see* Army of the Republic of Vietnam). The Air Force converted three aircraft into fixed-wing gunships: C-47 "Gooneybird" aircraft were equipped with 7.62mm Gatling machine guns and redesignated the AC-47,* also known as Puff the Magic Dragon; AC-119 "Flying Boxcars" were also equipped with 7.62mm Gatling guns; and C-130 "Hercules"* planes were converted to AC-130* gunships by the addition of 7.62mm Gatling guns, Vulcan Gatling guns, and 40mm Bofors cannons.

Sources: William W. Momyer, *Airpower in Three Wars*, 1978; Jack S. Ballard, *The United States Air Force in Southeast Asia: Fixed Wing Gunships, 1962–1972*, 1982.

GVN

See Republic of Vietnam

HAIG, ALEXANDER MEIGS JR.

Above: U.S. Army General Alexander Haig on January 1, 1978, when he was serving in Belgium as commander of the military forces of the North Atlantic Treaty Organization. Three years later, President Ronald Reagan asked Haig to serve as his secretary of state. In the chaos surrounding the shooting of the president in 1981, Haig created a minor constitutional crisis when he said, "I'm in charge," as if he were in line for succession to the presidency.

Alexander Meigs Haig Jr. was born on December 2, 1924. He graduated from West Point in 1947, and for a time in 1948 he worked on General Douglas MacArthur's* staff in Tokyo. There he learned a lifelong disdain for journalists and for civilian authority. After Korea, Haig spent a decade in obscure Army posts, and in 1961 he earned a master's degree in international relations at Georgetown University. The theme of his master's thesis was "the role of the military man in the making of national security policy." It advocated a military czar permanently at the president's side advising on military challenges.

In 1963 Haig was chosen by Joseph Califano to work as military assistant to Secretary of the Army Cyrus R. Vance.* When Vance was appointed deputy secretary of defense under Robert S. McNamara* in 1964, Haig remained with him, becoming deputy special assistant to both the secretary and deputy secretary of defense. He became McNamara's right hand, responsible for liaison between his office and the president's office. In 1964 McNamara and his aides were steadily involved in plans for covert raids against North Vietnam and in readying U.S. escalation. He was an advocate of a strong military presence in South Vietnam.

Haig arrived in Vietnam in July 1966 as G-3, an operations planning officer for the 1st Infantry Division* at Lai Khe just north of Saigon.* While there he was awarded three Distinguished Flying Crosses. As commander of the 1st Battalion of the 26th Infantry Regiment, he led a surprise assault on Ben Suc,* a Vietcong* refuge in the Iron Triangle.* In June 1967 Haig came home, was promoted to colonel, and received command of a cadet regiment at West Point. Late in 1968 he got a call from Henry Kissinger* to join the White House staff as his military advisor on the National Security Council. Among other duties, Haig screened all intelligence information to the president. Although few people knew his name, insiders began to recognize Haig as one of the most important people in Washington. By 1970 he had acquired direct access to

President Richard M. Nixon* as well as the authority to conduct presidential briefings in Kissinger's absence. On September 7, 1972, Nixon promoted Haig over the heads of 240 senior officers to four star general rank. At the same time he was designated vice chief of staff of the U.S. Army.*

Haig played a central part in the final settlement with Hanoi* by convincing Nixon that his survival in office was more important than how Vietnam turned out. In the peace negotiations of October 1972, Kissinger and Haig fought a war of telegrams over the settlement. Haig thought that Kissinger was going too far and giving up too much. Haig advocated the 1972 Christmas bombings (*see* Operation Linebacker II) of Hanoi and Haiphong and personally delivered the ultimatum to Nguyen Van Thieu* to accept the peace agreement. In May 1973 Haig became permanent assistant to President Nixon. His power was so extensive during the Watergate* crisis that Special Prosecutor Leon Jaworski called Haig the country's 37½th president.

Remarkably, Haig emerged from Watergate unscathed. Journalist Jules Witcover described his actions in getting Nixon to resign as a bloodless presidential coup. Haig continued as a national security advisor to President Gerald Ford* and then returned to power in Washington as secretary of state in the first Reagan administration. In 1986 Haig was giving serious consideration to making a run for the Republican presidential nomination in the election of 1988, but he had no political traction and abandoned the bid, eventually going to work for Commodore Computers. In January 2006 Haig participated in a White House conference of previous secretaries of state and defense, where they discussed foreign policy with leading figures in the Bush administration. FF

Sources: Roger Morris, *Haig: The General's Progress*, 1982; Alexander Haig, *Inner Circles: How America Changed the World*, 1992.

HAIPHONG HARBOR, MINING OF

Haiphong is the major port and third-largest city in North Vietnam. The bulk of North Vietnam's imports arrive through the port of Haiphong, which is connected by railroad with Hanoi.* During the Vietnam War Haiphong was a major supply depot and was heavily bombed from 1965 until 1968, when the bombing* was curtailed by President Johnson.* During the attacks much of the population was evacuated and the industry dispersed.

In 1972 the Nixon* administration sparked a major controversy when the president ordered the renewal of the bombing of Hanoi and Haiphong (April 16) and the mining of Haiphong Harbor as well as other harbors and inland waterways in North Vietnam (May 9). Also, U.S. naval forces intensified raids against coastal installations and put

Left: For fear of earning the wrath of the Soviet Union, Presidents Kennedy, Johnson, and Nixon refused to mine the harbor at Haiphong, the port through which most imports, including arms, entered North Vietnam. In 1972, however, during the course of North Vietnam's Eastertide Offensive, President Nixon finally mined the harbor. As part of Operation Linebacker, he also subjected warehouses and shipping areas in Haiphong to withering B-52 raids, as seen here on May 17, 1972.

Below: In 1968, workers clear a section of railroad track north of the Hai Van Pass. Hai Van Pass is a mountainous region and the road, Highway 1, winds back and forth to a height of 1,427 feet above sea level. The curving railway is 10,498 feet long and runs through seven tunnels.

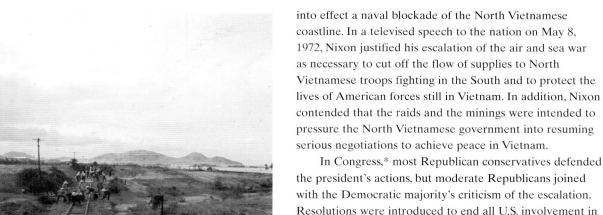

into effect a naval blockade of the North Vietnamese coastline. In a televised speech to the nation on May 8, 1972, Nixon justified his escalation of the air and sea war as necessary to cut off the flow of supplies to North Vietnamese troops fighting in the South and to protect the lives of American forces still in Vietnam. In addition, Nixon contended that the raids and the minings were intended to pressure the North Vietnamese government into resuming serious negotiations to achieve peace in Vietnam.

In Congress,* most Republican conservatives defended the president's actions, but moderate Republicans joined with the Democratic majority's criticism of the escalation. Resolutions were introduced to end all U.S. involvement in Southeast Asia (*see* War Powers Resolution, 1973). Across the country, Nixon's actions revived the dormant antiwar movement,* and protest demonstrations were renewed. JMR Jr.

Source: *Facts on File*, April–May 1972.

HAI VAN PASS

Highway 1 (*see* "Street Without Joy"), the main supply route along the north-south axis in South Vietnam, connected the port cities of Chu Lai and Da Nang* with Hue,* Quang Tri, and the areas south of the Demilitarized Zone.* Highway 1 ran through the Hai Van Pass at the boundary

Above: The journalist David Halberstam reported for the *New York Times* from South Vietnam in the early 1960s. His pessimistic articles about the progress of the war contrasted sharply with the glowing reports coming from the Pentagon. Halberstam received the Pulitzer Prize for his work in 1964. This photograph was taken in 1993.

Below: Morton Halperin, here in 1993, served as an advisor to Secretary of Defense Robert McNamara during the early 1960s. He gradually became a critic of the American war in Vietnam, arguing that indiscriminate use of firepower was actually making victory less likely to occur and that domestic politics, particularly the fear of appearing weak on Communism, was driving much of the escalation.

between Quang Nam and Thua Tien provinces. The supply line was critical to the American war effort, and over the years the Army invested considerable effort in keeping it open, particularly when bad weather made aerial resupply of American troops impossible.

Source: Harry G. Summers Jr., *Vietnam War Almanac*, 1985.

HALBERSTAM, DAVID

As a reporter for the *New York Times*, David Halberstam won a Pulitzer Prize for his coverage of Vietnam, where he was a correspondent, 1962–64. He was a penetrating critic of the war, but in the early stages of American military involvement he said that Vietnam was a legitimate part of America's global commitment, and as "a strategic country in a key area, it is perhaps one of only five or six nations in the world that are truly vital to U.S. interests." He also said, "We want stability for these people, whereas the Communists actively promote inconstancy. So, we cannot abandon our efforts to help these people." He insisted that Americans should understand the difficult and complex nature of the struggle in Vietnam, however, and he told the truth by American officials. These were the themes of his book, *The Making of a Quagmire*, published in 1965. Halberstam and some of his colleagues reported on the deteriorating military situation and the problems facing the South Vietnamese government. Halberstam was criticized for his reporting of these developments in Vietnam and along with other journalists was subjected to pressure from both Washington and the Vietnamese government. President Kennedy* suggested to *Times* publisher Arthur O. Sulzberger in October 1963 that Halberstam should be removed from the Vietnam assignment because he was "too close to the story." Sulzberger refused, although Halberstam did leave Vietnam in 1964.

Born in New York in 1934, Halberstam was a Harvard graduate who joined the *Times* in 1960. In 1967 he left the *Times*. He wrote articles for *Harper's* magazine, and later wrote several acclaimed books, including *The Best and the Brightest*, a critique of American policy in Vietnam and of American policymakers, as well as *The Powers That Be*, *The Reckoning*, and *The Fifties*. Considered one of America's most distinguished journalists and writers, David Halberstam died on April 23, 2007. HP

Sources: David Halberstam, *The Making of a Quagmire*, 1965, and *The Best and the Brightest*, 1972.

HALPERIN, MORTON

Morton Halperin was born in Brooklyn in 1938. He graduated from Columbia University in 1958 and earned a Ph.D. in political science from Yale in 1961. After working for the Center for International Affairs at Harvard between 1960 and 1966, Halperin went to work for the secretary of defense. The next year he became deputy assistant secretary of defense. Halperin was widely recognized as an expert in arms control, having written a number of books on the subject, including *Nuclear Weapons and Limited War*, 1960; *Strategy and Arms Control*, 1961; *A Proposal for a Ban on the Use of Nuclear Weapons*, 1961; *Arms Control and Inadvertent General War*, 1962; and *Limited War in the Nuclear Age*, 1963. Halperin quickly emerged as a critic of American policy in Vietnam, especially such domestic political imperatives as fear of appearing soft on Communism, which brought about the escalation of the war. He also observed that secrecy hampered full discussion of controversial policies and their possible consequences, which led Richard Nixon* into the 1970 invasion of Cambodia (*see* Operation Binh Tay) and the firestorm of protest following it. Halperin attributed the unrestrained use of herbicides and other chemical substances in Vietnam to the failure of policymakers to be precise in describing the limitations to be imposed on the use of such chemicals, as well as the tendency of those responding to the pressures of war to make maximum use of any weapon available.

In 1969 Halperin became a senior staff member on the National Security Council and a senior fellow of the Brookings Institute. Since 1974 Halperin has continued in his role as a critic of policymaking in Washington. He has concentrated on the growing discrepancy between the administration's desire that controversial policies and decisions be kept from the public in the name of national security and the public's right to know about such policies. JDC

Sources: *Contemporary Authors*, vols. 9–12, 1974; *American Men of Science: The Social and Behavioral Sciences*, vol. 7, 1968; Morton H. Halperin, *Bureaucratic Politics and Foreign Policy*, 1974.

HAMBURGER HILL

Hamburger Hill was the nickname for Dong Ap Bia, a mountain in the A Shau Valley* area of South Vietnam, southwest of Hue* near the Laotian* border. In May 1969 units of the Army of the Republic of Vietnam* (ARVN) and the U.S. 101st Airborne Division* fought against soldiers of the North Vietnamese Army* (NVA) in Operation Apache Snow.* The battle for Dong Ap Bia lasted from May 10 to May 20. It was atypical of the

This page: Medics rush an injured paratrooper to a medevac during fighting on Hamburger Hill in May 1969.

combat in the Vietnam War because it involved large troop units on both sides and because the enemy did not use the tactic of maneuver but instead chose to defend his positions on Dong Ap Bia. The result was a very bloody battle with high casualties* sustained by all units, thus prompting American troops to call the objective Hamburger Hill.

While the enemy's tactics were atypical, the United States characteristically emphasized firepower, including heavy artillery,* napalm,* and B-52* "Arc Light"* air strikes. The enemy's defensive skills against this tactic, however, together with his tenacity, meant that eventually his positions had to be assaulted by infantry, and the result was fierce combat, often hand to hand. After eleven days the enemy retreated to sanctuaries* in Laos. One week later Hamburger Hill was abandoned by the victorious American troops. This was a normal consequence of battles in Vietnam, especially in areas like the A Shau Valley, which were remote and sparsely populated. The basic strategy of both sides was attrition (*see* War of Attrition), not occupation of captured territory.

The Battle of Hamburger Hill was similar to other engagements during the war. Enemy losses were much higher than American casualties, the enemy resolved the battle by retreating without pursuit by American or ARVN forces, and the battlefield was abandoned shortly after the cessation of hostilities. Its timing made it newsworthy, however, and it attracted considerable media attention. In 1969 the new president, Richard Nixon,* was implementing Vietnamization,* a policy to reduce American ground combat involvement (and casualties) and shift that responsibility to the ARVN. Hamburger Hill, reported extensively by the print and broadcast media, seemed to contradict the intent of Vietnamization. It also came to symbolize the frustration of achieving an overwhelming battlefield success without any indication that the war was being won. To many, this frustration suggested that such battles were discrete, mutually exclusive, isolated events that were unrelated to any ultimate policy goal. Hamburger Hill became the subject of intense public debate, focusing on the decision to capture Ap Bia regardless of the casualties and irrespective of its marginal significance in terms of the reasons the United States was in Vietnam. STT

Sources: Samuel Lipsman et al., *The Vietnam Experience: Fighting for Time*, 1983; Shelby L. Stanton, *The Rise and Fall of an American Army: U.S. Ground Forces in Vietnam, 1965–1973*, 1985.

Left: Paratroopers jump out of a helicopter in May 1969 to assist in fighting at Dong Ap Bia, which became known as Hamburger Hill due to the heavy casualties the ARVN, U.S. 101st Airborne, and the NVA all suffered.

HAMLET EVALUATION SURVEY

Developed by Robert Komer* in 1967, the Hamlet Evaluation Survey was an elaborate, computerized system for measuring the number of South Vietnamese citizens living in areas "controlled" by the Republic of Vietnam.* Using eighteen political, economic, and military variables, the Hamlet Evaluation Survey classified villages into one of five categories, depending on the depth of their loyalty to Saigon.* At the end of 1967, according to the survey, more than two-thirds of the people of South Vietnam lived in villages loyal to the Republic of Vietnam. Just one more episode in the futile American pacification efforts (*see* Rural Reconstruction), the Hamlet Evaluation Survey was hopelessly optimistic and naive, and the Tet Offensive* in February 1968 exposed its gross inaccuracies.

Sources: Frances FitzGerald, *Fire in the Lake: The Vietnamese and the Americans in Vietnam*, 1972; Larry E. Cable, *Conflict of Myths: The Development of American Counter-insurgency Doctrine and the Vietnam War*, 1986.

HANOI

Located in the Red River Delta about seventy-five miles inland from the South China Sea, Hanoi is the capital of the Socialist Republic of Vietnam.* It was also the capital of French Indochina.* An industrial and transportation center, Hanoi was a graceful city, influenced by French architecture with spacious tree-lined boulevards. Its population in 1970 had reached 1,100,000 people.

Hanoi was the center of the post–World War II Vietnamese independence movement. Ho Chi Minh* proclaimed the Provisional Government of the Democratic Republic of Vietnam there on August 29, 1945, and three days later he proclaimed Vietnamese independence. Ironically, 500,000 people watched Ho quote the U.S. Declaration of Independence with American military personnel on the reviewing stand, American military aircraft flying overhead, and a band playing "The Star-Spangled Banner." In December 1946, after the French had returned in force, Ho Chi Minh and the Vietminh* blew up Hanoi's power station and attacked French outposts throughout the city. France* controlled Hanoi throughout the war, but as it progressed, French influence was increasingly confined to a small area around the city and in Haiphong. After the Battle of Dien Bien Phu* and the Geneva Accords* in 1954, the Vietminh regained control of Hanoi, making it the capital of the Democratic Republic of Vietnam.

Beginning in 1965 the United States launched massive bombing* campaigns against Hanoi, attacking fuel-storage facilities and transportation centers, especially the Paul Doumer Bridge and the rail yards across the Red River. In 1967 the United States launched air strikes against steel factories, power plants, and other industrial targets. Most industries as well as 800,000 of the city's population were relocated to rural areas. Hanoi was heavily bombed in 1972 in punishment for the Eastertide Offensive.* During the Christmas bombing of 1972 (*see* Operation Linebacker II), in which Richard Nixon* and Henry Kissinger* forced North Vietnamese leaders to fulfill the October Paris Peace Accords,* 36,000 tons of bombs were dropped on the city, killing 2,000 civilians and destroying the Bach Mai Hospital. SF

Sources: Paul Burbage et al., *The Battle for the Skies over North Vietnam, 1964–1972*, 1976; Lou Drendel, *Air War over Southeast Asia*, 1984; Danny J. Whitfield, *Historical and Cultural Dictionary of Vietnam*, 1976.

HANOI HANNAH

In the tradition of Tokyo Rose, Hanoi Hannah was a North Vietnamese radio announcer broadcasting pro-Communist propaganda into South Vietnam and hoping to destroy the morale of American troops there. Most U.S. soldiers reacted with contempt or amusement to her broadcasts, and even prided themselves on having had their units mentioned in her programs. Later in the war, by emphasizing and exaggerating American casualties* and reporting the antiwar* demonstrations back in the United States, Hannah probably helped some soldiers begin to question why they were risking their lives. She particularly singled out black soldiers,* attempting to exacerbate racial animosities and convince them that they were being killed for the advantage of white men. SF

Source: Terrence Maitland and Peter McInerney, *The Vietnam Experience: A Contagion of War*, 1983.

HANOI HILTON

One of numerous prisons that ultimately housed more than 700 American prisoners of war* (POWs) between August 1964 and February 1973, the "Hanoi Hilton" (Hoa Lo Prison) was built by the French near the center of Hanoi.* Sections of the Hilton were dubbed New Guy Village, Heartbreak Hotel, Little Vegas, and Camp Unity. These sections were further subdivided and named. It is an imposing facility, occupying a city block. Walls are 4 feet thick, 20 feet high, and were extended another 5 feet by electrified strands of barbed wire. Shards of glass were embedded on the top of the walls. Other prisons located in or near Hanoi included the "Zoo," "Alcatraz," the "Plantation," and the "Powerplant." The "Briarpatch," "Camp Faith," and "Camp Hope" (Son Tay) were all located within about thirty-five miles of Hanoi (*see* The Hanoi Hilton and Prisoners of War, p. 244).

Above: In 1954, tanks, armored personnel carriers, and artillery pieces rumble through the streets of Hanoi, with civilian bystanders waving flags and flowers and Vietnamese soldiers providing security. Ho Chi Minh's forces had seized control of the French colony of Tonkin, ending the French empire in northern Vietnam.

Left: The entrance to the Hoa Lo Prison in Hanoi, North Vietnam, in 1995. Between 1965 and 1972, most U.S. prisoners of war were incarcerated at Hoa Lo, which they nicknamed the "Hanoi Hilton."

Opposite page: During the course of the Vietnam War, the United States employed every weapon except nuclear bombs in its air assaults on North Vietnam. Bomb shelters were constructed throughout the major cities. Here residents of Hanoi emerge from shelters after the all-clear sirens sound.

Right: This aerial photograph of the "Hanoi Hilton" was taken on May 31, 1973. Several months earlier, the U.S. prisoners of war had been released and repatriated. During the war, in bombing campaigns over North Vietnam, U.S. pilots studiously avoided dropping ordnance near the prison.

HANOI HILTON

Below: Lieutenant General Paul D. Harkins in 1957. He earned the nickname "Ramrod" while he was deputy chief of staff of Patton's Third Army for his determination to fulfill Patton's desire to always keep moving.

Jeremiah Denton's* cell in New Guy Village consisted of "two solid concrete beds ... with metal-and-wood stocks at the foot of each. The one amenity was a small honey bucket [a pail that served as a toilet] ... The concrete bunks were about 3½ feet high and 2½ feet apart. The cell was 9 feet by 8 feet. The door had a small peephole and was flanked by windows which had been covered over by a thin layer of concrete." Sanitation was poor. Cells were infested with insects and rodents. The food, by normal standards, was not fit to eat. Medical treatment was poor to nonexistent and was provided only when a captive's condition became serious or the captive became cooperative.

The North Vietnamese constantly utilized various methods to break captives psychologically, primarily to elicit confessions or information of propaganda value. Captives were not permitted to organize with a recognized chain of command, as POWs generally do. Efforts were made to isolate prisoners and prohibit communications. Consequently, captives developed unobtrusive communication networks employing Morse and "tap" codes. Transmission methods included whistling softly, scratching sounds, even the cadence of sweeping with a broom. As communications networks and chains of command were established and ultimately discovered, prisoners were moved to different units and even to different prisons to break them up or punish the uncooperative. Prisoners were subjected to torture, but not for military information until later in the

war. Sometimes this occurred in their cells, but the Hilton and other prisons also had rooms especially for interrogation and torture. Torture took many forms, from various deprivations such as not being permitted to bathe, to beatings, extended darkness, isolation, shackling (often in contorted positions), and psychological torture.

While U.S. commanders were concerned that prisons might be hit inadvertently during the 1972 Christmas bombing (*see* Operation Linebacker II), prisoners welcomed the bombing and its attendant risks. As a settlement neared, conditions at the Hilton and other prisons improved markedly. Captives were given new clothes, were permitted to organize and to bathe and exercise regularly, and were given much-improved medical attention and food. SF

Sources: Jeremiah Denton, *When Hell Was In Session*, 1982; Benjamin F. Schemmer, *The Raid*, 1976.

HARKINS, PAUL DONAL

Paul D. Harkins was born in Boston on May 15, 1904. After graduating from West Point in 1929, Harkins took a cavalry assignment, served as deputy chief of staff of George Patton's Third Army in World War II, and then was chief of staff of the Eighth Army in Korea. General Paul Harkins served as the first commander of Military

Assistance Command, Vietnam* (MACV). He occupied that post between February 1962 and June 1964. Harkins was a strong supporter of Ngo Dinh Diem,* although the South Vietnamese president usually ignored his advice. Harkin's opposition to the coup that eventually toppled the Diem regime put him at odds with U.S. State Department officials in Saigon,* most notably Ambassador Henry Cabot Lodge.*

In the two decades following his departure from Vietnam, Harkins was criticized for his overly optimistic reports to Washington regarding the military and political situation there. His reports of success were so exaggerated that journalists in the Saigon press corps nicknamed him Blimpie. This occasionally brought him into conflict with American military officers in the field, who often held much more pessimistic views of the South Vietnamese situation. Harkins retired from active duty in 1964 when General William Westmoreland* replaced him at MACV. Paul Harkins died on August 21, 1984. SAK

Sources: *New York Times*, August 22–23, 1984; David Halberstam, *The Best and the Brightest*, 1972; George S. Eckhardt, *Command and Control, 1950–1969*, 1974.

HARRIMAN, WILLIAM AVERELL

William Averell Harriman was born in New York City on November 15, 1891, to one of America's most well-known families. After graduating from Yale in 1913, Harriman went to work for the Union Pacific Railroad. In 1917 he organized the Merchant Shipbuilding Company, made a fortune during World War I, and by the mid-1920s owned the largest merchant fleet in the country. He became chairman of the board of the Illinois Central Railroad in 1931 and the Union Pacific Railroad in 1932. During World War II Harriman represented the Lend-Lease program to the British and the Soviets, and he became ambassador to the Soviet Union* in 1943. He served briefly as ambassador to Great Britain* in 1946 before being named secretary of commerce in President Harry S. Truman's* cabinet. In 1948 Harriman was named as the official U.S. representative in Europe for the Marshall Plan. He was the U.S. representative to NATO in 1951, elected governor of New York in 1954, and during the Kennedy* administration served as an ambassador-at-large and assistant secretary of state for Far Eastern affairs. Between 1963 and 1965 Harriman was undersecretary of state for political affairs.

In 1962 Harriman had played a key role in negotiating the settlement in Laos,* and he had serious doubts about the efficacy of any military solution in Vietnam. Harriman had been a supporter of the containment policy* in Europe, but he saw Asia in different terms. By 1963 Harriman was privately condemning the corruption of the

Diem* regime and urging Kennedy to disassociate the United States from him. President Lyndon B. Johnson* appointed Harriman an ambassador-at-large in 1965 with responsibility for Southeast Asia. Harriman traveled throughout the world in 1965 and 1966 trying to gather support for the American war effort in Vietnam and trying to work out the details for peace talks. By that time his own faith in the war was dead. Early in 1968 Harriman took an active part in the Wise Old Men* group, which advised President Johnson to negotiate a settlement to the war and withdraw American troops. In May 1968, when the Paris peace talks* began, Harriman went there as the chief American negotiator. He remained in Paris until Henry Cabot Lodge* replaced him in January 1969. Throughout the Nixon* administration, Harriman urged American fidelity to a strict withdrawal timetable. W. Averell Harriman died on July 26, 1986.

Sources: Lee H. Burke, *Ambassador at Large: Diplomat Extraordinary*, 1972; *New York Times*, July 27, 1986; Walter Isaacson and Evan Thomas, *The Wise Men: Six Friends and the World They Made*, 1986.

HARTKE, RUPERT VANCE

Vance Hartke was born in Stendal, Indiana, on May 31, 1919. He took his undergraduate degree from Evansville College and a law degree from Indiana University, and between 1948 and 1958 he practiced law in Evansville. Hartke served as mayor of Evansville between 1956 and 1958, and he entered the U.S. Senate as a Democrat in 1958, serving until 1976. Hartke was an avid supporter of Lyndon B. Johnson's* Great Society* programs, and the president counted him as one of his most loyal followers in Congress* until early 1966, when Hartke began questioning American involvement in Vietnam. In January 1966, when Hartke signed a letter to the president with a number of his colleagues, asking Johnson to not resume the bombing* of North Vietnam and to work toward a diplomatic settlement, the president was enraged. He publicly criticized Hartke and actively worked to limit his patronage opportunities. Johnson also saw to it that several of Hartke's followers were fired from government jobs. It mattered little, and Hartke continued to question the depth of the American involvement in Southeast Asia. Hartke left the Senate in 1976 and moved to Virginia. Vance Hartke died on July 27, 2003.

Source: Susan Richards, *Vance Hartke: Democratic Senator from Indiana*, 1972; United States Senate, 2003.

Above: W. Averell Harriman was heir to the fabulous Northern Pacific Railroad fortune, a former ambassador to the Soviet Union, and foreign policy advisor to presidents John F. Kennedy and Lyndon B. Johnson. While serving as assistant secretary of state for Far Eastern Affairs in 1962, Harriman was the diplomat who negotiated the Geneva Accords of 1962, which temporarily ended the Communist insurgency in Laos.

Below: On December 19, 1967, Senator Vance Hartke, Democrat from Indiana, speaks at a press conference on Capitol Hill. Hartke earned the wrath of President Johnson early in 1966 by going public with his opposition to the Vietnam War. In spite of the president's opposition, Hartke won reelection in 1966.

THE HANOI HILTON AND PRISONERS OF WAR

Right: When the American prisoners of war were released on March 29,1973, they were first flown from Hanoi to Clark Air Base in the Philippines. A returning POW grips the railing and stares out a window of a C-141 Starlifter aircraft as it leaves North Vietnamese air space.

American prisoners of war constituted a political and diplomatic challenge during the Vietnam War. Beginning in 1964, when the first downed U.S. pilot was captured, to the signing of the Paris Peace Accords in 1973, return of the POWs constituted a central demand in all American negotiations with North Vietnam and the Vietcong, both of which exploited that bargaining chip for all it was worth. Eventually, the United States compromised on all of its other demands but remained firm on the return of all prisoners of war. Although North Vietnam insisted that it had adhered to the 1949 Geneva Convention on treatment of prisoners of war, its American POWs were routinely tortured and manipulated politically, and they suffered from malnutrition, inadequate medical care, and generally inhumane treatment. American POWs held by the Vietcong faced even more primitive conditions. On January 27, 1973, Henry Kissinger, assistant to the president for national security, concluded negotiations to end the Vietnam War. In Operation Homecoming, the Pentagon and the State Department supervised the repatriation of 566 military and twenty-five civilian prisoners of war. The repatriation process took place in three stages. In the first stage, all POWs were transferred to one of three release sites: POWs of the Vietcong were flown by helicopter to Saigon; those held in North Vietnam were released in Hanoi; and three POWs in China were released in Hong Kong. All POWs were then flown aboard U.S. military transports to Clark Air Base in the Philippines. In the second phase, at Clark,

former POWs were processed through a reception center, where debriefing and physical examinations were held. In the third phase, they were flown to military hospitals for recovery and rehabilitation. On February 12, 1973, the first group of POWs was released in Hanoi; the remainder were handed over to U.S. officials on March 29. A total of 114 American prisoners of war died during their captivity.

The United States uses the term "prisoner of war" to describe American military personnel captured by belligerent enemy nations. The term "missing in action" is reserved for military personnel who do not return from a combat mission and whose bodies have not been recovered. At the end of the war, 2,483 Americans remained unaccounted for, either captured or killed in North Vietnam, South Vietnam, Laos, or Cambodia. Since that time, the number has slowly decreased as remains have been discovered and repatriated to the United States for burial. During the 1990s formal diplomatic relations between the United States and the Socialist Republic of Vietnam accelerated recovery efforts. In the thirty years between 1975 and

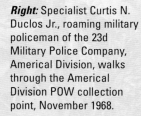

Right: Specialist Curtis N. Duclos Jr., roaming military policeman of the 23d Military Police Company, Americal Division, walks through the Americal Division POW collection point, November 1968.

2005, the remains of 647 missing American soldiers, Marines, and airmen were discovered, leaving 1,836 still unaccounted for.

For many years after the war, the question of prisoners of war and missing in action in Southeast Asia was a volatile political issue. The antiwar movement of the 1960s and early 1970s had created very ambivalent feelings in the United States about veterans of the Vietnam War, as if they had somehow been responsible for the decision to make war and the methods with which it was conducted. Many veterans had witnessed carnage in a war that, before it was over, had lost its purpose. Release of the Pentagon Papers in 1971 confirmed that American politicians during the Eisenhower, Kennedy, and Johnson administrations had outright lied about the Vietnam War or had released misleading information. Many veterans returned to the United States feeling cynical, as if their country had abandoned them.

That sense of abandonment soon blossomed into conspiracy theories about American military personnel still missing in action, fanning beliefs that many American veterans remained alive in Vietnam, Laos, and Cambodia, rotting as prisoners of war and victims of a government that no longer cared to find them. The Pentagon and the governments of Laos, Cambodia, and Vietnam denied any knowledge of American military personnel still alive in Indochina, but many Americans remained skeptical. The Pentagon Papers and Watergate had conjured up doubt among many Americans about the honesty of their leaders. Popular culture reflected the malaise, and the

missing-in-action controversy deepened it. During the 1980s a series of films convinced many people that North Vietnam had not released all American prisoners of war. Chuck Norris starred in *Missing in Action* (1983) as Special Forces leader James Braddock, an ex-POW who returns to Vietnam in 1975 as part of a fact-finding mission to locate any other surviving prisoners of war. When neither Vietnamese nor U.S. officials will cooperate,

Braddock is forced to take matters into his own hands. *Missing in Action 2: The Beginning* continues that theme, as does Sylvester Stallone in *Rambo* (1985) and Gene Hackman in *Uncommon Valor* (1983).

In 1993 more controversy erupted when Harvard professor Stephen Morris secured access to the archives of the former Soviet Union and located a document allegedly written by former North Vietnamese Army general Tran Van Quang. The document stated that in September 1972, when Secretary of State Henry Kissinger was negotiating an end to the war and the return of all prisoners of war, North Vietnam held 1,205 American POWs. Since only 591 American POWs had been released in March 1973, hundreds must have been left behind. The Pentagon doubted the accuracy of the document, but alleged

sightings of Americans surfaced periodically in the late 1980s. Congress launched an investigation, and in 1988 the House of Representatives reported that it had found "no evidence to support the belief that some Americans were still held captive in Indochina" and that "there was only a small hope that a small number of Americans might be alive." In 1996 Congress passed legislation requiring the Pentagon, every three years, to review the status of each American still listed as missing in action in Southeast Asia. Today, no recognized expert on the issue believes that any Americans remain captive in Vietnam, Laos, or Cambodia.

Sources: http://www.pbs.org/wgbh/amex/vietnam/trenches/mia.html; John G. Hubbell, *POW: A Definitive History of the American Prisoner of War Experience in Vietnam, 1964–1973,* 1976.

Below: Some American POWs were also incarcerated in the Nga Tu prison camp in Hanoi. In this March 29, 1973 photograph, taken just hours before their release, five POWs turn their backs on a North Vietnamese cameraman. They did not want to be photographed because they had been moved to this clean, well-lit cell just for the photograph. "We object to pictures," said one POW, "because this is not the way we lived."

Left: An American prisoner of war's memento, currently in the U.S. Naval Museum in Washington, D.C., contains toothpaste and a toothbrush, a spoon, matches, pencils, clothespins, and soap.

HATFIELD, MARK ODUM

Mark Hatfield was born in Dallas, Oregon, on July 12, 1922. He graduated from Willamette University in 1943 and took a master's degree from Stanford in 1948. Hatfield then taught political science at Willamette between 1950 and 1956. He was a state legislator in Oregon from 1951 to 1957, secretary of state from 1957 to 1959, and governor of Oregon from 1959 to 1967. Hatfield won election to the U.S. Senate as a Republican in 1966. Hatfield's career in the Senate was marked by a vigorous opposition to the Vietnam War. By 1967 he was criticizing the scale of the American military effort in Indochina,* and he also became a frequent critic of the Nixon* administration's handling of the war. In Hatfield's opinion, Nixon and Kissinger* were unnecessarily lengthening the American stay there. When Nixon authorized the invasion of Cambodia (*see* Operation Binh Tay), Hatfield spoke militantly against it and sponsored, along with Senator George McGovern,* a Senate amendment cutting off funds for the Vietnam War after December 31, 1971. The amendment never passed. Hatfield also opposed the military draft* and called for the establishment of a voluntary Army.

Sources: *Who's Who in America, 1984–1985*, 1985; Mark Hatfield, *Conflict and Conscience*, 1971, and *Amnesty: The Unsettled Question of Vietnam*, 1973.

Above: Republican Governor Mark Hatfield in his office in Salem, Oregon, on November 1, 1963. A liberal Republican, one of the last of that political breed, Hatfield became an inveterate opponent of the Vietnam War and a political thorn in the side of presidents Lyndon B. Johnson and Richard M. Nixon.

Below: Tom Hayden was one of the founders of Students for a Democratic Society (SDS), a radical political group of the 1960s. SDS called for an end to the Vietnam War, accused Democratic and Republican politicians of using U.S. foreign policy to promote capitalism, and called for a redistribution of wealth in the United States. Hayden eventually grew more conservative and mainstream in his politics. In 1979, he denounced nuclear power in a speech at Fordham University.

HATFIELD-McGOVERN AMENDMENT

Late in April 1970, President Richard Nixon* had approved a combined American–South Vietnamese invasion of Cambodia (*see* Operation Binh Tay) to attack Vietcong* and North Vietnamese sanctuaries* there. To many Americans, the invasion—Nixon called it an incursion— seemed a dangerous escalation of the war, and widespread protest demonstrations erupted across the country. Especially violent confrontations between students and National Guard troops occurred at Kent State University* in Ohio and Jackson State University in Mississippi. During the first week of May more than 100,000 protesters gathered in Washington, D.C., to denounce the invasion. Outraged at not being consulted about the invasion, the Senate symbolically protested by terminating the Gulf of Tonkin Resolution* in June 1970. Senator George McGovern* of South Dakota and Senator Mark Hatfield* of Oregon jointly sponsored an amendment requiring a total American withdrawal from South Vietnam by the end of 1971. Although the Hatfield-McGovern Amendment failed to pass in the Senate, it was an indication of the frustration that large numbers of Americans felt about the war.

Sources: George Herring, *America's Longest War: The United States and Vietnam, 1950–1975*, 1986; William Shawcross, *Sideshow: Kissinger, Nixon, and the Destruction of Cambodia*, 1979.

HAYDEN, THOMAS EMMETT

Thomas Hayden was born on December 12, 1940, in Royal Oak, Michigan, the only child of Catholic parents in a conservative working-class neighborhood. In December 1961, as a University of Michigan student, Hayden had helped found the Students for a Democratic Society* (SDS) and drafted the Port Huron Statement: "We are the people of this generation, bred in at least modest comfort, housed now in universities, looking uncomfortably to a world we inherit." At first SDS was not much more to the left than the liberal wing of the Democratic Party. But under the pressure of the civil rights movement and opposition to the Vietnam War, Hayden's politics gradually became more and more radical. By the fall of 1965, SDS was organizing against the draft* and was accused of sabotaging the war effort. In 1966 and 1967, SDS escalated its campus demonstrations and protest marches. Hayden met with North Vietnamese representatives in Czechoslovakia in 1967, where the release of American prisoners of war* (POWs) was discussed. He later flew to Cambodia* and escorted three released prisoners home.

In 1968 Hayden joined Rennie Davis* in planning the National Mobilization Committee's anti-Vietnam demonstrations at that year's Democratic National Convention. The protesters were assaulted by the Chicago police, but Hayden was later arrested and became one of the "Chicago 8"* defendants charged with conspiracy. Although he was convicted, the decision was later overturned on appeal. Following the trial Hayden joined actress Jane Fonda* on the antiwar circuit, and they were married in January 1973. After that Hayden began to change his radical image and entered California politics. He ran a surprisingly close race against Senator John Tunney in the senatorial primary in 1976, and in 1979 he and Fonda established the Campaign for Economic Democracy, a movement designed to secure popular control over major corporations. Dubbed the "Mork and Mindy" of the left in a column by George Will, they made appearances dressed conservatively and toned down their rhetoric from the militancy of the 1960s. Hayden won a seat in the California state assembly in 1980, and explained his political evolution by saying: "The radical or reformer sets a climate. The politician inherits the constituency that the reformer created. My problem is to be both." He served in the assembly until 1982, when he won a seat in the state senate. Hayden ran unsuccessfully for mayor of Los Angeles in 1997, and in 2000 he left the senate. FF

Sources: Charles Moritz, "Tom Hayden," *Current Biography*, 1976; Tom Hayden, *The American Future: New Visions Beyond Old Frontiers*, 1980, and *Rebel: A Personal History of the Sixties*, 2003; Nancy Zaroulis and Gerald Sullivan, *Who Spoke Up? American Protest Against the Vietnam War, 1963–1975*, 1984.

Left: At the Academy Awards ceremony on April 8, 1975, Bert Schneider and his co-producer accept an Oscar for Best Documentary Film. Their *Hearts and Minds* was an unrelenting indictment of the Vietnam War. Schneider then unexpectedly read a telegram from the Provisional Revolutionary Government of Vietnam that expressed gratitude to all Americans who had opposed the war in Vietnam. Later in the show, the singer Frank Sinatra read a statement that the Academy of Motion Picture Arts and Sciences did not endorse the telegram.

HEARTS AND MINDS

An Academy Award winner for Best Documentary in 1974, *Hearts and Minds* was a controversial film examining the U.S. involvement in Vietnam. By interviewing American policymakers, Vietnamese leaders, veterans, and Vietnamese peasants, the film looks at the war in terms of American culture, the World War II experience, and global politics. In one sense the film is balanced, devoting equal time to the war's supporters and critics. Harry S. Truman,* Dwight D. Eisenhower,* John F. Kennedy,* Lyndon B. Johnson,* Richard M. Nixon,* and William Westmoreland* present rationales supporting the war, while Clark Clifford,* Daniel Ellsberg,* and J. William Fulbright* oppose it. Navy lieutenant and POW (1966–73) George Coker (fifty-five bombing missions) explains the war in terms of Communist aggression, and former fighter-bomber pilot Captain Randy Floyd (ninety-eight bombing missions) explains it in terms of human beings. Other veterans, including paraplegic Robert Mueller and double amputee William Marshall, explain their views before, during, and after Vietnam.

In another sense, the film was not balanced. Graphic war footage includes the most famous and damning of the war. Colonel Nguyen Ngoc Loan,* Saigon* chief of police, is shown summarily executing a Vietcong* suspect during the 1968 Tet Offensive.* A young girl, Kim Phuc, her burns clearly visible, is shown running down a road nude, having torn off her burning clothes after the pagoda in which she had taken refuge was napalmed. While there are scenes of hamlets being bombed and put to flame by GIs as villagers beg for mercy, of Vietnamese being tortured, of disabled and mutilated Vietnamese and Americans, of Vietnamese recounting the destruction of their homes and loss of loved ones due to American bombardment, there are few scenes of Vietcong/North Vietnamese Army* violence, and virtually none of the injuries they inflicted on the civilian population. Critics of the film were outraged by what they saw as blatant bias. After footage in which a Vietnamese family demonstrably mourns the death of an ARVN soldier (*see* Army of the Republic of Vietnam), with his son crying and hugging his picture and his mother attempting to crawl into the grave with him, General William Westmoreland is shown saying, "The Oriental doesn't put the same high price on life as does the Westerner. Life is plentiful; life is cheap in the Orient. And as the philosophy of the Orient expresses itself, life is not important." Those who praised the film, however, felt that its spirit matched the nature of the American war effort in Vietnam. There is thought-provoking irony footage in celebrations of our own war for independence, or a minister before the "big game" praying for victory with a high school football team, or Colonel George S. Patton III's account of a memorial service for fallen comrades in which he concludes that his men are "a bloody good bunch of killers." SF

Source: "Hearts and Minds," *Variety*, May 15, 1974.

Above: An American GI's Zippo lighter engraved with the phrase, "give me your hearts, minds or I will wreck your fucking huts," commenting sarcastically on President Lyndon Johnson's speech in 1965 that victory will depend upon the hearts and minds of the Vietnamese people, as compared to the reality on the ground.

"HEARTS AND MINDS" (Phrase)

In 1965 President Lyndon B. Johnson* paraphrased John Adams' description of the American Revolution: "The Revolution was effected before the war commenced. The Revolution was in the minds and hearts of the people." About Vietnam Johnson said: "So we must be ready to fight in Vietnam, but the ultimate victory will depend on the hearts and minds of the people who actually live out there." Eventually, however, the United States did not win the hearts and minds of the Vietnamese people, and the war became a conflict over the hearts and minds of the American people.

Military apologists argued that the war was lost because Washington misperceived it as a guerrilla/civil war rather than a conventional war instigated, directed, and ultimately fought by North Vietnam. To them the emphasis on pacification (*see* Rural Reconstruction) was misplaced, resulting in the misallocation of resources away from fighting the war; an inappropriate strategy aimed at ferreting out guerrilla bands when main-force, hard-core North Vietnamese Army* units were the real problem; allowing invading forces sanctuaries* that guaranteed they could never be defeated; and a media focus that caused Americans to misunderstand and lose patience with the war. According to Harry G. Summers, the war was not in "the hearts and minds of the … people but the guns and bullets of the North Vietnamese Army."

Most observers, however, accepted the counter-arguments of military and pacification professionals like William Corson (*The Betrayal*, 1968) and Cincinnatus (*Self-Destruction*, 1981), who argued that "every strike that levels a village or cuts a road or kills innocent civilians contributes to the ultimate victory even if … the guerrillas lose both ground and men. For all such military operations, by their very nature and destructiveness, alienate the people among whom they occur." That sentiment was shared by people like CIA director William Colby and pacification expert Robert Komer.* Robert Taber (*The War of the Flea*, 1965) said that there "is only one way of defeating an insurgent people who will not surrender, and that is extermination. There is only one way to control a territory that harbours resistance, and that is to turn it into a desert. Where these means cannot, for whatever reason, be used, the war is lost."

But an unwillingness to understand, much less respect, either pacification or the Vietnamese people permeated the American command structure. American military personnel were either paternalistic or racist in their attitudes toward the Vietnamese; if U.S.-ARVN military violence did not turn the Vietnamese peasants against the United States, those attitudes surely did. Ultimately, the war became a battle for the American people's "hearts and minds." The Vietnamese could refuse defeat. They understood that Americans would tire of a war they did not and could not understand, that eventually enough body bags would return, that there were limits to the resources the United States could squander in Vietnam. When that day came, the Americans would leave, just as had the Chinese and the French before them. SF

Sources: Larry E. Cable, *Conflict of Myths: The Development of American Counter-insurgency Doctrine and the Vietnam War*, 1986; Andrew F. Krepinevich Jr., *The Army and Vietnam*, 1986; Frances FitzGerald, *Fire in the Lake: The Vietnamese and the Americans in Vietnam*, 1972.

Below: Crew chief Specialist Thomas L. Dannenburg of Riverhead, New York, opens fire with an M60 machine gun on a Vietcong position marked on a previous run by a red smoke grenade on March 16, 1966. Dannenburg was a member of Company A, 229th Helicopter Assault Battalion, 11th Aviation Group, 1st Cavalry Division.

HELICOPTER GUNSHIPS

Early U.S. helicopter operations in Vietnam met limited resistance from enemy small-arms fire, causing the U.S. Army* to begin arming helicopters in an attempt to suppress ground fire. A .30-caliber machine gun was mounted in the forward door of CH-21s* to give them the ability to suppress ground fire during landing operations. As the weapon had a limited arc of fire and the CH-21 suffered from poor maneuverability, this attempt was not very successful. The Army then decided to arm the new UH-1As* and organized a test unit, the Utility Tactical Transport Helicopter Company. Fifteen UH-1As were equipped with two .30-caliber machine guns and sixteen 2.75-inch rockets and sent to Thailand* for training. In November 1962 this unit was assigned to Tan Son Nhut Air Base* in Vietnam, where it began flying in support of U.S. Army CH-21 units.

Originally designated as "escorts," these helicopters were to pioneer the helicopter gunship role in Vietnam. As this role expanded, the term "escort" was dropped in favor of "gunship" or the nickname given to them by GIs, "hog." The UH-1As continued to provide most of the gunships used in Vietnam, although other helicopters also were used in this role. In a typical airmobile assault, gunships would make passes over landing zones to soften them up and draw enemy fire before the slicks* carrying troops came in.

As enemy ground weapons improved, the need for increased firepower from helicopter gunships became apparent. More sophisticated rocket packs, .50-caliber machine guns, and the M75 grenade launcher became standard equipment for the UH-1s; the CH-47,* capable of carrying more weight, was also turned into a gunship, using G.E. miniguns capable of firing 2,000 rounds per minute of 7.62mm shells either through the side windows or through the rear doors. As the need for increased firepower was recognized, the 1st Cavalry Division* received three heavily

modified CH-47s. These "go-go birds" were fitted with a grenade launcher capable of firing 200 rounds per minute of 40mm high explosive in the nose; rocket pods and cannons mounted on side sponsons; and .50-caliber machine guns firing through windows and the rear cargo hatch. In response to Vietcong* use of .50-caliber machine guns as antiaircraft weapons, a number of UH-1s were fitted with M24A 20mm cannons. These cannons enabled the UH-1s to stay out of range of enemy ground fire, while delivering 2,000 rounds per minute of fire.

The UH-1 provided the basic frame for the first helicopter specifically designed as a gunship, the AH-1G* Cobra. Using the basic components of the UH-1 allowed the Army to develop this gunship in only six months. Cobras began serving in Vietnam in 1967. Heavily armed with a variety of weapons and equipped with sophisticated, new "sight-guided" aiming systems, the Cobra proved a highly effective gunship. Cannons, grenade launchers, or machine guns could be mounted in turrets, giving them

Above: The XM21 weapons system, mounted here on a UH-1D helicopter, consists of a seven-round rocket pod and an M134 high rate of fire machine gun. Based on the principle of the traditional Gatling gun, the M134 had six gun barrels capable of firing up to 4,000 rounds per minute. Its impact on enemy infantry was devastating.

Opposite page: July 19, 1968: U.S. Marines with 2d Battalion, 3d Marines, move up Hill 366 on a search-and-clear mission 6,561 feet south of the DMZ. The helicopter overhead is a CH-46 troop transport.

the capability of swinging through a 230-degree arc. The weapons were aimed by the gunner "looking-in" the target, with the turret swinging to follow his head.

Overall, helicopter gunships proved their worth in Vietnam, providing ground forces with close support cover in a way fixed-wing aircraft could not. NJA

Sources: *Jane's All the World's Aircraft: 1970–1971*, 1971; Jim Mesko, *Airmobile: The Helicopter War in Vietnam*, 1985.

then destroyed a fourth CH-46. Panic-stricken Marines trying to escape the crashed helicopters were slashed to death by the whirling blades.

Sources: Edward Doyle and Samuel Lipsman, *The Vietnam Experience: America Takes Over, 1965–1967*, 1985; Willard Pearson, *The War in the Northern Provinces, 1966–1968*, 1975.

"HELICOPTER VALLEY"

Below: This CH-46 helicopter delivers supplies to the besieged Marine outpost at Khe Sanh in 1968. The CH-46 had the virtue of speed and could handle heavy cargo loads, allowing the Marines to relocate troops and supplies with remarkable efficiency.

"Helicopter Valley" was a nickname given to the Song Ngan Valley in 1966. Located in Quang Tri Province just south of the Demilitarized Zone,* Song Ngan Valley became famous on July 15, 1966, when a squadron of CH-46* helicopters carried the 3d Battalion, 4th Marines of the 3d Marine Division* as part of Operation Hastings* to stop North Vietnamese infiltration* of South Vietnam. The third wave of CH-46s faced a disaster when two of them collided and crashed. Another CH-46, desperately trying to avoid the collision, crashed into the jungle. North Vietnamese snipers

HELICOPTER WAR

The helicopter became the primary symbol of the U.S. military presence in Vietnam. No other weapons system attained the high degree of visibility or identification with the war that the helicopter did. The ubiquitous "Huey" (UH–1)* emerged as the unofficial symbol of U.S. involvement.

Helicopters were first used in Vietnam by the French, mainly for medical evacuation. The French had determined to begin using large numbers of helicopters for troop movements to offset the superior mobility of the Vietminh,* but the French defeat at Dien Bien Phu* ended those plans.

American combat involvement in Vietnam started and ended with helicopters. In December of 1961 the 8th and

11th Air Assault Division

363d Marine Heavy
Helicopter Squadron

48th Assault Helicopter Company
Gun Platoon

192d Assault Helicopter Company

Above: Use of the helicopter provided the most profound tactical innovation of the Vietnam War. The delivery of troops to a battle site could be coordinated with artillery bombardment and tactical air strikes, providing a combination of firepower and mobility unprecedented in military history. In 1965, a helicopter prepares to evacuate wounded soldiers near the Special Forces Camp near Du Co, South Vietnam.

57th Transportation companies arrived in Vietnam. Flying the Piasecki H-21 (later the Vertol and then Boeing-Vertol CH-21*), these units flew combat missions supporting the Army of the Republic of Vietnam* (ARVN), thus becoming the first U.S. troops to officially serve in a direct combat role. The units were followed by a U.S. Marine* helicopter squadron flying CH-34s* and by a U.S. Army* medical detachment using UH-1s for medical evacuation (*see* Medevac). In the fall of 1962, fifteen newly armed UH-1s arrived in Vietnam to serve as the first of the helicopter gunships of the war.

The first major offensive operation using American helicopters occurred on January 2, 1963, when ten CH-21s, escorted by five Huey gunships, were used to place ARVN forces in a ring around Ap Bac in an attempt to trap and eliminate a major enemy unit. Lacking fixed-wing* air cover, the units took heavy losses, including the loss of five helicopters. The enemy forces were able to withdraw from Ap Bac successfully. Thus the first airmobile assault of the Vietnam War failed. Lessons were drawn from this

failure, including the need to coordinate airmobile assaults with bombing and strafing runs by fixed-wing aircraft. As helicopter gunships improved, the need for fixed-wing support declined.

Faced with early failure in the attempt to use a new concept of airmobile fighting, the U.S. Army established a test division to work out more effective techniques. The division was established at Fort Benning, Georgia, as the 11th Air Assault Division. This division constantly exchanged personnel with units in Vietnam in an attempt to analyze and perfect airmobile techniques. In 1965 one of these units in Vietnam, the 173d Airborne Brigade,* teamed with a number of helicopter units in launching a series of airmobile assaults that were seen as highly successful. By October of 1965 the 11th Air Assault Division, now combined with major elements of the 2d Infantry Division and redesignated the 1st Cavalry Division (Airmobile),* was in place at An Khe in South Vietnam's Central Highlands. They constructed the world's largest helipad (known as the golf course, as it always had at least eighteen holes in it from rocket and mortar attacks), and the U.S. Army was ready to launch the helicopter war in earnest.

In November 1965 the 1st Cavalry fought its first major battles with the North Vietnamese Army* (NVA). The NVA launched an attack designed to draw out ARVN forces and ambush them in the Central Highlands.* The NVA then planned to drive across the center of South Vietnam, cutting the country in half. The 1st Cavalry forces, supporting the ARVN units, engaged the enemy in a series of battles known as the Battle of Ia Drang* Valley. NVA attempts to isolate American and ARVN units and hit them with superior forces were constantly thwarted by the 1st Cavalry's ability to move units rapidly with helicopters. At the end of the campaign, the NVA had lost 1,800 troops, while the 1st Cavalry lost 240 men and four helicopters. The pattern of conflict in the helicopter war had been established.

By the late 1960s the U.S. Army had 4,000 aircraft serving in Vietnam, including 3,600 helicopters. These were organized into four types of units. Airmobile divisions, starting with the 1st Cavalry Division and joined in 1968 by the converted 101st Airborne,* were fully equipped with their own helicopters under their direct control. Regular infantry divisions had organic aviation units attached to them, normally of battalion* strength. A number of helicopter companies were assigned directly to Military Assistance Command, Vietnam,* and a number of other helicopter units were assigned directly to special units such as engineer, signal, or support groups.

Operation Delaware,* conducted in the A Shau Valley* in 1966, represented a turning point in the helicopter war. This was the biggest airmobile operation to date, and was seen by U.S. forces as a major success. They lost more aircraft than expected, however, and it appeared that the NVA had, in a little more than a year, begun to adapt their tactics to fit within the helicopter war. In 1971 the United States was involved in the last major airmobile offensive operation of the war in Lam Son 719,* an attempt to clear the NVA from an area extending from Khe Sanh* into Laos.* Ground forces were provided by the ARVN, with U.S. support limited primarily to helicopters. Lam Son 719 failed to meet any of its objectives, with ARVN troops bogging down in heavy fighting.

The last major involvement of U.S. forces in Vietnam was defensive, and involved helicopter gunships. In the spring of 1972 the NVA launched major assaults supported by heavy armor, including Soviet T-54 tanks. A major factor in a successful ARVN defense was the presence of U.S. helicopter gunships armed with antitank weapons (*see* M72), including TOW missiles.

In 1975 South Vietnam collapsed. Americans at home witnessed the panic, as they had witnessed much of the helicopter war, on their television screens. Graphic images of hovering U.S. helicopters evacuating personnel from the American embassy, and of other helicopters, both U.S. and ARVN, crashing into the sea after dropping their passengers on ships, represented the end of American involvement in South Vietnam. A CH-53* involved in the evacuation crashed into the sea, killing two U.S. Marines—the last U.S. casualties of the Vietnam War.

American combat involvement in Vietnam began and ended with helicopters. Early attempts using U.S. helicopters and ARVN troops proved unsatisfactory; the same combination at the end of the war, as represented in Lam Son 719, proved equally ineffective. Yet the helicopter war concept of airmobile units did prove its value, and remains a key component of American military strategy. NJA

Sources: *The Encyclopedia of Air Warfare*, 1974; Jim Mesko, *Airmobile: The Helicopter War in Vietnam*, 1985.

HELMS, RICHARD McGARRAH

Richard Helms was born in St. Davids, Pennsylvania, on March 30, 1913. After graduating from Williams College in 1935, he became a staff correspondent for UPI and joined the *Indianapolis Times* in 1937. Helms stayed with the *Times* until 1942, when he was assigned by the United States Navy* to work with the Office of Strategic Services (OSS). After the war Helms stayed on with the OSS when it became the Central Intelligence Agency.* During the years of the Vietnam War between 1965 and 1973, Helms was deputy director and then director of the CIA. When the war reached its late stages in the early 1970s, Helms came under siege from critics protesting clandestine CIA activities in Indochina*—secret armies, assassination squads, sponsored coup d'etats, and domestic surveillance. As a result of congressional hearings, new legislation required the CIA to secure presidential approval of all covert operations, surrender documents to public scrutiny as long as they did not compromise agents in the field, stop surveillance of Americans abroad unless national security required it, and cease all domestic surveillance. Helms was forced to appear before a number of House and Senate committees in the mid-1970s as the legislation was evolving. Between 1973 and 1976 he also served as ambassador to Iran. Richard Helms died on October 22, 2002.

Sources: Thomas W. Powers, *The Man Who Kept the Secrets*, 1979; Morton H. Halperin et al., *The Lawless State: The Crimes of the U.S. Intelligence Agencies*, 1976; John Prados, *Presidents' Secret Wars: CIA and Pentagon Covert Operations Since World War II*, 1986; Richard Helms, *A Look Over My Shoulder: A Life in the Central Intelligence Agency*, 2003.

HERBICIDES

See Defoliants; Operation Ranch Hand

Above: During the Vietnam War, Richard Helms served as deputy director and then as director of the CIA. Among the most controversial of his efforts was the Phoenix Program, which targeted influential Vietcong officials for assassination. In South Vietnam, where political corruption was endemic, Phoenix Program assassins often killed political enemies of the Saigon regime.

HIGH NATIONAL COUNCIL

Between November 1963, with the assassination of Ngo Dinh Diem,* and Nguyen Van Thieu's* rise to power in June 1965, a succession of civilian and military governments assumed power in Saigon.* In September 1964 a military regime headed by General Nguyen Khanh* appointed a seventeen-member High National Council, representing a variety of political groups, to draft a new constitution. The constitution was ready on October 20, 1964, and the High National Council appointed Phan Khac Suu* as chief of state and Tran Van Huong* as prime minister. Buddhist* groups immediately began demonstrating against the High National Council; and on December 18, thirty young generals, led by Nguyen Khanh, formed an Armed Forces Council, dissolved the High National Council, and in January 1965 dismissed Prime Minister Huong.

Source: Harvey H. Smith et al., *Area Handbook for South Vietnam*, 1967.

Below: The Hmong (or Meo) people, a Montagnard group in the mountains of Laos, often cooperated with United States military personnel in fighting the North Vietnamese Army. After the war, thousands of Hmong, fearing retaliation from North Vietnam, fled Laos, emigrated from Vietnam, and ended up in the United States. In this photograph taken in the 1990s, three young Hmong women can be seen in traditional tribal clothing.

HIGHWAY 1

See "Street Without Joy"

"HILL OF ANGELS"

See Con Thien, Battle of

HILSMAN, ROGER

Roger Hilsman was born in Waco, Texas, on November 23, 1919. He graduated from West Point in 1943 and joined the Office of Strategic Services, working behind Japanese lines in Asia. After the war Hilsman stayed with the newly formed Central Intelligence Agency,* and in 1951 received a Ph.D. in international relations from Yale. Between 1950 and 1953 Hilsman worked on NATO development in Europe, spent the years between 1953 and 1956 with the Center for International Studies at Princeton, and then joined the Library of Congress. He wrote widely on foreign affairs, and his books *Strategic Intelligence and National Decisions* (1956) and *Alliance Policy in the Cold War* (1959) made him an influential figure in Washington. In 1961 Hilsman became director of the bureau of intelligence and research for the Department of State. As early as 1961 Hilsman was warning policymakers that military action alone would not solve guerrilla wars in underdeveloped countries; that popular support gained through economic development and political reform was indispensable. In

1963 Hilsman was promoted to assistant secretary of state for Far Eastern affairs. Along with Michael Forrestal,* Hilsman went to Vietnam on a fact-finding mission in 1963, and their Hilsman-Forrestal Report* concluded that the American commitment in Vietnam would be a difficult and long-term problem. Hilsman also urged John Kennedy* to exploit the growing rift between the Soviet Union* and China by seeking a normalization of relations with the People's Republic of China.*

After the assassination of President Kennedy, Hilsman resigned from the government to resume his academic career, teaching at Columbia University. In 1967 he published a well-received account of foreign policy during the Kennedy administration, *To Move a Nation*. A major contention was that Kennedy intended, after the election of 1964, to work for the neutralization of Vietnam, as had already been done in Laos,* and thus extricate the United States from that quagmire. Roger Hilsman is now retired and serves as professor emeritus at Columbia University. JMR Jr.

Sources: *Current Biography*, 1964; *Current Authors*, 1969; Roger Hilsman, *To Move a Nation*, 1967.

HILSMAN-FORRESTAL REPORT

Early in 1963, concerned about contradictory reports about Vietnam coming from military officials and journalists, President John F. Kennedy* dispatched State Department Far East expert Roger Hilsman* and White House staffer Michael Forrestal* to Vietnam on a fact-finding mission. In their report, they argued that American policies in Southeast Asia should be continued, but that the ARVN (*see* Army of the Republic of Vietnam) was weakened by severe corruption and morale problems, that Ngo Dinh Diem* was becoming increasingly isolated from the Vietnamese masses, and that the American commitment there would be longer than originally anticipated. The overall tone of the report, however, was optimistic and contributed to the escalation of the American effort in Vietnam.

Source: George C. Herring, *America's Longest War: The United States in Vietnam, 1950–1975*, 1986.

HMONG

The Hmong, also known as the Meo or Miao, were Laotian tribal people living in the mountains of North Vietnam and Laos.* They constituted about 15 percent of the Laotian population in the early 1970s, totaling more than 300,000 people. Speaking a Sino-Tibetan dialect, the Hmong were relatively late arrivals to Laos and Vietnam, migrating from China in the nineteenth century. Over the years the

Vietnamese and the French were in frequent conflict with them, and the Hmong were often recruited by all sides in the Vietnamese conflict. During the 1960s and 1970s the Central Intelligence Agency* raised a Hmong army, led by General Vang Pao, to attack the Ho Chi Minh Trail* as it passed through Laos, and over the years they sustained heavy casualties. After the end of the Vietnam War, large numbers of Hmong immigrated to the United States, settling primarily in the western states.

Sources: John Prados, *Presidents' Secret Wars: CIA and Pentagon Covert Operations Since World War II*, 1986; Keith Quincy, *Hmong: History of a People*, 2003.

Above: The Hoa Hao was a highly independent Buddhist sect in South Vietnam with more than 1 million adherents. They lived primarily in South Vietnam, particularly throughout the Mekong Delta. The Hoa Hao maintained its own militia, which became a potent political force in South Vietnam. In this 1948 photograph, a group of Hoa Hao women can be seen training with sabers for guerrilla warfare. In 1955, Ngo Dinh Diem ruthlessly crushed and disarmed the Hoa Hao.

HOA HAO

The Hoa Hao movement, a major but independent Buddhist sect prominent in the Mekong Delta,* was founded in 1919 by Huynh Phu So.* After a sickly youth, he entered a monastery in 1939; after he received what he termed a miraculous cure, he founded the sect. The movement had strong anti-French overtones, which the Japanese exploited between 1940 and 1945. A variant of Theravada Buddhism,* the Hoa Hao emphasized the importance of faith as opposed to experience, prayer four times daily, and veneration of Buddha, ancestors, and national heroes. By

Above: In this 1950 photograph, Ho Chi Minh can be seen just as he was attaining iconic political status in Vietnam. As the man responsible for expelling the French and achieving Vietnamese independence, Ho was revered in North Vietnam as well as in South Vietnam.

the late 1940s and 1950s the Hoa Hao had more than 1 million followers and were a force to be reckoned with in South Vietnam, the only political movement with roots in the Vietnamese peasantry sufficient to rival Communist influence. In April 1947 Communist guerrillas (*see* Vietcong) among the Vietminh* assassinated Huynh Phu So, and leadership of the movement shifted to Ba Cut, a powerful man who directed the Hoa Hao army in South Vietnam.

But it was just that Hoa Hao independence, particularly its military strength and independent army, which bothered other political elements in South Vietnam. The anti-Communist government of South Vietnam, like the Communist Vietminh, resented the independence of the Hoa Hao, and in 1955 it launched a military campaign against them. After extensive resistance, the Hoa Hao were subdued and conquered, and Ba Cut was arrested in April 1956 and executed in July. The Hoa Hao remained a strong religious presence in South Vietnam, but their status as an independent military power was over.

Source: Nguyen Long Thaonh Nam, *Hoa Hao Buddhism in the Course of Vietnamese History*, 2004.

HOANG VAN HOAN

Hoang Van Hoan was born in Nghe An Province in central Vietnam in 1905, and joined the Vietnam Youth Revolutionary League in 1926. Under pressure from the French, he fled to China and became a founding member of the Lao Dong Party* in 1930. Hoan was active in the Vietminh* after World War II and served as ambassador to the People's Republic of China* for several years in the 1950s. In 1958 Hoang Van Hoan became vice president of the National Assembly Standing Committee of the Democratic Republic of Vietnam.* Between 1951 and 1982 Hoan was also a member of the Central Committee and the politburo of the Democratic Republic of Vietnam.

Sources: Central Intelligence Agency, *Who's Who in North Vietnam*, 1969; Joseph Buttinger, *Vietnam: A Dragon Embattled*, Vol. 2, *Vietnam at War*, 1967.

HO CHI MINH

Ho Chi Minh was born as Nguyen Sinh Cung on May 19, 1890, in Nghe An Province of central Vietnam. His father, Nguyen Sinh Sac, had achieved mandarin status through diligent study but abandoned his family to become an itinerant teacher. Ho attended school in Hue,* where his lifelong quest for Vietnamese independence was first launched. Moving south in 1909, Ho Chi Minh, now calling himself Van Ba, taught school in a number of villages,

worked in Saigon,* and in 1911 signed on for work aboard a French freighter. In 1912 Ho left Vietnam and did not return for thirty years. He sailed around the world for three years, and lived one year in the United States—in Brooklyn. Known as Nguyen Tat Thanh, Ho then moved to London and from there to Paris, where he became a founding member of the French Communist Party in 1920. By then Ho Chi Minh was speaking and writing avidly on his major ideological theory—that anticolonial* nationalism and socioeconomic revolution were inseparable.

Suspicious of the Vietnamese nationalists among them, French security forces began tracking Ho Chi Minh's movements, and in 1924 he moved to Moscow, met the leaders of the Soviet Union,* studied for several months at the University of Oriental Workers, and then moved on to Canton. In southern China, Ho Chi Minh organized the Thanh Nien Cach Menh Dong Chi Hoi* (Revolutionary Youth League) to campaign for Vietnamese independence, and in 1930 he organized the Indochinese Communist Party (*see* Lao Dong Party). Throughout the 1930s Ho Chi Minh wandered widely throughout the world, spending time in China, the Soviet Union, Thailand,* and other parts of Asia. When the Japanese invaded Indochina* in 1940, Ho Chi Minh began allying himself with the Allied powers; Japanese domination of Vietnam, in his mind, was no better than that of the French Empire. Assuming the name Ho Chi Minh, he returned to Vietnam in May 1941 and established the Viet Nam Doc Lap Dong Minh Hoi* (League for Vietnamese Independence), or the Vietminh.* During World War II Ho cultivated his relationship with the United States, especially with OSS agents fighting against the Japanese in Indochina; when the war ended in 1945 Ho was widely recognized as the most prominent native leader in Vietnam. He declared Vietnamese independence on September 2, 1945, using language from the U.S. Declaration of Independence to punctuate his proclamation. When the French returned to Vietnam in 1946, Ho was prepared to work out an arrangement for Vietnamese independence within a French union—somewhat like the British Commonwealth—but his plans never materialized and broke down at the Fontainebleau Conference* in May 1946, when Ho traveled to Paris. By late 1946 the Vietminh were at war with French forces. Ho Chi Minh formed the Democratic Republic of Vietnam* in 1950, quickly won recognition from most Soviet-bloc countries, and finally won true independence in May 1954 when Vo Nguyen Giap* and the Vietminh defeated the French at Dien Bien Phu.*

Between 1954 and 1960 Ho Chi Minh consolidated his power in the North and waited to see if the government of Ngo Dinh Diem* in South Vietnam would collapse. When American military and economic assistance sustained the Diem regime, Ho organized the National Liberation Front, or Vietcong,* in 1960, began construction of the Ho Chi Minh Trail* through Laos* and Cambodia* into South

Vietnam, and began providing money and supplies to the Pathet Lao* in Laos and the Khmer Rouge* in Cambodia. Absolutely indefatigable in his drive for Vietnamese unification and independence, and often brutal in his implementation of revolution, Ho Chi Minh was the "father of his country." He died on September 2, 1969, and Vietcong and North Vietnamese Army* troops memorialized him in May 1975 when they invaded Saigon and renamed it Ho Chi Minh City.*

Sources: David Halberstam, *Ho*, 1971; Charles Fenn, *Ho Chi Minh: A Biographical Introduction*, 1973; Stanley Karnow, *Vietnam: A History*, 1983; William J. Duiker, *Ho: A Biography*, 2002.

Left: On April 30, 1975, the North Vietnamese juggernaut, launched just a few weeks before, reached Saigon and overthrew the government of the Republic of Vietnam. The Vietnam War was over, with America's enemy in possession of its key objectives — the reunification of South Vietnam with North Vietnam and the establishment of a Communist state there. In this photograph, triumphant North Vietnamese soldiers pose atop a Soviet tank on a main thoroughfare of Saigon.

HO CHI MINH CAMPAIGN (1975)

Under the direction of General Van Tien Dung,* the Ho Chi Minh campaign was the final assault on Saigon,* launched between April 26 and April 30, 1975. During late March and early April, Dung moved eighteen North Vietnamese Army* (NVA) divisions into place within a forty-mile radius of Saigon. Poised due east of Saigon were the 3d, 304th, 325th, and 324B divisions, with the objective of taking out the ARVN (*see* Army of the Republic of Vietnam) 1st Airborne Brigade at Ba Ria and the 951st ARVN Ranger Group and 4th Airborne Brigade near Long Thanh. Northeast of Saigon, Dung placed the 6th, 7th, and 314th divisions and assigned them the assault on Bien

Left: An ARVN tank burns on a Saigon street on April 30, 1975. North Vietnamese tanks are rumbling toward the government offices of the Republic of Vietnam and toward the U.S. embassy. Later in the day, they overran both and finally won the Vietnam War.

Hoa.* To the north, the 320B, 312th, and 338th divisions were assigned the conquest of the ARVN 5th Division at Ben Cat and the ARVN 9th Ranger Brigade at Lai Thieu. Northwest of Saigon, Dung had the 70th, 316th, 320th, and 968th divisions ready to pounce on the ARVN 25th Division at Trang Bang and Cu Chi. In the west, the 3d, 5th, 9th, and 16th NVA divisions were charged with an assault on the ARVN 22d Division at Tan An and Ben Luc and with a direct attack on the ARVN 7th and 8th ranger brigades outside of Saigon. In the southwest, the NVA 8th Division prepared to attack the ARVN 7th Division at My Tho.* Dung's attack plan worked flawlessly. The fighting was intense, but ARVN units kept falling back into an increasingly tight circle around Saigon. On April 29 Saigon was coming under intense artillery barrages, and NVA units had entered the outskirts of the city. The last Americans were evacuated on April 30, and the North Vietnamese took control of Saigon. The Ho Chi Minh campaign and the war were over.

Sources: Alan Dawson, *55 Days: The Fall of South Vietnam*, 1977; David Butler, *The Fall of Saigon: Scenes from the Sudden End of a Long War*, 1985.

HO CHI MINH CITY

When they finally overran South Vietnam in 1975, the North Vietnamese took control of Saigon* and quickly renamed it Ho Chi Minh City, in honor of Ho Chi Minh,* the father of Vietnamese nationalism, who had died in 1969.

Source: Stanley Karnow, *Vietnam: A History*, 1983.

Below: Triumphant soldiers of the North Vietnamese Army assemble in downtown Saigon to celebrate the fall of the government of South Vietnam on April 30, 1975. Many are waving the Vietminh flag, which will become the flag of the newly proclaimed Socialist Republic of Vietnam.

HO CHI MINH TRAIL

In May 1959 the Communist leadership in Hanoi* decided that the time had come to step up guerrilla efforts (*see* Vietcong) in South Vietnam, and they formed Group 559 to investigate enlarging the traditional series of trails through the mountains and jungles from the panhandle of North Vietnam into Laos,* southward into Cambodia,* and then leading into South Vietnam. In time Hanoi intended to use the so-called Ho Chi Minh Trail to take control of the war in the South and to conquer South Vietnam. By 1964 the Ho Chi Minh Trail remained primitive, requiring a physically arduous, exhausting trip to move supplies, and it was incapable of handling large numbers of troops. It took more than a month of hard marching to cover its several hundred miles.

When the United States commenced its vast logistical military buildup in 1964, North Vietnam began expanding the trail and increasing its capacity, and that effort continued until the final North Vietnamese victory in 1975. By 1965 the Ho Chi Minh Trail had become a well-marked series of jungle roads, capable of handling heavy trucks and other vehicles, replete with necessary support facilities, mostly built underground to escape American detection and air strikes. There were hospitals with sanitary operating rooms, fuel-storage tanks, and vast supply caches. While the North's logistical capability remained limited, North Vietnamese Army* (NVA) divisions required less than fifteen tons of supplies each day.

By 1967 the entire trail system had become a key to the war's progress. North Vietnam was moving more than 20,000 troops a month. U.S. Army Special Forces* operated advance camps near the trail outlets in the South; CIA-recruited Hmong* tribesmen sought to cut the trail in the North; and thousands of sorties* by a variety of aircraft sought to interdict the flow of men and materiel, though all without much success. A 1971 South Vietnamese Army invasion up Route 9 into Laos to cut the trail was a failure, resulting in a rout of the troops. By the end of the war the trail contained major fuel pipelines, and it was able to support more than a dozen full NVA divisions, an amazing feat. CD

Sources: James Clay Thompson, *Rolling Thunder*, 1980; Ralph Littauer and Norman Uphoff, eds., *The Air War in Indochina*, 1972; Jon M. Van Dyke, *North Vietnam's Strategy for Survival*, 1972.

HOFFMAN, ABBIE

Abbie Hoffman was born on November 30, 1936, in Worcester, Massachusetts. He graduated from Brandeis University in 1959 with a degree in psychology, studied for a time at the University of California at Berkeley, and

Left: The Ho Chi Minh Trail
will go down as one of
the greatest logistical
accomplishments in military
history. Despite constant,
heavy bombardment of the
Trail over the course of
seven years, the United
States never managed to
stop the infiltration of troops
and supplies from North
Vietnam, through Laos and
Cambodia, to South Vietnam.
This aerial photograph, taken
by a cameraman from the
U.S. Air Force on February
25, 1971, shows a section
of the Trail. The label DEST
TRK means "destroyed truck,"
and DMGD TRK means "dam-
aged truck." PRB DEST signi-
fies "probably destroyed."

began his political activism in 1960, protesting capital
punishment. Between 1963 and 1965 Hoffman was active in
the civil rights movement, and in 1964 he joined the Student
Non-Violent Coordinating Committee and worked actively
in Mississippi and Georgia. By late 1965, when he joined the
antiwar movement,* Hoffman's personality was characterized by a need to be noticed, frenetic activity, a mission-
ary/martyr complex, a large ego, frequent use of LSD and
marijuana, and a commitment to the counterculture. He
rejected mainstream values, preached revolution, and hoped
to discredit American values through ridicule, outrageous
behavior, and black humor.

By 1967 Hoffman was living on the Lower East Side of
New York City and directing his efforts against the Vietnam
War. He claimed to have serious goals but hoped to have
fun achieving them. He created pandemonium on the floor
of the New York Stock Exchange, for example, by throwing
dollar bills from the balcony and watching brokers scramble
after them. He combined farce with seriousness in his antiwar activities, on one occasion publicly trying to "exorcise"
the Pentagon of its evil spirits. Early in 1968 Hoffman participated in the occupation of Columbia University* and,
in August, played an important role in organizing the
demonstrations at the Democratic National Convention*
in Chicago. While in Chicago, Hoffman joined with Ed
Sanders, Jerry Rubin,* and Paul Krassner in founding the
Youth International Party—"Yippies"—in an attempt to

fuse the hippie and antiwar movements. The Yippies
sponsored songs, speeches, a "nude-in" in Chicago, and
nominated a pig named "Pigasus" as their presidential
candidate. Hoffman was arrested at the Chicago airport for
carrying a pocket knife. In 1969 Hoffman became one of
the famous "Chicago 8"* because of his arrest on charges of
conspiring to disrupt the Democratic convention. Although
he was acquitted on those charges, he was convicted of
contempt for his disruptive courtroom behavior. Eventually,
even those charges were dropped.

Hoffman then joined the campus lecture circuit,
speaking against the war, but in 1973 police arrested him for
selling cocaine to undercover agents. Hoffman jumped bail,
went underground, dyed his hair, and underwent plastic
surgery. His antiwar protests ended. Hoffman turned himself in to the authorities in 1980, entering a work release
program in 1981. After his release from the program,
Hoffman went back on the campus lecture circuit, averaging
seventy speeches a year. In 1986 he was working for Radio
Free USA and writing a book, *Steal This Urine Test*, a
manual on how to tamper with drug-test equipment. Late
in November 1986 he was arrested for protesting Central
Intelligence Agency* employment recruitment on the
campus of the University of Massachusetts at Amherst.
Abbie Hoffman died on April 12, 1989. JH

Source: Marty Jezer, *Abbie Hoffman: American Rebel*, 1993.

Below: Abbie Hoffman, leader
of the Youth International
Party, or "Yippies," on
September 18, 1968. He had
become known as one of
the "Chicago 8" for his
leadership of the antiwar
demonstrations in Chicago
during the Democratic
National Convention.

HONOLULU CONFERENCE OF 1965

Late in April 1965, with the military and political situation in South Vietnam deteriorating, the Joint Chiefs of Staff (*see* Chairman, JCS), Secretary of Defense Robert McNamara,* Ambassador to South Vietnam Maxwell Taylor,* and Assistant Secretary for Far Eastern Affairs William Bundy* met in Honolulu to develop a strategy for escalation of the American involvement in Indochina.* As a result of the conference, President Lyndon Johnson* agreed to use American combat forces to supplement the South Vietnamese Army. He decided to send approximately 40,000 additional American soldiers. They would be used in the "enclave strategy,"* which restricted their operations to within fifty miles of their base area. No troops would be sent to the Central Highlands.* Along with these nine United States Marine* and Army* battalions, Australia* agreed to send one battalion and South Korea* three. The possibility of future troop commitments was left open, as was the option of invading the Central Highlands. The commitment of large contingents of ground troops was a turning point in the war, a shift away from counterinsurgency* and an air war over the North to a large-scale ground war in the South. GFC

Source: Edward W. Knappman, ed., *U.S.-Communist Confrontation in Southeast Asia*, 1974.

HONOLULU CONFERENCE OF 1966

President Lyndon B. Johnson* announced on February 4, 1966, that he would consult with representatives of South Vietnam in Honolulu. The president was accompanied to the conference (February 6–8) by Secretary of Defense Robert McNamara,* Ambassador to South Vietnam Henry Cabot Lodge Jr.,* General William Westmoreland,* and Special Advisor General Maxwell Taylor.* At the conference, Johnson and his associates met with Nguyen Cao Ky* and Nguyen Van Thieu,* South Vietnam's top leaders. The American press argued that Johnson's decision to hold the

Below: President Lyndon B. Johnson traveled to Hawaii to meet with Nguyen Van Thieu and Nguyen Cao Ky, the leaders of the government of South Vietnam on October 17, 1966. The president was accompanied by his wife, Lady Bird Johnson, and at the airport in Honolulu, they received a traditional Hawaiian greeting.

conference was designed to counter Senator J. William Fulbright's* announcement on February 3, 1966, that the Senate Foreign Relations Committee* would open hearings on U.S. policies in Southeast Asia. At the conference, Johnson assured Ky and Thieu that American resolve was firm, but that the U.S. commitment would be politically easier to sustain if the South Vietnamese could reform their own government. During the conference they also discussed economic questions, the resumption of bombing* of North Vietnam, and the possibility of the People's Republic of China* entering the war. At the end of the meeting the participants released the Declaration of Honolulu, a joint communiqué in which both governments promised to work for peace, political reform, refugee* resettlement, economic growth, and control of inflation. It also called for defeat of the Vietcong* and self-determination for the people of South Vietnam. GFC

Source: Joseph Buttinger, *Vietnam: A Dragon Embattled*, Vol. 2, *Vietnam at War*, 1967.

HOOPES, TOWNSEND

Townsend Hoopes was born on April 28, 1922, in Duluth, Minnesota. He graduated from Yale in 1944. During the 1950s Hoopes was a consultant with the State Department, and in January 1965 President Lyndon B. Johnson* appointed Hoopes as his assistant secretary of defense. In October 1967 Hoopes became undersecretary of the United States Air Force.* When Secretary of Defense Robert S. McNamara* resigned in February 1968 and was replaced by Clark Clifford,* Hoopes gained influence and eventually helped convince Clifford that the Vietnam War was unwinnable and that the United States should disengage as quickly as possible. Hoopes helped supply information for the well-known *New York Times* story of March 12, 1968, reporting that the Joint Chiefs of Staff (*see* Chairman, JCS) were asking for another 206,000 troops and that administration officials were dismayed. In 1969 Hoopes recounted the period in *The Limits of Intervention*, the first of many books and articles by the prolific writer; his novel, *A Textured Web*, was published in 2002. Townsend Hoopes died on September 20, 2004. CD

Sources: Townsend Hoopes, *The Limits of Intervention*, 1969; *Washington Post*, September 25, 2004.

HOP TAC

"Hop Tac" was the nickname for the short-lived pacification program (*see* Rural Reconstruction) that General William Westmoreland* tried to implement around Saigon* in 1964. Shortly after arriving in South Vietnam and during his first year there, Westmoreland tried to "pacify" the guerrilla-held provinces around Saigon. The idea was to use South Vietnamese troops to move out from Saigon, eliminating all Vietcong* in the area and distributing American supplies to win the loyalties of the peasants. The French had earlier tried a similar policy—called *quadrillage*—which involved pacifying small quadrants of rural areas at a time and hoping to maintain their loyalties. Westmoreland's program was the first in a long string of American failures at guerrilla pacification. ARVN (*see* Army of the Republic of Vietnam) soldiers frequently deserted to escape confrontation with the Vietcong, especially after they had left the II Corps* area where their families lived. The South Vietnamese also failed to deliver the supplies that might have persuaded the peasantry to remain loyal. Westmoreland abandoned Hop Tac in mid-1965 after losing all of his faith in the abilities of South Vietnamese troops.

Sources: Frances FitzGerald, *Fire in the Lake: The Vietnamese and the Americans in Vietnam*, 1972; Larry E. Cable, *Conflict of Myths: The Development of American Counterinsurgency Doctrine and the Vietnam War*, 1986.

HO THI THIEN

Born in 1908 in Nha Trang, Ho Thi Thien gained international attention on May 30, 1966, when she committed suicide by immolation in front of the United Buddhist Church in Saigon.* Ho Thi Thien was a Buddhist nun protesting the political corruption and anti-Buddhist posture (*see* Buddhism) of the regime of Nguyen Cao Ky.*

Source: *New York Times*, May 30, 1966.

"HOT PURSUIT" POLICY

In 1965, when the war in Vietnam escalated, the North Vietnamese increased the infiltration of men and supplies along the Sihanouk Trail out of Cambodia* and the Ho Chi Minh Trail* out of Laos.* American military officers in Vietnam proposed a blockade of Sihanoukville (Phnom Penh) and military assaults on North Vietnamese and Vietcong* sanctuaries* in Cambodia. They also wanted approval to impose the "hot pursuit" policy, allowing American and South Vietnamese military units to follow retreating enemy forces across the border into Cambodia. At the time the Cambodian government, under the direction of Norodom Sihanouk,* was officially neutral, and the U.S. State Department was reluctant to widen the conflict. Consequently, President Lyndon B. Johnson* did not approve the Sihanoukville blockade, the attack on the sanctuaries, or the hot pursuit policy. The debate became a moot question, however, in 1970 when President Richard M. Nixon* approved the massive bombing (*see* Operation Menu) and military "incursion" into Cambodia

Below: A detail of a map of central Vietnam with the capital of Thua Thien Province, the city of Hue. Historically significant, Hue was badly damaged and almost destroyed during the Vietnam War. The Citadel, the seat of the Nguyen emperors, was hit with so much American firepower and bombs that little remains today.

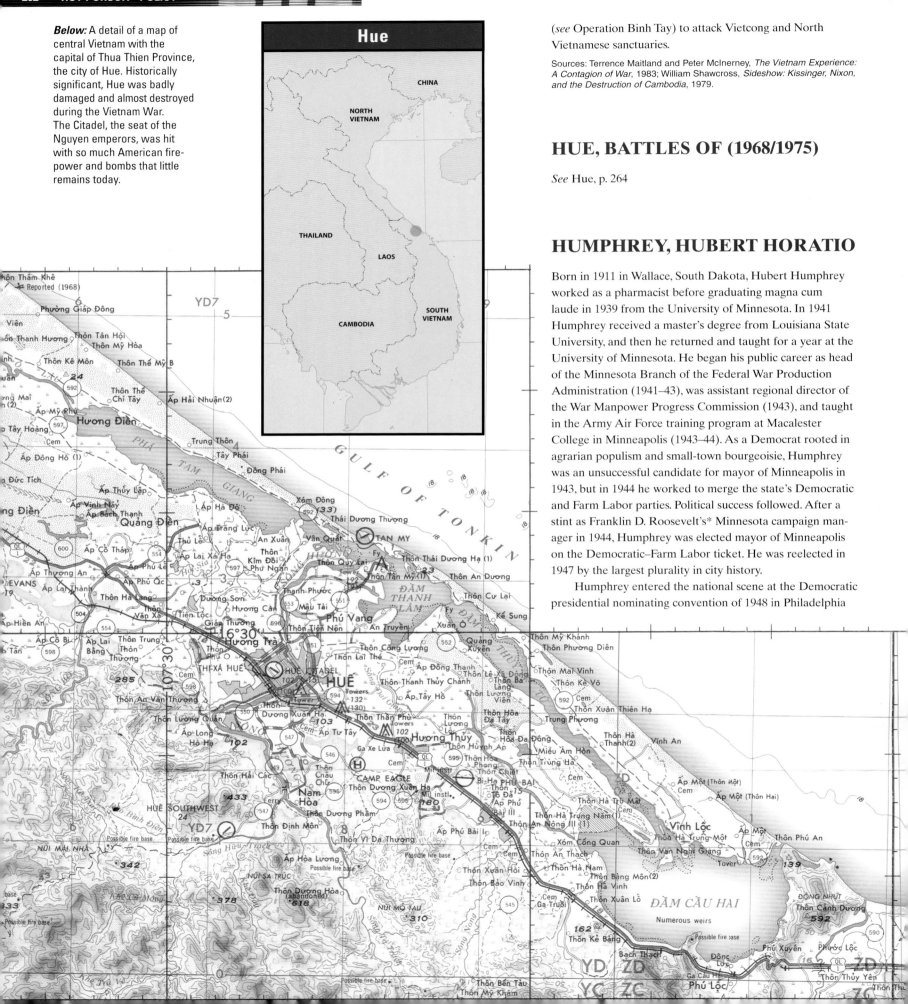

(*see* Operation Binh Tay) to attack Vietcong and North Vietnamese sanctuaries.

Sources: Terrence Maitland and Peter McInerney, *The Vietnam Experience: A Contagion of War*, 1983; William Shawcross, *Sideshow: Kissinger, Nixon, and the Destruction of Cambodia*, 1979.

HUE, BATTLES OF (1968/1975)

See Hue, p. 264

HUMPHREY, HUBERT HORATIO

Born in 1911 in Wallace, South Dakota, Hubert Humphrey worked as a pharmacist before graduating magna cum laude in 1939 from the University of Minnesota. In 1941 Humphrey received a master's degree from Louisiana State University, and then he returned and taught for a year at the University of Minnesota. He began his public career as head of the Minnesota Branch of the Federal War Production Administration (1941–43), was assistant regional director of the War Manpower Progress Commission (1943), and taught in the Army Air Force training program at Macalester College in Minneapolis (1943–44). As a Democrat rooted in agrarian populism and small-town bourgeoisie, Humphrey was an unsuccessful candidate for mayor of Minneapolis in 1943, but in 1944 he worked to merge the state's Democratic and Farm Labor parties. Political success followed. After a stint as Franklin D. Roosevelt's* Minnesota campaign manager in 1944, Humphrey was elected mayor of Minneapolis on the Democratic–Farm Labor ticket. He was reelected in 1947 by the largest plurality in city history.

Humphrey entered the national scene at the Democratic presidential nominating convention of 1948 in Philadelphia by leading the successful effort for a strong civil rights plank in the party platform. That fall Humphrey was elected to the U.S. Senate, defeating incumbent Republican Joseph H. Ball. Although somewhat brash and indefatigable in his advocacy of civil rights, Humphrey entered the Senate's inner circle, especially after his reelection in 1954 and 1960. His Senate career was devoted to the causes of civil rights, Medicare, and pro-labor legislation. Humphrey had been a founding member of the Americans for Democratic Action and served as its president in 1949 and 1950, so his liberal credentials were impeccable.

As an advocate of containment,* Humphrey was an early and ardent supporter of American intervention in Vietnam. He accepted the domino theory* and believed that the United States must take a stand in Southeast Asia if Communism was not to spread across the globe. Humphrey accepted a spot on Lyndon B. Johnson's* 1964 presidential ticket, and as vice president one of his prime duties was to marshal support for the increased direct involvement of U.S. armed forces in Vietnam. As the escalation continued between 1965 and 1968, Humphrey was often heckled as he became one of the few administration spokesmen willing to publicly defend the war effort.

Increasing domestic discontent over the war led to rival presidential bids by Democratic senators Robert F. Kennedy* and Eugene McCarthy* in 1968, both of whom challenged Johnson for the nomination. Johnson's withdrawal from the contest in March 1968 surprised the nation, including Vice President Humphrey, who fell heir to Johnson's formidable political support within the party. Shunning the open primaries, Humphrey built up support among the urban party machines and state party organizations, and after the assassination of Robert F. Kennedy and the disruptive nominating convention in Chicago, Humphrey became the Democratic candidate. Burdened by his association with a failing war policy, subject to intensive harassment on the campaign trail yet loyal to the president who was ultimately responsible for his candidacy, Humphrey finally made a last-minute effort in the campaign to distance himself from Johnson's war policy by calling for a negotiated settlement. Humphrey's moderate change of heart was one of many factors that narrowed the race with Republican candidate Richard M. Nixon* and third-party candidate George Wallace. Although a decided winner in the electoral vote, Nixon's victory margin in 1968 was only 43.4 percent of the popular vote to 42.7 percent for Humphrey and 13.5 percent for Wallace.

In 1970 Humphrey was reelected to the U.S. Senate. A short-lived effort to promote a 1972 presidential candidacy received no significant support within the party. Reelected to the Senate in 1976, Humphrey's main goal was full-employment legislation that designated the government as the employer of last resort. In a 1974 interview Humphrey commented on U.S. policy in Vietnam. He noted that very often big powers "miscalculate ... overestimating our power to control events .... Power tends to be a substitute for judgment and wisdom." Hubert Humphrey died of cancer on January 13, 1978. DB

Sources: *New York Times*, January 14, 1978; George Donth, *Leaders in Profile: The United States Senate*, 1975; Carl Solberg, *Hubert Humphrey: A Political Biography*, 1984.

HUYNH PHU SO

Born in the Mekong Delta* village of Hoa Hao in 1919, Huynh Phu So had a youth besieged by illness until he entered a monastery in 1939 where he experienced what he termed a miraculous cure. Using his considerable oratorical skills as well as expertise in herbal medicine and acupuncture, Huynh Phu So founded a new Buddhist sect, the Hoa Hao.* He quickly converted thousands of peasants south of Saigon,* stressing the importance of inner experience and the irrelevancy of external evidence. Each member of the Hoa Hao was expected to pray four times daily to Buddha, ancestors, and national heroes. Worried about his growing influence, the French arrested and imprisoned him in a mental hospital in 1940, where he converted his physician and a number of staff people. The French intended to exile him to Laos,* but by then the Japanese had taken over Indochina,* and Huynh Phu So was placed under house arrest in Saigon. The Japanese allowed him to see disciples and continue to direct his religious work. By then Huynh Phu So had an army of nearly 50,000. After World War II, Huynh Phu So established the Dan Xa, or Social Democratic Party, and the Hoa Hao had become a powerful political-religious sect in southern Vietnam. The movement continued to grow, and by the mid-1950s the Hoa Hao and Cao Dai* were very influential in the Mekong Delta, with strong sympathies among perhaps half of the area's 6 million people. In April 1947 Vietminh* guerrillas killed Huynh Phu So. No comparable leader appeared among the Hoa Hao to replace him.

Sources: Bernard Fall, "The Political Religious Sects of Vietnam," *Pacific Affairs* 28 (1955): 235–253; Joseph Buttinger, *Vietnam: A Dragon Embattled*, Vol. 2, *Vietnam at War*, 1967.

HUYNH TAN PHAT

Huynh Tan Phat was born in 1913 just outside of My Tho* in Dinh Tuong Province. He attended Hanoi University and became actively involved in anti-French nationalism. During the years of Ngo Dinh Diem's* reign over the Republic of Vietnam,* Huynh Tan Phat became active in the National Liberation Front (*see* Vietcong), becoming its secretary-general in 1964. In 1969 he became president of the Provisional Revolutionary Government of South Vietnam.* Huynh Tan Phat died on September 30, 1989, in Ho Chi Minh City.

Source: Danny J. Whitfield, *Historical and Cultural Dictionary of Vietnam*, 1976.

Above: In Youngstown, Ohio, Vice President Hubert H. Humphrey announces his candidacy for the presidency in 1968. In March, Lyndon B. Johnson had decided not to seek reelection. Humphrey eventually won the Democratic nomination but lost in the general election to the Republican candidate Richard M. Nixon.

HUE

Below: During the Tet Offensive of 1968, Vietcong and NVA troops overran the ancient city of Hue, formerly the imperial capital of Vietnam. Vietcong killing

squads then ruthlessly slaughtered residents known to have worked for the South Vietnamese government. Recapturing Hue from enemy troops took nearly a month of concerted action and heavy bombardment of the city by U.S. and ARVN forces. The city was destroyed. Here residents, refugees, and soldiers attempt to navigate a war-torn street to inspect the damage after South Vietnamese troops blasted their way through a gate of the Imperial Palace.

Right: An aerial view of Hue and the old Imperial Palace, taken in June 1968 after the Tet Offensive.

Heavy with historical significance, Hue has long been the center of Vietnamese cultural and religious life. It was also the capital of Thua Thien Province. The city is located in central Vietnam on Highway 1 and the Pearl River, approximately 670 miles north of Saigon and 420 miles south of Hanoi, in many ways the nexus of the Red River and Mekong deltas. It has no geographic outlet of its own to the South China Sea. The city is anchored by the Citadel, a fortress constructed by Gia Long in 1804 for the private use of the imperial family. The Citadel is protected by a moat and consists of three distinct walled enclosures. The outer wall is six miles in circumference and has ten gates. Inside is the Imperial Enclosure, where all official business of the empire was conducted. Finally, in the heart of the Imperial Enclosure is the Forbidden Purple City, the residence of the emperor, his family, and his concubines. The main gate to the Forbidden Purple City is the Ngo Mon Gate, or Noon Gate. At one time the Imperial Enclosure was adorned with pagodas, landscaped gardens, lakes, throne rooms,

and pavilions, decorated with elaborate mosaics and statues. After 1954 Hue was an independent municipality with a population of approximately 205,000 until South Vietnam fell to the Communists in 1975. Until his assassination in 1963, Ngo Dinh Can, the brother of President Ngo Dinh Diem, lived in Hue and ruled the city and the rest of South Vietnam all the way up to the 17th parallel, exercising the dictatorial powers of a virtual warlord. Historically, geography has rendered Hue a difficult city to defend. Bordered by Laos and the Annamese mountain chain to the west and the Demilitarized Zone to the north, Hue was relatively isolated. For centuries, foreign troops in Vietnam— Chinese, French, Japanese, and American—considered control of Hue to be of transcendent cultural and political significance, and the city often found itself at the vortex of military conflict.

During the Vietnam War, Hue twice found itself the site of vicious fighting, chaos, and destruction. Early in 1968, during the Tet Offensive, Hue became a target for Vietcong savagery. Early on the morning of January 31, 1968, the North Vietnamese Army (NVA) began pounding Hue with a punishing artillery assault, preparing the way for an invasion of the city, and NVA forces also cut off Highway 1 north and south of Hue, leaving the city hopelessly isolated. The Vietcong (VC) then attacked, and within a matter of hours the VC flag was fluttering above the Citadel. The symbol of Vietnamese independence had fallen and along with it all confidence in the

Left: Hospital corpsman D.R. Howe treats the wounds of Private First Class D.A. Crum of the 2d Battalion, 5th Marines, during Operation Hue City, February 6, 1968.

long-term viability of the government of South Vietnam. The Vietcong then engaged in the systematic liquidation of residents known to be friendly to Saigon, butchering thousands of people.

U.S. and Army of the Republic of Vietnam (ARVN) troops counterattacked almost immediately. General William Westmoreland subjected the city to unprecedented artillery and aerial bombardment. Elements of the 1st Air Cavalry Division, the 101st Airborne Division, the ARVN 1st Division, the U.S. 1st Marines, and ARVN rangers and marines fought their way into and out of Hue, frequently engaging in hand-to-hand combat with the Vietcong. Not until February 24, 1968 was the Citadel recaptured. By that time, Hue was in ruins. More than 116,000 of the city's 140,000 people were homeless, and as many as 10,000 people had been either assassinated outright by the Vietcong or killed by U.S. artillery fire. While sustaining 216 and 384 combat deaths respectively, U.S. and ARVN forces killed more than 5,000 Vietcong in Hue. In the end, the Battle of Hue of 1968 was a tactical defeat for the Vietcong, whose casualties were staggering; but in taking control of the city, if only for a few weeks, the Vietcong nevertheless scored a huge political victory.

In March 1975, Hue suffered again when North Vietnam launched its final assault on the South. On March 19, North Vietnamese troops in the B-4 Front groups and elements of the 341st Division assembled at My Chanh River north of Hue. The NVA 325C and 324B divisions stood ready to descend out of the Central Highlands to attack ARVN troops defending the city. By conquering Hue, the North Vietnamese Army would cut South Vietnam in half. General Ngo Quang Truong commanded ARVN forces. On March 20, 1975, General Ngo received confusing orders from President Nguyen Van Thieu of South Vietnam, which Ngo understood to mean that he should abandon Hue in order to hold the line at Da Nang. On March 24, Ngo evacuated ARVN troops from Hue, and North Vietnamese troops occupied the city.

Sources: Eric Hammel, *Fire in the Streets: The Battle for Hue, Tet 1968*, 1996; Keith Nolan, *The Battle for Hue*, 1996.

Below: On February 5, 1968, Marines occupy a building inside the city of Hue, where Vietcong and NVA troops had seized control during the Tet Offensive.

IA DRANG VALLEY, BATTLE OF (1965)

The Battle of the Ia Drang Valley began with a North Vietnamese attack on the Special Forces* camp at Plei Me in the Central Highlands* of Vietnam on October 19, 1965. The brand-new 1st Cavalry Division,* responsible for the security of the Central Highlands and the critical Highway 19 that ran through them toward the coast, was ordered to the relief of Plei Me, even though the division had not yet finished developing its airmobile tactics. The operation was code-named Silver Bayonet. Using airmobility, the division's 1st Brigade was able to fly over a North Vietnamese ambush and relieve the Special Forces camp. The North Vietnamese Army* (NVA) troops deployed in the ambush now had to flee back toward their base camps near the Cambodian border in the

Below: Besieged U.S. Special Forces and South Vietnamese troops at Plei Me in the Central Highlands of South Vietnam watch explosions from American fighter aircraft pummeling Vietcong and North Vietnamese positions on October 27, 1965. Enemy forces had surrounded the Special Forces camp.

Opposite page: Members of the 1st Cavalry Division march toward Chu Phong Mountain and the Ia Drang Valley. In November 1965, the Battle of the Ia Drang Valley captured the attention of politicians in both Washington, D.C., and Hanoi. For the first time, North Vietnamese regulars, not just Vietcong, engaged U.S. ground troops in extended battle. Although the Americans prevailed, the bloodshed on both sides stunned American and North Vietnamese leaders.

Chu Phong mountains. During their retreat they were harried constantly from the air by the 1st Cavalry Division.

In early November the division's 3d Brigade began a "search-and-destroy"* operation intended to break up the North Vietnamese concentration and destroy the NVA forces in the Ia Drang Valley and nearby mountains. On November 14 the 1st Battalion of the 7th Cavalry unwittingly landed in the midst of a large body of North Vietnamese troops, bringing on an intense and bloody two-day battle. Fighting was so fierce that relief forces had to land a considerable distance from the action, and for the first time American ground forces were directly supported by B-52* strikes. The 2d Battalion of the 7th Cavalry was ambushed while moving toward the scene of the original fighting, bringing on another daylong battle in which some American units, cut off and surrounded, were almost wiped out. The rest of the American forces managed to hang on to their positions with the assistance of air strikes and artillery fire. On November 18, the North Vietnamese broke off the action and withdrew. The 1st Cavalry Division returned to its base at An Khe on November 26. In the fighting, the division lost some 300 men killed. North Vietnamese dead totaled some 1,770 in the entire campaign.

The Battle of the Ia Drang Valley proved to be one of the most important of the Vietnam War. For the first time, U.S. forces faced elements of the North Vietnamese Army, and they were a formidable enemy. Although General William Westmoreland considered Ia Drang a decisive American victory, the fact that 300 U.S. soldiers died in the battle stunned Secretary of Defense Robert McNamara, who for the first time began to wonder if the war was going to be far more difficult than originally anticipated. Up until Ia Drang, American forces had been fighting Vietcong troops, brave to be sure but not nearly as well organized as North Vietnamese regulars. The battle was equally stunning to Vo Nguyen Giap and Ho Chi Minh. They had tasted the extraordinary level of American firepower and had lost nearly 2,000 men. Giap knew that North Vietnam could not sustain such massive losses indefinitely, so he implemented a tactical change in how NVA troops would engage the American army—only in close quarters. Giap called it "clutching the belts": fighting in such close proximity that U.S. troops could not call in tactical air support without bombing their own positions. Ia Drang dispelled all illusions that Vietnam was going to be a short and easy war. RSB III

Sources: Shelby L. Stanton, *The Rise and Fall of an American Army: U.S. Ground Forces in Vietnam, 1965–1973*, 1985; Thomas D. Boettcher, *Vietnam: The Valor and the Sorrow*, 1985; John Albright et al., *Seven Firefights in Vietnam*, 1970; Harold G. Moore and Joseph L. Galloway, *We Were Soldiers Once ... And Young: Ia Drang—The Battle That Changed the War in Vietnam*, 1993.

INCIDENT AT MUC WA

Incident at Muc Wa was the title of Daniel Ford's 1967 novel about the Vietnam War. The book centers on Corporal Stephen Courcey, a demolitions expert who has just arrived in Vietnam. Along with several other American soldiers, he establishes an outpost at Muc Wa. The novel proceeds to expose the absurdities of the war through tragicomedy. Courcey's girlfriend from the States shows up at Muc Wa as a war correspondent, but she is unable to meet him because he is off in the jungles with a visiting general and Army captain who are trying to earn their Combat Infantry Badges. The novel provides a caricature of stupid officers fighting a war for the wrong reasons. In the end, the troops at Muc Wa fight off a Vietcong* attack, and the Vietcong, in Ford's words, finally "exfiltrate" the area. In the end, Courcey is killed in action.

Sources: Daniel Ford, *Incident at Muc Wa*, 1967; Philip D. Beidler, *American Literature and the Vietnam Experience*, 1982.

Below: During the course of the Vietnam Wars — French and American — the Vietnamese displayed an extraordinary capacity to rebuild their infrastructure after artillery and aerial bombardment. This primitive 1929 bridge, constructed primarily of bamboo, was capable of allowing troops to march across and boats to pass beneath.

INDOCHINA

"Indochina" is the name Westerners have traditionally applied to parts of Southeast Asia, including Vietnam, Cambodia,* and Laos.* Under French rule its area was about 288,000 square miles, 10 percent larger than that of Texas. A spine of mountains runs from northwest to southeast from the Chinese border to the sea near Nha Trang,* with peaks rising from 8,524 feet north of Pleiku to 10,308 feet near China. Interspersed with plateaus, mountains also run from the coast at Nha Trang southwesterly to within 100 miles of Saigon.* Cambodia is largely a basin, surrounded on the north by the Dangrek Range, on the southwest by the Cardamom and Elephant ranges, and on the east by Vietnam's highlands and the Mekong Delta.* The north's significant river valley is that of the Song Koi, or Red. The Mekong River, which rises in China, flows southward through Laos, then forms the Laotian-Thai border, and finally flows through Cambodia and southern Vietnam to the South China Sea south of Ho Chi Minh City*

Left: In 1940, after the fall of France to Hitler's forces, Japanese troops began to occupy French Indochina in order to seize the rubber plantations there. They also began attacking rail traffic between Hanoi and southern China on the grounds that they needed to block the shipment of supplies to Chiang Kai-shek's Nationalist forces. A French Indochina-Yunnan Railroad train sits at a station in Hanoi. In previous weeks, over the protests of the United States, Japanese aircraft had repeatedly bombed the railroad line.

(Saigon). Light soil in the hills is easily eroded, but the river valleys are highly fertile. Traditional culture came to terms with the environment of heat, monsoon, and disease, depending on pigs, forest trees, rice, and water buffalo to help in cultivation.

Paleolithic man was present in northern Vietnam more than 10,000 years ago, neolithic man overspread the entire region from about 8000 to 5000 BC, and a Bronze Age culture ranged from coastal Indochina to Indonesia from about 500 to 300 BC. The people who were Proto-Vietnamese formed a kingdom known variously as Vat Lang and Au Loc, perhaps as early as 500 BC, and this was conquered by Han Dynasty Chinese by 111 BC. With brief moments of independence, it remained Chinese until AD 940, having come to be known as Nam-Viet. Despite a brief Ming Dynasty reconquest from 1407 to 1427, Vietnam emerged as a permanently independent entity. Buddhism* had become an increasing influence, though Confucianism* from China remained significant, especially for the mandarin rulers.

Indian influence had entered the southern part of Indochina by AD 100, being fairly strong in the kingdom of Champa,* established about that time. With internal troubles in India by the end of the sixth century AD, the Khmers* emerged as the strongest people in southern Indochina, with monumental architecture on the Indian model in the reign of Isarnavarman I (616–635). During the ninth century the Khmers established themselves near Tonle Sap (the "great lake"), founding Angkor and the empire that bore its name. Angkor endured repeated attacks by Champa and Thailand,* gradually decaying. The city itself was taken and looted by a Thai army in 1431, effectively ending the Khmer Empire. By this time Hinayana Buddhism was replacing the original god-king cult with its imported elements of the Hindu cult of Shiva. The Khmer collapse liberated the region now

known as Laos, most of which Angkor had controlled. The new kingdom of Lan Xang appeared, which had to fight off Burmese attacks and where Thai influence became dominant by the end of the eighteenth century.

By this time Vietnam, with an increasing population based on a successful rice culture, had completed its own conquest of the coastal region, which was won, slice by slice, from Champa and then Cambodia, the less imposing successor to Angkor. Vietnam reduced Cambodia to a vassal state, exacting tribute and dividing it into three residencies, each under a Vietnamese proconsul. There was an attempted Vietnamization of Cambodian culture, the monarchy was in effect abolished, and total conquest was prevented only by the imposition of French control of the region. (For that era, *see* France.) Vietnamese influence did not control more mountainous and Thai-influenced Laos, and, especially in the mountains, there remained tribes of other ethnic groups, ranging from the Sino-Tibetan Meo to the Malay Chams.

The population of Indochina at the end of the French era in 1954 was about 26,800,000, of whom some 21 million were Vietnamese, 3 million Cambodian, 1 million Moi and Kha, 600,000 Laotian, 600,000 Chinese,* 300,000 Man and Meo, 200,000 Muong, 100,000 Cham,* and 40,000 European. RWS

Sources: Bernard Philippe Groslier, *Indochina*, 1966; John F. Cody, "The French Colonial Regime in Vietnam," *Current History* 50 (1966): 72–78, 115; Ellen J. Hammer, *The Struggle for Indochina, 1940–1955*, 1966.

INDOCHINESE COMMUNIST PARTY

See Lao Dong Party

INDOCHINESE REFUGEES

Below: The fall of South Vietnam to the Communists precipitated a mass emigration of people afraid of North Vietnamese reprisals because of their cooperation with the United States. Many emigrants walked overland through South Vietnam, Cambodia, and Laos to refugee camps in Thailand, but most of them left in boats, which earned them the sobriquet "boat people." They risked dying from drowning, thirst, and pirates in the South China Sea. Some of them landed in Malaysia and Indonesia and then tried to make their way to the Philippines. Here refugees are crammed together on a boat out at sea.

The Vietnam War prompted the large-scale immigration of Indochinese refugees. Before the war, only a few thousand Vietnamese, Cambodians, and Laotians lived in the United States. During the 1950s and early 1960s, when the United States had military advisors in Vietnam, a few soldiers brought home Vietnamese wives, who became a tiny vanguard of the much larger migration to follow. In 1954 nearly 1 million Roman Catholics relocated from Communist North Vietnam to the spiritually more friendly climes of South Vietnam, where devout Catholic Ngo Dinh Diem presided over the country. Beginning in 1965 the introduction of U.S. ground troops into Vietnam and a massive escalation of American military and economic assistance stimulated unprecedented demographic change in South Vietnam, drawing Vietnamese peasants from the countryside to such cities as Saigon and Da Nang, where jobs were plentiful and wages high. The American war machine expended tens of billions of dollars and created millions of jobs. Almost overnight, Vietnam underwent an urbanization process that should have taken decades, pulling people from the cultural moorings of their ancestral villages.

As the war escalated, U.S. political and military policy rendered millions of Vietnamese homeless. Because the Vietcong could so easily disappear into the peasant population, American military planners had an increasingly difficult time distinguishing civilians from combatants. Artillery and air strikes aimed at enemy soldiers frequently damaged or destroyed entire South Vietnamese villages. To create "free-fire zones" where the American military could bombard an area without restraint, Vietnamese villagers had to be relocated to safe areas. On the logic that only Vietcong remained behind, the American military then laid waste to the region, destroying homes, livestock, and fields. With the conclusion of the bombardment, the peasants returned to burned-out, uninhabitable villages. Many left for the cities, and some secured visas and emigrated. Still, by 1975, only 20,038 Indochinese immigrants had settled in the United States.

The mass Indochinese migration to the United States, however, began in April 1975 when North Vietnamese troops conquered South Vietnam, spawning millions of Vietnamese refugees. The images of desperate South Vietnamese on the roof of the U.S. Embassy in Saigon scrambling to board evacuation helicopters seared itself into the American memory. Hundreds of thousands of South Vietnamese fled the country as political refugees in fear of reprisals for assisting Americans during the war. Some became known as boat people, who took to the South China Sea in small craft, hoping to be rescued by commercial ships and taken to the Philippines. Tens of thousands drowned at sea or fell victim to pirates plying the coastal waters. The U.S. Army evacuated thousands of Montagnard tribesmen from the Central Highlands of Vietnam and from Laos. Many Montagnards, especially the Hmong or Meo people, had cooperated with American soldiers in attacking the North Vietnamese Army (NVA), which stood ready to exact revenge.

Soon after the fall of Saigon, Khmer Rouge Communist forces overran Phnom Penh, Cambodia. The U.S. invasion of Cambodia in 1970 had forced the relocation of hundreds of thousands of Cambodians, who set out on foot for safer regions to the northwest. In 1975, when the Khmer Rouge Communists overran Phnom Penh and seized control of the government, the exodus continued. Led by genocidal maniac Pol Pot, the Khmer Rouge soon implemented a holocaust, killing more than a million Cambodians in an orgy of ideological violence. To escape the slaughter, many Cambodians fled across the border into Thailand, where United Nations and other international agency refugee camps awaited them. Tens of thousands of Cambodians spent years in those camps before being allowed to immigrate to the United States. A similar process repeated itself in Laos. In 1971 the South Vietnamese army, backed by heavy United States air support, had invaded Laos, hoping to sever the Ho Chi Minh Trail and cut the flow of supplies to NVA troops in Cambodia and South Vietnam. The NVA

Left: Vietnamese war refugees ride an Air Force helicopter to a safe area near Saigon after Vietcong attacked their village, March 1966.

Below: On December 11, 1978, Vietnamese refugees move from a boat anchored off the Malaysian shoreline to a smaller boat that will take them to a large refugee camp on the island of Palau Bidong. The boat, transferring refugees from smaller camps, had been in the South China Sea for twelve days.

managed to rout the invaders, but the invasion forced thousands of Laotians from their homes and toward such cities as Vientiane and Luang Prabang. In 1975, when the Pathet Lao Communists seized control of the government, thousands of Laotians fled the country for the safety of Thailand.

These Cambodians, Laotians, and Vietnamese enjoyed special status under U.S. immigration law, which treated political refugees far more favorably than economic refugees. The Indochinese refugees were able to secure the necessary papers to travel to the United States. From that base of 20,038 immigrants, the Indochinese American community grew rapidly. Eventually, more than 550,000 Vietnamese settled in the United States, along with 190,000 emigrants from Laos and 140,000 from Cambodia. Although small Indochinese communities could be found throughout the country, California eventually became home to most of them.

Sources: Nathan Caplan, John K. Whitmore, and Marcella Choy, *The Boat People and Achievement in America: A Study of Family Life, Hard Work, and Cultural Values*, 1989; William J. Duiker, *Vietnam Since the Fall of Saigon*, 1980; James M. Freeman, *Hearts of Sorrow: Vietnamese American Lives*, 1989; Ben Kiernan, *How Pol Pot Came to Power*, 1984; John Knudsen, *Boat People in Transition*, 1985; Bruce Grant, *The Boat People*, 1979; Bruce T. Downey and Douglas P. Olney, eds., *The Hmong in the West*, 1982; Hien Duc Do, *The Vietnamese Americans*, 1999; Sarah Streed, *Leaving the House of Ghosts: Cambodian Refugees in the Midwest*, 2002.

Above: The Ho Chi Minh Trail will surely go down as one of the greatest logistical accomplishments in military history. The United States, for all of its power, never managed to cut off the infiltration to South Vietnam of supplies and troops. An ARVN soldier searches a bunker storing supplies along the Ho Chi Minh Trail in Laos on February 14, 1971.

INFILTRATION

Throughout the years of the Vietnam War, one of the major U.S. challenges was stopping the infiltration of men and supplies into South Vietnam by the North Vietnamese. Between 1959 and 1975 North Vietnam sent supplies and reinforcements to the Vietcong* and North Vietnamese soldiers by three means: along the Ho Chi Minh Trail* down through the Laotian panhandle to the eastern border of Cambodia,* and then along smaller branches into the A Shau Valley,* Ia Drang Valley,* and War Zone C;* from Sihanoukville in neutral Cambodia by truck to bases along the Cambodian and Laotian border; and by small ships and junks down the coast of the South China Sea and then upriver in various regions of the Republic of Vietnam.* After 1970, when Lon Nol* deposed Prince Sihanouk* and realigned Cambodia with the United States, that infiltration route through Sihanoukville was shut off. Nevertheless, despite the elimination of that route and the

application of enormous American firepower along the Ho Chi Minh Trail and the South China Sea, North Vietnam still managed to ship supplies. Between 1959 and 1964 North Vietnam infiltrated more than 30,000 personnel into South Vietnam, and that number increased to 36,000 in 1965, 92,000 in 1966, and 101,000 in 1967. By 1968 North Vietnam was able to send more than 10,000 troops a month into South Vietnam—and enough food to feed them and ammunition to equip them—along the Ho Chi Minh Trail and through the American blockade of the South China Sea.

Source: William E. LeGro, *Vietnam from Ceasefire to Capitulation*, 1981.

INFLATION

See "Guns and Butter"

INTERNATIONAL COMMISSION OF CONTROL AND SUPERVISION

One of the provisions of the Paris Accords* of 1973 was the establishment of a four-nation International Commission of Control and Supervision (ICCS). It replaced the International Control Commission (ICC), a three-country body established by the Geneva Conference* of 1954. The ICC comprised Canada,* India, and Poland. The Paris Accords provided for those three nations to continue on the new ICCS, but India declined and was replaced by Indonesia. Hungary became the fourth member. Canada withdrew in August 1973 when it realized that the North Vietnamese were still intent on taking over South Vietnam. Iran then became the fourth member. The ICCS headquarters was located near Saigon* at Tan Son Nhut Air Base.* It had no power and became the butt of jokes among the Americans, South Vietnamese, and North Vietnamese vying for control in Southeast Asia.

Sources: Walter Scott Dillard, *Sixty Days to Peace*, 1982; Ramesh Thakur, *Peacekeeping in Vietnam: Canada, India, Poland, and the International Commission*, 1984.

INVASION OF CAMBODIA

See Operation Binh Tay

INVASION OF LAOS

See Lam Son 719

IRON TRIANGLE (WAR ZONE D)

The Iron Triangle was a National Liberation Front (NLF; *see* Vietcong) stronghold twenty miles northwest of Saigon* that had been built by the Vietminh* twenty years before in the war against French colonialism. Serving as a supply depot and staging area with a vast underground complex including command headquarters, dining halls, hospital rooms, munitions factories, and living quarters, it was never cleared by the French, nor was it successfully neutralized by the United States or the ARVN (*see* Army of the Republic of Vietnam). Located between Saigon, Tay Ninh, and Song Be cities, the Triangle comprised about 125 square miles and included portions of Bien Hoa, Binh Duong, Phuoc Long, Long Khanh, and Hau Nghia provinces. It was generally bounded by the Saigon River, the Song (river) Thi Thinh north of Bien Hoa, and the Than Dien Forest in Binh Duong Province. The area was heavily forested, consisting of jungle and rubber plantations and containing a few small villages and hamlets, the most strategic being Ben Suc,* which had been under NLF control since 1964.

In January 1967 the United States and the ARVN mounted the war's first major combined operation and the first U.S. corps-size operation. Operation Cedar Falls* deployed 32,000 troops against the Triangle. Its "search and destroy"* objective was to engage and eliminate enemy forces, destroy base camps and supplies, remove all noncombatants along with possessions and livestock to strategic hamlets,* and completely destroy four principal villages. Extensive underground complexes were found, and large quantities of supplies and papers were captured. The complete U.S. arsenal was employed—intensive bombing, flamethrowers, chemical warfare (defoliants and the first authorized major use of CS gas, or tear gas), and land-clearing Rome plows. Units participating in Cedar Falls included the 173d Airborne Brigade,* the 196th* and 199th* Infantry

Left: The Iron Triangle, just 20 miles northwest of Saigon, swarmed with Vietcong, and between 1963 and 1968 was often the site of bloody confrontations with U.S. and ARVN forces. On October 10, 1965, elements of the 173d Airborne Brigade conduct a search-and-destroy mission near Ben Cat in the Iron Triangle.

Above: Soldiers of the 173d Airborne Brigade patrol in the Iron Triangle in September 1965. The helicopters flew close by in support of the troops. Not until the Tet Offensive all but annihilated the Vietcong did U.S. and ARVN troops manage to secure control of the Iron Triangle. In 1975, North Vietnamese troops on their way to Saigon poured through the Iron Triangle.

brigades, elements of the 1st* and 25th* Infantry divisions, the 11th Armored Cavalry Regiment,* and the ARVN 5th Ranger Group.

There was little fighting, as the NLF fled to sanctuaries* in Cambodia* until the operation was finished. The destruction, however, chronicled in Jonathan Schell's *Village of Ben Suc*, was considerable. About 7,000 refugees* were created, and the region was made uninhabitable to anyone other than NLF/NVA forces. The operation's magnitude increased the NLF utilization of Cambodian sanctuaries; they did return to the Triangle to rebuild camps, however, which became springboards for the assault on Saigon during the Tet Offensive* of 1968. Subsequent operations against the Iron Triangle included Uniontown,* Atlas Wedge,* and Toan Thang.* SF

Sources: Stanley Karnow, *Vietnam: A History*, 1983; Shelby L. Stanton, *The Rise and Fall of an American Army: U.S. Ground Forces in Vietnam, 1965–1973*, 1985; Andrew F. Krepinevich Jr., *The Army and Vietnam*, 1986.

Left: First Vietminh and then the Vietcong became adept in the construction of underground bunkers, tunnels, and storage areas — so adept that French and later U.S. forces had difficulty locating them. Sergeant Richard Arvizu of the 11th Cavalry exits a hidden Vietcong bunker after searching it for enemy supplies and personnel.

Below: On this makeshift boat, troops from the 1st Infantry Division patrol a river in the Iron Triangle. Engineers connected two M4T6 bridge floats and mounted on them four .50-caliber machine guns on a rotating turret. The crew members carried machine guns and rifles. The craft was pushed along by a small powerboat.

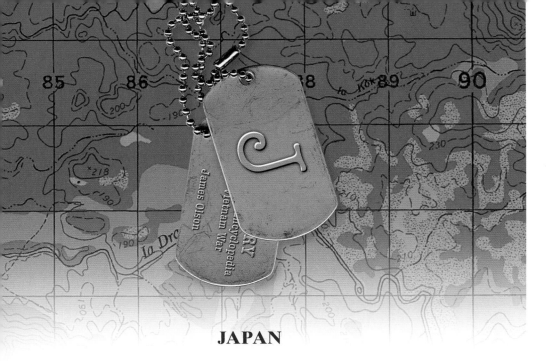

JAPAN

Japan played several important roles in the Vietnam conflict. Historically, the original drive for Vietnamese independence received substantial impetus from Japanese occupation during World War II. When Japan conquered Indochina* in 1941, it chose to leave French bureaucrats in nominal control, belying Japanese wartime propaganda of "Asia for the Asians" and greatly reinforcing Vietnamese anticolonialism.* Supported with U.S. supplies and advice, the Vietminh* had fought against Japanese occupation forces, becoming popular heroes in the process and the de facto government in the countryside. When the French

returned to power in 1946, the Vietminh simply turned their nationalist energies against them. Japan's rhetoric and occupation policies had accelerated the movement for Vietnamese independence.

Japan also served as a primary rationale for U.S. intervention in Vietnam after the French debacle at Dien Bien Phu* in 1954. China had become a Communist state in 1949; the Korean War had seemingly demonstrated the expansionist nature of Communism between 1950 and 1953; and a containment*-oriented American foreign policy worried about Communist aggression in Southeast Asia. If Vietnam fell to Communism, the United States argued, a sequence of disastrous events would follow: both Japan and the United States would lose access to Indochina's natural resources; Japanese economic expansion would be curtailed because Indochinese markets would be closed; and Japan would be forced into an accommodation with both the Soviet Union* and the People's Republic of China.* Japan was the United States' closest ally in Asia and had to be protected through American intervention in Vietnam. Finally, the United States had to prove to the Soviet Union, the Chinese, and the other nations of the world its commitment to stopping Communism.

During the war itself Japan played only a peripheral role. Despite the U.S.-Japanese security treaty of 1960, Japan resisted American blandishments to become more involved in the conflict. It viewed the American commitment in Vietnam as excessive and ultimately as a dangerous

Right: With the fall of France to Hitler's forces in the spring of 1940, Japan exploited the situation and occupied the northern half of Vietnam, much to the consternation of the United States. In July 1941, Japanese troops occupied southern Vietnam as well. The Vietminh had no more use for occupying Japanese forces than for French forces. On October 1, 1941, Japanese troops gather in South Vietnam, preparing to consolidate their power.

Left: Anti–Vietnam War protesters demonstrated against the construction of a U.S. Army hospital in Tokyo on March 8, 1968. The students were members of the Zengakuren, a left-wing political organization in Japan. Here bloodied riot police battle the students.

mistake. Japan's role in the conflict was confined to playing host to the Seventh Fleet* and various U.S. air wings, and permitting U.S. personnel to find necessary hospitalization and rest and recreation. Potent leftist elements periodically provoked domestic turmoil over such issues as hospitalized American soldiers in Japan conveying virulent tropical diseases to Japanese civilians, or the dangers of expanding airports, especially at Narita, which could then be used for American air operations against Vietnam. The leftists were never successful, however, in convincing the Japanese public that the United States was engaged in a racist war in Vietnam. Japan also adopted a conservative posture for fear of inciting its Communist neighbors in North Korea and China. Finally, Japan wanted to maintain commerce with North Vietnam. It was the presence of Japanese ships in Haiphong that restrained initial American plans to bomb and mine the harbor.

The irony, of course, is that the Vietnam War may have actually hastened the Japanese accommodation with the Soviet Union and the People's Republic of China. With Vietnam monopolizing U.S. diplomatic interests, with the articulation of the Nixon Doctrine* in 1969, and with the shock of not being consulted about Henry Kissinger's* secret initiatives to the People's Republic of China, Japan felt free, even compelled, to adopt a more independent diplomatic course in Asia. Although Japan remained solidly pro-Western, it was more wary about its relations with the United States and more independent in its dealings with the major powers. GMB

Sources: Stanley Robert Larsen and James Lawton Collins Jr., *Vietnam Studies: Allied Participation in Vietnam*, 1975; Frank Gibney, *Japan: The Fragile Superpower*, 1975; Edwin O. Reischauer, *Japan: Story of a Nation*, 1974; John K. Emmerson, *Arms, Yen, and Power*, 1971.

JASON STUDY

By the spring of 1966 Secretary of Defense Robert McNamara* was beginning to have serious misgivings about the nature of the war in Vietnam. Two of his closest civilian aides—John McNaughton and Adam Yarmolinksy—began searching for alternatives to the war, and in the summer of 1966, with the assistance of the Institute of Defense Analysis, a think tank, they organized a conference of perhaps fifty leading scholars at Wellesley, Massachusetts. They met there throughout the summer of 1966, and their collective report came to be known as the Jason Study. The major conclusion of the report was that American air strikes on Vietnam were having little effect and might even be counterproductive. Because much of North Vietnam's was a subsistence, agricultural economy, air strikes did not sufficiently disrupt its economic affairs. The flow of supplies into South Vietnam was not materially affected by air strikes, and the People's Republic of China* and the Soviet Union* quickly replaced any supplies lost. Worse still, the volume of supplies making their way into the South had actually increased since the bombing began, and the morale of the North Vietnamese had measurably stiffened. The Jason Study confirmed many of McNamara's growing suspicions about the war and converted him into an advocate of negotiation and an end to the bombing of North Vietnam.

Sources: Stanley Karnow, *Vietnam: A History*, 1983; Marc Jason Gilbert, *Why the North Won the Vietnam War*, 2002.

Above: Jacob Javits, Republican U.S. Senator from New York, went on to become the icon of liberal Republicanism in the United States and a critic of the Vietnam War. When this photograph was taken on January 1, 1956, Javits was serving as attorney general of New York under Governor Nelson Rockefeller.

Right: President Lyndon B. Johnson speaking at Johns Hopkins University in 1964.

JAVITS, JACOB KOPPEL

Jacob Javits was born in New York City on May 18, 1904. He took a law degree from New York University in 1927, practiced law privately, and served in the United States Army* during World War II. In 1946 Javits was elected to Congress,* and he won a seat in the U.S. Senate in 1956. A liberal Republican, Javits became a leading Republican critic of the Vietnam War. He supported both the Cooper-Church Amendment* and the Hatfield-McGovern Amendment,* and in 1970 he sponsored legislation to restrict the ability of the president to conduct war without congressional authorization. It was passed over Richard Nixon's* veto in 1973 and was known as the War Powers Resolution.* In 1980 Javits lost the Republican primary in New York. Since then he suffered from amyotrophic lateralsclerosis, or Lou Gehrig's disease. Jacob Javits died on March 7, 1986.

Sources: Jacob Javits, *Who Makes War: The President versus Congress,* 1973; Jacob K. Javits, *The Autobiography of a Public Man,* 1981.

JOHNS HOPKINS SPEECH

On April 7, 1966, amid widespread opposition to the Vietnam War, President Lyndon B. Johnson* delivered a speech at Johns Hopkins University and offered to hold "unconditional discussions" with the North Vietnamese about ending the conflict. Johnson also held out the proverbial diplomatic "carrot," offering a billion-dollar economic development program for the Mekong Delta.* The only hitch in the offer, of course, was Johnson's insistence that the United States would not negotiate with the National Liberation Front (*see* Vietcong) and was committed to the existence of a non-Communist, independent South Vietnam. DA

Sources: George C. Herring, *America's Longest War: The United States and Vietnam, 1950–1975,* 1986; *New York Times,* April 8, 1966.

JOHNSON, HAROLD KEITH

Harold Keith Johnson was born on February 22, 1912, in Bowesmont, North Dakota. He graduated from the United States Military Academy at West Point in 1933, and spent all of World War II in a Japanese prisoner-of-war camp after participating in the Bataan death march. Johnson saw active duty in the Korean War. He rose up through Army ranks until he was appointed Army chief of staff on July 6, 1964; he retired from the Army in 1968. Harold Johnson died on September 24, 1983.

Source: *New York Times,* September 25, 1983.

JOHNSON, LYNDON BAINES

Lyndon Baines Johnson was born on August 27, 1908, in the Hill Country of central Texas, and was raised in Johnson City. He attended Southwest State Teachers College, took a year off to teach school in Cotulla, Texas, and then graduated in 1930. Johnson taught school briefly in Houston before becoming assistant to the newly elected congressman from the Fourteenth District in Texas, Richard M. Kleberg. As a congressional aide, Johnson excelled at meeting people and cultivating relationships, especially with Congressman Sam T. Rayburn, the dean of the Texas delegation. After serving two years as the state director of the National Youth Administration, Johnson won his own seat in Congress,* and served there until 1949. He was elected to the U.S. Senate in 1948 in an election marked for its bitterness and fraud. Johnson became majority leader of the Senate in 1955 and earned a formidable reputation as a legislative strategist. After failing to win the Democratic presidential nomination in 1960, Johnson accepted a position as running mate with John F. Kennedy,* and he became vice president of the United States in 1961. When Kennedy was assassinated on November 22, 1963, Johnson became the thirty-sixth president of the United States.

As president, Johnson earned impeccable liberal credentials for his support of civil rights and antipoverty programs, but his "Great Society"* administration was politically destroyed in the jungles of Southeast Asia. Accepting the official U.S. view of the Vietnam War as one based on pure Communist aggression, Johnson ignored the anti-Western feelings and serious flaws of the Saigon* governments, and allowed himself to be trapped into escalation. He limited genuine consultation to the "hawks," most of whom also failed to grasp Vietnamese realities, and unlike Kennedy, Johnson did not know how to question

Left: President Lyndon B. Johnson with General William Westmoreland outside St. Barnabas Episcopal Church on August 14, 1966. Westmoreland had returned to Washington, D.C., to give the president a progress report on the war. The report was optimistic, although the general informed the president that U.S. troop levels needed to be increased.

Below: President Lyndon B. Johnson visits with Marine Gunnery Sergeant Clovis C. Coffman in the Enlisted Men's Mess Hall at Cam Ranh Bay on October 26, 1966. The president was visiting Vietnam to make his own assessment of progress and to encourage the troops.

their advice. His queries were confined to techniques and amounts; he assumed the correctness of American military involvement. Johnson also allowed his goals to escalate from stopping aggression to "winning," presumably by destroying both the enemy's forces and his will to continue.

Consequently, he obtained from Congress the Gulf of Tonkin Resolution* in August 1964, which authorized the president "to take all necessary measures to repel any armed attack against the forces of the United States and to prevent further aggression"—a virtual blank check. Johnson consistently reacted vigorously to attacks on American personnel or installations, beginning and increasing the bombing* of North Vietnam, sending ever more troops into South Vietnam, and allowing them to fight on the ground independently of ARVN forces (*see* Army of the Republic of Vietnam, p. 60). Johnson paid lip service to the idea of a negotiated settlement, but he ignored warnings by such advisors as George Ball,* who understood the power of Vietnamese nationalism. By 1968 Johnson had more than 540,000 troops in Vietnam, plus powerful naval forces off the coast and B-52s* bombing from bases on Guam and in Okinawa and Thailand.*

The enemy fought on, but Johnson refused to admit that his strategy of attrition (*see* War of Attrition) was not working. He replaced Robert McNamara* as secretary of

Right: On the president's trip to Vietnam in 1966, he worked the crowd of U.S. and ARVN military personnel. Johnson returned from the junket encouraged about the state of the war and confident that victory was inevitable.

defense when the latter began to turn "dovish." Late in January and early February 1968, the Vietcong* and the North Vietnamese Army* launched the Tet Offensive,* hitting Saigon* and thirty provincial capitals, and despite heavy casualties they earned a strategic victory by demoralizing American public opinion. When, after Tet, General William Westmoreland* requested 206,000 more American troops, Johnson asked Clark Clifford,* his new secretary of defense, to evaluate the request. Clifford asked Pentagon officials whether more troops would guarantee a victory in South Vietnam, and when they hedged their answers, he advised Johnson to seek peace. Johnson was enraged and almost fired Clifford. Stunned by his near defeat at the hands of Senator Eugene McCarthy* in the 1968 New Hampshire presidential primary, and depressed about the prospects of Senator Robert Kennedy* of New York seeking the Democratic presidential nomination, Johnson withdrew from the campaign at the end of March and announced a bombing halt and a willingness to seek a negotiated settlement. He then quibbled over such details as a meeting place for peace talks that, when they began in Paris in May, dragged on inconclusively until the end of his term. Johnson left the White House in January 1969 and retired to his Texas ranch, where he died on January 22, 1973. RWS

Sources: Robert W. Sellen, "Old Assumptions versus New Realities: Lyndon Johnson and Foreign Policy," *International Journal* 28 (Spring 1973), 205–229; Doris Kearns, *Lyndon Johnson and the American Dream*, 1976; Lloyd C. Gardner, *Pay Any Price: Lyndon Johnson and the Wars of Vietnam*, 1997; Herbert Schandler, *Lyndon Johnson and Vietnam: The Unmaking of a President*, 1983.

JOINT CHIEFS OF STAFF

See Chairman, Joint Chiefs of Staff

JOINT GENERAL STAFF

The Joint General Staff (JGS) was the South Vietnamese equivalent of the U.S. Joint Chiefs of Staff (JCS; *see* Chairman, JCS). JGS headquarters were in Saigon.* The major difference between the JGS and the JCS was that the JGS had direct operational control over the South Vietnamese forces. U.S. commanders of Military Assistance Command, Vietnam,* especially Generals William Westmoreland* and Creighton Abrams,* cooperated closely with, but did not control, the JGS.

Source: William C. Westmoreland, *A Soldier Reports*, 1976.

Left: On July 31, 1968, President Johnson received a tape-recorded message from his son-in-law Charles Robb, a Marine serving in Vietnam. Robb described the fighting in Vietnam for the president. For good reason, the president appears anguished and exhausted.

KATZENBACH, NICHOLAS

Nicholas Katzenbach was born in Philadelphia in 1922. He attended Princeton until joining the Army in 1942 and spent most of the war in Italian and German POW camps. When the war was over, he returned to Princeton and was allowed to graduate in 1945 by taking special examinations. Katzenbach then received a law degree from Yale in 1947. A Rhodes scholarship took him to Oxford between 1947 and 1949, and he then returned to the United States to practice law. In 1952 Katzenbach joined the law faculty at Yale, and between 1956 and 1960 he was professor of law at the University of Chicago Law School. With the election of John F. Kennedy* in 1960, Katzenbach came to Washington as an assistant attorney general, where he specialized in civil rights issues. He helped draft the Civil Rights Acts of 1964 and 1965. Katzenbach's reputation for composure under pressure was enhanced in December 1962 when he negotiated the release of prisoners captured by Cuba during the Bay of Pigs invasion in 1961.

When he became undersecretary of state in 1966, Katzenbach, who had no direct experience with foreign policy, spent his early months reading files and briefs and in discussion with his colleagues. Yet his experience in the Department of State was less successful than in the office of the attorney general. In an early session with the Senate Foreign Relations Committee,* Katzenbach provoked dismay among those who believed that he would continue in the tradition of his predecessor, George Ball,* who did not favor the escalation of the war. Katzenbach, when asked by the committee to interpret the 1964 Gulf of Tonkin Resolution,* argued that in its wording it supported President Johnson's* right to escalate the war as he saw fit. In this and other situations, Katzenbach's analytical approach and propensity to reconcile opposing viewpoints led his former admirers to see him as a mere functionary, unwilling to argue against a doubtful policy. Katzenbach became a senior vice president and general counsel for IBM in 1969, where he stayed until 1986. In 1992 Katzenbach was selected to lead the Bank of Credit and Commerce out of bankruptcy, and in 2004 he became a member of the board of directors of MCI. JDC

Sources: U.S. Navasky, "No. 2 Man at State Is a Cooler-Downer," *New York Times Magazine,* December 24, 1967; *Who's Who in Finance and Industry, 1985–86,* 1985; http://www.google.com/search?hl=en&q=Nicholas+Katzenbach&btnG=Google+Search.\

Above: During the Kennedy administration, Nicholas B. Katzenbach distinguished himself as an assistant attorney general handling civil rights controversies. Blessed with a keenly analytical mind and a gift for writing tight legal language, Katzenbach drafted the legislation that became the Civil Rights Acts of 1964 and 1965. On June 11, 1963, Katzenbach was a primary participant in one of the most famous incidents of the Civil Rights struggle. Alabama Governor George Wallace stood in front of Foster Auditorium at the University of Alabama in an attempt to stop desegregation of that institution by the enrolment of two black students, Vivian Malone and James Hood. This became known as the "Stand in the Schoolhouse Door." Wallace stood aside only after being confronted by Katzenbach, accompanied by federal marshals and the Alabama National Guard.

KAMPUCHEA

See Cambodia

KATTENBURG, PAUL

Born in Belgium in 1938, Paul Kattenburg immigrated to the United States in 1940 and earned degrees at the University of North Carolina (B.S.), Georgetown University (M.A.), and Yale (Ph.D.). Between 1952 and 1956 he served in the State Department as an Indochina* research analyst and between 1963 and 1964 as Vietnam desk officer. At a meeting of the National Security Council* on August 31, 1963, Paul Kattenburg became the first known American official to recommend withdrawal from Vietnam. He had traveled to South Vietnam many times on State Department business in the 1950s and early 1960s, and he became convinced that the regime of Ngo Dinh Diem* would never survive and that the Vietcong* would eventually prevail. His recommendation was summarily rejected by Dean Rusk* and Robert McNamara,* and Kattenburg was quickly cut off from the advisory–decision-making process on Vietnam. After he left public service, Kattenburg became the Charles L. Jacobsen Professor of Public Affairs at the University of South Carolina, where he remained until his retirement in 1986. Of his many articles and writings on the subject, *The Vietnam Trauma in American Foreign Policy, 1945–1975* (1980) is considered his most important work. Paul Kattenburg died June 12, 2004. SF

Sources: Stanley Karnow, *Vietnam: A History,* 1983; *New York Times,* June 25, 1971; University of South Carolina Libraries, *Paul Kattenburg Papers, 1938–2004,* 2005.

KENNAN, GEORGE FROST

Born in Milwaukee on February 16, 1904, George Kennan attended Princeton University and joined the Foreign Service of the State Department in 1926. He served as U.S. ambassador to the Soviet Union* in the early 1950s and became an expert on Russian affairs. In a 1947 article in the journal *Foreign Affairs*, Kennan became the father of the containment policy,* a foreign policy strategy to keep the Soviet Union behind its 1945 military boundaries. The Truman Doctrine, Marshall Plan, NATO, Berlin Airlift, and the other regional treaty organizations were all examples of containment. Since 1956 Kennan had worked as a professor of historical studies at the Institute for Advanced Studies at Princeton. Among his many books are *Russia Leaves the War*, *American Diplomacy 1900–1950*, and *Realities of American Foreign Policy*.

By the 1960s, however, Kennan was becoming a minority voice in foreign policy circles because of his conviction that the containment policy was being indiscriminately applied to too many unique situations. In Vietnam, he was convinced that nationalism, not Communism, was the moving force behind the rebellion, and from the beginning he opposed U.S. involvement in the war. He argued that it was a mistake for the United States to ally itself with a corrupt regime incapable of winning the confidence of most South Vietnamese. Kennan also harbored serious doubts about whether the United States could administer a military defeat to the Vietcong* and North Vietnamese using only conventional weapons. On February 10, 1966, Kennan testified before the Senate Foreign Relations Committee,* arguing that because the region was not of military or industrial importance, and because the area would remain philosophically independent of Russian or Chinese influence, the United States should withdraw as soon as possible. George Kennan spent the rest of his life actively commenting on American foreign policy; he died on March 17, 2005. KY

Sources: George Kennan, *Memoirs, 1950–1963*, 1972; David Halberstam, *The Best and the Brightest*, 1972; David Allen Mayers, *George Kennan and the Dilemma of American Foreign Policy*, 1988.

KENNEDY, EDWARD MOORE

Edward Moore Kennedy was born in Boston on February 22, 1932. He graduated from Harvard University in 1956 and then took a law degree at the University of Virginia in 1959. In 1962, with his brother John* serving as president of the United States and his other brother Robert serving as attorney general in the Kennedy cabinet, Edward Kennedy won election as a U.S. senator. In the Senate he staked out his own political ground with expertise in labor, judicial, and medical issues, but after the assassination of Robert Kennedy* in 1968, Edward inherited the mantle of his brother's anti-Vietnam commitment. He flirted with a run for the presidency in 1968, and his campaign book *Decisions for a Decade* outspokenly opposed the American commitment in Vietnam, condemned the "search and destroy"* strategy, and called for military defense of limited sanctuaries.* By 1969 Ted Kennedy was openly critical of the

Nixon* administration's continuing commitment to the struggle in Vietnam, and he also condemned the "gross corruption" of the government of the Republic of Vietnam.* But that year the incident at Chappaquiddick Island and the death of Mary Jo Kopechne all but destroyed Kennedy's presidential chances. He criticized the Nixon administration for the Cambodian invasion (*see* Operation Binh Tay) in 1970 and began calling for an immediate withdrawal of American forces from Southeast Asia. Kennedy tried to make presidential runs in the primaries of 1972, 1976, and 1980 but failed in each of them. He was reelected to the Senate in 1968, 1974, 1980, 1986, 2002, and 2006, has represented Massachusetts for forty-five years, and is currently the second-most senior member of the Senate.

Sources: John Galloway, *The Kennedys and Vietnam*, 1971; Edward M. Kennedy, *Decisions for a Decade*, 1968; Burton Hersh, *The Shadow Presidency: Ted Kennedy in Opposition*, 1997; http://kennedy.senate.gov/senator/index.cfm.

KENNEDY, JOHN FITZGERALD

John F. Kennedy was born in Brookline, Massachusetts, on May 29, 1917. He graduated from Harvard in 1940 and served in the Pacific with the U.S. Navy during World War II. He inherited the political mantle of the Kennedy family in Massachusetts, especially after his older brother Joseph was killed in Europe during the war, and in 1946 he was elected to Congress. He won a seat as a Democrat in the U.S. Senate in 1952, came close to winning a spot as Adlai Stevenson's vice presidential running mate in the election of 1956, and in 1960 defeated Richard Nixon* for the presidency.

Kennedy's involvement with Vietnam, in one way or another, had existed previously well into the 1950s. He was

Above: George Kennan, a former ambassador to the Soviet Union and architect of the containment policy, testifying before the Senate Foreign Relations Committee on February 6, 1970. In his testimony, Kennan endorsed a Johnson administration proposal by Senator Mark Gravel of Alaska that the United States and the Soviet Union engage in a series of cultural exchanges.

Below: Presidential candidate John F. Kennedy taking a break from campaigning in his Boston apartment in 1960.

Right: On November 22, 1963, President John F. Kennedy was assassinated while riding in a motorcade in Dallas, Texas. In this photo, taken seconds before bullets struck the president, he can be seen sitting in the backseat with his wife Jacqueline Kennedy. Governor John B. Connally of Texas and his wife Nellie Connally are seated behind the driver.

Below: Senator Edward Kennedy of Massachusetts at Logan International Airport in Boston on October 30, 1969. The Massachusetts Supreme Court had just agreed to a closed hearing about Kennedy's role in the drowning death of Mary Jo Kopechne. Her death and the scandal surrounding it ended Kennedy's fledgling candidacy for the presidency of the United States.

a relatively typical cold warrior, urging Eisenhower* to resist Communist expansion in Indochina.* When it was clear that the French would withdraw, Kennedy urged Eisenhower to back the government of Roman Catholic Ngo Dinh Diem* in South Vietnam. When Kennedy became president in 1961, he asked the U.S. Army* to develop counterinsurgency* forces and General Maxwell D. Taylor* to oversee the program. In 1963 Kennedy announced that "now is the time" and "Vietnam is the place" for a firm stand against Communist aggression. Kennedy also replaced Army chief of staff General George Decker with General Earle Wheeler,* who was more of a supporter of counterinsurgency tactics.

Believing in the domino theory* and committed to containment policies,* Kennedy was gradually drawn deeply into the Vietnamese quagmire. He ended up following a middle road, primarily because the advice he received from civilian and military advisors was so contradictory. By 1963 there were more than 16,000 U.S. economic and military advisors in South Vietnam, and the political and military situation was already deteriorating. Some U.S. officials in Washington and Saigon* urged support for an army coup in Vietnam; some urged stronger backing for Ngo Dinh Diem; a few people, like Chester Cooper,* urged withdrawal. Kennedy, tired of the manifest corruption of the Diem regime, opted for the coup but was surprised when news came of Diem's assassination. Years later, Kennedy supporters claimed that he was seriously considering a military withdrawal from Vietnam, but that he was waiting for the end of the 1964 election so Republicans would not be able to accuse him of being soft on Communism. Kennedy's critics, as well as Lyndon B. Johnson* loyalists, disagree, arguing that Kennedy was too much of a cold warrior to have considered such an option, and that he had steadily escalated the conflict in Indochina throughout his administration. John F. Kennedy was assassinated on November 22, 1963. CD

Sources: Arthur M. Schlesinger Jr., *A Thousand Days: John F. Kennedy in the White House*, 1965; David Halberstam, *The Best and the Brightest*, 1972; William J. Rust, *Kennedy in Vietnam*, 1985; Bruce Miroff, *Pragmatic Illusions: The Presidential Politics of John F. Kennedy*, 1976; Robert Dallek, *An Unfinished Life: John F. Kennedy, 1917–1963*, 2004.

KENNEDY, ROBERT FRANCIS

At age forty-two, while campaigning for the 1968 Democratic presidential nomination, Robert F. Kennedy was assassinated by Sirhan Sirhan in Los Angeles, dying on June 6, 1968. Born in Boston in 1925, he graduated from Harvard and the University of Virginia Law School. He managed the successful presidential campaign of his brother John* in 1960, and served as attorney general during his

Above: On March 18, 1968, Senator Robert F. Kennedy of New York announced his candidacy for the Democratic presidential nomination. An opponent of the Vietnam War, Kennedy was challenging Lyndon B. Johnson, the sitting Democratic president. In a few weeks, after Kennedy's candidacy gained momentum, Johnson announced his decision not to seek reelection. Kennedy's nomination seemed a given until his assassination on June 6, 1968.

Opposite page, above: Governor James Rhodes of Ohio ordered the National Guard to break up an antiwar demonstration on the campus of Kent State University on May 4, 1970. Guardsmen shot tear canisters into the crowd of students, and as the gas spread throughout the crowd, panic set in among the students and the guardsmen. Shots were fired, and when the gas cleared, four Kent State students lay dead. The antiwar movement had martyrs for its cause.

brother's presidency and then under President Lyndon Johnson.* In 1964 he resigned and was elected to the U.S. Senate from New York. He remained a senator until his death.

In 1962, when his brother was president, Robert Kennedy said, "We are going to win in Vietnam. We will remain here until we do win," although he played a very limited role in Vietnam policy while he was attorney general. He initially supported Johnson administration Vietnam policies; as a senator, however, he had increasingly dissented from Johnson's policies, particularly after the resumption of the bombing* of North Vietnam in 1966. Nonetheless, Robert Kennedy had refrained from making an open break with Johnson until he announced his candidacy for the presidency on March 16, 1968. He said that he wanted to end the bloodshed in Vietnam. "In private talks and in public I have tried in vain to alter our course in Vietnam before it further saps our spirit and our manpower, further raises the risks of wider war, and further destroys the country and the people it was meant to save." In his campaign he opposed further military escalation in Vietnam and U.S. bombing of the North. He did not enter the race, however, until after Eugene McCarthy* had made a strong showing against Lyndon Johnson in the New Hampshire primary. Two weeks later, Johnson said that he would not seek reelection. Just before he was murdered, Kennedy had won the California Democratic primary, and was making a strong bid for his party's presidential nomination. HP

Sources: Arthur M. Schlesinger Jr., *Robert Kennedy and His Times*, 1978; David Halberstam, *The Unfinished Odyssey of Robert Kennedy*, 1968; Evan Thomas, *Robert Kennedy: His Life*, 2000.

KENT STATE UNIVERSITY

After President Richard M. Nixon* announced that American and South Vietnamese soldiers had invaded Cambodia* on April 30, 1970, to eliminate Vietcong* base camps and stop the infiltration* of materiel and personnel from North Vietnam, students across the country demonstrated against the escalation of the war. On May 1, 1970, students at Kent State University in Ohio marched against the war and rioted, shattering windows, lighting fires, and damaging cars. The next night some of them set fire to the ROTC building on campus. When firefighters arrived to put out the blaze, some students seized the firehoses and turned them on the firefighters. Governor James Rhodes ordered in the National Guard, declared martial law, and announced that campus violence must come to an end. Rhodes felt that the rioters were part of a revolutionary group and he ordered that students not be allowed to assemble in groups on the campus until the disturbances were over.

Around noon on May 4, 1970, antiwar* protesters staged another rally. Campus police asked them a number of times to disperse, and when they refused, armed guardsmen advanced on them. A group of students began hurling chunks of concrete and rock at the guardsmen, and the guardsmen reacted with tear gas grenades. Apparently one of the guardsmen thought he heard a sniper shot, and he opened fire. Others joined him, some of them firing directly into the crowd of students. They fired a total of thirty-five rounds at students approximately sixty feet away. Four students died and fourteen were wounded. The incident triggered hundreds of college protest movements and a march on Washington, D.C., on May 9, 1970. The guardsmen were brought to trial but found not guilty. GFC

Sources: Weldon Brown, *The Last Chopper*, 1976; Clark Dougan and Steven Weiss, *The Vietnam Experience: A Nation Divided*, 1984; James Michener, *Kent State: What Happened and Why*, 1971; Richard E. Peterson and John Bilorsky, *May 1970: The Campus Aftermath of Cambodia and Kent State*, 1971; Philip Caputo, *13 Seconds: A Look Back at the Kent State Shootings*, 2005.

KHAM DUC AIRLIFT EVACUATION

As early as April 1968 intelligence analysts began to observe signs that the Kham Duc Special Forces* camp near the Laotian border fifty miles southeast of Da Nang* was being threatened in a way similar to that of the Khe Sanh* base. By early May it appeared that large contingents of Vietcong* and North Vietnamese units were preparing to attack, and beginning May 10, American commanders reinforced the installation. From May 10 to 11, 1968, American and allied forces at Kham Duc found themselves under intense artillery, mortar, and recoilless-rifle attacks. Losses on May 10 alone were heavy: fifteen killed, fifty-two wounded, and sixty-four missing in action. As a result of these losses, the prospect of increased activity by the enemy, and the relatively poor defensive potential of the base, General William Westmoreland* ordered the evacuation of Kham Duc.

The evacuation of the garrison at Kham Duc on May 12, 1968, was one of the most spectacular operations of the war. Intermittently throughout much of the day, United States Army* and Marine* helicopters lifted out survivors, while allied air strikes held off the enemy on all sides. While under constant attack, early in the morning a C-130* landed to pick up evacuees. It received heavy damage while on the landing strip and was able to carry out only three passengers because fuel was streaming from the fuselage through shrapnel holes. A C-123 transport, however, was able to make a successful morning pickup of several evacuees. In the early afternoon three C-130s attempted pickups. Enemy fire destroyed one after it took off with more than 100 civilian passengers; another, crippled in landing, was abandoned. Only the third made a successful landing

Left: The four students who were killed at Kent State University on May 4, 1970. A subsequent investigation revealed that the students had not made threatening moves on the guardsmen.

Right: Sandbagged trenches along the perimeter of Khe Sanh in March 1968. The American command in South Vietnam gave the defense of the base the nickname Operation Scotland.

and evacuation. Then, late in the afternoon, three additional C-130s succeeded in bringing out the last of the garrison. Of the 1,500 survivors of Kham Duc, the U.S. Air Force* flew out more than 500, nearly all in the final crucial minutes before the outpost fell.

One final evacuation mission took place when a C-130 landed at the now enemy-controlled Kham Duc landing strip to bring in a three-man Air Force control team. By the time the team realized that all allied forces had been withdrawn, the C-130 carrying them had already departed. To rescue this team a C-123 landed under heavy fire and successfully removed them. RDL

Source: Alan L. Gropman, *Airpower and the Airlift Evacuation of Kham Duc*, 1979.

KHE SANH

Below: In February 1968, during and after the Tet Offensive, the U.S. Marine outpost at Khe Sanh, South Vietnam, came under siege from North Vietnamese Army troops. On February 22, 1968, members of the H&S Company of the 1st Battalion, 26th Marines fire 81mm mortar rounds on enemy positions.

Khe Sanh is a town in Quang Tri Province located on Highway 9 between Laos* and Dong Ha.* It is just below the Demilitarized Zone* along the Laotian border. For seventy-five days late in 1967 and early in 1968, Khe Sanh was the site of one of the most publicized battles of the Vietnam War, where American and South Vietnamese forces inflicted a major military defeat on Vietcong* and North Vietnamese forces.

Sources: Moyers S. Shore II, *The Battle for Khe Sanh*, 1969; Bernard C. Nalty, *Air Power and the Fight for Khe Sanh*, 1973.

Left: Troops of Battery C, 1st Battalion, 13th Marines fire on enemy positions at Khe Sanh in late February 1968.

Below: An aerial view of Khe Sanh in 1968. During the battle of Khe Sanh, the U.S. Air Force launched a massive aerial bombardment campaign, Operation Niagara, to support the Marine base.

Above: After the fall of South Vietnam to North Vietnamese forces on April 30, 1975, Khmer Rouge forces overran Phnom Penh and placed Cambodia under Communist rule. Pol Pot, the Khmer Rouge leader, launched a murderous reign of terror that, over the course of several years, threatened to politically destabilize Southeast Asia. In 1979, North Vietnam invaded Cambodia to impose order on the country. NVA troops remained in the country for more than a decade, fighting the resistance movement. These are Khmer Rouge fighters in September 1989.

KHE SANH, BATTLE OF (1967–68)

See Operation Niagara

KHMER KAMPUCHEA KRON

With 700,000 people, the Khmer* were one of the largest minority groups in the Republic of Vietnam.* Most of them were concentrated in the Mekong Delta* region of southwestern South Vietnam. In the seventeenth century, ethnic Vietnamese had expanded out of Annam* into Khmer land and wrested it from them. Ever since, the ethnic and territorial rivalry between the Vietnamese and the Khmer of Cambodia* has been intense. "Kampuchea Kron" was the name given to the Khmer areas of southern Vietnam. During the 1950s an armed band of ethnic Cambodian soldiers, known as the Khmer Kampuchea Kron, began fighting against the regime of Ngo Dinh Diem,* demanding the return of Khmer land to Cambodia. By the early 1960s, U.S. Special Forces* had persuaded the Khmer Kampuchea

Kron to fight against the Vietcong* and North Vietnamese, and large numbers of the Khmer Kampuchea Kron were incorporated into Civilian Irregular Defense Group* military units. After the fall of South Vietnam in 1975, the Khmer Kampuchea Kron often fought as guerrillas against the troops of the Socialist Republic of Vietnam,* whom they viewed as aggressors out to destroy all of Cambodia (Kampuchea).

Sources: Michael Vickery, *Cambodia, 1975–1982*, 1984; Joan L. Schrock et al., *Minority Groups in the Republic of Vietnam*, 1967.

KHMER ROUGE

Khmer Rouge means "Red Cambodians," and is the term describing the Communist Party in Cambodia. The Khmer Rouge were first organized by Vietnamese Communists from both North and South Vietnam, and they waged guerrilla war against the neutral government of Prince Norodom Sihanouk.* Until 1969 the North Vietnamese gave only tacit support to the Khmer Rouge because

Left: When North Vietnam invaded Cambodia in 1979, bloody fighting erupted between NVA troops and the Khmer Rouge military. Many Khmer Rouge prisoners of war were interrogated in the old French Lycée in Toul Sleng, Vietnam — the school had been converted into a prison. This cell, complete with a shackle, hints at the treatment afforded the Khmer Rouge Communists, which was little better than that offered by North Vietnam to U.S. prisoners of war.

Above: A young Cambodian soldier armed with a Chinese-made AK-47 rifle sports the checkered red-and-white Khmer Rouge headband. The photograph was taken in May 1979 when Khmer Rouge soldiers battled invading North Vietnamese troops.

Sihanouk allowed them to ship military equipment and supplies through the Cambodian port at Kompong Som and across the country by truck to Communist bases along the Laotian and Cambodian borders with South Vietnam. But the North Vietnamese were angered when Prince Sihanouk agreed to Operation Menu,* the secret U.S. bombing of those bases in 1969. They subsequently increased their support of the Khmer Rouge, and substantially increased it in 1970 when General Lon Nol,* an American supporter, deposed Sihanouk. Between 1970 and 1975 the Khmer Rouge strengthened their position in Cambodia, isolating Lon Nol's Cambodian army to city fortresses and forcing its surrender in 1975.

Led by Pol Pot* (formerly Saloth Sar), the Khmer Rouge then imposed a genocidal reign of terror throughout Cambodia, depopulating the cities in the hope of creating an agrarian utopia, and murdering more than 2 million people in the process. By that time the Khmer Rouge had become a threat and an embarrassment to the North Vietnamese. In December 1978 the North Vietnamese conquered most of Cambodia, forcing the Khmer Rouge to withdraw to remote jungles to resume their guerrilla activities, this time against their Vietnamese enemies. Following ten years of Vietnamese occupation, nearly thirteen years of civil war, and almost a decade of factional fighting and United Nations–sponsored coalition governments, the remaining elements of the Khmer Rouge surrendered in 1999.

Sources: William Shawcross, *Sideshow: Kissinger, Nixon, and the Destruction of Cambodia*, 1979, and *The Quality of Mercy: Cambodia, Holocaust, and the Modern Conscience*, 1984; François Ponchaud, *Cambodia: Year Zero*, 1978; Ben Kiernan, "How Pol Pot Came to Power," Ph.D. diss., 1986, and *The Pol Pot Regime: Race, Power, and Genocide in Cambodia Under the Khmer Rouge, 1975–1979*, 2002; Central Intelligence Agency, *World Factbook*, 2006.

Right: A bellicose Nikita Khrushchev, premier of the Soviet Union, visited the United Nations on September 23, 1960. During his speech before the General Assembly, Khrushchev pounded the podium in a display of feigned anger and frustration designed more for the media than for U.S. policymakers.

KHMERS

The Khmers, an ethnic minority group numbering approximately 700,000 people twenty years following the end of the Vietnam War, are similar in history and culture to the people of Cambodia.* It was not until the eighteenth century, when Vietnamese control reached the Mekong Delta,* that the Khmers became part of Vietnam. They were concentrated northwest of Saigon* around Tay Ninh, southwest of Saigon around Phu Vinh, and throughout An Xuyen Province. While most Vietnamese are faithful to Mahayana Buddhism,* the Khmers are Hinayana Buddhists. Taller, darker, and less Mongoloid than the Vietnamese, the Khmers were distinguished in dress by tight, buttoned-down jackets and skirts with a lower end brought forward between the legs and tucked in at the waist. During the 1960s and 1970s tens of thousands of Khmers escaped the fighting in Vietnam by fleeing across the border into Cambodia. The Vietnamese tended to look down upon the Khmers as a primitive, less civilized people than themselves.

Source: Harvey Smith et al., *Area Handbook for South Vietnam*, 1967.

KHRUSHCHEV, NIKITA

Premier of the Soviet Union* between 1958 and 1964, Nikita Khrushchev was born in 1894 and gradually rose to power in the Communist Party after joining it in 1918. Khrushchev was a loyal follower of Josef Stalin, became a member of the Central Committee in 1934, and joined the politburo in 1939. After Stalin's death in 1953, Khrushchev won a power struggle with Georgy Malenkov and became first secretary of the Communist Party. He was ultimately removed as premier in 1964, primarily because of continuing Soviet problems with the People's Republic of China,* terrible agricultural harvests, and the apparent diplomatic defeat of the Soviet Union in the Cuban missile crisis of 1962. Khrushchev was troubled by the increasing American commitment in Vietnam during the early 1960s, but he genuinely did not want to see a major military conflict in Southeast Asia, primarily because he had no idea of what role China would play in it. In 1964, when the North Vietnamese came to Moscow with requests for huge increases in military support, Khrushchev agreed, but only

if the North Vietnamese would consider a negotiated settlement with the United States. But when Khrushchev was removed from office in October 1964, all hopes for negotiations died. Khrushchev then lived in obscurity until his death on September 11, 1971.

Sources: Carl A. Linden, *Khrushchev & the Soviet Leaders, 1957–1964*, 1966; William Taubman, *Khrushchev: The Man and His Era*, 2003.

Left: Private First Class Dan Bullock was killed in action on June 7, 1969, with multiple wounds from small arms fire. At the time, Bullock was only fifteen years old, the youngest American serviceman to die in the Vietnam War. Bullock had falsified his age when he enlisted in the Marine Corps.

KIA (KILLED IN ACTION)

"KIA" was the acronym for "killed in action." Technically, any serviceman or servicewoman who died as a result of wounds sustained in action with enemy forces was classified KIA. This included wounds inflicted in a variety of ways, both conventional (e.g., bullets, artillery shells, grenades, and mortar rounds) and unconventional (e.g., booby traps* and mines). This classification did not include deaths due to circumstances unrelated to combat, such as traffic accidents, homicides, snake bites, and aircraft crashes due to faulty maintenance. Consequently, while the Vietnam War Memorial* "wall" lists the names of more than 58,000 American servicemen and servicewomen who died in Southeast Asia between 1959 and 1975, nearly 11,000 were not technically killed in action. STT

Sources: Ronald J. Glasser, *365 Days*, 1971; Harry G. Summers Jr., *Vietnam War Almanac*, 1985.

THE KILLING AT NGO THO

The Killing at Ngo Tho is the title of Gene D. Moore's 1967 novel about the Vietnam War. The book centers on a Colonel Scott Leonard, who is a military advisor to General Huang Huu-Lac of the ARVN (*see* Army of the Republic of Vietnam). Their headquarters is at Ngo Tho, near the Cambodian* border. Leonard and Huang have a good working relationship, but when Vietcong* infiltrate the base, Leonard suspects treachery from Huang's staff. Leonard persuades the general to cooperate, and together they locate the traitor and destroy the Vietcong on the base.

Sources: Gene D. Moore, *The Killing at Ngo Tho*, 1967; Philip D. Beidler, *American Literature and the Experience of Vietnam*, 1982.

THE KILLING FIELDS

Released in 1984, *The Killing Fields* was directed by David Puttnam and starred Sam Waterston as *New York Times* journalist Sydney Schanberg, John Malkovich as a photojournalist, and Dr. Haing Ngor as Dith Pran, Schanberg's Cambodian associate. The film is set in Cambodia* in 1975 when the Khmer Rouge* overran Phnom Penh. Pran chooses to remain behind with Schanberg and then is unable to be evacuated with the foreign journalists. The rest of the film portrays Pran's struggle for survival and eventual escape from Pol Pot's* genocidal "Year Zero" campaign, in which the Khmer Rouge annihilated up to 2 million Cambodians by some estimates. Pran eventually escapes from Cambodia via Thailand,* and the film ends with Pran and Schanberg reuniting in a Thai refugee camp.

Source: Samuel G. Freedman, *"The Killing Fields," New York Times*, October 28, 1984.

THE KILLING ZONE

Written by William Crawford Woods, *The Killing Zone* was published in 1970. As David Halberstam* wrote in *The Best and the Brightest*, the Vietnam War was a consequence of liberal extremism, the belief that power and technology could achieve military as well as political ends. Vietnam was high-tech warfare, and in the end the United States discovered it had not been enough. In *The Killing Zone*, Woods writes of a training camp where an outdated profes-

Right: The film *The Killing Fields* (1984) portrayed the genocide wreaked on Cambodia by Pol Pot in the 1970s. The actor Dr. Haing Ngor portrays the *New York Times* cameraman Dith Pran, who was left behind in Cambodia after the fall of Phnom Penh and survived the carnage. The film won three Academy Awards.

sional soldier must train new recruits in the new age of warfare. But in the end there is a grisly camp accident in which several young soldiers are accidentally killed when a computer at the base incorrectly orders the use of live rounds in a training exercise. The novel exposes the intellectual arrogance of the programmers, systems analysts, accountants, statisticians, and experts who organized and conducted the Vietnam War.

Sources: William Crawford Woods, *The Killing Zone*, 1970; Philip D. Beidler, *American Literature and the Experience of Vietnam*, 1982.

KING, MARTIN LUTHER JR.

Martin Luther King Jr. was born on January 15, 1929, in Atlanta. He graduated from Morehouse College in 1948 and the Crozer Theological Seminary in 1951, and then took a Ph.D. in theology from Boston University in 1955. King rocketed into the national consciousness as leader of the Montgomery bus boycott in 1955 and 1956, and in 1957 he established the Southern Christian Leadership Conference to fight segregation. In 1960 King was one of the founding members of the Student Nonviolent Coordinating Committee. Inspired by the passive disobedience of Mahatma Gandhi in India, King applied those same tactics to the American South, leading demonstrations, sit-ins, boycotts, and protest marches. By 1965, when the Vietnam War escalation began, King was the premier civil rights leader in the United States.

From the very beginning of the conflict in Vietnam, King had serious misgivings about it, seeing it as a misguided effort on the part of the United States that the developing world would interpret as simply another attempt by the white, industrialized West to colonize the rest of the planet. King was also disturbed by the effect of the draft* on the black community and the inordinately large numbers of casualties black soldiers* were sustaining in 1965 and 1966. In 1967 King openly protested the Vietnam War and linked the civil rights and antiwar movements* together, a step that earned him the ire of President Lyndon Johnson* and most civil rights leaders. Other civil rights leaders, both black and white, worried that linking the two movements would only dissipate the force of the campaign for equality. But King was convinced that the Vietnam War was diverting financial and emotional resources away from domestic programs and into a futile effort abroad. By 1968 the rest of the country was slowly coming around to King's point of view, but his voice was stilled by an assassin on April 4, 1968.

Sources: Lenwood G. Davis, *I Have a Dream: The Life and Times of Martin Luther King Jr.*, 1973; Stephen B. Oates, *Let the Trumpet Sound: The Life of Martin Luther King Jr.*, 1982.

KISSINGER, HENRY ALFRED

Henry A. Kissinger was born in Fürth, Germany, on May 27, 1923; his family immigrated to the United States in 1938, fleeing Nazi persecution of German Jews. Kissinger joined the Army during World War II and spent time in occupied Germany after the conflict working in the military bureaucracy. He returned to the United States to pursue his education, eventually earning a Ph.D. from Harvard in 1954. Specializing in diplomacy, Kissinger wrote his doctoral dissertation on the Congress of Vienna (1815), displaying his appreciation for power politics and his disdain for the moralistic assumptions that, in his opinion, so frequently prevent long-term solutions to nationalistic rivalries. Kissinger taught at Harvard during the 1950s and early 1960s, and during those years he was a leading figure in the rise of "nuclear strategy" among intellectuals who considered thermonuclear weapons a reality that must be coordinated in any realistic defense policy. Kissinger's 1957 book *Nuclear War and Foreign Policy* argued that tactical nuclear weapons could be considered a highly useful tool in defense strategy. Filmmaker Stanley Kubrick used Kissinger as the model for the deranged Dr. Strangelove in his 1964 movie of the same name. Kissinger served as a consultant to both the Kennedy* and Johnson* administrations in the 1960s, and acquired a larger political profile between 1964 and 1968 as a foreign policy aide to Governor Nelson Rockefeller of New York, who was unsuccessfully pursuing the presidency. Before his inauguration in January 1969, President Richard M. Nixon* appointed Kissinger special assistant for national security affairs.

From the very beginning, both Kissinger and Nixon took the middle road about Vietnam, realizing that military victory was impossible but refusing to implement a unilateral withdrawal. They wanted to turn the war over to the South Vietnamese while maintaining the international credibility of the United States. Vietnamization,* the policy they proposed in June 1969, became the institutional reflection of their middle-of-the-road approach. Simultaneous with a gradual, phased withdrawal of American troops, the United States would hand over war materiel to the South Vietnamese while continuing to provide them naval and air support. Kissinger realized that the government of South Vietnam was notoriously corrupt and probably incapable of defeating the Vietcong* and North Vietnamese, so he intended, through the threat of military escalation and the carrot stick of U.S. economic assistance, to persuade North Vietnam to settle the conflict.

Between 1969 and 1973 Henry Kissinger was the central figure in the diplomatic effort to restore peace in Southeast Asia. He held secret talks with officials from North Vietnam, the National Liberation Front (*see* Vietcong), the Soviet Union,* and the People's Republic of China* while the official peace talks were going on in Paris. The negotiations were complicated by the rigidity of both

Above: The Reverend Martin Luther King Jr. emerged in the late 1950s and early 1960s as the leader and the moral conscience of the civil rights movement in America. In April 1964, one year before he expressed his opposition to the Vietnam War, King was photographed here at a restaurant in Atlanta, Georgia, meeting with staff from his Southern Christian Leadership Conference.

Below: Secretary of State Henry Kissinger on January 1, 1976. In 1973, Kissinger received the Nobel Peace Prize for his role in negotiating an end to the Vietnam War. The award stirred up controversy among liberals in the United States, who accused Kissinger of unnecessarily prolonging the Vietnam War.

Above: Robert Komer on November 21, 1967. A special assistant to the president and chief of pacification in Vietnam, Komer argued that William Westmoreland's strategy of attrition was inflicting collateral damage on South Vietnamese sufficient to destroy any hope of winning their political loyalties. Komer summarized his argument in a pithy phrase, "Double the military firepower, square the political error."

sides: the North Vietnamese insisted on a complete halt of American bombing* of North Vietnam, total withdrawal of U.S. troops from South Vietnam, removal of Nguyen Van Thieu* as president of South Vietnam, and participation of the National Liberation Front (NLF) in any new government in South Vietnam. The United States demanded a mutual withdrawal of American and North Vietnamese troops from South Vietnam, refused to abandon Nguyen Van Thieu, and insisted that the NLF be excluded from the political process in South Vietnam.

Progress in the peace talks did not really come until 1972. Adept at power politics, Kissinger was intent on exploiting the rivalry between the Soviet Union and the People's Republic of China, and he secretly visited Beijing in July 1971 to prepare for Nixon's famous February 1972 trip there. Similarly, Kissinger pursued a policy of detente with the Soviet Union, which Nixon followed up on with his summit meeting in Moscow in May 1972. By that time pressure to end the war in Vietnam was becoming overwhelming. Both Kissinger and Nixon realized that the conflict in Southeast Asia was retarding their efforts to reach an accommodation with China and the Soviet Union; and the antiwar movement* at home, particularly after the invasion of Cambodia* in 1970, was demanding an end to the conflict.

In the summer of 1972 the peace talks finally began to yield results, but only because of major modifications in the U.S. negotiating position. Kissinger was dealing head-to-head with Le Duc Tho,* North Vietnam's negotiator, and in October 1972 they reached an agreement. The United States agreed to halt the bombing of North Vietnam, allow the NLF to participate in the political process in South Vietnam, let North Vietnamese Army* (NVA) troops remain in place in South Vietnam, and withdraw all American troops. The North Vietnamese agreed to a prisoner-of-war* exchange and dropped their demand that Nguyen Van Thieu be removed from office in South Vietnam. When the North Vietnamese appeared in November 1972 to be stepping back from their October agreement, Nixon ordered the massive bombing of Hanoi* and Haiphong, as well as the mining of Haiphong Harbor.* In January 1973 Le Duc Tho agreed to uphold the October 1972 settlement. The two nations signed a formal agreement on January 27, 1973.

In September 1973 Nixon named Kissinger the new secretary of state, but by that time the Watergate* scandal had compromised the administration's ability to pursue either its domestic or foreign policy agenda. After Nixon's resignation in August 1974, Kissinger remained in office, serving as secretary of state under President Gerald Ford* and engineering the ill-advised attack on Cambodia in 1975 after the *Mayaguez** incident. Kissinger left the State Department in January 1977 when President Jimmy Carter and the Democrats assumed the reins of power. Since then Kissinger has lectured and written widely about American

foreign policy, served as chairman of the National Bipartisan Commission on Central America, and founded international consulting firm Kissinger Associates, of which he remains chairman.

Sources: William Shawcross, *Sideshow: Kissinger, Nixon, and the Destruction of Cambodia*, 1979; Seymour Hersh, *The Price of Power: Kissinger in the Nixon White House*, 1983; Henry A. Kissinger, *White House Years*, 1979, and *Years of Upheaval*, 1982; Jussi M. Hanhimaki, *Flawed Architect: Henry Kissinger and American Foreign Policy*, 2004; Henry Kissinger, *Ending the Vietnam War: A History of American Involvement and Extrication from the Vietnam War*, 2003; http://nobelprize.org/nobel_prizes/peace/laureates/1973/kissinger-bio.html.

KIT CARSON SCOUTS

Kit Carson Scouts were former Vietcong* guerrillas who had "rallied" to the government, often under the Chieu Hoi Program,* and who were willing to act as scouts for U.S. units. New scouts would be closely watched and regarded with suspicion, for they could not always be trusted. Some rallied only to work for the Vietcong as spies or to lead U.S. units into traps. Most were very reliable, however, risking and often losing their lives for the units they served. Consequently, good Kit Carson Scouts were highly prized and treated accordingly by their units. They had familiarity with the terrain and culture, understood Vietcong tactics in establishing ambushes, and could identify booby traps.* They also recognized Vietcong base and assembly areas from indicators Americans did not notice. Finally, Kit Carson Scouts were able to identify Vietcong collaborators in villages as well as Vietcong masquerading as civilians. SF

Source: Peter Goldman and Tony Fuller, *Charlie Company*, 1983.

KOMER, ROBERT WILLIAM

Robert William "Blowtorch Bob" Komer was born on February 23, 1922, in Chicago. He graduated from Harvard in 1942 and then received an M.B.A. there in 1947 after serving in the Army during World War II. Komer joined the Central Intelligence Agency* in 1947 and remained there until 1960. At the CIA, Komer was a Middle East expert. He was appointed to the National Security Council* in 1960, serving as a Middle East consultant, and in 1965 Komer became a deputy special assistant to President Lyndon B. Johnson.* One year later he was promoted to special assistant. Considered by journalist David Halberstam* to be one of "the best and the brightest," Komer invested all of his energies in the Vietnam conflict and became one of the most optimistic advisors on Johnson's staff, always insisting that the United States could win the war if only it could secure the support of the

Vietnamese people. During the war and after, Komer was known as "Blowtorch Bob," a name given to him by Henry Cabot Lodge, the American ambassador in South Vietnam, who said that arguing with Komer was like having a flamethrower aimed at the seat of one's pants.

Komer believed that military counterinsurgency* had to be combined with social and economic development, and in May 1967 the president sent him to Vietnam, where he was appointed civilian deputy to the commander of Military Assistance Command, Vietnam.* Working directly with General William Westmoreland,* Komer established the Civil Operations and Revolutionary Development Support* (CORDS) program to increase local support for the American war effort. Although Komer believed the ultimate answer in Vietnam was not a military one, his development program failed. After the Tet Offensive,* administration officials put more pressure on Komer for results, so he established the Accelerated Pacification Program* and the Phoenix Program,* which was a CIA-sponsored operation to assassinate Vietcong* and their sympathizers. Komer was appointed ambassador to Turkey in 1968, and he joined the Rand Corporation* as an analyst in 1969. Komer stayed with Rand until 1977, when the Democrats returned to the White House under Jimmy Carter. He was appointed as NATO advisor in 1977 and as undersecretary for policy in

the Defense Department in 1979. When Ronald Reagan came into the White House in 1981, Komer left government service to become a lecturer at George Washington University. Robert Komer died on April 9, 2000.

Sources: David Halberstam, *The Best and the Brightest*, 1972; *Who's Who in America, 1984–1985*, 1985; Guenter Lewy, *America in Vietnam*, 1978; Andrew F. Krepinevich Jr., *The Army and Vietnam*, 1986; John Prados, *Presidents' Secret Wars: CIA and Pentagon Covert Operations Since World War II*, 1986; Robert W. Komer, *Bureaucracy Does Its Thing: Institutional Constraints on US-GVN Performance*, 1972; Frank L. Jones, *Blowtorch: Robert Komer and the Making of Vietnam Pacification Policy*, 2005.

KOREA

During the Vietnam War the Republic of Korea sent more combat troops to South Vietnam than any other American ally. A South Korean liaison unit came to Vietnam in the summer of 1964, and between 1965 and late 1966 their Capital Division,* 9th Infantry Division, and 2d Marine Brigade arrived. South Koreans concentrated their combat efforts in II Corps.* By 1969 there were nearly 49,000 South Koreans fighting in South Vietnam. During the entire war the South Koreans suffered 4,407 combat deaths. The Capital and 9th divisions were withdrawn from South

Below: During the Vietnam War, the Republic of Korea (South Korea) supported the American effort with two divisions of combat troops. In 1966, an ROK soldier from the White Horse Division kneels beside a suspected Vietcong woman and her family in thick reeds near Bong Son, South Vietnam. The commotion has terrified the small boy behind her.

KOREAN TROOPS

Right: During the Vietnam War, Republic of Korea troops earned a reputation for ferocity in combat and ruthlessness in their treatment of suspected Vietcong. On March 9, 1968, with the Tet Offensive still in high gear, soldiers from the ROK Tiger Division interrogate a Vietcong prisoner.

Below: After a night battle in 1966, south of Quang Ngai, Quang Ngai Province in northern South Vietnam, a ROK Marine takes a break behind the protection of a headstone.

During the Vietnam War the Republic of Korea (South Korea) proved to be a firm ally of the United States. Between 1950 and 1953 U.S. and United Nations forces repelled the North Korean invasion of South Korea and then the invasion of South Korea by the People's Republic of China. A total of 1,789,000 American soldiers served in the Korean theater, with 33,741 killed in combat, 2,827 dead from accidents and illness, and 103,284 wounded. After the cease-fire in 1953 the United States kept a large contingent of soldiers in South Korea as a deterrent to any future North Korean aggression. In 1954 the United States and South Korea, along with several other European and Southeast Asian countries, formed the Southeast Asia Treaty Organization (SEATO), a mutual security arrangement against Communist aggression. In 1965, when the United States introduced ground troops into Vietnam, the Republic of Korea felt duty-bound to participate by virtue of the SEATO alliance and gratitude for U.S. assistance during its recent struggle for survival. South Korean officials had real doubts about the viability of the American presence in Vietnam, but the alliance dictated cooperation.

Republic of Korea troops, known as ROKs to American soldiers, deployed to Vietnam soon after the arrival of U.S. ground troops, with the Capital Division, nicknamed the Tiger Division, arriving in October 1965. The Capital Division deployed to II Corps and consisted

of one air cavalry regiment, two infantry regiments, three battalions of 105mm howitzers, and one battalion of 155mm howitzers. The 9th Division, nicknamed the White Horse Division, arrived in Vietnam on September 27, 1966, and also deployed to II Corps. Both divisions spent most of their time in II Corps, patrolling the coastal area to intercept supplies coming in from North Vietnam, keep the roads open between Phan Rang in the south to Qui Nhon in the north, and engage Vietcong and later North Vietnamese troops in combat. In addition to the White Horse and Tiger divisions, the Republic of Korea also sent to Vietnam its 2d Marine Brigade and a regimental combat team. At the peak of its deployment in 1969, the Republic of Korea had more than 49,000 ground troops in Vietnam. A total of 4,407 ROK troops died in combat. They remained in South Vietnam to the bitter end, even after U.S. ground troops had been withdrawn. The White Horse and Tiger divisions left Vietnam in March 1973.

Among U.S. soldiers, ROK troops earned reputations for bravery and ruthlessness. They were well trained, highly disciplined, and enjoyed excellent morale.

Left: The main camp of the ROK Marines in South Vietnam was located eight miles north of the coastal city of Qui Nhon. In this April 16, 1966, photograph, ROK Marines practice Taekwondo, a Korean version of karate.

Below: During the Eastertide Offensive in the spring of 1972, ROK troops found themselves in heavy combat with the North Vietnamese Army. This ROK soldier from the Tiger Division was wounded in the fighting on Route 10 near An Khe, South Vietnam, on April 15 and is being carried to safety by a comrade.

They brooked no opposition and were not often constrained by the Geneva conventions on war. They tended to treat Vietcong prisoners of war with contempt and brutality, and they had little sympathy for South Vietnamese peasants who assisted enemy troops or who broke the law. ROK commanders often summarily executed Vietcong prisoners of war, and they had no compunctions about brutalizing recalcitrant elements of the Vietnamese civilian population. When ROK commanders captured Vietnamese robbers and thieves, they sometimes hung them alive from meat hooks.

Just as indiscriminate American artillery bombardment alienated the civilian population, ROK ruthlessness sometimes played into the political hands of the Communists. Peasants knew that the ROK troops were allies of the United States and the South Vietnamese government, and when ROKs behaved with brutality, local peasants felt abused and even less loyal to Saigon. In a war for the "hearts and minds" of South Vietnamese peasants, ROK brutality played into the hands of the Vietcong and later the North Vietnamese, who at every opportunity reminded peasants of their suffering at the hands of ROK, U.S., and ARVN troops. As for the United States, its long-term relationship with the Republic of Korea was cemented by the American alliance with ROK soldiers.

Sources: Stanley Robert Larsen and James Lawton Collins Jr., *Allied Participation in Vietnam*, 1981; Shelby L. Stanton, *Vietnam Order of Battle*, 1981, and *The Rise and Fall of An American Army: U.S. Ground Forces in Vietnam, 1965–1973*, 1985.

Above: Soviet Premier Aleksei Kosygin joins President Lyndon B. Johnson in Glassboro, New Jersey, for a summit meeting on June 23, 1967. Just over Johnson's left shoulder is Secretary of Defense Robert S. McNamara; immediately behind the president is Andrei Gromyko, the Soviet Minister of Foreign Affairs, and next to Gromyko is Anatoly Dobrynin, the Soviet ambassador to the United States. Secretary of State Dean Rusk can be seen between the heads of Gromyko and Dobrynin.

Vietnam in March 1973. South Korea's loyalty to the American war effort in South Vietnam, even though most Korean officials did not think that the war was politically winnable, was a direct function of the close relationship existing between the two countries since the Korean War (1950–53).

Source: Stanley Robert Larsen and James Lawton Collins Jr., *Allied Participation in Vietnam*, 1981.

KOSYGIN, ALEKSEI NIKOLAYEVICH

A Soviet politician who assisted the North Vietnamese with weaponry during the 1960s, Aleksei Kosygin was born in St. Petersburg (now Leningrad) on February 20, 1904. After completing his schooling, he volunteered for the Red Army in 1919. In 1921 Kosygin was released from military service and thereupon entered the Leningrad Co-Operative Technicum, where he gained firsthand knowledge of the politics of Soviet Russia. Between 1929 and 1935 young Kosygin was a student at the Leningrad-Kirov Textile Institute. During the 1940s he became a protégé of Josef Stalin's and eventually became a deputy premier. In 1953,

however, he was removed from his deputy premiership after Stalin's death. But Khrushchev* brought him back, and in 1964 Kosygin was elected chairman of the USSR Council of Ministers.

In 1965 Kosygin became directly involved in North Vietnam's struggle against the United States. The Soviet premier departed from Moscow in February 1965 destined for Hanoi.* Before his departure from Moscow he had been reluctant to expand Soviet military aid to the North Vietnamese Communists. He tried to pressure the Hanoi leadership into accepting the possibility of negotiations to end the conflict. While Kosygin was in Hanoi, however, the United States launched air attacks on Dong Hoi (near Hanoi), which prompted the Soviet premier to reconsider his stance on the Vietnamese conflict.

Upon his return to Moscow, Kosygin told reporters that the United States was the aggressor in Vietnam—calling the American bombing* of North Vietnam "Hitlerite." The Soviet premier felt compelled to defend the USSR's "anti-imperialist" image and thus acquiesced to the Hanoi leader-ship's request for sophisticated military hardware. Within ten days after his return to Moscow, Soviet surface-to-air missiles (SAMs)* arrived in Hanoi. Kosygin also warned in press releases that the Soviet Union* could not have normal relations with the United States as long as it was involved in aggression in Vietnam. The Soviet Union continued to send more and more weapons to the North Vietnamese as the U.S. commitment to South Vietnam widened.

By 1967 the Johnson* administration was wearying of the Vietnam War, although not to the extent of abandoning their South Vietnamese allies. A series of letters were exchanged between Johnson and Ho Chi Minh.* These proposals were not firmly thought out, except for the idea of negotiations taking place. Lyndon Johnson insisted that only if North Vietnam ended its hostilities in the South would the United States be willing to end the bombing and enter negotiations to bring the war to a close. The Hanoi regime, on the other hand, refused even to consider talks until a bombing halt was in effect. In early February 1967 Kosygin visited London, where Prime Minister Harold Wilson tried to get the Soviet premier to bring pressure on Hanoi to negotiate. Before the meeting Johnson had indicated a willingness to compromise; now he insisted on a tougher line toward Hanoi, however. Only if the North ceased its operations in the South would the United States negotiate. Although Kosygin did pass along these proposals, the North Vietnamese remained silent and thus ended what Wilson called an "historic opportunity." Aleksei Kosygin would not again act as a broker in the conflict and continued to work at his desk in Moscow until his death on December 18, 1980. JSL

Sources: *Current Biography*, November 1965; Stanley Karnow, *Vietnam: A History*, 1983; *New York Times*, December 21, 1980; Robin Edmonds, *Soviet Foreign Policy, 1962–1973: The Paradox of a Superpower*, 1975; Leif Rosenberger, *The Soviet Union and Vietnam: An Uneasy Alliance*, 1986.

KRULAK, VICTOR H.

In command of Fleet Marine Force, Pacific* (FMFPac) from 1964 to 1968, Victor "Brute" Krulak was responsible for all United States Marine* units in the Pacific theater. Born in 1913, Krulak graduated from Annapolis in 1934, observed Japanese operations in China in the late 1930s, and commanded a parachute battalion in a diversionary attack on Choiseul Island during the Bougainville Campaign in 1943. Wounded and awarded a Navy Cross for valor, Krulak then served as a division operations officer on Okinawa and returned to China at the war's end to assist in the Japanese surrender. In Washington in the late 1940s he worked with staffs seeking to preserve Marine Corps autonomy during the unification battles, and during the Korean War he helped plan the Inchon landing (1950) and later served as chief of staff of the 1st Marine Division* until 1951.

From 1962 to 1964, as the special assistant for counterinsurgency* to the Joint Chiefs of Staff (*see* Chairman, JCS), Krulak gained a reputation as the "military's most skilled bureaucratic player in Washington at the time, a figure of immense import in the constant struggle over

Vietnam." Diminutive in size (5'4", 134 lbs) but not in military stature, he had no real operational authority as commander of FMFPac, but his fifty-four visits in-country and lengthy staff experience made him a force to reckon with among top commanders and their civilian counterparts in Washington. Krulak's memoir details the conflict of strategies characteristic of the command and political systems that oversaw the war effort.

In 1968 a faction of officers at Marine Headquarters pushed a Krulak nomination for commandant, but the general—along with fellow competitor Lewis Walt*—lost the battle to Leonard F. Chapman.* Krulak then retired, joined the Copely Newspaper Service, earned a Ph.D. from the University of San Diego (1970), and wrote a weekly syndicated column in addition to numerous articles and two books on international and military affairs. In 2004 Victor H. Krulak was the recipient of the Distinguished Graduate award, which honors United States Naval Academy alumni who have "provided a lifetime of service to the nation or armed forces…" DA

Sources: David Halberstam, *The Best and the Brightest*, 1972; Victor H. Krulak, *First to Fight: An Inside View of the U.S. Marine Corps*, 1984; History Division, United States Marine Corps, *Who's Who in the Marine Corps History*, 2005.

Above: Lieutenant General Victor H. Krulak of the U.S. Marine Corps greets Marines from the 9th Marine Expeditionary Brigade, the first U.S. combat troops to arrive in South Vietnam, in Da Nang on March 23, 1965.

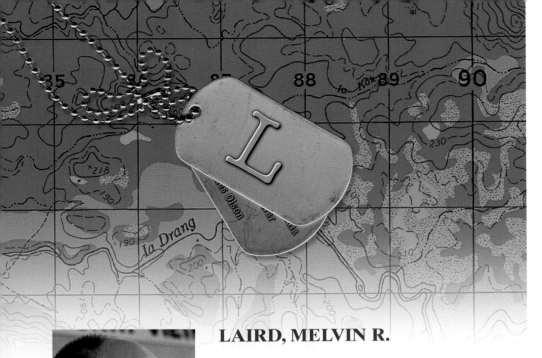

LAIRD, MELVIN R.

Born on September 1, 1922, Melvin R. Laird was a Republican congressman from Wisconsin (1953–69) and secretary of defense (1969–72) in the Nixon* administration. Melvin Laird was chosen by Nixon as secretary of defense because, as a veteran congressman, he had much influence in the U.S. Congress,* which Nixon believed could be used to diminish criticism from that quarter. Laird believed that he should have direct access to the president. Nixon's national security advisor, Henry Kissinger,* feared Laird's influence on Nixon and hence did not want the kind of access the secretary desired. Kissinger established an indirect channel between the White House and the Joint Chiefs of Staff (*see* Chairman, JCS) to offset some of Laird's power and influence.

Almost from the outset of his tenure as secretary of defense Laird began to lobby for troop reductions in Vietnam. He believed that Nixon's goodwill on Capitol Hill would run thin unless the president demonstrated his commitment in curtailing U.S. involvement in South Vietnam. And signs of congressional impatience were apparent in the spring of 1969. There was the normal partisan criticism, however; even the Senate Republican whip, Hugh Scott, called for the withdrawal of large numbers of troops from Vietnam. Nixon, on the other hand, had promised the American public "peace with honor" but could not accept huge troop reductions unless military conditions changed in South Vietnam.

By late 1969 Laird was pressing for a precise timetable of troop reductions, so that by the end of 1971 the United States would have only 206,000 soldiers in South Vietnam. Laird's insistence on troop reductions annoyed Kissinger, who worried that his bargaining position was being damaged by Laird. Kissinger went as far as warning Nixon that the South Vietnamese could not yet carry on the war themselves. Kissinger moreover had his assistants concoct or draft a contingency plan to knock the North Vietnamese out of the war. The proposal included massive bombing* attacks on North Vietnam. Laird intervened and warned

Nixon that if the plan was implemented, domestic opposition to the war would mount, particularly from congressional sources. Nixon shelved the idea, though it would be resurrected in the winter of 1972.

Laird meanwhile continued to press for disengagement, and coined the term "Vietnamization."* The defense secretary even visited South Vietnam and came away with the conviction that the South Vietnamese could defend themselves. Laird's appraisal was supported by Sir Robert Thompson,* the British guerrilla-warfare specialist. As protests mounted against Nixon's Vietnam policy, Laird responded to critics by saying that Vietnamization was the top priority of the administration. Laird avoided conflict and was convinced that the American public was tired of the war. When military officials pressed for massive incursions into Cambodia* in 1970, he urged restraint. He was vetoed, however, by Nixon and Kissinger. Laird would and did advise restraint in the winter of 1972, when Nixon decided on mining Haiphong Harbor* and using B-52* attacks to bring the North Vietnamese to the conference table. Laird decided to leave the Nixon administration at the end of the president's first term. Since 1974 Laird has served as the senior counselor for national and international affairs for the Reader's Digest Association. JSL

Sources: *Who's Who in America, 1984–85*; Allen E. Goodman, *The Lost Peace*, 1978; Melvin R. Laird, *The Nixon Doctrine*, 1972; http://www.wikipedia.org/wiki/Melvin_R._Laird.

LAM SON

Lam Son is a small village in Thanh Hoa Province and is the birthplace of Le Loi,* the famous Vietnamese nationalist who defeated a contingent of invading Chinese forces in 1428. Le Loi is one of the most famous names in Vietnamese history. During the Vietnam War, ARVN (*see* Army of the Republic of Vietnam) forces frequently used "Lam Son" as a code name to describe their military operations or their phase of joint military operations with U.S. forces. Operation Lam Son 719,* for example, was the code name for the 1971 ARVN invasion of Laos.* Lam Son 246 was the ARVN phase of Operation Somerset Plain,* the 101st Airborne Division's* assault on the A Shau Valley* in 1968. Lam Son 216 was the ARVN portion of Operation Delaware,* the 7th Cavalry's attack on the A Shau Valley that same year. Use of the code name Lam Son in ARVN operations was a symbolic act, designating South Vietnam as the "true" descendant of Vietnamese nationalism.

Sources: David G. Marr, *Vietnamese Anticolonialism, 1885–1925*, 1981; Joseph Buttinger, *The Smaller Dragon: A Political History of Vietnam*, 1958; Shelby L. Stanton, *The Rise and Fall of an American Army: U.S. Ground Forces in Vietnam, 1965–1973*, 1985.

Above: Melvin R. Laird conducting a press briefing at the Pentagon in November 1970. In 1969, President Richard M. Nixon appointed Laird, the former Republican Congressman from Wisconsin, as secretary of defense. Laird was then responsible for designing and implementing the Vietnamization program.

LAM SON 719

Lam Son 719 was the operational name for the disastrous Laotian invasion of February 1971. Nixon* and Kissinger* anticipated the heavy infiltration* of men and materiel during the 1971 dry season in preparation for a major North Vietnamese Army* (NVA) offensive during the 1972 elections.* Also hoping to test Vietnamization,* they proposed a major ARVN (see Army of the Republic of Vietnam) initiative for 1971. They initially proposed invading Cambodia* or North Vietnam, but General Creighton Abrams* and President Nguyen Van Thieu* favored severing the Ho Chi Minh Trail* in Laos* along Route 9.

The invasion proved to be an unmitigated disaster. Planning was confined to a few people in Washington and Saigon,* and the invasion units were given minimal notice and preparation time. Congressional restrictions prohibited

American ground troops in Cambodia and Laos, preventing American advisors from accompanying their units or coordinating artillery, helicopter, and tactical air support. Despite American predictions that four divisions would be necessary to secure the trail from the border to Tchepone (the objective), the ARVN committed only two divisions. The NVA had four seasoned divisions in opposition. The terrain was rugged, restricting ground movement and limiting flight patterns—all to the NVA's advantage. NVA artillery had greater range, and its troops' familiarity with the terrain gave them a fire-direction advantage. Finally, the weather was unusually rainy, impeding allied air support and resupply.

The ARVN's best units were committed—1st Infantry,* airborne,* marines,* and rangers. But NVA troops were not surprised, and they drew ARVN units away from U.S. artillery, lengthening ARVN supply lines and marshaling their own resources for a counterattack. Seizing the oppor-

Above: In 1971, with the support of some U.S. troops, the ARVN invaded Laos with the intent of securing Route 9 out of South Vietnam and reoccupying Khe Sanh as a forward supply base. The invasion was dubbed Operation Dewey Canyon II/ Lam Son 719. Here, U.S. soldiers provide support with an M551 Sheridan tank atop a hill on February 7, 1971. The operation proved to be a miserable failure, with the ARVN units barely escaping annihilation.

Above: When Dien Bien Phu fell to the Vietminh in 1954, the government of French Premier Joseph Laniel collapsed. Laniel, here in 1953, is reviewing some documents during a transportation strike in France.

tunity to annihilate the ARVN's best units, the NVA would have succeeded except for massive U.S. air strikes and American helicopter pilots' ability to extract beleaguered units. Lam Son 719 proved the failure of Vietnamization. The ARVN's best units suffered 50 percent casualties. Morale plummeted. It became obvious that the ARVN was hard-pressed to stand alone. The NVA buildup, moreover, was not stemmed; its 1972 offensive was furious, initially successful, and foreshadowed the Final Offensive of 1975 (*see* Ho Chi Minh Campaign). SF

Sources: Bruce Palmer Jr., *The 25-Year War: America's Military Role in Vietnam*, 1984; Nguyen Duy Hinh, *Lam Son 719*, 1981; David Fulghum and Terrence Maitland, *The Vietnam Experience: South Vietnam on Trial*, 1984; Keith William Nolan, *Into Laos. The Story of Dewey Canyon II/Lam Son 719*, 1986.

LAND REFORM

At the time of the Geneva Accords* of 1954, approximately 60 percent of Vietnamese peasants were landless and another 20 percent owned less than two acres of land. The desire to own land or acquire more land was almost universal in South Vietnam. Tenant farmers paid an average of 34 percent of their annual crop to landlords for use of the land. The Vietcong* had made a strong appeal to South Vietnamese peasants by distributing the land of absentee landlords in the early 1950s, but after Ngo Dinh Diem* took over in 1954, landlords regained control of their property. In areas they controlled, the Vietcong redistributed land and gained a stronger following from peasant farmers. Between January 1968 and December 1969, under the direction of President Nguyen Van Thieu,* the government of the Republic of Vietnam* began a modest land reform program in which 50,000 families received government land. Thieu also prohibited local officials from restoring land to former landlords. On March 26, 1970, the Republic of Vietnam, at Thieu's urging, passed the Land-to-the-Tiller Act, which provided for an end to rent payments and the issuing of ownership titles to the peasants currently working the land. The maximum amount of land that anyone could own was 37 acres. By 1972 the Land-to-the-Tiller Act had provided land titles to 400,000 formerly landless peasants, and the land they received totaled more than 1.5 million acres. The number of farm tenants in South Vietnam was reduced from 60 to 34 percent of the population. By 1973 all but 7 percent of the farmers in South Vietnam owned their own land. The Vietcong had for all intents and purposes lost a major issue that had been alienating the peasants from the government of the Republic of Vietnam.

Source: Guenter Lewy, *America in Vietnam*, 1978.

LANIEL, JOSEPH

Born in France in 1889, Joseph Laniel was educated at the École Gerson, Lycée Janson de Sailly, and the University of Paris. Active in the resistance movement during World War II, Laniel founded the Parti Républicain de la Liberté in 1946. Between 1940 and 1948 he served as secretary of state. Elected minister of state in 1952, Laniel rose to become prime minister of France* in June 1953, where he presided over the collapse of the French Indochinese empire. A right-wing politician, Laniel tried to implement the Navarre Plan* and accepted $400 million in American aid toward that end, but the defeat at Dien Bien Phu* ended his dreams. Laniel was firmly committed to Bao Dai* and did not want Vietnam divided, but he had no power to implement his wishes. His government collapsed before the Geneva Accords* were completed, and Laniel was replaced as prime minister by Pierre Mendès-France.* Joseph Laniel died on April 8, 1975.

Sources: *International Who's Who, 1964–1965*, 1965; *Who Was Who in America*, Vol. 6, 1976; Joseph Buttinger, *Vietnam: A Dragon Embattled*, Vol. 2, *Vietnam at War*, 1967.

LANSDALE, EDWARD GEARY

Born in 1908 and a graduate of UCLA, Edward Lansdale was an Air Force officer and an agent for the Central Intelligence Agency.* Lansdale had been an architect of the successful counterguerrilla and counterinsurgency* effort in the Philippines* in the early 1950s. Consequently, he was assigned to Vietnam in 1954, following the Geneva Accords* that ended the First Indochinese War between the Vietminh* and France.* His initial assignment was to plan, coordinate, and implement a psychological warfare ("psywar") campaign in North Vietnam in the 1954 to 1956 period. His campaign was a mixture of successes and failures, but it did contribute to the large exodus of people from North to South Vietnam. Following 1956, Lansdale became a close personal friend of Ngo Dinh Diem,* the president of the Republic of Vietnam.* He also became one of the very few Americans to whom Diem listened. This rapport between Diem and Lansdale was unofficial and bypassed normal channels of diplomatic relations, which resulted in great distrust of Lansdale by various diplomatic, military, and civilian representatives of the U.S. government. Lansdale's record in the Philippines, his successes in covert-action operations in Vietnam, and his relationship with a recalcitrant and often unresponsive Diem, however, made him a valuable policy conduit for both the Eisenhower* and Kennedy* administrations. Lansdale's views on the evolving situation in Vietnam in the 1950s and early 1960s were influential in Washington, even though they often conflicted with other perceptions from Americans in Vietnam who resented Lansdale's presence. Thus, Lansdale is significant because he manifested not only the clandestine, informal relations between the United States and South Vietnam that existed simultaneously and often in contradiction to the overt, official relations, but also the intense contest for influence over policy between the numerous American government agencies functioning in South Vietnam. Lansdale was basically the father of American counterinsurgency programs in Vietnam. Although he was considered a candidate for ambassador to South Vietnam by President John F. Kennedy, the appointment was vetoed by Secretary of Defense Robert McNamara.* Between 1965 and 1968 Lansdale served as a special assistant at the U.S. Embassy in Saigon. Edward Lansdale died on February 23, 1987. STT

Sources: John Prados, *Presidents' Secret Wars: CIA and Pentagon Covert Operations Since World War II*, 1986; Edward Geary Lansdale, *In the Midst of Wars: An American's Mission to Southeast Asia*, 1972; Jonathan Nashel, *Edward Lansdale's Cold War*, 2005.

LAO DONG PARTY

Ho Chi Minh,* although he was a Communist, understood the fragmented nature of Vietnamese society. He had, with his comrades Le Duc Tho,* Pham Van Dong,* Le Duan,* and Vo Nguyen Giap,* created the Indochinese Communist Party in 1929. The creation of this party, however, did not result in total cohesion among Vietnam's many political leaders. During the 1940s and after World War II, Ho Chi Minh determined that nationalism would be the catalyst to bring about the demise of French rule. He worked tirelessly to mobilize Vietnamese resistance against the French, and after 1941 it was his own Vietminh* that he believed would be the vehicle for ending French dominion in Vietnam.

But as a leader Ho understood by 1952 that neither the exclusive Communist Party nor the Vietminh were entirely capable of bringing all of Vietnamese society into union to end French rule. In 1952 he changed the name of the Communist Party to the Lao Dong, or Workers' Party. At the same time he merged it with the Lien Viet, or the National United Front. Ho believed that by these moves nationalist sentiment would rise throughout Vietnam. Through the apparatus of the Lao Dong Party, during the 1950s Ho introduced land reform, as well as education, health care, and other reforms, in the provinces held by the Vietminh. Even though he gained additional support among the Vietnamese populace, the demise of the French presence in Vietnam ultimately was decided on the battlefield at Dien Bien Phu.*

Probably the severest test of the Lao Dong Party came during the 1950s in North Vietnam over the program of collectivization. Peasants revolted against this program in several provinces. The Communists, however, crushed each revolt, believing that they were contrived from abroad. Ho Chi Minh urged moderation and even had the leader of the Lao Dong Party, Truong Chinh,* removed from his post. Le Duan* became the new leader or head of the Lao Dong Party, which he continued to head until his death in July 1986. Under the tutelage of Le Duan, however, the programs created by the Lao Dong Party were cautiously introduced to prevent future rebellions. In reality, the Lao Dong Party is the Communist Party, which wields great power in contemporary Vietnam. JSL

Sources: George C. Herring, *America's Longest War*, 1986; Donald Lancaster, *The Emancipation of French Indochina*, 1961; John T. McAlister Jr., *Vietnam: The Origins of Revolution*, 1969.

LAOS

Covering 92,429 square miles in mountainous Southeast Asia, Laos is one of the most underdeveloped nations in the world. Twenty years after the end of the Vietnam War, its population of 3,775,000 people were primarily engaged in rice cultivation, and more than 80 percent of them were illiterate. Eighty percent of today's population of 6,368,481 (2006 estimate) still relies on subsistence agriculture, though private enterprise and the decentralizing of government control have been slowly encouraged since 1986. The largest city and capital of Laos is Vientiane, with 189,600 people (2002 estimate), and the former capital city of the ancient kingdom of Laos is Luang Prabang, with a population of about 22,000. Approximately 90 percent of the population is ethnic Lao or Kha, while 9 percent are Hmong or Yao and the remaining 1 percent ethnic Vietnamese or Chinese. During the Vietnam War the country was engaged in a civil war between the Communist-backed Pathet Lao* and the forces of Souvana Phouma,* but along with Cambodia* and South Vietnam, Laos fell to the Communists in 1975.

In addition to its political role in the conflict, Laos proved strategically decisive. Its rugged mountains beneath a jungle canopy provided ideal concealment for North Vietnamese troops and supplies making their way down the Ho Chi Minh Trail* into Cambodia and South Vietnam. The Ho Chi Minh Trail connected North Vietnam with South Vietnam via the Laotian mountains and Central Highlands. Throughout the war, the U.S. military subjected the Ho Chi Minh Trail to massive aerial bombardment, but to no avail. Year after year, the trail expanded in terms of mileage and sophistication, with North Vietnamese troops and supplies moving virtually unimpeded. In 1971 South Vietnam staged an invasion of Laos designed to sever the Ho Chi Minh trail.

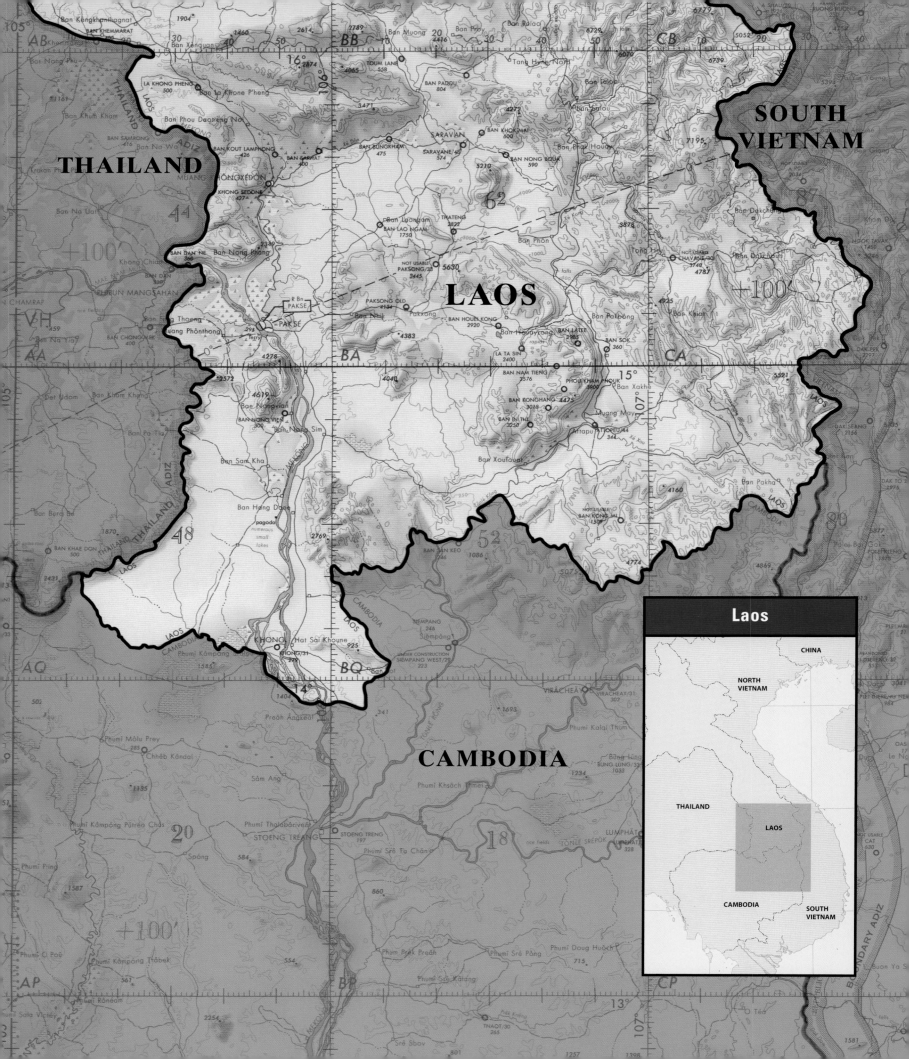

The expedition proved disastrous. ARVN troops became overextended, badly outrunning their supply lines. The North Vietnamese Army* nearly surrounded and cut off the ARVN units' line of retreat. Only massive American airpower directed at the NVA positions gave the ARVN an opportunity to escape back into South Vietnam and avoid annihilation. GLH

Sources: *Webster's Geographical Dictionary*, 1984; Charles A. Stevenson, *The End of Nowhere: American Policy Toward Laos Since 1954*, 1973; Martin Stuart-Fox, *A History of Laos*, 1997; Central Intelligence Agency, *World Factbook*, 2006.

duty in World War I as well as in Morocco between 1921 and 1926. He was promoted to general in 1939 but was imprisoned by the Germans in 1940. He escaped in 1943 and joined the Fighting French. After the war Tassigny became chief of staff and was the prime mover behind building the Vietnamese National Army.* Tassigny returned to France in 1951 because of illness and died there on January 11, 1952.

Sources: James J. Cooke, *France, 1789–1962*, 1975; Joseph Buttinger, *Vietnam: A Dragon Embattled.* Vol. 2, *Vietnam at War*, 1967.

Opposite page: A detail of the southernmost part of Laos, which borders Vietnam to the east, Cambodia to the south, and Thailand to the west.

LAOS, INVASION OF

See Lam Son 719

LATTRE DE TASSIGNY, JEAN JOSEPH DE

Jean Joseph de Lattre de Tassigny was born in 1889 in the Vendée at Mouilleron-en-Pareds, France.* He saw active

LA VANG BASILICA

The La Vang Basilica in Vietnam was completed in 1900 as a monument to the alleged appearance of the Virgin Mary to a group of persecuted Roman Catholics* in 1798. It was located about four miles outside of Quang Tri City in Quang Tri Province. The basilica was a favorite pilgrimage site for Vietnamese Catholics until its destruction during the Eastertide Offensive in 1972.*

Source: Danny J. Whitfield, *Historical and Cultural Dictionary of Vietnam*, 1976.

Left: An aerial photograph taken on October 14, 1968, of Fire Support Base Alpine, a recently activated U.S. Marine outpost located approximately 6 miles east of the Laotian border.

Above: General John D. Lavelle commanded the Seventh Air Force in Vietnam. He assumed command just as the last U.S. combat troops were being withdrawn from Vietnam, which left the U.S. Air Force with greater responsibility in attacking enemy troops and sites. Lavelle at the ceremony on July 29, 1972, at Tan Son Nhut Air Base outside of Saigon in which he assumed command.

LAVELLE, JOHN DANIEL

John D. Lavelle was born on September 9, 1916, in Cleveland. He graduated from John Carroll University in 1938 and spent World War II as a pilot in the Army Air Corps. After the war Lavelle rose up through Air Force ranks and in July 1971 took command of the Seventh Air Force* in Saigon.* Late in 1972 Lavelle was forced to testify before both the House and Senate Armed Services committees concerning his activities in 1971 and 1972. Although U.S. pilots were allowed to conduct "protective reaction strikes"* against North Vietnamese installations after October 31, 1968, Lavelle was charged with ordering dozens of unauthorized missions against North Vietnam. Lavelle argued before the committees that he was encouraged to carry out secret attacks against North Vietnam by his superiors, but no formal proof of his charges could be found. Because of the secret raids, Lavelle was relieved of his command of the Seventh Air Force in April 1972. John Lavelle retired from active duty later that year; he died on July 10, 1979.

Sources: Guenter Lewy, *America in Vietnam*, 1978; *New York Times*, July 11, 1979.

LBJ TAPES

In 1993 the Lyndon B. Johnson Presidential Library began releasing to the public selected conversations that President Lyndon B. Johnson* had conducted with trusted advisors in the Oval Office. Among the most controversial were discussions in early 1964 with Secretary of Defense Robert McNamara* and aide McGeorge Bundy.* On March 2, 1964, Johnson had been informed that the political situation in Vietnam was deteriorating rapidly, with the Vietcong* steadily gaining ground and the government of South Vietnam caught in a series of musical chair–like coups d'etat, the most recent just a few days before. Despite billions of dollars in military assistance from the United States, South Vietnam rested on a precipice, its long-term stability more uncertain than ever. Johnson found himself facing a real dilemma. With the presidential election of 1964* just nine months away, he did not want South Vietnam to fall to Communism. Such an event would arm his Republican opponent with a powerful election issue. The president had to do something, but none of his advisors offered any acceptable options. Johnson invited Bundy to discuss the matter, telling him, "There may be another coup, but I don't know what to do… If there is, I guess that war just… what alternatives do we have then? We're not going to send troops there, are we?"

Two months later, in May 1964, the president learned that, in 1963, more than 20,000 Vietnamese civilians had died, most of them victims of accidental American bombardment. The United States had managed to kill more innocent South Vietnamese civilians in 1963 than Vietcong. "Only" 5,000 had succumbed in 1962. Johnson wanted to know about the wisdom of going public with such news. He solicited the opinion of Robert McNamara, who replied, "I do think, Mr. President, that it would be wise for you to say as little as possible [about the war]. The frank answer is that we don't know what is going on out there."

Several weeks later, Johnson met again with Bundy. "I stayed awake last night thinking of this thing," he told Bundy. "It looks to me like we're getting into another

Right: Six weeks after winning the presidential election of 1968, President Lyndon B. Johnson asked Secretary of Defense Robert McNamara to meet with him at the LBJ Ranch outside of Johnson City, Texas. On December 22, 1968, McNamara delivered bad news about conditions in Vietnam.

Korea... I don't think we can fight them ten thousand miles away from home... I don't think it's worth fighting for... It's just the biggest damn mess I ever saw." LBJ's fear of losing the election, however, overcame his reservations about the war. By May 1964, approximately 400 American soldiers had died in Vietnam. By the time Johnson left office in January 1969, that number had jumped to nearly 31,000, all in a war "not worth fighting for."

Source: http://www.lbjlib.utexas.edu/ johnson/archives.hom/Dictabelt.hom/content.asp

LE DUAN

Secretary-general of the Communist Party of Vietnam* and noted revolutionary leader in twentieth-century Vietnam, Le Duan was born in Quang Tri Province in central Vietnam on April 4, 1907, and eventually found his way to Hanoi.* Le Duan, as a young man, was a political activist who advocated the end of French colonial rule in Indochina.* Because of his anti-French activities, he was imprisoned between 1931 and 1936 and then between 1940 and 1945. He also began to follow the leadership of Ho Chi Minh* and later became one of Ho's most trusted aides.

Because of his faithful service to the Vietminh* movement, Le Duan rose rapidly within the Communist Party hierarchy. In 1952 he headed the Vietminh military command in southern Vietnam and ultimately conducted a war of attrition against the French. With the defeat of the French in 1954, Le Duan was catapulted into prominence and in 1959 was made secretary-general of the Lao Dong Party* (Workers' Party); in 1960 he was named first secretary of the Lao Dong Party.

Meanwhile, as a consequence of the Geneva Conference* of 1954, Vietnam was divided temporarily into two political entities. Elections were promised but never held. A puppet regime under Ngo Dinh Diem* governed South Vietnam, while Ho Chi Minh, with Le Duan at his side, secured North Vietnam under the dominance of the Communist Party. By 1959 Vietnam once again was involved in conflict, but this time between revolutionaries in the South, who received aid from the North, and the Diem regime, which received assistance from the United States.

Le Duan advocated a total war against the Diem regime by the Vietcong.* He made a secret trip to the South in 1959 and found that the insurgents there faced annihilation unless they resorted to urban and rural terrorism. His report resulted in a redirection of the war in the South. Between 1959 and 1961 the Vietcong, as a consequence of directives from Hanoi, embarked on a massive campaign of terrorism and assassination in the South.

Le Duan continued to exert increasing influence on the conduct of the war. After a few years of limited guerrilla warfare in the South, Le Duan, along with other members of the Hanoi politburo, decided that in order to achieve victory they would have to adopt a conventional war akin to that which they had waged against the French. He noted in 1965 that whenever they had been offensive in warfare they had succeeded in driving out foreign aggressors, and Le Duan believed this would hold true with the Americans as well.

As the war progressed and American public opinion faltered, Le Duan became increasingly convinced that he and the Hanoi leadership would prevail in the South. With the end of the Johnson* administration, negotiations were held in Paris to end the conflict. For years both sides bantered around the conference table about the terms of a cease-fire. Meanwhile, Ho Chi Minh's health faltered, and on September 2, 1969, he died. Thus the mantle of power passed on to veteran nationalist fighters such as Le Duan, Pham Van Dong,* and Vo Nguyen Giap.* These men believed that the defeat of the United States and South Vietnam was their sacred mission. Le Duan finally realized his dream in 1975 with the fall of Saigon.* Le Duan died on July 10, 1986. JSL

Sources: *Who's Who in the World*, 1985; Jon M. Van Dyke, *North Vietnam's Strategy for Survival*, 1972; Vo Nguyen Giap, *Big Victory, Big Task*, 1967; *New York Times*, July 11, 1986.

LE DUC THO

Born in 1910 in Nam Ha Province in Tonkin,* Le Duc Tho was North Vietnam's principal negotiator at the Paris peace talks.* The son of a French functionary in the Vietnamese colonial government, Tho was educated in French schools before joining the revolution. He spent years in jail and hiding because of his revolutionary activities and helped found both the Indochinese Communist Party (*see* Lao Dong Party) and the Vietminh.* During the French Indochina War he was chief commissar for southern Vietnam and maintained primary responsibility for the region after U.S. intervention ended.

The Paris peace talks formally began on May 13, 1968, and deadlocked immediately. Tho insisted that the U.S. bombing of North Vietnam must stop before anything else could be negotiated. While his position was firm, Tho apparently had considerable discretion in how to pursue negotiations until Ho Chi Minh's* death in September 1969. After that, North Vietnamese decision making became collegial, and Tho reported to the collective leadership. Beginning on February 21, 1970, Tho met secretly with Henry Kissinger* for two years. Seeing the military and political struggles as part of the same overall conflict, Tho maintained a negotiating position throughout that any agreement must simultaneously resolve both issues. Furthermore, any armistice must include the replacement of Nguyen Van Thieu's* government with

Above: A close associate of Ho Chi Minh from the earliest days of the Indochinese Communist Party, Le Duan spent much of his adult life fighting France and the United States for the independence and reunification of Vietnam. In July 1967, Duan was serving as first secretary of the North Vietnam Labor Party.

Below: A committed Vietnamese nationalist and Communist, Le Duc Tho served steadily as the minister of foreign affairs for North Vietnam. He represented North Vietnam at the Paris peace negotiations, and his stubborn commitment to the withdrawal of all U.S. troops from South Vietnam as a prerequisite to serious negotiations proved enormously frustrating to President Richard M. Nixon and Secretary of State Henry Kissinger. This photograph of Le Duc Tho was taken in Paris on January 1, 1973, shortly before the signing of the Paris Peace Accords, which helped to end the war.

a coalition that included the National Liberation Front (*see* Vietcong).

In order to effect American withdrawal from Vietnam, Tho ultimately made concessions on these points. The principal provision of the October 1972 agreement allowed Thieu to retain power, with 150,000 North Vietnamese Army* troops remaining in South Vietnam. Thieu angrily rejected the agreement, and all sides sought "modifications." Renewed negotiations stalled in December. They were soon back on track, however, and an agreement almost identical to the October agreement was signed in Paris on January 27, 1973. Although the cease-fire never took place, Nixon* proclaimed "peace with honor." The settlement really provided only a face-saving "decent interval" before the Vietnamese finally settled the issue among themselves. With the agreements being roundly violated by all parties, Le Duc Tho and Henry Kissinger attempted in June 1973 to effect better observance of them, but there were no substantive results. Both men were awarded the Nobel Peace Prize, but Tho refused to accept it, contending that it would be inappropriate until there was genuine peace in Vietnam. In 1975 Le Duc Tho returned to South Vietnam to oversee the final assault on Saigon.* Between 1975 and 1986, he served on the politburo in Hanoi* and as the Lao Dong Party's* chief theoretician, but he resigned his post in December 1986 because of continuing economic troubles in the Socialist Republic of Vietnam.* Le Duc Tho died on October 13, 1990. SF

Sources: Stanley Karnow, *Vietnam: A History*, 1983; Joseph Buttinger, *Vietnam: A Dragon Embattled*, 2 vols., 1967; Henry Kissinger, *Years of Upheaval*, 1982; *Washington Post*, December 18, 1986; *New York Times*, October 14–15, 1990.

LE LOI

Le Loi was emperor of Vietnam from 1428 until his death in 1443. Le Loi led the independence movement that successfully expelled the Chinese in 1428. The emperor founded the dynasty that ruled Vietnam for more than three centuries until the Tay Son Rebellion* displaced them in the 1770s and 1780s.

Source: Joseph Buttinger, *The Smaller Dragon: A Political History of Vietnam*, 1958.

LEMAY, CURTIS EMERSON

Curtis E. LeMay was born on November 15, 1906, in Columbus, Ohio. He joined the Army Air Corps in 1928 and was commissioned as a second lieutenant in 1930. He rose to the rank of major general in 1943 when he commanded the 305th Bomber Group and 20th Bomber Command in the European theater during World War II, and received command of the 21st Bomber Command in the Marianas in 1945, advancing to commanding general of the Twentieth Air Force at Guam. LeMay became a legend because of his unorthodox methods. In Europe he had his bombers abandon the usual zigzag pattern of flight to avoid flak, so they could have more accurate runs; in the Pacific he removed the guns from the bombers in order to carry heavier payloads. In Japan, LeMay opposed dropping the atomic bombs because he believed that more firebomb raids would secure a surrender. After World War II, LeMay

Right: President John F. Kennedy met with General Curtis E. LeMay, chief of staff of the U.S. Air Force, at Eglin Air Force Base in Florida on May 4, 1962. LeMay had a well-earned reputation (earned during World War II) for strategic aggressiveness, a point of view that startled the new president.

rose through the ranks of the Air Force, becoming head of the Strategic Air Command in 1957 and Air Force chief of staff in 1961, a position he held until his retirement in 1965. LeMay came out of retirement to serve as George Wallace's vice-presidential running mate in the election of 1968,* and his position on Vietnam was hard-line. LeMay urged the United States to bring all of its firepower to bear, even nuclear weapons if necessary, on the North Vietnamese to end the war quickly. He famously said that the United States was capable of "bombing Vietnam back into the Stone Age" and that the North Vietnamese should be aware of such power. LeMay felt that any settlement in the Far East should protect free governments from Communist takeovers. Curtis LeMay died on October 1, 1990.

Sources: McKinley Kantor, *Mission with LeMay*, 1965; Barrett Tilman, *Curtis LeMay*, 2006.

LE THANH NGHI

Born in 1915, Le Thanh Nghi turned to anti-French nationalism as a student and was an early member of the Lao Dong Party* and the Vietminh.* In 1974 he became the deputy premier of the Democratic Republic of Vietnam, * and in 1976 assumed that same position in the new Socialist Republic of Vietnam,* later serving as vice president of the State Council. Le Thanh Nghi died on September 6, 2006.

Sources: *International Who's Who, 1981–1982*, 1982; *Who's Who in Socialist Countries*, 1978; *New York Times*, September 6, 2006.

LE VAN VIEN

Before World War II, Le Van Vien, also known as Bay Vien, was an illiterate chauffeur in the employ of the French colonialists. In the chaotic days at the end of the war, he organized a gang of Saigon* river pirates that eventually became known as the Binh Xuyen,* which was the name of the neighborhood in Cholon* where Le Van Vien had his headquarters. For two years he collaborated with the Vietminh* against the French. He was, in fact, deputy Vietminh commander for Cochin China* and was responsible for some notorious anti-French atrocities. In a characteristically expedient move, he switched sides in 1947 when the French agreed to recognize his gang as a "sect" similar to the Cao Dai* and Hoa Hao* religions. They also commissioned him as a colonel and later a general in the Vietnamese National Army.* In 1954 Emperor Bao Dai* gave Le Van Vien control of the national police.

The source of Le Van Vien's wealth and power was his control of the vice establishment in Saigon and Cholon. His huge gambling complex, the Grande Monde in Cholon, brought in millions of piasters that he shared

with Bao Dai. He owned the largest brothel in Asia, the so-called Hall of Mirrors, and had his own opium factory to supply his numerous opium dens. His empire also included Saigon's best department stores, a fleet of riverboats, and many houses and other real estate holdings.

After becoming prime minister in 1954, Ngo Dinh Diem* recognized Le Van Vien as the most immediate threat to his authority, and consequently the prime minister instigated a showdown with the vice lord in April 1955. The national army forced the Binh Xuyen out of Saigon. Le Van Vien escaped to France and never returned to Vietnam. DLA

Source: Bernard Fall, "The Political-Religious Sects of Viet-Nam," *Pacific Affairs* 28 (September 1955): 235–253.

LIGHT ANTITANK WEAPON
See M72

"LIGHT AT THE END OF THE TUNNEL"

First used by General William Westmoreland* at a televised press conference on November 17, 1967, to describe the imminent demise of Vietcong* resistance and an end to the war in Southeast Asia, the phrase "light at the end of the tunnel" eventually was converted by journalists into a sarcastic reference to American leadership, both political and military. Between 1967 and 1975 the phrase was used hundreds of times in magazine and newspaper articles to describe how misguided U.S. policies were and how American officials basically misunderstood the nature of the war. The phrase had a fitting climax in 1975 when a GI leaving Vietnam at the end of the conflict showed a poster to a United Press cameraman. The poster showed a light bulb shining from a tunnel.

Source: David Culbert, "Johnson and the Media," in Robert A. Divine, ed., *Exploring the Johnson Years*, 1981.

THE LIONHEADS

The Lionheads is the title of Josiah Bunting's 1972 novel about the Vietnam War. Written as a military history, the novel focuses on George Lemming, commanding general of the 12th Infantry Division (nicknamed the Lionheads). The time frame is March and April 1968, when U.S. forces were still reacting to the Tet Offensive.* It is a fairly standard account of military operations, with most critics commenting that the book was strong on explaining combat operations but weak on characterizations.

Sources: Josiah Bunting, *The Lionheads*, 1972; Philip D. Beidler, *American Literature and the Experience of Vietnam*, 1982.

Above: Walter Lippmann, the distinguished columnist for the *New York Times*, developed skepticism about the U.S. effort in Vietnam as early as the Gulf of Tonkin incident in 1964, and remained a critic throughout the war. Lippmann appears as a young man in this photograph taken aboard the ocean liner Conte di Savola on November 21, 1934.

LIPPMANN, WALTER

Walter Lippmann was born on September 21, 1889, in New York City. He graduated from Harvard in 1910 and in 1914 helped found the *New Republic*. Lippmann joined the editorial staff of the *New York Herald Tribune* in 1931, and over the years he became one of the country's most influential syndicated columnists. During the 1950s Lippmann worried about the moralisms that infected the cold war debate, preferring a foreign policy based on concrete political, economic, and strategic needs. He initially praised Lyndon Johnson's* handling of the war in Vietnam, especially after the Gulf of Tonkin incident* in 1964, but Lippmann was too much an advocate of a negotiated settlement to be content with the 1965 escalation of the American commitment. He also doubted whether Vietnam was really enough of a strategic interest to the United States to justify the resources the war was consuming. Between 1965 and 1973

Lippmann continued to call for de-escalation. Walter Lippmann died on December 14, 1974.

Sources: *New York Times*, December 15, 1974; Ronald Steele, *Walter Lippmann and the American Century*, 1980.

LITERATURE AND VIETNAM

See Literature and Vietnam, p. 314

LOC NINH, BATTLE OF (1967)

As part of his strategic preparation for the Tet Offensive* in 1968, General Vo Nguyen Giap* began attacking isolated American outposts in the fall of 1967. Located in Binh Long Province, nine miles east of the Cambodian border, was Loc Ninh, a military outpost defended by three Civilian Irregular Defense Group* companies, a company of Regional Forces,* and a Popular Forces* platoon. On October 29, 1967, two regiments of the 9th Vietcong Division left their base in Cambodia* and attacked the allied base at Loc Ninh. They encountered strong resistance from the local forces, and on November 1, ARVN (*see* Army of the Republic of Vietnam) forces and troops from the American 1st Brigade of the 1st Infantry Division* arrived to reinforce them. On November 7 the Vietcong abandoned the struggle, leaving 850 dead. Along with generally unsuccessful attacks at places like Dak To* and Song Be, the Vietcong* defeat at Loc Ninh encouraged American military officials to believe that at long last the enemy was trying to use conventional tactics. Actually, the attacks brought on a dispersal of allied forces out of the cities and into the countryside, just what Giap had hoped would occur, so that the upcoming Tet Offensive would have more impact.

Source: Edward Doyle and Samuel Lipsman, *The Vietnam Experience. America Takes Over, 1965–1967*, 1985.

LODGE, HENRY CABOT JR.

Henry Cabot Lodge Jr. was born on July 5, 1902, in Nahant, Massachusetts. He graduated from Harvard in 1924 and went to work as a journalist for the Boston *Evening Transcript* and then the *New York Herald Tribune*. Lodge traveled widely and spent time in Vietnam analyzing and writing about the nature of the French Empire there. In 1932 Lodge won a seat in the Massachusetts legislature, and in 1936 he was elected as a Republican to the U.S. Senate, serving there, except for a two-year military stint during World War II, until 1953. He lost his Senate seat in the election of 1952 to John F. Kennedy,* and in 1953 President

Dwight Eisenhower* named Lodge ambassador to the United Nations, a post Lodge held until 1960. He was Richard Nixon's* running mate in their unsuccessful presidential bid in 1960, and on June 27, 1963, John F. Kennedy named Lodge ambassador to the Republic of Vietnam.*

In many ways Lodge was a perfect choice. He had spent time visiting and writing about Indochina,* spoke fluent French, and as a Republican he might deflect GOP criticism of John F. Kennedy's foreign policies in Vietnam. Lodge was not long in Vietnam before he decided that Ngo Dinh Diem* had to go—his pride, arrogance, and unbridled ambition and greed would never allow him to effect the reforms necessary to prevent a Vietcong takeover. Lodge was enraged at Diem's attacks on the Buddhists* in August 1963, and he began advocating strongly the overthrow of the Diem government. Kennedy turned the matter over to Lodge after giving his approval, and after a good deal of intrigue the coup took place, with the Central Intelligence Agency* working with the military officers in the ARVN (*see* Army of the Republic of Vietnam) responsible for it. Lodge was horrified at the assassination of Diem.

During the next six months, when political instability plagued the South Vietnamese regime, Lodge tired of the struggle, and he resigned as ambassador in the spring of 1964. He was also planning a bid for the GOP presidential nomination in 1964. In 1965 President Lyndon B. Johnson* got Lodge to accept the ambassadorship to South Vietnam again, and he remained in Saigon* until 1967. Between 1967 and 1969 Lodge was ambassador-at-large for the United States and ambassador to West Germany.* He tried in vain to negotiate with the Vietcong* and North Vietnamese as head of the U.S. delegation to the Paris peace talks* in 1969 and 1970, but he resigned that post in 1970 to become special envoy to the Vatican. Lodge returned from the Vatican in 1975. Henry Cabot Lodge Jr. died on February 27, 1985.

Sources: William C. Widenor, *Henry Cabot Lodge and the Search for an American Foreign Policy*, 1980; *New York Times*, February 28, 1985.

LOH-6

In 1965 the United States Army* selected the Hughes Model 369 helicopter as the next generation of light observation helicopters. The LOH-6 began service in Vietnam in 1967 as the OH-6 Cayuse, nicknamed Loach.

The Loach had an enclosed aluminum semi-monocoque fuselage with side-by-side crew seats for two in front and fold-down seats for two in the rear. With the rear seats folded, four combat troops could ride in the rear cargo compartment. Powered by an Allison T63 shaft-turbine engine delivering 317 shaft horsepower, the Loach could cruise at 143 miles per hour. The aircraft could be armed with a variety of weapons, including twin machine guns, the M75 grenade launcher capable of firing 220 rounds per

Above: Henry Cabot Lodge, son of the isolationist Senator Henry Cabot Lodge of Massachusetts, had a distinguished political and diplomatic career. He served twice as U.S. ambassador to South Vietnam in the early 1960s. On March 1, 1967, Lodge was at Tan Son Nhut Air Base outside of Saigon to greet Arthur Goldberg, the U.S. ambassador to the United Nations.

Opposite page, inset: Singer Ann-Margret traveled several times with comedian Bob Hope to entertain U.S. troops in South Vietnam. For Hope's fifth annual Vietnam Christmas tour, 20,000 GIs gathered at Loc Ninh on December 22, 1968, to watch the show.

Opposite page, bottom: Late in 1967, Vo Nguyen Giap began the so-called "Border Battles" in preparation for the Tet Offensive, scheduled for early 1968. One of those battles took place at a U.S. Special Forces camp in Loc Ninh, South Vietnam. Much of the camp was destroyed on November 3, 1967, after sustained Vietcong mortar attacks. The Vietcong also attacked in human-wave assaults, and in seven days of combat, sustained more than 800 dead troops.

LITERATURE AND VIETNAM

THE GREEN BERETS

ROBIN MOORE

Brilliant, inspiring tales of the little known but crucially important arms of U.S. defense, the crack teams of the Special Forces – true-life heroes who have made the Green Beret a badge of honor in the jungles of Vietnam and the world over.

Because it was so bloody but undeclared, so overwhelming and so unpopular, the Vietnam War stamped its image on American culture. More than thirty years have passed since North Vietnamese troops overran Saigon, and a new generation of Americans still struggles to make sense of the war, as do their parents and grandparents. Literature, television, and film shaped the way in which tens of millions of Americans saw Vietnam. Few experiences in the United States have been more painful or confusing. In his 1983 novel *Vietnam-Perkasie: A Combat Marine Memoir*, W.D. Ehrhart captured a nation's angst: "I fought back passionately, in blind rage and pain, without remorse, conscience or deliberation. I fought back ... at the pentagon Generals and the Congress of the United States, and the *New York Times*; at the draft-card burners, and the Daughters of the American Revolution ... at the teachers who taught me that America always had god on our side and always wore white hats and always won; at the Memorial Day parades and the daily Pledge of Allegiance ... at the movies of John Wayne and Audie Murphy, and the solemn statements of Dean Rusk and Robert McNamara."

The literature of the Vietnam War actually predates the combat and the controversy. In 1955 novelist Graham Greene's *The Quiet American* described Alden Pyle, a well-intentioned American cold warrior intent on building democracy and foiling Communism in South Vietnam. British journalist Thomas Fowler tries to convince Pyle of his folly and criticizes the American tendency to describe good and evil in facile abstractions. Predicting failure for the United States in Vietnam, Fowler tells Pyle, "In five hundred years there may be no New York or London, but they'll be growing paddy in these fields ... Do you think the peasant sits and thinks of god and Democracy when he gets inside his mud hut at night?" *The Quiet American* also foresaw the havoc the Vietnam War would

BODY COUNT
WILLIAM TURNER HUGGETT
PUTNAM AWARD NOVEL

wreak on Vietnamese peasants. When one of his anti-Communist operations goes awry and several noncombatants are accidentally killed, Pyle smugly remarks, "They were only war casualties ... It was a pity, but you can't always hit your target. Anyway they died in the right cause ... In a way you could say they died for democracy." At the end of the novel, when Pyle's body washes up on a beach in Vietnam, Fowler's prophetic warnings come true.

In 1958 William J. Lederer and Eugene Burdick's *The Ugly American* took an opposite tack, seeing America's mission to rid the world of Communism as noble but naive, undermined by a State Department and diplomats composed more of political lackeys than by experts in the areas to which they are assigned. Although the lead character, the U.S. ambassador to the fictional nation of Sarkhan, is able and committed, the rest of the American diplomatic staff is shortsighted, and more interested in partying with local elites and the European diplomatic corps than winning the hearts and minds of peasants. Unlike The Quiet American, in which the very notion of fighting Communism is indicted, The Ugly American promotes that cause while indicting the competence of those charged with its implementation. In American literature, the debate over the merits of U.S. military action in South Vietnam was well under way long before the troops of the 3d Marine Expeditionary Corps landed in Da Nang, South Vietnam, in 1965. While *The Quiet American* questioned the prevailing faith that American money, power, and ideology could transform a Third World country, *The Ugly American* urged just the opposite—more American money, expertise, and power. During the war, American literature with few exceptions expressed the views of *The Quiet American*— that the Vietnam War was essentially not winnable from the outset.

Early in the war, several novels hailed the Green Berets and special operatives. Robin Moore's *Green Berets* appeared in 1965, almost simultaneously with the introduction of U.S. combat troops in Vietnam, and it was the first of what would eventually be only a handful of pro–Vietnam War novels, except for a host of pulp-fiction products. Set in South Vietnam, the novel treats Green

FLIGHT OF THE INTRUDER

A NOVEL

Stephen Coonts

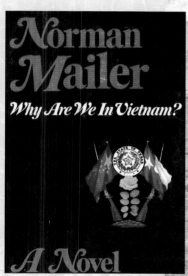

Norman Mailer

Why Are We In Vietnam?

A Novel

the quiet american

The great English writer's controversial story of a dedicated, stubbornly innocent young American diplomat in Asia—one of the most brilliant, disturbing novels of our time...
"Superb accomplishment!"
SATURDAY REVIEW

graham greene

Below: Photographer Larry Burrows captured this shot of Marines of the 9th Expeditionary Brigade coming ashore at Red Beach 2 in Da Nang in March 1965.

Below: Soldiers from the 1st Cavalry Division hover over a wounded comrade who is screaming in pain. A U.S. Army Special Forces camp at Plei Me in the Central Highlands of South Vietnam came under siege by North Vietnamese Army regulars on November 18, 1965, and the 1st Cavalry had been ordered to break the siege and relieve the Special Forces troops.

Berets as heroes, the vanguard for American values in a world verging on the precipice of Communism. Peter Derrig's *Pride of the Green Berets* (1966) reads like a Special Forces recruitment ad. Richard Newhafer's *No More Bugles in the Sky* (1966) has a group of veteran CIA pilots successfully bombing Chinese airfields north of the Vietnamese border to prevent the Vietcong from enjoying tactical air support. John Garfield's *Last Bridge* features a covert group of South Vietnamese soldiers operating behind enemy lines who successfully rescue an American POW.

Those books, however, were the last works of fiction with a positive slant on the conflict. In the ensuing decades, American writers generally portrayed the Vietnam War as an orgasm of violence and insanity. Several novels in 1967 launched what would become a wholesale, unrelenting literary assault on the Vietnam War. David Halberstam's *One Very Hot Day* describes a group of U.S. military advisors to the ARVN. Colonel Beaupre, the lead character, considers all of Vietnam a worthless hellhole and the ARVN little more than a clus-

ter of incompetents. Beaupre harbors no illusions about fighting Communism in the jungles of Vietnam. All he wants to do is survive the heat, humidity, insects, and Vietcong. Gene D. Moore's novel *The Killing at Ngo Tho* tells of ARVN treachery in assisting the Vietcong. John Sack's *M* tracks a company of U.S. soldiers from their training at Fort Dix, New Jersey, to Vietnam, where an Army specialist grows disillusioned with the corruption and cowardice of South Vietnamese allies and his inability to distinguish civilians from combatants. Victor Kokpakoff's *Prisoners of Quai Dong* focuses on a POW camp where Vietnamese guards torture and abuse their American captives and where everyone, captor and captive, is seen as a victim of the war. Daniel Ford's *Incident at Muc Wa* is a black comedy portraying incompetent officers fighting a wrongful war at a distant outpost set at a place called Muc Wa, while Norman Mailer's *Why Are We in Vietnam?* has nothing overtly to do with Vietnam but focuses on a cast of Texans on a hunting trip to the Brooks Range of Alaska, where they lay waste to the countryside and leave behind sheer carnage.

The Prisoners of Quai Dong

a novel by Victor Kolpacoff

IA DRANG—THE BATTLE THAT CHANGED THE WAR IN VIETNAM

WE WERE SOLDIERS ONCE... AND YOUNG

LT. GEN. HAROLD G. MOORE (Ret.) and JOSEPH L. GALLOWAY

The theme of desperate futility continues in 1968 and 1969. Tom Tiede's novel *Coward* (1968) is the story of Private Nathan Long, a soldier who becomes disillusioned with the Vietnam War and protests through picketing and going on hunger strikes. Court-martialed and sentenced to a combat tour of Vietnam, he is captured and tortured to death by the Vietcong. *Coward* has no heroes, not Americans or Vietnamese, and both sides are guilty of hideous atrocities. William Eastlake's bizarre *Bamboo Bed* (1969) begins with a suicide and is populated with a host of implausible fantasies. In *One to Count Cadence* (1969), James Crumley tells the story of self-destructive soldier Joe Morning, in a novel laced with gratuitous violence, brothels, and futility. William Crawford Woods' *The Killing Zone* (1970) pillories the American concept of techno-warfare, as soldiers die at an Army training camp when a computer mistakenly calls down live rounds on their position. William Pelfry's *Big V* (1972) is a fictional diary of Henry Winstead, a young draftee who finds nothing in Vietnam but meaningless violence and futility. In his novel *Body Count* (1973), William Huggett writes of Lieutenant Chris Hawkins, a Marine forced to assume command of a platoon from an inexperienced officer. Hawkins is a brave, competent officer who must deal with racial tensions, violence, and bewildering orders. The novel ends with a bloody assault on an NVA position and its abandonment only one day after victory.

Although the Vietnam War officially ended in 1975, its literary life thrived. Ron Kovic's memoir *Born on the Fourth of July* (1977) graphically portrays an idealistic young Marine who joins the Corps after seeing John Wayne in *The Sands of Iwo Jima*, and later becomes an antiwar activist to deal with his futility and loss upon returning to the States. Philip Caputo's *Rumor of War* (1977) also traffics in the loss of innocence, as a Marine who witnesses senseless brutality in Vietnam conspires in the killings of civilians. In *Dispatches* (1977), Michael Herr likewise portrays the black romanticism of the war and how it desensitized and dehumanized American soldiers and Vietnamese civilians. In 1978 James Webb's *Fields of Fire* and Tim O'Brien's *Going After Cacciato* followed in a similar vein.

Ten years after the last U.S. combat troops had left Vietnam, Patricia Walsh wrote *Forever Sad the Hearts*, a novel featuring Kate Shaw, a nurse anesthetist. Like so many others, she came to Vietnam believing in the American dream, only to see it die along with the hundreds of soldiers she saw succumb to combat wounds. She becomes increasingly disillusioned as the discrepancies widen between what she observes and what is reported. A young lieutenant captures the irony of the war,

telling Shaw while she works at a Vietnamese hospital, "You mean we shoot 'em and you fix 'em up? ... You're over here risking your life to save the people I'm risking my life to shoot." The patients whom Shaw was trying to heal had been wounded by the soldiers the government had paid to fight. John De Vecchio's *13th Valley* (1982) describes the Vietnam War as a swamp of racism, violence, and hubris. Stephen Wright's *Meditations in Green* (1983) pulls together all of the negative images. A young soldier goes to Vietnam full of dreams of glory as an interpreter of aerial photographs. He becomes appalled at the indiscriminate impact of carpet bombing on innocent civilians. To deal with his guilt, he turns to heroin and eventually slips into lunacy. Larry Heinman's *Close Quarters* (1983) tells of Philip Dosier, a soldier who mans an armored personnel carrier and randomly kills Vietnamese, steadfastly refusing to discriminate between civilians and soldiers.

In the 1980s and 1990s many Americans became obsessed with the idea that the United States had chosen not to win a winnable war and that a cynical government had knowingly left soldiers behind in Vietnam. Joe Weber's *Rules of Engagement* (1992) argued that the war was lost because the politicians placed too many restrictions on the military. Stephen Coonts' *Flight of the Intruder* has a similar theme, with Jake Grafton, an A-6 pilot who abandons the rules of engagement and attacks targets of his own choosing. In what critics called the "Ramboization" of the war, a spate of forgettable novels told of airmen, soldiers, and Marines rotting in North Vietnamese prisons long after the end of the war. Among the best of a bad lot is Allen Lieb's *Valley of the Shadow* (1992), J.C. Pollock's *Mission M.I.A.* (1982), and Brian Freemantle's *Vietnam Legacy* (1984). Today, in serious American fiction, Vietnam remains a war without redeeming qualities, fought for poorly defined objectives with an inappropriate and irresponsible expenditure of firepower. Americans have still not come to terms with Vietnam, and the war in Iraq will inspire no resolution. Once again the United States is fighting a war of its own choosing in a distant place, without allies and without clear objectives. Perhaps literary revisionists will someday take another look at Vietnam. Until then, the war will remain at once a testimony to American hubris and a credit to the soldiers who fought and died there.

Sources: Loren Baritz, *Backfire: A History of How American Culture Led Us into Vietnam and Made Us Fight the Way We Did*, 1987; Philip D. Biedler, *American Literature and the Experience of Vietnam*, 1982; Timothy J. Lomperis and John Clark Pratt, eds., *Reading the Wind: The Literature of the Vietnam War*, 1987; Philip H. Melling, *Vietnam in American Literature*, 1990; Mark P. Taylor, *The Vietnam War in History, Literature, and Film*, 2003.

Above: A Loach (OH-6) helicopter being prepared for a mission.

the Tet Offensive* of 1968, the post–Tet Offensive in 1969, and again, successfully, during the Final Offensive of 1975 (*see* Ho Chi Minh Campaign).

Sources: Al Santoli, *Everything We Had: An Oral History of the Vietnam War by Thirty-Three American Soldiers Who Fought It*, 1981; Shelby L. Stanton, *The Rise and Fall of an American Army: U.S. Ground Forces in Vietnam, 1965–1973*, 1985.

minute of 40mm shells, and the 7.62mm six-barrel machine gun capable of firing 2,000 rounds per minute.

With its relatively high speed and maneuverability, the Loach made an excellent flying command center, and was widely used for convoy control and as an airborne artillery spotter. The Loach was also widely used as a gunship* in support of ground operations. Overall, the Loach proved a versatile addition to the helicopter war in Vietnam. NJA

Source: *Jane's All the World's Aircraft: 1966–1967*, 1967.

LONG BINH

Long Binh was a major United States Army* supply facility constructed just outside the city of Bien Hoa,* about twenty miles north of Saigon.* The headquarters of II Field Force, Vietnam* and the III ARVN Corps were located at Long Binh, as was the Long Binh Jail—the "LBJ." Vietcong* attacked the Long Binh complex during

LONG RANGE RECONNAISSANCE PATROLS

Long Range Reconnaissance Patrols (LRRPs, pronounced "Lurps") were developed in response to specific combat conditions in Vietnam—a war without "lines" or "fronts" against a guerrilla army in rugged jungle terrain. The Vietcong* were found only when they wanted to be—when they initiated combat; therefore, finding Vietcong or North Vietnamese Army* (NVA) forces tended to be more difficult than defeating them. LRRPs were developed to overcome these problems. LRRPs were small units—ten to twelve men, although sometimes as large as a platoon* (about forty men)—patrolling a few days to a couple of weeks at a time. They neither occupied nor established fixed positions and usually were not resupplied. They traveled light, carried a minimum of food, and foraged off the land. To facilitate extended days in the field, lightweight freeze-dried LRRP rations were developed. They were preferred over traditional C-rations because they were lighter, less bulky, and tasted better.

Generally, LRRPs avoided enemy contact. Small in number and operating independent of larger units, LRRPs were not equipped to engage the enemy. Their missions included collecting intelligence on Vietcong/NVA base camps, supply areas, trail networks, and troop movements; making bomb-damage assessments; assisting in fire direction; capturing soldiers for interrogation; rescuing downed flight crews; laying booby traps;* and sabotage.

Initially, divisions developed their own LRRP units, usually one LRRP platoon with squads operating independently or in combination depending on the mission. Some divisions developed LRRP companies comprised of two platoons. The Special Forces,* under Project Delta,* made extensive use of LRRPs and established a training center at Nha Trang* for Special Forces as well as regular Army LRRPs. Special Forces LRRP teams typically consisted of two or three Americans plus indigenous personnel. The Australian Task Force included a squadron of Special Air Service commandos who served as LRRPs, and some ARVN divisions (*see* Army of the Republic of Vietnam) also developed LRRP units.

Two criticisms of the military's performance in Vietnam were that greater use was not made of LRRPs and that greater use was not made of rifle companies similarly operating in the field independently over extended periods of time with minimal or no resupply. For the most part, such units were highly successful. SF

Sources: Harry G. Summers Jr., *Vietnam War Almanac*, 1985; Shelby L. Stanton, *Green Berets at War*, 1985; Cincinnatus, *Self-Destruction*, 1981; Andrew F. Krepinevich Jr., *The Army and Vietnam*, 1986.

LON NOL

Born in French-controlled Cambodia* in 1913, Lon Nol was educated at a series of French colonial schools. Between 1935 and 1954 Lon Nol held a number of political and military positions in the French colonial administration and became close to Prince Norodom Sihanouk.* After independence the United States provided small amounts of assistance to Cambodia through a small military mission, resulting in close ties between Lon Nol, Minister of National Defense, and the United States. In 1966 Lon Nol became premier of Cambodia. Although a trusted member of Sihanouk's government, Lon Nol nevertheless criticized Sihanouk for allowing Vietcong* and North Vietnamese Army* troops to have sanctuaries* in eastern Cambodia. When Prince Sihanouk went to France* in January 1970, he entrusted the country to Prime Minister Lon Nol and Deputy Prime Minister Prince Sisowath Sirik Matak. Both were long on ambition, short on ability, and vehemently anti-Communist. Lon Nol, tired of Sihanouk's neutrality in the Indochinese conflict, engineered a coup in which the National Assembly ousted Sihanouk and placed Lon Nol in complete power.

Sihanouk charged that the March 1970 coup was instigated by the Central Intelligence Agency.* The accusation has not been proven, but Lon Nol was in contact with members of the Nixon* administration. Lon Nol nonetheless proved incapable of organizing the government. In inciting the coup, he unleashed historical conflicts between Cambodians and resident Vietnamese. Quickly losing control, anti-Vietnamese rage became rampages resulting in the deaths of several hundred Vietnamese. The American invasion of Cambodia in 1970 (*see* Operation Binh Tay) had further alienated the population, and they rallied to the Khmer Rouge.* By 1971 the Khmer Rouge controlled most of the country. In 1975 they triumphed, and when the government of Lon Nol collapsed on April 17 he fled to Hawaii. Lon Nol died on November 17, 1985. SF

Sources: Wilfred Burchett, *The Second Indochina War*, 1970; *Who's Who in the Far East and Australasia, 1970–1971*, 1971; William Shawcross, *Sideshow: Kissinger, Nixon, and the Destruction of Cambodia*, 1979; John Prados, *Presidents' Secret Wars: CIA and Pentagon Covert Operations Since World War II*, 1986.

LOWENSTEIN, ALLARD KENNETH

Born in Newark, New Jersey, on January 16, 1929, Allard K. Lowenstein was the principal figure in the "Dump Johnson" campaign of 1967 to 1968. Lowenstein received a B.A. from the University of North Carolina in 1949 and an LL.B. from the Yale Law School in 1954. Lowenstein had become president of the National Student Association in 1951, and remained prominent in that organization through the 1960s. In the early 1960s he gave legal aid to jailed civil rights workers in the South; recruited student volunteers for voter registration campaigns in Mississippi; advised the Reverend Martin Luther King Jr.* and the Southern Christian Leadership Conference; and actively supported the Student Nonviolent Coordinating Committee. He was a civilian observer of the 1966 elections in the Dominican Republic and the 1967 elections* in South Vietnam. When he returned from Vietnam, Lowenstein formed the Conference of Concerned Democrats and the Coalition for a Democratic Alternative to oppose President Lyndon B. Johnson's* Vietnam War policies and promote a "Dump Johnson" movement among Democrats. In November 1967 Lowenstein announced support for Senator Eugene McCarthy* for president and pledged to mobilize an army of youth volunteers. Lowenstein's Dump Johnson campaign was apparently a factor in the president's decision not to seek reelection in 1968. At the Democratic National Convention* in Chicago in 1968, Lowenstein led the Coalition for an Open Convention in opposing the nomination of Hubert H. Humphrey.* In the same year he was elected to the U.S. House of Representatives from Long Beach, Long Island. In Congress,* he supported liberal legislation and opposed the Vietnam War. As a result, Lowenstein was included on President Richard M. Nixon's* "enemies" list. He was defeated for reelection in 1970 after the New York legislature gerrymandered his district. He then served as chairman of Americans for Democratic Action from 1971 to 1973 and continued to be an active supporter of liberal causes during the 1970s. Allard Lowenstein was shot to death on March 14, 1980.

Sources: Roland Turner, ed., *The Annual Obituary 1980*, 1981; *New York Times*, March 15, 1980; Nancy Zaroulis and Gerald Sullivan, *Who Spoke Up? American Protest Against the Vietnam War, 1963–1975*, 1984.

LUCE, HENRY ROBINSON

Henry Robinson Luce was born in Tengchow, China, to missionary parents on April 3, 1898. He graduated from Yale in 1920 and helped establish *Time* magazine in 1927. A strong supporter of Chiang Kai-shek* and the conservative movement in Asia, Luce in particular and *Time* in

Above: In anticipation of its invasion of Cambodia, the U.S. staged a coup d'etat in Cambodia in order to remove Prince Norodom Sihanouk from power. Sihanouk had taken a neutral stance regarding the Vietnam War, and President Richard M. Nixon wanted a new government that would give permission for the invasion. Lieutenant General Lon Nol replaced Sihanouk in March 1970. This photograph of Lon Nol was taken on April 29, 1970.

Below: Congressman Allard Lowenstein, Democrat from New York, was an early supporter of the civil rights movement and one of the earliest Democratic critics of the Johnson administration's escalation of the war in Vietnam. Lowenstein is pictured here on October 26, 1970. He was assassinated on March 14, 1980.

Above: Henry Luce supported the American war effort in Vietnam. An influential member of the Republican Party, Luce held strong anti-Communist sentiments and played a large role in steering American foreign policy.

general, along with the associated magazines *Fortune* and *Life*, supported the American war effort in Vietnam, reporting news favorable to the cause and editorializing frequently in favor of the Johnson* administration. Henry Luce died on February 28, 1967, and under the new direction of Hedley Donovan *Time* magazine shifted its position and began criticizing the conduct of the war.

Sources: *New York Times*, March 1, 1967; John Kobler, *Luce*, 1968; W.A. Swanberg, *Luce and His Empire*, 1972.

LUONG NGOC QUYEN

Luong Ngoc Quyen was born in Hanoi* in 1885. He was a student in Japan and became a disciple of the ardent Vietnamese nationalist Phan Boi Chau.* He traveled widely throughout China, and in 1916 the British arrested him for spreading his anti-colonial views in Hong Kong and turned him over to the French. While in prison, Luong Ngoc Quyen engineered the unsuccessful Thai Nguyen rebellion north of Hanoi in 1917. The rebellion was crushed by the French and Luong died in the fighting, but in the process he became a martyr to Vietnamese nationalism.

Source: William J. Duiker, *The Rise of Nationalism in Vietnam, 1900–1941*, 1976.

LVT

LVTs, or Landing Vehicle Tracked, are amphibious transports principally used by the Marines. LVTs are also called Amtracs, a contraction of "amphibious tracked" vehicles, which were first developed before World War II. LVTs are meant to maneuver in the water, climb the beach, then traverse almost any sort of land terrain. During the Vietnam War they were modified into various types and were given their own designations. LVT followed by a "P,"for example, means the LVT is a personnel carrier. Other letter designations were "A" for armored, "C" for command, "E" for engineer, "H" for howitzer—generally a 105mm howitzer—"P(CMD)" for Personnel–Command, and "R" for recovery. This last was an LVT that rescued and hauled away disabled LVTs for repair and reuse.

LVTs could make about 7 miles per hour in water and 30 miles per hour on land; they were about 30 feet long and 10 feet high. Each required a crew of three. A commander and a machine gunner sat forward, looking out through periscopes. Unlike the common landing crafts used in World War II amphibious assaults, the Vietnam–era LVTs were enclosed at the top, further protecting the men inside. A common LVT in Vietnam was the LVTP5, which carried 32 combat-equipped men, and could range

Below: In December 1965 Staughton Lynd, professor of history at Yale University, defied a ban on U.S. citizens to travel to Vietnam. In response, the U.S. Department of State cancelled his passport. In this March 1966 photograph in front of the State Department building in Washington, D.C., Lynd displays his cancelled passport at an antiwar rally.

190 miles on roads. Empty, the LVTs were used to carry cargo to shore, or on land from point to point. The LVTCs carried less than a dozen men but a great deal of maps and communications equipment; they were distinguished from the outside by high antennas.

Owing to the geography of Vietnam, especially in the Mekong Delta, LVTs were put to use in attacks made along or across rivers. Especially notable actions for LVTs were Operation Double Eagle, a large search-and-destroy mission in the I Corps area (northern South Vietnam) in early 1966, and Operation Wolf Garden, efforts protecting the mouth of the Cua Viet River, also in the north. Additionally, LVTs were used extensively with Task Force Kilo in 1968 to repel forces near the DMZ. Occasionally, LVTs were used to evacuate wounded soldiers when medical helicopters could not land where the injured men were.

Sources: http://www.amtrac.org/3atlb/pages/papers/Riverine.html; www.amtrac.org; www.geocities.com/Pentagon; www.globalsecurity.org/military.

LYND, STAUGHTON

Born in 1929 to the famous sociologists Robert and Helen Lynd, Staughton Lynd graduated from Harvard in 1951, and in 1953, when faced with the draft,* he declared himself a conscientious objector; he was designated a noncombatant. In 1961 Lynd began teaching at Spelman College in Atlanta and earned a Ph.D. in history from Columbia in 1965. While in Atlanta, Lynd worked with Howard Zinn in 1962 to organize the Student Nonviolent Coordinating Committee and protested the actions of the Kennedy* administration during the Cuban missile crisis. Lynd was a civil rights activist throughout the early 1960s. In 1965 he was appointed an assistant professor of history at Yale.

Lynd's protest against the Vietnam War took two forms. The first was his refusal in 1965 to pay $300 in income tax, which he described as an act of civil disobedience. The second, and more dramatic, was a trip to North Vietnam in 1965 with Tom Hayden.* While in North Vietnam, Lynd described the war as immoral, illegal, and antidemocratic. The visit brought on a public, rhetorical battle with Yale president Kingman Brewster, who accused Lynd of "aiding the enemy." Lynd took a leave of absence from Yale, realizing he probably would not receive tenure, but then was unable to locate another position in higher education. He then went to law school at the University of Chicago and earned a degree in 1976. His law practice specializes in cases involving working-class people. JDC

Sources: John Corry, " 'We Must Say Yes to Our Souls'—Staughton Lynd: Spokesman for the New Left," *New York Times Magazine*, January 23, 1966; Joseph Lelyveld, "A Touch of Class," *New York Times Magazine*, August 14, 1977.

LZ

"LZ" is slang for "landing zone" or, in the military alphabet, "lima zula." While LZ technically referred to a landing area for any type of aircraft, it was almost always used to designate a place where helicopters could land, dispatch troops and/or cargo, receive troops and/or cargo, and depart. Because the battlefield terrain was typically covered by jungle or rain forest, LZs often had to be created by removing threatening obstacles to the thin-skinned helicopters. This was done in a variety of ways, depending on the circumstances. For instance, chain saws were frequently used, but if the forestation was too dense, a 15,000-pound bomb (known as the Daisy Cutter) could be dropped to create an instant LZ.

In Vietnam, the helicopter became the primary means of getting troops into battle, supplying them during their stay in the field, evacuating the wounded and dead, and finally removing the survivors after battle. Consequently, LZs became a focal point of combat activity. Upon initiation of contact with the enemy, the first objective was to make the LZ as secure and safe as possible. Likewise, the enemy could be expected to make the LZ so hazardous that helicopters could not accomplish their basic mission of combat-troop support. For helicopter crews flying into an LZ, the critical question was whether it was "hot" (actively contested by the enemy, in which case the helicopter was bound to be the principal target) or "cold" (safe and secure from enemy hostilities). STT

Source: Robert Mason, *Chickenhawk*, 1983.

Below: An aerial photograph of a recently cleared section of jungle near Tchepone, Laos. In preparation for the ARVN invasion of Laos in March 1971, a C-130 cargo plane dropped a 15,000-pound bomb to create a site for helicopter landings, an LZ. The bomb detonates above ground rather than on contact with the ground, so no crater is created.

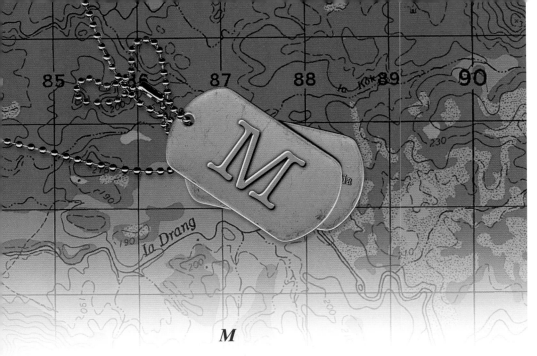

M

of Vietnam), the inability to distinguish between Vietcong* and civilians, and the unbelievably poor morale among U.S. soldiers. The novel climaxes in the tragic killing of a Vietnamese girl by an American grenade lobbed into a shelter to kill Vietcong.*

Sources: John Sack, *M*, 1967; Philip D. Beidler, *American Literature and the Experience of Vietnam*, 1982; Review of *M* by Neil Sheehan, *New York Times Book Review*, May 14, 1967.

M14 RIFLE

The M14 rifle was adopted by the United States Army* in 1957, with delivery beginning in 1959. The M14 was the result of a decadelong search for a replacement rifle for the M1 used in World War II. As such, the M14 was the Army's standard weapon at the start of the Vietnam era. It was rapidly replaced by the M16, however, as the basic infantry rifle and weapon of choice in Vietnam.

Development of the M14 reflected a century-old tradition of emphasizing marksmanship in the U.S. Army. The Army sought a heavy-caliber weapon, accurate at ranges up to 1,000 yards. Yet tactics that evolved in World War II and in the Korean War emphasized firepower over marksman-

Below: During the early stages of the Vietnam War, the M14 rifle was standard issue to U.S. soldiers. With its design based on the earlier M1 Garand, the M14 fired a NATO 7.62mm cartridge with a 20-round magazine. In April 1967, by order of Secretary of Defense Robert McNamara, the M16 replaced the M14 as the standard issue rifle.

In 1967 John Sack published his novel *M*, the first in a series of anti–Vietnam War novels. The novel focuses on M Company, a training unit of American soldiers, and follows them from basic training at Fort Dix, New Jersey, through several months of combat in Vietnam. Sack juxtaposes Specialist 4 Demirgian, a gung ho American soldier committed to the philosophical rationale of the war, with the corruption of ARVN troops (*see* Army of the Republic

ship, and the M14 was an uneasy compromise between the two.

A major factor in the development of the M14 was the decision to standardize weapons used by NATO forces. All infantry weapons developed were expected to share ammunition. The British military, finding that few British troops in World War II had attempted to fire on targets more than 300 yards away, and that, indeed, fewer still had bothered trying to aim their rifles, pushed for a small, lightweight assault rifle firing a small-caliber round with a high rate of fire. The British developed a fine weapon meeting these characteristics, the EM-2, and tried to push it as the standard infantry weapon for NATO. The U.S. Army, with a tradition of marksmanship, balked at the weapon, and forced NATO to adopt the 7.62mm (.30-caliber) round as a standard. The M14 was the American version of this rifle.

M16s* had also been adopted by the Army, in limited numbers, and their early success in Vietnam led the Army to reverse their position, dropping the M14 in favor of the M16—a lightweight assault rifle firing a small-caliber 5.56mm shell with a high rate of fire, much to the confusion and consternation of our NATO allies. NJA

Source: Thomas L. McNaugher, "Marksmanship, McNamara, and the M-16 Rifle: Innovation in Military Organizations," *Public Policy* 28 (Winter 1980): 1–38.

M16 RIFLE

The adoption of the M16 as the basic infantry weapon of the U.S. armed forces represented a break with more than a hundred years of military tradition, and was, in large part, a direct result of the war in Vietnam.

The M16 has been called one of the military success stories of the twentieth century. Now one of the best-known infantry weapons in the Western world, it was developed as a private venture by an unknown company employing only one

designer. Developed for Armalite by Eugene Stoner in the mid-1950s as the AR-15, the weapon was designed to take advantage of modern manufacturing techniques and materials. The metal components of the weapon were stamped, pressed, or forged rather than constructed using the traditional methods of machining and casting. Plastics were used in place of traditional wood. Mechanically, the M16 varied from other automatic or semiautomatic weapons. It is gas-operated, but rather than using the conventional piston, the gas is led through a tube directly into the bolt carrier. The drawback to this design is that it can lead to the action fouling up—something that happened frequently in the early days of its use in Vietnam. Furthermore, troops using the

weapon had a tendency to tape two clips together, so that when they emptied one they could simply pull out the clip, turn it over, and start firing again. This caused the clips to hang and jam the action. Kept clean and fed with single clips, however, the M16 proved to be a highly reliable weapon.

While it did prove to be a highly respected, reliable weapon, the M16 was not at first considered suitable for the American infantryman. The U.S. Army* adopted its first rifle as standard equipment in 1855 (earlier arms had been smoothbore weapons, lacking the accuracy capable with rifled barrels). From this time on the Army stressed accuracy over long distance—marksmanship—and over rate of fire in selecting weapons. The American infantryman was expected to be a sharpshooter, and therefore needed a weapon with hitting power at long range. In light of the

Left: A U.S. Marine armed with an M16 rifle fights his way house-to-house on February 4, 1968, during the reconquest of the city of Hue, South Vietnam.

Opposite page, bottom: On February 13, 1963, Private First Class Rehkamp of Cincinnati, Ohio, participated in an inspection of relocation camps as part of the strategic hamlet program and demonstrated use of the M14 rifle to curious South Vietnamese civilians.

Below: In 1967, the M16 rifle replaced the M14 as the standard rifle issued to U.S. soldiers and Marines. The Armalite (Colt) M16, designed by Eugene Stoner, a former Marine corporal, fired a 5.56mm round and was automatic. In its early versions, the M16 suffered from serious jamming and cleaning defects.

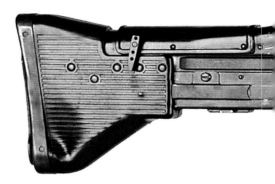

Civil War experience with rifled weapons, the Army published a training manual stressing that what counted was the number of hits, not the number of shots fired, and that such hits should be made out to a range of 1,000 yards or more. This led to an emphasis on heavy-caliber weapons. Then in the 1950s American military forces started to standardize their weapons and equipment with other NATO armed forces, so that ammunition could be interchangeable among allies. It was decided to adopt the British-developed 7.62mm cartridge as the basic cartridge for infantry weapons. Reflecting these two concerns, the U.S. Army developed the M14* as its next-generation infantry weapon, and started to supply field units with that weapon. It was in this context that the Armalite weapon was introduced.

In 1962 Defense Secretary Robert McNamara* sought to interest the Army in the M16. Having just developed the M14, the Army showed little interest in adopting the new weapon. The M16 fired a 5.56mm slug that gained its hitting power from its muzzle velocity of 3,250 feet per second. As the slug lost speed, its hitting power dropped, giving it an effective range of only about 400 yards. Furthermore, the lightweight slug was easily diverted from its path by any object it encountered, including twigs, therefore affecting its accuracy over long distances. Its strong point was not marksmanship but a high rate of fire. With its straight-line design (a line drawn through the barrel would hit the rifleman at the shoulder, instead of above as in traditional designs), the M16 could be held on target even in automatic

Below: In February 1968 U.S. Marines began the reconquest of the imperial city of Hue in South Vietnam; the fighting was house-to-house urban warfare. A fatigued Marine takes a break to clean his M16, a weapon troops often found unreliable.

fire, allowing the soldier to spray a target. In short, the M16 did not fit within the Army's traditions.

While the Army failed to adopt the M16, the U.S. Air Force* did so for its security forces. More importantly, the Army did purchase the weapon for special units, including some of the Special Forces.* These units saw the first direct combat action by U.S. troops in Vietnam, and they found the M16 far superior to the M14 for the type of fighting they were doing. In jungle fighting, firepower was far more important than marksmanship. Just 39 inches in length and weighing only 6 pounds 5 ounces, the M16 was an easy weapon to carry and bring into action quickly. In 1967 the Army reversed its long tradition and adopted the M16, much to the consternation of NATO. By this time, the weapon was being manufactured by Colt Arms. Several million M16s have been manufactured over the past three decades—the rifle is now the most widely used infantry weapon in the world, and is "the standard by which all military rifles of the future will be judged," according to the Military Analysis Network. NJA

Sources: Thomas L. McNaugher, "Marksmanship, McNamara, and the M-16 Rifle: Innovation in Military Organization," *Public Policy* 28 (Winter 1980): 1–38; *The Illustrated Encyclopedia of 20th Century Weapons and Warfare*, 1969; Federation of American Scientists newsletter, 2006.

M60 MACHINE GUN

The M60 machine gun was designed to replace both the .30-caliber Browning light machine gun and the .50-caliber heavy machine gun for the U.S. armed forces. Mounted on a tripod, the M60 served as a heavy machine gun, used primarily to defend fixed positions. As a light machine gun, the M60 used a folding bipod attached to the barrel. Although Vietnam saw its first major use, the weapon's design dates back to World War II, incorporating the belt-fed mechanism of the German MG-42 machine gun and the operating mechanism of the German MG-42 automatic rifle. Although it does not have selective-fire capabilities, the M60 does have a low cyclic rate of 600 rounds per minute, which permits firing single rounds. The weapon is gas-operated, with a muzzle velocity of 2,800 feet per second and a

maximum effective range of 3,500 yards. Far smaller and lighter than its predecessors at 42.4 inches in length and 18.75 pounds, the M60 is the first truly portable machine gun in the U.S. arsenal. Capable of being fired from the hip while moving, the M60 proved well suited to the type of fighting found in Vietnam. Today's M60E3 fires the standard 7.62mm NATO round and is used primarily as a support crew–served weapon. NJA

Sources: John Quick, *Dictionary of Weapons and Military Terms*, 1973; Federation of American Scientists newsletter, 2006.

Above: During World War II and in Korea, U.S. troops were armed with the Browning automatic rifle (BAR) and the .30-caliber light and heavy machine guns. During the Vietnam War, the M60 machine gun replaced the earlier weapons. The M60 fired belt-fed 7.62mm rounds and could be rested on a bipod, which allowed a soldier to engage in sustained firing of the weapon with less fatigue and greater accuracy.

Left: Private First Class Milton L. Cook of the 25th Infantry Division fires an M60 machine gun at Vietcong positions 10 miles north of Cu Chi in South Vietnam. On a search-and-destroy mission, Cook had come under fire from Vietcong snipers.

Above: In 1966 Specialist George R. Sanchez of the 101st Airborne Division fires an M72 rocket launcher at a Vietcong position. Soldiers on an infantry assault mission appreciated the M72 because of its light weight and its firepower.

Opposite page: Soldiers from Company B of the 4th Infantry Division as part of "Task Force Oregon" in early September 1967 participate in Operation Cook in Quang Ngai Province, approximately 320 miles northeast of Saigon. The troops have come under fire from Vietcong soldiers hiding in a village. A U.S. soldier targets the village with an M79 grenade launcher.

M72

The M72, or Light Antitank Weapon (LAW), was a high-explosive rocket used by U.S. and South Vietnamese forces to destroy Vietcong* and North Vietnamese bunkers. Lightweight and approximately 3 feet long, the M72 was perfectly suited for infantry assaults.

Source: Harry G. Summers Jr., *Vietnam War Almanac*, 1985.

M79

The M79 grenade launcher was introduced in the early 1960s, just as the war in Vietnam was heating up and starting to take more U.S. military attention. The M79 represented a vast improvement over earlier rifle-fired grenades. Looking like a single-barrel, break-open shotgun, the M79 was only 28.6 inches long and weighed just 6 pounds, 2 ounces, making it a highly portable weapon capable of being carried and fired by light infantry on the move. The M79 fired a 9-ounce, 40mm shell with various warheads, including antipersonnel, armor-piercing, and white phosphorus. With an effective range of 400 meters and far greater accuracy than the older rifle-fired grenades, the M79 gave the field soldier a potent weapon against enemy bunkers and troop concentrations. An automatic version, the M75, was capable of firing 220 rounds per minute with a range of 2,000 meters. The M75 was often mounted in a remote-control turret for helicopter use. NJA

Source: John Quick, *Dictionary of Weapons and Military Terms*, 1973.

Above: The M79 was a single-shot, shoulder-fired grenade launcher popular during the Vietnam War. It was nicknamed "Thumper" or "Blooper" because of its distinctive firing sound. The M79 was an attempt to increase firepower for the infantryman—more accurate with further range than rifle grenades, yet more portable than a mortar—but its single-shot nature was a strong drawback in battle.

Above: Former General of the Army Douglas MacArthur expressed extreme misgivings about the deployment of U.S. combat forces to South Vietnam. His warnings were not heeded. This 1945 image shows MacArthur on the eve of the signing of the peace treaty ending war with Japan.

Right: A group of American-led South Vietnamese civilian defense troops prepare to begin Operation Birmingham in search of Vietcong near Tay Ninh Air Base in South Vietnam on April 24, 1966. One of the South Vietnamese is helping a U.S. military advisor with his radio pack.

MAAG

See Military Assistance and Advisory Group

MACARTHUR, DOUGLAS

The child of a military family, Douglas MacArthur was born on January 26, 1880, on an Army base near Little Rock, Arkansas. He graduated from West Point in 1903, and then served with distinction in the Philippines, Mexico, and with the Rainbow Division in World War I. After the war, MacArthur became commandant of West Point. He was promoted to general in 1930, and in 1935 went to the Philippines as a military advisor. During World War II he was commander in chief of Army forces in the Pacific, and after the war virtually ruled Japan as head of the occupation forces. MacArthur drafted the new Japanese constitution and then established a democratic govern-ment and economic revival in Japan. MacArthur took command of United Nations forces in South Korea* in 1950 after the North Korean invasion, reversed the invasion with the amphibious assault at Inchon, and

then lost his command because of insubordination in 1951, after the Chinese entered the conflict and he refused to accept President Harry S. Truman's* vision of a limited conflict. MacArthur then retired from the Army. Before his death on April 5, 1964, MacArthur frequently expressed to his associates, as well as to President John F. Kennedy,* his misgivings about the United States becoming involved in a protracted guerrilla war in Southeast Asia.

Source: William Manchester, *American Caesar: Douglas MacArthur, 1880–1964*, 1978.

McCAIN, JOHN SIDNEY JR.

Commander in chief of Pacific naval forces (1968–72), John McCain Jr. was the youngest son of another full admiral, John McCain Sr. He was born on January 17, 1911, in Council Bluffs, Iowa. He grew up in Washington, D.C., where he attended Central High School. After completing high school he entered the United States Naval Academy at Annapolis at the tender age of sixteen. In 1931 he gradu-ated from Annapolis nearly at the bottom of his class.

McCain's first tour of duty was aboard the battleship *Oklahoma*, and he subsequently served on submarines between 1933 and 1938. After his stint on submarines he became an instructor of electrical engineering at the Naval Academy. With the outbreak of World War II, McCain entered combat aboard the USS *Skipjack*, a submarine, and subsequently commanded submarines in both the Atlantic and Pacific. After the war he became records director of the Bureau of Naval Personnel until 1949.

During the 1950s McCain successfully served aboard the USS *St. Paul* as its executive officer. His next assignments followed in succession: director of Navy undersea warfare research and development; commander of Submarine Squadron 6; commander of the attack transport USS *Monrovia*; director of progress analysis in the Office of the Chief of Naval Operations; commanding officer of the USS *Albany*; and chief legislative liaison for the secretary of the Navy. McCain was promoted to rear admiral in 1959 and to vice admiral four years later.

During the early 1960s McCain was part of the Atlantic Fleet's amphibious command, eventually rising to its entire command in 1965. Admiral McCain took part in the U.S. intervention in the Dominican Republic in 1965. He finally succeeded retiring admiral Ulysses S. Grant Sharp* as Commander in Chief, Pacific Command* on July 31, 1968. McCain was a hard-liner on the Vietnam War and believed that the Communists were using the Vietnamese conflict to further their expansionist aims. In the fall of 1972 it was McCain who urged that President Nixon* take drastic measures against North Vietnam. He supported the resumption of bombing* as well as the mining of Haiphong Harbor* to bring the North Vietnamese to

the conference table. McCain, before 1972, was a strong and vocal proponent of the Nixon administration's Vietnamization* program. Yet, by the fall of 1972, McCain was weary of his longtime service to the country and consequently decided to return to the Naval Academy as an instructor of electrical engineering. John McCain retired in 1972 and died on March 22, 1981. JSL

Sources: *Current Biography,* November 1970; *Washington Post,* March 24, 1981; *Congressional Record,* October 3, 1972; *New York Times,* March 23, 1981.

McCAIN, JOHN SIDNEY III

The son of John Sidney McCain Jr., John S. McCain III followed in the line of two four-star admirals. Born in 1936, he was educated at the Naval Academy at Annapolis as were his admiral father and grandfather. Graduating in 1958, he began two years of flight training in Pensacola, Florida, and became a pilot of attack planes in 1960.

Beginning in the summer of 1967, McCain flew more than twenty missions against Communist targets in Vietnam. Flying off the aircraft carrier *Oriskany* on his twenty-third mission on October 26, 1967, his A-4E Skyhawk was hit by a missile over Hanoi, destroying its right wing. McCain made a high speed upside ejection from his tumbling airplane, breaking his right knee and both arms. He landed in Truc Bach lake in Hanoi and sank to the bottom. His arms useless, he nearly drowned before inflating his floatation vest with his teeth. Surfacing, he was pulled from the lake and attacked by an angry mob that bayoneted and hit him with

Above: Journalists nicknamed Vice Admiral John S. McCain Jr. "Red-line McCain" because of his practice during press briefings of marking out "free-fire zones" in red lines on maps of South Vietnam. Eventually, most of South Vietnam was a free-fire zone with red lines criss-crossing the entire country.

Left: On July 29, 1967, the aircraft carrier USS *Forrestal* was launching air strikes against North Vietnam from the Gulf of Tonkin. A Phantom jet accidentally fired a Zuni missile, which struck Lieutenant John McCain III's A-4 Skyhawk on board. He escaped by climbing out of the cockpit and crawling along the nose of the jet and jumping off its refueling probe. He was struck in the legs and chest by shrapnel. The explosion and subsequent fire killed 134 U.S. Navy personnel. It was the Navy's worst carrier fire since World War II.

Right: President Richard Nixon greets the recently released prisoner of war John McCain at a White House reception honoring returned POWs on May 24, 1973.

Below: John McCain in Truc Bach Lake in Hanoi on October 26, 1967, being dragged out of the water by an angry mob of North Vietnamese Army (NVA) soldiers and North Vietnamese citizens after ejecting from his damaged airplane. From here he was taken to the "Hanoi Hilton" where he was a prisoner of war for the next five and a half years. This photo was radioed to Tokyo on October 27 by the North Vietnamese government.

a rifle butt. He was taken to the Hoa Lo Prison, nicknamed the "Hanoi Hilton" in Hanoi, in worse physical condition than any prisoner before him.

His captors denied him medical attention, but when they learned he was the son of an admiral—at the time serving in Europe—they began to tend his wounds and give him better treatment. They asked him to contribute compromising statements about the war to film crews, but he refused. In December 1967, McCain was transferred to a prison on the outskirts of Hanoi nicknamed "The Plantation." At first, he had contact with other American prisoners, but then he was placed in solitary confinement for two and a half years.

In July 1968, McCain's father was promoted to Commander in Chief, Pacific Command, thus given responsibility for all military functions in and around South Vietnam. McCain's captors offered him early release on this account, but McCain refused unless all POWs were released. He was repeatedly beaten from this time, aggravating his 1967 wounds.

In 1971 McCain's conditions improved and he was quartered with other prisoners. He was released in the spring of 1973 along with other POWs in keeping with the Paris Peace Accords signed earlier in the year. He returned home one of the most celebrated of the released POWs and was greeted by President Nixon. He underwent long physical therapies for his injuries and regained flight status, although some of his infirmities never properly healed.

McCain held various posts for the Navy throughout the 1970s but, owing in part to poor annual physical exams, resigned from the service in 1981. He ran for and won a seat from Arizona in the U.S. Congress in 1982. He was reelected in 1984 and then elected to the U.S. Senate from Arizona in 1986. He was reelected three more times to the Senate. In 2008, McCain won the GOP presidential nomination.

Sources: Robert Timberg, *John McCain: An American Odyssey*, 1999; Stuart Rochester and Frederick Kiley, *Honor Bound: American Prisoners of War in Southeast Asia 1961–1973*, 1999; www.Wikipedia.org.

McCARTHY, EUGENE JOSEPH

Elected to the U.S. House of Representatives in 1948 and to the Senate in 1958 from his native state of Minnesota, Eugene McCarthy became an outspoken opponent of the Vietnam War. Born in Watkins, Minnesota, on March 29, 1916, he was a schoolteacher and college professor before being elected to Congress. He served on the Senate Foreign Relations Committee,* and after supporting the Gulf of Tonkin Resolution* and generally refraining from criticism of Johnson* administration policies in Vietnam, by 1967 he had become a leading critic of the war.

On November 30, 1967, McCarthy announced as a candidate for the 1968 Democratic presidential nomination against President Johnson, emphasizing his support for a negotiated settlement of the war. He said that the war was draining "the material and moral resources of the country from our really pressing problems." Viewed as more of a scholar than a politician, McCarthy surprised the experts. He demonstrated the political potential of the antiwar movement* and was a rallying point for youthful opponents of the war. His strong showing against Johnson in the New Hampshire primary on March 12, 1968, was a major factor in Robert Kennedy's* decision to become a candidate for the presidential nomination and in Johnson's decision not to seek reelection. McCarthy remained in the race for the nomination through the Democratic National Convention in Chicago, where he was defeated by Vice President Hubert Humphrey.* McCarthy left the Senate after completing his second term in 1970. Eugene McCarthy continued to comment on political and social affairs until his death on December 10, 2005. HP

Sources: Eugene McCarthy, *The Year of the People*, 1969; Dominique Sandbrook, *Eugene McCarthy and the Rise and Fall of Postwar American Liberalism*, 2005.

McGEE, GALE WILLIAM

Gale McGee was born in Lincoln, Nebraska, on March 17, 1915. He graduated from the Nebraska State Teachers College in 1936 and eventually earned a Ph.D. in history from the University of Chicago. Between 1938 and 1948 he taught at a number of colleges until his appointment as professor of history at the University of Wyoming. McGee served as a legislative assistant to Democratic senator Joseph O'Mahoney in 1955 and 1956, and in 1958 he won election to the U.S. Senate. During the Vietnam War McGee was one of the Senate's most articulate "hawks," generally supporting the American military presence in Southeast Asia. McGee served in the Senate until 1977. He had been defeated in the election of 1976 by Malcolm Wallop. After his 1976 defeat, McGee served from 1977 to 1981 as a permanent representative to the Organization of American States. He is the author of *The Responsibility of World Power* (1968). Gale McGee died on April 9, 1992. JDC

Sources: *Current Biography*, 1961; "Democrats," *Time*, January 17, 1969; *The Almanac of American Politics, 1982*, 1982; *Biographical Directory of the United States Congress*, 2006.

Above: Beginning in 1966, U.S. Senator Eugene McCarthy, Democrat from Minnesota, expressed serious misgiving about the war in Vietnam. Late in 1967, McCarthy decided to challenge President Lyndon B. Johnson for the Democratic presidential nomination. Here McCarthy campaigns in the presidential primary election on June 2, 1968, in San Francisco, California.

Above: U.S. Senator Gale McGee, Democrat from Wyoming, on December 1, 1958, one month after his election. Normally a supporter of President Lyndon B. Johnson, McGee defected over conduct of the war in Vietnam.

Left: John McCain being released from his five and a half years as a prisoner of war in mid-March, 1973, at a routine turnover ceremony at Gia Lam Airfield in Hanoi.

McGOVERN, GEORGE STANLEY

Above: U.S. Senator George McGovern, an anti-Vietnam War Democrat from South Dakota, won the Democratic presidential nomination in 1972. In the general election, the Republican Richard M. Nixon won in a landslide. McGovern is picture here during the election campaign.

George Stanley McGovern was born in Avon, South Dakota, on July 19, 1922. He served as a pilot with the Army Air Force during World War II and received his B.A. from Dakota Wesleyan University in 1945. McGovern went on to earn an M.A. and a Ph.D. in history from Northwestern University in 1949 and 1953, respectively. He taught at Dakota Wesleyan between 1949 and 1953, and then served for two years as executive secretary of the South Dakota Democratic Party. McGovern was elected to Congress* in 1956, and in 1961 accepted President John F. Kennedy's* offer to direct the Food for Peace program. McGovern was elected to the U.S. Senate in 1963 and served there until 1981. In 1968, after the assassination of Robert F. Kennedy,* McGovern staged a belated run for the Democratic presidential nomination, emphasizing opposition to the war in Vietnam and the need to reinforce Great Society* programs. He lost the nomination to Hubert Humphrey,* but between 1968 and 1972 McGovern was a leading figure in the restructuring of the Democratic Party, de-emphasizing the power of the urban machines and the South in favor of women and minorities. McGovern won the Democratic presidential nomination in 1972, campaigning on the theme of an immediate, unilateral withdrawal from Vietnam, but he suffered a landslide defeat at the hands of President Richard M. Nixon* in the general election. McGovern then returned to South Dakota, where in 1974 he successfully ran for the U.S. Senate. Six years later, McGovern lost his bid for reelection. He unsuccessfully sought the Democratic presidential nomination in 1984. From 1998 to 2001, McGovern served as U.S. ambassador to the United Nations Food and Agricultural Agencies, and in 2001 he was appointed UN Global Ambassador for World Hunger.

Sources: George S. McGovern, *A Time of War, A Time of Peace*, 1968; *Who's Who in America, 1984–1985*, 1985; Theodore White, *The Making of the President, 1972*, 1973; Robert Sam Anson, *McGovern: A Biography*, 1972; Richard Michael Marano, *Vote Your Conscience: The Last Campaign of George McGovern*, 2003.

McNAMARA, ROBERT STRANGE

Robert S. McNamara was born on June 9, 1916, in San Francisco. He graduated from the University of California at Berkeley in 1937 and then received his M.B.A. from Harvard in 1939. An expert in systems management and statistics, McNamara served in administrative positions with the Army Air Corps during World War II, and after the war he joined the Ford Motor Company, where he rose rapidly through management ranks as one of the new generation of whiz kids. In 1960, at the age of forty-four, McNamara was named president of Ford Motor

Company. President-elect John F. Kennedy* had his eye on McNamara, however, and offered him the cabinet post of secretary of defense. McNamara came to Washington, D.C., in 1961 and remained there until his resignation from the Pentagon in 1968.

Robert McNamara proved to be one of the most influential figures in the history of the Vietnam War. Blessed with a keen, analytical mind and a supreme confidence in the efficacy of modern technology, McNamara became a primary architect of American policy in Vietnam, exercising both logistical and operational control over the war, presiding over the initial buildup, and eventually losing all faith in the American effort there. McNamara was a leading exponent of counterinsurgency,* the Gulf of Tonkin Resolution,* and the bombing* of North Vietnam in 1964 and 1965, as well as the large-scale commitment of ground troops to South Vietnam. To stop infiltration* from North Vietnam along the Ho Chi Minh Trail* and across the Demilitarized Zone,* McNamara called for the construction of an electronic barrier across Southeast Asia—a system of devices to alert the United States of any breach of security at any time. Dubbed McNamara's Wall (*see* Project Practice Nine) by skeptical journalists, the proposal was never implemented, but it did reveal the naivete of McNamara's faith in modern technology.

By 1966, however, McNamara had become increasingly skeptical of the American war effort in Vietnam. He was astonished at the resilience of the North Vietnamese and the relative lack of effect American bombing had, especially on their extraordinary ability to move men and materiel down the Ho Chi Minh Trail into South Vietnam. McNamara was also surprised at the level of casualties the Vietcong* and North Vietnamese Army* were willing to accept, and he knew, statistician that he was, how their commitment upset the basic philosophy behind the American war of attrition* there. Finally, McNamara grew positively disgusted with the corruption of South Vietnamese officials, the instability of their government, and their lack of sensitivity to democratic principles. Between 1961 and 1966 McNamara visited South Vietnam eight times, and by the end of 1966 he realized that American casualties were too high for the results achieved. No end of the war was in sight.

By 1967 McNamara was advocating a negotiated settlement to the conflict, pushing on President Lyndon Johnson* a diplomatic solution to the problem. Understandably, the president was upset. For years he had accepted the counsel and advice of these "experts," the "best and the brightest" in David Halberstam's* words, and now they were essentially admitting they had been wrong, after the troop totals had reached more than 500,000 soldiers and more than 30,000 Americans were dead. As McNamara's skepticism grew throughout 1967, so did Johnson's frustration, and in November 1967 he asked McNamara to resign his defense post. By that time McNamara was advocating an end to bombing the North, a cap on American troop strength in Vietnam, and gradually turning the war over to the South Vietnamese. After leaving the Department of Defense, McNamara became president of the World Bank, a position he held until his retirement in 1983. In 1995 the publication of McNamara's book *In Retrospect: The Tragedy and Lessons of Vietnam* stirred up enormous controversy from veterans groups, who held McNamara responsible for the deaths of tens of thousands of U.S. troops.

Sources: David Halberstam, *The Best and the Brightest*, 1972; Gregory Palmer, *The McNamara Strategy and the Vietnam War: Program Budgeting in the Pentagon, 1960–1968*, 1978; Robert S. McNamara, *In Retrospect: The Tragedy and Lessons of Vietnam*, 1995.

McNAMARA'S WALL

See Project Practice Nine

McNAUGHTON, JOHN THEODORE

Born on November 21, 1921, John McNaughton was one of Robert McNamara's* whiz kids brought into the Department of Defense to make it more efficient. McNaughton was a former Harvard Law School professor and one of McNamara's closest civilian advisors when the United States embarked on its Vietnamese venture. After President Johnson* received the Gulf of Tonkin Resolution in August 1964, McNaughton was among the hard-liners who urged serious action against North Vietnam. Of course, the Johnson administration decided that any military operations against North Vietnam would be taken after the November 1964 elections.

McNaughton agreed with Maxwell Taylor's* assertions that only direct intervention by the United States would save South Vietnam from almost certain takeover by the Communists. He recommended that combat units be introduced and that air bases be constructed in South Vietnam. McNaughton also suggested that naval forces be stationed

Below: Secretary of Defense Robert McNamara was the architect of U.S. policy in Vietnam. On July 18, 1965, four months after the deployment of U.S. Marines to South Vietnam, McNamara visited several Marine units near Le My, South Vietnam. McNamara rides in a jeep with Marine Lieutenant Colonel David Clement and Major General Lewis Walt, commander of Marine forces in Vietnam. Lance Corporal Felix A. Gallegos drives the jeep.

Above: U.S. Senator Mike Mansfield, Democrat from Montana, was among the earliest of the Senate Democrats to break with the Johnson administration over the Vietnam War. Mansfield's skepticism had surfaced several years before, during the Kennedy administration.

in the Gulf of Tonkin to provoke the North Vietnamese and hence give the United States justification to punish the Hanoi* regime. Although McNaughton was a hard-liner, he did urge some restraint so as not to damage Johnson's image with the American public. In March 1965, after U.S. combat forces had been deployed in South Vietnam, McNaughton asserted that only these forces, with accompanying reinforcements, could avert defeat of the South Vietnamese. He supported continuing escalation at least until American public opinion soured on the Vietnam War.

By late 1967, however, McNaughton began to question America's role in Vietnam. Throughout the summer of 1966, he had been part of a think tank institute that drafted the Jason Study.* This study found that U.S. actions in Vietnam had failed. Because of its primitive economy, North Vietnam had not been materially damaged by U.S. air raids. Instead of destroying their morale, the air raids had strengthened patriotism and nationalism among the Hanoi leadership. The study found in addition that the North Vietnamese had increased their infiltration* into the South. Such conclusions alarmed McNamara and made him more pessimistic about the U.S. involvement. McNaughton, in private conversations with McNamara, warned in the summer of 1967 that the Vietnam War was fast becoming so serious that its consequences "could cause the worst split in our people in more than a century." McNaughton, however, did not live to see his prophecy fulfilled. In July 1967, John McNaughton and his family were killed in an air crash, only a short time before he was to become the secretary of the Navy. JSL

Sources: "Career's End," *Newsweek*, July 31, 1967; *New York Times*, July 18, 1967; Stanley Karnow, *Vietnam: A History*, 1983.

MACV

See Military Assistance Command, Vietnam

MADDOX

See USS *Maddox*

MANSFIELD, MICHAEL JOSEPH

Successor to Lyndon Johnson* as majority leader of the U.S. Senate, Mike Mansfield served in that position from 1961 until 1977, the longest-serving majority leader in Senate history. Born in New York City on March 16, 1903, he grew up in Montana, enlisted in the Navy at age fifteen, and later served with the Marines. His military service took him to

Asia, and he developed a deep interest in the Far East. He taught Far Eastern history at the University of Montana before being elected to the U.S. House of Representatives as a Democrat in 1942. He served on the House Foreign Affairs Committee, and when elected to the Senate in 1952, he became a member of the Foreign Relations Committee.*

Mansfield was an early supporter of Ngo Dinh Diem* in Vietnam. When the majority leader visited Vietnam in 1962 at President Kennedy's* request, however, he returned with a pessimistic assessment of developments there. Under the Johnson* administration, he also made several visits to Southeast Asia and expressed increasing concern about the escalation of the war. He cautioned that the United States should learn from the French experience in Vietnam, and in 1965 he advised President Johnson against a major commitment of American troops. As his efforts to convince Johnson that a negotiated settlement rather than further military action was the proper course proved futile, Mansfield became a public opponent of the war. He was even more critical as the war continued under the Nixon* administration, and became a champion of the reassertion of congressional foreign policy powers. He backed the 1970 Cooper-Church* and Hatfield-McGovern* amendments, and in 1971 his amendment calling for withdrawal of U.S. military forces within nine months (subject to the release of American prisoners of war*) passed the Senate but was defeated in the House. He did not seek reelection in 1976, and in 1977 was named by President Carter as U.S. ambassador to Japan, a position he retained under the Reagan administration. Mike Mansfield died on October 5, 2001. HP

Sources: David Halberstam, *The Best and the Brightest*, 1972; Stanley Karnow, *Vietnam*, 1983; Don Oberdorfer, *Senator Mansfield: The Extraordinary Life of a Great American Statesman and Diplomat*, 2003.

MAO ZEDONG

Born in Hunan, China, in 1893, Mao Zedong came from peasant roots. As a young man he journeyed to Beijing and found employment as a library assistant at Beijing National University. There he was caught up in revolutionary fervor and joined the Chinese Communist Party. In the 1920s Mao began to articulate his view that the future of revolution in China rested with the peasantry and not with the working poor in major cities, for there were too few of them. After the famous Long March of 1934 to 1935, Mao established himself in Yenan in northwest China and became a folk hero during World War II because of his aggressive tactics against the Japanese. He led the Communists to victory in the Chinese Civil War and in 1949 became chairman of the Communist Party and of the People's Republic of China.*

Afraid that revolutionary principles and zeal were waning in China by the 1960s, Mao launched the Cultural Revolution in 1966 and fueled its fanatical attacks on

Above: Mao Zedong on August 18, 1966, reviewing for the first time the military forces of the "Great Proletarian Cultural Revolution" in Tiananmen Square.

Chinese intellectuals until 1969. China was thrown into such turmoil that it had little opportunity to assist the North Vietnamese and Vietcong,* beyond some weapons shipments, in their struggle against the United States. The long ethnic rivalry between Chinese* and Vietnamese in Southeast Asia would probably have precluded any unified front anyway. After 1969 more practical Chinese leaders brought the Cultural Revolution to an end, and Mao Zedong spent his last years in retirement. Mao Zedong died in 1976. CD

Sources: Daniel S. Papp, *Vietnam: The View from Moscow, Peking, Washington*, 1981; Jung Chang and Jon Halliday, *Mao: The Unknown Story*, 2005.

MARINE COMBINED ACTION PLATOONS (CAPs)

First formed in the fall of 1965 to support the South Vietnamese government's Revolutionary Development Program and the III Marine Amphibious Force's* (MAF) budding civic action policy, the Marine Combined Action Platoon (CAP) became an integral, well-publicized part of the "other war"—the effort to gain the confidence of villagers and thus deny the Vietcong* (VC) a critical base of support. Limited to defending airfields during the first several months of deployment, Marine patrols found booby traps,* mines, and snipers to be constant and costly reminders of an unseen VC presence. Responding with modest medical and construction projects based on Marine experiences in the Caribbean islands and Central America, Marine civic action programs eventually won enthusiastic support in Saigon* and Washington and tapped resources from all major I Corps* commands to build schools, roads, and hospitals.

Marine CAPs supplemented civic action programs by integrating U.S. Marine Corps* units with Republic of Vietnam* Popular Forces* (PFs), with which the American units would train, share rations and quarters, and fight side by side. Typically, a squad of Marines plus a Navy corpsman would be integrated into a PF platoon and assigned to a particular hamlet to "win hearts and minds"* and cultivate intelligence sources. The III MAF organized these units under a G-5, or civil affairs, section in Da Nang,* and the program grew rapidly, with four Combined Action Battalions deployed in Vietnam between October 1967 and July 1970. The last Marine CAP withdrew when Marine ground and air operations ceased in the spring of 1971.

The Marine CAPs represented a strategic alternative to the war of attrition* that General William Westmoreland* had decided to wage in Vietnam. Such Marine Corps general officers as Victor Krulak* and Lewis Walt* argued that because 90 percent of South Vietnamese peasants lived within ten miles of the South China Sea, the United States should concentrate its military resources especially in pacification*

programs administered by Marine CAPs. By providing security, health care, and economic-development projects there, the Marines could help win the political support of millions of Vietnamese peasants. Westmoreland rejected such proposals as too passive, however. He opted instead for search-and-destroy* operations, in which Marines and Army soldiers chased the enemy into the interior. From Westmoreland's perspective, the Marine proposal implied years of an American military presence in South Vietnam; he thought he could achieve a military victory in a much shorter period of time. History proved him wrong. Whether the Marine Corps' pacification-heavy strategy would have prevailed is debatable, but it certainly would have had a better chance than Westmoreland's war of attrition, which inflicted massive, unintended harm on South Vietnamese peasants. DA

Sources: *The Marines in Vietnam, 1954–1973*, 1983; Shelby L. Stanton, *Vietnam Order of Battle*, 1981; Larry E. Cable, *Conflict of Myths: The Development of American Counterinsurgency Doctrine and the Vietnam War*, 1986; Russell H. Stolfi, *U.S. Marine Corps Civil Action Efforts in Vietnam, March 1965–March 1966*, 1968.

Above: A Marine on a Combined Action Platoon (CAP) sets out on patrol with a German Shepherd.

Right: In January 1968, Marines from the 2d Battalion, 4th Marines, launch mortars during Operation Ballistic Armor in Thua Thien Province, I Corps, South Vietnam.

MARINE CORPS, UNITED STATES

In the decade between the Geneva Accords* of 1954 and the first overt commitment of U.S. combat troops (two Marine battalions at Da Nang*) in March 1965, Marines helped establish the Vietnamese Marine Corps and also served with the U.S. Military Assistance and Advisory Group* in Saigon;* two helicopter squadrons and a radio company sent to the theater in 1962; as advisors to Republic of Vietnam* infantry units; and in small security forces at allied air bases and at the U.S. Embassy. Before South

Vietnam collapsed in 1975, Marines who had spent at least part of the normal thirteen-month tour in-country numbered more than 450,000.

While mines, booby traps,* and sniper rounds accounted for a high percentage of early Marine casualties,* after the rapid buildup in I Corps* (1966–67) small-arms fire and shrapnel accounted for almost 90 percent of the deaths and wounds suffered by Marine personnel. Peaking at 85,520 Marines in-country in 1968 (almost one-third of the Marine Corps' total strength at the time), in six years Marine units lost almost 15,000 killed and 89,000 wounded in action,

Left: Leathernecks of the 1st Marine Division cross the Vu Gia River in June 1969.

FIGHTING THIRD

Above: A watercolor of a Marine grunt painted by Corporal Richard L. Yaco in 1968 was used on the cover of a commemorative brochure. This style is representative of much of the artwork produced during the Vietnam War era.

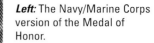

Above: Lance Corporal Jose Francisco Jimenez, posthumously awarded the Medal of Honor for heroism in Vietnam in August 1969, while serving as a fire team leader with Company K, 3d Battalion, 7th Marines, 1st Marine Division. Jimenez's unit came under heavy attack by North Vietnamese soldiers concealed in well camouflaged emplacements south of Da Nang, Quang Nam Province. He plunged forward toward the enemy, personally destroying several enemy personnel and silencing an antiaircraft weapon. He slowly maneuvered to within 10 feet of hostile soldiers who were firing automatic weapons from a trench and, in the face of vicious enemy fire, destroyed the position. Although he was by now the target of concentrated fire from hostile gunners intent upon halting his assault, he continued to press forward. Shouting encouragement to his companions, Jimenez continued his aggressive forward movement until he was killed in action.

compared with the 20,000 killed and 70,000 wounded while fighting the Japanese in World War II. Marines accounted for 28.4 percent of the casualties, 33.5 percent of those wounded and hospitalized, 4.7 percent of the POWs,* and 8 percent of the MIAs among American forces in the theater.

Fifty-seven Medals of Honor were awarded to twelve Marine officers and forty-five enlisted men, thirteen of whom survived to attend their ceremonies; and Marines captured 4,098 prisoners (not including Vietcong* suspects and civilian detainees) and 22,879 weapons, and reported killing approximately 86,000 enemy soldiers and guerrillas.

Marine units deployed to Vietnam included two divisions reinforced by two regimental landing teams, a reinforced air wing, several battalion landing teams afloat and on call with the Seventh Fleet,* plus small units detached to the U.S. Army* or guarding the U.S. Embassy and naval installations in the Saigon area. This force broke down into twenty-four infantry regiments, two reconnaissance battalions, two force reconnaissance companies, four armored battalions, more than ten battalions of artillery, four Combined Action Battalions, two antitank battalions, twenty-six aircraft squadrons (approximately 500 helicopters, fighters,* and fighter-bombers), and five battalions each of engineers and motor transport personnel. Two medical battalions and a hospital company supplemented the hundreds of U.S. Navy* doctors, corpsmen, and nurses* attached to Marine units.

While the Marine Corps' worldwide strength peaked at 317,400 in 1968 and thus fell short of the 485,113 figure set in World War II, more than 730,000 Marines served during the Vietnam era, compared with about 600,000 in the war against Japan.* Peacetime personnel policies remained in effect from 1965 to 1973 and accounted for the disparities in numbers between the two wars. In Vietnam, Marines served twelve- and thirteen-month tours, then rotated back to "the world." Except for those who extended for six-month increments or chose to reenlist, Marines were not required to serve for the duration of the conflict as in earlier years. Fleet Marine Force, Pacific Command* thus required some 9,000 to 10,000 troops to keep the Marine war going, and between 85,000 and 120,000* men and women enlisted, were drafted into, or left the Marine Corps in each of the six years before its units withdrew in the spring of 1971. DA

Sources: *The Marines in Vietnam, 1954–1973,* 1983; Shelby L. Stanton, *Vietnam Order of Battle,* 1981; J. Robert Moskin, *The U.S. Marine Corps Story,* 1982.

Left: The Navy/Marine Corps version of the Medal of Honor.

Below: In 1968 to 1969, the 9th Marines conducted thirty-seven military operations in Quang Tri Province of I Corps in South Vietnam. Marines at the Quang Tri Combat Base pause for a memorial service dedicated to their comrades killed in action. The Marines place their helmets on their rifles and bow their heads in tribute.

1st Marine Division

3d Marine Division

Above: A Marine drill instructor "explains" one of the finer points of becoming a Marine to a young recruit.

MARINE CORPS RECRUIT DEPOTS

When asked what makes their service special, Marines usually reply, "Boot camp"—during the Vietnam era eight to twelve weeks of intense indoctrination designed to supplant civilian values and introduce recruits to the rudiments of the Marine Corps* mission and tradition. Training began abruptly in a receiving barracks where shorn "boots" met their drill instructors (DIs), noncommissioned officers who then double-timed them through several days of showers, dental work, inoculations, and the issue of uniforms, rifles, 782-gear, and *The Guidebook for Marines*, parts of which had to be memorized and recited loudly and in unison.

The regimen changed occasionally during the war but at any time included Marine Corps history, physical fitness, marksmanship, and daily doses of close-order drill on "the grinder"—a few acres of sun-baked tarmac on which DIs called cadence and resorted to other techniques to instill discipline. A meticulous final inspection followed by a family-oriented graduation ceremony capped Marine Corps Recruit Depot (MCRD) training, and, no longer called boots, the Marines then received orders to an Infantry

Training Regiment (ITR) at Camp Lejeune, North Carolina, or Camp Pendleton, California.

MCRD, Parris Island, South Carolina: First established in 1911 at the Marine Barracks, Port Royal Naval Station, recruit training moved after two months to the Norfolk (Virginia) Naval Yard and then back to the barracks in 1915; the name of the base became Parris Island in 1919. Located amid salt marshes between Charleston and Savannah, the base is hot, humid, and under attack by sand fleas in summer, but rarely cold enough to suspend training during its damp winters.

MCRD, San Diego, California: Dubbed Hollywood Marines by those trained at Parris Island, San Diego recruits at least enjoyed a dry, moderate climate year-round. The Marine Corps first established Camp Howard on a nearby island in 1914 and moved to the mainland later that year, selecting a permanent site for the future recruit depot in 1919. In 1923 boot training shifted from Mare Island in San Francisco Bay to San Diego, where the supervision of recruits from western states continued through World War II, the Korean War, and the Vietnam War. DA

Source: V. Keith Fleming, "Welcome to the Marines: Boot Camp Training," in Ashley Brown, ed., *The U.S. Marines in Action*, 1986.

MARTIN, GRAHAM ANDERSON

Born in Mars Hill, North Carolina, on September 12, 1912, Graham Martin graduated from Wake Forest University in 1932 and joined the National Recovery Administration in 1933 as an aide to W. Averell Harriman.* After working in various New Deal agencies during the 1930s and serving in the Army Air Corps during World War II, Martin went to the State Department in 1947 as a foreign service officer. He was assigned to Paris for eight years, worked as a special assistant to Douglas Dillon, undersecretary of state, between 1957 and 1959, and became ambassador to Thailand* in 1963. He was successful there in building a strong military relationship between Americans and the Thais, and in 1969 Martin became ambassador to Italy. An avowed anti-Communist, Martin was named to replace Ellsworth Bunker* as ambassador to Vietnam in 1973.

Martin's stay in Vietnam was a disaster. He carried a powerful emotional burden as ambassador because his wife's son had been killed in the war, and Martin was much too abrupt for Nguyen Van Thieu,* who needed constant reassuring and praise. Martin also disregarded the problem of official corruption in the South Vietnamese government, which bled local villages and generated more support for the Vietcong.* Finally, Martin tended to exaggerate the strength of the American position in South Vietnam. Right up to the end, Martin believed that the South Vietnamese government in general and the city of Saigon* in particular could survive the North Vietnamese and Vietcong assault in the spring of 1975. Holding on to the embassy flag, Martin and his wife climbed to the roof of the U.S. Embassy on

April 29, 1975, and fled the country. Before his retirement from the State Department, Martin served as a special assistant to Secretary of State Henry Kissinger* and as an ambassador-at-large for the Pacific. Graham Martin died in 1990.

Sources: Tad Szulc, *An Illusion of Peace*, 1978; *New York Times*, April 2, 1973, May 2, 1976, and August 26, 1976.

MAT TRAN DAN TOC GIAI PHONG MIEN NAM

See Vietcong

MAYAGUEZ INCIDENT

On May 12, 1975, a Cambodian gunboat seized the SS *Mayaguez*, an American merchant ship, in transit from Hong Kong to Thailand.* The ship and its thirty-nine-member crew were taken seven miles to the Cambodian island of Poulo Wai. The Khmer* government of Cambodia* claimed that the *Mayaguez* was captured inside Cambodian territorial waters while engaged on a spy mission for the United States. President Gerald Ford* responded that the Cambodian action was an "act of piracy" and demanded the release of the ship and its crew. When appeals to the People's Republic of China* and the United Nations to use their influence to persuade

Above: In 1973, Graham Martin was appointed U.S. ambassador to the Republic of Vietnam (South Vietnam) after testifying before the United States Foreign Relations Committee. The Senate confirmed Graham's nomination, and he was serving in Saigon two years later when North Vietnamese forces conquered South Vietnam.

Left: Early in May 1975, forces of the new Communist government of Cambodia seized the American freighter *Mayaguez* in the South China Sea. President Gerald Ford tried a botched raid to liberate the crew. Diplomatic negotiations soon led to the release of the ship and its crew, and here the *Mayaguez* is pictured on its first voyage after the release. It is carrying cargo in Sembawang Port in Singapore.

Cambodia to release the crew appeared to fail, Ford prepared for a military response.

On May 14, 200 U.S. Marines* were landed on Koh Tang Island by helicopter assault to rescue the *Mayaguez* crew, who were presumed to be held there. The assault force encountered heavy Cambodian resistance and were able to advance no further than the beach. In a simultaneous operation a Marine boarding party from the USS *Holt* seized the empty *Mayaguez* (on May 13 the crew had been moved to the Cambodian mainland). While military operations were under way, the Cambodian government released the crew of the *Mayaguez* along with five Thai fishermen who had been captured earlier and charged with spying for the United States. The announcement of the release was made at 7:07 PM EDT on Cambodian radio, and by 11:00 PM the *Mayaguez* crew had been taken aboard the USS *Wilson* from a Thai fishing boat. Subsequently, at 11:16 PM President Ford ordered a halt to offensive operations and a withdrawal of all forces. Planned air strikes of the Cambodian mainland, however, were still carried out. Rescue of the Marines on Tang Island was delayed because heavy Cambodian gunfire drove off the evacuation helicopters. It was not until naval gunfire support could be used that the Marines were finally evacuated on the morning of May 15. The operation resulted in fifteen dead and fifty wounded.

Foreign and domestic reactions to the United States were generally favorable or neutral, although actual casualty figures were not immediately released. It later came to light that Secretary of State Henry Kissinger* kept a possible diplomatic option a secret from the National Security Council.* The Chinese apparently were using their influence to gain release of the crew and were expecting success. General Brent Scowcroft, deputy of national security affairs, later admitted that the United States had responded harshly in an attempt to show that although it had recently withdrawn from Southeast Asia, the country was prepared to protect its interests abroad. MD

Sources: Chris Lamb, "Belief Systems and Decision Making in the *Mayaguez* Incident," *Political Science Quarterly* 99 (Winter 1984–85): 681–702; Roy Rowan, *The Four Days of Mayaguez*, 1975; Ralph Wetterhahn, *The Last Battle: The Mayaguez Incident and the End of the Vietnam War*, 2001.

MEDEVAC

"Medevac" was an acronym for medical evacuation, almost always associated with the evacuation of casualties by helicopter during or after a battle. Consequently, the helicopters used for these missions also were called medevac helicopters, or simply medevacs. The use of the helicopter in a variety of missions was a distinguishing feature of the Vietnam War. For American and allied troops, that of the helicopter was perhaps the most nearly ubiquitous sound of the war. Usually, it evoked positive feelings for troops in the field, because the helicopter almost always meant relief in some form, be it additional troop reinforcements; supplies such as ammunition, food, and medicine; or evacuation of the wounded and/or dead. The medevac helicopter was an especially important factor in enhancing and sustaining troop morale in the field. Soldiers knew that if they were wounded, the probability was high that they would be transported quickly to a field hospital. Statistics suggest the validity of this assumption: nearly 98 percent of those wounded in action were evacuated from the battlefield alive, and no battlefield was more than one hour's flying time from a hospital. Medevac

Right: During ten days in May 1969, the 101st Airborne Division suffered 300 dead and wounded soldiers during its assault on Hamburger Hill in the A Shau Valley of South Vietnam. The heavy losses, occurring so soon after President Richard M. Nixon had announced the first withdrawal of U.S. forces from Vietnam, stirred up a storm of controversy in the United States. In this photograph, a wounded paratrooper is medevaced by a UH-1 Huey helicopter.

Left: In 1965, soon after their arrival in-country, elements of the 173d Airborne Brigade deployed for search-and-destroy operations against the Vietcong in War Zone C. An ambushed platoon waits for helicopter evacuation. The rescue helicopter is flying through pink smoke used to identify the troops' position.

Above: Operation Pecos, a U.S. Marine search-and-destroy mission, commenced on July 20, 1967, west of Da Nang, South Vietnam. Marines from the 1st Battalion of the 7th Marines carry a wounded Marine to a Marine Observation Squadron helicopter for evacuation.

helicopter crews often had to fly into "hot" landing zones to evacuate the wounded, and all of those involved in evacuating wounded under such conditions were at great risk to becoming casualties themselves. The use of the helicopter for medical evacuation contributed substantially to the military performance of American and allied troops during the Vietnam War, and medevacs resulted in many wounded being saved who might otherwise have died from their wounds. A synonym for medevac was "dustoff," used after the death of Lieutenant Paul B. Kelley in 1964. Kelley's radio call sign was "dustoff," and he was killed on a medevac mission. STT

Source: Robert Mason, *Chickenhawk*, 1983.

MEDICAL SUPPORT

Because of major improvements in medical support facilities and evacuation of the wounded from the battlefield, less than 19 percent of soldiers died from combat wounds in the Vietnam War, compared with 26 percent in the Korean War and 29 percent in World War II. Helicopters quickly evacuated wounded troops to base-camp hospitals, MASH units, field hospitals, and hospital ships stationed off the coast on the South China Sea. Also, because of major improvements in pharmaceutical care against infectious diseases, death or disability from malaria, hepatitis, and intestinal disorders was well below the rates of the Korean War and World War II.

Source: Spurgeon Neel, *Vietnam Studies: Medical Support of the U.S. Army in Vietnam, 1965–1970*, 1973.

Left: Lance Corporal Ralph Everett of Oakland, California, offers a smoke to his wounded comrade, U.S. Marine Corporal Wayne White of Anchorage, Kentucky, while they wait for White's evacuation on November 29, 1967.

Below: Late in July 1967, elements of the 3d Marine Division engaged North Vietnamese regulars in Operation Hickory III near the Demilitarized Zone separating North Vietnam from South Vietnam. On July 29, 1967, Marines from E Company 2/9 carry a wounded comrade to an H-34 helicopter for evacuation.

Right: U.S. Navy surgeons perform open heart surgery aboard the USS *Repose*, a hospital ship cruising in the South China Sea. The presence of such advanced medical facilities so close to combat zones dramatically reduced wounded/kill ratios of U.S. troops during the Vietnam War.

Below: In January 1967, a U.S. Navy doctor attached to the 3d Marine Division dispenses medicine to a South Vietnamese boy.

Opposite, top left: Marine Corporal Larry R. Miklos (center) is evacuated aboard a helicopter south of Da Nang on September 1, 1967. The helicopter is experiencing heavy machine gun fire from Vietcong troops.

Opposite, top right: Hospitalman Third Class Dan Franzen of Topeka, Kansas, attached to Marine Aircraft Group MAG-16, assists a wounded Vietcong prisoner being evacuated in a helicopter of Marine Medium Helicopter Squadron (HMM)-263 for treatment by U.S. medical personnel.

Opposite, bottom: Elements of the 3d Marine Division load a wounded comrade aboard a waiting landing vehicle tracked (LVT) for evacuation on May 20, 1967. The 3d Marines are conducting Operation Beau Charger in the southern half of the DMZ.

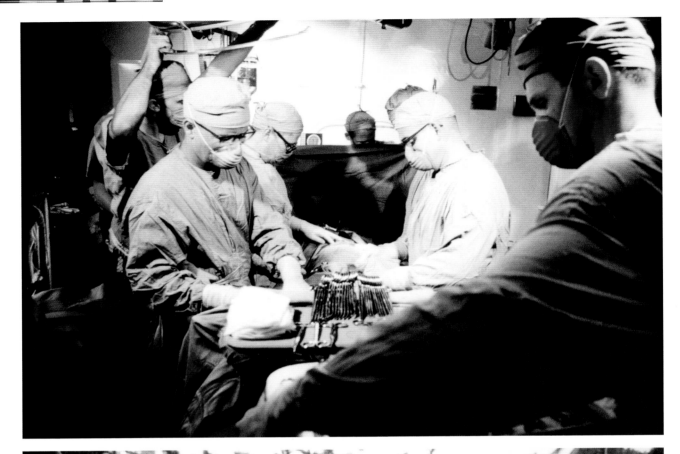

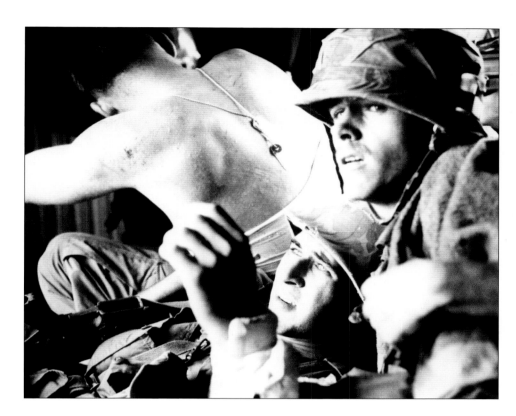

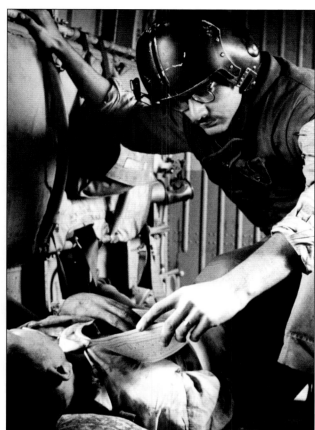

Above: Captain Ernest Medina led the U.S. Army infantry company involved in the My Lai massacre of approximately 500 South Vietnamese civilian men, women, and children on March 16, 1968. Medina denied ordering the slaughter, and at his court-martial, he was acquitted of murder. In this December 4, 1969, photograph, Medina answers questions at a press conference in Washington, D.C.

Right: On January 1, 1962, three years before the introduction of U.S. combat troops in South Vietnam, ARVN soldiers wade through a canal and flooded rice paddies in the Mekong Delta in hopes of luring hidden Vietcong troops into a firefight.

Opposite page: Elements of the U.S. 199th Light Infantry Brigade and ARVN Rangers conducted a joint campaign dubbed Operation Shelby in August 1967. Here helicopters of the 199th deliver the ARVN Rangers to a combat zone near a pineapple plantation in the Mekong Delta.

MEDINA, ERNEST L.

Ernest L. Medina was born in Springer, New Mexico, in 1936. His mother died when he was only a few months old and shortly thereafter his father sent him to Montrose, Colorado, where he was reared by his grandparents. To supplement his grandparents' meager income he worked as a soda jerk, a paperboy, and in a local supermarket.

When Medina was sixteen years old, he lied about his age to enlist in the National Guard, where he served until 1956, when at the age of twenty he entered the Army as a private. In March 1964, after serving eight years, Medina was commissioned a second lieutenant, graduating fourth out of a class of more than 200 from Officer Candidate School at Fort Benning, Georgia. After his second tour of duty in Germany, where he met his wife, Barbara, an East German refugee, he was ordered to Hawaii in December of 1966. Medina was promoted to captain and given command of Charlie Company, which was a part of the 11th Infantry Brigade (*see* 23d Infantry Division). In December of 1967 the 11th Brigade was flown to Vietnam.

While in Vietnam Medina received the Bronze and Silver stars for valor. On March 10, 1970, Medina was charged with murder, manslaughter, and assault as a result of the March 16, 1968, massacre at My Lai* hamlet. On September 22, 1970, a jury of five officers cleared him of all charges. Subsequently, Medina resigned his commission from the Army on October 15, 1971, explaining, "I cannot wear the uniform with the same pride I had before."

Medina then moved to Menominee, Michigan, where he worked in a helicopter-manufacturing company owned by F. Lee Bailey, the defense lawyer at his trial. MD

Sources: Seymour M. Hersh, *My Lai 4: Report on the Massacre and Its Aftermath*, 1970; Michael Bilton and Kevin Sims, *Four Hours in My Lai*, 1992.

MEKONG DELTA

The Mekong Delta area of Vietnam technically extends from Go Cong Province all the way down to the Ca Mau Peninsula, the area drained by the Mekong River as it reaches the South China Sea. Sometimes, the Vam Co, Saigon, and Dong Nai rivers are also included in the region known as the Mekong Delta, giving it a total area of more than 26,000 square miles. The Mekong Delta region is known for its elaborate system of rivers and canals as well as its rice cultivation. Formed by silt deposits, the soil is extremely fertile, and at the mouth of the Mekong River the sediment extends the shoreline by an average of 250 feet a year. The Mekong Delta region is inhabited primarily by ethnic Vietnamese, with large concentrations of Khmers* in the southwestern areas. The Mekong Delta was included in the IV Corps* Tactical Zone during the Vietnam War.

Source: Danny J. Whitfield, *Historical and Cultural Dictionary of Vietnam*, 1976.

Right: ARVN troops cross rice paddies in the Mekong Delta in 1967, with helicopters hovering overhead to help spot the enemy, provide additional firepower, and evacuate the wounded.

Below: Using canoes and hovercraft guided by helicopters overhead, soldiers inspect huts along the muddy waters of the Mekong Delta for evidence of Vietcong in 1966.

Left: In 1967 a machine gunner scans for hostiles below while his helicopter is on patrol over the Mekong Delta.

Below: On October 10, 1967, during a joint operation with the ARVN 21st Division, U.S. Navy Captain Paul H. Gray, commander of the 116 River Patrol Task Force, shoots up a Vietcong sampan in the Mekong Delta.

MEKONG RIVER PROJECT

Above: French Premier Pierre Mendès-France in September 1954.

Known officially as the Mekong River Basin Development Project, the Mekong River Project was launched in 1957 by the United Nations Economic Commission for Asia and the Far East. Designed after the successful Tennessee Valley Authority of the 1930s, the Mekong River Project involved Laos,* Cambodia,* Thailand,* and the Republic of Vietnam,* but Burma and the Democratic Republic of Vietnam* refused to participate. Surveys began in 1958 under the direction of the four-nation committee, headquartered in Bangkok. By the early 1970s the Mekong River Project had completed three dams for providing flood control and hydroelectric power.

Sources: Harvey H. Smith et al., *Area Handbook for South Vietnam,* 1967; "The Mekong Project," *Impact* 8 (1963): 168–180; Danny J. Whitfield, *Historical and Cultural Dictionary of Vietnam,* 1976.

MENDENHALL, JOSEPH

Born in Maryland in 1920 and a graduate of the Harvard Law School, Joseph Mendenhall was a career diplomat in the State Department, where he worked with the Marshall Plan and Vietnamese affairs. He served in the American embassy at Saigon* between 1959 and 1962; was director of Far Eastern affairs in Washington, D.C., between 1964 and 1965; was director of the U.S. Agency for International Development* (USAID) mission in Vientiane, Laos,* between 1965 and 1968; and served first as deputy then as acting assistant administrator of USAID Vietnam in Washington between 1968 and 1969. In 1963 President John F. Kennedy* sent Mendenhall and General Victor Krulak* to Saigon to assess the situation in Vietnam; Krulak decided that the war was being aggressively pursued and could be won, while Mendenhall determined that the regime of Ngo Dinh Diem* was near collapse. Mendenhall reported that educated, urban Vietnamese were more interested in eliminating Diem than in fighting the Vietcong* and that there was a "virtual breakdown of the civil government in Saigon." He warned of a religious war between Catholics* and Buddhists* and saw no chance of defeating the Vietcong unless "as a minimum, Nhu [Diem's brother] withdrew or was removed from the government." When Mendenhall and Krulak returned from Vietnam, JFK remarked, "You two did visit the same country, didn't you?" SF

Source: Stanley Karnow, *Vietnam: A History,* 1983.

MENDÈS-FRANCE, PIERRE

An unconventional political figure who became prime minister of France* at age forty-seven during the 1954 Geneva Conference,* Pierre Mendès-France believed that his country's position in world affairs depended on withdrawal from the war in Indochina.* He had been urging direct negotiations with Ho Chi Minh* and was opposed to the United States becoming militarily involved in Vietnam. In the National Assembly on June 10, 1954, he called for a complete change in French policy, "to make it sure that France's aim is not the intervention of the United States, but an honorable end of the terrible conflict … France should play for a straightforward peace with the Vietminh."

A week later the longtime critic of the Indochina war was chosen to head the government. He immediately pledged to obtain a cease-fire and imposed a deadline of four weeks, saying that he would resign otherwise. He told the French people, "If you want war we shall have to send draftees, your own sons, to the battlefields of Indochina. If you want peace, I shall bring you a cease-fire agreement by July 20 or resign." He met his deadline, the negotiations including some secret meetings with Zhou Enlai,* China's representative at the talks. The armistice agreement included the provisional partitioning of Vietnam at the 17th parallel (*see* Geneva Accords). Mendès-France remained in office for only a short time thereafter. His government fell in February 1955 during controversy over French policy in North Africa.

Born in Paris in 1907, he was first elected to the Chamber of Deputies in 1932 and held key positions in a number of French governments. Pierre Mendès-France died in 1982. HP

Sources: Jean Lacouture, *Pierre Mendès-France,* 1985; Alexander Werth, *Lost Statesman,* 1958.

MIA (MISSING IN ACTION)

See Prisoners of War

MICHIGAN STATE UNIVERSITY ADVISORY GROUP

Headed by Wesley Fishel, the Michigan State University Advisory Group (MSUAG) contracted with the South Vietnamese government to train civil servants, civil guards, and police, reforming the National Administration Institute along American lines, reorganizing Ngo Dinh Diem's* administration, studying social problems, and issuing reports and recommendations to South Vietnamese and American policymakers. The MSUAG functioned between 1954 and 1961. Fishel was a strong supporter of Ngo Dinh Diem. Given to social science jargon, Fishel extracted democratic principles from virtually all of Diem's oppressive and authoritarian actions and claimed that the internal Communist threat left Diem no choice. Shortcomings in South Vietnam's exercise of democracy were explained away with such statements as "the people of Southeast Asia are not, generally speaking, sufficiently sophisticated to understand what we mean by democracy." According to Fishel, South Vietnam needed strong leadership, not democracy. He defended its corruption on the grounds that all Asian governments were corrupt. Early in the 1960s the program was dissolved when Michigan State University refused to restrain returning scholars who openly criticized the South Vietnamese government. SF

Sources: Bernard Fall, *The Two Viet-Nams: A Social and Political Analysis*, 1963; Frances FitzGerald, *Fire in the Lake: The Vietnamese and the Americans in Vietnam*, 1972.

"MIKE" FORCES

See Mobile Strike Force Command

MILITARY AIRLIFT COMMAND

From its headquarters at Scott Air Force Base, Illinois, the Military Airlift Command (MAC) directed during the Vietnam era some 90,000 active-duty military personnel and civilians as well as more than 1,000 aircraft at more than 340 locations in 26 countries. Created as the Air Transport Command just before World War II, MAC was redesignated the Military Air Transport Service in 1947 and received its present designation in 1966. It held responsibilities throughout the era for airlift support of American forces throughout the world, and in supporting these requirements managed air bases not just within the mainland United States but also at such far-flung places as Clark Air Base, the Philippines;* Ramstein Air Base, Federal Republic of Germany; and Hickam Air Force Base, Hawaii.

Below: A U.S. Air Force C-133 aircraft loads equipment at Fort Campbell, Kentucky, on December 12, 1967. Operation Eagle Thrust, the largest and longest air movement of U.S. combat forces to Southeast Asia, deployed 10,000 paratroopers from the 101st Airborne Division. C-141 aircraft transported the troops and C-133s the equipment.

Below: Because of shortages of military aircraft, the Department of Defense's Military Airlift Command contracted with commercial aircraft companies to ferry soldiers to and from South Vietnam. In 1966, troops disembark from a Continental Airlines 707 jetliner at Tan Son Nhut Air Base in South Vietnam.

MAC's assigned airlift capability—all configured to handle passengers, supplies, and equipment—rested during the early Vietnam era essentially on an aging fleet of C-124 transports, slow C-133 aircraft, and C-130* and C-135 cargo aircraft that were more suited to tactical airlift roles. Some of the great difficulties MAC personnel faced in supporting Southeast Asia requirements with these aircraft were their relatively small cargo capacities and, especially, the lengthy flying times necessary to travel across the Pacific. For example, a roundtrip between Travis Air Force Base, California, a major departure port, and Saigon* in the prop-driven C-124 normally required about ninety-five flying hours.

As a result of the difficulties inherent in resupplying a large overseas force by air, MAC officials during the 1950s moved toward the replacement of these prop-driven transports with jet cargo aircraft. Accordingly, a milestone in Southeast Asia strategic airlift support was realized in April 1965 when the C-141 Starlifter* became operational. This jet cargo transport could carry 67,620 pounds of cargo across the Pacific at speeds in excess of 440 knots per hour. A second improvement came with the deployment of the C-5 Galaxy,* an enlarged version of the C-141, beginning in December 1969. These two aircraft greatly enhanced MAC's ability to supply American forces in Southeast Asia

over a massive logistics pipeline reaching halfway around the globe.

Charged with strategic airlift in support of military operations in Southeast Asia between American escalation in 1965 and withdrawal of forces in 1973, MAC used all types of aircraft at its disposal to develop and operate a complex airlift system that spanned more than 15,000 miles between the United States and American bases in the Pacific and on the Asian mainland. This reliance on strategic airlift stemmed from the disabilities of ship movements to support an ever-larger and more sophisticated military mission to South Vietnam. Moreover, the lack of suitable ports, roads, and railways hampered the ready distribution of personnel and war materiel in Southeast Asia. It was not uncommon, for instance, during the 1965 to 1966 force buildup for ships to wait to be unloaded in harbors for days or weeks.

In responding to the urgent Southeast Asian theater requirements during the American escalation of operations, the U.S. Air Force* quickly found that traffic to the Pacific grew from a monthly average of 33,779 passengers and 9,123 tons of cargo in fiscal year 1965 to 65,350 passengers and 42,296 tons of cargo in fiscal year 1967. Similar rises were experienced until 1969, when reductions in military support began to take place. Throughout the conflict in Southeast Asia, MAC personnel offered unique airlift support to American military forces in the theater. Only with the collapse of South Vietnam in 1975 did MAC airlift into that nation finally end. RDL

Source: Kenneth W. Patchin, "Strategic Airlift," in Carl Berger, ed., *The United States Air Force in Southeast Asia, 1961–1973, An Illustrated Account*, 1977.

MILITARY ASSISTANCE AND ADVISORY GROUP (MAAG)

The U.S. government created the Military Assistance and Advisory Group (MAAG), Indochina* in 1950 to process, monitor, and evaluate American military aid to the French forces fighting in Southeast Asia. As originally conceived, it numbered about sixty men and was headed by a general officer. The French commanders resented MAAG's presence, however, and hindered its operations. At first, the American group's mission was not to train or advise the Vietnamese National Army* (VNA), but by the time of the Battle of Dien Bien Phu* those activities were under consideration by both American and French officials. After the Geneva Conference (see Geneva Accords), specific Franco-American discussions began on the future relationship between MAAG and the VNA. In 1955, MAAG, Indochina became MAAG, Vietnam, and a separate MAAG was established in Cambodia.* In 1955 and 1956, MAAG, Vietnam took over from the French the training and organizing of the VNA. Using various legal pretexts to avoid overt violation of the limits set at Geneva on foreign troops, the number of American advisors grew to almost 700 in the late 1950s.

The task facing MAAG was enormous. The South Vietnamese Army that it inherited from the French was poorly trained, equipped, and led. Furthermore, the Vietnamese often viewed the American advisors as interlopers, just as they had the French colonialists. Despite these difficulties, by 1960 MAAG had shaped the South Vietnamese Army into what appeared on paper to be an efficient force. The reality, however, was that the army still lacked good leadership, and President Ngo Dinh Diem* constantly frustrated MAAG by selecting his commanders on the basis of loyalty rather than merit.

By the time John F. Kennedy* became president of the United States in 1961, the role and effectiveness of MAAG was under review. Following military doctrine developed during World War II and the Korean War, MAAG had prepared the South Vietnamese Army to fight a conventional war, with little attention paid to guerrilla tactics. The growing strength of the Communist insurgency in South Vietnam in the early 1960s necessitated a change in doctrine. As part of Kennedy's move toward a counterinsurgency* effort, the administration replaced MAAG with the Military Assistance Command, Vietnam* (MACV) in 1962. DLA

Source: Ronald H. Spector, *United States Army in Vietnam: Advice and Support: The Early Years, 1941–1960*, 1983.

MILITARY ASSISTANCE COMMAND, VIETNAM

Located at Tan Son Nhut Air Base* outside Saigon,* the U.S. Military Assistance Command, Vietnam (MACV) was a unified command subject to the direction of the Commander in Chief, Pacific.* The MACV commander was responsible for all American military activities in Vietnam. MACV was first established at Saigon on February 8, 1962, after President John F. Kennedy* had ordered an increase in U.S. military personnel. The Military Advisory and Assistance Group* (MAAG), which had been in Vietnam since November 1955, remained in charge of advising ARVN officials (see Army of the Republic of Vietnam), but on May 15, 1964, MACV succeeded MAAG in that responsibility as well. Between that reorganization on May 15, 1964, and its departure from Vietnam on March 29, 1973, MACV directed the United States Army, Vietnam;* Naval Forces, Vietnam;* the Seventh Air Force;* III Marine Amphibious Force;* the 5th Special Forces Group;* I Field Force, Vietnam;* II Field Force, Vietnam;* XXIV Corps;* and a variety of pacification programs (see Rural Reconstruction). Four people commanded MACV: General Paul Harkins* (February 1962–June 1964); General William Westmoreland* (June 1964–July 1968); General Creighton Abrams* (July 1968–June 1972); and General Frederick Weyand* (June 1972–March 1973).

Sources: Shelby L. Stanton, *Vietnam Order of Battle*, 1981; Bruce Palmer Jr., *The 25-Year War: America's Military Role in Vietnam*, 1984; George S. Eckhardt, *Command and Control, 1950–1969*, 1981.

MILITARY REGIONS

Until July 1970, U.S. military officials had divided South Vietnam into four major geographical areas, known as Corps Tactical Zones. They were designated I Corps,* II Corps,* III Corps,* and IV Corps.* After July 1970 a new designation was used. Military Region I, or MR I, was the new designation for I Corps. MR II referred to II Corps, MR III to III Corps, and MR IV to IV Corps.

Source: Harry G. Summers Jr., *Vietnam War Almanac*, 1985.

MILITARY SEALIFT COMMAND

The Military Sealift Command was a United States Navy* operation responsible for shipping fuel, food, clothing, and weapons to Vietnam in support of the American war effort. At its peak the Military Sealift Command operated more than 500 ships, including fuel tankers, LSTs, aircraft ferries, tugboats, and troop carriers. At the end of the war in 1975, the Military Sealift Command helped evacuate more than 40,000 refugees* from South Vietnam.

Source: Edward J. Marolda and G. Wesley Pryce III, *A Short History of the United States Navy and the Southeast Asian Conflict, 1950–1975*, 1984.

Right: Army troops line up to board USNS *General Nelson M. Walker* on November 12, 1965. *General Nelson M. Walker* became part of the Military Sealift Command operation in August 1965.

Below: Military Sealift Command landing operations during Deckhouse V, January 6–15, 1967. Two U.S. Marine Corps amphibious tractors are moving along the beach in the foreground, with a UH-1 helicopter approaching at right. USS *Washtenaw County* (LST-1166) is in the background. Deckhouse V was the first Special Landing Force (SLF) operation of 1967, and was significant for two reasons: it was a sizable, combined U.S. Marine and Vietnamese Marine amphibious operation; and it was the last SLF landing to take place beyond the boundaries of I Corps. The combined seaborne and heliborne force assaulted an area of suspected Vietcong concentrations on the coast between the Co Chien and Ham Luong reaches of the Mekong River. The operation produced unspectacular results. The combined force killed only twenty-one Vietcong, destroyed two small arms workshops, and captured forty-four weapons and forty-two tons of rice. Seven U.S. Marines died and one Vietnamese Marine died accidentally.

Above: USNS *General Nelson M. Walker* on April 16, 1967, as part of the Military Sealift Command. The ship operated as USS *Admiral H.T. Mayo* in World War II, first delivering released prisoners of war from France to Boston, then transporting troops from France to Okinawa and bringing servicemen home from the Western Pacific. The ship was active in the Korean War and carried out troop lifts to Southeast Asia from August 1965 until the end of 1967. The ship was taken to the scrap yard in January 2005.

Above: Landing ship tanks (LSTs) unloading near Da Nang on July 25, 1966. More than fifty LSTs served in Vietnam and many served in direct support of the Mobile Riverine Forces. They often moved slowly up and down the rivers of Vietnam, supplying troops with food, ammunition, fuel, and medical supplies.

Right: Vietnamese Mobile Guerrilla Forces prepare to go on patrol as part of Operation Birmingham in Tay Ninh Province on April 24, 1966. The area was bounded on the west and north by Cambodia and on the south by the Song Vam Co River and Tay Ninh City. The two reinforced brigades were launched to locate and destroy VC forces and base camps in the area of operations. They moved rapidly to successive areas by helicopter to exploit new intelligence on VC troop and supply installations. Planning was continuous and orders were issued for operations in new areas as the situation developed.

MISSING IN ACTION

Distributed by MGM/United Artists in 1983 and 1984, *Missing in Action* starred Chuck Norris as Special Forces* leader James Braddock, who had escaped from a Vietnamese prisoner of war* (POW) camp after ten years' imprisonment. After the war is over in 1975, Braddock returns to Vietnam as part of an American fact-finding mission, but is frustrated with the lying and posturing of the sadistic General Tran (played by James Hong), who denies knowledge of any remaining American prisoners in Vietnam. Braddock leaves the mission, heads into Thailand* where he purchases enough weapons to become a one-man army, and then returns to Vietnam and rescues a group of American POWs. *Missing in Action*, precursor to *Rambo*, was one of the genre of action films in the 1980s celebrating the sacrifices American soldiers made during the Vietnam War.

Source: http://www.imdb.com/title/tt0087727/.

MISSING IN ACTION 2: THE BEGINNING

Released by MGM/United Artists in 1985, *Missing in Action 2: The Beginning* starred Chuck Norris as American Special

Forces* soldier James Braddock, who is captured and spends ten years in a Vietnamese prisoner of war camp before escaping. Dubbed a "prequel" to *Missing in Action*, *Missing in Action 2* tells the story of Braddock in the period before the scenes depicted in the first film. Like *Rambo*, *Missing in Action*, as well as *Uncommon Valor* and *Missing in Action 2*, portrays the American effort in Vietnam as a noble one spoiled only by politicians back home who refused to give American soldiers the total support they needed to win.

Source: http://www.imdb.com/title/tt0089604/.

MOBILE GUERRILLA FORCES

Designed to fight the Vietcong* insurgency, the Mobile Guerrilla Forces (MGFs) evolved out of the special reconnaissance projects—Projects Delta,* Omega,* and Sigma*—established in 1965 and 1966. Each MGF consisted of a twelve-man "A-Team" of Special Forces,* a 150-man mobile guerrilla company, and a thirty-four-man combat reconnaissance platoon. The MGF operated for extended periods of time in Communist-controlled regions of South Vietnam and Cambodia.* Basically, they were hit-and-run units giving the North Vietnamese and

Vietcong* a taste of their own tactical medicine. The MGF operations were known as Blackjack Missions and existed between October 1966 and July 1967, when they became part of the Mobile Strike Forces.

Source: Francis J. Kelly, *U.S. Special Forces, 1961–1971*, 1973.

MOBILE RIVERINE FORCE

Because of the extent of the Mekong Delta,* nearly 90 percent of the lines of communication in South Vietnam were by river and canals. More than 50,000 junks operated in the Mekong Delta, providing Vietcong* guerrillas with the ability to ship supplies and move about virtually undetected. To interdict that guerrilla effort, the United States Navy* implemented Operation Game Warden* in 1965 and established Task Force 116 under the command of Captain Burton B. Witham Jr. to carry it out. In 1967 Task Force 117 was established to attack the Vietcong in the Mekong Delta and the Rung Sat Swamp* area. Eventually, several hundred armed small craft—31-foot fiberglass PBRs, air-cushion vehicles,* reconditioned World War II landing craft, motorized junks, LCM-6 mechanized landing craft, and amphibious troop carriers—operated with Task Forces 116 and 117. In June 1967 the Mobile Riverine Force was established by joining the existing naval riverine forces with the U.S. Army* 9th Infantry's riverine forces. Blessed with 5,000 highly mobile troops, the Mobile Riverine Force was capable of moving the soldiers upriver more than 150 miles within a day. The Mobile Riverine Force was headquartered first at Vung Tau* in III Corps* but moved to a Seabee*-constructed base at Dong Tam about 5 miles from My Tho* in the Mekong Delta. Between 1969 and 1971 the Mobile Riverine Force was turned over to the ARVN (*see* Army of the Republic of Vietnam) as part of Vietnamization.*

Sources: William B. Fulton, *Riverine Operations, 1966–1969*, 1973; Victor Croizat, *The Brown Water Navy: The River and Coastal War in Indo-China and Vietnam, 1948–1972*, 1984.

Below: The U.S. naval ship *Benewah* was the base for the Mobile Riverine Force (MRF) in September 1967 and was used as a troop ship, berthing all the troops of the MRF. It was equipped with a floating pier for smaller boats and a helipad to accommodate air traffic.

Right: The U.S. Navy played an important role in searching for Vietcong troops by patrolling the rivers and deltas of South Vietnam. In this 1968 photo, a Navy armored barge crew of the 9th Infantry Division patrols the Mekong River near My Tho.

Right: As part of its Riverine Operations, the U.S. Navy patrolled the internal waterways of South Vietnam. In June 1967, one of the U.S. Navy's Monitors, which was considered a "battleship" of the riverine assault forces, fires 40mm shells at Vietcong positions in the nearby jungles to support U.S. ground combat troops.

Below: A U.S. Navy Mobile Riverine Force (Naval Task Force 117) pushes away from the pier to form up on the My Tho River and attack Vietcong positions on September 26, 1967. The force consists of ATCs and Monitors.

Right: Troops from a U.S. Navy strike force slog their way through the Plain of Reeds in South Vietnam, trying to implant electronic sensors that will detect Vietcong movements and relay the information to American forces on October 18, 1969.

Opposite page, right: Captain Vernon Gillespie of the U.S. Special Forces leads a small group of Montagnard soldiers on patrol through a jungle stream on November 1, 1964.

Opposite page, left: These Montagnard soldiers were photographed on November 12, 1969, at the U.S. Special Forces Camp at Duc Lap, South Vietnam, 2 miles from the Cambodian border. At the time, North Vietnamese troops had imposed a month-long siege of the camp.

Opposite page, bottom: During the Vietnam War, the Vietcong, the North Vietnamese, and the United States recruited support among the Montagnard people of Laos and South Vietnam. This 1962 photograph features Montagnard irregular forces. They were generally not issued uniforms and wore old abandoned French uniforms or simple tribal loincloths.

MOBILE STRIKE FORCE COMMAND

In June 1965 the Military Assistance Command, Vietnam* established Mobile Strike Force Commands in each of the four Corps Tactical Zones and at the 5th Special Forces Group* headquarters at Nha Trang.* Each of these "Mike" forces consisted of a Special Forces* twelve-man A-Team, several Civilian Irregular Defense Group* battalions, a reconnaissance company, and a Nung* or Cambodian airborne company. They were all under the direction of Special Forces commanders. The Mobile Strike Force Commands operated until the withdrawal of the 5th Special Forces Group from South Vietnam in 1971.

Sources: John S. Bowman, ed., *The Vietnam War Almanac*, 1985; Shelby L. Stanton, *Green Berets at War*, 1985; Andrew F. Krepinevich Jr., *The Army and Vietnam*, 1986.

MOMYER, WILLIAM WALLACE

William W. Momyer was born on September 23, 1916, in Muskogee, Oklahoma. He graduated from the University of Washington in 1937, joined the Army Air Corps in 1938, and saw action in North Africa and Italy during World War II. Momyer rose through the ranks of the United States Air

Force* officer corps after World War II, and in 1966 was given command of the Seventh Air Force* in Vietnam, where he supervised the air war over Southeast Asia. Momyer left South Vietnam in the summer of 1968 and retired from the Air Force in 1973.

Sources: William W. Momyer, *Airpower in Three Wars*, 1978; John Morrocco, *The Vietnam Experience. Thunder From Above: Air War, 1941–1968*, 1985; http://www.af.mil/bios/bio.asp?bioID=6504.

MONTAGNARDS

The Montagnards, or "mountain people," were indigenous tribes occupying the Central Highlands* of Vietnam. Before World War II the Montagnards were isolated from the conflict in Indochina,* except for periodic tribute payments they made to a series of emperors. During the nineteenth and early twentieth centuries French imperial officials continued the policy of general neglect. But when the Vietminh* began their assault on the French Empire again in 1946, General Vo Nguyen Giap* declared the Central Highlands* crucial to the expulsion of the French and the conquest of the South. Through the 1940s, 1950s, and 1960s, competing armies tried to woo the Montagnards, and the North Vietnamese proved more successful than the South Vietnamese or the Americans. After 1954 Ho Chi Minh* brought more than

10,000 Montagnards to Hanoi* for training as teachers, medical assistants, soldiers, and political agents; established open, self-governing zones in the North for the mountain people; and gave the tribes representation in the National Assembly. The South Vietnamese took another approach, trying to assimilate the Montagnards through relocation, reservations, and cultural pressure. The fact that South Vietnam also put Catholic refugees* on Montagnard land only further alienated the mountain people. Some Montagnard tribes, like the Hre and the Rhade, were loyal to the United States and South Vietnam, but they were exceptions rather than

the rule. By 1975 the Montagnards had suffered the loss of their land and cultural isolation, and were facing the disintegration of their village lifestyle. More than 200,000 of them had died in the conflict, and 85 percent of all Montagnards had been displaced from their tribal lands. Still facing persecution in Vietnam, small numbers of Montagnard refugees began resettling in the United States in 1986, many in North Carolina.

Sources: Gerald C. Hickey, *Free in the Forest: An Ethnohistory of the Vietnamese Central Highlands, 1954–1976*, 1982; Robert L. Mole, *The Montagnards of South Vietnam: A Study of Nine Tribes*, 1970; Raleigh Bailey et al., *The Montagnards: Their History and Culture*, 2004.

Right: A Montagnard soldier attached to the U.S. Special Forces Camp at Tieu Atar, South Vietnam, prepares to do guard duty with a child strapped to his back on October 30, 1969. Tieu Atar was the site of a Montagnard refugee camp.

MOORE, ROBERT

Robert Moore was born October 21, 1909, in Charlotte, North Carolina, and graduated from the United States Naval Academy in 1932. He fought in both the Atlantic and Pacific during World War II, and by 1961 he had achieved the rank of rear admiral. In 1964 Moore was transferred to the attack aircraft carriers with the Seventh Fleet* in the South China Sea. He was aboard the USS *Ticonderoga** during the Gulf of Tonkin incident* in July and August 1964, and he assumed command of the task force that President Lyndon Johnson* ordered to bomb North Vietnam. Robert Moore retired from the Navy in 1967.

Sources: *Who's Who in America*, 1966, 1966; Eugene C. Windchy, *Tonkin Gulf*, 1971.

MOORER, THOMAS HINMAN

Thomas Moorer was born in 1912 in Mount Willing, Alabama. He graduated from the United States Naval Academy and served on warships between 1933 and 1935 and in aviation squadrons between 1936 and 1943. Moorer commanded a bombing squadron in 1943, and between 1943 and 1945 he served as a gunnery and tactical officer on the staff of the commander of the Naval Air Force. Moorer had

a variety of assignments in the late 1940s and early 1950s, serving as executive officer on the aircraft carrier *Midway* and receiving the rank of captain in 1952. Between 1953 and 1962 Moorer was successively on the staff of the commander of the Naval Air Force, Atlantic Fleet; aide to the assistant secretary of the Navy; commander of the USS *Salisbury Sound*; and a strategic planner for the chief of naval operations. He was promoted to rear admiral in 1958 and in 1962 became commander of the Seventh Fleet.* Moorer became commander in chief of the Atlantic Fleet and head of NATO in 1965. In 1967 he was named chief of naval operations and, in 1970, chairman of the Joint Chiefs of Staff (*see* Chairman, JCS). He was a soft-spoken, competent leader who relied on his diplomatic and problem-solving skills. Thomas Moorer retired in 1974; he died on February 5, 2004. JDC

Sources: *International Who's Who, 1984–1985*, 1984; "Armed Forces," *Time* 96 (February 26, 1965): 16, and *Time* 85 (July 6, 1970): 21; Henry Kissinger, *White House Years*, 1979; Richard K. Betts, *Soldiers, Sailors and Cold War Crises*, 1977; Lawrence J. Korb, *The Joint Chiefs of Staff: The First Twenty-Five Years*, 1976; Thomas Hinman Moorer, *The Reminiscences of Admiral Thomas Hinman Moorer*, 1981; http://www.arlingtoncemetery.net.

MORATORIUM DAY DEMONSTRATIONS (1969)

The Moratorium Day demonstrations on October 15, 1969, constituted the largest public protest at that time in American history. The demonstrations were organized by the Vietnam Moratorium Committee, which was founded on June 30, 1969, to galvanize a majority position against the war through a nationwide demonstration in October, with plans for one additional day of demonstrations on each successive month until there were satisfactory peace negotiations and a firm American commitment to withdraw from Vietnam. This timetable of demonstrations was conceived by peace campaign veterans Sam Brown,* Marge Sklencar, David Hawk, and David Mixner in an effort to counter the anarchic and violent protest seen in the Chicago demonstrations in 1968 (*see* Democratic National Convention), and to take the antiwar movement* into the communities where people who had never protested before could respectably offer their opposition to the war in Vietnam. At the same time, the reconstituted New Mobilization Committee to End the War in Vietnam was preparing for renewed antiwar demonstrations. Working in an uneasy collaboration, the two groups developed a moderate and mainstream approach, whereby organizers generated a grassroots structure in dozens of cities across the nation, garnered bipartisan endorsements from a multitude of senators and congressional representatives, and got their message to the people through ads in the *New York Times* and at press conferences. Millions of people participated in the October 15

Above: Admiral Thomas Moorer pictured here on August 7, 1967. At the time he was chief of U.S. naval operations.

Left: On October 15, 1969, antiwar protesters staged a demonstration in Detroit, Michigan, as part of the nationwide Moratorium Day demonstrations. To keep him warm, the mother of three-year-old George Griffenhan has wrapped him in the U.S. flag.

Above: Antiwar protesters assemble for a rally in Washington Square Park in New York City on October 15, 1969. Hundreds of similar demonstrations took place throughout the city and the United States that day.

Below: U.S. Senator Wayne Morse, elected as a Republican from Oregon who later switched parties, was one of the earliest major political figures to break with the Johnson administration over the war when he voted against the Gulf of Tonkin Resolution in 1964. On February 8, 1966, Morse sits as a member of the Senate Foreign Relations Committee. He is questioning retired Army Lieutenant General James Gavin.

moratorium. The activities, in an effort to suspend "business as usual," varied: many people, including some GIs in Vietnam, wore black armbands to show their opposition to the war; others flashed their car headlights; some passed out leaflets door to door; more than 100,000 people massed on the Boston Commons; New York City mayor John Lindsay decreed the event a day of mourning and ordered the city's flags to be flown at half-staff; the two largest unions, the Teamsters and the Auto Workers, joined with the Chemical Workers to support the moratorium; a quarter of a million people marched in Washington, D.C.; and Coretta Scott King led a candlelight vigil through the capital. Countless speakers, from Benjamin Spock* to former Supreme Court justice Arthur Goldberg* to activist David Dellinger* and diplomat Averell Harriman,* all voiced their opposition to the war. The White House attempted to dampen the sense of goodwill and unity the moratorium demonstrated by releasing a message of support for it by North Vietnamese premier Pham Van Dong,* but the enormous numbers and the moderate nature of the protest demonstrated overwhelming nationwide opposition to the war. President Nixon's* "silent majority" speech* two weeks later attempted to downplay mainstream opposition to the war, but the moratorium demonstrations in November surpassed the October 15 demonstrations in number. The Vietnam Moratorium Committee was disbanded in April 1970. LKA

Sources: Nancy Zaroulis and Gerald Sullivan, *Who Spoke Up? American Protest Against the War in Vietnam, 1963–1975*, 1984; Charles DeBenedetti, *The Peace Reform in American History*, 1980.

MORSE, WAYNE LYMAN

Known as a maverick who frequently stood alone and refused to compromise, Wayne Morse was elected to the U.S. Senate in 1942 and served through 1968. Born in Madison, Wisconsin, on October 20, 1900, he received a law degree from the University of Oregon. Elected to the Senate from Oregon as a Republican, he became an independent in 1952 and in 1955 joined the Democrats.

He was an early and outspoken critic of U.S. military involvement in Vietnam, but his irascible style and reputation as a gadfly left him without much influence. He argued vigorously against the 1964 Gulf of Tonkin Resolution.* Morse was the first to suggest that the Johnson* administration was not revealing the full story of the Gulf of Tonkin incident.* He charged that the United States was acting as a "provocateur" in Vietnam. Morse criticized the administration for not referring the matter to the United Nations. He asserted that the place to settle the controversy "is not by way of the proposed predated declaration of war, giving to the President the power to make war without a declaration of war. The place to settle it is around the conference tables."

Morse argued that the resolution represented an illegal abridgment of the Constitution, and warned at the time of its passage that President Johnson would interpret it broadly. He said that those senators who voted for it "will live to regret it." But he was joined only by Senator Ernest Gruening* in voting against the resolution. He later predicted that the Tonkin controversy would continue for decades.

During the remainder of his last term in the Senate, Morse repeatedly opposed Johnson administration policies in Vietnam and in 1967 failed in an effort to repeal the Gulf of Tonkin Resolution. Morse lost a reelection bid in 1968. Wayne Morse died on July 2, 1974. HP

Sources: Anthony Austin, *The President's War*, 1971; *Congressional Record*, August 6–7, 1974; *New York Times*, July 21, 1974; Mason Drukman, *Wayne Morse: A Political Biography*, 1977.

MORTARS

Mortars are muzzle-loaded, either smooth- or rifle-bored, high-angle fired weapons. Small, light, and easier to move than artillery, the mortars used in Vietnam varied in range up to a maximum of 5,650 meters for the 4.2 inch ("four-deuce"), usually mounted on vehicles or emplaced at firebases, with U.S. forces also deploying the smaller, troop-carried 81mm and 60mm at the battalion and company levels, respectively. Commonly used mortar ammunition included high explosive (either impact or proximity fused) for use against troops and light materiel; white phosphorus ("willy-pete") for screening, signaling, and incendiary action; illumination; and tactical gas rounds.

This page: Australia sent troops to assist the U.S. military effort in Vietnam. Here in June 1965, members of the 1st Battalion of the Royal Australian Regiment fire 81mm rounds at Vietcong sappers trying to penetrate the perimeter around the Bien Hoa Air Base near Saigon.

Above, left: A Marine adjusts the coordinates on his mortar tube to target attacking North Vietnamese regulars during Operation Ballistic Armor in Thua Thien Province in February 1968.

Above, right: In 1966, the 3d Marine Division was operating in Quang Tri Province of I Corps in northern South Vietnam. These Marines fire 60mm mortar rounds at enemy troops during Operation Utah.

Right: Corporal Bryan Walsh of California (left) and Lance Corporal R.F. Brinson fire a mortar to clear a fire support base on Hill 510, approximately 35 miles southwest of Da Nang, South Vietnam, on June 18, 1970. They are members of 2d Battalion, 11th Marines.

The Vietcong* and North Vietnamese Army* often captured allied ordnance, and their 82mm mortar, rather than the more cumbersome 120mm model, became a choice weapon because it also fired U.S.-made 81mm rounds. With sympathetic villagers to pace off the dimensions of U.S. positions, Communist gunners proved accurate and elusive. Relying on the weapon's high-angle trajectory, skilled mortarmen would "hang" several rounds in the air toward a target, then quickly disassemble and move or bury their mortar before enemy radar or visual sighting could direct and adjust effective counterbattery fire. DA

Source: Edgar C. Doleman Jr., *The Vietnam Experience: Tools of War*, 1984.

MU GIA PASS

Located in Quang Binh Province, the Mu Gia Pass was part of the Truong Son Mountain Range and a strategic route for North Vietnamese supplies making their way into South Vietnam during the years of the war. Throughout the 1960s the pass was subjected to massive American bombing in an attempt to cut off the flow of supplies.

Source: Danny J. Whitfield, *Historical and Cultural Dictionary of Vietnam*, 1976.

MUSIC

Music has always been important to a warrior; it reminds him of sweethearts and of home, expresses what he is fighting for, soothes him on the march, and bridges him through bouts of boredom. This was no less true of the millions of American servicemen who served far from home in a land and a culture quite alien to their own. In this case, however, music also stoked a young man's tendency to rebellion and fueled a skeptical view of the war and the military.

The Vietnam War coincided with an unusual and dynamic period of American popular music, from the early '60s to the early '70s. The very early '60s seemed a conservative reaction against the sexuality of Elvis Presley; songs were fairly tame coming from Paul Anka, Frankie Avalon, and the "bobbie sox" set. But then the civil rights movement heated up and folk singers like Pete Seeger and Bob Dylan began popularizing protest songs. In 1963, the Beatles bowled over a great deal of American music.

As the war heated up, protest songs shifted some attention from civil rights to Vietnam. Joan Baez and Judy Collins blasted the escalating conflict in song; Peter, Paul, and Mary made a national hit out of *Where Have All the Flowers Gone?* ("just as the flowers are picked, so the soldiers die"). Bob Dylan chimed in with *Blowin' in the Wind* ("How many times must the cannon balls fly before they are forever banned?")

But pro-war forces did not surrender the airwaves to the protesters. Staff Sergeant Barry Sadler's *Ballad of the Green Berets,* which celebrated the heroism and sacrifice of the American volunteer Special Forces, was the number one hit of 1966. Glenn Campbell's *Galveston* echoed the lament of any faithful soldier risking his life far from home. *Okie from Muskogee* was a paean to bedrock American patriotism.

But suffusing all of these was a kind of music even more elemental and perhaps more welcomed by Americans during their Vietnam tours: rebellious and sexual rock 'n' roll. Although without any overt war theme, such songs as *I Can't Get No Satisfaction* and *We Gotta Get Out of This Place* were songs of defiance and frustration felt by many American GIs. By the late '60s, drug-related songs fueled both the drug culture in America and among servicemen in Vietnam. The Doors' *Light My Fire* is a notable example, and so is Jimi Hendrix's *Purple Haze*, both released in 1967. Hendrix also tapped into the African American rebellion against the draft, the military, and the war merely by being such a counterculture icon. But African American rebellion was more concretely pronounced in Edwin Starr's 1970 *War* ("What is it good for? Absolutely nothing").

As the war intensified, the protest songs became more pointed. Arlo Guthrie's *Alice's Restaurant Massacree* championed draft dodging. Pete Seeger's *Waste Deep in the Big Muddy* blasted the military mentality. Joni Mitchell's

Left: Private First Class Ronnie R. Cole and Corporal Gary M. Durkham of Indianapolis, Indiana, prepare to fire an 81mm mortar from Fire Support Base Sam in I Corps, South Vietnam on September 12, 1970. They are members of the 1st Marine Division.

Right: During Operation Yellowstone in January 1968, members of Company A, 3d Battalion, 22d Infantry of the 25th Infantry Division gather around a guitar player and sing a few songs.

Woodstock cried for peace ("I dreamed I saw the bombers … turning into butterflies above our nation"). There was also Country Joe and the Fish's outrageous *I-Feel-Like-Fixin'-to-Die Rag* ("What are we fighting for? Don't know and I don't give a damn"), practically unthinkable that it would be allowed airtime in any other country at war, but it reflected the sentiments of many who faced the draft even as America's policy was to wind down the involvement there.

In the final years of the war, as far more Americas were departing than arriving, music seemed to want to put the war behind it. The biggest hit of 1971 was Three Dog Night's *Joy to the World.* In 1973 it was Tony Orlando's *Tie a Yellow Ribbon*, which was the anxious meditation about the homecoming of a former convict, but could just as well have been that of a returning Vietnam vet. Tony Orlando's convict is overwhelmingly welcomed; Vietnam vets met a much more ambiguous reception.

Sources: Don and Jeff Breithaupt, *Precious and Few: Pop Music in the Early Seventies*, 1996; www.battlefield-notes.com; www.ichiban1.org.

Right: During Operation Yellowstone in January 1968, members of Company A, 3d Battalion, 22d Infantry of the 25th Infantry Division gather around a guitar player and sing a few songs.

MUSTE, ABRAHAM JOHANNES

Below: A.J. Muste, a lifelong pacifist, was among the earliest and the most consistent critics of the Vietnam War. Muste returned from a self-appointed peace mission to Hanoi, North Vietnam, on January 16, 1967. Muste urged peace negotiations with the Vietcong and North Vietnamese to end the war.

A.J. Muste was born in the Netherlands on January 8, 1885, and immigrated to the United States in 1891. He attended Hope College in Michigan and in 1909 became a minister in the Dutch Reformed Church. Inspired by Quaker writings and the suffering of the industrial poor, Muste was an avowed pacifist by 1915. He joined the Fellowship of Reconciliation,* a nondenominational pacifist group, in 1915. From 1926 to 1929 Muste served as national chairman of the Fellowship of Reconciliation, and from 1940 to 1953 served as its executive secretary. He openly opposed both World War I and II. In 1957 Muste helped found the Committee for Nonviolent Action, which protested nuclear proliferation through mass demonstrations, and was elected its first national chairman.

When the United States increased its involvement in Vietnam, Muste was one of the earliest critics. He was the keynote speaker at one of the first antiwar* rallies, held on December 20, 1964, in New York City. Throughout 1965 and 1966 Muste appeared at dozens of antiwar rallies, vigils, and demonstrations, and in 1966 he was expelled from South Vietnam after leading a demonstration in Saigon.* In November 1966, at the age of eighty-two, Muste became chairman of the Spring Mobilization to End the War in

Below: A.J. Muste, a lifelong pacifist, was among the earliest and the most consistent critics of the Vietnam War. Muste returned from a self-appointed peace mission to Hanoi, North Vietnam, on January 16, 1967. Muste urged peace negotiations with the Vietcong and North Vietnamese to end the war.

Vietnam.* A.J. Muste visited North Vietnam and spoke with Ho Chi Minh* in January 1967; he died not long afterward, on February 11, 1967. JR

Sources: Jo Ann Robinson, *Abraham Went Out*, 1981; *New York Times*, February 12, 1967; Nancy Zaroulis and Gerald Sullivan, *Who Spoke Up? American Protest Against the War in Vietnam, 1963–1975*, 1984.

MY LAI

See My Lai Massacre, p. 372

MY THO

My Tho is the capital city of Dinh Tuong Province. Located along Highway 4 between Saigon* and Ca Mau, My Tho was first founded by Chinese refugees* fleeing from Taiwan. With a population of nearly 100,000, My Tho became one of South Vietnam's autonomous principalities in September 1970. During the Tet Offensive* in 1968, Vietcong* forces occupied My Tho, and in response U.S. bombers and artillery reduced a full third of the city to rubble.

Source: *Webster's Geographical Dictionary*, 1984.

Below: A "purple haze" rises from a landing zone to mark the spot for a medevac to pick up wounded 1st Cavalry Division soldiers during operations in the A Shau Valley, April 30, 1968.

MY LAI MASSACRE

Above: Lieutenant Hugh Thompson testified November 23, 1970, at the court-martial of William Calley, the platoon leader in Company C, Task Force Barker, Americal Division, who was most responsible for the slaughter of more than 500 South Vietnamese civilian men, women, and children on March 16, 1968, at the village of My Lai in Quang Ngai Province, South Vietnam.

Right: Ron Haeberle, a U.S. Army photographer attached to Company C, Task Force Barker, Americal Division, snapped hundreds of photographs of the events at My Lai village on March 16, 1968. In this photograph, helicopters deliver soldiers to My Lai that morning.

On the morning of March 16, 1968, a group of American soldiers—Charlie Company of the 11th Infantry Brigade of the Americal Division—attacked the village of My Lai in Quang Ngai Province, South Vietnam. They had hoped to surprise the Vietcong 48th Battalion, which had been operating in the area with impunity. Tensions ran high. The Tet Offensive was now in its sixth week, and the soldiers of Charlie Company had been on patrol almost constantly. They had lost a number of soldiers to mines and booby traps during that period, but they had been unable to engage their Vietcong enemy, which seemed to melt into the local peasant population just before U.S. troops arrived at a prospective battle site. The soldiers had come to resent the local population, which seemed sympathetic to the Vietcong, making the job of American troops infinitely more dangerous. The 11th Brigade was under the command of Colonel Oran K. Henderson, who answered to General Samuel Koster, head of the Americal Division.

Medina described the mission and reminded the men that the attack would provide an opportunity to avenge their fallen comrades. The anticipated engagement would be intense, bloody, and deadly.

When the helicopters arrived, however, they attracted no small-arms fire. The bucolic village and its still-sleepy villagers seemed more concerned about breakfast than combat, but the American troops were tense and itching for a fight. Over the course of the next four hours, they summarily executed more than 500 Vietnamese men, women, and children. The soldiers also engaged in an orgy of rape and mutilation. Midway into the slaughter, the troops stopped for lunch before resuming the blood-letting. Lieutenant William Calley's platoon did most of the killing, with Calley enthusiastically participating. At one point, Chief Warrant Office Hugh Thompson, hovering in a helicopter above My Lai, noticed Calley shooting a huddled group of Vietnamese. Outraged at what he knew was a war crime, Thompson landed the helicopter between Calley and the villagers and told the lieutenant that unless the killing stopped immediately, he would machine-gun the platoon. Calley ceased firing, and Thompson returned to brigade headquarters where he reported the incident to a chaplain and to Colonel Oran Henderson, expecting a thorough investigation, as required by Army regulations. When the shooting ended, My Lai resembled

a charnel house of bloody corpses. Charlie Company experienced one casualty—a self-inflicted leg wound—and recovered only two weapons, proof positive that they had not engaged the Vietcong but only a group of civilian noncombatants. The 48th was nowhere in sight. The after-action report, however, described an American combat victory at My Lai, and a news story about the "battle" made its way into *Stars and Stripes*. Colonel Oran Henderson did not conduct an investigation, and My Lai quickly drifted back into obscurity, one village in a country of thousands of villages, in a war without fronts.

More than a year later, however, multiple copies of a single letter began arriving at the White House, Congress,

Colonel Henderson wanted the Vietcong 48th Battalion eliminated, a task he handed over to Lieutenant Colonel Frank Barker, who assembled several companies into "Task Force Barker." Captain Ernest Medina headed C Company, or Charlie Company. He was an excellent combat officer and highly respected by his troops. Barker told Medina that on the morning of March 16, they would attack an area dubbed Pinkville, home to the 48th Vietcong. Because the villagers would be at the local market, the troops could assume that anybody left behind was Vietcong. On the evening of March 15, Medina assembled his three platoons—one of them under the command of Lieutenant William Calley—for a pre-operation briefing.

Left: In addition to the killings of peasant villagers at My Lai on March 16, 1968, U.S. soldiers systematically burned down huts and buildings, poisoned wells, and destroyed livestock.

The entire incident soon became a cause célèbre in the United States. Antiwar activists accused the Nixon administration in general and the Army in particular of cavalierly handling an incident that may very well have been one of many massacres in an immoral war. Veterans groups rallied to William Calley, however, seeing a military conspiracy to make him the scapegoat for My Lai. President Nixon, more responsive to veterans than to antiwar activists, periodically tested the political waters, keeping Calley

and the Pentagon describing a horrific incident in 1968 at the village of My Lai in Quang Ngai Province. Ronald Ridenhour, a Vietnam veteran who had heard rumors of the massacre, wrote the letters, in which he told of how a unit of American soldiers had slaughtered hundreds of innocent Vietnamese. The U.S. Army assigned its own lawyers to investigate whether a war crime had occurred, and they asked Lieutenant General William R. Peers to head a formal investigation of the incident and any associated cover-up. Peers confirmed both—a massacre and then a cover-up at every level of the Army chain of command. Although many soldiers participated in the massacre, only two—Captain Ernest Medina and Lieutenant William Calley—were formally charged with war crimes and put on trial. At his trial, Medina pled ignorance, insisting that he had been unaware of the killings, a claim that defied logic. How could an "excellent combat officer," in the vicinity all morning long, not be aware that his troops were killing 500 people? At his trial, Calley confessed that he had killed civilians, but only on Medina's orders. Calley said that in the briefing the night before, Medina had told the troops to waste the village, to kill everything in sight. Medina denied issuing such instructions, but the testimony at trial was confusing.

Several troops present at the briefing agreed with Calley's version of events, but others said that Medina had issued no such orders. The military tribunals eventually acquitted Medina of war crimes, but convicted Calley and sentenced him to life in a military stockade at hard labor. As for the cover-up, General Samuel Koster and Colonel Oran K. Henderson saw their military careers come to an ignominious end.

out of the stockade and under house arrest and then, in several steps over an eighteen-month period, reducing his life sentence to time served. Calley eventually went free.

In his official report on My Lai, General Peers came to several conclusions about the incident. The soldiers of Charlie Company had not been adequately trained about rules of engagement and war crimes—how to identify criminal orders from superior officers and their own individual responsibility to disobey such orders. At the brigade and division levels, commanding officers had been more concerned about their careers than their duty and had failed to investigate the incident and bring its perpetrators to justice. Many of the soldiers themselves, after months of stress and frustration, had developed ethnocentric feelings of resentment and superiority toward all Vietnamese—combatants as well as civilians—which dehumanized them and increased the likelihood of improper behavior toward them. In many ways, My Lai became a symbol for the entire Vietnam War.

Sources: Michael Bilton and Kevin Sims, *Four Hours in My Lai*, 1993; James S. Olson and Randy Roberts, *My Lai: A History in Documents*, 1997.

Below: In February 1970, as Lieutenant William Calley prepared to go on trial for his crimes at My Lai, Vo Thi Lien, a thirteen-year-old survivor of My Lai, appears at a press conference in London at the behest of the British Communist League. On the left is Madame Le Dhi Lao, a member of the National Liberation Front, and Kha Nguyen, their interpreter.

NAPALM

Napalm is jellied gasoline. Its name is an acronym of naphthenic and palmitic acids, which are used in its manufacture. Although employed in World War II and the Korean War, napalm became infamous in Vietnam, where it was used in three capacities. Perhaps its most visual use was when being dropped from aircraft in large canisters that tumbled lazily to earth. Exploding on impact, napalm engulfed large areas in flame, sucking up all the oxygen and emitting intense heat, thick black smoke, and a smell that no one exposed to it will ever forget. Dropping napalm from high-speed jet aircraft was not very accurate, resulting in numerous instances of "friendly" (allied) and/or civilian casualties. A second use of napalm was in flamethrowers—by both U.S.–ARVN (*see* Army of the Republic of Vietnam) and Vietcong*–North Vietnamese Army* forces—which were very effective in clearing bunkers. If the flames could not be directed to penetrate the bunker, they could bathe the bunker in fire, consuming all the oxygen and suffocating

Below: U.S. tactical fighter jets unload napalm bombs on enemy positions, which explode near U.S. troops on patrol on January 1, 1966.

Above: A Vietnamese Air Force T-28, in tactical support of ARVN troops, drops napalm bombs on Vietcong positions near Da Nang, South Vietnam on January 1, 1962. The photo was taken by *Life* photographer Larry Burrows, who died in 1971 when the helicopter he was traveling in to photograph the South Vietnamese Army's invasion of Laos was hit by antiaircraft fire and crashed.

those inside. Flamethrowers also were used in destroying "enemy" villages. Napalm was used in base camp and fire-base perimeter defense. Barrels of napalm would be buried under concertina wire (coils of barbed wire standing two to three feet high and stretched around the perimeter). As troops massed to breach the wire, the barrels would be detonated, incinerating anyone in the immediate area—and dampening the attackers' enthusiasm. A terrifying, effective weapon, napalm's properties are such that it clings to whatever it touches. Smothering it is the only effective way to put it out. Trying to wipe it off only spreads it around, expanding the burn area. The rapid consumption of oxygen can cause suffocation, and the intense heat can produce severe burns without actual contact. The noise, smoke, and smell are terrifying in themselves. SF

Source: Edgar C. Doleman Jr., *The Vietnam Experience: Tools of War*, 1984.

NATIONAL COORDINATING COMMITTEE TO END THE WAR IN VIETNAM

The Madison, Wisconsin–based National Coordinating Committee to End the War in Vietnam (NCC) was a short-lived umbrella organization formed in August 1965 to mobilize nationwide activity against the war in Vietnam and to coordinate the more than thirty disparate local antiwar groups that had sprung up in protest of President Johnson's* escalation of the war in February 1965. Its roots lay in the Assembly of Unrepresented People, an organization that linked social injustice to the war in Vietnam. The NCC sponsored the International Days of Protest in October 1965, which involved about 100,000 people nationwide and included a massive rally at Berkeley with a teach-in at the Oakland Army Base, a parade of 20,000 to 25,000 people down Fifth Avenue in New York, and the first draft-card burning since Johnson had signed the order making such burnings a felony. The NCC, which included an uneasy coalition of the Old and New Left, antiwar liberals, and different pacifist groups, disbanded in January 1966 because of splits within the organization about whether to remain an umbrella group or to reorganize as a national organization making immediate withdrawal from Vietnam the group's basic priority. The NCC's last action was to call for another International Day of Protest in March 1966. The large size and global scope of the second International Day of Protest showed the increasing power of the antiwar movement* and the growing unpopularity of the war. LKA

Sources: Nancy Zaroulis and Gerald Sullivan, *Who Spoke Up? American Protest Against the War in Vietnam, 1963–1975*, 1984; Charles DeBenedetti, *The Peace Reform in American History*, 1980.

NATIONAL COUNCIL OF RECONCILIATION AND CONCORD

One provision of the Paris Peace Accords* was creation of a tripartite National Council of Reconciliation and Concord. The accords called for a withdrawal of all American troops from Vietnam within sixty days of the cease-fire, return of all prisoners of war,* and establishment of the National Council of Reconciliation and Concord. The National Council, composed of representatives of the United States, the Democratic Republic of Vietnam,* the Republic of Vietnam,* and the Provisional Revolutionary Government of South Vietnam,* would then negotiate a political settlement throughout Vietnam. That, of course, was the stickiest negotiating point and one that was never concluded. The National Council never got off the ground in 1973, and any hope for a final political settlement died with the North Vietnamese offensive in 1975.

Sources: Guenter Lewy, *America in Vietnam*, 1978; George C. Herring, *America's Longest War: The United States in Vietnam, 1950–1975*, 1985; Walter Scott Dillard, *Sixty Days to Peace*, 1982.

NATIONAL LEADERSHIP COUNCIL

Between the assassination of Ngo Dinh Diem* in November 1963 and the rise of the ruling junta of Nguyen Cao Ky* in June 1965, South Vietnam had experienced wave after wave of political instability. On June 12, 1965, Generals Nguyen Van Thieu,* Nguyen Cao Ky, and Nguyen Huu Co* declared the establishment of a National Leadership Council to rule the Republic of Vietnam.* The three military leaders subsequently expanded the National Leadership Council to ten members and elected Nguyen Cao Ky chief executive of the council. Ky eventually used his position as head of the council to become the new premier of the Republic of Vietnam. The National Leadership Council functioned until the regular elections in 1967,* when Nguyen Van Thieu became the new president of the Republic of Vietnam.

Source: Frances FitzGerald, *Fire in the Lake: The Vietnamese and the Americans in Vietnam*, 1972.

NATIONAL LIBERATION FRONT

See Vietcong

NATIONAL SECURITY ADVISOR

In 1947, as the cold war and fear of Communism gained momentum in the United States, Congress* passed the National Security Act, which consolidated the Armed Services into a new Department of Defense, established the Central Intelligence Agency,* and formed the National Security Council (NSC).* The national security advisor is the head of the NSC administrative staff and is known as the assistant to the president for national security affairs. During the years of the Vietnam War four men served as the national security advisor. Gordon Gray served under President Dwight Eisenhower* and left the position in January 1961. McGeorge Bundy* took over under President John F. Kennedy* and served until April 1966, when Walt W. Rostow* assumed the post. With the election and then the inauguration of Richard Nixon* in January 1969, Rostow left the National Security Council and was replaced by Henry Kissinger.* Kissinger served there until November 1975.

Sources: George C. Herring, *America's Longest War: The United States and Vietnam, 1950–1975*, 1985; Paul L. Kattenburg, *The Vietnam Trauma in American Foreign Policy, 1945–1975*, 1980.

NATIONAL SECURITY COUNCIL

Created by the National Security Act of 1947, the National Security Council (NSC) consisted of the president, the vice president, the secretaries of defense and state, and the director of the Office of Emergency Planning. Under presidents John F. Kennedy* and Lyndon B. Johnson,* the NSC had little power because these two presidents essentially bypassed it in policy-making, but between 1969 and 1977 the NSC became the major foreign policy body in the United States. President Richard M. Nixon* named Henry Kissinger* as national security advisor, and Kissinger added the head of the Central Intelligence Agency* and the Joint Chiefs of Staff (*see* Chairman, JCS) to the NSC on an informal basis. Nixon allowed the NSC to supplant completely the Department of State in Vietnam War decisions, and it remained that way until mid-1973, when Kissinger replaced William P. Rogers* as secretary of state.

Sources: Richard A. Johnson, *The Administration of United States Foreign Policy*, 1971; Tad Szulc, *The Illusion of Peace*, 1978.

Below: Soldiers of Company B, 2d Battalion, 47th Infantry, 3d Brigade of the 9th Infantry Division display a captured National Liberation Front/Vietcong flag found while searching house to house along the Saigon perimeter in the area south of the Kinh Doi Canal and in the cluster of villages south of the Y Bridge in May 1968.

NAVAL BOMBARDMENT

Between the summer of 1965 and early fall of 1972, the U.S. Seventh Fleet* occupied positions off the coast of North and South Vietnam. Task Force 70.8, part of the Seventh Fleet, was charged with shore-bombardment operations. Except for a six-month stay of the battleship USS *New Jersey* (1968–69), Task Force 70.8 was composed primarily of cruisers and destroyers. The ships provided artillery support for U.S. and South Vietnamese troops, and attacked important targets within range in North Vietnam. Most of Task Force 70.8 shore bombardment took place in I Corps.*

Source: Edward J. Marolda and G. Wesley Pryce III, *A Short History of the United States Navy and the Southeast Asian Conflict, 1950–1975*, 1984.

NAVAL FORCES, VIETNAM

Below: In 1966, the heavy cruiser USS *Saint Paul* fires its big guns in support of U.S. infantry operations against the Vietcong. The *Saint Paul* was part of the U.S. Seventh Fleet operating in the South China Sea off the coast of South Vietnam.

The office of the commander of Naval Forces, Vietnam existed between April 1, 1966, and March 29, 1973, to direct the U.S. naval effort along the coast of the South China Sea. Naval Forces, Vietnam supervised Task Forces 115, 116, and 117 (*see* Mobile Riverine Force), involving coastal surveillance and river operations, as well as the Coast Guard* patrols and the Seabees.* Seventh Fleet* operations farther off the coast, however, were under the direct command of the Commander in Chief, Pacific Command,* in Hawaii.

Source: Edward J. Marolda and G. Wesley Pryce III, *A Short History of the United States Navy and the Southeast Asian Conflict, 1950–1975*, 1984.

NAVARRE PLAN

A career Army officer, Henri Navarre was appointed commander of French forces in Indochina* in May 1953. Major General René Cogny became his deputy. Together they developed the so-called Navarre Plan to end the crisis in Vietnam. The plan proposed a major strengthening of the Vietnamese National Army,* the addition of nine new French battalions to the Indochinese theater, withdrawal of scattered French forces, and the launching of a major offensive in the Red River Delta against the Vietminh.* The United States agreed to support the Navarre Plan in 1953 with nearly $400 million in assistance. Eventually, Navarre committed his augmented forces to the village of Dien Bien Phu* in northwestern Vietnam, hoping the Vietminh would stage a frontal attack on the French valley outpost. The rest was history. General Vo Nguyen Giap* inflicted a complete defeat on the French Army and destroyed the French Empire in Indochina.

Sources: Joseph Buttinger, *Vietnam: A Dragon Embattled*, Vol. 2, *Vietnam at War*, 1967; Jules Roy, *The Battle of Dien Bien Phu*, 1965.

Left: U.S. Navy gunners on the fantail of the USS *Benewah* fire their 40mm guns at Vietcong positions in the coastal jungles on April 16, 1968. The *Benewah* was an APB — an Amphibious Propelled Barracks.

Left: In July 1967, U.S. Navy riverine patrols participated in Operation Concordia in the Mekong River Delta of South Vietnam. A member of the crew mans a forward 40mm gun aboard a Monitor.

Right: U.S. Navy ordnance men load a bomb on an A-4 Skyhawk aircraft on February 19, 1972. They are working aboard USS *Hancock*, an American aircraft carrier in the South China Sea.

Below: The catapult officer aboard USS *Hancock* gives the "turn-up" engine signal to the pilot of an A-1H Skyraider in preparation for a bombing run over North Vietnam on May 6, 1966. The *Hancock* is part of the U.S. Navy Seventh Fleet operating in the South China Sea.

NAVY, UNITED STATES

The United States Navy played a direct role in the conflict in Vietnam from 1964 to 1975. The Seventh Fleet* was responsible for naval operations in the South China Sea and over Indochina.* During the war the Navy performed three major functions. First, aircraft attack carriers flew tens of thousands of sorties* over North Vietnam, South Vietnam, Laos,* and Cambodia.* The F-4 Phantom,* A-4 Skyhawk,* A-1 Skyraider,* and A-6 Intruder* were the primary naval aircraft involved in the attacks on the Vietcong* and North Vietnam. Second, cruisers and destroyers, and for a while the battleship *New Jersey*, were responsible for naval artillery bombardment in support of U.S., South Korean,* and ARVN troops (*see* Army of the

Left: Two F-8 Crusader II fighter-bombers streak across the skies over North Vietnam on March 18, 1967. They are part of Fighter Squadron 53 and have just been launched from the aircraft carrier USS *Hancock.*

Below: During Operation Market Time in 1965, a U.S. Navy PCF-21 boat patrols the coast of South Vietnam to interdict supplies headed for the Vietcong.

Right: In July 1967, a U.S. Navy Armored Troop Carrier (ATC) participating in riverine operations during Operation Concordia prepares to assume a blocking position in order to direct fire in support of U.S. Army troops fighting the Vietcong.

Below: A U.S. Navy Swift boat patrols near Phu Quoc Island in the Gulf of Thailand. It is part of Operation Market Time, a U.S. Navy effort to interdict North Vietnamese supplies infiltrating South Vietnam via the coast.

Republic of Vietnam). Finally, a host of smaller craft were responsible for patrolling the coast of the South China Sea and the major river systems in South Vietnam to interdict enemy supplies. During the course of the war naval personnel suffered 1,574 killed in action and 4,180 wounded.

Source: Edward J. Marolda and G. Wesley Pryce III, *A Short History of the United States Navy and the Southeast Asia Conflict, 1950–1975*, 1984.

NEOCONSERVATIVE REVISIONISM

During the course of the Vietnam War frustration steadily mounted over the morality of the war. Liberal critics considered the war badly misconceived, with American policymakers confusing Communism and nationalism in Southeast Asia. They downplayed Ho Chi Minh's* political ideology, arguing that he employed Communism only as a means to an end, a way to secure the resources needed to achieve his ultimate goal—the independence and reunification of Vietnam. For most critics of the war, the U.S. intervention in Vietnam was ill-conceived at best and immoral at worst, the wrong war in the wrong place at the wrong time, a conflict that callously inflicted misery, pain, and death on millions of people. Pro-war policymakers, on the other hand, considered the war essential to stop the advance of Communism in Southeast Asia and around the world.

One political constituency in the United States believed in the war's purpose but criticized its conduct, protesting not on moral but on strategic and tactical grounds. As the war stretched on with no end in sight, and with strict rules of engagement limiting American troop movements and bombing targets, conservative Republicans and conservative southern Democrats complained of having to fight a limited war. Such U.S. senators as Republican Barry Goldwater* of Arizona and Democrat Richard Russell* of Georgia called on President Lyndon B. Johnson* and then Richard M. Nixon* to liberate the American military from politically imposed restraints; marshal and concentrate all of its power and, if necessary, pursue retreating enemy troops into Laos* and Cambodia;* mine the North Vietnamese harbor at Haiphong;* and invade North Vietnam. For fear of inciting a nuclear confrontation with the Soviet Union* or a Korean War–like invasion of Chinese troops, Presidents Johnson and Nixon refused to employ all of the conventional military options at their disposal and, in the end, lost a war they could have won. For the next thirty years, however, the consensus of political opinion sided with liberal critics who considered the war unnecessary and with strategic analysts still convinced that a widening of the ground war into Laos, Cambodia, and North Vietnam would have been the height of folly.

In the 1980s and 1990s, however, the tide began to change. Although the vast majority of academics remained bitter critics of the war, a group soon to be identified as "neoconservative revisionists" found more and more publication outlets for their point of view—that the war was noble in purpose, necessary to the long-term security of the United States, and could have been won had U.S. politicians not been so paranoid about repercussions in the Soviet Union and the People's Republic of China.* Neoconservative revisionists insisted that the Soviet Union would not have intervened in Vietnam because the region was, at best, marginal to its national security interests, and that China, embroiled in the chaos of Mao Zedong's* Cultural Revolution, could not have sustained a Korean War–like invasion of South Vietnam.

Some of the impetus for a reevaluation of the war came from the memoirs of American military officials anxious to redeem themselves in the eyes of the American people by shifting blame for losing the war to the politicians. In his memoir *A Soldier Reports* (1976), William C. Westmoreland* argued that the war could have been won had he been allowed to invade Laos and Cambodia in order to pursue escaping enemy troops, sever the Ho Chi Minh Trail,* and invade North Vietnam to force the people to defend their own country instead of wreaking havoc throughout Indochina. In his 1978 book *Strategy for Defeat: Vietnam in Retrospect*, Admiral Ulysses S. Grant Sharp made essentially the same argument. As CinCPac—Commander in Chief, Pacific Command—Sharp directed all naval operations in the Philippines,* the Pacific, and the South China Sea, and he believed that had Presidents Johnson and Nixon been more aggressive in the application of American airpower, North Vietnam would have been forced to the negotiating table long before 1972.

In 1978 Guenter Lewy wrote the first comprehensive revisionist view of the Vietnam War. Lewy insisted that the United States had failed to grasp the revolutionary nature of the war, and that the gradualist approach to escalation had unnecessarily delayed the full deployment of U.S. resources in Southeast Asia. The United States did not pay enough attention to the loyalties of South Vietnamese peasants, and the war could have been won had as much money been invested in pacification as in military firepower. Lewy also argued that antiwar critics vastly exaggerated the number of South Vietnamese civilian casualties.

In 1982 former lieutenant colonel Harry G. Summers Jr. claimed in his book *On Strategy: A Critical Analysis of the Vietnam War* that the United States committed serious strategic and tactical mistakes that lost the Vietnam War. On the political level, Summers insisted that the United States should have declared war on North Vietnam; only then could the Johnson and Nixon administrations have been able to inspire sacrifice and support from the American public. A former Army officer and Vietnam veteran, Summers also believed that the United States fought against the wrong enemy, concentrating too many resources on battling the Vietcong and too little on the real enemy—North Vietnam. Had North Vietnam been invaded and punished ruthlessly from the air, the Vietcong would have been essentially cut off in South Vietnam and unable to pursue the fight without their ally. The United States wasted tens of billions of dollars and tens of thousands of lives with a no-win strategy.

In the 1990s and early 2000s the neoconservative revision continued, now bolstered by a new faith in the military and in conventional warfare emerging from the American victory over Iraq in the First Gulf War. C. Dale Walton's *Myth of Inevitable U.S. Defeat in Vietnam* (2002) argued that the United States had badly exaggerated the risk of Soviet or Chinese intervention in Vietnam and concurred with Harry Summers' argument that U.S. invasions of Cambodia, Laos, and North Vietnam would have produced an American victory. Defeat in Vietnam was hardly inevitable—just the consequence of poor strategic choices. In 1999 Michael Lind wrote *Vietnam: The Necessary War*, looking upon Vietnam as one battle in the larger cold war, which the United States won definitively when the Soviet Union disintegrated in 1991. Lind viewed Vietnam as a necessary "proxy war" in that larger struggle.

Sources: William Westmoreland, *A Soldier Reports*, 1967; Ulysses S. Grant Sharp, *Strategy for Defeat: Vietnam in Retrospect*, 1978; Harry G. Summers Jr., *On Strategy: A Critical Analysis of the Vietnam War*, 1982; Michael Lind, *Vietnam: The Necessary War*, 1999; C. Dale Walton, *Myth of Inevitable U.S. Defeat in Vietnam*, 2002.

NEUTRALITY

The question of neutrality was a difficult one during the Vietnam War, especially as it related to Laos* and Cambodia.* Both Laos and Cambodia claimed neutrality in the conflict between the United States and Vietnam, but at the same time the North Vietnamese consistently used both countries to move troops and supplies into South Vietnam. North Vietnam began constructing the Ho Chi Minh Trail* in 1959, and eventually it reached all through the panhandle of southern Laos and the eastern parts of Cambodia and into South Vietnam. The United States ostensibly honored the neutrality of Laos and Cambodia but throughout the conflict worked to stop the enemy flow of supplies. International law requires neutral nations to prevent their own exploitation by a belligerent, which both Laos and Cambodia failed to do, and the United States eventually justified all of its interventions there—the White Star Mobile Training Teams* between 1959 and 1962, Operation Barrel Roll* in 1964, Operation Steel Tiger* and Operation Tiger Hound in 1965, Operation Rolling Thunder* in the 1960s, and the 1970 and 1971 "incursions" into Cambodia and Laos—on the grounds that if a neutral

nation did not stop a belligerent from using its territory for hostile purposes, the other belligerent was then not obligated to respect political neutrality. "Neutrality" proved to be an empty word during the Vietnam War.

Source: Arnold R. Isaacs, *Without Honor: Defeat in Vietnam and Cambodia*, 1983.

NEUTRALIZE

"Neutralize" was one of the first and most commonly used euphemisms used to describe assassination. The term originated considerably before Vietnam, however, and was frequently used in a context both broader than and different from assassination: that of physical targets or enemy positions to be destroyed by aerial bombardment or artillery. In Vietnam the term was also used to designate "unfriendly" hamlets hiding Vietcong,* subjecting those hamlets to destruction. If pacification efforts (*see* Rural Reconstruction) continually failed, a decision might be made to "neutralize" the hamlet by relocating the inhabitants to a government-controlled area, perhaps a New Life Hamlet,* and destroying the original hamlet, often by burning it down, giving rise to the phrase "zippo war."* Often the results of such neutralizations were negative in that innocent civilians were killed either because of mistaken identity or false or erroneous information providing the basis for targeting. SF

Sources: Jonathan Schell, *The Village of Ben Suc*, 1967; Richard Hammer, *One Morning in the War*, 1970.

NEW LIFE HAMLETS

Part of the Civil Operations and Revolutionary Development Support* pacification program (*see* Rural Reconstruction), New Life Hamlets were one of a succession of hamlet development programs beginning with Strategic Hamlets* and continuing through "Ap Doi Moi" (Really New Life Hamlets), which followed the New Life Hamlet program. Each was intended to deprive the Vietcong* "fish" of the civilian "sea" by relocating civilians from the countryside to secured, fortified hamlets. Revolutionary Development (RD) cadres lived and worked among hamlet residents and tried to teach them about the Republic of Vietnam,* hoping to earn their respect and build their loyalty. In practice, the New Life Hamlet program was riddled with corruption. It ignored the sacred nature of the land and the people's worship of their ancestors—to the Vietnamese, to leave ancestral land was to die. Resources were inadequate or unavailable. Pacification priorities were always subordinate to military needs, and security was uniformly inadequate. The RD cadres, even when present and not corrupt, were undertrained. Paid and supplied by Saigon,* they were dependent on and had to please Saigon officials, not the villagers. Hastily constructed in Vietcong areas, the hamlets were usually infiltrated. In sum, the program was poorly conceived and even more poorly executed. SF

Source: Larry E. Cable, *Conflict of Myths: The Development of American Counterinsurgency Doctrine and the Vietnam War*, 1986.

NEWPORT

The major American troop buildup between 1965 and 1968 required enormous logistical resources. By 1968 nearly 45 percent of all American military personnel in South Vietnam were support troops, and more than 5 million tons of goods were shipped into the country. Because of inadequate port facilities, American merchant ships in 1965 usually waited at least twenty days to be unloaded. To eliminate that backlog, the United States constructed major deepwater ports at Cam Ranh Bay,* Da Nang,* Qui Nhon,* and Newport, near Saigon.* The port at Newport just outside Saigon relieved the congestion there after its construction was completed in 1967. Under the direction of the Army transportation corps, Newport handled more than 150,000 tons of supplies each month.

Sources: Carroll H. Dunn, *Base Development in South Vietnam, 1965–1970*, 1972; Edwin B. Hooper, *Mobility, Support, Endurance: A Story of Naval Operational Logistics in the Vietnam War, 1965–1968*, 1972.

NEW YORK TIMES CO. v. UNITED STATES, 403 U.S. 713 (1971)

In this decision, the U.S. Supreme Court upheld the First Amendment right of the *New York Times* and the *Washington Post* to publish excerpts from a U.S. Defense Department study marked TOP SECRET and entitled *History of U.S. Decision-Making Process on Vietnam Policy*, popularly known as the Pentagon Papers.* The *New York Times* began to publish excerpts from the Pentagon Papers on Sunday, June 13, 1971. On the evening of June 14, after White House consultation, U.S. attorney general John Mitchell asked the *New York Times* to stop publishing excerpts from the Pentagon Papers on the grounds that their publication violated the Espionage Act. The *Times* refused to comply, saying that "it is in the interest of the people of this country to be informed of the material contained in this series of articles." The Department of Justice obtained a temporary restraining order against the *Times*. The newspaper appealed to the U.S. Supreme Court on June 24. While the *Times* was restrained from publishing excerpts from the Pentagon Papers, the *Washington Post* began to publish portions of the study. The *Post* distributed extracts to some 345 client publications through the *Washington Post–Los Angeles Times* News Service. The Department of Justice obtained a temporary restraining order against the *Post*, and then appealed to the U.S. Supreme Court when the U.S. Court of Appeals for the District of Columbia ruled that the *Post* had a constitutional right to publish the material. Extracts from the Pentagon

Below: The "showcase" Binh Hoa New Life Hamlet in Lai Thieu, South Vietnam, in July 1968. The refugees are mostly women, and the drab, two-walled houses are constructed of cement and sheet metal.

Above: South Vietnam President Ngo Dinh Diem at his desk in Independence Palace in Saigon in February 1958. He vowed to fight Communism, lift the new nation from poverty, and free it from U.S. assistance.

Papers were also published by the *Boston Globe*, the *Los Angeles Times*, the *St. Louis Post-Dispatch*, the *Christian Science Monitor*, and a number of other newspapers during June 22 to 29. The Department of Justice obtained a restraining order against the *St. Louis Post-Dispatch* on June 26. On that day, the U.S. Supreme Court heard public oral arguments from Solicitor–General Erwin Griswold for the United States, Alexander Bickel for the *Times*, and William Glendon for the *Post*. In an extraordinary flourish of activity, the Court rendered a 6–3 decision on June 30 and issued a short per curiam opinion for the Court, with Justices Burger, Harlan, and Blackmun dissenting. The decision was accompanied by nine opinions. The per curiam opinion held that the United States had not overcome the heavy presumption against the constitutional validity of any prior restraint on the press. Justices Black and Douglas took a nearly absolute view of a First Amendment prohibition of prior restraint on newspapers. Justices Brennan, Marshall, Stewart, and White acknowledged that there could be conditions that would justify a prior restraint on press publication of national security information. Such conditions were not, in their view, present in this case. Chief Justice Burger objected to the "unseemly haste" with which the Court handled the cases of the *Times* and the *Post*. Justices Harlan and Blackmun also objected to the "frenzied train of events [that] took place in the name of the presumption against prior restraints created by the First Amendment." The dissenting justices believed that publication of the Pentagon Papers should have been delayed until an assessment could be made of their potential effect on national defense and security. The *New York Times* and the *Washington Post* hailed the decision as a victory for freedom of the press and resumed publication of excerpts of the Pentagon Papers on July 1. JK

Source: Sanford J. Ungar, *The Papers and the Papers*, 1972.

NEW ZEALAND

A charter member of the Southeast Asia Treaty Organization,* New Zealand was reluctant to become too deeply involved in the Vietnam War, simply on the grounds of limited resources and limited political support at home, and because the war was more than 2,000 miles away. Nevertheless, New Zealand did make a troop commitment to the conflict. Eventually, New Zealand sent about 1,000 soldiers and artillery support troops to South Vietnam, because it wanted to prove its allegiance to American collective security arrangements in the Pacific and because it genuinely did not want to see a Communist takeover of Vietnam, Cambodia,* or Laos.*

Sources: Stanley Robert Larsen and James Lawton Collins Jr., *Allied Participation in Vietnam*, 1975; Shelby L. Stanton, *Vietnam Order of Battle*, 1981.

NGHE TINH UPRISING

Communism appeared for the first time in Vietnam in Nghe An and Ha Tinh provinces in 1930 and 1931. The worldwide depression had driven down the price of rice more than 50 percent, and tax revolts were spreading throughout the countryside. Peasants in Nghe An Province joined with discontented factory workers, protesting capitalism and French imperialism. They formed a "Red Soviet" in Nghe An Province on September 12, 1930. Public demonstrations were widespread until French aircraft attacked a crowd of 6,000 protesters, killing more than 200 of them. The protests then went underground, but the movement weakened because of the famine that hit Vietnam in 1930 and 1931. The French went after leaders of the Indochinese Communist Party (*see* Lao Dong Party) with a vengeance, arresting 1,000 of them and executing 80. The uprising is known as the Nghe Tinh Uprising because of its strength throughout Nghe An and Ha Tinh provinces.

Source: William J. Duiker, *The Rise of Nationalism in Vietnam, 1900–1941*, 1976.

NGO DINH CAN

Ngo Dinh Can was the younger brother of Ngo Dinh Diem* and Ngo Dinh Nhu,* and from the Ngo family compound in Hue* he ruled central Vietnam as a virtual warlord or feudal baron. The dividing line between the two brothers' domains was Phan Thiet Province. The youngest brother, Ngo Dinh Luyen, resided abroad as South Vietnam's ambassador to Great Britain.*

Unlike his brothers, Can did not have a Western education, never traveled abroad, and seldom left his native Hue, where he lived with the clan's widowed matriarch. He lived in a simple, reclusive style, despite many reports that he had used his position for personal enrichment. Employing his own secret-police network, Can exercised a severe, even brutal, domination over central Vietnam. His local authority was largely independent of Saigon, and at times he was at odds with his brothers. Overall, however, the brothers worked together to maintain their power. Following the assassination of Diem and Nhu in 1963, the new regime arrested, tried, and executed Can. DLA

Sources: Robert G. Scigliano, *South Viet-Nam: Nation Under Stress*, 1963; Terrence Maitland and Stephen Weiss, *The Vietnam Experience: Raising the Stakes*, 1982.

NGO DINH DIEM

See Ngo Family, p. 388

NGO DINH LUYEN

See Ngo Family, p. 388

NGO DINH NHU

Born in 1910, Ngo Dinh Nhu was educated at the École des Chartes in Paris and then worked in the French colonial bureaucracy until penalized for his nationalist activities. A master at organization, Nhu orchestrated Saigon* demonstrations in September 1954 advocating a "third force" alternative to French colonialism or Ho Chi Minh.* The Can Lao Nhan Vi Cach Mang Dang* was his primary effort at mass organization. Unfortunately, Nhu's "personalism" was based on a misinterpretation of French thinking and was so alien to Vietnamese thought and culture that no one understood it. The party was organized along the lines of Communist cells, complete with fascist-style storm troopers and an elaborate intelligence network. Nhu used the party to maintain the authority of the Ngo family rather than building democratic institutions or national unity.

Nhu recommended and administered the Strategic Hamlet Program.* Like everything else in the Diem regime, it was poorly administered and riddled with corruption. Obsessed with numbers, Nhu pushed the construction of strategic hamlets more rapidly than they could be assimilated, often in unsecured areas. Government promises for equipment, material, and money were not kept. Villagers often had to pay bribes to receive promised supplies. The Vietcong* quickly subverted many hamlets; others simply disintegrated.

Nhu was head of the secret police, and also commanded Vietnamese Special Forces,* effectively his personal army. With these resources Nhu frustrated numerous efforts to depose his brother Ngo Dinh Diem,* who always viewed internal dissent as more threatening than the Vietcong. The corruption, brutality, and intrigue caught up with the Diem regime in 1963 when Nhu took on the Buddhists.* After Nhu's Special Forces attacked Buddhist pagodas, the United States notified plotting generals that it would accept a coup. On November 1 the generals moved. Diem and Nhu were murdered that next day. SF

Sources: Stanley Karnow, *Vietnam: A History*, 1983; Thomas D. Boettcher, *Vietnam: The Valor and the Sorrow*, 1985; Denis Warner, *The Last Confucian*, 1963.

MADAME NGO DINH NHU

Born as Tran Le Xuan ("Beautiful Spring") in 1924 to a completely Gallicized Vietnamese family that had enriched itself in service to the French colonialists, Tran Le Xuan dropped out of Hanoi's* Lycée Albert Sarraut. She was fluent in French but never learned to write in Vietnamese. In 1944 Tran Le Xuan married Ngo Dinh Nhu,* and because his brother Ngo Dinh Diem* never married, she was essentially the first lady of the Republic of Vietnam.* Powerful in her own right, Madame Nhu issued decrees having the force of law banning divorce, adultery, prostitution, dancing, boxing, beauty contests, and fortune-telling, among other things. Considering herself a feminist, she lectured on women's issues and commanded her own paramilitary organization, the Women's Solidarity Movement.

Madame Nhu saw herself as the reincarnation of the Trung sisters, ancient leaders in the struggle for independence from China,* but she was more a reincarnation of Marie Antoinette. Incredibly insensitive to and uncaring about anyone outside the ruling clique or the sufferings that Diem's inept, corrupt, and increasingly brutal government imposed on the people, when Buddhist monks, including Thich Quang Duc,* and a nun immolated themselves in protest of Diem's government, Madame Nhu airily referred to them as Buddhist "barbeques." Ngo Dinh Nhu encouraged her outrageousness by adding that "if the Buddhists want to have another barbecue, I will be glad to supply the gasoline." Such statements helped consolidate U.S. opposition to Diem, paving the way for the November 1963 coup. In November 1963 Madame Nhu was traveling in the United States, campaigning for support for the Diem regime, when Diem and her husband were assassinated. She then traveled to Rome a widow, spending more recent years on the French Riviera. SF

Sources: Frances FitzGerald, *Fire in the Lake: The Vietnamese and the Americans in Vietnam*, 1972; Stanley Karnow, *Vietnam: A History*, 1983; Thomas D. Boettcher, *Vietnam: The Valor and the Sorrow*, 1985; *New York Times*, October 28–31 and November 1–2, 1963.

NGO DINH THUC

See Ngo Family, p. 388

NGUYEN

The Nguyen were the dynastic family in control of Annam* and Cochin China* during the seventeenth and eighteenth centuries. In the sixteenth century the Trinh family, another warlord group, took control of Vietnam from the Le clan, and by 1620 the Nguyen clan had separated from the Trinh* family and dominated Annam. Throughout the 1600s the

Above: Ngo Dinh Nhu, brother of and advisor to President Ngo Dinh Diem, in April 1961.

Below: Madame Ngo Dinh Nhu, first lady of the Republic of Vietnam, at a press conference in Washington, D.C., on October 21, 1963.

NGO FAMILY

Below: President Ngo Dinh Diem and U.S. military advisor Colonel Hal McCown tour the president's summer home in Pleiku in August 1963.

In 1954 the Geneva Accords divided Vietnam at the 17th parallel, into the Democratic Republican of Vietnam (North Vietnam) and the Republic of Vietnam (South Vietnam). It was a foregone conclusion to all conference participants that Ho Chi Minh would become head of state for North Vietnam, but finding a head of state for South Vietnam was far more difficult. Throughout Vietnam, North and South, Ho Chi Minh was acknowledged among the vast majority of Vietnamese as the father of their country, the man who had marshaled the forces of nationalism and expelled the French from Indochina. Since the Geneva Accords called for reunification elections in 1956, with the two heads of state vying for control of a united Vietnam, Ho Chi Minh had the advantage of name recognition among peasants, and the fact that he was a Communist meant little to them. For American policymakers, however, Ho Chi Minh posed a real dilemma. In any fair election, he was destined to win and Vietnam to fall to Communism unless a viable leader for South Vietnam could be identified and installed. To have any chance at all in the election he had to be a genuine nationalist with a record of anti-French activities, and to satisfy the demands of the United States he had to be anti-Communist.

The Eisenhower administration thought they had their man in Ngo Dinh Diem. The Ngo family had been prominent in Vietnam since the tenth century, establishing a short-lived dynasty in the city of Hue. For the next six centuries, the Ngo enjoyed power and status as mandarins in Vietnam's imperial court. Early in the eighteenth century, they converted to Roman Catholicism and became Vietnam's most prominent Christian family. Deeply religious, they periodically endured intense perse-

cution at the hands of zealous Buddhists, especially in the 1880s, when Buddhist monks burned at the stake hundreds of Ngo family members. One member of the family—Ngo Dinh Kha—happened to be studying for the priesthood and escaped the carnage. Upon hearing that his parents, grandparents, brothers, sisters, aunts, uncles, and cousins were dead, he returned to Vietnam. He married and fathered nine children, the third of whom was born Jean Baptiste Ngo Dinh Diem on January 3, 1901.

Extremely devout but just as eccentric, Diem studied briefly for the priesthood but decided to secure a secular education instead, while maintaining for the rest of his life a vow of celibacy. He attended the French Lycée in Hue, and in 1921 graduated at the top of his class from the French College for Administration in Hanoi. He returned to Hue as a civil servant and steadily rose through the bureaucratic ranks, pleasing his French taskmasters. They were especially happy in 1929 when he uncovered a Communist plot to overthrow Emperor Bao Dai. As a reward, Bao Dai appointed Diem minister of the interior, a cabinet-level post of great influence. Diem quickly became disenchanted, however, seeing Bao Dai and all of the civil servants, including himself, as nothing more than French puppets. He resigned in 1933, establishing his anti-French nationalist credentials, and retired to the family compound in Hue.

Diem became virulently anti-Communist in 1945 when the Vietminh kidnapped his older brother Ngo Dinh Khoi, an outspoken anti-Communist and former governor of Quang Ngai Province. Anxious that Khoi might become a rival to Ho Chi Minh, the Vietminh convicted him in a kangaroo court and sentenced him to death. They buried him alive, along with his young son. Ngo Dinh Diem then fled Vietnam, with Vietminh spies close on his heels. He spent several years in a Maryknoll Seminary in Lakewood, New Jersey, hiding out from the Vietminh and cultivating relationships with prominent Roman Catholics, including Senators Mike Mansfield of Montana and John F. Kennedy of Massachusetts. In the early 1950s the Eisenhower administration began scouring the globe for a Vietnamese to challenge Ho Chi Minh; they eventually found Ngo Dinh Diem, who seemed to possess all the necessary attributes—a history of devout Christianity, anti-French nationalism, and intense anti-Communism. In 1955 Diem left New Jersey for Saigon, where he became president of the newly established Republic of Vietnam.

The United States saw Diem as the harbinger of democracy in Southeast Asia. He was; but like his four-

teenth-century ancestor, Diem yearned for a Ngo family dynasty, and he worked to resurrect it in South Vietnam. From his position as president, he appointed his younger brother Ngo Dinh Nhu as head of the secret police. In turn, Nhu established thirteen separate units of the secret police and dispersed them throughout the country, where they investigated, harassed, and even murdered political dissenters. Nhu became a virtual warlord of Saigon and southern South Vietnam. His wife, Tran Le Xuan, also known as Madame Ngo Dinh Nhu, served as virtual first lady of South Vietnam, since Diem had never married. Madame Nhu headed up her own paramilitary organization, the Women's Solidarity Movement, and exercised police powers independent of her husband and brother-in-law.

Ensconced in the family compound in Hue, little brother Ngo Dinh Can lived with his mother and had no official position. But with his own personal secret police and private army, he ruled Hue and the surrounding region as warlord, commanding troops of his own and browbeating into submission local political authorities. He served as de facto governor of Hue and the northern regions of South Vietnam, enjoying as much power there as Nhu exercised in Saigon and points south, and brooking no opposition. From Phan Thiet Province north to the 17th parallel, Can held dictatorial power.

Finally, Ngo Dinh Thuc was the senior surviving Ngo brother. Political in the best sense of the word and blessed with a spiritual temperament, Thuc had entered the Roman Catholic priesthood and rose steadily through its ranks. During World War II he became a monsignor and then bishop of the diocese of Binh Long. In 1957 Pope Pius XII named Thuc archbishop of Hue, which

made him the presiding Roman Catholic authority of Vietnam. The Ngo family now ruled the political and religious establishments of South Vietnam. That power did not stop there. In 1956 Diem appointed his younger brother Ngo Dinh Luyen as South Vietnam's ambassador to Great Britain. Politically, economically, diplomatically, and religiously, the Ngo family governed South Vietnam.

The Ngo family dynasty, however, never emerged, because Diem's rule lasted only nine years. He imposed a virtually fascist dictatorship over South Vietnam, establishing a reputation for corruption and ruthlessness that gradually alienated the Buddhist majority as well as such ethnic minorities as the Cham, Chinese, Khmers, and Montagnards. The Vietcong exploited the deepening resentment among Vietnamese peasants for Diem and his family, steadily gaining power and threatening to overthrow the government. The United States tried in vain to prop up Diem, but his stubborn megalomania doomed the effort. In November 1963 the Kennedy administration quietly let Diem's rivals know that the United States would not react to a coup d'etat. Within three weeks, Ngo Dinh Diem and Ngo Dinh Nhu had been assassinated. The new regime in Saigon arrested, tried, and executed Ngo Dinh Can. At the time of the assassinations, Ngo Dinh Thuc was at the Vatican answering charges of corruption in his administration of the archbishopric of Hue. He never returned to Vietnam. Madame Nhu happened to be traveling in the United States when her husband was assassinated. She subsequently lived in Rome and Paris. Ngo Dinh Luyen remained in London.

Sources: David Halberstam, *The Making of a Quagmire*, 1965; Anthony T. Buscaren, *The Last of the Mandarins: Diem of Vietnam*, 1965; Denis Warner, *The Last Confucian*, 1963.

Below: The Ngo Dinh family, the presidential family of South Vietnam, in 1963: (left to right) Ngo Dinh Le Thuy, seventeen, her mother, Madame Ngo Dinh Nhu, Diem's brothers Archbishop Ngo Dinh Thuc and head of secret police Ngo Dinh Nhu, President Ngo Dinh Diem, and Nhu's two sons, Trac, twelve, and Quyhn, eight, and daughter Le Quyan, two.

Above: General Nguyen Huu Co, the minister of defense for South Vietnam, appears at a military review celebrating the first anniversary of the regime of Nguyen Cao Ky on June 19, 1966.

Trinh tried unsuccessfully to bring the Nguyen back under control, but they were never able to penetrate the large walls the Nguyen had constructed near the 17th parallel (*see* Geneva Accords). Gradually the Nguyen moved south, colonizing the Mekong Delta* and bringing the Cham* and Khmer* people under Annamite culture. By the 1700s the Nguyen had taken over parts of Thailand,* Laos,* and Cambodia,* and were anxious to dominate all of Indochina.* The Tay Son Rebellion* temporarily displaced them in the late eighteenth century, but under Nguyen Gia Long* they reestablished their control. Indeed, because the Tay Son Rebellion had crushed the Trinh family in the north, Gia Long was able to unite all of Vietnam under a Nguyen dynasty, which remained in power until the abdication of Bao Dai* in 1955. Only the arrival of the French Empire, and later the Japanese and Americans, stopped Nguyen expansion. Although the Nguyen had nationalist sympathies and resented foreign control over Vietnam, they tended to cooperate with foreign rulers—French, Japanese, or American—in order to maintain their own positions of wealth and influence. Blessed with a Confucian,* elitist mentality, they continued to occupy important political positions in South Vietnam during the 1950s, 1960s, and 1970s. The most prominent family representative then was Nguyen Cao Ky,* head of the South Vietnamese Air Force.*

Source: Joseph Buttinger, *The Smaller Dragon: A Political History of Vietnam*, 1958.

NGUYEN CAO KY

Nguyen Cao Ky was born on September 8, 1930, in Son Tay, Tonkin,* near Hanoi.* Ky was drafted into the Vietnamese National Army in 1950, served with distinction, and rose to the rank of lieutenant. He was trained as a pilot in France* and Algeria in 1953 and 1954, and during the regime of Ngo Dinh Diem* he became an officer, eventually a lieutenant general, in the South Vietnamese Air Force.* Flamboyant and possessing an iron will, Ky first came to prominence in 1964 when he threatened to conduct an air strike against the headquarters of Nguyen Khanh* because of all the squabbling during the Khanh military regime. Ky finally agreed to cooperate after a dressing-down by U.S. ambassador Maxwell Taylor,* and in 1965 Ky became prime minister, sharing power with General Nguyen Van Thieu.* A dedicated elitist with decidedly Western tastes, Ky imposed brutal restrictions on the Buddhists*—far more than even Ngo Dinh Diem had imposed—and invited their wrath. Throughout 1966 the Buddhists demanded Ky's ouster, but he continued in power. In 1967 he agreed, with considerable support from the United States, to let Thieu become the sole head of state, with Ky serving as vice president. Although Ky had promised Lyndon Johnson* that he would strive to bring about a "social revolution" in Vietnam, he had no intention of upsetting the status quo of corruption and power that was enriching him and his family. Between 1967 and 1971 Ky's influence was gradually

Right: On February 4, 1966, General Nguyen Cao Ky, the premier of South Vietnam, joins his wife, in matching flight suits and scarves, in touring a battle site near Bong Son where joint U.S.-ARVN military operations killed more than 700 Vietcong.

eclipsed as Thieu consolidated his own power, and in 1971 Thieu disqualified Ky from challenging him for the presidency of South Vietnam. Nguyen Cao Ky fled South Vietnam before the Final Offensive (*see* Ho Chi Minh Campaign) and opened a liquor store in southern California. Ky made headlines in 2004 as the first South Vietnamese leader to visit Vietnam since the war, and he returned again early in 2005 to announce his decision to relocate permanently. SF

Sources: David Halberstam, *The Best and the Brightest*, 1972; Nguyen Cao Ky, *Twenty Years and Twenty Days*, 1976; George C. Herring, *America's Longest War: The United States in Vietnam, 1950–1975*, 1986; http://en.wikipedia.org/wiki/Nguyen_Cao_Ky.

NGUYEN CHANH THI

Nguyen Chanh Thi was born in central Vietnam in 1923 and became a career military officer in the Army of the Republic of Vietnam.* In 1960, as a colonel, Thi worked surreptitiously in an unsuccessful coup attempt against Ngo Dinh Diem.* Although loyal to the concept of an independent South Vietnam, Nguyen Chanh Thi was also a Buddhist* who resented Diem's attacks on the order. By 1965 Thi had risen to command I Corps,* and there he formed a close relationship with Buddhist* leader Thich Tri Quang.* As Buddhist opposition to the government of Nguyen Cao Ky* mounted, Thi became more and more vulnerable. In 1966 Ky dismissed Thi as I Corps* commander, put him under house arrest in Saigon,* and triggered countrywide Buddhist protest demonstrations. Nguyen Chanh Thi was then exiled to the United States, and died on June 23, 2007.

Source: "Central Figures in the Struggle for Leadership of Vietnam," *U.S. News & World Report* (March 28, 1966): 14.

NGUYEN CHI THANH

Nguyen Chi Thanh, the North Vietnamese commander in charge of operations in South Vietnam, was born in 1914 in central Vietnam. He attended school in Hanoi* and became a schoolteacher before World War II, but he joined the Vietminh* after the war and began fighting first the French and then the Americans in South Vietnam. In 1965 Thanh was infiltrated into South Vietnam to take control of North Vietnamese and Vietcong* troop movements. He operated out of Tay Ninh Province, where he headed the Central Office for South Vietnam.* Thanh was committed to defeating South Vietnamese and American troops through conventional means on an early timetable, but as his forces accumulated heavy losses in 1965 and 1966,

General Vo Nguyen Giap* switched to more emphasis on guerrilla operations and a political victory over the Americans. Nguyen Chi Thanh died on July 8, 1967, in a Hanoi hospital.

Source: *New York Times*, July 9, 1967.

NGUYEN CO THACH

Nguyen Co Thach, a veteran North Vietnamese politician, was active in anti-French activities as a student in the 1930s, and with the Vietminh* in the 1940s and 1950s. He began a diplomatic career in 1954 with the creation of the Democratic Republic of Vietnam.* Between 1956 and 1960 Thach served as ambassador to India and headed the Vietnamese delegation to the Geneva convention in 1962. After the fall of South Vietnam in 1975, Thach became assistant and then minister of foreign affairs for the Socialist Republic of Vietnam.* He was removed from his post by the ruling Politburo in 1991. Nguyen Co Thach died on April 10, 1998.

Source: *International Who's Who, 1982–1983*, 1983.

NGUYEN DUY TRINH

Nguyen Duy Trinh was born in the village of Nghi Loc, Nghe An Province, in 1910. He joined the New Vietnam Revolutionary Party as an eighteen-year-old student in 1928, and was a member of the Communist Party as early as 1930. Trinh was imprisoned for anti-French activities in 1928 in Saigon,* was released in 1930, and was imprisoned in Kontum again between 1932 and 1945. Upon his release at the end of World War II, Trinh immediately organized anti-French uprisings in Vinh and Hue,* and in 1951 was selected as a member of the Central Committee of the

Below: The American actress and antiwar activist Jane Fonda meets in Hanoi with Vice Prime Minister of North Vietnam Nguyen Duy Trinh on July 21, 1972. Fonda's visit earned her the lasting enmity of American Vietnam War veterans.

Above: In 1975 Nguyen Huu Tho was serving as the president of the central committee of the Provisional Revolutionary Government of South Vietnam, the successor to the Communist National Liberation Front.

Vietnam Workers' Party. After the expulsion of the French from Indochina* in 1954, Trinh became secretary of the Central Committee of the Vietnam Workers' Party, and deputy prime minister of North Vietnam in 1960, where he served until 1975. Trinh served concurrently as minister of foreign affairs between 1965 and 1975. After the fall of South Vietnam in 1975, Trinh became a member of the politburo of the Socialist Republic of Vietnam.* Nguyen Duy Trinh died in 1985.

Source: *Who's Who in the Socialist Countries*, 1978.

NGUYEN HUU CO

Nguyen Huu Co was a native of South Vietnam, born in 1925. He rose quickly through the ranks of the Army of the Republic of Vietnam,* and was one of thirteen generals who replaced Ngo Dinh Diem* following a coup in 1963. After two years of political instability for South Vietnam, Co was one of the ten generals who helped put Nguyen Cao Ky* in power in 1965. Co was widely known as an excellent field commander who was also hopelessly corrupt, accumulating a fortune by accepting payments from draft dodgers and selling military appointments. Nguyen Huu Co was serving as defense secretary and deputy premier when he was ousted from power and exiled to Taiwan in 1967.

Source: "Clean-Up Time," *Newsweek* (February 6, 1967): 44–45.

NGUYEN HUU THO

Below: At the time of this photograph in January 1975, Nguyen Luong Bang was serving as the vice president of North Vietnam.

Nguyen Huu Tho was born on July 10, 1910, in the Cholon* suburb of Saigon.* A French-educated Saigon attorney, Tho was a revolutionary with middle-class credentials. Between 1945 and 1954 he fought against French forces in Vietnam, protested American involvement in the conflict as early as 1950, and spent two years in prison for anti-French activity from 1950 to 1952. He was arrested again in 1961 for establishing the Saigon-Cholon Peace Movement, then escaped from the control of the Diem* government and became chairman of the central committee of the National Liberation Front (*see* Vietcong) in 1962. By June 1970 Tho was chairman of the consultative council of the Provisional Revolutionary Government of South Vietnam,* and entered Saigon with North Vietnamese forces in 1975. After stepping down as acting president of the Socialist Republic of Vietnam (1980–1981), Tho became chairman of the National Assembly, a post he held until 1987. Nguyen Huu Tho died on December 24, 1996.

Source: *International Who's Who, 1976–1977*, 1976; http://www.coldwarfiles.org.

NGUYEN KHANH

Born in 1927, Nguyen Khanh grew up to be an incorrigible, untrustworthy schemer. He quit school in 1943 and afterward joined the Vietminh* in their campaign against the Japanese and the French, but the Vietminh soon expelled him. Khanh then defected to the French, who trained him for an officer's position in the Vietnamese National Army.* In 1954 Khanh came to the support of Ngo Dinh Diem,* but in 1963 he also participated in the coup against him. Khanh then participated in a bloodless coup in January 1964 that put him in control of the government of South Vietnam. For the next year South Vietnam deteriorated under his convoluted leadership, with the Vietcong* gaining strength and his own government torn apart by corruption and internecine political warfare. In February 1965 Generals Nguyen Cao Ky* and Nguyen Van Thieu* ousted Khanh for good. He was exiled to the United States and took up residence in Palm Beach, Florida. Today Khanh heads the Government of Free Vietnam, an anti-Communist organization based in Westminster, California. SF

Sources: *Who's Who in the Far East and Australasia, 1964–1965*, 1965; Stanley Karnow, *Vietnam: A History*, 1983; Frances FitzGerald, *Fire in the Lake: The Vietnamese and the Americans in Vietnam*, 1972; Daniel Ellsberg, *Secrets: A Memoir of Vietnam and the Pentagon Papers*, 2002.

NGUYEN LUONG BANG

Nguyen Luong Bang was born in Hai Hung Province in North Vietnam in 1904. He worked as a sailor before joining Ho Chi Minh's* Revolutionary Youth League (*see* Thanh Nien Cach Menh Dong Chi Hoi) in 1925. Bang was a founding member of the Indochinese Communist Party (*see* Lao Dong Party) in 1930. Between 1931 and 1943 he spent most of his time in French prisons, escaping in 1932 but being recaptured in 1933. Bang escaped again in 1943 and fled to China.* Between 1952 and 1956 he was the ambassador to the Soviet Union* for the Democratic Republic of Vietnam.* Bang became vice president of the Democratic Republic of Vietnam in 1969.

Source: U.S. State Department, *Who's Who in North Vietnam*, 1972.

NGUYEN NGOC LOAN

General Nguyen Ngoc Loan achieved infamy with the filmed summary execution of a Vietcong* suspect in Saigon* during the Tet Offensive* in 1968. Widely reported in the United States, it contributed to the American people's increasing revulsion with the war. Loan attempted to

Left: On February 16, 1965, an American helicopter pilot sighted a suspicious, camouflaged vessel moored along the coast of Phu Yen province in South Vietnam. This aerial view shows a 100-ton-capacity Vietnamese navy tank landing ship (LST). Russian-made weapons and ammunition have been unloaded between the ship and the boulders jutting out on the beach.

Below: Lieutenant General Nguyen Khanh, commander-in-chief of the Armed Forces of South Vietnam, on February 20, 1965, inspects a cache of Russian-made weapons and ammunition stored in a coastal cave in Phu Yen province. He is accompanied by ARVN and U.S. officers.

justify the execution, explaining that the man had murdered a friend and his family. Nevertheless, the execution was in keeping with his reputation for ruthlessness, corruption, and brutality.

A northern-born Catholic, Loan first came into prominence in 1966 as a colonel while serving as Saigon's chief of police—a lucrative position that enabled him to control Saigon's extortion racket. Faced with the "Buddhist crisis," Nguyen Cao Ky* placed Loan in charge of subduing rebellious I Corps* Buddhists. With loyal troops reinforced by tanks and airborne units, Loan attacked Da Nang* pagodas that lodged resisting Buddhists* and military units. In a series of firefights ending on May 22, Loan regained control of the city, killing hundreds of rebel troops and about a hundred civilians in the process. He then proceeded to lay siege to Hue,* prompting self-immolations by nine Buddhist priests and nuns in protest. After Loan pacified Hue, Ky instigated a public relations campaign to soften resulting resentments. Prominent members of the uprising were treated leniently. Colonel Loan was ordered to clean up Hue, and he jailed hundreds, who remained behind bars for years without trial. Loan's efforts were rewarded with promotion to general and chief of the national police shortly thereafter. Loan fled to the United States after the fall of South Vietnam in 1975. Nguyen Ngoc Loan died in Burke, Virginia, on July 14, 1998. SF

Sources: Frances FitzGerald, *Fire in the Lake: The Vietnamese and the Americans in Vietnam*, 1972; *New York Times*, February 1–2, 1968; *New York Times*, July 16, 1998.

Below: In one of the most infamous photographs of the Vietnam War, Brigadier General Nguyen Ngoc Loan, South Vietnamese Police Chief, summarily executes a Vietcong officer on the streets of Saigon during the Tet Offensive on February 1, 1968. For the antiwar movement in the United States, the photograph became an emblem of South Vietnamese corruption.

NGUYEN PHU DUC

Nguyen Phu Duc was born on November 13, 1924, in Son Tay, and he was educated at the University of Hanoi* and the Harvard Law School. During the 1960s Nguyen Phu Duc was a diplomat in active support of the South Vietnamese government. He served as special assistant for foreign affairs to President Nguyen Van Thieu* in 1968; acted as envoy to Thailand,* Laos,* Indonesia, and the United States between 1969 and 1972; and participated in the Paris peace talks* of 1968 and 1973. Duc was named minister of foreign affairs in 1973, and between 1974 and 1975 he was ambassador to Belgium.

Source: *International Who's Who, 1982–1983*, 1983.

NGUYEN THI BINH

Nguyen Thi Binh was born in 1927 to a middle-class Saigon* family. As a student she became a strident nationalist, opposing first French rule, then Japanese occupation, and finally the American presence. Between 1951 and 1954 Nguyen Thi Binh spent three years in a French prison for anti-French and anti-American activities, and after 1954 she was a bitter opponent of the regime of Ngo Dinh Diem.* Nguyen Thi Binh joined the National Liberation Front

Left: President Richard M. Nixon and Secretary of State Henry Kissinger meet at the White House with Nguyen Phu Duc, chief foreign policy advisor to President Nguyen Van Thieu of South Vietnam on November 29, 1972. Duc is sitting next to President Nixon. South Vietnam reluctantly agreed to endorse the ceasefire agreement Kissinger negotiated with North Vietnam.

(NLF; *see* Vietcong) soon after its creation in December 1960, and in 1962 she had risen to membership in its central committee. Binh traveled around the world explaining the NLF position and opposing U.S. involvement in the war. At the same time she worked as a representative, and between 1963 and 1966, as head of the Women's Liberation Association, a group promoting the rights of Vietnamese women in the struggle for revolution. In 1968 Binh appeared in Paris as head of the NLF delegation at the peace talks.* For the next four years Binh served as the public NLF spokesperson, and after the collapse of the South Vietnamese government in 1975, she was named minister of education for the Socialist Republic of Vietnam.* In 1992, Nguyen Thi Binh was elected the vice president of the Socialist Republic of Vietnam.

Sources: John S. Bowman, ed., *The Vietnam War Almanac*, 1985; *Encyclopedia of the Third World, vol. 3: 1929–1931*, 1982; http://www.onlinewomeninpolitics.org.

NGUYEN VAN BINH

Nguyen Van Binh was born on September 1, 1910, in Saigon* and was educated at the Roman Catholic Seminary of Saigon and in Rome. He was ordained a Roman Catholic priest in 1937 and served in parishes in Duc Hoa and Can Dat. He was ordained a bishop in 1955 and served for six years as the apostolic vicar of Can Tho* until being named

archbishop of Saigon in 1961 (Ho Chi Minh City after 1976), a position he held until his death in July 1995.

Source: *Who's Who in the Far East and Australasia, 1981–1982*, 1982; http://www.catholic-hierarchy.org.

NGUYEN VAN HINH

In an effort to counter the military strength of the Vietminh,* the French began in 1951 the creation of the Vietnamese National Army* (VNA). General Nguyen Van Hinh, as chief of staff, was the commander of this force from its inception until November 1954. Hinh was the son of Nguyen Van Tam, a prominent Vietnamese collaborator with the French and one of Emperor Bao Dai's* prime ministers. Like his father, Hinh was a French citizen. He was also an officer in the French armed forces, had a French wife, and preferred the French way of life. In the eyes of the Vietnamese he was French, and his command of the VNA made a mockery of the notion of an independent Vietnamese army. Because of its colonialist stigma, the VNA under Hinh never became the efficient and inspired anti-Vietminh force that the French and many Vietnamese desired.

In 1954 Hinh openly challenged Ngo Dinh Diem's* authority as prime minister. Defying demands by Diem that he leave the country, the general plotted with gangsters and religious sects around Saigon to oust the prime minister.

Below: Nguyen Thi Binh, here on July 11, 1969, headed the delegation of the National Liberation Front at the Paris peace negotiations of 1968. She stubbornly remained committed to the right of the National Liberation Front to participate in the government of South Vietnam.

Above: Nguyen Van Thieu, chief of state of South Vietnam, oversees a military review celebrating the first anniversary of the Ky government on June 19, 1966.

Below: President Nguyen Van Thieu visited President Richard Nixon in San Clemente, California on April 4, 1973. Nixon bids adieu to Thieu, who is about to be flown away in the presidential helicopter.

Diem responded with his own enticements to the sects. Hoping to maintain a stable government in Saigon* to combat the Communists in the North, the Americans warned that a coup by Hinh would mean the end of U.S. assistance to South Vietnam. Faced with that prospect, Bao Dai ordered Hinh to come to France,* and the general reluctantly complied. Hinh returned once to Vietnam in 1955 when Diem's authority seemed threatened, but soon fled the country when Diem's forces prevailed. Hinh was then given a high position in the French Army. DLA

Source: Joseph Buttinger, *Vietnam: A Dragon Embattled*, Vol. 2, *Vietnam at War*, 1967.

NGUYEN VAN LINH

Nguyen Van Linh was born in 1913 in North Vietnam. A longtime member of the central committee of the Lao Dong Party,* Nguyen Van Linh was a bitter opponent of the French Empire as well as the subsequent Japanese and American occupations of Vietnam. Between 1976 and 1981 Linh served as secretary of the Communist Party of Vietnam, and as general secretary from 1986 to 1991. Nguyen Van Linh died in 1998.

Source: *International Who's Who, 1982–1983*, 1983; Communist Party of Vietnam Online Newspaper, 2006.

NGUYEN VAN THIEU

Nguyen Van Thieu was born in 1923 in the village of Tri Thuy in Ninh Thuan Province. Thieu distinguished himself against the Vietminh* after graduating from the Vietnamese Military Academy as an infantry lieutenant in 1949. Thieu also graduated from the United States Command and General Staff College in 1957. His major commands in the Army of the Republic of Vietnam* (ARVN), beginning in 1959, included the 21st Infantry Division, commandant of the National Military Academy, the ARVN 1st Infantry Division,* and the 5th Infantry Division. He led a brigade of the 5th Division against Diem's presidential guard during the 1963 coup. Thieu continued to rise in power after the overthrow of Ngo Dinh Diem* and was instrumental, along with General Nguyen Cao Ky,* in bringing General Nguyen Khanh* to power in January 1964. By February 1965 Ky and Thieu had positioned themselves to take over the government. Surprisingly, the Ky-Thieu government was South Vietnam's longest lasting. Although Ky originally was premier and Thieu was chief of state and commander in chief of the armed forces, Thieu outmaneuvered Ky to become the presidential candidate (with Ky as his vice president) in the 1967 elections.

While Thieu would have been more acceptable to the United States than Ky was in 1965, they were about equally acceptable by 1967. The primary American concern was that they not run against each other, splitting the military and raising prospects for a civilian government or more coups.

A Thieu-Ky ticket ensured military unity and their victory. Thieu managed only 35 percent of the vote, however, with a surprise peace candidate running an unexpectedly strong second in elections marred by double voting by military personnel and stuffed ballot boxes. When Ky attempted to run against him for president in 1971, Thieu outmaneuvered Ky again, disqualifying his candidacy on a technicality. Eliminating Ky prompted General Duong Van "Big" Minh* to withdraw, leaving Thieu to run unopposed and to head the government until just before its collapse in April 1975.

Thieu bitterly opposed the proposed 1972 peace agreement. Calling it a sellout, he delayed its signing until January 1973. To gain Thieu's assent, some minor modifications were effected. More importantly, Nixon* made secret promises regarding future American military support. In August 1974 Nixon resigned rather than face impeachment, and Gerald Ford* became president. Congress* passed the War Powers Resolution* and other legislation restricting American involvement in Southeast Asia. When Thieu asked the United States to honor Nixon's promises, President Ford had neither the authority nor the sense of obligation to provide assistance. For the first time, Thieu and South Vietnam stood alone.

The stability of Thieu's regime did not result from his establishing a popular government. Like its predecessors, it was noted for corruption, incompetence, and oppression. Stability resulted only from Thieu's keeping the Vietnamese military command either unable or unwilling to mount a successful coup. This depended largely on his maintaining the confidence of the United States. At bottom it was the American military and American money that kept South Vietnam afloat, as demonstrated by its rapid disintegration once that support was terminated. Some criticized the United States for not coming to Thieu's assistance in 1975; a strong case can be made, however, that because South Vietnam had failed to build a viable government after a massive twenty-five-year effort, there were no meaningful prospects for ever building one. Nguyen Van Thieu lived for many years in Great Britain; he died there on September 29, 2001. SF

Sources: Who's Who in the Far East and Australasia, 1974–1975, 1975; Stanley Karnow, Vietnam: A History, 1983; Edward Doyle and Terrence Maitland, The Vietnam Experience: The Aftermath, 1975–1985, 1985; New York Times, September 30–October 1, 2001.

NHA TRANG

Nha Trang, fifteen miles north of Cam Ranh Bay* in Khanh Hoa Province, was a major logistic base for the supply of American military forces and headquarters for the 5th Special Forces Group* and I Field Force, Vietnam.* Nha Trang had a population of 194,969 in 1971. It was made an autonomous municipality in October 1970. Fast becoming a popular international tourist designation, its population has reached approximately 300,000.

Sources: Harvey H. Smith et al., Area Handbook for South Vietnam, 1967; Danny J. Whitfield, Historical and Cultural Dictionary of Vietnam, 1976; Nha Trang Administrative Board Statistics, 2005.

9th INFANTRY DIVISION

The 9th Infantry Division was created in 1940 and during World War II saw combat in North Africa, Italy, France, and Germany. Known as Old Reliables, the 9th was deactivated in 1946, reactivated in 1947, deactivated in 1962, and reactivated again in 1966 and deployed to Vietnam on December 16 of that year. In 1967 the 9th Division fought in Dinh Tuong and Long An provinces, the Saigon* area

Below: Private First Class Peter A. Haag of Company B, 2d Battalion, 47th Infantry, 3d Brigade, 9th Infantry Division, is engaging in a house-to-house search for Vietcong survivors of the Tet Offensive on May 13, 1968.

Right: In the early morning of April 27, 1968, Armored Troop Carriers (ATC) of the 9th Infantry Division's Mobile Riverine Force move up the My Tho River in South Vietnam during Operation Truong Cong Dinh. Their mission is to pick up troops of the Mobile Riverine Force who have been fighting the Vietcong.

Below: U.S. troops from the 9th Infantry Division patrol through the debris and ruins of a village on the outskirts of Saigon after the Tet Offensive of 1968. The soldiers from Company B, 2d Battalion, 47th Infantry, are combing house-to-house for Vietcong. They are south of the Y Bridge over the Kinh Doi Canal.

during the Tet Offensive* and post-Tet campaigns of 1968, and widely throughout IV Corps* in 1969. One brigade of the 9th Infantry Division participated in the Mobile Riverine Force,* which searched for and fought against Vietcong* units in the Mekong Delta.* During its stay in Vietnam the 9th Infantry Division was commanded by four men: Major General George S. Eckhardt (December 1966–June 1967); Major General George G. O'Connor (June 1967–February 1968); Major General Julian J. Ewell (February 1968–April 1969); and Major General Harris W. Hollis (April 1969–August 1969). The 1st and 2d brigades of the 9th Infantry Division left Vietnam on August 27, 1969, while the 3d Brigade remained behind, assigned to the 25th Infantry Division.* The 3d Brigade left Vietnam on October 11, 1970.

Sources: Shelby L. Stanton, *Vietnam Order of Battle*, 1981, and *The Rise and Fall of an American Army: U.S. Ground Forces in Vietnam, 1965–1973*, 1985.

9th MARINE AMPHIBIOUS BRIGADE

When the North Vietnamese Army* (NVA) attacked in force across the Demilitarized Zone* in late March 1972, the 9th Marine Amphibious Brigade (MAB) deployed troops and aircraft off the coast ready to attack NVA-controlled areas south or north of the 17th parallel (*see* Geneva Accords), support ARVN forces (*see* Army of the Republic of Vietnam), and if necessary evacuate U.S. military personnel and materiel from South Vietnam's northern provinces. The deployment of the 9th MAB revived the Marine Corps'* traditional amphibious role, and with Marine aircraft sent ashore to provide support for ARVN infantry, the 9th MAB also dispatched a battalion landing team (BLT) to provide security for the air bases at Bien Hoa and Nam Phong.

In 1975 the Seventh Fleet* and the 9th MAB conducted Operation Frequent Wind* (April 29–30) to evacuate U.S. personnel and friendly South Vietnamese from Saigon.* The 9th MAB provided several ground security units and sixty-eight transport helicopters to lift thousands off the roof of the U.S. Embassy and out of Tan Son Nhut Air Base,* and two of the brigade's officers died when their CH-46* helicopter crashed into the South China Sea on the last day of the Vietnam War. But the 9th MAB took more casualties two weeks later when—two hours after the unannounced release of the crew of the SS *Mayaguez* (*see Mayaguez* Incident)—elements of one of its BLTs unwittingly landed on Koh Tang Island and met fierce resistance from Cambodian forces. The Marine Corps' role in Indochina* thus ended in a bloody but futile daylong battle. DA

Sources: Edwin H. Simmons, "Marine Corps Operations in Vietnam, 1969–1972," and Richard E. Carey and David A. Quinlan, "Frequent Wind," in *The Marines in Vietnam, 1954–1973*, 1983; J. Robert Moskin, *The U.S. Marine Corps Story*, 1982.

Left: On March 8, 1965, the first U.S. combat troops arrived in South Vietnam — 3,500 Marines. Landing on the beaches near Da Nang are Marines from the 3d Battalion of the 9th Marine Expeditionary Brigade. Though they took up positions on the beach, anticipating combat, they encountered no Vietcong during the landing, only young South Vietnamese women welcoming them ashore.

Above: Paul Nitze helped shape cold war defense policy over the course of numerous presidential administrations. He was awarded the Legion of Merit by President Harry S. Truman in 1946 and the Presidential Medal of Freedom in 1985 by President Ronald Reagan for his contributions to the freedom and security of the United States. For more than forty years, Nitze was one of the chief architects of U.S. policy toward the Soviet Union.

Right: Landing craft from the 9th Marine Expeditionary Brigade deliver heavy equipment to the beaches of Da Nang, South Vietnam, on March 8, 1965. Marines from the 9th represented the first U.S. combat troops to arrive in South Vietnam.

9th MARINE EXPEDITIONARY BRIGADE

The August 1964 Gulf of Tonkin incident* led to the transformation of the 9th Marine Expeditionary Brigade (MEB) from a paper organization into the deployable 6,000-man air and ground force from which two infantry battalions made the initial sea and air landings to secure Da Nang's* air base in March 1965. Despite this commitment of combat troops, the landing directive from Washington and Military Assistance Command, Vietnam* stated that the Marines "will not, repeat, will not, engage in day-to-day actions against the Vietcong," and overall responsibility for both offensive and defensive operations in the vicinity temporarily remained with ARVN commanders (*see* Army of the Republic of Vietnam).

In early May, however, the 9th MEB established two more bases on the coast at Chu Lai and Phu Bai, fifty-seven miles south and thirty miles north of Da Nang, respectively. Sensitive to reviving memories of the 1954 French debacle through use of the term "expeditionary," the 9th MEB became the III Marine Amphibious Force* on May 7. DA

Sources: Jack Shulimson and Edward F. Wells, "The Marine Experience in Vietnam, 1965–71: First In, First Out," in *The Marines in Vietnam, 1954–1973*, 1983; Philip Caputo, *A Rumor of War*, 1977.

NITZE, PAUL HENRY

Paul H. Nitze was born in Amherst, Massachusetts, on January 16, 1907. He graduated summa cum laude from Harvard in 1928 and shortly thereafter became a vice president for the investment banking firm of Dillon, Reed, and Company. In 1940 Nitze became assistant to James V. Forrestal, undersecretary of the Navy. In 1941 he was named financial director of the Office of the Coordinator of Inter-American Affairs, then under Nelson Rockefeller's direction. During World War II Nitze served on the Board of Economic Warfare and the Foreign Economic Administration, and after the war he was vice chairman of the U.S. Strategic Bombing Survey. Nitze moved to the State Department in 1946, helped develop the Marshall Plan, and in 1949 succeeded George Kennan* as head of the State Department's policy planning staff. In 1956 Nitze wrote *U.S. Foreign Policy, 1945–1955*.

In 1960 President John F. Kennedy* appointed Nitze assistant secretary of defense for international security affairs, where he specialized in disarmament and military assistance plans. Nitze was secretary of the Navy between 1963 and 1967, and deputy secretary of defense between 1967 and 1969. In that position he helped draft the San Antonio Formula* and served on the Ad Hoc Task Force on Vietnam,* where he advised against further escalation of the war for fear of intervention from the People's Republic of China.* Nitze resigned from the Defense Department when Richard Nixon* entered the White House in January 1969, although he served until 1974 as a member of the U.S. delegation to the Strategic Arms Limitation Talks. In 1981 Nitze was named head of the U.S. delegation to the Intermediate Range Nuclear Forces Negotiations with the Soviet Union, in 1984 as arms control advisor to Secretary of State George Schultz, and as ambassador-at-large in 1985 by President Ronald Reagan. Paul Nitze died on October 19, 2004. JDC

Sources: David Callahan, *Dangerous Capabilities: Paul Nitze and the Cold War*, 1990; *New York Times*, October 20, 2004.

NIXON, RICHARD MILHOUS

Richard M. Nixon was born on January 9, 1913, in Yorba Linda, California. He graduated from Whittier College in 1934 and then took a law degree at Duke in 1937. Nixon practiced law in Whittier, California, between 1937 and 1942, and was active in the Naval Reserve during World War II. He won a seat in Congress, as a Republican, in 1946, and then rose to prominence in 1949 pushing the treason case against Alger Hiss for the House Un-American Activities Committee. A conservative, anti-Communist Republican, Nixon won a seat in the U.S. Senate in 1950. In 1952 Dwight D. Eisenhower* selected Nixon as his

Left: Richard Nixon first visited Vietnam in 1953 as part of an extensive tour of Asia undertaken on behalf of President Eisenhower. Between 1961 and 1968, Nixon visited South Vietnam four times. Here, in 1965, Nixon lunches with Brigadier General Frederick Karch, assistant commander of the 3d Marine Division, at the 1st Battalion, Fourth Marine Regiment field mess in Chu Lai, Vietnam.

Below: On November 3, 1969, President Richard M. Nixon delivered his famous "Silent Majority Speech," in which he argued that most Americans supported the administration's policy in Vietnam. The next day in the Oval Office, with former Michigan governor George Romney, the president luxuriates in the piles of supportive telegrams.

Right: President Richard M. Nixon authorized the U.S. invasion of Cambodia on April 30, 1970. The invasion reawakened the dormant antiwar movement. In this photograph, Nixon explains the invasion from the White House in a televised speech to the nation. He insists that it is an "incursion," not an "invasion."

Below: President Richard M. Nixon made a surprise trip to South Vietnam to visit with South Vietnamese officials and U.S. troops on July 30, 1969. Here he wades through a crowd of troops near a combat zone.

vice-presidential running mate, and Nixon survived a controversy over personal use of campaign funds to become vice president of the United States. In 1960 he lost a narrow election for president to Democrat John F. Kennedy,* and in 1962 he lost a bid for the governorship of California to incumbent Democrat Pat Brown. Most observers assumed that Nixon's political career was over, but while practicing law he spoke widely on behalf of Republican candidates and causes, and in 1968 he won the GOP presidential nomination. By then the Democratic Party was self-destructing over Vietnam, and in the general election, promising a new plan to end the war, Nixon narrowly defeated Hubert Humphrey.*

Although Nixon's political career had taken a hard-line, ideological tone over the years, especially in foreign policy, he proved to be a pragmatic president willing to explore a variety of initiatives. Until 1967 he had supported the American commitment in Vietnam, but he became more critical as the election politics of 1968 heated up. By the time he took office in 1969, Nixon, along with his national security advisor, Henry Kissinger,* was convinced that the war must come to an end. But they wanted no ignominious withdrawal either. Anything less than an "honorable" peace would compromise their grand design to reach an accommodation with the People's Republic of China* and the Soviet Union* without abandoning traditional allies.

The Nixon-Kissinger approach to peace came to be known as Vietnamization* and rested on several major assumptions: (1) the government of Nguyen Van Thieu* was stable and was prepared to assume more responsibility for conduct of the war; (2) South Vietnamese troops would gradually replace American troops in combat operations, and American troops would simultaneously be withdrawn; (3) the American withdrawal must not bear the slightest taint of defeat; (4) there must be no coalition government with the Vietcong* in the South; (5) all prisoners of war* (POWs) would have to be returned; and (6) the withdrawal of all North Vietnamese troops from South Vietnam would have to be carried out before the United States would terminate its support of the Republic of Vietnam.*

In the ongoing peace talks in Paris* as well as the secret diplomacy of Henry Kissinger, the North Vietnamese refused to cooperate, insisting on an unconditional withdrawal of all American troops and creation of a coalition government, without Nguyen Van Thieu, in South Vietnam. Nixon then initiated the large-scale bombing of infiltration* routes in Cambodia (see Operation Menu) and strategic targets in North Vietnam, but it had little impact on the negotiations. The pace of Vietnamization quickened. Most American combat troops were removed between 1969 and 1972, and massive amounts of materiel were handed over to South Vietnam. In 1970 Nixon launched an "incursion" into Cambodia (see Operation Binh Tay) by American and ARVN troops (see Army of the Republic of Vietnam) to attack Vietcong and North Vietnamese sanctuaries* there, but the invasion triggered a storm of protest as well as the tragedy at Kent State University.* In 1971 he ordered an invasion of Laos (see Lam Son 719) to sever North Vietnamese supply lines, but it too did little to stop the flow of men and materiel.

In March 1972, conscious of the upcoming presidential election and anxious to fulfill his promise of ending the war, Nixon was ready to make some concessions, and the North Vietnamese were equally ready to intensify their commitment to the fall of the South. They launched a massive invasion of South Vietnam, and in response Nixon unleashed the massive bombing of the Democratic Republic of Vietnam.* Late in 1972 negotiations finally became serious, but only because the United States surrendered on most major points. Nixon was anxious to reach a settlement before the election. He agreed to a coalition government in South Vietnam, complete withdrawal of American troops, leaving North Vietnamese troops in place, and exchanges of all prisoners of war. The treaty was concluded late in October, and Nixon won reelection in November, defeating George McGovern.* In December 1972, when North Vietnam appeared to be dragging its feet on the POW issue, Nixon ordered a new round of massive Christmas bombings (see Operation Linebacker II), and North Vietnam finally acquiesced. In March 1973, in what will surely be remembered as the high point of the Nixon administration, the American POWs came home. After that, the Watergate* quagmire gradually destroyed the Nixon presidency, forcing his resignation in August 1974. Nixon spent the rest of his life as an anxious elder statesman, gradually achieving a measure of redemption and writing several books on foreign policy and about his experiences in politics. Richard M. Nixon died on April 22, 1994.

Sources: Fawn Brodie, *Richard Nixon: The Shaping of His Character*, 1983; Henry Kissinger, *Years of Upheaval*, 1982; Theodore S. White, *Breach of Faith. The Fall of Richard Nixon*, 1976; Richard Nixon, *RN: The Memoirs of Richard Nixon*, 1978, and *No More Vietnams*, 1985; Melvin Small, *The Presidency of Richard Nixon*, 2003.

Above: Frederick Nolting served as U.S. ambassador to South Vietnam during the early years of the Kennedy administration. Here he is speaking to the press in Saigon on July 1, 1961.

NIXON DOCTRINE

Facing enormous political pressure because of economic problems, squeezes on the federal budget, antiwar opposition, and a new spirit of neo-isolationism, President Richard Nixon* announced the Nixon Doctrine in a talk with journalists on Guam on July 25, 1969. While maintaining the protection of Southeast Asia and Japan under the "nuclear umbrella," the United States insisted that Asian soldiers, rather than American troops, would have to carry the burden of land warfare in the future. The Nixon Doctrine would not go into effect until after American disengagement from Vietnam, and would not modify any existing U.S. commitments to the Southeast Asia Treaty Organization* or any bilateral commitments to Japan,* South Korea,* Taiwan (see Chiang Kai-shek), or the Philippines.* Critics charged that the Nixon Doctrine was based on a continuation of the containment policy* and actually made the United States more dependent on its Asian allies and more vulnerable to political instability in the area. President Nixon invoked the doctrine in 1971 to justify increased American economic and military assistance to Iran.

Source: Earl C. Ravenal, "The Nixon Doctrine and Our Asian Commitments," *Foreign Affairs* 49 (1971): 201–217.

NOLTING, FREDERICK ERNEST

Born on August 24, 1911, in Richmond, Virginia, Frederick Nolting received a B.A. from the University of Virginia in 1933, an M.A. from Harvard in 1941, and a Ph.D. from the University of Virginia in 1942. After service in the Navy during World War II, Nolting joined the State Department, serving in a series of minor positions until his appointment to the NATO delegation in 1955. Dwight D. Eisenhower* named him the alternate permanent representative to NATO in 1957, and then appointed him ambassador to South Vietnam in 1961. Nolting developed a close and supportive relationship with President Ngo Dinh Diem* and

Below: Soldiers of the North Vietnamese Army conduct target practice and war games in Bach Dang, North Vietnam, near the city of Hanoi on July 19, 1966.

Right: This North Vietnamese SKS 39mm caliber carbine rifle was introduced by the Soviet Union in 1946 and had only limited production in North Vietnam. It is identified by the factory mark of a "1" inside a five-pointed star. SKS carbines fire semi-automatic and have a ten round magazine capacity. The sights can be adjusted to a maximum distance of 1,000 meters, but are crude and so are only accurate for individual targets to about 500 meters.

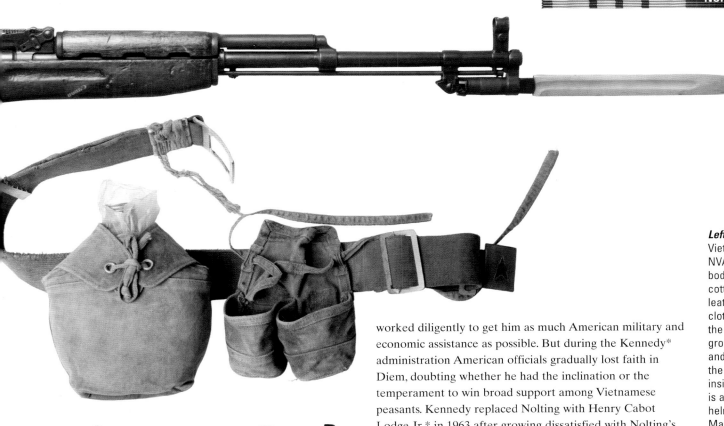

worked diligently to get him as much American military and economic assistance as possible. But during the Kennedy* administration American officials gradually lost faith in Diem, doubting whether he had the inclination or the temperament to win broad support among Vietnamese peasants. Kennedy replaced Nolting with Henry Cabot Lodge Jr.* in 1963 after growing dissatisfied with Nolting's unwavering support of Diem and his unwillingness to clearly describe the deterioration of Diem's political position. Nolting resigned from the State Department and joined the investment firm of Morgan Guaranty Trust Company. He stayed there until 1970, when he joined the faculty of the University of Virginia to direct the White Burkett Miller Center for Public Affairs. Frederick Nolting died in 1989.

Sources: David Halberstam, *The Best and the Brightest*, 1972; *Who's Who in America, 1978–1979*, 1979.

NORTH VIETNAM

See Democratic Republic of Vietnam

NORTH VIETNAMESE ARMY

At the outset of the war in Vietnam, most American soldiers anticipated a fairly quick end to the conflict because they expected the North Vietnamese Army (NVA) to be little match for U.S. firepower. By 1975, however, the American military respected the NVA as one of the finest armies, man for man, in the world. In 1950 the NVA, though not yet officially named, consisted of three infantry divisions of perhaps 35,000 troops. They were commanded by Vo Nguyen Giap.* That army engaged the French and finally defeated them in 1954 at the Battle of Dien Bien Phu.*

Left: Equipment of the North Vietnamese Army. The green NVA sun helmet has a plastic body covered by a green cotton cloth and a black leather chinstrap, with a cloth covered ventilator at the top and four aluminum grommets. The sweatband and webbing are intact inside the helmet and the NVA metal insignia (a star in a wreath) is affixed to the front of the helmet. It was picked up by Major David Carraway in a cave in Nui Ba Der (Black Virgin Mountain) in the III Corps tactical zone in 1969. The brown sun helmet is made of cardboard covered inside and out with tan drill and has an olive brown plastic impregnated rain cover marked "QT-222, 23 December 1968, Quang Ngai, V.N." The webbing belt has a square aluminum buckle with a star cut into it. Some NVA soldiers painted the star red. Attached to the belt are a canteen and a grenade pouch. NVA grenades were usually "homemade" (the guerilla origins of the NVA showing), and were usually of the "stick" type. The typical pouch held two of these, with the handles secured by ties. However, pouches holding much larger numbers of grenades were also found. The Type 54 pistol, 7.62mm caliber, is an exact copy of the Soviet Union's Tokarev TT-33 and was called a Chicom because it was supplied by Communist China. The barrel of this gun was damaged when it was struck by a U.S. 5.56mm rifle bullet at Phuoc Loc.

Right: North Vietnamese members of the Joint Military Commission (JMC) after disembarking from a C-130 aircraft at Tan Son Nhut Air Base, South Vietnam, in February 1973.

The NVA was formally organized in 1954 after the Geneva Accords.* By 1964 the NVA totaled fifteen infantry divisions armed with World War II–vintage weapons. During the next decade, supplied by the Soviet Union* and the People's Republic of China,* the NVA grew to nearly 600,000 men organized into eighteen infantry divisions. In 1968 the NVA had used PT-76 Soviet tanks; by 1975 it had a total of four armored regiments equipped with nearly 1,000 Soviet-made T-34, T-54, T-59, and PT-76 tanks. The NVA also consisted of ten artillery regiments, twenty independent infantry regiments, twenty-four antiaircraft regiments, and fifteen SAM* regiments. Despite early denials, more than half of the NVA was deployed in South Vietnam, Laos,* and Cambodia* in the late 1960s and early 1970s, and the other half invaded South Vietnam in 1975 for the final conquest (*see* Ho Chi Minh Campaign).

Sources: Anthony Robinson, ed., *The Weapons of the Vietnam War*, 1983; International Institute for Strategic Studies, *The Military Balance 1963–64*, 1963, and *The Military Balance 1974–75*, 1975; Edward Emering, *Weapons and Field Gear of the North Vietnamese Army*, 1998.

NUNG

The Nung were a Sino-Tibetan minority group of more than 300,000 people living in North Vietnam. A small number, perhaps 15,000, resided in the Central Highlands* of South Vietnam. Originating in the western Canton River area of China, the Nung migrated to Tonkin* in the nineteenth century and intermarried with Muong and Thai people. In 1955 Ngo Dinh Diem* raised three battalions of Nung soldiers to fight the Binh Xuyen* and Hoa Hao* sect. During the 1960s the 5th Special Forces Group* continued to train and equip the Nung tribesmen, and eventually came to consider them a superb fighting force against the Vietcong* and North Vietnamese Army.* Some 612,000 remain in Vietnam, with about 120,000 in China, 48,000 in Laos,* and 20,000 in Myanmar.

Sources: Alan Houghton Brokrick, *Little China: The Annamese Lands*, 1942; Shelby L. Stanton, *Vietnam Order of Battle*, 1981; Joseph Buttinger, *Vietnam: A Dragon Embattled*, Vol. 2, *Vietnam at War*, 1967; http//:www.vnpeoples.org/Nung.

NURSES (WOMEN) IN VIETNAM

See Women in Vietnam

NVA

See North Vietnamese Army

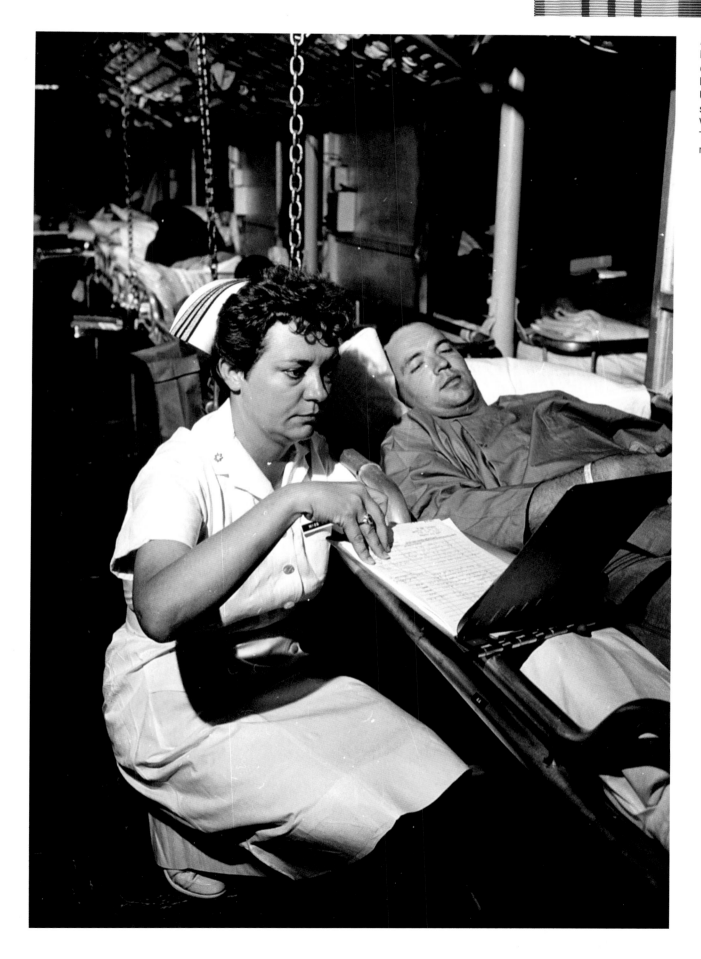

Left: Lieutenant Commander Dorothy Ryan checks the chart of Marine Corporal Roy Hadaway aboard the USS *Repose*, a hospital ship off the coast of South Vietnam on April 22, 1966. There were twenty-nine nurses aboard the ship.

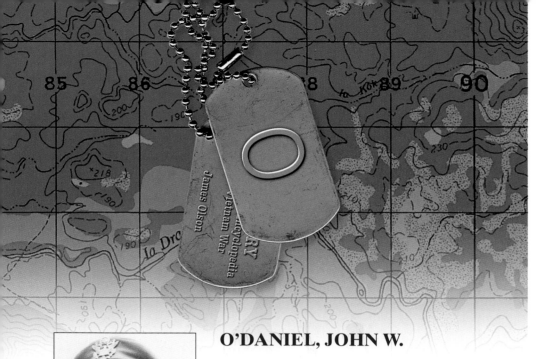

Diem* and for the potential of the South Vietnamese military. After his retirement from the U.S. Army in 1955, he became one of the founders of the American Friends of Vietnam,* a highly effective lobby for American support of the Diem government. DLA

Source: Ronald H. Spector, *Advice and Support: The Early Years, 1941–1960*, 1983.

OFFICE OF CIVIL OPERATIONS

A forerunner of CORDS (Civil Operations and Revolutionary Development Support),* the Office of Civil Operations was established in November 1966 by Ambassador Henry Cabot Lodge Jr.* to pursue the goal of pacification (*see* Rural Reconstruction) in South Vietnam. At that time, pacification fell under the general direction of the embassy in the Republic of Vietnam,* but when CORDS was established in May 1967, that effort passed to the control of Military Assistance Command, Vietnam.*

Sources: Larry E. Cable, *Conflict of Myths: The Development of American Counterinsurgency Doctrine and the Vietnam War*, 1986; Andrew F. Krepinevich Jr., *The Army and Vietnam*, 1986.

101st AIRBORNE DIVISION (AIRMOBILE)

From the very beginning of the conflict to the end of American combat operations in Vietnam, the 101st Airborne Division (Airmobile) was one of the elite U.S.

O'DANIEL, JOHN W.

Lieutenant General John W. O'Daniel was chief of the U.S. Army Military Assistance and Advisory Group* (MAAG), Indochina, from March 1954 to October 1955. "Iron Mike" O'Daniel was a hard-charging combat veteran of both world wars and the Korean War.

In 1953 he was commander of the U.S. Army, Pacific, when the Joint Chiefs of Staff (*see* Chairman, JCS) selected him to head a special mission to Vietnam to assess French needs for military aid. He made a second inspection trip later in 1953 before becoming chief of MAAG in 1954. His initial reports on the French effort in Indochina* were positive. After the French defeat at Dien Bien Phu,* however, he became one of the key American officials in implementing the transfer of South Vietnamese military training and support responsibilities from France* to the United States. While in Vietnam, he developed a high regard for Ngo Dinh

Above: In 1954, General John "Iron Mike" O'Daniel became commander of the Military Assistance and Advisory Group (MAAG), which supervised the transfer of responsibility for training South Vietnamese troops from France to the United States. MAAG was the predecessor to Military Assistance Command, Vietnam (MACV).

Right: Members of the 502d Infantry, 1st Brigade, 101st Airborne Division complete construction of a bunker at Fire Support Base Bastogne, to be used as a field hospital, in April 1968.

military units. The 1st Brigade of the 101st arrived in Vietnam on July 29, 1965, and fought in the II Corps* Tactical Zone. In 1966 the brigade fought in Phu Yen and Kontum provinces. The 1st Brigade became part of Task Force Oregon (see 23d Infantry Division), along with the 3d Brigade of the 25th Infantry Division* and the 196th Light Infantry Brigade,* to fight in Quang Ngai and Quang Tin provinces and allow the U.S. Marines* to move north, closer to the Demilitarized Zone.* On November 18, 1967, the 1st Brigade rejoined the 101st Airborne Division.

The 101st Airborne Division deployed to Vietnam on November 19, 1967. Known as the Screaming Eagles, the 101st had an illustrious history, especially at the Battle of the Bulge in World War II. By 1967 the division was completing its transition from parachutist to airmobile tactics. At first committed to III Corps,* the 101st was moved to Hue* during the Tet Offensive,* and in April and May 1968

the unit ranged widely throughout Thua Thien and Quang Tri provinces. In mid-1968 the 3d Brigade fought around Dak To* and then joined the 25th Infantry Division in defense of Saigon.* It was redeployed to I Corps* in September 1968. The 101st participated in Operation Texas Star* throughout 1970, and in 1971 joined the ARVN (see Army of the Republic of Vietnam) in Operation Jefferson Glenn,* the last American offensive action of the war. Later in 1971 the 101st supported the ARVN in Lam Son 719*—the ill-fated invasion of Laos.* The 101st Airborne Division left Vietnam on March 10, 1972.

Sources: Shelby L. Stanton, *Vietnam Order of Battle*, 1981, and *The Rise and Fall of an American Army: U.S. Ground Forces in Vietnam, 1965–1973*, 1985; Willard Pearson, *The War in the Northern Provinces, 1966–1968*, 1975; John J. Tolson, *Airmobility, 1961–1971*, 1973; Edward F. Murphy, *Dak To: The 173rd Airborne Brigade in South Vietnam's Central Highlands*, 2002.

Below: Soldiers from the 327th Infantry of the 101st Airborne Division, as part of Operation Van Buren, begin to cross a rice field in search of Vietcong troops on January 23, 1966.

199th LIGHT INFANTRY BRIGADE

The 199th Light Infantry Brigade was formed at Fort Benning, Georgia, in 1966, and arrived in South Vietnam in December of that year. The brigade assumed responsibility for Operation Fairfax,* defending the approaches to Saigon,* until late 1967. In December 1967 the brigade undertook Operation Uniontown,* a sweep into War Zone D (see Iron Triangle) near Bien Hoa.* During the Tet Offensive* the brigade defended Bien Hoa airfield together with the Long Binh* post complex and the headquarters of II Field Force, Vietnam.* Elements of the brigade, however, were used to recapture the Pho Tho racetrack in Saigon and, together with other American and South Vietnamese troops, held the area during two days of house-to-house fighting. During most of 1968 the 199th Light Infantry Brigade continued to patrol the area around Bien Hoa in support of a series of joint American-Vietnamese operations known as Operation Toan Thang* (or "Total Victory"). The brigade also supported the invasion of Cambodia (see Operation Binh Tay) in May 1970. The 199th Light Infantry Brigade was withdrawn from South Vietnam in the fall of 1970 and was deactivated at Fort Benning in October. The 199th sustained more than 3,200 casualties during its stay in South Vietnam. RSB III

Sources: Shelby L. Stanton, *Vietnam Order of Battle*, 1981, and *The Rise and Fall of an American Army: U.S. Ground Forces in Vietnam, 1965–1973*, 1985; Robert J. Gouge, *These are My Credentials: The 199th Light Infantry Brigade in the Republic of Vietnam, 1966-1970*, 2004.

Below: During Operation Fairfax in May 1967, soldiers from the 199th Light Infantry Brigade have just completed a search of the village of Long Trung 5 miles northeast of Saigon. A member of Company A climbs a muddy bank after crossing a river on the way to base camp.

196th LIGHT INFANTRY BRIGADE

Raised at Fort Devens, Massachusetts, in 1965, the 196th Light Infantry Brigade arrived in South Vietnam in August 1966. The brigade's first major combat came during Operation Attleboro* in October and November 1966. In the spring of 1967 the brigade was assigned to a divisional task force in the I Corps* Tactical Zone named Task Force Oregon (see 23d Infantry Division). Task Force Oregon became the American Division (see 23d Infantry Division) in September 1967. When the American Division was withdrawn from South Vietnam in 1971, the 196th Light Infantry Brigade was reconstituted as a separate provisional brigade. This provisional brigade was withdrawn from South Vietnam in June 1972. It was the last American combat brigade to leave the country. The 196th Light Infantry Brigade participated in the following operations and battles: Attleboro, Cedar Falls,* Junction City,* Malheur,* Hill 63 (1967), Nhi Ha (1968), Tien Phuoc (1969), and Frederick Hill. During its tour in South Vietnam the 196th Light Infantry Brigade sustained nearly 7,000 casualties. RSB III

Sources: Shelby L. Stanton, *Vietnam Order of Battle*, 1981, and *The Rise and Fall of an American Army: U.S. Ground Forces in Vietnam, 1965–1973*, 1985.

173d AIRBORNE BRIGADE

The 173d Airborne, formed in 1963 and stationed in Okinawa as the Pacific's ready-action strike force, was the first major United States Army* combat unit in Vietnam. The brigade arrived in-country on May 7, 1965. It was supposed to serve in South Vietnam only temporarily until a brigade of the 101st Airborne* could be deployed from the United States, but that was changed by the brigade's completion of early combat operations. Aside from periodic duty in III Corps,* the 173d operated primarily in northern II Corps.* The 2d Battalion of the 173d conducted the only major U.S. airborne assault of the war in III Corps in 1967 during Operation Junction City.* Unlike most infantry brigades, which have three battalions, the 173d had only two. Occasionally it was augmented with a "round out"

Major Battles/Operations

1966

28 Nov - 5 Jan, 1967	Canary
17 Dec - 2 Feb, 1967	Uniontown I

1967

12 Jan - 14 Dec	Fairfax/Rang Dong
1 Mar - 1 May	Enterprise
17 Nov - 17 Dec	Strike
17 Dec - 17 Feb, 1968	Manchester

1968

13 Jan - 23 Jan	Altoona
31 Jan - 18 Feb	Tet Offensive/ Battle of Saigon
7 Mar - 16 Mar	Valley Forge
8 Mar - 7 Apr	Wilderness
16 Mar - 28 Mar	Uniontown II/ Box Springs
30 Mar - 31 Jan, 1969	Haverford
1 Jun - 16 Feb, 1969	Toan Thang/ Complete Victory

1969

4 Feb - 12 Feb	Strangler I
13 Feb - 16 Feb	Strangler II
12 Mar - 14 Mar	LuLu
24 Nov - 28 Nov	Ransom Raider

1970

6 May - 27 Jun	Cambodian Invasion
1 Jul - 15 Oct	Keystone Robin
15 Oct	Inactivated at Fort Benning

Order of Battle/Division Base Camp

199th LIB Hq. — Long Binh/Cat Lai, Bien Hoa, Long Binh/ Duc Hoa, Xuan Loc, Long Binh/Gia Ray

Infantry

2nd Bn. 3rd Infantry	3rd Bn. 7th Infantry
4th Bn. 12th Infantry	5th Bn. 12th Infantry

Artillery
2nd Bn. 40th Artillery

Support

Troop D, 17th Cavalry	Co. F 51st Inf (LRRP)
Co. M, 75th Infantry Rangers	7th Support Bn.
87th Engineer Company	313th Signal Company
152nd Military Police Platoon	503rd Chemical Det.

179th Military Intelligence Det.
44th Military History Det.
49th Scout Dog Detachment
40th Public Information Det.
856th Army Security Agency Det.

Attached
3rd Squadron, 11th Armored Cavalry

199th Light Infantry Brigade
Vietnam
1966 - 1970

Left: Troops from the 4th Battalion of the 173d Airborne Brigade load wounded comrades aboard a UH-1D after assaulting Hill 875 15 miles southwest of Dak To in the Central Highlands on November 23, 1967.

Below: Specialist 4 Archie L. Gaffee (left) and Specialist 4 Robert Crane (right) plot a fire mission as Sergeant Alfred Bohannon (center) looks on. It is May 5, 1965, and the 173d Airborne Brigade has arrived in South Vietnam.

Right: Troops from the 173d Airborne Division patroling War Zone D of South Vietnam in 1965.

Below: A soldier from the 17th Cavalry, 173d Airborne Brigade, fires an M60 into enemy positions near Landing Zone English in South Vietnam, February 1969.

battalion, such as the 1st Battalion of the Royal Australian Regiment. In 1969 the brigade's battalions were mated with the 22d and 24th ARVN (see Army of the Republic of Vietnam) infantry divisions for joint operations.

The 173d was affectionately known as the Sky Soldiers and as the Herd or Two Shades of Soul because of its camaraderie and excellent relations between black and white troops. It won a Presidential Unit Citation in 1967 for taking the infamous Hill 875 from the North Vietnamese Army* on Thanksgiving Day in 1967 just outside of Dak To.* Establishing itself quickly as a battle-seasoned unit with aggressive leadership, the 173d took great pride in its abilities. It participated in many operations, including Marauder, Crimp, Attleboro,* Hawthorne,* Cedar Falls,* Junction City, Greeley, and MacArthur.* It also paid for its aggressiveness. The 173d Airborne Brigade sustained more casualties in its seven years in Vietnam than did the entire divisions of either the 82d* or 101st Airborne during World War II. The 173d Airborne Brigade left Vietnam on August 25, 1971. SF

Sources: Shelby L. Stanton, *Vietnam Order of Battle*, 1981, and *The Rise and Fall of an American Army: U.S. Ground Forces in Vietnam, 1965–1973*, 1985; Harry G. Summers Jr., *Vietnam War Almanac*, 1985; Edward Murphy, *Dak To: The 173rd Airborne Brigade in South Vietnam's Central Highlands*, 2002.

ONE TO COUNT CADENCE

One to Count Cadence is the title of James Crumley's 1969 Vietnam War novel. The story centers on a 10-man communications detachment stationed first at Clark Air Base in the Philippines* and then in Vietnam during the early stages of the war. A Sergeant "Slag" Krummel is the narrator, and his foil is Joe Morning, a classic, self-destructive loser. The novel exposes the gratuitous violence of military life—bars, brothels, fights, and profanity—as well as the futility of the war in Vietnam. The novel concludes with the communications team, decimated by combat in Vietnam, returning to the Philippines, where Morning joins the Huk rebellion.

Sources: James Crumley, *One to Count Cadence*, 1969; Philip D. Beidler, *American Literature and the Experience of Vietnam*, 1982.

ONE VERY HOT DAY

One Very Hot Day is the title of David Halberstam's* 1967 Vietnam War novel. Written at an early stage of American involvement in the escalated war, *One Very Hot Day* traces three characters—the American captain Beaupre, the Vietnamese lieutenant Thuong, and the black American ranger captain Redfern—on one day in the hot, wet, sticky, despair-ridden atmosphere of the Vietnam War. When one of Beaupre's men, a Lieutenant Anderson, dies in an ambush, Beaupre is unable to find any reason for the death, any meaning to a dead American in some nowhere-place called Ap Than Thoi. A likable young American soldier had died for nothing on a hot day in the middle of nowhere. Such is the theme of *One Very Hot Day*.

Sources: Philip D. Beidler, *American Literature and the Experience of Vietnam*, 1982; David Halberstam, *One Very Hot Day*, 1967.

OPERATION ABILENE

Operation Abilene was a sweep of Phuoc Tuy Province mounted by elements of the 1st Infantry Division* in April 1966. Such sweeps were intended to put pressure on the Vietcong* and demonstrate the U.S. Army's* willingness to take the offensive into the jungle. RSB III

Source: Shelby L. Stanton, *The Rise and Fall of an American Army: U.S. Ground Forces in Vietnam, 1965–1973*, 1985.

OPERATION ALA MOANA

Operation Ala Moana was the code name for the combat operations of the 25th Infantry Division* in December 1966. General William Westmoreland* wanted to keep the Vietcong* away from major rice-producing areas near Saigon* and in the Ho Bo Woods in III Corps.* Operation Ala Moana was launched on December 1, 1966, and continued into 1967, although most of the combat action shifted then to Hau Nghia Province. Operation Ala Moana was a preliminary to Operation Cedar Falls.*

Source: Shelby L. Stanton, *The Rise and Fall of an American Army: U.S. Ground Forces in Vietnam, 1965–1973*, 1985.

OPERATION APACHE SNOW

Operation Apache Snow was the code name for the combat activities of the 9th Marine Regiment and elements of the 101st Airborne (Airmobile) Division* in Thua Thien Province of I Corps* between May 10 and June 7, 1969. The most important and controversial phase of Operation Apache Snow was the Battle of Ap Bia, or Hamburger Hill.

Source: Shelby L. Stanton, *The Rise and Fall of an American Army: U.S. Ground Forces in Vietnam, 1965–1973*, 1985.

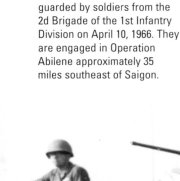

Below: A Vietcong prisoner is guarded by soldiers from the 2d Brigade of the 1st Infantry Division on April 10, 1966. They are engaged in Operation Abilene approximately 35 miles southeast of Saigon.

OPERATION ATLAS WEDGE

Operation Atlas Wedge was the code name for the engagement between Colonel George S. Patton's 11th Armored Cavalry* and elements of the North Vietnamese Army* (NVA) 7th Division in the abandoned Michelin rubber plantation near Saigon* between March 17 and 26, 1969. The 11th Armored Cavalry destroyed huge bunkers in the area and fought intense battles with the North Vietnamese before the NVA withdrawal.

Source: Shelby L. Stanton, *The Rise and Fall of an American Army: U.S. Ground Forces in Vietnam, 1965–1973*, 1985.

OPERATION ATTLEBORO

Operation Attleboro, conducted in War Zone C* between September 14 and November 24, 1966, was the first field test of the U.S. Army's doctrine of "search and destroy."* Initiated by the 196th Light Infantry Brigade,* Operation Attleboro had the objective of discovering the location(s) of the Vietcong* or North Vietnamese base areas, and forcing the enemy to fight. There was no important contact in this operation until October 19, when the brigade discovered a major base area and severe fighting erupted. By November 6 the American units involved included (in addition to the 196th Light Infantry Brigade) the 1st and 2d battalions of the 27th Infantry Regiment (25th Infantry Division),* the 173d Airborne Brigade,* and two brigades of the 1st Infantry Division.* By November 15 the 9th Vietcong Division was able to successfully disengage. The U.S. Army* reported 1,106 enemy casualties. RSB III

Sources: Shelby L. Stanton, *The Rise and Fall of an American Army: U.S. Ground Forces in Vietnam, 1965–1973*, 1985; S.L.A. Marshall, *Ambush: The Battle of Dau Tieng, Also Called the Battle of Dong Ming Chau, War Zone C, Operation Attleboro, and Other Deadfalls in South Vietnam*, 1969.

OPERATION BABYLIFT

With the imminent takeover of South Vietnam by Communist forces in 1975, President Gerald R. Ford* announced that the United States would evacuate some 2,000 Vietnamese orphans to the United States. At a press conference in San Diego on April 3, 1975, he commented: "I have directed … that C-5A aircraft and other aircraft especially equipped to care for these orphans during the flight be sent to Saigon. I expect these flights to begin within the next 36 to 48 hours. These orphans will be flown to Travis Air Force Base in California, and other bases on the West Coast, and cared for in those locations."

Hours after the presidential statement, the dramatic humanitarian airlift, named Operation Babylift, began. On

April 4, 1975, the first Babylift aircraft, a Military Airlift Command* C-5 en route from Clark Air Base, the Philippines,* landed at Tan Son Nhut Air Base* in Saigon;* unloaded its military cargo; and was on its way back to the Philippines with 314 persons on board. Unfortunately, what started out as a routine flight ended in tragedy when the aircraft crashed approximately fourteen minutes after takeoff. Of the 314 aboard, 138 were killed. It was a tragic beginning that fortunately was not repeated in other flights.

Although Babylift got off to a bad start, the operation gathered momentum thereafter and was conducted without further mishap. By noon the next day, five C-141s* and

Above: Sergeant Arnold S. Owens of Battery A, 2d Battalion, 33d Artillery stands atop ammunition boxes and directs the fire of a 105mm howitzer during Operation Attleboro on November 18, 1966.

other aircraft had moved 141 orphans and 137 evacuees and escorts from Saigon to Clark Air Base. During subsequent days the flow of aircraft to and from Saigon continued at a steady pace as Vietnamese refugees* were transported to homes in the United States. Between April 5 and May 9, 1975, Operation Babylift aircraft evacuated 2,678 Vietnamese and Cambodian orphans to the homes of sponsors in the United States. RDL

Sources: "Global Humanitarian Airlift," Military Airlift Command Fact Sheet, February 1983; Dick J. Burkard, *Military Airlift Command: Historical Handbook, 1941–1984*, 1984.

OPERATION BARREL ROLL

Operation Barrel Roll was the code name given to American air operations over northern Laos* from December 1964 to February 1973. The aircraft involved included both United States Navy* and Air Force* fighters,* as well as Air Force bombers (including B-52s*) and fixed-wing gunships.* For political reasons, the U.S. government did not inform the public of these operations until U.S. aircraft were lost, at which time it was announced that the Americans were flying escort missions at the request of the Royal Laotian government. RSB III

Sources: John S. Bowman, ed., *The Vietnam War: An Almanac*, 1985; R. Frank Futrell et al., *Aces and Aerial Victories: The United States Air Force in Southeast Asia*, 1976.

OPERATION BEAU CHARGER

See Project Practice Nine

OPERATION BINH TAY

Operation Binh Tay was the code name for combined U.S.-ARVN (*see* Army of the Republic of Vietnam) combat activities in Cambodia* in 1970. On May 6, 1970, as part of the Cambodian "incursion," the 4th Infantry Division* combined with the 49th ARVN Regiment in attacking Vietcong* and North Vietnamese Army* positions in Cambodia. On May 16, 1970, the 4th Infantry Division turned Binh Tay completely over to ARVN troops, which continued the operation until mid-June without making significant enemy contact.

Sources: Shelby L. Stanton, *The Rise and Fall of an American Army: U.S. Ground Forces in Vietnam, 1965–1973*, 1985; William Shawcross, *Sideshow: Kissinger, Nixon, and the Destruction of Cambodia*, 1979; Tom Carhart, *Battles and Campaigns in Vietnam*, 1984.

OPERATION BLUE LIGHT

See C-141 Starlifter

OPERATION BOLO

Operation Bolo was the code name given to the United States Air Force* effort to eliminate North Vietnamese MiG-21 strength. Because American aircraft were prohibited from attacking the airfields from which the MiGs operated (until April 1967), it was necessary to lure the MiGs into the air. F-4C aircraft were equipped with F-105* electronic pods in an effort to confuse North Vietnamese radar. The operation was mounted on January 2, 1967, from Ubon Air Base in Thailand.* Seven MiG-21s were shot down and the remainder temporarily withdrawn from action. No American aircraft were lost. RSB III

Source: R. Frank Futrell et al., *Aces and Aerial Victories: The United States Air Force in Southeast Asia*, 1976.

OPERATION BRAVO

Late in October 1963, as the political support for his regime was rapidly disappearing, Ngo Dinh Diem* hatched an elaborate plot to shore up his crumbling position. Known as Operations Bravo I and Bravo II, the plan involved staging a fake revolt in Saigon,* with Diem and his brother Ngo Dinh Nhu* fleeing to the countryside. The rebels would conduct demonstrations, orchestrate "revolutionary" broadcasts from the Saigon radio station, and even assassinate several local officials. All this, known as Bravo I, would continue for several days. Bravo II would then go into effect, with Diem and Nhu marching back into Saigon and crushing the "rebellion," proving that only they were capable of keeping the Republic of Vietnam* out of Communist hands. Although both Diem and Nhu thought that the operation was under way early in November, military officials responsible for conducting Operations Bravo I and II were actually plotting, with tacit American support, a coup d'etat against the regime. The coup was successful, and Ngo Dinh Diem and Ngo Dinh Nhu were assassinated. Operations Bravo I and II had failed.

Sources: Stanley Karnow, *Vietnam: A History*, 1983; Denis Warner, *The Last Confucian*, 1963; Tran Van Don, *Our Endless War*, 1972.

OPERATION BUFFALO

Operation Buffalo was the code name for a brief combat action by elements of the 3d Marine Division* near the Demilitarized Zone* in I Corps.* The operation lasted between July 2 and July 14, 1967, and resulted in just over 700 enemy casualties.

Sources: Shelby L. Stanton, *Vietnam Order of Battle*, 1981; Willard Pearson, *The War in the Northern Provinces, 1966–1968*, 1975.

OPERATION CEDAR FALLS

A major "search and destroy"* effort by U.S. troops in January 1967, Operation Cedar Falls, named after the hometown of an early Vietnam War recipient of the Medal of Honor (posthumously), was aimed at the Iron Triangle,* located only 20 miles northwest of the outskirts of Saigon.* A 60-square-mile area of rice paddies, dense jungle, rubber plantations, and an extremely sophisticated complex of underground tunnels, the Iron Triangle had been controlled by the Vietcong* (VC) since the late 1950s and was characterized as a "dagger pointed at the heart of Saigon." Destruction of the VC infrastructure in the Iron Triangle was the basic military objective of Cedar Falls. The fundamental plan of the operation was the "hammer and anvil" tactic, in which a blocking force of American troops would be landed by helicopter at one edge of the area and then a second force (the "hammer") would drive the enemy against this "anvil." In order for this tactic to work, the entire area had first to be cleared of innocent civilians so that a free-fire zone* could be created. In this way, *any* Vietnamese in the area would be assumed to be Vietcong.

Operation Cedar Falls began on January 8, 1967, with the forced evacuation and total destruction of Ben Suc,* an Iron Triangle village that was a haven for VC. The next phase was saturation bombing and artillery fire, after which the infantry swept the Iron Triangle using the hammer-and-anvil tactic. The tunnel complex was a particular target, and approximately 500 tunnels, running for some twelve miles underground, were discovered and destroyed. Operation Cedar Falls lasted eighteen days and was declared a success. The VC lost 775 veteran soldiers, while American losses

Above: During Operation Buffalo on July 10, 1967, 1 mile northeast of Con Thien in South Vietnam, tanks from the 3d Tank Battalion and troops from K Company of the 3d Battalion, 9th Marines prepare to coordinate their assault activities.

Right: Soldiers from the 1st Squadron of the 4th Cavalry, using flame throwers on "Zippo Track" armored personnel carriers, incinerate Vietcong positions during Operation Cedar Falls in the Iron Triangle of South Vietnam. The M113 tanks were nicknamed Zippo because of their tendency to combust when hit.

Below: A CH-47 helicopter hovers in the Iron Triangle of South Vietnam unloading troops from the 3d Platoon, Company C, 1st Engineering Battalion, 1st Infantry Division on January 8, 1967. The soldiers are about to clear a landing zone with chain saws and explosives to accommodate resupply helicopters during Operation Cedar Falls.

were approximately 250. The enemy bastion was seized, and the Vietcong were eliminated from the Iron Triangle. The major allied units involved in the operation were the 1st* and 25th* Infantry divisions,* the 173d Airborne Brigade,* the 11th Armored Cavalry,* and several ARVN units (*see* Army of the Republic of Vietnam). Because basic strategy in the conflict did not include occupation of captured territory, however, allied troops did not remain in the Iron Triangle after Cedar Falls. Given the enemy's tenacity and resiliency, within six months the Vietcong had returned in strength, while the local inhabitants were more hostile and resentful of the allies; they had also become more supportive of the enemy than before the occupation. The Iron Triangle became a major staging area for the Tet Offensive* attacks on Saigon beginning on January 31, 1968, illustrating the frustration that characterized American military successes throughout the war: to defeat the enemy thoroughly only to find him reappearing nonetheless sometime after the engagement. STT

Sources: Jonathan Schell, *The Village of Ben Suc,* 1967; Bernard William Rogers, *Cedar Falls–Junction City: A Turning Point,* 1974.

OPERATION CHAOS

See Central Intelligence Agency

Left: A helicopter delivers B Company of the 2d Battalion, 8th Cavalry, 1st Air Cavalry Division during Operation Delaware, an assault on North Vietnamese forces in the A Shau Valley of South Vietnam in April 1968.

OPERATION COMMANDO HUNT

Commando Hunt was the code name for combined United States Navy,* Marine,* and Air Force* air assaults on infiltration* routes along the Ho Chi Minh Trail* in the Laotian panhandle. The air strikes began in 1968 and continued until January 1973, but they had little or no effect on the volume of materiel and the number of troops brought into South Vietnam by the North Vietnamese.

Sources: Tom Carhart, *Battles and Campaigns in Vietnam*, 1984; John Morrocco, *The Vietnam Experience. Rain of Fire: Air War, 1969–1973*, 1985.

OPERATION DEFIANT STAND

Operation Defiant Stand was the code name for a combined U.S. Navy,* U.S. Marine Corps,* Korean marines, and ARVN (*see* Army of the Republic of Vietnam) amphibious assault on Barrier Island south of Da Nang.* The Vietcong* responded with only light resistance when the landing force swept across the island on September 7, 1969.

Source: Shelby L. Stanton, *The Rise and Fall of an American Army: U.S. Ground Forces in Vietnam, 1965–1973*, 1985.

OPERATION DELAWARE

Operation Delaware was the code name for a combined U.S. Army*–ARVN (*see* Army of the Republic of Vietnam) combat operation in the A Shau Valley.* The ARVN portion of the operation was dubbed Operation Lam Son 216. Elements of the 1st Cavalry Division (Airmobile),* 101st Airborne Division (Airmobile),* the 196th Light Infantry Brigade,* the ARVN 1st Division, and the ARVN Airborne Task Force Bravo participated in the operation, which took place between April 19 and May 17, 1968. Although the operation resulted in nearly 900 enemy casualties, American forces sustained heavy helicopter losses and never really dealt a deathblow to Vietcong* and North Vietnamese Army* forces in the A Shau Valley.

Sources: Shelby L. Stanton, *Vietnam Order of Battle*, 1981, and *The Rise and Fall of an American Army: U.S. Ground Forces in Vietnam, 1965–1973*, 1985; Willard Pearson, *The War in the Northern Provinces, 1966–1968*, 1975.

OPERATION DEWEY CANYON

Operation Dewey Canyon was the code name for the combat activities of the 9th Marine Regiment in I Corps* between January 22 and March 18, 1969. The Marine objective was to cut a North Vietnamese Army* (NVA) supply route that came into Vietnam from Laos* and moved through the Da Krong Valley and the A Shau Valley.* During the course of Operation Dewey Canyon, Marines flew more than 13,000 sorties* in air support of the campaign, and the 9th Marine Regiment discovered more than 500 tons of NVA weapons and ammunition, along with inflicting more than 1,335 casualties on the North Vietnamese.

Sources: Shelby L. Stanton, *Vietnam Order of Battle*, 1981, and *The Rise and Fall of an American Army: U.S. Ground Forces in Vietnam, 1965–1973*, 1985; Keith William Nolan, *Into Laos. The Story of Dewey Canyon II/Lam Son 719*, 1986.

OPERATION DOUBLE EAGLE

Operation Double Eagle was launched by U.S. Marines* in I Corps* on January 28, 1966. The 4th Marines and the 7th Marines, two regiments garrisoned at Chu Lai in Quang Tin Province, joined the 2d ARVN Division (*see* Army of the Republic of Vietnam) to drive south into Quang Ngai Province, where they hoped to trap a large contingent of Vietcong*–North Vietnamese Army* (NVA) troops between them and the U.S. Army 1st Cavalry Division* and 22d ARVN Division's operations in Binh Dinh Province. The Marines made an amphibious assault at Thach Tru, a coastal point approximately twenty miles south of Quang Ngai, and then drove inland. For the next five weeks, the Marines searched in vain for significant Vietcong/NVA contacts, encountering little more than occasional sniper fire. Early in March, the Marines called off Operation Double Eagle.

Sources: Shelby L. Stanton, *The Rise and Fall of an American Army: U.S. Ground Forces in Vietnam, 1965–1973*, 1985; Willard Pearson, *The War in the Northern Provinces, 1966–1968*, 1975; Jack Shulimson, *U.S. Marines in Vietnam: An Expanding War 1966*, 1982.

OPERATION EAGLE PULL

Operation Eagle Pull was the code name for the U.S. effort to evacuate American diplomatic and military officials from Cambodia* in 1975. With the Khmer Rouge* surrounding and invading Phnom Penh, the capital city

Right: During Operation Double Eagle in January 1966, helicopters from the Marine Aircraft Group (MAG) 36 deliver Marine riflemen to a landing zone approximately 35 miles south of Chu Lai in South Vietnam. The Marines are heading off on a search-and-destroy mission.

of Cambodia, naval helicopters from the Seventh Fleet,* leaving from ships in the South China Sea, landed on the embassy grounds and removed 276 people, most of them Cambodian and American embassy employees and their families.

Sources: Arnold R. Isaacs, *Without Honor: Defeat in Vietnam and Cambodia*, 1983; William Shawcross, *Sideshow: Kissinger, Nixon, and the Destruction of Cambodia*, 1979.

Left: On April 14, 1975, in the South China Sea, as Khmer Rouge troops overrun the capital city of Phnom Penh, Cambodia, a Navy HC-3 helicopter makes a transfer from the supply ship USS *Mars* to the USS *Hancock*, which has been participating in Operation Eagle Pull.

OPERATION EL PASO

Operation El Paso was the code name for combat activities of the U.S. 1st Infantry Division* and the ARVN (*see* Army of the Republic of Vietnam) 5th Infantry Division in Binh Long Province of III Corps.* Early in May 1966, American intelligence officers received news of an impending attack by the Vietcong* (VC) 9th Division on the Special Forces* base at Loc Ninh. Operation El Paso I was designed to locate the VC 9th Division, but it was largely a fruitless endeavor. So on June 2, 1966, the 1st Division went deep into War Zone C* in search of the Vietcong. By that time Military Assistance Command, Vietnam* (MACV) hoped that the mission would prevent the Vietcong from conduct-

Below: During Operation Eagle Pull on April 12, 1975, Marines from F Company, 2d Battalion, 4th Marines run to embark CH-53 helicopters landing on a soccer field in Phnom Penh, Cambodia. The Marines are providing security for the evacuation of U.S. employees and diplomatic personnel from Cambodia. The helicopters have come from the USS *Hancock*.

ing offensive operations during the monsoon season. Operation El Paso II ended on July 13, 1966, by which time MACV claimed to have killed 855 Vietcong.

Source: Shelby L. Stanton, *The Rise and Fall of an American Army: U.S. Ground Forces in Vietnam, 1965–1973*, 1985.

OPERATION ENHANCE PLUS

Operation Enhance Plus was the code name for a crash program late in 1972 to transfer huge volumes of military equipment to the South Vietnamese. In October 1972, when it became apparent that a negotiated settlement with the Vietcong* and North Vietnamese was possible, Secretary of State Henry Kissinger* had the Pentagon launch Operation

Enhance Plus, a six-week program to deliver $2 billion in military equipment, as well as control over American military bases in South Vietnam, to the government of Nguyen Van Thieu.* Kissinger also asked Thieu to take military control of as much territory in South Vietnam as possible, all of this based on the premise that U.S. military influence there would shortly be discontinued. Operation Enhance Plus supervised the equipment transfer. By the end of 1972, with goods shipped in from the United States, Taiwan (*see* Chiang Kai-shek), South Korea,* and the Philippines,* South Vietnam had acquired one of the largest aircraft and naval armadas in the world.

Sources: Stanley Karnow, *Vietnam: A History*, 1983; Nguyen Duy Hinh, *Vietnamization and the Cease-Fire*, 1980; Henry Kissinger, *Years of Upheaval*, 1982.

Right: Handlers from the 49th Scout Dog Platoon search a home in the village of Long Trung for Vietcong during Operation Fairfax in May 1967. Long Trung is located approximately 5 miles northeast of Saigon. The 49th Scout Dog Platoon is part of the 199th Light Infantry Brigade.

OPERATION ENTERPRISE

Operation Enterprise was the code name for combined U.S.-ARVN (*see* Army of the Republic of Vietnam) military activities in Long An Province in 1967 and 1968. Launched on February 13, 1967, Operation Enterprise was designed to clear the Vietcong* (VC) out of Long An Province. The 9th Infantry Division,* several ARVN elements, and groups of Regional Forces* and Popular Forces* participated in the operation, which continued until March 11, 1968. Although Military Assistance Command, Vietnam* claimed more than 2,000 VC casualties, the campaign had not achieved its objective of clearing the VC out of Long An Province. They remained popular in provincial villages and retained a powerful presence throughout the area, even after the losses that the Tet Offensive* had brought on them.

Sources: Shelby L. Stanton, *Vietnam Order of Battle*, 1981, and *The Rise and Fall of an American Army: U.S. Ground Forces in Vietnam, 1965–1973*, 1985.

OPERATION FAIRFAX

Operation Fairfax was the code name given to combined United States Army* and ARVN (*see* Army of the Republic of Vietnam) combat operations outside Saigon* in 1967. It was an early experiment in Vietnamization,* in which ARVN forces were supposed to gradually assume responsibility for the campaign. The 199th Light Infantry Brigade* joined the 5th ARVN Ranger Group, and both units patrolled the region surrounding Saigon. The main objective of Operation Fairfax was to enable the South Vietnamese to assume responsibility for defending Saigon. The operation began in January 1967, and by November ARVN troops had assumed primary responsibility for the combat patrols. The Tet Offensive* in January 1968, however, demonstrated clearly that ARVN troops had not achieved the capability of defending the country's capital city against Vietcong* attack.

Source: Shelby L. Stanton, *The Rise and Fall of an American Army: U.S. Ground Forces in Vietnam, 1965–1973*, 1985.

OPERATION FARMGATE

In April 1961 the United States Air Force* created the 4400th Combat Crew Training Squadron, also called Jungle Jim, and stationed it at Elgin Air Force Base in Florida. In October 1961 half of the 4400th Combat Squadron received a new code name—Farmgate—and were deployed to an old French air base at Bien Hoa, just fifteen miles northeast of Saigon.* Farmgate trained Vietnamese pilots to fly A-1H

Skyraiders,* dropped propaganda leaflets over Vietcong* territory, and supplied Vietnamese ranger camps and Civilian Irregular Defense Group* camps along the Laotian and Cambodian borders. At first, Farmgate pilots provided only covert support to Vietnamese operations; they had to fly with Vietnamese copilots in Vietnamese aircraft.

The American pilots chafed under their restrictions, and by 1964 almost ninety of them were flying combat missions for South Vietnam. When Captain Edwin G. Shank was shot down and killed while piloting a T-28 aircraft in May 1964, the press got wind of the combat operations and criticized the Department of Defense. Operation Farmgate continued after the press revelations, but Secretary of Defense Robert McNamara* strictly confined its duties to training missions.

Source: John Morrocco, *The Vietnam Experience. Thunder from Above: Air War, 1941–1968*, 1985.

OPERATION FRANCIS MARION

Operation Francis Marion was the code name for operations by the 4th Infantry Division* in the Ia Drang Valley* from April to October 1967. The 4th Infantry Division had the responsibility of patrolling the Cambodian border to prevent North Vietnamese forces from pushing into the Central Highlands.* During Operation Francis Marion elements of the 4th Infantry Division fought in eight battles and numerous smaller skirmishes. The heaviest fighting took place in May, June, and July. On May 18, Company B of the 1st Battalion, 8th Infantry, lost twenty-nine killed and thirty-one wounded in an ambush; and over a two-day period from May 20 to 22, the 1st Battalion, 8th Infantry, as well as the 3d Battalion, 12th Infantry, were subjected to a series of fierce assaults by North Vietnamese regulars. In October 1967 Operation Francis Marion was incorporated into Operation Greeley, and the combined operations were renamed Operation MacArthur.* RSB III

Source: Shelby L. Stanton, *The Rise and Fall of an American Army: U.S. Ground Forces in Vietnam, 1965–1973*, 1985.

OPERATION FREEDOM DEAL

See Operation Menu

OPERATION FREQUENT WIND

Operation Frequent Wind was the code name for the U.S. Navy's* evacuation of American personnel and Vietnamese

Right: At the end of April 1975, as North Vietnamese troops overrun Saigon, the United States implements Operation Frequent Wind to evacuate U.S. personnel and South Vietnamese civilians. CH-53 helicopters deliver employees and refugees to the USS *Hancock*.

civilians from Saigon* in April 1975. The U.S. aircraft carriers *Enterprise* and *Coral Sea* supplied the necessary air cover, and Operation Frequent Wind commenced on the morning of April 29, 1975. The two primary evacuation locations were Tan Son Nhut Air Base* and the U.S. Embassy in Saigon. More than 7,100 American and South Vietnamese military and civilian personnel were helicoptered out of Saigon to ships of Task Force 76 of the Seventh Fleet.* The Military Sealift Command* and ships of the South Vietnamese Navy,* along with hundreds of sampans and junks, also ferried thousands of Vietnamese civilians and military personnel out of South Vietnam. When Operation Frequent Wind was over, more than 80,000 people had been evacuated from South Vietnam and taken to the Philippines* and Guam.

Sources: Thomas G. Tobin et al., *Last Flight from Saigon*, 1978; Edward J. Marolda and G. Wesley Pryce III, *A Short History of the United States Navy and the Southeast Asian Conflict, 1950–1975*, 1984.

OPERATION GAME WARDEN

Launched in December 1965, Operation Game Warden was the code name of the United States Navy* program to patrol approximately 3,000 miles of rivers and canals in South Vietnam, especially in the Mekong Delta,* to prevent the Vietcong* and North Vietnamese from moving personnel and materiel along the inland waterways. Task Force 116 of the U.S. Navy, also known as the Riverine Assault Force (*see* Mobile Riverine Force), conducted the operation. The task force used air-cushion vehicles,* helicopters, minesweepers, fiberglass boats, and LST landing ships to attack the Vietcong and North Vietnamese on the rivers and streams of South Vietnam.

Sources: William B. Fulton, *Riverine Operations, 1966–1969*, 1973; Victor Croizat, *The Brown Water Navy: The River and Coastal War in Indochina and Vietnam, 1948–1972*, 1984.

OPERATION GREELEY

See Operation MacArthur

OPERATION HARVEST MOON

Operation Harvest Moon was the code name for a joint U.S. Marine* and ARVN (*see* Army for the Republic of Vietnam) operation intended to trap the Vietcong* in the Phuoc Ha Valley in December 1965. The operation began on December 8 when the 11th ARVN Ranger Battalion and the 1st Battalion of the 5th ARVN Regiment were ambushed and overrun by the Vietcong. A Marine counterattack began on December 9, encountering fierce resistance and forcing the deployment of eventually three Marine battalions. From December 12 to 14, B-52* strikes were made in support of the ground effort, and follow-up ground forces encountered little immediate resistance, although the 2d Battalion of the 7th Marines was ambushed on December 18 and suffered heavy casualties before a

combination of artillery and close air support forced the Vietcong to disengage. RSB III

Sources: Shelby L. Stanton, *The Rise and Fall of an American Army: U.S. Ground Forces in Vietnam, 1965–1973*, 1985; Jack Shulimson and Charles M. Johnson, *U.S. Marines in Vietnam: The Landing and the Buildup 1965*, 1978.

OPERATION HASTINGS

Operation Hastings was the code name for a grueling battle between a joint U.S. Marine*–South Vietnamese force and the 324B North Vietnamese regular division in July 1966. Six Marine battalions and five ARVN battalions (*see* Army of the Republic of Vietnam) were ultimately committed to the struggle, which began on July 7. The most intensive fighting took place on July 28 in the Song Ngan Valley, which the Marines had nicknamed Helicopter Valley* after a number of helicopters were either shot down or crashed there. Operation Hastings was a typical Marine operation of 1966, in which the Marines attempted

Left: Major General Lewis Walt discusses elements of Operation Harvest Moon with the commanding officer of E Company, 2d Battalion, 7th Marines on December 9, 1965. Operation Harvest Moon consisted of ARVN and U.S. Marines working jointly to isolate, trap, and annihilate Vietcong troops in the Phuoc Ha Valley of South Vietnam.

Right: During Operation Hastings in late July 1965, Marines encountered heavy fire in a landing zone. Troops from I Company, 3d Battalion, load wounded comrades onto a helicopter for medical evacuation from Song Ngan Valley in I Corps.

to defend the I Corps* Tactical Zone by attacking any large-scale enemy troop concentration they discovered, using helicopter mobility to bring in large numbers of troops quickly. Although some of the Marine encounters are labeled as distinct operations, the fighting was more or less continuous. Operation Hastings officially ended on August 3, but was immediately succeeded by Operation Prairie.* RSB III

Sources: Shelby L. Stanton, *The Rise and Fall of an American Army: U.S. Ground Forces in Vietnam, 1965–1973*, 1985; Willard Pearson, *The War in the Northern Provinces, 1966–1968*, 1975; S.L.A. Marshall, *Battles in the Monsoon: Campaigning in the Central Highlands, South Vietnam, Summer 1966*, 1966.

surrounded by the 24th NVA Regiment (*see* North Vietnamese Army), Operation Hawthorne was launched on June 2, 1966, and concluded on June 20, 1966. Along with the 1st Battalion of the 42d ARVN Regiment and the 21st ARVN Ranger Battalion (*see* Army of the Republic of Vietnam), the 1st Brigade succeeded in reaching the outpost and withdrawing the isolated troops. More than 460 air strikes, including 36 B-52* sorties,* were called in on NVA troops. On June 20, 1966, the NVA 24th Regiment withdrew from the area, having sustained approximately 530 casualties.

Sources: Shelby L. Stanton, *Vietnam Order of Battle*, 1981, and *The Rise and Fall of an American Army: U.S. Ground Forces in Vietnam, 1965–1973*, 1985; S.L.A. Marshall, *Battles in the Monsoon: Campaigning in the Central Highlands, South Vietnam, Summer 1966*, 1966.

OPERATION HAWTHORNE

Operation Hawthorne was the code name for combat activities of the 1st Brigade of the 101st Airborne Division* in Kontum Province during June 1966. Designed to rescue the Tou Morong Regional Force, which was

OPERATION HICKORY

See Project Practice Nine

Left: During Operation Hickory in May 1967, Marine infantrymen and tanks of the 2d Battalion of the 26th Marines move through flatlands in the Demilitarized Zone north of I Corps in search of Vietcong troops and North Vietnamese regulars.

Below: On February 14, 1973, U.S. aircraft brought home the first of the U.S. prisoners of war from North Vietnam. The first group included U.S. Navy and U.S. Air Force personnel. Two POW airmen smile at Hickam Air Force Base in Honolulu, Hawaii, where they landed temporarily before flying on to the mainland.

OPERATION HOMECOMING

On January 27, 1973, Henry Kissinger,* assistant to the president for national security affairs, concluded a cease-fire with representatives of North Vietnam that provided for the withdrawal of American military forces from South Vietnam. Part of the agreement also provided for the release of nearly 600 American prisoners of war* (POWs) held by North Vietnam and its allies. This gave rise to Operation Homecoming, the return of POWs from Southeast Asia to their homes in the United States. The operation was divided into three phases. First, there was to be the initial reception of prisoners at three release sites: prisoners held by the Vietcong* were to be flown by helicopter to Saigon;* those held in North Vietnam were to be released at Hanoi;* and three POWs in China were to be freed in Hong Kong. All groups were to be flown to Clark Air Base, the Philippines.* Second, at Clark Air Base these individuals were to be processed through a reception center, debriefed, and examined by physicians. Third, the former POWs were to be flown to military hospitals for recovery. Beginning on February 12, 1973, the first of these POWs were released at Hanoi, and the last were turned over to American officials on March 29. In all, 591 POWs were released. RDL

Source: Carl Berger, "American POWs and Operation Homecoming," in Carl Berger, ed., *The United States Air Force in Southeast Asia, 1961–1973: An Illustrated Account*, 1984.

Right: Captain Harold T. Fields, 1st Air Cavalry Division, and an interpreter question a Vietnamese civilian on October 6, 1966. At the time, elements of the 1st Air Cavalry were deeply involved in Operation Irving, a mission designed to flush out and destroy two battalions of North Vietnamese regulars from concealed mountain positions 25 miles north of Qui Nhon in South Vietnam.

Opposite page: On February 22, 1967, the U.S. Army and ARVN conducted Operation Junction City against Vietcong forces in War Zone C of Tay Ninh Province, South Vietnam. Here, soldiers from Battery C, 2d Battalion, 32d Artillery insert a round into a 175mm howitzer.

OPERATION IRVING

Operation Irving was the code name for the 1st Cavalry (Airmobile) Division's* activities in Binh Dinh Province of II Corps* between October 2 and October 24, 1966. Charged with clearing Vietcong* and North Vietnamese Army* elements out of the Phu Cat Mountain area, Operation Irving combined the 1st Cavalry with Republic of Korea* troops. When the operation was concluded on October 24, Military Assistance Command, Vietnam* claimed that Irving had inflicted 681 casualties on the enemy.

Sources: Shelby L. Stanton, *Vietnam Order of Battle*, 1981, and *The Rise and Fall of an American Army: U.S. Ground Forces in Vietnam, 1965–1973*, 1985; Kenneth D. Mertel, *Year of the Horse—Vietnam: First Air Cavalry in the Highlands*, 1968.

OPERATION JEFFERSON GLENN

Launched on September 5, 1970, and continuing until October 8, 1971, Operation Jefferson Glenn was the code name for the combined activities of the 101st Airborne Division* and the ARVN 1st Infantry Division (*see* Army of the Republic of Vietnam) in Thua Thien Province. During the 399 days of the operation, allied forces established several firebases in the coastal lowlands of Thua Thien Province and fought against regular North Vietnamese Army* troops. Gradually, the 101st Airborne disengaged and turned the fighting over to ARVN troops. The North Vietnamese and Vietcong* sustained more than 2,000 casualties before the operation was terminated. Operation Jefferson Glenn was the last major U.S. ground combat operation in the Vietnam War.

Sources: Shelby L. Stanton, *Vietnam Order of Battle*, 1981, and *The Rise and Fall of an American Army: U.S. Ground Forces in Vietnam, 1965–1973*, 1985.

OPERATION JUNCTION CITY

Operation Junction City was the code name for the 1967 combined United States Army*–ARVN (*see* Army of the Republic of Vietnam) search-and-destroy* campaign in War Zone C* of Tay Ninh Province. At its time, Junction City was the largest military operation of the war, involving twenty-two American and ARVN battalions—elements of the 1st,* 4th,* and 25th* Infantry divisions,* the 196th Light Infantry Brigade,* the 11th Armored Cavalry,* and the

Right: During Operation Junction City in April 1967, U.S. Army troops with the 1st Infantry Division pause to clean their weapons before resuming their pursuit of the Vietcong 9th Division.

173d Airborne Brigade.* Military Assistance Command, Vietnam* launched Operation Junction City on February 22, 1967, one month after the conclusion of Operation Cedar Falls.* Junction City continued until May 14, 1967. It was successful in attacking Vietcong* (VC) strongholds in War Zone C. By the end of the operation, the VC had taken nearly 3,000 casualties. But instead of making the VC vulnerable by eliminating their secure areas in War Zone C, Junction City had different results. The VC 9th Division simply withdrew from War Zone C and moved across the Cambodian border, where they could regroup and be resupplied. That added a new strategic dimension to the war. The question of how to deal with the Cambodian sanctuaries* preoccupied American policymakers through-out the war.

Sources: Shelby L. Stanton, *Vietnam Order of Battle*, 1981, and *The Rise and Fall of an American Army: U.S. Ground Forces in Vietnam, 1965–1973*, 1985; Bernard William Rogers, *Cedar Falls–Junction City: A Turning Point*, 1974.

OPERATION KINGFISHER

Operation Kingfisher was the code name for a three-month operation by the 3d Marine Division* in the I Corps* Tactical Zone beginning in July 1967. This operation was one of a number of Marine operations that summer designed to interrupt North Vietnamese Army* infiltration* of the Demilitarized Zone* and to support efforts to build a manned and electronic barrier across South Vietnam that was expected to prevent, or reduce in effectiveness, any large-scale movement of enemy troops. This barrier project was initially code-named Project Practice Nine,* was renamed Project Illinois City in June 1967, and was finally called Project Dye Marker a month later. The cost of Operation Kingfisher was 340 U.S. Marines killed and 3,086 wounded. RSB III

Sources: Allan R. Millett, *Semper Fidelis: The History of the United States Marine Corps*, 1980; Shelby L. Stanton, *The Rise and Fall of an American Army: U.S. Ground Forces in Vietnam, 1965–1973*, 1985.

OPERATION KEYSTONE

See C-141 Starlifter

OPERATION LEXINGTON III

Operation Lexington III was the code name for battles of the 1st Battalion of the 18th Infantry Division in the Rung Sat* Special Zone between April 17, 1966, and June 9, 1966. Although Operation Lexington III resulted in the destruc-tion of large numbers of Vietcong* sampans, movement in the waist-deep mangrove swamps prevented the large-scale engagement of ground troops. The onset of the summer monsoons brought Operation Lexington III to an end.

Source: Shelby L. Stanton, *The Rise and Fall of an American Army: U.S. Ground Forces in Vietnam, 1965–1973*, 1985.

OPERATION LINEBACKER I

On Good Friday, March 30, 1972, three North Vietnamese Army* (NVA) divisions crossed the Demilitarized Zone* (DMZ) and invaded the Republic of Vietnam.* Before the Easter weekend was over, 120,000 NVA regulars with 200 armored vehicles were in South Vietnam. Launched to strengthen Hanoi's negotiating position at Paris, the invasion prompted the second major bombing* campaign over North Vietnam by the United States. Named Linebacker I, the operation continued for nearly nine months and involved nearly all U.S. Air Force* assets in the theater. B-52* Arc Light* bombing missions against infiltration* routes and staging areas increased, and B-52 forces already in the theater were strengthened by additional aircraft deployments to Guam. At the same time, tactical airpower forces were also reinforced. Over the next few weeks, U.S. Marine* air squadrons deployed to several staging bases; Navy* carrier support doubled; and Air Force tactical air units rejoined the war from Korea* and the United States. The major priority of returning tactical air units was to support South Vietnamese forces directly, so that the ground battle in South Vietnam could be stabilized.

On April 2, 1972, President Richard Nixon* authorized air strikes against military targets and logistic supply points north of the DMZ to the parallel at 17°25'; this was increased to 18°N on April 4 and to 19°N on April 6. On April 9, fifteen B-52s struck railroad and supply depots at Vinh, the first use of B-52s in North Vietnam since October 28, 1968. Three days later, eighteen B-52s struck Bai Thuong airfield. On the weekend of April 15 to 16, Navy and Air Force aircraft bombed military storage areas surrounding Hanoi* and Haiphong.

As with most military operations, these attacks had several purposes. They disrupted the flow of war supplies supporting the invasion of South Vietnam; warned Hanoi that if it persisted in the invasion, it would face mounting raids in the North; and demonstrated continuing American support for the government of South Vietnam. Furthermore, these attacks were intended to persuade the North Vietnamese to seek a political, rather than a purely military, resolution of the conflict.

When the initial Linebacker I bombing operations brought further North Vietnamese intransigence, President Nixon announced that the North Vietnamese ports of Haiphong, Cam Pha, Hon Gai, and Thanh Hoa, as well as

smaller inlets harboring North Vietnamese patrol boats, would be mined. The mines were laid on May 9 and activated two days later. Simultaneously, Nixon announced that Linebacker I air operations throughout North Vietnam would continue until a formal cessation of hostilities could be secured. Throughout the spring and summer of 1972, Linebacker I operations continued. In the fall, North Vietnam indicated a willingness to negotiate, and on October 22, 1972, Nixon ended Linebacker I. RDL

Sources: W. Hays Parks, "Linebacker and the Law of War," *Air University Review* 34 (January–February 1983): 2–30; R. Frank Futrell et al., *Aces and Aerial Victories: The United States Air Force in Southeast Asia, 1965–1973*, 1976; John Smith, *The Linebacker Raids: The Bombing of North Vietnam, 1972*, 2000.

OPERATION LINEBACKER II

On October 22, 1972, when it seemed that the Paris peace talks* were leading to an agreement, the United States halted air operations above the 20th parallel. This end of Operation Linebacker I* provided a breathing spell for the North Vietnamese, who quickly strengthened air defenses in Hanoi* and Haiphong. By mid-December, Hanoi had repaired rail lines to China* and adjusted its supply routing to compensate for the naval mine blockade. The restored rail lines were capable of handling 16,000 tons of supplies per day, or 2.5 times Hanoi's needs. Simultaneous with the cessation of bombing,* negotiations between North Vietnam and the United States stalled amid indications that Hanoi might renew its offensive in South Vietnam. By early December an agreement that had appeared so near five weeks earlier was in shambles. President Richard Nixon* then launched Operation Linebacker II, a final eleven-day bombing campaign (the "Christmas bombing") that was one of the heaviest aerial assaults of the war. The U.S. Air Force* used F-105,* F-4,* F-111,* and for the first time B-52* aircraft to attack Hanoi and Haiphong. Tactical aircraft flew more than 1,000 sorties* and the B-52s about 740, most of them against rail yards, power plants, communication facilities, air defense radar sites, docks and shipping facilities, petroleum stores, ammunition supply depots, air bases, and transportation facilities.

The North Vietnamese retaliated with most of their inventory of about 1,000 surface-to-air missiles (SAMs)* and a heavy barrage of antiaircraft fire. The countermeasures were ineffective. Only twenty-seven U.S. aircraft were lost; however, eighteen B-52s were destroyed or badly damaged by missiles. In spite of this, the air attacks continued, and by December 28 North Vietnamese defenses had been all but obliterated. During the last two days of the campaign American aircraft flew over Hanoi and Haiphong without suffering any losses. The North

Above: Troops from Company D, 1st Battalion, of the 173d Airborne Brigade pause to fill their canteens with water from a fast-moving stream on November 26, 1967. Such water was likely to contain fewer dangerous bacteria than water from stagnant ponds. The soldiers have just completed an assault on Hill 800 approximately 12 miles northwest of Dak To in the Central Highlands of South Vietnam. They are part of Operation MacArthur.

Right: Specialist 4 Francisco Diaz of Newark, New Jersey, is point man with the 2d Battalion, 8th Mechanized Infantry, 4th Infantry Division. In this photo taken June 27, 1967, Diaz stands with his AN/PRT-4 and AN/PRR-9 radios, prepared to relay intelligence to his squad leader. Diaz is part of Operation MacArthur.

Vietnamese lost eight aircraft in aerial fighting during the Linebacker II campaign, as well as suffering substantial collateral damage in the raids.

Partially as a result of Linebacker II's success, negotiations resumed with Henry Kissinger* and Le Duc Tho* in Paris on January 8, 1973. While the diplomats talked, American air attacks were restricted and confined to south of the 20th parallel. U.S. Air Force, Navy,* and Marine* fighters* flew about twenty sorties per day with B-52s, adding thirty-six to the daily total. On January 23, 1973, the Paris negotiators signed a nine-point cease-fire agreement to be effective on January 28, 1973. The airpower displayed in Linebacker II had played a significant role in extracting this agreement to end the war. RDL

Sources: W. Hays Parks, "Linebacker and the Law of War," *Air University Review* 34 (January–February 1983): 2–30; R. Frank Futrell et al., *Aces and Aerial Victories: The United States Air Force in Southeast Asia, 1965–1973*, 1976; John Smith, *The Linebacker Raids: The Bombing of North Vietnam, 1972*, 2000.

OPERATION MACARTHUR

Operation MacArthur was the code name for combat operations of the 4th Infantry Division* in the western highlands of South Vietnam between October 12, 1967, and January 31, 1969. It began as Operation Greeley back in June 1967 when two paratrooper battalions of the 173d Airborne Brigade* were airlifted into Dak To* to relieve a Special Forces* camp there. Elements of the 1st Cavalry Division,* the 42d ARVN Regiment, and the 5th and 8th ARVN Airborne battalions (*see* Army of the Republic of Vietnam) were also engaged in the early campaign. Operation Greeley became part of Operation MacArthur in October 1967. Operation MacArthur then became the battle for Dak To in 1967. U.S. and ARVN forces ultimately prevailed at Dak To, driving the North Vietnamese Army* (NVA) back into Laos,* but in 1968 the NVA returned, and Operation MacArthur continued until early in 1969. When the operation ended, Military Assistance Command, Vietnam* claimed a total of 5,731 enemy casualties.

Sources: Shelby L. Stanton, *Vietnam Order of Battle*, 1981, and *The Rise and Fall of an American Army: U.S. Ground Forces in Vietnam, 1965–1973*, 1985.

OPERATION MALHEUR

Operation Malheur was the code name for two operations of Task Force Oregon (*see* 23d Infantry Division) in the spring of 1967. To help fight Vietcong* and North Vietnamese Army* (NVA) elements in the southern reaches of I Corps,* General William Westmoreland* decided early in 1967 to bring together three separate Army brigades. Dubbed Task Force Oregon, the division-size unit consisted of the 1st Brigade of the 101st Airborne Division,* the 196th Light Infantry Brigade,* and the 3d Brigade of the 25th Division.* Westmoreland hoped that Task Force Oregon would increase security in the coastal areas, keep Route 1 open to commercial and military traffic, and relieve pressure in the northern reaches of Binh Dinh Province. Operation Malheur I, the first combat operation of the task force, was launched on May 11, 1967. It continued through July 1967 in the area of Duc Pho. Although the task force engaged in numerous firefights and called in repeated air strikes, it had little more success than uncovering large amounts of Vietcong and NVA food and ammunition. Operation Malheur II, launched late in July and concluded early in August 1967, was equally unsuccessful in engaging any large enemy forces. Task Force Oregon, however, did meet Westmoreland's objective of increasing security in southern I Corps and maintaining the integrity of Route 1.

Sources: Shelby L. Stanton, *Vietnam Order of Battle*, 1981, and *The Rise and Fall of an American Army: U.S. Ground Forces in Vietnam, 1965–1973*, 1985; Willard Pearson, *The War in the Northern Provinces, 1966–1968*, 1975.

OPERATION MARKET TIME

Operation Market Time was the code name for United States Navy* operations in the South China Sea to prevent the North Vietnamese from supplying the Vietcong* and North Vietnamese Army* by coastal infiltration.* Operation Market Time began on March 11, 1965, and placed a picket line of ships from the U.S. Navy, U.S. Coast Guard,* and South Vietnamese Navy* along the 1,000-mile coast of the South China Sea in South Vietnam. They regularly boarded and inspected the more than 50,000 junks operating off the coast and along the major rivers. General William Westmoreland* estimated that Operation Market Time was so successful that between 1965 and the end of 1966 the Vietcong lost the ability to resupply themselves by sea. In 1965, 70 percent of their supplies came in through the South Vietnamese coast and 30 percent along the Ho Chi Minh Trail,* but by 1967 only 10 percent of their supplies were being infiltrated from the coast.

Source: Edward J. Marolda and G. Wesley Pryce III, *A Short History of the United States Navy and the Southeast Asian Conflict, 1956–1975*, 1984.

OPERATION MASHER/WHITE WING

In January 1966 Major General Harry W.O. Kinnard received orders to use his 1st Cavalry Division (Airmobile),* stationed near An Khe, to eliminate Vietcong* and North Vietnamese Army* forces from four valleys in northeastern Binh Dinh Province. The 1st Cavalry Division was assisted by the ARVN (*see* Army of the Republic of Vietnam) Airborne Brigade, the ARVN 22d Division, and the 1st Regiment of the Republic of Korea's Capital Division.* Known as the Bong Son campaign, the mission was code-named Operation Masher. That code name was changed to Operation White Wing on February 4, 1966. The operation lasted from late January to March 6, 1966, by which time the North Vietnamese had abandoned

Below: U.S. Navy Swift boats operate in the Gulf of Thailand off the coast of Vietnam as part of Operation Market Time.

Above: In January 1966, during Operation Masher, this soldier from the 1st Cavalry Division prepares to explore an underground bunker. Operation Masher targeted Vietcong and North Vietnamese forces in northeastern Binh Dinh Province, South Vietnam.

Command, Vietnam* to launch a larger combat operation in the area, which led to Operation Apache Snow.*

Sources: Shelby L. Stanton, *Vietnam Order of Battle*, 1981, and *The Rise and Fall of an American Army: U.S. Ground Forces in Vietnam, 1965–1973*, 1985.

OPERATION MAYFLOWER

Operation Mayflower was the code name for a diplomatic initiative President Lyndon B. Johnson* launched on May 13, 1966, in an attempt to bring the North Vietnamese to the negotiating table. He stopped the bombing* of North Vietnam and instructed Foy Kohler, the U.S. ambassador to the Soviet Union,* to meet with the North Vietnamese delegation in Moscow to propose peace negotiations. The North Vietnamese summarily refused to even meet with Kohler, and on May 15, 1968, Johnson terminated Operation Mayflower and resumed the bombing.

Sources: Stanley Karnow, *Vietnam: A History*, 1983; *New York Times*, May 13–15 and 17–19, 1966.

OPERATION MENU

On March 18, 1969, the United States Air Force* began Operation Menu, a series of secret, illegal B-52* bombings of National Liberation Front (NLF; *see* Vietcong) and North Vietnamese Army* (NVA) sanctuaries* in eastern Cambodia.* It continued for fifteen months until the Cambodian invasion (May 1970), when it was renamed Operation Freedom Deal and expanded to include "targets" throughout Cambodia. Freedom Deal continued until Congress* prohibited funds for bombing Cambodia, effective August 15, 1973. By the end of operations, 16,527 sorties* had been flown and 383,851 tons of bombs dropped.

General Creighton Abrams* had wanted to attack the sanctuaries for some time; President Lyndon Johnson,* however, repeatedly refused permission. When Richard Nixon* became president in January 1969, these requests were resubmitted with the justifications that striking sanctuaries would reduce NLF-NVA offensive capabilities and that the Central Office for South Vietnam* (COSVN; the NLF-NVA command structure) had been located and could be destroyed by either ground or air attack. After initial hesitation, Nixon approved, for reasons of his own. The bombing was to "signal" Hanoi* that Nixon was "tougher" than Johnson and to lend credence to the "mad man" image he wanted to create among North Vietnamese leaders.

"Menu" was a series of attacks (meals) against NLF-NVA base areas, including "Breakfast"—Base Area 353, 25 square kilometers near the Fishhook,* inhabited by 1,640

the region. They would return, however, and the United States would subsequently launch Operations Davy Crockett, Crazy Horse, Irving,* and Thayer to attack them again.

Sources: Shelby L. Stanton, *The Rise and Fall of an American Army: U.S. Ground Forces in Vietnam, 1965–1973*, 1985; Willard Pearson, *The War in the Northern Provinces, 1966–1968*, 1975; *The 1st Air Cavalry Division: Vietnam, August 1965 to December 1969*, 1970.

OPERATION MASSACHUSETTS STRIKER

Operation Massachusetts Striker was the code name for the 101st Airborne (Airmobile) Division's* activities in the A Shau Valley* between March 1 and May 8, 1969. In its sweep operations through the valley, the 101st discovered an enormous North Vietnamese Army* (NVA) logistic base, complete with ammunition dumps, underground oil depots, motor-pool repair facilities, and a field hospital, all concealed in the jungles. The discovery of such a large NVA logistic investment persuaded Military Assistance

Cambodians (U.S. military population estimates) and the supposed headquarters of COSVN; "Lunch"—Base Area 609, located on the Laotian-Cambodian-Vietnamese borders and inhabited by 198 Cambodians; "Snack"—Base Area 351, 101 square kilometers in the Fishhook, including one town and 383 Cambodians; "Dinner"—Base Area 352, located in the Fishhook, including one town and 770 Cambodians; and "Dessert"—Base Area 350, located north of the Fishhook with 120 Cambodians. The military did not recommend bombing Base Areas 354, 704, and 707 because they had substantial Cambodian populations. Nonetheless, Base Area 704 was authorized as "Supper," with 247 B-52* missions flown against it. In March 1970 Nixon authorized the expanded bombing of Laos,* including B-52 raids against the Plain of Jars.

Officially, Military Assistance Command, Vietnam* claimed that the base areas were not inhabited by Cambodian civilians, but private military reports indicated an awareness of civilian presence and expectations of civilian casualties. These reports contended that although casualties should be light because the base areas were sparsely populated and Cambodians lived apart from the NLF-NVA, "some Cambodian casualties would be sustained ... [and] the surprise effect of attacks would tend to increase casualties ... [due to] probable lack of protective shelter around Cambodian homes." The number of Cambodians killed is unknown.

Nixon, very concerned that Operation Menu not become public knowledge, ordered elaborate security measures that included the falsification of military records, an offense punishable by court-martial under Article 107 of *The Uniform Code of Military Justice*, so there was absolutely no record of the bombings having occurred. Nixon and Henry Kissinger's* justification was that secrecy was necessary to protect Cambodia's Prince Norodom Sihanouk,* who had given his "tacit consent." They did not provide evidence to support this proposition, however, and Prince Sihanouk vehemently denied that he had consented, tacitly or otherwise. SF

Sources: William Shawcross, *Sideshow: Kissinger, Nixon, and the Destruction of Cambodia*, 1979; John Morrocco, *The Vietnam Experience. Rain of Fire: Air War, 1969–1973*, 1984.

OPERATION NEUTRALIZE

Operation Neutralize was the code name for the combined United States Air Force,* Army,* and Navy* operation to relieve the siege of Con Thien* in September and October of 1967. To relieve the 3d Marine Division* at Con Thien from the assault by the North Vietnamese Army* (NVA) 325C and 324B divisions, General William Momyer,* commander of the Seventh Air Force,* developed the SLAM* (seek, locate, annihilate, and monitor) approach. It involved coordinated heavy fire support, using naval artillery bombardment, tactical air support, B-52* bombing, and artillery fire, which was leveled at NVA forces outside Con Thien. Launched on September 11, 1967, Operation Neutralize lasted until October 31, 1967, during which 4,000 aircraft sorties* unloaded 40,000 tons of bombs on an area about the size of Manhattan. North Vietnamese forces could not withstand the firepower, and they ended the siege of Con Thien at the end of October.

Sources: Terrence Maitland and Peter McInerney, *The Vietnam Experience: A Contagion of War*, 1983; John Morrocco, *The Vietnam Experience. Thunder from Above: Air War, 1941–1968*, 1985.

OPERATION NEVADA EAGLE

Operation Nevada Eagle was the code name for the activities of the 101st Airborne Division (Airmobile)* in Thua Thien Province of I Corps* between May 17, 1968, and February 28, 1969. During those eight and a half months of combat, often involving heavy booby-trap* casualties and search-and-destroy* sweeps, the 101st Airborne claimed to have inflicted 3,299 casualties on Vietcong* and North Vietnamese Army* forces.

Sources: Shelby L. Stanton, *Vietnam Order of Battle*, 1981, and *The Rise and Fall of an American Army: U.S. Ground Forces in Vietnam, 1965–1973*, 1985.

OPERATION NIAGARA

Operation Niagara was the code name for a joint United States Air Force,* Navy,* and Marine* air assault on Khe Sanh* between January 14 and March 31, 1968. North Vietnamese Army* (NVA) forces had put the Marine base at Khe Sanh under siege, and President Lyndon B. Johnson* feared that a defeat there would resemble the French debacle at Dien Bien Phu* fourteen years earlier. Committed to maintaining the Marine base at Khe Sanh, the United States launched Operation Niagara. Air Force, Navy, and Marine pilots flew more than 5,000 tactical fighter-bomber (*see* Fighters) and B-52* sorties* over Khe Sanh during the next ten weeks, unloading more than 100,000 tons of bombs on NVA forces and eventually forcing the North Vietnamese to end the siege.

Sources: Carl Berger, ed., *The United States Air Force in Southeast Asia, 1961–1973*, 1977; Rober Pisor, *The End of the Line: The Siege of Khe Sanh*, 1982; Moyers S. Shore II, *The Battle for Khe Sanh*, 1969.

OPERATION NIAGARA

In early 1967 North Vietnam began planning what would in one year be known as the Tet Offensive. Vo Nguyen Giap, after considerable debate within the politburo in Hanoi, decided to launch a huge military offensive throughout South Vietnam. He knew that General William Westmoreland, like French general Henri Navarre in 1954, itched for a major conventional battle

Right: U.S. Marines disembark from a helicopter at the far western edge of the Demilitarized Zone in October 1968. They are part of a 6,000-man force charged with the mission of sweeping out North Vietnamese regulars near Khe Sanh.

with the North Vietnamese Army (NVA), one in which superior American firepower would destroy the enemy. Westmoreland inadvertently played into Giap's hands by deploying 6,000 Marines to Khe Sanh, a small village tucked away in western Quang Tri Province, approximately eighteen miles south of the Demilitarized Zone and eight miles east of the Laotian border. Westmoreland wanted the Marines to interdict supplies flowing south along the Ho Chi Minh Trail. Hoping to set a trap for Westmoreland, Giap began concentrating NVA troops at strategic locations along the Laotian and Cambodian borders with South Vietnam. He positioned the NVA 325C Division northwest of Khe Sanh. Giap also placed his 304th Division to the

southwest of Khe Sanh, with elements of the NVA 320th and 324th divisions prepared to reinforce the others if necessary. NVA forces surrounding Khe Sanh exceeded 40,000 troops.

Westmoreland informed President Lyndon B. Johnson that the enemy was finally staging the long anticipated, Dien Bien Phu–like offensive. The president asked military planners to build a model of Khe Sanh in the White House situation room so that he could follow the looming battle on a day-to-day basis. On January 21, 1968, North Vietnamese artillery opened fire on Khe Sanh. Acting as if Vo Nguyen Giap fought only template battles, Westmoreland interpreted the artillery fire as the preliminary to an infantry assault on Khe Sanh, just as at Dien Bien Phu fourteen years before. Westmoreland then unleashed Operation Niagara to pummel NVA positions with everything in the American arsenal, including B-52 bombing campaigns. The NVA in turn subjected the Marines to mortar fire and repeated infantry patrols to probe their defenses. Johnson and Westmoreland anxiously waited for the final NVA assault, where American firepower would annihilate the enemy.

Right: Marine Private First Class Robert DuBois of Brooklyn, New York, shaves the head of Corporal Efrain Torres, also of New York on March 8, 1968. They are outside a bunker in Khe Sanh, South Vietnam, where North Vietnamese forces have placed the Marines under siege. Thousands of North Vietnamese troops, while assaulting the Marine position at Khe Sanh, were killed by U.S. tactical aircraft and B-52 bombers engaging in tactical air operations.

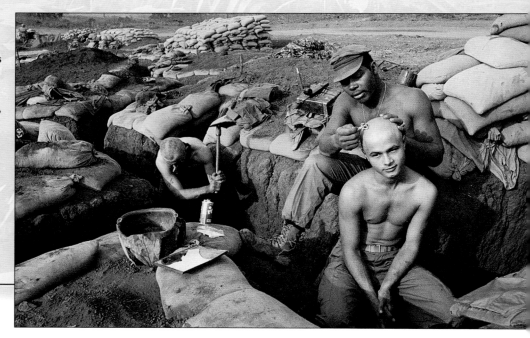

Left: In February 1968, during the North Vietnamese siege of the Marine base at Khe Sanh, a Marine takes a moment to relax in a bunker.

to the back pages, although fighting there continued between the Marines and NVA troops. One month later, as the Tet Offensive eased in intensity, Westmoreland launched Operation Pegasus to relieve the Marines at Khe Sanh. The 1st Cavalry Division reopened Route 9 into Khe Sanh just as Giap ended the siege. NVA troops exited the region for redeployment to other areas of South Vietnam. In mid-June the Marines left Khe Sanh for redeployment to other parts of Quang Tri Province, leaving Khe Sanh what it once had been—a sleepy redoubt in the middle of nowhere, an epic confrontation that never occurred, a monument to the most frustrating war in United States history. When the dead were counted, the United States had lost 205 Marines, and Westmoreland placed the number of dead NVA soldiers at between 10,000 and 15,000 men.

Sources: Robert Pisor, *The End of the Line: The Siege of Khe Sanh*, 1982; Eric Hammel, *Khe Sanh: Siege in the Clouds*, 2004; John Prados and Ray W. Stubbe, *Valley of Decision: The Siege of Khe Sanh*, 2004; Ronald J. Drez and Douglas Brinkley, *The Voices of Courage: The Battle for Khe Sanh, Vietnam*, 2005.

Over the course of the next six weeks, Westmoreland staged more than 50,000 Air Force and naval aircraft sorties against the NVA 325C, 304th, 320th, and 324th divisions, eventually detonating more than 200 million pounds of explosives on the five square miles surrounding Khe Sanh. The Marines dug in; journalists swarmed on Khe Sanh, hoping to witness an epic battle, "another Dien Bien Phu"; and President Johnson, often in his pajamas in the middle of the night, paced around the situation room studying the scale model of Khe Sanh. The Marines waited, Johnson waited, and Westmoreland waited, but the final attack never came.

Vo Nguyen Giap had never intended to attack in some culminating, epic battle to end the Vietnam War. Westmoreland may have been thinking about Dien Bien Phu, but for Giap it was ancient history. It was 1968, not 1954, and he had other plans. Khe Sanh was a feint, a ploy, a trick to confuse Westmoreland. As a preliminary for the Tet Offensive, in which Vietcong troops would attack provincial capitals throughout South Vietnam, Giap staged what later became known as the border battles—at Khe Sanh, Con Thien, and Loc Ninh—designed to pull U.S. soldiers and Marines out of the cities and provincial capitals, where the Vietcong were about to strike en masse. Large numbers of American soldiers, instead of being in the cities, would find themselves along the Cambodian and Laotian borders in battles that were only sideshows to the real fight. For the Marines under siege there, Khe Sanh was no picnic, but the battle itself, while symbolizing courage under combat, also became an icon to Vo Nguyen Giap's military genius.

On January 31, 1968, the launching of the Tet Offensive throughout South Vietnam relegated Khe Sanh

Below: During Operation Pegasus in 1968, U.S. forces operated to relieve the siege of the Marines at Khe Sanh. American troops have just captured Hill 471 along Highway 9. A wary American relaxes for a moment, but keeps a tight grip on his weapon.

OPERATION PAUL REVERE

Operation Paul Revere was the code name for four combat operations (I, II, III, and IV) of the 4th Infantry Division,* 25th Infantry Division,* and 1st Cavalry Division (Airmobile)* in Pleiku Province in 1966. Operation Paul Revere I commenced on May 19, 1966, and Operation Paul Revere IV concluded on December 30, 1966. Fighting with the North Vietnamese Army* 1st Division was conducted near the Cambodian border throughout the campaigns, but American forces were unable to cross the border in pursuit of North Vietnamese forces. When the Paul Revere operations were concluded at the end of the year, the 4th and 25th Infantry divisions, along with the 1st Cavalry (Airmobile), were claiming more than 4,000 enemy casualties.

Sources: Shelby L. Stanton, *Vietnam Order of Battle*, 1981, and *The Rise and Fall of an American Army: U.S. Ground Forces in Vietnam, 1965–1973*, 1985; Willard Pearson, *The War in the Northern Provinces, 1966–1968*, 1975; Tom Carhart, *Battles and Campaigns in Vietnam*, 1984.

OPERATION PEGASUS

Operation Pegasus was the code name for the 1st Cavalry Division (Airmobile)* operation to relieve the siege of Khe Sanh* in April 1968. U.S. Marine* and ARVN (*see* Army of the Republic of Vietnam) units assisted in

the operation. The ARVN dimension was code-named Operation Lam Son 207. Operation Pegasus was launched on April 1, 1968, and concluded on April 15, 1968, when the siege of Khe Sanh was broken.

Sources: Shelby L. Stanton, *The Rise and Fall of an American Army: U.S. Ground Forces in Vietnam, 1965–1973*, 1985; *The 1st Air Cavalry Division: Vietnam, August 1965 to December 1969*, 1970.

OPERATION PENNSYLVANIA

Operation Pennsylvania was the code name for an unofficial but State Department–approved visit to Hanoi* by Herbert Marcovich, a French biologist, and Raymond Aubrac, a worker with the Food and Agriculture Organization. Aubrac knew Ho Chi Minh* personally and offered to visit with him in Hanoi. Henry Kissinger* knew of the visit and acted as a go-between for the State Department and Aubrac. Aubrac and Marcovich went to Hanoi in July 1967, visited with Ho Chi Minh and Pham Van Dong,* and returned expressing positive hopes for a negotiated settlement, although little came of the visit. The North Vietnamese were committed to reunification of the two countries, and were willing to negotiate if that goal was a real possibility. In 1967 it was not, at least given the diplomatic position of the United States.

Sources: Stanley Karnow, *Vietnam: A History*, 1983; Henry Kissinger, *White House Years*, 1979.

Right: During Operation Pegasus in 1968, the 1st Cavalry Division conducted a sustained campaign to relieve the siege of the Marines at Khe Sanh. In this photograph taken on March 30, 1968, a CH-47 Chinook helicopter unloads the supplies needed to set up a Tactical Operations Center (TOC) at a new base camp 12 miles east of Khe Sanh.

Left: Soldiers from the 1st Cavalry Division, as part of Operation Pegasus, observe tactical air assaults on North Vietnamese on a far hill line from the Special Forces Camp at Lang Vei on April 14, 1968.

Below: Private First Class Manuel A. Diaz of San Juan, Puerto Rico, a rifleman with Company C, 2d Battalion, 7th Infantry, 3d Brigade, examines a Chinese-made 90mm recoilless rifle during Operation Pegasus on April 6, 1968.

OPERATION PERSHING

Operation Pershing was the code name for the combat activities of the 1st Cavalry Division (Airmobile)* in Binh Dinh Province of II Corps.* Launched on February 11, 1967, Operation Pershing was designed to attack the Vietcong* (VC) and the North Vietnamese Army* (NVA) 610th Division. Operation Pershing continued for nearly a year, inflicting more than 5,400 casualties on VC and NVA forces. The 1st Cavalry Division's activities had been so successful that when the Tet Offensive* erupted in February 1968, Binh Dinh Province was one of the quietest areas in South Vietnam.

Sources: Shelby L. Stanton, *The Rise and Fall of an American Army: U.S. Ground Forces in Vietnam, 1965–1973*, 1985; Willard Pearson, *The War in the Northern Provinces, 1966–1968*, 1975; *The 1st Air Cavalry Division: Vietnam, August 1965 to December 1969*, 1970.

OPERATION PIRANHA

Operation Piranha was the code name for a joint U.S. Marine* and ARVN (*see* Army of the Republic of Vietnam) amphibious-heliborne assault on Vietcong* positions on the Batangan Peninsula in September 1965. It was an attempt to repeat the success of Operation Starlite* and was marked by the destruction of a major Vietcong stronghold. RSB III

Source: Shelby L. Stanton, *The Rise and Fall of an American Army: U.S. Ground Forces in Vietnam, 1965–1973*, 1985.

OPERATION PRAIRIE

Operation Prairie was the code name for the combat activities of the 3d Marine Division* in the Con Thien* and Gio Linh regions of I Corps* in 1966 and early 1967. The Marines were concerned with stopping the North Vietnamese Army* (NVA) 324B Division from crossing the Demilitarized Zone* and invading Quang Tri Province. Operation Prairie, following on the heels of Operation Hastings,* was launched on August 3, 1966, and continued until January 31, 1967. A second stage of Operation Prairie commenced on February 1, 1967, and concluded on March 18, 1967. In both stages of the operation, the 3d Division killed more than 2,000 NVA soldiers. The Marines succeeded in driving the North Vietnamese back across the Ben Hai River,* but the NVA units only regrouped, reequipped, and recrossed back into South Vietnam later in 1967.

Sources: Shelby L. Stanton, *Vietnam Order of Battle*, 1981, and *The Rise and Fall of an American Army: U.S. Ground Forces in Vietnam, 1965–1973*, 1985; Willard Pearson, *The War in the Northern Provinces, 1966–1968*, 1975; Jack Shulimson, *U.S. Marines in Vietnam: An Expanding War 1966*, 1982.

OPERATION RANCH HAND

Operation Ranch Hand, the code name for a United States Air Force* mission to spray herbicides in Southeast Asia between 1961 and 1971, arose out of the military necessity of destroying the jungle cover and food of the Vietcong.* Herbicides, or weed-killing chemicals, had long been used in American agriculture, spread both by ground and aerial methods. Many American military leaders also recognized the potentials of such chemicals for combat situations, but refrained from using them either because of legal restrictions made in treaty or because of possible in-kind retaliations. In 1961 President Ngo Dinh Diem* of South Vietnam ended this long-standing proscription, however, and asked the U.S. Air Force to conduct such defoliant operations in his nation.

Diem's request launched a debate over the morality of using herbicides that raged for years. On one side, some policymakers argued that herbicides offered an economical and efficient means of defoliating* enemy hiding areas. Others, however, doubted the chemicals' effectiveness, suggested that their use would needlessly alienate South Vietnamese villagers, and argued that the chemicals posed serious ecological problems for all living organisms coming in contact with them. Virtually all individuals noted that the use of such defoliants could lead to terrific adverse publicity; almost certainly it would foster charges of barbarism and brutality. Accepting these risks, President John F. Kennedy* approved the use of herbicides in Southeast Asia in November 1961.

Operation Ranch Hand officially commenced in January 1962. The U.S. Air Force's Tactical Air Command was initially directed to deploy six C-123 transports modified with crop-dusting equipment and sufficient supplies for four-month operations to South Vietnam to conduct this mission. After movement to Bien Hoa* Air Base outside Saigon,* the Ranch Hand pilots flew their first familiarization flights over targeted areas on January 10 and 11, 1962. The first Air Force operational Ranch Hand missions took place on January 13, 1962, as two C-123 aircraft sprayed land near Route 15 south and east of Saigon.

At first the use of herbicides was very carefully governed by Military Assistance Command, Vietnam* (MACV), but gradually limitations were relaxed and the spraying became more frequent and covered larger areas. In addition to the use of defoliants in South Vietnam, the Air Force conducted Ranch Hand missions in Laos* between December 1965 and September 1969. From the beginning of this operation until its official termination in February 1971 by General Creighton W. Abrams Jr.,* MACV commander, the Air Force disseminated 19.22 million gallons of herbicides in South Vietnam, according to a 1974 National Research Council study. Approximately 5.96 million acres in the nation had been sprayed during the

Opposite page: Soldiers from Troop B, 1st Squadron, 9th Cavalry, 1st Cavalry Division are on patrol in Binh Dinh Province of II Corps in South Vietnam during Operation Pershing on July 21, 1967. They pause in the stream, waiting for word from a point man in a clearing ahead.

operation, including 36 percent of its mangrove forests. An additional 417,420 gallons were sprayed on 65,972 hectares in Laos between 1965 and 1969. RDL

Source: William A. Buckingham Jr., *Operation Ranch Hand: The United States Air Force and Herbicides in Southeast Asia, 1961–1971*, 1982.

OPERATION ROLLING THUNDER

Operation Rolling Thunder was the code name for American bombing* attacks on strategic targets within North Vietnam. The raids began in an effort to persuade the North Vietnamese to cease their support of the war in the South by forcing them to pay a direct and increasing cost. Since American political leaders hoped to persuade the North Vietnamese quickly and at little cost to either side, President Lyndon B. Johnson* rejected a plan for a concentrated sixteen-day campaign and opted instead for a program of gradually escalated raids beginning in March 1965. There were seven phases to the Rolling Thunder campaign, separated by halts to see whether the North Vietnamese

were willing to begin negotiations, and usually marked by changes in the type and geographic location of the targets being attacked.

Before May 1965 only targets south of the 20th parallel could be attacked. When phase 2 began in May, American pilots were still ordered to hit no targets within thirty miles of Hanoi* or the Chinese borders, or within ten miles of Haiphong. For a brief period in early 1966 American air strikes were once again confined to the area just north of the 17th parallel (*see* Geneva Accords), but in April 1966 the operational area was expanded to all of North Vietnam, while the target list was expanded to include oil storage facilities near Hanoi. Phase 5, which began in February 1967, consisted of intensive bombing attacks on Hanoi-area factories, railroad yards, power plants, and airfields. Following another Christmas halt, attacks on Hanoi resumed in January 1968, but American aircraft were hampered by bad weather and by the need to support ground operations in the South in the wake of the Tet Offensive.* On April 1, 1968, all attacks north of the 19th parallel ceased, and all Rolling Thunder raids stopped on November 1. Throughout the Rolling Thunder campaign, target selection was closely controlled by the White House (from a list

Right: Marines from the 1st Battalion of the 4th Marines fire from a mountaintop on North Vietnamese positions in the valley below during Operation Scotland II on October 10, 1968. The Marines are located southeast of Khe Sanh in Quang Tri Province, South Vietnam.

of potential targets supplied by the Joint Chiefs of Staff; *see* Chairman, JCS). During the entire campaign American aircraft dropped more than 640,000 tons of bombs; 922 American aircraft were lost. RSB III

Sources: R. Frank Futrell et al., *Aces and Aerial Victories: The United States Air Force in Southeast Asia*, 1981; John Morrocco, *The Vietnam Experience. Thunder from Above: Air War, 1941–1968*, 1985; Donald L. Gilmore with D.M. Giangreco, *Eyewitness Vietnam: Firsthand Accounts from Operation Rolling Thunder to the Fall of Saigon*, 2006.

Marine Division continuing its operations around Khe Sanh. Operation Scotland II lasted until February 28, 1969. Operations Scotland and Scotland II accounted for a total of nearly 4,900 NVA casualties.

Sources: Shelby L. Stanton, *Vietnam Order of Battle*, 1981, and *The Rise and Fall of an American Army: U.S. Ground Forces in Vietnam, 1965–1973*, 1985; Willard Pearson, *The War in the Northern Provinces, 1966–1968*, 1975.

Below: These Marines from the 3d Marine Division are part of Operation Scotland on January 25, 1968. They maintain constant surveillance, watching for hostile action on the part of North Vietnamese regulars.

OPERATION SCOTLAND

Operation Scotland was the code name for two 3d Marine Division* actions in I Corps* in 1967 and 1968. Launched on November 1, 1967, Operation Scotland centered on the Khe Sanh* region of Quang Tri Province. It continued until March 31, 1968, inflicting 1,561 casualties on Vietcong* and North Vietnamese Army* (NVA) forces. Operation Scotland came to an end when Operation Pegasus* began on April 1, 1968. Elements of the 3d Marine Division and the 7th Cavalry engaged North Vietnamese regulars near Khe Sanh. South Vietnamese paratroopers joined the action. Operation Pegasus was the code name for the relief of the siege of Khe Sanh. When Operation Pegasus ended in April 1968, Operation Scotland II began, with the 3d

OPERATION SEA DRAGON

A United States Navy* counterpart to the Air Force's* Rolling Thunder* campaign, Operation Sea Dragon was the code name for an operation to cut North Vietnamese supply lines, October 1966–October 1968. Cruisers and destroyers dominated the operation, except for a brief stay by the battleship *New Jersey*. The naval ships ranged up and down the coast of North Vietnam, shelling shore batteries, supply routes, and communication stations, and sinking small North Vietnamese ships running supplies south. Operation Sea Dragon came to an end when President Lyndon B. Johnson was trying to secure a negotiated settlement at the Paris peace talks.*

Source: Edward J. Marolda and G. Wesley Pryce III, *A Short History of the United States Navy and the Southeast Asian Conflict, 1950–1975*, 1984.

Right: In August 1968, troops from the 101st Airborne Division load supplies aboard a UH-1D helicopter at Fire Base Berchtesgaden as part of Operation Somerset Plain, which was designed to attack and destroy North Vietnamese regulars in the A Shau Valley, South Vietnam.

OPERATION SHINING BRASS

Operation Shining Brass was the code name for the first U.S. Special Forces* infiltration of Laos* to locate and disrupt the Ho Chi Minh Trail.* In October 1965 a Special Forces team conducted the operation, calling in a number of F-105 air strikes after locating an ammunition depot. They withdrew after several days, satisfied that they had located the Ho Chi Minh Trail and destroyed an ammunition cache but disappointed that they had not encountered any Vietcong* or North Vietnamese soldiers, except for sniper fire.

Sources: Terrence Maitland and Peter McInerney, *The Vietnam Experience: A Contagion of War*, 1983; Shelby L. Stanton, *The Green Berets at War*, 1985; Charles M. Simpson, *Inside the Green Berets: The First Thirty Years*, 1983; Francis J. Kelly, *U.S. Army Special Forces, 1961–1971*, 1973.

OPERATION SILVER BAYONET

See Ia Drang Valley, Battle of

OPERATION SOMERSET PLAIN

Operation Somerset Plain was the code name for a combined 101st Airborne Division* and ARVN (*see* Army of the Republic of Vietnam) 1st Regiment combat operation in the A Shau Valley* in August 1968. The ARVN portion of the operation was code-named Lam Son 246. Little contact was made with North Vietnamese Army* forces, and the allied troops evacuated the area on August 18 and 19, 1968.

Source: Shelby L. Stanton, *The Rise and Fall of an American Army: U.S. Ground Forces in Vietnam, 1965–1973*, 1985.

OPERATION STARLITE (STARLIGHT)

Operation Starlite was the code name for a U.S. Marine* combined land-air-amphibious operation aimed at destroying the 1st Vietcong* Regiment on the Van Tuong Peninsula in August 1965. The operation began on August 18 when the 3d Battalion of the 3d Marine Division* came ashore, while the 2d Battalion of the 4th Marine Division* flew into landing zones to the west. Fighting was fierce as the Marines moved from one Vietcong defensive position to the next. Nevertheless, by August 19 the 1st Vietcong Regiment was pinned down along the coast and destroyed through a combination of ground fire, air strikes, and naval battery fire. Operation Starlite marked the first large battle between American forces and Vietcong main force groups. Its success encouraged the Marines to follow up with a similar operation (code-named Operation Piranha*) the following month. RSB III

Sources: Shelby L. Stanton, *The Rise and Fall of an American Army: U.S. Ground Forces in Vietnam, 1965–1973*, 1985; Jack Shulimson and Charles M. Johnson, *U.S. Marines in Vietnam: The Landing and the Buildup 1965*, 1978.

OPERATION STEEL TIGER

Operation Steel Tiger was the code name for U.S. air operations over the Ho Chi Minh Trail* in the northern Laotian panhandle. Operation Steel Tiger began in April 1965 and involved both U.S. Air Force* and Navy* aircraft flying from bases in Thailand* and South Vietnam, as well as from aircraft carriers in the South China Sea. Although all types of aircraft flew on these interdiction missions, including B-52* bombers, the most effective aircraft were Air Force fixed-wing gunships,* particularly the AC-130* Spectre.

A subsidiary operation intended to interdict the Ho Chi Minh Trail in the southern Laotian panhandle was code-named Operation Tiger Hound, which began in December 1965. In 1968 both operations were stepped up to cover the entire Ho Chi Minh Trail. At that time the code name was changed to Operation Commando Hunt.* Commando Hunt campaigns were numbered in series, and American military officials estimated that some 20,000 trucks were destroyed in Commando Hunt 5. Although at times the flow of men and supplies along the Ho Chi Minh Trail was slowed to a trickle by the air campaigns, the trail was never completely closed. RSB III

Sources: William W. Momyer, *Airpower in Three Wars*, 1978; Thomas D. Boettcher, *Vietnam: The Valor and the Sorrow*, 1985; John Morrocco, *The Vietnam Experience. Thunder from Above: Air War, 1941–1968*, 1985, and *The Vietnam Experience. Rain of Fire: Air War, 1969–1973*, 1984.

OPERATION SUNRISE

Operation Sunrise was the code name for an early attempt at pacification (*see* Rural Reconstruction). In March 1962 South Vietnamese leader Ngo Dinh Diem* launched a pilot project in Binh Duong Province north of Saigon.* ARVN troops (*see* Army of the Republic of Vietnam) attempted to establish five strategic hamlets* and move peasants off their ancestral homelands to the new communities in the Ben Cat district. The peasants were reluctant to move, however, because of religious ties to ancestral land, coercive ARVN methods, government corruption and unwillingness to deliver the promised payments and resources, and the fact that the hamlets were located far from market areas where rice could be sold. Operation Sunrise was a failure.

Sources: Stanley Karnow, *Vietnam: A History*, 1983; Frances FitzGerald, *Fire in the Lake: The Vietnamese and the Americans in Vietnam*, 1972.

Below: During Operation Starlite, U.S. Marines conducted a joint land-air-amphibious operation against the positions of the 1st Vietcong Regiment on the Van Tuong Peninsula in South Vietnam on August 19, 1965. The smoke comes from the aerial burning of a South Vietnamese village.

Below: Soldiers from the 1st Battalion, 27th Infantry Division participate in Operation Toan Thang I outside Saigon on May 13, 1968. As part of a search-and-destroy mission, they are wading across a deep canal with weapons held high to keep them dry.

OPERATION TALON VISE

See Operation Frequent Wind

OPERATION TEXAS

Operation Texas was the code name for a combined Army of the Republic of Vietnam* (ARVN) and U.S. Marine* combat operation to relieve the North Vietnamese Army* siege of a South Vietnamese Regional Forces* outpost at An Hoa, approximately fifteen miles south of Chu Lai in Quang Ngai Province. On March 19, 1966, the Vietcong 1st Regiment attacked the An Hoa base, and Marine helicopters quickly brought reinforcements and evacuated the wounded. On March 20 the 3d Battalion of the 7th Marines and the 5th ARVN Airborne Battalion joined in the engagement. The 2d Battalion of the 4th Marines* came in later, trapping the enemy between the base and the new Marine positions. The Vietcong* were annihilated.

Sources: Shelby L. Stanton, *The Rise and Fall of an American Army: U.S. Ground Forces in Vietnam, 1965–1973*, 1985; Willard Pearson, *The War in the Northern Provinces, 1966–1968*, 1975.

OPERATION TEXAS STAR

Operation Texas Star was the code name for combined U.S.-ARVN (*see* Army of the Republic of Vietnam) military operations in I Corps* between April 1 and September 5, 1970. In cooperation with the ARVN 1st Infantry Division, the 101st Airborne Division (Airmobile)* conducted pacification (*see* Rural Reconstruction) and development programs as well as offensive operations against North Vietnamese Army* forces in Quang Tri and Thua Thien provinces. At the conclusion of Operation Texas Star, Military Assistance Command, Vietnam* claimed 1,782 casualties inflicted on the North Vietnamese.

Source: Shelby L. Stanton, *Vietnam Order of Battle*, 1981.

OPERATION TIGER HOUND

See Operation Steel Tiger

OPERATION TOAN THANG

Operation Toan Thang was the code name for a massive allied combat operation outside Saigon* in 1968. The Tet Offensive,* with its attacks on Saigon, had shown how vulnerable and tentative the American presence in South Vietnam still was, and U.S. military officials were determined to prevent any repetition of the successful Vietcong* raids on the capital. Military Assistance Command, Vietnam* (MACV) launched Operation Toan Thang on April 8, 1968, using seventy-nine U.S. and ARVN battalions (see Army of the Republic of Vietnam). The units formed a security ring around Saigon and set out to destroy all Vietcong and North Vietnamese Army* (NVA) troops in what was known as the Capital Military District. When the NVA and Vietcong launched the mini Tet Offensive in May 1968, Operation Toan Thang successfully prevented any major successful attacks on Saigon, except for the detonation of 100 pounds of explosives outside a Saigon radio and television complex. When Operation Toan Thang was concluded on May 31, 1968, when the mini Tet Offensive ended, MACV claimed to have inflicted 7,645 casualties on Vietcong and NVA forces.

Sources: Shelby L. Stanton, *Vietnam Order of Battle*, 1981, and *The Rise and Fall of an American Army: U.S. Ground Forces in Vietnam, 1965–1973*, 1985; Tom Carhart, *Battles and Campaigns in Vietnam*, 1984.

OPERATION TRAN HUNG DAO

Operations Tran Hung Dao I and Tran Hung Dao II were conducted by the South Vietnamese during and just after the Tet Offensive* of 1968. Both involved several Vietnamese marine, ranger, and airborne battalions fighting Vietcong* in the Saigon* area. The ARVN (see Army of the Republic of Vietnam) 5th Ranger Group encountered particularly bitter fighting in Cholon.* Tran Hung Dao I commenced on February 5 and concluded on February 17, 1968, and Tran Hung Dao II started on February 17 and finished on March 8, 1968, the day after the last Vietcong resistance in Cholon had been eliminated. In both operations, ARVN forces claimed credit for 1,666 enemy casualties. Although Operations Tran Hung Dao I and II had successfully repelled Vietcong forces from Saigon and Cholon, they had also indicated how vulnerable South Vietnam still was to guerrilla activity.

Sources: Shelby L. Stanton, *Vietnam Order of Battle*, 1981; Don Oberdofer, *Tet!*, 1971.

Above: Purple smoke identifies a landing spot for a UH-1D helicopter picking up the commanding officer of Company D, 4th Battalion, 12th Infantry, 199th Light Infantry Brigade on October 2, 1968. Operation Toan Thang II has been launched in defense of Saigon.

OPERATION UNION

Operations Union I and II were code names for combat activities of the 1st Marine Division* in Quang Nam and Quang Tin provinces during 1967. The Vietcong* were particularly strong between Chu Lai and Da Nang* in the Phuoc Ha Valley, as was the North Vietnamese Army* (NVA) 2d Division. Operation Union I, involving the 1st and 3d battalions of the 1st Marines and the 3d Battalion of the 5th Marines,* began on April 21, 1967, and continued until May 17, 1967. Operation Union II commenced on May 25, 1967, and concluded on June 5, 1967. The Marines claimed to have inflicted 1,566 casualties on the enemy in both operations before the NVA retreated.

Sources: Shelby L. Stanton, *Vietnam Order of Battle*, 1981, and *The Rise and Fall of an American Army: U.S. Ground Forces in Vietnam, 1965–1973*, 1985.

OPERATION UNIONTOWN

Operation Uniontown was the code name for the combat activities of the 199th Light Infantry Brigade* in Bien Hoa Province. Launched on December 17, 1967, Operation Uniontown had as its objective a clearing of the Vietcong* from the Bien Hoa area. Operation Uniontown became part of the larger American reaction to the Tet Offensive* in February 1968, and when the operation was concluded on March 8, 1968, the 199th Infantry Brigade claimed 922 Vietcong casualties. As for clearing the Vietcong from Bien Hoa Province, Operation Uniontown dealt them a savage, but not a lethal, blow.

Source: Shelby L. Stanton, *Vietnam Order of Battle*, 1981.

OPERATION UTAH

Operation Utah was the code name for a combined U.S. Marine* and ARVN (*see* Army of the Republic of Vietnam) assault in Quang Ngai Province between March 4 and March 8, 1966. North Vietnamese Army* (NVA) regular troops of the 36th NVA Regiment were operating south of Chu Lai. Five Marine battalions from the 1st,* 4th,* and 7th Marines air-assaulted into an area just outside Quang Ngai City, and after several days of heavy fighting they drove the NVA out of the region, inflicting more than 600 casualties on the enemy.

Sources: Shelby L. Stanton, *Vietnam Order of Battle*, 1981, and *The Rise and Fall of American Army: U.S. Ground Forces in Vietnam, 1965–1973*, 1985; Jack Shulimson, *U.S. Marines in Vietnam: An Expanding War 1966*, 1982.

OPERATION VULTURE

Late in March 1954 General Paul Ely,* the French chief of staff, flew to Washington to request American air support in Indochina* if the Chinese intervened on the side of the Vietminh.* Admiral Arthur W. Radford,* chairman of the Joint Chiefs of Staff (*see* Chairman, JCS), then unveiled to Ely what he called Operation Vulture, a series of American air strikes around Dien Bien Phu* aimed at severing Vietminh communications, destroying their artillery, and ending the siege there. Radford told Ely that the French would have to make a formal request for such assistance. If such a request came through, 200 American aircraft from the carriers *Essex* and *Boxer*, both stationed in the South China Sea, would conduct the air strike. But when Operation Vulture encountered congressional opposition, President Dwight Eisenhower,* over Radford's objections, argued that he would allow the air strike only with formal congressional approval as well as verbal support from NATO allies. At that point the French withdrew their request, afraid that any multinational approach would reduce their control over the military campaign in Indochina. Operation Vulture never came to pass.

Sources: Philippe Devillers and Jean Lacouture, *End of a War: Indochina, 1954*, 1969; Bernard B. Fall, *Hell in a Very Small Place: The Siege of Dien Bien Phu*, 1967; Melvin Gurtov, *The First Vietnam Crisis: Chinese Communist Strategy and United States Involvement, 1953–54*, 1967; John Prados, *The Sky Would Fall: Operation Vulture, the U.S. Bombing Mission in Indochina*, 1983.

OPERATION WHEELER/WALLOWA

Operation Wheeler/Wallowa was the code name for the yearlong operations of the Americal Division (23d Infantry Division*) in Quang Nam and Quang Tin provinces of I Corps.* Launched on November 11, 1967, Operation Wheeler/Wallowa continued until November 11, 1968, and resulted in more than 10,000 Vietcong* and North Vietnamese Army* casualties.

Sources: Shelby L. Stanton, *Vietnam Order of Battle*, 1981; Willard Pearson, *The War in the Northern Provinces, 1966–1968*, 1975.

OPERATION WHITE STAR

Operation White Star was the code name for the 1959 U.S. Special Forces* program to organize Hmong* (Meo) tribesmen in Laos* to serve as a resistance force against Vietcong* and North Vietnamese infiltration* and supply routes in Laos along the Laotian-Vietnamese border. Operation White Star formally ended in 1962 after the

Geneva agreements settling the Laotian controversy, but the Special Forces continued to work closely with Hmong tribesmen throughout the 1960s.

Sources: Douglas Blaufarb, *The Counterinsurgency Era: U.S. Doctrine and Performance*, 1977; Shelby L. Stanton, *Green Berets at War*, 1985; John Prados, *Presidents' Secret Wars: CIA and Pentagon Covert Operations Since World War II*, 1986.

OPERATION YELLOWSTONE

Operation Yellowstone was the code name for combat operations of the 25th Infantry Division* in War Zone C* between December 8, 1966, and February 24, 1967. Although troops encountered frequent Vietcong* mortar attacks, ground combat was relatively light, except for some intense confrontations early in January. The major consequence of Operation Yellowstone, aside from the 1,254 casualties the 25th Infantry Division claimed to have inflicted on the Vietcong, was to confirm that Tay Ninh Province (War Zone C) continued to be a major stronghold of the Vietcong.

Source: Shelby L. Stanton, *The Rise and Fall of an American Army: U.S. Ground Forces in Vietnam, 1965–1973*, 1985.

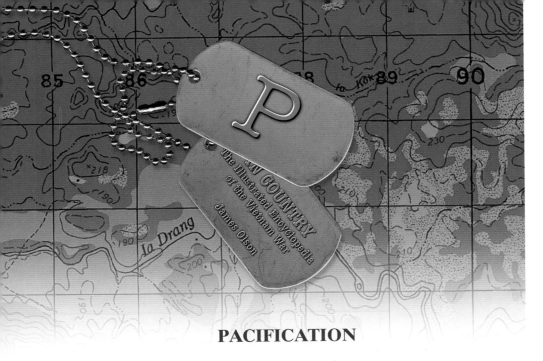

PACIFICATION

See Rural Reconstruction

PACIFIC COMMAND

Pacific Command, or PACOM, was located in Hawaii. It was a unified command headquarters responsible for joint military operations in Asia and the Pacific. Four individuals served as commander in chief of the Pacific Command during the Vietnam War: Admiral Harry D. Felt until June 1964; Admiral Ulysses S. Sharp* until July 1968; Admiral John S. McCain* until September 1972; and Admiral Noel Gayler until the end of the war.

Sources: George S. Eckhardt, *Command and Control, 1950–1969*, 1974; Bruce Palmer Jr., *The 25-Year War: America's Military Role in Vietnam*, 1984.

Below: Admiral John S. McCain Jr., commander in chief of Pacific Command, briefs pilots of Fighter Squadron 143 aboard the aircraft carrier USS *Constellation* in the Gulf of Tonkin on December 20, 1969. The briefing was part of a Christmas tour of U.S. Naval Forces in Vietnam that McCain had undertaken.

PARIS PEACE ACCORDS (1973)

In the aftermath of the so-called Christmas bombing (*see* Operation Linebacker II) of Hanoi* and Haiphong in December 1972, American Henry Kissinger* and North Vietnamese Le Duc Tho* resumed peace talks on January 8 in Paris, and after two weeks of intensive negotiations finally settled on an agreement on January 23. Two days later, on January 25, 1973, cease-fire agreements were formally signed in Paris, and another chapter in the fighting in Indochina* had closed.

The agreement of January 1973 differed little from an abortive one of October 1972 that had been unacceptable to South Vietnamese president Nguyen Van Thieu.* The agreement called for a cease-fire, American troop withdrawal, prisoner exchanges (especially of the American pilots shot down over North Vietnam), but permitted Vietnamese troops on both sides to remain in place. That tacit recognition of Communist military strength meant that the South Vietnamese government had to maintain its territorial integrity without American ground support against an enemy with more than 100,000 main force troops in the South. The agreement also called for an eventual compromise government reflecting the military balance in the South.

Years later the North Vietnamese claimed that the United States reneged on the agreement, claiming in secret protocols—for which there is no proof save for their claims—that Richard Nixon* agreed to supply billions of dollars in economic assistance to rebuild the North. Still, it is clear that the North Vietnamese never intended to live by the agreements, merely waiting for the propitious time to invade the South. Nixon accepted the agreement and felt that he could intervene with airpower and military supplies if necessary, believing that such intervention would maintain the balance of power in Vietnam. CD

Sources: Allan E. Goodman, *The Lost Peace: America's Search for a Negotiated Settlement of the Vietnam War*, 1978; Walter Scott Dillard, *Sixty Days to Peace*, 1982; Seymour Hersh, *The Price of Power: Kissinger in the Nixon White House*, 1983.

PARIS PEACE TALKS

Formal discussions between representatives of the United States and the Democratic Republic of Vietnam* began in Paris on May 13, 1968, and continued intermittently until January 25, 1973, when Henry Kissinger* and Le Duc Tho* signed the Paris Peace Accords* ending the war. The talks developed out of a painful reassessment of American policy by President Lyndon B. Johnson* in the aftermath of the Communist Tet Offensive* in 1968. After receiving Secretary of Defense Clark Clifford's* report in mid-March that the United States could not win the war,

Johnson stunned a nationwide audience on March 31, 1968, announcing he would seek peace in Vietnam and not seek renomination or reelection in 1968. After several weeks of preparatory talks, the Paris peace talks commenced on May 13, 1968.

From the outset, the talks were fraught with difficulties. The chief American negotiator was W. Averell Harriman* until January 1969, followed by Henry Cabot Lodge.* Le Duc Tho headed the North Vietnamese delegation throughout the negotiations. Nguyen Thi Binh* headed the National Liberation Front (NLF; *see* Vietcong) delegation. During Johnson's presidency the United States approached the talks believing that it held the advantage in Vietnam and thus continually insisted on mutual withdrawal of American and North Vietnamese forces, leaving the Saigon* government in control. The North Vietnamese and NLF, of course, refused to accept such an arrangement. The impasse in the two negotiating positions was symbolized by a monthlong debate over the size and shape of the table that the two sides would sit at once formal negotiations began. Later, during the Nixon* administration, the United States operated from a belief that, whether it held the advantage or not, it had to remain firm to impress on the Soviet Union* and the People's Republic of China* that the United States had not lost its will to resist Communist aggression. Meanwhile, the North Vietnamese remained unyielding in their negotiating position. They wanted all foreign military forces removed from Indochina,* and they would not admit to any division of Vietnam. Eventually this test of

wills would prove uneven: the United States would weaken, while the North Vietnamese leadership would accept tremendous losses in manpower and the devastation of their homeland to stay the course.

By 1971 Henry Kissinger and Richard Nixon had decided to pursue secret negotiations to end the war. The Paris peace talks were too public, and because the United States was willing to make concessions to the North Vietnamese and NLF point of view, Kissinger and Nixon felt that secret negotiations would better preserve American credibility. Those secret negotiations reached fruition in the fall of 1972, and the final arrangement was signed on January 25, 1973. CD

Sources: Allan E. Goodman, *The Lost Peace: America's Search for a Negotiated Settlement of the Vietnam War*, 1978; Walter Scott Dillard, *Sixty Days to Peace*, 1982.

PARROT'S BEAK

The "Parrot's Beak" illustrates the complexities, both political and logistic, surrounding the war in Vietnam. The Parrot's Beak is a region of Cambodia* jutting into South Vietnam west of Saigon* and north of the Mekong River. Vietcong* and North Vietnamese units established a presence in the region early in the Vietnam War, giving them a safe haven close to major population centers in South Vietnam. After becoming independent from France,*

Below: Government troops and villagers read a newspaper with a headline reporting the ceasefire on June 15, 1973, as it goes into effect. Though January 27, 1973, is generally recognized as the enactment date of the Paris Peace Accords, the talks continued out of necessity. Sporadic fighting continued in some regions. U.S. ground forces were removed from Vietnam by March 29, 1973, but bombing continued in North Vietnam. Due to continued allegations of ceasefire violations by all sides, Kissinger and Le Duc Tho met in Paris in May and June of 1973 to get the implementation of the peace agreement back on track. On June 13, 1973, the United States and the DRV signed a joint communiqué pledging mutual support for full implementation of the Paris Accords. These government troops were searching, house-to-house, to prevent the Communists from infiltrating a small hamlet along Highway 1, west of Saigon.

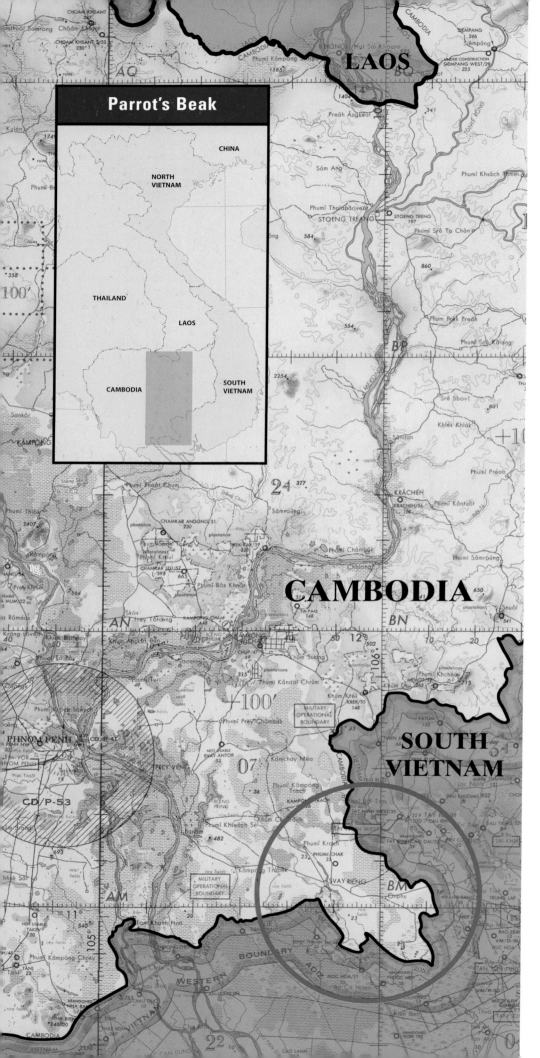

Parrot's Beak

Cambodia had been ruled by Prince Norodom Sihanouk.*
Early in his rule, Sihanouk had sought close ties with the
United States to offset Cambodia's two centuries-old
enemies: Thailand* and Vietnam. As American interests
became increasingly identified with South Vietnam,
Sihanouk sought closer ties with the People's Republic of
China* as a means of countering Vietnamese influence.
At the same time, he allowed the North Vietnamese to
establish a presence along the Cambodian-Vietnamese
border, with a major presence in the Parrot's Beak.
Sihanouk believed that the Chinese would restrain them
from violating Cambodian sovereignty. This strategy came
apart as China sank into increased isolation during Mao
Zedong's* Cultural Revolution.

In late 1967 the North Vietnamese were building up
forces inside Cambodia in preparation for 1968's Tet
Offensive.* General William Westmoreland* pressed
President Lyndon Johnson* to approve American ground
assaults against the enemy in Cambodia. Sihanouk began
once again to court American support. In an interview
with the *Washington Post* in December 1967, Sihanouk
stated he would grant the United States the right of "hot
pursuit" against the North Vietnamese and Vietcong
inside Cambodia—as long as no Cambodians were harmed.
Sihanouk suggested that Johnson send Senator Mike
Mansfield,* whom he labeled "a just and courageous man
whom we consider a friend," to Cambodia to discuss the
issue. Johnson, however, was reluctant to expand the war,
and nothing came of this overture.

After Richard Nixon's* inauguration, the question of
sanctuaries* in Cambodia became a major policy issue.
General Creighton Abrams,* Westmoreland's successor,
reported that the Communists had recently moved 40,000
fresh troops into the area, and were supplying them largely
by sea through the port of Sihanoukville, on the Gulf of
Siam. In February 1969, Nixon ordered the bombing of
Cambodia in retaliation for increased Communist attacks
from that area. The bombing, dubbed Operation Menu,*
was seen as a short-term operation. In fact, it continued
for fourteen months.

The operation was conducted in total secrecy, with only
a few sympathetic members of Congress* informed of the
actions. Then an enterprising *New York Times* correspondent broke the story. Finally acknowledged in 1973, the
air strikes fueled demands for impeachment of Nixon in
Congress, and helped win the support needed to pass the
War Powers Resolution Act.*

As a result of American air action in the Parrot's Beak,
the North Vietnamese began preparing for Sihanouk to turn
against them completely by arming and training guerrillas
of the Khmer Rouge,* the Cambodian Communist movement. At the same time, Sihanouk was losing the support
of the Cambodian military and middle class. In 1970, while
Sihanouk was in France, he was removed by Lon Nol,*

setting Cambodia on a long downward road from which it has yet to fully recover. NJA

Sources: Shelby L. Stanton, *The Rise and Fall of an American Army: U.S. Ground Forces in Vietnam, 1965–1973*, 1985; William Shawcross, *Sideshow: Kissinger, Nixon, and the Destruction of Cambodia*, 1979; Stanley Karnow, *Vietnam: A History*, 1983.

"PASSAGE TO FREEDOM"

In 1954, when the Geneva Accords* divided Indochina* at the 17th parallel into North and South Vietnam, Roman Catholic leaders in the North openly urged Catholic peasants to relocate to South Vietnam, where they thought the Church would have a more hospitable reception. Approximately 900,000 Roman Catholics* relocated to South Vietnam. The South Vietnamese government, headed by northerner Ngo Dinh Diem,* received the refugees* with open arms, and the United States assisted the relocation by providing a task force of fifty ships to help move the people. Reception centers, financed by the United States and the South Vietnamese government, offered the refugees food, clothing, and medical assistance. The program to relocate the refugees was called the Passage to Freedom by U.S. officials.

Source: Gertrude Samuels, "Passage to Freedom," *National Geographic* 107 (June 1955): 858–874.

PATHET LAO

Nominally led by Prince Souphanouvong, the Pathet Lao ("Land of the Lao") evolved from Ho Chi Minh's* Indochinese Communist Party (*see* Lao Dong Party). Educated in France* as an engineer, Prince Souphanouvong affiliated with the Vietminh* while working in Vietnam. The deplorable conditions resulting from French colonial rule made Souphanouvong a radical nationalist in favor of armed revolt. With Vietminh assistance, he helped build nationalist political and military organizations that briefly governed Laos* in 1945. During the First Indochina War the Pathet Lao worked closely with the Vietminh. At Dien Bien Phu* Pathet Lao forces occupied blocking positions to prevent French reinforcements. Although the Vietminh argued determinedly for Pathet Lao and Khmer Issarak* (pro-Vietminh Cambodian nationalists) representation at the 1954 Geneva conference (*see* Geneva Accords), France and the United States absolutely refused. Pressured by China* and the Soviets, the Vietminh yielded amid charges by Laotian and Cambodian nationalists that they had been sold out to gain Western acceptance of Vietminh control of at least northern Vietnam. Pathet Lao exclusion resulted in a Laotian settlement that reflected neither its political nor military strength.

Throughout the 1950s and into the 1960s, Prince Souvanna Phouma* and his half brother Prince Souphanouvong tried to establish a unified government. Their efforts were sabotaged repeatedly by American determination to deny the Pathet Lao any participation in the national government. The unwillingness of Premier Souvana Phouma to deploy the Royal Laotian Army against the Pathet Lao promoted U.S. funding of a rightist mercenary army, led by General Phoumi Nosavan, which attacked both the Pathet Lao and the Royal Laotian Army. To American dismay, the brothers joined forces, defeating Phoumi's mercenaries, and provoking the "Laotian crisis" and the 1962 Geneva agreements on Laos.

Continued American intervention prevented Pathet Lao participation in the coalition government agreed upon at Geneva. The Pathet Lao retreated to two northern provinces and the eastern border, where North Vietnamese Army* forces controlled the Ho Chi Minh Trail.* The United States initiated a "secret war" against both the trail and the Pathet Lao through extensive bombing (more than 2 million tons—slightly less tonnage than was dropped in all of World War II), establishing Special Forces* camps, and raising a mercenary army among Meo Hmong* tribesmen. These actions effectively partitioned Laos until a Pathet Lao–dominated coalition government was established in 1974. It was replaced by the Lao People's Democratic Republic in December 1975. SF

Sources: Philippe Devillers and Jean Lacouture, *End of A War*, 1969; Peter Poole, *Eight Presidents and Indochina*, 1978; Wilfred Bruchett, *The Second Indochina War*, 1970; Bernard Fall, *The Two Viet Nams*, 1967; Paul F. Langer and Joseph J. Zasloff, *North Vietnam and the Pathet Lao: Partners in the Struggle for Laos*, 1970; Charles A. Stevenson, *The End of Nowhere: American Policy Toward Laos Since 1954*, 1973.

PATHFINDERS

Trained at the Airborne School at Fort Benning, Georgia, Pathfinders (known as black hats because of their black baseball caps) were the U.S. Army's equivalent of combat air traffic controllers. Working in small teams, they were parachuted or helicopter-inserted into hostile terrain to direct air traffic. They were utilized anytime an operation employed substantial numbers of aircraft, including airborne or heliborne combat assaults, major search-and-destroy* operations, establishing forward artillery firebases, or extracting large enemy caches. Because ground travel was time-consuming and forfeited the element of surprise, and because roads were subject to mining and ambush, the United States relied heavily on airmobile operations. The skies were often crowded with gunships,* helicopters, and helicopter-gunships; and without Pathfinders serious accidents were likely. Pathfinders' responsibilities included identifying drop zones for airborne operations and landing

Opposite page: A map of the Parrot's Beak, Cambodia, showing how it juts into Vietnam near Saigon. Vietcong and NVA units established a presence in this area of Cambodia early in the Vietnam War, allowing close access to Saigon.

zones—or LZs*—for heliborne operations; supervising the clearing and securing of LZs for heliborne operations; determining flight approaches to these zones; establishing and operating navigational aids; coordinating various types of aircraft and the sorties* of aircraft over their operational area; and occasionally fire direction for tactical aircraft and artillery, especially final preparation fires prior to heliborne combat assault operations. Pathfinders were used most extensively by airborne and airmobile forces, including the 82d,* the 101st,* and ARVN (*see* Army of the Republic of Vietnam) airborne divisions,* the 173d Airborne Brigade,* and the U.S. Marines.* SF

Sources: Bernard W. Rogers, *Cedar Falls–Junction City: A Turning Point*, 1974; John J. Tolson, *Airmobility, 1961–1971*, 1973; Shelby L. Stanton, *The Green Berets at War*, 1985.

PENTAGON PAPERS

On Sunday, June 13, 1971, the *New York Times* began publishing a series of articles based on a several-thousand-page, secret Defense Department account of American involvement in Indochina.* Within a few days the Justice Department obtained a temporary restraining order barring further publication on the grounds of national security, and the so-called Pentagon Papers became another flash point between liberals and conservatives in the great Vietnam debate. In 1967 Secretary of Defense Robert McNamara* had ordered a history of U.S. involvement in Indochina, and the project was completed in 1968. In 1971 the secret history became public knowledge. The previous year, one of the coauthors of the history, a Rand Corporation* employee named Daniel Ellsberg,* had begun photocopying thousands of pages and giving them to J. William Fulbright,* chairman of the Senate Foreign Relations Committee.* The next year Ellsberg provided a complete set to the *New York Times*. Efforts by the Nixon* administration could not dissuade the paper from publishing excerpts of the history.

By a vote of six to three, the U.S. Supreme Court overturned the temporary restraining order on June 30, 1971, and permitted publication, noting that the freedoms of speech and press were at stake. Publication of the Pentagon Papers became a cause célèbre primarily because they revealed duplicity in the Johnson* administration—government officials telling the public one thing and actively pursuing different military and political policies, in particular being involved in Indochina sooner and to a greater extent than the public had once assumed. CD

Sources: John P. Roche, "The Pentagon Papers," in *Sentenced to Life*, 1974; Peter Schrag, *Test of Loyalty*, 1974; Daniel Ellsberg, *Secrets: A Memoir of the Vietnam War*, 2002.

PENTAGON PAPERS TRIAL

The Pentagon Papers Trial was the popular name given to the 1972–73 trial of Daniel Ellsberg* and Anthony J. Russo.* The defendants were charged with conspiracy, espionage, and conversion of government property (theft) for photocopying in 1969 substantial portions of a forty-seven-volume study commissioned by U.S. Secretary of Defense Robert S. McNamara* in 1967 and titled *History of U.S. Decision-making Process on Vietnam Policy*, otherwise known as the Pentagon Papers.* Criminal charges against Ellsberg came after the *New York Times* and other newspapers published excerpts of the Pentagon Papers in June and July 1971. Contrary to common belief, Ellsberg and Russo were not indicted for giving the Pentagon Papers to any newspapers. They were indicted for temporarily removing the Pentagon Papers from the premises of the Rand Corporation* in Santa Barbara, California, and for photocopying the documents at an advertising agency owned by Russo's friend Lynda Sinay. Ellsberg was first indicted on June 25, 1971. He surrendered to federal authorities in Boston on June 28.

A new indictment was returned in secret on December 29, 1971, charging Ellsberg and Russo with fifteen counts of conspiracy, espionage, and theft. Listed as unindicted coconspirators were Lynda Sinay and Vu Van Thai, a former South Vietnamese ambassador to the United States. The charges against Ellsberg carried maximum penalties of 115 years' imprisonment and $120,000 in fines. Those against Russo carried maximum penalties of thirty-five years' imprisonment and $40,000 in fines. During the trial, however, federal district court judge William Byrne directed an acquittal on one espionage count against Ellsberg and Russo. The trial began in Los Angeles on July 10, 1972, with initial selection of the jury. On July 24, Judge Byrne revealed that the United States had filed a wiretap transcript of a conversation by a member of the defense team, but ruled that the contents need not be disclosed because they did not bear on the case. The Supreme Court upheld the judge in November. Jury selection began in January 1973. Several key questions animated the four-month trial: (1) Can citizens be prosecuted for conspiracy to obstruct the executive branch's function of controlling the dissemination of classified documents when there is no statute authorizing the president to classify general national security information or making it a crime to duplicate or release such information to the public? (2) Can a citizen lawfully be prosecuted for duplicating or disseminating information that was improperly marked TOP SECRET? (3) Because the defendants had not given the Pentagon Papers to a foreign nation, could they be prosecuted for espionage? (4) Can citizens be prosecuted for espionage for leaking classified information if their only intent is to inform the public of what they believe is government misconduct? (5) Did photocopying the documents constitute theft? (6) What was stolen—physical documents or information? (7) Who owned the copied documents: the federal government, the Rand Corporation, or the three former Defense Department officials who possessed the documents and gave Ellsberg permission to study them?

Key testimony in the trial centered on these questions as well as the judge's instruction that the government prove that the published information injured the United States or helped a foreign nation. On May 11, 1973, however, at the close of testimony, Judge Byrne dismissed all charges against Ellsberg and Russo and declared a mistrial because of "improper government conduct" that offended a "sense of justice." Among other things, a White House unit, with Central Intelligence Agency* assistance, had burglarized the office of Ellsberg's psychiatrist in 1971 in search of information damaging to Ellsberg; FBI wiretap transcripts of telephone conversations by Ellsberg in 1969 and 1970 had disappeared; and presidential assistant John Ehrlichman had offered Judge Byrne the directorship of the FBI during

the trial. A poll of jurors after the mistrial indicated that most would have voted for acquittal. JK

Sources: Peter Schrag, *Test of Loyalty*, 1974; Daniel Ellsberg, *Secrets: A Memoir of the Vietnam War*, 2002.

PEOPLE'S LIBERATION ARMY

See People's Republic of China

PEOPLE'S REPUBLIC OF CHINA

On October 1, 1949, Mao Zedong's* victorious Communist forces proclaimed the People's Republic of China in

Below: This retouched photograph of Mao Zedong, chairman of the People's Republic of China, was taken in his private rail car on January 1, 1963, near Hebei, China.

Beijing, the traditional capital. The next twenty-five years would be as tumultuous as the preceding twenty-five years of civil war. After the Chinese intervention in the Korean War, the United States attempted to freeze the People's Republic out of the international community, erecting a series of regional security pacts and mutual defense treaties among surrounding nations. In return, the Chinese predicted the demise of capitalism and American global hegemony, declaring "wars of national liberation"* throughout the world. Their own People's Liberation Army was a model. Although the People's Liberation Army eventually became huge and questionable in quality, it was unsurpassed in its ability, through tightly controlled discipline and mass appeal, to politicize large numbers of people. Mao Zedong predicted that mass uprisings and guerrilla wars in capitalist countries would bring about the revolution that Karl Marx had predicted.

Ho Chi Minh's* People's Army of Vietnam was modeled on the People's Liberation Army, but other than that there was little resemblance. Although the United States feared the intervention of the Chinese in the Vietnam conflict, just as had happened in Korea,* the People's Republic of China was not inclined to do so. For centuries an intense and often bloody rivalry had raged between the Vietnamese and the Chinese, and the North Vietnamese would have viewed any Chinese military intervention into Indochina as simply a pretext for renewing the domination of the peninsula they had once enjoyed. Also, in 1962 Mao

had plunged the Chinese people into the Great Proletarian Cultural Revolution. Mao gained control of the army and let loose a rampaging horde of young Red Guards to terrorize government officials, scientists, and teachers. The Cultural Revolution so destabilized Chinese society that a concerted military effort in Indochina was not really possible. Finally, by 1971 the Chinese began to fear Soviet and even Vietnamese power more than American power, which seemed to be ebbing. With increasingly powerful Vietnamese forces to their south and Soviet forces aligned all along their long northern borders, Chinese leaders decided to seek a rapprochement with the United States. Richard Nixon* and Henry Kissinger* exploited that decision and normalized diplomatic relations in 1972. Although the Chinese provided some weapons and economic assistance to the North Vietnamese during the course of the war, they never posed the threat to the United States that they had twenty years earlier in Korea. CD

Sources: *China, Vietnam, and the United States*, 1966; King C. Chen, *Vietnam and China, 1938–1954*, 1969; Stanley Karnow, *Vietnam: A History*, 1983.

PEOPLE'S REVOLUTIONARY PARTY

See Lao Dong Party

Below: Representatives of North Vietnam and South Vietnam sign the agreement reuniting the nation as the Socialist Republic of Vietnam on November 22, 1975. Seated to the left is Truong Chinh, representing North Vietnam, and to the right is Pham Hung, representing South Vietnam. The meeting was held in Saigon, which had been renamed Ho Chi Minh City.

PEOPLE'S SELF-DEFENSE FORCE

The People's Self-Defense Force (PSDF) was an unpaid, part-time militia in the Republic of Vietnam* designed to prevent Vietcong* infiltration* and village dominance. Although the Republic of Vietnam claimed that there were more than 4 million members of the PSDF in 1972, those numbers were highly inflated because they included all men between the ages of sixteen and fifty. Commitment to the PSDF was often weak, and the Vietcong were known for infiltrating the group.

Sources: Guenter Lewy, *America in Vietnam*, 1978; Ngo Quang Truong, *Territorial Forces*, 1981.

PEOPLE'S WARS

See Wars of National Liberation

PF

See Popular Forces

PHAM HUNG

Pham Hung was born in Hanoi in 1911. He joined the Communist Party just after turning twenty and spent the next forty years fighting against the succession of French, Japanese, and American forces occupying Vietnam. By 1963 Hung was a member of the central committee of the Lao Dong Party.* When the final assault on South Vietnam began in 1975, Hung was the senior North Vietnamese politburo member in the South. General Van Tien Dung* was military commander of the final assault, and Hung was the chief political commissar. He became part of the Provisional Revolutionary Government* in 1975 and of the ruling politburo of the new Socialist Republic of Vietnam.* Pham Hung was prime minister of Vietnam from 1987 to 1988. He died on March 10, 1988.

Source: *Who's Who in the Socialist Countries*, 1978; *Nhan Dan*, April 30, 2005.

PHAM NGOC THAO

Pham Ngoc Thao was born in 1922 to Roman Catholic parents. While still a student Thao began absorbing anti-French attitudes, and after World War II he joined the Vietcong.*

When the Geneva Accords* were concluded in 1954, Thao decided to stay in South Vietnam, and he became a captain in the army. Loyal to General Nguyen Khanh* and opposed to Ngo Dinh Diem,* Thao enjoyed a brief popularity in 1964 when Khanh was in control of the military junta in Saigon,* but after Khanh's resignation later in the year, Thao was exiled to the United States as press attaché to Ambassador Tran Thien Khiem.* When Thao tried to return to South Vietnam in 1965 to lead a coup against the government, he disappeared under mysterious circumstances and was never seen again. Most political observers in Saigon assumed that General Nguyen Van Thieu* had seen to Thao's death.

Sources: *Newsweek* 65 (March 1, 1965): 21–22; Frances FitzGerald, *Fire in the Lake: The Vietnamese and the Americans in Vietnam*, 1972.

PHAM VAN DONG

Pham Van Dong was born on March 1, 1906, in Quang Nam Province. At the time Quang Nam Province was part of the French protectorate of Annam.* Dong's family had an educated, mandarin background, and he was educated at the French lycée academy at Hue,* where two of his classmates were Vo Nguyen Giap* and Ngo Dinh Diem.* As a student Dong became active in nationalist groups and eventually

Below: A bloodless coup d'etat in Saigon on February 1, 1965, ousted Premier Nguyen Khanh of South Vietnam. ARVN Colonel Pham Ngoc Thao engineered the coup.

defined himself as a revolutionary bent on the expulsion of the French. In 1930 French authorities arrested him for sedition, and he spent the next eight years in prison. He finally fled to China,* where he met Ho Chi Minh* and became one of the founding fathers of the Lao Dong Party.* For the next four decades, along with Ho Chi Minh and Vo Nguyen Giap, Dong was among the triumvirate that dominated North Vietnamese politics.

Pham Van Dong was active in the Vietminh* in their struggle against the Japanese during World War II and the French between 1946 and 1954, and he served as the leader of the Vietnamese delegation to the Geneva Conference (*see* Geneva Accords) in 1954. Dong was Ho Chi Minh's prime minister from 1950 to Ho's death in September 1969, and after Ho's death Dong emerged as the most public figure in North Vietnam. Between 1969 and 1975 Dong released several diplomatic initiatives, always insisting on an American withdrawal, and frequently gave interviews to the Western press. Pham Van Dong played a key role in the Paris Peace Accords* of 1973, in which the United States agreed to withdraw from

South Vietnam while leaving in place all North Vietnamese forces. After the conquest of South Vietnam in 1975, Pham Van Dong was appointed prime minister of the Socialist Republic of Vietnam.* He remained at that post until December 1986, when a series of economic setbacks in the Socialist Republic of Vietnam forced his resignation. Pham Van Dong died on April 29, 2000.

Sources: *Who's Who in the Socialist Countries*, 1978; Joseph Buttinger, *Vietnam: A Dragon Embattled*, Vol. 2, *Vietnam at War*, 1967; *Washington Post*, December 18, 1986; *New York Times*, April 30–May 1, 2000.

Right: North Vietnamese Premier Pham Van Dong, a longtime associate of Ho Chi Minh, poses on the steps of the presidential palace in Hanoi on January 1, 1967.

PHAN BOI CHAU

Originally named Phan Van San, Phan Boi Chau was born in 1867 in the central province of Nghe An, Vietnam. After passing the mandarin examinations in 1900, Phan Boi Chau began organizing resistance movements against the French. At first he wanted the restoration of a royal Vietnamese government, and he threw his support behind Prince Cuong De,* a direct descendant of Gia Long* of the Nguyen* dynasty. After the Japanese victory over Russia in 1904, Chau felt that the support of Japan* was necessary to Vietnam, so both he and Cuong De went to live in Japan and study. Phan Boi Chau met with Japanese leaders, who urged him to send young men to Japan for military and political training, and in 1907 he organized the "Exodus to the East," a program that sent more than 200 young Vietnamese to study in Japan.

By then, however, Chau was growing more sympathetic with Chinese philosophers committed to democratic reform, and his royalist schemes to restore Cuong De to the Vietnamese throne waned. Instead of a return to the inflexibility of the mandarin bureaucracy, Vietnamese independence would come only through mass participation. He attempted a rebellion against the French that failed late in 1907, and led to the execution of thirteen of his followers. He had remained in Japan during the revolt but fled to Siam after the French began demanding his extradition. Phan Boi Chau and his resistance group, Duy Tan Hoi (founded in 1904), continued to play an important role in Vietnamese nationalism. He was imprisoned between 1912 and 1917 for establishing a new nationalist group, the Viet Nam Quang Phuc Hoi, and for the unsuccessful assassination attempt on Albert Sarraut. Phan Boi Chau was a major figure in Vietnamese rebellion against the French, because his political organizations rallied mass insurgency and his East Asia United League at least gave the Vietnamese a visible profile among nationalists in Japan, China,* Korea,* India, and the Philippines.*

French agents constantly tracked Phan Boi Chau after the 1907 revolt, but he maintained his freedom, albeit a furtive one, until 1925 when they caught up with him in

Shanghai. Charged with sedition, he was extradited to Hanoi,* tried and convicted, and placed under house arrest in Hue.* Phan Boi Chau died fifteen years later, in 1940.

Sources: *Webster's New Biographical Dictionary,* 1983; David G. Marr, *Vietnamese Anticolonialism, 1885–1925,* 1971; Joseph Buttinger, *Vietnam: A Dragon Embattled,* Vol. 1, *From Colonialism to the Vietminh,* 1967.

PHAN CHAU TRINH

Born in central Vietnam in 1872, Phan Chau Trinh came from a wealthy, scholarly, landowning family. His father was loyal to Emperor Ham Nghi and fought in the Scholar's Revolt, but he was killed in 1885 by other dissidents who considered him a traitor. Phan Chau Trinh studied the Chinese classics under the tutorship of his brother, and by 1901 he had earned the most prestigious mandarin degree. He met Phan Boi Chau* in 1903 and in 1905 resigned his position in the mandarin bureaucracy. He quickly split company with Phan Boi Chau, however, because he had no faith in Japanese benevolence, and instead of viewing the French as the major enemy of Vietnamese independence he blamed the mandarin bureaucracy and the imperial family. Phan Chau Trinh preferred the French to the Nguyen* clan.

Allying himself with French anticolonialists,* Phan Chau Trinh called for the destruction of the mandarin bureaucracy and its replacement with a modern educational and legal system. He also advocated the industrialization of Vietnam. Phan Chau Trinh eschewed the radical violence of Phan Boi Chau, but his trust in the power of French liberals proved naive. French officials arrested him for revolutionary activity* in 1908 and kept him in prison until 1911, when he went to live in France.* For the next ten years Phan Chau Trinh met with French liberals and journalists, and became a symbol of Vietnamese nationalism, but he lacked broad peasant support. Phan Chau Trinh died in 1926.

Sources: Joseph Buttinger, *The Smaller Dragon: A Political History of Vietnam,* 1958; *Webster's New Biographical Dictionary,* 1983.

PHAN DINH PHUNG

Born in 1847, Phan Dinh Phung became one of the most prominent of the nineteenth-century Vietnamese nationalists. He rose to power at the imperial court of Tu Duc. Although he was banished from the imperial court because of his eventual opposition to the accession of Ham Nghi to the imperial throne, Phan Dinh Phung organized his own guerrilla army, retreated into the mountains of central Vietnam, and for nearly a decade regularly attacked the French throughout a region extending from Thanh Hoa Province in the north to Quang Binh in the south. Phan Dinh Phung died of dysentery in 1896, but his life and

career became a rallying point and patriotic memory for three generations of Vietnamese nationalists.

Sources: *Webster's New Biographical Dictionary,* 1983; Stanley Karnow, *Vietnam: A History,* 1983; Joseph Buttinger, *Vietnam: A Dragon Embattled,* Vol. 1, *From Colonialism to the Vietminh,* 1967.

PHAN HUY QUAT

From February 16 to June 12, 1965, Phan Huy Quat was prime minister of South Vietnam. An able and reform-minded civilian politician, he served as a transitional leader between General Nguyen Khanh* and Air Marshal Nguyen Cao Ky.* Born in 1901 in northern Vietnam, Phan Huy Quat received a medical degree in Hanoi* in 1937 and operated a maternity clinic there until 1945. Quat became one of the founders of the Dai Viet Quoc Dan Dang,* or Nationalist Party of Greater Vietnam. In the early 1950s he held several cabinet posts including minister of defense. Ngo Dinh Diem* viewed Quat as a serious rival and refused to give him a cabinet post after 1954. In 1955 the United States came very close to endorsing Quat as a replacement for Diem. Phan Huy Quat was one of the signers of the "Caravelle" petition urging reform in April 1960 and was arrested but later released by Diem's government in November 1960.

After Diem's assassination in 1963, Quat was finally included in South Vietnam's cabinet. Early in 1965 the Armed Forces Council forced Nguyen Khanh from power, and the military group supported the selection of Quat as prime minister. Quat attempted to structure a representative cabinet and to cultivate the goodwill of the military, but he was unable to overcome the factional intrigues among Buddhists,* Catholics,* and other groups in Saigon.* When Quat finally came to an impasse with elderly chief of state Phan Khac Suu,* the military forced Quat to resign, and Nguyen Cao Ky* became prime

Below: President Lyndon B. Johnson meets in the White House with Phan Huy Quat, the foreign minister of the Republic of Vietnam (South Vietnam) on June 4, 1964.

minister. Phan Huy Quat was a well-known opponent of Communism. After Hanoi's victory in 1975, attempts to get him out of Vietnam proved unsuccessful, and he was killed. DLA

Source: Robert Shaplen, *The Lost Revolution*, 1965.

PHAN KHAC SUU

Phan Khac Suu was born in My Tho* in the Mekong Delta* in 1905. The son of a prosperous farmer, Suu studied engineering in Paris during the 1920s. He returned to Saigon* in 1930 and took an engineering job with the French government, but at night he was actively engaged in anti-French nationalist activities. The French imprisoned him at Poulo Condore* between 1940 and 1945. Suu was a devout member of the Cao Dai* religious sect, and he served briefly in 1954 as minister of agriculture under Ngo Dinh Diem.* After cooperating in the abortive coup against Diem in 1960, Suu spent three more years in prison. He was released after Diem's assassination in 1963, and became chief of state of South Vietnam (1964–65) and president of the Constituent Assembly (1966–67). During the last years before his death in 1970, Phan Khac Suu was an opponent of Generals Nguyen Cao Ky* and Nguyen Van Thieu.*

Source: *New York Times*, May 25, 1970.

Right: Phan Khac Suu after his election as president of the Constituent Assembly of South Vietnam on January 1, 1966. Suu was an inveterate opponent of both Nguyen Cao Ky and Nguyen Van Thieu.

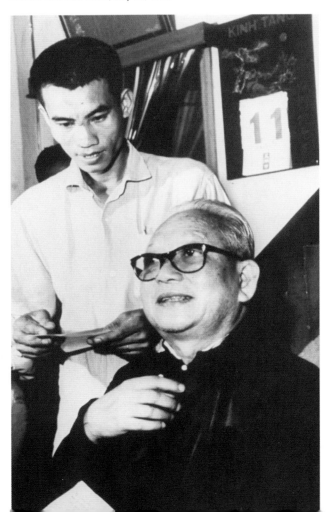

PHAN QUANG DAN

Phan Quang Dan was born on November 6, 1918, in Nghe An. He received an M.D. degree from the University of Hanoi in 1945 and later studied at the Sorbonne in Paris and at Harvard University. An intense anti-Communist, Phan Quang Dan was a political advisor to Bao Dai* in the late 1940s. He relocated to South Vietnam after 1954 and taught at the Medical School of Saigon.* He practiced medicine in a working-class neighborhood in Saigon and won election to the Constituent Assembly in 1955. An outspoken opponent of Ngo Dinh Diem,* Dan was not allowed to assume his seat in the assembly and instead spent time undergoing torture as a political prisoner. Later in the 1960s, Phan Quang Dan spoke out against the corruption of the Thieu-Ky government even while opposing the Communists.

Sources: *Asia Who's Who*, 1960; Frances FitzGerald, *Fire in the Lake: The Vietnamese and the Americans in Vietnam*, 1972; Joseph Buttinger, *Vietnam: A Dragon Embattled*, Vol. 2, *Vietnam at War*, 1967.

PHILIPPINES

The Philippines played a dual role in the Vietnam War. The location of the giant military complexes of Subic Bay Naval Base and Clark Air Base within the Philippines virtually assured that this country would serve as the primary non-U.S. staging area for the war. Virtually all naval aircraft and ordnance passed through Subic. It served as the main repair station for the Seventh Fleet,* playing host to 1,600 military personnel and 9,000 sailors at any one time. Similarly, Clark Air Base saw such an increase in traffic that a reserve air base on Mactan Island was made operational in order to handle some of the volume. Clark became the hub for all U.S. military air traffic in the western Pacific and the operational center of the Thirteenth Air Force.

The second role for the Philippines was support for the war effort. Manila had always been a strong champion of South Vietnam, which the Philippines considered the key to the future political direction of Southeast Asia. In June 1964 Defense Minister Tran Thien Khiem* of South Vietnam visited the Philippines, in return for which Manila sent thirty-four Filipino doctors to Saigon.* Later in 1964 the Philippines reiterated its support for the defense of Southeast Asia in general and Vietnam in particular under the SEATO agreements. In September 1965 Manila served as the center for the American-sponsored Asian People's Anti-Communist League, which condemned North Vietnamese aggression in South Vietnam. In October 1966 the Philippines hosted a summit of all the nations that had troops in South Vietnam to assess the prospects for peace there. North Vietnam, of course, refused to attend.

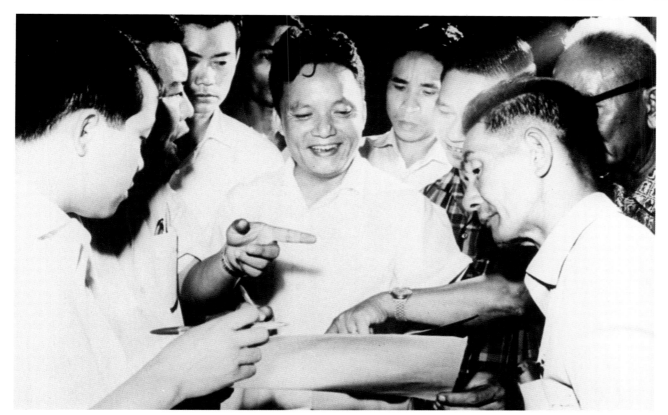

Left: Phan Quang Dan, the Sorbonne- and Harvard-educated, iconoclastic political figure in South Vietnam during the 1960s, was equally critical of the Communists and the corruption of the regimes of Nguyen Cao Ky and Nguyen Van Thieu.

Increasing American military involvement in South Vietnam led to the "Many Flags Program" of 1965, in which the United States asked for troop commitments from its allies. Australia,* New Zealand,* and South Korea* quickly responded. President Lyndon B. Johnson* especially wanted Filipino participation. The new president of the Philippines, Ferdinand Marcos, initially refused; but after visits from Vice President Hubert Humphrey,* Senator Mike Mansfield,* Secretary of State Dean Rusk,* and Ambassador W. Averell Harriman,* he relented. On February 19, 1966, Marcos announced that a combat engineering battalion of 2,000 men would be sent to Vietnam. The battalion served until October 4, 1969, when increasing Filipino opposition to the Vietnam War forced its withdrawal. Marcos's support for the war, however, was not motivated simply by feelings of national security. He negotiated aggressively for $39 million in additional American aid as well as sizable contributions of equipment to the Philippine military. Marcos also made sure that Filipino troops had full access to U.S. military PXs, which they exploited, and that the United States employ Filipino civilians in Vietnam.

The Philippines also contributed to the Vietnam War in another, less direct way. During the 1950s the United States had supported the highly successful Filipino fight against the Communist-led Hukbalahap (Huk) insurrection. This included engineering the ascendancy of the strongly pro-U.S. Ramon Magsaysay to the Philippine presidency. As Paul Nitze* noted in 1965, the Philippine experience demonstrated conclusively that guerrillas could be suppressed. In a very

real sense, the Philippines became a model for the American role in South Vietnam.

After the end of the war and the triumph of North Vietnam in 1975, the Philippines became even more important to U.S. interests. The Socialist Republic of Vietnam* permitted a large Soviet naval presence in Cam Ranh Bay* and a significant Soviet air presence at Da Nang.* Subic Bay and Clark military facilities were considered a counterweight of inestimable importance. The twenty-year presidency of Ferdinand Marcos ended in 1986, and the United States closed the last of its military bases in the Philippines in 1992. GMB

Sources: William J. Pomeroy, *An American Made Tragedy: Neo-Colonialism and Dictatorship in the Philippines*, 1974; James Gregor, *Crisis in the Philippines: A Threat to U.S. Interests*, 1984; Man Mohini Kaul, *The Philippines and South East Asia*, 1978; Central Intelligence Agency, *World Factbook*, 2006.

PHOENIX PROGRAM

A joint effort by the government of (South) Vietnam (GVN; *see* Republic of Vietnam) and the Central Intelligence Agency* to gather intelligence on the Vietcong* infrastructure (VCI) and to coordinate a counterinsurgency* effort against that VCI, the Phoenix Program was actually an attempt to use the same techniques and tactics that had proved effective for the Vietcong. The three basic objectives of Phoenix were to identify Vietcong (VC), gain the support and cooperation of local Vietnamese in combating the VC, and eventually reduce the military and political activities of the enemy. Phoenix was characterized primarily by its bureaucratic nature. To be successful, it had to decrease the endemic political contests that so characterized South Vietnam. A unified and coordinated effort was necessary before the GVN could gain legitimacy and loyalty, which were essential factors in diminishing the enemy's political and military effectiveness.

Phoenix was aimed at the VC "shadow government" (policymakers and policy implementers). Its first task was to identify individual members of the VCI. It then sought to "neutralize"* those individuals, through arrest, conversion, or death. While basically a GVN program, Phoenix relied heavily on American support. The CIA provided essential advice and personnel for the intelligence-gathering aspects of the program. The Civil Operations and Revolutionary Development Support* (CORDS) assisted in the effort to coordinate Phoenix activities both among the numerous and varied GVN governmental units and with the village and hamlet officials.

The Phoenix Program faced major obstacles. Coordination was a continuing difficulty, corruption was prevalent, and the quota system adopted for identifying members of the VCI meant that any Vietnamese was at risk. Begun in 1968 under the direction of Robert Komer*

Right: On March 22, 1966, President Lyndon B. Johnson named Robert Komer to a new post as a full-time special assistant to the president to offer advice on "peaceful reconstruction in Vietnam."

and William Colby,* Phoenix lasted until 1972 and was only marginally successful. Although these years coincided with a precipitous decline in VC activity and effectiveness, Phoenix was not a major factor in that decline. Rather, the debilitation of the VC was due to normal losses of a military nature, especially after the Tet Offensive,* which was a disaster for the Vietcong, who lost approximately 80 percent of their military forces in a six-week period of massive conventional attacks.

Phoenix did result in the identification and neutralization of more than 20,000 individuals in South Vietnam. Inconsistent record keeping, abuse of the program in resolving personal disputes, the use of Phoenix to maintain a favored position by removing political adversaries, and the quota system, however, meant that many of those neutralized were not Vietcong. STT

Sources: John Prados, *Presidents' Secret Wars: CIA and Pentagon Covert Operations Since World War II*, 1986; Douglas Valentine, *The Phoenix Program*, 2000; John L. Cook, *The Advisor: The Phoenix Program in Vietnam*, 2000; Stuart Herrington, *Stalking the Vietcong. Inside Operation Phoenix: A Personal Account*, 2004; www.thememoryhole.org/phoenix/.

PHU BAI

Located forty-five miles north of Da Nang* near Hue,* Phu Bai was an important American military installation between 1965 and 1972. An air and Marine base was established at Phu Bai in the spring of 1965. In April the 9th Marine Expeditionary Brigade,* along with the 3d Battalion of the 4th Marines,* was stationed at Phu Bai, along with ten UH-34* helicopters. Eventually Phu Bai became home to Marine Air Group 39, with its seventy-five helicopters and fixed-wing aircraft. Phu Bai fell to the Vietcong* after the American withdrawal from Vietnam.

Sources: Edward Doyle and Samuel Lipsman, *The Vietnam Experience: America Takes Over, 1965–1967*, 1985; Carroll H. Dunn, *Base Development in South Vietnam 1965–1970*, 1972.

PHUOC BINH

Phuoc Binh (also known as Song Be, after the Be River), capital of Phuoc Long Province, was located in the northern tip of II Corps,* at the foot of the Central Highlands* in mountainous terrain. Almost due west of Snoul, Cambodia,* a major Vietcong* and North Vietnamese Army* (NVA) supply base, Phuoc Binh was a frequent target for enemy attack. Surrounded by mountains that were never cleared of Vietcong-NVA forces, the city and military compounds were shelled so frequently that the area was appropriately called Rocket Alley.

Left: Phu Bai Airfield was located on the coast of the South China Sea between Da Nang and Hue, South Vietnam. This aerial view of Phu Bai Airfield was taken in 1967.

Left: A new bridge is being constructed to replace the bridge submerged in water in Phu Bai. The new bridge is being constructed by U.S. Navy Mobile Construction Battalion 121.

Above: Léon Pignon, a high commissioner for Indochina, was a rabid proponent of French colonialism in Vietnam and a sworn enemy of the Vietminh. Here he is at his desk in Saigon on April 1, 1950.

Opposite page, top: In November 1965, U.S. Cavalry troops participated in the airmobile attack on North Vietnamese regulars in the Ia Drang Valley of South Vietnam. Combat engineers travel through forested areas of Chu Phong mountain near Pleiku in the Central Highlands.

Opposite page, bottom: The actor Charlie Sheen starred in the 1986 Oliver Stone film *Platoon.* The film, still considered the best of the Vietnam War genre of films by many critics, launched Sheen's career in Hollywood. Sheen's father, Martin, had also starred in a hugely successful Vietnam War movie, *Apocalypse Now.*

In May 1965 Phuoc Binh was defended by an ARVN (*see* Army of the Republic of Vietnam) ranger battalion and an American Special Forces* detachment. A Vietcong attack put the rangers to rout; the Special Forces held their compound only after hand-to-hand combat. In October 1967, as a prelude to the 1968 Tet Offensive,* Vietcong and NVA forces mounted a series of attacks in rural areas, including Phuoc Binh, to draw U.S. forces away from the population centers that would be the real objective. The Phuoc Binh attack was successfully repelled, but the city was attacked again during the Tet Offensive, and it was virtually destroyed in the fighting.

Engineers, supported by U.S. infantry, opened the road from Long Binh* to Phuoc Binh early in 1969 for the first time in three years. Phuoc Binh's remoteness, coupled with difficult terrain and proximity to the Iron Triangle,* made continuous Vietcong-NVA interdiction of the main highway easy, necessitating allied resupply by air. Phuoc Binh was the first provincial capital to fall during the 1975 Final Offensive (*see* Ho Chi Minh Campaign). The province was lightly defended, making it an ideal diversion for the main offensive in II Corps. Phuoc Binh's fall reportedly was facilitated by ARVN corruption so great that infantry units had to pay artillery units for fire support. SF

Sources: Shelby L. Stanton, *The Rise and Fall of an American Army: U.S. Ground Forces in Vietnam, 1965–1973,* 1985; Stanley Karnow, *Vietnam: A History,* 1983; Bruce Palmer Jr., *The 25-Year War,* 1984.

PHUOC LONG

See Phuoc Binh

PIASTER

Before World War II, the currency used throughout French Indochina* was the piaster, a money directly tied to the franc. Issued by the Bank of Indochina, the piaster was the first currency used nationwide in Vietnam. A severe inflation hit the piaster during the Japanese occupation of World War II because the Vichy France* government issued large volumes of unsecured piasters. The French revalued the piaster to 17 francs in 1946, an official rate of 21 piasters to the U.S. dollar, but it actually sold on the free market for 65 piasters to the dollar. A new piaster was issued in 1949 after the unification of Vietnam, Laos,* and Cambodia,* but it was devalued in 1952. In 1954 the Republic of Vietnam* withdrew from the franc zone, and in 1955 the South Vietnamese government began issuing a new, independent piaster, whose value was supported by the United States.

Source: Harvey H. Smith et al., *Area Handbook for South Vietnam,* 1967.

PIGNON, LÉON

Léon Pignon was born on April 19, 1908, and was educated at the École Coloniale. During the 1930s he worked for the Ministry for the Colonies and spent time in Tonkin.* Strongly committed to the idea of the French Empire, Pignon always saw independence for Vietnam as the height of folly. Pignon spent time in a German prison during World War II, and after the war was federal commissioner for foreign affairs from 1946 to 1947 and commissioner of the republic in Cambodia* from 1947 to 1948. He succeeded Georges d'Argenlieu* and Emile Bollaert as high commissioner for Indochina* from 1948 to 1950. Pignon hated the Vietminh* and would not hear of negotiating with them. Between 1950 and 1954 he served as a delegate to the United Nations Trusteeship Council, and between 1954 and 1959 as director of political affairs for the Ministry of French Overseas Territories. Léon Pignon died on April 4, 1976.

Sources: *International Who's Who 1976–77,* 1977; Joseph Buttinger, *Vietnam: A Dragon Embattled,* Vol. 2, *Vietnam at War,* 1967.

PLAIN OF REEDS

The Plain of Reeds was a flat, brush-covered region covering nearly 2,500 square miles in Kien Phong and Kien Tuong provinces and parts of Dinh Tuong, Long An, and Hau Nghia provinces. The Vietcong* used the Plain of Reeds as a base area for military operations against American and South Vietnamese forces.

Source: Danny Whitfield, *Historical and Cultural Dictionary of Vietnam,* 1976.

PLATOON

Commanded by a lieutenant, a platoon is an organizational unit composed of two or more squads.* A sergeant is usually second in command.

Source: Shelby L. Stanton, *Vietnam Order of Battle,* 1981.

PLATOON

Platoon is a gritty, grunt's-eye view of the Vietnam War. Directed by Oliver Stone, a Vietnam veteran, the film focuses on the war in 1967, as two sergeants, one brutal and the other compassionate, struggle for influence and as a new recruit witnesses combat and atrocities committed by and against his platoon. Unlike the surrealism of *Apocalypse*

Now,* the jingoism of *Rambo,** and the overt antiwar attitudes of *Coming Home,** *Platoon* was widely recognized by critics during its late 1986 release as the best and most realistic of the Vietnam War films.

Source: "Vietnam Images," *USA Today*, January 2, 1987.

PLEIKU

Located in the Central Highlands* and bordered by Cambodia,* Pleiku City is the capital of Pleiku Province and was II Corps* Tactical Zone headquarters. Pleiku City also was a regional market for mountain tribes, and its strategic location made it the center of a large U.S.-ARVN (*see* Army of the Republic of Vietnam) military complex. The province endured heavy fighting throughout the war. On February 7, 1965, National Liberation Front (NLF; *see* Vietcong) forces attacked Camp Holloway and Pleiku's airfield, killing 9 and wounding 128 Americans. Coupled with NLF attacks on American personnel at Qui Nhon,* this served as Lyndon Johnson's* justification for regularizing the air war and committing U.S. combat units to South Vietnam. Why the NLF attacked Pleiku and why the United

Right: In the late summer and fall of 1965, both North Vietnamese Army (NVA) and Vietcong units established a combined front in the Central Highlands of Vietnam. In late October, the 33rd Regiment of the NVA attacked Plei Me Special Forces Camp approximately 40 miles south of Pleiku City in the Pleiku Province. Plei Me was garrisoned with a 12-man U.S. Special Forces Team and 350 Montagnard mercenaries. The siege continued for several days. An ARVN relief force was sent out from Pleiku and ambushed enroute by the NVA 32nd Regiment. 1st Cavalry Artillery supported the ARVN column, the ambushers were beaten off, and the siege was lifted. Here, wounded American soldiers of the Special Forces are evacuated by helicopter from the camp in Plei Me on November 1.

States responded as it did are debatable. Some say the attack was the logical consequence of guerrilla warfare. Others see an attempt by North Vietnam to gain leverage with the Soviets, and as a "coup" for China. Some, citing Johnson's "I've had enough of this," see the American response as resulting from having been pushed too far. Others, citing McGeorge Bundy's* "Pleikus are like street-cars" (one comes along every few minutes), contend that the Americanization of the war had already been decided—the attack was only a pretext.

The first major battle between U.S. and North Vietnamese Army* (NVA) forces occurred in Pleiku Province's Ia Drang Valley* in November 1965. Elements of the 1st Cavalry Division* and the NVA 32d, 33d, and 66th regiments were locked in heavy combat for three days before NVA forces withdrew. Pleiku City was rocketed and mortared in the summer of 1967 as the NLF and NVA prepared for the 1968 Tet Offensive.* It also was the scene of heavy fighting during Tet. In the Final Offensive (*see* Ho Chi Minh Campaign), the NVA made a diversionary attack against Pleiku and Kontum while three divisions prepared for the main assault against Ban Me Thuot.* After Ban Me Thuot fell, Nguyen Van Thieu* ordered Pleiku's abandonment. The rout had begun. SF

Sources: Shelby L. Stanton, *The Rise and Fall of an American Army: U.S. Ground Forces in Vietnam, 1965–1973*, 1985; Jean Lacouture, *Vietnam Between Two Truces*, 1966; George C. Herring, *America's Longest War: The United States in Vietnam, 1950–1975*, 1986.

"POINT"

"Point" was a term used during the Vietnam War to describe an individual or unit advancing in front of the main body of troops. The purpose of the "point" was to draw enemy fire and allow the main body of soldiers to then counterattack.

Source: Al Santoli, *Everything We Had: An Oral History of the Vietnam War by Thirty-Three American Soldiers Who Fought It*, 1981.

POL POT

Born in Cambodia* as Saloth Sar in 1928, Pol Pot left his peasant background and as a teenager during the 1940s joined the forces of Ho Chi Minh* in fighting both the Japanese and the French. He became secretary of the Cambodian Communist Party in 1963, and during that same year he retreated into the Cambodian jungles and formed the Khmer Rouge* guerrillas. They opposed the government of Norodom Sihanouk,* and the American invasion of Cambodia in 1970 (*see* Operation Binh Tay) greatly swelled their numbers, giving them the strength to depose the government of Lon Nol* in 1975. At that point Pol Pot initiated a genocidal campaign matched only by Adolf Hitler's World War II assault on Jews and East Europeans. Dreaming of a preindustrial, agricultural utopia, Pol Pot decided to eliminate cities, intellectuals, professionals, and the Cambodian middle class. He completely evacuated the capital city of Phnom Penh and declared "Year Zero." During the next three years the Khmer Rouge obliterated libraries, temples, cities, schools, and colleges, and turned the entire country into a large concentration camp. An estimated 2 million people perished in his crusade for his version of utopia. In 1978 the Vietnamese invaded Cambodia and deposed Pol Pot, creating the People's Republic of Kampuchea in its place. Pol Pot retreated into the jungles with what was left of the Khmer Rouge and continued guerrilla warfare against the new government. He was diagnosed with Hodgkin's disease in 1984 and resigned from the Communist Party a year later, though he remained a political force and power within the Khmer Rouge until suffering a stroke in 1995. Pol Pot died on April 15, 1998.

Sources: Michael Vickery, *Cambodia, 1975–1982*, 1984; John Barron and Paul Anthony, *Murder of a Gentle Land*, 1977; Ben Kiernan, "How Pol Pot Came to Power," Ph.D. diss., 1986; William Shawcross, *Sideshow: Kissinger, Nixon, and the Destruction of Cambodia*, 1979, and *The Quality of Mercy: Cambodia, Holocaust, and the Modern Conscience*, 1984; *New York Times*, April 15–18, 1998; Philip Short, *Pol Pot: Anatomy of a Nightmare*, 2004.

POPULAR FORCES

The Popular Forces were paramilitary units, along with the Regional Forces,* and helped constitute the Territorial Forces* of South Vietnam. Unlike the Regional Forces,

they were nonuniformed, static units charged with village and hamlet defense, first activated in 1955 and under the operational control of the province chief. In 1964 they became part of the South Vietnamese Army, commanded by the Joint General Staff.* After 1969, when U.S. military units began their gradual withdrawal from Vietnam, the Popular Forces were often removed from their home villages and attached to main ARVN (*see* Army of the Republic of Vietnam) units for combat with the Vietcong* and North Vietnamese. Together with the Regional Forces, the Popular Forces suffered more than 80,000 killed between 1965 and 1973.

Source: Ngo Quang Truong, *Territorial Forces*, 1981.

PORTER, WILLIAM JAMES

Born in England in 1914, William Porter became a specialist in the Middle East, eventually obtaining a clerk's position at the American diplomatic mission in Baghdad, and for the next ten years serving in Beirut, Baghdad, Damascus, and Jerusalem. Porter became ambassador to Algeria in 1962, and was assigned in 1965 as deputy ambassador to South Vietnam. This unusual position was created so that Porter, an experienced diplomat, could work with the ambassadors assigned to that post.

   Porter's assignment was to bring order to the so-called pacification program (*see* Rural Reconstruction) recently established in South Vietnam. The object was to attract the

Above: In June 1970, a U.S. Army photographer snapped this picture at Troy Bridge, south of Phu Bai in South Vietnam, of a civilian's identification paper being checked by members of the 162nd Popular Forces platoon.

Left: Pol Pot, the megalomaniacal leader of the Khmer Rouge, dictator of Cambodia, and engineer of the holocaust that took 2 million of his fellow citizens' lives, is pictured here on December 12, 1979. Pot had been deposed and fled to the jungles to escape invading North Vietnamese troops, and a Japanese photographer located him at his hideout on the Thai-Cambodian border.

Above: William J. Porter was serving as deputy U.S. ambassador to South Vietnam in 1965 during the early stages of the introduction of American ground combat troops and the subsequent escalation of the fighting. This photograph was taken on September 9, 1965.

loyalty of the Vietnamese people through the efforts of trained workers in health, education, and agriculture strategically located throughout the country. The program was not working efficiently, however, because there were different agencies involved, including the Central Intelligence Agency,* the United States Information Agency, and the Agency for International Development,* which were duplicating one another's efforts. Porter's attempt to coordinate the program was short-lived because, after eighteen months, it was transferred from the embassy to the Military Assistance Command,* and Porter was reassigned as ambassador to South Korea.

Porter's most significant role in the Vietnam War was as provider of information and advice to President Lyndon Johnson* and as negotiator in the Paris peace talks.* Porter, drawing on his earlier experience with insurgency in Morocco and Algeria, pointed out that in the uprisings in those two countries, there had been considerable popular support. The Vietcong,* he noted, had not mobilized such support. His reports buttressed Johnson's belief that a policy of escalation was in order because the struggle against the Vietcong could be won.

In 1970 the aggressive diplomatic style that Porter had developed stood him in good stead, for he was called on to explain to a Senate subcommittee the expenditure, kept secret, of $1 billion on the 50,000 troops sent to South Vietnam since 1965. Again, in the following year, he drew on his skill at negotiation when asked to explain to the South Vietnamese the withdrawal of 20,000 of the 50,000 American troops located in Vietnam.

In 1971 Porter was named as a delegate to the Paris peace talks with North Vietnam then in progress. His task was to work out detailed arrangements to buttress the broad agreements between Henry Kissinger* and Le Duc Tho,* the North Vietnamese negotiator. Porter's most significant contribution to the Paris talks was his unwillingness to allow his opponents to use them as a stage for propaganda statements. His unconventional approach helped to break the deadlock that had stalled progress in these negotiations. According to a *Time* magazine report, Porter "changed the once patient and restrained U.S. style in Paris" by taking the verbal offensive and talking tough. In 1973 President Richard Nixon* named him as undersecretary of state for political affairs, and in 1974 as ambassador to Canada. William Porter's last post, 1975–77, was as ambassador to Saudi Arabia. William James Porter died in 1988. JDC

Sources: *Current Biography Yearbook*, 1974; "People," *Time*, (January 17, 1972): 26–27; *International Who's Who, 1983–1984*, 1983.

POST-TRAUMATIC STRESS DISORDER

Between 1954 and 1975 more than 2.8 million Americans served in Vietnam, and nearly 1 million of them saw combat. Because of its unique nature—a guerrilla conflict (*see* Vietcong), a war of attrition,* intense opposition at home, and the youthful age of the average soldier (nineteen)—the Vietnam War exacted a high toll from its participants. Most of the American combatants experienced to one degree or another a serious psychological disorder characterized by emotional numbness, severe flashbacks, and recurring nightmares, periodic panic and depression, and, sometimes, violent behavior. In earlier wars the disorder had other names—"shell shock" in World War I, "battle fatigue" in World War II, "operational exhaustion" in the Korean War—but the Vietnam variety was more severe because the war was such a traumatic event in American society overall. Risking their lives, sometimes killing and maiming civilians, the Vietnam veterans then came home to a hostile country convinced that their sacrifice had been a waste at best and murder at worst. In 1980, with the third edition of its *Diagnostic and Statistical Manual of Mental Disorders*, the American Psychiatric Association named the Vietnam veteran disease PTSD, or Post-Traumatic Stress Disorder. In December 1979 the Veterans Administration opened the first Vet Center staffed with social workers, psychologists, and paraprofessionals. By January 1985 there were 135 Vet Centers across the country and more than 200,000 veterans had sought treatment.

Source: John Langone, "The War That Has No Ending," *Discover* 6 (June 1985): 44–54.

POULO CONDORE

Poulo Condore is an island approximately seventy-five miles off the southeast coast of the Ca Mau Peninsula in the South China Sea. In February 1861 a French invasion force reached Vietnam, and by July they had seized Saigon.* After one year the French were firmly in control of the three surrounding provinces: Dinh Tuong, Gia Dinh, and Bien Hoa. In June 1862 Emperor Tu Duc agreed to a peace treaty. He had little choice, since a dynastic rebellion against him had erupted in Tonkin.* As part of the treaty, France* gained control of Poulo Condore, $4 million, religious freedom, free access to port facilities at Tourane (Da Nang),* and the right to veto any foreign alliances that Vietnam tried to establish. The French constructed an infamous prison on Poulo Condore to incarcerate politically rebellious nationalists. Such prominent anti-imperialists as Phan Chu Trinh,* Pham Van Dong,* and Le Duc Tho* all spent years in the underground cells, suffering from heat, hunger, and disease. After the expulsion of the French, the South

Left: An artillery forward observer and his radio-telephone operator here take a break after a contact mission in the Mekong Delta of South Vietnam. The year is 1969, and they are members of the 2d Battalion, 60th Infantry, of the 9th Infantry Division.

Below: This sobbing Marine radioman is comforted by a chaplain on July 7, 1968. A member of the 1st Battalion, 3d Marines, he survived a direct mortar hit that killed his platoon leader.

Vietnamese government used the prison to hold Vietcong* guerrillas, Communist sympathizers, and North Vietnamese prisoners of war. By that time Poulo Condore was known by its Vietnamese name: Con Son Island. The island became infamous in 1970 when revelations of the "tiger cages"*— the prison cells at the Con Son Correctional Center— received international press coverage.

Sources: Stanley Karnow, *Vietnam: A History*, 1983; *New York Times*, July 8, 1970.

THE PRISONERS OF QUAI DONG

The Prisoners of Quai Dong is the title of Victor Kolpacoff's 1967 novel describing a prison camp in North Vietnam inhabited by American prisoners of war* (POWs) and their North Vietnamese captors. Through the lens of an interrogation room, where Americans are regularly tortured to extract confessions, Kolpacoff eventually describes everyone there—American POWs, Vietnamese officials, and innocent witnesses—as equally prisoners of the Vietnam War itself.

Sources: Victor Kolpacoff, *The Prisoners of Quai Dong*, 1967; Philip D. Beidler, *American Literature and the Experience of Vietnam*, 1982.

Opposite page, top: U.S. Navy Lieutenant Commander John "Mike" McGrath was a pilot shot down over North Vietnam. He spent six years as a prisoner of war, most of the time at the infamous "Hanoi Hilton," where the POWs endured brutal conditions. In 1975, McGrath recounted his experiences in his book *Prisoner of War: Six Years in Hanoi*, which was published by the Naval Institute Press. In these sketches, McGrath shows a POW with ankles and wrists secured to prevent the straightening or stretching of joints in the shoulders, hips, back, elbows, and knees (right). The POWs could be left in such a posture for hours and even days, which produced excruciating pain and long-term arthritic conditions. Another sketch depicts a POW being beaten on the buttocks with a rubber hose (left).

Right: On August 5, 1964, Lieutenant Everett Alvarez, a U.S. Navy pilot, was shot down in a raid on North Vietnamese patrol boat installations. In this photograph taken by a Japanese cameraman, Alvarez has just been captured and is being escorted by a North Vietnamese sailor. Alvarez would spend more than eight years in North Vietnamese prison camps.

PRISONERS OF WAR

Seven hundred and seventy-one American servicemen were captured and interned by Communist forces during the Vietnam conflict. Of these, 113 died in captivity and 658 were released, most in 1973 in conformity with the Paris Peace Accords of early that year. In previous conflicts, most American prisoners were low ranking persons, but during the Vietnam War, most were aviators and thus relatively high ranking. Some were held prisoner for close to a decade, longer than any American POWs before them.

The North Vietnamese and Vietcong tried to use the POWs as propaganda pawns, attempting to goad them into confessions of remorse for their actions on behalf of the South Vietnamese or otherwise displaying sympathy for the North Vietnamese. To this end, they voluntarily released some prisoners back to the Americans. They also tortured prisoners to force confessions or reveal military information. They routinely kept prisoners in solitary confinement, withheld medical attention and sufficient diet, and forced the prisoners to live in disgusting conditions.

For the most part, the American POWs did not succumb to the propaganda aims but rather endured torture and deprivations according to their own codes of honor and the demands of the U.S. Code of Military Conduct. In prison camps, they communicated as best they could with one another, supported one another, and worked at maintaining morale despite being given no news about the war and America except as pleased and benefited their captors. Prisoners in and around Hanoi cheered when Americans resumed bombing targets nearby despite the obvious risk to themselves.

As deplorable as the camps in North Vietnam were, captives in the South faced even more harsh conditions. Sometimes on the move, confined to primitive conditions, more at the mercy of the heat, rain, insects, and other predatory life of the region, they suffered greatly. Five percent of prisoners in the North died in captivity; in the South, the number was around 20 percent.

The Communist forces released almost 600 American prisoners from both the North and the South in the spring of 1973. The captors had improved the prisoners' diet just before release and issued new clothing, so that Americans at first did not appreciate the conditions these captives had endured. But in the months and years following, the tales of physical and psychological torture came to light, and with it a greater appreciation for the devotion to duty shown by those who had suffered such abuse and deprivation.

Sources: Stuart I. Rochester and Frederick Kiley, *Honor Bound: American Prisoners of War in Southeast Asia 1961–1973*, 1999; Samuel Lipsman and Stephen Weiss, *The False Peace 1972–74*, 1985.

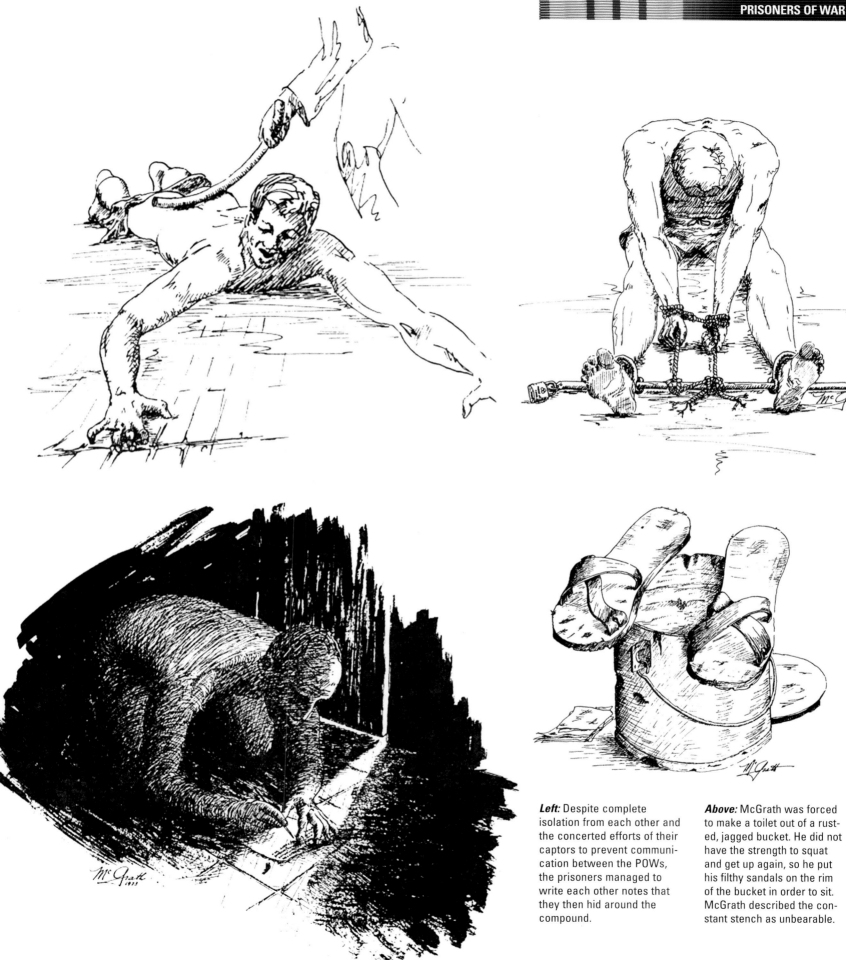

Left: Despite complete isolation from each other and the concerted efforts of their captors to prevent communication between the POWs, the prisoners managed to write each other notes that they then hid around the compound.

Above: McGrath was forced to make a toilet out of a rusted, jagged bucket. He did not have the strength to squat and get up again, so he put his filthy sandals on the rim of the bucket in order to sit. McGrath described the constant stench as unbearable.

PROJECT DELTA

In May 1964 the Studies and Observation Groups* launched Project Leaping Lena, a program to train Civilian Irregular Defense Group* and elite Vietnamese troops in long-range reconnaissance patrol* (LRRP) tactics. One year later the LRRP training program was reassigned to the 5th Special Forces Group,* which redesignated it Project Delta. Composed of 450 troops divided into twelve reconnaissance teams; twelve Roadrunner teams (indigenous South Vietnamese who dressed as Vietcong* or North Vietnamese and infiltrated their units); a security company composed of ethnic Nung* troops; and the 91st ARVN Ranger Battalion (see Army of the Republic of Vietnam), they gathered intelligence on North Vietnamese and Vietcong units, evaluated bomb and artillery damage, and conducted raids. Also known as Detachment B-52, after September 1966 Project Delta included the training of regular U.S. infantry units in LRRP tactics as well.

Source: Francis J. Kelly, *U.S. Army Special Forces, 1961–1971*, 1973.

PROJECT DYE MARKER

See Project Practice Nine

PROJECT ILLINOIS CITY

See Project Practice Nine

PROJECT OMEGA

Encouraged by the success of Project Delta* in 1965, General William Westmoreland* had the 5th Special Forces Group* launch Project Omega in August 1966. Also known as Detachment B-50, Project Omega consisted of approximately 900 Civilian Irregular Defense Group* troops and 125 U.S. personnel. It was headquartered at Ban Me Thuot* in II Corps.* Project Omega gathered intelligence on enemy positions, called in air strikes and evaluated bombing damage, and conducted special raids against the North Vietnamese and Vietcong.* Project Omega evolved into the Mobile Guerrilla Force* concept in 1967 and was absorbed into the Studies and Observation Groups* program in November 1967.

Source: Francis J. Kelly, *U.S. Army Special Forces, 1961–1971*, 1973.

PROJECT PRACTICE NINE

Project Practice Nine was the code name for the Department of Defense's plan to install an electronic infiltration barrier across Vietnam, just south of the Demilitarized Zone* (DMZ), from the South China Sea to Laos.* Popularly known as the Electric Fence or McNamara's Wall, the barrier was to consist of a strip of bulldozed jungle laced with mines, electronic sensors, booby traps,* and other obstacles. The Defense Department was convinced that construction of the barrier would eliminate the need for larger troop reinforcements in I Corps,* so William Westmoreland* and Military Assistance Command, Vietnam* (MACV) endorsed the concept. The Marine Corps,* however, was totally opposed. The Marines thought it would be too expensive and probably unworkable—that the technology would not really stop infiltration.* Worse, they were convinced that Project Practice Nine would drastically change their role in the war, taking them away from mobile assaults to requiring Marines to defend static positions along the barrier. But the Defense Department rejected the Marine arguments, and in the spring of 1967 the 3d Marine Division* began preparing for construction of the barrier.

In preparing for barrier construction, the 3d Marine Division had to launch sweep-and-clear operations in May 1967. On May 18 a combined Marine-ARVN (see Army of the Republic of Vietnam) force attacked into the southern reaches of the DMZ. Five ARVN battalions invaded Laos in the Lam Son 54 portion of the operation. The 1st Battalion of the 3d Marines pushed into the DMZ in Operation Beau Charger, and in the west Operation Hickory saw the 2d and the 3d Battalion of the 9th Marines, the 2d Battalion of the 26th Marines, the 3d Battalion of the 4th Marines,* and the 2d Battalion of the 3d Marines engaged in the sweep. They were fighting the 31st, the 32d, and the 812th regiments of the North Vietnamese Army* (NVA). The Marines evacuated large numbers of civilians from the area, engaged in hard fighting with the NVA, and destroyed massive bunker and tunnel complexes. The initial sweep operations were concluded at the end of May. In June 1967 Project Practice Nine was renamed Project Illinois City, and it was renamed again in July 1967, this time as Project Dye Marker. Although some test stages of the barrier were constructed, Secretary of Defense Robert McNamara's* dream of a wall all the way across Vietnam never came to be. It was too ambitious, too expensive, and too naive, all of which became abundantly clear in 1968 with the Tet Offensive* and the siege of Khe Sanh.*

Sources: Shelby L. Stanton, *The Rise and Fall of an American Army: U.S. Ground Forces in Vietnam, 1965–1973*, 1985; Gregory Palmer, *The McNamara Strategy and the Vietnam War: Program Budgeting in the Pentagon, 1960–1968*, 1978; Lloyd Norman, "McNamara's Fence: Our Eyes and Ears Along the DMZ," *Army* 18 (August 1968): 28–33.

PROJECT SIGMA

Encouraged by the success of Project Delta* in 1965, General William Westmoreland* had the 5th Special Forces Group* launch Project Sigma in August 1966. Known as Detachment-56, Project Sigma consisted of approximately 900 Civilian Irregular Defense Group* troops and 125 U.S. personnel. It was headquartered at Ho Ngoc Nau outside Saigon.* Project Sigma gathered intelligence on enemy positions, called in air strikes and evaluated bombing damage, and conducted special raids against the North Vietnamese and Vietcong.* Project Sigma evolved into the Mobile Guerrilla Force* concept in 1967 and was absorbed into the Studies and Observation Groups* program in November 1967.

Source: Francis J. Kelly, *U.S. Army Special Forces, 1961–1971*, 1973.

PROTECTIVE REACTION STRIKES

On October 31, 1968, as part of a general, informal agreement reached in Paris between negotiators for the United States and North Vietnam, U.S. Navy and Air Force "offensive" strikes against the Democratic Republic of Vietnam* were halted. The United States continued reconnaissance flights over North Vietnam, however, and when those flights were fired on, the U.S. Air Force* began sending armed escorts with them. Those escorts fired on the antiaircraft installations attacking the reconnaissance planes, although the U.S. strikes had to be confined to areas south of the 19th parallel. In April 1970 the United States authorized air strikes on North Vietnamese SAM* and antiaircraft installations protecting the Ho Chi Minh Trail* from American bombing.* Those strikes had to occur south of the 20th parallel. Department of Defense spokesmen referred to them as protective reaction strikes. Other "protective reaction strikes" were used in 1970 to stop North Vietnamese infiltration* across the Demilitarized Zone.* More than 1,100 sorties* occurred in 1970 as part of the protective reaction program.

Sources: John Morrocco, *The Vietnam Experience. Rain of Fire: Air War, 1969–1973*, 1984; Peter Mersky and Norman Polmar, *The Naval Air War in Vietnam*, 1981.

PROVISIONAL REVOLUTIONARY GOVERNMENT OF SOUTH VIETNAM

The Provisional Revolutionary Government of South Vietnam was the name taken by the National Liberation Front (NLF; *see* Vietcong) in 1969. It was the Communist government in South Vietnam until 1975, when North Vietnamese forces reunited the country. Its primary spokesperson was Nguyen Thi Binh,* longtime foreign minister for the NLF.

Sources: Douglas Pike, *History of the Vietnamese Communist Party*, 1978, and *The Viet Cong Strategy of Terror*, 1970.

PROXMIRE, WILLIAM

When Republican Senator Joe McCarthy died in 1957, Wisconsin voters replaced him with Democrat William Proxmire, a former state assemblyman and three-time gubernatorial loser. Born in 1915 in Illinois, Proxmire attended the Hill School, majored in literature at Yale and finance at Harvard, rose to master sergeant before receiving a commission in the Army Counter Intelligence Corps in World War II, and in 1946 married Elsie Rockefeller (John D.'s granddaughter) before earning an M.A. in public administration at Harvard.

In the Senate, Proxmire quickly gained a reputation as a maverick—he opposed both "excessive" military spending and liberal domestic legislation (except civil rights), and even attacked small projects dear to his party's leadership. He supported intervention in Vietnam through 1965 and, according to an authorized biography, "was flying with the fiercest of hawks." Proxmire criticized Lyndon Johnson's* handling of the war in 1966, and after the Tet Offensive* in early 1968 he broke completely with administration policy. "Tet," he said later, "made me very suspicious." Unsuccessful attempts to legislate an end to the war followed, with Proxmire urging that funding cease for B-52* and defoliation* missions. Through the Nixon* years he continued to speak against the war and also led Senate opposition to the C-5A cargo plane. While Proxmire's transition from hawk to dove roughly paralleled shifting public opinion toward the war, a skeptical approach to Pentagon spending remained a consistent feature of his work during thirty-two years in the Senate, from which he retired in 1989. William Proxmire died on December 15, 2005. DA

Sources: *Who's Who in American Politics, 1985–1986*, 1986; George C. Herring, *America's Longest War: The United States and Vietnam 1950–1975*, 1986; *New York Times*, 1957–1975, and December 16–17, 2005.

PSYCHOLOGICAL OPERATIONS

During the war in Vietnam the United States Information Agency (USIA), directing the Joint U.S. Public Affairs Office, and several military units invested an enormous

Below: During the Vietnam War, U.S. military operations included the Chieu Hoi program, an effort to entice Vietcong troops away from the National Liberation Front and to commit their loyalty to the Republic of Vietnam (South Vietnam). In July 1970, U.S. Air Force Sergeant Clinton W. Brown (left) and Staff Sergeant Doyle I. Hanni (right) open boxes of Chieu Hoi pamphlets to be airdropped over known Vietcong territory. The two men are part of the 9th Special Operations Squadron.

amount of resources in "psyops," or psychological operations: propaganda campaigns aimed at the North Vietnamese, the Vietcong,* and the South Vietnamese. Between 1965 and 1972 the United States dropped 50 billion leaflets over North and South Vietnam, and over the Ho Chi Minh Trail* in Laos* and Cambodia*—all with the goal of building an anti-Communist nationalism, supporting the Chieu Hoi program,* or breaking the will of the North Vietnamese to resist. They inundated South Vietnam with posters, banners, newspaper articles, magazines, brochures, comic books, bumper stickers, and matchbook covers, all urging the Vietcong and the North Vietnamese to end the fighting. The USIA also filled the available airwaves with anti-Communist radio broadcasts.

Military operations were also extensive. The Psychological Operations Directorate of Military Assistance Command, Vietnam* coordinated propaganda campaigns. The U.S. Air Force* dropped leaflets and the Navy* handed out brochures during routine searches of merchant ships and used loudspeaker broadcasts from patrol craft. The U.S. Army* eventually had four psyops battalions—the 6th Psychological Operations Battalion in III Corps,* the 7th Psychological Operations Battalion in I Corps,* the 8th Psychological Operations Battalion in II Corps,* and the 10th Psychological Operations Battalion in IV Corps.* Each battalion had its own printing plant, photographic and tape-recording production equipment, and loudspeaker trucks.

Sources: Robert W. Chandler, *War of Ideas: The U.S. Propaganda Campaign in Vietnam*, 1981; Shelby L. Stanton, *Vietnam Order of Battle*, 1981.

Left: A 14th Air Commando Wing C-47 Skytrain showers known Vietcong territory with thousands of leaflets inviting them to switch loyalties and abandon the Communist cause on December 6, 1966. Aircraft of the 14th Air Commando Wing unit were capable of dropping more than a million and a half leaflets over Vietnam on a single flight.

Below: U.S. Army psychological operations worked to secure the loyalties of South Vietnamese peasants to the Saigon government and to switch the loyalties of the Vietcong. Here two Army troops pack leaflets into a M129E1 leaflet bomb that will be dropped over enemy territory in April 1968.

PUEBLO

See USS *Pueblo*

"PUFF THE MAGIC DRAGON"

See AC-47 Gunship

PUNJI STAKES

Until 1965 the Vietcong* made or captured 90 percent of its weaponry, necessitating the imaginative utilization of natural resources, including bamboo. Punji stakes were lengths of bamboo cut into strips, sharpened to a point, and hardened over flame. These hardened sticks, which could penetrate the soles of combat boots and which might be coated with feces or some other infection-causing substance, were used as passive as well as offensive weapons. They were also excellent substitutes for concertina (coils of barbed wire) in defending fixed positions. Punji stakes were often driven into the bottoms of shallow holes, then carefully

Right: A U.S. Marine paces carefully through a punji-staked gully in the I Corps area of South Vietnam, south of the Demilitarized Zone on January 28, 1966.

Below: The Vietcong used punji stakes as booby traps to protect encampments and villages. In this 1962 photograph, thousands of punji stakes are pounded into the ground surrounding a strategic hamlet.

camouflaged so that an unsuspecting soldier would step on them, impaling his foot. The holes were often dug near obstacles, channeling a soldier's foot to that spot. Sharp sticks were also driven into rice paddies, to be stepped on as troops moved through them, or mounted onto saplings that were then bent over and camouflaged. An unwary soldier would activate a trip mechanism, releasing the sapling, which would fly up, piercing him with sticks. When mounted on platforms suspended in trees, activating the trip mechanism caused the platform to sail down, the sticks perforating the victim.

Such booby traps* were highly effective because they took both a physical and psychological toll on troops. The Vietcong were more interested in wounding soldiers than killing them because wounded soldiers required more attention. Units stopped their movement; medevacs* were called in for more seriously wounded soldiers, giving away an entire unit's position. Booby traps were a major advantage for the Vietcong and often helped to compensate for their lack of firepower. SF

Sources: George McTurnan Kahin and John W. Lewis, *The United States in Vietnam*, 1967; Al Santoli, *Everything We Had: An Oral History of the Vietnam War by Thirty-Three American Soldiers Who Fought It*, 1981; Edgar C. Doleman Jr., *The Vietnam Experience: Tools of War*, 1984.

Right: In April 1972, during the Eastertide Offensive, large numbers of North Vietnamese Army soldiers swept into Quang Tri Province in northern South Vietnam. Only a handful of U.S. combat troops remained in South Vietnam, and resistance to the invasion fell to ARVN troops, such as those pictured here.

Opposite: Four years earlier, in 1968, U.S. Army troops from the 1st Cavalry Division fought in Quang Tri Province to quell the Tet Offensive. U.S. Army soldiers sit on the porch of a home in a village about 5 miles south of Quang Tri in Quang Tri Province.

QUANG TRI, BATTLE OF (1972)

On March 30, 1972, as part of the Eastertide Offensive,* four North Vietnamese divisions attacked across the Demilitarized Zone* into Quang Tri Province. The North Vietnamese Army* (NVA) had moved long-range 130mm artillery just north of the Cam Lo–Cua Viet River bringing Quang Tri City and an area five miles south of the city under bombardment. NVA forces, backed by that artillery and amphibious PT-76 tanks, brought Quang Tri City under siege from three separate directions. Internecine rivalries between the Army of the Republic of Vietnam* (ARVN) and South Vietnamese Marine Corps* commanders, as well as friction between U.S. advisors and ARVN officers, weakened the defensive effort. Cloud cover during the first two weeks of April inhibited American

air support, and even though the weather cleared in mid-April and B-52* strikes were heavy, the North Vietnamese crossed the Cam Lo–Cua Viet River barrier and invaded on a broad front. NVA artillery were also striking hard at ARVN forces south of Quang Tri City. On April 27, 1972, the cloud cover returned, and the NVA 304th Division attacked Quang Tri City. Thousands of South Vietnamese refugees* began fleeing the city along Highway 1 (*see* "Street Without Joy") toward Hue,* and the North Vietnamese targeted the 130mm guns on the road. By April 30 the North Vietnamese were indiscriminately shelling the capital city; on May 1 they took the city. The rest of the province fell under North Vietnamese control two days later.

But the Eastertide Offensive then stalled and degenerated into a stalemate. Not until the end of the summer did the South Vietnamese, buoyed by massive B-52 air support, launch the counteroffensive. In house-to-house combat, the South Vietnamese recaptured Quang Tri City on September 15, 1972, suffering more than 5,000 casualties in the process. The fighting and bombing almost completely obliterated Quang Tri City.

Source: G.H. Turley, *The Easter Offensive: Vietnam, 1972*, 1985.

QUEEN'S COBRAS

"Queen's Cobras" was the name used to describe the crack infantry regiment sent to South Vietnam by Thailand* in the fall of 1967. The troops fought alongside American soldiers in III Corps* before their removal almost one year later.

Source: Harry G. Summers Jr., *Vietnam War Almanac*, 1985.

QUI NHON

Qui Nhon was the capital city of Binh Dinh Province in South Vietnam. At the peak of the fighting in Vietnam during the late 1960s, Qui Nhon had a population of more than 188,000. Located on the coast just off Highway 1 (*see* "Street Without Joy"), Qui Nhon is 420 miles north of Saigon.* Before the arrival of large numbers of American ground troops, Qui Nhon was a small fishing and commercial port. Military engineers deepened the harbor, constructed supply and petroleum depots, and transformed Qui Nhon into a major supply base. Service

Below: Two members of Thailand's Queen's Cobra Regiment have the grim task of guarding a pile of mangled Vietcong bodies after a battle 15 miles east of Saigon in December 1967.

Left: Soaked from the seasonal monsoon rains north of Qui Nhon, South Vietnam, these soldiers from the U.S. Army's 1st Cavalry Division take a break on a search-and-destroy mission as part of Operation Thayer on January 5, 1967. For troops on patrol, the monsoons made it difficult and sometimes impossible to stay dry and keep warm.

Below: Elements of the1st Brigade of the U.S. Army's 1st Cavalry Division trudge through the mud on a search-and-destroy mission as part of Operation Thayer north of Qui Nhon, South Vietnam on January 17, 1967.

Above: U.S. Marine Corporal Dave Taylor of State College, Pennsylvania, stands over a huddled group of South Vietnamese elderly men, women, and children on September 10, 1965. Taylor's platoon had conducted a sweep looking for Vietcong, and the absence of men in the village north of Qui Nhon meant danger for the Marines because of the heightened likelihood of ambush and sniper attacks.

support for the nearly 100,000 American, South Vietnamese, and Korean* troops operating in the northern reaches of II Corps* came from Qui Nhon. The Capital Division* of the South Korean Army had its headquarters in Qui Nhon. The port and supply depot was part of the American effort to keep land routes open between the coast and the Central Highlands.* With sixteen precincts and four villages, the population of Qui Nhon in 1999 was approximately 240,000.

Sources: Harvey H. Smith et al., *Area Handbook for South Vietnam*, 1967; Shelby L. Stanton, *Vietnam Order of Battle*, 1981; Carroll H. Dunn, *Base Development in South Vietnam, 1965–1970*, 1972; *People's Committee of Binh Dinh Province*, 2006.

Left: A wary Marine guards an older Vietnamese woman in a Qui Nhon village on September 11, 1965. During the Vietnam War, the Marines experienced difficulty distinguishing between combatants and civilians, and they learned to stay alert for unseen dangers, especially civilians who might secretly be Vietcong or Vietcong sympathizers.

Opposite page, bottom: During the same sweep of villages north of Qui Nhon, South Vietnam, Corporal John Glover of Miami, Florida, comes upon a sick, elderly Vietnamese man and carries him to a Marine aid station. Glover's companion keeps a careful eye for snipers. The village being searched was known for heavy Vietcong infiltration, although most of the men had fled the area before the Marine sweep.

RADIO HANOI

See Hanoi Hannah

RAMBO

Written and directed by Sylvester Stallone, *Rambo* (*see Rambo* and Other Vietnam Films, p. 486) is a sequel to Stallone's 1983 hit film *First Blood*. In *Rambo*, Stallone plays the role of a Vietnam veteran imprisoned for wrecking a small Oregon town after the local police chief and deputies harassed him. Richard Crenna, playing the role of Rambo's former Green Beret commander, springs him, literally, from a rock pile for a special mission in "Nam." Single-handedly, Rambo reenters Vietnam and rescues a group of American prisoners of war* (POWs) still languishing in bamboo-cage cells. As it turns out, the rescue project had been intended only as a political gesture by politicians back home, to do something about the POW-MIA issue. Rambo surprises them by winning another Medal of Honor, bringing home his comrades, and threatening the mission chief, whom he considers a stooge for the politicians who lost the first war in Vietnam. Riding a crest of American patriotism and nationalism, *Rambo* was a runaway box-office smash in 1985, the most successful of the Vietnam-genre films spawned in the 1980s.

Source: http://en.wikipedia.org/wiki/Rambo.

RADFORD, ARTHUR WILLIAM

As chairman of the U.S. Joint Chiefs of Staff (JCS; *see* Chairman, JCS) in 1954, Admiral Arthur W. Radford played a central role in the determination of American options during the decisive French battle of Dien Bien Phu.* Radford was born on February 27, 1896, and was a 1916 graduate of the Naval Academy. After World War I he became an aviator, and his own career advancement and the growth of naval aviation formed a virtually parallel history. During World War II he commanded a carrier group and a carrier division. After the war he rose to the command of the Pacific Fleet and to the chairmanship of the JCS in August 1953.

Radford had great confidence in the key role of airpower in modern warfare, and he was a forceful advocate of this view in the Eisenhower* administration's deliberations on Vietnam in 1954. In March of that year the Vietminh* army began its attack on the French garrison at Dien Bien Phu. Washington already was considering the implications of a French defeat, and as the battlefield conditions worsened, a decision on how to help the French was urgently needed. French Chief of Staff General Paul Ely* came to Washington and conferred directly with Radford. The admiral discussed a plan, Operation Vulture,* in which American carrier-based aircraft could inflict a massive air strike on the Vietminh forces besieging Dien Bien Phu. Upon his return to Paris, Ely believed that Radford had made a commitment to the plan, but Radford insisted that he had only raised the possibility. President Eisenhower refused to authorize an American bombardment without allied support, and in early May the Vietminh overran the outpost. Radford was chairman of the JCS until his retirement in August 1957. Arthur Radford died in 1973. DLA

Sources: Arthur W. Radford, *From Pearl Harbor to Vietnam: The Memoirs of Admiral Arthur W. Radford*, 1980; John Prados, *The Sky Would Fall: Operation Vulture, the U.S. Bombing Mission in Indochina, 1954*, 1983.

RAND CORPORATION

The Rand Corporation is a nonprofit think tank designed to analyze issues of national importance to the United States. Rand emerged at the end of World War II when it was organized as an adjunct of Douglas Aircraft Company in Santa Monica, California. The name was derived from combining parts of the words Research and Development. Rand separated from Douglas Aircraft in 1948 and was incorporated under the laws of California as a private, nonprofit corporation. Rand concentrated on "operational research," first focusing on the operational employment of existing weapons systems and later broadening out into more general tasks concerned with the allocation of resources for national security purposes. By the 1950s Rand was developing "systems analysis" as its major focus for such clients as the U.S. Air Force, Department of Defense, and the State Department. During the 1960s Rand's major focus was the Vietnam War. It provided copious studies of Saigon* politics, the National Liberation Front (*see* Vietcong), the organization of combat villages,

Left: A South Vietnamese Navy LSU-501 prepares to disembark Cambodian refugees at Vung Tau, South Vietnam on July 23, 1970. The U.S. invasion of Cambodia generated heavy bombing campaigns that wreaked widespread destruction and generated hundreds of thousands of refugees.

command structures in North Vietnam, weapons effectiveness, and negotiation strategies. Rand studies were heavily employed by American officials in developing military and political policy in Southeast Asia. LC

Sources: L.R. Smith, *The Rand Corporation*, 1966; Mike Gravel, ed., *Pentagon Papers*, 1971.

in reeducation camps, most of whom died there. The government of Pol Pot in Kampuchea was even more brutal, relocating more than 2 million citizens into camps before executing them in a genocidal orgy.

Sources: Nguyen Long with Harry Kendall, *After Saigon Fell*, 1981; Ginette Sagan and Stephen Denney, *Violations of Human Rights in the Socialist Republic of Vietnam*, 1983; Michael Vickery, *Cambodia, 1975–1982*, 1984.

REEDUCATION CAMPAIGNS

The term "reeducation" has become a euphemism for concentration camps, imprisonment, and brainwashing by totalitarian states in the twentieth century. After the end of the Vietnam War in 1975, both the Socialist Republic of Vietnam* and the Pol Pot* government in Kampuchea (now Cambodia*) implemented widespread reeducation campaigns to punish and/or reorient citizens closely associated with the U.S. war effort or the governments of the Republic of Vietnam* and Lon Nol* in Cambodia. In Vietnam, more than 400,000 Vietnamese were placed

REFUGEES

See Indochinese Refugees

REGIMENT

A regiment is a basic military organizational unit in the U.S. Marine Corps,* and in the U.S. Army's* armored cavalry units. During the Vietnam War the 11th Armored Cavalry

RAMBO AND OTHER VIETNAM FILMS

This page: The Vietnam War seized control of the American heart and soul, and Hollywood captured its widespread influence, here portrayed in the visage of actor Mel Gibson (upper left) in the 1990 film *Air America*; Robert Duvall and Martin Sheen (bottom), in the 1979 film *Apocalypse Now*, and Gene Hackman (upper right), in the 1988 film *Bat 21*.

During World War II the film industry worked hand in hand with the federal government to promote the effort by producing movies that cast the United States and its allies in a good light, usually portraying American soldiers, sailors, airmen, and Marines in heroic terms and the war itself as a noble struggle between good and evil. That culture of heroic virtue characterized films with World War II themes throughout the 1950s and early 1960s, with such actors as John Wayne, Robert Stack, Tyrone Power, and Errol Flynn playing the roles of military heroes and becoming identified as such in the minds of many Americans. Hollywood was prepared to do the same for the Vietnam War, but the political winds shifted quickly as antiwar sentiments deepened.

Film historians look to *The Ugly American* (1963) as the first Vietnam War film. Based on William Lederer and Eugene Burdick's 1958 best-selling novel of the same name, *The Ugly American* features Marlon Brando as Harrison Carter MacWhite, U.S. ambassador to the fictionalized nation of Sarkhan, a Vietnam-like country beset by poverty and a Communist insurgency. Like the novel, the film is an indictment of the U.S. Foreign Service and its tendency in the 1950s and early 1960s to use ambassadorships as political rewards. Usually illiterate in the language of their host country and ignorant of its history and culture, American diplomats spend their time drinking and partying with other European diplomats and local elites, while the Communists recruit followers among the peasants. For any hope of success against wars of liberation in underdeveloped countries, reform of the State Department was a must. Although *The Ugly American*

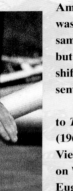

was not per se an anti–Vietnam War film, it nevertheless predicted failure for the United States in the developing world barring significant changes in policy.

During the next five years Hollywood bided its time as Americans debated the merits of the war, but as the conflict stretched out, without any end in sight, the cast of public opinion was set. In 1968 Hollywood released two

Left: Actor Matthew Modine starred in Stanley Kubrick's *Full Metal Jacket*, a high profile 1987 film that trails a Marine platoon from boot camp to the horrors of Hue, South Vietnam, during the Tet Offensive of 1968, when the Marines had to recapture the city from Vietcong and NVA forces.

films about Vietnam, one an indictment of the war effort and the other an endorsement. In the B-movie *Angels from Hell*, Vietnam veterans appear as narcissistic motorcycle bikers who have traded helicopters and M16s for Harleys but remain just as prone to violent rampages that often hurt innocent people. *Satan's Sadists* (1969), *The Losers* (1970), and *Chrome and Hot Leather* (1971) continued the Vietnam-veteran-turned-amoral-biker motif. Evil in its very nature, the war had changed for the worse the men charged with its conduct.

Juxtaposed with *Angels from Hell* was John Wayne's *The Green Berets*, released several months after the Tet Offensive had soured much of the American public on the war. *The Green Berets* is a World War II–genre film, with John Wayne as a Green Beret colonel fighting the expansion of Communism in Southeast Asia. Critics panned *The Green Berets* as naive and silly at its best and malignantly diabolical at its worst, and it remains today one of the few pro–Vietnam War films ever released.

In 1970, the year of Kent State and the Jackson State University killings and the American invasion of Cambodia, four anti–Vietnam War films were playing in U.S. theaters. Ironically, none of them was actually set in Vietnam. *The Wild Bunch* (1969), starring William Holden, Robert Ryan, and Ernest Borgnine, depicted turn-of-the-century train robbers of the Southwest being pursued by hired railroad detectives. As it was in Vietnam, it is often difficult to distinguish the good guys from the bad, and innocent civilians are frequently caught in the crossfire. In *Little Big Man*, Dustin Hoffman plays Jack Crabb, a white man who moves back and forth during his boyhood and adolescence between white society and that of Cheyenne Indians, deciding that the Indians have virtue and integrity, while whites are violent and corrupt. In one scene, U.S. cavalry troops lay waste to an Indian village, killing every man, woman, and child in a slaughter reminiscent of Wounded Knee and chillingly anticipating the soon-to-be-published news reports of the My Lai massacre. *Catch-22* and *M*A*S*H*, both 1970 films, are dark, antiwar comedies set in World War II and Korea, respectively, in which military officers appear haplessly inept and stupid. In *Catch-22*, based on Joseph Heller's

Above: In the 1993 film *Heaven and Earth*, Tommy Lee Jones stars as a Vietnam veteran who brought home from the war a Vietnamese wife and child. The film, directed by Oliver Stone, addresses the problem of veterans and Indochinese immigrants and their emotional adjustment to life in the United States after the war.

Right: In 1986, Clint Eastwood portrayed a crusty Marine gunnery sergeant veteran of World War II, Korea, and Vietnam in the film *Heartbreak Ridge*. In the film, the "gunny" trains a platoon of green Marines and leads them into battle during the U.S. invasion of Grenada in 1983. The film marked a turning point for veterans of the war, whose own popularity had suffered because of the unpopularity of the war. In *Heartbreak Ridge*, the Marines are portrayed as iconic American heroes.

novel of the same name, the lead figure hates the insanity of the war and tries to escape it by feigning insanity himself, a ploy that fails because it is normal—sane—to want to escape from insane situations. *M*A*S*H* revolves around the antics of a Mobile Army Surgical Hospital, where the physicians come to see war as irrational, its planners as immorally ambitious or fanatically patriotic, and its perpetrators as the hapless victims of forces beyond their control.

North Vietnam's conquest of South Vietnam finally ended the conflict and provided filmmakers an opportunity to vent their frustrations about a war that stole the lives of more than 58,000 Americans and several million Vietnamese. What began as a noble effort to stem the tide of Communism evolved into a bloody nightmare of confusion, alienation, and excess, in which democracy, Communism, nationalism, and American domestic politics coagulated into a foreign policy catastrophe. Two films in 1976—*Taxi Driver* and *Tracks*—launched Americans into decades of self-recrimination and second-guessing about Vietnam. In *Taxi Driver*, Robert De Niro played a demented Vietnam veteran whose experience in Southeast Asia has warped him into a killer. *Tracks* starred Dennis Hopper as an Army sergeant escorting home the body of a fallen comrade. During the journey, nobody wants to listen to his story. Vietnam has already become tainted, a conflict with no heroes, only victims. At the end of the film, as the casket is lowered into its grave, Hopper jumps in too, only to emerge in jungle fatigues with an M16, screaming, "You want to go to Nam? I'll take you there!"

In the late 1970s American introspection about Vietnam spawned a host of films, all of them consumed with outrage, bewilderment, and profound sorrow over how the war could have gone so wrong. *Go Tell the Spartans* (1978) starred Burt Lancaster as a U.S. military advisor training South Vietnamese troops. The film addresses most of the problems that plagued the U.S. military effort in Vietnam—the venality of South

Vietnamese politicians and military officers, peasant sympathy for the Vietcong, excessive use of firepower in areas inhabited by noncombatants, and the frustration of conquering an area one day and abandoning it the next. *The Boys in Company C* (1978) exposed the absurdities of the war, with American soldiers using heroin and marijuana, fragging their officers, and faking body counts.

Two other 1978 films returned to the impact of the war on Vietnam veterans. In *Coming Home*, Jon Voight plays Luther Martin, a bitter, angry paraplegic who can find no real significance in his personal sacrifice. The war left him a cripple without a cause. This veteran, however, is not a ticking time bomb, as in *Taxi Driver* and *Tracks*, but a healer in need of healing, a man who condemns the war and finds hope that in his paralysis he can help prevent future Vietnams. *The Deer Hunter* also shows the impact of the war on soldiers and their friends and

families. Set in a western Pennsylvania steel town and in Vietnam, *The Deer Hunter* stars Robert De Niro as Michael, a loner comfortable with blood and violence, a man who kills a deer with one shot and finds shortcomings in his friends. In Vietnam, Michael is comfortable with the death and terror surrounding him, but he also discovers compassion and risks his life to save a friend. He returns from the war purged of aggression, more able to relate to women, and no longer interested in deer hunting. At a funeral service for a friend killed in Vietnam, Michael and his companions spontaneously sing "God Bless America," with Michael now a whole person reconciled to himself and his country.

Francis Ford Coppola in 1979 inaugurated a celluloid frontal assault on the Vietnam War. In *Apocalypse Now*, Marlon Brando played Colonel Walter Kurtz, a mysterious and insane Green Beret who has abandoned the war and retreated upriver deep into Cambodia, where he has established a shadowy, surreal fiefdom. Captain Willard (Martin Sheen) is assigned the mission of finding and extracting Kurtz. Along the way, Willard encounters absurdity after absurdity, including go-go dancers and Playboy bunnies being airlifted into the

war zone, American soldiers surfing the waves of the South China Sea during battle, and an American officer (Robert Duvall) citing the virtues of napalm with the oft-quoted statement, "I love the smell of napalm in the morning." Based loosely on Joseph Conrad's novella *Heart of Darkness*, Coppola's *Apocalypse Now* portrays Vietnam as a cesspool of death, immorality, and insanity.

Two 1987 films continue the theme of carnage, waste, and futility. In *Gardens of Stone*, James Caan and James Earl Jones play battle-hardened veterans charged with the burial detail at Arlington National Cemetery—the "Gardens of Stone." Caan's character is caught on the horns of a deadly dilemma: whether or not to dissuade a zealous young soldier from wanting to serve his country by testing his mettle in Vietnam. The young man eventually deploys to Vietnam, where his letters home reflect his increasing disillusionment with the war, as well as a loss of faith, innocence, and conviction. When the veterans receive the dreaded news that their young soldier has been killed in combat and that his body will soon be their charge, they slump in grief and disappointment, convinced of the Vietnam War's ultimate futility.

Stanley Kubrick's *Full Metal Jacket* tells a similarly dark tale, following a platoon of Marines from boot camp to combat in the city of Hue during the Tet Offensive. Along the way a crazed Marine murders his drill instructor, while other Marines are portrayed as racist killers. One comments, "Anyone who runs is a VC. Anyone who stands still is a well-disciplined VC." The film lacks subtleties and metaphors, except in that it ends with the Marines leaving Hue singing Walt Disney's "Mickey Mouse Club" theme song.

Other films of the 1980s rehabilitated the reputation of Vietnam veterans, treating them as normal people caught up in extraordinary events, suffering and dying for their country and then being abandoned by their own government. In *First Blood* (1982), Sylvester Stallone appeared as John Rambo, a Medal of Honor recipient and Green Beret Vietnam veteran. On a trip

Above: John Irwin directed the 1989 film *Hamburger Hill.* The film heralded the courage of U.S. soldiers in the face of the ambiguous nature of the war and the political controversies surrounding what seemed to many to be a senseless battle and loss of life.

Above left: In the 1989 film *In Country*, Bruce Willis confronts painful memories as a Vietnam War veteran searching for the names of fallen comrades at the Vietnam War Memorial in Washington, D.C.

Left: Mel Gibson starred in the 2002 film *We Were Soldiers,* based on the 1992 book *We Were Soldiers Once... And Young,* the true story of 450 soldiers of the 1st Battalion, 7th Cavalry, who were dropped by helicopter into a clearing in the Ia Drang Valley and immediately surrounded by 2,000 North Vietnamese soldiers.

Above: *The Quiet American*, a 2002 film set in Vietnam before the American escalation of the war in the 1960s, starred Michael Caine and Brendan Fraser. The film reflected the novel's skepticism about the prospects for a war in Indochina, as well as the postwar cynicism of the American public.

Below: The plight of Vietnam vets after their return became a topic of continuing interest throughout the 1970s and 1980s. *Some Kind of Hero*, starring Richard Prior and Margot Kidder, massaged the theme of anxiety and regret among those who served and returned to an ungrateful country.

onment. He returns to Vietnam in 1975 as part of a fact-finding mission to locate surviving prisoners of war. When the Vietnamese government obfuscates and the U.S. government acquiesces, Braddock purchases weapons in Thailand and then heads back to Vietnam to rescue a group of American POWs. *Missing in Action 2: The Beginning* (1985) continued to portray that theme, as did Gene Hackman in *Uncommon Valor* (1983) and Sylvester Stallone in *Rambo: First Blood Part II* (1985). Although *Good Morning Vietnam* (1987) cast a lighter shade on the conflict, its depiction of military disc jockey Adrian Cronhauer ridiculing the war daily over the airwaves broadcast the same message.

Perhaps the key Vietnam War movie of the 1980s was about Cambodia—*The Killing Fields*, which tells the story of *New York Times* reporter Sidney Schanberg (Sam Waterson) and his photographer, Dith Pran (Haing Ngor). The film highlights Khmer Rouge madness and their slaughter of 2 million Cambodians. The United States is held indirectly responsible for widening the Vietnam War into Cambodia. The 1980s ended with Oliver Stone's second Vietnam War film, *Born on the Fourth of July*, with Tom Cruise as Ron Kovic, a wounded U.S. Marine from Long Island, New York, who returns home a paraplegic, endures scandalous conditions in a Veterans Administration hospital, and goes on to become a leading figure in the antiwar movement.

to the Pacific Northwest, he learns that a former comrade has died of cancer, a victim of Agent Orange and a callous government. Harassed and beaten by local cops resentful of his long hair, Rambo escapes and conducts his own war against the town, surrendering only to a former commanding officer from Vietnam. The enemy in *First Blood* is clearly the government, the federal government that trained and then abandoned soldiers and the local governments and town folk who abused them. At the end of *First Blood*, Rambo tells his former commanding officer, "Nothing is over, nothing! You just don't turn it off. It wasn't my war—you asked me, I didn't ask you—and I did what I had to do to win, but somebody wouldn't let us win."

The theme of an ungrateful country abandoning its soldiers found expression in a number of other films. Chuck Norris starred in *Missing in Action* (1983) as Special Forces leader James Braddock, who had escaped from a Vietnamese POW camp after ten years of impris-

After the Gulf War of 1989 to 1990 and the collapse of the Soviet Union, Hollywood revived American patriotism and the image of the military, both of which had sagged since the Vietnam War. In 1998 *Saving Private Ryan* and *The Thin Red Line* hailed the bravery of American soldiers during World War II as did *Windtalkers* (2002). *Courage Under Fire* (1996), *Three Kings* (1999), and *Jarhead* (2005) did the same for Gulf War veterans. Among the most recent Vietnam War films, *We Were Soldiers* (2002) portrays the Battle of the Ia Drang Valley in 1965, where U.S. troops engaged Vietcong guerrillas and North Vietnamese regulars in a fierce battle with broad strategic and tactical implications. Troops on both sides appear as simple, brave men fighting for causes in which they believe. *We Were Soldiers* is free of metaphor, didactic images, and moral judgments about the war.

Sources: Michael A. Anderegg, ed., *Inventing Vietnam: The War in Film and Television*, 1999; Linda Dittmar and Gene Michaud, *From Hanoi to Hollywood: The Vietnam War in American Film*, 1991; Mark P. Taylor, *The Vietnam War in History, Literature, and Film*, 2003; Lawrence H. Suid, *Scenes of Conflict: Hollywood, the Pentagon, and the Films of the Vietnam War*, 1990.

In 1989, Brian De Palma's film *Casualties of War* exposed the ironies and futilities of Vietnam, as well as the bond that formed between soldiers in combat. The film starred Michael J. Fox and Sean Penn.

Selected Vietnam War Filmography

1969 (2005)

84 Charlie Mopic (1989)

Air America (1990)

American Commandos (1985)

The Anderson Platoon (1968)

Apocalypse Now (1979)

Bat 21 (1988)

Birdy (1984)

Born on the Fourth of July (1989)

The Boys in Company C (1978)

A Bright and Shining Lie (1998)

Casualties of War (1989)

Cease Fire (1985)

Coming Home (1978)

The Cu Chi Tunnels (2001)

The Deer Hunter (1978)

Distant Thunder (1988)

First Blood (1982)

Flight of the Intruder (1991)

Full Metal Jacket (1987)

Gardens of Stone (1987)

Go Tell the Spartans (1978)

Good Morning Vietnam (1987)

The Green Berets (1968)

Hamburger Hill (1987)

The Hanoi Hilton (1987)

Hearts and Minds (1974)

Heaven and Earth (1993)

In Country (1989)

Indochene (1992)

The Iron Triangle (1989)

Jacknife (1989)

Jacob's Ladder (1990)

The Killing Fields (1984)

The Long Road Home: Vietnam Revisited, 1969 (1999)

The Lost Command (1966)

Missing in Action (1984)

Missing in Action 2: The Beginning (1985)

Off Limits (1988)

Operation Dumbo Drop (1995)

Platoon (1986)

Platoon Leader (1988)

Purple Hearts (1993)

Regret to Inform (1998)

The Siege of Firebase Gloria (1989)

Some Kind of Hero (1982)

Tigerland (2001)

Uncommon Valor (1983)

We Were Soldiers (2002)

Regiment* was the only Army regiment in-country. It consisted of three armored cavalry squadrons and an air cavalry troop. Three infantry battalions* constitute a Marine regiment. Between 1965 and 1975 the Marines used ten regiments in the Vietnam War: the 1st, 5th, and 7th regiments of the 1st Marine Division;* the 3d, 4th, and 9th regiments of the 3d Marine Division;* the 26th and 27th regiments of the 5th Marine Division;* and the 11th and 12th artillery regiments.

Source: Harry G. Summers Jr., *Vietnam War Almanac*, 1985.

Below: In this 1968 photograph, a soldier from the Regional Forces, an element of the Army of the Republic of Vietnam (ARVN), stands guard at an ARVN outpost.

REGIONAL FORCES

The Regional Forces, part of the Territorial Forces* of the South Vietnamese Army, were paramilitary troops organized at the province level to protect villages, hamlets, and such fixed positions as bridges and ferries. The Regional Forces were first activated in 1955 under the control of the Interior Department of South Vietnam to protect critical positions in the Mekong Delta,* and by 1960 they were defending more than 9,000 posts, more than half of which were in the Delta. At first called the Civil Guard, in 1960 the Regional Forces were transferred to the Defense Department and in 1964 to the South Vietnamese Army. Instead of being controlled by the province chief, they were under the command of the Joint General Staff.* The basic combat unit of the Regional Forces was the company,* and by 1973 the Regional Forces totaled more than 1,800 companies. Between 1965 and 1973 the Regional Forces and the Popular Forces* had more than 80,000 killed.

Sources: Ngo Quang Truong, *Territorial Forces*, 1981; Harvey H. Smith et al., *Area Handbook for South Vietnam*, 1967.

Left: Frederick Reinhardt (left) in 1941 when he was third secretary of the U.S. diplomatic delegation to the Soviet Union. He is speaking with U.S. Ambassador to Russia Laurence Steinhardt. The photo was taken by Margaret Bourke-White for Time Life Pictures.

REINHARDT, GEORGE FREDERICK

G. Frederick Reinhardt was born on October 21, 1911, in Berkeley, California. After graduating from the University of California in 1933, he went on to Cornell University, where he earned a master's degree in 1935. Reinhardt attended the Cesare Alfien Institute of Diplomacy in Florence, Italy, in 1937, and then received an appointment to the U.S. Foreign Service. During the 1930s Reinhardt had minor posts in Austria, Latvia, Estonia, and the Soviet Union,* and during World War II he was a staff aide with General Dwight Eisenhower.* Between 1945 and 1948 he served as first secretary and consul general in Moscow and then held a variety of positions with the State Department in Washington until 1955. Reinhardt became ambassador to the Republic of Vietnam* in 1955 and held the post until 1957. He later held ambassadorships to the United Arab Republic, Yemen, and Italy. Reinhardt retired from public life in 1968. G. Frederick Reinhardt died on February 22, 1971.

Sources: John E. Finding, *Dictionary of American Diplomatic History*, 1980; *New York Times*, February 23, 1971.

REPUBLIC OF KOREA

See Korea

REPUBLIC OF VIETNAM

The term "Republic of Vietnam"* was the name given to the government of South Vietnam. After the Geneva Accords* of 1954 had divided North from South Vietnam at the 17th parallel, Ngo Dinh Diem* became prime minister in a government headed by Emperor Bao Dai.* After consolidating his power, Diem called for a national referendum on October 23, 1955, to determine whether Bao Dai should remain emperor or whether the country should become a republic under Diem's leadership. Diem reported after the referendum that 98 percent of the people of South Vietnam wanted a republic. So on October 26, 1955, Diem proclaimed the establishment of the Republic of Vietnam and named himself president. A new constitution was promulgated on October 26, 1956.

Source: Harvey H. Smith et al., *Area Handbook for South Vietnam*, 1967.

Below: A U.S. Navy Command Communication boat engages in a search-and-destroy mission in Vung Tau Bay and along the Thi Vai River, South Vietnam, in late October 1967. The boat was part of Naval Task Force 117.

REVOLUTIONARY PERSONALIST LABOR PARTY

See Can Lao Nhan Vi Cach Mang Dang

REVOLUTIONARY YOUTH LEAGUE

See Thanh Nien Cach Menh Dong Chi Hoi

RHEAULT CONTROVERSY

In 1969 Colonel Robert Rheault, commander of the 5th Special Forces Group,* was arrested for ordering the execution of Thai Khac Chuyen, a Special Forces employee who Rheault discovered was a double agent for the Vietcong.* Because of the highly secret nature of the project Chuyen was working, the Central Intelligence Agency* refused to release classified information, and the case against Rheault had to be dismissed. He resigned from the Special Forces in 1969.

Source: Charles M. Simpson III, *Inside the Green Berets: The First Thirty Years*, 1983.

RIVERINE ASSAULT FORCE (TASK FORCE 116)

See Mobile Riverine Force

RIVERINE PATROL FORCE (TASK FORCE 117)

See Mobile Riverine Force

"THE ROCKPILE"

On July 4, 1966, about ten miles from the southern boundary of the Demilitarized Zone* (DMZ) and sixteen miles west of Dong Ha, a small Marine reconnaissance patrol made note of "a sort of toothpick-type mountain stuck out in the middle of an open area" with a "sheer cliff straight up and down." The 700-foot "Rockpile," often manned by a Marine squad, became a key post from which to observe North Vietnamese Army* activity in the central and western sectors of northern I Corps.* Located at a fork in the Cam Lo River, the Rockpile was supplied by helicopter, and within a kilometer of Route 9 it dominated the landscape between Camp Carroll to the east and Khe Sanh* to its southwest. Marines launched numerous operations from the Rockpile area, and the peak was a familiar landmark for those fighting the DMZ war. DA

Sources: Jack Shulimson, *Marines in Vietnam: An Expanding War, 1966*, 1982; Edward Doyle and Samuel Lipsman, *The Vietnam Experience: America Takes Over, 1965–1967*, 1985.

Above: A river patrol craft (RPC) ferries a squad of soldiers from B Company, 1st Battalion, 16th Infantry Regiment to the bank of a river, where they will disembark and commence a search-and-destroy mission, March 10, 1968, in Gia Dinh Province, South Vietnam. The Tet Offensive had already peaked.

ROGERS, WILLIAM PIERCE

William P. Rogers was born at Norfolk, New York, on June 23, 1913. He graduated from Colgate University in 1934, and in 1937 earned a law degree at Cornell University, where he edited the law review. Rogers worked briefly with a Wall Street firm in 1937 before joining the staff of New York County district attorney Thomas E. Dewey, who was about to launch his campaign against racketeers. While serving on Dewey's staff, Rogers gained extensive experience as a trial lawyer. He was an officer with the United States Naval Reserve in the Pacific during World War II. After the war Rogers returned to Dewey's staff briefly and then went to work as counsel to several congressional committees. During those years he came to know congressman and later senator Richard Nixon* and worked on the Alger Hiss case. In 1950 Rogers returned to private law practice and continued as a Nixon advisor. When Dwight D. Eisenhower* was elected president in 1952, Rogers became deputy attorney general. In October 1957 he became attorney general in the Eisenhower cabinet.

Between 1960 and 1968 Rogers practiced law, but when Nixon entered the White House in 1969, Rogers became secretary of state. While naming Rogers to the State Department, however, Nixon also named Henry Kissinger* to the post of special White House assistant on foreign affairs. From the beginning, Kissinger's influence

Right: President Richard Nixon with his Secretary of State William P. Rogers on December 1, 1968. Rogers had been a close advisor to then-Vice President Nixon throughout the Eisenhower administration.

was dominant. Nixon tended to be suspicious and secretive, and he distrusted the "Ivy League types" at the State Department. Moreover, Rogers was always upstaged by Kissinger; the making of foreign policy had definitely shifted to the White House. Thus, William Rogers was often put in the position of explaining and defending policies before Congress* and the nation that had been formulated by Nixon and Kissinger with little or no input from the State Department. This was especially true in the areas of Sino-Soviet and Vietnam policy. Rogers himself was often the subject of unkind chatter on the Washington cocktail circuit. But he continued to serve until 1973, when he resigned to return to his private law practice. In 1986 he was chosen by the Reagan administration to head the investigation of the *Challenger* disaster. William P. Rogers died on January 2, 2001. JMR Jr.

Sources: *Current Biography*, 1969; Thomas G. Paterson, *American Foreign Policy*, 1983; *U.S. News and World Report*, February 24, 1986; *New York Times*, January 3, 2001; http://www.state.gov/secretary/former/40814.htm.

ROMAN CATHOLICISM

Roman Catholicism came to Vietnam in the sixteenth and seventeenth centuries with the arrival of Portuguese, French, and Spanish missionaries. Dominican priests from Portugal arrived in the Mekong Delta* in 1550 and in Quang Nam Province in central Vietnam in the 1580s. French Jesuits, the most prominent of whom was Alexandre de Rhodes, worked throughout Vietnam in the seventeenth century, and by 1700 there were nearly 1 million converts there. Perhaps 25 percent of them were in Tonkin,* with the rest in Annam* and Cochin China.* During the eighteenth century Confucians* and Buddhists throughout Vietnam campaigned against Catholicism as an alien religion tied closely to European imperial expansion, and persecution of Catholics was widespread.

With the French conquest of Vietnam in the nineteenth century, Catholicism was liberated from nationalist opposition, built a native clergy, and received great support from the French colonial bureaucracy. After 1954, when Ngo Dinh Diem* took control of the government of South Vietnam, Catholicism got an even stronger foothold in the country. The French had encouraged Catholicism as a counter to Buddhism,* and Diem filled his government with Roman Catholics. Diem's brother Ngo Dinh Thuc* was the archbishop of Hue* and leader of the Catholic clergy in Vietnam. Although the dominant position of Catholics in the government of South Vietnam declined after the assassination of Diem in 1963, they still exerted extraordinary influence because of their dominance of the officer corps of the South Vietnamese military, the higher levels of the government bureaucracy, and the professions. Overall,

Roman Catholics were better educated and more prosperous than the country's non-Catholics.

There were actually two Catholic communities in South Vietnam during the years of the Vietnam War. Of the 1.5 million Roman Catholics in the country, approximately 900,000 of them in the 1960s were refugees* from the Red River Delta area of North Vietnam. Led by Father Hoang Quynh, they were more anti-Buddhist and anti-Communist than their southern counterparts. Father Hoang Quynh's lay organization, the Luc Luong Dai Doan Ket, or Greater Unity Force, was an activist organization in South Vietnam. Southern Catholics were led by Paul Nguyen Van Binh,* the archbishop of Saigon.* Southern Catholics were more sympathetic to Buddhist grievances, not nearly as militant as the northerners, and received less support from the Diem regime. As a whole, however, Catholics in Vietnam were pro-Western and anti-Communist, and wanted little compromise with the Vietminh* and later the Vietcong.* The northern Catholic refugees came into the South after the Geneva Accords* in 1954, and migrated in village units with their local priest. The government established 319 refugee villages for them. Nearly 400,000 refugees settled in villages

in the Mekong Delta, 60,000 in the Central Lowlands, and 70,000 in the Central Highlands.* Others ended up in the slums of Saigon or Cholon.* Northern Catholics were consequently more impoverished than their southern brethren.

The northern refugees were for the most part poorly educated peasants who had lived in exclusively Roman Catholic villages in North Vietnam and who had rarely had contact with non-Catholics. Catholics born in South Vietnam lived mainly in cities and coastal areas of the northern provinces. In Saigon the Catholic community was upper middle class and virtually controlled the military, civil service, and professions. South Vietnam by the 1960s was divided into 13 dioceses with 700 local parishes. In the late 1960s there were more than 1,700 priests, 4,000 nuns, and 625 seminarians in the country. The Church enrolled 400,000 students in parochial schools, maintained a college at Dal Lat,* and operated 26 hospitals, 7 leper sanitariums, and 55 orphanages.

Sources: Harvey H. Smith et al., *Area Handbook for South Vietnam*, 1967; Virginia Thompson, *French Indochina*, 1937; Joseph Buttinger, *Vietnam: A Dragon Embattled*, 2 vols., 1967; Pierro Gheddo, *The Cross and the Bo-Tree: Catholics and Buddhists in Vietnam*, 1970; Peter C. Phan, *Mission and Catechesis: Alexandre de Rhodes and Inculturation in Seventeenth Century Vietnam*, 1998.

Above: U.S. Marines on patrol outside Da Nang, South Vietnam, pass by a Roman Catholic Church on January 1, 1968. The Tet Offensive began at the end of the month.

Above: George Romney, the governor of Michigan and moderate Republican candidate for president in 1968, is seen here on December 25, 1967, on a tour of South Vietnam. He is visiting Fire Support Base "Thunder Four," 50 miles northeast of Saigon and 18 miles southeast of the Cambodian border. Thunder Four served as headquarters for elements of the 1st Infantry Division in South Vietnam.

ROME PLOW

Manufactured by the Rome Caterpillar Company of Rome, Georgia, the Rome plow was used to clear jungle areas during the Vietnam War, especially potential ambush locations along supply routes. The huge tractor had a large, cutting blade more curved than most bulldozer blades and extending out at the bottom. The blade was sharp and powerful enough to cut easily through tree trunks up to 36 inches in diameter, and a spike at one edge of the blade could split even larger trees.

Source: John H. Hay Jr., *Tactical and Materiel Innovations*, 1974.

ROMNEY, GEORGE

George Romney was born on July 8, 1907, in the Mormon colonies in Chihuahua, Mexico. He attended the University of Utah and George Washington University in the 1920s but never graduated. In 1929 Romney went to work as a tariff specialist for Senator David Walsh of Massachusetts, and in 1930 he became a lobbyist for the Aluminum Company of America (ALCOA). Romney spent the next twenty-three years working for ALCOA, as well as the Automobile Manufacturers Association, and in 1954 he became president of American Motors. In 1962 Romney ran on the Republican ticket and won the governorship of Michigan. He was reelected in 1964 and 1966. Romney had a reputation as a moderate to liberal Republican, and in 1968 he made a run for the Republican presidential nomination. At the time he was harboring serious reservations about the war in Vietnam, and after traveling there on a fact-finding mission, he returned to the United States and, during the New Hampshire presidential primary campaign, claimed that the Pentagon had tried to "brainwash" him. Although subsequent events would prove he was correct, use of the term "brainwash" hurt him politically in New Hampshire—Richard Nixon* won the primary, the Republican nomination, and the White House. In January 1969 Nixon named Romney to his cabinet as secretary of housing and urban development; Romney retired from public life in 1973. George Romney died on July 26, 1995.

Sources: Clark Mollenhoff, *George Romney, Mormon in Politics*, 1968; Theodore White, *The Making of the President, 1968*, 1969.

ROOSEVELT, FRANKLIN DELANO

Franklin D. Roosevelt, the thirty-second president of the United States, was born in Hyde Park, New York, on January 30, 1882. Raised amid family wealth, he developed a paternalistic liberalism, graduated from Harvard in 1904, and studied law at Columbia University. He was admitted to the New York bar in 1907 and practiced law privately. After serving a term in the state legislature between 1911 and 1913, Roosevelt was appointed assistant secretary of the Navy, a post he occupied until 1920. Roosevelt was James Cox's running mate in the presidential election of 1920, but they lost by a landslide to the Republican ticket of Warren G. Harding and Calvin Coolidge. After being stricken with polio in 1921, Roosevelt spent much of the rest of the decade trying to restore his health, and in 1928 he was elected governor of New York. He served in Albany until 1933, when he entered the White House as president of the United States. Roosevelt's presidency was one of the most important in U.S. history; his New Deal attempted to ease the Great Depression of the 1930s, and his leadership of the country during World War II made him a beloved figure until his death on April 12, 1945.

Midway through World War II, Roosevelt realized that colonialism was dead and that the United States would best be served by aligning itself with the forces of nationalism in the developing world. He had little faith in Charles de Gaulle and thought that France* had badly mismanaged its affairs in Indochina.* By 1944 Roosevelt was advocating placing Indochina under an international trusteeship. Early in 1945, however, as the British contemplated returning to their former colonies in Asia, Roosevelt amended his point of view, and at the Yalta Conference in 1945 agreed to a proposal calling for trusteeships only with the approval of the mother country. The Yalta agreement killed any hope for a trusteeship over Indochina. After Roosevelt's death in 1945, Harry S. Truman* took over as president of the United States. Truman shared none of Roosevelt's concerns about imperialism and colonialism, and American policy during his administration shifted strongly toward French policies in Indochina.

Sources: George C. Herring, *America's Longest War: The United States in Vietnam, 1950–1975*, 1986; Chester Bain, *Vietnam: The Roots of Conflict*, 1967; Frances FitzGerald, *Fire in the Lake: The Vietnamese and the Americans in Vietnam*, 1972.

Below: President Franklin D. Roosevelt addresses the nation from the White House on November 4, 1938, during the heated congressional elections. Even his sincere, soothing voice could not prevent a Republican rout of the Democrats.

ROSTOW, WALT WHITMAN

W.W. Rostow, an economist with extensive service in the federal government, began advising John F. Kennedy,* then a senator from Massachusetts, on foreign policy in 1958 and was active in Kennedy's successful 1960 presidential campaign. Kennedy appointed Rostow deputy special assistant to the president for foreign security affairs in the incoming administration, and as such Rostow participated throughout 1961 in the formulation of U.S. policy toward Laos* and Vietnam. He generally advocated a strong diplomatic and military role in opposing Communist insurgents operating in Asia. Later, Rostow moved to the State Department, where he was placed in charge of long-range analysis and planning in a broad range of foreign policy areas.

Beginning in June 1964 Rostow began to exert direct influence on President Lyndon B. Johnson* by serving as one of his principal advisors on Southeast Asia. During this period W.W. Rostow developed his unique foreign policy perspective on Vietnam and like situations, which came to be called the Rostow thesis. Essentially, he argued that externally supported insurgencies could be stopped only by military action against the source of external support. As a result, he urged a series of escalating military measures

designed to impart the maximum possible psychological blow and thereby force a cessation of the external support. This policy approach flowed from Rostow's belief that modernization—expressed in his important 1960 study, *The Stages of Economic Growth*—created certain dislocations and discontents that, although transitional, could be used by Communists to gain support. He commented that it was necessary to hold off any Communist challenge until full modernization was achieved.

Consistent with this general approach to the problem in Southeast Asia, Rostow argued in June 1964 that the United States commit both military force and a strong public stance against North Vietnamese support for rebel forces in Laos and South Vietnam. Although not without critics, "The outlook embodied in the 'Rostow thesis' came to dominate a good deal of Administration thinking on the question of pressures against the North in the months ahead," according to the Pentagon Papers.*

Although Rostow had previously worked in the background, on March 31, 1966, President Johnson appointed him special assistant to the president for national security affairs, succeeding McGeorge Bundy.* In this post Rostow worked closely with Johnson for the remainder of the administration on virtually all foreign policy issues. One of these involved the bombing of the North Vietnamese industrial base. In May 1966, for instance, Rostow argued for the "systematic and sustained bombing" of petroleum-product facilities in North Vietnam. This goal was realized in the bombing campaigns* that followed in the Hanoi* and Haiphong areas.

Throughout the remainder of the Johnson administration Rostow continued to support the large-scale bombing program, although the president chose to limit aerial attacks during the latter months of his term. During this time overtures were reportedly made on Rostow's behalf to MIT and several other leading universities to secure for him a teaching position after the administration's end. Eventually, he accepted a position as professor of economics and history at the University of Texas at Austin, where a Lyndon B. Johnson School of Public Affairs was planned. In the final hours of his presidency, Johnson awarded Rostow and nineteen others the Medal of Freedom, the country's highest civilian honor. Rostow lived in Austin, Texas, and taught economics and history until his death on February 13, 2003. RDL

Sources: W.W. Rostow, *The Stages of Economic Growth: A Non-Communist Manifesto*, 1960, and *The Diffusion of Power, 1957–1972*, 1972; Seyom Brown, *The Faces of Power: Constancy and Change in United States Foreign Policy from Truman to Johnson*, 1968; Eric F. Goldman, *The Tragedy of Lyndon Johnson*, 1969; George C. Herring, *America's Longest War: The United States and Vietnam, 1950–1975*, 1986.

ROWE, JAMES NICHOLAS

A Special Forces* advisor and early prisoner of war* in Vietnam, James N. Rowe was born in 1938 at McAllen, Texas. He graduated from the United States Military Academy in 1960, B.S., and was commissioned second lieutenant, United States Army.* An early volunteer for the Special Forces* (Green Berets), Rowe was sent to Vietnam in 1963 as an advisor to an Army of the Republic of Vietnam* (ARVN) unit. On October 29, 1963, Lieutenant Rowe accompanied his ARVN unit on a raid of a Vietcong village in the Mekong Delta.* But the plan of attack went awry when the Vietcong (VC) declined to react in the prescribed manner. As a contingent of the ARVN unit surged through the village firing into the huts, the VC were expected to flee into the forest, where an ambush awaited them. But the VC moved in the opposite direction, regrouped, and counterattacked. The ARVN unit soon found itself in desperate straits. When help failed to arrive from other units in the area, the ARVN troops were cut off and decimated. Lieutenant Rowe and two other Green Berets were among the survivors taken prisoner.

For the next five years Rowe was held a captive in the field, forced to live the life and share the squalor and privation of his captors. Three attempts to escape failed, resulting in punishment and closer confinement for a period. Finally, on December 31, 1968, Lieutenant Rowe was able to break away from his captors in the confusion when American helicopter gunships* attacked the VC. Fortunately, a gunship crewman spotted him in a clearing, and he was rescued.

In 1971 Rowe (by then a Major) published a detailed autobiographical account of his service and captivity in Vietnam. Reaction to his book reflected the intensity of the domestic discord over the Vietnam War. On the one hand, Rowe was hailed as a genuine hero and his book was commended for its "shattering impact," a revelation of the evils of Communism. But other reviewers called it self-serving and parochial, a revelation of American attitudes of superiority and disdain for the Vietnamese people. One reviewer cast doubts on the author's integrity, questioning how Rowe could have recalled all the minute details of his service and captivity years after the fact. The details of his imprisonment were called boring. The comments no doubt reflected the reviewer's attitude toward the war more than toward Rowe himself.

Rowe continued to serve in the Army until 1974, when he resigned. In 1975 he ran on the Republican ticket for state office in Texas, but lost. He then turned his attention to writing as a career. In 1981 Colonel Rowe was recalled to active duty, and in 1987 was assigned to the Philippines to provide counterinsurgency training to its military. James N. Rowe was killed there on April 21, 1989, while returning to the U.S. Embassy. JMR Jr.

Sources: James N. Rowe, *Five Years to Freedom*, 1971; *Contemporary Authors*, 1st rev., vols. 37–40, 1979, pp. 469–71; *U.S. Veteran Dispatch*, 1995.

RUBIN, JERRY

Jerry Rubin was born on July 14, 1938, in Cincinnati. He graduated from the University of Cincinnati in 1961, and in 1964 he was active in Mario Savio's Free Speech Movement at the University of California at Berkeley. As the free speech movement was transformed into an anti-Vietnam campaign, Rubin emerged as a radical leader and organizer of the Vietnam Day Committee (VDC), a prominent antiwar group. VDC demonstrations took on the image of radical insurgency in 1966 when protesters tried to block trains carrying Vietnam-bound soldiers to training and embarkation posts. Early in 1968 Rubin joined with Abbie Hoffman* in forming the Youth International Party, or "Yippies," to promote counterculture ideas and oppose the war in Vietnam. The Yippies sponsored large and disruptive demonstrations in Chicago during the Democratic National Convention* in August 1968, and Rubin was arrested as one of the Chicago 8.* His behavior at the subsequent trial, where he was charged with conspiracy to riot, was outra-

geous, and he was found guilty of contempt. Convicted of conspiracy, Rubin appealed, and won in the federal appeals court in 1972. When the war ended in 1973 Rubin's public personality lost some of its attraction, and he disappeared from the public scene. By the early 1980s Jerry Rubin was a successful stockbroker on Wall Street, the ultimate symbol of the transformation of 1960s Yippies into 1980s Yuppies. Jerry Rubin died on November 28, 1994, in Los Angeles.

Sources: Jerry Rubin, *Growing Up at 37*, 1976; Thomas Powers, *Vietnam: The War at Home*, 1984; Nancy Zaroulis and Gerald Sullivan, *Who Spoke Up? American Protest Against the Vietnam War, 1963–1975*, 1984; *New York Times*, November 29, 1994.

RUNG SAT SWAMP

The Rung Sat Swamp consisted of the swampland deltas of the Saigon and Dong Nai rivers. Vietcong* sappers harassed the flow of supplies to Saigon by placing mines in the deep river shipping lanes. The Rung Sat Swamp was the area from which the sappers operated.

Source: Harry G. Summers Jr., *Vietnam War Almanac*, 1985.

RURAL DEVELOPMENT PROGRAM

See Rural Reconstruction

RURAL RECONSTRUCTION

By 1968 a "two pincers" strategy dominated the American war effort. The "violence" pincer consisted of attacking main force North Vietnamese Army* (NVA) and National Liberation Front (NLF; *see* Vietcong) units, pushing them into uninhabited regions, breaking their ties with local NLF guerrilla and political cadres, and eliminating local NLF infrastructures. Allied main force units would address the first three "violence" objectives, while local units and the Phoenix Program* would address the fourth. The second pincer would be Rural Reconstruction, a comprehensive pacification program developed by Colonel Nguyen Be. Rather than attempting to win people to the government's side, Rural Reconstruction was intended to put the government on the side of the people. The program failed for three basic reasons: (1) U.S.-GVN (*see* Republic of Vietnam) commitment to "conventional" military thinking; (2) inability to change the attitudes of civilian officials; and (3) the resulting corruption and misallocation of resources. At the program's heart were fifty-nine-member Rural

Reconstruction cadres trained largely by former Vietminh.* Cadres had the following assignments: (1) to live in villages cleared of NLF military units; (2) to gain villagers' trust and cooperation by hearing their grievances against the government; (3) to recommend or take action redressing those grievances; (4) to assist villagers in education, health, public works, and agricultural projects; and (5) to root out the NLF political and local guerrilla infrastructure. Gaining villagers' confidence was often difficult because of GVN corruption and memories of past pacification programs such as Strategic Hamlets.* Villagers often feared that the cadres would force them to build new strategic hamlets or force them to do other work, such as erecting defensive positions for the Regional Forces.*

Cadre teams were also created too rapidly. Many were inadequately trained. Many were assigned to inadequately secured villages only to be driven out or killed by the NLF. Adequate security was dependent on ridding the area of main force units and training Popular Forces* to protect villages against local guerrilla attack; such forces generally were poorly trained and poorly armed. In some instances local officials refused to arm them at all. Unable to defend themselves, much less their assigned village, they often ran away from any perceived threat. This was a major failure, as studies of the effectiveness of previous pacification programs indicated that an inability to establish adequate security precluded any meaningful decision on whether pacification programs could work (apparently overlooking the possibility that necessary security could not be established because the populace was simply unwilling to be "pacified"). Village chiefs and GVN officials often failed to cooperate with cadres by refusing to furnish necessary resources or to act on cadre recommendations. Complaints about corruption in particular went unheeded. Military considerations almost always took precedence over reconstruction priorities; at times the military destroyed reconstruction projects during its operations. Without the cooperation of either villagers or GVN officials, cadre members' morale plummeted. One-fourth deserted within their first year.

While the primary objective of the American effort in Vietnam officially was always pacification, the allocation of resources and the options considered indicated clearly that pacification programs were secondary to the military effort, demonstrating a curious Catch-22 logic. The United States insisted that the underlying problems were political and required a political solution. Before a political solution could be found, however, stability and order had to be established. Consequently, political solutions had to be postponed until a military solution to the insurgency produced stability and order. At that point energies could be directed to the development of political solutions that redressed the original causes of instability.

Ultimately, Rural Reconstruction evolved into military control with a few welfare programs. This is not because the military mentality dominated thinking on Vietnam; the military position dominated largely by default. American non-military planning was woeful, and policymakers were ignorant of the history and culture of the Vietnamese people. Furthermore, the Vietnamese High Command and GVN officials themselves were virtually out of touch with their own people. French- or American-educated, living primarily in Saigon,* Vietnamese officials and commanders knew little about the people and conditions of the countryside. The NLF excelled because of its intimate knowledge of both. Rural Reconstruction was designed to copy the tactics of the NLF. That effort failed because reconstruction cadres ultimately were dependent on Saigon and the United States, whereas NLF cadres were dependent on the people, a difference in dependency not lost on the Vietnamese peasant. SF

Sources: David Halberstam, *The Making of a Quagmire*, 1964; Frances FitzGerald, *Fire in the Lake: The Vietnamese and the Americans in Vietnam*, 1972; Larry E. Cable, *Conflict of Myths: The Development of American Counterinsurgency Doctrine and the Vietnam War*, 1986; Andrew F. Krepinevich Jr., *The Army in Vietnam*, 1986.

RUSK, DAVID DEAN

Dean Rusk was born on February 9, 1909, in Cherokee County, Georgia. He grew up barefoot and poor in rural Georgia, graduated from Davidson College in 1931, and then attended Oxford University as a Rhodes scholar. Rusk joined the U.S. Army during World War II, received a commission as an infantry officer, and saw combat as operations officer under General Joseph Stilwell in the China-Burma theater. Between 1946 and 1962 Rusk worked for the State Department as an assistant secretary of state for Far Eastern affairs, becoming a dedicated anti-Communist and advocate of the containment policy.* Rusk became head of the Rockefeller Foundation in 1952 and remained there until 1960, when president-elect John F. Kennedy* nominated him as his new secretary of state.

Known as "the Buddha," Rusk rarely spoke up in general meetings and had a penchant for loyalty, giving it to his superiors and expecting it from his subordinates. At first Rusk hoped to leave Vietnam to the Department of Defense as essentially a military question, but by 1963 he had lost hope in the ability of Ngo Dinh Diem* to govern South Vietnam. Throughout 1963 Rusk became increasingly outspoken that Diem had to initiate serious reforms or be removed from office. In the process, Rusk became a more and more visible advocate of a hard-line approach to Vietnam, taking a Cold Warrior position.

During the years of the Johnson* administration, Rusk's reputation as a hawk became even more obvious. He opposed any negotiated settlement to the conflict, especially as long as the Vietcong* and North Vietnamese held any military advantages in the field, and he favored an

Opposite page: Jerry Rubin dons a toy machine gun and participates in an antiwar demonstration at the Cannon House Office Building in Washington, D.C., on October 7, 1968. Rubin is also wearing a red and blue cape bearing a yellow star, the colors of the Vietcong, and waving the peace sign.

Above: President Lyndon B. Johnson confers with Secretary of State Dean Rusk on October 31, 1968. To Rusk's right sits Undersecretary of State Nicholas Katzenbach. Seated behind Johnson is General William Westmoreland, head of the Military Assistance Command, Vietnam.

aggressive bombing campaign* against North Vietnam. Unlike Secretary of Defense Robert S. McNamara* and his successor Clark Clifford,* Rusk never wavered in support of American policies in Vietnam, at least never publicly. He refused to accept the growing conviction in 1967 that the Vietnam conflict was essentially an internal civil war originating in a nationalist rebellion, preferring instead to see it in Cold War terms as a clear case of Communist aggression, this time orchestrated by the People's Republic of China.* Rusk consistently supported military demands for increasing troop commitments to Vietnam, including the request after the Tet Offensive* for another 200,000 soldiers. He urged President Lyndon B. Johnson* to stay the course with the war despite the increasing strength of the antiwar movement* at home and the counsel of the "Wise Old Men"* that the United States disengage, and was disappointed with the president's decision late in March 1968 not to seek reelection. Rusk became closely associated in the public mind with administration policy in Vietnam, perhaps paying a price of sorts upon leaving office in January 1969 when most prestigious universities refused even to consider him for a faculty appointment. Ultimately, he accepted a post at the University of Georgia, where he taught international law from 1970 to 1984. Dean Rusk died on December 20, 1994. CD

Sources: David Halberstam, *The Best and the Brightest*, 1972; Arthur M. Schlesinger Jr., *A Thousand Days: John F. Kennedy in the White House*, 1965; Richard J. Walton, *Cold War and Counterrevolution: The Foreign Policy of John F. Kennedy*, 1972; Doris Kearns, *Lyndon Johnson and the American Dream*, 1976; Warren Cohen, *Dean Rusk*, 1980; Thomas W. Zeiles, *Dean Rusk: Defending the American Mission Abroad*, 1999.

RUSSELL, RICHARD BREVARD

A native Georgian, Richard Russell was born on November 2, 1897, and received a law degree from the University of Georgia in 1918. He practiced law for three years before being elected as a Democrat to the state legislature. Ten years later, at the age of thirty-three, he became the youngest governor in the history of Georgia. Russell then won a seat in the U.S. Senate in the election of 1932, where he remained for the next thirty-eight years. He became a master of parliamentary maneuver and a formidable debater. Although Russell fought social welfare and civil rights legislation, he nevertheless held great respect among liberal senators because of his ability and integrity. By 1952 Russell was a major figure in the Democratic Party. He lost the presidential nomination to Adlai Stevenson that year, but as chairman of the Senate Armed Services Committee and of the military expenditures subcommittee of the Appropriations Committee, Russell wielded vast influence over military policy.

As early as 1954, Russell warned Dwight D. Eisenhower* against sending arms and advisors to bolster French forces in Indochina.* He once told John Foster Dulles* that he was "weary of seeing American soldiers being used as gladiators to be thrown into every arena around the world." When Eisenhower decided to make the commitment, Russell said that he would "support the flag," but that "it is going to be a long drawn-out affair costly in both blood and Treasure." Russell remained faithful to his word. As long as American forces were fighting in Vietnam, he supported the policies of successive presidents. But he regretted the intervention, calling it "one of the great tragedies of our history."

Throughout the summer and fall of 1970, Senator Richard Russell's health deteriorated. He entered Walter Reed Medical Center on December 8, 1970, and died there on January 21, 1971, at the age of seventy-three. JMR Jr.

Sources: *Current Biography*, 1949; *New York Times*, January 22, 1971.

RUSSO, ANTHONY J. JR.

Born in Suffolk, Virginia, on October 14, 1936, Anthony (Tony) Russo was codefendant with Daniel Ellsberg* in the Pentagon Papers Trial,* 1972–73. Russo attended the Virginia Polytechnic Institute, where he received a B.S. in aeronautical engineering in 1960 and participated in the cooperative engineering program at NASA's Langley Space Laboratory. In 1961 he entered Princeton University and earned an M.S. in aeronautical engineering in 1963 and a public affairs master's degree from the Woodrow Wilson School of Public and International Affairs in 1964. There he assisted Oskar Morgenstern in the Econometrics Research Program and studied foreign policy under Richard Falk, Edmundo Flores, George Kennan,* and Klaus Knorr. In June 1964 Russo joined the Rand Corporation.* He then spent twenty-four months in South Vietnam, February 1966–January 1968, where he interviewed prisoners for Rand's "Viet Cong Motivation and Morale" study for the U.S. Department of Defense. Russo also participated in a statistical assessment of the U.S.-sponsored crop-destruction program (*see* Defoliants). These research experiences led Russo to begin questioning U.S. policy in Vietnam. Independently, Russo also published a study to show that, contrary to some earlier research, local and peasant support for the National Liberation Front (*see* Vietcong) tended to be strongest in South Vietnam's poorest provinces and hamlets (*see* Russo, "Economic and Social

Correlates of Government Control in South Vietnam," in Ivo K. Feierabend et al., eds., *Anger, Violence, and Politics*, 1972). Russo was dismissed by the Rand Corporation for "budgetary reasons" in July 1968, but he was allowed to remain on staff to complete pending work. Russo left Rand in January 1969 to join the firm of Social Engineering Technology in Los Angeles. He also became involved in poverty and civil rights work in Los Angeles. In December 1970 he joined the Research and Information Systems Office of the Los Angeles County Probation Department.

Tony Russo and Daniel Ellsberg first met at the Rand villa in Saigon* in 1965, but they did not become friends until 1968 when occupying offices across the hall from each other at Rand's headquarters in Santa Monica, California. When Ellsberg sought a way to copy the Pentagon Papers* in 1969, Russo arranged for the rental of a Xerox machine at an advertising agency owned by his friend Lynda Sinay. Russo then assisted Ellsberg in photocopying the "secret" documents. He was first questioned by the Federal Bureau of Investigation about his role in the publication of the Pentagon Papers on June 19, 1971, but refused to answer FBI questions. On June 23 Russo was subpoenaed to testify before a federal grand jury in Los Angeles. Despite a grant of immunity, Russo refused to testify unless his testimony could be made public. On August 16 he began serving a forty-seven-day jail term for contempt of court. During portions of his imprisonment, according to Russo, he was shackled and beaten, placed in solitary confinement, and otherwise abused for leading a twenty-one-day hunger strike in protest of government actions against inmates at the Attica state prison in New York. On October 1, U.S. District Court judge Warren J. Ferguson released Russo from prison and ordered the government to provide Russo with a transcript of any testimony he might be required to give to the grand jury. Assistant U.S. attorney David R. Nissen held the order to be "unlawful" and refused to comply with it. Russo again declined to testify before the grand jury. On December 29 the grand jury issued a new indictment in the Pentagon Papers case, which added new charges against Ellsberg and also included criminal charges against Russo. The trial of Ellsberg and Russo opened in Los Angeles on July 10, 1972. In October 1972, during a stay in the trial, Russo testified at the third annual session of the Commission of Enquiry into U.S. War Crimes in Indochina, held in Copenhagen, Denmark. On May 11, 1973, U.S. District Court judge William Matthew Byrne dismissed all charges against Ellsberg and Russo and declared a mistrial in their case because of "improper government conduct." After the trial, Russo continued his antiwar activity, sought to organize a nationwide campaign to impeach President Richard M. Nixon,* and ultimately returned to social work. JK

Sources: Mike Gravel, ed., *Pentagon Papers*, 1971; Peter Schrag, *Test of Loyalty*, 1974.

Dinh Diem* named Saigon the capital city of South Vietnam. When North Vietnamese and Vietcong* forces overran Saigon in 1975, they renamed it Ho Chi Minh City.*

Sources: Virginia Thompson, *French Indochina*, 1968; Ellen J. Hammer, *Vietnam, Yesterday and Today*, 1966; *Saigon Times Weekly*, September 16, 2006.

SALEM HOUSE

See Daniel Boone Operations

SAIGON

Saigon was the capital city of South Vietnam during the Vietnam War. Originally settled by Cambodians, Saigon has for centuries been a major port city in Southeast Asia. It is located approximately forty-five miles up the Ben Nghe River, or Saigon River, from the South China Sea. The French began using the name Saigon in 1861 when they moved into the city and prepared for their takeover of the rest of the country. By 1980 the city had a population of nearly 2 million people concentrated into twenty-seven square miles, making it one of the most population-dense areas in the world; the population in 2004 had reached approximately 5 million. Right next to Saigon is the city of Cholon,* composed mostly of ethnic Chinese.* In 1956 Ngo

SALISBURY, HARRISON EVANS

Harrison Evans Salisbury was born on November 14, 1908, in Minneapolis. Between 1930 and 1948 Salisbury worked for the United Press and traveled widely in his assignments. After joining the staff of the *New York Times* in 1948, Salisbury was assigned as Moscow bureau chief and remained there until 1953; he became assistant managing editor of the *Times* in 1964. Late in 1966 Salisbury traveled to North Vietnam to report on the effects of the American bombing.* His reports were controversial on two levels: first, he confirmed North Vietnamese claims that civilian casualties from the American bombing were quite high; second, he argued that the bombing efforts were only increasing the resolve of the North Vietnamese to continue

Right: South Vietnamese workers put the finishing touches on a national memorial in downtown Saigon in November 1966. The statue depicts an ARVN soldier going into battle. The memorial, which included other statues, was dedicated to the military leaders, soldiers, and politicians responsible for the independence of the Republic of Vietnam (South Vietnam).

Left: Workers begin to clear rubble from a bombed out section of Cholon, the area of Saigon inhabited largely by Chinese, on February 15, 1968. Just two weeks earlier, the Vietcong had launched the Tet Offensive, which included mortar attacks and the infiltration of Saigon. The American counterattack was equally destructive to the city.

Left: More than 100,000 Roman Catholic schoolboys stage an anti-Communist and pro-American demonstration in downtown Saigon on June 12, 1966. The banner they wield expresses appreciation to the soldiers from four countries—the United States, South Korea, Australia, and New Zealand—the allies of South Vietnam, fighting the Vietcong.

Below: The Soviet Union supplied North Vietnam with large quantities of surface-to-air missiles during the Vietnam War. The surface-to-air missiles pictured here are Soviet-made SA-2s, code-named Guideline. The Soviet Union supplied enough SA-2s to give North Vietnam a formidable antiaircraft capability.

the war effort. During the 1960s and 1970s Salisbury continued to write widely for the *Times*, and became widely known as the patriarch of American journalism. He authored several books, including *Heroes of My Time*, published posthumously in 1993. Harrison E. Salisbury died on July 5, 1993.

Sources: Harrison E. Salisbury, *Behind the Lines: Hanoi, December 23, 1966–January 7, 1967*, 1967; *Who's Who in America, 1976–1977*, 1977; Clayborne Carson et al., eds., *Reporting Civil Rights. Part Two: American Journalism 1963–1973*, 2003.

SAN ANTONIO FORMULA

On September 29, 1967, in San Antonio, Texas, President Lyndon B. Johnson* delivered a speech in which he offered to stop the bombing* of North Vietnam if Ho Chi Minh* would agree to begin serious negotiations for a peaceful settlement of the conflict, and if Ho would promise not to use the bombing halt as an opportunity to increase the North's infiltration* of troops and supplies into South Vietnam. In diplomatic and journalistic circles, the president's offer became known as the San Antonio Formula. Hanoi never responded positively to the offer, even though Johnson reiterated it on March 31, 1968, after the Tet Offensive* and his own decision not to seek reelection. For six months Johnson unilaterally stopped all bombing of North Vietnam above the 19th parallel, but the North Vietnamese did not seriously consider a negotiated settlement at the time.

Sources: Guenter Lewy, *America in Vietnam*, 1978; *New York Times*, September 30, 1986.

The SA-2 had a blinding speed of Mach 3.5 and carried a 2,000-pound warhead. An SA-2 brought down its first U.S. aircraft, an F-4C Phantom, in July 1965. To the advantage of U.S. pilots, the SA-2 at launch and burn emitted a fiery, smoke-laden trail that allowed for evasive action. On average, thirteen missiles were required to bring down a single U.S. aircraft.

SAM

The acronym SAM described surface-to-air missiles employed by the North Vietnamese against United States Navy* and Air Force* bombers and fighter-bombers (*see* Fighters). The standard SAM was the Soviet SA-2 Guideline, a two-stage missile equipped with a 285-pound warhead with a maximum range of thirty miles. The first SA-2 Guidelines were deployed in the summer of 1965, and by the end of the war more than 200 SA-2 sites were operational, most of them protecting Hanoi* and Haiphong. Because of the U.S. "Wild Weasel"* program and various other electronic jamming efforts, the North Vietnamese used 150 SA-2s for every American aircraft they destroyed.

Source: Anthony Robinson, "Air Forces in Vietnam," in John S. Bowman, ed., *The Vietnam War: An Almanac*, 1985.

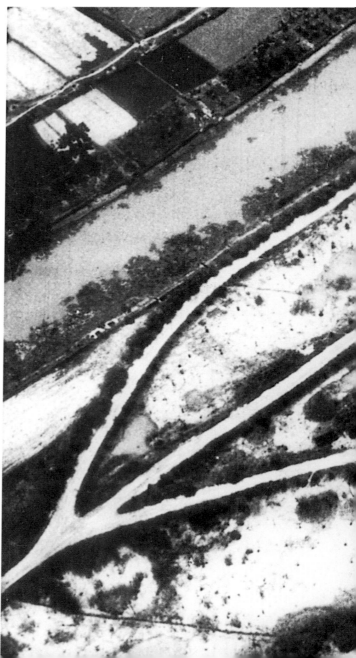

SAN ANTONIO FORMULA

SANCTUARIES

Throughout the war in Vietnam the North Vietnamese and Vietcong* used "hit and run" tactics and often fled across the border into sanctuaries in neutral Laos* and Cambodia.* Although the inability of a neutral nation to prevent a belligerent from exploiting its territory allows, according to international law, the other belligerent to use force on neutral territory, the United States had a difficult time with the issue. Periodically, regular American military units would cross the borders in "hot pursuit,"* and Studies and Observation Groups* teams regularly operated in Cambodia and Laos, as did naval and Air Force units in the bombing of infiltration* routes; but not until the Cambodian invasion of 1970 (see Operation Binh Tay) and the Laotian invasion of 1971 (see Lam Son 719) did the United States openly assault North Vietnamese and Vietcong strongholds across the borders. Although those invasions posed serious threats to the integrity of the sanctuaries, the subsequent withdrawal of American and South Vietnamese forces allowed the North Vietnamese and Vietcong to return to their original positions.

Sources: Guenter Lewy, *America in Vietnam*, 1978; Harry G. Summers Jr., *On Strategy: A Critical Analysis of the Vietnam War*, 1982; William Shawcross, *Sideshow: Kissinger, Nixon, and the Destruction of Cambodia*, 1979; Keith William Nolan, *Into Laos: The Story of Dewey Canyon II/Lam Son 719*, 1986.

"SANITIZE"

"Sanitize" was one of a number of euphemisms developed to refer to assassination. It became infamous in conjunction with the Central Intelligence Agency's* Phoenix Program,* in which as many as 20,000 South Vietnamese were killed because of suspected ties to the National Liberation Front (see Vietcong). Still, the term was widely used before the Phoenix Program to describe political assassinations carried out by South Vietnamese and American personnel. Critics

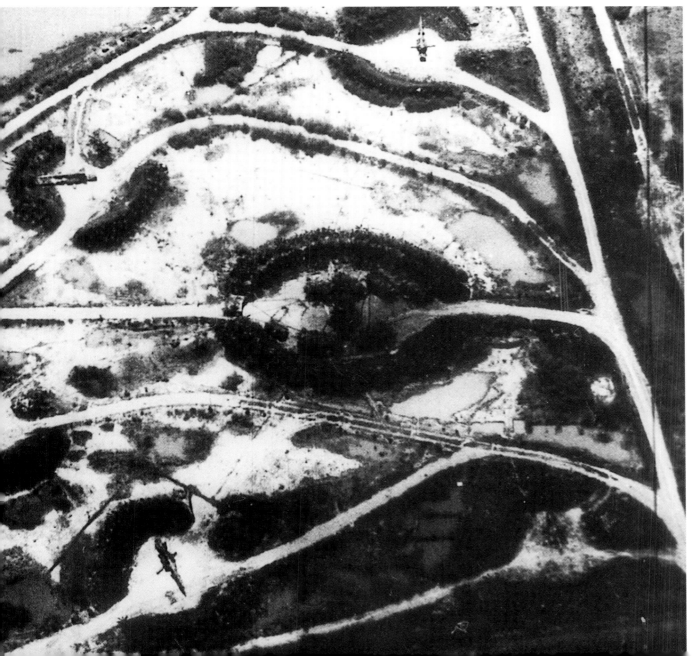

Left: An aerial reconnaissance photo of a SAM battery beside a canal in the Red River Delta area of North Vietnam. Six SA-2 Guideline missile launch sites are visible. Electronic support equipment and a Fan Song fire control radar system are enclosed in the large berm at center right. The berm would be the target for the Wild Weasels. If they could destroy it, the battery would be forced to use the SA-2's ineffective optically directed guidance system.

charged that use of the term was indicative of the war's degrading and dehumanizing nature. The act of killing people who may or may not have been "innocent" was masked by a sterile, antiseptic term that occluded its reality even from those actively involved in the deaths. Critics saw development of such terminology as insidious, part of what they perceived as the larger fabric of lies surrounding the war and of how its very nature served to debase and degrade both those who participated in it and the United States as a nation. SF

Sources: Loren Baritz, *Backfire*, 1985; Guenter Lewy, *America in Vietnam*, 1978.

SCHLESINGER, ARTHUR MEIER JR.

Arthur M. Schlesinger Jr. was born in Columbus, Ohio, on October 15, 1917. The son of distinguished historian Arthur M. Schlesinger, he attended public schools, Phillips Exeter Academy, and Harvard. His senior thesis, a biography of Orestes A. Brownson, was published in 1939. Schlesinger joined the Harvard faculty that same year. He won the Pulitzer Prize for his book *The Age of Jackson* (1945). His trilogy *The Age of Roosevelt* in the late 1950s firmly established Schlesinger as one of America's most outstanding historians. In 1961 President John F. Kennedy* appointed Schlesinger as a special advisor, a post in which he served until Kennedy's assassination in 1963. Schlesinger's book *A Thousand Days*, though essentially an apology, was nevertheless a cogent description of the "Age of Camelot."

Schlesinger, although a supporter of the antipoverty and civil rights thrusts of Lyndon B. Johnson's* Great Society* reforms, broke with the administration over Vietnam. In 1966 Schlesinger wrote *The Bitter Heritage*, a history of American involvement in South Vietnam, in which he accused American policymakers of confusing Communism and nationalism, backing an essentially fascist dictator in the person of Ngo Dinh Diem,* and using conventional tactics in a futile guerrilla war (*see* Vietcong). Schlesinger denied the reality of the domino theory* and doubted that the Chinese (*see* People's Republic of China), traditionally enemies of the Vietnamese, had any intention of intervening. After leaving the Kennedy administration, Schlesinger continued teaching and writing. He was a professor emeritus of history at the City University of New York, where he taught until 1994. Arthur M. Schlesinger Jr. died on February 28, 2007.

Sources: Arthur M. Schlesinger Jr., *The Bitter Heritage: Vietnam and American Democracy, 1941–1966*, 1966; *Directory of American Scholars, History*, 1984; *New York Times*, May 26, 2004.

SCHLESINGER, JAMES RODNEY

James Schlesinger was born in New York City on February 15, 1929. He graduated from Harvard University in 1950 and then took an M.A. and a Ph.D. there in economics in 1952 and 1956. Between 1955 and 1963 Schlesinger taught at the University of Virginia. He spent the next six years with the Rand Corporation.* During his years at Virginia and Rand, Schlesinger wrote two important books: *The Political Economy of National Security* (1960) and *Issues in Defense Economics* (1967). Schlesinger became assistant director of the Bureau of the Budget in 1969, chairman of the Atomic Energy Commission in 1971, head of the Central Intelligence Agency* in 1973, and secretary of defense later in 1973. He served in that position throughout the Watergate* crisis involving President Richard M. Nixon* and the fall of the Republic of Vietnam* in 1975. Schlesinger left the Pentagon in 1975, served for a time as a visiting scholar at Johns Hopkins University, and then became secretary of energy under President Jimmy Carter in 1977. Schlesinger left the Carter administration in 1979 and became a senior advisor to the Center for Strategic and International Studies at Georgetown University. After retiring to private life, Schlesinger went to work as a senior advisor to Lehman Brothers, Kuhn Loeb, Inc. In January 2006 he was appointed a member of the Arms Control and Nonproliferation Advisory Board; in May he was named co-chairman of a Defense Science Board study on Department of Defense energy strategy.

Sources: *Who's Who in America, 1984–1985*, 1985; http://en.wikipedia.org/wiki/James_Schlesinger.

SEABEES

Naval construction units, known as Seabees, were active in the Vietnam conflict from the very beginning of the American presence there. As early as 1954, Amphibious Construction Battalion 1 engineers were constructing refugee camps in South Vietnam, and between 1962 and 1965 they built camps for the 5th Special Forces Group.* During that period they were also heavily engaged in civic action programs, building airstrips, bridges, dams, roads, housing, and schools. Naval Mobile Construction Battalions, each staffed with 24 officers and 738 enlisted men, began arriving at Da Nang* in May 1965 as part of the 30th Naval Construction Regiment. The 3d Naval Construction Brigade arrived in Vietnam on June 1, 1966. The 32d Naval Construction Regiment was sent to Vietnam on August 1, 1967, assigned to the Hue*–Phu Bai region. Most Seabee activities took place in I Corps,* where teams constructed waterfront facilities, storage areas, ammunition dumps, roads, and bridges. The Seabees were based at Da Nang,* Chu Lai,

Left: Offloading vehicles onto a pontoon causeway off Chu Lai, circa early May 1965. An airfield is being built from interlocking aluminum and steel mats and will be fully completed by the end of June. Construction on the new air base, located on Dangquat Bay, about 60 miles southeast of Da Nang, began May 8 after some 6,000 Marines and Seabees made an amphibious landing from U.S. Navy ships. Marine Corps F-4 Phantoms and A-4 Skyhawks began flying air strikes against North Vietnam on June 1 from an 8,000-foot-long aluminum airstrip.

Below: Crewmen aboard a Riverine inshore patrol craft (PCF) conduct a raid on the Cua Long River as part of Operation SEALORDS on November 11, 1968. The crewmen can be seen firing at suspected Vietcong on the banks of the river.

Hue–Phu Bai, Dong Tam, and Quang Tri. At their peak strength in 1968, Seabees totaled more than 10,000 men. The last Seabee unit to leave Vietnam was the 3d Naval Construction Brigade, which departed on November 1, 1971.

Sources: Shelby L. Stanton, *Vietnam Order of Battle*, 1981; Richard Tregakis, *Southeast Asia. Building the Bases: The History of Construction in Southeast Asia*, 1975.

SEALORDS

SEALORDS was an acronym for South East Asian Lake Ocean River Delta Strategy launched on October 8, 1968. In February 1969, as part of the Vietnamization* program, the United States Navy* began handing over to South Vietnam a fleet of nearly 250 patrol craft and 500 motorized junks that had formerly been part of the Mobile Riverine Force* and Task Forces 116 and 117. The Army of the Republic of Vietnam,* assisted by U.S. naval advisors, took

control of the patrol craft, and the program was renamed SEALORDS. Virtually all of the craft fell into the hands of the Vietcong* and North Vietnamese in 1975.

Sources: Edward J. Marolda and G. Wesley Pryce III, *A Short History of the United States Navy and the Southeast Asian Conflict, 1950–1975*, 1984; William B. Fulton, *Riverine Operations, 1966–1969*, 1973.

SEAL TEAMS

Early in 1961 teams of U.S. Special Forces* units began arriving in South Vietnam to train the Vietnamese in counterinsurgency.* The first Special Forces teams were Army units, but the U.S. Navy* also established its own counterinsurgency groups, known as sea, air, and land (SEAL) teams. The first SEAL groups arrived in South Vietnam in 1966 and deployed to the swamps of the Mekong Delta,* where they engaged in a variety of activities. SEAL teams infiltrated Vietcong* areas in small boats or as frogmen, parachuted in or were landed by helicopters, conducted "hunter-killer" raids, worked with Studies and Observation Groups* intelligence teams, and operated from fast-moving airboats and Seawolf helicopters. The SEALs were supported by the Navy's Task Force 116 (*see* Mobile Riverine Force).

Source: Edward J. Marolda and G. Wesley Pryce III, *A Short History of the United States Navy and the Southeast Asian Conflict, 1950–1975*, 1984.

Above: A member of a Navy SEAL (Navy Sea-Air-Land) team stands guard using a Stoner automatic weapon on March 26, 1968. Other members of the team are busy setting up explosives to destroy Vietcong bunkers on Tan Dinh Island in South Vietnam as part of Operation Bold Dragon III.

Right: A mechanized landing craft (LCM) carries a Navy SEAL team down the Bassac River in the Mekong Delta, South Vietnam on March 26, 1968. A flotilla of river patrol boats (PBR) accompanies them as Operation Bold Dragon III commences. They are headed for a Vietcong stronghold on Tan Dinh Island.

Left: In October 1968, U.S. sailors, aboard a personnel landing craft, fire an 81mm mortar at Vietcong positions.

Below: Staff Sergeant Thomas C. Robinson takes a break while on a search-and-destroy mission against the Vietcong in the jungles of Long Thanh east of Saigon late in April 1966. Robinson leads 1st Platoon, Company C, 1st Battalion, 18th Infantry Regiment of the 1st Cavalry Division.

SEARCH-AND-DESTROY STRATEGY

"Search and destroy" was the euphemism for the strategy of attrition that the United States employed in Vietnam between 1965 and 1968. Developed primarily by Generals William Westmoreland* and William Depuy, search and destroy relied on the naive assumption that superior American technology and firepower would eventually inflict casualties so severe that the Vietcong* and the North Vietnamese Army* (NVA) would be unable to sustain the war. Instead of the enclave strategy* that would confine the United States to a defensive posture, "search and destroy" meant seeking out the enemy and, with artillery, airpower, and ground forces, destroying their base areas and personnel. Once the main NVA regiments had been eliminated, the United States hoped that the South Vietnamese would be able to deal effectively with the Vietcong.

But the search-and-destroy strategy rested on a major assumption—that the United States would be able to inflict massive losses on the North Vietnamese without itself experiencing unacceptable casualty levels. That assumption, however, was contradicted by two basic facts in Vietnam: first, the Vietcong and North Vietnamese retained the strategic initiative and could pick and choose their battles, including the timing of attacks and the resource investment;

Above: Specialist 4 Orman Osborn slogs through a stream during a search-and-destroy patrol north of Phu Loi, South Vietnam on March 20, 1968. He makes sure to keep the M60 on his shoulder dry. The patrol is about to come upon a small Vietcong base camp.

Opposite page: Troops from F Company, 2d Battalion, 9th Marines patrol through the thick, tall stalks of a sugar cane field on the hunt for Vietcong troops on January 8, 1966. The dense foliage makes for a difficult and dangerous mission.

second, more than 200,000 young men reached draft age in North Vietnam each year, allowing the North to resupply its military units. Both of these facts together guaranteed that the United States would at best be able to fight them only to a standstill. The irony, of course, was that the Vietcong and North Vietnamese were also banking on their ability to inflict unacceptable losses on the United States, until the patience of the American public wore out and U.S. troops were withdrawn. Their scenario proved to be the correct one. The Tet Offensive* of 1968 was a political disaster in the United States, forcing Lyndon B. Johnson's* decision not to seek reelection and convincing large numbers of Americans that the war in Vietnam was not worth the effort and that the United States might not be capable of "winning" by any means. The election of 1968* turned out to be the strategic watershed of the Vietnam War. Between 1969 and 1973 the United States pursued a policy of staged withdrawal, rather than trying to "search and destroy" the enemy. The war of attrition* had failed.

Sources: Robert Shaplen, *The Road from War: Vietnam, 1965–1970*, 1970; George C. Herring, *America's Longest War: The United States in Vietnam 1950–1975*, 1986; W. Scott Thompson and Donaldson D. Frizzell, *The Lessons of Vietnam*, 1977; Harry G. Summers Jr., *On Strategy: A Critical Analysis of the Vietnam War*, 1982.

SEARCH-AND-RESCUE OPERATIONS

During the course of the war the United States Air Force* (USAF) rescue service recovered several thousand American and allied fighting men who went down in the jungles, mountains, and waters of Southeast Asia. The first USAF rescue team, consisting of three officers and three airmen, arrived in South Vietnam on temporary duty on January 10, 1962. Based at Tan Son Nhut Air Base,* near Saigon,* this unit's mission was to organize a search-and-rescue (SAR) control center and network throughout the country. In April 1962 the six-man cadre was officially designated Detachment-3, Pacific Air Rescue Center, with overall responsibility for rescue operations within the theater. Its job was especially difficult at first, for the detachment had no aircraft and had to rely on American advisors to provide helicopter assistance for air-rescue missions.

In addition to not having its own aircraft, the detachment lacked most of the basic equipment needed for an effective SAR system. For example, in the early days of its operations the SAR center sent requests for help to opera-

tional units by bicycle, a method faster and more reliable than trying to use the existing Vietnamese telephone network. Its reliance on the U.S. Army* and later the U.S. Marines* for helicopter support also created problems, because they were not prepared for rescue missions and had other duties that they considered of higher priority.

Very quickly after the establishment of the rescue center in Vietnam, it became clear to Air Force officials that specialized aircraft and devices were needed to operate effectively over the jungle and mountainous terrain of Southeast Asia. As a result, in November 1963 the commander of the Air Rescue Service pressed for the acquisition of the CH-3 single-rotor cargo amphibious helicopter for use in the theater. It had a forward speed of about 150 miles per hour, the ability to remain aloft for more than four hours, and a range of approximately 500 miles. He reported that the Air Service was not equipped to do the

Below: Airman First Class William J. Flowers of Milwaukee, Wisconsin, poses in front of an HH-3E ("Jolly Green Giant") helicopter at Da Nang Air Base in South Vietnam. Flowers is assigned to the 38th Aerospace Rescue and Recovery Squadron's Detachment 7. During a seven-day period in February 1967, Flowers participated in the rescue of nineteen people.

Below: Four U.S. Air Force pararescuemen, working in the Mekong Delta of South Vietnam, display the gear used in their work. From left to right, they are Sergeant Lonnie G. Conner of Axton, Virginia; Airman First Class Lonnie N. Davidson of Newman, Illinois; A1C Larry D. Nickolson of Pixley, California; and A1C John C. Wilkins of Marine City, Michigan. The equipment consists of a rescue sling (bottom), scuba gear, medical kit (center), a forest penetrator (left of Nickolson), and, in the background, one of Detachment 10, 38th Aerospace Rescue and Recovery Squadron's HH-43 ("Huskie") helicopters.

Opposite page: II Corps was the Central Highlands military region in South Vietnam, an area of approximately 5,400 square miles. The highland area stretched roughly from Ban Me Thuot in Darlac Province north to Kontum Province and the southern border of I Corps. II Corps was sparsely populated, primarily by Montagnard tribesmen.

Recognized early by North Vietnamese Army (NVA) strategists as a key to the conquest of Vietnam, an NVA attempt to cut Vietnam in two in 1965 with an attack from Cambodian sanctuaries across the Central Highlands to the sea was foiled by the U.S. First Cavalry Division in the Battle of Ia Drang.

They repeated this same strategy with an attack on Ban Me Thuot on March 10, 1975. In the face of this attack, South Vietnamese President Nguyen Van Thieu made the decision on March 14, 1975, to withdraw his overextended forces from the highlands to coastal enclaves. By March 31, 1975, the NVA 320th Division reached Tuy Hoa on the coast of the South China Sea. South Vietnam had been cut in two, and a month later Saigon fell to the NVA.

job in Southeast Asia and that, by "utter default," Air Force combat crews were "made dependent upon ill-equipped and ill-trained... U.S. Army and Marine Corps helicopter resources diverted to accomplish our mission... Their noble efforts have wrought confusion and even disaster when engaged in some attempts to prosecute Air Service missions."

In response, Headquarters USAF ordered a number of combat-modified CH-3s. Pending their manufacture, however, the Air Force was forced to use existing HH-43s and HU-16s, decent helicopters but not as well suited to jungle operations as the CH-3. In March 1964 three USAF HH-43 units were transferred from the Philippines* and Okinawa to Southeast Asia. In June 1964 the first temporary-duty contingent—two HH-43s and thirty-six personnel—was sent to Nakhon Phanom, Thailand.* That same month the 31st Air Rescue Squadron at Clark Air Base, the Philippines, deployed two HU-16 amphibious helicopters to Da Nang,* South Vietnam, to provide rescue service for American airmen downed in the Gulf of Tonkin. Two HU-16s from the 33d Air Rescue Squadron were also deployed to Korat Air Base, Thailand, to support USAF operations there and in Laos.* By January 1, 1965, five helicopter detachments were operating in the theater: at Bien Hoa and Da Nang, South Vietnam, and at Udorn, Nakhon Phanom, Takhli, and Korat, Thailand.

Air rescue in Vietnam entered a new phase in January 1966 when the Air Force activated the 3d Aerospace Rescue and Recovery Group at Tan Son Nhut Air Base to serve as the primary rescue agency in Southeast Asia. The group eventually directed the activities of four rescue squadrons and ten rescue detachments based throughout South Vietnam and Thailand. These units were solely responsible for the recovery of 3,883 pilots between 1964 and mid-August 1973. Of this number, 2,807 American—926 Army, 680 Navy, and 1,201 Air Force—aircrew members were rescued. The rescue units also saved 555 allied military pilots, 476 civilians, and 45 other unidentified persons. During the course of the war in Vietnam, 71 American search-and-rescue men were killed and 45 aircraft destroyed while conducting recovery operations. RDL

Source: Earl H. Tilford Jr., *Search and Rescue in Southeast Asia, 1961–1975*, 1980.

II CORPS

The second allied Combat Tactical Zone in South Vietnam, II Corps included the Central Highlands* and contiguous central lowlands, and was known politically as the Central Vietnam Highlands, one of the four major administrative political units of South Vietnam in the 1960s and early 1970s. Also known as Military Region 2 (MR 2), II Corps'

military and administrative headquarters was in Pleiku,* and the region consisted of the following provinces: Kontum, Binh Dinh, Pleiku, Phu Bon, Phu Yen, Darlac, Khanh Hoa, Quang Duc, Tuyen Duc, Ninh Thuan, Lam Dong, and Binh Thuan. The major ARVN (*see* Army of the Republic of Vietnam) units operating in II Corps were the 22d and 23d divisions.

Sources: Harvey H. Smith et al., *Area Handbook for South Vietnam*, 1967; Shelby L. Stanton, *Vietnam Order of Battle*, 1981.

II FIELD FORCE, VIETNAM

Headquartered at Bien Hoa, II Field Force, Vietnam was in the Republic of Vietnam* between March 1966 and May 1971, assisting ARVN forces (*see* Army of the Republic of Vietnam) in III* and IV Corps,* protecting Saigon,* controlling U.S. military operations in the Mekong Delta,* and directing the invasion of Cambodia (*see* Operation Binh Tay) in 1970. A corps*-level military organization, II Field Force, Vietnam was commanded by the following individuals: Major General Jonathan Seaman (March 1966– March 1967); Lieutenant General Bruce Palmer Jr. (March 1967–July 1967); Lieutenant General Frederick C. Weyand* (July 1967–August 1968); Lieutenant General Walter Kerwin Jr. (August 1968– April 1969); Lieutenant General Julian Ewell (April 1969–April 1970); and Lieutenant General Michael S. Davison (April 1970–May 1971).

Source: Shelby L. Stanton, *Vietnam Order of Battle*, 1981.

SECRETARY OF DEFENSE

In 1946 Congress passed the National Security Act, which coordinated the Army, Navy, and Air Force into a Department of Defense, with a secretary of defense enjoying cabinet status. The secretary of defense is in the direct chain of military command, between the president of the United States and the Joint Chiefs of Staff (*see* Chairman, JCS). During the course of direct American involvement in the Vietnam War, seven men served as secretary of defense. Neil H. McElroy was serving under Dwight Eisenhower* when the U.S. commitment began to escalate, and in December 1959 Thomas S. Gates Jr. replaced him. When John F. Kennedy* took over the White House in 1961, Robert S. McNamara* became the new secretary of defense. He served under Kennedy and Lyndon B. Johnson* until Johnson let him go in March 1968, replacing him with Clark M. Clifford.* When Richard M. Nixon* took over the White House in January 1969, Clifford left the Pentagon, and Melvin Laird* became the new

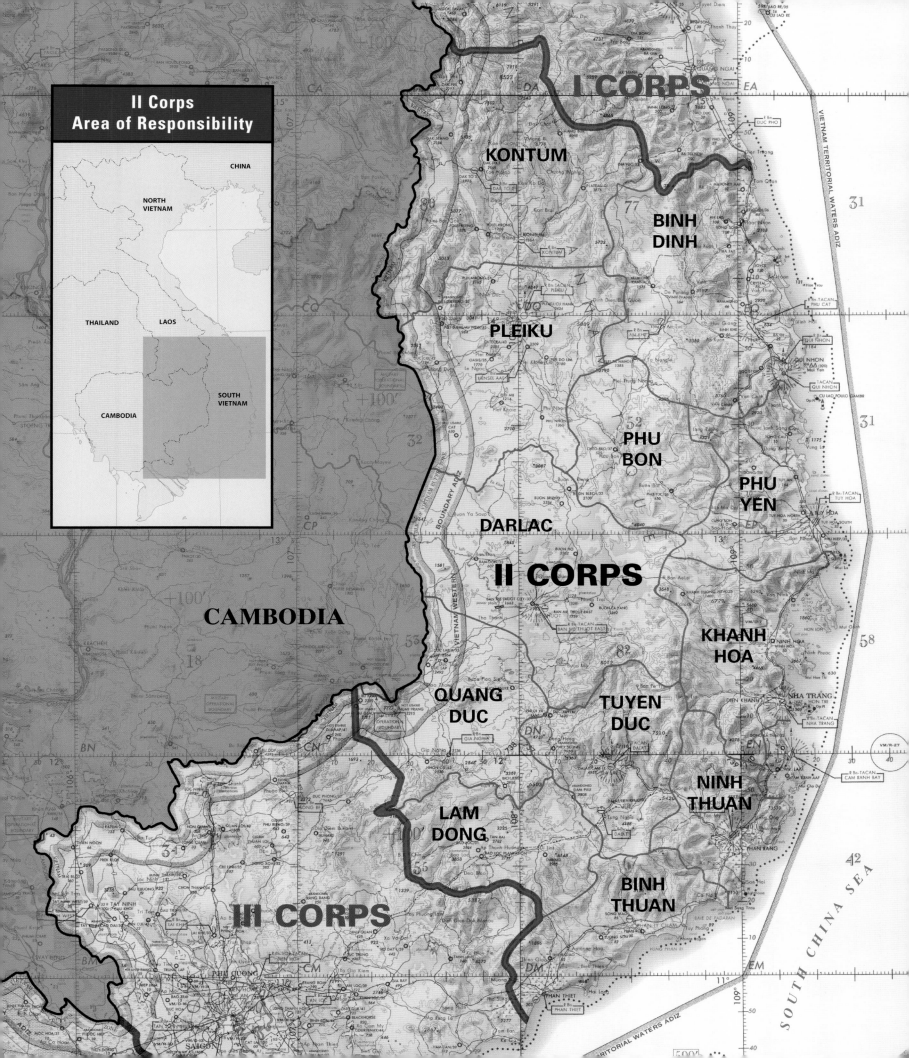

**II Corps
Area of Responsibility**

CHINA

NORTH
VIETNAM

THAILAND LAOS

CAMBODIA

SOUTH
VIETNAM

I CORPS

KONTUM

BINH
DINH

PLEIKU

PHU
BON

PHU
YEN

DARLAC

II CORPS

CAMBODIA

KHANH
HOA

QUANG
DUC

TUYEN
DUC

NINH
THUAN

LAM
DONG

III CORPS

BINH
THUAN

SOUTH CHINA SEA

secretary of defense. Laird resigned in January 1973, and Elliot Richardson took over. Richardson resigned in July 1973, and James Schlesinger* assumed the post and remained there until the war ended.

Sources: Guenter Lewy, *America in Vietnam*, 1978; Douglas Kinnard, *The Secretary of Defense*, 1980.

SECRETARY OF STATE

The secretary of state enjoys a cabinet-level position and is the chief foreign policy officer for the United States. During the years of the war in Vietnam, five men served as secretary of state. John Foster Dulles* (1953–59) and Christian Herter (1959–61) served under President Dwight Eisenhower;* Dean Rusk* (1961–69) served under presidents John F. Kennedy* and Lyndon B. Johnson;* William P. Rogers* (1969–73) served under President Richard M. Nixon;* and Henry Kissinger* (1973–77) served under Presidents Nixon and Gerald Ford.*

Source: Guenter Lewy, *America in Vietnam*, 1978.

SENATE FOREIGN RELATIONS COMMITTEE

Long considered one of the most prestigious of Senate committees, the Foreign Relations Committee has traditionally been identified with bipartisan support of foreign policy. Its leadership has frequently cooperated closely with whatever administration has happened to be in power. J. William Fulbright,* the Arkansas Democrat who became chairman in 1959 and remained in that position through 1974, was floor manager for the Gulf of Tonkin Resolution* when it passed the Senate in 1964. By 1965, however, Fulbright and others on the committee were having strong second thoughts about Johnson* administration Vietnam policies, and the committee became a focal point for the gradually emerging opposition in Washington. Early in 1966 the committee held nationally televised hearings on the war policy. Chairman Fulbright called both administration officials and outside experts to testify, and the hearings served as the first national forum on Vietnam.

As the committee continued to examine Vietnam policy, a confrontational attitude developed between it and the executive branch, and the committee became the stronghold of those favoring a more assertive congressional role in foreign policy. From 1967 to 1968 the committee conducted an inquiry into the events leading up to the 1964 Gulf of Tonkin Resolution and raised many questions about the accounts provided by the Johnson administra-

tion. In March 1968, following the Tet Offensive* and at a pivotal political point, the committee again held highly publicized hearings on Johnson administration policies. When Nixon* took office in 1969, the committee maintained its pressure for an end to American military involvement in Southeast Asia, and particularly opposed the administration's 1970 incursion into Cambodia (*see* Operation Binh Tay) as well as the American bombing in Cambodia (*see* Operation Menu). Although the committee was a forum for vigorous discussion, and several of its members became leading dissenters from executive branch policies on Vietnam, the Foreign Relations Committee did not until 1973–74 begin to impose major legislative restrictions on U.S. activities in Southeast Asia. HP

Sources: Anthony Austin, *The President's War*, 1971; Thomas M. Franck and Edward Weisband, *Foreign Policy by Congress*, 1979; Haynes Johnson and Bernard Gwertzman, *Fulbright: The Dissenter*, 1968; Edward P. Haley, *Congress and the Fall of South Vietnam and Cambodia*, 1982.

17th PARALLEL

See Geneva Accords of 1954

SEVENTH AIR FORCE

The presence of the United States Air Force* (USAF) in Vietnam began in 1961 when the 4400th Combat Crew Training Squadron was deployed to Bien Hoa. Crew member activities were code-named Farmgate,* and using B-26 bombers, C-47* transports, T-28D Nomads, and A-1E Skyraiders* they trained Vietnamese pilots and provided close air support for ARVN operations (*see* Army of the Republic of Vietnam). Until April 1966, USAF operations in Vietnam were under the direction of the 2d Air Division, but the massive buildup of 1965 required command reorganization; on April 1, 1966, the Seventh Air Force, stationed at Tan Son Nhut Air Base* outside Saigon, took over. The Seventh Air Force had tactical-fighter wings at Bien Hoa in III Corps,* Cam Ranh Bay* and Phan Rang in II Corps,* and Da Nang* in I Corps.* During the war seven individuals commanded the Seventh Air Force: Lieutenant General Joseph Moore (April–July 1966); General William Momyer* (July 1966–August 1968); General George S. Brown* (August 1968–September 1970); General Lucius Clay (September 1970–August 1971); General John Lavelle* (August 1971–April 1972); General John W. Vogt* (April 1972–October 1972); and Lieutenant General Timothy O'Keefe (October 1972–March 1973).

Source: Carl Berger, ed., *The United States Air Force in Southeast Asia, 1961–1973*, 1977.

SEVENTH FLEET

The Seventh Fleet was responsible for all U.S. naval operations in the western Pacific in general and Southeast Asia in particular between 1965 and 1973. During the years of the Vietnam conflict, the Seventh Fleet was commanded by Vice Admiral Roy L. Johnson (June 1964–March 1965); Vice Admiral Paul P. Blackburn (March 1965–October 1965); Rear Admiral Joseph W. Williams (October 1965–December 1965); Vice Admiral John J. Hyland (December 1965–November 1967); Vice Admiral William F. Bringle (November 1967–March 1970); Vice Admiral Maurice F. Weisner (March 1970–June 1971); Vice Admiral William P. Mack (June 1971–May 1972); and Vice Admiral James Holloway (May 1972 to the end of the war). In the Seventh Fleet, Task Force 77 was the aircraft carrier* attack unit; Task Force 76 was the amphibious unit; Task Force 73 was the logistics support unit; Task Force 70.8 was the group of destroyers and cruisers responsible for shore bombardment; and Task Force 117 was the Riverine Assault Force (*see* Mobile Riverine Force).

Source: Edward J. Marolda and G. Wesley Pryce III, *A Short History of the United States Navy and the Southeast Asian Conflict, 1950–1975*, 1984.

SHANGHAI COMMUNIQUÉ OF 1972

Issued by Richard Nixon* during his precedent-breaking diplomatic mission to the People's Republic of China* in 1972, the Shanghai Communiqué promised that the United States would reduce its military presence on Taiwan as soon as diplomatic tensions began to ease. The promise encouraged the Chinese goverment that the United States was finally preparing to recognize it as the legitimate representative of the Chinese people, but the North Vietnamese were extremely suspicious. The last thing they wanted was improved relations between the United States and China. Mao Zedong* had been pressing North Vietnam to consider a reduced military effort in South Vietnam, and the North Vietnamese interpreted the Shanghai Communiqué as part of a larger Chinese-American conspiracy to reduce their influence in Southeast Asia.

Source: Stanley Karnow, *Vietnam: A History*, 1983.

Below: The USS *New Jersey* prepares for action off the coast of Vietnam with the Seventh Fleet's Task Force 77 in 1968.

SHARP, ULYSSES S. GRANT

U.S. Grant Sharp was born on April 2, 1906, in Chinook, Montana. After graduating from the United States Naval Academy in 1927, Sharp rose through the officer ranks. He commanded a minesweeper during World War II and in June 1964 became Commander in Chief, Pacific Command* (CinCPac), with its 400 ships, 3,500 aircraft, and 500,000 men and women spread out over 85 million square miles. Sharp oversaw the Vietnam buildup through the Tet Offensive* early in 1968; he frequently advocated more intensive bombing* of North Vietnam, asserting that "toughness" was "the only policy that the Communists understand." Sharp retired in July 1968, and his memoir, *Strategy for Defeat* (1978), gives his alternative to the military policy that U.S. forces implemented in Vietnam as well as a general prescription for the future. DA

Sources: U.S. Grant Sharp, *Strategy for Defeat*, 1978; *Who's Who in America, 1964–1965*, 1965; Edward J. Marolda and G. Wesley Pryce III, *A Short History of the United States Navy and the Southeast Asian Conflict, 1950–1975*, 1984; http://www.sandiego-online.com/issues/august97/profile.shtml.

"SHORT-TIMER"

A "short-timer" was an individual who had a relatively short time remaining on his or her assignment to duty in Southeast Asia. Unlike in previous wars, when troops had been in the service "for the duration," during the Vietnam War troops were assigned to the Southeast Asia combat theater for a limited period, either 12 months (U.S. Army)* or 13 months (U.S. Marines).* When the soldier's 365 days in the combat zone ended, he was reassigned. As a result, each individual knew the precise date on which he would be eligible to leave the combat zone, and those with relatively little time left to serve in Southeast Asia were called short-timers. The term acquired a wartime ethos and became the subject of countless hours of discussion. Short-timers became the focal points of envy in every unit and manifested their high status by publicly demonstrating how soon they would be reassigned. Two common ways of showing how "short" an individual was were by calendars drawn on helmet covers and the "short-timer's stick," which was

Right: In 1965, Admiral Ulysses S. Grant Sharp straps himself into a helicopter during a tour of U.S. Navy and Marine installations in South Vietnam. Seated next to Sharp is Brigadier General Keith B. McCutcheon, commander of the First Marine Aircraft Wing, and next to McCutcheon is Major General Lewis W. Walt, commander of the III Marine Amphibious Force.

notched, so that each day a knob could be removed until there were no knobs remaining. STT

Source: Al Santoli, *Everything We Had: An Oral History of the Vietnam War by Thirty-three American Soldiers Who Fought It*, 1981.

THE SHORT-TIMERS

The Short-Timers is the title of Gustav Hasford's 1979 novel about the Vietnam War. An extraordinarily violent book, the novel focuses on William "Joker" Doolittle, a Marine combat reporter in Vietnam who refuses promotion to sergeant and insists on wearing a peace button. With his time running "short"—only forty-nine days remaining on his tour—Doolittle's insubordination rankles a superior officer and he finds himself reassigned to a vulnerable combat unit. Supposedly fighting for freedom, the soldiers appear more as prisoners of the Vietnam War themselves.

Sources: Gustav Hasford, *The Short-Timers*, 1979; Philip D. Beidler, *American Literature and the Experience of Vietnam*, 1982.

SHOUP, DAVID MONROE

An aspiring poet with the world's largest private collection of sake cups and bottles, David M. Shoup became commandant of the Marine Corps* when President Dwight Eisenhower* elevated him over several senior generals in 1959. Born in Indiana in 1904, Shoup attended DePauw University on an academic scholarship, and after receiving his commission in 1927 spent the prewar years at sea, in naval yards, and in China. After duty in Iceland in 1941, Shoup was wounded while serving as a division operations officer on Guadalcanal (1942) and earned a second Purple Heart, plus the Medal of Honor, while commanding the initial assault at Tarawa (1943).

Although Shoup missed service in Korea, top staff and command billets marked his rise to commandant, and once confirmed by the Senate he began issuing pithy, handwritten "Shoupisms" that challenged tradition, and he abolished "swagger sticks," "drumming out" Marines convicted by courts-martial, gun salutes preceding his post inspections, and the custom of allowing senior officers to select staffs

Above: As part of the process of Vietnamization, a tank is returned to an American base that is about to be handed over to the Army of the Republic of Vietnam on September 30, 1971, in Tay Ninh. The U.S. Senate, in a rebuff to President Richard M. Nixon, has just voted for a complete withdrawal of U.S. forces from Indochina by the spring of 1972. The message painted on the tank reflects the feelings of the crew.

Above: David M. Shoup was awarded the Medal of Honor as a colonel in World War II for his command at Tarawa Atoll in November 1943. Though suffering from a painful leg wound from an exploding enemy shell soon after landing at Betio Island, Shoup went on to rally his troops and lead them across the fringing reefs to charge the heavily fortified island. He was largely responsible for the final decisive defeat of the Japanese forces at Tarawa.

Shoup became commandant of the Marine Corps in 1959 when President Eisenhower elevated him over several senior generals. He retired after President Kennedy was assassinated and became a prominent critic of the Vietnam War.

that would follow them from post to post for years. Shoup also presided over the Marine transition from pure amphibious doctrine to the vertical assault, participated in the Bay of Pigs and Cuban missile crisis decisions, and, alone among the Joint Chiefs of Staff (*see* Chairman, JCS), favored the Nuclear Test Ban Treaty of 1963.

Shoup retired after the Kennedy assassination, and he held positions with an insurance firm and presidential commissions on amateur athletics and the Selective Service before emerging as a prominent Vietnam War critic in May 1966. "I don't think the whole of Southeast Asia, as related to the present and future safety and freedom of the people of this country," he told a Los Angeles college audience, "is worth the life or limb of a single American." Although often identified as an activist, Shoup published only one article, testified twice before Congress,* and gave a few short interviews to the press. In declining health, he loaned his name if not his skills to the peace movement and mostly confined his arguments to practical military concerns. "I was among the first," he said during a final interview in 1971, "to say we could not win because we were not permitted to go to the heart of the war—to North Vietnam. As soon as we get out, North Vietnam will be able to move right in and take over. After all that killing—it is frustrating, frustrating." David M. Shoup died in 1983, less than eight years after the fall of Saigon.* DA

Source: Dudley Acker Jr., "The World According to Shoup," unpublished manuscript, Northern Arizona University, April 1985.

SIGMA II

In 1963, as the political and military situation in South Vietnam was deteriorating, the Joint Chiefs of Staff (*see* Chairman, JCS) staged a series of war games carrying the code name Sigma I. The outcome confirmed some of their worst fears: that a military victory over the Vietcong* in South Vietnam would require more than 500,000 American combat troops. In September 1964 the Joint Chiefs of Staff conducted another war game scenario for South Vietnam, this time with national security advisor McGeorge Bundy* participating. Known as Sigma II, the games were designed to assess the impact of a major air offensive against North Vietnam. The results were no more encouraging than those of Sigma I. Indeed it seemed, from the results of Sigma II at least, that the United States had little chance of preventing a Vietcong* victory. Nevertheless, political and diplomatic events during the next eight months pushed the United States closer and closer to military intervention on a large scale.

Source: Stanley Karnow, *Vietnam: A History*, 1983.

SIHANOUK, NORODOM

Born in 1922 in Cambodia,* Norodom Sihanouk was crowned king of Cambodia by French officials in 1941. He functioned as a puppet ruler until 1954 when, after the French defeat at Dien Bien Phu,* Cambodia was given its independence. Between 1954 and 1970 Sihanouk tried to maintain Cambodian neutrality between the People's Republic of China* and the Vietnamese, and between the United States and the major Communist powers, but it proved to be an impossible task. When the American buildup in South Vietnam began in 1965, Sihanouk started leaning toward the Vietnamese, but that only lasted until North Vietnamese Army* (NVA) troops began exploiting his neutrality. In 1969 Sihanouk acquiesced to American requests for the secret bombing of NVA installations in Cambodian territory, and in March 1970, while he was visiting the Soviet Union* and asking government officials to assist him in expelling the NVA troops, he was deposed by Lon Nol.* Sihanouk then moved to Peking, hoping but failing to get Chinese support in his attempt to regain power. Throughout the 1970s and 1980s, Norodom Sihanouk periodically tried to regain his throne in Cambodia but repeatedly failed. After thirteen years in exile, Prince Sihanouk returned to Cambodia in November 1991, and in 1993 he again became king. In poor health, Sihanouk abdicated in October 2004, and his son Norodom Sihamoni was appointed the new king of Cambodia.

Sources: *International Who's Who, 1971–1972*, 1972; William Shawcross, *Sideshow: Kissinger, Nixon, and the Destruction of Cambodia*, 1979; Ben Kiernan, "How Pol Pot Came to Power," Ph.D. diss., 1986; Wikipedia: The Free Encyclopedia, 2006.

SILENT MAJORITY SPEECH

President Richard Nixon's* November 3, 1969, "silent majority" speech was made in response to the massive antiwar protest of the Moratorium Day demonstration* of October 15 and in anticipation of the moratorium days set for mid-November. In this televised speech, Nixon both attacked the antiwar movement* as subversive of his administration's policies and outlined a plan of action for the future. He made a patriotic appeal to "the great silent majority" of Americans to support his search for a "just and lasting peace" as an alternative to an immediate withdrawal that, he stated, would lead to "a collapse of confidence in American leadership, not only in Asia but throughout the world." Nixon outlined the history of American involvement in Vietnam since his inauguration, and stated that the previous administrations had "Americanized the war," but his administration would henceforth "Vietnamize the search for peace." To this end, he described a plan of withdrawal of American forces from Vietnam to correspond with the buildup and strengthening of South Vietnam's forces. He then attacked the antiwar movement as a "vocal minority" and stated that "North Vietnam cannot defeat or humiliate the United States. Only Americans can do that." Despite the White House claim of 80,000 letters and telegrams of support following the speech, the Moratorium Day demonstrations of mid-November exceeded their October counterparts in attendance. Nevertheless, Nixon's appeal to patriotism and his promise of Vietnamization* and the consequent return of American troops marked the beginning of the end of the massive antiwar demonstrations of the Vietnam era. LA

Sources: Richard Nixon, *RN: The Memoirs of Richard Nixon*, 1978; Nancy Zaroulis and Gerald L. Sullivan, *Who Spoke Up? American Protest Against the War in Vietnam, 1963–1975*, 1984.

SKYCRANE

See CH-54 Skycrane

SLAM

SLAM was the acronym for "seek, locate, annihilate, monitor," a concept developed by General William M. Momyer,* commander of the Seventh Air Force.* First introduced during Operation Neutralize* in September 1967 at the siege of Con Thien,* SLAM involved an overall coordination of B-52* air strikes, tactical air support, naval bombardment,* artillery assaults, and ground fire. B-52 Stratofortresses struck first and were followed by tactical air attacks, naval gunfire, and artillery barrages, all concentrated in small areas. For the next five years, SLAM was the standard operating approach to concentrating American firepower.

Sources: Terrence Maitland and Peter McInerney, *The Vietnam Experience: A Contagion of War*, 1983; William W. Momyer, *Airpower in Three Wars*, 1978.

Below: Soldiers from the 478th Aviation Company of the 1st Cavalry Division adjust the linkage on the left engine and install a dust cap on the left landing gear of a CH-54A Skycrane ("Flying Crane") helicopter at Nha Trang, South Vietnam on April 28, 1967.

Right: A UH-1D Iroquois helicopter delivers soldiers from the 101st Airborne Division to a point near the Demilitarized Zone dividing South Vietnam from North Vietnam on October 16, 1969.

SLICK

The Vietnam War became a helicopter war for American forces, and a common way for an infantryman to go into action was by slick. "Slick" was the term used to refer to an assault helicopter used to carry troops into combat during airmobile operations. The UH-1* became the premier helicopter for this maneuver. Troops could ride beside the wide doors of the aircraft, normally in two rows on each side, and could exit quickly when landing in a "hot LZ"*—a landing zone under fire. Often, a UH-1 would not touch down during slick operations; instead, it would hover a couple of feet above the ground while troops evacuated the aircraft. Troops learned to feel for the UH-1 "bounce" as it came in quickly and went into a hover over an LZ, and they would exit on the bounce, so that slicks spent very little time close to the ground. NJA

Source: Jim Mesko, *Airmobile: The Helicopter War in Vietnam*, 1985.

SMART BOMBS

Because of the increasingly devastating effectiveness of North Vietnamese antiaircraft defenses, the United States developed the so-called smart bombs, which could be dropped from safe distances and would then head toward their targets with the assistance of laser beams, television cameras, and computers. There were two types of smart bombs—laser-guided bombs and computer-directed, electro-optically guided bombs. The first laser-guided "Paveway" bomb was tested in 1966, and in 1967 the first electro-optically guided bomb, known as the Walleye, was used over North Vietnam. The Walleye, a 2,000-pound bomb with a camera and computer attached to its front, could be dropped more than thirty miles from its target and could be carried by any combat jet. During the Christmas bombing of 1972 (*see* Operation Linebacker II), when the United States wanted to make sure that the

North Vietnamese lived up to the agreement they had accepted in October, smart bombs were used extensively over North Vietnam, achieving an accuracy rate unknown of earlier in the war.

Source: Edgar C. Doleman Jr., *The Vietnam Experience: Tools of War*, 1984.

SMITH, WALTER BEDELL

W. Bedell Smith was born in Indianapolis on October 5, 1895. After serving in the state national guard of Indiana between 1910 and 1915, Smith made a career in the U.S. Army,* seeing action in France during World War I and attaining the rank of lieutenant general during World War II. He was chief of staff to Dwight D. Eisenhower* during the North African campaign in 1942 and 1943. After the war, Smith served as ambassador to the Soviet Union* from 1946 to 1949, director of the Central Intelligence Agency* from 1950 to 1953, and undersecretary of state during the Eisenhower administration. Smith headed the American delegation to the Geneva Conference (*see* Geneva Accords) on Vietnam in 1954, and then retired from government service to accept a vice chairmanship of the American Machine and Foundry Company. The author of two books (*My Three Years in Moscow*, 1950, and *Eisenhower's Six Great Decisions*, 1956), W. Bedell Smith died on August 9, 1961.

Sources: *Who Was Who in America, 1961–1968*, 1968; *New York Times*, August 10, 1961.

Below: In mid-April 1966, at the end of a search-and-destroy mission in the Long Thanh area east of Saigon, UH-1 helicopters arrive to carry members of the 1st Infantry Division back to the brigade area.

Síng trường thiện xa chỉ dùng để bắn Bọn chỉ huy
và cô văn Mỹ

SNIPERS

In a war of relatively few pitched battles, but rather of small combats day after day, of countless patrols over the same territory, and with strategies attuned both to psychological effects and attrition, sniping during the Vietnam conflict became a notable tactic. Sniping was used by both sides. It could slow an advancing force, pin it down so that other weaponry could be brought to bear, instill terror into an enemy thus lowering its morale, and reduce enemy activity—including sniping—in an area of operation.

U.S. forces did not have an active sniper program when they began to arrive as battle units in 1965. But the Marines soon began to develop one and training began in Vietnam with persons who were outstanding marksmen, combat veterans, and recommended by their commanding officers. Eventually, Marine snipers formed sniper platoons of three squads of five two-man teams that were assigned to regiments. A team comprised a shooter and a spotter, who usually used a powerful telescope and carried a conventional

Above: Each Vietcong sniper rifle came equipped with a cartridge box (below) and instructions for use. The instructions read, "This sniper rifle is to be used to shoot unit commanders and American advisors only."

Opposite page, bottom: American sharpshooters in Hue, South Vietnam, monitor the streets below their tower for Vietcong targets on February 3, 1968.

Left: Throughout the Vietnam War, the .30-caliber, bolt-action, single-shot sniper rifle with telescopic lens was used effectively on targets sometimes more than 1,000 yards away.

Below: Soldiers from the 173d Airborne Brigade captured this Soviet sniper rifle, model 91/30, 7.62mm caliber while cleaning out a Vietcong supply base.

Above: A sniper team from the 1st Cavalry Division used this XM21 sniper rifle (with its special scope case) in South Vietnam. Designed by James Leatherwood, the rifle was equipped with an adjustable ranging telescope (ART). It was a National Match M14 converted to sniper configuration at Rock Island Arsenal in Illinois. The ART had a variable power magnification, 3 to 9, for ranging between 300 and 900 meters. When the scope is set on 3-power and aimed at a target 300 yards away, two vertical markers above and below the crosshairs mark out a distance of thirty inches, the approximate distance between a soldier's belt buckle and the top of his helmet. The sniper can then place the crosshairs at the target's chest. The magnification ring provides the same feature at other ranges up to 900 meters.

rifle in case the two men were attacked. Marine sniper teams ventured into the countryside with the protection of up to fourteen Marines, or fewer, or none if they were especially intent on stealth and surprise. Snipers were sometimes looked upon with scorn—as cold-blooded killers—but also with envy as soldiers carrying the war to the enemy, and they usually were relieved of routine duties. Marine snipers preferred Winchester 70 rifles and Remington 700s, often painted with camouflage to match the camouflage of the snipers' uniforms.

U.S. Army snipers started somewhat later and generally used modified M14s, which became known as M21s and XM21s, for their work. At first they were not so free to range from conventional units as Marine snipers, but rather were used as sharpshooting riflemen with platoons. As the war progressed both Marine and Army snipers were highly trained. Snipers could not only perform their regular shooting duties, but also acted as artillery spotters because they were closer to the enemy, and as intelligence gatherers, watching enemy movements and collecting papers off enemy soldiers they had shot.

The North Vietnamese also trained snipers. They generally used Russian-made Mosin-Nagant rifles fitted with 4-power PE telescopic sights and trained for weeks

before going into the field. They often worked in groups of three, setting one ahead and two on the flanks of an American unit line of march. The lead shooter would aim for a commander, radio operator, or heavy weapons specialist, then the others would open up from the flanks. NVA snipers also liked to slip behind an American patrol and pick off the last man or penetrate between units at night and shoot at both, hoping to set off massive friendly fire between the two groups of soldiers.

The Americans tried various counter-sniping tactics, including sending out snipers to find and shoot enemy snipers. Snipers sometimes became known by their methods. The Communists put a bounty of $10,000 onto the "white feather sniper," who was the Marines' top scoring sniper, Marine Sergeant Chuck Mawhinney. He had 101 confirmed kills and liked to wear a white feather in the band of his boonie hat. The Marines' second-highest ranking sniper was Sergeant Carlos Hathcock with ninety-three confirmed kills. The bounty on his head was $30,000. Both survived their tours of duty and went on to train new snipers.

Sources: Andy Dougan, *Through the Crosshairs: A History of Snipers*, 2004; Adrian Gilbert, *Sniper*, 1994; Charles Henderson, *Marine Sniper*, 1986; Martin Pegler, *Sniper: A History of the U. S. Marksman*, 2007, Martin Pegler, *Out of Nowhere: A History of the Military Sniper*, 2004.

Below: Corporal Tom Romo of San Antonio, Texas, narrows in on a Vietcong soldier about 1,200 yards away in April 1968. Spotting is Private Jim McConnell of Sparks, Nevada.

SOCIALIST REPUBLIC OF VIETNAM

Ho Chi Minh* had proclaimed the establishment of the Democratic Republic of Vietnam* on January 14, 1950, when his Vietminh* forces were struggling for power with the French. At the Geneva Conference (*see* Geneva Accords) of 1954, North Vietnam became officially known as the Democratic Republic of Vietnam, while South Vietnam was designated the Republic of Vietnam.* But when North Vietnamese forces finally conquered South Vietnam in 1975, they changed the name of the entire country to the Socialist Republic of Vietnam, by which it is currently known.

Source: Stanley Karnow, *Vietnam: A History*, 1983.

SONG NGAN VALLEY

See Helicopter Valley

SON TAY RAID

In the summer of 1970 Secretary of Defense Melvin Laird* presented President Richard Nixon* with a Pentagon plan for a daring raid to rescue more than 100 Americans from the Son Tay prison installation located twenty-three miles west of Hanoi.* Only a few months earlier, in April, the United States' invasion of Cambodia* had torn the nation apart. The one issue that still bound the American people was their growing concern for the prisoners of war* (POWs) and servicemen classified as missing in action. Nixon had been receiving reports that American POWs were dying from torture and ill-treatment. In Nixon's view the raid, if successful, would not only be humanitarian, it would also give him some clout at the Paris peace talks;* these were stalled, partly because of the POW issue. Therefore, he approved the raid.

Planning for the mission was headed by Army brigadier general Donald D. Blackburn, special assistant for counterinsurgency activities for the Joint Chiefs of Staff (*see* Chairman, JCS), and Army colonel E.E. "Ed" Mayer, head of the Special Operations Division within SACSA (Special Assistant for Counterinsurgency and Special Activities). The plan they developed entailed a helicopter assault on the Son Tay prison compound by a fifty-six-man force. One helicopter would have to crash-land inside the compound to give the assault team enough time to eliminate the guards. The remaining helicopters would land outside the compound. Two would contain security forces to prevent the camp from being reinforced; they would also use satchel charges to breach the walls of the compound. The other helicopters would be empty to accommodate the 70 to 100 expected POWs. To divert enemy attention away from Son Tay, U.S. Navy* and Air Force* planes would pretend to attack Haiphong Harbor. Although not in the original plan, F-105s* were to be used to escort the helicopters in and to act as bait for North Vietnamese surface-to-air missiles. The raid was to last no longer than thirty minutes, because that was how long it had been determined it would take the North Vietnamese to respond with overwhelming force.

Right: A pilotless, low-flying drone in 1970 photographed this eastern-aspect image of the Son Tay prison 23 miles west of Hanoi in North Vietnam in preparation for the unsuccessful rescue mission.

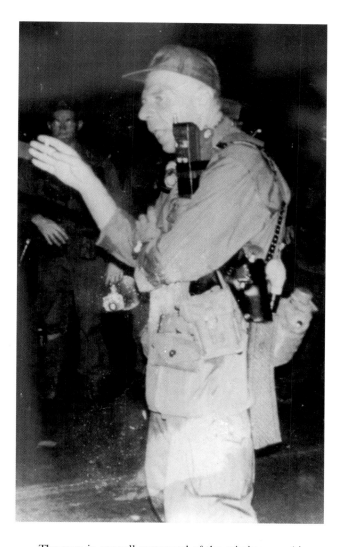

The man in overall command of the mission was Air Force brigadier general Leroy J. Manor, while Army colonel Arthur D. Simons would lead the actual raid on the prison compound. The fifty-six men who were to compose the newly designated Joint Contingency Task Force Ivory were carefully selected Special Forces* and Ranger volunteers. The task force underwent six months of training and three months of rehearsal at Eglin Air Force Base in Florida. Intelligence for the mission relied heavily on photos from SR-71 high-altitude flyovers and low-altitude drones. Neither of these methods was able to confirm that POWs were still being held at Son Tay. Prior to the raid, in fact, intelligence was received from a Central Intelligence Agency* contact, Nguyen Van Hoang, a senior North Vietnamese official who dealt with POW interrogations, that the prisoners had been moved to a new camp called Dong Hoi, fifteen miles to the east. The move had been made on July 14, 1970, because of severe flooding. Although this intelligence was available, it was decided to proceed with the raid.

Following a flight from Thailand* the raiders were above Son Tay prison camp at a little after 2:00 AM on November 21. The raid went off with only a few hitches. One mistake proved fortuitous, however. The helicopter containing Colonel Simons and the support group landed in the wrong compound. They landed in what had been identified as a "secondary school" but in fact contained Russian or Chinese troops who were training North Vietnamese air-defense technicians. Simons' group was able to eliminate the "primary external ground threat" to the Son Tay assault team. The Americans suffered no casualties, with the exception of one man slightly injured during the helicopter crash-landing. Although they found the camp empty of American POWs, General Manor praised the operation as "a complete success with the exception that no prisoners were rescued."

The raid did produce some positive results, however. Prisoners who had previously been scattered throughout the countryside were now concentrated in a prison in Hanoi, called the Hanoi Hilton.* This move had a positive effect on prisoner morale, if not treatment. The raid also caused serious concern among the North Vietnamese and their allies because it revealed their vulnerability to this type of raid. MD

Source: Benjamin F. Schemmer, *The Raid*, 1976.

SORTIES

The term "sortie" is used to describe one round-trip for cargo planes or one attack by gunships,* fighters,* fighter-bombers, or strategic bombers. During the Vietnam War United States Air Force,* Navy,* and Marine Corps* pilots launched more than 300,000 fighter-bomber sorties and 2,380 B-52 sorties.

Source: Harry G. Summers Jr., *Vietnam War Almanac*, 1985.

SOUTHEAST ASIAN INSURGENCIES

World War II dealt a deathblow to what remained of the European empires. France, Great Britain, and the Netherlands no longer had the financial resources to control distant colonies. Nationalist groups began to demand independence. Among them were Communist groups that yearned for independence and hoped, once independence had been secured, to impose a Marxist-Leninist model of government. In the former Dutch East Indies, nationalists proclaimed the independence of "Indonesia" in 1945, but the Dutch did not recognize it until 1949. A period of liberal democracy ensued until 1957, when Sukarno

Left: Colonel Arthur D. "Bull" Simons of New York City discloses the SOG Son Tay mission to raiders in Thailand. The description was greeted with thunderous applause.

Right: Dick Meadows of the U.S. Army Special Forces set and detonated the explosives that destroyed this helicopter during the raid on the Son Tay prison, where many American POWs had been incarcerated.

Right: At a White House ceremony in 1970, President Richard M. Nixon decorates a group of SOG raiders. From left to right are Air Force Brigadier General Leroy J. Manor of Morrisonville, New York, who commanded the overall operation; Air Force Technical Sergeant Leroy Wright of Little Falls, Minnesota; Specialist First Class Tyrone Adderly of Philadelphia; Colonel Arthur D. "Bull" Simons of New York City; and President Richard M. Nixon.

proclaimed martial law and imposed a virtual dictatorship. The Communist Party of Indonesia, identified by the acronym PKI, launched an insurgent movement aimed at gaining power. Financial chaos and gross corruption provided fertile ground for Communist political gains, and the PKI steadily increased in power. Early in the 1960s, when it appeared the PKI might come to power in Indonesia, the Kennedy administration flirted with the idea of military intervention but eventually decided against such action.

In the Philippines, a U.S. colony until full independence was achieved in 1946, the government faced a Communist insurgency of its own. Known as the Huk Rebellion, the insurgency promoted an anti-American, pro-Soviet ideology that found little support among Filipinos, rich or poor, whose political and even cultural ties to the United States remained quite strong. Under the leadership of J. Lawton Collins, the U.S. Army launched a pacification campaign in the Philippines designed to improve the economic lot of the poorest Filipinos and to rob the Huks of their political constituency. The campaign succeeded, and the Huk Rebellion was crushed.

In 1946 the Malaya Union had become a crown colony of Great Britain,* and was proclaimed the Federation of Malaya in 1948. The colonial government soon found itself fighting a powerful Communist insurgency led by Chin Peng and his Communist Party of Malaya (CPM). Like Chin Peng, however, most of the Communists were ethnic Chinese, generally loathed by the dominant ethnic Malays. The British government exploited that traditional ethnic rivalry in crushing the insurgency. As ethnic Chinese, the Communist insurgents could not melt into the peasant population or find much economic support there. In 1957 Great Britain extended independence to the Federation of Malaya, which became known as the nation of Malaysia.

In Indochina,* France* soon found itself foundering in the face of concerted nationalist sentiments in its colonies of Laos,* Cambodia,* and Vietnam. At the end of World War II, France had hoped to reassert its colonial authority in Southeast Asia, but it was not to be. Only a shell of its former greatness, France could not stop the independence movements. In 1954 the Geneva Conference met to address the future of French Indochina, but Ho Chi Minh* and his Vietminh* army held the diplomatic cards. When the Vietminh overran the French outpost at Dien Bien Phu* in 1954, the French Empire in Indochina disintegrated. Cambodia, Laos, and Vietnam became independent nations. Almost immediately, however, Communist insurgencies emerged in all three countries. In Cambodia, the Communists channeled their energies into the Khmer Rouge* (Red Khmer) movement that sought to overthrow the new Cambodian government, and in South Vietnam, or the Republic of Vietnam,* the Vietcong* worked to undermine the new pro-American government of Ngo Dinh Diem.* The Pathet Lao* Communists worked to destabilize the government of Laos. Those insurgent movements continued throughout the era of the Vietnam War, and in 1975, when Communists came to power in South Vietnam, the Pathet Lao triumphed in Laos, as did the Khmer Rouge in Cambodia.

Source: Matthew Worley, *In Search of Revolution: International Communist Parties in the Third Period*, 2004.

SOUTHEAST ASIA TREATY ORGANIZATION (SEATO)

Similar to the North Atlantic Treaty Organization (NATO) and the Central Treaty Organization (CENTO), the Southeast Asia Treaty Organization (SEATO) was created in 1954 as part of the Manila Pact, a regional defense scheme for the South Pacific. Although SEATO calls for member consultation in the event of military or political emergencies, it does not include the unified military command or joint forces so important to NATO. The Senate ratified the treaty by an 82 to 1 vote, and SEATO became an important link in U.S. global containment policy.* Along with the United States, SEATO included Great Britain,* the Philippines,* France,* Australia,* New Zealand,* Pakistan, and Thailand.* Conspicuous by their absence from the organization were India, Burma, and Indonesia, each of which preferred a nonaligned status in the conflict between the United States and the Soviet Union.* Although President Lyndon Johnson* used SEATO membership to justify the American commitment in Vietnam, President Richard Nixon,* in the Nixon Doctrine,* denied that such membership guaranteed the commitment of U.S. troops to Asian conflicts. Nevertheless, membership in SEATO greatly increased U.S. involvement in Asian politics. Under the pressure of the conflict in Vietnam, in which SEATO nations had originally supported the American struggle against the Vietcong* and North Vietnamese, strains appeared in SEATO, and the organization dissolved in 1977. KY

Source: Walter LaFeber, *America, Russia, and the Cold War, 1945–1975*, 1975.

SOUTH KOREA

See Korea

SOUTH VIETNAM

See Republic of Vietnam

SOUTH VIETNAMESE ARMY

See Army of the Republic of Vietnam

SOUTH VIETNAMESE MARINE CORPS

The South Vietnamese Marine Corps, first organized in April 1965, consisted of one division divided up into the 147th, 258th, and 369th brigades and nine battalions. They worked closely with United States Marine Corps* units in I Corps* but suffered from many of the same liabilities as the Army of the Republic of Vietnam*—low morale as well as corruption among the officer corps. By 1972 there were more than 13,000 troops in the South Vietnamese Marine Corps.

Source: Harry G. Summers Jr., *Vietnam War Almanac*, 1985.

SOUTH VIETNAMESE NATIONAL POLICE

In addition to maintaining law and order and administering the country's criminal justice system, the South Vietnamese National Police were directly charged with counterinsurgency efforts against the Vietcong.* Beginning in 1967 the United States decided that strengthening the National Police would help the pacification (*see* Rural Reconstruction) process by replacing military with civilian authority. Between 1965 and 1972 the size of the National Police increased from 52,000 to nearly 121,000 people. The National Police Field Forces and the Provincial Reconnaissance Units were offices of the National Police. Trained by American advisors, the police units were not above the use of terrorism themselves to deal with the Vietcong. Of all the organizations wielding political and military authority in South Vietnam, the National Police were probably the most corrupt and the least respected.

Below: On February 20, 1963, two years before the introduction of U.S. ground combat troops to South Vietnam, two U.S. military advisors accompany several soldiers who are delivering pro-government, anti-Vietcong pamphlets to South Vietnamese civilians living near an ARVN base.

Left: South Vietnamese Marines aboard landing crafts in the well of the amphibious transport dock USS *Duluth* as they prepare for an amphibious assault as part of Operation Song Thanh on May 25, 1972.

Below: South Vietnamese Marines aboard tracked landing vehicles (LVT) depart into the South China Sea for an amphibious assault as part of Operation Song Thanh. In the distance, the heavy cruiser USS *Newport News* provides shore bombardment prior to the landing.

Below: South Vietnamese Navy officer candidates gather in Newport, Rhode Island, after having successfully completed officer candidate school on July 22, 1970. Secretary of the Navy John H. Chafee presented them with their diplomas.

Wages were extremely low, and because South Vietnamese military units held conscription priority, the National Police had a difficult time recruiting or training effective leaders. As its units became riddled with Vietcong infiltrators, late in 1969 a reform movement of the National Police began, one which limited the brutal treatment of arrestees and provided for the dismissal of corrupt officers, but it was too little and too late to change its reputation.

Source: Guenter Lewy, *America in Vietnam*, 1978.

SOUTH VIETNAMESE NAVY

At the beginning of the war, the South Vietnamese Navy consisted of approximately 500 small junks that had been plying the coast of the South China Sea since 1960. By 1969,

after four years of large-scale American participation in the conflict, the South Vietnamese Navy had added 460 other ships, ranging from 640-ton PCEs, to patrol the coast, down to small riverine craft—LSTs and fiberglass-and-aluminum patrol boats. In 1969, when the Mobile Riverine Force* was discontinued, the South Vietnamese Navy received another 242 patrol craft. Finally, as part of Vietnamization* between 1969 and 1972, the United States Navy* handed over another 800 ships and craft to the South Vietnamese Navy— minesweepers, patrol craft, Coast Guard cutters, seaplane tenders, and destroyer escorts. By the time the United States withdrew from Vietnam late in 1972, the South Vietnamese Navy—with 1,500 ships, 40,000 officers and sailors, and 13,000 marines—was one of the largest in the world. It was not, however, one of the most powerful. Morale within the South Vietnamese military in general, including the navy, was poor, and the dumping of so many ships and so much sophisticated technology, without proper training, was more than the Vietnamese could handle. Efficiency was extremely low, and the navy was unable to seriously cripple the Vietcong* or North Vietnamese final assault on the Republic of Vietnam.*

Sources: John S. Bowman, ed., *The Vietnam War Almanac*, 1985; Edward J. Marolda and G. Wesley Pryce III, *A Short History of the United States Navy and the Southeast Asian Conflict, 1950–1975*, 1984.

Left: Ensign Do-Minh Hao of the South Vietnamese Navy trains during an imaginary mission on November 9, 1970. Supervising him is Ensign David E. Garvin of Portland, Oregon. They are in the combat information center of the tank landing ship USS *Whitfield County.* Hao is one of five Vietnamese Navy ensigns receiving a seven-week official orientation aboard the *Whitfield County.*

Below: Engineman Seaman Truong Van Con of Saigon, South Vietnam, trains with the U.S. Coast Guard. He is operating the throttles of the high-endurance cutter *Yakutat* in 1970 as part of the Vietnamization program.

SOUVANNA PHOUMA

Prince Boun Khong fathered twenty children, among them Prince Souvanna Phouma (a middle child) and his half brother Prince Souphanouvong (the youngest), who were raised after Boun Khong's death by his oldest son, Prince Phetsart. All three were educated in France* as engineers— Phetsart as a mechanical engineer, Souvanna as a marine, electrical, and civil engineer, and Souphanouvong as a road and bridge engineer. For years they were the only engineers in Laos,* a relatively primitive country of less than 3 million ethnically diverse people. About half the population is Lao, and the remaining is composed of a variety of tribal groups including the Meo (Hmong),* who have clashed with the Lao historically.

Although each was a nationalist opponent of French colonialism, the brothers pursued independence in different ways. Having acquired a taste for Western life, Souvanna Phouma favored a negotiated independence. Because there were no paved roads anywhere in Laos and the French were building neither roads nor bridges, Souphanouvong built roads in Vietnam, where he witnessed the abominable living conditions for peasants on French-owned rubber plantations and in labor camps. He developed contempt for French colonialism, as well as ties with the Vietminh.* Phetsart for his part took a middle position, working to maintain an alliance between his two brothers in the face of what became a determined American effort to split them apart.

In August 1945, Souphanouvong, with the support of his brothers, expelled the French and established an independent government with Phetsart and Souvanna Phouma as ministers. The French, however, after reasserting themselves in Vietnam and Cambodia,* launched a three-pronged offensive, defeating Lao forces. While Souphanouvong organized Lao resistance groups in the countryside, which cooperated with the Vietminh and participated at the siege of Dien Bien Phu,* Souvanna Phouma and Phetsart lived in exile in Thailand.* Eventually, the French enticed Souvanna Phouma to return to Vientiane to form a provisional government, while Phetsart remained in Thailand, refusing all French entreaties.

Souphanouvong's ties with the Vietminh made him a Communist to American officials, who conspired with the French to exclude him from the 1954 Geneva Conference. But the Geneva Accords* called for negotiations between all three factions in Laos—the French collaborator rightists under Phoumi Nosovan, Souvanna Phouma's neutralists, and Souphanouvong's Pathet Lao* ("Land of the Lao"). The brothers quickly reached an agreement on a government of "national reconciliation," something they would do repeatedly between 1954 and 1964. Phoumi Nosovan was uncooperative.

Unfortunately for Laos, the United States in professing a desire for a neutral government was determined that it would be a pro-Western neutralism. The Pathet Lao, in addition to being denied a voice in the government, were to be destroyed. Thus, Souvanna Phouma and his brother could not be permitted to enter into an alliance that unquestionably would control Laos. This prompted a secret war directed by the Central Intelligence Agency* with the active assent of the State Department and the U.S. Army.* Between 1954 and 1960 the United States spent more than $300 million in Laos (more than $100 for every inhabitant, more than Laos' annual per capita income), with $239 million for military purposes and $7 million for economic development. In 1959 the United States paid $100 per vote in the National Assembly to bring down the coalition government, throwing Souvanna Phouma out of office.

The 1961 Laotian "crisis" resulted from a Souvanna Phouma and Souphanouvong attempt to defeat the mercenary army of the corrupt and incompetent Phoumi Nosovan. The 1962 Geneva Conference, convened to thwart the alliance, produced an agreement giving the Pathet Lao a minor voice in a new government headed by Souvanna Phouma, calling for neutrality, an end to American military activities, expulsion of all foreign military personnel, a prohibition against Laotian military alliances, and election of a National Assembly. This government was subverted by American intrigue, including the assassination of uncooperative political leaders.

While all parties violated the agreements, it is clear that the United States never intended anything more than a pretense of compliance. The Pathet Lao utilized North Vietnamese Army* (NVA) advisors and protected the eastern border so that North Vietnam could infiltrate men and supplies south. While only a trickle of northerners and small amounts of supplies moved down the Ho Chi Minh Trail* between 1959 and 1964, main force NVA units and substantial amounts of materiel were moved through Laos after 1965. Meanwhile, the U.S. "secret war" included 5,000 to 12,000 military and CIA personnel and 5,000 Tai soldiers illegally stationed in Laos to lead a mercenary army of Hmong tribesmen against the Pathet Lao, and another 1,000 military personnel running secret training bases in Thailand. Under the pretext of attacking NVA infiltration* routes, the United States began bombing Laos in 1964, before the Gulf of Tonkin incident.* The justification for this was that the Pathet Lao would threaten Thailand if they came to power, a weak claim for three reasons. First, there is no way that a primitive society such as Laos' could threaten a highly developed nation such as Thailand, which had a population ten times larger. Second, even the Pathet Lao army, which was generally regarded as better disciplined and more effective than either the neutralist or rightist armies, was poorly trained, poorly equipped, and poorly disciplined. Laotians simply do not have much heart for war, which is one reason the United States had to resort to building a Meo army. Finally, Laos has yet to threaten Thailand since the Pathet Lao came to power in 1975.

The result, lasting until 1975, was a de facto partitioning with an increasingly rightist government in Vientiane headed (most of the time) by Souvanna Phouma, and Souphanouvong's Pathet Lao controlling two northern provinces, the northeastern border, and about one-third of the population. In February 1971 the South Vietnamese invaded southern Laos in a disastrous attempt to sever the Ho Chi Minh Trail.* The invasion, as well as the American withdrawal from Vietnam and the surging Khmer Rouge* strength in Cambodia, undermined the government of Souvanna Phouma, and in 1975 the Pathet Lao took over in all of Laos, deposing Souvanna Phouma. SF

Sources: Roger Hilsman, *To Move a Nation*, 1967; Wilfred Burchett, *The Second Indochinese War: Cambodia and Laos*, 1970; Peter Poole, *Eight American Presidents and Indochina*, 1973; Arthur M. Schlesinger Jr., *A Thousand Days: John F. Kennedy in the White House*, 1965; John Prados, *Presidents' Wars: CIA and Pentagon Covert Operations Since World War II*, 1986.

SOVIET UNION

The origins of the Vietnam War reach back to the cold war assumption on the part of the United States that the Soviet Union was expansionist and inspiring many of the anti-colonial rebellions occurring throughout the world. The containment policy* was designed to deal with Soviet aggression, and it resulted in the Truman Doctrine, Marshall Plan, Berlin airlift, NATO, and the Korean War. The irony is that the Soviet Union was preoccupied with Europe after World War II, and Josef Stalin viewed Ho Chi Minh's* campaign in Vietnam as more nationalistic than communistic. The Soviet Union did not extend diplomatic recognition to the Democratic Republic of Vietnam* (DRV) until 1950; Vietnam was very much outside the Soviet area of interest. Therefore, Moscow provided rhetorical support but little else to the Vietminh.*

In 1954 the Soviet Union co-chaired, along with Great Britain,* the Geneva Conference (*see* Geneva Accords) to settle the Vietnamese question. Actually, the Soviets pursued a pro-Western course at Geneva. At the time, they were currying French opinion because French Communists had done well in recent elections. Also, they wanted to

Below: Pro-Vietnam and anti-United States posters on display during a May Day parade in Moscow in 1969.

dissuade France* from joining the American-led European Defense Community, with its plans for rearming West Germany.* Finally, the Soviets were interested in reaching an accommodation, if possible, with the United States. For these reasons the Soviet Union worked for an armistice acceptable to the French and agreed to a partitioning of Vietnam between a Communist North and a non-Communist South. Later, when South Vietnam and the United States balked on holding the prescribed elections, the Soviet Union carefully sidestepped Ho Chi Minh's pleas for assistance.

Soviet interest in Indochina* intensified, however, as the independence of the People's Republic of China* increased in the 1950s. Vietnam became an important counterweight to expanding Chinese influence. Gradually, the Soviet Union began to increase its delivery of military equipment, training personnel, and economic assistance to North Vietnam, and by the late 1960s Moscow was far and away the largest supplier of North Vietnam and the Vietcong.* This assistance exceeded $1 billion a year by 1970. At the same time the Soviet Union hoped that the American preoccupation with Vietnam would distract the United States from European concerns.

North Vietnam was unusually astute in maintaining a diplomatic balance between the Soviet Union and China, neatly playing them off against each other in a diplomatic minuet. For the Soviets, North Vietnam was maddeningly independent, especially in 1968 when Ho Chi Minh condemned the invasion of Czechoslovakia. Still, the DRV leaned more toward Moscow than Peking, not only because Moscow was a more reliable supplier of materiel but also because of ancient fears of Chinese expansion into Indochina. In addition, the Cultural Revolution in the People's Republic of China left China too weak and internally preoccupied to be very reliable.

The United States never appreciated the independence of Vietnamese Communism. Presidents Lyndon B. Johnson* and Richard Nixon* both sought to have the Soviet Union restrain North Vietnam, assuming that Moscow had direct influence in Hanoi.* What few understood was that Hanoi would pursue policies sanctioned neither by Moscow nor Peking, and in fact notoriously irritated the Soviets throughout the war by taking their aid, expressing gratitude for it, but keeping them in the dark about DRV war plans.

As the war concluded in 1975, the Soviets were considered the diplomatic victors internationally. The border skirmishes between the Vietnamese and the Chinese increased Soviet influence, and they secured important military bases at Da Nang* and Cam Ranh Bay.* They could now challenge American military superiority in the Indian Ocean and the western Pacific. Moreover, the Soviet line about the inevitable decline of American power received a major boost with the Vietnam defeat.

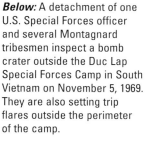

Below: A detachment of one U.S. Special Forces officer and several Montagnard tribesmen inspect a bomb crater outside the Duc Lap Special Forces Camp in South Vietnam on November 5, 1969. They are also setting trip flares outside the perimeter of the camp.

Finally, the Soviets appreciated the new "realism" in American foreign policy that grew out of Vietnam, a development that they believed gave them a freer hand in Angola, Afghanistan, and Ethiopia. Indeed, a war that began in order to staunch the tide of Soviet Communism had a very different result. GMB

Sources: George McT. Kahin, *Intervention: How America Became Involved in Vietnam*, 1986; Daniel S. Papp, *Vietnam: The View from Moscow, Peking, Washington*, 1981; Robin Edmonds, *Soviet Foreign Policy, 1962–1973: The Paradox of a Superpower*, 1975; Leif Rosenberger, *The Soviet Union and Vietnam: An Uneasy Alliance*, 1986.

SPECIAL FORCES

See Green Berets

SPOCK, BENJAMIN McLANE

Born in New Haven, Connecticut, on May 2, 1903, Benjamin Spock was a prominent figure in the antidraft and anti–Vietnam War movements of the 1960s. He received a B.A. from Yale University in 1925 and an M.D. from Columbia University in 1929. While on active duty as a psychiatrist in the U.S. Naval Reserve (1944–46), he wrote *The Common Sense Book of Baby and Child Care* (1946), which, through subsequent editions, became one of the best-selling books in publishing history. In the early 1960s, Dr. Spock began to speak out against nuclear weapons testing. He supported a full-page advertisement in the *New York Times* in 1962 titled "Dr. Spock Is Worried." The ad warned of the dangers of radioactive contamination of milk and other foods from nuclear bomb tests. From 1963 to 1967 he served as co-chairman of the National Committee for a Sane Nuclear Policy (SANE). By 1963 he had also become a public opponent of U.S. military involvement in Vietnam. He supported President Lyndon B. Johnson* as the peace candidate in 1964, but when Johnson increased U.S. military operations in Vietnam in February 1965, Dr. Spock wrote to the president in protest and began to appear at many public demonstrations against the war. In 1967 he retired as supervising pediatrician of the Family Clinic at Case Western Reserve University to devote himself full-time to antiwar and antidraft activity. Dr. Spock joined a delegation that turned in 992 draft* cards to the U.S. Department of Justice in Washington, D.C., in October 1967; he was then arrested in December 1967 for an act of civil disobedience outside the armed forces induction center on Whitehall Street in Manhattan. He also signed a nationally distributed "Call to Resist Illegitimate Authority." In 1968 he and four others— William Sloane Coffin Jr.,* Michael Ferber, Mitchell Goodman, and Marcus Raskin—were indicted for conspiring to violate Selective Service laws. In July, Dr. Spock was found guilty, fined $5,000, and sentenced to two years in prison. The conviction, however, was overturned by the U.S. Court of Appeals for the First Circuit. At the end of the trial, Dr. Spock said, "There is no shred of legality or constitutionality to this war; it violates the United Nations Charter, the Geneva Accords,* and the United States' promise to obey the laws of international conduct. It is totally, abominably illegal." Dr. Spock continued to protest the Vietnam War, and ran for president in 1972 on the People's Party ticket. (He received 78,801 votes.) After the war, he continued to oppose nuclear arms and U.S. military involvement abroad, and remained an active and prominent member of SANE. On December 7, 1978, he was fined $200 and sentenced to two months in jail for his participation in a protest against construction of the nuclear power plant at Seabrook, New Hampshire. On June 2, 1981, Dr. Spock and eleven others were arrested for refusing to leave the White House after a public tour, stopping instead to pray in protest of budget cuts proposed by the Reagan administration. Benjamin Spock died on March 15, 1988. JK

Sources: Jessica Mitford, *The Trial of Dr. Spock*, 1969; Lynn Z. Bloom, *Doctor Spock: Biography of a Conservative Radical*, 1972; *New York Times*, March 16–17, 1988.

SPRING MOBILIZATION TO END THE WAR IN VIETNAM

The Spring Mobilization to End the War in Vietnam was organized on November 26, 1966, to sponsor antiwar* demonstrations in the spring of 1967. Veteran peace activist A.J. Muste* was chairman of the group, and its four vice chairmen were David Dellinger,* editor of *Liberation*; Edward Keating, publisher of *Ramparts*; Sidney Peck, a professor at Case Western Reserve University; and Robert Greenblatt, a professor at Cornell University. In January 1967 they named the Reverend James Luther Bevel, a close associate of Martin Luther King Jr.'s,* as director of the Spring Mobilization to End the War in Vietnam. During the next four months organizers prepared for mass demonstrations, one scheduled for New York City and the other for San Francisco, and on April 15, 1967, the demonstrations were held. More than 125,000 marched in New York City against the war—including Martin Luther King Jr., James Luther Bevel, and Benjamin Spock*—and another 60,000 marched in San Francisco. Up to its time, the Spring Mobilization was the largest antiwar demonstration in U.S. history.

Sources: Thomas Powers, *Vietnam: The War at Home*, 1984; Clark Dougan and Steven Weiss, *The Vietnam Experience: A Nation Divided*, 1984; Nancy Zaroulis and Gerald Sullivan, *Who Spoke Up? American Protests Against the War in Vietnam, 1963–1975*, 1984.

Above: A squad from B Battery, 8th Battalion, 4th Artillery fire the "Big Gun" 175 in support of Marine operations in the battle for Hill 65 in South Vietnam. The Army unit is from Fort Sill, Oklahoma.

SQUAD

A squad is a basic organizational institution in the United States Army* and Marine Corps.* A sergeant usually commands the squad, composed of two teams of four men each. A tank and its crew is considered the squad for an armored unit, as is the howitzer or long-range gun and its crew in an artillery unit.

Source: Harry G. Summers Jr., *Vietnam War Almanac*, 1985.

SQUADRON

The term "squadron" refers to a cavalry unit of battalion* size in the United States Army.* Usually commanded by a lieutenant colonel, a squadron has approximately 1,000 officers and men, divided into three troops. A squadron is also a basic organizational institution in the United States Air Force* and Navy,* where it consists of two or three groups of five aircraft each.

Source: Harry G. Summers Jr., *Vietnam War Almanac*, 1985.

SRV

See Socialist Republic of Vietnam

STENNIS, JOHN CORNELIUS

John Cornelius Stennis was born on August 3, 1901, in Kemper County, Mississippi, and served as a circuit judge (1937–47) and as a member of the U.S. Senate (1947–89). Originally, Stennis had severe reservations about the U.S. commitment in Vietnam. During the early 1950s he voiced concern over U.S. support of the French and the Ngo Dinh Diem* regime during the late 1950s. Stennis, however, became a hard-liner once the Gulf of Tonkin incident* occurred.

Although he questioned from time to time the actions taken by the Johnson* administration in Vietnam, Stennis recoiled from the notion of a U.S. pullout or military defeat. He echoed the sentiments of many Americans who believed that once involved in an overseas war the United States could accept nothing less than total victory. After Johnson's commitment of troops to Vietnam in 1965, Stennis is purported to have stated that "America's purpose [in Vietnam] is to win." Because of his hard-line view, Stennis even suggested that Johnson's Great Society* programs might have to be curtailed to win the Vietnam War.

Stennis's view of a military victory in Vietnam endeared him to the Pentagon, with its vast assortment of senior officers. As a member of the Senate Armed Services Committee, he wielded much power, which he used to assist in the Pentagon's prosecution of the Vietnam War. Beginning in the spring of 1967, Stennis began to criticize the Johnson administration's handling of the conflict, and Senate hearings ensued. The hearings, which were held before Stennis and the Senate Armed Services Committee, revealed a lack of success in winning the Vietnamese conflict, although Robert McNamara* and other officials presented evidence of progress.

Stennis came away from the hearings determined that the Johnson administration, not America's military officials, had failed in Vietnam; hence he advocated more latitude for military commanders in the field. Lyndon Johnson, however, was not about to give up his constitutional powers as commander in chief. Johnson privately ridiculed Stennis and others on the committee for trying to push him deeper into war. The president nonetheless avoided direct confrontation with the committee, because he realized that public opinion polls indicated that a great many Americans favored tougher measures in Vietnam.

The Tet Offensive* of 1968 shattered Stennis's belief that the war could be won. When General William Westmoreland* suggested that more troops might be needed, Stennis and hard-line senators openly questioned the winnability of the war. Stennis and others warned Secretary of Defense Clark Clifford* that Congress* had serious doubts about the conduct of the war. Thereafter, Stennis would support a pullout of American troops, although not without first assisting the South Vietnamese in gaining the requisite skills to defend themselves. John C. Stennis died on April 23, 1995. JSL

Sources: *Who's Who in America, 1984–1985*, 1985; Ernest R. May, *"Lessons" of the Past*, 1973; Stanley Karnow, *Vietnam: A History*, 1983; *Biographical Directory of the United States Congress*, 1995.

STRATEGIC AIRLIFT

When the large-scale deployment of military forces to South Vietnam began in 1965, the U.S. Air Force's* Military Airlift Command* (MAC) found itself assigned the task of providing the urgent transportation of personnel and certain supplies from the United States to Southeast Asia. The American reliance on strategic airlift stemmed from the necessity of projecting forces over long distances within a relatively short period of time and from the inability of the U.S. Navy* and merchant transports to move personnel and supplies efficiently to the other side of the world. This requirement gave rise to the creation of an extensive strategic-airlift operation between American West Coast bases and Southeast Asia.

The task of getting essential supplies, personnel, and units to Vietnam was staggering. Air Force officials found that traffic to the Pacific grew from a monthly average of 33,779 passengers and 9,123 tons of cargo in fiscal 1965 to 65,350 passengers and 42,296 tons of cargo in fiscal 1967. During 1967, moreover, strategic airlift carried most of the cargo, while chartered commercial airliners carried most of the passengers. Not to be overlooked were the thousands of combat personnel flown by these aircraft to Honolulu and nine other cities in the Pacific for rest and recuperation leaves (R&R). The R&R flights began in fiscal 1966 with 14,970 passengers. The numbers increased to 521,496 in 1967 and to 774,386 in fiscal 1968.

To expedite the flow of critically required cargo from aerial ports during the Vietnam buildup, the Air Force developed a series of intercontinental airlift routes, each with well-equipped and efficiently managed personnel and equipment-handling facilities. It also employed a series of priority designations: among them a "999," which identified the highest-priority cargo, and the "Red Ball" (an airlift reference to the famous World War II truck express in Europe), which tagged priority U.S. Army* spare parts for inoperative combat equipment. The MAC began its Red Ball Express on December 8, 1965, guaranteeing shipment within 24 hours of receipt at the aerial port. The 1,000th Red Ball mission departed Travis Air Force Base, California, on May 1, 1967.

On several occasions during the war, the Air Force was called on to undertake the deployment of major Army units under special conditions. The first of these, designated Operation Blue Light, came late in 1965 when strategic-airlift transports moved the 3d Brigade, 25th Infantry Division,* from Hawaii to Pleiku,* Vietnam, to offset a buildup of Communist forces in the area. These aircraft flew 231 sorties* over a 26-day period and moved 3,000 troops and 4,700 tons of equipment the 6,000 miles to Pleiku by January 23, 1966.

In mid-1969 emphasis shifted to the return of units to the United States in accordance with the president's policy of gradual American withdrawal from Vietnam, beginning with 25,000 troops before August 31. The MAC strategic-airlift fleet carried out the redeployments through a series of operations called Keystone. In the first of these operations, C-141* transports airlifted 15,446 of the 25,000 troops plus 47.5 tons of materiel. As the president directed other incremental withdrawals over the next several years, these airlift managers responded accordingly.

As American participation in the war was phased out, MAC devoted considerable strategic-airlift capacity to equipment being delivered to South Vietnamese forces. Following the peace agreements in January 1973, the command turned its attention to the withdrawal of the remaining American military personnel and materiel from Vietnam. This task involved several thousand tons of materiel and more than 20,000 personnel. RDL

Source: Carl Berger, ed., *The United States Air Force in Southeast Asia, 1961–1973*, 1984.

Above A sentry on stilts protecting a strategic hamlet circa 1962.

Right: A South Vietnamese farmer smiles as he sits with his four young children at one of the gates to the Cu Chi strategic hamlet in October 1962.

STRATEGIC HAMLET PROGRAM

Launched in 1962, the Strategic Hamlet Program had high hopes for depriving the Vietcong* "fish" of their peasant "sea." Designed by Sir Robert Thompson,* the architect of similar counterinsurgency* programs in Malaya and the Philippines,* the Strategic Hamlet Program would bring peasants in from scattered villages to hamlets surrounded by moats and fences and protected by well-trained military forces. In these strategic hamlets, peasants would be won over to the government of the Republic of Vietnam* by fair elections, land reform, good schools, and improved medical facilities. The Vietcong would then have no one to exploit and no villages in which to hide; they would be forced to come out into the open, where ARVN (*see* Army of the Republic of Vietnam) and American forces would destroy them.

The theoretical hopes of the Strategic Hamlet Program were dashed on the rocks of reality. By the end of 1962 the government claimed to have established more than 3,500 hamlets, but they were hardly secure from Vietcong attack or infiltration.* In the Mekong Delta* the program required the massive relocation of peasants away from their ancestral homelands, which only further alienated them from the South Vietnamese government. Ngo Dinh Diem* never implemented the promised land reform, and large volumes of U.S. assistance money were diverted by corrupt government officials away from hamlet medical, educational, and welfare programs and into their own pockets. The Vietcong were able, by simply massing their forces, to overrun any strategic hamlet at will. The program proved to be so unpopular that it may have actually increased the Vietcong appeal among peasants. After the assassination of Ngo Dinh Diem in November 1963, the program was abandoned.

Sources: Roger Hilsman, *To Move a Nation*, 1967; Larry E. Cable, *Conflict of Myths: The Development of American Counterinsurgency Doctrine and the Vietnam War*, 1986; Frances FitzGerald, *Fire in the Lake: The Vietnamese and the Americans in Vietnam*, 1972; Tran Dinh Tho, *Pacification*, 1980.

"STREET WITHOUT JOY"

Highway 1 is Vietnam's north-south highway. During both Indochina* wars opposing forces tried to control it. Running south to north, Highway 1 went from Saigon* to Bien Hoa,* Phan Rang, Nha Trang,* Tuy Hoa, Qui Nhon,* Quang Ngai, Chu Lai,* Quang Nam, Da Nang,* Hue,* and Quang Tri,* and then across the Demilitarized Zone* to Dong Hoi, Vinh, Ninh Binh, and Hanoi.* The stretch from Hue north to Quang Tri City ran through major Vietminh* and later Vietcong* strongholds. French soldiers, used to costly and futile efforts to clear the road, referred to it sardonically as *la rue sans jolie*, "the street without joy." American soldiers easily understood that perspective. SF

Sources: Terrence Maitland and Steven Weiss, *The Vietnam Experience: Raising the Stakes*, 1982; Danny J. Whitfield, *Historical and Cultural Dictionary of Vietnam*, 1976; Bernard Fall, *Street Without Joy: Insurgency in Vietnam*, 1961.

STUDENTS FOR A DEMOCRATIC SOCIETY (SDS)

Students for a Democratic Society (SDS) was a leading campus-based, antidraft and anti–Vietnam War organization of the mid-1960s. SDS was established in January 1960, primarily by students who had been affiliated with the Socialist Party. After an organizing conference in May 1960 at the University of Michigan, SDS obtained a $10,000 grant from the United Auto Workers (UAW). SDS then opened an office in New York City, with Tom Hayden* serving as the first SDS field secretary. The primary purposes of SDS were to support the civil rights movement and to engage in community organizing in poor neighborhoods in northern cities.

SDS began to gain strength and notoriety after its June 1962 conference at a UAW camp in Port Huron, Michigan. At that conference, SDS issued the first major manifesto of the New Left, the *Port Huron Statement*, which called for a more participatory democratic society and an and to the nuclear arms race. The statement also criticized other aspects of U.S. foreign policy associated with the cold war. By 1964, especially after the Gulf of Tonkin incident* in August, elements within SDS began to organize campus demonstrations and teach-ins* against the Vietnam War and to circulate "We Won't Go" petitions among draft-age men. SDS organized a demonstration against the Vietnam War that brought more than 20,000 protesters to Washington, D.C., on April 17, 1965. Membership in SDS grew rapidly during 1965, to about 124 chapters by the end of the year. After endorsing the "black power" position of CORE and SNCC in June 1966, SDS, a mostly white student organization, turned its full attention to campus protests against the war, the draft,* and corporate capitalism. By December 1966, when it adopted a militant draft resistance position, SDS had about 250 chapters, approximately 25,000 chapter members, and some 6,000 national members. SDS was soon plagued, however, by internal dissension, independent-minded local chapters, many members who were stimulated more by the new counterculture than by politics, a futile search for a new revolutionary working class, and a concerted attempt by the "Marxist-Maoist" Progressive Labor Party to take over SDS.

Above: U.S. Secretary of Defense Robert S. McNamara and staff visit strategic hamlet Plei Mrong in 1963.

During 1967 antiwar and antidraft demonstrations on and off campuses became more frequent, increasingly militant, and occasionally violent. Students seized campus buildings; sought to drive recruiters for the military, Central Intelligence Agency,* and Dow Chemical Company off campuses; picketed or attacked military induction centers; rioted; and sometimes bombed buildings or set them aflame. During Stop the Draft Week in October 1967, Carl Davidson, a national SDS leader, said, "We must tear them [induction centers] down, burn them down if necessary." Nearly three-quarters of the nation's universities had experienced demonstrations by the end of the 1967–68 academic year, at which time SDS had about 300 chapters. The militance of protests escalated further during 1968. From March through May 1968 the SDS chapter at Columbia University,* led by Mark Rudd, initiated several seizures of campus buildings, which led to violent confrontations with New York City police and a campuswide strike that shut down the university. Under SDS pressure, Columbia agreed to sever its ties to the Institute of Defense Analysis, abandon plans to build a gymnasium in Morningside Park, and drop charges against most of the student demonstrators. Nationally, SDS helped to organize a series of militant demonstrations held in parks and streets outside the Democratic National Convention* in Chicago in late August 1968. The National Commission on the Causes and Prevention of Violence later concluded that the violence associated with the Chicago demonstrations was caused by a "police riot," not by the demonstrators. The Chicago demonstrations helped to boost SDS membership, which apparently reached its peak in December 1968 when

SDS may have had as many as 400 chapters. The SDS national convention, however, held in Ann Arbor, Michigan, on December 26, 1968, was split by factionalism and by a growing desire to adopt "revolutionary violence" as the means to end the draft and the Vietnam War. Seeing themselves allied with "third world revolutionaries," sizable factions within the SDS leadership began to encourage or engage in violent protests.

In March 1969 the SDS national "war council," meeting in Austin, Texas, resolved to promote "armed struggle as the only road to revolution" in "the heartland of a world-wide monster" (i.e., the United States). Out of this council grew a violent group, the Weathermen, which brought 600 people to Chicago in October 1969 to engage in violent protests, called the Days of Rage. By fall 1969, however, SDS was disintegrating rapidly, and the leadership for organizing massive protest demonstrations against the Vietnam War had already passed to other organizations, particularly the Moratorium Day and the New Mobilization committees.

Right: In October and November 1969, Project Delta carried out Operation Trojan Horse, in which elements of the 101st Airborne Division conducted covert activities along northwestern reaches of Vietnam, near the borders with Laos and Cambodia. Troops from Detachment B-52 rappel into triple canopy jungle. The soldier is carrying a spool of communication wire for use as a landline in setting up an ambush site. One way to stretch the range of their observations was to have troops relay the signal for an ambush by employing a series of clicks on field phones.

The Weathermen, some local SDS chapters, and various SDS factions continued to function through the early 1970s, but SDS, which had never been a highly coherent national organization, ceased to exist as a coordinated nationwide entity by early 1970. JK

Source: Kirkpatrick Sale, *SDS: Ten Years Toward A Revolution*, 1973.

STUDIES AND OBSERVATION GROUPS (SOG)

In January 1964, Military Assistance Command, Vietnam* organized the Studies and Observation Groups (SOG), supposedly to evaluate the success of the military advisor program but actually to perform clandestine operations throughout Southeast Asia. The SOG program was directed by the special assistant for counterinsurgency and special activities, who reported directly to the Joint Chiefs of Staff (*see* Chairman, JCS). By 1966 SOG included more than 10,000 personnel, of which 2,000 were Americans and

8,000 were South Vietnamese and Montagnard* troops. They were divided into a number of different groups. The Psychological Studies Group, operating out of Hue* and Tay Ninh, made false radio broadcasts from powerful transmitters. The Air Studies Group—complete with UH-1F* and CH-34 helicopters, a C-130* squadron, and a C-123 squadron—specialized in dropping and recovering special intelligence groups into Laos,* Cambodia,* and North Vietnam. The Maritime Studies Group concentrated its efforts on commando raids along the North Vietnamese coast and the Mekong Delta.* The Gulf of Tonkin incident* in July and August 1964 was triggered by SOG operations. The Ground Studies Group carried out the greatest number of missions, including monitoring the location of American POWs,* assassinations, kidnapping, rescue of airmen downed in enemy territory, early long-range reconnaissance patrols,* and harassment and booby-trapping* of infiltra-tion* routes. SOG operations were headquartered in Kontum, Ban Me Thuot,* and Da Nang.*

Sources: Larry E. Cable, *Conflict of Myths: The Development of American Counter-insurgency Doctrine and the Vietnam War*, 1986; Andrew F. Krepinevich Jr., *The Army and Vietnam*, 1986.

Above: Huey helicopters from the 155th Assault Helicopter transport an SOG reconnaissance team near the Cambodian border with South Vietnam.

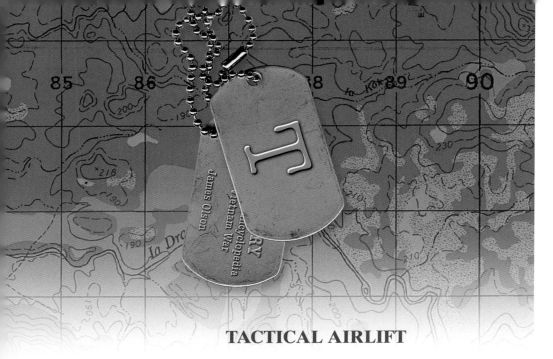

TACTICAL AIRLIFT

One of the hallmarks of modern American warfare has been airmobility to, around, and from the battlefield. As a result of this basic means of waging war, the United States Air Force* early sent tactical airlift transports to Vietnam; four C-47s* arrived at Bien Hoa* Air Base, near Saigon,* on November 16, 1961, as part of the first Air Force detachment. These C-47 airlifters performed diverse missions—supporting flights by other Air Force aircraft, providing airdrops of Vietnamese paratroops, and conducting night flareship operations. Their most demanding task, however, was to resupply U.S. Army Special Forces* detachments at remote locations throughout South Vietnam.

In 1963 the number of C-47s in Vietnam was increased to six, but airlift tasks gradually shifted to large, twin-engine C-123 Providers. Although the C-123 had been tagged as "obsolescent" as early as 1955, sixteen were deployed to Vietnam in December 1961 as part of Project Mule Train to provide "tactical airlift support of South Vietnamese armed forces." The first four Providers reached Tan Son Nhut Air Base* on January 2, 1962, with the remaining aircraft following during the next two years. All were assigned to the 315th Air Commando Wing, and until 1965 these aircraft were the principal airlift element in South Vietnam.

Beginning in 1965 the C-130 Hercules* began to dominate tactical airlift activities in Vietnam. Equipped with four turboprop engines, the C-130 could move a 15-ton payload, about three times the capacity of the C-123. Although used to transport personnel and materiel between bases in the western Pacific and the Asian mainland before 1965, C-130 in-country missions from South Vietnamese bases became routine in April 1965. At first beginning with a handful of C-130 aircraft and a small mission assignment, by December 1965 the in-country force had grown to thirty-two aircraft and by February 1968 it stood at ninety-six C-130s.

Also used for tactical airlift in Vietnam during this period were six squadrons of C-7A Caribou transports (*see* Caribou Aircraft). These aircraft were initially flown by the

United States Army,* and several had been deployed to Vietnam since the spring of 1962. By 1966 the force had expanded to six companies and operated under the scheduling and mission control of specified Army corps and divisions. In April 1966 the two services agreed to transfer the Caribous to the Air Force in keeping with a decision to centralize all land-based fixed-wing aircraft under the control of the Air Force.

Aerial transport aircraft played key roles in virtually all operations of the Vietnam conflict, as seen in the operations of the 1st Brigade, 101st Airborne Division,* during the spring and summer of 1966, for example. The 1st Brigade made five successive moves, each requiring more than 200 C-130 missions and each operation largely sustained by aerial resupply. The C-130s first airlifted the brigade from Tuy Hoa to Phan Thiet early in April; next, to the highlands airstrip at Nhon Co later that month; then north to Dak To* soon after; and finally back to Tuy Hoa in July.

Perhaps the greatest test of tactical airlift capability came during the 1968 Tet Offensive.* The early attacks at Tan Son Nhut Air Base and on many of the upcountry airstrips temporarily dislocated the airlift system. Transport crews, however, managed to fly numerous emergency troop and resupply missions on behalf of hard-pressed garrisons. By February 3, the fourth day of the attacks, the tactical airlift force had regained its prerogative, and resupply operations played a critical role in the defeat of the Communist offensive. At the critical siege of Khe Sanh,* for instance, tactical airlift ensured that the defense of the firebase was successful.

Over the years between 1962 and 1973, the Air Force's tactical airlift forces delivered more than 7 million tons of passengers and cargo within South Vietnam. By comparison, American and British transports carried slightly more than 2 million tons during the Berlin airlift and about 750,000 tons during the Korean War. The Air Force lost 53 C-130s in the Southeast Asia war, more than half of them in 1967 and 1968. C-123 losses also totaled 53, and C-7 losses numbered 20. Of these 126 aircraft, enemy action accounted for 61, including 17 destroyed by sapper or shelling attacks on the ground. The other 65 were lost in accidents mainly associated with the difficult conditions at forward airstrips. All but 10 of the losses occurred in South Vietnam. RDL

Source: Ray L. Bowers, *The U.S. Air Force in Southeast Asia: Tactical Airlift*, 1983.

TACTICAL AREA OF RESPONSIBILITY

TAOR is a military acronym referring to "Tactical Area of Responsibility." It refers to a specific area of land where responsibility for security and military operations is assigned to a single commander. The TAOR is used as a measure of control for assigning forces, coordinating support, and evaluating progress.

Source: Edward Doyle and Samuel Lipsman, *The Vietnam Experience: America Takes Over, 1965–1967*, 1985.

TAI

The Tai were a Laotian ethnic minority living in the region surrounding Dien Bien Phu* in Tonkin.* They made a living raising rice and trading for opium with the Hmong.* The Tai were frequently recruited to assist first the French and later the Americans in resisting the North Vietnamese and Vietcong* during the struggle for power in Indochina* after World War II.

Sources: Edgar O'Ballance, *The Indochina War 1945–1954: A Study in Guerrilla Warfare*, 1964; Charles A. Stevenson, *The End of Nowhere: American Policy Toward Laos Since 1954*, 1973.

TAIWAN

See Chiang Kai-shek

TANG PHUC

Tang phuc are the white mourning clothes worn by the Vietnamese after the death of a relative.

Source: Ann Crawford, *Customs and Culture of Vietnam*, 1966.

TAN SON NHUT AIR BASE

Located just on the fringe of Saigon,* Tan Son Nhut Air Base handled the bulk of South Vietnamese commercial and military air traffic throughout the war. Tan Son Nhut was the headquarters of the South Vietnamese Air Force,* and after 1962, headquarters for the U.S. 2d Air Division. It was in charge of all American air operations in South Vietnam. Between 1966 and 1973 the Seventh Air Force* assumed control of those operations. Tan Son Nhut was also known as Pentagon East because the headquarters of the U.S. Military Assistance Command, Vietnam* (MACV) was located there. On April 29, 1975, after the evacuation of several thousand Americans and Vietnamese, military demolition teams destroyed MACV headquarters. The air

base was later rebuilt by North Vietnamese and Soviet engineers to serve the commercial and military needs of Ho Chi Minh City,* formerly Saigon.

Sources: Harvey H. Smith et al., *Area Handbook for South Vietnam*, 1967; Thomas G. Tobin, *Last Flight from Saigon*, 1978.

TASK FORCE 116

See Mobile Riverine Force

TASK FORCE 117

See Mobile Riverine Force

TASK FORCE OREGON

See 23d Infantry Division

TAYLOR, MAXWELL DAVENPORT

Maxwell D. Taylor was born on August 26, 1901, in Keysteville, Missouri. After graduating from West Point in 1922, Taylor taught at the military academy between 1927 and 1932, and during World War II was generally credited with playing a major role in the development of airborne

Below: U.S. Army Military Police stand guard on the flight line at Tan Son Nhut Air Base in South Vietnam on April 14, 1966. The Vietcong had just mortared the base, and the aircraft needed to be protected from Vietcong sappers and suicide bombers intent on destroying them. The Vietnamese Air Force C-47 behind the jeep was destroyed by a direct hit. The petrol, oil, and lubricants depot burns in the background.

Above: The Vietcong attacked Bien Hoa Air Base outside Saigon with more than 100 rounds of 81mm mortar fire on November 1, 1964. They managed to damage or destroy twenty-eight U.S. B-57 Canberra jet bombers. In response, the U.S. dramatically reinforced security on the base. In this photograph, Maxwell D. Taylor, U.S. Ambassador to South Vietnam, inspects the base with General William Westmoreland, commander of U.S. forces in South Vietnam.

warfare. He was with the 82d Airborne Division in North Africa and Sicily and commanded the 101st Airborne Division at the Normandy invasion. After the war Taylor spent four years, between 1945 and 1949, as commandant of West Point. He commanded the Eighth Army in Korea, and became commander in chief of the Far East Command in 1955. In June of that year Taylor became chief of staff of the U.S. Army,* serving until 1959. During the late 1950s, afraid that the Army would be eclipsed by the nuclear power of the U.S. Air Force,* Taylor began advocating the "flexible response" theory, arguing that a deterrence policy based exclusively on nuclear weapons would leave the United States unable to deal with conventional crises around the world. Taylor wrote *The Uncertain Trumpet* in 1959, calling for a diversified military capability and counterinsurgency* focus.

President John F. Kennedy* read his book, and on July 1, 1961, Taylor became the president's military advisor. Kennedy sent Taylor and W.W. Rostow* to Vietnam in October 1961 on a fact-finding mission, and their report advocated the commitment of several thousand combat troops to assist the government of Ngo Dinh Diem* in stopping the Vietcong.* Between 1962 and 1964 Taylor served as chairman of the Joint Chiefs of Staff (*see* Chairman, JCS), and then spent a year as ambassador to South Vietnam. He worked desperately in 1964 and 1965 to return South Vietnam to civilian rule after the assassination of Diem, and late in 1965 he became a special advisor to President Lyndon B. Johnson.* Johnson made Taylor a member of the Senior Advisory Group studying the Vietnam problem in 1968, and Taylor became a strong advocate of a continued American military presence in the country. Taylor left government service in 1969 to serve as chairman of the Foreign Intelligence Advisory Board. Maxwell Taylor died on April 19, 1987. GFC

Sources: Maxwell D. Taylor, *The Uncertain Trumpet*, 1959, and *Swords and Plowshares*, 1972; *Who's Who in America, 1976–1977*, 1977; David Halberstam, *The Best and the Brightest*, 1972; *New York Times*, April 20, 1987.

TAYLOR-ROSTOW MISSION OF 1961

In October 1961 President John F. Kennedy* sent an investigative team, led by General Maxwell D. Taylor* and his deputy, Walt W. Rostow,* to survey the military and political situation in South Vietnam. They found very poor morale there and the government of Ngo Dinh Diem* weak and losing support among peasants in the countryside. Taylor and Rostow recommended an increase in military aid, greater numbers of military advisors, and the placement of an 8,000-man logistical task force to serve as soldiers and/or economic and political workers. Both men felt that the increase in American commitment would not lead to concomitant increases in Communist strength because they assumed that North Vietnam was too vulnerable to American airpower. The Kennedy administration accepted their recommendations, and the Taylor-Rostow mission played an important role in the early escalation of the conflict.

Sources: Maxwell D. Taylor, *Swords and Plowshares*, 1972; Paul Y. Hammond, *Cold War and Detente*, 1975; Walt W. Rostow, *The Diffusion of Power, 1957–1972*, 1972.

TAY SON REBELLION

By the late eighteenth century, Vietnamese peasant resentment about high taxes, poverty, and the struggle for power between the Trinh* family in the North and the Nguyen* dynasty in the South had dramatically increased. In 1773 the three Tay Son brothers—Ho Nhac, Ho Lu, and Ho Hue—led a rebellion against the Nguyen dynasty and captured Saigon.* At the same time, the Trinh used the Nguyen defeat to take control of Hue.* But in 1786 Ho Hue Tay Son turned on the North and seized control of the Trinh capital of Hanoi.* After repulsing an invading Chinese army in 1788, the Tay Son were rulers of all of Vietnam. They quickly replaced Chinese with Vietnamese as the language of government and tried to break Chinese commercial influence. Their promises of redistribution of property to peasants, however, were never fulfilled. The three Tay Son brothers all died early in the 1790s and left behind no stable group to rule the country. Gia Long,* the surviving member of the Nguyen clan, then led a resistance movement against Tay Son rule, which succeeded in 1802.

Source: Joseph Buttinger, *The Smaller Dragon: A Political History of Vietnam*, 1958.

TCHEPONE

See Lam Son 719

TEACH-INS

In early February 1965, when the United States began to bomb North Vietnam, a group of faculty members at the University of Michigan wrote to President Lyndon B. Johnson* protesting the escalation of the conflict. After Johnson ordered 3,000 Marines into Da Nang* on March 10, a teach-in was organized for 8 PM on March 24, 1965. Some 3,000 Michigan students attended the first teach-in, where faculty members discussed the nature of the conflict; the major speaker was Arthur Waskow of the Institute for Policy Studies in Washington. In the six weeks after the teach-in at the University of Michigan, faculty members across the country were holding similar meetings as forums for opposing the escalation of the conflict. Those teach-ins continued on college campuses throughout the war, and a national teach-in was held on May 15, 1965, on 122 campuses across the country. Tom Hayden* and Jane Fonda* adopted the teach-in approach to reach soldiers in the "Free the Army" (FTA) campaign, with more informal teach-ins held for military personnel at coffeehouses and other places near military posts. SF

Sources: Thomas Powers, *Vietnam: The War at Home*, 1984; Nancy Zaroulis and Gerald Sullivan, *Who Spoke Up? American Protest Against the War in Vietnam, 1963–1975*, 1984; Larry Waterhouse and Mariann Wizard, *Turning the Guns Around*, 1971.

Below: ARVN troops travel in personnel carriers on February 7, 1971, as part of Operation Dewey Canyon II/Lam Son 719, which was designed to clear North Vietnamese troops from Route 9 into Laos and to reoccupy Khe Sanh as a forward supply base. For ARVN troops, the invasion of Laos proved to be an unmitigated disaster.

TELEVISION AND THE VIETNAM WAR

In terms of journalism, politics, and popular culture, television and the Vietnam War had a symbiotic relationship, influencing each other in subtle as well as dramatic ways. Between 1964 and 1975 the war was broadcast nightly into the living rooms of tens of millions of Americans, shaping their attitudes toward the conflict and the decisions of policymakers. Television journalism came into its own in the jungles of Vietnam and served as the primary venue through which Americans acquired information about the war. Critics, of course, insisted that television had a bias for the dramatic over the complex, telescoped events, and suffered a serious liberal bias, and many held television responsible for the loss of the Vietnam War. Television journalists responded predictably, arguing that most reporting was balanced and accurate, that the print media was just as subject to mistakes and bias, and that all of them depended heavily upon government reports as sources.

Right: CBS television news anchor Walter Cronkite, a cigarette in his mouth and typewriter on his lap, on board an American Airlines aircraft on the tarmac in New York City on June 12, 1960.

The Battle of Khe Sanh and the Tet Offensive of 1968 generated the most controversy over the role of television in wartime. At Khe Sanh, television journalists like Walter Cronkite and Marvin Kalb fell all over themselves comparing the siege with Dien Bien Phu and alerting Americans to what was sure to be a seismic event in the history of the war. They bought into General William Westmoreland's view of the conflict and were completely ignorant of what Vo Nguyen Giap had accomplished at Khe Sanh—drawing U.S. troops into distant border battles, of which Khe Sanh was only the most famous, while the Vietcong staged a massive assault on towns and cities throughout South Vietnam. Vo Nguyen Giap might as well have written some of the copy that Cronkite and Kalb read on the air. The North Vietnamese general had hoodwinked the major networks just as thoroughly as he had hoodwinked Westmoreland.

The Tet Offensive itself, however, became the most controversial journalistic event of the war. It was, from the perspective of the Communists, an unmitigated tactical disaster. The expected uprising of the people of South Vietnam against their own government never materialized, and the U.S. Army and Marine Corps had responded to the surprise attack swiftly and thoroughly. When the fog of battle cleared, some 100,000 Vietcong guerrillas had been killed, effectively destroying the VC as a military force. Westmoreland had achieved a stunning victory, and he chose to claim as much from the U.S. Embassy in Saigon, standing over the bodies of several dead Vietcong who had managed to breach the compound. What Westmoreland saw as a tactical victory, however, turned into a colossal strategic defeat. For years he had been promising victory, insisting that the Vietcong were growing steadily weaker and that their capacity for waging war had been seriously compromised. Then, in a matter of hours, the Vietcong demonstrated their continuing strength. Not even the American embassy was secure. When *CBS News* anchor Walter Cronkite reported that the war had ground to a stalemate, President Lyndon B. Johnson lost the last of his political traction. Political support for the war within the United States evaporated. In a matter of months, Johnson decided not to seek reelection in 1968. General Westmoreland and many other political and military leaders held the media responsible for the loss of American political willpower.

Television also demonstrated how the Vietnam War affected American popular culture. Early in the 1960s, before the introduction of U.S. ground troops in Vietnam, television still trafficked in the glories of World War II, when America's enemies had seemed so malignant and so visible. In September 1965 prime-time television featured such pro-military programs as *Combat!*, *Convoy*, and *12 O'Clock High*, with such pro-military comedies as *Mr. Roberts*, *McHale's Navy*, *Hogan's Heroes*, *F Troop*, and *Gomer Pyle, U.S.M.C.* As the Vietnam War grew ever more controversial, programming changed. By 1967 only five prime-time television programs had military themes. With the fall 1968 lineup, only *Hogan's Heroes* and *Gomer Pyle* survived.

In addition to reducing military programming in commercial television, the Vietnam War altered the focus of many existing popular series. On September 17, 1966, *Mission: Impossible* debuted on CBS. During its early years *Mission: Impossible* featured a team of American spies who weekly engaged in foreign intrigue, promoting U.S. national security interests through covert actions against Communist bloc and third world governments. As the Vietnam War became increasingly unpopular, however, *Mission: Impossible* writers refocused the series, abandoning the overthrow of foreign governments for attacks on organized crime within the United States. On the evening news each night, Americans watched the Vietnam War—a colossal example of foreign intervention—deteriorate politically, and they lost interest in fictional television programs that glorified similar interventions. The popular sci-fi series *Star Trek*, which also debuted in 1966, featured a crew of astronauts exploring distant galaxies. They operated under a firm rule of engagement: that they not interfere with the internal political affairs of the new societies they encountered.

Antiwar themes surfaced in a number of television programs. *Rowan and Martin's Laugh-In* regularly featured actress Goldie Hawn bedecked in peace symbols, while the Smothers Brothers variety entertainment program regularly targeted the Vietnam War for criticism. In September 1967 the brothers headlined folksinger Pete Seeger, who sang the antiwar ballad "Waste Deep in the Big Muddy." In subsequent shows they provided a platform for antiwar activist/singer Joan Baez to perform, and they aired an interview with antiwar pediatrician Dr. Benjamin Spock. In 1969 CBS canceled *The Smothers Brothers* for political reasons. In Norman Lear's *All in the Family*, meanwhile, Archie Bunker and his son-in-law argued frequently over the merits of the war. Such debates continued in Lear's popular sitcom *Maude*.

By the mid-1970s, with U.S. troops out of Vietnam and the Communists triumphant, television programming reflected profound disillusionment with the war. One of the most popular series in television history—*M*A*S*H*—debuted on CBS in September 1972, just as the Vietnam War entered its final stages. Based on the 1970 antiwar film of the same name, *M*A*S*H* was a

dark comedy revolving around the 4077th Mobile Army Surgical Hospital during the Korean War. Released at the time of the Kent State University killings and the U.S. invasion of Cambodia, *M*A*S*H* ridiculed war and the military, portraying most officers as bumbling incompetents or bloodthirsty killers interested only in promoting their own careers regardless of how many civilians or soldiers had to be sacrificed in that pursuit. War was evil and futile and its policymakers deluded. For more than a decade, until its last episode on January 21, 1983, tens of

Below: Lance Corporal Greg Penta of the 3d Marine Division fires a .50-caliber machine gun at North Vietnamese troops surrounding Khe Sanh in northern South Vietnam on February 26, 1968.

millions of viewers tuned in to *M*A*S*H*, whose antiwar values entered American popular culture.

It was not until the late 1980s that television was ready to treat the Vietnam War as anything less than twisted and malignant. In 1987 *Tour of Duty* premiered, the first weekly dramatic series devoted to the war, and it fell largely into the earlier genre of World War II films, with soldiers doing their best and fighting for their country, in this case infantry troops from a fictional Bravo Company fighting in Vietnam in 1967. *Tour of Duty* remained on the small screen until the spring of 1990. Between 1988 and 1991 the series *China Beach* dramatically portrayed the trials of nurses in Vietnam during the war, and it too was much closer to *Tour of Duty* in its point of view than it was to *M*A*S*H*. Finally, in 2005 *The Unit*, a *Mission: Impossible* clone, highlighted covert military operations and attracted a large television audience.

Sources: Peter Baestrup, *Big Story: How the American Press and Television Reported and Interpreted the Crisis of Tet 1968 in Vietnam and Washington*, 1983; Michael Arlen, *Living Room War*, 1999; Jorge Lewinski, *The Camera at War*, 1978; Saran Farenick, "Television and the Vietnam War," in James S. Olson, ed., *The Vietnam War: A Handbook of the Literature and Research*, 1993; Suzy Kalter, *The Complete Book of M*A*S*H*, 1988.

Opposite page, top: ARVN troops and armored personnel carriers battle Vietcong soldiers in the streets of northern Saigon on May 6, 1968. The Tet Offensive will soon enter its final stages.

Opposite page, bottom: A female Vietcong soldier fires a rocket-propelled grenade in southern Cuu Long Delta during the Tet Offensive in the spring of 1968.

Below: Marine Corporal Bruce Lint of Connecticut plays the guitar for his buddies to help pass the time at Khe Sanh in northwestern South Vietnam, on February 19, 1968, during the Tet Offensive.

"TERMINATE WITH EXTREME PREJUDICE"

"Terminate with extreme prejudice" was a Central Intelligence Agency* euphemism used to refer to killing people, especially civilians suspected of belonging to or supporting the National Liberation Front (*see* Vietcong). Critics said that such terminology was part of a government propaganda effort by the United States to manipulate the general population into supporting an unjust and immoral war by hiding its grisly nature. Although others disagreed, one needs only to watch any number of documentaries on the war and listen to the mangled speech of government officials defending U.S. policy in Vietnam to get the feeling that the obfuscation was intentional. SF

Sources: WGBH Educational Foundation, *Vietnam, A Television History*, 1983; CBS, *1984 Revisited with Walter Cronkite*, 1984.

TERRITORIAL FORCES

The South Vietnamese Territorial Forces, including the Regional Forces* and the Popular Forces,* were responsible for local population security in villages throughout the Republic of Vietnam.* The Territorial Forces were first organized after the Geneva Accords,* and they expanded in size from 102,000 people in 1955 to 532,000 in 1972. By that time they represented just over half of South Vietnam's military forces.

Sources: Ngo Quang Truong, *Territorial Forces*, 1981; Andrew F. Krepinevich Jr., *The Army in Vietnam*, 1986.

TET

Tet is the most important Vietnamese festival and celebrates the lunar new year. In the belief that the first week of the new year will determine family fortunes for the rest of the year, Vietnamese freshly paint their houses for Tet and buy new clothes. The holiday is characterized by family visits to pagodas, churches, and cemeteries; sacrifices to deceased family members; firecrackers, drums, and gongs; and family visitations.

Source: Ann Crawford, *Customs and Culture of Vietnam*, 1967.

TET OFFENSIVE

On January 30, 1968, Vietcong* units launched attacks throughout I* and II Corps,* and by January 31, 1968, Vietcong and North Vietnamese soldiers were assaulting American and South Vietnamese forces throughout the country. In addition to attacking thirty-six of forty-four provincial capitals and five of six major cities, the Vietcong attacked the U.S. Embassy in Saigon,* Tan Son Nhut Air Base,* the presidential palace, and South Vietnam general staff headquarters. In the summer of 1967 the North Vietnamese had commenced planning for the January 1968 offensive. They decided to launch diversionary raids in the Central Highlands* and northern border areas, the most famous of which was the months-long siege of U.S. Marines* at Khe Sanh.* The purpose of the raids was to deceive American intelligence; during the campaigns in the highlands and northern provinces Vietcong were slowly moving into the provincial capitals and major cities to prepare for the Tet attacks. While all this was going on, both the North Vietnamese and the National Liberation Front (*see* Vietcong) called for a cease-fire during the Tet* holiday celebrations. By the time of the holiday, however, they had moved 100,000 soldiers and vast amounts of supplies undetected into the cities.

On two levels, the Tet Offensive was a tactical disaster for the Vietcong and North Vietnamese. The offensive failed in that the South Vietnamese Army had held, and American troops, airlifted into the critical areas, quickly regained control, except in Hue,* where the fighting continued for weeks. Nor had the South Vietnamese risen up en masse and rallied to their "Vietcong liberators." Finally, the Vietcong and North Vietnamese may have suffered as many as 40,000 battlefield deaths, compared with 1,100 for the United States and 2,300 for the South Vietnamese. The Vietcong were so decimated by the fighting that they never regained their strength, and after the Tet Offensive the war in Vietnam was largely a struggle between mainline U.S., ARVN (see Army of the Republic of Vietnam), and North Vietnamese regulars.

But if the Tet Offensive was a tactical defeat for the Vietcong and North Vietnamese, it was also a colossal strategic victory. Throughout 1966 and 1967 American military and political leaders had been talking of the progress in the war, how the enemy would not long be able to sustain such enormous losses, how there was a "light at the end of the tunnel,"* how the war would soon be over. The Tet Offensive, by exposing the determination of the Vietcong

and North Vietnamese, as well as their continuing vitality, demoralized American public opinion. Television reporters broadcast home the incredible sight of General William Westmoreland,* standing beside several dead Vietcong *inside* the U.S. Embassy compound, describing the American victory. The Tet Offensive led quickly to the near defeat of President Lyndon B. Johnson* in the New Hampshire Democratic primary and his withdrawal from the race in March 1968. After Tet, American policy toward Vietnam had little to do with winning the war, only with finding an "honorable" way out. CD

Sources: Don Oberdorfer, *Tet! The Turning Point*, 1983; Robert Pisor, *The End of the Line: The Siege of Khe Sanh*, 1982; Pham Van Son and Le Van Duong, eds., *The Viet Cong Tet Offensive 1968*, 1969.

THAI HOANG VAN

Thai Hoang Van was born in 1906 in Thai Binh Province. He studied at the Hoang Pho Military Academy and joined the Communist Party in 1930, becoming a founding member of the Vietminh* in 1945. He was promoted to brigadier general in the Vietminh army in 1946, and to major general in the People's Army of Vietnam, North Vietnam, in 1959. Thai Hoang Van served as deputy minister of national defense in 1961, and in 1965 became commander of Military Region 5, which was the northern region of South Vietnam. During the 1960s and early 1970s Thai Hoang Van was a member of the Central Committee of the Lao Dong Party* and of the Central Military Party Committee.

Source: Borys Lewytzkyj and Juliuz Stroynowski, *Who's Who in the Socialist Countries*, 1978.

THAILAND

Thailand, with 198,115 square miles and a population of more than 64 million, is drained by the Menam River Valley, and has a southern arm extending down the Malay Peninsula. Eastern Thailand is drained by the Mekong River, which is the boundary between much of Thailand and Laos.* Originally, Thailand was a buffer state between British interests in Burma and French interests in Indochina.* Although 95 percent of the Thais are Buddhist, including the 5 million ethnic Chinese,* the Malay minority along the southern extension are Muslim.

About 25 percent of Thailand remains forested, especially the northern and eastern regions, down from more than 60 percent in the 1980s. From these forests come such valuable woods as teak, ebony, boxwood, and rosewood, but a rapidly expanding economy has raised conservation concerns due to deforestation. Traditional agricultural is

handicapped by elevation, slope, soil leaching, and winter drought. The major breadbasket of Thailand is along the Menam River Valley. The central alluvial plains of the Menam are capable of producing at least two crops a year of rice, tobacco, and peanuts. Rice cultivation is found on most of the farmland and is a major export, together with textiles and rubber products. Unlike most Asian nations, Thailand produces a rice surplus each year. The Thais usually supplement their diet with fish. Bangkok, located in the delta on the lower Chao Phraya, has a population of more than 9 million and is the commercial, financial, and political center of the country.

During the war in Vietnam, Thailand was a close American ally. Although the Thais had traditionally been friendly with the Vietnamese, they were suspicious of Communist intentions, feared the fall of Cambodia* and Laos to guerrillas, and wanted above all else to preserve their independence. By 1969 the Thais had a total of nearly 12,000 combat troops in Vietnam, including the elite Queen's Cobras* and the Black Panther Division of the Royal Thai Army Volunteer Force. The U.S. 46th Special Forces* Company assisted Thai forces in resisting Communist guerrilla activity along the Laotian border and in the south on the Malay Peninsula. The last of the Thai troops left Vietnam in April 1972.

The United States also had a strong military presence in Thailand, including the 8th, 355th, 366th, and 388th Tactical Fighter Wings and the 307th Strategic Wing. Strategic bombing operations over North and South Vietnam often originated in Thailand.

Sources: Stanley Robert Larsen and James Lawton Collins Jr., *Allied Participation in Vietnam*, 1975; Shelby L. Stanton, *Vietnam Order of Battle*, 1981; U.S. Central Intelligence Agency, *World Factbook*, 2006; http://www.iucn.org; www.asiainfo.org.

THANH NIEN CACH MENH DONG CHI HOI

Known as the Revolutionary Youth League, the Thanh Nien Cach Menh Dong Chi Hoi was organized by Ho Chi Minh* shortly after his arrival in China in 1924. Ho organized students in southern China into small cell groups to agitate for revolution through writing and speeches. The group ceased to function after Ho fled to Moscow in 1927.

Source: William J. Duiker, *The Rise of Nationalism in Vietnam, 1900–1941*, 1976.

THICH NU THANH QUANG

Born in 1911, Thich Nu Thanh Quang was a native of South Vietnam and a Buddhist nun. Quang gained international attention on May 28, 1966, when she committed suicide in front of the Dieu De Pagoda in Hue.* After dousing herself with five gallons of gasoline, she lit a match and remained motionless in a kneeling position for nine seconds before collapsing in flames. Before her suicide, Quang had drafted a letter to President Lyndon Johnson* calling for the United States to abandon its support for the political regime of Nguyen Cao Ky.* Her death triggered a series of mass Buddhist protests throughout the country.

Source: *New York Times*, May 29, 1966.

THICH QUANG DUC

Thich Quang Duc was a 66-year-old Buddhist monk whose self-immolation on June 11, 1963, profoundly affected the attitude of the Kennedy* administration toward Ngo Dinh Diem* and dramatically signified the Buddhist crisis in South Vietnam. Quang Duc burned himself to death at a busy Saigon* intersection in full view not only of passersby but also the media, which the Buddhists (*see* Buddhism) had alerted before the incident. The result was maximum exposure, especially in the United States. While self-immolation was a traditional form of protest in many parts of Asia, the event violated the sensibilities of the policymakers in Washington and was a critical factor in convincing them that Diem was incapable of governing the Republic of Vietnam.* Thus, the incident also reflected the sophistication of the Buddhist anti-Diem movement in understanding the importance of the press as a convenient method of expressing its position. Quang Duc's action also reflected the increasing inability of the Diem government to deal with the pervasive pluralism that characterized South Vietnam in this period. With his mandarin mentality, Diem responded to dissatisfaction with his regime by enacting more repression. The result of this escalation was a growing stubbornness by Diem and more self-immolations by Buddhist monks, as well as other anti-Diem demonstrations. Thus, Thich Quang Duc's suicide marked the beginning of the end of the Diem regime. STT

Sources: Stanley Karnow, *Vietnam: A History*, 1983; *New York Times*, June 12–13, 1963.

Below: In protest of what he considered to be the corrupt, anti-Buddhist policies of the South Vietnamese government of Ngo Dinh Diem, Buddhist monk Thich Quang Duc doused himself in gasoline and immolated himself with a match on June 11, 1963. The image hit the wire services and appeared in newspapers around the world. The suicide was in Saigon's central market place.

Opposite: III Corps was the densely populated, fertile military region between Saigon and the Central Highlands. It stretched from the Mekong Delta to the rugged mountains around Song Be near the II Corps border.

THICH TRI QUANG

Historically, Vietnamese Buddhist monks have taken part in public affairs *only* during crises in which they have claimed with some legitimacy to speak for the Vietnamese people. At those times, they have demonstrated formidable abilities to organize and mobilize mass protests against those they held responsible for the crisis. Thich Tri Quang, a charismatic Buddhist monk born in 1922, mobilized Buddhists (*see* Buddhism) three times in the 1960s. Profound nationalists, the Buddhists objected to foreign dominance and foreign influence in Vietnam. Therefore, they opposed the American presence almost as much as they opposed Communism. Although Tri Quang worked with the Vietminh* in the struggle against France,* he broke with them because they claimed to represent all Vietnamese, with an alien ideology, when only the Buddhists could truly represent them. Tri Quang advocated a "middle way," based on traditional values, between the foreign-influence doctrines of Catholicism and Communism.

Tri Quang organized Buddhist opposition to Ngo Dinh Diem,* a Catholic. Animosity between Catholics and Buddhists stemmed from their theological differences and from the French favoritism of Catholics and persecution of Buddhists. When some 900,000 northern Catholics moved south after the 1954 Geneva Conference (*see* Geneva Accords) and Diem became president, relations worsened. In May 1963, Tri Quang moved against Diem. Monks took to the streets demanding Diem's resignation, a return to traditional ways, and an end to the Catholic domination of the government. They maintained pressure until Diem was overthrown.

Recognizing Tri Quang's power, U.S. ambassador Henry Cabot Lodge* recommended that he hold office in the post-Diem government. It was not to be. In the convoluted politics of General Nguyen Khanh's* tenuous rule, Tri Quang mobilized Buddhists first to force Khanh's resignation and then to bring him back. After 1964 the Buddhists were relatively quiet, until 1966 when Nguyen Cao Ky* fired I Corps* commander General Thi, who had developed a close relationship with Tri Quang. Buddhist protests paralyzed the government and forced Ky to call elections. Determined U.S. support, however, enabled Ky to survive and break the monk's power. Tri Quang, placed under house arrest, began a long fast and almost died. Distrusted by the North Vietnamese, Thich Tri Quang was exiled to a monastery in 1975. SF

Sources: Frances FitzGerald, *Fire in the Lake: The Vietnamese and the Americans in Vietnam*, 1972; Stanley Karnow, *Vietnam: A History*, 1983; George McTurnan Kahin and John W. Lewis, *The United States in Viet Nam*, 1967.

III CORPS

The third allied Combat Tactical Zone in South Vietnam was III Corps. During the 1960s and early 1970s the country was divided into four major administrative and military regions, and III Corps extended from the northern Mekong Delta* to the southern Central Highlands. Also known as Military Region 3 (MR 3), III Corps had its headquarters in Saigon,* and consisted of the following provinces: Tay Ninh, Binh Long, Phuoc Long, Phuoc Tuy, Long An, Binh Duong, Long Khanh, Binh Tuy, Gia Dinh, Hau Nghia, and Bien Hoa. The 18th and 25th divisions of the ARVN (*see* Army of the Republic of Vietnam) played prominent roles in the military defense of III Corps, as did the 2d Armored Cavalry and the 81st Airborne Rangers.

Sources: Harvey H. Smith et al., *Area Handbook for South Vietnam*, 1967; Shelby L. Stanton, *Vietnam Order of Battle*, 1981.

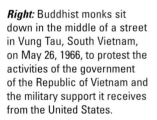

Right: Buddhist monks sit down in the middle of a street in Vung Tau, South Vietnam, on May 26, 1966, to protest the activities of the government of the Republic of Vietnam and the military support it receives from the United States.

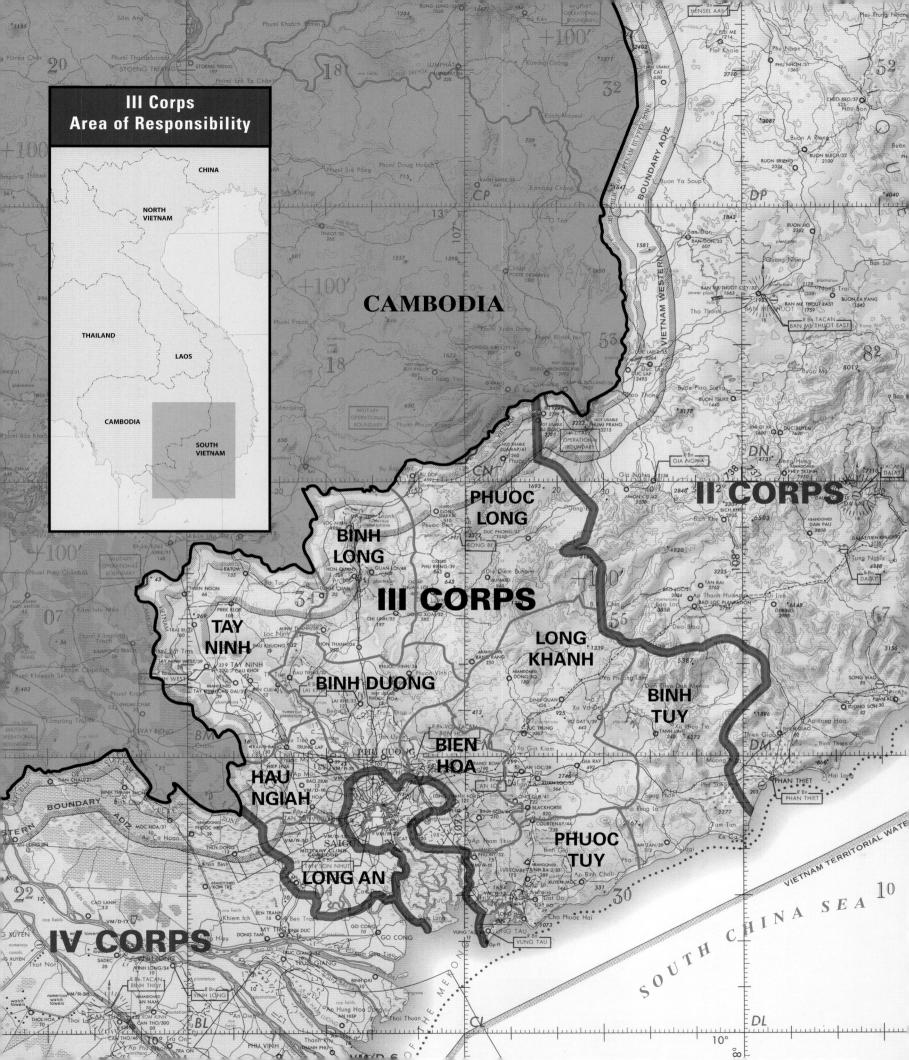

**III Corps
Area of Responsibility**

CHINA

NORTH
VIETNAM

THAILAND

LAOS

CAMBODIA

SOUTH
VIETNAM

CAMBODIA

II CORPS

PHUOC
LONG

BINH
LONG

III CORPS

TAY
NINH

LONG
KHANH

BINH DUONG

BINH
TUY

BIEN
HOA

HAU
NGIAH

PHUOC
TUY

LONG AN

IV CORPS

SOUTH CHINA SEA

VIETNAM TERRITORIAL WATE

3d MARINE AMPHIBIOUS BRIGADE (MAB)

When the III Marine Amphibious Force* departed Da Nang* in April 1971, the 3d Marine Amphibious Brigade (3d MAB) took its place at headquarters under Major General Alan J. Armstrong. The brigade began planning on March 1 for beginning operations set with a target date for April 14. Assuming responsibility for more than 13,600 Marines who remained in Vietnam, the 3d MAB included a Marine regiment, fixed-wing and helicopter gunships,* and the remainder of a force-logistics command. Remnants of the Marine civic action program were deactivated shortly, and the 3d MAB formally ceased to exist and was out of Vietnam by June 26, leaving behind a scattering of naval-gunfire teams along the Demilitarized Zone,* a Marine advisory unit, a few officers at Military Assistance Command, Vietnam* and guards for the U.S. Embassy in Saigon*—in a "transitional support" group of some 500 Marines. DA

Source: Edwin H. Simmons, "Marine Corps Operations in Vietnam, 1969–1972," in *The Marines in Vietnam, 1954–1973,* 1983.

III MARINE AMPHIBIOUS FORCE (MAF)

A corps headquarters established at Da Nang* in May 1965, the III Marine Amphibious Force (III MAF) replaced the 9th Marine Expeditionary Brigade* (9th MEB) and grew by 1968 to include two reinforced Marine divisions, one air wing, a U.S. Army* corps, plus several Republic of Vietnam* and South Korean* units. With tactical responsibility for the five northern provinces of South Vietnam, I Corp's* seven Marine commanders often disagreed with Military Assistance Command, Vietnam* (MACV) strategy, and this strain characterized the relationship until the Army's XXIV Corps* took over command of the region in March 1970.

The role of the III MAF in Vietnam reflected yet another of the war's ironies. Trained and equipped for rapid deployment as shock troops, the Marines were wedded to earlier contingency plans calling for a force that could be supplied over a beach, and once committed they were held in relatively static defense positions around coastal enclaves* and later along the Demilitarized Zone* (DMZ). Meanwhile, MACV ordered an Army division retrained for Mobile Riverine Force* operations in the Mekong Delta,* an area and operational approach perhaps more suitable to the Marines' traditional purpose.

The III MAF's Tactical Area of Responsibility* (TAOR) thus became a 30- to 70-mile-wide zone that stretched from the DMZ south some 225 miles, to Sa Huynh at a spur in the Annamite mountain chain. In 1965 an estimated 2.6 million (85 percent ethnic Vietnamese) lived in the 10,000-square-mile TAOR, mostly fishermen and farmers clustered in hamlets along the flat coastal plains or in small alluvial valleys lying inland between steep mountain slopes. These inhabitants were culturally and historically different from those, say, in Saigon,* and also included Montagnard* tribesmen in the hills and business-oriented Chinese,* Indians, and a few remaining French in Da Nang, Hue,* and other urban areas.

At first assigned to defend the Da Nang airfield and a nearby ridgeline, the III MAF believed that no more than 2,000 Vietcong* operated in the densely populated agricultural area of Quang Nam Province (150,000 civilians within

Right: The laundry at the Marine base at Khe Sanh in 1968.

Left: A member of the III Marine Amphibious Force shaves at a buffalo (a water tank on wheels) on September 30, 1967.

Left: An aerial view of Khe Sanh on February 27, 1968, particularly the area occupied by the First Battalion, 9th Marines of the III Marine Amphibious Force. The Marines were under siege by the North Vietnamese Army.

Right: Private H.W. Whiting patrols in the jungles near the Demilitarized Zone as part of Operation Prairie on November 2, 1966. Whiting is a member of F Company, 2d Battalion, 5th Marines of the III Marine Amphibious Force.

Below: Marines try to pull and push a "Mule" (a widely used term in Vietnam to describe a four-wheel, half-ton vehicle with a platform mounted on two axles), mounted with a 106mm recoilless rifle, up a riverbank near Route 9 east of Khe Sanh on April 3, 1968. The Marines are members of F Company, 2d Battalion, 1st Marines, III Marine Amphibious Force. They are engaged in Operation Pegasus.

81mm mortar range of the Marines), and thus stressed pacification (*see* Rural Reconstruction) in its contribution to MACV planning. Although never completely rejecting General William Westmoreland's* decision to "search and destroy"*—the III MAF's early operations were labeled clear and hold*—Marine staffs objected to the drift toward a "big unit" war and won support from Fleet Marine Force, Pacific Command* (FMFPAC) in Hawaii and the Marine commandant in Washington, both prevailing upon the Commander in Chief, Pacific Command* (CinCPac) and the Joint Chiefs of Staff (*see* Chairman, JCS) to slightly but never substantially alter MACV's reliance on increased firepower. Indeed, by 1966 the Marine effort became two distinct wars—one in the South stressing pacification, another at the southern boundary of the DMZ seeking to stop North Vietnamese Army* infiltration* and find and destroy large enemy units.

The III MAF never quarreled with the lack of a pacification effort in the sparsely populated northern area of its TAOR, but it did object strenuously to Secretary of Defense Robert McNamara's* 1966 concept of an unmanned barbed-wire and electronic-sensor barrier along the DMZ (*see* Project Practice Nine). ("Hell," remarked a grunt in rare agreement with staff officers, "they'll just walk around it.") Although the project began in the Gio Linh–Con Thien* sector, the III MAF eventually prevailed and ordered construction of what it argued was a more feasible "mobile defense/conventional barrier," and by 1967 it had completed most of the strongpoints that dotted the northern tier of Quang Tri Province until they were abandoned in favor of a "mobile mode" after the 1968 siege of Khe Sanh.*

Meanwhile, the III MAF's war with MACV intensified. While Marines retook Hue and defended Khe Sanh* in the wake of the Tet Offensive,* General Westmoreland re-examined the command structure in I Corps, and briefly in February to March 1968 he installed an interim headquarters, MACV(Fwd), at Phu Bai under General Creighton Abrams* to coordinate with the III MAF the conduct of all operations in I Corps' two northern provinces. Bemoaning throughout the war what it described as "fluctuating command direction" from Saigon, the III MAF became particularly incensed with another 1968 decision by MACV, approved by CinCPac, to end the Marines' relative autonomy over air-ground operations and give the Seventh Air Force* "mission direction" over the 1st Marine Aircraft Wing based at Da Nang.

During Vietnamization* the Marine presence in I Corps dwindled more rapidly than the Army's, and after XXIV Corps assumed command of all operations in 1970, the III MAF confined its concerns to seven operations in Quang Nam Province and ten special-landing forays to the south of Da Nang. Just short of six years in-country, the III MAF headquarters yielded its command to the 3d

Marine Amphibious Brigade* and left Da Nang on April 14, 1971.

Between 1965 and 1971 the III MAF was commanded by six individuals: Major General William R. Collins (May 1965–June 1965); Major and then Lieutenant General Lewis W. Walt* (June 1965–February 1966 and March 1966–June 1967); Major and then Lieutenant General Keith B. McCutcheon (February 1966–March 1966 and March 1970–December 1970); Lieutenant General Robert E. Cushman Jr.* (June 1967–March 1969); Lieutenant General Herman Nickerson Jr. (March 1969–March 1970); and Lieutenant General Donn J. Robertson (December 1970–April 1971). DA

Above: On February 18, 1968, in the midst of the Tet Offensive, Marines move house-to-house to recapture the city of Hue from the Vietcong. This Marine is firing at a sniper.

Sources: *The Marines in Vietnam, 1954–1973*, 1983; Lewis W. Walt, *Strange War, Strange Strategy*, 1976; Victor H. Krulak, *First to Fight: An Inside View of the U.S. Marine Corps Story*, 1982; Shelby L. Stanton, *Vietnam Order of Battle*, 1981; Allan R. Millett, *Semper Fidelis: The History of the United States Marine Corps*, 1980; J. Robert Moskin, *The U.S. Marine Corps Story*, 1982.

3d MARINE DIVISION

Below: Leathernecks of the 2d Battalion, 9th Marines, 3d Marine Division, prepare to fire an 81mm mortar in defense of a landing zone as a Marine transport helicopter comes in for a landing on August 27, 1968. The LZ, southwest of Vandegrift Combat Base, was the night position for the Marines as they conducted a search-and-clear mission.

The March 1965 deployment of two battalions from the 3d Marine Division on Okinawa to guard the Da Nang* air base marked the first overt commitment of U.S. combat forces to South Vietnam's defense. Composed eventually of the 3d, 4th, and 9th Marine regiments, plus the 5th Marine Division's* 26th Marines, the 3d Marine Division's headquarters moved north to the Hue* area in October 1966, to Quang Tri eighteen months later, then finally to Dong Ha* in June 1968.

Medals of Honor were awarded to twenty-nine Marines and one Navy corpsman who served with the division. Units from the 3d Marine Division became chiefly responsible for setting up a defensive barrier along the Demilitarized Zone* (DMZ), and fought and operated out of Gio Linh and Con Thien,* both within five kilometers of the DMZ and together with Dong Ha and Cam Lo forming "Leatherneck Square"; occupied Camp Carroll, the Rockpile,* and Ca Lu along Route 9; and successfully defended Khe Sanh* in the spring of 1968.

The division, which had not seen action since landing on Bougainville, Guam, and Iwo Jima during World War II, received a Presidential Unit Citation and Vietnamese Cross of Gallantry with Palm, redeployed to Okinawa in late November 1969, and in 1975 provided troops involved in the Phnom Penh, Da Nang, and Saigon* evacuations, as well as the units that attacked Koh Tang Island during the *Mayaguez** affair. DA

Sources: *The Marines in Vietnam, 1954–1973*, 1983; R. Robert Moskin, *The U.S. Marine Corps Story*, 1982; Allan R. Millett, *Semper Fidelis: The History of the United States Marine Corps*, 1980; William Turner Huggett, *Body Count*, 1973.

Above: Troops of the 1st Battalion, 3d Marines unload equipment at Da Nang Air Base three hours before their operation is to commence on March 8, 1965.

Left: Photographer Sergeant Bruce A. Atwell and a 106mm recoilless rifle team of the 3d Marine Division come under a North Vietnamese rocket attack on February 9, 1968. Sergeant Atwell was wounded and evacuated to safety.

Above: Hugh Thompson attempted to stop the massacre at My Lai, landing his helicopter between the U.S. soldiers and the Vietnamese civilians and threatening to shoot the soldiers.

THOMPSON, HUGH C. JR.

Hugh Thompson was born in Atlanta on April 15, 1943, and was raised in Lafayette, Louisiana. He joined the U.S. Navy in 1961 and served for three years before mustering out. In 1964 Thompson joined the U.S. Army* and became a helicopter pilot in Vietnam, rising to the rank of chief warrant officer. On March 16, 1968, while flying over My Lai village in Quang Ngai Province, Thompson noticed the bodies of Vietnamese civilians strewn widely over a field. On closer examination, he saw U.S. soldiers gunning them down in what would soon become known as the My Lai* massacre. Thompson immediately realized that he was witnessing a war crime, since no orders had been given to provide medical assistance to the injured. He landed the helicopter between the soldiers and the Vietnamese civilians and trained an M60* machine gun on the American troops, informing them that unless they stopped the slaughter, he would shoot them. The killing stopped, and Thompson immediately reported what he had seen to commanding officers, who did not investigate his accusations.

In December 1969, when *Life* magazine published photographs of the village dead, My Lai became a scandal of epic proportions. Some initial attention came to Thompson for his actions, but as the scandal deepened, he was ostracized in the Army, as if he had been disloyal. In protest of the lack of will in the Army to fully investigate the incident, Thompson refused to accept the Distinguished Flying Cross for his service in Vietnam. Not until 1996 did the Army make things right, giving Thompson the Soldier's Medal, an award for courage in a non-combat situation. Thompson and his gunner Larry Colburn returned to My Lai and met with villagers in 1998. Hugh Thompson died on January 6, 2006.

Sources: Michael Bilton and Kevin Sim, *Four Hours in My Lai*, 1992; *New York Times*, January 7, 2006.

THOMPSON, ROBERT

Born in England on April 16, 1916, Robert Thompson served in a variety of positions in Malaysia during the 1930s and then spent six years in the Royal Air Force during World War II. He returned to Malaysia after the war and served as deputy and later secretary of defense between 1957 and 1961. During his years in Malaysia he became a recognized expert in counterinsurgency* against Communist guerrillas. At the request of the United States, Thompson was brought to South Vietnam in 1961 as head of the British mission there, where he remained until 1965, playing an important role in advising American military and political officials on how to deal with the Vietcong.* Thompson tried to apply the lessons the British had learned in Malaysia to Vietnam, urging the United States to establish the Strategic Hamlet Program* and to win the "hearts and minds"* of the people. He warned the United States about relying too heavily on a military solution to the problem in Vietnam, but his advice was not really heeded. Also, Thompson placed too much faith in the government of the Republic of Vietnam.* The British had succeeded with their counterinsurgency in Malaysia in part because they were the government of a colony, but the United States had to deal with a native South Vietnamese government, one run by the likes of Ngo Dinh Diem* and Nguyen Khanh.* Extraordinary corruption and lack of vision doomed the counterinsurgency effort. Early in the 1970s, Thompson spent some time as a consultant to the Nixon* administration and approved of the concept of Vietnamization. Robert Thompson spent the rest of his life writing and consulting about counterinsurgency programs and pacification until his death in 1992.

Sources: Robert Thompson, *Revolutionary War in World Strategy, 1945–1949*, 1970, and *Peace Is Not at Hand*, 1974; Larry E. Cable, *Conflict of Myths: The Development of American Counterinsurgency Doctrine and the Vietnam War*, 1986.

365 DAYS

365 Days is the title of Ronald J. Glasser's 1971 book on the Vietnam War. Telling his story from the perspective of a medical officer in Japan* treating wounded American soldiers there, Glasser picked the title from each of the wounded men's preoccupation with the number 365—the number of days in a Vietnam tour of duty. The book deals primarily with the unbelievable sense of futility expressed by dying and wounded teenagers.

Sources: Ronald J. Glasser, *365 Days*, 1971; Philip D. Beidler, *American Literature and the Experience of Vietnam*, 1982.

THURMOND, STROM

Strom Thurmond, a Republican senator from South Carolina throughout the Vietnam era, had long been in the political arena. After having served as both state senator and circuit court judge, in 1946 Thurmond was elected governor of South Carolina on the Democratic ticket. In 1948, after the Democratic National Convention had adopted a civil rights plank for its platform, the breakaway States Rights Party (sometimes referred to as the Dixiecrats) selected Thurmond as its presidential candidate. Unsuccessful in this bid, Thurmond was able to enter the Senate in 1954. Ten years later he transferred his allegiance to the Republican Party, so that he could work openly for the candidacy of conservative Barry M. Goldwater,* the Republican senator from Arizona, during the presidential election of 1964.

Although best known for his conservative southern stand in opposition to antidiscrimination measures and civil rights legislation, Thurmond also favored a militantly anti-Communist foreign policy and large defense appropriations. Indeed, the South Carolina senator was one of the few to associate himself with the causes of ideological right-wing organizations like the John Birch Society and the Young Americans for Freedom in the early 1960s. During the presidency of Lyndon Johnson,* Thurmond was among the five leading Republican supporters of a tough anti-Communist foreign policy in the Senate.

To offset what he regarded as unrelenting Communist expansionism, Thurmond favored the unrestrained use of military force in Vietnam. He charged in August 1966, as one example, that the administration was following a "no win" policy in Southeast Asia and urged the use of increased force to ensure the continued existence of South Vietnam. The following April he criticized an East-West treaty governing the peaceful exploration and use of outer space as "another step in the artificial and unrealistic atmosphere of detente with Communism."

In 1968 Thurmond backed Richard M. Nixon* for the Republican presidential nomination and was credited with persuading most southern Republican delegates to the party's national convention to support Nixon instead of another candidate. As a result, Thurmond wielded considerable influence in the White House during the Nixon administration. Harry Dent, Thurmond's former aide, was a political advisor to the president, and about twenty other friends and associates of the senator's received significant administrative jobs. Thurmond supported President Nixon's efforts to conclude the conflict in Southeast Asia through a negotiated peace, but he nevertheless continued to urge constant opposition to Communist activity throughout the world. Strom Thurmond, the longest-serving and oldest senator in U.S. history, died on June 26, 2003. RDL

Sources: Seyom Brown, *The Faces of Power: Constancy and Change in United States Foreign Policy from Truman to Johnson*, 1968; Eric F. Goldman, *The Tragedy of Lyndon Johnson*, 1969; George C. Herring, *America's Longest War: The United States and Vietnam, 1950–1975*, 1979; Jack Bass and Marilyn Thompson, *Strom*, 2005.

TICONDEROGA

See USS *Ticonderoga*

TIGER CAGES

"Tiger cages" were small stone compartments used by the South Vietnamese to confine prisoners of war* (POWs) at the Con Son Correctional Center on Con Son Island (*see* Poulo Condore). The cages measured 5 by 9 feet and had

Below: The aircraft carrier USS *Ticonderoga* underway in the Gulf of Tonkin in April 1968.

bars on top. According to official releases of the Saigon* government, prisoners were humanely treated and confined only temporarily in the tiger cages, and all were obstinate troublemakers. But in July 1970 the Red Cross reported that the prisoners were abused and that South Vietnam was violating the Geneva Convention. Chained to walls day and night, denied adequate food, water, and exercise, the prisoners often died or lost the use of their legs. While South Vietnam claimed that the prisoners were common criminals, the Red Cross disagreed, saying that the prisoners were mostly North Vietnamese POWs or Buddhist dissidents. On July 7, 1970, congressmen Augustus Hawkins and William Anderson condemned the prison after touring it. In February 1971 the U.S. Mission in Saigon announced that the State Department would provide $400,000 to construct 288 isolation cells to replace the notorious tiger cages and that all POWs would be removed from the Con Son facility. LC

Source: Edward W. Knappman, ed., *South Vietnam: U.S.–Communist Confrontation in Southeast Asia*, vols. 6 & 7, 1973.

TIGER DIVISION

The Tiger Division was the Capital Division* of the Republic of Korea* Army. The Tiger Division was first deployed to South Vietnam in September 1965, and spent most of the war fighting in II Corps.* Headquartered at Qui Nhon,* the Tiger Division's primary activity involved protecting the major American installations along the coast in II Corps and keeping transportation lanes open between those installations and the U.S. air bases at Phu Cat and Phan Rang.

Sources: Shelby L. Stanton, *Vietnam Order of Battle*, 1981, and *The Rise and Fall of an American Army: U.S. Ground Forces in Vietnam, 1965–1973*, 1985; Harry G. Summers Jr., *Vietnam War Almanac*, 1985.

TO HUU

Originally known as Nguyen Kim Thanh, To Huu was born in Thua Thien Province in 1920 and educated in Hue.* He became a devoted Communist as a student and eventually was known as the poet laureate of North Vietnam. Huu had held a variety of positions in the government of the Democratic Republic of Vietnam,* including minister of culture, but was forced to resign his post as deputy prime minister after a failed attempt at monetary reform in 1985 resulted in economic disaster. To Huu died on December 9, 2002.

Sources: Danny J. Whitfield, *Historical and Cultural Dictionary of Vietnam*, 1976; *New York Times*, December 11, 2002.

Right: A soldier of the Tiger Division of the Republic of Korea Army leads a young Vietcong boy who is being taken prisoner in 1968.

Left: On the attack carrier USS *Oriskany* in the Gulf of Tonkin in November 1967, an enlisted flight deck director guides an A-3B Skywarrior onto the steam catapult. Skywarriors were used primarily as aerial tankers, providing in-flight refueling for fighter and attack aircraft flying missions over North Vietnam.

TON DUC THANG

Ton Duc Thang, also known as Ton That Thien, was a native of South Vietnam, born in 1888. While attending school in Saigon* in 1910, Thang met Ho Chi Minh* and became a dedicated anti-French, Vietnamese nationalist. For his political activities against the empire, the French placed Thang in the notorious prison at Poulo Condore* between 1929 and 1945. After World War II he immediately began working with the Vietminh,* and served in various leadership positions in the Lao Dong Party.* After Ho Chi Minh's death in 1969, Thang moved up from vice president of the Democratic Republic of Vietnam* to president, but it was only a figurehead position, which he filled until his death in 1980.

Sources: "Meet Uncle Tom," *Newsweek* (October 6, 1969); "North Viet Nam," *Time* (October 3, 1969); William J. Duiker, *The Rise of Nationalism in Vietnam, 1900–1941*, 1976; *Encyclopaedia Britannica*, 2006.

Left: Crewmen on a destroyer in the Gulf of Tonkin work with an H-3 Sea King helicopter. The Sea King was responsible for rescue and recovery of downed pilots over North and South Vietnam, among other missions.

TONKIN

Geographers generally divide Vietnam into three major regions: Tonkin in the north, Annam* in the center, and Cochin China* in the south. The ancestors of the Vietnamese migrated out of southern China (*see* People's

Republic of China) and settled first in Tonkin and later in Annam. Not until the nineteenth century did they displace Cambodians from Cochin China in the south. Drained primarily by the Red River, much of Tonkin is a fertile delta capable of supporting a dense population. In addition to the Red River, the Clear, Black, and Thai Binh rivers cut through Tonkin, depositing a rich loam soil. The major city of Tonkin is Hanoi,* a com-

Right, inset: A plane captain gives a thumbs-up to an A-4 Skyhawk on the flight deck of the aircraft carrier USS *Kitty Hawk* as it operates in the Gulf of Tonkin in January 1967.

mercial and manufacturing center, with the nearby port city of Haiphong connected to the Thai Binh River. The Red River Delta is a huge rice field. Because the Red River regularly floods, Tonkin is covered with an elaborate system of dikes* and canals. During the Vietnam War the United States considered but never used air strikes to attack the canals and dikes, primarily because the strikes would have destroyed a civilian food supply and constituted a war crime according to international law. Inland from the Red River Delta, Tonkin becomes a series of hills and then mountains at the Chinese and Laotian borders. In these mountains, tribes of Montagnards* ("mountain people") are widely scattered. These mountain areas are also rich in such ore deposits as iron, zinc, tin, and coal.

Sources: Pierre Gourour, *The Peasants of the Tonkin Delta*, 1955; Edward Doyle and Samuel Lipsman, *The Vietnam Experience: Setting the Stage*, 1981.

TON THAT DINH

Born a southerner in 1930, Ton That Dinh rose to power in the Republic of Vietnam* because of his close personal relationship with Ngo Dinh Diem.* Diem viewed Dinh with trust and paternalism, and in 1961 he had made Dinh the youngest general in the Army of the Republic of Vietnam* (ARVN). Dinh converted to Roman Catholicism early in the 1960s and was an active member of Ngo Dinh Nhu's* Personalist Labor Party. Ambitious for a prominent political position in Ngo Dinh Diem's cabinet, Dinh turned to plotters against the regime after Diem refused. In November 1963 he played a leading role in the coup d'etat that toppled Diem's government and led to his assassination. Suspected of still being loyal to the Diem faction, however, Dinh was arrested by General Nguyen Khanh,* but was held only temporarily. When Nguyen Cao Ky* took control of the government, Dinh was again in command of an ARVN

Opposite: Pilots make final pre-flight checks as their aircraft are prepared for launch from the deck of the aircraft carrier USS *Oriskany* in the Gulf of Tonkin in September 1967.

corps, but he lost favor during the Buddhist crisis of 1966 when he resented the tactics that Ky used to crush the protest. In the summer of 1966 Dinh lost command of his corps and was exiled from the Republic of Vietnam.

Sources: Joseph Buttinger, *Vietnam: A Dragon Embattled*, 2 vols., 1967; Frances FitzGerald, *Fire in the Lake: The Vietnamese and the Americans in Vietnam*, 1972.

THE TRAITORS

The Traitors is the title of John Briley's 1969 Vietnam War novel. It centers on an American patrol ambushed and captured by the Vietcong.* At a detention camp an American defector tries to brainwash them, eventually persuading two of the captives to participate in a harebrained scheme to free an imprisoned Buddhist from a political prison in South Vietnam on the naive hope that he will be able to end the war.

Sources: John Briley, *The Traitors*, 1969; Philip D. Beidler, *American Literature and the Experience of Vietnam*, 1969.

TRAN BUU KIEM

Tran Buu Kiem was born in 1921 in Can Tho and took a law degree at Hanoi University. A fervent anti-French nationalist, Kiem organized student protest movements against the French Empire and became active as a leader on the central committee of the National Liberation Front (*see* Vietcong) in the 1950s and 1960s. Kiem served on the delegation to the Paris peace talks* in 1968 and was minister to the president of the Provisional Revolutionary Government of South Vietnam.*

Source: *International Who's Who, 1982–1983*, 1983.

TRAN DO

Born in North Vietnam in 1922, Tran Do served as deputy commander of North Vietnamese and Vietcong* forces in South Vietnam during the 1960s and early 1970s. He lived with his troops in underground bunkers and jungle camps, established no headquarters, and always remained on the move, confusing and frustrating American forces trying to capture him. Although the South Vietnamese resented the leadership of northerners in their campaign against the governments of Ngo Dinh Diem,* Nguyen Cao Ky,* and Nguyen Van Thieu,* Do managed to prevent such factionalism from seriously hindering the war effort. Tran Do planned and executed the Tet Offensive* in 1968 that,

although resulting in tens of thousands of casualties for the Vietcong and North Vietnamese, was a political deathblow to the American war effort.

Source: John S. Bowman, ed., *The Vietnam War Almanac*, 1985.

TRAN KIM TUYEN

A native of North Vietnam, Tran Kim Tuyen attended medical school, practiced medicine for a time in Hanoi,* and then fled to South Vietnam in 1954 as part of the large-scale Catholic relocation across the Demilitarized Zone.* In South Vietnam, Tuyen became head of the feared Office of Political and Social Studies, a Central Intelligence Agency*–established secret police force loyal to Ngo Dinh Diem.* Tuyen became disaffected with Diem late in the 1950s, primarily because he believed that Diem's weak and corrupt government would guarantee a Communist takeover. In 1962 and 1963 Tuyen began plotting the overthrow of the Diem government, but when Diem found out, he effectively exiled Tuyen, naming him diplomatic counsel to Egypt. Tuyen never reached Egypt but ended up in Hong Kong, where he continued to oppose Diem. After the fall of the Diem government, Tuyen returned to South Vietnam but played no prominent political role. Tran Kim Tuyen fled to Great Britain* just before the fall of Saigon* in 1975.

Source: Stanley Karnow, *Vietnam: A History*, 1983.

TRAN THIEN KHIEM

Tran Thien Khiem, a South Vietnamese diplomat and an ambassador to the United States, was born on December 15, 1925. Khiem joined the Vietnamese Army as a young man, rising quickly through the ranks. In 1960, after stopping an attempted coup against Ngo Dinh Diem,* Khiem became army chief of staff and a powerful figure in South Vietnamese politics. Three years later, however, Khiem was a leading figure in the successful coup d'etat and assassination of Ngo Dinh Diem. In 1964 Khiem joined with General Nguyen Khanh* in deposing General Duong Van Minh.* Khiem was then named defense minister and commander in chief of the new government. The Khanh government was soon shaky, however, and Khiem was plotting against it. For a brief time in 1964 Khiem joined Khanh and Duong Van Minh in a triumvirate government until the forces of air force general Nguyen Cao Ky* took over. Khiem was then sent into honorable exile, first as ambassador to the People's Republic of China* between October 1964 and October 1965, and then from 1965 to 1968 as ambassador to the United States.

Khiem returned to Saigon* in 1968 as minister of the interior, and for five months in 1969 he served as deputy prime minister. He became prime minister in 1969 and remained in that post until 1975. General Khiem was considered a leading figure in the lucrative South Vietnamese heroin traffic, a trade that included most other prominent officials in the government. In April 1975, as North Vietnamese and Vietcong* forces were moving into Saigon, Khiem escaped to Taiwan.

Sources: *International Who's Who, 1976–1977*, 1976; Stanley Karnow, *Vietnam: A History*, 1983.

TRAN VAN CHUONG

Tran Van Chuong was born in 1898 and was educated at the University of Paris. He set up a law practice in Hanoi* in 1925 and became a prominent member of the French-Vietnamese establishment. His daughter, Tran Le Xuan, married Ngo Dinh Nhu* (*see* Ngo Dinh Nhu, Madame), and in 1954 Tran Van Chuong became minister of state for the Republic of Vietnam.* He then served as ambassador to the United States between 1954 and 1963. He resigned in protest in August 1963 when Ngo Dinh Diem* began his attacks on the Buddhists, and in the fall of 1963 Tran Van Chuong followed his daughter around the United States contradicting her statements of support for the Diem government. After the assassination of Diem later that year, Tran Van Chuong remained in the United States, living in Washington, D.C.

Sources: *Who's Who in the Far East and Australasia, 1974–1975*, 1975; Stanley Karnow, *Vietnam: A History*, 1983.

TRAN VAN DO

Tran Van Do was minister of foreign affairs in Ngo Dinh Diem's* first cabinet in 1954. A physician and a man of distinguished reputation in Vietnam, Do was head of the State of Vietnam's delegation to the Geneva Conference at the time of the completion of the Geneva Accords* in 1954. At Geneva, he made a determined but futile effort to prevent the partitioning of Vietnam and, in the name of his government, denounced the final accords.

Do had been a longtime and close associate of Ngo Dinh Diem's. Do's brother, Tran Van Chuong,* was the father of Madame Ngo Dinh Nhu* and became Diem's ambassador to the United States. Do split with Diem in the spring of 1955, however, because he objected to Diem's unwillingness to broaden his government beyond the Ngo family circle. Do was one of the signers of the "Caravelle" petition in 1960 that urged Diem to initiate political reforms. After Diem's death, Tran Van Do served once

again as foreign minister, in the cabinet of Prime Minister Phan Huy Quat.* DLA

Source: Bernard B. Fall, *Viet-Nam Witness, 1953–66*, 1966.

TRAN VAN DON

General Tran Van Don was one of the leaders of the South Vietnamese Army who helped Ngo Dinh Diem* secure power and who later helped remove Diem from office. Although he lived most of his life in Vietnam, Don was born in France* in 1917 while his father was attending medical school. As a French citizen, he found himself in the French Army during World War II, and, largely through circumstance, he became a career military officer. When the French decided during their war with the Vietminh* to create a Vietnamese National Army* (VNA), Don, who was then a colonel, became chief of staff for General Nguyen Van Hinh,* whom the French placed in command of the VNA. It was with the support of such key officers as Colonel Don that Ngo Dinh Diem was able to secure VNA support in 1955 in subduing the private and sectarian military forces in South Vietnam.

Under Diem, Don became a general and rose to command of I Corps, with headquarters at Hue.* Like other military officers, however, he became increasingly disillusioned with Diem and the entire Ngo family. In 1963 Don was one of the principal conspirators in the coup that ended with Diem's assassination. With the rise to power in 1965 of younger military officers such as Nguyen Cao Ky* and Nguyen Van Thieu,* Don was among the senior officers forced to retire. Elected to the South Vietnamese senate in 1967, Don remained an influential figure in South Vietnam. On April 29, 1975, the day before North Vietnam's seizure of Saigon,* Tran Van Don chose to seek exile in the United States. DLA

Source: Tran Van Don, *Our Endless War: Inside Vietnam*, 1978.

TRAN VAN HUONG

Tran Van Huong was born on December 1, 1903. He worked as a schoolteacher before joining the Vietminh* resistance movement against the French. Huong served as mayor of Saigon* in 1954 and again in 1964, until he became prime minister of South Vietnam in a civilian government orchestrated by General Nguyen Khanh.* Huong encountered bitter opposition from various Buddhist factions and was in office only three months. After the Tet Offensive* in 1968, General Nguyen Van Thieu* appointed Huong prime minister again. He lasted in that post until 1969. In 1971 Huong became vice president of South Vietnam and remained in that position until April 21, 1975, when Thieu abdicated. Tran Van Huong was president of South Vietnam for nine days until he surrendered authority to General Duong Van Minh* on the eve of the North Vietnamese victory.

Sources: George C. Herring, *America's Longest War: The United States in Vietnam, 1950–1975*, 1986; *International Who's Who, 1976–1977*, 1976.

TRAN VAN LAM

Tran Van Lam was born on July 30, 1913, in Cholon.* He was educated at Hanoi University as a pharmacist and spent his career in Saigon.* Lam was elected to the Saigon City Council in 1952 and served in the National Assembly between 1956 and 1961. Between 1961 and 1964 Tran Van Lam was the ambassador to Australia* and New Zealand* for the Republic of Vietnam.* He returned to South Vietnam in 1964, and in 1968 was appointed minister of foreign affairs, where he served until 1973 when he became speaker of the Senate. He remained in that position until the collapse of South Vietnam in 1975.

Source: *Who's Who in the Far East and Australasia*, 1974.

TRAN VAN TRA

Tran Van Tra was born in Quang Ngai in central Vietnam in 1918. He worked on the railroads until the end of World War II, when he joined the Vietminh* to oppose the return of the French Empire. Successful at politics, Tra became a senior officer of the Vietminh, received political and military training in the Soviet Union* and People's Republic of China,* and in 1963 assumed command of Vietcong* forces in South Vietnam. He led the attack on Saigon* during the Tet Offensive* of 1968. Tra joined the armistice commission after the January 1973 cease-fire, but two months later he was back in Hanoi* planning the final assault on the South. He then was transferred to Loc Ninh, a command post about seventy-five miles north of Saigon, where he continued to plan the assault. In 1975 Tra was a leader of the conquest of Saigon when ARVN forces (*see* Army of the Republic of Vietnam) collapsed. After he published in 1982 a critical account of internal dissension among Communist leaders during the Vietnam conflict, Tra was purged from the Communist Party. Tran Van Tra died on April 20, 1996.

Sources: John S. Bowman, ed., *The Vietnam War Almanac*, 1985; *New York Times*, April 21–22, 1996.

TRINH

The Trinh were the family dynasty in control of Tonkin* in the northern portion of Vietnam. By the 1590s Trinh Kiem was the power behind the throne of the Le dynasty in Tonkin, and the Trinh ruled Tonkin until 1786, when leaders of the Tay Son Rebellion* invaded and seized Hanoi.* When the Tay Son government collapsed in 1802, the Trinh were unable to return to power in Hanoi because the Nguyen* dynasty, under Gia Long,* had unified Cochin China,* Annam,* and Tonkin under one rule.

Source: Joseph Buttinger, *The Smaller Dragon: A Political History of Vietnam*, 1958.

TROOP

The term "troop" usually refers to a cavalry unit of company* size, though it is often used to refer to any one or a group of soldiers. Usually commanded by a captain, a troop is made up of two or more platoons.* During the war in Vietnam there were also reconnaissance troops, armored cavalry troops, and air cavalry troops.

Source: Harry G. Summers Jr., *Vietnam War Almanac*, 1985.

TRUMAN, HARRY S.

Harry S. Truman, the thirty-third president of the United States, was born on May 8, 1884, in Lamar, Missouri. After graduating from high school he worked the family farm near Independence, Missouri, before joining the Army in 1917. Truman saw combat with the 129th Field Artillery of the 35th Division at St. Miniel and the Meuse-Argonne offensives. After the war he operated a clothing store and studied law in night school. Active in the politics of Tom Pendergast's Kansas City machine, Truman became a Jackson County judge in 1922, served as presiding judge between 1926 and 1934, and won election to the U.S. Senate in 1934. Truman was reelected in 1940 but served in obscurity until he chaired the Senate Committee to Investigate the National Defense Program. Franklin D. Roosevelt* selected Truman as his running mate to replace Henry A. Wallace in 1944, and when Roosevelt died of a stroke on April 12, 1945, Truman became president of the United States.

Unlike Roosevelt, however, Truman had no philosophical opposition to colonialism nor any real interest in Indochina.* Truman was content to let France* return to control of her colonial empire. So instead of pursuing Roosevelt's plan to establish intermediary "trusteeship" status over former European colonies, Truman wanted the European powers to resume their imperial positions as a way of fighting Communist expansion in the world. Truman also had a distinct distrust for Ho Chi Minh* because of his ties to Moscow, and instead of viewing Ho as a legitimate nationalist, Truman could see him only as a Communist. Although the United States adopted a position of pro-French neutrality toward the war in Indochina during the late 1940s and early 1950s, President Truman provided for covert economic and military assistance to the French. Hundreds of millions of dollars of Marshall Plan assistance to France were also diverted to the colonial enterprises in Indochina and Africa. When Harry S. Truman left office in January 1953, the United States was clearly a French supporter in the Indochina war. Fear of Communism had replaced opposition to imperialism as the main focus of American third world policy.

Sources: Alfred Steinberg, *The Man from Missouri: The Life and Times of Harry S. Truman*, 1962; George C. Herring, *America's Longest War: The United States and Vietnam, 1950–1975*, 1986.

TRUONG CHINH

Truong Chinh was born in 1907 in Nam Dinh. He joined the Revolutionary League of Vietnamese Youth in 1927 and was expelled from the Nam Dinh School for his anti-French, revolutionary activities. Chinh joined the Communist Party in 1930 and was imprisoned by the French. After his release in 1936, Chinh worked as a journalist until 1939 when the French imprisoned him again. He escaped prison and fled to Yenan late in 1939, returning to Vietnam in 1941. Between 1941 and 1945 Chinh was the secretary-general of the Central Committee of the Communist Party of Indochina (*see* Lao Dong Party). During the 1950s he was active in the Labor Party of Vietnam, and was appointed deputy prime minister of North Vietnam in 1958. Chinh's relationship with Ho Chi Minh* was a close one, with Chinh acting as Ho's chief Marxist theorist. Chinh was viewed, however, as a moderate and an advocate of negotiation whenever possible. After the fall of South Vietnam in 1975, Chinh rose to greater power in the Socialist Republic of Vietnam,* eventually becoming the second-most-powerful individual in the country. He resigned as party chief and president in December 1986 after severe economic problems in the Socialist Republic of Vietnam eroded his political base. Truong Chinh died in 1988.

Sources: *Who's Who in the Socialist Countries*, 1978; Frances FitzGerald, *Fire in the Lake: The Vietnamese and the Americans in Vietnam*, 1972; *Washington Post*, December 18, 1986.

Below: A radio transmission operator (RTO) and his commander stand on an isolated landing zone, watching helicopters of the 1st Air Cavalry Division fly overhead. The troops are part of Operation Pershing, a search-and-destroy mission on the Bong Son Plain and An Lao Valley. The two American soldiers are waiting for the second wave of troops to land.

TRUONG DINH DZU

In 1967 an obscure Buddhist lawyer ran an unexpectedly strong second to the presidential ticket of Nguyen Van Thieu* and Nguyen Cao Ky.* Truong Dinh Dzu took 17 percent of the vote in a field of ten candidates to Thieu's 35 percent, an unheard-of result in the quagmire of South Vietnamese politics. Candidates who were "pro-Communist," "neutralist," or allied with "militant Buddhists" were excluded from the election, and Dzu had kept his platform relatively secret. But he was allowed to run because he had Central Intelligence Agency* contacts and because he advocated a bombing* "pause" rather than a "halt" in North Vietnam, and because he initially opposed negotiations with the National Liberation Front (*see* Vietcong). Nevertheless, Truong Dinh Dzu, in the absence of stronger peace candidates, became the token peace candidate, and his 17 percent electoral finish was an embarrassment to the government. In a country where the "will of heaven" determines political authority, the election weakened Thieu's legitimacy. In response he jailed and later exiled Truong Dinh Dzu. SF

Sources: Frances FitzGerald, *Fire in the Lake: The Vietnamese and the Americans in Vietnam*, 1972; Stanley Karnow, *Vietnam: A History*, 1983; Edward Herman and Frank Brohead, *Demonstration Elections*, 1984.

TRUONG NHU TANG

Truong Nhu Tang was born in 1923 in the Saigon* suburb of Cholon.* Educated at the University of Paris, he became a successful banker in South Vietnam, directing the Viet-Nam Bank for Industry and Commerce and the Viet-Nam Sugar Company in Saigon. During the late stages of the government of Ngo Dinh Diem* in the early 1960s, Tang became disenchanted with the corruption and American involvement. In 1964 he became a director of the People's Movement for Self-Determination, and in 1966 president of the Viet-Nam Youth Union. He was imprisoned in 1967 and 1968 for advocating peace with the Vietcong,* and in 1968 Tang joined the National Liberation Front (see Vietcong). In 1969 he was named minister of justice for the Provisional Revolutionary Government of South Vietnam,* and remained in that position until the fall of South Vietnam in 1975. Truong Nhu Tang then became minister of justice for the southern part of the new Socialist Republic of Vietnam.*

Source: *International Who's Who, 1976–1977*, 1976.

TUNNEL RATS

"Tunnel rats" was military slang for describing American soldiers specially trained to attack Vietcong* and North Vietnamese Army* underground positions. In South Vietnam there were hundreds of miles of tunnels that the Vietcong used to protect living areas, storage depots, ordnance factories, hospitals, and supplies from American air and artillery strikes. The most elaborate tunnels, first constructed by the Vietminh* in the 1940s, were located around Cu Chi, approximately twenty-five miles northeast

Right: Tunnel rats of Company B, 2d Battalion, 8th Cavalry Regiment, 1st Brigade, 1st Cavalry Division prepare to enter a tunnel after dropping fragmentation grenades into it during Operation Pershing.

Left: During Operation Cedar Falls, engineers with the 173d Airborne Brigade take explosives into a Vietcong tunnel in the Thanh Dien Forest of the Iron Triangle in an attempt to destroy the tunnel.

Above: Sergeant Ronald A. Payne of the 25th Infantry Division crawls through a tunnel with a flashlight and a handgun in search of Vietcong and their equipment during Operation Cedar Falls.

Left: Soldiers of Company B, 2d Battalion, 28th Infantry, 1st Infantry Division inspect an enemy cache of arms and equipment recovered from one of the Vietcong tunnels during Operation Cedar Falls. Fifty-eight 81mm mortar rounds, twenty-one 60mm mortar rounds, ten rifle grenades, and three cans of charges have been loaded onto a jeep trailer.

of Saigon* along Highway 1 (*see* "Street Without Joy"). The area around Cu Chi, also known as the Iron Triangle,* became the most bombed, gassed, defoliated, and devastated area in the history of combat because of American attempts to destroy the tunnel network.

Source: Tom Mangold and John Penycate, *The Tunnels of Cu Chi*, 1985.

Below: Replacement troops coming into the 25th Infantry Division at Cu Chi receive training at the Lightning Mines, Boobytraps, and Tunnel Training Center in a jungle near the base camp. The troops must successfully complete a course that is riddled with both explosives and non-explosive boobytraps at the end of nine hours of instruction.

20th ENGINEER BRIGADE

The 20th Engineer Brigade served in South Vietnam between August 1967 and September 1971. It consisted of eighteen battalions* in the 34th and 79th Engineer Groups and was stationed at Bien Hoa.* The 20th Engineer Brigade confined its construction work to III Corps* and IV Corps* operations.

Source: Shelby L. Stanton, *Vietnam Order of Battle*, 1981.

25th INFANTRY DIVISION

Nicknamed the Tropic Lightning Division, the 25th Infantry Division served in the southwest Pacific during World War II and in Korea* from 1951 to 1953. The division's 3d Brigade deployed to Vietnam from Hawaii in December 1965, with the rest of the division following in January and April 1966. (The original components of the 3d Brigade were transferred to the 4th Infantry Division* in August 1967. In return, the 25th Infantry Division received the 3d Brigade of the 4th Infantry Division. The original 3d Brigade of the 25th Infantry Division was reunited with the division following the withdrawal from Vietnam in 1970.)

During most of its time in Vietnam, the 25th Infantry Division served in the Saigon* vicinity and along the Cambodian border of III Corps.* Until August 1967, the division's 3d Brigade served in the western highlands around Pleiku.* In August this brigade became part of the 4th Infantry Division. The rest of the division participated in

operations intended to clear the Iron Triangle* in early 1967, and returned to that area with several other American units as a part of Operation Junction City.* During the Tet Offensive* of 1968 the division assisted in the defense of Saigon, and was engaged in bitter fighting while protecting Tan Son Nhut Air Base.* During most of late 1968 and 1969 the division was responsible for the security of the area around Cu Chi, and elements of the division were often involved in hard fighting in defense of base areas. In 1970 the division participated in the invasion of Cambodia* (*see* Operation Binh Tay) before turning over responsibility for the security of its area to the Army of the Republic of Vietnam.* Most of the 25th Infantry Division left Vietnam in December 1970. The division's 2d Brigade remained in Vietnam until April 1971. During the course of the Vietnam War, the 25th Infantry Division suffered 34,500 casualties, twice the number it suffered in World War II and Korea combined. SF and RSB III

Sources: Shelby L. Stanton, *Vietnam Order of Battle*, 1981, and *The Rise and Fall of an American Army: U.S. Ground Forces in Vietnam, 1965–1973*, 1985.

XXIV CORPS

Headquartered at Phu Bai in I Corps,* the XXIV Corps was first activated in Vietnam after the Tet Offensive* in 1968. Until 1970, when the 3d Marine Division* left Vietnam, XXIV Corps was subordinate to the III Marine Amphibious Force.* In March 1970 the headquarters of the XXIV Corps was shifted to Da Nang,* and XXIV Corps then assumed control of Marine and South Vietnamese military operations in I Corps. Deactivated at the end of June 1972, during its nearly four years in I Corps the XXIV Corps had responsibility at various times for all or parts of the following units: the 1st Cavalry Division,* the 82d* and 101st* Airborne divisions, the 5th Infantry Division,* the 108th Artillery Group, and the III Marine Amphibious Force.* The following lieutenant generals commanded the XXIV Corps: William B. Rosson (February–July 1968); Richard Stilwell (July 1968–June 1969); Melvin Zais (June 1969–June 1970); James W. Sutherland (June 1970–June 1971); and Welborn G. Dolvin (June 1971–June 1972).

Source: Shelby L. Stanton, *Vietnam Order of Battle*, 1981.

Above: A young Vietnamese child and a U.S. soldier of the 25th Infantry Division test a swing set in a new playground at the American base in Cu Chi, Vietnam. The playground, part of an improvement project, was built by members of the 25th in July 1966.

23d INFANTRY DIVISION

In February 1967, in order to support U.S. Marine* operations along the Demilitarized Zone,* the U.S. Army* formed an ad hoc division-size unit known as Task Force Oregon. Support troops were provided by various units, and the combat units consisted of one brigade from each of the two divisions already in Vietnam (the 101st Airborne Division* and the 25th Infantry Division),* plus the independent 196th Light Infantry Brigade.* In September 1967 the "borrowed" brigades were returned to their parent divisions and replaced by the 11th Infantry Brigade and the 198th Infantry Brigade. At that time Task Force Oregon was renamed the Americal Division (resurrecting a name first used in World War II when the Army formed a new division on New Caledonia). Officially, the Americal Division was known as the 23d Infantry Division, but the American high command preferred to use the designation Americal, calling it the only named division on active service.

The Americal Division's area of responsibility consisted of the three southern provinces in I Corps.* From November 1967 to November 1968 the division conducted numerous

Below: U.S. helicopters drop Company C soldiers of the 11th Infantry Brigade, 23d Infantry Division at My Lai in March 1968. The photo was taken by Army photographer Ronald L. Haeberle, whose photos of the massacre shocked the world.

sweeps and patrols throughout this region as part of a year-long operation code-named Wheeler/Wallowa.* Also during this period, units of the 11th Infantry Brigade committed a series of atrocities while conducting operations in Quang Ngai Province. The worst of these incidents occurred on March 16, 1968, at the hamlet of My Lai* in Son My village where some 300–500 South Vietnamese civilians were killed by American soldiers.

The division continued to patrol its region during 1969 and 1970, fighting numerous small-unit engagements. The

American Division was deactivated in November 1971, and the 196th Infantry Brigade returned to independent status. During its period of service the American Division suffered more than 17,500 casualties. RSB III

Sources: Shelby L. Stanton, *Vietnam Order of Battle*, 1981, and *The Rise and Fall of an American Army: U.S. Ground Forces in Vietnam, 1965–1973*, 1985; Willard Pearson, *The War in the Northern Provinces, 1966–1968*, 1975.

UH-1

The Bell UH-1 helicopter is one of aviation's true success stories. Thousands of the aircraft have been built in a number of variations, serving a multitude of roles. Called the Iroquois by the United States Army,* the aircraft is much better known by its nickname, Huey, derived from its initial designation of HU-1. In its multitude of roles in Vietnam, the Huey became a familiar sight on the television screens of America. Hardly a night passed without the evening news showing Hueys in dustoff,* slick,* or other missions.

Bell was chosen in 1955 to provide the Army with a utility helicopter capable of serving as a frontline medical evacuation (*see* Medevac) aircraft, a general utility aircraft, and an instrument training aircraft. Deliveries to the U.S. Army began in 1959. In 1961 a more powerful version, the UH-1B, was introduced. In 1967, starting with the UH-1D series, the airframe length was increased, giving the Huey a much roomier passenger/cargo compartment capable of carrying more troops or supplies. In 1968 Bell developed a specialized version of the aircraft with a stronger airframe and more powerful engine. The Huey tug, as it was called, was capable of lifting loads of up to three tons, nearly double that of a conventional Huey.

The UH-1 carried out a variety of missions in Vietnam, and it carried them all out well. As a troop transport, the Huey could carry from eleven to fourteen fully equipped combat troops. As a medical evacuation helicopter, the Huey carried six litters and a medical attendant. Conventional Hueys could carry 3,880 pounds of supplies, either internally or in a sling under the fuselage. As a gunship,* the Huey could carry a variety of armaments, including rocket packs on each side of the fuselage, a nose-mounted M5 40mm grenade launcher capable of firing 220 rounds per minute, or two side-mounted XM-140 30mm cannons.

Powered by a 1,400 shaft horsepower Avco Lycoming engine, the Huey had a cruising speed of 127 miles per hour and a range of 318 miles. Fast and highly maneuverable, the Huey proved far superior to the CH-21* or CH-34* as an assault helicopter. Combat troops normally rode in the wide doors on each side of the aircraft, and could exit quickly, greatly reducing the time the helicopter was on the ground.

Right: UH-1 Hueys lined up at the maintenance facility at Vinh Long Airfield in Vinh Long, South Vietnam, on October 19, 1969. The facility was operated by soldiers of the 1st Cavalry Division.

Opposite page: On October 16, 1969, troops from the 101st Airborne Division jump from a UH-1D helicopter. They are preparing for a tactical sweep against North Vietnamese forces near the Demilitarized Zone. Vietcong troops, largely wiped out during the Tet Offensive of 1968, no longer operate in the area.

Often, troops jumped from a Huey just above the ground as it "bounced" in ground effect and then took off, with the entire ground time reduced to a matter of seconds.

The Huey continues to serve a major role in military organizations throughout the non-Communist world. The U.S. Army retained 2,700 improved UH-1H models beyond the year 2000 to serve in a variety of roles, including resupply, troop transport, command, electronic warfare, and medical evacuation. NJA

Sources: *Jane's All the World's Aircraft, 1970–1971*, 1971; *Jane's All the World's Aircraft, 1985–1986*, 1986.

UNCOMMON VALOR

One of the many POW-genre films of the early 1980s, *Uncommon Valor* was released in 1983 and starred Gene Hackman as Colonel Jason Rhodes and Robert Stack as a Texas multimillionaire, both of whom are intent on financing and carrying out a mission to rescue their sons, who they believe are still prisoners of war* in Vietnam. Hackman recruits several of their sons' former comrades, and they stage a rescue. The film tells the story of the recruitment and training of the rescue squad and the successful mission.

Source: http://www.imdb.com/title/tt0086508/.

Below: A crew chief from the 62d Aviation Company works on the engine of a UH-1 helicopter in Can Tho, South Vietnam, in 1970.

UNITED STATES AGENCY FOR INTERNATIONAL DEVELOPMENT

In the Foreign Assistance Act of September 4, 1961, Congress* recommended that the United States adopt programs assisting foreign countries in economic development and external and internal security, and two months later President John F. Kennedy* established the Agency for International Development (AID) by executive order. New York lawyer Fowler Hamilton became the first AID administrator, succeeded in 1962 by economist David E. Bell. During the 1960s AID represented a shift in American foreign assistance away from Europe and toward the third world. In addition to loans and grants, AID assigned American specialists abroad. By the end of 1962 AID had more than 5,000 employees overseas, and they were training another 8,000 foreign nationals. By 1965 AID was spending more than $2 billion a year, and loans were beginning to replace grants as a major form of assistance. AID missions were established in seventy foreign countries, and most workers were assigned to projects in agriculture, education, and public health. By that time the number of AID employees had reached more than 15,000.

During the early years of the Vietnam buildup, AID became increasingly involved in anti-Communist programs—public safety, civic action, and rural and community development. Its 1967 budget earmarked more than $550 million for Vietnam. AID workers tried unsuccessfully to establish farming cooperatives, self-help projects, and village elections. As the war became more and more controversial at home, the public image of AID deteriorated, especially as revelations of Central Intelligence Agency* involvement in AID appeared. Between 1968 and 1975, AID personnel strength dropped from 18,000 people to less than 6,000. In addition to continuing its development activities, AID began running refugee assistance programs around the world. It also conducted Operation Babylift* in 1975, when thousands of refugees* were removed from Vietnam. After new legislation passed through Congress in 1973, AID programs shifted away from industrially oriented capital expenditures to popular participation programs in public health, education, and agriculture.

Sources: Rober E. Asher, *Development Assistance in the Seventies: Alternatives for the United States*, 1970; Paul G. Clark, *American Aid for Development*, 1972; John Prados, *Presidents' Secret Wars: CIA and Pentagon Covert Operations Since World War II*, 1986.

UNITED STATES AIR FORCE

See Air Force, United States

UNITED STATES ARMY, VIETNAM

The United States Army, Vietnam was a logistical command headquarters between July 1965 and March 1973. It functioned at Saigon* and later Long Binh.* The deputy commander of Military Assistance Command, Vietnam* supervised the United States Army, Vietnam.

Source: Harry G. Summers Jr., *Vietnam War Almanac*, 1985.

USS *C. TURNER JOY* (DD-951)

The *C. Turner Joy* is a Forrest Sherman–class destroyer of 4,200 tons and a crew of 360 people. The destroyer has three 5-inch guns, two 3-inch guns, six torpedoes, and depth charges. Commissioned on August 3, 1959, the *C. Turner Joy* completed two western Pacific deployments and was in the midst of its third in August 1964 when it went to the assistance of the USS *Maddox*,* another destroyer, under attack by North Vietnamese torpedo boats. After firing, along with the carrier USS *Ticonderoga*,* on the boats and destroying one of them, the *C. Turner Joy* retired to an area 100 miles off the North Vietnamese coast and continued patrolling. On August 4, 1964, both the *C. Turner Joy* and the *Maddox* picked up on radar what they believed to be small surface craft approaching at extreme range in poor weather. Fire from the destroyers and aircraft from the *Ticonderoga* sank two of the boats and damaged two others, although the attacking boats were never positively identified. In retaliation for this "Gulf of Tonkin incident,"* President Lyndon B. Johnson* ordered air strikes against four North Vietnamese torpedo houses and supporting facilities. Congress* passed the Gulf of Tonkin Resolution,* which legally cleared the way for direct U.S. involvement in the Vietnam War. Throughout the rest of the war, the *C. Turner Joy* conducted shore bombardment (*see* Naval Bombardment) and screening patrols in the South China Sea. The destroyer was decommissioned in 1982. CA

Sources: *Jane's Fighting Ships, 1976–1977*, 1978; Tom Carhart, *Battles and Campaigns in Vietnam*, 1984.

Below: The destroyer USS *C. Turner Joy* is underway off the coast of Oahu, Hawaii, on November 24, 1969. In August 1964, the USS *C. Turner Joy* was involved in the incident that led to the Gulf of Tonkin Resolution and the escalation of the U.S. war in Vietnam.

USS *MADDOX* (DD-731)

Commissioned on June 2, 1944, the USS *Maddox* was an Allen M. Sumner–class destroyer that carried six 5-inch guns and ten 21-inch torpedoes. The *Maddox* was assigned to the Third Pacific Fleet and supported the Luzon invasion in late 1944 and early 1945, as well as the Okinawa and Japanese home islands campaigns in the summer of 1945. As part of the Seventh Fleet* in the South China Sea in the summer of 1964, the *Maddox* came under attack by three North Vietnamese patrol boats. With help from the destroy-er *C. Turner Joy** and the carrier *Ticonderoga*,* the *Maddox* destroyed one of the patrol boats and damaged two others. Two days later, on August 4, 1964, the *Maddox* picked up radar information of five attacking patrol boats, and the same three U.S. ships engaged them for more than two hours. The Gulf of Tonkin incident* was used by President Lyndon Johnson* to order air strikes against North Vietnam and to justify a major escalation of the war. The *Maddox* completed two additional tours in Vietnamese waters in 1965 and 1966, supporting carriers and bombarding the shore. In 1969 the USS *Maddox* was decommissioned. CA

Sources: U.S. Navy Department, *Dictionary of American Naval Fighting Ships*, 1969; Tom Carhart, *Battles and Campaigns in Vietnam*, 1984.

USS *PUEBLO*

Early in the morning of January 23, 1968, forces from the North Korean Navy seized the USS *Pueblo*, a highly sophisticated American intelligence ship. The seizure reportedly occurred fifteen miles off the North Korean coast, well beyond the twelve-mile territorial limit, with eighty-three Americans on board the *Pueblo*. One was killed in the attack and four wounded. North Korea claimed that the ship was seized in waters seven miles off the coast, in what was a violation of their territorial sovereignty. Even if the territorial violation had been accurate, the North Korean action was a severe reaction, since American and Soviet intelligence ships regularly worked the Asian coasts and occasionally wandered off course. Such occurrences usually warranted only orders to leave. Although the United States immediately ordered 350 aircraft to air bases in South Korea as a show of force, the crew of the *Pueblo* spent eleven months in captivity and were beaten, tortured, and forced to sign false confessions. Because the diplomatic controversy over the *Pueblo* lasted throughout 1968—along with the Tet Offensive,* election of 1968,* My Lai,* and the assassinations of Martin Luther King Jr.* and Robert Kennedy*—American energies were distracted, and a more vigorous response, one which held out at least the possibility of military action against Korea,* was out of the question. The quagmire in Vietnam had limited the American capacity to deal with other crises in the world. SS

Source: F. Carl Schumacher and George C. Wilson, *Bridge of No Return*, 1971.

USS *TICONDEROGA*

The *Ticonderoga* was an *Essex*-class aircraft carrier commis-sioned on May 8, 1944. After participating in the Pacific campaigns against Japan in 1945, the *Ticonderoga* spent two years bringing American servicemen home from Japan.* Decommissioned on January 9, 1947, it was converted for jet operations and recommissioned on September 11, 1954.

Right: The USS *Pueblo*, a U.S. Navy environmental research ship, gathering intelligence off the coast of North Korea in 1968 before its capture and the seizure of its crew. The North Koreans hijacked the ship on the high seas, the first incident of a U.S. Navy ship being captured by a foreign military force in more than 150 years. The provocative act inspired only a tepid response by the United States because of its preoccupation with the Vietnam War.

On August 1, 1964, while operating in international waters in the Gulf of Tonkin, the *Ticonderoga* received reports from the destroyer *Maddox** of attacks by three torpedo boats. The carrier deployed four aircraft to attack the boats. Two days later the *Ticonderoga* assisted the destroyer *C. Turner Joy** as it was being attacked by torpedo boats. The Gulf of Tonkin incident* led to the Gulf of Tonkin Resolution* by Congress* authorizing air strikes against North Vietnam, and, along with the USS *Constellation*, the *Ticonderoga* flew sixty sorties* against four North Vietnamese bases and oil storage facilities, destroying twenty-five torpedo boats and causing severe damage. Between November 1965 and August 1969, the *Ticonderoga* completed five combat tours in the Far East and its aircraft flew more than 35,000 sorties* against North and South Vietnamese targets. The *Ticonderoga* was decommissioned on September 1, 1973, and sold for scrap. CA

Sources: Tom Carhart, *Battles and Campaigns in Vietnam*, 1984; U.S. Navy Department, *Dictionary of American Naval Fighting Ships*, Vol. 3, 1978.

U THANT

U Thant was born in Burma in 1909 and became secretary of the Ministry of Information in 1949, where he served until 1957. In that year Thant received appointment as the Burmese ambassador to the United Nations. During the next four years he proved himself as a strong neutralist with great diplomatic skills. In 1961 Thant became secretary-general of the UN. He presided over the General Assembly during the most intense years of the Vietnam War, frequently urging a negotiated settlement of the conflict and occasionally playing a direct role in negotiating such a settlement. Thant's major attempt at a settlement came in 1964 when he tried to work with Premier Nikita Khrushchev* in bringing the North Vietnamese to the negotiating table. His efforts were stillborn until 1968, when he helped in working out some of the details of the Paris peace talks.* U Thant resigned as secretary-general of the UN in 1971; he died in 1974.

Sources: Stanley Karnow, *Vietnam: A History*, 1983; *Encyclopaedia Britannica*, 2006.

Above: The USS *Ticonderoga*, an attack aircraft carrier, patrols in the Gulf of Tonkin in 1964, just before the Gulf of Tonkin incident and congressional passage of the Gulf of Tonkin Resolution.

peace talks* on Vietnam. When Richard Nixon* entered the White House in 1969, Vance's role in foreign policy faded, except for periodic consultation assignments with Secretary of State Henry Kissinger,* but in 1977 the new president, Jimmy Carter, named Vance secretary of state. As secretary, Vance advocated diplomatic recognition and restoration of relations with the government of Vietnam. He resigned from the post after the abortive American attempt to rescue the Iranian hostages in 1980, and served for years as a member of the Council on Foreign Relations. Cyrus Vance died on January 12, 2002.

Sources: David McLellan, *Cyrus Vance*, 1985; *New York Times*, January 13, 2002.

Above: Cyrus Vance at first supported the Vietnam War, but changed his views by the late 1960s, advising the president to pull out of South Vietnam. He received the Presidential Medal of Freedom in 1969.

VANCE, CYRUS ROBERTS

Cyrus Vance was born on March 27, 1917, in Clarksburg, West Virginia, and received an undergraduate and a law degree from Yale in 1939 and 1942 respectively. After service in the Navy during World War II, Vance began practicing law in New York City, and became general counsel for the Department of Defense in 1961. In 1962 President John F. Kennedy* named Vance secretary of the Army. Vance was a close friend of Lyndon B. Johnson's,* and he became deputy secretary of defense in 1964. He toured Vietnam in 1966 and publicly defended administration policy, and from 1968 to 1969 Vance served on the negotiating team at the Paris

VANN, JOHN PAUL

John Paul Vann was born in Norfolk, Virginia, on July 2, 1924. In 1943 he joined the Army Air Corps, went to flight and navigation school, and in 1945 became a second lieutenant. When the Army Air Corps became the U.S. Air Force* in 1947, Vann chose to remain in the U.S. Army.* During the Korean War,* Vann was head of logistics for the 25th Infantry Division.* When China invaded Korea, he was given command of a ranger company. After subsequent tours of duty in Europe, Vann was promoted to lieutenant colonel in 1961. In 1962 he was sent to South Vietnam as

Right: In 1967, Lieutenant Colonel John Paul Vann, one of the first U.S. military advisors to the Army of the Republic of Vietnam, discusses strategy with an ARVN counterpart. Vann was a loyal soldier and patriot who nevertheless offered a devastating critique of U.S. policy in Vietnam. He remained in Vietnam in a civilian position until his death in 1972.

a U.S. advisor to an ARVN (*see* Army of the Republic of Vietnam) division. Vann was awarded the Distinguished Flying Cross for the Battle of Ap Bac,*but he was extremely critical of ARVN performance and voiced his feelings to the media. He left the Army in 1963, convinced that the Vietcong* would prevail because of incompetence and corruption in the ARVN. Vann returned to Vietnam in 1965 as a civilian working for the Agency for International Development.* Highly gifted militarily, he became chief advisor to the U.S. Army in II Corps,* which gave him virtual command of all U.S. military personnel in the area, an unprecedented responsibility for a civilian. John Paul Vann died in an aircraft crash on June 6, 1972.

Source: Neil Sheehan, *A Bright and Shining Lie: John Paul Vann and America in Vietnam*, 1988.

VAN TIEN DUNG

Van Tien Dung, the protégé of General Vo Nguyen Giap,* who led the final assault on South Vietnam in 1975, was born on May 1, 1917, in Ha Deng Province, Tonkin,* of peasant ancestry. Dung joined the revolutionary movement in the mid-1930s, fought against the French before and during World War II, and against the Japanese occupation forces of Indochina* after 1940. General Giap took notice of the peasant soldier and moved him up through the army ranks, appointing Dung chief of staff in 1953 and giving him logistical command of the assault against French forces at Dien Bien Phu* in 1954. Dung was second in command to Giap throughout the 1960s, and early in the 1970s became the youngest member of the politburo in North Vietnam. Giap named Dung commander of the campaign against South Vietnam in 1975. Dung's book *Our Great Spring Victory* describes the assault on and collapse of the South Vietnam government. Dung replaced Giap as minister of national defense in February 1980. Van Tien Dung died in 2002.

Sources: Van Tien Dung, *Our Great Spring Victory*, 1976; U.S. Central Intelligence Agency, *Who's Who in North Vietnam*, 1969; Stanley Karnow, *Vietnam: A History*, 1983.

VIETCONG

In 1954, after the Geneva Conference (*see* Geneva Accords) on Indochina,* Ho Chi Minh,* just as he had promised, ordered his forces to withdraw back into North Vietnam, where he would wait for the results of the promised elections to reunite the country in 1956. Included in the withdrawing troops were those Vietminh* originally from southern Vietnam. Some of them undoubtedly stayed in the South, but they were few in number and restrained

by Hanoi.* But five years later, with the government of Ngo Dinh Diem* firmly in control of the Republic of Vietnam* and the elections canceled, Ho Chi Minh decided to rejoin the battle in the South. He permitted southern Communists to return home, recruit new supporters, and prepare for the "revolutionary struggle." Southern Communists engaged in a frenzy of assassination and

Below: Two U.S. Marines stand guard over four Vietcong prisoners on a beach in the northern reaches of South Vietnam. It is June 1965, and the troops are part of the 3d Marine Division.

Left: A black cotton, pajama-style shirt typically worn by Vietcong guerrillas.

Right: Vietcong guerrillas patrol a water zone in the Plain of Reeds in preparation for an ambush of U.S. and ARVN soldiers on March 2, 1966.

Below: Early guns of the Vietcong. The top gun is a .30 caliber copy of a U.S. Thompson M1928. This weapon was donated to the National Military Academy of Vietnam museum in 1962. The National Military Academy of Vietnam no longer exists. It was located, during the Vietnam War, at Dalat, in the mountains of Vietnam, and was considered a quiet and beautiful location. Until 1968, it had essentially had no experience with the war. Vietcong attacks during the 1968 Tet Offensive on Dalat were minor and easily defeated. The bottom gun is a home-made shotgun patterned after a submachine gun. It has bolt action and uses hand-loaded shot cartridges. It was used mainly for psychological purposes against the South Vietnamese villagers. It dates from the days (1959 to 1963) when the Vietcong were desperate for any kind of modern weapon, or modern-looking weapon, and before they were supplied with Soviet or Chinese-made assault rifles such as the AK-47. General William C. Westmoreland gave this weapon to the museum in 1967.

Left: In 1966, Marines from the 3d Marine Division captured this Vietcong soldier and his training weapon, a replica of the M1 carbine.

Below: More Vietcong weapons and paraphernalia, including a rocket launcher (bottom) and a pistol. Above the weapons is a fedora-style hat, worn by many Vietcong soldiers, composed of layers of blue cloth stitched tightly together, with a three-inch crown and a two- to three-inch wide brim. Embroidered in red on the front of the brim are the letters SANG ("noble"). A metal megaphone used by Vietcong officers during the training of troops and to announce battle calls and attacks.

terrorism to destabilize the Saigon* regime. On December 20, 1960, Ho Chi Minh organized the National Liberation Front (NLF) of South Vietnam, with Nguyen Huu Tho* serving as chairman. The purpose of the NLF was to foment a general uprising in the Republic of Vietnam in order to bring about a Communist revolution that would unite the South with the North. It remains arguable how firmly southern Communists controlled the NLF and how firmly Hanoi controlled the southern Communists. During the Kennedy* administration the southern insurgents became stronger. South Vietnamese president Ngo Dinh Diem, seeking to deride the insurgency, called the guerrillas the Vietcong (short for Vietnamese Communists). American troops later called them VC or Charlie. But the VC soon appeared more than a match for Diem's government forces. At the Battle of Ap Bac* in January 1963, for example, the Vietcong were outnumbered 10 to 1 but managed to inflict a humiliating defeat on ARVN forces (*see* Army of the Republic of Vietnam). By late 1963 American intelligence analyses found that the Vietcong controlled more villages in the South than did the Saigon government.

The Vietcong high-water mark was reached in 1963 to 1964. In 1965 President Lyndon B. Johnson* began committing the first deployments of what would become more than half a million troops and a vast array of weaponry. Hanoi responded with its own buildup of North Vietnamese regular troops. The Vietcong were battered by American forces and taken over gradually by North Vietnamese Army* cadres. The Tet Offensive* in January and February 1968, although a political disaster for the United States, was a deathblow for the independence of the Vietcong. By the end of 1968 the Vietcong had suffered deep and disastrous losses, while North Vietnamese troops were largely responsible for the war effort in South Vietnam. In 1969 the Provisional Revolutionary Government of South Vietnam* superseded the Vietcong and NLF. CD

Sources: Douglas Pike, *Viet Cong: The Organization and Techniques of the National Liberation of South Vietnam*, 1966, and *History of the Vietnamese Communist Party*, 1978; Truong Nhu Tang, *A Viet Cong Memoir*, 1985.

Above: The Vietcong battle flag was captured during operations in Tay Ninh Province in July 1969 by soldiers from the Third Platoon of Company D, 1st Battalion, 12th Cavalry, 1st Cavalry Division. The triangular, half-red and half-blue flag with the five-pointed yellow star measures 13.5 inches on the staff and 15.5 inches on the fly.

Below: Vietcong nurses typically wore clothing such as this black cotton blouse with buttons and snaps on the front; this green cotton brassiere with elastic back and non-adjustable shoulder straps; and this green and white plaid cotton scarf. This particular scarf is hand-embroidered with "Doan Kim Luyen 12 69." The clothing was in a knapsack captured in Cambodia in 1970.

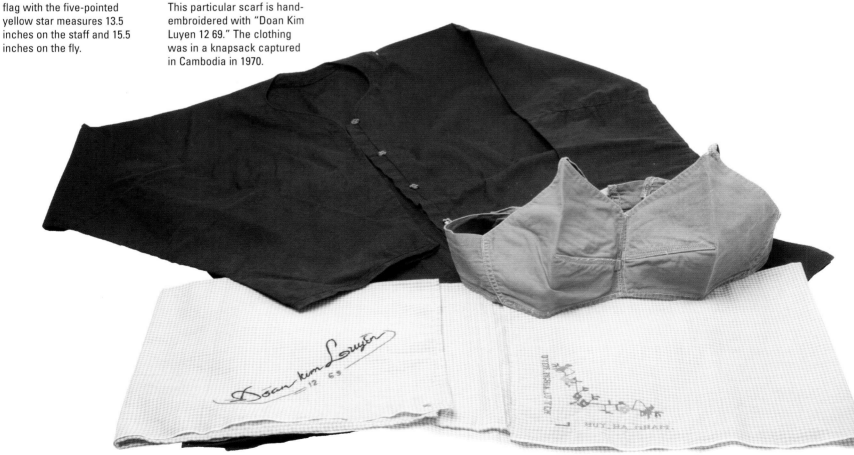

Left: From the street in a South Vietnamese urban environment, Vietcong soldiers fire a machine gun at an American aircraft during a raid.

VIETMINH

"Vietminh" is the shortened and most commonly used name for the Viet Nam Doc Lap Dong Minh Hoi, or League for the Independence of Vietnam. The Vietminh was a patriotic-front organization created at the Eighth Plenum of the Indochinese Communist Party (ICP; see Lao Dong Party) in May 1941. Under the direct guidance of Ho Chi Minh,* the front provided a vehicle for the party to mobilize the anti-French and anti-Japanese nationalism of the Vietnamese people. At the same time, the party made a conscious decision to de-emphasize ideology and class war until national independence was achieved.

The creation of the Vietminh also represented a shift in military strategy by the ICP to guerrilla (see Vietcong) warfare, and it was largely through rural insurgency that the Vietminh led the resistance first against the Japanese and then against the French. The anticolonial war of the Vietminh gained its most spectacular success with the surrender of the French garrison at Dien Bien Phu* in May 1954. It was with representatives of the Vietminh that the French negotiated the Geneva Accords* of 1954 that led to de facto recognition of Ho Chi Minh's government in Hanoi* and to the eventual military withdrawal of the French from Vietnam.

Long before Dien Bien Phu and Geneva, however, the Communist identity of the Vietminh leadership was clearly apparent in Vietnam. In 1951, in an effort to maintain and attract broad support for the liberation struggle, the Communist Party dropped the name Vietminh and adopted the name Lien Viet Front. Despite this move, "Vietminh" remained during the 1950s the designation most commonly used in South Vietnam for the Communists. Around the time of the creation of the National Liberation Front (see Vietcong) in South Vietnam in 1960, the name "Vietcong" replaced "Vietminh" as the term used outside of North Vietnam for the Vietnamese Communists. DLA

Sources: William J. Duiker, *The Communist Road to Power in Vietnam*, 1981, and *Ho*, 2002.

VIET NAM CACH MENH DONG MINH HOI (Vietnam Revolutionary League)

The origins of the Vietminh* can be traced to an anti-Communist Chinese nationalist warlord, Chang Fa-kwei, who had jailed Nguyen Ai-Quoc (Nguyen the Patriot) for Communist activities. The Chinese had had designs on Vietnam for centuries, and the end of World War II presented new opportunities. Chang and two other warlords, Lu-Han and Lung-Yun, wanted control over Tonkin.* The Viet Nam Quoc Dan Dang* (VNQDD), a pro-Chinese, Vietnamese nationalist organization formed by Chiang Kai-shek,* as well as other non-Communist nationalist organizations, were weak, with aging leadership, and in no position to serve Chinese interests. Nguyen Ai-Quoc led the well-organized Indochinese Communist Party (ICP; see Lao Dong Party). Ai-Quoc's willingness to set aside ideological differences with Chang and collaborate in forming the Viet Nam Cach Menh Dong Minh Hoi (a coalition of Vietnamese nationalist organizations that became known more simply as the Vietminh) typified his willingness to compromise Communist principles in order to strengthen his own organization.

Chang released Ai-Quoc from prison and funded the new coalition. Ai-Quoc promptly changed his name to Ho Chi Minh* ("He Who Enlightens") because he was too well known as a Communist. Because the ICP comprised a small minority of the Vietnam Revolutionary League, Chang mistakenly believed that he could prevent Ho from dominating the organization. Ho returned to Vietnam and, with Vo Nguyen Giap,* organized Vietnamese resistance to Japan. They established ties with the United States' OSS (Office for Strategic Services), rescued downed Allied pilots, collected intelligence, harassed Japanese forces, and planned to seize control of Vietnam before the Allies could execute plans to accept the Japanese surrender in Indochina.*

Though many more in number, the non-Communist members of the Revolutionary League were no match for Ho's leadership. On September 2, 1945, with American military personnel on the reviewing stand and warplanes flying overhead in salute, Ho Chi Minh proclaimed the independence of Vietnam under the governance of the Vietminh. SF

Sources: Bernard Fall, *The Two Viet-Nams: A Political and Military Analysis*, 1963; William J. Duiker, *The Rise of Nationalism in Vietnam, 1900–1941*, 1976.

VIET NAM DOC LAP DONG MINH HOI

See Vietminh

VIETNAMESE AIR FORCE

In 1951 the French established a small unit in the Army Air Corps that formed the beginning nucleus of the South Vietnamese Air Force. Primarily engaged in observation, liaison, and small-cargo transport, the Vietnamese Air Force used Morane Saulnier MS500 Criquets; it became an independent military unit in 1955 after the withdrawal of

Left: The South Vietnamese crew of an H-34 helicopter complete a briefing at Tan Son Nhut Air Base in South Vietnam and prepare to embark on a mission in November 1966.

Left: In August 1971, as part of President Richard Nixon's Vietnamization program, Americans from the 17th Special Operations Squadron at Phan Rang Air Base train South Vietnamese counterparts on the operation of the AC-119 gunship.

Right: The two streamers are the U.S. Marine Corps' versions of the Civil Actions Medal and the Gallantry Cross.

Opposite page, top: The Army Distinguished Service Order was bestowed for meritorious or heroic deeds related to wartime operations and was awarded for both combat and non-combat service. It was considered the equivalent of the Legion of Merit. The Staff Service Medal was awarded for staff service evidencing outstanding initiative and devotion to duty. The Technical Service Medal was awarded to military servicemen and civilians working as military technicians who showed outstanding professional capacity. The Training Service Medal was awarded to instructors at military schools and civilians who contributed significantly to training. The Armed Forces Honor Medal was awarded for contributions to the formation and organization of the RVN Armed Forces.

Opposite page, bottom: A lieutenant general of the 7th ARVN Army reads a commendation awarded to Major General Ellis W. Williams (center) of the 25th Infantry Division. Major General Harris W. Hollis (right) wears the National Order of Vietnam, the Gallantry Cross (with Palm), and the Armed Forces Honor Medal. He will take over command of the 25th Infantry Division from Major General Williams.

the French from Indochina.* At that time its equipment included Grumman F-8F Bearcat fighters, Cessna L-19 aircraft for reconnaissance, and C-47 and AAC-1 Toucan aircraft for transport. Beginning in 1960 the United States began supplying the Vietnamese Air Force with A-1 Skyraiders* and T-28Ds. The U.S. Air Force* began training Vietnamese pilots on jet aircraft—primarily Northrop F-5As (*see* F-5) in 1966, and early in 1967 established the 522d Squadron at Bien Hoa.* Eight Vietnamese Air Force squadrons were eventually established using F-5As or F-5Es. The squadrons also used A-37 Dragonflys. The A-1s were replaced by A-37s between 1967 and 1969.

Between 1969 and 1973 the Vietnamese Air Force was greatly expanded as part of Richard Nixon's* Vietnamization* process. By December 1972 there were 42,000 men and 49 squadrons in the Vietnamese Air Force. It had nearly 2,100 aircraft—primarily A-37 and F-5 squadrons; AC-47 and AC-119 gunships;* O-1 FAC aircraft; C-7, C-119, C-123, and C-130* transports; and UH-1* and CH-47* helicopters. The real weaknesses in the Vietnamese Air Force were lack of trained maintenance personnel, shortages of spare parts, and serious problems of morale.

Sources: Dong Van Kuyen, *The RVNAF*, 1980; Carl Berger, ed., *The United States Air Force in Southeast Asia, 1961–1973*, 1977; John S. Bowman, ed., *The Vietnam War Almanac*, 1985.

VIETNAMESE AWARDS

The U.S. Secretary of Defense granted a request for approval of foreign awards to U.S. military personnel on February 7, 1966. As a result, the Republic of Vietnam* designed medals, including the Vietnam Campaign Medal among numerous others, to be awarded to U.S. Armed Forces personnel by the government of the Republic of Vietnam beginning March 24, 1966.

The Vietnam Campaign Medal, established in 1966, was awarded to members of the U.S. Armed Forces who had served for six months in South Vietnam between 1965 and 1973 or who did not complete the length of service required but were wounded, captured, or killed in action. The Vietnam Campaign Medal was equivalent to the United States' Vietnam Service Medal and was the most commonly awarded Vietnamese decoration to foreigners.

The Republic of Vietnam Campaign Medal has a bar with the date "1960" followed by a dash and a blank space. The government of South Vietnam planned to post the beginning and ending date of the war, with the ending date indicating that South Vietnam triumphed over North Vietnam. However, because the South Vietnamese government fell, an ending date was never established.

Other frequently bestowed Vietnam awards include the Vietnam Civil Actions Medal and the Vietnam

NATIONAL ORDER
OF VIETNAM

ARMY DISTINGUISHED
SERVICE ORDER

STAFF SERVICE
MEDAL

TECHNICAL SERVICE
MEDAL

TRAINING SERVICE
MEDAL

GALLANTRY
CROSS

GALLANTRY CROSS
(WITH PALM)

ARMED FORCES
HONOR MEDAL

VIETNAM CAMPAIGN
MEDAL

CIVIL ACTIONS MEDAL
(FIRST CLASS)

Gallantry Cross, both of which were awarded extensively to both Vietnamese military service members and to the members of foreign militaries. The Vietnam Civil Actions Medal was a mid-level service award given for outstanding civic service to the state. The Vietnam Civil Actions unit citation was most often awarded to units of the U.S. Marine Corps that had participated in local police actions to suppress civil unrest in certain areas of South Vietnam.

The Gallantry Cross was awarded to any military personnel who had accomplished deeds of valor or displayed heroic conduct while fighting an enemy force. The Vietnam Gallantry Cross Unit Citation with Palm was issued to every allied nation that provided military support to Vietnam between March 1, 1961, and the fall of Saigon* in April 1975. The U.S. military began authorizing the Vietnam Gallantry Cross in March 1968 with retroactive presentation of the decoration to 1961. In 1974, the Vietnam Gallantry Cross unit citation was authorized to every military unit of the U.S. Army that had served under the Military Assistance Command from 1961 to 1974. This effectively granted the unit version of the award to any member of the U.S. Army who had served for any period of time in the Republic of Vietnam. Members of other services were not affected and still required individual or unit orders for the Vietnam Gallantry Cross Unit Citation to be awarded.

The highest honor that could be bestowed upon an individual by the Republic of Vietnam government was the National Order of Vietnam, a combined military-civilian decoration. It was awarded to any person who performed "grandiose works, remarkable deeds, exhibited bravery, or for those who have honored and served the country by lofty virtues and outstanding knowledge." During the Vietnam War, the National Order of Vietnam was bestowed on several members of the U.S. military, most of whom were senior military and political advisors to the South Vietnamese government. The decoration could also be awarded posthumously.

Sources: www.usamilitarymedals.com.

its training, but the defeat at Dien Bien Phu* in 1954 ended those plans. In 1955 the new leader of the Republic of Vietnam,* Ngo Dinh Diem,* took over the VNA, and it became the nucleus of the Army of the Republic of Vietnam.*

Sources: George C. Herring, *America's Longest War: The United States and Vietnam, 1950–1975*, 1986; Bernard Fall, *The Two Viet-Nams: A Political and Military Analysis*, 1963.

VIETNAMESE NATIONALIST PARTY

See Viet Nam Quoc Dan Dang

VIETNAMESE NATIONAL ARMY

During the late 1940s and early 1950s the Truman* administration urged the French to establish a Vietnamese army to assist them in fighting the Vietminh.* The French were reluctant to do so, but finally decided in 1950 to go ahead with the idea. Although they had a goal of 115,000 troops for the Vietnamese National Army (VNA), it totaled only 38,000 soldiers by the end of 1951. Plus the army was poorly trained and deeply infiltrated by the Vietminh. The Navarre Plan* of 1953 called for increasing the size of the VNA and improving

VIETNAM INDEPENDENCE LEAGUE

See Vietminh

VIETNAMIZATION

In 1969 the new U.S. president, Richard Nixon,* wanted to extricate the nation from the Vietnam quagmire. When

Right: A U.S. Air Force staff sergeant trains Sergeant Nguyen Van Heip on how to load a minigun with live ammunition aboard an AC-119 gunship at Phan Rang Air Base in South Vietnam in August 1971. The training is part of the Vietnamization program to transfer U.S. military equipment to South Vietnam.

Left: Two Vietnamese airmen examine the forward-looking infrared sensor system of a U.S. Air Force AC-119 gunship. Training them are members of the U.S. Air Force 17th Special Operations Squadron at Phan Rang Air Base in South Vietnam.

Hanoi* appeared unwilling to negotiate and when military analysts convinced him that there were few immediate levers to move the North Vietnamese to the peace table, Nixon turned to a three-prong policy: American troop withdrawal, consequently lowered draft* calls permitting creation of a lottery system, and—the key to the entire process—turning the ground fighting over to the Army of the Republic of Vietnam,* so-called Vietnamization, which became the basis for the Nixon Doctrine* that Asians, not Americans, should fight Asian wars.

The policy was not new. In the 1950s the French had their own policy of turning fighting over to native units, called jaunissement, or yellowing. And certainly the rationale for commitment of U.S. forces to the conflict in 1965 to 1968 had been, eventually, to use the breathing room to build an effective South Vietnamese Army and to turn the burden of combat on the ground over to it.

Still, the U.S. government pursued Vietnamization with great vigor, and by the end of 1970 the South Vietnamese Army was among the largest and best equipped in the world. In those cases in which their officers were competent and brave, the units were excellent and capable of holding the line. But the record was mixed. A larger army meant larger draft calls and severe dislocations in the Vietnamese economy. Desertion rates remained high. And the quality of officers remained uneven, sometimes excellent but all too often mediocre.

Vietnamization had three major tests. In 1971 Nixon ordered a hastily planned South Vietnamese invasion of Laos (*see* Lam Son 719); it went badly. In 1972 North Vietnam launched a strong offensive that crushed and routed many South Vietnamese units; only massive application of U.S. airpower managed to restore the balance. Then in March 1975 the North Vietnamese attacked with nearly twenty divisions and within two months had crushed the South. CD

Sources: Stanley Karnow, *Vietnam: A History*, 1983; George C. Herring, *America's Longest War: The United States in Vietnam, 1950–1975*, 1986; Nguyen Duy Hinh, *Vietnamization and Cease-Fire*, 1985.

VIETNAM LOBBY

See American Friends of Vietnam

VIET NAM QUOC DAN DANG

The Viet Nam Quoc Dan Dang, or Vietnamese Nationalist Party, was established in Canton, China, in 1925 to oppose Ho Chi Minh's* forces in Vietnam. In 1927 Nguyen Thai Hoc, a schoolteacher, secretly established a branch of the party in Hanoi.* Patterned after the Kuomintang in China, the Vietnamese Nationalist Party wanted to modernize Vietnam and expel the French. An unsuccessful uprising at Yen Bay, northwest of Hanoi, in 1930 severely hurt the party, and many of its members fled to Yunnan in southwest China. Although the Vietnamese Nationalist Party was generally inactive during the Ngo Dinh Diem* years, its leader then, Nguyen Tuong Tam, opposed Diem and called for the end of Buddhist suppression. Tam committed suicide in 1963. After the fall of Diem in November of that year, the Vietnamese Nationalist Party became a major force in South Vietnam, opposing Communism and calling for democratic socialism and an end to discrimination against Buddhists (*see* Buddhism). By the late 1960s there were four major factions in the Vietnamese Nationalist Party, the largest of which was centered in the Mekong Delta* with 95,000 members. Most of them were Buddhists led by Nguyen Hoa Hiep and Tran Van Tuyen. A second group of 50,000 was based in Quang Ngai Province as well as in the provinces of Quang Nam and Quang Tin. It was led by Nguyen Dinh Bach and Bui Hoanh, who was the political administrator of Quang Ngai Province. Buddhist militant Thich Tri Quang* was influential in this faction. A third group, numbering about 10,000 people, consisted of Roman Catholic refugees* from North Vietnam and was led by Le Hung. Another group had only 1,000 members, also influential among Roman Catholic refugees.

Sources: William J. Duiker, *The Rise of Nationalism in Vietnam, 1900–1941*, 1976; Harvey H. Smith et al., *Area Handbook for South Vietnam*, 1967.

VIETNAM REVOLUTIONARY LEAGUE

See Viet Nam Cach Menh Dong Minh Hoi

VIETNAM VETERANS AGAINST THE WAR

Vietnam Veterans Against the War (VVAW) was founded in 1967 after six veterans who marched together in an antiwar* demonstration decided that veterans needed their own antiwar organization. Its membership ultimately included several thousand veterans and a few government infiltrators. The VVAW participated in most major antiwar activities, including at the 1968 Democratic National Convention* in Chicago. Government officials saw VVAW from its inception as a special threat because Vietnam veterans had a unique credibility. Furthermore, officials feared the group's capacity for violence, though VVAW

demonstrations were always among the most peaceful and orderly. With Jane Fonda's* financial assistance, VVAW conducted the Detroit "Winter Soldier Investigation"* (February 1971), in which numerous veterans testified about "war crimes" that they either witnessed or perpetrated. Selected testimonies were published in The Winter Soldier Investigation (1972). Speaking at the hearings, prompted in part by VVAW outrage over the assertion that the My Lai* massacre was an aberration resulting from soldiers having "gone berserk," executive secretary Al Hubbard stated: "The crimes against humanity, the war itself, might not have occurred if we, all of us, had not been brought up in a country permeated with racism, obsessed with Communism, and convinced beyond a shadow of a doubt that we are good and most other countries are inherently evil." The government and its supporters denounced the proceedings and made several attempts to discredit the testimony given.

On April 19, 1971, the VVAW began "Dewey Canyon III." (Dewey Canyon* I and II were U.S. military operations in Laos.*) The campaign included more than 1,000 veterans, led by men in wheelchairs and mothers of men killed in combat, who held a memorial service at the Tomb of the Unknown Soldier, and then were refused permission to lay wreaths on graves of fallen comrades at Arlington Cemetery (though after much haggling 200 were permitted in to lay wreaths the next day). They camped on the mall

in defiance of a court order, which was rescinded after it was realized that it would be poor public relations to arrest peaceful combat veterans. On April 23, 1971, more than 1,000 veterans threw medals they had won in Vietnam over police barricades and onto the Capitol steps.

Subsequent activities included several protests in December 1971 of the heaviest bombing of North Vietnam since 1968, and demonstrations at the 1972 Republican convention in Miami, for which eight VVAW members (and two sympathizers) were tried on contrived criminal conspiracy charges. In July 1974 about 2,000 members demonstrated in Washington, demanding universal amnesty for draft* resisters and deserters, implementation of the Paris peace treaty, ending aid to Nguyen Van Thieu* and Lon Nol,* Richard Nixon's* impeachment, and a universal discharge with benefits for all Vietnam veterans.

In all its activities, the VVAW had an overriding goal: to make the nation realize, in the words of cofounder Jan Barry, "the moral agony of America's Vietnam War generation"—whether "to kill on military orders and be a criminal, or to refuse to kill and be a criminal." SF

Sources: Myra MacPherson, Long Time Passing: Vietnam and the Haunted Generation, 1984; Nancy Zaroulis and Gerald Sullivan, Who Spoke Up? American Protest Against the War in Vietnam, 1963–1975, 1985; Andrew E. Hunt, The Turning Point: A History of Vietnam Veterans Against the War, 2001.

Above: Antiwar protesters carry a banner, "Vietnam veterans against the war," outside the Democratic National Convention in Miami, Florida, in July 1972.

Right: The Vietnam War Memorial with names of U.S. military killed or missing in Vietnam, as photographed on August 12, 2003.

VIETNAM WAR MEMORIAL

After watching the film *The Deer Hunter** in 1979, Vietnam veteran Jan C. Scruggs first conceived of the idea for a Vietnam War Memorial. Scruggs had little success promoting the idea until the CBS Evening News did a prime-time spot on the campaign. Robert Doubek and John Wheeler, two attorneys in Washington, D.C., who were both veterans, heard about the spot and soon organized the Vietnam Veterans Memorial Fund to raise money and construct the memorial. With the assistance of Senator Charles Mathias Jr. of Maryland, they formed a National Sponsoring Committee that included Bob Hope, former president Gerald Ford,* Rosalynn Carter, Senator George McGovern,* and General William Westmoreland.* On April 30, 1980, the Senate unanimously approved a bill setting aside two acres on the mall near the Lincoln Memorial. The House approved the measure more than a month later, and on July 1, 1980, President Jimmy Carter signed the bill into law.

A national competition for memorial designs received 1,421 entries by the deadline of March 31, 1981, and the winner was Maya Lin, a Yale architecture student. Her proposal for a black-granite sculpture, rising out of the ground and then descending back again in angular form, with the names of more than 58,000 dead or missing American soldiers inscribed on it, soon raised a storm of protest. Some Vietnam veterans resented the fact that an Asian-American woman had designed it, while others thought it memorialized the shame of the war. Still, by January 4, 1982, more than 650,000 people had donated more than $5 million, and Secretary of the Interior James Watt issued a building permit following a compromise agreement to include a sculpture of three soldiers by Frederick Hart. Hart's sculpture was finished on September 20, 1982, and the entire memorial was dedicated on November 13, 1982. At that time a total of 58,022 names were inscribed on the memorial. In 1986 another 108 names were added, that of 95 servicemen killed on combat missions outside the formal war zone and 13 others who died of their wounds after leaving the war zone. RLS

Sources: Joel L. Swerdlow, "To Heal a Nation," *National Geographic* 167 (May 1985): 555–573; Jan C. Scruggs and Joel L. Swerdlow, *To Heal a Nation: The Vietnam Veterans Memorial*, 1985.

VOGT, JOHN W. JR.

John Vogt was born on March 19, 1920, in Elizabeth, New Jersey. An Army Air Corps pilot during World War II, Vogt rose through the ranks of the United States Air Force* officer corps during the 1950s, and between 1965 and 1968 served as deputy for plans and operations at the Pacific Air Force headquarters in Honolulu. Vogt took command of the Seventh Air Force* in 1972. As part of the American withdrawal from Vietnam, Vogt moved the Seventh Air Force out of Tan Son Nhut Air Base* to Thailand* in March 1973. He stepped down as commander of the Seventh Air Force in October 1973 to become commander in chief of the Pacific Air Force. John Vogt retired from the Air Force in 1975 after a stint as commander in chief of the United States Air Force in Europe.

Source: Harry G. Summers Jr., *Vietnam War Almanac*, 1985.

VO NGUYEN GIAP

Vo Nguyen Giap was born in 1912 in Quang Binh Province and studied in Hanoi* at the Lycée Albert Sarraut and at the University of Hanoi Law School. As a teenager Giap was politically active in the Revolutionary Party of New Vietnam, and in 1933 joined the Indochinese Communist Party (*see* Lao Dong Party). In 1939 he was forced into exile for his anti-French activities, and his wife died in 1941 in a French jail. By that time Giap was thoroughly familiar with the interests of Ho Chi Minh,* and in 1941 he helped Ho organize the Vietminh.* Between 1941 and 1945 Giap was active in the mountains of northern Tonkin* and southern China* putting together an army and harassing French and Japanese units. Ho Chi Minh promoted Giap to general and commander in chief of the Democratic Republic of Vietnam* in 1946.

As military leader of the Vietminh, Giap put together an army of nearly 300,000 revolutionary troops and militia, and in 1953 he launched a drive into Laos,* having already gained control of most of central and northern Vietnam outside the coastal lowland areas. The new French commander, Henri Navarre (*see* Navarre Plan), reversed himself and chose to commit 10,000 troops to an isolated plateau, Dien Bien Phu,* in northwest Vietnam, astride Giap's line of communications. Giap then reversed his own course, cut off the French, secretly brought artillery up into the surrounding mountains (a tactic the French considered impossible), massed 50,000 troops of his own, and established a siege of Dien Bien Phu. The French surrendered on May 7, 1954, and gave up their Indochinese empire.

Giap also led the military campaign against the United States and South Vietnam during the 1960s and 1970s. A believer in direct military confrontation as opposed to guerrilla action, Giap frequently orchestrated frontal attacks on U.S. positions, with disastrous results. The Tet Offensive* all but destroyed the Vietcong,* and forced North Vietnamese Army* troops to carry the burden of the war. Still, Tet had been a strategic victory even if a tactical defeat. In 1972 Giap planned and tried to implement the Eastertide Offensive,* assuming that with the United States all but out of South Vietnam, the country was ripe for attack. Throughout most of the country ARVN (*see*

Army of the Republic of Vietnam) troops held their positions, and, buttressed with massive B-52* strikes from the United States, they were able to regain all that they had lost in the initial stages of the offensive. The North Vietnamese suffered more than 100,000 casualties, and in the wake of the defeat Giap was replaced by his chief of staff, Van Tien Dung,* who led the final assault on South Vietnam in 1975. In 1980 Giap retired as minister of defense of the Socialist Republic of Vietnam.* CD

Sources: Vo Nguyen Giap, *Dien Bien Phu*, 1962, *Big Victory, Big Task*, 1967, and *Unforgettable Days*, 1978; G.H. Turley, *The Eastertide Offensive: Vietnam 1972*, 1985; *Who's Who in the Socialist Countries*, 1978; John W. Keegan, *Victory at Any Cost: The Genius of Vietnam's General Vo Nguyen Giap*, 2005.

VUNG TAU

Vung Tau, the fifth-largest city in South Vietnam with nearly 40,000 people, was also the southernmost major port facility in the country. Located in Phuc Tuy Province in III Corps,* Vung Tau was more than 400 miles south of Hue.* It was formerly known as Saint Jacques. The port at Vung Tau was the main support center for the southern area of South Vietnam, and was situated at the entrance to the Mekong River system leading into Saigon.* Vung Tau was also the support area for the Mobile Riverine Force.* Today Vung Tau, with its extensive beaches, is a popular tourist destination, and its estimated population had reached 240,000 in 2005.

Sources: Harvey H. Smith et al., *Area Handbook for South Vietnam*, 1967; Carroll H. Dunn, *Base Development in South Vietnam, 1965–1970*, 1972; Wikipedia: The Free Encyclopedia, 2005.

VU VAN MAU

Vu Van Mau was born in Hanoi* on July 25, 1914. He attended law school at Hanoi University and at the University of Paris and began practicing law in Hanoi in 1949. He became a professor of law at Hanoi University in 1950 and dean of the law school in 1954. After the division of Indochina* in 1954, Mau moved to the South and became minister of foreign affairs in the government of Ngo Dinh Diem.* In 1963 Vu Van Mau resigned in protest when Diem's police forces began attacking Buddhist strongholds. He even shaved his head in the fashion of Buddhist monks to protest the discrimination and persecution. After the fall of the Diem government, Mau returned to private law practice. Vu Van Mau settled in France in 1988; he died in Paris on August 20, 1998.

Sources: *Asia Who's Who*, 1960; *New Standard*, September 11, 1998.

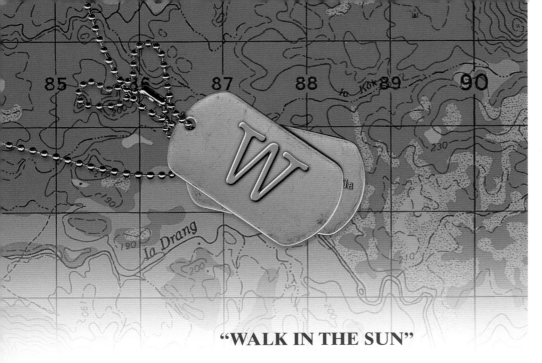

All of their senses were finely honed, so that reaction came instinctively. But such a high level of alert consumed enormous amounts of nervous energy. A "walk in the sun" provided a tremendous, if temporary, sense of relief from the omnipresent burden of intense vigilance. SF

Sources: Shelby L. Stanton, *Vietnam Order of Battle*, 1981; Al Santoli, *Everything We Had: An Oral History of the Vietnam War by Thirty-three American Soldiers Who Fought It*, 1981.

"WALK IN THE SUN"

"Walk in the sun" was a phrase soldiers used to denote some type of ground troop movement free of the risk of combat. These were rare, cherished events when troops could move freely without having to be constantly alert for ambush or booby traps.* The need to be constantly alert to every detail of the environment, to any aberration in the nature of the terrain or vegetation, to smells in the air, to any changes in the noise of the jungle—to a sudden quiet or the sound of startled animals or birds—had a grinding and exhausting effect on the men who stalked the jungles.

WALT, LEWIS

Lewis Walt was born on February 16, 1913, in Wabaunsee County, Kansas. He graduated from the Colorado School of Mines in 1936 and that summer accepted a commission as a lieutenant in the Marine Corps. Walt saw combat on Tulagi, Guadalcanal, New Britain, and Peleliu during World War II, and he served with the 5th Marines in Korea. He took command of the 3d Marine Division* in 1965 and led the III Marine Amphibious Force* in Vietnam. In 1967 Walt returned to the United States, and after a stint as assistant commandant of the U.S. Marine Corps,* he retired in 1971. Lewis Walt died on March 26, 1989.

Sources: Lewis W. Walt, *Strange War, Strange Strategy*, 1976; Edwin H. Simmons, "Marine Corps Operations in Vietnam: 1965–66, 1967, 1968, 1969–72," in *The Marines in Vietnam, 1954–1972*, 1974.

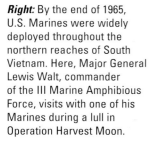

Right: By the end of 1965, U.S. Marines were widely deployed throughout the northern reaches of South Vietnam. Here, Major General Lewis Walt, commander of the III Marine Amphibious Force, visits with one of his Marines during a lull in Operation Harvest Moon.

WARNKE, PAUL CULLITON

A native of Webster, Massachusetts, Paul Warnke was born on January 31, 1920, and graduated from Yale in 1941 and the Columbia University Law School in 1948. Warnke practiced law in Washington, D.C., until 1966, when he was named general counsel for the Department of Defense. Between 1967 and 1969 he served as assistant secretary of defense for international security affairs. During those years Warnke came to be a vigorous opponent, within the Defense Department, of the Vietnam War. He was convinced that it was the wrong war in the wrong place, and that the United States would be unable to prevail. Warnke had great influence over Secretary of Defense Clark Clifford,* and General William Westmoreland* would later blame Warnke for converting Clifford from a hawk to a dove about Vietnam. Later, Warnke became one of Clifford's law partners. When Richard Nixon* won the election of 1968, Warnke found himself exiled with the rest of the Democrats; so he returned to private practice and continued to work on antiwar programs for the Democratic National Committee. Warnke returned to government service in 1977 during the Carter administration as director of the Arms Control and Disarmament Agency and as chief negotiator of the second Strategic Arms Limitation Treaty (SALT II). Warnke's appointment was quite controversial because of his open opposition to the Vietnam War and because he opposed deployment of the B-1 bomber and the Trident nuclear submarine. Although Warnke had no illusions about Soviet benevolence, he did believe that both the United States and the Soviet Union had the capacity to destroy each other many times over and that weapons reduction was essential to world peace. Warnke continued to work on the SALT II treaty until his resignation in October 1978. He also served for years as a member of the Council on Foreign Relations. Paul Warnke died on October 31, 2001.

Sources: *Current Biography*, 1977; Stanley Karnow, *Vietnam: A History*, 1983; Paul Warnke, "Apes on a Treadmill," *Foreign Policy* 18 (1975): 12–30; *New York Times*, November 1, 2001.

WAR OF ATTRITION

The primary, indeed the only, strategy the U.S. military pursued in Vietnam was that of "attrition," the wearing away of enemy forces to the point where they were either unable or unwilling to continue fighting. At that point victory would be achieved. Given this strategy, the goal was to find the most economical tactics—"economical" in maximizing enemy losses while minimizing allied losses. In pursuing this plan, a number of substrategies were tried and retried, giving rise to tactics like "enclaves,"* "oil spots," "search and destroy,"* "search and clear," "strategic hamlets,"* "new life hamlets,"* and "really new life hamlets." Pacification (see Rural Reconstruction) was given only lip service by the United States, as evidenced by the miniscule resources allocated for pacification compared with the resources allocated for military combat operations. General William Westmoreland* believed in attrition, pronouncing in 1967 that the "crossover" point had been reached—that the Vietcong* and North Vietnamese were now losing personnel faster than they could replace them. The Tet Offensive* of 1968 proved Westmoreland wrong but gave him a new basis for justification: Tet enemy losses were so great that the United States now had a stranglehold on enemy troop strength. He soon learned, however, that such a stranglehold did not really exist.

Eventually the strategy of attrition suffered from at least two serious flaws. First, U.S. military planners had not foreseen the enormous casualties that the North Vietnamese were willing to accept. American forces were highly effective in their mission of inflicting losses upon the enemy, but attrition alone was not sufficient to destroy North Vietnam's will to wage war. Second, the American military failed to take into consideration American public opinion; U.S. casualties proved to be unacceptable to the public. In retrospect, it can be argued that the most strategically decisive attrition figures were American rather than North Vietnamese. North Vietnam was able and willing to absorb extremely heavy military losses in pursuit of its objectives. American casualties, although a smaller percentage than North Vietnamese Army* losses, were nevertheless sufficient to cause the American public to question the wisdom of a distant war in an alien land. SF and SAK

Sources: Stanley Karnow, *Vietnam: A History*, 1983; John E. Mueller, "The Search for the 'Breaking Point' in Vietnam: The Statistics of a Deadly Quarrel," *International Studies Quarterly* 4 (December 1980): 497–519; Russell F. Weigley, *The American Way of War*, 1973; Harry G. Summers Jr., *On Strategy: A Critical Analysis of the Vietnam War*, 1982; Andrew F. Krepinevich Jr., *The Army and Vietnam*, 1986.

WAR POWERS RESOLUTION (1973)

By 1973 congressional reaction began to sharpen to the cumulative effect of having been ignored and deceived by the executive branch on the question of the Vietnam-Indochina* war. By midsummer there was ample evidence that the Nixon* administration had consistently and deliberately falsified statistics, data, and reports to Congress* to hide the extent of questionable activity in Vietnam, Cambodia,* and Laos.* Such revelations spurred Congress into belated action, and in July the House and Senate finally agreed on passage of a War Powers Resolution to restrain the president and reassert the authority of Congress over the power to make war, despite the opposition of administration loyalists in Congress and the threat of a presidential veto.

The measure did not apply to the war in Indochina, however, because the president and the Congress had already agreed to a date for the cutoff of funds there. But in the future, the bill required that the president must report to Congress within 48 hours if (a) he committed American forces to a foreign conflict, or (b) he "substantially" increased the number of combat troops in a foreign country. Unless Congress approved the president's action within 60 days, the commitment would have to be terminated. At the insistence of the Senate, however, a loophole was inserted allowing the deadline to be extended another 30 days if the president certified that more time was necessary to complete the safe evacuation of American forces. Congress could also order an immediate withdrawal within the 60- or 90-day period by passing a concurrent resolution, which was veto-proof.

President Richard M. Nixon* vetoed the War Powers Resolution, but after nine attempts both the House and the Senate voted to override the veto on November 7, 1973, and the measure became law. JMR Jr.

Sources: *Facts on File*, 1973; *United States Code: Congressional and Administrative News*, 93d Congress, 1st Session, 1973, pp. 2346–2366; *United States Statutes at Large*, 1973, vol. 87, 1974, pp. 555–559.

WAR RESISTERS LEAGUE

The War Resisters League (WRL), headquartered at 339 Lafayette Street, New York City, is "a secular pacifist organization that advocates Gandhian nonviolence to create a democratic society without war, racism, sexism, and exploitation." Members pledge that, "War is a crime against humanity. I therefore am determined not to support any kind of war, international or civil, and to strive for the removal of all the causes of war." WRL publishes a magazine called The Nonviolent Activist. WRL is also linked to a wider organization, War Resisters International. Founded in 1923 by Jessie Wallace Hughan as a secular counterpart to the Fellowship of Reconciliation, WRL played an important role in the antidraft, anti–war tax, and anti–Vietnam War protests of the 1960s and 1970s. As early as Lincoln's birthday in 1947, WRL had helped to sponsor demonstrations around the United States in which some 400–500 men destroyed their draft cards or mailed them to President Harry Truman.* Dwight Macdonald spoke on behalf of WRL at a New York rally at which 63 men burned their draft cards. Under attack during the McCarthy era, WRL was supported by such notable figures as Albert Einstein, who wrote in 1953: "The War Resisters League is important because ... The existence of such a moral elite is indispensa-

ble for the preparation of a fundamental change in public opinion, a change that, under present day circumstances, is absolutely necessary if humanity is to survive."

In the late 1950s and early 1960s, WRL actively supported ban-the-bomb demonstrations, civil disobedience against civil-defense drills, and civil rights protests. By 1963, under the leadership of Dave Dellinger* and David McReynolds, WRL focused its protests on the escalation of the Vietnam War and the rise in Selective Service inductions. Dave Dellinger and A.J. Muste* edited *Liberation*, an influential, radical magazine initially supported by WRL and published from 1956 to 1975. On May 16, 1964, WRL cosponsored a demonstration in New York City at which twelve men burned their draft* cards. In December 1964, WRL cosponsored the first nationwide demonstration against the Vietnam War. According to WRL, its membership grew from 3,000 to 15,000 between 1964 and 1973. From 1965 through 1983, WRL's Workshop in Nonviolence published a widely read "movement" magazine called WIN. WRL was the major organizer of Stop the Draft Week in late 1967 as well as a cosponsor or endorser of many "teach-ins"* and demonstrations, including the May Day demonstrations of 1971. WRL organized draft-counseling networks to assist young men who wished to obtain conscientious objector status, refuse registration or induction, or flee into exile. WRL also spearheaded a major campaign to promote refusal of payment of income taxes and of a federal tax on telephone charges levied to raise revenue for the Vietnam War. On April 18, 1974, the Internal Revenue Service seized $2,537.43 in taxes not paid by WRL employees during 1969 to 1971. Similar IRS seizures have occurred periodically since then. Since the Vietnam War, WRL has remained active in promoting nonviolent action and in opposing subsequent wars in Central America, Iraq, and elsewhere. WRL announced its disapproval of the Soviet invasion of Afghanistan in 1979 to 1980 and strongly protested the Israeli invasions of Lebanon in 1982 and 2006. JK

Sources: Thomas Powers, *Vietnam: The War at Home*, 1984; Pauline Maier, *The Old Revolutionaries*, 1980; Nancy Zaroulis and Gerald Sullivan, *Who Spoke Up? American Protest Against the War in Vietnam, 1963–1975*, 1984; Judith Pasternak, *War Resisters League Board*, 2006.

WARS OF NATIONAL LIBERATION

On January 6, 1961, Soviet premier Nikita Khrushchev* delivered a speech in Moscow in which he predicted that the world was moving toward socialism and that "wars of national liberation" were the primary vehicle of that movement. Furthermore, he pledged Soviet support for indigenous rebellions to overthrow fascists and capitalists.

President John F. Kennedy* interpreted the speech as a formal statement of the Soviet Union's* intention to use surrogate forces to promote its interests rather than to engage in direct engagements with the United States. Kennedy saw the Communist movements in Latin America, Africa, and Southeast Asia as part of that larger Soviet strategy, and he devised new counterinsurgency* strategies to oppose them. Vietnam became the test case for Kennedy's counterinsurgency program to thwart a war of national liberation.

Sources: Bruce Miroff, *Pragmatic Illusions: The Presidential Politics of John F. Kennedy*, 1976; Bower J. Bell, *The Myth of the Guerrilla*, 1971.

WAR ZONE C

The term "War Zone C" was used by the United States Army* to describe a region near the Cambodian border in III Corps* where Vietcong* activity was particularly strong. War Zone C included portions of Tay Ninh, Binh Long, and Binh Duong provinces.

Sources: Bernard William Rogers, *Cedar Falls–Junction City: A Turning Point*, 1974; Andrew F. Krepinevich Jr., *The Army and Vietnam*, 1986.

WAR ZONE D

See Iron Triangle

"WASTED"

Many people, especially combat soldiers, came to see the entire U.S. effort and the resulting loss of life in Vietnam as a waste. "Wasted," which referred to killing people, evolved from this sentiment. A soldier who killed an enemy soldier in combat might describe the incident in colorful, profane language by saying he "wasted the — —"* (expletive deleted) with his M16* or M79.* "Wasted" might also be used to describe the mercy killing of a wounded soldier, either enemy or allied, who was obviously mortally wounded, or the summary execution of a prisoner of war.* The term is most frequently associated, however, with what is considered to be an unnecessary killing—the accidental or intentional killing of civilian noncombatants or the killing of another soldier. SF

Sources: Thomas D. Boettcher, *Vietnam: The Valor and the Sorrow*, 1985; Vietnam Veterans Against the War, *The Winter Soldier Investigation: An Inquiry into American War Crimes*, 1972.

Left: In 1966, during Operation Sioux City, paratroopers from the 173d Airborne Brigade take a break in War Zone D to read *Stars and Stripes* and catch up on military and world news. They have just completed two days of patrols.

WATER BUFFALO

The water buffalo was the most important domesticated animal in the Vietnamese economy. Throughout all of Vietnam there were more than 2 million water buffalos, most of which were used as draft animals by Vietnamese farmers.

Source: Danny J. Whitfield, *Historical and Cultural Dictionary of Vietnam*, 1976.

WATERGATE

On June 22, 1972, Washington, D.C., police caught several men attempting to wiretap Democratic Party National Headquarters in the Watergate Building. At their arraignment the next morning, one of the burglars, James McCord, revealed that he had worked for the Central Intelligence Agency* and was currently working for the Richard Nixon* reelection campaign. Under the impact of extraordinary investigative reporting by people like Bob Woodward and Carl Bernstein of the *Washington Post* and Seymour Hersh of the *New York Times* during 1973 and early 1974, as well as a Senate investigating committee, it became clear that the highest officials in the Nixon administration had orchestrated a series of illegal and unethical campaign programs, and that the president himself had ordered a cover-up of the entire affair. Eventually the House Judiciary Committee voted two articles of impeachment against Richard Nixon, on charges of obstructing justice and abuse of power, and the Supreme Court voted 8 to 0 that Nixon turn over key tapes to the Watergate special prosecutor, Leon Jaworski. Richard Nixon resigned the presidency on August 9, 1974, as the revelations over Watergate totally eliminated the president's credibility as well as his capacity to act directly in matters of foreign policy. U.S. troops had all been removed from South Vietnam by the time the Watergate crisis erupted, and the Nixon administration was politically unable to marshal any resources to sustain the Republic of Vietnam* against North Vietnamese attack. CD

Sources: Henry Kissinger, *White House Years*, 1979; Theodore H. White, *Breach of Faith*, 1976.

WEST GERMANY

West Germany, long conceded to be America's strongest ally in Europe, next only to Great Britain,* had little to do with Vietnam. Officially, West Germany supported the anti-Communist policy in South Vietnam, but privately German leaders had serious reservations about the American commitment there. More important is the question of the impact of Vietnam on West Germany. The American preoccupation with Vietnam drew attention away from Europe, and, by default, West Germany assumed a much more significant role in NATO. There is also some evidence that Soviet restraint in Vietnam was tacitly bought by U.S. assurances of preventing West Germany from gaining joint nuclear control over weapons stationed on its soil. The denouement of the war contributed to a decline in American prestige in Europe and to a more independent stance by western European nations. West Germany's increasing trade and political contacts with eastern bloc countries attested to its new independence. GMB

Sources: Viola Herms Drath, ed., *Germany in World Politics*, 1979; Wolfram Hanreider, *The Stable Crisis: Two Decades of German Foreign Policy*, 1970; Terence Prittie, *Willy Brandt: Portrait of a Statesman*, 1974.

WESTMORELAND, WILLIAM CHILDS

William C. Westmoreland was born on March 26, 1914, in Spartanburg County, South Carolina, to a distinguished family. He entered the United States Military Academy in 1932 and graduated in 1936 as First Captain (the senior

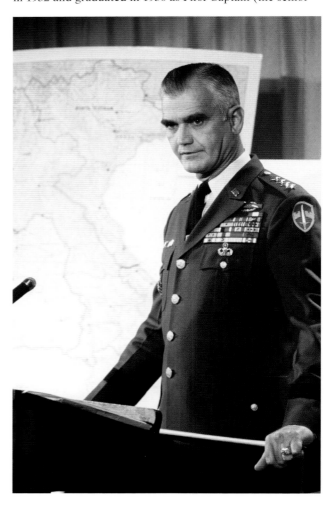

Right: General William Westmoreland, in the United States to address a joint session of Congress, convenes a briefing for journalists in the Pentagon on November 22, 1967. Westmoreland had just received a report from his deputy field commander that the allied situation in the Dak To area was "in excellent hands" and morale was high. Based on the report, Westmoreland commented that the bloody battle in the Central Highlands of Vietnam "is the beginning of the great defeat for the enemy," but those words would soon haunt him.

cadet in the corps). During World War II, Westmoreland served in North Africa, Sicily, France, and Germany, and during the Korean War he commanded the 187th Airborne Infantry Regimental Combat Team. Before his appointment in 1964 as Military Assistance Command, Vietnam* (MACV) commander, Westmoreland had commanded the 101st Airborne Division* and served a stint as superintendent of West Point. As MACV commander, he decided to seek a holding action combined with spoiling attacks to prevent a major enemy offensive, while the United States constructed the necessary logistical infrastructure to support a larger military force in the South. Later, as that force became larger, Westmoreland turned to a strategy of attrition. He sent U.S. and ARVN (*see* Army of the Republic of Vietnam) forces on "search and destroy"* missions, sometimes with success, sometimes without, seeking to kill, wound, capture, or cause to desert more enemy troops than the enemy could resupply. With the enormous firepower of the American military, Westmoreland thought that his war of attrition* was succeeding by the end of 1967.

The Communist Tet Offensive* of 1968 proved to be Westmoreland's downfall. The massive attack on South Vietnam's urban areas seemingly belied his claims of approaching victory. Although American and ARVN forces all but annihilated the Vietcong,* the Tet Offensive was a strategic victory for the Communists because the American public, forced to choose between Westmoreland's positive analysis of the outcome and the media's view of the strength of the attack, moved decidedly against the war. Creighton Abrams* replaced Westmoreland as MACV commander in July 1968. After serving as Army chief of staff during the Nixon* administration, Westmoreland retired from active duty in 1972. He flirted with South Carolina and national politics in the late 1970s, but the Vietnam War proved to be too much of an albatross.

Westmoreland was back in American headlines in 1982 when the CBS News documentary *The Uncounted Enemy: A Vietnam Deception* accused him of manipulating data on enemy troop strength in 1967 to paint a brighter picture of the military situation in South Vietnam. In response Westmoreland filed a libel suit against CBS, but an out-of-court settlement in 1985 ended the issue without any payments by either party. William C. Westmoreland died on July 18, 2005. CD

Sources: William C. Westmoreland, *A Soldier Reports*, 1976; David Halberstam, *The Best and the Brightest*, 1972; Andrew F. Krepinevich Jr., *The Army in Vietnam*, 1986; Larry E. Cable, *Conflict of Myths: The Development of American Counterinsurgency Doctrine and the Vietnam War*, 1986; *New York Times*, July 19, 2005.

Right: Actor Mel Gibson in a scene from the 2002 film *We Were Soldiers*, a depiction of the Battle of the Ia Drang Valley in 1965. Gibson plays Lieutenant Colonel Harold G. Moore. Standing behind him is Sam Elliott, who plays Sergeant Major Basil Plumley.

WE WERE SOLDIERS

Based on Harold G. Moore and Joseph L. Galloway's 1992 book *We Were Soldiers Once … And Young: Ia Drang— The Battle That Changed the War in Vietnam*, the film *We Were Soldiers* was released in 2002. It starred Mel Gibson as Lieutenant Colonel Harold G. Moore, commander of the 1st Battalion, 7th Cavalry, and follows him and his men during the Battle of the Ia Drang Valley* from October 23 to November 26, 1965. The battle represented the first major engagement of the Vietnam War between regular U.S. ground troops and main force Vietcong* troops. In the genre of Vietnam War films, *We Were Soldiers* clearly reflects post–Gulf War American attitudes toward the military. Unlike earlier films like *Coming Home*, *Apocalypse Now*, and *The Deer Hunter* (*see Rambo and Other Vietnam Films*), in which Americans are portrayed as ruthless killers and hapless victims of the conflict, *We Were Soldiers* is populated with ordinary people, from ordinary families, caught up in a war that had no nobility beyond the camaraderie of men in combat and love of country even under the most difficult of circumstances. The Vietcong troops are portrayed in the same light, as human beings fighting for their country. When the troops of the 1st Battalion come home after Ia Drang, they return to their communities as heroes—good men who served when their country called.

Source: Harold G. Moore and Joseph L. Galloway, *We Were Soldiers Once … And Young: Ia Drang—The Battle That Changed the War in Vietnam*, 1992.

WEYAND, FREDERICK CARLTON

Frederick C. Weyand was born on September 15, 1916, in Arbuckle, California. He graduated from the University of California at Berkeley in 1939 and joined the Army, serving in the Burma area during World War II and as an infantry officer in Korea. In 1966 Weyand took command of the 25th Infantry Division,* and early in 1967 he became head of II Field Force, Vietnam.* Weyand left Vietnam in 1968, spent some time as a military advisor to the Paris peace negotiations in 1969, and in 1970 returned to Vietnam as Military Assistance Command, Vietnam* (MACV) deputy commander. In June 1972 he replaced General Creighton Abrams* as MACV commander and presided over the American withdrawal from South Vietnam. Weyand became Army chief of staff in 1974 and retired from active duty in 1976.

Sources: Frederick Weyand, "Vietnam Myths and American Military Realities," *Commanders Call*, July/August 1976; Clark Dougan and David Fulghum, *The Vietnam Experience: The Fall of the South*, 1985.

WHEELER, EARLE GILMORE

A former chairman of the Joint Chiefs of Staff (*see* Chairman, JCS), Earle Wheeler was born on January 13, 1908, and after high school decided to attend West Point, graduating in 1932. Between 1932 and 1936 he was the company officer with the 29th Infantry. He then saw service in Tientsin, China, from 1937 through 1938. During the first half of World War II, Wheeler trained new divisions that eventually saw action in the European theater. In 1944 he was reassigned in Europe, where he saw service in logistics. After World War II he was posted to the National War College, and by 1962 was a full general. In that same year he became deputy chief of the U.S. European Command and then Army chief of staff. In 1964 Earle Wheeler was appointed chairman of the Joint Chiefs of Staff.

After U.S. warships were attacked in the Gulf of Tonkin in 1964, Wheeler began to press President Lyndon Johnson* for drastic measures. Wheeler was particularly alarmed at the deterioration of the Saigon* regime after Ngo Dinh Diem's* ouster and subsequent assassination. The chairman received reports, from Pentagon and Central Intelligence Agency* officials, which indicated that the collapse of the South Vietnamese regime might result in a complete Communist takeover of Southeast Asia—the domino theory.* By 1965, along with other administration officials, Wheeler was urging direct U.S. intervention in South Vietnam, and as the U.S. presence grew in Vietnam, he supported U.S. ground forces engaging the enemy in the field. The chairman had good relations with Congress,* especially with Senators John Stennis* and Henry Jackson.

By early 1967 the U.S. commitment to Vietnam had grown to massive proportions. The American public began to sour on the war as casualties mounted, and the U.S. media televised in gruesome and realistic detail the ferocity of the conflict. Congress began to reassess its commitment to the war, and members of Johnson's administration also questioned the rationale for the continuing involvement in Vietnam. In the summer of 1967, President Johnson held a special meeting to assess the Vietnam War. In that meeting Johnson asked Wheeler when would the United States succeed and what would be the ultimate troop commitment to achieve that victory. To both questions Wheeler replied with a request for additional manpower and a call-up of the reserves. Johnson and his White House aides were shocked. While William Westmoreland* portrayed optimism, General Wheeler had presented them with a protracted war with no end in sight. President Johnson decided not to run for reelection and offered overtures for de-escalation.

President Richard Nixon* came into office in 1969 pledged to "peace with honor" in Vietnam. Melvin Laird* with Wheeler began the process of Vietnamization.* General Wheeler, however, believed in slow disengagement to give the South Vietnamese armed forces enough time to adjust to the transition. In 1970 Wheeler successfully lobbied Nixon for incursions of U.S. combat forces into Cambodia (*see* Operation Binh Tay) to destroy North Vietnamese sanctuaries.* He told Nixon that if these actions were successful, the South Vietnamese would be able to take over the war faster. Earle Wheeler retired in 1970; he died in December 1975. JSL

Sources: *Current Biography*, November 1965; Stanley Karnow, *Vietnam: A History*, 1983; *New York Times*, December 19, 1975.

WHITE HORSE DIVISION

Throughout the Vietnamese conflict, the South Koreans maintained a substantial commitment in support of the U.S. military effort. The "White Horse Division" was the nickname of the Republic of Korea's 9th Infantry Division. The 9th was in Vietnam between September 27, 1966, and March 16, 1973, and was headquartered in Ninh Hoa.

Source: Shelby L. Stanton, *Vietnam Order of Battle*, 1981.

WHITE STAR MOBILE TRAINING TEAM

In July 1959, President Dwight D. Eisenhower* authorized the use of U.S. Special Forces* groups, known as White Star Mobile Training Teams, to help train the Laotian Army. Between 1959 and 1962, when they were withdrawn after the negotiated settlement with the Pathet Lao,* the teams worked with both the Laotian Army and Hmong* tribal groups in Laos,* trying to assist them in resisting the guerrilla tactics of the Pathet Lao. At its peak in 1962, the program had more than 500 American soldiers working in Laos.

Sources: Charles A. Stevenson, *The End of Nowhere: American Policy Toward Laos Since 1954*, 1973; John Prados, *Presidents' Secret Wars: CIA and Pentagon Covert Operations Since World War II*, 1986.

WHY ARE WE IN VIETNAM?

Why Are We in Vietnam? is the title of Norman Mailer's 1967 novel. Although the novel's setting is Texas, New York City, and the Brooks Range of Alaska, it is an antiwar story without ever being directly set in Vietnam. A cast of characters—D.J. Jellicoe, Rusty Jellicoe, Alice Lee Jellicoe, Medium Asshole Pete, Medium Asshole Bill, and Tex Hude—end up in the Brooks Range of Alaska on a hunting trip. There, in a pristine and naturally savage environment, they use all the hunting technology they can muster and literally slaughter wolves, caribou, bighorn sheep, and bears. The carnage is extraordinary and, in Norman Mailer's mind, symbolic of what American military technology was doing to the life and habitat of Southeast Asia.

Sources: Norman Mailer, *Why Are We in Vietnam?*, 1967; Philip D. Beidler, *American Literature and the Experience of Vietnam*, 1982.

Above: General Earle Wheeler was a primary architect of U.S. military policy in Vietnam during the early 1960s. He was convinced that the U.S. could win the war militarily. Here he is on January 25, 1968, just days before the onset of the Tet Offensive. At the time, he was serving as chairman of the Joint Chiefs of Staff.

Right, inset: Members of the 354th Tactical Fighter Squadron, the first Wild Weasel pilots, stationed at Takhli Royal Thailand Base, Thailand, in July 1966. Of the sixteen men, four would be killed in action, two would be taken as prisoners of war, and three would be wounded in action.

Right: Three camouflaged U.S. Air Force F-105 Thunderchiefs, called Thuds, on a mission in May 1966. Armed with 2.75in. white phosphorous rockets and AGM-45 Shrike antiradar missiles, they are en route to targets in North Vietnam.

WILD WEASEL

The term "Wild Weasel" referred to a new weapons system for tactical fighter aircraft. "Weasel" was used to describe the system's ability to ferret out and destroy enemy surface-to-air missiles (SAMs)* and antiaircraft installations. Usually, the Weasel was an F-105* equipped with electronic devices capable of tuning in on SAM radar beams. While other aircraft attacked the designated enemy targets, the Wild Weasels went after the SAM and antiaircraft installations. While the aircraft and technology have changed, the Wild Weasel mission has essentially remained the same in the modern U.S. Air Force.

Sources: Dewey Waddell and Norm Wood, eds., *Air Power—Vietnam*, 1978; William Momyer, *Air Power in Three Wars*, 1978.

WILLIAMS, SAMUEL T.

Lieutenant General Samuel T. Williams was chief of the U.S. Army Military Assistance and Advisory Group* (MAAG), Vietnam, from October 1955 to August 1960. He enlisted in the Texas National Guard as a private in 1916 and was commissioned a second lieutenant, infantry, in 1917. He served as a platoon and company commander in World War I and was decorated several times for valor. In World War II he commanded an infantry regiment and was an assistant division commander in the Normandy invasion. During the Korean War he commanded the 25th Infantry Division and was deputy commander of a Korean Army Corps. He was commanding general of the Fourth Army at the time of his selection as chief of MAAG, Vietnam.

Known within the Army as Hanging Sam, Williams was a sharp-tongued commander who demanded strict discipline and maximum effort from his subordinates. His no-nonsense style appealed to Ngo Dinh Diem,* and Williams established a good relationship with the South Vietnamese president. Like most American officers of his generation, he thought in terms of conventional, not guerrilla, warfare. He organized and equipped the South Vietnamese Army to protect the South from invasion from the North and to provide internal security against essentially conventional tactics. Even when Diem's government began to experience increasing attacks by guerrilla forces in 1960, Williams tended to view this insurgency as a diversionary move by the regime's enemies in Hanoi.* He retired in 1960 after forty-three years of active service and settled in San Antonio, Texas, where he continued to write and speak on military topics. DLA

Source: Ronald H. Spector, *Advice and Support: The Early Years, 1941–1960*, 1983; Harold S. Meyer, *Hanging Sam: A Military Biography of General Samuel T. Williams: From Pancho Villa to Vietnam*, 1990.

WING

"Wing" is a term describing a unit of up to 500 aircraft in the U.S. Marine Corps,* commanded by a major general. In the U.S. Air Force* and Navy,* a wing is a smaller organizational institution. A naval air wing is commanded by a captain and consists of approximately 75 aircraft, usually in the form of two fighter squadrons,* four attack squadrons, and reconnaissance aircraft. An Air Force wing is under the command of a colonel and consists of three squadrons of 25 aircraft each, as well as a wing headquarters and supply and engineering squadrons.

Source: Harry G. Summers Jr., *Vietnam War Almanac*, 1985.

WINTER SOLDIER INVESTIGATION

Late in 1969, as the revelation of the My Lai* atrocities caused intense public debate over the nature of the war in Vietnam, the Vietnam Veterans Against the War* (VVAW) wanted to make it clear that My Lai was by no means the only example of war crimes committed there. The American public had been conditioned by the brutality of the Nazis and the Japanese during World War II, and the "brainwashing" of the North Koreans, to assume that only other countries committed war crimes. Between January 31 and February 2, 1971, VVAW convened the "Winter Soldier Investigation" in Detroit. For three days 116 veterans testified of war crimes they had either committed or witnessed. There were also panel

discussions on weaponry, medical care, prisoners, racism, the ecological devastation of Vietnam, and the psychological effects of the war on American soldiers.

Source: Vietnam Veterans Against the War, *The Winter Soldier Investigation*, 1972.

"WISE OLD MEN"

"Wise Old Men" was used in the last days of the Lyndon B. Johnson* administration to describe a group of experienced American diplomats and former public officials who advised the president on the Vietnam War. The group included W. Averell Harriman,* Dean Acheson,* Paul Nitze,* George Kennan,* John McCloy, Robert Lovett, and Charles Bohlen, all of whom had a lifetime of experience in European affairs but knew little about Vietnam. Among some antiwar liberals, the term "Wise Old Men," or "WOMs," was a derisive name for establishment liberals who had caused the war. But early in 1968 the Wise Old Men began to turn against the war, and in a dramatic meeting on March 25, 1968, they advised Johnson to end the conflict. Less than a week later Johnson announced his decision not to seek reelection.

Source: Walter Isaacson and Evan Thomas, *The Wise Men: Six Friends and the World They Made*, 1986.

WITHDRAWAL

In April 1969, just three months after Richard Nixon* took office as president, U.S. troop strength in Vietnam reached its peak of 543,000. He had promised a disengagement from South Vietnam when he was campaigning for president in 1968, and during a visit to Vietnam in July 1969 Nixon ordered General Creighton Abrams,* commander of American military forces, to reduce U.S. casualties and initiate Vietnamization*—turning the war over to South Vietnamese military forces. Abrams then developed a fourteen-stage withdrawal process, designed to begin in August 1969 and end in November 1972. By January 1970 troop strength had dropped to 473,000 as Abrams saw to the removal of U.S. Marines* first along with some of the Army infantry divisions. Troop levels steadily declined, to 404,000 in July 1970, 336,000 in January 1971, 225,000 in July 1971, 133,200 in January 1972, and 45,600 in July 1972. The last of the combat troops, the 3d Battalion of the 21st Infantry, left South Vietnam in August 1972. The final withdrawal of all American troops took place in March 1973, except for a handful of soldiers left with the Defense Attaché Office.*

Sources: Shelby L. Stanton, *Vietnam Order of Battle*, 1981; Guenter Lewy, *America in Vietnam*, 1978.

Right: Three U.S. Army nurses at a field hospital at Nha Trang, north of the U.S. naval base at Cam Ranh Bay, on July 15, 1965.

AMERICAN WOMEN IN VIETNAM

The Pentagon estimates that approximately 11,000 military women deployed to Vietnam during the war. Most were nurses who served in all branches except theMarine Corps. Air Force nurses went through two months of flight school and two more weeks with their own instructor after they arrived in Vietnam. Most Air Force nurses worked the evacuation flights of wounded military personnel to Japan, Okinawa, Hawaii, the Philippines, and the United States. As many as 150 received orders to serve on ground bases in Vietnam. U.S. Navy nurses were required to have two years of military nursing experience before heading to Vietnam. Navy nurses spent their tour at the Da Nang Navy Hospital or aboard the USS *Repose* or the USS *Sanctuary*, hospital ships on the South China Sea. Army nurses spent eight to ten weeks in training at Fort Sam Houston before deployment.

Army nurses began arriving in Vietnam in the spring of 1965 when President Lyndon B. Johnson sent regular U.S. ground troops to Vietnam. The 3d Medical Field Hospital deployed to Ton Son Nhut Air Base in April 1965, and the 58th Medical Battalion reached Long Binh in May. In July the 9th Field Hospital arrived in Nha Trang. One month later, so did the 85th Evacuation Hospital. The 43d Medical Group and the 523d Field Hospital arrived in September, and the 1st Medical Battalion, 2d Surgical Hospital, 51st Field Hospital, and 93d Evacuation Hospital arrived in November. Eventually, the Army sent forty-seven medical units to Vietnam.

Nursing was often the most emotionally hazardous duty of the war. For the course of a year, day after day,

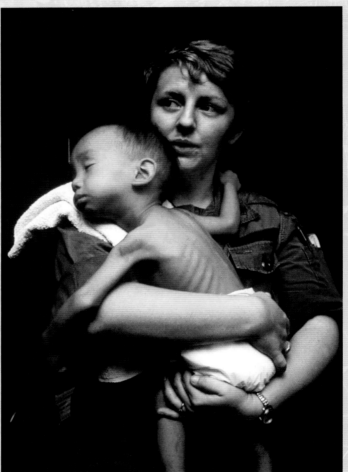

nurses found themselves exposed to human suffering at its most malignant. Frequently they encountered young men with massive, almost unbelievable wounds. The combination of helicopters and field hospitals allowed many soldiers to survive wounds that in any previous war would have been fatal. In her 1987 book *In the Combat Zone*, Kathryn Marshall recounts a nurse describing soldiers hit by napalm and phosphorous bombs. Some "burn victims were essentially denuded," she said. "We used to talk about fourth-degree burns—you know, burns are labeled first, second, and third degree, but we had people who were burnt all the way through." Another nurse remembered wounds so large "you could put both of your hands in them." She also remembered wounds so horrific they transcended existing medical terminology. "Horriblectomies were when they'd had so much taken out or removed. Horridzoma meant the initial grotesque but also the repercussions of the injury." Another nurse had recalled "the screams of teenaged boys whose bodies had been blown to bits, moaning for their mothers, begging for relief, praying for death. Pretty soon it just became another day's work for me. Otherwise I would have gone nuts."

Military women served in a variety of other capacities. Assigned to the Women's Army Corps (WAC), they became secretaries and clerks at MACV or worked in logistics. Some served in the Signal Corps. Army women could also be found working as air traffic controllers, intelligence officers, decoders, and cartographers. For the most part, their duties kept them confined to Saigon and the surrounding region. When necessary, WACs also

Right: During the Vietnam War, U.S. military nurses cared for sick and wounded American soldiers, sailors, Marines, and airmen, but they also invested considerable time and energy in the care of South Vietnamese civilians who had been wounded or displaced by the war. In this photograph, a U.S. nurse cares for an emaciated South Vietnamese child.

volunteered in local hospitals and orphanages. Worried that the Vietcong might target the women, the Army kept them carefully protected. Eight military women were killed in Vietnam, but only one—First Lieutenant Sharon Ann Lane—died as a result of enemy fire. The other seven died in automobile, helicopter, and plane crashes.

Thousands of civilian women volunteered to work in Vietnam. The American Red Cross employed 1,120 women in-country during the war. Many educated women without nursing credentials worked for Supplemental Recreation Activities Overseas (SRAO), helping soldiers. So-called Donut Dollies, on missions to maintain troop morale, managed clubs or visited troops in the field, serving an estimated 280,500 soldiers during the war. Other civilian women staffed the twenty-two USO clubs in Vietnam. A variety of religious groups—American Friends Service Committee, Mennonite Central Committee, and Catholic Relief Services—sent missionaries and volunteers to work with the South Vietnamese in health and education programs. Hundreds of women worked for such civilian contractors as Bechtel, Brown and Root, and Martin Marietta, supplying goods and services in Vietnam to the military. Finally, approximately 80 female journalists reported from Vietnam during the war. In all, more than 50,000 women served in civilian and military capacities.

When they returned from Vietnam, women faced unique challenges. Many nurses had worked sixteen-hour shifts routinely, and during the busiest times performed services usually reserved for physicians. As military officers they enjoyed a level of respect and deference unknown in civilian life. Upon resuming work in civilian hospitals, many found themselves bored and resentful of the condescending attitudes of local physicians. They had witnessed horrific suffering, and many experienced post-traumatic stress syndrome (PTSS), but the Veterans Administration virtually ignored them, providing support groups for troubled male soldiers but not for women. Many women also suffered PTSS from sexual harassment and sexual assault in Vietnam. Unfortunately, the Veterans Administration still did little for them.

Women veterans suffered that anonymity for a number of years, but as their anger mounted, especially over the absence of VA services aimed at women, they organized. Nurse veterans formed the Women's Veterans Project within the Vietnam Veterans of America and lobbied for VA health, educational, and financial benefits. They also found hope in the drive to establish a memorial in Washington, D.C., for women veterans. Former Army nurse Dian Carlson Evans served in Vietnam from 1968 to 1969, and her idea for a women's memorial germinated in 1983. She struggled for years to secure the necessary congressional approval and to raise $2.5 million. By 1991 she had the money and the authorization, and Glenna Goodacre received a commission to design the memorial. Goodacre produced a larger-than-life bronze sculpture of three women cradling a wounded GI. The more than 10,000 women nurses had treated more than 153,000 wounded soldiers. The memorial was unveiled and dedicated on Veterans Day in 1993.

Sources: Kathryn Marshall, *In the Combat Zone: An Oral History of American Women in Vietnam, 1966–1975*, 1987; June A. Willenz, *Women Veterans: America's Forgotten Heroines*, 1984; Lynda Van Devanter and Christopher Morgan, *Home Before Morning*, 1983; Olga Gruzit-Hoyt, *A Time Remembered: American Women in the Vietnam War*, 1999; Diane Canwell and Jon Sutherland, *American Women in the Vietnam War*, 2005; Stephanie Salazar, "American Women in Vietnam," unpublished manuscript, Department of History, Sam Houston State University.

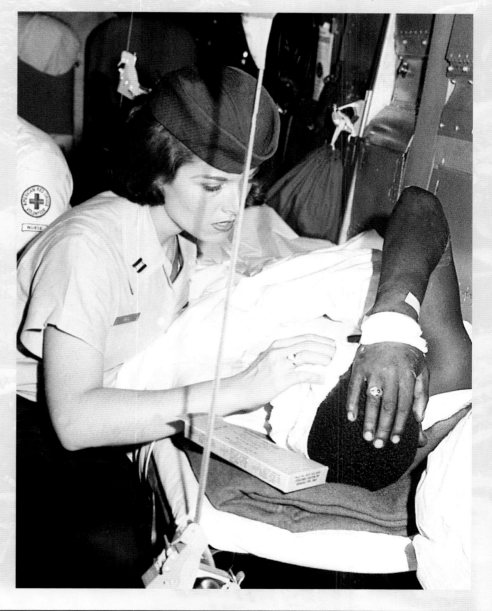

Below: A nurse attends to a wounded American soldier as they prepare to depart from Tan Son Nhat Air Base for the United States in January 1967.

The North Vietnamese broke through Xuan Loc with Soviet T54 tanks and headed straight toward Bien Hoa, and from there made the southern turn into Saigon at the end of the month. Although defeated at Xuan Loc, ARVN 18th Division troops had proved battle-worthy—the only contingent of South Vietnamese troops to perform well during the 1975 campaign.

Source: Clark Dougan and David Fulghum, *The Vietnam Experience: The Fall of the South*, 1985.

XUAN LOC, BATTLE OF (1975)

By mid-April 1975 nine North Vietnamese Army* (NVA) divisions were bearing down on Saigon* from three directions: from Tay Ninh in the northwest, south along Highway 4, and east along Highway 1 (*see* "Street Without Joy"). Xuan Loc was located thirty-five miles northeast of Saigon on the road to Bien Hoa* Air Base. The 341st NVA Division led the attack on Xuan Loc, which was defended by the 18th ARVN Division (*see* Army of the Republic of Vietnam). The fighting was bitter and intense, and the ARVN troops fought well, holding off the NVA assault on Saigon for two weeks. Xuan Loc was reduced to rubble in the struggle, and its population fled in a mass exodus.

Below: South Vietnamese refugees scramble to be evacuated from South Vietnam aboard a Chinook helicopter on April 14, 1975. The chopper has landed on Highway 1. Invading North Vietnamese troops are coming from the north on Highway 1 and are determined to overrun South Vietnam.

XUAN THUY

Xuan Thuy, a veteran North Vietnamese diplomat, was born in 1912. He was among the earliest of the Vietnamese nationalists, resisting the French Empire through the Vietminh,* being imprisoned and tortured by French officials, but surviving to become the foreign minister of North Vietnam between 1963 and 1965. Between 1968 and 1970 Xuan Thuy headed the North Vietnamese delegation at the Paris peace talks,* always insisting with uncompromising firmness on a unilateral American withdrawal from South Vietnam, recognition of the National Liberation Front (*see* Vietcong) as the legitimate government of South Vietnam, and dissolution of the South Vietnamese government. In 1970 North Vietnam dispatched Le Duc Tho* to Paris to continue the negotiations with Henry Kissinger,* and Xuan Thuy served as Tho's chief deputy. Xuan Thuy participated in the signing of the peace treaty between the United States and North Vietnam in January 1973; he died on June 18, 1985, in Hanoi.*

Sources: *New York Times*, June 19, 1985; U.S. Central Intelligence Agency, *Who's Who in North Vietnam*, 1969.

Below: In mid-April 1975, two Chinook helicopters hover over Highway 1, trying to evacuate supplies, troops, and family members of the ARVN 18th Division from Xuan Loc, South Vietnam. North Vietnamese troops have invaded South Vietnam and the fall of Saigon is imminent.

Below: On May 8, 1972, amidst North Vietnam's Eastertide (Easter) Offensive, President Richard Nixon has responded with Operation Linebacker, a massive bombing campaign over North Vietnam and South Vietnam. In this photograph, a crewman aboard the aircraft carrier USS *Constellation* prepares to load two 500-pound bombs onto U.S. Navy fighter bombers, which are headed for targets 15 miles west of Hanoi. The USS *Constellation* was conducting operations from Yankee Station.

YANKEE STATION

Located at 17°30'N 108°30'E, "Yankee Station" was the place-name for the U.S. Seventh Fleet's* staging area in the South China Sea. After 1966, Task Force 77, the carrier strike group in the Seventh Fleet, used Yankee Station as the reference point for its operations.

Source: Harry G. Summers Jr., *Vietnam War Almanac*, 1985.

YEAR ZERO

See Pol Pot

Left: On May 3, 1972, with the Eastertide Offensive raging ashore in South Vietnam, the aircraft carrier USS *Constellation* operates in the South China Sea southeast of Saigon at Yankee Station.

Below: U.S. Navy jets are catapulted from the deck of the USS *Constellation* on April 26, 1972. The aircraft are targeting North Vietnamese troops that have invaded South Vietnam during the Eastertide Offensive.

ZHOU ENLAI

A leading figure in the development of the People's Republic of China,* Zhou Enlai was born in China in 1896. Enlai joined the Chinese Communist Party in 1921 when he was a student in France, and in 1924 he returned to China and joined Sun Yat-sen's Kuomintang. In 1927 he was appointed director of the military department of the Chinese Communist Central Committee, and later that year he escaped Chiang Kai-shek's* purge of Communists in the Kuomintang. A close associate of Mao Zedong's,* Enlai became a leading figure in the Chinese Revolution of 1949.

Between 1949 and 1958 Enlai, a skilled negotiator, served as foreign minister of the People's Republic of China, and between 1949 and his death in 1976 he was also premier.

In his approach to the war, he was suspicious about a united Vietnam. For 2,000 years China and Vietnam had been engaged in a struggle for power, and Zhou Enlai preferred a Southeast Asia divided into a number of nation-states instead of one dominated by the Vietnamese, whom he considered imperialistic and aggressive. Enlai therefore supported a negotiated settlement of the conflict, even though the Chinese provided military supplies to the Vietminh,* the Vietcong,* and the North Vietnamese Army.* Enlai also wanted to improve Chinese relations with the United States as a way of gaining leverage with the Soviet Union,* and the war in Vietnam complicated that endeavor. When Richard Nixon* began normalizing American relations with China in 1971 and 1972, the North Vietnamese were convinced that the Chinese were out to betray them. Although massive Chinese assistance and a Chinese invasion of North and South Vietnam to fight the United States was an American fear in the 1960s, such a development was unthinkable to Zhou Enlai. He was not that ideologically locked into the cold war to respond in such rigid ways. Zhou Enlai died on January 8, 1976.

Sources: Henry Kissinger, *White House Years*, 1979; Stanley Karnow, *Vietnam: A History*, 1983; *Webster's New Biographical Dictionary*, 1983; Douglas S. Papp, *Vietnam: The View from Moscow, Peking, Washington*, 1981; Julia Ching, *Zhou Enlai: A Political Life*, 2006.

Right: While ARVN soldiers burn down a Vietcong hideout, U.S. Army Special Forces Captain Vernon Gillespie contacts base camp via radio. It was a common tactic during the Vietnam War to burn villages thought to harbor Vietcong. The use of the Zippo lighter to set fire to village homes led to the term "zippo war."

Left: Lieutenant Daniel Hill ignites a hut in a Vietcong-infested village as part of Operation Van Buren in South Vietnam on January 23, 1966. He is a soldier of B Company, 2d Battalion, 327th Infantry of the 101st Airborne Division. Their joint mission with South Korean troops was to deny the Vietcong a valuable stock of rice.

Below: Examples of Vietnam-era Zippos engraved with personal thoughts and mantras.

"ZIPPO WAR"

The Zippo has long been the lighter of choice for outdoorsmen because of its dependable flame, even under windy conditions, and it was popular for similar reasons among American troops in Vietnam. During search-and-destroy* missions, U.S. soldiers often used their Zippo lighters to burn the homes of villagers in Vietcong-controlled areas. Television footage and magazine photographs of American soldiers torching peasant homes with the lighters gave rise to the term "zippo war." On the other hand, the Vietcong often booby-trapped Zippos by filling them with explosive materials and leaving them conspicuously in bars or other places frequented by American troops. Thinking another GI had forgotten it, a soldier would pick it up, only to have it explode in his hand when he tried to light it. The term "zippo" was also used to describe a flamethrower, especially the M2A17 portable flamethrower. SF

Sources: Shelby L. Stanton, *Vietnam Order of Battle*, 1981; Edgar C. Doleman Jr., *The Vietnam Experience: Tools of War*, 1984.

Left: Private First Class Ernest Espinosa of San Francisco pours diesel fuel into a portable flamethrower on August 21, 1967.

Appendix A
The Minority Groups of South Vietnam, 1970

Group	Culture	Population	Primary Residence
Chinese	Chinese	1,100,000	Cholon and the major cities
Khmer	Cambodian	700,000	Mekong Delta
Jarai	Montagnard	150,000	Pleiku and Phu Bon
Rhade	Montagnard	100,000	Darlac, Phu Bon, Tuyen Duc, and Khanh Hoa
Koho	Montagnard	100,000	Lam Dong and Tuyen Duc
Hre	Montagnard	100,000	Quang Ngai
Bahnar	Montagnard	75,000	Kontum, Pleiku, and Binh Dinh
Roglai	Montagnard	57,000	Khanh Hoa, Ninh Thuan, Binh Thuan, and Binh Tuy
Bru	Montagnard	40,000	Quang Tri
Katu	Montagnard	40,000	Quang Nam and Quang Tin
M'Nong	Montagnard	40,000	Quang Duc
Sedang	Montagnard	40,000	Kontum
Cham	Indian	40,000	Thua Thien
Stieng	Montagnard	30,000	Phuoc Long and Binh Long
Cua	Montagnard	20,000	Quang Ngai and Quang Nam
Chru	Montagnard	15,000	Tuyen Duc
Chrau	Montagnard	15,000	Long Khanh, Binh Tuy, Phuoc Tuy, and Bien Hoa
Pacoh	Montagnard	15,000	Thua Thien
Rengao	Montagnard	15,000	Kontum
Halang	Montagnard	10,000	Kontum
Jeh	Montagnard	10,000	Quang Nam, Quang Tin, and Kontum
Hroy	Montagnard	10,000	Phu Yen and Phu Bon
Duan	Montagnard	3,500	Kontum
Takua	Montagnard	3,000	Quang Nam and Quang Tin
Monom	Montagnard	2,000	Kontum
Strieng	Montagnard	1,000	Kontum

Sources: Gerald C. Hickey, *Free in the Forest: An Ethnohistory of the Central Highlands, 1954 to 1976*, 1982; Minority Rights Group, *The Montagnards of South Vietnam*, 1973.

Appendix B
The Population and Provinces of South Vietnam, 1971

Province	Corps Zone	Area*	Population	Capital City
An Giang	IV	734	605,497	Long Xuyen
An Xuyen	IV	1,941	279,113	Quan Long
Bac Lieu	IV	988	352,230	Bac Lieu City
Ba Xuyen	IV	997	436,668	Khanh Hung
Bien Hoa	III	929	496,638	Bien Hoa City
Binh Dinh	II	3,640	754,150	Qui Nhon
Binh Duong	III	784	257,900	Phu Cuong
Binh Long	III	1,010	42,000	An Loc
Binh Thuan	II	1,930	284,929	Phan Thiet
Binh Tuy	III	1,427	74,315	Ham Tan
Cam Ranh**	II		104,666	
Chau Doc	IV	801	576,818	Chau Doc City
Chuong Thien	IV	884	285,517	Vi Thanh
Da Nang**	I		437,668	
Dinh Tuong	IV	598	478,586	My Tho
Darlac	II	6,552	244,772	Ban Me Thuot
Gia Dinh	III	552	1,345,425	Gia Dinh City
Go Cong	IV	196	198,088	Go Cong City
Hau Nghia	III	496	234,756	Khiem Cuong
Hue**	I		199,893	
Khanh Hoa	II	2,292	250,000	Nha Trang
Kien Giang	IV	2,000	386,094	Rach Gia
Kien Hoa	IV	804	618,870	Truc Giang
Kien Phong	IV	923	497,729	Cao Lanh
Kien Tuong	IV	1,720	519,000	Muc Hoa
Kontum	II	3,930	117,046	Kontum City
Lam Dong	II	2,125	89,106	Bao Loc
Long An	III	632	381,861	Tan An
Long Khanh	III	1,723	161,605	Xuan Loc
My Tho**	IV		100,000	
Nha Trang**	II		194,969	
Ninh Thuan	II	1,324	203,404	Phan Rang
Phong Dinh	IV	616	337,159	Can Tho
Phu Bon	II	1,847	69,765	Cheo Reo
Phuoc Long	III	2,045	47,210	Phuoc Long City
Phuoc Tuy	III	850	124,844	Phuoc Tuy City
Phu Yen	II	2,020	334,184	Tuy Hoa
Pleiku	II	3,260	214,912	Pleiku City
Quang Duc	II	2,300	38,305	Gia Nghia
Quang Nam	I	2,527	575,686	Hoi An
Quang Ngai	I	2,207	731,471	Quang Ngai City
Quang Tin	I	1,876	405,421	Tam Ky
Quang Tri	I	1,583	310,000	Quang Tri City
Qui Nhon**	II		188,717	
Sa Dec	IV	315	316,877	Sa Dec City
Saigon**	III		1,804,880	
Tay Ninh	III	1,515	386,738	Tay Ninh City
Thua Thien	I	1,919	555,514	Hue
Tuyen Duc	II	1,898	116,205	Tung Nghia
Vinh Binh	IV	873	411,190	Phu Vinh
Vinh Long	IV	658	563,282	Vinh Long City
Vung Tau**	III		86,636	

*Area in square miles.
**Independent municipality.

Sources: Judith Banister, *The Population of Vietnam*, 1985; Danny J. Whitfield, *Historical and Cultural Dictionary of Vietnam*, 1976; *Encyclopedia of the Third World, Volume III: 1929*, 1982.

Appendix C
Vietnam War Acronyms and Slang Expressions

AAA: antiaircraft artillery

Abn: airborne (paratrooper or parachutist-qualified)

ACAV: armored cavalry assault vehicle

Admin: administration

Advance Guard Youth: a Vietnamese student organization that became a nationalistic group by World War II

AF: Air Force

AFB: Air Force base

AFLC: Air Force Logistics Command

AFL-CIO: American Federation of Labor and Congress of Industrial Organizations

AG: Adjutant General

Agency: Central Intelligence Agency

Agitprop: agitation propaganda designed to indoctrinate Vietnamese civilians, Vietcong, and NVA with anti-Communist values

AHC: an assault helicopter company

AID: Agency for International Development

Airborne: people or materiel dropped by parachute

Air cav: air cavalry, referring to helicopter-borne infantry

Air mattress: an affectionate nickname for the 3d Brigade of the 82d Airborne Division

Airmobile: people or materiel delivered by helicopter

AK: an AK–47 rifle

ALCOA: Aluminum Company of America

All-Afro: another nickname for the 3d Brigade of the 82d Airborne Division. The nickname was taken from the AA (officially meaning "All American") on the division's shoulder patch.

Alpha bravo: slag expression for ambush, taken from the initials AB

AM or AMBL: airmobile

Americal: 23d Infantry Division

Amtrack: an amphibious vehicle, equipped with armor, used primarily by United States Marines to transport troops and materiel

Angel: helicopter that hovers near a carrier to pick up pilots who crash

A-O: area of operations

Ao Dai: long dress worn over black or white baggy pants by Vietnamese women. The Ao Dai is split at the hips, creating a front and back panel. Among men the Ao Dai reaches only the knees, instead of the ankles as it does for women.

Ap: Vietnamese word meaning hamlet

APC: an armored personnel carrier

Ap Doi Moi: "New Life" hamlet

ARA: aerial rocket artillery

Arc Light: code name for B-52 bombing missions along the Cambodian border

Arm: armored

Article 15: a nonjudicial punishment handed out by an officer to enlisted personnel

Arty: artillery

ARVN: (Arvin) the South Vietnamese Army (Army of the Republic of Vietnam)

ASAP: (A-sap) as soon as possible; a request for extreme urgency in a military assignment

ASH: assault support helicopter

ATC: air traffic control

A Teams: 12-man Green Beret units

ATFV or ATFG: Australian Task Force, Vietnam

AWC: an aerial weapons company

AWOL: absent without leave

Banh Chunq: a traditional Vietnamese dish prepared for the Tet holidays. It is a cake made from rice, soybeans, and pork, wrapped in banana leaves, and steamed for several hours.

Banh Da: a traditional Vietnamese cookie made from rice paste and sesame seeds. It is either dried or toasted until very crisp.

Banh Duc: a traditional Vietnamese dish of rice flour mixed with a small amount of limestone powder and water. It is a jelled rice after cooling.

Banh Giay: a traditional Vietnamese rice cake usually served on ceremonial occasions

BAR: a Browning automatic rifle

Base area: an area of installations, defensive fortifications, or other physical structures used by the enemy

Baseball: a baseball-shaped grenade about 2 1/2" in diameter

Base Camp: a semipermanent field headquarters and center for a given unit usually within that unit's tactical areas responsibility. A unit may operate in or away from its base camp. Base camps usually contain all or part of a given unit's support elements.

Battalion days in the field: days when battalions were patrolling in the field. It was used to measure a battalion's efficiency.

BC: body count; the number of enemy dead on a given battlefield

BCD: bad conduct discharge

Bde: brigade

Beans: a meal; chow

Beaten zone: where most bullets will hit when a machine gun is fired into bush

Beehive: antipersonnel artillery rounds filled with thousands of small metal darts

Believer: a dead soldier, usually the enemy

The Bell Telephone Hour: interrogation or torture of VC suspects using electric shocks generated by a field telephone

Berm, berm line: hedgerow or foliated built-up area which divided rice paddies; also, a rise in the ground such as dikes or a dirt parapet around fortifications

Betel nut: a nut Vietnamese chew with lime and tobacco. It has a numbing effect, sometimes causing drool. The chewer frequently spits out a red juice.

B–5 Front: Communist military command operating in Quang Tri and Thua Thien provinces in I Corps

B–40 rocket: a shoulder-held RPG launcher

Big shotgun: a 106mm recoilless rifle using antipersonnel canister ammunition

Big stuff: artillery fire support on air force ordnance

Binh Tram: an NVA logistical unit responsible for defense and maintenance for a section of the Ho Chi Minh Trail

Bird: any aircraft, usually helicopters

Bird dog: a light fixed-wing observation aircraft, but in particular the army O–1A or E planes

BK amputee: below-the-knee amputation of the leg

Black Hats: an affectionate term for Pathfinders

Black Magic: nickname for the M16A1 rifle

Bladder: a heavy-duty, rubberized collapsible petroleum drum ranging from 2,000 to 50,000 gallons

Bladder Bird: a C–123 or C–130 aircraft equipped with rubberized collapsible drum and 350-GPM pumps; also called Cow or Flying Cow

Blade time: used when referring to available helicopter support. Units were generally allocated a specific amount of "blade time" daily for command and control and logistical support.

Blanket Division: an affectionate nickname for the 1st Cavalry Division. The name came from its large shoulder patch.

Blivet: a 250- or 500-gallon rubberized fabric collapsible drum (*see* bladder)

Bloody One: a nickname for the 1st Infantry Division. It came from the red numeral "1" on the division shoulder patch. Also known as the Big Dead One.

BLT: battalion landing team

Bluper: an M79 grenade launcher

Bn: battalion

Boat People: refugees fleeing Vietnam by boat after 1975

Bode: a Cambodian

Bo doi: a uniformed NVA soldier

Body bags: plastic bags used for retrieval of bodies on the battlefield

Bolter: plane that misses the arrest wire when landing on an aircraft carrier

Booby trap: an explosive charge hidden in a harmless object which explodes on contact

Boondocks, boonies, bush: expressions for the jungle, or any remote area away from a base camp or city; sometimes used to refer to any area in Vietnam

Bouncing Betty: a trip-wire mine, designed to explode at groin height

Bring smoke: to direct intense artillery fire or air force ordnance on an enemy position

BS: border surveillance

Bubble: the two-man OH–13 Sioux helicopter

Buddy system: placing South Vietnamese units under U.S. sponsorship for training. Also used when an American soldier recently arrived in Vietnam was paired up with an experienced soldier.

Bush: an infantry term for the field or the "boonies"

Bushmasters: any elite unit skilled in jungle operations

Bust caps: Marine term for rapid firing of an M16 rifle

Butcher brigade: a derogatory nickname given to the 11th Infantry Brigade after the My Lai massacre

C–4: a very stable plastic explosive carried by infantry soldiers

CAG: Combined Action Groups; pacification teams organized by the communists as a base camp. Usually contained fortifications, supply depots, hospitals, and training facilities.

Cambodian Liberation Army: also called Khmer Liberation Army. Communist armed forces of National United Front of Kampuchea (FUNK).

C and C: command and control helicopter used by reconnaissance or unit commanders

C and S: cordon and search. An operation to seal off and search an area or village

CAP: Capital Division (Republic of Korea). Also, Combined Action Platoons.

Capital Military Zone: Saigon and the immediate surrounding area

Caribou: the CV–2 twin-engine cargo airplane used by the Army until turned over to the Air Force in December 1966

CAS: (Cass) Saigon office of the Central Intelligence Agency

Cat: caterpillar tractor

Caterpillar: an administrative or logistical convoy on a normally secure road

Cav: a nickname for air cavalry

Cbt: combat

CBU: cluster bomb unit

CENTO: Central Treaty Organization

CG: commanding general

Cha Gio: Vietnamese dish of pork, noodles, vegetables, and crab, wrapped in rice paper and deep fried.

Charlie, Charles, Chuck: Vietcong, short for the phonetic representation Victor Charlie.

Charlie rats: Army combat rations (C-rations). The term "Charlie" was both the phonetic alphabetization of the "C" in C-rations and signified the enemy or enemy activity.

Cha Tom: Vietnamese dish of sugar cane sticks grilled in a shrimp paste

Che: a sweet dish sold by street vendors in Vietnam. Che is a dessert pudding of beans, noodles, and coconut.

Checkerboard sweep: a specific technique employed dividing a fixed area into blocks, into one of which a ground element is inserted while mechanized/armor elements operate around the periphery to saturate the area and prevent an enemy escape.

Checkmate: a security roadblock

Chem: chemical

Cherry: a new troop replacement

Chicom: (Cheye-com) a term describing a Chinese Communist or weapons manufactured in China

Chickenplate: bulletproof breastplate

Chieu Hoi: (Choo Hoy) "Open arms." Program under which GVN offered amnesty to VC defectors.

Chinh huan: North Vietnamese indoctrination sessions for all Communist party members

Chinook: the CH-47 cargo helicopter; also called Shithook or Hook

Chogie, cut, a chogie: to move out quickly. Term brought to Vietnam by soldiers who had served in Korea.

Chopper: helicopter

Chops: chief of operations

CIA: Central Intelligence Agency or simply "The Agency" or "The Company"

CIC: Combat Information Center

CIB: Combat Infantry Badge for actual time in combat

CIDG: (Sidgee) Civilian Irregular Defense Group

CINCPAC: Commander in Chief, Pacific

CIO: Congress of Industrial Organizations

CIP: Counterinsurgency Plan. A 1961 plan calling for additional U.S. aid to support a 20,000-man increase in the ARVN and to train, equip, and supply a 32,000-man addition to South Vietnam's Civil Guard.

Civic action: a combination of MEDCAPS (medical civic action programs), ICAPS (intelligence civic action programs), and other civil affairs activities

Claymore: a popular fan-shaped antipersonnel land mine

CLCV: Clergy and Laity Concerned About Vietnam

Clearance: permission from military and political authorities to engage the enemy in a particular area

Clear and hold: an American military tactic in which U.S. troops captured and then attempted to permanently hold an area

Close air support: air strikes against enemy targets that are close to friendly forces, requiring detailed integration of each air mission with the fire and movement of those forces

Cloverleaf: a patrol technique in which subordinate elements move out from a central area and "loop" back toward the main advance unit's direction starting point. It was used as a technique of advance by units in unknown terrain.

Clutch belt: an ammunition cartridge belt worn by marines

CO: commanding officer

Co: company

Cobra: the AH–1G attack helicopter

Code of Conduct: military rules for U.S. soldiers taken prisoner

Combat sky spot: radar-controlled air strike

Comm: communications

Commo: communications of signal capacity, personnel, or equipment

Concertina barbed wire: coiled barbed wire used as infantry obstacles

Condolence Award: compensation paid to the family of a dead ARVN trooper

Cong: short for Vietcong

Connex: a large metal box used for shipping and storage

Contact: slang expression to describe firing on the NVA or Vietcong or being fired upon by them

CONUS: continental United States

CORDS: Civil Operations and Rural Development Support

CORE: Congress of Racial Equality

Corps: two or more divisions, responsible for the defense of a Military Region

COSMUSMACV: Commander, U.S. Military Assistance Command, Vietnam

COSVN: Central Office of South Vietnam

Cow: C–123 or C–130 aircraft equipped with a rubberized collapsible drum and 350-GPM pumps. Also called Bladder Bird, Flying Cow.

COWIN: Conduct of the War in Vietnam. A report commissioned in 1971 by the U.S. Army Deputy Chief of Staff for Military Operations.

CP: command post

C-ration: box of canned food used in military operations

CRB: Cam Ranh Bay

CRID: (Crid) Republic of Korea Capitol Infantry Division. Americans called it the Tiger Division.

Crispie critter: enemy soldier killed through burning to death

Crunchies: infantrymen; also, "ground pounders" and "grunts"

CS: Composite Service. Also riot control gas agent, such as a CS-grenade, used widely to clear out enemy tunnel works. Also a type of tear gas.

C's: C-rations or combat rations; canned army meals for field use

CTZ: Corps Tactical Zones (*see* I, II, III, and IV Corps)

Cu Chi National Guard: nickname of the 25th Infantry Division. Its division headquarters and most of its troops were stationed at Cu Chi throughout the war.

CWC: civilian war casualties

Cyclo: a motorized three-wheel passenger vehicle

Daisy Cutter: a 15,000-pound bomb designed to clear helicopter landing zones in heavy jungle areas

DAO: Defense Attaché Office. Part of the U.S. Embassy to South Vietnam, it replaced the Military Assistance Command, Vietnam.

Dead space: an area which cannot be covered by fire or observation due to the nature of the terrain

Deep serious: the worst possible position, such as being nearly overrun

Defcon: defensive contact artillery fire. Usually plotted at night by artillery forward observers "ringing the perimeter with steel."

Delta Tango: phonetic alphabetization of DT, meaning defensive targets

DePuy foxhole: defensive position ensuring interlocking defensive fire named after Major General William E. DePuy, commanding the 1st Infantry Division in Vietnam in 1966

DEROS: (Dee-ros) date eligible for return from overseas; the date a person's tour in Vietnam was estimated to end.

DeSoto: destroyer naval patrols in the South China Sea

Det-cord: detonating cord used for explosives

DIA: Defense Intelligence Agency

Di di mau: move quickly

Dink: a racist reference to enemy forces or Vietnamese civilians

Diome nickel: a 105mm howitzer

Div: division

DMS boot: direct molded-sole jungle boot

DMZ: demilitarized zone

DNG: Da Nang

Doc: affectionate title for enlisted medical aidman

DOD: Department of Defense

Dong: Vietnamese monetary unit; one piaster

Double force: buddy operations combining U.S. and ARVN forces

Doubtfuls: indigenous personnel who cannot be categorized as either Vietcong or civil offenders. It also can mean suspect personnel spotted from ground or aircraft.

Doughnut dollies: Red Cross girls

Doughnut six: chief of Red Cross girls. Six was the customary military number of a commander on any level when using the radio.

Dozer-infantry: team of tank-dozers, bulldozers, Rome plows, and infantry which use jungle-busting techniques in difficult terrain

DRAC: Delta Regional Assistance Command

The Drag: squad behind the main maneuver element to ensure rear safety

Dragon Ship: AC–47 aircraft fitted out with Gatling-type machine guns. Also called Puff, Puff the Magic Dragon, and Spooky.

Drum: metal container for fuel

DRV: Democratic Republic of Vietnam

Dua Dam: Vietnamese funeral procession—complete with altar, horse-drawn hearse and coffin, and marchers bearing wreaths, banners, and flags

Dud: any explosive that fails to detonate when activated

Duster: a nickname for the M42 tracked vehicle mounting twin 40mm antiaircraft guns used as ground support

Dustoff: a nickname for a medical evacuation helicopter or mission

DX: direct exchange of equipment for repair and replacement

DZ: drop zone in airborne operations

Eagle flights: large air assault of helicopters

ECM: electronic countermeasures, such as jamming and deception

EDT: Eastern Daylight Time

Electric Strawberry: a nickname for the 25th Infantry Division because of the division's shoulder patch representation of "Tropic Lightning"

Elephant grass: tall, sharp-edged grass found in the highlands of Vietnam

EM: enlisted man

En: engineer

ENGR CMD/COM: Engineer Command

ENI: enemy-initiated incident

E-Nine, E–9: a sergeant major, the highest enlisted rank

Errand boy: daily scheduled courier flight; also called Pony Express

Escort: armed helicopter escort

ETS: date of departure from overseas duty station

Extraction: voluntary or involuntary withdrawal by air of troops from any operational area via helicopter

FAC: (Fack) Forward air controller

FAE: fuel air explosive

FAL-FAR: pro-U.S. Royal Armed Forces of Laos

FANK: Forces Armées Nationales Khmeres

fatigues: standard combat uniform, green in color

Fatikees: nickname for jungle fatigues

FBI: Federal Bureau of Investigation

FEC: French Expeditionary Corps

FFV: Field Force, Vietnam

Field of fire: area that a weapon or group of weapons can cover effectively with fire from a given position

Fireballing: concentration of large amounts of artillery fire in an area

Fire base: temporary artillery firing position often secured by infantry

Firefight: exchange of small arms fire between opposing units

Firefly: helicopter team consisting of one helicopter equipped with a searchlight or arc lamps and two gunships

Fire support base: a semifixed artillery base established to increase fire coverage of an area and provide security for the firing unit

I Corps: northernmost military region in South Vietnam

Flack jacket: heavy fiberglass-filled vest worn for protection from shrapnel

Flare: illumination projectile; hand-fired or shot from artillery, mortars, or air

Flare ship: any aircraft used primarily to drop illumination flares

Flower power: nickname for the 9th Infantry Division. It came from the Octofoil design on the division shoulder patch.

Flying Cow: C–123 or C–130 aircraft equipped with rubberized collapsible drum and 350-GPM pump. Also called Cow, Bladder Bird.

Flying Crane: the CH–54 heavy helicopter

FMFPAC: Fleet Marine Force, Pacific Command

FNG: most common name for newly arrived person in Vietnam. It was literally translated as a "fuckin' new guy."

FOB: forward operating base. A combined command post and logistical base established in the field, usually by a battalion but also widely used by Special Forces.

Foo-gas: see Phougas

FOR: Fellowship of Reconciliation

Forest penetrator: device lowered and raised by cable from a helicopter and used for extracting a person from heavy jungle

Forward support area: a fixed or semifixed area utilized as a forward logistical base

Four Corners: the town of Di An, where the 1st Infantry Division was stationed. It also came to mean any small town near a U.S. military base.

IV Corps: the southernmost military region in South Vietnam, located in the Mekong Delta

FPJMC: four-party joint military commission

FPJMT: four-party joint military team

Frag: to kill or attempt to kill one's own officers or sergeants, usually with a fragmentation grenade; also the common term for any grenade

Freak: short term used for radio frequency

Free fire zone: any area in which permission was not required prior to firing on targets

FRI: (Fry) friendly initiated incident

FSB: fire support base. Semipermanent base established to provide artillery support for allied units operating within range of the base.

FTA: Free the Army

FULRO: United Front for the Struggle of Oppressed Races; resistance organization in the highlands of Vietnam made up of Montagnards, Cham, and ethnic Khmer. FULRO continues to fight against the Communist government.

FUNK: National United Front of Kampuchea. Popular front established in 1970 and nominally headed by Prince Norodom Sihanouk, dedicated to the overthrow of the Lon Nol government in Phnom Penh.

Funky Fourth: a nickname of the 4th Infantry Division

FWMAF: Free World Military Assistant Forces. The term referred to allies of South Vietnam.

GAO: General Accounting Office

Ghost: take off; take it easy in a unit; do nothing; being absent; shirking duty

Ghost time: free time off duty

Go-go ship: an armed CH–47 helicopter

Gom dan: "gathering" or "herding in." Term used by Vietnamese Communists to describe resettlement of rural villagers in cities and GVN-sponsored refugee camps.

Gooks: slang expression brought to Vietnam by Korean War veterans. The term refers to anyone of Asian origin.

Gooney bird: nickname for the C–47 aircraft

GOP: Grand Old Party (Republican)

GPM: gallons per minute

Gravel: type of mine

Green: used to signify "safe," such as a Green LZ (safe landing zone)

Greenbacking: employing mercenaries

Green Berets: members of Special Forces of the U.S. Army. They were awarded the green beret headgear as a mark of distinction.

Ground Pounder: infantryman

Grunt: a popular nickname for an infantryman in Vietnam; supposedly derived from sound one made when lifting up his rucksack

Guerrilla: soldiers of a resistance movement who are organized on a military or paramilitary basis

Guerrilla warfare: military operations conducted in enemy-held or hostile territory by irregular, predominantly indigenous forces

Gung ho: very enthusiastic and committed

Gun jeep or truck: armored vehicle equipped with machine guns

Gunney: marine gunnery sergeant

Gunship: an armed helicopter or adapted fixed-wing aircraft

GVN: Government of South Vietnam

Gypsy operation: frequent displacement of small unit bases

Ha: HAWK missile

Hamlet: a small rural village

Hammer and anvil: an infantry tactic of surrounding an enemy base area, then sending in other units to drive the enemy out of hiding

Hanoi Hilton: nickname American prisoners of war used to describe the Hoa Loa Prison in Hanoi

Hard hat: full-time VC soldier, as opposed to a reservist or guerilla

Hardspot: ambush by a tank element

Hasty defense: defense normally organized while in contact with the enemy

Hawks: nickname for the battalion reconnaissance platoon

HE: high explosive, such as HE artillery rounds

He: Hercules missile

Heavy arty: B–52 bombing strikes

Heavy gun team: three armed helicopters operating together

Heavy stuff: heavy artillery such as 8-inch or 175mm cannon, but also meaning fire support from the battleship *New Jersey*

Hedgehogs: isolated outposts in which the French high command concentrated troops

Heliborne: aloft in a helicopter

Helix: air force spotter

The Herd: nickname of the 173d Airborne Brigade, the first major combat unit sent into Vietnam

Herringbone: tactical formation for mechanized and armor units during halts (or during ambush), when the unit is moving in column. The armored vehicles turn alternately to the sides of the road to orient their main armament and heaviest armor obliquely to the flanks.

HES: Hamlet Evaluation System

HH: heavy helicopter

H & I: harassing and interdictory fire by artillery

High angle hell: mortar fire

High points: CIA and MACV term for brief periods (usually about three days) of intense enemy activity, such as attacks against population centers or military posts

HJ: Honest John missile

Hmong: a dominant Laotian hill tribe. Most of them opposed the North Vietnamese and Pathet Lao.

Hog flight: helicopter(s) mounting the 40mm cannon M5 nose-mounted armament for direct-fire weapon support

Hoi Chanh: one who joined the Chieu Hoi program

Home plate: airfield or carrier where an aircraft is based

Honcho: individual in charge; also meaning to supervise

Hook: nickname for the CH–47 Chinook helicopter

Hootch: house or living quarters or a native hut

Hop Tac: Vietnamese for "cooperation." Name of unsuccessful pacification program begun in 1964, concentrated in one seven-province area around Saigon.

Horse pill: the antimalaria tablet taken weekly by U.S. personnel in Vietnam

Hot: dangerous, such as Hot LZ (where aircraft are receiving enemy fire)

Hotel Alpha: phonetic alphabetization of HA meaning "haul ass," move out immediately

Hotel Echo: phonetic alphabetization of HE, high-explosive artillery or mortar rounds

Hot Pursuit: policy allowing American military to chase Vietcong and NVA soldiers across the border into Cambodia

HP: horsepower

HQ: headquarters

Huey: nickname for the UH-series helicopters

Hug: close with the enemy or to be pinned down in close quarters with the enemy

Hump: rotation of 25 percent or more of a unit within a thirty-day period; also called "rotational hump." It also meant to carry or march.

ICC: International Control Commission

ICCS: International Commission of Control and Supervision

ICP: Indochinese Communist Party

ICSC: International Commission for Supervision and Control

IDA: Institute for Defense Analysis

Illum: to illuminate, as with flares or searchlights

Incoming: receiving enemy mortar or rocket fire

in country: Vietnam

Indirect fire: bombardment by mortars or artillery in which shells travel to an unseen target

Infusion: program for transfer of personnel within or between commands to reduce rotational hump

In, Inf: infantry

Insertion: secret helicopter placement of combat troops in an operational area

Intelligence & Interdiction (I&I): night artillery to disturb enemy sleep, curtail their movement, and weaken their morale

In the field: any forward combat area or any area outside of a town or base camp

Irregulars: armed individuals and groups not members of the regular armed forces, police, or other internal security forces

IRS: Internal Revenue Service

ITR: Infantry Training Regiment

Jacob's Ladder: a rope ladder dropped by a Chinook helicopter and used to climb down through difficult foilage or onto rough terrain

JCS: Joint Chiefs of Staff

Jesus nut: mythical nut that holds the rotors onto a helicopter

JGS: Joint General Staff, South Vietnamese counterpart of the JCS

JMC: Joint Military Commission. Consisted of representatives of the DRV, the PRG, the U.S., and the RVN. It was to ensure that the concerned parties implemented and abided by the Paris agreement.

JMT: four-party Joint Military Team. Established in 1973; consisted of representatives of the DRV, the PRG (Provisional Government of South Vietnam), the U.S., and the RVN. It was to account for prisoners and MIAs on all sides.

Jolly Green Giant: heavily armed Air Force C–47 aircraft supporting troops or an Air Force HH–53 heavy rescue helicopter

Jumping Junkies: derogatory nickname for paratroopers or parachutist-qualified troops

Jungle-busting: use of a tank or armored vehicle to cut trails through the jungle or other heavy vegetation

JUSPAO: Joint United States Public Affairs Office

Kalishnikov: AK–47 rifle

K-bar: combat knife

Keystone, Keystoning: Operation Keystone was the code word for the incremental process in which the United States Army withdrew from Vietnam. These were divided into Keystone Eagle, Cardinal, Bluejay, Robin, Oriole, Mallard, Owl, etc., and spanned the period July 1969–November 1972.

K-Fifty: Chinese Communist 7.62mm submachine gun

KHA: Killed in Hostile Action. Since the United States was not engaged in a "declared war," the use of the official term "KIA (Killed in Action)" was not authorized by Department of Defense. KIA came to mean enemy dead.

Khmer Rouge: "Red Khmers." The forces of the Cambodian Communist Party.

KIA: killed in action

Killer team: marine mobile ambush team

Kill-zone: area around an explosive device in which 95 percent fatalities are predicted

Kit Carson Scout: an ex-VC/NVA soldier employed by U.S. units as a scout

KKK: Khmer Kampuchea Kron, a pro-U.S. Cambodian exile group

Klick: short for kilometer

KP: kitchen police

KPNLF: Khmer People's National Liberation Front; the major non-Communist Cambodian political and resistance organization fighting against Vietnamese occupation forces

Laager: positioning of helicopters in a secure forward area so that weapons systems may be used in defense. Also, all-around night-defensive position established by mechanized vehicles.

Land tail: that part of an air-transported unit not committed to combat by air but which joins the unit via land movement

Lao Dong party: Vietnam Worker's party, Marxist-Leninist party of North Vietnam

LAPE: low altitude parachute extraction

LAW: (Law) M72 light antitank weapon. A shoulder-fired, 66mm rocket with a one-time disposable fiberglass launcher.

LBJ Ranch: (L-B-J) the Long Binh Stockade. The last word was changed to make a pun on the initials of President Lyndon Baines Johnson.

LCM: mechanized landing craft used in harbors and inland waterways

Leatherneck: a Marine

Lifer: career soldier

Lift: a single helicopter trip carrying cargo from a loading area to a landing zone

Light at the End of the Tunnel: term describing the imminent demise of the Vietcong and North Vietnamese

Lightning bug: helicopter equipped with searchlights; also called "firefly"

Limited conventional war: U.S. Department of Defense designation for conflict involving American units larger than four thousand men. Used by Pentagon to reclassify Vietnam War from a guerrilla war.

The Line: being on duty with an infantry unit in the field

Line Haul: long-distance military truck convoys; also called Long Haul

Little Appalachia: nickname for the headquarters of the 1st Infantry Division; derived from the poor living conditions in some parts of the Appalachian Mountains in the United States

LJ: Little John missile

Local force: Vietcong combat unit subordinate to a district or province headquarters

Log bird: logistical resupply helicopter

Log run: aerial logistical resupply mission

LOH: (Loach) light observation helicopter, notably the OH–6A

Long green line: column of infantry advancing through jungle terrain

LORAPL: Long Range Planning Task Group. Created in July 1968 by General Abrams to review U.S. strategy in Vietnam over the previous four years and recommend changes. Headed by Lieutenant Colonel Dr. Donald S. Marshall.

LP: listening post forward off a defensive perimeter

LRP or LRRP: (Lurp) long-range reconnaissance patrol

LST: troop-landing ship

Lt.: Lieutenant

LTG: Lieutenant General

Luc Luong Dac Biet: (LLDB) South Vietnamese Special Forces

Lurps: long-range reconnaissance patrol members. Also, an experimental lightweight food packet consisting of a dehydrated meal and named after the soldiers it was most often issued to.

LZ: landing zone

MAAG: Military Assistance and Advisory Group

MAB: Marine Amphibious Brigade

MAC: Military Airlift Command

MACOI: MACV Office of Information

MAC-SOG: Military Assistance Command Studies and Observation Group

MACV: (Mac-vee) Military Assistance Command, Vietnam

Mad minute: concentrated fire of all weapons for a brief period of time at maximum rate; also called "Mike-mike"

MAF: Marine Amphibious Force

Main Force: Vietcong and North Vietnamese military units

Maj.: Major

Mama-san: mature Vietnamese woman

marching fire: fire delivered by infantry in an assault, especially with automatic rifles and machine guns fired from the hip or rapidly firing rifles from the shoulder while advancing

MAT: Mobile Advisory Team. Usually a six-member team of two U.S. Army officers, three enlisted men, and an interpreter responsible for training territorial forces (RF and PF).

Mat Tran: the National Liberation Front

Maverick: a stolen government vehicle

MASH: Mobile Army Surgical Hospital

MCRD: Marine Corps Recruit Depots

MEB: Marine Expeditionary Brigade

Mech: mechanized infantry

MEDCAP: (Med-cap) Medical Civil Action Program

Medevac: medical evacuation by helicopter; also called "Dustoff"

Meeting engagement: collision between two advancing forces, neither of which is fully deployed for battle

M14: rifle used in early portion of Vietnam conflict

MG: machine gun

MGF: mobile guerrilla force, composed of highly trained indigenous personnel commanded by U.S. Special Forces, who operated as a guerrilla force in Vietcong-controlled areas.

MIA: Missing in Action

MiG: Soviet fighter plane

Mighty Mite: blower used to force smoke and tear gas throughout tunnel systems

Mike Force, MSF: Special Forces Mobile Strike Force; composed of indigenous personnel and used as a reaction or reinforcing unit

Mission: an operational flight by several aircraft; also the embassy or legation

Mission Council: organized by U.S. Ambassador Maxwell Taylor, it met weekly to coordinate activities among all U.S. agencies in Vietnam. After Henry Cabot Lodge replaced Taylor, OCO (later CORDS) oversaw the Mission Council.

Mission ready: any equipment, but especially helicopters, completely capable of performing assigned missions

MIT: Massachusetts Institute of Technology

M1: World War I–vintage American rifle

Moonshine: a flare-carrying aircraft

Mort: mortar

MP: Military Police

Mpc: military pay certificates, used instead of American currency in war zones to discourage black marketeering

mph: miles per hour

MR: Military Region

MSFC: Mobile Strike Force Command

M16: the standard American rifle used in Vietnam after 1966

M60: American-made machine gun

M79: single-barreled grenade launcher used by infantry

MSU Advisory Group: Michigan State University team

Mxd: mixed artillery of 105mm/155mm types

Napalm: incendiary used in Vietnam by French and Americans both as defoliant and antipersonnel weapon

Nap-of-the-earth: flight as close to the earth's surface as terrain will permit

NASA: National Aeronautics and Space Administration

National Council of Reconciliation and Concord: institution provided for by the Paris agreement to promote implementation of the agreement, ensure democratic liberties, and organize elections

National Revolutionary Movement: Diem's followers, dominated by his brothers Nhu and Can

Native sport: hunting for Vietcong

NATO: North Atlantic Treaty Organization

NCC: National Coordinating Committee to End the War in Vietnam

NCO: noncommissioned officer, usually a squad leader or platoon sergeant

NDP: night defensive position

Nem: traditional Vietnamese dish in which ground pork is mixed with powdered rice and packed as a sausage into banana leaves

Neutralize: to render an enemy force, installation, or operation ineffective by military action

New Mobe: the New Mobilization Committee to End the War

Next: soldier due for rotation to United States in a few days; also "Short"

NG: National Guard

NH: Nike-Hercules missile

NLF: National Liberation Front, officially the National Front for the Liberation of the South

No-doze mission: airborne broadcast of psychological operations tapes of appeals, music, and propaganda during the hours of darkness

No Fire Zone: an area in which any use of military fire must be cleared by the appropriate authority

Non: the ubiquitous conical hat worn by men and women in Vietnam. Usually it is made from latania leaves.

NORS: (Nors) not operationally ready—reason, support

No sweat: with little effort or no trouble

NSA: National Security Agency. An intelligence-gathering agency established in 1952, NSA is responsible to the executive branch and specializes in code breaking and electronic surveillance.

NSC: National Security Council. Responsible for developing defense strategies for the United States. Situated in the White House, it exerts general direction over the CIA.

Number One: the best, prime

Number Sixty: the M60 machine gun

Number Ten: the worst. "Number ten-thou" meant the very worst.

Nungs: Chinese tribal troops from the Highlands of North Vietnam. They provided special troops to the U.S. Special Forces.

Nuoc-mam: a pungent Vietnamese concentrated fish-sauce used to flavor rice

NVA: North Vietnamese Army

NZ: New Zealand

OCO: Office of Civilian Operations. Created to have command responsibility over all civilian agencies operating in Vietnam, forming in effect a pacification high command, under jurisdiction of the U.S. Embassy. Transformed into CORDS in 1967. (*See also* CORDS.)

OCS: Officers' Candidate School

Oil spot: pacified area

One-buck: code designation for units held in readiness in the United States for deployment in Vietnam on 48-hour notice

One-oh-worst: derisive nickname for the 101st Airborne Division (Airmobile) based on its numerical designation

On station: armed helicopter flight in position to support a ground commander

Ontos vehicle: lightly armored tracked vehicle equipped with six mounted 106mm recoilless rifles. In the Vietnam War it was used primarily to support infantry.

OPLAN: Operations Plan

Option IV: U.S. military plan for helicopter evacuation from Saigon

Ord: ordnance

OSS: Office of Strategic Services. Created in 1942, the OSS was an intelligence-gathering operation which became a forerunner of the CIA.

Out-country: the Southeast Asian conflict outside South Vietnam (i.e., Laos and North Vietnam, sometimes Thailand, Cambodia, and China)

PACAP: Pacific Air Force

P's: piasters, the Vietnamese monetary unit

P–38: can opener for canned C-rations

Pacification: several programs of the South Vietnamese and U.S. governments to destroy the Vietcong in the villages, gain civilian support for the GVN, and stabilize the countryside

PACOM: Pacific Command

Pathet Lao: the Laotian Communists, who from their inception have been under the control of the Vietnamese Communist Party

PAVN: (Pavin) People's Army of Vietnam. The North Vietnamese Army; also known as the NVA

PE: Pershing missile

Peers Inquiry: Report of the Department of the Army Review of the Preliminary Investigation into the My Lai Incident, May 14, 1970. The inquiry was directed by Lt. Gen. W.R. Peers.

Penny nickel nickel: a 155mm howitzer

Pentagon East: the Military Assistance Command, Vietnam headquarters complex at Tan Son Nhut Air Base

Perim: perimeter surrounding a fire base or position or even base camp

PF: Popular Forces

PFC: Private First Class

Phougas: drums of jellied gasoline fired defensively as a fixed-fire weapon; also spelled "foo-gas"

Piaster: South Vietnamese currency

Piss tube: a mortar

PLA: People's Liberation Army

Platoon: approximately forty-five men belonging to a company

Pods: rubberized 500-gallon containers

Point man: lead soldier in a unit cutting a path through dense vegetation if needed and constantly exposed to the danger of tripping bobby traps or being the first in contact with the enemy

Poison Ivy: nickname for the 4th Infantry Division. The name came from the design of its shoulder patch and its official designation as the Ivy Division.

poncho liner: nylon insert to the military rain poncho, used as a blanket

Pony Soldiers: members of a long range-patrol or any soldier in the 1st Cavalry Division

POW: prisoner of war

Prep: preparation or prestrike by air force, artillery, or armed helicopter fire placed on an LZ or objective prior to attack or landing

PRGVN: Provisional Revolutionary Government of South Vietnam

Prick: nickname for the PRC–25 lightweight infantry field radio

Province chief: governor of a state-sized administrative territory in South Vietnam, usually a high-ranking military officer

PRP: People's Revolutionary party; Communist party that dominated the NLF. Founded on January 15, 1962, as the successor to the Lao Dong party in South Vietnam.

PSDF: People's Self-Defense Fund

Psychedelic Cookie: nickname for the 9th Infantry Division derived from the Octofoil design of its shoulder patch

Psyops: psychological operations; planned use of propaganda to influence enemy thinking

Psywar: psychological warfare

PTSD: post-traumatic stress disorder

Puff the Magic Dragon, Puff: a C–47 up-gunned air force support aircraft; also called "dragon ship"

Puking Buzzards: derisive term for the 101st Airborne Division gleaned from the design of the screaming eagle on its shoulder patch

Punji stake: razor-sharp bamboo stake sometimes coated with poison or feces and usually hidden under water, along trails, at ambush sites, or in deep pits

Purple-out zone: emergency evacuation

PX: post exchange

PZ: pickup zone for helicopter loading, troop assembly, and troop extraction

QM: Quartermaster

QNH: Qui Nhon

quad–60: four 60-caliber machine guns mounted as one unit

Rabbits: white American soldiers, according to black vernacular

Rallier: an individual who voluntarily surrenders to the South Vietnamese

Ramp alert: fully armed aircraft on the ground at a base or forward strip ready for takeoff in about fifteen mintues

R&R: rest-and-recreation vacation taken during a one-year duty tour in Vietnam. Out-of-country R&R was at Bangkok, Hawaii, Tokyo, Australia, Hong Kong, Manila, Penang, Taipei, Kuala Lampur, or Singapore. In-country R&R locations were at Vung Tau or China Beach.

RD: Revolutionary Development

RD cadres: Revolutionary Development cadres; South Vietnamese who were trained to use Vietcong political tactics to carry out GVN pacification

React: for one unit to come to the aid of another under enemy fire

Recon: reconnaissance

Recon-by-fire: a method of reconnaissance in which fire is placed on suspected enemy positions to cause the enemy to disclose his presence by movement or return fire

Red haze: reconnaissance flight to detect heat emissions from the ground

Redleg: nickname for an artilleryman

Red LZ: landing zone under hostile fire. (*See also* "Hot.")

Reeducation camps: political prisons and labor camps of varying degrees of severity throughout Vietnam

Rehab: rehabilitate or recuperate

REMF: Rear Area Mother Fucker. Nickname given to men serving in the rear by front-line soldiers.

Retrograde: any movement, voluntary or involuntary, to the rear

Rev-dev: troop nickname for revolutionary development programs

RF/PF: Regional and Popular Forces of South Vietnam; also known as "Ruff-Puffs"

RLT: regimental landing team

Roadrunner: road-clearing operation with mission of catching local guerrillas by surprise; also, a Special Forces trail-watch team

Rock 'n' roll: to put an M16A1 rifle on full automatic fire

Rocket belt: encircling zone around friendly locality from which enemy large-caliber (122mm, 140mm, etc.) rocket attacks could be launched

ROKs: (Rocks) Republic of Korea soldiers and marines

Rome plow: specially mounted bulldozer blade used in forest or jungle clearing and heavy-duty land clearing

RON: (Ron) Remain overnight position. Known also as "NL" for night location.

Rotate: to return to the United States at the end of a tour of duty in Vietnam

ROTC: Reserve Officers' Training Corps

Round Eye: slang term used by American soldiers to describe another American or an individual of European descent

RPG: Russian-manufactured antitank grenade launcher; also, rocket-propelled grenade

RR: either recoilless rifle or radio relay

RTO: radio telephone operator who carried the "lightweight" infantry field radio

Ruck, Rucksack: backpack issued to infantry in Vietnam

Ruff-Puffs: South Vietnamese Regional Forces and Popular Forces (RF/PF); paramilitary forces usually of squad or platoon size recruited and utilized within a hamlet, village, or district

RVN: Republic of Vietnam (South Vietnam)

RVNAF: Republic of Vietnam Armed Forces

SAC: Strategic Air Command

Saddle: final air attack position

Saigon tea: an "alcoholic" beverage consisting primarily of Coca-Cola

Saigon warrior: derisive term for troops stationed in Saigon

SALT: Strategic Arms Limitation Treaty

Salty dog: a "battle loss item" lost as a result of enemy action

SAM: Soviet-made surface-to-air missile

Sampan: a Vietnamese peasant's boat

SANE: Committee for a Sane Nuclear Policy. Moderate American disarmament group active in the 1960s.

sanitize: a euphemism for assassination which became widely used in conjunction with the CIA's Phoenix Program

Sappers: North Vietnamese Army or Vietcong demolition commandos

SAR: search and rescue

SAS: Students Afro-American Society

SA–2: a Russian-built surface-to-air missile with an effective altitude of 59,000 feet and a speed of Mach 2.5

Scared Horse: nickname for the 11th Armored Cavalry Regiment, derived from the design on its shoulder patch displaying a rearing horse

Science Fiction: nickname for the U.S. Army Special Forces

Scoutships: OH–13 or OH–23 helicopters used for surveillance or reconnaissance

Screaming Chickens: nickname for the 101st Airborne Division derived from the eagle emblem of the divisional shoulder patch as well as a disparagement of the division motto "Screaming Eagles"

SDS: Students for a Democratic Society. Founded in 1962, SDS became the largest radical student organization in the country, focusing its energies on community organization of the poor and opposition to the Vietnam War.

Seabees: naval construction engineers. Derived from "C.B."—Navy construction battalion.

SEAIR: Southeast Asian Airlift

SEAL: Navy special-warfare force members

Seal bins: 500-gallon rubberized containers

SEALORDS: South East Asian Lake Ocean River Delta Strategy

Search and clear: offensive military operations to sweep through areas to locate and attack the enemy

Search and destroy: offensive operations designed to find and destroy enemy forces rather than establish permanent government control; also called "Zippo missions"

SEATO: Southeast Asia Treaty Organization

II Corps: Central Highlands military region in South Vietnam

782-gear: individual equipment owned by a unit and issued to a Marine while assigned to that unit. In boot camp that included a bucket, cleaning equipment, a poncho, and a shelter half. The name is derived from the number of the form on which it was originally issued.

Seventeenth parallel: temporary division line between North and South Vietnam established by the Geneva Accords of 1954

70th Corps: NVA military command activated in 1970 to control defense of base areas in Laos

SF: U.S. Army Special Forces; also called Green Berets

SHP: shaft horsepower

SG: Sergeant missile

Shadow: AC–119 with three miniguns used for aerial fire support

Shake 'n' bake: sergeant who earned his rank quickly through NCO schools or other means with less than the normal amount of time in service

Shit burning: the sanitization of latrines by kerosene incineration of excrement

Short, short-time: individual with little time remaining in Vietnam

Short rounds: rounds of ammunition or bombs falling short of the target. Also the inadvertent or accidental delivery of ordnance to friendly forces or civilians.

Shotgun, shotgunner: armed guard on or in a vehicle who watches for enemy activity and returns fire if attacked. Also a door gunner on a helicopter.

Skycrane: huge double-engine helicopter used for lifting and transporting heavy equipment

Slapflare: a cylindrical, hand-held flare

Slick: helicopter used to lift troops or cargo with only protective armaments systems

Smokey Bear: C–47 aircraft used to drop illuminating flares or a helicopter-mounted smoke generator

SNAFU: Situation normal (all fucked up)

SNCC: Student Non-Violent Coordinating Committee

Sneaky Petes: U.S. Army Special Forces or Rangers

Snoop 'n' poop: Marine search-and-destroy offensive mission

SOG: Studies and Observations Group

Sortie: one aircraft making one takeoff and landing to conduct the mission for which it was scheduled

Spec. 4: Specialist 4th Class, Army rank similar to corporal

Special Forces: U.S. soldiers, popularly known as Green Berets, trained in techniques of guerrilla warfare

Special operations: military operations requiring specialized or elite forces

Spectre: AC–130 equipped with Vulcan machine guns and 105mm howitzer

Sperm: Marine light observation helicopter

Spider hole: Vietcong guerrilla foxhole

Spook: civilian intelligence agent

Spooky: AC–47 aircraft with Gatling guns and illumination flares

SP pack: cellophane packet containing toiletries and cigarettes issued to soldiers in the field

Spray: to open fire, usually on automatic

SRV: Socialist Republic of Vietnam

Stand-down: period of rest and refitting in which all operational activity, except for security, is stopped

Starlight: night reconnaissance or surveillance mission employing a light-intensifier scope

Starlight scope: an image intensifier using reflected light from the stars or moon to identify targets

State: U.S. Department of State

Stopper: support fire immediately available to impede enemy movement across a defensive line or area

Strac: ready in the best possible condition. Derived from STRAC (Strategic Army Command), where units were kept at peak readiness in the United States itself.

Strip alert: fully armed aircraft at a base or forward strip ready to take off within five minutes

Sugar reports: mail from home or specifically from a girlfriend

Surv: surveillance aircraft

TAC: Tactical Air Command

Tac air: tactical air support

Tail-end Charlie: the last man in a given file

Talk-quick: a secure voice communications system

Talon Vise: original name of the military contingency for the U.S. evacuation of Saigon; see Operation Frequent Wind

Tango-boat: U.S. landing boat modified for use in the Mekong Delta

Tank farm: group of storage tanks

TAOR: tactical area of operational responsibility

Terminate with Extreme Prejudice: a CIA euphemism for assassination

Tet: Vietnamese Lunar New Year holiday period

III Corps: military region between Saigon and the Highlands

III MAF: III Marine Amphibious Force

Thump-gun: nickname for the M79 40mm grenade launcher, a popular squad weapon

Thunder run: movement of armored columns up and down a road or trail with the vehicles firing alternately to each side

Tiger cages: term describing cells at the Con Son Correction Center on Con Son Island

Tigers: battalion patrol and ambush element

Tiger suits: striped camouflage jungle fatigues

Tonkin: northern section of Vietnam

Top: First Sergeant of a company; also known as the First Shirt

TOT: time on target; an artillery term meaning artillery rounds from different batteries dropped onto a target simultaneously

Track: slang expression for an APC

Tri-Thien Front: North Vietnamese military region comprising Quang Tri and Thua Thien provinces. Unlike other Communist military districts in South Vietnam, it was controlled directly by North Vietnam and not indirectly through COSVN.

Truong Son Corridor: supply lines paralleling the Ho Chi Minh Trail but located within South Vietnam

Tunnel rat: a U.S. soldier who searched enemy tunnel systems with a flashlight

Turtle: a replacement, so named because it seemed like forever until he arrived

XXIV Corps: U.S. Army command activated in 1968 to operate in I Corps Tactical Zone

UCLA: University of California at Los Angeles

Uncle Ho: Ho Chi Minh

USAF: U.S. Air Force

USAID: U.S. Agency for International Development

USARMYFMR: U.S. Army Forces Military Region

USARPAC: U.S. Army, Pacific

USARV: U.S. Army, Vietnam

USIA: U.S. Information Agency. Established in 1953 with the purpose of international dissemination of information about the United States Overseas, the agency was referred to as the USIS.

USMC: U.S. Marine Corps

USO: United Service Organizations

Utilities: Marine slang for their combat fatigues

VA: Veterans Administration

VC: Vietcong

VIC: Vietcong infrastructure

VDC: Vietnam Day Committee

Victor Charlie: phonetic alphabetization of VC, the popular name for the Vietcong

Vietcong: Communist forces fighting the South Vietnamese government

Vietminh: Viet Nam Doc Lap Dong Minh Hoi, or the Vietnamese Independence League

Vietnamization: President Nixon's program to gradually turn the war over to the South Vietnamese while phasing out American troops

VMS: Vietnam Moratorium Committee

VNA: Vietnam National Army

VNAF: Vietnamese Air Force (South)

VNMC: South Vietnamese Marine Corps

VNN: South Vietnamese Navy

VNSF: South Vietnamese Special Forces

VNQDD: Viet Nam Quoc Dan Dang, or Nationalist party of Vietnam

VVA: Vietnam Veterans of America

VVAW: Vietnamese Veterans Against the War

WAAPM: wide area antipersonnel munition

Walk in the sun: ground troop movement free of the risk of combat

Waste: to kill or destroy

Web gear: canvas belt and shoulder straps used for packing equipment and ammunition on infantry operations

Wheel jockeys: truck drivers on convoy or line-haul operations

Whiskey Papa, Willie Peter, W-P: phonetic alphabetization for white phosphorus mortar or artillery rounds and grenades

Whistler: artillery fuse deliberately set to scare troops up front

The White Lie Ward: the Da Nang hospital ward for hopeless cases

White Mice: South Vietnamese police. The nickname came from their uniform white helmets and gloves.

WIA: wounded in action

Widow-maker: nickname for the M16 rifle

Wild Weasel: new weapons system for tactical fighter aircraft allowing for the detection and destruction of enemy surface-to-air missiles and antiaircraft installations

Willie Peter: popular nickname for white phosphorus mortar or artillery rounds or grenades

Winchester: radio communication meaning "out of ammunition"

WOMs: Wise Old Men

The world: the United States

WRL: War Resisters League

W-P: white phosphorus mortar/artillery rounds or grenades

XO: executive officer second in command to the senior officer

Yards: Montagnard soldiers

Zap: to shoot at and hit, wound, kill, or destroy

Zippo: flamethrower

Zippo mission: search-and-destroy mission

Zoo: the jungle

Zonked: drugged

Sources

Dougan, Clark, et al. *The Vietnam Experience: Nineteen Sixty-Eight*, 1983.

Dougan, Clark, et al. *The Vietnam Experience: The Fall of the South*, 1985.

Doyle, Edward, et al. *The Vietnam Experience: America Takes Over, 1965–67*, 1982.

Doyle, Edward, et al. *The Vietnam Experience: Passing the Torch*, 1981.

Fulghum, David, et al. *The Vietnam Experience: South Vietnam on Trial*, 1984.

Lewy, Guenter. *America in Vietnam*, 1978.

Lipsman, Samuel, et al. *The Vietnam Experience: Fighting for Time*, 1983.

Maitland, Terrence, et al. *The Vietnam Experience: A Contagion of War*, 1983.

Maitland, Terrence, et al. *The Vietnam Experience: Raising the Stakes*, 1982.

Santoli, Al. *To Bear Any Burden: The Vietnam War and Its Aftermath in the Words of Americans and Southeast Asians*, 1985.

Santoli, Al. *Everything We Had: An Oral History of the Vietnam War by Thirty-Three American Soldiers Who Fought It*, 1981.

Stanton, Shelby L. *Vietnam Order of Battle*, 1981

Terry, Wallace. *Bloods: An Oral History of the Vietnam War by Black Veterans*, 1984.

Whitfield, Danny J. *Historical and Cultural Dictionary of Vietnam*, 1976.

Specialist 4 Charles McDivitt
from Company B, 1st Battalion,
16th Infantry of the 1st Infantry
Division balances on a log
over a stream while on
patrol in Gia Dinh Province
on March 10, 1968.

Appendix D
A Chronology of the Vietnam War, 1945–1975

1945

Sept. 02	Ho Chi Minh proclaims the Democratic Republic of Vietnam.
Sept. 26	A. Peter Dewey, head of the OSS mission in Saigon, is shot by Vietminh troops, becoming the first American to die in the Vietnam War.

1946

Mar. 06	Franco-Vietnamese Accords signed.
June 01	The Fontainebleau Conference convenes.
Dec. 19	The Vietminh attack French forces in Tonkin, formally beginning the First Indochina War.

1948

June 05	The French name Bao Dai head of state of Vietnam.

1949

Mar. 08	Élysée Agreement signed.
Oct. 01	Mao Zedong proclaims the People's Republic of China.

1950

Jan. 14	Ho Chi Minh again proclaims establishment of the Democratic Republic of Vietnam.
June 27	President Harry S. Truman announces increased U.S. military assistance to Vietnam.
Aug. 03	United States Military Assistance and Advisory Group arrives in Saigon.
Dec. 30	United States signs a Mutual Defense Assistance Agreement with France, Vietnam, Cambodia, and Laos.

1952

Nov. 04	Dwight D. Eisenhower is elected president.

1953

July 27	Korean War armistice is signed.

1954

Mar. 13	Vietminh attack the French fortress at Dien Bien Phu.
Mar. 20	Admiral Arthur Radford proposes Operation Vulture to assist the French in defending Dien Bien Phu.
Apr. 07	President Dwight D. Eisenhower uses the domino analogy to explain the political significance of Indochina.
Apr. 25	Winston Churchill and the British refuse to participate in Operation Vulture.
Apr. 29	President Eisenhower announces that the United States will not provide air support to the French garrison at Dien Bien Phu.
May 07	The Vietminh conquer Dien Bien Phu.
May 08	The Geneva Conference opens.
July 20	France signs a cease-fire ending hostilities in Indochina.
Aug. 01	The first of nearly one million refugees from North Vietnam cross into South Vietnam.
Sept. 08	United States signs the Manila Treaty forming the Southeast Asia Treaty Organization.

1955

Mar. 28	Ngo Dinh Diem attacks the Binh Xuyen.
June 05	Ngo Dinh Diem attacks the Hoa Hao.
July 06	Ngo Dinh Diem repudiates the Geneva Agreements and refuses to plan for open elections throughout the country.
Oct. 26	Ngo Dinh Diem proclaims the Republic of Vietnam with himself as president.

1957

May 5–19	Ngo Dinh Diem visits the United States.

1959

Apr. 04	President Eisenhower makes his first commitment to maintain South Vietnam as a separate nation.
Apr. 22	Christian A. Herter replaces John Foster Dulles as secretary of state.
July 01	General Lyman Lemnitzer replaces General Maxwell Taylor as chief of staff, U.S. Army.
July 08	First American servicemen (Major Dale Bius and Master Sergeant Chester Ovnard) killed by Vietcong attack at Bien Hoa.
Dec. 01	Thomas S. Gates Jr. replaces Neil H. McElroy as secretary of defense.
Dec. 31	Approximately 760 U.S. military personnel in Vietnam.

1960

Oct. 01	General George Decker replaces General Lyman Lemnitzer as chief of staff, U.S. Army.
Dec. 20	National Liberation Front established.
Dec. 31	Approximately 900 U.S. military personnel in Vietnam.

1961

Jan. 21	John F. Kennedy succeeds Dwight D. Eisenhower as president. Dean Rusk succeeds Christian A. Herter as secretary of state. Robert S. McNamara succeeds Thomas S. Gates Jr. as secretary of defense. McGeorge Bundy succeeds Gordon Gray as national security adviser.
Jan. 28	Kennedy approves a Vietnam counterinsurgency plan.
Mar. 23	Kennedy insists that a Laotian cease-fire must precede negotiations to establish a neutral Laos.
May 9–15	Vice President Lyndon Johnson visits South Vietnam and recommends a strong American commitment there. Geneva Conference on Laos opens.
June 09	President Ngo Dinh Diem asks for U.S. military advisers to train the South Vietnamese Army.
July 01	General Maxwell Taylor is appointed military adviser to president John F. Kennedy.
Oct. 01	Ngo Dinh Diem requests a bilateral defense treaty with the United States.
Nov. 03	General Maxwell Taylor concludes that U.S. military, financial, and political aid will bring victory without a U.S. takeover of the war. He advises Kennedy to send 8,000 U.S. combat troops to Vietnam.
Dec. 15	Kennedy restates U.S. commitment to an independent South Vietnam.
Dec. 31	U.S. military personnel in Vietnam now number 3,205.

1962

Feb. 06	MACV (U.S. Military Assistance Command, Vietnam) established in Saigon under the command of General Paul Harkins. The major buildup of American forces begins.
Feb. 14	Kennedy authorizes U.S. military advisers in Vietnam to return fire if fired upon.
Mar. 22	United States launches the Strategic Hamlet (rural pacification) Program.
May 15	United States sends 5,000 marines and 50 jet fighters to Thailand to resist Communist aggression in Laos.

July 23	Geneva Accords on Laos signed.
Oct. 01	General Earle Wheeler replaces General George Decker as chief of staff, U.S. Army. General Maxwell Taylor replaces General Lyman Lemnitzer as chairman, Joint Chiefs of Staff.
Dec. 31	U.S. military personnel now in Vietnam number 11,300.

1963

Aug. 21	South Vietnam troops attack Buddhist pagodas.
Aug. 22	Henry Cabot Lodge replaces Frederick Nolting as U.S. ambassador to Vietnam.
Aug. 24	State Department instructs Henry Cabot Lodge to eliminate the influence of Ngo Dinh Nhu in the South Vietnamese government.
Nov. 01	Military coup overthrows the government of President Ngo Dinh Diem.
Nov. 02	Diem and his brother Ngo Dinh Nhu assassinated.
Nov. 22	President John F. Kennedy assassinated.
Dec. 31	U.S. military personnel in Vietnam now number 16,300.

1964

Feb. 07	Johnson removes American dependents from South Vietnam.
June 20	General William Westmoreland replaces General Paul Harkins as head of MACV.
June 23	General Maxwell Taylor replaces Henry Cabot Lodge as U.S. ambassador to South Vietnam.
June 30	Admiral Ulysses S. Grant Sharp replaces Admiral Harry D. Felt as CINCPAC.
July 03	General Harold Johnson replaces General Earle Wheeler as chief of staff, U.S. Army.
Aug. 02	U.S. destroyer *Maddox* allegedly attacked by North Vietnamese patrol boats in the Gulf of Tonkin.
Aug. 04	U.S. destroyer *Turner Joy* claims attack by North Vietnamese patrol boats.
Aug. 07	U.S. Congress passes Gulf of Tonkin Resolution.
Oct. 01	U.S. Army 5th Special Forces Group arrives in Vietnam.
Nov. 01	Vietcong attack Bien Hoa Air Base. Six U.S. B–57 bombers destroyed; five American service personnel killed.
Nov. 02	Johnson defeats Senator Barry Goldwater in presidential election.
Dec. 24	Vietcong kill two U.S. soldiers in an attack on the Brinks Hotel in Saigon.
Dec. 31	U.S. military personnel in Vietnam now number 23,300.

1965

Feb. 07	Vietcong launch a widespread attack on American military installations in South Vietnam.
Mar. 02	Operation Rolling Thunder begins.
Mar. 08	First American combat troops (U.S. Third Marine regiment) arrive in Vietnam to defend Da Nang.
Mar. 24	First teach-in held at the University of Michigan.
Apr. 06	Johnson permits U.S. ground combat troops to conduct offensive operations in South Vietnam.
Apr. 17	Students for a Democratic Society hold antiwar rally in Washington, D.C.
May 15	National Teach-In held throughout the country.
June 08	State Department reports that Johnson has authorized the use of U.S. troops in direct combat if the South Vietnamese Army requests assistance.
June 18	Arc Light Operations begin.
July 08	Henry Cabot Lodge succeeds Maxwell Taylor as U.S. ambassador to South Vietnam.
Aug. 18	Operation Starlight begins.
Aug. 21	Operation Starlight ends.
Oct. 15-16	Antiwar protests in forty American cities.
Oct. 23	Operation Silver Bayonet begins.
Nov. 14-16	Battle of the Ia Drang Valley.
Nov. 20	Operation Silver Bayonet ends.

| Dec. 25 | Johnson suspends bombing of North Vietnam (Operation Rolling Thunder) and invites North Vietnam to negotiate. |
| Dec. 31 | U.S. military personnel in Vietnam now number 184,300; 636 U.S. military personnel killed in action to date; 22,420 allied troops in Vietnam. |

1966

Jan. 19	Operation Van Buren begins.
Jan. 24	Operation Masher/White Wing/ Thank Phong II begins.
Jan. 31	Bombing of North Vietnam (Operation Rolling Thunder) resumes.
Feb. 04	Senate Foreign Relations Committee opens televised hearings on the Vietnam War.
Feb. 06	President Lyndon Johnson convenes the Honolulu Conference.
Feb. 21	Operation Van Buren ends.
Mar. 01	Senate refuses to repeal the Gulf of Tonkin Resolution.
Mar. 04	Operation Utah/Lien Ket 26 begins.
Mar. 06	Operation Masher/White Wing/Thang Phong II ends.
Mar. 08	Operation Utah/Lien Ket 26 begins.
Mar. 20	Operation Texas/Lien Ket 28 begins. President Lyndon Johnson convenes the Guam Conference.
Mar. 24	Operation Texas/Lien Ket 28 ends.
Apr. 01	Walt Rostow replaces McGeorge Bundy as national security adviser.
Apr. 07	President Lyndon Johnson offers the Johns Hopkins Speech.
May 01	U.S. forces bombard Vietcong targets in Cambodia.
May 10	Operation Paul Revere/Than Phong 14 begins.
June 02	Operation Hawthorne/Dan Tang 61 begins. Operation El Paso II begins.
June 21	Operation Hawthorne/Dan Tang 61 ends.
June 29	United States bombs oil facilities in Haiphong and Hanoi.
July 04	Operation Macon begins.
July 07	Operation Hastings/Deckhouse II begins.
July 13	Operation El Paso II ends.
July 30	Operation Paul Revere/Than Phong 14 ends.
Aug. 01	Operation Paul Revere II begins.
Aug. 03	Operation Hasting/Deckhouse II ends. Operation Prairie begins.
Aug. 06	Operation Colorado/Lien Ket 52 begins.
Aug. 21	Operation Colorado/Lien Ket 52 ends.
Aug. 25	Operation Paul Revere II ends.
Aug. 26	Operation Byrd begins.
Sept. 14	Operation Attleboro begins.
Sept. 23	Operation Maeng Ho 6 (South Korean Capital Division) begins.
Oct. 02	Operation Irving begins.
Oct. 18	Operation Paul Revere IV begins.
Oct. 24	Operation Irving ends.
Oct. 25	Operation Thayer II begins.
Oct. 26	Johnson visits U.S. troops in Vietnam.
Oct. 27	Operation Macon ends.
Nov. 09	Operation Maeng Ho 6 ends.
Nov. 24	Operation Attleboro ends.
Nov. 30	Operation Fairfax begins.
Dec. 30	Operation Paul Revere IV ends.
Dec. 31	U.S. military personnel now in Vietnam number 385,300; 6,644 U.S. military personnel killed in action to date; 52,500 allied military personnel in Vietnam.

1967

Jan. 01	Operation Sam Houston begins.
Jan. 06	Operation Palm Beach begins.
Jan. 08	Operation Cedar Falls begins.

Jan. 26	Operation Cedar Falls ends.
Jan. 31	Operation Prairie ends.
Feb. 01	Operation Prairie II begins.
Feb. 11	Operation Pershing begins.
Feb. 12	Operation Thayer II ends.
Feb. 13	Operation Enterprise begins.
Feb. 17	Operation Lien Ket 81 begins.
Feb. 22	Operation Lien Ket 81 ends.
	Operation Junction City begins.
Mar. 07	Operation Oh Jac Kyo I (South Korean) begins.
Mar. 18	Operation Prairie II ends.
Apr. 05	Operation Sam Houston ends.
	Operation Francis Marion begins.
Apr. 15	One hundred thousand antiwar protesters rally in New York.
Apr. 18	Operation Oh Jac Kyo I ends.
Apr. 21	Operation Union begins.
May 01	Ellsworth Bunker replaces Henry Cabot Lodge as U.S. ambassador to South Vietnam.
May 09	Robert Komer appointed deputy to the MACV commander.
May 14	Operation Junction City ends.
	Operation Kole Kole begins.
May 17	Operation Union ends.
May 19	U.S. planes bomb a power plant in Hanoi.
May 25	Operation Union II begins.
May 31	Operation Palm Beach ends.
June 05	Operation Union II ends.
July 02	Operation Buffalo begins.
June 07	Congressional Joint Economic committee estimates the war will cost $4 to $6 billion more in 1967 than the $20.3 billion requested by Johnson.
June 14	Operation Buffalo ends.
June 16	Operation Kingfisher begins.
Sept. 03	Nguyen Van Thieu elected president of South Vietnam.
Sept. 04	Operation Swift begins.
Sept. 05	Operation Dragon Fire begins.
Sept. 15	Operation Swift ends.
Sept. 19	Operation Bolling begins.
Sept. 27	Operation Shenandoah II begins.
Sept. 29	Johnson offers to stop bombing of North Vietnam if they will immediately come to the negotiating table (San Antonio Formula).
Oct. 12	Operation Francis Marion ends.
	Operation MacArthur begins.
Oct. 21	Fifty thousand antiwar activists protest at the Pentagon.
Oct. 30	Operation Dragon Fire ends.
Oct. 31	Operation Kingfisher ends.
Nov. 01	Operation Scotland begins.
Nov. 11	Operation Wheeler/Wallowa begins.
Nov. 19	Operation Shenandoah II ends.
Dec. 07	Operation Kole Kole ends.
Dec. 08	Operation Yellowstone begins.
Dec. 14	Operation Fairfax ends.
Dec. 17	Operation Uniontown begins.
	Operation Maeng Ho 9 begins.
Dec. 19	Operation Muscatine begins.
Dec. 31	U.S. military personnel now in Vietnam number 485,600; 16,021 U.S. military personnel killed in action to date.

1968

Jan. 03	Senator Eugene McCarthy announces his decision to seek the Democratic presidential nomination.

Jan. 19	Operation Pershing ends.
Jan. 20	Operation McLain begins.
	Operation Byrd ends.
Jan. 21	Operation Lancaster II begins.
	Operation Nicaragua begins.
	NVA siege of Khe Sanh begins.
Jan. 22	Operation Pershing II begins.
	Operation Jeb Stuart begins.
Jan. 30	Operation Maeng Ho 9 ends.
	Tet Offensive begins.
Jan. 31	Vietcong and NVA capture Hue.
	General Leonard F. Chapman replaces General Wallace M. Greene as Marine Corps commandant.
Feb. 01	Richard M. Nixon announces his candidacy for the presidency.
Feb. 05	Operation Tran Hung Dao begins.
Feb. 16	Operation Maeng Ho 10 begins.
Feb. 17	Operation Tran Hung Dao ends.
	Operation Tran Hung Dao II begins.
Feb. 24	Operation Yellowstone ends.
Feb. 25	ARVN and U.S. troops reconquer Hue.
Feb. 26	Operation Houston begins.
Feb. 27	Westmoreland requests 206,000 more troops.
	CBS anchorman Walter Cronkite predicts over the evening news that the war cannot be won.
Feb. 29	Operation Pershing II ends.
	Operation Napoleon/Saline begins.
Mar. 01	Operation Maeng Ho 10 ends.
Mar. 08	Operation Uniontown ends.
	Operation Tran Hung Dao ends.
Mar. 11	Operation Enterprise ends.
	Operation Saratoga ends.
	Operation Quyet Thang begins.
Mar. 12	Eugene McCarthy wins the New Hampshire Democratic presidential primary.
Mar. 16	Senator Robert Kennedy announces his decision to seek the Democratic presidential nomination.
	My Lai massacre takes place.
Mar. 17	Operation Duong Cua Dan begins.
Mar. 25–26	Senior Advisory Group on Vietnam recommends deescalation of the American commitment in Vietnam.
Mar. 30	Operation Cochise Green begins.
Mar. 31	Operation Scotland ends.
	Operation Jeb Stuart ends.
	Lyndon Johnson announces his decision not to run for reelection.
Apr. 01	Operation Pegasus/Lam Son 207 begins.
	Operation Carentan II begins.
Apr. 07	Operation Quyet Thang ends.
Apr. 08	Operation Toan Thang begins.
	Operation Burlington Trail begins.
Apr. 15	Operation Pegasus/Lam Son 207 ends.
	Operation Scotland II begins.
Apr. 19	Operation Delaware/Lam Son 216 begins.
Apr. 23	Columbia University demonstrations begin.
Apr. 26	Two hundred thousand people in NYC demonstrate against the war.
Apr. 27	Vice President Hubert Humphrey announces his decision to seek the Democratic presidential nomination.
May 03	Johnson announces that formal peace talks will take place in Paris.
May 04	Operation Allen Brook begins.
May 12	Vietnam peace talks open in Paris.
May 17	Operation Carentan II ends.
	Operation Delaware/Lam Son 216 ends.

Operation Jeb Stuart III begins.

Operation Nevada Eagle begins.

May 18 Operation Mameluke Thrust begins.

May 31 Operation Toan Thang ends.

June 06 Robert Kennedy is assassinated.

June 10 Operation Muscatine ends.

July 01 General Creighton Abrams replaces General William Westmoreland as head of MACV.

July 03 General William Westmoreland replaces General Harold Johnson as chief of staff, U.S. Army.

July 17 Operation Quyet Chien begins.

July 30 Operation Truong Cong Dinh ends.

Operation Duong Cua Dan ends.

July 31 Admiral John McCain replaces Admiral U.S. Grant Sharp as CINCPAC.

Aug. 02 Operation Lam Son 245 begins.

Aug. 24 Operation Allen Brook ends.

Operation Tien Bo begins.

Aug. 28 Antiwar protests and riots in Chicago during the Democratic National Convention.

Sept. 09 Operation Tien Bo ends.

Sept. 11 Operation Lam Son 261 begins.

Sept. 12 Operation Houston ends.

Oct. 16 Operation Lam Son 271 begins.

Oct. 23 Operation Mameluke Thrust ends.

Oct. 24 Operation Henderson Hill begins.

Oct. 31 Johnson announces end of bombing of North Vietnam.

Operation Rolling Thunder ends.

Nov. 03 Operation Jeb Stuart III ends.

Nov. 05 Richard Nixon defeats Hubert Humphrey in the 1968 presidential election.

Nov. 11 Operation Wheeler/Wallowa ends.

Operation Burlington Trail ends.

Nov. 23 Operation Lancaster II ends.

Dec. 01 Operation Speedy Express begins.

Dec. 06 Operation Henderson Hill ends.

Operation Taylor Common begins.

Dec. 08 Operation Le Loi I begins.

Dec. 09 Operation Napoleon/Saline ends.

Dec. 31 U.S. military personnel in Vietnam now number 536,000; 30,610 U.S. military personnel killed in action to date; 65,600 allied troops in Vietnam.

1969

Jan. 01 Operation Quyet Thang begins.

Operation Rice Farmer begins.

Jan. 22 Operation Dewey Canyon begins.

Richard Nixon inaugurated as president.

William Rogers becomes secretary of state.

Melvin Laird becomes secretary of defense.

Henry Kissinger becomes national security adviser.

Jan. 31 Operation Bolling ends.

Operation MacArthur ends.

Operation McLain ends.

Operation Cochise Green ends.

Feb. 10 Operation Le Loi I ends.

Feb. 24 Operation Quyet Thang 22 begins.

Feb. 27 Operation Quang Nam begins.

Feb. 28 Operation Kentucky ends.

Operation Scotland II ends.

Operation Nevada Eagle ends.

Mar. 01 Operation Oklahoma Hills begins.

Operation Wayne Grey begins.

Mar. 04 Operation Quyet Chien ends.

Mar. 07 Operation Taylor Common ends.

Mar. 10 Operation Quyet Thang 22 ends.

Mar. 18 Operation Dewey Canyon ends.

Operation Menu begins.

Mar. 20 Operation Quyet Thang 25 begins.

Mar. 26 Women Strike for Peace demonstration in Washington, D.C.

Mar. 31 Operation Quyet Thang 25 ends.

Apr. 14 Operation Wayne Grey ends.

Apr. 15 Operation Washington Green begins.

Apr. 18 Operation Dan Thang 69 begins.

Apr. 22 Operation Lam Son 277 begins.

Operation Putnam Tiger begins.

Apr. 24 Operations Lam Son 245, 261, and 271 end.

Apr. 30 The number of U.S. military personnel in Vietnam reaches 543,300.

May 01 Operation Virginia Ridge begins.

May 10 Operation Apache Snow begins.

May 14 Nixon proposes peace plan for Vietnam involving mutual troop withdrawal.

May 15 Operation Dan Quyen 38-A begins.

May 16 Lamar Plain begins.

May 29 Operation Oklahoma Hills ends.

May 31 Operation Speedy Express ends.

June 07 Operation Apache Snow ends.

Operation Dan Quyen 38-A ends.

June 08 Nixon announces the removal of 25,000 troops from Vietnam.

June 20 Operation Quang Nam ends.

Operation Lam Son 277 ends.

July 16 Operation Virginia Ridge ends.

July 21 Operation Idaho Canyon begins.

July 25 Richard Nixon proclaims the Nixon Doctrine.

Aug. 13 Operation Lamar Plain ends.

Aug. 25 Operation Lien Ket 414 begins.

Aug. 26 Operation Lien Ket 531 begins.

Aug. 27 U.S. 9th Infantry Division withdraws from Vietnam.

Aug. 31 Operation Rice Farmer ends.

Sept. 03 Ho Chi Minh dies.

Sept. 22 Operation Putnam Tiger ends.

Sept. 25 Operation Idaho Canyon ends.

Sept. 29 Operation Quyet Thang 21/38 begins.

Oct. 15 National Moratorium antiwar demonstrations staged throughout the United States.

Nov. 01 Operation Dan Tien 33D begins.

Nov. 12 Operation Dan Tien 40 begins.

Nov. 15 The New Mobilization Committee to End the War in Vietnam sponsors a demonstration of 250,000 in Washington, D.C.

Nov. 16 My Lai massacre described in the press.

Nov. 30 U.S. 3d Division withdraws from Vietnam.

Dec. 07 Operation Randolph Glen begins.

Dec. 11 U.S. 3d Brigade, 82d Airborne Division, withdraws from Vietnam.

Dec. 28 Operation Dan Tien 33D ends.

Operation Dan Tien 40 ends.

Dec. 31 Operation Quyet Thang ends.

Operation Dan Thang 69 ends.

Operation Lien Ket 414 ends.

Operation Lien Ket 531 ends.

Operation Quyet Thang 21/38 ends.

U.S. military personnel strength in Vietnam declines to 475,200; 40,024 U.S. military personnel killed in action to date. Allied personnel in Vietnam totals 70,300.

1970

Feb. 20	Henry Kissinger opens secret peace negotiations in Paris.
Mar. 18	Prince Norodom Sihanouk of Cambodia deposed by General Lon Nol.
Mar. 31	Operation Randolph Glen ends.
Apr. 01	Operation Texas Star begins.
Apr. 15	U.S. 1st Infantry Division withdraws from Vietnam.
Apr. 29	Operations in Cambodia begin.
Apr. 30	United States invades Cambodia.
May 04	National Guard troops kill four students at Kent State University during demonstrations against the Cambodian invasion.
June 30	Operations in Cambodia end.
Sept. 05	Operation Texas Star ends.
	Operation Jefferson Glenn/Op ORD 13–70 begins.
Oct. 11	U.S. 3d Brigade, 9th Infantry Division, leaves Vietnam.
Nov. 21	Unsuccessful raid on the Son Tay Prison in North Vietnam.
Dec. 07	U.S. 4th Infantry Division leaves Vietnam.
Dec. 08	U.S. 25th Infantry Division withdraws from Vietnam.
Dec. 22	U.S. Congress prohibits U.S. combat forces or advisers in Cambodia and Laos.
Dec. 31	U.S. military personnel strength in Vietnam reaches 334,600; 44,245 U.S. military personnel killed in action to date. Allied military personnel declines to 67,700.

1971

Jan. 01	Operation Washington Green ends.
Jan. 30	Operation Lam Son 719 begins.
	Operation Dewey Canyon II begins.
Jan. 31	Winter Soldier Investigation begins in Detroit.
Feb. 07	Operation Dewey Canyon II ends.
Mar. 03	U.S. 5th Special Forces Group leaves Vietnam.
Mar. 05	U.S. 11th Armored Cavalry Regiment withdraws from Vietnam.
Mar. 29	Lt. William L. Calley Jr. found guilty of murder.
Apr. 06	Operation Lam Son 719 ends.
Apr. 14	U.S. III Marine Amphibious Force withdraws from Vietnam.
Apr. 20	Demonstrators in Washington, D.C., and San Francisco call for an end the war.
Apr. 29	U.S. 1st Cavalry Division withdraws from Vietnam.
Apr. 30	U.S. 2d Brigade, 25th Infantry Division, withdraws from Vietnam.
May 3–5	People's Coalition for Peace and Justice demonstrates against the war in Washington, D.C.
June 13	*New York Times* starts publishing the Pentagon Papers.
June 30	Supreme Court allows publication of the Pentagon Papers.
Aug. 25	U.S. 173d Airborne Brigade withdraws from Vietnam.
Aug. 27	U.S. 1st Brigade, 5th Infantry Division, withdraws from Vietnam.
Aug. 31	Royal Thai Army withdraws from Vietnam.
Oct. 08	Operation Jefferson Glenn/OP ORD 13–70 ends.
Nov. 12	Nixon confines U.S. ground forces to a defensive role.
Nov. 29	Americal Division divided into individual units.
Dec. 26	Nixon orders resumption of bombing of North Vietnam.
Dec. 31	U.S. military strength declines to 156,800; 45,626 U.S. military personnel killed in action to date. Allied military personnel in Vietnam declines to 53,900.

1972

Feb. 21	Nixon seeks détente with the People's Republic of China by visiting Beijing.
Mar. 10	U.S. 101st Airborne Division leaves Vietnam.
Mar. 23	United States suspends Paris peace talks until North Vietnam and the NLF enter into "serious discussions."

Mar. 30	Eastertide Offensive begins.
Apr. 07	Battle of An Loc begins.
Apr. 15	U.S. bombing of Hanoi begins again.
Apr. 15–20	Widespread antiwar demonstrations across the United States.
Apr. 27	Paris peace talks resume.
May 01	North Vietnamese conquer Quang Tri.
May 04	United States suspends the Paris peace talks.
May 08	U.S. Navy mines North Vietnamese ports.
June 18	NVA forces an end to the battle of An Loc.
June 22	Watergate break-in and arrests.
June 26	U.S. 3d Brigade, 1st Cavalry Division, withdraws from Vietnam.
June 29	U.S. 196th Infantry Brigade withdraws from Vietnam.
July 01	General Bruce Palmer Jr. becomes acting chief of staff, U.S. Army.
July 13	Paris peace talks resume after ten weeks.
Aug. 23	U.S. 3d Battalion, 21st Infantry, withdraws from Vietnam.
Sept. 15	ARVN forces recapture Quang Tri.
Sept. 26–27	Henry Kissinger conducts secret talks with North Vietnamese diplomats in Paris.
Oct. 16	General Creighton Abrams becomes chief of staff, U.S. Army.
Oct. 17	Peace talks begin in Laos.
Oct. 19–20	Kissinger meets with President Nguyen Van Thieu in Saigon to secure South Vietnamese support for the pending Paris Peace Accords.
Nov. 07	Nixon is reelected president in a landslide over Senator George McGovern.
Nov. 20–21	Kissinger and Le Duc Tho put finishing touches on the Paris Peace Accords.
Dec. 13	Paris peace talks stall.
Dec. 18–29	Operation Linebacker II conducted.
Dec. 31	U.S. military strength declines to 24,000; 45,926 U.S. military personnel killed in action to date. Allied personnel drops to 35,500. SVNAF personnel killed in action to date numbers 195,847.

1973

Jan. 8–12	Kissinger and Le Duc Tho convene more private negotiations.
Jan. 15	Nixon halts all U.S. offensive action against North Vietnam.
Jan. 27	Peace pact signed in Paris by the United States, South Vietnam, North Vietnam, and the National Liberation Front.
Jan. 30	Elliot L. Richardson becomes secretary of defense.
Feb. 12	First of American POWs released by North Vietnam.
Feb. 21	Peace agreement signed in Laos.
Mar. 16	ROK Capital Division and 9th Infantry Division withdraw from Vietnam.
Mar. 29	MACV headquarters removed.
	Last of American POWs released by North Vietnam.
June 13	Implementation accord signed in Paris by the United States, South Vietnam, North Vietnam, and the National Liberation Front.
June 24	Graham Martin becomes U.S. ambassador to South Vietnam.
	Congress prohibits all bombing in Cambodia after August 15.
July 02	James Schlesinger becomes secretary of defense.
Aug. 14	Arc Light Operations end.
	All direct American military operations end in all of Indochina.
Sept. 22	Henry Kissinger becomes secretary of state.
Nov. 07	War Powers Resolution becomes laws despite a presidential veto.
Dec. 31	American military personnel in South Vietnam drops to 50. To date, 46,163 U.S. military personnel killed in action. No allied military personnel remain in Vietnam.

1974

Aug. 09	Nixon resigns the presidency.
	Gerald Ford is inaugurated as president of the United States.
Aug. 20	Congress reduces aid to South Vietnam from $1 billion to $700 million.
Sept. 04	General Creighton Abrams dies.
Sept. 16	Ford offers clemency to draft evaders and military deserters.

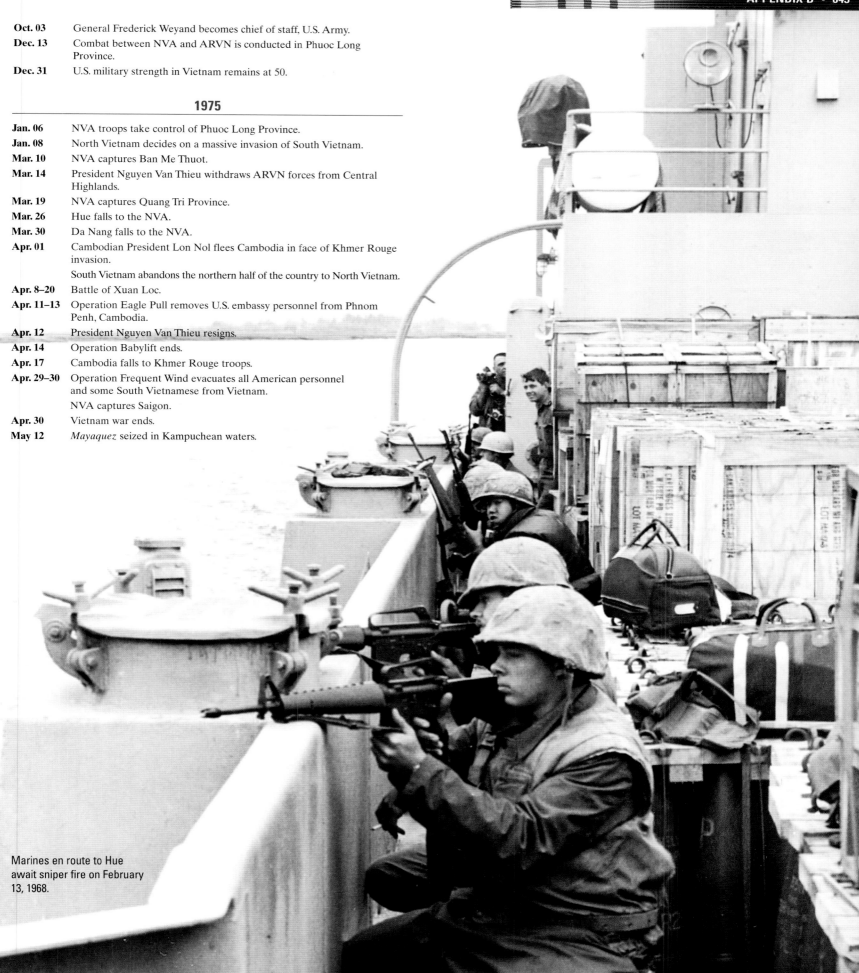

Oct. 03	General Frederick Weyand becomes chief of staff, U.S. Army.
Dec. 13	Combat between NVA and ARVN is conducted in Phuoc Long Province.
Dec. 31	U.S. military strength in Vietnam remains at 50.

1975

Jan. 06	NVA troops take control of Phuoc Long Province.
Jan. 08	North Vietnam decides on a massive invasion of South Vietnam.
Mar. 10	NVA captures Ban Me Thuot.
Mar. 14	President Nguyen Van Thieu withdraws ARVN forces from Central Highlands.
Mar. 19	NVA captures Quang Tri Province.
Mar. 26	Hue falls to the NVA.
Mar. 30	Da Nang falls to the NVA.
Apr. 01	Cambodian President Lon Nol flees Cambodia in face of Khmer Rouge invasion.
	South Vietnam abandons the northern half of the country to North Vietnam.
Apr. 8–20	Battle of Xuan Loc.
Apr. 11–13	Operation Eagle Pull removes U.S. embassy personnel from Phnom Penh, Cambodia.
Apr. 12	President Nguyen Van Thieu resigns.
Apr. 14	Operation Babylift ends.
Apr. 17	Cambodia falls to Khmer Rouge troops.
Apr. 29–30	Operation Frequent Wind evacuates all American personnel and some South Vietnamese from Vietnam.
	NVA captures Saigon.
Apr. 30	Vietnam war ends.
May 12	*Mayaquez* seized in Kampuchean waters.

Marines en route to Hue await sniper fire on February 13, 1968.

Appendix E
Selected Bibliography of the Vietnam War

Air War

Ballard, Jack S. *The United States Air Force in Southeast Asia: Development and Employment of Fixed Wing Gunships, 1962–1972.* 1982.

Bell, Dana. *Warbirds Illustrated. Air War over Vietnam.* vol. II. 1982.

Berger, Carl, ed. *The United States Air Force in Southeast Asia, 1961–1973, An Illustrated Account.* 1977.

Bowers, Ray L. *The U.S. Air Force in Southeast Asia: Tactical Airlift.* 1983.

Buchanan, Albert R. *The Navy's Air War: A Mission Completed.* 1946.

Buckingham, William A. Jr. *Operation Ranch Hand: The United States Air Force and Herbicides in Southeast Asia. 1961–1971.* 1982.

Burbage, Paul, et al. *The Battle for the Skies Over North Vietnam, 1964–1972.* 1976.

Corum, Delbert, et al. *The Tale of Two Bridges.* 1976.

Dong Van Khuyen. *The RVNAF.* 1980.

Drendel, Lou. *Huey.* 1983; *Air War over Southeast Asia.* 1984; *B–52 Stratofortress in Action.* 1984.

Eastman, James N. Jr., Walter Hanak, and Lawrence J. Paszek, eds. *Aces and Aerial Victories: The United States Air Force in Southeast Asia, 1965–1973.* 1976.

Fox, Roger P. *Air Base Defense in the Republic of Vietnam, 1961–1973.* 1979.

Futrell, R. Frank, et al. *Aces and Aerial Victories: The United States Air Force in Southeast Asia, 1965–1973.* 1976.

Futrell, Robert F. *The United States Air Force: The Advisory Years, 1961 to 1965.* 1981.

Gropman, Alan L. *Airpower and the Airlift Evacuation of Kham Duc.* 1979.

Harvey, Frank. *Jane's All the World's Aircraft, 1964–1965.* 1965; *Air War–Vietnam.* 1967.

Lavalle, A.J.C., ed. *Airpower and the 1972 Spring Invasion.* 1976.

Lavalle, A.J.C. *The Battle for the Skies Over North Vietnam.* 1976; *Last Flight from Saigon.* 1978.

Littauer, Raphael, and Norman Uphoff, eds. *The Air War in Indochina.* 1972.

McCarthy, James R., and Allison McCarthy. *George B. Linebacker: A View from the Rock.* 1986.

McDonald, Charles, and A.J.C. Lavalle, eds. *The Vietnamese Air Force 1951–1975: An Analysis of Its Role in Combat.* 1976.

Mason, Robert C. *Chickenhawk.* 1983.

Mersky, Peter, and Norman Polmar. *The Naval Air War in Vietnam: 1965–1975.* 1981.

Mesko, Jim. *Airmobile: The Helicopter War in Vietnam.* 1985.

Mikesh, Robert C. *B–57 Seven Canberra at War: 1964–1972.* 1980.

Momyer, William W. *Airpower in Three Wars.* 1978.

Momyer, William W., and Louis L. Wilson Jr. *The Vietnamese Air Force, 1951–1975: An Analysis of Its Role in Combat.* 1986.

Morrocco, John. *The Vietnam Experience. Rain of Fire: Air War, 1969–1973.* 1984; *The Vietnam Experience. Thunder From Above: Air War, 1941–1968.* 1984.

Nalty, Bernard C. *Air Power and the Fight for Khe Sanh.* 1973; *An Illustrated Guide to the Air War over Vietnam.* 1981.

Nalty, Bernard C., George M. Watson, and Jacob Neufield. *The Air War over Vietnam.* 1971.

Osborne, Arthur M. "Air Defense for the Mining of Haiphong." *U.S. Naval Institute Proceedings,* Series 100 September 1974.

Prados, John. *The Sky Would Fall: Operation Vulture; The U.S. Bombing Mission in Indochina, 1954.* 1983.

Rausa, Rosario. *Skyraider: The Douglas A–1 "Flying Dump Truck."* 1982.

Robbins, Christopher. *Air America.* 1979.

Schneider, Donald K. *Air Force Heroes in Vietnam.* 1986.

Smith, Myron J. Jr. *Air War Southeast Asia, Nineteen Sixty-One to Nineteen Seventy-Three: An Annotated Bibliography and 16mm Film Guide.* 1979.

Thompson, James Clay. *Rolling Thunder: Understanding Policy and Program Failure.* 1980.

Tilford, Earl H. Jr. *Search and Rescue in Southeast Asia, 1961–1975.* 1980.

Tobin, Thomas G., et al. *Last Flight from Saigon.* 1978.

Tolson, John J. *Airmobility, 1961–1971.* 1973.

Windchy, Eugene C. *Tonkin Gulf.* 1971.

Antiwar Movement

Anson, Robert Sam. *McGovern: A Biography.* 1972.

Bannan, John F., and Rosemary S. Bannan. *Law, Morality, and Vietnam: The Peace Militants and the Courts.* 1978.

Baskir, Lawrence M. and William A. Strauss. *Chance and Circumstance: The Draft, the War, and the Vietnam Generation.* 1978.

Bender, David L., ed. *The Vietnam War: Opposing Viewpoints.* 1984.

Bloom, Lynn Z. *Doctor Spock: Biography of a Conservative Radical.* 1972.

Chatfield, Charles, ed. *Peace Movements in America.* 1973.

Chomsky, Noam. *American Power and the New Mandarins.* 1969; *At War with Asia.* 1970.

Cohen, Mitchell, and Dennis Hale, eds. *The New Student Left: An Anthology.* 1966.

Cortright, David. *Soldiers in Revolt.* 1976.

Critchfield, Richard. *The Long Charade: Political Subversion in the Vietnam War.* 1968.

Dellinger, David. *Revolutionary Non-Violence.* 1970.

Destler, I. M., Leslie H. Gelb, and Anthony Lake. *Our Own Worse Enemy.* 1984.

Doan Van, Taoi and David Chanoff. *The Vietnam Gulag.* 1986.

Dougan, Clark, and Samuel Lipsman. *The Vietnam Experience: A Nation Divided.* 1984.

Ellsberg, Daniel. *Papers on the War.* 1972.

Friedman, Leon, and Burt Neuborne. *Unquestioning Obedience to the President: The ACLU Case Against the Legality of the War in Vietnam.* 1972.

Johnson, James Turner. *Just War Tradition and the Restraint of War.* 1981.

King, Martin Luther Jr. *Where Do We Go from Here: Chaos or Community?* 1967.

Larner, Jeremy. *Nobody Knows: Reflections on the McCarthy Campaign of 1968.* 1970.

McCarthy, Eugene. *The Year of the People.* 1969.

Meconis, Charles A. *With Clumsy Grace: The American Catholic Left, 1961–1975.* 1979.

Menashe, Louis, and Ronald Radosh. *Teach-ins: U.S.A.* 1967.

Meyer, Ernest L. *Hey Yellowbacks; The War Diary of a Conscientious Objector.* 1972.

Michener, James. *Kent State: What Happened and Why.* 1971.

Peterson, Richard E., and John Bilorsky. *May 1970: The Campus Aftermath of Cambodia and Kent State.* 1971.

Polenberg, Richard. *One Nation Divisible.* 1980.

Powers, Thomas. *The War at Home: Vietnam and the American People.* 1973; *Vietnam, the War at Home: The Antiwar Movement, 1964–1968.* 1984.

Prugh, George S. *Law at War: Vietnam, 1964–1973.* 1975.

Quigley, Thomas E., ed. *American Catholics and Vietnam.* 1968.

Rosenberg, Milton J., Sidney Verba, and Philip E. Converse. *Vietnam and the Silent Majority.* 1970.

Sale, Kirkpatrick. *SDS.* 1973.

Schandler, Herbert Y. *The Unmaking of a President: Lyndon Johnson and Vietnam.* 1977.

Skolnick, Jerome H., et al. *The Politics of Protest.* 1969.

Staff of the Columbia *Daily Spectator. Up Against the Ivy Wall: A History of the Columbia Crisis.* 1969.

Surrey, Davis S. *Choice of Conscience: Vietnam Era Military and Draft Resisters in Canada.* 1982.

Thomas, Norman M. *Is Conscience a Crime?* 1972.

Walzer, Michael. *Just and Unjust Wars: A Moral Argument with Historical Illustrations.* 1977.

Zaroulis, Nancy, and Gerald Sullivan. *Who Spoke Up? American Protest Against the War in Vietnam, 1963–1975.* 1984.

Biographies

Ambrose, Stephen E. *Eisenhower. Vol. 2, President and Elder Statesman, 1952–1969.* 1984.

Blakey, Scott. *Prisoner at War: The Survival of Commander Richard A. Strattan.* 1978.

Cohen, Warren. *Dean Rusk.* 1980.

Eisele, Albert. *Almost to the Presidency: A Biography of Two American Politicians.* 1972.

Evans, Rowland, and Robert Novak. *Lyndon B. Johnson: The Exercise of Power.* 1966.

Fenn, Charles. *Ho Chi Minh: A Biographical Introduction.* 1973.

Geyelin, Philip. *Lyndon B. Johnson and the World.* 1969.

Goldman, Eric. *The Tragedy of Lyndon Johnson.* 1969.

Halberstam, David. *The Unfinished Odyssey of Robert Kennedy.* 1968; *Ho.* 1971.

Hammer, Richard. *The Court-Martial of Lieutenant William Calley.* 1971.

Hersh, Seymour. *The Price of Power: Kissinger in the Nixon White House.* 1983.

Hoopes, Townsend. *The Devil and John Foster Dulles.* 1973.

Kalb, Bernard, and Marvin Kalb. *Kissinger.* 1974.

Kearns, Doris. *Lyndon Johnson and the American Dream.* 1976.

Johnson, Haynes, and Bernard Gwertzman. *Fulbright: The Dissenter.* 1968.

Lacouture, Jean. *Ho Chi Minh: A Political Biography.* 1968.

Lewis, David. *King: A Critical Biography.* 1970.

McGovern, James R. *Black Eagle: General Daniel "Chappie" James, Jr., USAF.* 1985.

Mazlish, Bruce. *Kissinger: The European Mind in American Policy.* 1976.

Miller, Merle. *Lyndon: An Oral Biography.* 1980.

O'Neill, Robert J. *General Giap: Politician and Strategist.* 1969.

Powell, Lee J. *William Fulbright and America's Lost Crusade: Fulbright's Opposition to the Vietnam War.* 1984.

Pruessen, Ronald W. *John Foster Dulles: The Road to Peace.* 1982.

Rust, William J. *Kennedy In Vietnam.* 1985.

Schlesinger, Arthur M. Jr. *A Thousand Days: John F. Kennedy in the White House.* 1965; *Robert Kennedy and His Times.* 1978.

Sorenson, Theodore C. *Kennedy.* 1965.

Steele, Ronald. *Walter Lippmann and the American Century.* 1980.

Warner, Denis. *The Last Confucian.* 1963.

Wills, Garry. *The Kennedy Imprisonment: A Meditation on Power.* 1982.

Cambodia and Laos

Ablin, David A., and Marlowe Hood, eds. *The Cambodian Agony.* 1986.

Barron, John, and Paul Anthony. *Murder of a Gentle Land.* 1977.

Branfman, Fred. "Presidential War in Laos, 1964–1970." In N. Adams and A. McCoy, eds. *Laos: War and Revolution.* 1970.

Briggs, Lawrence P. *Ancient Khmer Empire.* 1951.

Brown, MacAlister, and Joseph J. Zasloff. *Apprentice Revolutionaries: The Communist Movement in Laos, 1930–1985.* 1986.

Burchett, Wilfred. *The China-Cambodia-Vietnam Triangle.* 1982.

Burns, Richard D., and Milton Leitenberg. *The Wars in Vietnam, Cambodia, and Laos, 1945–1982: A Bibliographic Guide.* 1984.

Caldwell, Malcolm, and Tan Lek. *Cambodia in the Southeast Asian War.* 1973.

Chandler, David P. *A History of Cambodia.* 1983.

Chandler, David P., and Ben Kiernan, eds. *Revolution and Its Aftermath in Kampuchea: Eight Essays.* 1983.

Chang, Pao-Min. *Kampuchea between China and Vietnam.* 1985.

Charny, Joel, and John Spragens Jr. *Obstacles to Recovery in Vietnam and Kampuchea.* 1984.

Dommen, Arthur J. *Laos: The Keystone of Indochina.* 1985.

Etcheson, Craig. *The Rise and Demise of Democratic Kampuchea.* 1984.

Goldstein, Martin E. *American Policy Toward Laos.* 1973.

Haley, P. Edward. *Congress and the Fall of South Vietnam and Cambodia.* 1982.

Hersh, Seymour. *Cover-Up.* 1972.

Hildebrand, George, and Gareth Porter. *Cambodia: Starvation and Revolution.* 1976.

Isaacs, Arnold R. *Without Honor: Defeat in Vietnam and Cambodia.* 1983.

Kiernan, Ben. "How Pol Pot Came to Power." Ph.D. diss., 1986.

Langer, Paul F., and Joseph J. Zasloff. *North Vietnam and the Pathet Lao: Partners in the Struggle for Laos.* 1970.

Leifer, Michael. *Cambodia: The Search for Security.* 1967.

Marshall, S.L.A. *West to Cambodia.* 1983.

Nguyen Duy, Hinh. *Lam Son 719.* 1981.

Osborne, Milton. *Politics and Power in Cambodia.* 1973; *Before Kampuchea: Preludes to Tragedy.* 1985.

Ponchaud, François. *Cambodia: Year Zero.* 1978.

Poole, Peter A. *The Expansion of the Vietnam War Into Cambodia: Action and Response by the Governments of North Vietnam, South Vietnam, Cambodia and the United States.* 1985.

Porter, Gareth, and George C. Hildebrand. *Cambodia: Starvation and Revolution.* 1976.

Ratnam, Perala. *Laos and the Super Powers.* 1980.

Rowan, Roy. *The Four Days of Mayaguez.* 1975.

Sananikone, Gudone. *The Royal Lao Government and U.S. Army Advice and Support.* 1981.

Shaplen, Robert. *Bitter Victory.* 1986.

Shawcross, William. *Sideshow: Kissinger, Nixon, and the Destruction of Cambodia.* 1979; *The Quality of Mercy: Cambodia, Holocaust, and the Modern Conscience.* 1984.

Simon, Sheldon W. *War and Politics in Cambodia: A Communications Analysis.* 1974.

Stevenson, Charles A. *The End of Nowhere: American Policy Toward Laos Since 1954.* 1973.

Sutsakhan, Sak. *The Khmer Republic at War and the Final Collapse.* 1980.

Tran Dinh Tho. *The Cambodian Incursion.* 1979.

Vickery, Michael. *Cambodia, 1975–1982.* 1984.

Vongsavanh, Solitchay. *RLA Military Operations and Activities in the Laotian Panhandle.* 1981.

Diplomacy

Albinski, Henry. *Politics and Foreign Policy in Australia.* 1970.

Ball, George W. *Diplomacy in a Crowded World.* 1976.

Baral, Jaya K. *The Pentagon and the Making of U.S. Foreign Policy: A Case Study of Vietnam, 1960–1968.* 1978.

Bator, Victor. *Vietnam, a Diplomatic Tragedy: Origins of U.S. Involvement.* 1965; *Drawing the Line: The Origin of the American Containment Policy in East Asia,* 1982.

Betts, Richard K. *Soldiers, Statesmen and Cold War Crises.* 1977.

Blum, Robert. *Drawing the Line: The Origin of the American Containment Policy in East Asia.* 1982.

Brown, William A. *The Soviet Role in Asia.* 1983.

Chayes, Abram, et al. *Vietnamese Settlement: Why 1973 Not 1969?* 1973.

Chen, King C. *Vietnam and China, 1938–1954.* 1969.

Cole, Allen, ed. *Conflict in Indochina and Its International Repercussions.* 1956.

Dacy, Douglas. *Foreign Aid, War and Economic and Development: South Vietnam, 1955–1975.* 1988.

Dillard, Walter Scott. *Sixty Days to Peace.* 1982.

Donovan, John C. *The Cold Warriors: A Policy-Making Elite.* 1974.

Drachman, Edward R. *United States Policy Toward Vietnam, 1940–1945.* 1970.

Edmonds, Robin. *Soviet Foreign Policy, 1962–1973: The Paradox of a Superpower.* 1975.

Franck, Thomas M., and Edward Weisband. *Foreign Policy by Congress.* 1980.

Fulbright, J. William. *The Crippled Giant.* 1962; *The Arrogance of Power.* 1967.

Goodman, Allan E. *The Lost Peace: America's Search for a Negotiated Settlement of the Vietnam War.* 1978.

Herrington, Stuart A. *Peace with Honor?* 1983.

Honey, P. J. *Communism in North Vietnam: Its Role in the Sino-Soviet Dispute.* 1963.

Hsiao, Gene T., ed. *The Role of External Powers in the Indochina Crisis.* 1973.

Jordan, Amos A., and William J. Taylor Jr. *American National Security: Policy and Process.* 1981.

Kraslow, David, and Stuart Lorry. *The Secret Search for Peace in Vietnam.* 1968.

Larsen, Stanley Robert, and James Lawton Collins Jr. *Allied Participaton in Vietnam.* 1975.

Lawson, Eugene K. *The Sino-Vietnamese Conflict.* 1984.

Morganthau, Hans. *Vietnam and the United States.* 1973.

Papp, Daniel S. *Vietnam: The View from Moscow, Peking, Washington.* 1981.

Porter, Gareth. *A Peace Denied.* 1975.

Ray, Hemen. *China's Vietnam War.* 1983.

Rosenberger, Leif. *The Soviet Union and Vietnam: An Uneasy Alliance.* 1986.

Rosie, George. *The British in Vietnam: How the Twenty-five Years War Began.* 1970.

Ross, Douglas A. *In the Interests of Peace: Canada and Vietnam, 1954–1973.* 1984.

Sutter, Robert G. *Chinese Foreign Policy after the Cultural Revolution: 1966–1977.* 1978.

Szulc, Tad. *The Illusion of Peace: Foreign Policy in the Nixon Years.* 1978.

Taylor, Charles. *Snow Job: Canada, the United States and Vietnam (1954–1973).* 1974.

Thakur, Ramesh. *Peacekeeping in Vietnam: Canada, India, Poland, and the International Commission.* 1984.

Thies, Wallace. *When Governments Collide: Coercion and Diplomacy in the Vietnam Conflict, 1964–1968.* 1980.

Fall of the South

Butler, David. *The Fall of Saigon.* 1985.

Cao Van Vien. *The Final Collapse.* 1983.

Dawson, Alan. *55 Days: The Fall of South Vietnam.* 1977.

Dougan, Clark, and David Fulghum. *The Vietnam Experience: The Fall of the South.* 1985.

Fulghum, David, and Terrence Maitland. *The Vietnam Experience. South Vietnam on Trial.* 1984.

Haley, Edward P. *Congress and the Fall of South Vietnam and Cambodia.* 1982.

Hosmer, Stephen, et al. *The Fall of South Vietnam.* 1978.

Nguyen Long, with Harry Kendall. *After Saigon Fell.* 1981.

Pilger, John. *The Last Day.* 1975.

Porter, Gareth. *A Peace Denied: The United States, Vietnam, and the Paris Agreement.* 1975.

Snepp, Frank. *Decent Interval.* 1977.

Tobin, Thomas G., et al. *Last Flight from Saigon.* 1978.

Van Tien Dung. *Our Great Spring Victory.* 1977.

Warner, Denis. *Certain Victory: How Hanoi Won the War.* 1977.

First Indochina War

Bodard, Lucien. *The Quicksand War: Prelude to Vietnam.* 1967.

Devillers, Philippe, and Jean Lacouture. *End of a War: Indochina, 1954.* 1969.

Fall, Bernard. *The Viet Minh Regime.* 1956; *Street Without Joy: Insurgency in Vietnam, 1946–1963.* 1961; *Hell in a Very Small Place: The Siege of Dien Bien Phu.* 1966.

Gurtov, Melvin. *The First Vietnam Crisis: Chinese Communist Strategy and United States Involvement, 1953–54.* 1967.

Halberstam, David. *The Making of a Quagmire.* 1964.

Hammer, Ellen. *The Struggle for Indochina.* 1954.

Lancaster, Donald. *The Emancipation of French Indochina.* 1961.

Langlais, Pierre. *Dien Bien Phu.* 1963.

O'Ballance, Edgar. *The Indochina War 1945–1954: A Study in Guerrilla Warfare.* 1964.

Patti, Archimedes L. A. *Why Vietnam? Prelude to America's Albatross.* 1980.

Rose, Lisle Abbott. *Roads of Tragedy: The United States and the Struggle for Asia, 1945–1953.* 1976.

Roy, Jules. *The Battle of Dien Bien Phu.* 1965.

Werth, Alexander. *France 1940–1955.* 1956.

French Empire

Cady, John. *The Roots of French Imperialism in Indochina.* 1954.

Doyle, Edward, and Samuel Lipsman. *The Vietnam Experience: Setting the Stage.* 1981.

Ennis, Thomas. *French Policy and Developments in Indochina.* 1956.

Long, Ngo Vinh. *Before the Revolution: The Vietnamese Peasants Under the French.* 1973.

Marr, David G. *Vietnamese Anticolonialism, 1885–1925.* 1981.

Osborne, Milton E. *The French Presence in Cochinchina and Cambodia: Rule and Response (1859–1905).* 1969.

Taylor, Keith Weller. *The Birth of Vietnam.* 1983.

Thompson, Virginia. *French Indochina.* 1937.

General Histories

Austin, Anthony. *The President's War.* 1971.

Berman, Larry. *Planning a Tragedy: The Americanization of the War in Vietnam.* 1982.

Boettcher, Thomas D. *Vietnam: The Valor and the Sorrow.* 1985.

Bonds, Ray, ed. *The Vietnam War.* 1979.

Bonds, Ray. *The Vietnam War: The Illustrated History of the Conflict in Southeast Asia.* 1983.

Bowman, John S., ed. *The Vietnam War: An Almanac.* 1985.

Braestrup, Peter, ed. *Vietnam As History.* 1984.

Buttinger, Joseph. *Vietnam: The Unforgettable Tragedy.* 1977.

Cairns, James Ford. *The Eagle and the Lotus: Western Intervention in Vietnam, 1847–1968.* 1969.

Charlton, Michael, and Anthony Moncrief. *Many Reasons Why: The American Involvement in Vietnam.* 1978.

Chester, Lewis, Godfrey Hodgson, and Bruce Page. *An American Melodrama.* 1969.

Cooper, Chester L. *The Lost Crusade: America in Vietnam.* 1970.

Doyle, Edward, and Samuel Lipsman. *The Vietnam Experience: Passing the Torch.* 1981.

Fall, Bernard. *The Two Vietnams: A Political and Military Analysis.* 1967.

Fishel, Wesley R., ed. *Vietnam: Anatomy of a Conflict.* 1968.

FitzGerald, Frances. *Fire in the Lake: The Vietnamese and the Americans in Vietnam.* 1972.

Gallucci, Robert L. *Neither Peace Nor Honor: The Politics of American Military Policy in Vietnam.* 1975.

Gattleman, Marvin E., et al., eds. *Vietnam and America: A Documented History.* 1985.

Halberstam, David. *The Best and the Brightest.* 1972.

Hammer, Ellen Joy. *Vietnam, Yesterday and Today.* 1966.

Hammond, William Michael. *The Vietnam War.* 1979.

Harriman, W. Averell, and Elie Abel. *Special Envoy to Churchill and Stalin, 1941–1946.* 1975.

Harrison, James P. *The Endless War: Fifty Years of Struggle in Vietnam.* 1982.

Herring, George C. *America's Longest War: The United States in Vietnam, 1950–1975.* 1986.

Higgins, Marguerite. *Our Vietnam Nightmare.* 1965.

Kahin, George McTurnan, and John W. Lewis. *The United States in Vietnam: An Analysis in Depth of the History of American Involvement in Vietnam.* 1967.

Kalb, Marvin, and Elie Abel. *Roots of Involvement: The U.S. in Asia, 1784–1971.* 1971.

Karnow, Stanley. *Vietnam: A History.* 1983.

Kattenburg, Paul L. *The Vietnam Trauma in American Foreign Policy, 1945–1975.* 1980.

Kendrick, Alexander. *The Wound Within: America in the Vietnam Years, 1945–1974.* 1974.

Kenny, Henry J. *The American Role in Vietnam and East Asia.* n.d.

LeGro, William E. *Vietnam: From Cease-fire to Capitulation.* 1981.

Lewy, Guenter. *America in Vietnam.* 1978.

Maclear, Michael. *The Ten Thousand Day War: Vietnam, 1945–1975.* 1981.

O'Ballance, Edgar. *The Wars in Vietnam: 1954–1973.* 1975; *The Wars in Vietnam: 1954–80.* 1981.

Palmer, Bruce Jr. *The 25-Year War: America's Military Role in Vietnam.* 1984.

Palmer, David R. *Summons of the Trumpet: U.S.-Vietnam in Perspective.* 1978.

Patti, Archimedes. *Why Vietnam? Prelude to America's Albatross.* 1981.

Raskin, Marcus G., and Bernard Fall, eds. *The Viet-Nam Reader: Articles and Documents on American Foreign Policy and the Viet-Nam Crisis.* 1965.

Scigliano, Robert. *South Viet-Nam: Nation Under Stress.* 1964.

Shaplen, Robert. *The Lost Revolution: The U.S. in Vietnam, 1946–1966.* 1966.; *The Road from War: 1965–1970.* 1970.

Smith, Harvey H., et al. *Area Handbook for North Vietnam.* 1967; *Area Handbook for South Vietnam.* 1967.

Smith, R. B. *An International History of the Vietnam War: Revolution Versus Containment, 1955–61.* 1983.

Sobel, Lester A., ed. *South Vietnam: US-Communist Confrontation in Southeast Asia.* Seven volumes. 1966–1973.

Stavins, Ralph, Richard J. Barnet, and Marcus G. Raskin. *Washington Plans an Aggressive War.* 1971.

Summers, Harry G. Jr. *Vietnam War Almanac.* 1985.

Turley, William S. *The Second Indochina.* 1986.

Whitfield, Danny J. *Historical and Cultural Dictionary of Vietnam.* 1976.

Zasloff, Joseph J., and Allan E. Goodman, eds. *Indochina in Conflict: A Political Assessment.* 1972.

Insurgency and Counterinsurgency

Andrews, William R. *The Village War: Vietnamese Communist Revolutionary Activities in Dinh Tuong Province, 1960–1964.* 1973.

Beckwith, Charles, and Donald Knox. *Delta Force.* 1983.

Bell, J. Bower. *The Myth of the Guerrilla: Revolutionary Theory and Malpractice.* 1971.

Blaufarb, Douglas S. *The Counterinsurgency Era: U.S. Doctrine and Performance 1950 to Present.* 1977.

Cable, Larry E. *Conflict of Myths: The Development of American Counterinsurgency Doctrine and the Vietnam War.* 1986.

Cao Van Vien. *The U.S. Adviser.* 1980.

da Silva, Peer. *Sub Rosa: The CIA and the Uses of Intelligence.* 1978.

Duiker, William. *The Communist Road to Power.* 1981.

Fall, Bernard. *The Viet Minh Regime.* 1956; *Street Without Joy: Insurgency in Vietnam, 1946–1963.* 1961.

Goodman, Allen E. *The Making of a Quagmire.* 1964.

Greene, Graham. *The Quiet American.* 1956.

Henderson, William. *Why the Vietcong Fought: A Study of Motivation and Control in a Modern Army in Combat.* 1979.

Herrington, Stuart A. *Silence Was a Weapon: The Vietnam War in the Villages.* 1982.

Hosmer, Stephen T. *Viet Cong Repression and Its Implications for the Future.* 1970.

Johnson, Chalmers. *Autopsy on People's War.* 1973.

Kelly, Francis J. *U.S. Army Special Force, 1961–1971.* 1973.

Komer, Robert W. *Bureaucracy Does Its Thing: Institutional Constraints on US-GVN Performance.* 1972.

McGarvey, Patrick J. *Visions of Victory: Selected Vietnamese Communist Military Writings, 1964–1968.* 1969.

Mecklin, John. *Mission in Torment.* 1965.

Mus, Paul, and John T. McAlister Jr. *The Vietnamese and Their Revolution.* 1970.

Nighswonger, William A. *Rural Pacification in Vietnam.* 1966.

O'Meara, Andrew P. *Infrastructure and the Marxist Power Seizure: An Analysis of the Communist Model of Revolution.* 1973.

Osborne, Milton E. *Strategic Hamlets in South Vietnam: A Survey and a Comparison.* 1965.

Pike, Douglas. *Viet Cong: The Organization and Techniques of the National Liberation Front of South Vietnam.* 1966; *War, Peace, and the Viet Cong.* 1969; *The Viet Cong Strategy of Terror.* 1970.

Popkin, Samuel L. *The Rational Peasant: The Political Economy of Rural Society in Vietnam.* 1979.

Prados, John. *Presidents' Secret Wars. CIA and Pentagon Covert Operations Since World War II.* 1986.

Race, Jeffrey. *War Comes to Long An: Revolutionary Conflict in a Vietnamese Village.* 1972.

Sansom, Robert L. *The Economics of Insurgency in the Mekong Delta*. 1970.

Shackleton, Ronald A. *Village Defense: Initial Special Forces Operations in Vietnam*. 1975.

Smith, R. Harris. *OSS: The Secret History of America's First CIA*. 1972.

Stimpson, Charles M. III. *Inside the Green Berets: The First Thirty Years*. 1983.

Stanton, Shelby L. *Green Berets at War*. 1985.

Stolfi, Russell H. *U.S. Marine Corps Civil Action Efforts in Vietnam, March 1965–March 1966*. 1968.

Tanham, George Kilpatrick. *Communist Revolutionary Warfare: From the Vietminh to the Viet Cong*. 1967.

Thompson, Robert. *Defeating Communist Insurgency*. 1966; *Revolutionary War in World Strategy, 1945–1949*. 1970; *Peace Is Not at Hand*. 1974.

Tran Dinh Tho. *Pacification*. 1979.

Tran Van Don. *Our Endless War: Inside Vietnam*. 1978.

Tran Van Tra. *Ending the 30 Years War*. 1982.

Trullinger, James Walker Jr. *Village at War: An Account of Revolution in Vietnam*. 1980.

Truong Chinh. *Primer for Revolt: The Communist Takeover in Vietnam*. 1963.

Turner, Robert F. *Vietnamese Communism: Its Origins and Developments*. 1975.

West, Francis J. *The Village*. 1972.

Land War

Albright, John, John A. Cash, and Allan W. Sandstrum. *Seven Firefights in Vietnam*. 1970.

Anderson, Charles R. *The Grunts*. 1976.

Candlin, A.H.S. "The Spring Offensive in Vietnam." *Army Quarterly and Defense Journal*. July 1972.

Carhart, Tom. *Battles and Campaigns in Vietnam*. 1984.

Cincinnaus. *Self-Destruction: The Disintegration and Decay of the United States Army During the Vietnam Era*. 1978.

Collins, James Lawton Jr. *The Development and Training of the South Vietnamese Army, 1950–1972*. 1975.

Cook, John L. *The Advisor*. 1973.

Dickson, Paul. *The Electronic Battlefield*. 1976.

Doleman, Edgar C. Jr. *The Vietnam Experience: The Tools of War*. 1984.

Dunn, Carroll H. *Base Development in South Vietnam, 1965–1970*. 1972.

Dunstan, Simon. *Vietnam Tracks: Armor in Battle, 1945–1975*. 1982.

Ezell, Edward Clinton. *First Air Cavalry Division in Vietnam*. 1967; *The First Air Cavalry Division: Vietnam, August 1965 to December 1969*. 1970; *The First Marine Division and Its Regiments*. 1981; *The Great Rifle Controversy*. 1984.

Garland, Albert N. *Infantry in Vietnam: Small Unit Actions in the Early Days 1965–66*. 1982.

Garland, Albert N., ed. *A Distant Challenge: The U.S. Infantryman in Vietnam, 1967–1972*. 1983.

Gershen, Martin. *Destroy or Die: The True Story of My Lai*. 1971.

Hay, John H. Jr. *Tactical and Material Innovations*. 1975.

Heiser, Joseph M. Jr. *Logistic Support*. 1974.

Hymoff, Edward. *The First Cavalry Division*. 1985; *The Infantry Brigade in Combat: First Brigade, 25th Infantry Division ("Tropic Lightning") in the Third Viet Cong-North Vietnamese Army Offensive, August 1968*. 1984.

Johnson, Harold K. "The Enclave Concept: A 'License to Hunt.'" *Army*. April 1968.

Krepinevich, Andrew F. Jr. *The Army and Vietnam*. 1986.

Krulak, Victor H. *First to Fight: An Inside View of the U.S. Marine Corps*. 1984.

Mahler, Michael D. *Ringed in Steel: Armored Cavalry. Vietnam, 1967–68*. 1986.

Mangold, Tom, and John Penycate. *The Tunnels of Cu Chi*. 1985; *The Marines in Vietnam, 1954–1973*. 1974.

Marshall, S.L.A. *Ambush: Battles in the Monsoon: Campaigning in the Central Highlands, South Vietnam, Summer 1966*. 1966; *Bird: The Christmastide Battle*. 1968; *The Battle of Dau Tieng, Also Called The Battle of Dong Ming Chau, War Zone C, Operation Attleboro, and Other Deadfalls in South Vietnam*. 1969; *The Fields of Bamboo: Dong Tre, Trung Luong, and Hoa Hoi: Three Battles Just Beyond the China Sea*. 1971; *Vietnam: Three Battles*. 1982.

Mertel, Kenneth D. *Year of the Horse—Vietnam: First Air Cavalry in the Highlands*. 1968.

Meyerson, Harvey. *Vinh Long*. 1970.

Miller, Kenneth E. *Tiger, The LURP Dog*. 1983.

Millet, Allan R. *Semper Fidelis: The History of the United States Marine Corps*. 1980.

Neel, Spurgeon. *Vietnam Studies: Medical Support of the U.S. Army in Vietnam, 1965–1970*. 1973.

Ngo Quang Truong. *The Easter Offensive of 1972*. 1980; *Territorial Forces*. 1981.

Nolan, Keith William. *The Battle for Hue: Tet, 1968*. 1983.

Ott, David Ewing. *Field Artillery, 1954–1973*. 1975.

Parker, William D. *U.S. Marine Corps Civil Affairs in I Corps, Republic of Vietnam, April 1966–April 1967*. 1970.

Pearson, Willard. *The War in the Northern Provinces, 1966–1968*. 1975.

Peers, W. R. *The My Lai Inquiry*. 1979.

Pimlott, John, ed. *Vietnam: The History and the Tactics*. 1982.

Pisor, Robert. *The End of the Line: The Siege of Khe Sanh*. 1982.

Ploger, Robert R. *U.S. Army Engineers, 1965–1970*. 1974.

Rienzi, Thomas M. *Vietnam Studies: Communications-Electronics, 1962–1970*. 1972.

Robinson, Anthony, ed. *The Weapons of the Vietnam War*. 1983.

Rogers, Bernard William. *Cedar Falls—Junction City: A Turning Point*. 1974.

Schell, Jonathan. *The Village of Ben Suc*. 1967.

Shore, Moyers S. II. *The Battle for Khe Sanh*. 1969.

Shulimson, Jack. *U.S. Marines in Vietnam: An Expanding War 1966*. 1982.

Shulimson, Jack, and Charles M. Johnson. *U.S. Marines in Vietnam: The Landing and the Buildup 1965*. 1978.

Spector, Ronald H. *United States Army in Vietnam: Advice and Support: The Early Years, 1965–1973*. 1985.

Staff of the *Infantry* Magazine, ed. *A Distant Challenge: The U.S. Infantryman in Vietnam, 1967–1970*. 1971.

Stanton, Shelby L. *Vietnam Order of Battle*. 1981; *The Rise and Fall of an American Army: U.S. Ground Forces in Vietnam, 1965–1973*. 1985.

Starry, Donn A. *Mounted Combat in Vietnam*. 1979.

Stolfi, Russell H. *U.S. Marine Corps Civil Action Efforts in Vietnam, March 1965–March 1966*. 1968.

Stuckey, John D., and Joseph H. Pistorius. *The Third Marine Division and Its Regiments*. 1983; *Mobilization of the Army National Guard and Army Reserve: Historical Perspective and the Vietnam War*. 1984.

Tolson, John J. *Airmobility, 1961–1971*. 1973.

Tregakis, Richard. *Southeast Asia: Building the Bases; The History of Construction in Southeast Asia*. 1975.

Turley, G. H. *The Easter Offensive: Vietnam 1972*. 1985.

West, Francis J. *Small Unit Action in Vietnam, Summer 1966*. 1967.

Whitlow, Robert H. *U.S. Marines in Vietnam: The Advisory and Combat Assistance Era, 1954–1964*. 1977.

Legacy of Vietnam

Alley, Rewi. *Refugees from Viet Nam in China*. 1980.

Chanda, Nayan. *Brother Enemy. The War After the War: A History of Indochina Since the Fall of Saigon*. 1986.

Duiker, William J. *Vietnam Since the Fall of Saigon*. 1980.

Elliott, David W. P., ed. *The Third Indochina Conflict*. 1981.

Gelb, Leslie, and Richard Betts. *The Irony of Vietnam: The System Worked*. 1979.

Grant, Bruce. *The Boat People*. 1979.

Isaacs, Arnold R. *Without Honor: Defeat in Vietnam and Cambodia*. 1983.

Lake, Anthony, ed. *The Legacy of Vietnam*. 1976.

Nguyen Long. *After Saigon Fell*. 1981.

Nguyen Van Canh, with Earle Cooper. *Vietnam Under Communism, 1975–1982*. 1983.

Palmer, Dave R. *Summons of the Trumpet: U.S.-Vietnam in Perspective*. 1984.

Podhoretz, Norman. *Why We Were in Vietnam*. 1982.

Sagan, Ginette, and Stephen Denney. *Violations of Human Rights in the Socialist Republic of Vietnam*. 1983.

Salisbury, Harrison E., ed. *Vietnam Reconsidered: Lessons from a War*. 1984.

Schultz, Richard H. Jr., and Richard A. Hunt. *Lessons from an Unconventional War*. 1982.

Thompson, W. Scott, and Donaldson Fuzell, eds. *The Lessons of Vietnam*. 1977; *Vietnam: 10 Years Later*. 1984.

Wheeler, John. *Touched with Fire: The Future of the Vietnam Generation*. 1984.

Literature and Film

Adair, Gilbert. *Vietnam on Film*. 1981; *Hollywood's Vietnam*. 1983.

Baber, Asa. *The Land of a Million Elephants*. 1970.

Balaban, John. *After Our War*. 1974.

Balk, H. Wesley. *The Dramatization of 365 Days*. 1972.

Beidler, Philip D. *American Literature and the Experience of Vietnam*. 1982.

Berry, D. C. *Saigon Cemetery*. 1972.

Berry, Jan, and W. D. Ehrhart, eds. *Demilitarized Zones: Veterans after Vietnam*. 1976.

Blacker, Irwin R. *Search and Destroy*. 1966.

Briley, John. *The Traitors*. 1969.

Bryan, C.D.B. *Friendly Fire*. 1976.

Bunting, Josiah. *The Lionheads*. 1972.

Casey, Michael. *Obscenities*. 1972.

Cassidy, John. *A Station in the Delta*. 1979.

Clark, Alan. *The Lion Heart*. 1969.

Coe, Charles. *Young Man in Vietnam*. 1968.

Coleman, Charles. *Sergeant Back Again*. 1980.

Coonts, Stephen. *Flight of the Intruder*. 1986.

Corson, William R. *The Betrayal*. 1968.

Crumley, James. *One to Count Cadence*. 1969.

Duncan, David Douglas. *War Without Heroes*. 1970.

Duncan, Donald. *The New Legions*. 1967.

Durden, Charles. *No Bugles, No Drums*. 1976.

Eastlake, William. *The Bamboo Bed*. 1969.

Ehrhart, W. D., ed. *Carrying the Darkness: American Poetry of the Vietnam War*. 1985.

Emerson, Gloria. *Winners and Losers*. 1976.

Ford, Daniel. *Incident at Muc Wa*. 1967.

Glasser, Ronald J. *365 Days*. 1971.

Groom, Winston. *Better Times Than These*. 1978.

Hasford, Gustav. *The Short-Timers*. 1979.

Heath, G. Louis, ed. *Mutiny Does Not Happen Lightly: The Literature of the American Resistance to the Vietnam War*. 1976.

Heinemann, Larry. *Close Quarters*. 1977.

Herr, Michael. *Dispatches*. 1977.

Hollenbeck, Peter, et al. *Vietnam Literature Anthology*. 1985.

Hughes, Larry. *You Can See a Lot Standing under a Flare in the Republic of Vietnam*. 1969.

Huggett, William Turner. *Body Count*. 1973.

Just, Ward. *To What End*. 1968; *Military Men*. 1970.

Karlin, Wayne, Basil T. Paquet, and Larry Rottman, eds. *Free Fire Zone*. 1973.

Kolpacoff, Victor. *The Prisoners of Quai Dong*. 1967.

Kopit, Arthur. *Indians*. 1969.

Kovic, Ron. *Born on the Fourth of July*. 1976.

Kowet, Don. *A Matter of Honor*. 1984.

Kozloff, Max, ed. *Artists and Writers Protests Against the War in Vietnam: Anthology of 18 Authors*. 1967.

Lifton, Robert Jay. *Home from the War*. 1973.

Lomperis, Timothy J. *Reading the Wind: The Literature of the Vietnam War*. 1986.

Lowenfels, Walter, ed. *Where Is Vietnam?* 1967.

Lowry, Timothy S. *And Brave Men, Too*. 1985.

McCarthy, Gerald. *War Story: Vietnam War Poems by an Ex-Marine*. 1977.

McCarthy, Mary. *The Seventeenth Degree*. 1974.

Mailer, Norman. *Why Are We in Vietnam?* 1967.

Maiman, Joan M., et al. *Vietnam Heroes: A Tribute: An Anthology of Poems by Veterans and Their Friends*. 1982.

Mayer, Tom. *Weary Falcon*. 1971.

Moore, Gene D. *The Killing at Ngo Tho*. 1967.

Moore, Robin. *The Green Berets*. 1965.

Morrison, C. T. *The Flame in the Icebox*. 1968.

O'Brien, Tim. *If I Die in a Combat Zone*. 1973; *Going after Cacciato*. 1978.

Parks, David. *G.I. Diary*. 1965.

Pelfrey, William. *The Big V*. 1972.

Rabe, David. *The Basic Training of Pavlo Hummel and Sticks and Bones*. 1973; *Streamers*. 1977.

Roth, Robert. *Sand in the Wind*. 1973.

Rottmann, Larry, ed. *Winning Hearts and Minds: Poems by Vietnam Veterans*. 1972.

Rowe, John. *Count Your Dead*. 1968.

Russ, Martin. *Happy Hunting Ground*. 1968.

Sack, John. *M*. 1967.

Schulze, Gene. *Third Face of War*. 1969.

Sloan, James Park. *War Games*. 1971.

Stone, Robert. *Dog Soldiers*. 1974.

Tiede, Tom. *Coward*. 1968.

Tegaskis, Richard. *Vietnam Diary*. 1963.

Topham, J., ed. *Poems of the Vietnam War*. 1985.

Vance, Samuel. *The Courageous and the Proud*. 1970.

Webb, James. *Fields of Fire*. 1978.

Weigel, Bruce. *A Romance*. 1979.

Wilson, James C. *Vietnam in Prose and Film*. 1982.

Woods, William Crawford. *The Killing Zone*. 1970.

Memoirs and First-Person Accounts

Anderson, Charles B. *The Grunts*. 1976.

Baer, Gordon, and Nancy Howell-Koehler. *Vietnam: The Battle Comes Home*. 1984.

Baker, Mark. *Nam: The Vietnam War in the Words of the Men and Women Who Fought There*. 1981.

Ball, George W. *The Past Has Another Pattern*. 1982.

Bernard, Edward. *Going Home*. 1973.

Bleier, Rocky, and Terry O'Neill. *Fighting Back*. 1980.

Brant, Toby L. *Journal of a Combat Tanker Vietnam, 1969*. 1986.

Brennan, Matthew. *Brennan's War: Vietnam, 1965–1969*. 1986.

Bridwell, Ric. *Manchu Delta*. 1986.

Briscoe, Edward G. *Diary of a Short-Timer in Vietnam*. 1970.

Broughton, Jack. *Thud Ridge*. 1969.

Brown, John M. *Rice Paddy Grunt: Unfading Memories of the Vietnam Generation*. 1986.

Browne, Malcom. *The New Face of War*. 1986.

Burchett, Wilfred G. *Vietnam: Inside Story of the Guerrilla War*. 1965.

Cao Van Vien and Dong Van Khuyen. *Reflections of the Vietnam War*. 1980.

Caputo, Philip. *A Rumor of War*. 1977.

Carter, Jimmy. *Keeping Faith*. 1982.

Cassidy, John. *A Station in the Delta*. 1982.

Chanoff, David, and Doan Van Toai. *Portrait of the Enemy*. 1986.

Clark, Johnnie M. *Guns Up!* 1986.

Cleland, Max. *Strong at the Broken Places*. 1980.

Colby, William E., and Peter Forbath. *Honorable Men: My Life in the CIA*. 1978.

Collins, James Lawton Jr. *The Development and Training of the South Vietnamese Army, 1950–1972*. 1975.

Cook, John L. *The Advisor*. 1973.

Currey, Richard. *Crossing Over: A Vietnam Journal*. 1980.

Dengler, Dieter. *Escape from Laos*. 1979.

Denton, Jeremiah A. *When Hell Was in Session*. 1976.

Donovan, D. *Once a Warrior King: Memories of an Officer in Vietnam*. 1985.

Downs, Frederick. *The Killing Zone: My Life in the Vietnam War*. 1978.

Drury, Richard S. *My Secret War*. 1979.

Ehrhart, W. D. *Vietnam-Perkasie: A Combat Marine Memoir*. 1983.

Ehrhart, William. *Marking Time*. 1986.

Eisenhower, Dwight D. *White House Years*. 1963.

Ellsberg, Daniel. *Papers on the War*. 1972.

Enthoven, Alain C., and K. Wayne Smith. *How Much is Enough? Shaping the Defense Program, 1961–1969*. 1971; *The Eyewitness History of the Vietnam War: 1961–1975*. 1983.

Fall, Bernard, ed. *Ho Chi Minh on Revolution*. 1968.

Garrett, Richard. *P.O.W.* 1981.

Giap, Vo Nguyen. *Dien Bien Phu*. 1962; *Big Victory, Big Task*. 1967; *Unforgettable Days*. 1978.

Goldman, Peter, and Tony Fuller. *Charlie Company: What Vietnam Did to Us*. 1983.

Grauwin, Paul. *Doctor at Dienbienphu*. 1955.

Hakes, Thomas L. *A Soldier's Diary of Thoughts, Memories and Letters*. 1987.

Haldeman, Joe. *War Year*. 1972.

Halstead, Fred. *Out Now! A Participant's Account of the American Movement Against the Vietnam War*. 1978.

Harriman, W. Averell. *America and Russia in a Changing World: A Half Century of Personal Observation.* 1971.

Harriman, W. Averell, and Elie Abel. *Special Envoy to Churchill and Stalin, 1941–1946.* 1975.

Herbert, Anthony B. *Soldier.* 1973.

Herr, Michael. *Dispatches.* 1984.

Herrington, Stuart A. *Peace with Honor? An American Reports on Vietnam, 1973–1975.* 1983.

Hilsman, Roger. *To Move a Nation: The Politics of Foreign Policy in the Administration of John F. Kennedy.* 1967.

Ho Chi Minh. *Prison Diary.* 1966.

Hoopes, Townsend. *The Limits of Intervention.* 1969.

Hosmer, Stephen T., ed. *The Fall of South Vietnam: Statements by Vietnamese Military and Civilian Leaders.* 1978.

Hubbell, John G., et al. *POW.* 1976.

Javits, Jacob. *Who Makes War? The President Versus Congress.* 1973.

Johnson, Lyndon Baines. *The Vantage Point: Perspectives of the Presidency, 1963–1969.* 1971.

Jones, James. *Viet Journal.* 1973.

Joyner, William, et al. *Vietnam Heroes: That We Have Peace.* 1983.

Kamazi, I. *Nam Book.* 1981.

Kauffman, Joel. *The Weight.* 1980.

Ketwig, John. *And a Hard Rain Fell: A Soldier's True Story of His Stay in Vietnam.* 1985.

Kirban, Salem. *Goodbye, Mr. President.* 1974.

Kirk, Donald. *Tell It to the Dead: Memories of a War.* 1975.

Kissinger, Henry. *White House Years.* 1979; *Years of Upheaval.* 1982.

Klein, Joe. *Payback: Five Marines after Vietnam.* 1984.

Lansdale, Edward Geary. *In the Midst of Wars: An American's Mission to Southeast Asia.* 1972.

Lee, Larry. *American Eagle: The Story of a Navajo Vietnam Veteran.* 1977.

Lewis, Lloyd B. *The Tainted War: Culture and Identity in Vietnam War Narratives.* 1985.

Linedecker, Clifford. *Kerry: Agent Orange and an American Family.* 1982.

Lodge, Henry Cabot. *The Storm Has Many Eyes: A Personal Narrative.* 1973.

McCarthy, Eugene. *The Year of the People.* 1969.

McCauley, Anna K. *Miles from Home.* 1984.

McDonough, James R. *Platoon Leader.* 1985.

Marshall, Samuel L. *Bird: The Christmastide Battle.* 1968; *Ambush.* 1982; *Campaigning in the Central Highlands, Vietnam, Summer 1966.* 1984.

Mason, Robert C. *Chickenhawk.* 1984.

Mecklin, John. *Mission in Torment.* 1965; *Selected Works.* Vols. 1–4. 1966–67.

Mulligan, James A. *The Hanoi Commitment.* 1981.

Nasmyth, Virginia, and Spike Nasmyth. *Hanoi Release John Nasmyth.* 1984.

Nguyen Cao Ky. *Twenty Years and Twenty Days.* 1976.

Nguyen Ngoc, Ngan. *The Will of Heaven.* 1981.

Nixon, Richard M. *RN: The Memoirs of Richard Nixon.* 1978; *No More Vietnams.* 1985.

Noel, Chris, et al. *Matter of Survival.* 1987.

O'Brien, Tim. *If I Die in a Combat Zone.* 1979.

Page, Tim. *Tim Page's Nam.* 1983.

Palmer, Dave R. *Summons of the Trumpet.* 1984.

Parrish, John A. *Twelve, Twenty & Five: A Doctor's Year in Vietnam.* 1986.

Porter, Gareth, ed. *Vietnam: The Definitive Documentation of Human Decisions.* 1979.

Regan, David J. *Mourning Glory: The Making of a Marine.* 1980.

Ridgway, Matthew B. *Soldier: The Memoirs of Matthew B. Ridgway.* 1956.

Risner, Robinson. *The Passing of the Night: My Seven Years as a Prisoner of the North Vietnamese.* 1974.

Roche, John P. *Sentenced to Life: Reflections on Politics, Education, and Law.* 1974.

Roskey, William. *Muffled Shots: A Year on the DMZ.* 1987.

Rostow, W. W. *The Diffusion of Power, 1957–1972.* 1972.

Rowan, Stephen A. *They Wouldn't Let Us Die: The Prisoners of War Tell Their Story.* 1975.

Rowe, James N. *Five Years to Freedom.* 1971.

Rubin, Jerry. *Do It!* 1970; *Growing (Up) at 37.* 1976.

Sack, John. *Lieutenant Calley: His Own Story.* 1971.

Salinger, Pierre. *With Kennedy.* 1966.

Salisbury, Harrison. *Behind the Lines: Hanoi, December 23, 1966–January 7, 1967.* 1967.

Santoli, Al. *Everything We Had: An Oral History of the Vietnam War by Thirty-Three American Soldiers Who Fought It.* 1981; *To Bear Any Burden: The Vietnam War and Its Aftermath in the Words of Americans and Southeast Asians.* 1985.

Schanberg, Sydney. *The Death and Life of Dith Pran.* 1985.

Scholl-Latour, Peter. *Death in the Rice Fields: An Eyewitness Account of Vietnam's Three Wars, 1945–1979.* 1985.

Sharp, U.S.G. *Strategy for Defeat: Vietnam in Retrospect.* 1978.

Sharp, U.S.G. and William Westmoreland. *Report on the War in Vietnam.* 1968.

Simpson, Charles M. III. *Inside the Green Berets: The First Thirty Years.* 1983.

Snepp, Frank. *Decent Interval: An Insider's Account of Saigon's Indecent End.* 1977.

Sorenson, Theodore C. *Kennedy.* 1965.

Stockdale, Jim, and Sybil Stockdale. *In Love and War: The Story of a Family's Ordeal and Sacrifice During the Vietnam Years.* 1984.

Taylor, Maxwell D. *The Uncertain Trumpet.* 1959; *Swords and Plowshares.* 1972.

Terry, Wallace. *Bloods: An Oral History of the Vietnam War by Black Veterans.* 1984.

Thompson, Robert. *No Exit from Vietnam.* 1970; *Peace Is Not at Hand.* 1974.

Tran Van Dinh. *This Nation and Socialism Are One: Selected Writings of Le Duan.* 1977.

Triotti, John. *Phantom over Vietnam: Fighter Pilot, USMC.* 1984.

Truong Nhu Tang, with David Chanoff and Doan Van Toai. *A Viet Cong Memoir.* 1985.

Vance, Cyrus. *Hard Choices.* 1983.

Vance, Samuel. *Courageous and the Proud.* 1970.

Van Devanter, Lynda, and Christopher Morgan. *Home Before Morning: The Story of an Army Nurse in Vietnam.* 1983.

Walter, Keith. *A Piece of My Heart: Stories of Twenty-Six American Women Who Served in Vietnam.* 1986.

Webb, Kate, *On the Other Side: 23 Days with the Viet Cong.* 1972.

Westmoreland, William C. *A Soldier Reports.* 1976.

Whittington, Ruben B. *Moonspinners, Vietnam 65–66.* 1986.

Williams, William Appleman, et al., eds. *America in Vietnam: A Documentary History.* 1985.

Willwerth, James. *Eye in the Last Storm.* 1972.

Zalin, Grant. *Survivors: American POWs in Vietnam.* 1985.

Zumwalt, Elmo, et al. *My Father, My Son.* 1986.

Zumwalt, Elmo R. Jr. *On Watch.* 1976.

MIAs/POWs

Calvin, Rodney. *First Heroes: American MIAs-POWs Left Behind in Vietnam.* 1987.

Clarke, Douglas L. *The Missing Man, Politics and the MIA.* 1979.

Grooth, Winston, and Duncan Spencer. *Conversations with the Enemy.* 1983.

Hubbell, John G. *P.O.W.: A Definitive History of the American Prisoner-of-War Experience in Vietnam, 1964–1973.* 1976.

Kim, Samuel. *The American POWs.* 1978.

O'Daniel, Larry J. *Missing in Action.* 1979.

Reader's Digest. *POW: A Definitive History of the American Prisoner of War Experience in Vietnam, 1964–1973.* 1976.

Schlemmer, Benajmin. *The Raid.* 1976.

Zalin, Grant. *Survivors: American POWs in Vietnam.* 1985.

Minorities

Binkin, Martin, et al. *Blacks in the Military.* 1982.

Byrd, Barthy. *Home Front: Women and Viet Nam.* 1986.

Goff, Stanley, and Robert Sandfors. *Brothers: Black Soldiers in the Nam.* 1982.

Holm, Jeanne. *Women in the Military.* 1982.

Mullen, Robert W. *Blacks and Vietnam.* 1981.

Taylor, Clyde, ed. *Vietnam and Black America: An Anthology of Protest and Resistance.* 1973.

Terry, Wallace. *Bloods: An Oral History of the Vietnam War by Black Veterans.* 1984.

Vance, Samuel. *Courageous and the Proud.* 1970.

Willenz, June A. *Women Veterans: America's Forgotten Heroines.* 1984.

Naval War

Butler, James. *River of Death—Song Vam Sat.* 1979.

Croizat, Victor. *The Brown Water Navy: The River and Coastal War in Indo-China and Vietnam, 1948–1972.* 1984.

Fulton, William B. *Riverine Operations, 1966–1969*. 1973.

Galloway, John. *The Gulf of Tonkin Resolution*. 1970.

Goulden, Joseph C. *Truth Is the First Casualty*. 1969.

Hooper, Edwin B. *Mobility, Support, Endurance: A Story of Naval Operational Logistics in the Vietnam War, 1965–1968*. 1972.

Hooper, Edwin B., Dean C. Allard, and Oscar P. Fitzgerald. *The United States Navy and the Vietnam Conflict: The Setting of the Stage to 1959*. 1976.

Luckow, Ulrik. "Victory Over Ignorance and Fear: The U.S. Minelaying Attack on North Vietnam." *Naval War College Review*. January-February 1982.

Marolda, Edward J., and G. Wesley Pryce III. *A Short History of the United States Navy and the Southeast Asian Conflict, 1950–1975*. 1984.

Mersky, Peter, and Norman Polmar. *The Naval Air War in Vietnam: 1965–1975*. 1981.

Naval Facilities and Engineering Command. *Southeast Asia: Building the Bases. The History of Construction in Southeast Asia*. 1975; *Riverine Warfare: The U.S. Navy's Operations on Inland Waterways*. 1968.

Triotti, John. *Phantom over Vietnam: Fighter Pilot, USMC*. 1984.

Tulich, Eugene. *The United States Coast Guard in Southeast Asia During the Vietnam Conflict*. 1975.

Van Vleet. *Naval Aviation in Viet Nam*. 1985.

Windchy, Eugene C. *Tonkin Gulf*. 1971.

Press/Media

Arlen, Michael. *Living Room War*. 1969.

Bailey, George A. "Television War: Trends in Network Coverage of Vietnam 1965–1970." *Journal of Broadcasting*, 20 (Spring 1976); "Interpretive Reporting of the Vietnam War by Anchormen." *Journalism Quarterly* 53, no. 2 (Summer 1976).

Bailey, George A., and Lawrence W. Lichty. "Rough Justice on a Saigon Street: A Gatekeeper Study of NBC's Tet Execution Film." *Journalism Quarterly* 49, no. 2 (Summer 1972).

Barnouw, Erik. *The Image Empire*. 1970.

Braestrup, Peter. *Big Story: How the American Press and Television Reported and Interpreted the Crisis of Tet 1968 in Vietnam and Washington*. 1983; *Battle Lines: Report of the Twentieth Century Fund Task Force on the Military and the Media*. 1985.

Brewin, Bob, and Sydney Shaw. *Vietnam on Trial: Westmoreland vs. CBS*. 1986.

Gitlin, Todd. *The Whole World Is Watching*. 1980.

Goulden, Joseph C. *Truth Is the First Casualty*. 1968.

Gravel, Mike, ed. *The Pentagon Papers*. 1971.

Hallin, Daniel C. *The Uncensored War: The Media and Vietnam*. 1986.

Herz, Martin F., and Leslie Rider. *The Prestige Press and the Christmas Bombing, 1972: Images and Reality in Vietnam*. 1985.

Lunn, Hugh. *Vietnam: A Reporter's War*. 1986.

Mills, Nick. *The Vietnam Experience: Combat Photographer*. 1983.

Mueller, John E. *War, Presidents, and Public Opinion*. 1973.

Turner, Kathleen J. *Lyndon Johnson's Dual War: Vietnam and the Press*. 1985.

Strategy and War Management

Baldwin, Hanson W. *Strategy for Tomorrow*. 1970.

Baral, Jaya. *The Pentagon and the Making of U.S. Foreign Policy*. 1978.

BDM Corporation. *A Study of Strategic Lessons Learned in Vietnam*. 1980.

Berman, Larry. *Planning a Tragedy: The Americanization of the War in Vietnam*. 1982.

Collins, John M. *U.S. Defense Planning: A Critique*. 1982.

Eckhart, George S. *Command and Control, 1950–1969*. 1974.

Fallows, James. *National Defense*. 1981.

Gabriel, Richard, and Paul Savage. *Crisis in Command*. 1978.

Hoang Ngoc Long. *Strategy and Tactics*. 1980.

Kinnard, Douglas. *The War Managers*. 1977; *The Secretary of Defense*. 1980.

Korb, Lawrence J. *The Joint Chiefs of Staff: The First Twenty-Five Years*. 1976.

Luttwack, Edward N. *The Pentagon and the Art of War*. 1985.

Mueller, John E. "The Search for the 'Breaking Point' in Vietnam: The Statistics of a Deadly Quarrel." *International Studies Quarterly* 4 (December 1980).

O'Brien, William V. *The Conduct of Just and Limited War*. 1981.

O'Neill, Robert J. *The Strategy of General Giap Since 1964*. 1969.

Palmer, Gregory. *The McNamara Strategy and the Vietnam War: Program Budgeting in the Pentagon, 1960–1968*. 1978.

Pettit, Clyde Edwin. *The Experts*. 1975.

Pimlott, John, ed. *Vietnam: The History and the Tactics*. 1982.

Summers, Harry G. Jr. *On Strategy: A Critical Analysis of the Vietnam War*. 1982.

Van Dyke, Jon M. *North Vietnam's Strategy for Survival*. 1972.

Walt, Lewis W. *Strange War, Strange Strategy*. 1976.

Tet Offensive

Brodie, Bernard. *The Tet Offensive*. 1976.

Dougan, Clark, and Steven Weiss. *The Vietnam Experience: Nineteen Sixty-Eight*. 1983.

Nolan, Keith W. *Battle for Hue: Tet, 1968*. 1983.

Oberdorfer, Don. *Tet!* 1971; *TET: The Turning Point of the Vietnam War*. 1983.

Pham Von Son and Le Van Duong, eds. *The Viet Cong Tet Offensive 1968*. 1969.

Veterans and Soldiers

Baskir, Lawrence M., and William A. Strauss. *Chance and Circumstance: The Draft, the War, and the Vietnam Generation*. 1978.

Boyle, Richard. *Flower of the Dragon: The Breakdown of the U.S. Army in Vietnam*. 1972.

Brandon, Heather. *Casualties: Death in Vietnam, Anguish and Survival in America*. 1984.

Card, Josephina J. *Lives After Vietnam*. 1983.

Cohen, Eliot A. *Citizens and Soldiers: The Dilemmas of Military Service*. 1985.

Cortright, David. *Soldiers in Revolt*. 1976.

Goldstein, Joseph, Burke Marshall, and Jack Schwartz, eds. *The My Lai Massacre and Its Cover-up: Beyond the Reach of the Law?* 1978.

Hanser, William L. *America's Army in Crisis*. 1973.

Hendin, Herbert, and Ann P. Haas. *Wounds of War*. 1984.

Hersh, Seymour. *My Lai 4*. 1970.

King, Edward. *The Death of the Army*. 1972.

Klein, Robert. *Wounded Men, Broken Promises*. 1981.

Kubey, Craig, et al. *The Viet Vet Survival Guide: How to Cut Through the Bureaucracy and Get What You Need and Are Entitled To*. 1985.

Lifton, Robert Jay. *Home from the War*. 1973.

MacPherson, Myra. *Long Time Passing: Vietnam and the Haunted Generation*. 1984.

Moskos, Charles. *The American Enlisted Man*. 1970.

Peers, W. R. *The My Lai Inquiry*. 1979.

Sonnenberg, Stephen M., et al., eds. *The Trauma of War: Stress and Recovery in Viet Nam Veterans*. 1985.

Starr, Paul. *The Discarded Army*. 1973.

Whiteside, Thomas. *The Withering Rain*. 1971.

Wilcox, Fred A. *Waiting for an Army to Die: The Tragedy of Agent Orange*. 1983.

Vietnamese Culture and Ethnicity

Crawford, Ann (Caddel). *Customs and Culture of Vietnam*. 1966.

Dumoutier, Gustave. *Annamese Religions*. 1955.

Dutt, Sukumar. *Buddhism in East Asia*. 1966.

Embree, John F. *Ethnic Groups of Northern Southeast Asia*. 1950.

Gheddo, Pierro. *The Cross and the Bo-Tree: Catholics and Buddhists in Vietnam*. 1970.

Gregerson, Marilyn J. "The Ethnic Minorities of Vietnam," *Southeast Asia: An International Quarterly* 20. Winter 1972.

Groslier, Bernard Philippe. *The Art of Indochina*. 1962.

Hickey, Gerald Cannon. *Village in Vietnam*. 1964; *The Highland People of South Vietnam: Social and Economic Development*. 1967; *Free in the Forest: An Ethnohistory of the Vietnamese Central Highlands, 1954–1976*. 1982; *Sons of the Mountains: Ethnohistory of the Vietnamese Central Highlands to 1954*. 1982.

Hoskins, Marilyn W., and Eleanor Shepherd. *Life in a Vietnamese Urban Quarter*. 1971.

Iredell, F. Raymond. *Vietnam: The Country and the People*. 1966.

Karnow, Stanley. *Life, Southeast Asia*. 1962.

McAlister, John T. *Southeast Asian Tribes, Minorities and Nations*. 1967.

Mole, Robert L. *The Montagnards of South Vietnam: A Study of Nine Tribes*. 1970.

Nguyen Dinh-Hoa, ed. *Some Aspects of Vietnamese Culture*. 1972.

Oliver, Victor L. *Cao Dai Spiritualism: A Study of Religion in Vietnamese Society*. 1976.

Rawson, Philip. *The Art of Southeast Asia*. 1967.

Schrock, Joan L., et al. *Minority Groups in the Republic of Vietnam*. 1967.

Vietnamese History

Bain, Chester. *Vietnam: The Roots of Conflict*. 1967.

Bastin, John Sturgis. *The Emergence of Modern Southeast Asia*. 1967.

Bone, Robert C. *Contemporary Southeast Asia*. 1962.

Buttinger, Joseph. *The Smaller Dragon: A Political History of Vietnam*. 1958; *Vietnam: A Dragon Embattled*. 2 vols. 1967; *Vietnam: A Political History*. 1968.

Cady, John Frank. *Southeast Asia: Its Historical Development*. 1958.

Chen, King C. *Vietnam and China, 1938–1954*. 1969.

Chesneaux, Jean. *The Vietnamese Nation: Contribution to a History*. 1966.

Coedes, George. *The Making of Southeast Asia*. 1966; *The Indianized States of Southeast Asia*. 1968.

Cotter, Michael G. "Towards a Social History of the Vietnamese Southward Movement." *Journal of Southeast Asian History* 9 (March 1968), 12–24.

Donnell, John C., and Charles A. Joiner, eds. *Electoral Politics in South Vietnam*. 1974.

Duncanson, Dennis J. *Government and Revolution in Vietnam*. 1968.

Duiker, William J. *The Rise of Nationalism in Vietnam, 1900–1941*. 1976.

Goodman, Allen E. *Politics in War: The Bases of Political Community in South Vietnam*. 1973.

Hall, Daniel. *A History of Southeast Asia*. 1955.

Hall, D.B.E. *A History of Southeast Asia*. 1968.

Hammer, Ellen Joy. *Vietnam, Yesterday and Today*. 1966.

Harrison, Brian. *Southeast Asia, A Short History*. 1954.

Hawthorne, Lesleyanne, ed. *Refugee: The Vietnamese Experience*. 1982.

Joiner, Charles A. *The Politics of Massacre: Political Processes in South Vietnam*. 1974.

Lacouture, Jean. *Vietnam: Between Two Truces*. 1966.

McAlister, John T. Jr. *Vietnam: The Origins of Revolution*. 1970; *The Vietnamese and Their Revolution*. 1970.

McAlister, John T. Jr., and Paul Mus. *The Vietnamese and Their Revolution*. 1970.

McAleavy, Henry. *Black Flags in Vietnam: The Story of the Chinese Intervention*. 1968.

Marr, David G. *Vietnamese Anticolonialism, 1885–1925*. 1971.

Ngo Vinh Long. *Before the Revolution: The Vietnamese Peasant Under the French*. 1973.

Nguyen Phuc-Tan. *A Modern History of Vietnam, 1802–1954*. 1964.

Pike, Douglas. *History of the Vietnamese Communist Party*. 1978.

Samuels, Gertrude. "Passage to Freedom in Vietnam." *National Geographic* 107 (June 1955), 858–74.

Scigliano, Robert. *South Viet-Nam: Nation Under Stress*. 1963; *South Viet-Nam Since Independence*. 1963.

Steinberg, David J., ed. *In Search of Southeast Asia*. 1971.

Thai, Van-Kiem. *Viet Nam Past and Present*. 1956.

Turner, Robert F. *Vietnamese Communism: Its Origins and Developments*. 1975.

Warner, Denis. *The Last Confucian*. 1963.

Crewmen of the 3d Marine Division on Swift boat 80 load an 81mm mortar to fire inland on Vietcong positions 2 miles south of the DMZ along the coast of the South China Sea.

About the Editor and Contributors

G. Dudley Acker Jr. is an adjunct professor of military history at Northern Arizona University in Flagstaff.

Linda K. Alkana is a faculty member and undergraduate advisor in the department of history at California State University at Long Beach.

Charles Angel teaches history at North Harris College.

Nolan J. Argyle is a professor of political science at Valdosta State College in Valdosta, Georgia. He is the author of *The Bridge at Kilometer 575* and *Tax Expenditure Analysis: A Concept Whose Time Has Come*.

Gary M. Bell is dean of the Honors College at Texas Tech University, Lubbock, Texas.

David Bernstein is a former member of the department of history at California State University at Long Beach.

Linda Casci teaches social studies at McCullough High School in The Woodlands, Texas.

Gloria Collins teaches at Aldine High School in Houston, Texas.

Joanna D. Cowden teaches history at California State University at Chico..

Charles M. Dobbs chairs the department of history at Iowa State University, and is the author of *The United States and East Asia* and *The Unwanted Symbol. American Foreign Policy, the Cold War and Korea: 1942-1950*.

Samuel Freeman is a professor of political science at the University of Texas-Pan American in Edinburgh, Texas.

Frances Frenzel teaches at Madisonville High School, Madisonville, Texas.

E. James Hindman is professor of history and president emeritus at Angelo State University in San Angelo, Texas.

Gerald Holder was a member of the department of geography at Sam Houston State University in Huntsville, Texas.

Sean Kelleher was a member of the department of political science at the University of Texas, Permian Basin.

John Kincaid is the Robert B. and Helen S. Meyner Professor of Government and Public Service at Lafayette College in Easton, Pennsylvania.

Roger D. Launius is a member of the Division of Space History at the Smithsonian Institution's National Air and Space Museum in Washington, D.C.

John S. Leiby teaches history at Paradise Valley Community College, Phoenix, Arizona. He is the author of *Report to the King: Colonel Juan Camargo y Cavallero's Historical Account of New Spain, 1815* and *Colonial Bureaucrats and the Mexican Economy: Growth of a Patrimonial State, 1763-1821*.

Terry Martin teaches at Willis High School in Willis, Texas.

James S. Olson is a professor of history at Sam Houston State University in Huntsville, Texas. He is the author, co-author, editor, or co-editor of more than thirty books, including *Where the Domino Fell: America and Vietnam, 1945 to 2006*. His book *Bathsheba's Breast: Women, Cancer, and History* was nominated by the Johns Hopkins University Press for the Pulitzer Prize in History and was recognized by the *Los Angeles Times* as one of the best non-fiction books in America for 2002.

Hoyt Hughes Purvis is a faculty member in the Honors College of the University of Arkansas.

John A. Ricks III is a professor of history at Valdosta State College in Valdosta, Georgia.

Joseph M. Rowe Jr. is a professor of history at Sam Houston State University, Huntsville, Texas.

Robert W. Sellen was a faculty member in the department of history at Georgia State University.

Sally Smith teaches history at McCullough High School in The Woodlands, Texas.

Stafford T. Thomas is an emeritus faculty member at California State University at Chico.

John E. Wilson teaches history at Conroe High School in Conroe, Texas.

Kim Younghaus researched defoliants while a graduate student at Sam Houston State University.

Troops off-load from a CH-21 Workhorse in a landing zone 10 miles north of the An Binh airstrip on April 19, 1963.

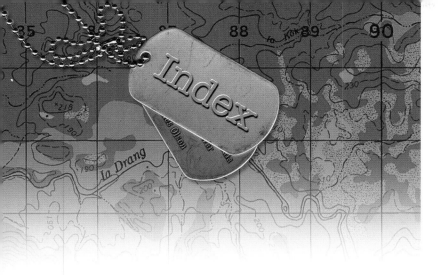

Image Credits

Alamy: © Ralph A. Clevenger: background: 60-61, 82-83, 94-95, 162-163, 214-215, 224-225, 244-245, 264-265, 270-271, 298-299, 314-317, 372-373, 388-389, 436-437, 486-491, 554-555, 618-619

Art Archive: Department of Defense Washington: 158 bottom; US Naval Museum Washington: 245 left; Department of Defense Washington: 445; US Navy: 511 bottom

Associated Press: © Henri Huet: 74; 82 top right, 175 bottom; © Rick Merron: 201 bottom; © Nick Wheeler: 241 bottom; © Bettmann: 242 bottom; 243 top; © Bettmann: 243 bottom; 244 top; © Bettmann: 245 top, 247 top, 250; © Tim Page: 252; © Bettmann: 253; © Christophe Boisvieux: 254; © Bettmann: 256; © Jacques Pavlovsky/Sygma: 257, 258; © Bettmann: 259, 260; © Wally McNamee: 263; © Kyoichi Sawada/Bettmann: 264 top; © Bettmann: 265 bottom; © Kyoichi Sawada/Bettmann: 266; © Tim Page: 267; © Bettmann: 268, 269; © Alain Dejean/Sygma: 270; © Bettmann: 271 bottom, 272; © Tim Page: 274; © Bettmann: 276 bottom, 277, 278 top; © Jack Kightlinger: 281; © Bettmann: 283 top; 283 bottom; © Bettmann, 284, 285, 286, 287; © Jacques Langevin/Sygma: 290; © Bettmann: 291 top; © Tim Page: 291 bottom; © Bettmann: 292; © Wally McNamee: 293 top; © Bettmann: 293 bottom, 295 top, 296; © Tim Page: 297, 298 bottom; © Bettmann: 299, 300; © Wally McNamee: 302 bottom; © Bettmann: 303, 308 top; © Yoichi Okamoto: 308 bottom; © Bettmann: 309 top, 310; © Bettmann: 312 top left and right; © John Stewart/Bettmann: 312 bottom; 313 top, 316 right, 319 bottom, 320 bottom, 321; © Dana Stone/Bettmann: 323 top; © Bettmann: 325 bottom, 328 top; © Ron Sachs/Sygma: 330; © Bettmann: 331 top; © Wally McNamee: 332; © Martin Stuart-Fox/Bettmann: 333; 334 top; © Bettmann: 340, 341; © Shunsuke Akatsuka/Bettman: 342; © Tim Page: 343; © Bettmann: 348 top, 350 bottom, © Bill Hall/Bettmann: 351 bottom; © Bettmann: 352, 353; © Tim Page: 360 top left; © Bettmann: 360 bottom left, 362, 363 left, 364, 365, 366, 370 bottom left, 370-371, 372 top; © Hulton-Deutsch Collection: 373 bottom; © Bettmann: 385, 386, 387 bottom, 388, 389 bottom; © Dick Halstead/Bettmann: 390 top; © Bettmann: 390 bottom, 395 top; © Bettmann: 396, 400 top, 401 bottom, 402, 408 bottom right, © Tim Page: 412 top; © Bettmann: 430; 434; © Dana Stone/Bettmann: 436 bottom; © Christian Simonpietri/Sygma: 437 top; © Dana Stone/Bettmann: 437 bottom; © Bettmann: 451, 456, 459, 462; © Tim Page: 465 top; © Bettmann: 467 bottom, 468, 470, 478-479, 480; © Kyoichi Sawada/Bettmann: 481; © Bettmann: 482, 483, 484; © Bill Hall/Bettmann: 498; © Bettmann: 499, 500, 502, 522, 529 bottom, 542, 547, 553, 554, 556, 557 top, 560; © Hulton-Deutsch Collection: 570; © Bettmann: 581; © Larry Downing/Reuters: 604; © Bettmann: 610, 619, 620; © David Hume Kennerly/Bettmann: 622 bottom; © Bettmann: 622-623 top, 623

From the Collection of Bradford Edwards, photographed by Hans Kemp, © 2007 Asia Ink and Visionary World: 247 bottom, 625 right

Courtesy Everett Collection: Wisconsin Historical Society: 140, 617

Getty Images: © Larry Burrows/Time & Life Pictures: 19; © Co Rentmeester/Time & Life Pictures: 21; © Jon Brennis/Time & Life Pictures: 45 top, bottom left; © Larry Burrows/Time & Life Pictures: 58; © Francis Miller/Time & Life Pictures: 71 top; © Carl Mydans/Time & Life Pictures: 73 top; © Dick Swanson/Time & Life Pictures: 75 top; © Jim Sharpe/Time & Life Pictures: 77; © Howard Sochurek/Time & Life Pictures: 81; © Hulton Archive: 83 top; © Time & Life Pictures: 83 bottom; © Larry Burrows/Time & Life Pictures: 116; © William Vandivert/Time & Life Pictures: 158 top; © Diana Walker/Time & Life Pictures: 164; © Keystone/Hulton Archive: 175 top; © Leonard McComb/Time & Life Pictures: 185 left; © Larry Burrows/Time & Life Pictures: 193; © RDA/Hulton Archive: 211 top; © AFP/AFP: 213; © Marvin Lichner/Time & Life Pictures: 228 top; © MPI: 231 top; © Hulton Archive: 232-233; © David Hume Kennedy: 234; © Arnold Newman: 236 top; © Terry Ashe/Liaison: 236 bottom; © Lee Lockwood/Time & Life Pictures: 240; © Nat Farbman/Time & Life Pictures: 246 top; © Bill Pierce: 246 bottom; © Jack Birns/Time & Life Pictures: 255; © Eliot Elisofan/Time & Life Pictures: 278 left; © Francis Miller/Time & Life Pictures: 278 right, 282; © STF/AFP: 295; © Mark Ellidge/Keystone Features: 298 top; © Thomas D. McAvoy/Time & Life Pictures: 304; © Roger Viollet/Francoise DeMulder: 309 bottom; © Larry Burrows/Time & Life Pictures: 315 right; © Ian Brodie/Hulton Archive: 319 top; © Alfred Eisenstaedt/Time & Life Pictures: 320 top; © Authenticated News/Hulton Archive: 326 left; © Paul Schuter/Time & Life Pictures: 331 middle; © STF/AFP: 334 bottom; © Co Rentmeester/ Time & Life Pictures: 335; © Hulton Archive: 337 left; © Larry Burrows/Time & Life Pictures: 348 bottom, 351 top, 363 top right; © Ronald S. Haeberie/Time & Life Pictures: 372 bottom; © Ronald S. Haeberie/Time & Life Pictures: 373 top; © Larry Burrows/Time & Life Pictures: 375 inset; © John Dominis/Time & Life Pictures: 387 top; © Larry Burrows/ Time & Life Pictures: 389 top; © STF/AFP: 391; © Time & Life Pictures: 392; © Robert Cohen/ RDA: 395 bottom; © Arthur Schatz/Time & Life Pictures: 402 bottom; © John Dominis/ Time & Life Pictures: 403; © STF/AFP: 404-405 bottom; © Dick Swanson/ Time & Life Pictures: 418 top; © AFP: 455; © Robert W. Kelley/Time & Life Pictures: 457; © Lee Lockwood/Time & Life Pictures: 458; © Larry Burrows/Time & Life Pictures: 460, 461; © Carl Mydans/Time & Life Pictures: 464; © AFP: 466; © Margaret Bourke-White/Time & Life Pictures: 493; © Walter Bennett/Time & Life Pictures: 496; © Keystone: 541; © Larry Burrows/Time & Life Pictures: 546 top; © Express/Hulton Archives: 546 bottom; © AFP: 557 bottom; © Patrick Christain: 577; © Ronald S. Haeberie/Time & Life Pictures: 582-583; © Francis Miller/Time & Life Pictures: 590 left; © MPI: 590 bottom; © Keystone: 592 top; © Central Press: 595; © Gig: 612; © John Olson/Time & Life Pictures: 618; © Dirck Halstead/Time & Life Pictures: 621; © Larry Burrows/Time & Life Pictures: 624

Courtesy of D.M. Giangreco: 44 bottom, 508-509

The Granger Collection, New York: 79 top

Courtesy of Jim Henthorn/ www.nexus.net/ ~911gfx/sea-ao.html: background map: 105, 207, 306, 452, 519, 561

The Image Works: © George Gardner: 603

The Kobal Collection: © Enigma/Goldcrest: 294; © Orion: 465; © Eagle/Tri-Star: 486 top; © Tri-Star: 486 middle; © Zeotrope/United Artists: 486 bottom; © Warner Bros.: 487, 488 top; © Malpaso/Warner Bros.: 488 bottom; © Warner Bros.: 489 top; © RKO Radio Pictures: 489 middle; © Stephen Vaughan/Paramount: 489 bottom; © Phil Bray/Miramax/Dimension Films: 490 top; © Paramount: 490 bottom; © Columbia Tri-Star: 491

Reprinted by permission from John M. McGrath. *Prisoner of War: Six Years in Hanoi.* **(Annapolis, MD, Naval Institute Press. © 1975)**: 471

Courtesy National Museum of the Marine/ Marine Corps Historical Center: 324-325 top, 327 inset

Marine Corps University Research Center Archives: 528-529

© Map Resources: inset map: 207, 195, 262, 306, 452, 519, 561

National Archives: SP5 Bryan K. Grigsby: 1 bottom; Lt John C. Carter: 2-3; SP4 Gerald Brown: 6-7; SSgt W.F. Schrider: 8-9; 10-11; Sgt Alfred Batungbacal: 12-13; SSgt R. Wickley: 14; 15; SP4 Talmadge Harbison: 17; 18, 20; Yoichi Okamoto/Lyndon Bayne Johnson Library: 22; SSgt R. Wilson: 23 top; SSgt Edward J. McCrossan: 23 bottom; Karl H. Schumacher: 25; SP4 Richard H. Goff: 26 left; SP4 Robert Glenn Hovis: 26 right; SSgt Edward J. McCrossan: 28, 29 top; 29 bottom, 30; SFC Howard C. Breedlove: 32 bottom, 33 bottom; 34, 35 bottom; SP4 Kenneth L. Powell: 36 bottom; 37, 38-39, 39 top left and bottom inset; SP5 Lawrence J. Sulivan: 40; 42 inset; Lt John C. Carter: 42-43; SP4 Talmadge Harbison: 46; Cpl M.J. Coats: 47; 48; Sgt A.V. Huffman: 49 top; Sgt PFC C.D. Thomas: 49 bottom; 53; Cpl Curry: 55 top; Sgt M.F. Belmont: 55 bottom; Sgt Mullins: 56; SP5 Zack Richards: 56 bottom; Sgt K.B. McVeigh: 57 top; Sgt Vojack: 57 bottom; SP5 Gilbert L. Meyers: 60; SP5 Michael P. Laley: 61; SP4 G.A. Cooper: 62 top; SP5 Anthony B'Recht: 62 bottom; 63 top; SP5 C.D. Turner: 63 bottom; PFC Jose C. Rivera: 64; 65 inset: PFC Laslo Kondor: 66 top; Sgt Lyle V. Boggess: 66 bottom; 67 bottom, 68, 69; SFC Howard C. Breedlove: 82 left; PFC Andrew J. Szurgot Jr: 84 left; 84-85, 87; SP4 Dennis J. Kurpius: 88 bottom; M/Sgt Al Chang: 89 bottom left; 91; Yoichi Okamoto/Lyndon Bayne Johnson Library: 95, 96 bottom; R.J. DelVecchio: 97 top; Cpl R. Sanville: 97 bottom; SSgt Hector Robertin: 98; 100, 101 bottom, 103 bottom; H.C. Wolford Jr: 106 bottom; 107 top, 108 bottom; PFC Thomas L. Larsen: 109 bottom;

A U.S. Army soldier directs an approaching Huey helicopter to pick up injured soldiers after a paradrop in October 1966.

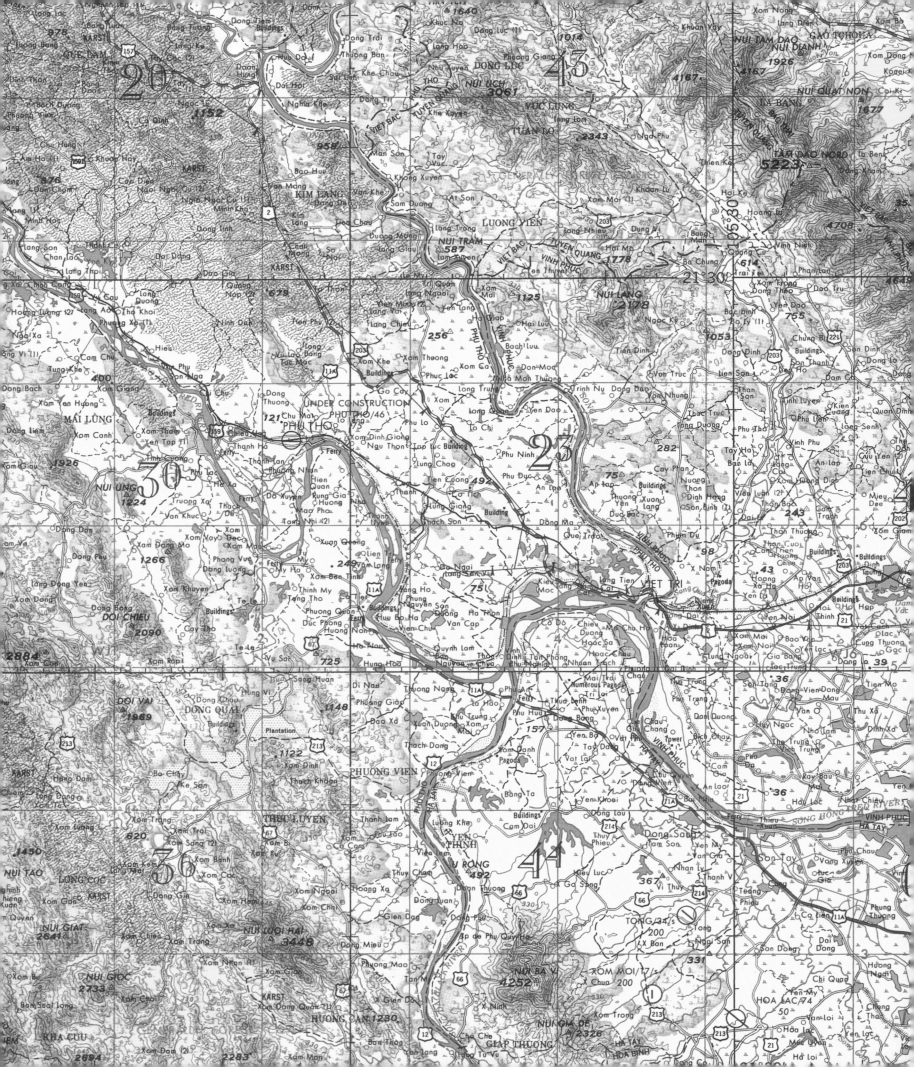